MINNESOTA BUSINESS GUIDEBOOK TO LAW & LEADING ATTORNEYS

1ST EDITION PUBLISHED NOVEMBER 1994

© COPYRIGHT 1994 BY AMERICAN RESEARCH CORPORATION. ALL RIGHTS RESERVED.

No part of this publication may be reproduced, stored in a retrieval system or transmitted in any form or by any means, electric, mechanical, photocopying, recording or otherwise without the permission of the publisher.

The information contained herein is presumed to be accurate at the time of publication. The publisher is not liable for damages from errors or omissions. This publication is designed to provide accurate and authoritative information in regard to the subject matter covered. It is published with the understanding that the publisher is not engaged in providing legal advice, legal service, or instructions on the practice of law. For legal advice, consult an attorney, such as those listed in this book.

ISBN 1-885573-01-4
ISSN 1076-1276
SAN 298-2986
UPC 7-9417573014-4

AMERICAN RESEARCH CORPORATION
527 MARQUETTE AVENUE, SUITE 2100
MINNEAPOLIS, MN 55402
Phone: (612) 334-3445
Fax: (612) 334-3447

 This book is printed using soy-based inks on paper which is 50% recycled with a minimum of 10% post-consumer fiber. Entire book is recyclable.

PURPOSE:

The purpose of the *Business Guidebook to Law & Leading Attorneys* is to provide businesses with the legal information they need and the names of reputable and qualified Minnesota attorneys who can help with a variety of legal issues.

TABLE OF

PART ONE: ABOUT THIS *GUIDEBOOK*
Acknowledgments vii
Introduction viii
Methodology ix
Alphabetical Listing of Nominated Attorneys..x
Using the *Business Guidebook*..xiv

PART TWO: MINNESOTA'S LEGAL SYSTEM AND BASICS OF LAW
1. **Selecting & Managing Counsel**..1
   What to Look for in an Attorney, Questions to Ask, Understanding Legal Fees, Controlling Costs, How to Handle Disputes, What to Expect from an Attorney, Clients' Rights.
2. **Contract Law**..11
   Requirements for a Legally Binding Contract, Legal Consequences of Breaking a Contract, Resolving Contract Disputes.
3. **Minnesota's Legal & Judicial System**...17
   Minnesota Laws and Courts, When to Hire an Attorney, How Courts Decide Cases, Appeals.
4. **Process of a Lawsuit** 21
   What to Expect from a Lawsuit, Recovering Costs and Attorney Fees, Damage Awards, Out-of-Court Settlements.
5. **Alternative Dispute Resolution**..27
   Alternatives to Going to Court, Finding a Provider, How Alternative Dispute Resolution Can Save Time and Money.

PART THREE: AREAS OF BUSINESS LAW AND LEADING ATTORNEYS
6. **Agricultural Law**...31
   Production Contracts, Limited Liability Companies, Farm Bankruptcies, International Agricultural Agreements.
7. **Arts, Entertainment, Advertising & Media Law**..41
   Contracts Frequently Used by Artists and Entertainers, Restrictions on Advertising, Free Speech, Defamation, Obscenity, Sweepstakes, Disclaimers, Privacy Rights Against the Media.
8. **Banking Law** 55
   Federal and State Laws Regulating Banks and their Relationships with Companies, Lender Liability.
9. **Bankruptcy & Workout Law** 63
   Chapter 7, Chapter 11, Fraudulent Conveyances, Alternatives to Bankruptcy, Workouts, Reorganization.
10. **Business Tax Law**...81
    Tax Incidents of Corporations, Partnerships, and Sole Proprietorships, State, Local, Sales, Use, FICA, and Unemployment Taxes.
11. **Closely Held Business Law** 97
    Sole Proprietorships, Partnerships, Professional Corporations, Limited Liability, Buy-Sell Agreements, Business Succession.
12. **Commercial Litigation** 113
    General Business Litigation Issues, What Courts Handle Different Types of Disputes, When Does a Transactional Matter become Litigious.
13. **Commercial Real Estate Law** 135
    Landlord and Tenant Rights and Responsibilities, Purchasing, Leasing, Mortgage Financing, Development Financing.
14. **Criminal Law** 159
    White Collar Crime, Antitrust Laws, Corporate Criminal Liability, RICO, Fraud, Computer Crime.

iv

CONTENTS

15. Employee Benefits Law..175
Compensation, 401(k) Plans, Employee Stock Ownership Plans (ESOPs), IRA's, Keogh Plans, Employee Rights, ERISA, Cafeteria Plans, Pension Plans.

16. Employment Law..181
Employee and Employer Rights and Responsibilities, Wage and Hour Regulations, Independent Contractors, Social Security, Sexual Harassment, Discrimination, OSHA.

17. Environmental Law..203
Water Rights, Superfund, Toxic Torts, Asbestos, Underground Storage Tanks, Recycling, Air Pollution, Solid Wastes, Stray Voltage, Electromagnetic Fields, EPA, MPCA.

18. Federal, State & Local Government Law..223
Public Finance, Government Contracts, Lobbying and Legislative Remedies.

19. Franchise & Dealership Law..241
State & Federal Disclosure Requirements, Statutory, Contract & Common Law Remedies for Unlawful Termination.

20. Health Law..261
Patient Rights, Integrated Service Networks, Medicaid, Medicare, Government Regulation of Health Care Facilities.

21. Immigration Law..277
Immigrants, Visa Categories, Employer Responsibilities, Obtaining Permission to Stay in the US.

22. Intellectual Property Law..287
Copyright, Trademarks, Patents, Licensing Agreements, Trade Secrets, Computer Software.

23. International Business Law..303
International Contract Negotiations, Litigating Foreign Disputes, Import-Export Regulations.

24. Labor Law..315
Employee and Employer Rights and Responsibilities, Collective Bargaining and Other Union Negotiations, NLRB, Major Labor Relations Acts, Union Certification Drives.

25. Nonprofit Corporations Law..329
Creating a Nonprofit Corporation, Liability, Tax Considerations.

26. Personal Injury Defense Law..337
Product Liability, Warranties, Strict Liability, Negligence, Intentional Torts, Dram Shop Laws, Workers' Compensation, Corporate Liability.

27. Probate, Estate Planning & Trusts Law..367
Wills, Trusts, Tax Considerations, Retirement Planning, Estate Planning, Business Considerations.

28. Professional Malpractice Defense Law..383
Medical, Engineering, Accounting, Legal, and Other Professional Malpractice.

29. Publicly Held Corporations Law..397
Structuring the Corporation, S Corporations, Corporate Liability, Tax Considerations, Directors' Fiduciary Responsibilities.

30. Securities & Venture Finance Law..417
Stocks, Bonds, Securities Markets, Over-the-Counter Stocks, Regulatory Concerns, Securities Acts, Minnesota Blue Sky Laws, Exemptions from Regulation.

PART FOUR: APPENDIXES AND INDEXES

A. Legal Resources..433
B. State Bar Associations around the Country..455
C. Attorneys & Law Firms by Region..459
D. Subject Matter Index..501
E. Listing Attorneys Index..506

AMERICAN RESEARCH CORPORATION WOULD LIKE TO THANK THE FOLLOWING ATTORNEYS FOR EDITORIAL ASSISTANCE IN THE DEVELOPMENT OF THE MINNESOTA BUSINESS GUIDEBOOK

Arts, Entertainment, Advertising & Media Law: *Laura Danielson, Barbara Gislason*
Bankruptcy Law: *Phillip Kunkel, James Baillie, Sam Verducci*
Criminal Law: *John Sheehy, Ronald I. Meshbesher*
Employment Law: *Marshall Tanick*
Immigration Law: *Laura Danielson, Jerome Ingber, Richard Breitman, H. Sam Myers*
Personal Injury Defense Law: *John Carey, Edward Matonich, Gerald Maschka, John Person, Mark Kosieradzki*
Tax Law: *Jerome Geis*

MINNESOTA BUSINESS GUIDEBOOK TO LAW & LEADING ATTORNEYS

Editor in Chief: *Brett R. Johnson*
Associate Publisher: *Scott C. Anderson*
Managing Editor: *Joseph Mitzel, J.D.*
Director of Marketing: *Elaine M. Keller*
Production Manager: *Marti Davis*
Assistant Production Manager: *Leslie R. Minkler*
Administrative Assistant: *Debbie Rosenblum*
Proofreader: *Katy M. Podolinsky*
Copy Editor: *Debra Goodwin-Wellever*

AMERICAN RESEARCH CORPORATION WOULD LIKE TO THANK THE FOLLOWING FOR ASSISTANCE IN THE DEVELOPMENT OF THE MINNESOTA BUSINESS GUIDEBOOK

Attorney Surveys: *Scott Anderson, Christine Gorman, Marya Morstad, Elizabeth Grambsh, Stephanie Gunderson, Matt Van Dyke*
Product Research: *George Creel*
Marketing/Advertising: *Peter Smith, Smith Communications, Laurie Meyer, J.D.*
Promotions: *Sara Campbell, Jill Hoffman*
Graphics & Design: *Wayne Thompson, Brian Barber, Amy Fastenau*
Client Focus Groups: *Brian Sullivan, Ira Morgenstern, Daniel Prins, Joan Wrabetz, John Trautz, Steve Bernstein, Julia Knight, Peter Remes, Curtis Beckman, John Scholz*
Attorney Focus Groups: *Kris Sharpe, Lewis Remele Jr., Rolf Engh, Joe Finley Jr., Keith Halleland, Leon Steinberg, John Levy*
Editors: *Patrick Howe, Timothy Walker*
Copy Editors: *Ginna Watson*
Administration: *Randall Barry, Monika Robinson, Milicent Calinog*
Planning: *Todd Baxter*
Videography: *Ian Corbin*

AMERICAN RESEARCH CORPORATION

President & CEO: *Brett R. Johnson*
Vice President: *Gerald R. Sorensen*
Associate Publisher: *Scott C. Anderson*
Managing Editor: *Joseph Mitzel, J.D.*
Director of Marketing: *Elaine M. Keller*
Production Manager: *Marti Davis*
Assistant Production Manager: *Leslie R. Minkler*
Administrative Assistant: *Debbie Rosenblum*
Director of Research: *Joseph G. Bruening, J.D.*
Research Assistants: *Joan Bettinger, Kathleen M. Shea, Merrie-Buff Johnson, Jerilyn Johanson*
Proofreader: *Katy M. Podolinsky*
Copy Editor: *Debra Goodwin-Wellever*
Systems & Technology: *Kurtis Lange, Ginny Shea*

ACKNOWLEDGMENTS

American Research Corporation is pleased to present The Minnesota *Business Guidebook to Law & Leading Attorneys*. This resource is intended to provide the reader with a better understanding of common legal issues affecting businesses today and give decision makers an intelligent approach to finding the right lawyer. Along with its sister publication, The Minnesota *Consumer Guidebook to Law & Leading Attorneys*, the *Guidebooks'* objective is to give Minnesota businesses and consumers greater and more efficient access to the law and the legal community.

Many thanks are in order, beginning with the 2000-plus attorneys who completed mail surveys and took time to offer thoughtful recommendations in our phone surveys. In putting this book together, we learned a great deal about the Minnesota legal community and gained tremendous respect for the quality of our state's attorneys. Our only regret is that the survey process, however rigorous, cannot possibly recognize the thousands of able and talented practitioners who were overlooked. In this sense, the list found in this *Guidebook* is not complete. Nor could it ever be. It is, however, an excellent resource and a wonderful place to start. Our greatest appreciation is reserved for the attorneys whose biographical profiles appear at the end of each chapter. They recognize the need for improved information, and they see the impact that such information can have in helping businesses avoid legal difficulties and operate more efficiently. Without their support, this book would not be possible.

Brett R. Johnson
Publisher

INTRODUCTION

The Minnesota *Business Guidebook to Law & Leading Attorneys* is a resource for the business community to use in addressing legal issues more efficiently and more intelligently. Along with the basics on the legal system, the Minnesota *Business Guidebook* provides information on major issues in specific areas of Minnesota and federal law. At the end of most chapters are biographies of attorneys recommended by their peers in specific areas of law.

The *Guidebook's* purpose is to equip readers with the information they need to address a specific legal problem, and to provide them with a short list of attorneys, licensed to practice in Minnesota, who are among the most qualified to help.

Our editors (attorneys themselves) and researchers are continually collecting relevant legal information, which they summarize and distill to provide readers a concise reference source on Minnesota law and legal resources. This *Guidebook* cannot replace (or diminish the importance of) legal counsel. We are, however, a starting point—a guidepost. Used properly, the *Guidebook* can help you obtain a better legal result.

Selecting the right attorney may be the single, most important factor in a favorable legal outcome. Thus, we recommend you read the Selecting and Managing Counsel Chapter and take time to review the biographies carefully before selecting attorneys to interview. Most of those listed here excel in multiple areas and are referenced in chapters other than the chapter in which their full biography appears. The Leading Attorneys Index at the back of the book provides the names of all listed attorneys and the locations of their biographies. The Legal Resources Appendix covers additional legal resources such as government agencies that provide technical assistance to business. Together, they provide a wealth of information and resources organized by region and interest.

The *Guidebook's* leading attorney sections, appearing at the end of most chapters, provide professional biographies of highly regarded legal experts—Minnesota attorneys other attorneys would recommend if a friend or family member needed legal help. This information is designed to help you find the most appropriate legal counsel.

The attorneys who qualified to appear in this book were chosen through a survey conducted by the American Research Corporation.

Briefly, we asked a large sample of Minnesota attorneys to name the legal specialists whom they hold in highest regard. The resulting nominated group, representing less than five percent of all Minnesota attorneys, was offered the opportunity to participate in this referral guide through a biographical profile. Those who chose to do so paid a standard fee to underwrite the cost of publishing and distributing this book. More information on the methodology of the survey is provided below.

This is not a ranking or a "best of" list. Certainly there are numerous highly qualified and reputable attorneys not listed. We can say, however, that all the attorneys listed in this book are *among* the most highly qualified and reputable in Minnesota as determined by their peers in an extensive statewide survey.

The production of this *Guidebook* is an ongoing effort; there will be future editions containing biographies of attorneys not included in earlier versions as well as updates on Minnesota law and other useful resources. Based on reader feedback, we will make other changes to the *Guidebooks* to ensure that they remain useful and become the important legal education resource that we envision.

> We asked Minnesota attorneys to whom they would refer a close friend or relative in need of specialized legal assistance.

METHODOLOGY

The leading attorneys listings found at the end of most chapters are designed to provide biographical information on qualified, reputable Minnesota attorneys. These peer-selected listings are the result of surveys conducted with Minnesota attorneys. To create this list, 1800 attorneys licensed to practice law in Minnesota were mailed questionnaires during the summer of 1992 that asked, "If a close friend or relative needed legal help in a certain area of law, to whom would you refer them?"

These phase-one survey recipients were selected using a random sort by zip code to ensure geographic balance. After self-nominations were removed, an attempt was made to contact each nominee. We spoke with approximately 600 of these attorneys from whom we sought names of individuals in their practice area (where the

> This list represents only a small percentage of the reputable and qualified attorneys in Minnesota.

attorney is regarded as excellent) whom they held in highest regard. Additional calls were then made to those recommended during this second phase. All partner or same-firm nominations were removed if the attorney did not receive other independent non-firm referrals.

A third phase involved contacting those attorneys regarded as oustanding by their peers as indicated by multiple independent referrals during the second phase. Altogether, over 2000 Minnesota attorneys were interviewed. A complete list of all 831 attorneys is found below.

Note: This list includes attorneys from both the Minnesota *Business Guidebook to Law & Leading Attorneys* and the Minnesota *Consumer Guidebook to Law & Leading Attorneys*.

ALPHABETICAL LISTING OF NOMINATED ATTORNEYS

Abdo, Kenneth J.
Ahern, Michael J.
Alsop, David D.
Altman, Lawrence R.
Amundson, Luther M.
Anderson, Douglas P.
Anderson, John M.
Andresen, Charles H. (Huck)
Andresen, Craig W.
Anthony, Joseph W.
Aronson, Robert D.
Aronson, Terrence M.
Arthur, Lindsay G.
Arundel, Edward M.
Arzt, Philip K.
Ashley, Barbara Z.
Bachman, Walter
Baer, Carl
Baer, Timothy R.
Baillie, James L.
Bains, Herman H.
Ball, Ian Traquair
Bannigan, John F. Jr.
Bans, Charles
Barnard, Allen D.

Barnett, Timothy M.
Bartle, Emery W.
Baudler, Bryan
Beck, Peter K.
Belfry, K. Scott
Bennett, Robert
Berens, Michael
Berg, Larry J.
Berg, Nancy Z.
Bergerson, Stephen R.
Bergfalk, Jerrold F.
Bergquist, Edward W.
Berndt, Daniel E.
Berquist, Charles C.
Bird, Charles A.
Bjorklund, Mary J.
Bland, J. Richard
Blethen, Bailey W.
Bluth, Joseph P.
Boelter, Philip F.
Bohl, Phillip W.
Bohrer, Edward J.
Borden, Thomas R.
Bowman, Richard A.
Bradt, Gene P.

Brand, Martha C.
Brand, Steve A.
Brandt, John E.
Breen, Richard H.
Breitman, Richard L.
Brennan, David R.
Briol, Mark J.
Brody, William J.
Brown, Frederick C. Jr.
Brown, Lawrence C.
Brown, Ronald J.
Bruno, Frederic
Brynestad, Lorens Q.
Bucher, Paul W.
Bujold, Tyrone P.
Burk, Robert S.
Burns, Ann B.
Burns, Richard R.
Burns, William M.
Busch, Kevin M.
Bye, Don L.
Byrne, Daniel F.
Byron, John P.
Cahill, James D.
Cahill, Peter A.

Cambronne, Karl L.
Campbell, Craig R.
Carey, John W.
Carlson, Alan G.
Carlson, Jack W.
Carlson, Steven E.
Carpenter, Kevin S.
Carroll, John R.
Carron, Reid
Ceisel, Colia F.
Cella, Catherine A.
Chalmers, Carolyn
Chamberlain, Paul W.
Chase, Joseph F.
Christiansen, Jay D.
Christoffel, James F.
Christy, Angela M.
Ciresi, Michael V.
Clinton, Jack W.
Cole, Daniel J. Jr.
Cole, Phillip A.
Colich, Michael J.
Collins, Theodore J.
Commers, Lawrence R.
Comstock, Rebecca A.
Conlin, Thomas M.
Connelly, John J.
Constantine, Katherine A.
Cooper, Peter L.
Cooper, Stephen W.
Cope, John F.
Corwin, Gregg M.
Cosgriff, William J.
Crandall, William A. III
Crawford, Rollin H.
Cromett, Michael F.
Crosby, Robert L.
Culhane, Martin A. III
Cunningham, G. Alan
Cutler, Kenneth L.
Dady, J. Michael
Dailey, James J.
Damon, Matthew E.
Danielson, Laura J.
D'Aquila, Barbara Jean
Davies, R. Scott
Davis, Stephen J.
Dawson, James M.
Dayton, Charles K.
Deaner, Ted E.
Degnan, John M.
DeSanto, John E.
Devoy, Kimball J.
Dickel, Morris
Diehl, John E.
Dolan, Michael J.
Dolan, William T.
Dordell, Wayne P.
Dosland, C. Allen
Downing, Lawrence D.
Doyle, Terence N.
Drahos, Carl C.
Druck, James B.

Dudderar, Frederick A.
Dueholm, James A.
Dunlap, John C.
Dunlap, Mary H.
Dunlevy, Shawn M.
Dunn, James F.
Durkin, Marian M.
Eastwood, J. Marquis
Eckman, Stephen S.
Edell, Robert T.
Edgerton, Ward G.
Edstrom, Dean R.
Efron, Stanley
Eide, David B.
Eidsness, Alan C.
Eisberg, John F.
El-Ghazzawy, Karim G.
Eller, Daniel A.
Elliott, Christopher E.
Engh, N. Rolf
Engh, Paul
Erhart, John J.
Erickson, James C.
Estebo, Orrin S.
Fabel, Thomas L.
Fabyanske, Marvin T.
Fairbairn, David R.
Fargione, Michael
Feeney, Leo F.
Feinberg, Thomas D.
Ferrell, Charles S.
Fetsch, Michael F.
Field, Harold D. Jr.
Finley, Joseph M.
Fisher, Linda H.
Fishman, Phillip F.
Fitzgerald, David F.
Fitzgerald, Richard J.
Fitzmaurice, James
Flaherty, Patrick F.
Flaskamp, William D.
Fleming, Terrence J.
Flom, Gerald T.
Flynn, George W.
Flynn Peterson, Kathleen
Ford, Michael J.
Forsberg, David C.
Forschler, Richard A.
Foster, William D.
Frans, Myron L.
Frécon, Alain
Frederick, Harold A.
Freeman, Todd I.
Freitag, Gregory G.
French, John D.
Friedberg, Joseph S.
Friedemann, Konrad J.
Friederichs, Norman P.
Frieders, Jill I.
Friedman, Fred T.
Frommelt, Roger H.
Fruth, Terence M.
Fuller, Steven M.

Fuller, Steven S.
Furness, Catherine B.
Gage, F. Kelton
Gagnon, Craig W.
Galvin, Michael J. Jr.
Garon, Philip S.
Garrett, Thomas H. III
Gartner, Ludwig B. Jr.
Geis, Jerome A.
Gersick, Barry A.
Ginsburg, Roy A.
Gislason, Barbara J.
Gislason, Daniel A.
Glennon, Edward M.
Goetz, John C.
Goff, Richard D.
Goldberg, Daniel J.
Goldstein, Robert M.
Gordon, Avron L.
Gordon, John B.
Gordon, Roger D.
Gordon, Stephen D.
Gottesman, Joel H.
Gould, John D.
Graff, N. Walter
Graham, Kathleen M.
Grasmoen, Cheryl L.
Gray, Earl P.
Greco, Deanne M.
Greenberg, Malin D.
Greene, Clifford M.
Greene, William L.
Greenswag, Douglas B.
Grindal, H. Theodore
Grinnell, Paul E.
Grooms, Lloyd W.
Grorud, David C.
Gunhus, Gunder D.
Gurstel, Norman K.
Guy, William L. III
Hackel, Joan M.
Hagemann, Andrew E. Jr.
Haik, Raymond A.
Halagan, Robert S.
Halla, Trudy J.
Hallberg, Mark A.
Halleland, Keith J.
Halverson, Jan D.
Hamel, Mark E.
Hamre, Curtis B.
Hanley, Bruce H.
Hanley, William J.
Hansen, Karen M.
Hansen, Robyn L.
Hanson, Bruce E.
Hanson, Lee W.
Hanson, Samuel L.
Hanson, Steven A.
Harper, William D.
Harries, Gilbert W.
Harris, John E.
Hashmall, David L.
Hauer, Robert J. Jr.

Haug, William A.
Haugen, Orrin M.
Haugh, William E. Jr.
Hawkins, Charles L.
Hay, Nick
Haynes, David N.
Haynor, Charles R.
Hayward, Edward J.
Healy, John D. Jr.
Heaney, Timothy M.
Hedeen, William T.
Hedin, Douglas A.
Heiberg, Robert A.
Heilman, Edward G.
Heinzerling, Karl K.
Hemphill, Stuart R.
Hendrixson, Peter S.
Henneman, Larry R.
Hennessy, Patrick B.
Henson, Robert F.
Herman, John H.
Herr, David F.
Herzog, W. Scott
Heuel, Daniel J.
Hibbs, John S.
Hippe, Benjamin R.
Hippee, William H. Jr.
Hobbins, Robert L.
Hoch, Gary W.
Hoff, George C.
Hoffman, Robert L.
Hoffman, Thomas E.
Hogan, Barry P.
Holbrook, John D.
Holper, Richard D.
Hols, David R.
Horton, Donald E.
Houston, John R.
Hughes, Kathleen A.
Hughes, Kevin J.
Hughes, Laurence B.
Hummel, Lynn J.
Hunegs, Richard G.
Huntrods, R. Ann
Hutchinson, David C.
Hvass, Charles T. Jr.
Hyde, Maclay R.
Iannacone, Michael J.
Ingber, Jerome B.
Irvine, Peter M.
Irvine, Robert W.
Iverson, Jon K.
Jarpe, Geoffrey P.
Jaycox, Jack S.
Jeffries, Richard N.
Jensen, Gordon L.
Jensen, Roger A.
Jepson, William E.
Jesse, Franklin C. Jr.
Johanneson, John C.
Johannson, Kenneth F.
Johnson, Brian N.
Johnson, Craig W.

Johnson, Dennis R.
Johnson, Eugene L.
Johnson, G. Robert
Johnson, Jeffrey S.
Johnson, Joel D.
Johnson, Larry W.
Johnson, Michael D.
Johnson, Reese C
Johnson, Thomas L.
Johnstone, William A.
Jonason, William A.
Kalla, Mark J.
Kampf, William I.
Kane, Thomas P.
Kantor, David
Kaplan, Elliot S.
Kaplan, Samuel L.
Kaplan, Sidney
Karp, Michael C.
Kaster, James H.
Katz, A. Larry
Keating, James R.
Keegan, David C.
Kelley, David W.
Kelley, Douglas A.
Kelly, John D.
Kelly, Thomas M.
Kelly, Timothy D.
Kennedy, Charles R.
Kennedy, David J.
Keppel, William J.
Kershner, H. Morrison
Keyes, Jeffrey J.
Kief, Paul A.
Killen, John J.
King, D. Randall
King, Lawrence R.
King, Robert J. Jr.
King, Thomas R.
Kirby, John D.
Kissoon, Kathleen W.
Knapp, John A.
Knowles, Faye
Knutson, Roger N.
Koch, Gary W.
Koneck, John M.
Korman, Dennis J.
Korman, James R.
Kosieradzki, Mark R.
Kraft, John H.
Krause, Raymond C.
Krekelberg, Charles A.
Krueger, Patrick M.
Kuderer, Elton A.
Kueppers, Frederick A. Jr.
Kuller, Hart A.
Kunkel, Phillip L.
Kuntz, Timothy J.
LaFave, E. Joseph III
Laine, Edward M.
Lallier, Thomas J.
Lange, Gregory J.
Langevin, Judith B.

Lano, Neal A.
Lantz, W. Charles
Lapp, William S.
Lareau, Richard G.
Larsen, Dexter A.
Laurie, Gerald T.
LaVerdiere, Richard A.
Lawrence, Douglas M.
Lazar, Raymond M.
LeFevere, Charles L.
Leonard, Brian F.
Lervick, John C.
Levine, John D.
Levy, John C.
Libbey, Keith A.
Lies, Thomas W.
Lillehaug, David L.
Linstroth, Paul J.
Litman, Stephen R.
Litsey, Calvin L.
Little, Bruce H.
Lockhart, Greer E.
Logstrom, Bridget A.
Long, Frances L.
Love, Brian J.
Lovett, Thomas G. IV
Lowther, Patrick A.
Lubben, David J.
Lucas, Joan H.
Lucas, Robert E.
Ludcke, George O.
Lund, Kevin A.
Lundquist, John W.
McCoy, Timothy J.
McCullough, D. Patrick
McDonald, David C.
McDonald, John R.
McDowell, Gary D.
McGunnigle, George F. Jr.
McInerney, Daniel J. Jr.
MacIntosh, G. Thomas II
McIntyre, J. Lawrence
Mack, Warren E.
McKay, Susan A.
Mackenzie, Reed K.
McLaughlin, David C.
McLean, Edward D.
Madson, Eric O.
Magie, Robert H. III
Magnuson, Eric J.
Magnuson, Gerald E.
Magnuson, Roger J.
Mahoney, Jerry C. D.
Mahoney, Patrick E.
Mahoney, Richard P.
Malkerson, Bruce D.
Malone, Robert G.
Manahan, James H.
Manka, Gary L.
Mansfield, Seymour J.
Marben, Kurt J.
Maring, David S.
Marrin, James F.

Martin, James T.
Martin, Kathleen M.
Martin, Phillip H.
Martin, Richard H.
Maschka, Gerald L.
Maser, Kris L.
Mason, John M.
Massopust, Richard H. Jr.
Mathison, Leigh D.
Matonich, Edward J.
Mattos, Patricia G.
Maus, Terence L.
Mauzy, William J.
Mavity, William J.
Mayerle, Thomas M.
Maynard, Hugh M.
Mellum, Gale R.
Merley, Dennis J.
Meshbesher, Ronald I.
Meyer, Helen M.
Meyer, Michael L.
Meyer, Theodore J.
Meyer, William G.
Meyerle, Kathleen A.
Michaels, Franklin
Mickelsen, Ruth A.
Miller, David B.
Miller, Eric R.
Miller, Thomas F.
Mishek, Mark G.
Mitau, Lee R.
Mohr, Gordon G. (Jeff)
Mohs, Daniel M.
Molle, John E.
Moore, Malcolm L.
Moore, Robert M. Jr.
Moos, Rebecca Egge
Mooty, John W.
Moratzka, Timothy D.
Morris, Frederick W.
Morris, Ralph K.
Morrow, Joan S.
Moskal, David J.
Mottaz, Thomas D.
Muck, Thomas R.
Muir, Ross
Mulligan, Allan E.
Mullin, William E.
Munger, Harry L.
Munic, Martin D.
Murphy, Brian J.
Murphy, Michael E.
Myers, Howard S. (Sam) III
Nauen, Charles N.
Nawrocki, Lawrence M.
Neff, Scott C.
Neils, Roger D.
Neilson, James M.
Nelson, Gary M.
Nelson, Janice M.
Nelson, Steven C.
Nelson, Sue A.
Nelson, Susan R.

Nelson, Thomas F.
Neuville, Thomas M.
Newman, Kathleen M.
Nichols, Donald H.
Nikolai, Thomas J.
Nilan, Michael T.
Nord, Larry M.
Nordhougen, Curtis A.
Norman, Kenneth J.
Norwich, Donald P.
Nowlin, Forrest D. (Dick)
Nygaard, Richard J.
Nys, John N.
O'Brien, Daniel W.
O'Brien, J. Dennis
O'Brien, James E.
O'Brien, Maurice W. (Bill)
O'Brien, William J.
Odlaug, Bruce G.
O'Gorman, Patricia A.
O'Leary, Daniel B.
O'Leary, J. Brian
O'Loughlin, Terence J.
Olson, Floyd B.
Olup, Linda A.
O'Neill, Brian B.
Opperman, Vance K.
Orenstein, David A.
Orenstein, Melvin I.
Ornstein, David R.
Osterman, Lawrence
O'Toole, Dennis L.
Palmer, Rebecca
Parsons, Charles A. Jr.
Patchin, Michael J.
Patrick, Howard A.
Patton, Harold R.
Payne, James A.
Pearson, Curtis A.
Pedersen, James F.
Pemberton, Richard L.
Pentelovitch, William Z.
Perl, Justin H.
Person, John W.
Persson, Darrold E.
Peterson, Bruce A.
Peterson, David T.
Peterson, Desyl L.
Peterson, Gary M.
Peterson, H. Jeffrey
Peterson, Richard A.
Peterson, Roger A.
Pfaffly, Philip A.
Plunkett, Hugh V. III
Plunkett, J. Patrick
Polk, Michael S.
Popham, Wayne G.
Powell, Romaine R.
Prescott, Jack L.
Prichard, Michael
Pritzker, Fred H.
Provo, John W.
Quaintance, Charles Jr.

Quam, John C.
Quinlivan, John D.
Quinlivan, Michael R.
Radio, Thomas J.
Rajkowski, Frank J.
Ramstad, Charles J.
Ramstad, James O.
Ramstad-Hvass, Sheryl
Ranum, Robert K.
Rapoport, Larry G.
Ravich, Paul H.
Regan, John E.
Regan, Thomas M.
Regnier, Pierre N.
Reid, Douglas D. Jr.
Reif, Thomas J.
Reinhart, Robert R. Jr.
Reister, Raymond A.
Remele, Lewis A. Jr.
Remington, Ann
Resnick, Phillip S.
Rhode, Susan C.
Richards, Carver
Richter, Scott E.
Riedy, John M.
Ries, Charles W.
Riley, James M.
Riley, Peter W.
Ringstrom, Bruce N.
Rischmiller, Reid G.
Robbins, Jeffrey C.
Roby, Joseph J. Jr.
Roche, Kevin H.
Rockwell, James W.
Rodenberg, John R.
Roe, Roger R. Jr.
Roegge, James F.
Rohricht, Thomas E.
Ronning, Richard L.
Rosenstein, Elinor C.
Rosholt, Stephen C.
Ross, Burton G.
Ross, Richard A.
Roston, David G.
Roth, Randi Ilyse
Rotman, Lewis J.
Rubenstein, Andrea F.
Rubenstein, James A.
Runchey, Barbara J.
Russell, Robert L.
Ryan, Lehan J.
Rysavy, Donald E.
Saeks, Allen I.
Samples, James M.
Sampson, Ellen G.
Sand, David B.
Sandberg, Peter C.
Sanders, Thomas P.
Satorius, Daniel M.
Sawicki, Z. Peter
Sayre, Grover C. III
Schade, William M.
Scheerer, Paul J.

Schlesinger, Robert N.
Schmidt, Cecil C.
Schmidt, Henry W.
Schmitz, Peter J.
Schmitz, Stuart E.
Schmoker, Richard C.
Schneider, Mark W.
Schnell, Brian B.
Schnell, Robert L. Jr.
Schroeder, Clinton A.
Schulz, John R.
Schupp, Timothy R.
Schwebel, James R.
Scoll, Jonathan P.
Seaton, Douglas P.
Seed, Peter H.
Seeger, Ronald L.
Sefkow, Robert J.
Segal, Susan L.
Seiler, Steven J.
Sellergren, David C.
Setterlund, Jack E.
Severson, Robert K.
Sharpe, W. Smith (Kris) Jr.
Sheahan, Michael J.
Sheehy, Lee E.
Sheran, John M.
Sherman, Morris M.
Shnider, Bruce J.
Shulman, Daniel R.
Shulman, David A.
Sieben, Harry A. Jr.
Sieben, Michael R.
Sieben, William R.
Signorelli, Mark T.
Silverman, Robert J.
Simonett, Martha M.
Simonson, James S.
Sinclair, James D.
Sipkins, Peter W.
Skatvold, Paul O.
Smith, Louis N.
Smith, Nick
Smith, Ralph T.
Snider, Jerry W.
Snyder, Michael C.
Snyder, Stephen J.
Sobol, Brian L.
Sobolik, Dennis M.
Soth, William R.
Soucie, Fred M.
Soule, George W.
Spellacy, Kevin A.
Spence, Russell M.
Spencer, David J.
Spevacek, Charles E.
Sprenger, Paul C.
Stacker, Howard G.
Stageberg, Mark N.
Stageberg, Roger V.
Starns, Byron E.
Steffen, John K.
Stein, Robert A.

Steinberg, Leon I.
Stenmoe, Gregory J.
Stephenson, James P.
Stephenson, Robert H.
Stewart, James H.
Stewart, Michael R.
Stewart, T. Chris
Stingley, Susan B.
Stone, John F.
Stoneking, Gary E.
Stout, John H.
Strangis, Ralph L.
Straughn, Robert O.
Strauss, Robert F.
Strawbridge, Douglas A.
Streitz, Robert J.
Strinden, Jon E.
Struthers, Margo S.
Stuart, Barbara G.
Stumo, Mary E.
Stuurmans, Jan
Sudeith, Russell J. Jr.
Sullivan, David P.
Sullivan, Timothy A.
Sumners, John S.
Sussman, Ross A.
Svoboda, Gerald L.
Swaden, Martin L.
Swanum, Vernon D.
Sweetland, Heather L.
Swelbar, Gaylord W.
Swenson, Donald C.
Tanick, Marshall H.
Tarkow, Howard B.
Tarvestad, Anthony M.
Taylor, Frank A.
Telstad, Cindy K.
Tennis, Greig R.
Tewksbury, Michael D.
Thibodeau, Thomas R.
Thiel, John W.
Thomas, John C.
Thompson, Elizabeth A.
Thompson, Joe E.
Thompson, Peter J.
Thomson, Douglas W.
Thomson, James J. Jr.
Thoreen, Gerald L.
Thorsen, Madge S.
Thorson, Frederick L.
Thorwaldsen, Paul R.
Tiegel, Lisa R.
Timmer, Steven J.
Tinkham, Thomas W.
Tobin, Timothy P.
Torgerson, Paul M.
Torvik, Stephen
Trenti, John A.
Trousdale, Elmer B.
Trucano, Michael
Truesdell, Lynn G.
Tully, Ralph H.
Tyra, Kenneth T.

Undem, John D.
Unger, Michael W.
Vaa, Galen J.
Van de North, John B. Jr.
Van Drake, Stephen R.
Van Putten, Marinus W. Jr.
Van Valkenburg, Paul
Vanasek, Alan R.
Vessey, James B.
Vidas, Robert O.
Villaume, Frank E. III
Villaume, Philip G.
Vogel, Peter L.
Vogt, Thomas M.
Vollertsen, Nancy L.
Wade, Terry L.
Wallner, Robert M.
Walsh, Ronald J.
Weber, Robert G.
Weikart, Neil A.
Weil, Cass S.
Weinstine, Robert R.
Weiss, Honnen S.
Weissman, Gary A.
Weitz, Mark S.
Welch, Jane S.
Wellman, Steven C.
Wellvang, Steven A.
Wendland, Craig W.
Wernick, Mark S.
Westman, Nickolas E.
Westra, Mark W.
Weyandt, Gregory M.
Wheaton, John R.
White, Robert T.
Whitehead, G. Marc
Wicks, John R.
Wilhoit, Richard A.
Wille, Karin L.
Williams, Douglas J.
Williams, Richard A. Jr.
Wilmes, Gregory L.
Wilson, C. Thomas
Wilson, M. Sue
Wilson, Richard G.
Windhorst, John W. Jr.
Winer, Edward L.
Winthrop, Sherman
Wold, Peter B.
Wolf, Thomas
Woodward, Albert A.
Worke, Renee L.
Wray, Mary Anne
Wray, Tsippi
Wylie, Richard T.
Yanowitz, Alan J.
Young, Stephen R.
Zalk, Robert H.
Zech, Paul J.
Zeglovitch, Robert
Zimmer, Michael A.
Zuber, Nicolas J.
Zwakman, John C.

xiii

USING THE BUSINESS GUIDEBOOK

The *Business Guidebook to Law & Leading Attorneys*' first five chapters discuss general legal topics including: Selecting and Managing Counsel, Minnesota's Legal and Judicial Systems, and Process of a Lawsuit. These introductory chapters are followed by 25 chapters on specific areas of law with profiles of nominated attorneys who practice in each of these specific areas.

If the services of an attorney are necessary, we advise that you review the biographical profiles at the end of each chapter to identify attorneys whose expertise matches your need.

Appendix A: *Legal Resources,* lists a wealth of helpful resources throughout Minnesota for businesses with specialized needs.

Appendix B: *State Bar Associations around the Country,* can be used as a resource to learn about law and lawyers in other jurisdictions.

Index C: *Attorneys & Law Firms by Region,* provides the names and respective firms of peer-recommended attorneys throughout Minnesota.

Attorneys whose biographical profiles appear in the *Guidebook* have indicated their interest in discussions with prospective clients who have specific legal needs that match the experience summarized in their profile. The following is a guide to the format of biographical profiles:

Because many attorneys practice in multiple areas of law, the short listings are attorneys who practice in this area but whose full biographical profile appears in another section of the Guidebook.

Bullet (•) indicates attorney was nominated in this specfic area of law.

STEPHEN Z. ERGAN: Ergan Roberts & Wilson - 221 North First St. P.O. Box 665 - Anytown, US 55454 - Phone: (111) 343-8989, Fax: (111) 343-8023 - *See Complete biographical profile in Real Estate Law Chapter.*

• **ROBERT T . GANNON:** Marx & Thomas - 3000 Norwest Center - Anytown, US 55454 - Phone: (111) 554-8809, Fax: (111) 544-8097 - *See Complete biographical profile in Intellectual Property Law Chapter.*

Full biographical profile of the attorney's practice and expertise.

Employment history, professional associations and community provide insight into the attorney's background and interests.

Information about the attorney's firm, his or her partners, and associates can provide insight into the other resources the attorney can draw upon.

• **SUSAN T. JOERG:** Susan Joerg practices primarily family law concentrating in all aspects of matrimonial law. She has successfully represented individual clients in issues arising out of divorce and legal separation proceedings, spousal maintenance, child support, child custody and visitation, domestic and child abuse, antenuptial agreements, paternity and third party child custody proceedings. Emanating from her focus on child custody, Ms. Joerg has also developed a significant practice representing mental health professionals in disputes with their respective state licensing boards.
Education: JD 1980 University of Minnesota; BA 1976, Smith College
Employment History: 1990-present, Masters & Joerg; Partner 1987-90, Mey, Alling & Killman; Private practice 1981-87; Attorney 1980-81, Anytown City Attorney's Office.
Representative Clients: Lutheran Social Services; Catholic Charities; City of Lakes Mental Health Center; Newton Extended Care, Inc.
Professional Associations: American Academy of Matrimonial Lawyers; Minnesota Academy of Matrimonial Lawyers (Secretary); ABA; MSBA (Liaison to the Minnesota Continuing Legal Education Committee from the Diversity Committee and Family Law Policy Committee, Family Law Committee); HCBA (Diversity Committee, Ethics Committee (Chair), Family Law Section (Cochair), Executive Committee (Cochair)); American Women Lawyers; Midwest Custody Project.
Community Involvement: United Board of Directors (1990-present); Anystate Dept. of Human Services Committee regarding placement of children (1989-93); Director Women's Venture (1992-present); YMCA (Board of Directors 1987-present).
Firm: Formed in January 1991, Masters & Joerg brought to the community unique knowledge and varied expertise in all areas of family and children issues. The firm has over 25 years combined experience representing clients in matters of dissolution, custody, adoption, delinquency, paternity, appeals, and personal estate planning. The firm strengthens its commitment to the community through active participation in Bar activities, teaching, and speaking at public forums and seminars.

Abbreviations for degrees, associations, and courts are used throughout. See abbreviation key at beginning of each profile section.

SUSAN T. JOERG

Masters & Joerg
400 Fourth Avenue North
Suite 230
Anytown, US 55415
Phone: (111) 555-2220
Fax: (111) 555-2244

Admitted: 1980 Anystate; 1979 US Dist. Ct. (MN)
Birthdate: 09/01/50

Indicates in which court attorney is licensed to practice and when he or she was admitted to practice law.

xiv

CHAPTER
1

SELECTING & MANAGING COUNSEL

It is surprising how few businesses take an informed approach to selecting legal services. A lot of executives are intimidated, and do not use the same principles they use when making other major business decisions. As a result, they often make inappropriate choices and wind up unhappy. There is a right way to select and manage counsel and it does affect how satisfied a business will be with the representation it receives. Given the importance of the issues our society trusts lawyers to handle and the amount of money spent on their services, businesses have a right to be satisfied with the representation they receive.

No one should fall into the trap of believing the tired old saying that, "lawyers are all alike." Lawyers are not all alike. Every lawyer must have a four-year college degree before being admitted to law school. However, the degree can be in any area, so a particular lawyer might have a degree in English, accounting, biology, or any other academic subject. In law school, students study many required subjects but they also have the opportunity to study areas of special interest, such as environmental law, family law, or tax law. After law school, law students must pass a state bar exam to practice law in that state. The United States is broken down into many different systems of courts, known as bars. Each bar sets its own requirements for lawyers who practice there. A lawyer who is not a member of the Minnesota bar cannot practice law in Minnesota absent special permission. Bars may also have special categories of lawyers who are certified to practice in a particular area.

The businessperson who exercises care in choosing a lawyer intelligently can be satisfied because there is a right way to choose legal services and it does make a difference. The following three-step process can help businesses find the right attorney for their legal needs.

STEP 1: PREPARING A LIST

The first step anyone faces in choosing a lawyer is to generate a list of potential prospects. This is usually an easy step. There are thousands of lawyers in Minnesota alone, and most people know of at least one lawyer to whom they could refer someone. The quality of these referrals varies greatly, however, depending on the source.

ADVERTISING

Ever since the U.S. Supreme Court lifted the ban on attorney advertising, there has been an explosion in the amount of print and broadcast advertising done by the thousands of Minnesota lawyers eager to reach new clients. However, not all forms of lawyer advertising are permitted. For example, a lawyer is never allowed to solicit business from an accident victim in the hospital unless specifically invited there by the victim. But while some forms of advertising are banned, the range of permissible forms of advertising is quite broad and can include some fairly outlandish forms of self-promotion.

Given the amount of advertising that some lawyers do, the average person could easily rattle off the names of at least a few lawyers who practice in his or her community. The trouble, of course, is that the best known attorneys are not necessarily the best practitioners of their profession. While it may be easiest to look up the section on attorneys in the phone book or call a telephone number broadcast on radio or television, it often pays to use other sources of information. A local bar association can be a source of names. Some industrial trade organizations have attorney referral networks. Of course, it is hoped that this book will be of great use in helping businesspersons find competent, peer-referred attorneys to handle their legal affairs. Consulting one or more of the lawyers listed at the end of the chapters is an excellent way to start the search for a good lawyer.

PERSONAL REFERRALS

Another good source of attorney names is personal referrals. Friends and relatives are often able to recommend a lawyer. Business associates may also be a good source of names. A trusted accountant, insurance agent, or employer might also be able to recommend a competent lawyer. The benefit of a recommendation from a business associate is that, unlike a recommendation from a friend or relative, accountants, insurance agents, and employers regularly consult with attorneys on a broad variety of issues and may be in a better position to steer a novice toward the best lawyer for his or her needs.

Regardless of who recommends a name, ask specific questions about the lawyer. How does the person know the lawyer? Has the person ever consulted the lawyer? If so, for what reason? What are the lawyer's strengths and weaknesses? Does he or she return phone calls promptly and keep the client informed of the process of the case? What outcome was the lawyer able to get? Is the lawyer a member of the Minnesota bar? A referral that seems promising at first may not help much if it turns out that the lawyer practices a different area of law, the lawyer is not a member of the Minnesota bar, or if the person recommending the lawyer knows very little about him or her.

REFERRAL SERVICES

Anyone who would be more comfortable talking with someone who shares a similar background should not hesitate to seek out such an attorney. Some women may turn to other women to handle their legal affairs because they believe that another woman could empathize with the unique legal problems women face. A person of color might prefer to give business to another person of color, or someone in the gay and lesbian community might believe that a person from their community can best represent their interests. Law schools have made tremendous strides in recruiting more diverse student bodies in the past two decades and consequently, the ranks of lawyers today have swelled with competent practitioners of every race, gender, ethnicity, and lifestyle. In order to make the legal community more responsive to our changing society, several organizations have sprung up here in Minnesota that refer callers to lawyers sensitive to the needs of women, Hispanic-Americans, African-Americans, Asian-Americans, gays, lesbians, and others. A person who would feel more comfortable hiring a lawyer from a particular background should not hesitate to seek out names from one of these special referral organizations. Most of these organizations have no fee associated with their services or their fees are paid by the lawyer, not the businessperson.

Once the businessperson has a list of a few potential lawyers it is time to think about the next step—researching the attorneys on the list.

STEP 2: RESEARCHING THE ATTORNEYS ON THE LIST

Once a person has gathered the names of a number of possible attorneys, there are many issues to consider. Some questions can be answered by a quick phone call to the lawyer's office but others can only be answered by talking to other people. Some of the more important issues to research about the lawyers on the list include:

REPUTATION

An attorney's reputation for technical skill is important, but only the individual can determine its relevance to a particular legal matter. Consider that a lawyer who has built a sterling reputation for his or her competent handling of complex litigated probate disputes may be overqualified to draft a simple will. Similarly, a lawyer whose head is full of knowledge gained from representing large corporations may need to start researching from scratch if asked to represent a small start-up company. Savvy individuals with a variety of legal concerns often employ different lawyers to work on different matters because they realize no lawyer can be all things to all people for every type of legal question. Certainly if the case involves a lot of money or the company's reputation is at stake, as is the case when a company is accused of white collar crime, then the business wants to find the very best attorney there is to handle the matter. For more routine matters, where smaller dollar amounts are at stake, a less experienced lawyer may actually be a better fit, not to mention, more affordable.

As important as a lawyer's technical reputation is, his or her ethical reputation may be even more important. It pays to ask around about a lawyer's ethical reputation, for a lawyer's reputation is well known among other professionals. To find out about an attorney's reputation, the individual should ask others with similar needs or problems for references—perhaps someone who has gone through a similar situation. Lawyers should be willing to provide references or a list of past clients, and the potential client can then check with those past clients. Beware of lawyers with poor ethical reputations. The state of Minnesota maintains the Office of Lawyers Professional Responsibility Board (520 Lafayette Road, Suite 100, St. Paul, MN 55155-4196, (612) 296-3952). The Board investigates charges of unethical conduct against attorneys and has authority to recommend disbarment. Potential clients may contact the Lawyers Professional Responsibility Board to learn if an attorney has ever been publicly disciplined. A lawyer who does not follow the rules of his or her own profession may not handle the case properly either.

Despite the considerable criticism they get in the media, lawyers are held to very high ethical standards. For every example of misconduct reported in the media, there are literally thousands of honest and reputable attorneys that will do the right and ethical thing. Putting effort into choosing a lawyer can go a long way to eliminate the risks of retaining an unethical attorney.

SPECIALIZATION

Following trends in other professions, many lawyers today devote themselves to one area of law and present themselves as "experts" in that area. Because it is wise to get an attorney whose experience matches a company's particular need, many decision makers will be tempted to hire a lawyer described as an expert in his or her area of law. This may not always be the best course of action. The state of Minnesota only has certification standards for specialization in real estate and civil trials. Minnesota recognizes two national certifications for bankruptcy and criminal law. Outside these four areas, no lawyer should claim to be a specialist, specialized, or certified in any area of law, but some lawyers might use similar terminology. One attorney may call herself a tax expert because she has handled tax matters for over twenty years, while another attorney may call himself a tax expert because, although he only passed the bar last month and is still quite inexperienced, he plans to devote himself exclusively to tax matters. Clearly one expert is not equal to another. Buyer beware!

Another important point to keep in mind is that not all legal matters require the attention of a specialist. Just as one would not automatically turn to a medical specialist for a common cold, one need not turn to a legal specialist for every routine legal matter. Chances are good that if a local attorney engaged in the general practice of law has done a fine job on a variety of legal matters in the past, he or she can be counted on to handle routine legal matters in the future. Also, because most specialists will be clustered in larger cities, a business in a small community may choose to hire a generalist practicing locally for the ease and convenience of being able to work with a member of the community.

FIRM SIZE

Another important issue to consider is whether to go with a solo practitioner, a lawyer in a small firm, or a lawyer in a large firm. Recognize that in most cases it is an individual attorney who will work on a particular file and with whom the client will have the most interaction. An individual may not immediately notice a difference between a solo practitioner, a lawyer at a small firm, and a lawyer at a large firm. A solo practitioner or a lawyer practicing in a small group may be able to provide more personalized attention to a file but a larger firm can bring a depth of resources that most small firms cannot. Lawyers at large firms typically charge more for their services, however, so an individual may not want or need to pay extra for a relatively straightforward legal problem. Again, it all depends on the needs of the particular individual.

LOCATION

A lawyer's location is another obvious consideration. A lawyer in the client's hometown may not always be the best choice. If many meetings will take place in a city other than where the client lives, it may be advantageous to hire an attorney who lives in the other city. Most larger firms in Minnesota are centrally located in downtown office buildings in major cities. While these locations may provide the most convenient access to courthouses, banks, and corporate headquarters, they may not be the most convenient for the individual client. Most lawyers charge for transportation time and the time necessary for them to get to and from meetings and court appearances, so it may be wise to choose someone located near the courthouse or any other location where meetings will take place. If a particular matter will not require many meetings or trips to the courthouse, the convenience of a downtown office may be unnecessary. Of course, because nice office space downtown is usually more expensive than office space in a suburb or small town, downtown lawyers may have higher overhead expenses that they have to pass along to their clients.

STEP 3: INTERVIEWING THE ATTORNEYS

Once a businessperson has narrowed down his or her list to a few attorneys, he or she should then phone them individually and seek a personal consultation with each one. It is wise to ask on the phone whether the lawyer charges a fee for the initial consultation. As with any major purchase, a consumer of legal services is not obligated to hire the first attorney he or she sees.

INITIAL CONSULTATION

It is not reasonable for a business to expect free advice from a lawyer, but good attorneys will welcome the opportunity to spend time with a potential client answering questions and being compared with their peers because they know their knowledge and experience will show through. The initial consultation is no time to be shy. Years ago, many lawyers liked to think that they were above the need to market their practice or to pursue clients. Some law firms reflexively recoiled from the suggestion that a potential client would ask them to show why their firm was the best to handle a matter. Times have changed and lawyers today are accustomed to sitting down with potential clients to discuss representation.

An initial consultation can be more productive if the individual takes contracts, photographs, other relevant documents, and a list of questions to the meeting. At the initial interview the individual should be open and honest with the attorney. It is best not to embellish or hide facts because they may dilute the strength of a case. Some facts, such as the events in dispute occurring some time ago, may make a case impossible to win because of the statute of limitations, and the lawyer can explain that any money spent pursuing the claim would be money wasted. Some facts are less damaging than the individual assumes, and the lawyer can minimize their effect by acting quickly. The attorney may feel that a conflict of interest prevents him or her from representing the client. For example, the lawyer already represents the opposite party in a dispute. Most of what an individual tells a lawyer in an interview is confidential and protected by the attorney-client privilege.

Consulting a lawyer does not obligate the business to employ or to retain that lawyer. Most initial consultations are either free of charge or available for a small nominal fee, especially should the businessperson decide not to employ the attorney consulted. Some attorneys will charge for the initial consultation if they are subsequently hired.

It is important to note an important distinction between consulting an attorney and retaining that attorney. Only retaining an attorney obligates him or her to act on behalf of the client. Many Minnesotans have learned this lesson the hard way. They thought that consulting a lawyer about their legal problem meant that their case was being handled so they stopped taking steps to pursue a claim. Meanwhile the lawyer they consulted allowed the statute of limitations to run out on the claim because the lawyer believed that he or she had not been retained to act on the client's behalf. Many legal malpractice suits have centered on whether an original office visit with a lawyer constituted a consultation or a hiring. The lesson to learn is that before leaving a lawyer's office, the individual and the lawyer should be absolutely clear as to whether the lawyer has or has not been hired.

PERSONAL CHEMISTRY

So much of being a good attorney has to do with responsiveness, understanding of a client's particular situation, and the ability to communicate. The lawyer who has bad rapport with a client may not be an effective representative of the client's interests. Because each person is different, the chemistry between a client and an attorney is one of the most important elements of their relationship. Smart shoppers should ask many questions. Is the lawyer listening to the client's story or does he or she interrupt in the middle of sentences? Does he or she present a variety of options to pursue or does she insist there is only one right way to do everything? Does the lawyer try to dominate the conversation? Are the attorney's business philosophy and approach to risk-taking compatible with the client's attitude? Is the attorney open to working with in-house counsel to lower bills? Is this someone the client wants to spend time with? Gut feelings at this stage of the process can tell someone much about what it would be like to hire this person. After the decision is made to hire an attorney, the client has a right to expect that the attorney will spend time explaining the progress of matters he or she is working on and to involve the client at appropriate times. If the attorney is difficult to work with early on, it is a good bet the relationship will be tense later.

MALPRACTICE INSURANCE

It may be an uncomfortable subject to raise with an attorney whom one has just met for the first time, but it is important to determine whether he or she carries malpractice insurance. The financial losses stemming from a poorly handled case can be quite large. If the lawyer does not carry malpractice insurance, it may be impossible to recover any losses should the lawyer commit legal malpractice.

EXPERIENCE

Many individuals naïvely assume that the longer a lawyer has been in practice the more experience he or she has. This assumption is frequently unfounded. Relevant experience in a particular area of law is far more important than the total number of years that a person has practiced law. A young attorney whose practice has been narrowly focused on one area of law may have far more insight into how a problem should be handled than an attorney with more years of practice in a broad variety of legal matters. In addition, because laws change so quickly, in some cases a recent graduate may have greater knowledge of a particular area of law than a more senior attorney. The potential client should ask pointed questions about a lawyer's specific experience handling similar cases.

In some large firms, a senior partner may agree to handle a matter, then assign most of the work to less experienced associates. It pays to ask such an attorney who is going to work on a file, and discuss that person's experience and his or her success in representing cases or doing similar work. Still other lawyers may be eager to take on a case in an area of law in which they have little experience, reasoning that they can simply learn the relevant law as they go along. Not having experience in the relevant area of law need not rule out a lawyer. A lawyer inexperienced in one area of law may still be a terrific choice to handle a case, but it is appropriate to ask how long it will take the lawyer to learn the relevant laws and whether the client is expected to pay for the educational time.

ESTIMATE OF TIME

The lawyer ought to be able to estimate a timetable for completing the case. This will depend on many variables, including the complexity of the matter, whether the lawyer expects to go to trial, how cooperative all parties are, and the lawyer's workload. Asking for a timetable is likely to bring a number of these issues out into the open. A relatively simple matter may take a long time to complete if a particular lawyer is too busy to devote his or her full attention to it. A lawyer with very little experience may reveal that inexperience if he or she cannot describe the steps necessary to complete a task and estimate how long each will take.

COST

Money should be discussed at the initial meeting with an attorney. It is important to know for what will and what will not be charged and at what rates. Although a lawyer may not be able to give an exact cost, most lawyers with experience should be able to provide a ballpark estimate of their fees.

An individual should not feel uncomfortable comparison shopping for a lawyer. Hiring an attorney can be a major outlay of resources so, like any other expenditure, a businessperson should find out such details as how and how often bills are sent out, whether the firm requires a retainer, and whether the firm has minimum billing increments. Find out how often the lawyer sends out status reports about a case or matter. Finally, as with any business arrangement, get your agreement in writing. Lawyers have several different ways that a client may pay the fees for their services:

Flat Fees

The simplest fee payment option is the flat fee. A lawyer charging a flat fee simply quotes a fee for which he or she will do the work. Flat rates were traditionally quite rare. A lawyer often has no way of knowing for certain how complex a matter is until investigating it and can be understandably adverse to committing to a flat fee in advance. Recently the flat fee has been growing in popularity. Much of this growth is client-driven and stems from clients' desire to better predict and control the rising cost of legal representation. Today, lawyers are increasingly willing to discuss the possibility of a flat fee for relatively simple legal matters such as regulatory compliance filings or friendly acquisitions. The client should bear in mind, however, that some lawyers who advertise low flat fees for simple matters rarely ever find that a client has a simple matter. Sometimes the low advertised flat fees are merely a ploy to get a potential client in the door in hopes that, once in the office, the client can be convinced that his or her needs are actually far more complex and therefore justify much higher fees.

Hourly Rates

For many matters a lawyer will charge an hourly rate for time spent on a file. The hourly rate is usually a reflection of the lawyer's competence, experience, and overhead expenses. The lowest hourly rate is not necessarily the best deal for the business. An experienced lawyer with higher rates will usually be able to complete a matter more quickly than a less experienced lawyer with lower rates. A common complaint about hourly rates is that they give the lawyer no incentive to handle a matter in a timely fashion. After all, who wants to work quickly and efficiently if it means making less money? Paying for legal services at hourly rates is a time-honored tradition at American law firms which is unlikely to disappear soon, and can unfortunately open the door to much disagreement over how long it should have taken a lawyer to complete a task. Because law firms are under increasing pressure from clients to hold down their bills, today many attorneys are willing to discuss "blended rates," an arrangement whereby a partner's billing rate is blended with an associate's lower billing rate. Before agreeing to hire a lawyer to work for an hourly rate, it is appropriate to request a written estimate of the hours that will probably be needed, as well as an estimate of how much money will be necessary for miscellaneous expenses.

Retainer Fees

There are actually two kinds of retainer fees used in the legal community. The first is a variation of the flat fee. Rather than paying a lawyer a flat fee to handle a specific matter, some wealthy individuals or large corporations will simply pay an attorney a lump sum each year to retain that attorney for the year. In return for this kind of retainer fee, the lawyer agrees to be on call for any legal problems that arise or to manage routine day-to-day legal affairs. The average business does not have a sufficient volume of legal questions to require this type of set-up.

The more common retainer fee is actually just an advance on the hourly rate, described above. If it is the first time that a lawyer has represented a particular client or if there is any question about the client's ability to pay, the lawyer may insist upon the payment of a large retainer up front. This money is then placed in a special account and the costs of legal services provided are then deducted from that account. A client who agrees to pay this type of retainer is still entitled to periodic written statements detailing how much has been deducted from the account for legal services and, of course, the client is entitled to any money remaining in the account when legal representation has been concluded.

Contingent Fees

Another common legal fee arrangement is the contingent fee. Years ago, contingent fees were unheard of in the business context, but today more businesses are seeking these agreements from their legal counsel. The contingent fee is most common among personal injury attorneys who charge for their services by taking a percentage (the going rate is one-third) of whatever damages are recovered or the amount of money saved for the client, whether through an out-of-court settlement or a jury award. The percentage that a lawyer asks for depends on the difficulty of the issues, the amount of money at stake, and the skill and experience of the attorney. Essentially, when an individual asks a lawyer to take a case on a contingency basis, the lawyer is being asked to gamble on the outcome of the case. A case with only a very slight chance of success can consume a great deal of the lawyer's time and energy and yield no fee if the case is lost. In that case, an individual may need to offer a lawyer a larger percentage of the award in order to convince him or her to take that risk. Conversely, an individual with a case that is very likely to result in a large award and that presents few procedural difficulties may be able to bargain down the contingent fee to a smaller percentage of the award.

A person may be better off with a more experienced attorney because, although the fee will be higher, so will the award. If a less experienced attorney handles a lawsuit, and wins a $300,000 award, the client keeps $200,000 and the lawyer gets $100,000. But if an attorney whose superior legal talents result in an award of $600,000, the client keeps $400,000 and the attorney gets $200,000. Hiring the less experienced attorney would therefore cost the business the extra $200,000 it would have received if the more experienced lawyer had handled the case.

There are several reasons to be especially careful when hiring a lawyer to work on a contingent fee basis. Many law firms specializing in these kinds of cases make their money by handling a large number of cases and settling them quickly. Given the typical contingent fee arrangement, some lawyers are motivated to accept early settlement offers.

By settling early, these firms make a lot of money very quickly. This tactic is popular with some lawyers as they take a cut of the settlement at a time when they have few expenses and because they have not spent the time and money to fully prepare a case. Be wary of such firms. The client has the right to refuse any settlement offer made and should consider doing so, especially if the case is a strong one that may cause a jury to award a large sum of money. Remember that the law gives an individual only one chance to make a case before a jury. Only under very special circumstances can someone go back to court to ask a jury for more money just because the original award money ran out after a period of several years.

Although contingent fee agreements are quite popular with some attorneys, they are inappropriate in some types of cases, and ethics rules forbid lawyers from accepting a contingent fee arrangement in criminal cases and some divorce cases.

Variable Contingent Fees

A third payment option becoming fairly popular among some lawyers is the variable contingent fee arrangement. In this situation, the attorney's fees vary depending upon when the case is settled.

Typical arrangements specify that the attorney collects 20 percent if the case settles before initiating a formal lawsuit, 25 percent if the case settles within a year after a lawsuit is filed, and 33 percent of any damage award received any time after a year. With this type of arrangement, the lawyer has an incentive not to settle too early because the fee will be greater if a larger settlement can be won by going to trial.

It is wise to clarify the exact terms of a variable contingent fee arrangement before signing it. Almost all contingent fee agreements stipulate that the attorney's expenses are first deducted from any award won, and the remainder of the money is then split on the one-third/two-third basis. Thus the statement common in the advertisements of many lawyers, "no fee unless we win your case," does not mean that a client pays nothing for legal representation. A lawyer's fee will be a percentage of any award and therefore may be nothing, but win or lose, a client is almost always responsible for the attorney's costs. A client must make sure, therefore, that he or she fully understands what kinds of costs he or she is expected to pay before signing a contingent fee agreement. In an attempt to eliminate any misunderstanding about this, in 1993 the Minnesota Supreme Court changed the Lawyers' Rules of Professional Conduct to require attorneys who intend to charge fees to cover their expenses to disclose that fact in their advertisements.

Miscellaneous Expenses

Many disputes that clients have with lawyers over money stem from a misunderstanding of the difference between "fees" and "expenses." Regardless of which of the types of fee plans discussed above a client chooses, most lawyers will charge for their expenses in addition to their fees and regardless of the outcome of the case. Many a contingent fee client, lured by an attorney claiming, "no fees unless we recover for you," has been shocked to find out, after failing to recover any money on their claim, that they owe money to their lawyer. The client may indeed pay no fees unless the case is successful but may still be responsible for sizable expenses incurred handling the case, regardless of its outcome. For example, an attorney might charge for travel time, secretarial overtime, delivery services, court costs, filing fees, deposition fees, expert witness fees, investigation expenses, and the initial consultation. Many law firms bill incidentals such as photocopying and postage at rates far higher than what those services would cost at an independent copy center or post office, so it is important to discuss specific details. Also ask about referral fees. Some lawyers refer clients only to other lawyers who will split the fees with them. Thus the individual who employs a lawyer referred by another lawyer may be inadvertently paying for two attorneys but getting the services of only one.

BENEFITS OF THE PROCESS

The point of this three-step process is to educate businesses to become more sophisticated consumers of legal services, including referral services. The three-step process described above should begin with a list of names and, after diligent research and meetings, conclude with one name standing out among the others as the best choice. A decision maker should be able to cross some names off the list before actually meeting the lawyers, because after researching the names it will become apparent that some attorneys are inappropriate for the legal matter at hand. It is even possible that every name on the list will be crossed off for one reason or another, and the businessperson will have to return to step one and seek more names. For example, if it becomes apparent that a particular legal matter will require the services of a lawyer who litigates matters regularly in a courtroom and all of the attorneys on the list rarely see the inside of a courtroom, a businessperson should go back to a referral agency or to this book and specifically look for names of lawyers whose practices include litigation.

Chapter 1: Selecting & Managing Counsel

Unless the business is under extreme pressure to resolve a legal matter immediately, it is far better to spend time in choosing a good lawyer than to try and undo a poor decision later. If a businessperson chooses well, the job of working with counsel should be far easier. It is always the prerogative of the client to change lawyers before a legal matter has been concluded, but doing so can be costly and time consuming. If a client fires his or her attorney before a matter is settled, the attorney is owed for the reasonable value of the time that has been spent on the matter, even if a contingent fee agreement stated that the attorney would be paid only if the case were won. All of the files on the matter belong to the client and must be turned over to the client on termination of the lawyer's services.

CONTRACT LAW

A contract is a legally binding agreement between parties to do or not do something. Businesses need to enter into contracts for many reasons, so a good understanding of contract law is essential to succeed in business. There are several factors to look at to determine whether a contract has been made. Once a contract has been created, it must be determined if there are any issues that call into question its validity. Finally, if there has been a breach of the contract, there is a question of whether damages have occurred.

This chapter summarizes the elements of a contract, who can enter into contracts on behalf of a company, factors that may affect validity of a contract, and recovering damages if a contract is breached. One should always read and understand a document before agreeing to be held to its contents. Before one enters into a contract with major implications, an attorney experienced in the subject matter of the contract should be consulted.

CONTRACT COMPONENTS

There are three elements that must be present for a contract to exist: an offer, acceptance, and consideration.

OFFER

The first step to a contract is an offer. An offer is a statement, written or spoken, by a party of his or her intention to be held to a commitment upon acceptance of the offer. Many business owners have gotten into legal disputes because, during business negotiations, a customer believed an offer had been made when the business believed the parties were still only discussing possible options. A businessperson should carefully consider whether his or her statements or the statements of other parties constitute offers. There are a number of factors to look at to determine whether a statement constitutes an offer.

- Is the person making the offer serious? A business executive who jokingly states that he or she will sell a successful business in exchange for a good bottle of single malt scotch is not making an offer. On the other hand, a business executive who writes up an offer on a bar napkin may be perfectly serious. Courts look at the context in which the statement was made to determine whether it was a valid offer.

Chapter 2: Contract Law

- Does the statement show a willingness of the party to be held to its contents? A person requesting a price quote or opening negotiations is not making an offer. An advertisement is usually viewed as an invitation to an offer rather than an offer by itself.

- Does the statement contain definite terms with regard to the subject matter? Is the subject matter identified, are parties identified, is the price set, are quantities determined, and is time for performance stated? There should be enough information contained in the statement that, if needed, a court would be able to enforce the contract or determine the damages.

ACCEPTANCE

The second requirement for a valid contract is acceptance of the offer. In order for an acceptance of an offer to be effective, it must be made while the offer is still open. In some situations, the company making the offer gives a definite time frame (My company will sell you this computer software for $2000 but you must decide whether to buy it within two days). Other ways an offer may end include: the person making the offer withdraws the offer, the person who receives the offer rejects it, or reasonable time passes after the offer is made. If the subject matter of the offer is destroyed before acceptance, the offer terminates.

Unless an offer specifies otherwise, an offer can be accepted though the mail. An important rule known as the "mailbox rule" says that an acceptance is effective once it is put in the mailbox. If the offeror attempts to withdraw the offer after the acceptance is mailed but before it is received, the person accepting the offer can hold the offeror to the contract. For this reason, anyone making an offer should be aware that it might be accepted, by means of the mailbox rule, before the offeror knows of the acceptance. This can be problematic if the original offeror assumed the offer was rejected and has already found another buyer. To avoid possible confusion, some businesses will specify in an offer that acceptance of the offer is only effective upon receipt of the acceptance.

If a person changes the conditions of an offer in responding to the offer, the offer is rejected and the changed conditions constitute a counteroffer (I want to buy the software, but I will pay only $1500 for it). In this scenario, the person who made the original offer can respond to the counteroffer by accepting or rejecting it, or proposing yet another offer.

There are two ways a person can accept an offer, either by promising to do something, or by performing the desired act. In the first type, a customer promises to pay $2000 for computer software. This is a bilateral contract. In the second type, a business owner offers a contractor $1000 to replace ceiling tiles and the contractor replaces the tiles; the contractor accepted the offer by performing the act requested. This is a unilateral contract.

CONSIDERATION

Consideration is a legal concept which describes something of value that is given in exchange for a performance or a promise to perform. The presence of consideration distinguishes contracts from gifts. Consideration can be a promise to do something there is no legal obligation to do, or a promise to not do something there is a legal right to do. Promises to exchange money, goods, or services are forms of consideration. All parties in an agreement must give consideration in order to create a contract, but courts typically do not look at the adequacy of consideration unless there is evidence of some type of wrongdoing by the party benefiting most from the contract.

DEFENSES TO CONTRACT

Once it is determined that there is a contract, it must be determined whether there are any defenses which call into question the validity of the contract. There are some defenses which make the contract unenforceable (void) and other defenses which may give the parties the option to enforce the contract or not (voidable).

LEGALITY OF THE CONTRACT

Although two persons may exchange an offer, acceptance, and consideration, if the subject matter of the contract is illegal, an enforceable contract does not exist. For example, if a person offers to pay another person money for illegal drugs, this is a void contract.

CAPACITY OF THE PARTIES

In order to be bound to a contract, the parties must be competent to enter into the legal arrangement. Underage persons, persons who are mentally ill, and intoxicated persons are usually not bound by the contracts they enter. However, a minor may have the option of enforcing the contract.

AGENCY

Businesses sometimes challenge the validity of a contract by alleging that the person who signed for the company was not an agent of the company and therefore had no authority to act on the company's behalf. Agency is the legal status in which one person, the agent, has authority to conduct business for another party, the principal. Unless their business is very small, most business owners must rely on other people to conduct business and enter into contracts on behalf of the business. Because a principal is bound by contracts entered into by his or her agents, business operators should be familiar with the laws of agency.

An agent's authority to enter into contracts on behalf of the business can be actual, implied, or apparent. Actual authority is authority that the principal has intentionally given to an agent who has accepted it. The clearest example of creating actual authority is where a business owner hires someone to negotiate purchases for the company. Implied authority results because of the agent's relationship with the principal or the principal's business, from custom, or by acquiescence. For example, a principal might not have intentionally authorized an employee to make credit purchases for the business, but if the principal has repeatedly paid off debts incurred by the employee, he or she may inadvertently have created implied authority in that employee. Apparent authority can result when the principal acts in a way that would cause third parties reasonably to assume that the agent had authority. For example if a business owner is aware than an employee is claiming authority to act on behalf of the business, the principal may have an obligation to clarify that the employee is not authorized to enter into a contract on behalf of the business.

MISTAKE, DURESS, AND FRAUD

A mutual mistake by both parties to a contract on an important issue makes the contract unenforceable. However, a mistake by only one party does not necessarily make the contract void.

Duress is the use of force or pressure by one party to make the other party agree to the contract. The force does not have to be physical—one could be put under mental duress. The use of duress makes the contract voidable by the party under duress.

Fraud is the intentional misrepresentation of an important issue of the contract. The presence of fraud in a contractual proceeding makes the contract voidable by the party upon whom the fraud was perpetrated.

STATUTE OF FRAUDS

Contracts, in many instances, do not have to be in writing to be legally binding. However, a rule known as the Statute of Frauds requires that some contracts must be written to be valid. Contracts involving the sale of real estate, contracts concerning the sale of goods worth more than $500, contracts that cannot be performed within one year, contracts to pay off someone else's debts, leases for more than one year, and contracts concerning a marriage must be in writing.

PAROL EVIDENCE RULE

Although not a defense to a contract, the parol evidence rule may affect the contents of a contract and how a contract is enforced. The parol evidence rule applies once parties have come to a final, written contract. Once there is a final, written contract between the parties, the parol evidence rule forbids the introduction in a court proceeding of any previous agreements between the parties on the subject matter of the contract. The parol evidence rule permits the judge or jury in a contract dispute to look only at the written contract and not any previous discussions between the parties. The impact of the parol evidence rule is that all factors which are important to the agreement and that have been decided by the parties should be stated in the final, written contract. The parol evidence rule does not forbid the introduction of subsequent agreements between the parties.

CONTRACT TERMINATION

Once there is a valid contract between parties, it can end in several ways. A contract may have a limited time span and finish at the end of the stated time. If a person is hired to work for two weeks, the contract concludes at the end of two weeks. In many instances where there is a specific time frame stated in the contract, parties to the contract may have the option to extend the contract for a longer period of time. Contracts may also be project, not time, specific. Goods or services may be contracted for a project and upon the completion of the project, the contract for these goods or services ends. Parties to a contract may mutually agree to rescind the contract. In that case, the parties may agree on the duties and responsibilities of each party after the rescission.

A contract also may end because of a breach. A breach occurs when a person does not fulfill his or her responsibilities as promised in the contract. A breach may be minor or major. A minor breach is one that affects small, minor details of the agreement and may not affect the outcome of the contract. However, a major breach is one that does affect the subject matter of the contract and may affect the outcome of the contract. This is also known as a breach of a material issue. When there has been a breach in a contract, the question of damages is raised.

DAMAGES

The damages due to a party when there is a contract breach depend on many factors, including: which party breaches, what damages were incurred, what the contract states with regard to damages, whether the breach is material or not, and the subject matter of the contract. When a person is harmed by a breach, courts usually award only foreseeable damages. Foreseeable damages are those damages which the parties anticipate or should anticipate at the time the contract is formed.

MONEY DAMAGES

In most cases when an injury results from a contract breach, the injured party receives money damages. The court places the person in the position he or she would have been in if the contract had been performed. For example, if a business owner contracts with a roofer to put a new roof on a warehouse for $50,000, the roofer might stop in the middle of the job and refuse to finish the new roof. If the business owner finds another roofer to finish the job at an additional cost of $15,000, the damages are $15,000.

Although a person is normally entitled to the money difference between what was promised and what it costs to complete the promise, the injured party must mitigate to collect damages. Mitigation means the injured party takes reasonable steps to limit the extent of the injury and finish the job. So in the previous example, the business owner must make reasonable efforts to find another party to finish the roof and must take reasonable steps to protect inventory in the warehouse from exposure due to the lack of a roof. If the business owner refuses to look for another roofer and consequently inventory in the warehouse is ruined, the breaching roofer will probably be able to successfully defend against paying for the cost of the ruined goods.

SPECIFIC PERFORMANCE

There are some situations where money damages are inadequate. Typically in contracts involving the sale of land, awarding money damages for a breach does not put the nonbreaching party in the same position he or she would have been if the contract were fulfilled. Because real estate is unique, one cannot simply go out and buy property which is the same as originally contracted. In cases such as this, a remedy called specific performance may be awarded by the court. The court may order the breaching party to perform the duties required by the contract. The use of specific performance is rare. Only in cases where the subject matter of the contract is unique, and it is difficult to put a monetary amount on the damage incurred as a result of the breach, is specific performance ordered. Specific performance is not awarded in personal service contracts. So in the previous example, the court would not order the original roofer to complete the job.

LIQUIDATED DAMAGES

In an attempt to set monetary damage amounts in cases where it may be difficult, some contracts have provisions that specify the amount of damages in event of a breach. Such predetermined damages are called liquidated damages. An example is when a company puts down earnest money for space in a mall and later decides not to open a store at the mall. In a real estate contract with a liquidated damage provision, the business owner may forfeit the earnest money to the mall owners as a damage award.

RESCISSION

In most contract disputes, a court puts the nonbreaching party in the position he or she would have been in if the contract had not been breached. However, there are times when the court may place the party in the position he was in before the contract was executed. This remedy is known as rescission. In cases where there was a mutual mistake on the subject matter of the contract, the parties may be returned to their positions before the contract. In this case, if the parties have exchanged goods or money, those items are returned to the other party. This remedy may also be selected in cases where one party intentionally misrepresents a material fact.

MANDATORY ARBITRATION AND FORUM SELECTION

Parties to a contract will often agree in advance to arbitrate any disputes arising from the contract rather than going to court. Arbitration agreements usually specify that each party chooses one arbitrator and a third arbitrator is chosen by the first two arbitrators. Mandatory arbitration can save time and money, but business owners may want to have an attorney review the mandatory arbitration clause before signing a contract that includes one. Arbitration is discussed more fully in the Alternative Dispute Resolution Chapter.

Parties may also choose to include a forum selection clause in a contract. A forum selection clause stipulates that any legal action stemming from the contract will be brought in a particular court and that a particular jurisdiction's laws will govern. With a forum selection clause, a Minnesota business might be able to insure that it could defend itself in a Minnesota court applying Minnesota laws against any lawsuit arising from the contract. Such a clause could save the Minnesota business time and money should any disputes arise.

CHAPTER 3

MINNESOTA'S LEGAL & JUDICIAL SYSTEM

It may be useful for a person thinking about initiating a legal action to understand the legal and judicial system that exists in Minnesota. One of the most confusing aspects of the judicial system is that there are two separate systems: state and federal. The majority of cases are filed in state courts. This chapter discusses the state and federal systems and summarizes the jurisdictions of both. The Process of a Lawsuit Chapter outlines how a case goes through the state civil and criminal process. Claims which arise on Native American lands may be subject to tribal courts and not the state or federal courts.

As one may remember from civics class, there are three branches of government: legislative, executive, and judicial. The legislative branch creates the laws, the executive branch enforces the laws, and the judicial branch interprets the laws. Laws are also called statutes or codes. The executive branch can create rules or regulations to govern its administrative procedures and the judicial branch may also interpret these regulations.

When a case is brought before a court, the court applies the law to the facts of the case and a decision is made. There are many sources of law the court uses in making its decision: the Constitutions of both the United States and the state of Minnesota, statutes, regulations and prior decisions of its own or of other higher courts (case law). The way in which a court answers a legal question is binding on all other lower courts within that jurisdiction when faced with the same legal question. For example, if the Minnesota Supreme Court decides a legal question, all state courts in Minnesota must follow that decision. However, state courts in Wisconsin would not have to follow the Minnesota decision because they are in a different jurisdiction.

REPRESENTATION

Perhaps the first question a business person may ask is, "Do I really need a lawyer to handle my legal affairs?" The best answer is almost always yes. Occasionally, a business is able to rely on non-lawyers to handle some legal matters. For example, some companies hire paralegals to draft routine contracts. For most legal matters, however, hiring a lawyer is essential. Obviously, when a business is sued or thinking of bringing a lawsuit, the business should have an attorney representing its interests. In rare instances, a businessperson may be permitted to represent himself or herself. For example, landlords can appear in conciliation court without a lawyer. In the majority of cases, however, a company hires counsel to represent itself and in some cases, must be represented by counsel.

Chapter 3: Minnesota's Legal & Judicial System

JURISDICTION

When a person decides to file a legal action, he or she must decide in which court system to file the case. The court in which a person files a case depends on which court has jurisdiction over such cases. Jurisdiction determines whether a particular court has the power and authority to decide a case. This is subject matter jurisdiction. If a court does not have subject matter jurisdiction, it may not decide a case. A court must also have personal jurisdiction over the defendant in a case. There are different ways to have personal jurisdiction, including if a defendant resides or has a business within the court's geographical region. For example, a Minnesota plaintiff cannot bring an action in Minnesota district court against a defendant who lives and works in another state, if that defendant has no contact with the state of Minnesota. Jurisdiction is set in law, constitutions, or case law. It is possible to have courts with overlapping jurisdiction and a person has a choice of in which court to file an action.

There are three types of subject matter jurisdiction: exclusive, general, and limited. Exclusive jurisdiction means that only a particular court can decide a case. An example of exclusive subject matter jurisdiction is bankruptcy court. Only in a federal bankruptcy court can a person file a bankruptcy action. State courts have no jurisdiction in bankruptcy cases. General jurisdiction means that a court has the ability to hear and decide a wide range of cases. Unless a law or constitutional provision denies them jurisdiction, courts of general jurisdiction can handle any kind of case. The Minnesota district courts are general jurisdiction courts. Limited jurisdiction means that a court has restrictions on the cases it can decide. Conciliation court is a court of limited jurisdiction because it can only hear and decide cases which claim damages of $7500 or less.

VENUE

Venue is frequently confused with jurisdiction. While jurisdiction asks whether a court system has authority to hear a case, venue asks which court within a jurisdiction should hear and decide a case. In Minnesota, a case is usually brought in the county in which the claim originates or where one or more defendants resides. For example, if a person is hit by a car in Duluth, and the car was driven by a person from St. Paul, an action against the driver could be filed in either St. Louis County (Duluth) or in Ramsey County (St. Paul). Change of venue can be requested by either of the parties. For example, a corporate defendant in Rochester might request a change of venue to Moorhead because adverse publicity in Rochester makes it impossible for the corporation to get a fair trial in Rochester or because most of its files are located in Moorhead. The defendant could not request that the trial be moved to Milwaukee because the Wisconsin court lacks jurisdiction.

STATE AND FEDERAL COURTS

As previously mentioned, there are two separate court systems: state and federal. Which court system a person enters depends on a number of factors: whether a court has exclusive jurisdiction over the subject matter of the case, the amount of damages involved, and the locations of the parties in the case.

STATE COURTS

Minnesota has three levels to its court system: district courts, Court of Appeals, and the Supreme Court. There are two special courts which are not in the judicial system and were created by the executive branch to address specific areas—Tax Court and Workers' Compensation Court.

Business Guidebook to Law & Leading Attorneys

Minnesota has divided its 87 counties into ten judicial districts. Each judicial district is composed of anywhere from one to 17 counties. Each district court hears cases in each county within its district at some time. As previously mentioned, the district court has general subject matter jurisdiction and handles a wide variety of cases, both civil and criminal. The district courts are courts of original jurisdiction, that is, cases start there. That is where trials are held, witnesses testify, evidence is presented, and judgments are rendered. Depending on the size of the district, some have created specific divisions to handle certain matters such as probate and family. Conciliation court is a division of district court and appeals from conciliation court are heard there. A person who loses a case in district court may appeal it. Appeals from district court are typically brought to the Minnesota Court of Appeals.

The Minnesota Court of Appeals was created in 1983 to assist the Minnesota Supreme Court with its workload. Unlike the district courts which hear trials with witnesses, jurors, and evidence, the Court of Appeals' primary function is to determine whether there has been an error at the district court level, and if so, to remedy it. The Court of Appeals reviews the transcript from the district court and may also consider written and oral arguments. The Court of Appeals can reverse or affirm a district court ruling or send it back to the district court for additional action. The Court of Appeals hears most appeals from the district courts unless the law specifically states that a particular appeal goes directly to the Minnesota Supreme Court. The Court of Appeals is made up of 16 judges who are divided into rotating three-judge panels. These panels travel throughout the state hearing appeals. Appeals from this court are sent to the Minnesota Supreme Court.

The Minnesota Supreme Court is the highest court in the state. Like the Court of Appeals, it does not hold trials but reviews transcripts, takes written and oral arguments, and determines whether there has been an error at the district court level. It may also reverse, affirm, or remand a case. The Supreme Court is the rule-making body for the state courts and has administrative responsibility for the operation of the state court system. The Minnesota Supreme Court is composed of seven justices who hear appeals in St. Paul. A Minnesota Supreme Court decision is a final decision in Minnesota and may be appealed to the United States Supreme Court only if there is a federal issue involved.

Federal Courts

The federal court system hears both civil and criminal cases and is also broken down into three levels. There are generally three ways a case can be filed in federal court: the case involves a federal law, the case raises a question of United States Constitution interpretation, or the case involves parties from more than one state and the amount in question is more than $50,000.

The federal government has divided the United States into federal judicial districts. The state of Minnesota makes up one federal judicial district. The federal district court for Minnesota has offices in Minneapolis, St. Paul, and Duluth. Like the state district courts, the federal district court holds trials in cases over which it has jurisdiction. Appeals from the federal district court go to the Eighth Circuit Court of Appeals.

Included in the federal system is the bankruptcy court. Federal bankruptcy courts have exclusive jurisdiction over bankruptcy matters. There are four bankruptcy court offices in Minnesota—Minneapolis, St. Paul, Duluth, and Fergus Falls.

The federal government groups the United States' federal judicial districts into circuits, and each circuit has a court of appeals. Minnesota is in the Eighth Circuit along with Arkansas, Iowa, Missouri, Nebraska, North Dakota, and South Dakota. The Eighth Circuit Court of Appeals hears the appeals from federal district courts within the circuit. As in the Minnesota Court of Appeals, the Eighth Circuit Court of Appeals does not try cases, but only reviews cases from lower courts within the circuit. The Eighth Circuit Court of Appeals has an office in St. Paul and its main office in St. Louis, Missouri. Appeals from the Eighth Circuit Court of Appeals are heard at the United States Supreme Court.

The United States Supreme Court hears appeals from the circuit courts of appeal and states' Supreme Courts, and other cases in which it has jurisdiction—cases between states, for example. The court is made up of nine justices and is based in Washington, D.C. The Supreme Court has very broad discretion to decide which cases it will review and only a small percentage of the cases appealed to the United States Supreme Court are actually heard. As with other appellate courts, the refusal to hear an appeal lets stand the lower court's ruling.

CHAPTER 4

PROCESS OF A LAWSUIT

The American legal system uses an adversary model to settle disputes. This model allows opposing parties to present their cases to an impartial third party who renders a decision. The adversary process determines the facts of the case, determines the governing law, applies the law to the facts, and provides a judgment.

Our legal system makes several distinctions between civil and criminal cases. Civil cases resolve private conflicts between people, businesses, and the government. Criminal cases involve the enforcement of a law by the government. Most lawsuits, whether civil or criminal, are resolved before trial. Disputes may be resolved before any legal action is filed, after legal action is filed in court, or while a trial is in process but before the judge or jury renders a decision. Most cases have to be filed within the time limits set by law. These limits are known as the statutes of limitation. The time limitations vary depending on the type of legal claim filed. If a case is not filed within the time period set by law, one loses the right to file a lawsuit.

This chapter outlines the process of a case through the civil and criminal court system. It also outlines the trial process. Finally, it discusses the use of conciliation court.

The Minnesota's Legal & Judicial System Chapter discusses the state and federal court systems in Minnesota. Also, see specific subject matter chapters for more information, including the Criminal Law Chapter and the Personal Injury Defense Law Chapter. The Alternative Dispute Resolution Chapter discusses options for resolving disputes outside the courtroom.

CIVIL PROCESS

Civil cases make up the majority of cases filed. Examples of civil cases include: personal injuries, contract disputes, landlord-tenant disputes, adoptions, and marriage dissolutions (divorce). In civil cases where damage is done to a party, that party can claim money damages. However, depending on the case, a party may ask for something other than money damages. For a discussion of damages in contract disputes, see the Contract Law Chapter. A person may ask the court to issue an injunction against another party. An injunction bars a person from doing a specific act. The court may issue a restraining order restricting the defendant's actions until the case is resolved. For example, if a person signs a contract to buy a house from the homeowner and the owner turns around and sells the house for a second time to another person, the first buyer may ask the court to restrain the seller from completing the sale to the second buyer until the case between the first buyer and the seller is resolved.

On rare occasions, civil cases may be filed as class actions. Class actions arise when there is a common question of law and fact for a large number of persons. There is a special process to go through for a class action to be established. This certification process can be lengthy. Recent examples of class actions brought in Minnesota include breast implant cases and real estate dual agency cases.

The burden of proof in a civil case is on the party who initiates the case, the plaintiff. The plaintiff must prove his or her case by a preponderance of evidence. This means that the party in a case who presents the more convincing evidence wins the case. The plaintiff's evidence must be more convincing than the evidence presented by the opposing party, the defendant.

Civil juries may include only six jurors and are not required to reach a unanimous verdict. If five of the six jurors agree on a case resolution, it may be enough for a verdict. A person is limited to bringing one legal action for damages arising from the same circumstances.

CIVIL PRETRIAL PROCESS

As previously mentioned, a civil case is a private dispute between two or more parties. The following is an outline of the steps one may take if a civil action is filed in a Minnesota district court.

The plaintiff has his or her attorney prepare a document called a complaint. The complaint states what the dispute is about, why the defendant is responsible, and asks the court to take a stated action, such as awarding damages. The complaint, along with a summons, is delivered to the party against whom the the action has been filed. A summons is a written order stating that a defendant must answer the plaintiff's complaint. There are several procedural requirements for serving a summons. The party served is the defendant. The defendant has a specific period of time to respond to the complaint. The defendant's written response is an answer. The answer admits or denies allegations in the complaint, states any defenses to the plaintiff's complaint, and asks the court to decide in favor of the defendant. The defendant may also state any claims he or she has against the plaintiff. These claims by the defendant against the plaintiff are called counterclaims. The plaintiff is given a specific period in which to respond to the defendant's counterclaims. If the defendant does not respond to the complaint, the plaintiff can win the case by default. The complaint, answer, and any counterclaims are called the pleadings. These documents are eventually filed in district court.

If it appears that based on all the information presented, one side clearly has the advantage, that side will often file a motion for summary judgment, which requests that the judge dismiss the case if he or she decides that there is no triable issue of fact. At this same time one party may file a motion to dismiss the case. There are a number of grounds on which a party may move to dismiss a case. For example a party may claim the court does not have jurisdiction, or that the action was brought too late under the statute of limitations, which vary in length depending on the type of case in Minnesota.

There are several steps before a case goes to trial. To assist the parties in preparing their cases and learning about the other side's case, a process called discovery occurs. During discovery, each side may ask the other to answer written questions, interrogatories, provide copies of documents, or answer questions orally under oath, the deposition. If the defendant is a corporation or partnership it must designate someone to speak on its behalf. A deposition is usually held in an attorney's office and recorded by a stenographer. A deposition can be used to impeach a witness during the trial if testimony at trial is different from the testimony given at the deposition. Each side may also make motions to the court asking it to settle legal questions that arise. If a settlement is not arranged during this pretrial process the parties proceed to trial. An outline of the trial process follows the Criminal Pretrial Process section.

CRIMINAL PROCESS

Unlike a civil case, which is a private dispute, criminal cases involve persons who are charged by the government with a violation of the law. Examples of criminal cases are assault, burglary, embezzlement, rape, and murder. Crimes in Minnesota are divided into categories ranging from the most serious crimes to less serious crimes. The most serious crimes are called felonies. Murder and arson are felonies. A person convicted of a felony may be sent to prison for a year or more and receive a fine. The next level of crime is called a gross misdemeanor. A person convicted of a gross misdemeanor may be sent to jail for up to a year and receive a fine. The next level of crime is a misdemeanor. A person convicted of a misdemeanor may be sent to jail for up to 90 days and receive a fine. Other violations, such as parking and moving violations, are called petty misdemeanors. A person guilty of these offenses cannot be sent to jail but can be fined.

The burden of proving a case against a defendant in a criminal proceeding is on the party bringing the charges, the prosecutor. A criminal defendant does not have to prove his or her innocence; the prosecutor must prove that the defendant is guilty. Decisions in a criminal proceeding are based upon a different standard than civil cases. In order for a person to be found guilty of a crime, the prosecution must prove the defendant is guilty beyond a reasonable doubt. The judge or jury must have no reasonable doubt to find a defendant guilty.

The number of jurors in a criminal case is 12, and unlike a civil proceeding, all jurors must reach a guilty or not guilty verdict. If a jury fails to reach a unanimous verdict, it is called a hung jury and a mistrial is declared. If a mistrial is declared, a new trial may be held.

Minnesota has sentencing guidelines that judges follow when sentencing a convicted offender. The guidelines are based on the seriousness of the crime committed and the offender's criminal history.

CRIMINAL PRETRIAL PROCESS

The following is an outline of the pretrial procedures for a felony criminal case filed in Minnesota district court.

When a crime is committed, the police conduct an investigation. When a person has been identified as the probable perpetrator of the crime, the evidence linking that person to the crime is presented to either a prosecutor, in this case, the county attorney, or in some instances, a grand jury. The prosecutor can file a complaint against the defendant or the grand jury can indict a person. Based upon the complaint or indictment, a warrant for arrest or a summons to appear in court is issued to the suspect. Once a suspect is arrested, he or she is charged with the crime. If police wish to question a suspect, he or she must be given Miranda warnings, advising the suspect that he or she does not have to answer the questions and has the right to an attorney. If the defendant is held in jail, he or she makes a court appearance at which bail is set. The amount of bail set depends on several factors including the likelihood that the defendant will return for future proceedings, the seriousness of the crime, and the risk to others should the defendant be released.

Most defendants want to be represented by an attorney, although they have a right to represent themselves. If a defendant wants to be represented by an attorney but cannot afford one, the court appoints a public defender to represent the defendant. At the next court appearance, the judge reviews the evidence against the suspect to make sure there is probable cause to believe the defendant committed the offense. At the same hearing, the defendant is arraigned. The judge reads the charges to the defendant, and the defendant answers either guilty or not guilty. If the defendant pleads guilty, the next step is sentencing. If the defendant pleads not guilty, his or her next appearance in court is called an omnibus hearing. This hearing resolves constitutional issues raised by the defendant. Issues raised here include legality of a search, coercion of a confession, or unconstitutional arrest. A judge rules on the issues raised. Charges may be dropped against a defendant based on the rulings of the judge at the omnibus hearing. At any stage in the proceeding, the defendant and prosecutor can engage in plea bargaining. During plea bargaining, a defendant may agree to plead guilty to a lesser criminal charge in exchange for dropping the more serious charge. If there is a guilty plea, there is a hearing to determine whether to accept the plea. Like a guilty plea at an earlier stage, the next step is sentencing.

Before a defendant is sentenced, there is a pre-sentence investigation. As stated before, Minnesota judges have guidelines to follow when sentencing criminals. There are some instances when a judge may stray from the guidelines, but the judge must state his or her reasons for not following the guidelines.

If a defendant does not plead guilty during pre-trial process and charges are not dropped by the prosecutor, the next step is a trial.

TRIAL PROCESS

Whether a case is civil or criminal, the basic outline of a trial is similar. The decision maker in a trial can be either a judge or a jury. There are rights to a jury trial in many cases, but this right may be waived by the parties. If a jury trial is requested, the first step is selecting a jury. A group of persons selected for jury duty is brought into the courtroom and asked questions by the judge and attorneys for both sides. The questioning is to determine whether a person can be a fair and impartial juror. A person who cannot be fair may be removed for cause. Others may be eliminated from the jury by the attorneys without reason. This is known as a peremptory challenge. Each attorney has a limited number of peremptory challenges that he or she may make. When a jury is selected, the members are sworn in.

The next step is the opening statement. The opening statement allows each side to tell the jurors about the case, what to expect, and what each side intends to prove. The plaintiff in a civil case and the prosecutor in a criminal case give their opening statements first.

After the opening statements, testimony begins. The plaintiff or prosecutor, whichever the case may be, calls witnesses to the stand and begins questioning them. The questioning of a witness by the party who asked him or her to testify is called direct examination. The opposing side also has the opportunity to question the witnesses; this questioning is called cross-examination. After cross-examination, the first party may question the witness again in rebuttal.

After the plaintiff or prosecution is done presenting its case, it is the defendant's turn. This time, the defense calls and questions witnesses, and the prosecution cross-examines them. Attorneys for either side may make objections to questions that the opposing side asks or evidence the opposing side wants to introduce. There are rules on what information is admissible in court, and the judge follows these rules when resolving any objections.

After both sides have presented their case, attorneys give closing arguments. In closing, each attorney summarizes the facts of the case and states why his or her side should prevail. Finally, the judge gives instructions to the jury on the law to be applied in the case. After receiving the judge's instructions, the jury retires to decide the issues in the case. As mentioned before, a jury need not reach a unanimous decision in a civil case, but it is required to reach a unanimous verdict in a criminal case. If a party believes that there was an error at trial, he or she can appeal the decision to a higher court. However, a prosecutor cannot appeal a not guilty verdict. Discussion of courts of appeals is contained in the Minnesota's Legal and Judicial System Chapter.

CONCILIATION COURT

Conciliation court is generally thought of as being of interest primarily to consumers because conciliation court cases involve relatively small amounts of money. Businesses should be familiar with conciliation courts, however, because they are often defendants in actions brought in conciliation court. Any person age 18 or older, company, governmental agency, or organization can be a party to an action in conciliation court. Conciliation court has limited jurisdiction and only hears cases where the amount of damages claimed is $7500 or less. A person does not need to be represented by an attorney in conciliation court and attorney participation is limited. The procedures have been simplified so that a plaintiff can represent himself or herself. Common issues resolved in conciliation court include damage to rental property, nonpayment of debts, and dishonored checks.

A person who wishes to file a claim in conciliation court fills out a standard conciliation court form in the county where the defendant lives or where the claim arose. Upon filling out the form, he or she must sign it before a notary public or a court deputy. The person must also pay the filing fee. The amount of the fee depends on the amount claimed. If a plaintiff wins his case, the court can ask the defendant to reimburse the plaintiff for this fee.

After the form is filled out and the fee is paid, the court administrator's office mails notice of the hearing to the plaintiff and defendant. When a defendant receives a conciliation court notice, he or she has the option of filing a counterclaim against the plaintiff. The defendant pays a fee for any counterclaims. If the counterclaim is more than $7500, the case will be transferred to district court. If a defendant fails to appear at the hearing, the plaintiff may win the case by default.

At the hearing, the plaintiff and defendant appear before a judge. The judge asks the plaintiff to state his or her case, then the defendant. After the judge has heard both parties, he or she may ask the parties questions. The judge does not make a decision at the time of the hearing. When the judge makes a decision, notice of the decision is mailed to both parties. A party who is dissatisfied with the judge's decision may appeal the decision to the district court. At the district court, a new trial is held.

A party who wins a conciliation court case must collect the money himself or herself. The court cannot collect the judgment for the prevailing party. There is a separate procedure to follow for collection. A conciliation judgment is valid for ten years.

RECOVERING FEES

In the American legal system, each side is generally responsible for its own legal costs. This means that in business litigation, the prevailing party generally pays its own legal fees. Exceptions to this rule are sometimes provided by statute or by agreement between the parties. For example, some civil rights laws award legal fees to a prevailing party who sues an employer for illegal discrimination.

Occasionally, business contracts will include provisions requiring the losing party to pay the prevailing party's legal fees in any dispute arising out of the contract. Such legal fee provisions generate a great deal of disagreement in the legal profession. Some lawyers insist upon them in every contract they draft, while other lawyers counsel their clients never to sign a contract that contains one. It is important to realize that legal fee provisions are a sword that can cut both ways. The loser winds up paying the winner's legal fees, but there is no way to know whether the side that drafts the provision will be the winner in any disagreement. However one feels about them, legal fee provisions are now included in most printed leases, promissory notes, and other business contracts. Because legal fees can be very expensive, it is worth considering carefully the possible effect of such a provision before signing an agreement that contains a legal fee provision.

SETTLING OUT OF COURT

A business person should never lose sight of one option that remains open throughout the dispute resolution process—settlement. Often the client needs to keep settlement in mind because most lawyers are trained to solve problems in court rather than out of court. A lawyer who has invested time and energy into preparing for trial may be unlikely to recommend settlement. In addition, lengthy litigation usually means higher fees for the lawyer. Human nature being what it is, lawyers may not be quick to point out when their own services are no longer necessary. The client may need to remind his or her lawyer that the primary objective is a satisfactory resolution of the dispute as soon as possible, not necessarily total victory at any cost.

It is a wise idea to include settlement strategies in early discussions with the attorney one hires to handle a matter. As time passes and legal fees mount, settlement may become an increasingly attractive option to proceeding to court. If clear goals are set from the start, and those goals are periodically reviewed, it will often be easier to settle later. If the parties do reach a settlement agreement, each side's attorney should be involved in drafting and reviewing the settlement papers before signing. It is possible for a party to agree to settle a matter without admitting fault and without compromising its position in any other disputes.

CHAPTER

5

ALTERNATIVE DISPUTE RESOLUTION

By Dwight Oglesby*

For hundreds of years clients, judges, and lawyers have complained about the cost, inefficiency, acrimony, and risk of litigation. Everyone involved with civil litigation professes to deplore its harmful side effects, but until recently no one has done much about it. The judiciary is leading the call for change, even as clients are demanding it. Most lawyers agree that change would be positive. The time for that change is upon us.

The purpose of this chapter is to help business decisionmakers understand the current status of alternatives to litigation and deal with a litigation system that, like all established systems, will resist the change that seems to be coming. In the modern civil litigation environment, the knowledgeable decisionmaker can and must insist on using options that have the potential to reduce some of the present problems of litigation. Courts in many states, including Minnesota, are encouraging alternatives to traditional litigation and lawyers must either endorse the new approach or risk losing the business of increasingly knowledgeable and assertive clients.

WHAT IS ALTERNATIVE DISPUTE RESOLUTION?

Simply stated, alternative dispute resolution (ADR) is the process of resolving disputes without going to trial in front of a judge or jury. ADR is typically cheaper and more confidential than the public trial process. In recent years caseloads in most courts have grown significantly, causing major delays and frustrations to clients, but to date ADR has been used in only a minority of cases. The reason for this inconsistency is historical, institutional and financial.

Before courts became overcrowded, law schools trained lawyers exclusively in the adversarial method. The adversarial system of jurisprudence is based on the concept that justice will emerge best if competing adversarial parties, represented by lawyers, present their admittedly biased version of a case to a judge or jury. The evidence is then subjected to the vital process of cross-examination in which each side has the opportunity to expose the flaws in an opponent's position. There is much more to modern litigation in its present advanced and complex state of evolution, but the fundamental adversarial concept is pretty straightforward. In fact, the system works quite well in some cases, particularly when cost and relationships between opponents is not a major concern. In many cases, however, the cost of litigation combat is prohibitive and the fighting and acrimony inherent in the process destroys relationships that could otherwise be preserved, be they personal, family or business. This longstanding litigation system is familiar to judges and litigators and has been in place for many years. Changing that established system is difficult.

Sophisticated parties, particularly corporations which are constantly in litigation, are now realizing the huge cost involved in that process and are looking for alternatives to the traditional combative approach. The training and traditions of lawyers and the courts is a powerful enough force against change but there is another one as well—the financial pressure of legal fees and other costs. No matter how dependable and honest a lawyer may be, the fact of the matter is that the existing litigation system can be very profitable for lawyers. Litigation must, of necessity, finance the huge support system surrounding it. This support system includes transcribers of testimony, paralegals, printers, accountants, and expert witnesses who will testify about and support opposing views on virtually any subject known to civilization.

Change is coming, however, from the top. In states like Minnesota, the courts have adopted rules that require lawyers and judges to make sure that clients understand that there are alternatives to traditional litigation. In each civil case in Minnesota, the parties must file a plan of ADR with the court. This plan must be approved by the trial judge. The parties and their lawyers must then make a good faith effort to settle the case.

Clients now are going to have to decide how to proceed with ADR when their lawyers present it to them. This chapter provides an overview of ADR options and can help businesspersons make decisions in consultation with their lawyers. The chapter addresses how to choose the type of ADR that will be most effective in a particular matter and discuss the characteristics of an effective mediator, arbitrator, or other neutral party who can help in ADR. There will be many exceptions to the general statements of this chapter, however, and readers should always make ADR decisions only with the advice and counsel of their lawyers, whose enthusiastic participation is essential to the success of any alternative to traditional litigation.

ADR AND THE SETTLEMENT PROCESS

The vast majority of lawsuits settle prior to trial, usually after a case has worked its way to near the head of the judge's docket and near to the trial date. That is the point at which judges, attorneys, and clients give settlement the most time and attention. It is also the point at which substantial fees have been paid, discovery is complete, and opposing arguments have been heard. In addition, sufficient time often has passed for emotional wounds to heal and for clients to have begun addressing new issues in their lives or businesses. ADR is one device to speed the settlement along.

Typically, ADR accelerates the point in the process at which settlement occurs. ADR may be used to avoid litigation entirely, but failing that, ADR is an effective way to decrease the time and money spent in litigation. This can result in large savings and better results than having a judge or jury make a decision for the parties.

The most frequently used methods of ADR are mediation, arbitration, and mediation-arbitration. Additional types of ADR include mini-trials, moderated settlement conferences, neutral fact findings, consensual special magistrates and summary jury trials. All of these have their place in the ADR process, but this article focuses on the role of mediation and arbitration to highlight their advantages and disadvantages.

THE ROLE OF JUDGES IN ADR

Judges properly want to devote their time to hearing arguments, reviewing briefs and trying those cases which cannot settle. ADR can help them manage their caseloads by enabling them to devote their time to those cases which need input of a judicial nature, as contrasted with cases that simply need concentrated settlement efforts.

ADR clears cases through the system more rapidly, freeing judges to focus their expertise and energies on issues which are the most complex, significant or resistant to settlement. The faster cases move through the system due to settlement, the better the judicial system's reputation, because the parties resolve their own matters and reduce delays. ADR is a powerful tool for judges to use in managing their caseloads and ADR usually reduces the total costs for litigants.

ARBITRATION

Most clients and lawyers have some familiarity with arbitration, which is simply a private trial in which a third party decides the outcome of a case after lawyers present evidence. In many cases, a panel of arbitrators is chosen to hear evidence. The panel then issues an opinion which usually is binding on the parties. Appeal rights are typically limited unless some very onerous showings are made, such as a conflict of interest, fraud, or other dishonesty. A simple mistake of law or fact is typically not enough to qualify for appeal. Because an appeal is rarely available, the parties have the benefit of certainty after an arbitration, but they risk living with an errant decision.

Because of the absence of appeal, the choice of arbitrators is crucial. The General Mills Corporation, for example, has for many years required all its suppliers and contractors to submit disputes to arbitration. There is, however, a strict requirement that arbitrators have a background in and knowledge of the business. In other words, an arbitrator skilled only in securities law would not be used to resolve a dispute over the price of flour.

Experience confirms the wisdom of using arbitrators who are knowledgeable about the subject of the dispute. In one case, complex engineering and cost accounting issues were arbitrated by a panel which included a senior partner in a law firm and a retired agribusiness executive. The panel simply did not have the experience to make a ruling without a lengthy and expensive educational process. This lack of experience increased the costs dramatically and the prevailing party received an award only after two years of hearings and $250,000 in legal fees. Having several million dollars at risk without possibility of appeal is a harrowing experience which most clients and lawyers want to avoid.

Nevertheless, there are many cases in which arbitration is appropriate if speed is desired and the parties are willing to risk living with a third party's decision. The securities and construction industries, for example, have utilized arbitration very successfully for many years.

It should be noted, however, that there has recently been significant criticism of companies which require the use of arbitration to settle internal disputes as a condition of employment. For example, plaintiffs in sexual harassment cases are claiming that the arbitrators chosen tend to be older men who are not sensitive to the concerns of women or sexual minorities. Many companies are reconsidering their approach to arbitration to resolve employment disputes.

The decision to use arbitration often is determined by a careful assessment of risk and a mutual recognition that each party shares some of the responsibility for the dispute. It works well when the form of ADR is matched properly with the type of dispute, but litigants should be aware that ADR is not a panacea for litigation.

MEDIATION

Mediation is different from arbitration in that the parties craft their own settlement terms with the assistance of a neutral mediator. The mediation process is flexible and can be tailored to each individual situation. In a typical commercial dispute mediation, attorneys for the parties present a brief statement of the case. This is an excellent opportunity for the parties to listen to each other's positions and size up each other's lawyers. It usually occurs after enough time has passed for tempers to have cooled, enabling litigants to be practical about the future costs and risks of litigation. While all of the parties usually meet together at the outset, they will often meet privately with the mediator after the initial case statements. This encourages candor and helps the mediator identify factual discrepancies and substantive issues.

A mediation is often the first chance for the parties to tell a disinterested party their version of the issues. Parties usually want to tell a neutral party their version of the facts and get a reaction before serious negotiating begins. Once they do so, pent up anger and frustration is less likely to block settlement efforts.

Creativity in settlement discussions is typically best when the decisionmakers participate directly in the process rather than sending a proxy. They know and understand the elements of the dispute with an intimacy that only comes from living through the dispute. Lawyers are essential to this process because they can point out the legal risks of tentative settlement proposals and help the litigants focus their energy and creativity on solutions that meet both their substantive and legal needs.

In a typical commercial case, the mediator will shuttle between conference rooms, trying to identify the core issues, while obtaining agreement on tangential issues. In this way, a mediator can take the pulse of the parties and, after a few hours, begin to help the parties propose various settlement options. In addition, the mediator can take a variety of steps which may break an apparent impasse. For example, the parties can be called together as a group to talk through the problem or the attorneys can meet separately to thrash out legal issues and test the strength of their own convictions about the success of arguments to be made. The parties can meet in private or with the mediator to determine if breakthroughs are possible. Sometimes an apology or expression of willingness to understand an adversary's position can be the needed catalyst for a successful mediation.

Absent such emotional breakthroughs, the mediation process can be a hard-boiled dollars and cents risk/reward evaluation. In an informal mediation setting, this can be particularly productive because various options can be tried on for size and rejected for better alternatives. The mediation becomes a classic negotiation with the risks of litigation being balanced against the benefits of a thoughtful settlement agreement. Only the litigants can accomplish this but they do it best with the active participation of their lawyers.

The kind of person litigants should choose as a mediator will vary, of course, depending on the dispute at hand and the personalities involved. A mediator should be a good listener and creative in proposing solutions. It is essential also for a mediator to be able to listen well and be able to identify the issues which are truly important and fundamental. A good mediator will identify and articulate the fundamental underlying interests of the parties and help the parties shed themselves of the roadblocks created by emotion or misplaced assumptions.

A mediator should also be someone with sufficient experience to command the respect of the parties and their lawyers. A recommendation by a judge is often useful. The parties should consider several options and be willing to interview several mediators before making a decision with the advice and counsel of their lawyers.

A significant benefit of mediation is that the litigants maintain confidentiality and control over the terms of settlement as well as the settlement process itself. This can be very important if the parties want to avoid a public airing of their disputes. Mediation also gives the parties an opportunity to size up their cases and their lawyers in an informal and confidential setting. And, as important as anything, mediation is often the first time the parties really listen to each other in a meaningful way. Because mediation is not binding unless the parties reach agreement, the only risk is time spent and the unlikely possibility that some fact fatal to one party's position will be disclosed inadvertently.

MEDIATION-ARBITRATION

Often referred to as "med-arb," mediation-arbitration is a hybrid combination of mediation and arbitration. Typically, the parties will agree to mediate to impasse or settlement. If they reach impasse, they then submit the dispute to binding arbitration of either the entire dispute or unresolved issues, using the mediator or a new person as the arbitrator.

---

* Dwight Oglesby is an owner of Kaufman Dispute Resolution, Ltd. He is the former Senior Vice President and General Counsel of DEI (previously the parent company of Minnegasco and Dyco Petroleum Corporation). Prior to that he was Senior Vice President and General Counsel of Munsingwear and an attorney, Vice President, and Secretary of the Pillsbury Company.

CHAPTER 6

AGRICULTURAL LAW

The word "change" is most frequently heard in discussions involving American agriculture today. The agriculture industry in this country is going through a period of unprecedented change as producers and processors struggle to deal with rapidly evolving technologies, increased mechanization, changing corporate ownership rules, international trade agreements, and a host of other issues unique to agriculture. Long considered a quiet, calm subcategory of the American legal system, the practice of agricultural law is changing swiftly as its practitioners strive to adapt their practices to the changing nature of the industry. Producers and processors alike need to keep themselves informed of how changes in agricultural law will affect them and the role they might play in directing that change. This chapter addresses agricultural production contracts, corporate ownership of farms, international agricultural agreements, and farm bankruptcies. The Intellectual Property Law Chapter describes the process for obtaining a plant patent. The Contract Law Chapter discusses general contract issues, and the Environmental Law Chapter discusses general environmental laws that impact farmers.

AGRICULTURAL PRODUCTION CONTRACTS

An agricultural production contract is an agreement between a producer and a processor, usually entered into before planting or the birth of an animal, that obligates the producer to sell his or her agricultural output to a particular processor. Agricultural production contracts are an increasingly important and popular way for agricultural producers and processors to do business in Minnesota. Drafting an agricultural production contract involves many of the same considerations discussed in the Contract Law Chapter. However, there are additional concerns unique to agricultural production contracts. When drafted well, an agricultural production contract can be a beneficial arrangement for both producer and processor. When drafted poorly, one or both risk tremendous financial losses and business disruption. Given their growing popularity, agricultural production contracts are rapidly changing the face of American agriculture and have received increased scrutiny from state legislatures.

THE FOOD PROCESSORS' PERSPECTIVE

The United States food processing industry has undergone tremendous change in the decades since the Second World War. Most small food processors have gone out of business while some other processors have grown enormously and spread nationally and in some cases, internationally. The increasing size of food processors has been both the cause and effect of increased capital-intensive, fast-paced mechanization in the food processing industry. Increased economies of scale in the food processing industry require full capacity utilization of equipment. This need for full capacity utilization in turn creates a need to line up supplies of raw materials well in advance of harvest. Production contracts are a way that processors seek to ensure quantity, quality, and timeliness of food inputs into the production process.

THE FOOD PRODUCERS' PERSPECTIVE

Food producers are as interested in stability and reliability in their business as food processors are in theirs. The agriculture business is notoriously plagued by bad weather, crop failures, fluctuating commodity prices, and soaring production costs. Theoretically, food producers seek agricultural production contracts out of a desire for stability and predictability. Realistically, many producers feel they have no choice but to enter into agricultural production contracts. The purchasers of their products sometimes insist on agricultural production contracts and producers feel they have no choice but to agree. Producers need not have such a fatalistic outlook, however. While most food processors prefer to do business using agricultural production contracts, most are willing to bargain over the terms.

CATEGORIES OF AGRICULTURAL PRODUCTION CONTRACTS

An agricultural production contract will generally follow one of three different forms—market specification contract, production management contract, or resource providing contract.

Market Specification Contract

The simplest form of the agricultural production contract is the market specification contract that states price, quantity, and quality of a product that will be traded at some future time. A market specification contract reduces uncertainties both for producer and processor while leaving the producer relatively free to meet its obligations however it sees fit. The biggest drawback of market specification contracts is that they often ignore the possibility of bad weather or crop failure. Agriculture is a notoriously unpredictable business and a farmer who agrees to deliver a certain crop at a set time may be inviting liability if subsequent events make performance impossible.

Production Management Contract

A more complicated form of the agricultural production contract is the production management contract. Like a market specification contract, a production management contract specifies price, quantity and quality, but also dictates how the producer will produce the goods. Production management contracts are becoming increasingly popular as processors try to produce unique, specialty products for niche markets. Production management contracts are especially popular with mass market processors, such as fast food companies, that demand uniform products for national markets. Drawbacks to production management contracts include all those mentioned above for market specification contracts and the additional burden that the farmer sacrifices some independence in deciding how best to manage the affairs of his or her farm.

Resource Providing Contract

The most complex form of the agricultural production contract is the resource providing contract. Under a resource providing contract, the processor provides all or part of the inputs to be used in producing the output to ensure that output will meet the processor's quality standards. Drawbacks to resource providing contracts include all those mentioned above for market specification contracts and production management contracts and the additional burden of being forced to do business with the processor in obtaining inputs for the production process. Producers must be very careful to understand their obligations under the resource providing contract and evaluate the probability that, even after he or she has purchased products from the processor, for instance seed and fertilizer which went into producing the crop, the processor usually retains the right to buy or not to buy the final product from the producer if that final product fails to meet the processor's standards.

MINNESOTA REQUIREMENTS FOR AGRICULTURAL PRODUCTION CONTRACTS

Theoretically, agricultural production contracts ought to benefit both parties; a win-win proposition. Many experts feel that historically, agricultural production contracts have benefited processors more than producers. In too many cases, agricultural production contracts have been drafted not to share the risk of crop failure, but merely to shift the risk of crop failure to producers. In response to past abuses, many states have enacted laws designed to protect the interests of farmers who sign agricultural production contracts. Agricultural production contracts for crops grown in Minnesota must comply with Minnesota's Agricultural Contracts Statute, one of the strictest laws in the country for protecting the interests of food producers. The Minnesota Agricultural Contracts Statute has five principal features:

- Arbitration or mediation clauses must be included in agricultural contracts governed by the law

- Termination rights are limited for any production contract that requires the producer to make a capital investment in buildings or equipment that cost $100,000 or more and have a useful life of five or more years

- Parent company responsibility is imposed on companies that make contracts through their subsidiaries

- Uniform Commercial Code's implied promise of good faith is imposed on all parties to the contract

- Minnesota's Commissioner of Agriculture is authorized to adopt additional rules prohibiting unfair trade practices

The first of these requirements, an arbitration or mediation clause, is discussed more fully in the Alternative Dispute Resolution Chapter. Parties to the contract can choose arbitration or mediation and can choose to designate the Minnesota Commissioner of Agriculture to conduct arbitration or mediation, or refer the matter to an outside service provider. Regardless of who conducts it, the arbitration or mediation must conform to the Minnesota Uniform Arbitration Act or the Minnesota Civil Mediation Act, respectively.

GENERAL DRAFTING ISSUES IN AGRICULTURAL PRODUCTION CONTRACTS

Four general issues should be treated carefully when drafting agricultural production contracts—quality, acceptance, title, and nonperformance.

Quality

To address the issue of quality the parties determine standards that will decide whether the producer has met the quality target set forth in the contract. Third party grading standards, such as a government grade, are most common, but the contract should anticipate the possibility of changes to those standards after formation of the contract but before delivery.

Acceptance

Acceptance refers to acceptance or non-acceptance of a product. The agricultural production contract should state that the involved parties determine how, when, and where acceptance will occur. An agricultural production contract should clarify which party pays for any required testing, who owns any rejected product, if and how any rejected product can be sold to third parties, and how and when a rejected product must be removed from the processor's facility.

Title

The issue of title refers to when title passes. A closely related issue is who bears the risk of loss before and after title passes. Some processors actually want risk of loss to remain with the producer for some period of time after title passes to the processor. Obviously, such a provision is almost never a good idea from the producer's standpoint.

Nonperformance

The nonperformance provision should clearly state each party's responsibilities upon crop failure, animal loss, or other factors that prevent one party's performance. Most such clauses include a requirement that the party unable to fulfill its side of the bargain must give notice of the nonperformance within a specified period of time, in a specified manner, to a specified person or office.

INTERNATIONAL AGRICULTURAL AGREEMENTS

Two primary factors determine the financial well-being of most farmers—the market prices they receive for their products and support payments received from the government. Both market prices and support payments are largely determined at the federal level by Congress and the President because agriculture is one of the most highly regulated sectors of the economy. In line with the increased internationalization of other sectors of the economy, the agricultural economy is being affected by increased international competition and pressure from foreign countries to open American domestic markets to more imported goods. American farmers are enjoying the benefits of increased access to many formerly closed foreign markets, yet, at the same time, more foreign agricultural products are finding their way into the domestic market, driving down domestic prices.

Many of this country's agriculture support programs are under increasing pressure at international negotiating sessions. Economists argue that price supports are a form of unfair subsidy and an inefficient way to help needy farmers. Political support for some agriculture support programs is waning under pressure to erase deficits and balance budgets. International agreements like the General Agreement on Tariffs and Trade (GATT) and the North American Free Trade Agreement (NAFTA) are likely to lead to the demise or significant alteration of many existing government support programs for agriculture while they open new foreign markets to American farmers.

It is difficult to predict the future of international agriculture agreements, but agricultural organizations are mobilizing to ensure their voices are heard in debates over agricultural policy. All segments of the agriculture industry are sure to be involved in the political process as they struggle to deal with change and seek the best in an uncertain international political climate for agriculture. Agricultural lawyers can help businesses engaged in agriculture get involved in the process, influence negotiations, and prepare for changes that do come about.

CORPORATE FARMING

How farmers are permitted to own their land is an important issue in Minnesota agriculture. The Minnesota State Legislature has found that "it is in the interest of the state to encourage and protect the family farm as a basic economic unit, to ensure it as the most socially desirable mode of agricultural production and to enhance and promote the stability and well-being of rural society in Minnesota and the nuclear family." For these reasons, the state forbids most corporations, limited liability companies, pension funds, investment funds, or limited partnerships to directly or indirectly engage in farming, or to obtain an interest in any real estate used for farming or capable of being used for farming. The law allows some minor exceptions for corporate farms used for research, encumbrances taken for purposes of security, land acquired by gift, and land used to raise breeding stock. In addition, some corporate-owned land was "grandfathered" into the law. Significant exemptions from the law permit agricultural land to be owned by:

- Family farm corporations
- Authorized farm corporations
- Family farm partnerships
- Authorized farm partnerships or general partnerships

Each of these four forms of organization has detailed conditions attached to it. An agricultural law attorney with experience in these matters can help farmers set up their businesses so as to avoid running afoul of these laws.

FARM BANKRUPTCIES

The federal Bankruptcy Code contains several provisions available only to family farmers. These provisions are known as Chapter 12 and are designed to allow family farmers to remain in the business of farming while reorganizing and attempting to pay off their debts. Chapter 12 offers the family farmer several advantages over other bankruptcy reorganization chapters because it recognizes the seasonal nature of most agricultural income, the difficulty of predicting in advance how much a farmer will profit from a crop, and the fact that most farmers need much more credit than do most individuals. Chapter 12 was originally scheduled to be repealed on October 1, 1993, but the repeal date was pushed back to October 1, 1998. All cases commenced or pending under Chapter 12 by October 1, 1998 and all matters or proceedings relating to such cases will proceed and be determined as if Chapter 12 had not been repealed.

FARMERS ELIGIBLE TO FILE FOR CHAPTER 12

Chapter 12 is only an option for farmers who receive at least half of their income from farming operations and have no more than $1.5 million in debt. At least 80 percent of that debt must be related to the farming operations, not including debt on the farmer's principal residence. The Bankruptcy & Workout Law Chapter discusses basics of bankruptcy for businesses that do not qualify to proceed under the farm bankruptcy provisions of the federal Bankruptcy Code.

MECHANICS OF A CHAPTER 12 BANKRUPTCY

A Chapter 12 bankruptcy filing is similar to a Chapter 11 corporate reorganization bankruptcy or a Chapter 13 personal reorganization bankruptcy. After a farmer files for Chapter 12, a "stay" is imposed and all actions of creditors to collect debt from the debtor must cease. If a creditor believes it deserves special protection, it can seek relief from the stay, requiring the debtor to give adequate protection to the creditor. Adequate protection under Chapter 12 is similar to adequate protection in other forms of bankruptcy but the terms are far more favorable to the farmer.

After filing for bankruptcy, the farmer has 90 days to file a plan of reorganization with the bankruptcy court. The reorganization plan must reveal all the farmer's debt and detail how he or she plans to repay the debt over three to five years. If the plan meets all of the requirements of Chapter 12, the bankruptcy court must approve it at a hearing held within 45 days after it is filed. Creditors are given an opportunity to file objections to the plan, but cannot veto it.

After filing for Chapter 12 the farmer almost always is allowed to continue operating the farm. An interested party can request that the farmer be removed from the farm, but a bankruptcy judge will only do so if the farmer is guilty of fraud, dishonesty, incompetence, or gross mismanagement of his or her affairs.

The reorganization plan is supervised by a court-appointed trustee. During the plan, the farmer makes periodic payments to the trustee who then pays creditors according to the terms of the plan. Should the farmer be removed for one of the above mentioned reasons, the trustee steps in to manage the farm. At the end of the plan period, the court discharges any remaining debts, with certain limited exceptions, and the debtor is given a "fresh start."

RESOURCES

Farmer-Lender Mediation: Questions and Answers. A pamphlet produced by the Minnesota Attorney General's Office and available free from local State Agricultural Extension offices.

United States Department of Agriculture, 14th and Independence Avenue NW, Washington, D.C. 20250: Public Affairs, (202) 720-4623; Extension Service, (202) 720-7173; Natural Resources & Environment, (202) 720-7173; Farmers Home Administration, (202) 720-4323.

Minnesota Attorney General, Agriculture/Labor Law Division, State Capitol, St. Paul, MN 55155, (612) 296-0693.

Minnesota Agriculture Department, 90 West Plato Boulevard, St. Paul, MN 55107: Agriculture Planning and Development, (612) 296-1486; Dairy & Livestock Services (612) 296-1586; Food Inspection Division, (612) 296-1591; Grain Inspection Division, 316 Grain Exchange, Minneapolis, 55415 MN (612) 341-7190.

Minnesota Extension Service, 240 Coffey Hall, University of Minnesota—St. Paul Campus, 1420 Eckles Avenue, St. Paul, MN 55108, (612) 625-8713.

Chapter 6: Agricultural Law

AGRICULTURAL LAW LEADING ATTORNEYS

Selected by Attorneys for
GUIDEBOOK
Law & Leading Attorneys
MINNESOTA

The attorneys profiled in this section were nominated by their peers in a statewide survey conducted in 1993 in which several thousand Minnesota attorneys were asked to name the lawyer to whom they would send a friend or family member in need of legal assistance in the area of *Agricultural Law*.

Because the survey resulted in a list of less than five percent of Minnesota's practicing attorneys, this should not be construed as a complete list. Nevertheless, it is an excellent source of highly qualified and reputable attorneys, who, if unable to assist can in most cases make quality referrals.

The attorneys profiled below were recommended by their peers in a statewide survey.

A list of all attorneys nominated in this category is found at the end of this section. For information on the survey methodology see page ix.

Please note that the shorter, two line attorney listings in this section are of attorneys who practice in this area but whose full biographical profile appears in another section of this book. A bullet "•" preceeding name indicates the attorney was nominated in this particular area of law. For information on the format of these profiles, consult the section "Using the *Business Guidebook*" found on page xiv. Note that the following abbreviations are used throughout these profiles:

App.	- Appellate	ABA	- American Bar Association
Cir.	- Circuit	ATLA	- American Trial Lawyers Association
Ct.	- Court	HCBA	- Hennepin County Bar Association
Dist.	- District	MDLA	- Minnesota Defense Lawyers Association
Hon.	- Honorable	MSBA	- Minnesota State Bar Association
JD	- Law degree (Juris Doctor)	MTLA	- Minnesota Trial Lawyers Association
LLB	- Law degree	NBTA	- National Board of Trial Advocacy
LLM	- Master in Law degree	RCBA	- Ramsey County Bar Association
Sup.	- Supreme		

BRYAN BAUDLER - Baudler, Baudler, Maus & Blahnik - 110 North Main Street - Austin, MN 55912 - Phone: (507) 433-2393, Fax: (507) 433-9530 - *See complete biographical profile in Personal Injury Defense Law Chapter.*

MORRIS DICKEL

Dickel, Johannson, Taylor, Rust & Tye, P.A.
407 North Broadway
P.O. Box 605
Crookston, MN 56716

Phone: (218) 281-2400
Fax: (218) 281-5831
800 number: (800) 584-7077

Admitted: 1953 Minnesota
Birthdate: 11/22/29

•**MORRIS DICKEL:** Mr. Dickel practices civil law with an emphasis on agricultural clients in the areas of litigation, farm incorporations, and estate planning and probate, including extensive experience in passing on agricultural entities from one generation to the next—including estate and gift tax planning. The firm has incorporated several hundred farm corporations.
Education: LLB 1953, University of Minnesota; BSL 1951, University of Minnesota.
Employment History: Partner 1957-present, Dickel, Johannson, Taylor, Rust & Tye, P.A.; Associate 1954-56, John Padden.
Representative Clients: Red River Valley Sugar Beet Growers Assn.; Red River Valley Farmers Insurance Pool; more than 150 farm corporations.
Professional Associations: Board of Law Examiners (1971-84); MSBA (Board of Governors 1985-91); Polk County Bar Assn.; ABA.
Community Involvement: Jaycees (past President); Lions Club (past President); one of the founders of Glenmore Foundation (a chemical dependency treatment center).
Firm: The firm has served clients in northwestern Minnesota and eastern North Dakota since 1932, providing a broad range of legal services. The firm is listed in *Best's Directory of Recommended Insurance Attorneys*, 1994. See additional listings in Closely Held Business Law and Probate, Estate Planning & Trusts Law Chapters.

Agricultural Law Leading Attorneys

•**RALPH K. MORRIS:** Since 1966, Mr. Morris has devoted substantially all of his legal practice to representation of clients involved in various aspects of agriculture. Although this ranges from individual farmers and ranchers to retail food processors, most of his experience relates to grower and producer-owned agricultural marketing and supply cooperatives. Legal services range from advice concerning articles, bylaws, and corporate structure to unique cooperative tax provisions, including Section 521 and Subchapter T of the Internal Revenue Code. In addition, Mr. Morris has served as legal counsel in structuring and negotiating joint venture arrangements involving grower-owned cooperatives and other food processing entities. Services in these projects include features unique to marketing of agricultural products under state and federal law, including grower contracts and federal farm policy regulations. Mr. Morris also has devoted substantial time to legal work involving financing of growers and grower-owned ventures. Mr. Morris has served as the president and chair of the Board of Directors of his law firm, Doherty, Rumble & Butler, P.A.
Education: LLB 1966, Stanford University; AB 1962 cum laude, senior honors thesis, Harvard University.
Representative Clients: American Crystal Sugar Company; Harvest States Cooperatives; Rocky Mountain Gen. Cooperative; Tri-State Generation & Transmission Assn.; American Dairy Assn. of Minnesota; Midwest Agri-Commodities Company; Associated Milk Producers, Inc.; Minn-Dak Farmers Cooperative; United Sugars Corp.; CENEX, Inc.; Minnesota Corn Processors; Western Fuels Assn.
Professional Associations: RCBA; MSBA.
Community Involvement: American Farmland Trust (Board member; Program Committee Chair); Harvard Alumni Assn.; John Brandt Foundation (Board of Trustees).
Firm: The law firm of Doherty, Rumble & Butler, P.A., has approximately 100 lawyers with offices in Minneapolis, Denver, and Washington, D.C., as well as St. Paul. Mr. Morris has assembled a team of lawyers within the firm to assist in ventures involving agricultural and cooperative matters. These specialists in areas such as securities law have made a commitment to remain generally familiar with agricultural and cooperative issues. With this team of specialists in the firm, Mr. Morris is able to coordinate and represent clients on all aspects of a grower-owned or agricultural project.

RALPH K. MORRIS

Doherty, Rumble & Butler
Professional Association
2800 Minnesota World Trade Center
30 East Seventh Street
St. Paul, MN 55101-4999

Phone: (612) 291-9282
Fax: (612) 291-9313

Admitted: 1966 Minnesota
Birthdate: 08/15/40

JOHN R. RODENBERG - Berens, Rodenberg & O'Connor, Chartered - 519 Center Street, P.O. Box 428 - New Ulm, MN 56073 - Phone: (507) 354-3161, Fax: (507) 354-7297 - *See complete biographical profile in Personal Injury Defense Law Chapter.*

•**RANDI ILYSE ROTH:** Ms. Roth specializes in agricultural law, with an emphasis on issues involving the Farmers Home Administration, issues arising out of agricultural production contracts, race discrimination in federal agricultural programs, and general federal administrative law. Other members of Farmers' Legal Action Group have expertise in many additional areas of agricultural law. Ms. Roth has been working in agricultural law full-time since 1986. She has traveled extensively to provide training on these topics and has written educational pieces that have enjoyed wide usage nationwide. She is the author of *Farmers' Guide to FDIC*, primary author of *Farmers' Guide to FmHA* (all editions), and has written numerous articles published in *Farmers' Legal Action Report*.
Education: JD 1984 cum laude, Northwestern University; BA 1979 magna cum laude, Yale University.
Employment History: Executive Director 1994, Farmers' Legal Action Group, Inc.; Interim Executive Director 1993, Farmers' Legal Action Group, Inc.; Staff Attorney 1986-93, Farmers' Legal Action Group, Inc.; Staff Attorney 1984-86, Legal Assistance Foundation of Chicago.
Representative Clients: All clients of Farmers' Legal Action Group, Inc., are financially distressed family farmers or organizations that represent financially distressed family farmers.
Professional Associations: American Agricultural Law Assn.
Community Involvement: Beth Jacob Congregation (Vice President of Operations); B'nai B'rith Hillel at the University of Minnesota (Board member); Talmud Torah of St. Paul (Board member).
Firm: Farmers' Legal Action Group, Inc. (FLAG), assists financially distressed family farmers by providing four categories of services in many areas of farm law: education, litigation, support, and legislative and administrative technical assistance. FLAG publishes numerous books and articles regarding a variety of farm law topics and distributes them nationwide. In addition, FLAG provides training for attorneys, advocates, and farmers nationwide. FLAG engages in class action impact litigation. FLAG helps its organizational clients in the federal and state legislative and administrative arenas by means such as drafting model legislation and commenting on proposed regulations. *See additional listings in Bankruptcy & Workout Law and Federal, State & Local Government Law Chapters.*

RANDI ILYSE ROTH

Farmers' Legal Action Group, Inc.
1301 Minnesota Building
46 East Fourth Street
St. Paul, MN 55101

Phone: (612) 223-5400
Fax: (612) 223-5335
800 number: (800) 233-4534

Admitted: 1984 Illinois;
1989 Minnesota;
1984 US Dist. Ct. (N. Dist. IL);
1989 US Dist. Ct. (MN);
1989 US Ct. App. (8th Cir.)
Birthdate: 02/18/57

Chapter 6: Agricultural Law

DENNIS M. SOBOLIK

Brink, Sobolik, Severson, Vroom & Malm, P.A.
217 Birch Avenue South
P.O. Box 790
Hallock, MN 56728

Phone: (2182) 843-3686
Fax: (218) 843-2724
800 number: (800) 962-6281

Admitted: 1959 Minnesota; 1981 North Dakota
Birthdate: 09/16/31

•**DENNIS M. SOBOLIK:** Mr. Sobolik represents agri-related businesses in all aspects of agricultural law, including real estate; probate, estate planning, and trusts; and farm corporation law. He also represents banks in all aspects of lender liability, purchase and sale of banks, and other aspects of bank collections.
Education: JD 1959, University of North Dakota; BS 1958, University of North Dakota.
Employment History: 1959-present, Brink, Sobolik, Severson, Vroom & Malm, P.A.; County Attorney 1972-1990, Kittson County; Assistant County Attorney 1963-72, Kittson County; County Attorney 1962-63, Kittson County.
Representative Clients: Numerous banks, agri-related businesses, farm corporations, and individual farmers in northwestern Minnesota and northeastern North Dakota. Names of representative clients furnished upon request.
Professional Associations: Kittson County Bar Assn.; 14th District Bar Assn. (President 1971-72); MSBA (Board of Governors 1972-84); ABA; ATLA; MTLA (Board of Governors 1973-74).
Community Involvement: Gustavus Adolphus College (Board of Regents 1982-89); Karlstad State Bank (Board Chair 1983-93); Crookston National Bank (Board Chair 1986-present).
Firm: The law firm of Brink, Sobolik, Severson, Vroom & Malm, P.A., organized by Lyman A. Brink (deceased), has rendered services to clients in northwestern Minnesota and northeastern North Dakota continuously since 1934. During that time, it has expanded from a sole practitioner office to a firm with seven attorneys all of whom are licensed to practice in all courts in Minnesota and North Dakota. Services include an exceptional in-house library and computerized research capabilities. In addition, the firm uses an aircraft to provide statewide service throughout Minnesota and North Dakota. Brink, Sobolik, Severson, Vroom & Malm maintains offices in Karlstad and Argyle, MN. Referrals from other attorneys represent a substantial part of the firm's present work load. *See additional listings in Banking Law and Probate, Estate Planning & Trusts Law Chapters.*

JOHN B. VAN DE NORTH JR. - Briggs and Morgan, P.A. - W-2200 First National Bank Building - St. Paul, MN 55101 - Phone: (612) 223-6600, Fax: (612) 223-6450 - *See complete biographical profile in Environmental Law Chapter.*

Complete listing of all attorneys nominated in Agricultural Law

PAUL W. BUCHER, Dunlap & Seeger, P.A., Rochester; **MORRIS DICKEL,** Dickel, Johannson, Taylor, Rust & Tye, P.A., Crookston; **GARY W. KOCH,** Gislason, Dosland, Hunter & Malecki, P.A., New Ulm; **CHARLES A. KREKELBERG,** Williams Nitz Krekelberg Sorkness & Seeger, Pelican Rapids; **PHILLIP L. KUNKEL,** Hall, Byers, Hanson, Steil & Weinberger, P.A., St. Cloud; **DAVID C. MCLAUGHLIN,** Pfluegel Helseth McLaughlin Anderson & Brutlag, Ortonville; **RALPH K. MORRIS,** Doherty, Rumble & Butler Professional Association, St. Paul; **BRIAN J. MURPHY,** Quarnstrom Doering Pederson Leary & Murphy, P.A., Marshall; **CURTIS A. NORDHOUGEN,** Dosland, Nordhougen, Lillehaug & Johnson, P.A., Moorhead; **RANDI ILYSE ROTH,** Farmers' Legal Action Group, Inc., St. Paul; **ROBERT L. RUSSELL,** Svingen, Athens & Russell, Fergus Falls; **DENNIS M. SOBOLIK,** Brink, Sobolik, Severson, Vroom & Malm, P.A., Hallock; **C. THOMAS WILSON,** Gislason, Dosland, Hunter & Malecki, P.A., New Ulm.

CHAPTER 7

ARTS, ENTERTAINMENT, ADVERTISING & MEDIA LAW

The primary concern of artists and entertainers is the creation of their art. But creating art should not be their only concern, because making a living as an artist or entertainer is also a business. Artists and entertainers must be sure to fully understand the legal aspects of the business relationships they enter into with agents, production companies, book publishers, managers, music clubs and record companies. They should also be concerned about the laws that regulate any relationships they form with other artists. To ignore these laws or to fail to get important business relationships defined in writing is virtually to guarantee problems as one's career advances.

This chapter describes arts and entertainment law, along with media and advertising law, because in the real world they are often related. For example, because artists and entertainers express their ideas and works to the public, they often encounter free speech issues, a major component of media law. In addition, this chapter outlines some of the elements of copyright and trademark law as they apply to artists who want to protect their rights to the artistic messages they create.

ARTS AND ENTERTAINMENT LAW

Arts and entertainment law is a broad area of legal specialization, so there is probably no such thing as a typical arts and entertainment lawyer. An attorney practicing in this area can concentrate his or her practice in just a few or in many of the legal issues that an artist or entertainer may encounter. An arts and entertainment lawyer's practice may include helping artists set up corporations or partnerships, settling copyright infringement cases, negotiating business deals, and drafting contracts between artists and record companies, production companies, book publishers or agents. This section outlines the areas of arts and entertainment law most likely to be encountered by an artist or performer.

TYPES OF CONTRACTS

The following is a list of the most common contracts an artist or entertainer is likely to encounter in his or her career.

Shopping Agreement
This is an agreement that an artist or a group of artists (such as a music group) makes with an agent or manager, who then shops around trying to get the individual or group a contract. This

agreement should spell out how long the contract is in effect (i.e. how much time the person will search on the artist's behalf). The time period should be long enough to give both parties time to evaluate each other's ability to work together, but not so long that the parties are stuck with an arrangement that does not suit them. This agreement should also spell out how the agent or manager is paid (usually a 10 to 20 percent commission), and who pays expenses. If the agreement stipulates that payment is on a commission basis, the document should clearly specify the terms.

Management or Booking Contract

When an individual artist or group wants to be managed and/or promoted by another party, a written contract should be entered into to spell out all the rights and responsibilities each party has to the other. The artist should carefully scrutinize all aspects of such a contract, especially if it is a long-term contract, to ensure that its terms are of value and that his or her rights are protected. Items to look for include: specific commitments the agency will make to protect and respect the artist's artistic freedom, specific commitments by the agency to promote the artist's career and/or provide with income or employment, how the agency will settle disputes over booking deals, and how the contract will be modified if the group changes its members, its name, or its artistic style.

Performance Agreement

Minnesota law stipulates that if the terms of a contract last for more than a year such as in a series of performances, the contract must be in writing. But to make sure that each party understands the full extent of its obligations and the rights of the other parties, all performance contracts should be in writing. Proving what was in an oral contract is very difficult to do, so settling a dispute over an oral contract is equally difficult. If an artist has a good relationship with someone for whom he or she has performed often, then a written performance contract can probably just state the basics: who performs, where and when the performance will take place, manner of performance, hours of performance, agreed compensation and manner and form of promotion and advertising. However, anyone agreeing to perform for the first time at a place or for a person or organization should sign a contract with a few more elements, including who pays attorney's fees if a dispute arises and whether disputes can be settled by arbitration or mediation. Performers should also make sure that the person signing the contract is an authorized representative of the person or organization shown in the contract as the party responsible for making payment after the performance.

Mutual Release Agreement

Mutual release agreements outline how to manage the legal and financial aspects of a group's breakup. Having a mutual release agreement is especially important if the departure of a member is not voluntary. Elements that should be clearly specified include whether the departing member has any rights to use some the group's material, whether the departing member receives any future royalties and which party, if any, has the right to continue using the group's name.

Entertainment Agency Contract

Minnesota Statutes require that any person involved in procuring, offering, or promising employment or engagements for three or more artists or groups of artists at any one time, or who has a written contract or a verbal agreement with an establishment or an individual to provide artists for one or more engagements, must be licensed as an entertainment agency by the Minnesota Department of Labor and Industry. Entertainment agencies are also required to submit to the Department of Labor and Industry the forms of contracts they will use and a schedule of fees to be charged and collected.

Artists can contact the Department of Labor and Industry, (612) 296-2175, to verify that a prospective agent is duly licensed within the State of Minnesota.

ORGANIZING THE BUSINESS

Probably the most important agreement or contract that artists sign is a document outlining their relationships with each other as they perform or create together. Handling the legal and financial details of a departure is made easier when the relationships among the artists forming a group have been clearly outlined beforehand. Some of the legal options artists have when creating formal relationships with each other are the topic of the next section.

General Partnership

For both artists and business people, a common arrangement is a general partnership in which all partners share in managing the partnership. A general partnership agreement should include the name of the partnership and whether it is protected or protectable by trademark, the members of the partnership, the partnership's location and duration, each partner's investment and participation in profits and loses, procedure for admitting new partners and liquidating the interests of departing members, amount of time to be contributed by each partner, and each partner's managerial and other responsibilities. Other elements of a general partnership agreement that may also be of special concern to artistic groups include naming a managing partner and setting a method for resolving disputes, setting conditions under which a partner can withdraw from the partnership, defining the grounds for expelling a partner, and specifying a period of time in which a departing partner cannot compete with the remaining partners.

A major drawback of a general partnership is that each partner can be held personably liable for the losses of the entire partnership. This means that if the partnership accumulates a large business debt, or if the partnership loses a large lawsuit, each partner may be forced to contribute some of his or her personal money to help pay off the debt. This drawback can be avoided by forming one of the different types of legal corporations, described in the next section.

Corporation

Although forming a general partnership agreement is a very common choice of a group of artists who perform or create together, artists also have the option of organizing as a corporation. To do this requires a little more organization and commitment by the group, because managing even a simple corporation requires a greater time commitment and closer attention to paperwork. However, depending on a group's specific circumstances, incorporating may be the best route to take, because two possible advantages of incorporating include lower taxes and reduced liability.

A corporation is a legal entity that operates separately from its owners, the shareholders. For most arts groups, all of the shareholders are also officers of the corporation. This is in contrast to the types of corporations most people are familiar with—public corporations with shares that can be traded on a public stock market. Artists rarely form public corporations, so only those small corporations with privately held shares are discussed here. In such closely held corporations, the officers of the corporation (president, vice president, secretary and treasurer) are the members of the group and they hold all the stock issued by the corporation.

The corporation may be structured so as to qualify as an S corporation, which gives significant tax advantages to the owners of the corporation. Simply put, an S corporation is not taxed, although any profits distributed to owners are taxed as personal income. In some other types of corporations, the corporation's profits are taxed and the earnings passed along to shareholders are taxed again.

Unlike a general partnership, the owners of a corporation are not generally liable for the debts of the corporation because of the legal separation between a corporation and its owners. Thus, if a corporation goes heavily into debt, bill collectors can generally only go after the assets of the corporation and cannot try to collect from the personal accounts of the corporation's shareholders. This exemption from liability disappears, however, if it can be proved in court that the shareholders engaged in fraud or otherwise seriously mismanaged the corporation.

TRADEMARK

A trademark is a word, name, symbol or design used by manufacturers and merchants to identify their products and distinguish them from other products. More to the point of this chapter, music groups, theater groups or individual artists or entertainers also have significant investments in their names as a way to distinguish their work from the works of other artists. Trademarks protect the owner of a product from others who would make a similar product and try to sell it using someone else's good name or reputation.

For an artist or group of artists, this protection is very valuable; a fact perhaps best illustrated by recalling that the name "Picasso" has been held to be a trademark. To make sure that the value in a name—value that an artist creates through hard work and talent—is not appropriated by someone else, the artist can register the name with the state or the federal government. Filing with the federal government protects the mark beyond the state's borders.

Although anyone can do an informal, preliminary search to determine whether a particular name is available to be registered as a trademark, it is best to hire the services of a lawyer experienced in trademark law to do a comprehensive search and to properly register the mark. A search by an attorney affords financial and legal protection. Although it may cost a little bit of money to hire an attorney to conduct this search, it is much better to know beforehand if anyone else has the name rather than after having spent money promoting and using a mark that belongs to someone else.

A name does not have to be registered in order to claim it as a trademark. This is so because a trademark automatically arises from repeated, regular use of a name. However, if the owner ever wants to claim that someone else is infringing on the use of a name, he or she will have a harder time doing this if the name was not previously registered as a trademark.

Registering a name as a trademark is the first step in protecting exclusive rights to it. Whether a person registers a trademark with the state or with the federal government, he or she gets a certificate of registration that is valid for 10 years. The registration can be renewed after 10 years. Whenever the artist stops regular, repeated use of a trademark, he or she is open to the possibility that someone else can begin legally using it. Also, the holder of the trademark must police the mark to make sure that others who try to use it are notified of the holder's exclusive rights to the trademark. If the holder does not act to stop others from infringing on a trademark, he or she can lose the exclusive right to use the trademark.

COPYRIGHT

A copyright is a federal protection that affords creators of original works of authorship the rights to exclusively reproduce, distribute, sell, perform or publicly display the copyrighted work. If someone writes a play or a book, drafts a song, paints a picture, sculpts artwork, makes a computer program, movie, or photograph, he or she already has the copyright to that work by virtue of having created it. Registering the work with the U.S. Copyright Office is mostly a legal formality, but there are reasons for doing so anyway. The most important reason is that if the creator of a work registers a copyright on a work within three months of its creation or at any time before an alleged infringement of the work, he or she may be able to collect statutory damages and attorney's fees in addition to actual damages in an infringement lawsuit.

While a lawyer likely would not be needed simply to register a copyright, an attorney should be consulted whenever engaging in any sort of copyright infringement case. However, a copyright holder may also want to engage an attorney if he or she is ever hired to create a work of art for someone else. An attorney in this case can ensure that an employment contract clearly states who has copyright for the work.

MEDIA LAW

As stated in the introduction to this chapter, media and advertising law and arts and entertainment law are related in the real world because many artists find themselves involved in free speech issues. Although free speech may sound like a straightforward issue, its practical applications have been the subject of much case law and are almost perpetually debated in the courts, which must try to balance individual and community rights. This section on media law focuses on some of the significant concerns in media law including defamation, obscenity, libel, and slander.

DEFAMATION

Freedom of speech is not absolute. Defamatory speech, speech that negatively reflects on someone else's reputation, is one type of speech that is limited. The two kinds of defamation are libel and slander. Libel occurs when the defamation is done in writing; slander occurs when the defamation is spoken. In order to sue for defamation, a plaintiff must prove that the information was false. The courts treat private persons differently than public figures in deciding defamation. Public figures have to prove not only that the information is false, but that the speaker or publisher either knew the words were false, or spoke or published the words with a reckless disregard for whether they were false or not.

At the time of Alfred the Great, the minimum penalty for defamation was loss of one's tongue. Modern laws offer somewhat lesser punishments. Minnesota law provides for both criminal and civil cases against libel, but the criminal statues have not been used for many years and it is likely that they are unconstitutional. In Minnesota, there is a somewhat different test when the defendant is a member of the media. The desire to provide for freedom of the press makes it more difficult to win a libel case against a media defendant.

There are usually two defenses against libel: truth and consent. In general, if a statement is true it is not actionable as libel or slander even though it may harm one's reputation. Any person who offers his or her consent to the transmission or publication of defaming information cannot then sue for libel or slander. Also, a statement of opinion cannot ordinarily be the basis of a libel suit. Furthermore, a person must be identified in order for defamation to have occurred. The identification occurs either when a person is directly named or when he or she is described so specifically as to be recognizable. In general, false statements that hurt the reputation of a business, accuse someone of a crime or impugn chastity are likely to be found to be defamatory. Clearly, the safest approach in publishing or broadcasting negative information about someone else is to make sure it is factually accurate. Another way to protect oneself from a defamation lawsuit is to limit negative remarks to dead people, who under the law do not have reputations and therefore cannot be defamed. In addition, people who are not in the public spotlight, or whose livelihoods do not otherwise depend on a favorable public perception, cannot generally be greatly damaged by defamatory remarks.

In determining damage awards, courts also take into account how many people heard the slander or read the libel. The more people who heard or read the defamation, the greater a damage award is likely to be. State and federal laws almost never allow for punishment that would prevent a libel or slander from occurring. That is, one cannot go to court and use libel law to prevent someone else from publishing a defamatory book. But because defamation law does allow for civil action after the libel or slander has occurred, many times the subject of the potentially defamatory material is successful in preventing the defamation by threatening to go to court if the material is published.

OBSCENITY

Material that has been deemed to be obscene is illegal to distribute or produce in any way. It is also illegal to participate in an obscene performance if a person knew or should have known that the performance material was obscene. The fines for violating these laws can be as high as $10,000 for the first offense. It is also illegal to use minors in sexually explicit representations and to show sexually explicit materials to minors.

Ever since the U.S. Supreme Court's famous 1973 decision in an obscenity case, determining whether material is obscene depends on this test: (a) Whether the average person applying contemporary community standards would find that the work, taken as a whole, appeals to the prurient interest, (b) whether the works depict or describe, in a patently offensive way, sexual conduct, and (c) whether the work, taken as a whole, lacks serious literary, artistic, political, or scientific value.

Many people find this test vague. Obscenity is particularly difficult to define, and deciding in court whether a particular piece of material or performance was obscene depends greatly on the particular judge or jury deciding the case. As a result, lawyers are justifiably reluctant to give specific advice on how to avoid crossing the line from acceptable sexual material into obscenity. At best, all they can do is recite the legal definition and discuss some of the details of a court's previous decisions.

ADVERTISING

Advertising issues can affect all business people, whether or not they think they are directly involved in the advertising, entertainment or media industries. Good communication with the public is one of the most important assets a business can have, whether it involves placing advertisements, dealing with the government or talking to the media.

Advertisements include a wide range of items—from television spots to catalogs. Advertisements are invitations to the public for offers on products or services. Advertisements are not considered offers under contract law, but are announcements that goods are available and offers from the public are solicited. Although advertisements do not constitute offers, they can raise liability issues in several different ways. Both the state of Minnesota and the federal government have laws regulating advertisements.

Minnesota Law

Under Minnesota's Deceptive Trade Practices Act, a person in the course of business engages in a deceptive trade practice when he or she:

- Passes off goods or services as those of another

- Causes likelihood of confusion or misunderstanding as to the source, approval, or certification of goods or services

- Causes likelihood of confusion or misunderstanding as to the affiliation, association, or connection with or certification by another

- Uses deceptive representations or designations of geographical origin in connection with goods or services

- Represents that goods or services have sponsorship approval, ingredients, uses, benefits that they do not have or that a person has sponsorship, approval, affiliation that the person does not have

- Represents that goods are new if they are used, reconditioned, or altered

- Represents goods or services are of a particular quality or standard of which they are not

- Disparages goods, services, or the business of another by false or misleading representations of fact

- Advertises goods or services with the intent not to sell them as advertised

- Advertises goods or services with intent not to supply reasonably expected public demand unless the advertisement discloses the limited quantity

- Makes false or misleading statements of fact concerning the reasons for, existence, or amounts of price reductions

- Engages in any other conduct which creates confusion or misunderstanding

Minnesota has a specific statute regarding false statements in advertising. This law states that any person, firm, corporation, or business, with the intent to sell or dispose of goods or services, who publishes or disseminates an advertisement that contains any material assertion, representation, or statement of fact that is untrue, deceptive, or misleading is guilty of a misdemeanor.

In addition, the Minnesota Prevention of Consumer Fraud Act states the use by any person of fraud, false pretense or promise, misrepresentation, misleading statement, or deceptive practice with the intent that others rely on it in connection with a sale is unlawful.

Minnesota law states that in addition to any civil penalties one may receive from violating these statutes, he or she may also receive a penalty if the conduct was perpetrated against a senior citizen or a disabled person.

Advertisements may also lead to product liability. Words, photographs, or a combination of the two may create liability if a product does not meet the claims stated or shown. An advertisement does not have to use the word "warranty" for a warranty to be created. For example, if an advertisement shows a photograph of a product being used in a particular fashion and the product fails when a consumer uses the product in that manner, the consumer may bring an action for failure of the product to meet its warranty.

Chapter 7: Arts, Entertainment, Advertising & Media Law

FEDERAL LAW

There are several federal statutes that regulate advertising. It is unlawful for a person, partnership, or corporation to disseminate any false advertisement. Unfair or deceptive acts or practices affecting commerce are also unlawful. Under the federal Lanham Act, any person, who in connection with any goods or services, uses any word, term, name, symbol, device, or any combination thereof or any false designation of origin, false or misleading description or representation of fact that is likely to cause confusion, mistakes, or deception shall be liable for civil damages. Also, a person can be liable for damages if his or her commercial advertising or promotion misrepresents the nature, characteristics, qualities, or geographical origin of goods, services, or commercial activities. Advertising agencies have been held liable under this statute when the advertising agency participates in the creation, development, and propagation of a false advertising campaign when it has knowledge of its falsity.

Advertisements may also cause copyright infringement claims. Advertisements may parody other advertisements or copyrighted works. A copyright owner has the exclusive right to control the reproduction, distribution, performance, display, and creation of derivative works. However, the Fair Use doctrine permits the limited use of a copyrighted work without the owner's permission. There are four factors to consider when determining whether use is fair use:

- Purpose and character of use, including whether the use is of a commercial nature or for nonprofit educational purposes

- Nature of the copyrighted work

- Amount of the work used in relation to the copyright work as a whole

- Effect of the use upon the potential market or value of the copyrighted work

Courts have used these four factors and reached various results. In some cases, courts have held that advertisements constituted fair use, and in other cases courts have held that copyright infringement occurred. Courts must decide whether the use constitutes a parody, which may constitute fair use, or if the use is using copyrighted material for purely commercial reasons. There is a presumption that a commercial use of copyrighted work is not fair use. However, the fact that the use is commercial is only one of the four factors to consider. When courts look at the nature of the copyrighted work, there is stronger protection for some works. Advertisements do not receive as much protection as literary works. So an advertisement parodying another advertisement may be acceptable, while an advertisement using a copyrighted song may be unacceptable.

CONTESTS, SWEEPSTAKES, & GAME PROMOTIONS

In addition to the state and federal laws described above, a complex set of rules governs contests, sweepstakes, and game promotions. Such promotions are a popular way of promoting a product or service, but if done improperly, they can plunge an advertiser into a morass of legal problems. One recent game promotion in England, sponsored by an American vacuum cleaner manufacturer, was so poorly planned it cost the company millions of dollars in legal fees and settlements with angry customers. Clearly, it pays to have game promotions carefully scrutinized before launching a new advertising campaign built upon prizes. Often, a properly worded disclaimer can prevent a lot of headaches.

One of the highest hurdles facing advertisers is that, while most states prohibit lotteries, each state has its own definition of what constitutes a lottery. If an advertiser is not careful, it can quickly run afoul of state laws against lotteries. Many states also have unique laws requiring posted rules, distribution of lists of winners, record retention, and postings of odds. In addition, the United States Postal Service, the Federal Communications Commission, and all major television networks have their own rules for contest advertisements, sweepstakes, and game promotions. Only an experienced advertising attorney can adequately advise on all these issues.

RESOURCES

The Practical Musician: A Legal Guidebook to the Music Industry. Minnesota Continuing Legal Education, 40 Milton Street North, St. Paul, MN 55104, (612) 227-8266, (800) 759-8840.

Resources and Counseling for the Arts, 75 West Fifth Street, Suite 429, St. Paul, MN 55102, (612) 292-4381.

A Guide to Intellectual Property Protection. This publication contains a detailed discussion of patent, trademark and copyright issues and is available free from the Minnesota Small Business Assistance Office—500 Metro Square, 121 Seventh Place E, St. Paul, MN 55101-2146, (612) 296-3871 or (800) 657-3858.

Chapter 7: Arts, Entertainment, Advertising & Media Law

ARTS, ENTERTAINMENT, ADVERTISING & MEDIA LAW LEADING ATTORNEYS

Selected by Attorneys for GUIDEBOOK
Law & Leading Attorneys
MINNESOTA

The attorneys profiled in this section were nominated by their peers in a statewide survey conducted in 1993 in which several thousand Minnesota attorneys were asked to name the lawyer to whom they would send a friend or family member in need of legal assistance in the area of *Arts, Entertainment, Advertising & Media Law.*

Because the survey resulted in a list of less than five percent of Minnesota's practicing attorneys, this should not be construed as a complete list. Nevertheless, it is an excellent source of highly qualified and reputable attorneys, who, if unable to assist can in most cases make quality referrals.

The attorneys profiled below were recommended by their peers in a statewide survey.

A list of all attorneys nominated in this category is found at the end of this section. For information on the survey methodology see page ix.

Please note that the shorter, two line attorney listings in this section are of attorneys who practice in this area but whose full biographical profile appears in another section of this book. A bullet "•" preceeding name indicates the attorney was nominated in this particular area of law. For information on the format of these profiles, consult the section "Using the *Business Guidebook*" found on page xiv. Note that the following abbreviations are used throughout these profiles:

App.	- Appellate	ABA	- American Bar Association
Cir.	- Circuit	ATLA	- American Trial Lawyers Association
Ct.	- Court	HCBA	- Hennepin County Bar Association
Dist.	- District	MDLA	- Minnesota Defense Lawyers Association
Hon.	- Honorable	MSBA	- Minnesota State Bar Association
JD	- Law degree (Juris Doctor)	MTLA	- Minnesota Trial Lawyers Association
LLB	- Law degree	NBTA	- National Board of Trial Advocacy
LLM	- Master in Law degree	RCBA	- Ramsey County Bar Association
Sup.	- Supreme		

KENNETH J. ABDO

Abdo & Abdo, P.A.
710 Northstar West
625 Marquette Avenue
Minneapolis, MN 55402

Phone: (612) 333-1526
Fax: (612) 342-2608

Admitted: 1983 Minnesota; 1983 US Dist. Ct. (MN)
Birthdate: 07/30/56

•**KENNETH J. ABDO:** Mr. Abdo is an attorney, a principal shareholder, and Vice President of Abdo & Abdo, P.A. He concentrates in business, entertainment, intellectual property, employment, and contract law and negotiates and counsels on a wide range of entertainment contracts and matters. Mr. Abdo is an adjunct professor of Art, Entertainment & Sports Law at William Mitchell and Hamline University law schools where he lectures on music, film, media, sports, trademark, and copyright. He also lectures and writes for various legal and public audiences. His writing includes two chapters in *The Practical Musician*, 1993.
Education: JD 1982, William Mitchell (staff writer, *William Mitchell Law Review*; Moot Court Society); BA 1979, University of Minnesota (Phi Beta Kappa; Omicron Delta Kappa).
Employment History: A former professional musician and disc jockey, Mr. Abdo has been with Abdo & Abdo, P.A., as a law clerk and practicing attorney since 1979.
Representative Clients: Businesses and individuals in the entertainment business, including radio and television talent and stations, actors, for profit and nonprofit theatres, music recording studios, independent film and music projects, comedians, agents, managers, writers, musicians, film and theatre production companies, special event production companies, literary publishing, sports, and entertainer licensing and merchandising.
Professional Associations: ABA (Planning Committee, Forum on Entertainment and Sports Industry annual conference); MSBA (Chair 1991-93, Arts and Entertainment Law Section; Chair 1993-present, Music Law Committee; Cochair 1992-present, annual Seminar on Entertainment and Sports Law).
Community Involvement: The Cricket Theatre (Board Chair); Board member: Concerts for the Environment; Midwest Center for Arts, Entertainment and Law; Minneapolis Athletic Club; Youth Forum Minnesota.
Firm: Since 1936 Abdo & Abdo, P.A., has provided personalized legal services for businesses and individuals. The firm's five attorneys provide legal counsel focused on the specific needs of small and medium-sized businesses including start-ups, maintenance, mergers, acquisitions, partnerships, securities, real estate, employment, intellectual property (copyrights and trademarks), entertainment, debtor, creditor, and general and complex litigation. They also serve the legal needs of individuals, professionals, and business owners in the areas of employment, contracts, wills, probate, and estate planning. *See additional listing in Intellectual Property Law Chapter.*

•**STEPHEN R. BERGERSON:** An officer, shareholder, and cochair of Fredrikson & Byron's Advertising, Media & Entertainment Law Group. Mr. Bergerson is a former ad agency account executive and professional musician who practices advertising, entertainment, and promotion law. His expertise is in advertising review, sweepstakes compliance, television network clearance, trademarks and copyright clearance and protection, drafting and negotiating photo releases and agency/client, music licensing, talent, noncompete and confidential disclosure agreements and resolving related disputes. He has twenty years of experience representing large and small marketers and their advertising, sales promotion, direct marketing and public relations agencies throughout the country. Mr. Bergerson is an adjunct professor at the University of St. Thomas and at Metro State University, is a nationally known speaker, lecturer, and seminar leader, and is the author of over 125 articles. He has received the American Advertising Federation Medal of Merit, Minnesota Advertising Federation Distinguished Service and Government Relations awards, WCCO Radio Good Neighbor Award, and the William Mitchell College of Law Award of Excellence. He is listed in *Who's Who in American Law*, *Who's Who Worldwide*, and *Who's Who in America*.
Education: JD 1974, William Mitchell; BA 1970 with honors, University of Minnesota.
Employment History: Currently, Fredrikson & Byron; 1983-90, Kinney & Lange; 1979-83, Ramier & Gries; 1974-79, Joseph Robbie Law Offices; Account Executive 1971-74, Campbell-Mithun Advertising.
Representative Clients: Campbell-Mithun-Esty; Martin Williams; Carmichael Lynch; McCracken Books; Haagen Daz; Wilson-Griak; Kamstra Communications; Business Incentives; Carlson Marketing Group; Gage Marketing; NSP; Colle & McVoy; Chuck Ruhr Advertising; Miller Meester.
Professional Associations: American Advertising Federation (Chair, State Legislative Council and Ad Standards Committees, Legal Affairs Committee, past chair Eighth District); board member and chair, Alternative Dispute Resolution Committee, Better Business Bureau; general counsel and past president, Advertising Federation of Minnesota; past president, Minnesota Advertising Review Council; general counsel, Minnesota Assn. of Independent Commercial Producers; Editorial Advisory Board, *Advertising Compliance Service*; former coordinator, Four A's Institute of Advanced Advertising Studies.
Firm: Fredrikson & Byron's Advertising, Media & Entertainment Law Group offers clients an unusual breadth and depth of expertise in the areas of advertising, sales promotion, direct marketing and public relations, film, video, literary, music, sports, cable and broadcast television, First Amendment, libel, and public access. Mr. Bergerson's cochairs are John Stout, Paul Landry, and Adrian Herbst, all of whom also have professional backgrounds in their areas of practice. *See additional listing in Intellectual Property Law Chapter.*

STEPHEN R. BERGERSON

Fredrikson & Byron, P.A.
1100 International Centre
900 Second Avenue South
Minneapolis, MN 55402

Phone: (612) 347-7025
Fax: (612) 347-7077

Admitted: 1974 Minnesota
Birthdate: 06/19/45

RICHARD R. BURNS - Hanft, Fride, O'Brien, Harries, Swelbar & Burns, P.A. - 1000 First Bank Place, 130 West Superior Street - Duluth, MN 55802 - Phone: (218) 722-4766, Fax: (218) 720-4920 - *See complete biographical profile in Probate, Estate Planning & Trusts Law Chapter.*

•**LAURA J. DANIELSON** - Patterson & Keough, P.A. - 1200 Rand Tower, 527 Marquette Avenue South - Minneapolis, MN 55402 - Phone: (612) 349-5740, Fax: (612) 349-9266 - *See complete biographical profile in Immigration Law Chapter.*

DAVID R. FAIRBAIRN - Kinney & Lange, P.A. - 625 Fourth Avenue South, Suite 1500 - Minneapolis, MN 55415-1659 - Phone: (612) 339-1863, Fax: (612) 339-6580 - *See complete biographical profile in Intellectual Property Law Chapter.*

Chapter 7: Arts, Entertainment, Advertising & Media Law

BARBARA J. GISLASON

Barbara J. Gislason & Associates
219 SE Main Street - Suite 506
Minneapolis, MN 55414

Phone: (612) 331-8033
Fax: (612) 331-8115

Admitted: 1980 Minnesota;
1980 US Dist. Ct. (MN);
1983 US Ct. App. (8th Cir.);
1988 US Sup. Ct.
Birthdate: 03/19/52

•**BARBARA J. GISLASON**: A pioneer in the evolution of art and entertainment law in Minnesota, Ms. Gislason handles a variety of legal issues which often require the talents of four or five attorneys at bigger firms. She is especially effective in negotiating resolution of client conflicts in and out of state and is effective in communicating with clients, opposing counsel, and judges.
Education: JD 1980, William Mitchell; BA 1974, Carleton College.
Employment History: 1992-present, The Gislason Agency (literary agent); 1985-present, Barbara J. Gislason & Associates; Panel Arbitrator/Referee 1987-94, Hennepin County Dist. Court; Adjunct Professor 1985-90, Minneapolis College of Art and Design; Adjunct Professor 1983-84, Hamline University School of Law; Associate 1980-85, Babcock, Locher, Neilson & Mannella.
Representative Clients: Midwest Watercolor Society; Black Lights Entertainment; Flanders Contemporary Art; Midwest Fashion Design Consortium; Coffee House Press; Voice Plus; Chameleon Design; Opera 101; radio and television personality Barbara Carlson; art broker Holly Hastings; playwright John Davidson; educational developer Arlene Sonday; human rights activist Kate Millett; musician David Wolfensen; photographer Sandy May.
Professional Associations: MSBA (Chair 1991-92, Computer Law Section International Committee; Chair 1990-91, Art & Entertainment Law Section; Chair 1989-90, Art Law Committee; Chair 1991, Bar-Media Symposium; Chair 1987-88, Computer Law Section Litigation Committee); MN Intellectual Property Law Assn. (Chair 1989-91, Copyright Committee).
Community Involvement: Midwest Center for Arts, Entertainment & the Law (Board member 1993-94); Opera 101 (Board member 1993-94); MN State Board of Law Examiners (Advisory Panel 1989-93); Alexandra House for battered women (Legal Panel 1984-93); MN Opera Assn. (Board member 1990-92); MN State Arts Board (Advisory Panel 1990-91).
Firm: Barbara J. Gislason & Associates, founded in 1985, with offices in Hennepin and Anoka Counties, represents clients in art and entertainment, employment, and family law matters. Barbara Gislason's knowledge in computer, copyright, trademark, and media law and her experience in contract negotiation, mediation, arbitration, and civil litigation affords clients superior value. Barbara Gislason offers clients a hands-on personalized approach often lost in bigger firms. In 1992, she opened a literary agency to provide additional service to the creative community. *See additional listings in Employment Law and Intellectual Property Law Chapters.*

•**STUART R. HEMPHILL** - Dorsey & Whitney - Pillsbury Center South, 220 South Sixth Street - Minneapolis, MN 55402-1498 - Phone: (612) 340-2734, Fax: (612) 340-2868 - *See complete biographical profile in Intellectual Property Law Chapter.*

EUGENE L. JOHNSON - Dorsey & Whitney - Pillsbury Center South, 220 South Sixth Street - Minneapolis, MN 55402-1498 - Phone: (612) 340-2625, Fax: (612) 340-2868 - *See complete biographical profile in Intellectual Property Law Chapter.*

•**JOHN A. KNAPP** - Winthrop & Weinstine, P.A. - 3200 Minnesota World Trade Center, 30 East Seventh Street - St. Paul, MN 55101 - Phone: (612) 290-8400, Fax: (612) 292-9347 - *See complete biographical profile in Federal, State & Local Government Law Chapter.*

CALVIN L. LITSEY

Faegre & Benson
2200 Norwest Center
90 South Seventh Street
Minneapolis, MN 55402

Phone: (612) 336-3000
Fax: (612) 336-3026
800 number: (800) 328-4393

Admitted: 1983 Minnesota
Birthdate: 11/22/55

•**CALVIN L. LITSEY:** Mr. Litsey, a member of Faegre & Benson's Media, Communications and Entertainment Law Group and its Intellectual Property Group, concentrates his practice in entertainment law and intellectual property law, providing transactional and litigation expertise to the firm's entertainment, media, advertising, and intellectual property clients. Mr. Litsey's experience includes advising individuals and corporations on the adoption, ownership, acquisition, transfer, protection, and licensing of rights in trademarks, logos and designs, advertising and promotional materials, music, photographs, films, multimedia works, literary works, computer software, CD-ROMs, and merchandise. He also furnishes business formation, financing, and intellectual property counseling and negotiates and drafts agency, production, recording, licensing, merchandising, advertising, broadcasting, and sponsorship agreements. Mr. Litsey also represents clients in connection with a wide variety of copyright, trademark, trade secret, unfair competition, breach of contract, and false advertising lawsuits. In addition to practicing law, Mr. Litsey writes and lectures on intellectual property and entertainment law issues and teaches entertainment law as an adjunct professor at the University of Minnesota Law School.
Education: JD 1983 magna cum laude, Order of the Coif, University of Minnesota (Articles Editor, *Minnesota Law Review*); BA 1978 magna cum laude, Yale University.
Employment History: Partner 1991-present, Associate 1984-91, Faegre & Benson; Law Clerk 1983-84, Hon. Harlington Wood, Jr., US Court of Appeals, Seventh Circuit (Chicago, IL).
Representative Clients: Dayton-Hudson Corp.; International Multifoods Corp.; Cowles Media; Norwest Corp.; Wagner Spray Tech Corp.; Martin/Williams Advertising; The Minnesota Orchestral Assn.; The Science Museum of Minnesota; Target Stores; Troupe America; Walker Art Center; Columbia Pictures; MCA; Motion Picture Assn. of America; Musicland Group, Inc.
Professional Associations: ABA (Patent, Trademark and Copyright Law Section); The Copyright Society; MSBA (Litigation, Computer Law, and Art and Entertainment Sections). *See additional listing in Intellectual Property Law Chapter.*

Arts, Entertainment, Advertising & Media Law Leading Attorneys

•**BRUCE H. LITTLE:** Mr. Little practices arts, entertainment, and media law as an outgrowth of his general litigation practice in the area of copyright, trademark, and patents. Reported decisions include *Moore v. Columbia Pictures, et al.* and *National Car Rental v. Computer Associates International*. Mr. Little is author of "Scope of Use - The Licensing Perspective," 1993 Minnesota State Bar Association Continuing Legal Education (CLE), "Liability of Software Suppliers for Negligence or Defects," 1993 International Computer Law Conference, "Understanding Section 117 and Other Issues of Unauthorized Use by Software Owners and Licensees," 1992 Minnesota State Bar Association CLE, and is coauthor of "Who Owns the Design: The Law of Copyright or Contract," 1988, Minnesota Institute of Legal Education. Mr. Little is married and has two children.
Education: JD 1984, University of Illinois (*University of Illinois Law Review*); BS 1976, University of Illinois.
Employment History: Attorney 1986-present, Popham, Haik, Schnobrich & Kaufman; Attorney 1984-86, Peterson & Ross (Chicago).
Representative Clients: MCA Records; La'Face Records; Winterland Productions; Desert Wind Films; Western Publishing, Inc.; Restaurants Unlimited; Computer Associates International.
Professional Associations: ABA (Intellectual Property Section; Litigation Section (Eighth Circuit Reporter, Intellectual Property Committee); Computer Law Committee); MSBA (Computer Law and Arts and Entertainment Law Sections); American Intellectual Property Lawyers Assn.; Minnesota Intellectual Property Lawyers Assn.
Community Involvement: Interfaith Hospitality Network; St. Joseph's H.O.P.E.; Minnesota Assn. of Rehabilitation Facilities; Greater Minneapolis Day Care Assn.
Firm: Popham, Haik, Schnobrich & Kaufman, Ltd., is a firm of more than 230 attorneys with offices in Denver, Miami, Minneapolis, Washington, D.C., and international affiliations in Beijing, China and Leipzig and Stuttgart, Germany. The firm represents clients nationally and internationally on intellectual property issues and issues relating to corporate and business law, administrative law, and litigation. *See additional listing in Intellectual Property Law Chapter.*

BRUCE H. LITTLE

Popham, Haik, Schnobrich & Kaufman, Ltd.
222 South Ninth Street
Suite 3300
Minneapolis, MN 55402

Phone: (612) 333-4800
Fax: (612) 334-8888

Admitted: 1986 Minnesota;
1984 Illinois;
1984 US Dist. Ct. (N. Dist. IL);
1986 US Dist. Ct. (MN);
1986 US Ct. App. (8th Cir.);
1993 US Sup. Ct.
Birthdate: 08/15/54

•**JOHN W. PROVO** - Popham, Haik, Schnobrich & Kaufman, Ltd. - 222 South Ninth Street, Suite 3300 - Minneapolis, MN 55402 - Phone: (612) 333-4800, Fax: (612) 334-8888 - *See complete biographical profile in Probate, Estate Planning & Trusts Law Chapter.*

Z. PETER SAWICKI - Kinney & Lange, P.A. - 625 Fourth Avenue South, Suite 1500 - Minneapolis, MN 55415-1659 - Phone: (612) 339-1863, Fax: (612) 339-6580 - *See complete biographical profile in Intellectual Property Law Chapter.*

•**LEE E. SHEEHY** - Popham, Haik, Schnobrich & Kaufman, Ltd. - 222 South Ninth Street, Suite 3300 - Minneapolis, MN 55402 - Phone: (612) 333-4800, Fax: (612) 334-8888 - *See complete biographical profile in Federal, State & Local Government Law Chapter.*

Chapter 7: Arts, Entertainment, Advertising & Media Law

JOHN H. STOUT

Fredrikson & Byron, P.A.
1100 International Centre
900 Second Avenue South
Minneapolis, MN 55402

Phone: (612) 347-7012
Fax: (612) 347-7077

Admitted: 1967 Minnesota
Birthdate: 12/13/40

•**JOHN H. STOUT:** An officer, shareholder, and cochair of Fredrikson & Byron's Advertising, Media and Entertainment, and International Business Groups. Mr. Stout is a finance lawyer whose practice focuses on film (he has worked on financings for more than 50 independent feature films), video, music, and communications clients (particularly multimedia, cable, and wireless televisions matters). He works on a variety of organizational, financing, joint venture, acquisition, and commercial contract projects for a wide range of corporate clients. Mr. Stout also advises on directors and officers issues.
Education: JD 1967, University of Michigan; BA 1962, Carleton College.
Representative Clients: American Playhouse, New York; Paisley Park Enterprises; World Satellite Network; James Productions; Digital Cafe; numerous production companies, producers, directors, writers, and talent in the film, video, and music business.
Professional Associations: ABA (Business Law Section, Committee on Institutional Investors, and Forum Committee on Sports and Entertainment Law); MSBA (Entertainment & Sports Law Section); Minnesota Secretary of State Corporate Advisory Committee; National Assn. of Corporate Directors (member and director).
Community Involvement: Cofounder, past chair, and current director, Minnesota Film Board; resource panelist, Independent Feature Project, New York and Minneapolis; 1992, recognized by the Minnesota legislature for his efforts to develop the local motion picture industry; cofounder, past chair, and director, Metropolitan Economic Development Association, a minority business development organization; cofounder, chair, and director, Milestone Growth Fund, a minority business investment fund; Minnesota Minority Business Advocate of the Year 1990, Small Business Administration; Distinguished Achievement Award, Carleton College; named to the Twin Cities Volunteer Hall of Fame (*Mpls./St. Paul* magazine) for his work with the arts and minority businesses.
Firm: Mr. Stout is one of seven attorneys in Fredrikson & Byron's Advertising, Media and Entertainment Law Group. He works with Steve Bergerson (advertising law), Paul Landry (music), Adrian Herbst and Theresa Harris (cable television and communications), Chet Taylor (cable television and sports), Corinna Vecsey (cable television, literary and publishing), and legal assistant, Mary Kay Robertson (cable television). All of these attorneys have backgrounds in their areas of practice: Mr. Stout as a film producer and investor; Mr. Bergerson as a musician and advertising agency account executive; Mr. Landry and Mr. Taylor as professional performers; Mr. Herbst as a city council member familiar with cable television franchise administration; and Ms. Vecsey as an editor and employee of a publishing house. *See additional listings in Publicly Held Corporations Law and Securities & Venture Finance Law Chapters.*

JOHN S. SUMNERS - Merchant, Gould, Smith, Edell, Welter & Schmidt, P.A. - 3100 Norwest Center, 90 South Seventh Street - Minneapolis, MN 55402-4131 - Phone: (612) 332-5300, Fax: (612) 332-9081 - *See complete biographical profile in Intellectual Property Law Chapter.*

MARSHALL H. TANICK - Mansfield & Tanick, P.A. - 1560 International Centre, 900 Second Avenue South - Minneapolis, MN 55402-3383 - Phone: (612) 339-4295, Fax: (612) 339-3161 - *See complete biographical profile in Employment Law Chapter.*

•**DOUGLAS J. WILLIAMS** - Merchant, Gould, Smith, Edell, Welter & Schmidt, P.A. - 3100 Norwest Center, 90 South Seventh Street - Minneapolis, MN 55402-4131 - Phone: (612) 332-5300, Fax: (612) 332-9081 - *See complete biographical profile in Intellectual Property Law Chapter.*

Complete listing of all attorneys nominated in Arts, Entertainment, Advertising & Media Law

KENNETH J. ABDO, Abdo & Abdo, P.A., Minneapolis; **STEPHEN R. BERGERSON,** Fredrikson & Byron, P.A., Minneapolis; **LAURA J. DANIELSON,** Patterson & Keough, P.A., Minneapolis; **BARBARA J. GISLASON,** Barbara J. Gislason & Associates, Minneapolis; **ROBERT M. GOLDSTEIN,** Robert M. Goldstein, P.A., St. Paul; **STUART R. HEMPHILL,** Dorsey & Whitney, Minneapolis; **JOHN A. KNAPP,** Winthrop & Weinstine, P.A., St. Paul; **JOHN C. LEVY,** Parsinen, Bowman & Levy, P.A., Minneapolis; **CALVIN L. LITSEY,** Faegre & Benson, Minneapolis; **BRUCE H. LITTLE,** Popham, Haik, Schnobrich & Kaufman, Ltd., Minneapolis; **MALCOLM L. MOORE,** Moore & Hansen, Minneapolis; **LAWRENCE OSTERMAN,** Attorney at Law, Minneapolis; **JOHN W. PROVO,** Popham, Haik, Schnobrich & Kaufman, Ltd., Minneapolis; **DANIEL M. SATORIUS,** Abdo & Abdo, P.A., Minneapolis; **LEE E. SHEEHY,** Popham, Haik, Schnobrich & Kaufman, Ltd., Minneapolis; **JOHN H. STOUT,** Fredrikson & Byron, P.A., Minneapolis; **DOUGLAS J. WILLIAMS,** Merchant, Gould, Smith, Edell, Welter & Schmidt, P.A., Minneapolis.

CHAPTER 8

BANKING LAW

Banks are financial intermediaries that link those who have money—depositors—with those who need money—borrowers. Banks play an important role in modern, industrial economies by gathering deposits, repackaging them into a staggering variety of financial instruments and reselling them to borrowers. The important position that banks have in modern economies is also one of the easiest positions to abuse. Recognizing the potential for abuse and mismanagement inherent in the banking system and the negative effect that a weak banking system has upon the larger economy, state and federal authorities have created an extensive set of regulations that make the banking industry one of the most heavily regulated sectors of the economy. No other industry, through its day-to-day operations, affects as many other businesses as banking does. Many business managers feel frustrated when dealing with banks because they fail to understand the regulatory straightjackets that banks are sometimes put in by federal or state regulators or they do not understand the fear that many bankers understandably now have of borrower lawsuits. The relationship that a company has with its bankers is important to its success in business. Understanding the laws that affect bankers and their relationships with borrowers can better one's chances of getting a business loan, receiving more favorable terms, and having satisfying business relations with banks.

This chapter discusses the strict regulatory environment in which banks operate and potential sources of lender liability. International Letters of Credit are discussed in the International Business Law Chapter. Several different types of bank loans primarily of interest to new companies are discussed in the Securities & Venture Finance Law Chapter. Workouts for troubled loans are discussed in the Bankruptcy & Workout Law Chapter.

NATIONAL VERSUS STATE BANKS

Commercial banks can be chartered either as national banks or state banks. The individuals who start a bank are free to choose the type of bank charter that best fits their needs. National bank charters are granted by the Department of the Treasury's Office of the Comptroller of the Currency in Washington, D.C. State bank charters are granted by the individual state's banking commission. Here in Minnesota, the State Commerce Department, located in St. Paul, processes applications for state bank charters. Whether applying for a state or federal charter, applicants are required to provide extensive information about their financial history, their proposed management structure, the banking needs of the community, and their intentions for serving the community wherein the bank will be located.

National bank charters are more expensive to procure although for most purposes, state banks and national banks have identical rights and privileges once formed. One important difference between national and state banks is that membership in the Federal Reserve System (the "Central Bank" of the United States) and coverage by the Federal Deposit Insurance Corporation (FDIC) are automatic for national banks. State banks must make separate applications to join the Federal Reserve System and the FDIC. Applications for FDIC coverage and Federal Reserve System membership require much of the same information required in the original charter application.

REGULATING BANKS

Once a bank is chartered, state and federal regulators have a number of tools to use to control bank operations. The goal of most banking regulation is to prevent the widespread bank failures that plagued the country during the Great Depression. Much tighter supervision of commercial banks and federal guarantees of most bank deposits have promoted much greater business confidence in the banking system and prevented the widespread bank panics that gripped the U.S. economy periodically in its early history.

REGULATORY AGENCIES

The Comptroller of the Currency has jurisdiction over the thousands of national banks in the country. The Office of the Comptroller issues national charters and has authority to examine and supervise national banks. The Office of the Comptroller's numerous functions are carried out through six regional administrative offices located throughout the country. The state of Minnesota is assigned to the Midwestern Region District, which has its principal offices in Kansas City, Missouri. The Minneapolis Field Office, 920 Second Avenue South, Minneapolis, MN 55402, is a good source of information about federal bank regulations. The Office of the Comptroller also maintains duty stations in Minneapolis (3 stations), Alexandria, Duluth, and Fargo ND. Bank examinations can also be carried out by representatives of the FDIC and the Federal Reserve.

The Minnesota Commerce Department, Financial Examinations, Banks Division, 133 East 7th Street, St. Paul, MN 55101, regulates branch banking in Minnesota, sets maximum interest rates in certain categories of loans and otherwise supervises state chartered banks.

Banks can also be subject to control by a host of other federal and state regulatory agencies. The Department of Justice has authority to prevent bank mergers that it believes may create a trend toward monopoly in a given area. The Securities and Exchange Commission requires banks that sell stock to the public to file periodic reports with the Commission. Banks that choose to participate in a variety of government loan programs are subject to scrutiny by the Veterans Administration, the Departments of Labor, Interior, Housing and Urban Development, or Health and Human Services. In addition, banks, like other businesses, are affected by state and federal regulations regarding equal employment opportunity, discrimination in lending, fair credit reporting, truth in lending, and collection practices for delinquent loans.

PERIODIC REPORTS

Periodically, all banks are required to submit detailed financial condition reports to bank regulators. These reports must be submitted quarterly by larger banks and at lest semi-annually by some smaller banks. Special reporting requirements are imposed on troubled banks and near continuous reporting is required for banks thought likely to fail.

BANK EXAMINATIONS

In addition to having to file periodic reports, banks are subject to periodic visits by teams of inspectors to ensure the banks are being run in compliance with all applicable laws, that sound banking principles are being observed, and that the bank is not discriminating unfairly against any class of people. Often, these inspections are unannounced. Inspectors check all bank records, physically inspect documents, test computer systems, review loan procedures and policies, and count cash. Two areas of particular interest to bank examiners are the status of outstanding loans and the balance of the bank's loan portfolio.

Status of Outstanding Loans

Bank examiners evaluate the strengths of loans that a bank has made and make predictions of the likelihood that the loans will be repaid. Each bank receives a grade on the strength of its overall loan portfolio. To evaluate loans, examiners check the collateral pledged for each loan and the cash flow of the borrower repaying the loan. Accurate loan documentation is essential to this stage of the examination and as a result, a bank can be quite strict in insisting upon proper documentation from even its best customers.

Portfolio Balance

A bank's loan portfolio is also evaluated for balance. Theoretically, a bank's loan portfolio is stronger if loans are spread out over a wide variety of loan categories such as real estate, manufacturers, service providers, and automobile fleets. A balanced loan portfolio is better able to withstand periodic economic fluctuations in any given industry than a loan portfolio heavily weighted toward one particular industry.

The Uniform Interagency Bank Rating System

More than one regulatory agency may have authority to examine a given bank, but because multiple examinations would be costly for the government and overly burdensome for banks, examiners use the Uniform Interagency Bank Rating System, a uniform set of standards, to grade banks. The Uniform Interagency Bank Rating System grades banks in five different areas—capital adequacy, asset quality, management ability, earnings performance, and liquidity. These five elements are commonly referred to by their acronym, CAMEL. Every bank is rated on a scale of 1 to 5 for each element of CAMEL, with 1 being the highest rating and 5 being the lowest. A rating of 1 is excellent. A rating of 2 is good, with minor problems. A rating of 3 signifies a bank has trouble in that particular area and will usually cause authorities to take corrective action against the bank to remedy the problem. A rating of 4 signifies more trouble and usually triggers more serious corrective action. A rating of 5 is reserved for banks with a very high possibility of imminent failure and will usually trigger the search for candidates with which to merge the troubled bank.

LIMITS PLACED UPON BANK LOANS

Both federal and state laws control the interest rates that banks can charge to borrowers. Regulations provide a range of interest rates that are permissible. A bank is then free to charge different borrowers different rates within those ranges depending upon the bank's perception of each business' ability to pay back the loan, the cost of funds the bank pays its depositors, and the competitive pressures of the financial marketplace. Federal and state laws also set lending limits on the amount that can be lent to a particular individual or business. These lending limits are determined primarily by the bank's capital assets.

LIMITS PLACED UPON THE USE OF BANK FUNDS

Both federal and state laws place a variety of restrictions on what a bank can do with its own funds. These rules are extremely complex and only an experienced professional can adequately advise bank management. A few general comments can be made:

Real Estate

National banks and many state banks are prohibited from investing in real estate except to the extent that the investment is used for the bank's own needs. Total investment in the bank's own real estate cannot exceed the amount of its capital stock.

Securities

National Banks and many state banks are prohibited from investing in nearly all equity securities. Limited exceptions permit investment in subsidiaries performing bank functions, U.S. Treasury securities and general obligations of state and municipal governments.

Investments in Other Industries

Banks are generally prohibited from investing in nonfinancial sectors of the economy such as manufacturing and health care. Within the financial services sector, banks are prohibited from making some investments in insurance or securities underwriting. These limits are coming under increasing scrutiny, however, and Congress is currently considering whether to scrap some of these restrictions.

LENDER LIABILITY

A big worry for lenders today is potential liability for the loans they make. There was a time when bank officers felt free to step in and tell a business how it ought to be run whenever that business failed to make timely loan payments. Then a wave of lawsuits brought by business owners convinced juries that bank interference with business decisions had been the cause of business failures. Failed businesses sometimes won very substantial verdicts or settlements from their banks. Early successes spawned a rash of copycat lawsuits challenging every conceivable action a bank might have taken before the business failed. Banks have lost lawsuits alleging bad faith for failing to loan enough money, for loaning too much money, for calling in a loan too early, and for failing to call a loan in early enough.

A bank always needs to resist the temptation to take control of a business too quickly because if the bank becomes so involved in the debtor's business that it "controls" the business, the creditor can become liable for any liabilities incurred by the business. This possibility is particularly serious because the definition of when a creditor "controls a debtor" is hazy and difficult to define. There is no simple formula to apply and courts look to all the creditor's actions in the broadest context in answering the question. Lenders need to be extremely careful about using their influence to get the borrower to take actions detrimental to the company but beneficial to the bank. Attorneys experienced in this area of law are frequently called upon to advise their bank clients on how to ensure better payment of loans without unnecessarily incurring liability. The advice of experienced counsel is strongly recommended.

If all this were not enough to cause the average banker to lose sleep, today's bankers also need to worry about lawsuits brought by the government for environmental cleanup costs at the sites of borrowers' operations. Financial management of a debtor's business can have especially high risks in the realm of environmental matters. In one notorious case, the *Fleet Factors* decision, the court held that a lender could be held liable for Superfund cleanup costs at the debtor's facility if the lender "had the ability to influence the hazardous waste decisions of its borrower" even though the lender had never actually participated in the decision-making process. The court's position that mere ability to influence a borrower's hazardous waste handling decisions can trigger lender liability for cleanup sent shock waves through the banking community. The Environmental Protection Agency (EPA) has tried to assuage the fears of many bankers by promulgating new rules it uses to determine when banks can become responsible for environmental cleanup costs. However, many people in the banking industry are not comfortable with the new rules and fear the potential for liability is still great. Banks and bank clients concerned with how their actions might be interpreted by a court assigning responsibility for environmental cleanup costs should consult counsel experienced in interpreting EPA lender liability rules.

Lender liability lawsuits are having a dramatic effect on the way lenders and borrowers interact with each other. Many longstanding relationships that once were consistently cordial are becoming increasingly adversarial. Even a borrower in excellent financial condition may find it increasingly difficult to secure loans if it has a history of business litigation. Banks now feel threatened by possible lawsuits from regulators and borrowers. Understandably, they may be reluctant to offer business advice or to introduce business managers to new business contacts.

RESOURCES

Minnesota Commerce Department, Financial Examinations, Banks Division, 133 East 7th Street, St. Paul, MN 55101, (612) 296-2715.

United States Department of the Treasury, Comptroller of the Currency, Bank Supervision and Policy, 250 E Street SW, Washington, D.C. 20219.

Lender Liability: A Practical Guide. James R. Butler Jr., A. Barry Capello, Arne E. Forry, Frances Komoroske, Bureau of National Affairs, Inc., Rockville, MD, 1987.

How to Get a Business Loan (Without Signing Your Life Away). Joseph R. Mancuso, Prentice Hall Press, New York, NY, 1990

Getting a Business Loan: Your Step-by-Step Guide. Orlando J. Antonini, Crisp Publications, 1993.

Negotiating a Bank Loan You Can Live With. Arthur G. Pylis III, Probus Publishing Co., Chicago, IL, 1991.

Doing Business with Banks, A Common Sense Guide for Small Business Owners. Gibson Heath, USA Press Inc., Lakewood, CO, 1991.

Borrowing for Your Business, Winning the Battle for the Banker's "Yes." George M. Dawson, Upstart Publishing Co. Inc., Dover, NH, 1991.

Chapter 8: Banking Law

BANKING LAW LEADING ATTORNEYS

Selected by Attorneys for
GUIDEBOOK
Law & Leading Attorneys
MINNESOTA

The attorneys profiled in this section were nominated by their peers in a statewide survey conducted in 1993 in which several thousand Minnesota attorneys were asked to name the lawyer to whom they would send a friend or family member in need of legal assistance in the area of *Banking Law*.

Because the survey resulted in a list of less than five percent of Minnesota's practicing attorneys, this should not be construed as a complete list. Nevertheless, it is an excellent source of highly qualified and reputable attorneys, who, if unable to assist can in most cases make quality referrals.

The attorneys profiled below were recommended by their peers in a statewide survey.

A list of all attorneys nominated in this category is found at the end of this section. For information on the survey methodology see page ix.

Please note that the shorter, two line attorney listings in this section are of attorneys who practice in this area but whose full biographical profile appears in another section of this book. A bullet "•" preceeding name indicates the attorney was nominated in this particular area of law. For information on the format of these profiles, consult the section "Using the *Business Guidebook*" found on page xiv. Note that the following abbreviations are used throughout these profiles:

App.	- Appellate		ABA	- American Bar Association
Cir.	- Circuit		ATLA	- American Trial Lawyers Association
Ct.	- Court		HCBA	- Hennepin County Bar Association
Dist.	- District		MDLA	- Minnesota Defense Lawyers Association
Hon.	- Honorable		MSBA	- Minnesota State Bar Association
JD	- Law degree (Juris Doctor)		MTLA	- Minnesota Trial Lawyers Association
LLB	- Law degree		NBTA	- National Board of Trial Advocacy
LLM	- Master in Law degree		RCBA	- Ramsey County Bar Association
Sup.	- Supreme			

•**CARL BAER** - Kief, Fuller, Baer, Wallner & Rodgers, Ltd. - P.O. Box 780, 514 America Avenue - Bemidji, MN 56601 - Phone: (218) 751-2221, Fax: (218) 751-2285 - *See complete biographical profile in Commercial Litigation Chapter.*

•**STEVEN E. CARLSON** - Dorsey & Whitney - 3 Gracechurch Street - London, England EC 3V OAT - Phone: 011-4471-929-3334, Fax: 011-4471-929-3111 - *See complete biographical profile in International Business Law Chapter.*

•**JAMES F. CHRISTOFFEL** - Christoffel, Elliott & Albrecht, P.A. - 100 South Fifth Street, Suite 1250 - Minneapolis, MN 55402 - Phone: (612) 672-0900, Fax: (612) 341-2835 - *See complete biographical profile in Commercial Real Estate Law Chapter.*

•**KATHERINE A. CONSTANTINE** - Dorsey & Whitney - Pillsbury Center South, 220 South Sixth Street - Minneapolis, MN 55402-1498 - Phone: (612) 340-8792, Fax: (612) 340-2643 - *See complete biographical profile in Bankruptcy & Workout Law Chapter.*

•SHAWN M. DUNLEVY: Mr. Dunlevy practices in the areas of banking law, bankruptcy, business law, commercial law, corporate law, creditor remedies, debtor and creditor law, lender support litigation, and loan workouts. He primarily represents lenders on troubled commercial loans—reviewing commercial loan files and providing legal audits; providing recommendations on maximizing recovery and minimizing exposure; negotiating, structuring, and documenting workout and restructuring agreements; representing lenders in foreclosure, replevin, bankruptcy, and debt collection actions. He also represents lenders in new loan transactions and renewal of existing loans. Mr. Dunlevy has substantial involvement in consumer work on behalf of institutional lenders, consisting primarily of foreclosure, replevin, bankruptcy, and debt collection actions. He has prepared and presented a significant number of seminars for attorneys, banks, credit unions, finance companies, trade associations, and businesses. Mr. Dunlevy served as a bankruptcy trustee for ten years, dealing with a wide variety of procedural and substantive issues, and an equally wide variety of individual and business debtors.
Education: JD 1980, University of North Dakota; BA 1975 cum laude, University of North Dakota.
Employment History: Currently, Fryberger, Buchanan, Smith & Frederick, P.A.; prior to graduating from law school, was employed by a family-owned manufacturing and construction business.
Representative Clients: Commercial State Bank of Two Harbors; First American Bank of Brainerd; General Motors Acceptance Corporation; Itasca State Bank of Grand Rapids; Kanabec State Bank; Northern State Bank of Virginia; Norwest Corporation; Security State Bank of Hibbing; Republic Bank, Inc.; Western National Bank of Duluth.
Professional Associations: 11th District Bar Assn.; MSBA; ABA; State Bar of Wisconsin; US Bankruptcy Ct. (Bankruptcy Trustee 1982-92 (5th Div.)).
Firm: Please see firm profile in Appendix C. *See additional listings in Bankruptcy & Workout Law and Commercial Litigation Chapters.*

SHAWN M. DUNLEVY

Fryberger, Buchanan, Smith & Frederick, P.A.
302 West Superior Street
Suite 700
Duluth, MN 55802

Phone: (218) 722-0861
Fax: (218) 722-9568

Admitted: 1980 Minnesota; 1986 Wisconsin; 1981 US Dist. Ct. (MN); 1986 US Dist. Ct. (W. Dist. WI); US Bankruptcy Ct.
Birthdate: 10/15/53

•CHRISTOPHER A. ELLIOTT - Christoffel, Elliott & Albrecht, P.A. - 100 South Fifth Street, Suite 1250 - Minneapolis, MN 55402 - Phone: (612) 672-0900, Fax: (612) 341-2835 - *See complete biographical profile in Bankruptcy & Workout Law Chapter.*

•ROGER D. GORDON - Winthrop & Weinstine, P.A. - 3000 Dain Bosworth Plaza, 60 South Sixth Street - Minneapolis, MN 55402 - Phone: (612) 347-0700, Fax: (612) 347-0600 - *See complete biographical profile in Publicly Held Corporations Law Chapter.*

•DOUGLAS B. GREENSWAG - Leonard, Street and Deinard Professional Association - 150 South Fifth Street, Suite 2300 - Minneapolis, MN 55402 - Phone: (612) 335-1527, Fax: (612) 335-1657 - *See complete biographical profile in Bankruptcy & Workout Law Chapter.*

•JEFFREY S. JOHNSON - Barna, Guzy & Steffen, Ltd. - 400 Northtown Financial Plaza, 200 Coon Rapids Boulevard - Minneapolis, MN 55433 - Phone: (612) 780-8500, Fax: (612) 780-1777 - *See complete biographical profile in Commercial Real Estate Law Chapter.*

•DAVID KANTOR - Leonard, Street and Deinard Professional Association - 150 South Fifth Street, Suite 2300 - Minneapolis, MN 55402 - Phone: (612) 335-1500, Fax: (612) 335-1657 - *See complete biographical profile in Commercial Real Estate Law Chapter.*

•DAVID W. KELLEY - Leonard, Street and Deinard Professional Association - 150 South Fifth Street, Suite 2300 - Minneapolis, MN 55402 - Phone: (612) 335-1500, Fax: (612) 335-1657 - *See complete biographical profile in Commercial Real Estate Law Chapter.*

•W. CHARLES LANTZ - Dorsey & Whitney - 201 First Avenue SW, Suite 340 - Rochester, MN 55902 - Phone: (507) 288-3156, Fax: (507) 288-6190 - *See complete biographical profile in Commercial Real Estate Law Chapter.*

•DOUGLAS M. LAWRENCE - Moss & Barnett, A Professional Association - 4800 Norwest Center, 90 South Seventh Street - Minneapolis, MN 55402 - Phone: (612) 347-0349, Fax: (612) 339-6686 - *See complete biographical profile in Bankruptcy & Workout Law Chapter.*

•BRIAN F. LEONARD - O'Neill, Burke, O'Neill, Leonard & O'Brien, Ltd. - 100 South Fifth Street, Suite 1200 - Minneapolis, MN 55402 - Phone: (612) 332-1030, Fax: (612) 332-2740 - *See complete biographical profile in Bankruptcy & Workout Law Chapter.*

•JOHN R. MCDONALD - Robins, Kaplan, Miller & Ciresi - 2800 LaSalle Plaza, 800 LaSalle Avenue - Minneapolis, MN 55402 - Phone: (612) 349-8500, Fax: (612) 339-4181 - *See complete biographical profile in Bankruptcy & Workout Law Chapter.*

•**DAVID B. MILLER** - Faegre & Benson - 2200 Norwest Center, 90 South Seventh Street - Minneapolis, MN 55402 - Phone: (612) 336-3000, Fax: (612) 336-3026 - *See complete biographical profile in Securities & Venture Finance Law Chapter.*

•**HOWARD A. PATRICK** - Robins, Kaplan, Miller & Ciresi - 2800 LaSalle Plaza, 800 LaSalle Avenue - Minneapolis, MN 55402 - Phone: (612) 349-8500, Fax: (612) 339-4181 - *See complete biographical profile in Bankruptcy & Workout Law Chapter.*

•**THOMAS E. ROHRICHT** - Doherty, Rumble & Butler Professional Association - 2800 Minnesota World Trade Center, 30 East Seventh Street - St. Paul, MN 55101-4999 - Phone: (612) 291-9333, Fax: (612) 291-9313 - *See complete biographical profile in Publicly Held Corporations Law Chapter.*

•**ALLEN I. SAEKS** - Leonard, Street and Deinard Professional Association - 150 South Fifth Street, Suite 2300 - Minneapolis, MN 55402 - Phone: (612) 335-1548, Fax: (612) 335-1657 - *See complete biographical profile in Commercial Litigation Chapter.*

ROBERT J. SEFKOW

Pemberton, Sorlie, Sefkow, Rufer & Kershner
110 North Mill Street
P.O. Box 866
Fergus Falls, MN 56538-0866

Phone: (218) 736-5493
Fax: (218) 736-3950

Admitted: 1974 Minnesota
Birthdate: 09/18/49

•**ROBERT J. SEFKOW:** Mr. Sefkow practices banking, corporate, and commercial law, including financing, collection, workout and bankruptcy, purchase and sale of businesses, corporate formation, and related real estate and commercial litigation services.
Education: JD 1974, University of Wisconsin; BS 1971, University of Minnesota.
Employment History: Currently, Pemberton, Sorlie, Sefkow, Rufer & Kershner.
Representative Clients: Community First National Bank of Fergus Falls; American National Bank of Brainerd; Lake Region Hospital Corp.
Professional Associations: ABA; MSBA (Chair 1988-89, Business Law Section; 1980-81, 302A Task Force); State Bar of Wisconsin.
Firm: Founded in 1882, Pemberton, Sorlie, Sefkow, Rufer & Kershner and its predecessor firms have been serving clients in Minnesota and North Dakota for more than 110 years. Firm members have been active in the profession on a statewide level. Former firm member Roger Dell served as Chief Justice of the Minnesota Supreme Court from 1953 to 1962. Former partner Gerald S. Rufer served as president of the Board of Law Examiners for many years. Richard L. Pemberton was president of the Minnesota State Bar Association in 1986-87, and currently serves as chair of the Minnesota Racing Commission. The firm's 12 attorneys are able to provide specialized services commonly associated with big city practices. *See additional listings in Bankruptcy & Workout Law and Commercial Litigation Chapters.*

•**ROBERT K. SEVERSON** - Brink, Sobolik, Severson, Vroom & Malm, P.A. - 217 Birch Avenue South, P.O. Box 790 - Hallock, MN 56728 - Phone: (218) 843-3686, Fax: (218) 843-2724 - *See complete biographical profile in Commercial Litigation Chapter.*

•**DENNIS M. SOBOLIK** - Brink, Sobolik, Severson, Vroom & Malm, P.A. - 217 Birch Avenue South, P.O. Box 790 - Hallock, MN 56728 - Phone: (218) 843-3686, Fax: (218) 843-2724 - *See complete biographical profile in Agricultural Law Chapter.*

Complete listing of all attorneys nominated in Banking Law

CARL BAER, Kief, Fuller, Baer, Wallner & Rodgers, Ltd., Bemidji; STEVEN E. CARLSON, Dorsey & Whitney, London; JAMES F. CHRISTOFFEL, Christoffel, Elliott & Albrecht, P.A., Minneapolis; KATHERINE A. CONSTANTINE, Dorsey & Whitney, Minneapolis; SHAWN M. DUNLEVY, Fryberger, Buchanan, Smith & Frederick, P.A., Duluth; CHRISTOPHER A. ELLIOTT, Christoffel, Elliott & Albrecht, P.A., Minneapolis; ROGER D. GORDON, Winthrop & Weinstine, P.A., Minneapolis; DOUGLAS B. GREENSWAG, Leonard Street and Deinard Professional Association, Minneapolis; JEFFREY S. JOHNSON, Barna, Guzy & Steffen, Ltd., Minneapolis; DAVID KANTOR, Leonard, Street and Deinard Professional Association, Minneapolis; DAVID W. KELLEY, Leonard, Street and Deinard Professional Association, Minneapolis; W. CHARLES LANTZ, Dorsey & Whitney, Rochester; DOUGLAS M. LAWRENCE, Moss & Barnett, A Professional Association, Minneapolis; BRIAN F. LEONARD, O'Neill, Burke, O'Neill, Leonard & O'Brien, Ltd., Minneapolis; JOHN R. MCDONALD, Robins, Kaplan, Miller & Ciresi, Minneapolis; DAVID B. MILLER, Faegre & Benson, Minneapolis; HOWARD A. PATRICK, Robins, Kaplan, Miller & Ciresi, Minneapolis; THOMAS E. ROHRICHT, Doherty, Rumble & Butler Professional Association, St. Paul; ALLEN I. SAEKS, Leonard, Street and Deinard Professional Association, Minneapolis; ROBERT J. SEFKOW, Pemberton, Sorlie, Sefkow, Rufer & Kershner, Fergus Falls; ROBERT K. SEVERSON, Brink, Sobolik, Severson, Vroom & Malm, P.A., Hallock; DENNIS M. SOBOLIK, Brink, Sobolik, Severson, Vroom & Malm, P.A., Hallock.

CHAPTER 9

BANKRUPTCY & WORKOUT LAW

Every year, for many businesses in America, the answer to financial problems is to declare bankruptcy, a legal proceeding in federal court that allows a business to be released from the obligation of paying some or all of its debts. It is often said that bankruptcy gives a debtor a fresh start, but filing bankruptcy is not a panacea for all financial problems because it is not painless. Declaring bankruptcy can seriously damage a company's credit rating, making it difficult to establish credit or take out loans. Without good credit, some companies simply cannot operate. Many companies can work themselves out of even very serious debt without ever going near a bankruptcy court, so declaring bankruptcy should not be an automatic first step for a business experiencing financial problems. This chapter discusses bankruptcy options available for businesses. For more information on personal bankruptcy, see the *Consumer Guidebook to Law & Leading Attorneys*, Bankruptcy Law Chapter.

BACKGROUND

Bankruptcy law is almost entirely federal law. The United States Constitution grants to the federal government the exclusive right to make bankruptcy laws. Pursuant to this authority, the federal government created the Bankruptcy Code, Bankruptcy Rules of Procedure, and a system of bankruptcy courts to handle bankruptcies throughout the country. This is not to say that bankruptcy law is uniform throughout the nation, however. Although the federal government has final authority to make all bankruptcy laws, in some instances the Bankruptcy Code grants to individual states the power to deviate from or to supplement federal rules in very limited circumstances. For instance, the Bankruptcy Code allows a debtor to keep certain assets, known as exempt assets, that creditors cannot reach to satisfy a debt. The Bankruptcy Code gives individual states the authority to expand the categories of exempt assets if they choose. Thus, although bankruptcy law is federal law rather than state law, the amount and type of assets that are beyond the reach of creditors differ depending upon the state in which the debtor files for bankruptcy. Attorneys experienced in handling business bankruptcies can advise a business on where best to file for bankruptcy to receive the most favorable treatment from the local bankruptcy court.

THE MOST COMMON BUSINESS BANKRUPTCIES

The Bankruptcy Code creates different categories of bankruptcy, known as chapters, appropriate for different debtors. The most common forms of business bankruptcy are Chapter 7 and Chapter 11.

CHAPTER 7

The vast majority of bankruptcy cases filed are Chapter 7 cases. Chapter 7, often called "liquidation bankruptcy," is commonly used by individuals who simply want to walk away from their debt, but it may also be used by businesses that want to terminate their operations and liquidate their assets. When a debtor files Chapter 7, the bankruptcy court appoints a person to administer the case. This person, called the trustee, is a private citizen, not an employee of the court. The debtor turns over some or all of his or her debts and assets to the trustee, and the trustee then liquidates the property by selling it off and dividing the resulting cash among the creditors. The trustee can sue and be sued on behalf of the estate.

Petition and Schedules

A Chapter 7 case begins when the debtor files a petition with the bankruptcy court. Any individual, partnership, or corporation can file Chapter 7 regardless of the amount of debt or whether the debtor is solvent or insolvent. The petition should be filed with the court serving the area where the debtor lives or where his or her principal place of business or assets are located.

Along with the petition, or shortly thereafter, the debtor files with the court several schedules listing current income and expenditures, a statement of financial affairs, all executory contracts, existing or potential lawsuits by or against the debtor, and any recent transfers of assets. If a debtor does not reveal a debt in these schedules, the bankruptcy court cannot discharge or cancel that debt. Any debt omitted from these schedules is called a non-scheduled debt and is not affected by the bankruptcy.

Stay

Filing the petition automatically stops (stays) all of the listed creditors from trying to collect the money owed them. The stay arises automatically, without any judicial action, although the court usually notifies creditors of the filing of the petition. The stay is effective from the time of filing, even if the creditors do not receive notice until much later. As long as the stay is in effect, creditors generally cannot start or continue actions against the debtor to collect on the debt. Lawsuits, garnishment actions, and even telephone calls to the debtor must cease. See Stay section, page 66.

Creditors Meeting

After the debtor files a Chapter 7 petition, the court appointed trustee administers the case and liquidates assets. The trustee usually calls a meeting of the debtor, the debtor's attorney, and the creditors. The debtor must attend this meeting. Creditors may attend in order to ask questions and examine documents concerning the debtor's financial affairs and property. In most Chapter 7 bankruptcies, all of the debtor's assets are either exempt or subject to valid liens, so there are no assets for creditors to pursue. In these cases, known as "no asset" cases, it is likely that no creditors will attend the creditors meeting. If it appears that a case will have assets to pursue, usually creditors do attend this meeting to gather information about the case because they plan to ask the bankruptcy judge to declare some of the debts non-dischargeable, they plan to challenge the exempt status of some asset, or they plan to file claims. After the creditors meeting, the creditors can file a claim against the debtor with the court. If the debtor has non-exempt assets free of security interests, these are used to satisfy valid claims.

Liquidation, Discharge, and Reaffirmation

A Chapter 7 bankruptcy concludes when the trustee sells the debtor's property, distributes the cash to the creditors, and discharges the remaining debt. The trustee's primary role is to sell off the debtor's non-exempt assets in a way that maximizes the amount the creditors receive for their claims. Revenues from assets subject to security interests, such as property subject to a mortgage, are used to satisfy the debt on the particular asset. The discharge extinguishes the debtor's remaining liability on the debt. Certain items are non-dischargeable and thus unaffected by the bankruptcy. Non-dischargeable assets include most tax obligations, liability for damages resulting from willful or malicious acts, debts incurred by giving false financial information, or debts incurred for luxury goods or services just before bankruptcy.

Creditors can ask the court to deny an individual debtor a discharge. The grounds for denial of discharge are extremely narrow and requests for denial are rarely granted. Grounds for denial include failing to adequately explain the loss of assets, perjury or failing to obey lawful orders of the court, and fraudulently transferring, concealing, or destroying property that should be in the estate.

Because a secured creditor has rights that permit him or her to seize pledged property, a debtor may want to reaffirm a debt even after it has been discharged if the debtor wants to keep the property. A reaffirmation is an agreement between the debtor and the secured creditor that the creditor will not exercise his or her right to take back the asset so long as the debtor makes payments. A debtor must wait six years before filing for Chapter 7 again.

CHAPTER 11

Chapter 11 is frequently referred to as "reorganization bankruptcy." Individuals are permitted to file for Chapter 11, but it is generally used for business reorganizations. Under this chapter of the Bankruptcy Code, a debtor is given time to satisfy its debts while still continuing to operate its business. The major justification for Chapter 11 is that the value of a business as an operating entity is almost always greater than it would be were the business forced to cease operations and its assets sold off. In a Chapter 11 reorganization the debtor is given "breathing room" in which to restructure its debt while continuing to provide jobs for its employees, pay creditors, and produce a return for investors. During the repayment period, the company is usually allowed to continue operating under the current owner unless the creditors can show that the management is unfit to run the company.

Petition

Chapter 11 usually commences when the debtor business voluntarily files a bankruptcy petition. Involuntary petitions are discussed below. The voluntary petition should follow official forms available from legal stationary stores. In the petition, the business includes information concerning its name, place of operation, location of principal assets, a debtor's plan or notice of intent to file a plan, and a request for relief. By filing for Chapter 11, the business automatically becomes a "debtor in possession," a debtor that possesses and controls its assets even though undergoing reorganization under Chapter 11. Unlike Chapter 7 bankruptcy cases, a trustee is not automatically appointed in Chapter 11 cases. Instead, in Chapter 11 cases, the bankruptcy judge has discretion to decide whether it is necessary to appoint a trustee. Generally, trustees are not appointed in Chapter 11 cases. If appointed, the trustee assumes control of the business that filed for Chapter 11.

Stay

Filing the petition automatically stops (stays) all of the listed creditors from trying to collect the money owed them. The stay arises automatically, without any judicial action, although the court usually does notify creditors of the filing of the petition. The stay is effective from the time of filing, even if the creditors do not receive notice until much later. As long as the stay is in effect, creditors generally cannot start or continue actions against the debtor to collect on the debt. Lawsuits, garnishment actions, and even telephone calls to the debtor must cease. In some situations, such as when a creditor has clear title to a particular property and the property is not necessary to the reorganization, a secured creditor can petition the court for relief from the automatic stay to recover the property.

Plan

The debtor also files a written disclosure statement and plan of reorganization with the court. For 120 days after the filing, the debtor has an exclusive right to file a plan. After the exclusive right expires, a creditor or the case trustee can file a competing plan. Chapter 11 cases can drag on in court for years, but the creditors' right to file a competing plan acts as an incentive for the debtor to file a plan within the exclusive period. The disclosure statement contains detailed information about the debtor's assets and liabilities and is meant to be used by the creditors to evaluate the debtor's plan of reorganization. The plan must classify outstanding claims and detail how each class of claims will be treated. The plan also must show that the creditors will receive more money if the business is allowed to continue operation than they would if the assets of the company were liquidated. All creditors whose contractual rights will be modified or who will be paid less than they are owed are given a right to vote on the plan. In order for it to be accepted by the creditors, each class must approve the plan with a majority vote. The plan must also be approved by the court. If the court approves the plan, but some of the creditors do not, the court can force the reluctant creditors to accept it. If a plan is not approved, the company can be liquidated

COMMON BANKRUPTCY ISSUES

A number of issues are common in both Chapter 7 and Chapter 11 bankruptcies.

INVOLUNTARY BANKRUPTCY

Unlike the situations described above where the debtor decides whether to file bankruptcy, in an involuntary bankruptcy, creditors force the debtor into bankruptcy. Under certain conditions, creditors can petition the Bankruptcy Court to initiate a Chapter 7 or 11 bankruptcy against a debtor. The court will only accept such a petition if it is signed by at least three creditors who are owed a total of at least $5000 in unsecured debt. If a debtor has fewer than 12 unsecured creditors, however, just one unsecured creditor owed at least $5000 can file an involuntary bankruptcy petition.

Involuntary bankruptcy is rare, but if someone does file a petition against a debtor in Bankruptcy Court, the debtor has an opportunity to file an answer to the petition and refute any charges made against it by creditors in the petition. If the judge sides with the debtor, the court dismisses the petition and can make the creditors pay reasonable attorney's fees and any money the debtor loses in defending the case. In addition, if the judge decides that the petition was filed in bad faith, the court may also order the creditors to pay punitive damages to the debtor.

Conversion, Dismissal, and Suspension

The petitioner's original choice of bankruptcy chapter is not permanent. Once begun, a case may be voluntarily or involuntarily converted to a new chapter. Requirements for conversion vary from chapter to chapter, but once converted from a chapter, a case may not be converted back to the previous chapter. The bankruptcy court has authority to suspend or dismiss a case. The court can suspend or dismiss a case "for cause," for failure to pay filing fees, or "if the interests of creditors and the debtor would be better served by such dismissal or suspension."

Transfers to Avoid Losing an Asset in Bankruptcy

Some transfers that are valid in regular business relationships are invalid when one party is in or approaching bankruptcy. The Bankruptcy Code empowers a bankruptcy trustee to invalidate a number of transfers made prior to a bankruptcy filing.

Fraudulent Conveyances

The Uniform Fraudulent Transfer Act is designed to remove any temptation a debtor may have to hide property, for example, by giving it to a relative before declaring bankruptcy. Any transfer of the debtor's assets made within 90 days of filing for bankruptcy or within one year if a relative or business associate is involved is carefully scrutinized by the Bankruptcy Court. If the court determines that the debtor was attempting to defraud creditors by selling property at a below-market price, the court can order the property or other assets be given over to the trustee. Anything that was sold at a reasonable market value before a bankruptcy filing cannot be recovered by the court under the rules of the Uniform Fraudulent Transfer Act.

Preferences

A preference occurs when a debtor unfairly treats one creditor more favorably than another creditor similarly situated. For instance, if a debtor with only $100 owes $100 each to creditors A and B and pays A completely, leaving nothing for B, then A has received a preference and B has been harmed by the preference given to A. Bankruptcy condemns preferences if the following conditions exist:

- Transfer is for the benefit of a creditor

- Transfer is made for debt owed prior to the initiation of bankruptcy

- Debtor is insolvent at the time of transfer

- Transfer is made either 90 days before filing of the bankruptcy or one year before filing if made to an insider such as a relative or director of a corporate debtor

- Transfer lets a creditor receive more than it would have in a hypothetical Chapter 7 liquidation of the debtor's estate

Creditors receiving preferences can be forced to "disgorge" them by returning the assets to the debtor's estate so that other creditors can share them equally.

EFFECTS OF DECLARING BANKRUPTCY

The old adage that it is better to know how to swim before jumping into deep water applies to any business considering filing bankruptcy. One of the most obvious effects of declaring bankruptcy can be serious damage to one's business credit rating. Because a bad credit rating can follow a business for a long time, even relatively simple bankruptcies are not painless.

Another drawback to bankruptcy is public exposure. One of the first events in many bankruptcies is a meeting between the debtor and all its creditors. At this meeting, the creditors and a court-appointed trustee are allowed to examine all the debtor's financial records, such as bank statements and loan documents, and ask questions about how money has been spent. For a business with anything unsavory to hide, a bankruptcy proceeding can be incriminating. For some businesses, the public exposure of bankruptcy may permit competitors to get an unfair inside look at how the business is run.

Finally, bankruptcy can be expensive. Understandably, bankruptcy attorneys are very careful about a clients' ability to pay legal bills. Most bankruptcy attorneys usually collect enough money in advance from their near-bankrupt clients to handle a typical bankruptcy filing. Any contest with creditors will push fees higher, to a level that many businesses may be unable to pay. In addition, the trustee in charge of a bankruptcy case is paid by commission, a percentage of the money that he or she distributes to pay creditors.

ALTERNATIVES TO BANKRUPTCY

Any business in financial trouble has undoubtedly received many letters from creditors demanding payment on debts owed. Even a very demanding creditor may have a change of heart once a debtor mentions the possibility of filing bankruptcy, because creditors know that bankruptcy means that they may only get a fraction of what is owed them.

If a business is confident that its financial problems are only temporary, it may want to consider asking major creditors to accept reduced payments for a short period or asking for a short delay in making payments. Provided that the debtor has not already given creditors reason to doubt its sincerity, e.g., by completely ignoring their letters or by consistently breaking promises, chances are good that creditors will agree on one of these plans.

As mentioned above, creditors know that bankruptcy means they will probably get just a small fraction of the total sum owed them. Creditors also know that if they sue to collect their money, they will undergo the hassle of going to a judge to get a court order to force the debtor to pay. This is time-consuming and costly. All these factors make it more likely that a creditor will agree to a repayment plan.

WORKOUTS

The term "workout" is used to describe a somewhat nebulous process whereby a business and its creditors get together to realign their financial expectations of each other. Workouts can be traumatizing and all parties involved typically come away with less than they had going into the process, but a successful workout can be better for all involved than bankruptcy. If a business's financial prospects dramatically worsen, creditors may need to accept a lower rate of interest or payments drawn out over a longer period of time, or they may see the business collapse entirely. Creditors, shareholders, labor unions, management, and suppliers need to realize that diminished returns from a financially troubled company may be preferable to the returns from a defunct company. The primary advantages of workout over bankruptcy are that workout gives the parties greater control over the process (no interference from bankruptcy court) and it can dramatically cut legal fees.

Workout sometimes commences voluntarily when far-sighted management, realizing that commitments will not be met, approaches creditors to obtain more favorable terms. Dramatic events, such as litigation losses, environmental catastrophes, and changes in business or economic conditions can also trigger the need for workout.

Workout and bankruptcy proceedings are often interrelated. For example, the threat of filing for bankruptcy may provide needed impetus for recalcitrant parties to agree to a workout plan. Similarly, if a business is able to agree to a plan of workout with most, but not all, of its creditors and investors, then a Chapter 11 petition may be used as a tool to force the remaining creditors to go along with the terms of the workout.

To the uninitiated, workout may seem like a game with no rules or a trip without a map. In part, this is true; the parties have a great deal of flexibility to come to new terms between themselves. Theoretically, they can do whatever they want. Realistically, however, the possibility of filing for Chapter 11 creates a set of "pseudo-rules" for workouts that establish parameters for negotiations. Parties know that if they refuse to go along with a plan similar to what would be approved in a hypothetical Chapter 11 case, bankruptcy proceedings can be initiated, and a plan enforced against their will. Similarly, if a debtor and one creditor come to a workout agreement that unfairly disadvantages other creditors, the remaining creditors might initiate involuntary bankruptcy proceedings and have the workout plan invalidated as a preference.

The biggest concern for lenders going into workout negotiations is potential lender liability. A creditor always needs to resist the temptation to take control of the business because if a creditor becomes so involved in the debtor's business that it controls the business, the creditor may become liable for any damages incurred. This possibility is particularly serious because the definition of when a creditor "controls a debtor" is hazy and difficult to define. There is no simple formula to apply and courts look to all the creditor's actions in the broadest context. Financial management of a debtor's business can have especially high risks in environmental matters. In one notorious case (the *Fleet Factors* decision), a court held that a lender could be held liable for Superfund cleanup costs of the debtor's facility if the lender "had the ability to influence the hazardous waste decisions of its borrower" even though the lender had never actually participated in the decision-making process. Mere ability to influence can equal lender liability.

RESOURCES

Bankruptcy in Minnesota. This free booklet is available by sending a self-addressed, stamped envelope to: Pamphlets, Minnesota State Bar Association, 514 Nicollet Mall, Suite 300, Minneapolis, MN 55402.

Minnesota Small Business Assistance Office, 500 Metro Square, 121 Seventh Place E, St. Paul, MN 55101-2146, (612) 296-3871 or (800) 657-3858. The organization publishes *A Guide to Starting a Business in Minnesota*, a helpful resource that is available for no charge.

BANKRUPTCY & WORKOUT LAW LEADING ATTORNEYS

The attorneys profiled below were recommended by their peers in a statewide survey.

The attorneys profiled in this section were nominated by their peers in a statewide survey conducted in 1993 in which several thousand Minnesota attorneys were asked to name the lawyer to whom they would send a friend or family member in need of legal assistance in the area of *Bankruptcy & Workout Law.*

Because the survey resulted in a list of less than five percent of Minnesota's practicing attorneys, this should not be construed as a complete list. Nevertheless, it is an excellent source of highly qualified and reputable attorneys, who, if unable to assist can in most cases make quality referrals.

A list of all attorneys nominated in this category is found at the end of this section. For information on the survey methodology see page ix.

Please note that the shorter, two line attorney listings in this section are of attorneys who practice in this area but whose full biographical profile appears in another section of this book. A bullet "•" preceeding name indicates the attorney was nominated in this particular area of law. For information on the format of these profiles, consult the section "Using the *Business Guidebook*" found on page xiv. Note that the following abbreviations are used throughout these profiles:

App.	- Appellate	ABA	- American Bar Association
Cir.	- Circuit	ATLA	- American Trial Lawyers Association
Ct.	- Court	HCBA	- Hennepin County Bar Association
Dist.	- District	MDLA	- Minnesota Defense Lawyers Association
Hon.	- Honorable	MSBA	- Minnesota State Bar Association
JD	- Law degree (Juris Doctor)	MTLA	- Minnesota Trial Lawyers Association
LLB	- Law degree	NBTA	- National Board of Trial Advocacy
LLM	- Master in Law degree	RCBA	- Ramsey County Bar Association
Sup.	- Supreme		

JAMES L. BAILLIE

Fredrikson & Byron, P.A.
1100 International Centre
900 Second Avenue South
Minneapolis, MN 55402

Phone: (612) 347-7013
Fax: (612) 347-7077

Admitted: 1967 Minnesota; 1969 US Ct. App. (8th Cir.); 1980 US Ct. App. (5th Cir.)
Birthdate: 08/27/42

•**JAMES L. BAILLIE:** Mr. Baillie is chair of Fredrikson & Byron's Bankruptcy Group. His areas of practice are business litigation, debtor-creditor remedies, and commercial law with special emphasis on Chapter 11 reorganization, loan workouts, and financial restructuring. Mr. Baillie has extensive experience in negotiating, analyzing companies, and managing crisis situations. He is one of six Minnesota bankruptcy lawyers listed in *The Best Lawyers in America*. He received the first ABA National Pro Bono Publico Award in 1984. His representative lectures include "How to Do a Motion in Bankruptcy Court," 1993 Minnesota Continuing Legal Education Bankruptcy Institute; "Hostile Purchases of Assets and Creditors' Plans," 1992 Minnesota Continuing Legal Education Bankruptcy Institute; "Waiver of Debtor Rights in Workout Agreements: Enforceability and Advisability," 1993 National Conference of Bankruptcy Judges; "The Role of the PBGC in Restructuring," 1991 Institute for International Research; "The Role of the Board in Turn Arounds," 1990 National Association of Corporate Directors.
Education: JD 1967, University of Chicago; AB 1964, University of Chicago.
Employment History: Judicial Clerk 1967-1968, Hon. Miles W. Lord, Judge, US District Court, District of Minnesota.
Representative Clients: Munsingwear; Endotronics.
Professional Associations: ABA (Coeditor, *Bankruptcy Litigation*, Litigation Section, Bankruptcy and Insolvency Committee newsletter; Board of Editors, *Business Law Today*, Business Law Section magazine; Chair, ABA Standing Committee on Lawyers' Public Service Responsibility); MSBA (Chair 1985-88, Bankruptcy Section; Chair 1982-85, Committee on Legal Assistance to the Disadvantaged); HCBA (Chair 1977-1979, Debtor-Creditor Committee).
Firm: James Baillie is chair of Fredrikson & Byron's Bankruptcy Group which includes nine attorneys and focuses on bankruptcy and debtor-creditor matters. It is the largest and among the most respected practices of this type in the region. Mr. Baillie works closely with Faye Knowles, Clinton Cutler, Ann Ladd, Jon Nuckles, David Marshall, William Connors, Kimberly Nordby, and John Koneck. *See additional listing in Commercial Litigation Chapter.*

Bankruptcy & Workout Law Leading Attorneys

•**JAMES F. CHRISTOFFEL** - Christoffel, Elliott & Albrecht, P.A. - 100 South Fifth Street, Suite 1250 - Minneapolis, MN 55402 - Phone: (612) 672-0900, Fax: (612) 341-2835 - *See complete biographical profile in Commercial Real Estate Law Chapter.*

•**KATHERINE A. CONSTANTINE:** Ms. Constantine practices in the area of bankruptcy and workout law and banking law, with an emphasis on creditor representation. Her practice includes the representation of indenture trustees, secured lenders, and unsecured creditors in restructurings, reorganizations, liquidations, and avoidance actions. She also represents lenders in loan transactions and purchasers in the acquisition of assets from bankruptcy estates. Ms. Constantine has been with the firm since 1986 and a partner in the Banking and Commercial Department since 1989. In addition to her work with Dorsey & Whitney, Ms. Constantine offers her time as a lecturer for Minnesota Continuing Legal Education.
Education: JD 1980, Georgetown University (Associate Editor 1979-80, *The Tax Lawyer*); BSFS 1977 magna cum laude, Georgetown University (Phi Beta Kappa).
Employment History: Partner 1989-present, Associate 1986-88, Dorsey & Whitney; Associate 1983-85, Fabyanske Svoboda & Westra P.A.; Associate 1980-83, Nichols, Kruger, Starks and Carruthers.
Representative Clients: First Trust National Association; First Bank National Association; Minneapolis Employees Retirement Fund; City of Brooklyn Center; Riverside Bank; Texaco; Northern States Power Company.
Professional Associations: MSBA (Bankruptcy Section); HCBA; ABA; American Bankruptcy Institute; Minnesota Women Lawyers.
Community Involvement: Active member of the Kenwood neighborhood advisory council and school volunteer.
Firm: Dorsey & Whitney is the largest law firm in Minnesota and one of the largest firms in the United States with over 350 lawyers in 12 offices. The depth and breadth of the experience of its lawyers enables it to provide a broad range of services to meet the diverse legal needs of its client base, which includes Fortune 500 companies, public agencies, banks and other financial institutions, nonprofit organizations, individual investors, family owned businesses, and high-tech and low-tech, growth oriented companies. *See additional listing in Banking Law Chapter.*

KATHERINE A. CONSTANTINE

Dorsey & Whitney
Pillsbury Center South
220 South Sixth Street
Minneapolis, MN 55402-1498

Phone: (612) 340-8792
Fax: (612) 340-2643

Admitted: 1980 Minnesota;
1980 US Dist. Ct. (MN);
1985 US Ct. App. (8th Cir.)
Birthdate: 04/01/55

•**TED E. DEANER:** Mr. Deaner has represented lenders for 34 years. His experience includes developing and writing loan procedures and forms for the documentation of loans and handling all phases of loan collection such as workouts, restructures, real and personal property foreclosures, bankruptcies, and lender liability issues. He also practices commercial real estate law and is developing his practice in the areas of employment policies and procedures for employers, especially personnel policies, hiring, firing, sexual harassment, and ADA issues. Mr. Deaner is certified as a Real Property Law Specialist by the Minnesota State Bar Association and is a certified course trained general arbitrator and mediator. He is an author and lecturer on topics of concern to lenders and other creditors.
Education: JD 1960, University of Minnesota; BSL 1958, Amherst College, University of Minnesota.
Representative Clients: Several Farm Credit System institutions as well as regional and local banks.
Professional Associations: MSBA (Real Property Law Section (Governing Council 1992-present); Business Law Section; Agricultural Law Section; Economics of Law Practice Committee (Chair 1974-75)); MN Board of Continuing Legal Education (1980-81); Olmsted County Bar Assn. (President 1980-81); ABA (Business Law Section Committee on Commercial Financial Services and Subcommittee on Agricultural Financing; Law Practice Management Section; Advisory Board, Real Property and Probate and Trust Law Section's Forum Committee on Rural Lawyers and Agribusiness); American Agricultural Law Assn. (Board member 1989-92).
Firm: O'Brien, Ehrick, Wolf, Deaner & Maus has roots reaching back to 1933 when it was founded by F. J. O'Brien as a sole practitioner. In addition to Mr. Deaner, who is a Certified Real Property Specialist, the firm's current partners include four others who are certified as Civil Trial Specialists by the Minnesota State Bar Association. Family law partner Jill Frieders is a Fellow of the American Academy of Matrimonial Lawyers. Good library resources and computerization augment the firm's services to its clients. *See additional listings in Employment Law and Commercial Real Estate Law Chapters.*

TED E. DEANER

O'Brien, Ehrick, Wolf, Deaner & Maus
Marquette Bank Building
Suite 611
P.O. Box 968
Rochester, MN 55903

Phone: (507) 289-4041
Fax: (507) 281-4778

Admitted: 1960 Minnesota;
1961 US Dist. Ct. (MN);
1990 US Ct. App. (8th Cir.);
1978 US Sup. Ct.
Birthdate: 01/23/36

FREDERICK A. DUDDERAR

Hanft, Fride, O'Brien, Harries, Swelbar & Burns, P.A.
1000 First Bank Place
130 West Superior Street
Duluth, MN 55802

Phone: (218) 722-4766
Fax: (218) 720-4920

Admitted: 1981 Minnesota; 1979 Indiana
Birthdate: 04/04/54

•**FREDERICK A. DUDDERAR:** Mr. Dudderar represents both secured creditors and business debtors in matters pertaining to loan enforcement and restructuring, including workout arrangements and Chapter 11 bankruptcy reorganization. His practice also includes debtor-creditor litigation and commercial law and arbitration.
Education: JD 1979, Valparaiso University; BA 1976, Indiana University.
Employment History: Currently, Hanft, Fride, O'Brien, Harries, Swelbar & Burns, P.A.; Law Clerk 1981-82, Minnesota Supreme Court; Law Clerk 1979-81, Indiana Court of Appeals, Fourth District.
Representative Clients: First Bank North, N.A.; First Bank Minnesota, N.A.; Norwest Bank Minnesota North, N.A.; Minnesota Power & Light Company; Archer Brothers, Inc.; Pioneer National Bank; Johnson-Wilson Builders Company; Lakehead Sign Company; Lutsen Resort Company; Commissioner, Iron Range Resources and Rehabilitation.
Professional Associations: MSBA; ABA.
Community Involvement: Legal Aid Service of Northeastern Minnesota (Board Chair 1991-present); Superior Hiking Trail Assn. (Board member 1991-93).
Firm: Founded in 1899, Hanft, Fride, O'Brien, Harries, Swelbar & Burns, P.A., is a full service law firm engaged primarily in business and trial work. The firm's 17 attorneys serve clients throughout Minnesota, northern Wisconsin, and beyond. S*ee additional listings in Closely Held Business Law and Commercial Litigation Chapters.*

•**SHAWN M. DUNLEVY** - Fryberger, Buchanan, Smith & Frederick, P.A. - 302 West Superior Street, Suite 700 - Duluth, MN 55802 - Phone: (218) 722-0861, Fax: (218) 722-9568 - *See complete biographical profile in Banking Law Chapter.*

CHRISTOPHER A. ELLIOTT

Christoffel, Elliott & Albrecht, P.A.
100 South Fifth Street
Suite 1250
Minneapolis, MN 55402

Phone: (612) 672-0900
Fax: (612) 341-2835

Admitted: 1981 Minnesota; 1981 Iowa; 1981 US Dist. Ct. (MN); 1981 US Bankruptcy Ct. (MN)
Birthdate: 08/05/57

•**CHRISTOPHER A. ELLIOTT:** Mr. Elliott handles business bankruptcy, creditor/debtor litigation, financial restructuring, and commercial law. His work involves representation of business debtors in bankruptcy proceedings. Mr. Elliott has been lead counsel in bankruptcy proceedings involving debtors with assets exceeding $150 million.
Education: JD 1981, University of Iowa; BS 1978, University of Iowa.
Employment History: Founding Partner 1989-present, Christoffel, Elliott & Albrecht, P.A.; Associate/Shareholder 1983-1989, Fabyanske, Svoboda, Westra & Davis, P.A.; Law Clerk 1982-1983, Hon. Kenneth G. Owens, Chief Judge, US Bankruptcy Court, District of Minnesota; Law Clerk 1981-1982, Hon. Bruce M. Snell, Jr., Judge, Iowa Court of Appeals.
Professional Associations: HCBA; RCBA; MSBA; The Iowa State Bar Assn.
Firm: Mr. Elliott is one of the original partners of Christoffel, Elliott & Albrecht, P.A., founded in 1989. In addition to Mr. Elliott's areas of expertise, the firm concentrates on banking, real estate, commercial law, and commercial litigation. James Christoffel represents all types of lending clients including national banks, state chartered banks, asset based lenders, venture capital funds, construction lenders, permanent lenders, and equipment lessors. Gary Albrecht leads the firm's commercial litigation practice which includes representation of lenders, investors, and telecommunication industry clients. *See additional listings in Banking Law and Commercial Real Estate Law Chapters.*

DOUGLAS B. GREENSWAG

Leonard, Street and Deinard Professional Association
150 South Fifth Street, Suite 2300
Minneapolis, MN 55402

Phone: (612) 335-1527
Fax: (612) 335-1657

Admitted: 1983 Minnesota
Birthdate: 05/22/57

•**DOUGLAS B. GREENSWAG:** Mr. Greenswag practices principally in the area of commercial bankruptcy and workouts as counsel for creditors, debtors, and equity holders. The matters handled by Mr. Greenswag range from small family businesses up to transactions involving about $500 million in debt. He is certified as a Business Bankruptcy Specialist by the American Bankruptcy Board of Certification. Mr. Greenswag is a frequent lecturer on bankruptcy to Minnesota Continuing Legal Education, Minnesota Institute for Legal Education, National Business Institute, and the Minnesota Chamber of Commerce and Industry. Some of his lecture topics include protecting secured creditors in Minnesota and defending preferences and good faith issues in Chapter 11 reorganization plans.
Education: JD 1983 magna cum laude, University of Iowa; BA 1979 cum laude, Colgate University.
Employment History: 1983-present, Shareholder 1990-present, Leonard, Street and Deinard.
Representative Clients: Transamerica Commercial Finance Corp.; Lull Industries, Inc.; Columbia Gas Transmission Corp.; National City Bank; Ball, Ball & Brosamer, Inc.; James E. Ramette, Bankruptcy Trustee; Fleet Credit Corp.; RD Management Corp.
Professional Associations: ABA (Bankruptcy and Litigation Sections); MSBA (Bankruptcy Section); American Bankruptcy Institute; HCBA.
Community Involvement: Capital Community Services (Board member).
Firm: Leonard, Street and Deinard is a full service commercial law firm of approximately 125 attorneys. The firm includes a specialized section devoted to business bankruptcies and workouts, of which Mr. Greenswag is a member. *See additional listing in Banking Law Chapter.*

•**RICHARD D. HOLPER:** Mr. Holper is a shareholder in Holper Welsh & Mitchell, Ltd., and practices in the areas of financing, financial and real estate restructuring, asset-based commercial and real estate lending, commercial litigation, and business and real estate reorganization. He lectures frequently and writes in the area of bankruptcy. He is author of "The Impact of Bankruptcy Reform Act upon Certain Provisions of the Uniform Commercial Code," 3 *Hamline L. Rev.*, 1 (Rev. 1986); editor, 1980-92, of *Bankruptcy Law Letter* (Warren, Gorham, & Lamont, Inc.); and contributing author to *Uniform Commercial Code Deskbook*. In addition, he is listed in *The Best Lawyers in America* (Minnesota Bankruptcy 1989-1993).
Education: JD 1971 summa cum laude, University of Louisville (Editor-in-Chief, *Law Review*; Delta Theta Phi); BA 1965 with distinction, Marquette University.
Employment History: Shareholder 1992-present, Holper Welsh & Mitchell, Ltd.; Managing Partner 1990-92, Robins, Kaplan, Miller & Ciresi (Chicago office).
Representative Clients: Premier Salons International, Inc.; Bioplasty, Inc.; Cascade Medical, Inc.; First Bank National Assn.; ITT Commercial Finance; The First National Bank of Chicago.
Professional Associations: ABA; American College of Bankruptcy (Fellow); American Bankruptcy Institute (Board member 1986-89); Commercial Law League of America (1974-present); MSBA (Chair 1982-85, Bankruptcy Section); State Bar of Wisconsin; Illinois State Bar Assn.; National Assn. of Accountants in Insolvencies (Associate member 1982-86).

RICHARD D. HOLPER

Holper Welsh & Mitchell, Ltd.
750 Pillsbury Center
200 South Sixth Street
Minneapolis, MN 55402

Phone: (612) 373-2200
Fax: (612) 373-2222

Admitted: 1971 Minnesota; 1982 Wisconsin; 1990 Illinois; 1971 US Dist. Ct. (MN); 1971 US Ct. App. (8th Cir.); 1982 US Dist. Ct. (W. Dist. WI); 1982 US Dist. Ct. (E. Dist. WI); 1990 US Dist. Ct. (N. Dist. IL)
Birthdate: 01/03/43

•**MICHAEL J. IANNACONE:** Mr. Iannacone handles bankruptcy cases under Chapters 7, 11, 12, and 13, workouts and collections, representing debtors or lenders and also serving as a Bankruptcy Trustee. He is appointed by the Department of Justice, Office of the United States Trustee to act as a Trustee in approximately 600 cases per year and to act as operating Trustee in Chapter 11 cases.
Education: JD 1975, William Mitchell; BA 1970, Harvard University.
Employment History: Solo practitioner in St. Paul since 1976.
Representative Clients: Served as Chapter 11 Trustee for the French Accent; Chapter 7 Trustee for Schaak Electronics, Hoffmann Electric, and Kullberg-White; represented debtor in *In re Substad*, which upheld exempt status of over $200,000 of IRA funds; represented farmers and lenders during the farm crises of the middle 1980s.
Professional Associations: National Assn. of Bankruptcy Trustees; RCBA; MSBA; ABA.
Community Involvement: Woodbury Athletic Assn. (volunteer coach); Southeast Metro Sharks swim meets (head timer).
Firm: The Iannacone Law Office has one associate attorney, Heather L. Iannacone, who practices primarily in the trustee litigation and administration areas. *See additional listing in Commercial Litigation Chapter.*

MICHAEL J. IANNACONE

Iannacone Law Office
101 East Fifth Street
Suite 1614
St. Paul, MN 55101

Phone: (612) 224-3361
Fax: (612) 297-6187

Admitted: 1975 Minnesota; 1975 US Dist. Ct. (MN)
Birthdate: 07/17/48

DAVID KANTOR - Leonard, Street and Deinard Professional Association - 150 South Fifth Street, Suite 2300 - Minneapolis, MN 55402 - Phone: (612) 335-1500, Fax: (612) 335-1657 - *See complete biographical profile in Commercial Real Estate Law Chapter.*

DAVID W. KELLEY - Leonard, Street and Deinard Professional Association - 150 South Fifth Street, Suite 2300 - Minneapolis, MN 55402 - Phone: (612) 335-1500, Fax: (612) 335-1657 - *See complete biographical profile in Commercial Real Estate Law Chapter.*

Chapter 9: Bankruptcy & Workout Law

FAYE KNOWLES

Fredrikson & Byron, P.A.
1100 International Centre
900 Second Avenue South
Minneapolis, MN 55402

Phone: (612) 347-7054
Fax: (612) 347-7077

Admitted: 1978 Minnesota;
1983 US Dist. Ct. (MN);
1983 US Ct. App. (8th Cir.)
Birthdate: 01/19/49

•**FAYE KNOWLES:** Ms. Knowles is a shareholder, practicing with Fredrikson & Byron's Commercial Litigation/Bankruptcy Group. In addition, she serves on the firm's nine-member Board of Directors. She has a high level of experience in bankruptcy, debtor-creditor remedies, and commercial law. Before joining Fredrikson & Byron she was a partner in a small civil practice firm and brings a wide range of experience to commercial disputes. Ms. Knowles has excellent negotiating skills and the ability to quickly understand a company's business in order to analyze its potential for turnaround. Ms. Knowles is a frequent continuing legal education lecturer for local, state, and national education organizations on topics of bankruptcy and debtor-creditor law.
Education: JD 1978 cum laude, University of Minnesota (Appellate Advocacy Instructor 1977-78); BA 1971 cum laude, Carleton College.
Employment History: 1988-present, Fredrikson & Byron P.A.; Associate 1978-82, Partner 1983-88, Arnold & McDowell, Minneapolis (primary practice included bankruptcy, debtor-creditor remedies, corporate, partnership, franchise, and employment law).
Professional Associations: Federal Bar Assn.; MSBA (Board of Governors 1991-present; Chair 1991-92, Bankruptcy Section; Board member 1990-present, MSB Foundation; Editor 1985-86, *Minnesota Bankruptcy Bulletin*); HCBA (Debtor-Creditor Committee; Chair 1989-91, Bar Memorial Committee; Governing Council); American Bankruptcy Institute (Committees on Professional Compensation and Uniform Local Rules); American Bankruptcy Board of Certification (Board of Directors and Secretary 1992-present; Standards Committee 1992-present); Local Bankruptcy Rules Advisory Committee.
Firm: Ms. Knowles practices in Fredrikson & Byron's Bankruptcy Group, which focuses on bankruptcy and debtor-creditor matters. It is the largest and one of the most respected practices of this type in the state. This practice group is comprised of highly experienced bankruptcy attorneys, including James Baillie, Clinton Cutler, Ann Ladd, Jon Nuckles, David Marshall, Kimberly Nordby, William Connors, and John Koneck. *See additional listings in Commercial Litigation and Publicly Held Corporations Law Chapters.*

•**JOHN M. KONECK** - Fredrikson & Byron, P.A. - 1100 International Centre, 900 Second Avenue South - Minneapolis, MN 55402 - Phone: (612) 347-7038, Fax: (612) 347-7077 - *See complete biographical profile in Commercial Real Estate Law Chapter.*

HART KULLER

Winthrop & Weinstine, P.A.
3200 Minnesota World Trade Center
30 East Seventh Street
St. Paul, MN 55101

Phone: (612) 290-8400
Fax: (612) 292-9347

Admitted: 1976 Minnesota;
1976 US Bankruptcy Ct.
Birthdate: 12/05/51

•**HART KULLER:** Mr. Kuller handles bankruptcy and reorganization proceedings, mergers and acquisitions, and corporate and real estate finance. Mr. Kuller also lectures at professional institutes. His recent presentations include "Impossibility and Frustration of Performance," Contract Law in Minnesota, 5/27/93; "Recent Developments in Bankruptcy Case Law," Bankruptcy Litigation Institute Course Book, 4/28/92.
Education: JD 1976 cum laude, University of Minnesota; BA 1973 with honors, Northwestern University.
Employment History: Shareholder, Winthrop & Weinstine; 1976-79, Stacker & Ravich.
Professional Associations: HCBA; MSBA; ABA; American Bankruptcy Institute.
Firm: Winthrop & Weinstine has an active practice in commercial bankruptcy cases, workouts, financial restructurings, and reorganizations. The firm has been involved with substantially all major Chapter 11 cases brought before the United States Bankruptcy Court for the District of Minnesota. *See additional listings in Publicly Held Corporations Law and Commercial Real Estate Law Chapters.*

Bankruptcy & Workout Law Leading Attorneys

•PHILLIP L. KUNKEL: Mr. Kunkel practices commercial financing, real estate financing, foreclosures, workouts, and business bankruptcy law, primarily handling banking and bankruptcy matters for lenders. He is the author of several publications relating to bankruptcy and agricultural law and possesses extensive teaching and lecturing experience on the topics of workouts, commercial financing, and bankruptcy for William Mitchell, Hamline University, and University of Minnesota law schools. He is also a continuing legal education lecturer in Minnesota, North Dakota, Iowa, Arkansas, Colorado, Illinois, Missouri, and Washington.
Education: JD 1977 cum laude, University of Minnesota; BA 1974 magna cum laude, St. John's University.
Employment History: 1988-present, Hall, Byers, Hanson, Steil & Weinberger, P.A.; Attorney 1979-87, Moratzka, Dillon & Kunkel; Clerk 1977-79, Judge Kelly, First Judicial District.
Representative Clients: First American National Bank; Zapp National Bank.
Professional Associations: ABA (Business Bankruptcy and Commercial Financial Services Committees); MSBA (Bankruptcy Section; Banking Law Committee); American Agricultural Law Assn. (President 1988-89); American Bankruptcy Institute.
Community Involvement: St. John's University Alumni Assn.; Youth Soccer and Basketball (Coach); United Way.
Firm: The law firm of Hall, Byers, Hanson, Steil & Weinberger was founded in 1931 by Lawrence M. Hall, former Speaker of the Minnesota House of Representatives, and has operated continuously to the present time. Since the founding of the firm, the legal system and the practice of law have grown in size and complexity. To meet this growth, Hall, Byers, Hanson has also grown in size and ability to handle a wide variety of complex legal matters. At present the firm employs 40 persons, consisting of 16 attorneys and 24 support staff. Minneapolis address: 2904 Plaza VII, 45 South Seventh Street, Minneapolis, MN 55402. Phone: (612) 339-2553, Fax: (612) 339-4775. *See additional listing in Commercial Real Estate Law Chapter.*

PHILLIP L. KUNKEL

Hall, Byers, Hanson, Steil & Weinberger, P.A.
1010 West St. Germain
Suite 600
St. Cloud, MN 56301

Phone: (612) 252-4414
Fax: (612) 252-4482

Admitted: 1977 Minnesota; 1985 US Ct. App. (8th Cir.); 1985 US Sup. Ct.
Birthdate: 05/21/52

•DOUGLAS M. LAWRENCE: Mr. Lawrence concentrates his practice in the areas of asset-based lending, real estate finance, and bankruptcy and workouts, with an emphasis on commercial and mortgage loan transactions and workouts. Mr. Lawrence represents financial institutions and their clients on credit and real estate related matters ranging from small business loans to leveraged buyouts and from commercial real estate acquisitions to the resolution of troubled real estate loans. Prior to entering private practice, Mr. Lawrence was the vice president and associate general counsel for ITT Diversified Financial Corporation, and general counsel of its Capital Resources Group. During his 13-year tenure with ITT, Mr. Lawrence closed in excess of $400 million in asset-based financing on loans secured by motor freight, railcar, aircraft, construction, mobile equipment, industrial plant, equipment and fixtures, letters of credit, and real estate. Many of these transactions involved various types of income-producing property such as office towers, warehouses, condominiums, and shopping centers, on both fee and ground lease interests. Mr. Lawrence has significant interstate financial experience and has closed or restructured transactions on both coasts and in most regional financial centers. Since entering private practice, he has successfully restructured three major factor defaults without financial or environmental loss to the lender and without closure of the facility. He also has significant environmental law experience dealing with the identification, cost estimation, and cleanup of environmentally sensitive sites. In 1994 he acted as lead counsel on a $60 million loan secured by approximately 40 mortgages of various priority in four states for one of the largest refuse haulers in the Midwest. Mr. Lawrence has been a speaker and cochair of workshops addressing such topics as loan documentation and lender liability. He is the author of "Recent Developments in the Federal and State Superfund Laws," (*Hennepin Lawyer*) and is certified as a Real Property Law Specialist by the Minnesota State Bar Association.
Education: JD 1977, William Mitchell; Candidate MBA, Metropolitan State University; BA 1973, University of Minnesota.
Employment History: August 1994-present, Moss & Barnett; 1991-July 94, O'Connor & Hannan; 1977-90, ITT Financial Corp.; 1964-77, various retail and other positions.
Representative Clients: ITT Financial Corp.; System Sales Corp.; Resource Capital Corp.; Towle Real Estate.
Community Involvement: St. Paul United Way; Aikido Yoshinkai of Minneapolis/St. Paul.
Firm: See firm profile in Appendix C. *See additional listing in Banking Law Chapter.*

DOUGLAS M. LAWRENCE

Moss & Barnett, A Professional Association
4800 Norwest Center
90 South Seventh Street
Minneapolis, MN 55402

Phone: (612) 347-0349
Fax: (612) 339-6686

Admitted: 1977 Minnesota; 1981 US Dist. Ct. (MN); 1991 US Tax Ct.
Birthdate: 10/10/48

BRIAN F. LEONARD

O'Neill, Burke, O'Neill, Leonard & O'Brien, Ltd.
100 South Fifth Street
Suite 1200
Minneapolis, MN 55402

Phone: (612) 332-1030
Fax: (612) 332-2740

Admitted: 1973 Minnesota;
1986 Wisconsin;
1973 US Dist. Ct. (MN)
1976 US Ct. App. (8th Cir.);
1981 US Sup. Ct.
Birthdate: 01/27/48

•**BRIAN F. LEONARD:** Mr. Leonard represents financial institutions, businesses, and individuals in business and financial transactions, workout and business reorganizations, bankruptcy cases, and civil and bankruptcy litigation. This includes representation of numerous debtors, creditors, and creditors committees in Chapter 11 cases, and numerous creditors, debtors, and trustees in Chapter 7 cases. He represents secured lenders in commercial and real estate foreclosures and related litigation, liquidation proceedings, and secured creditor remedies litigation. Mr. Leonard also works extensively in business and asset acquisition and sales, and in negotiation and preparation of documentation for commercial loan transactions and restructuring thereof. Mr. Leonard has also served as operating trustee in many Chapter 11 business bankruptcy cases. He has lectured for many continuing legal education seminars and has been an adjunct professor at the University of Minnesota Law School.
Education: JD 1973, University of Minnesota (staff, *Minnesota Law Review*); BA 1970, University of North Dakota.
Employment History: Partner/Shareholder 1973-present, O'Neill, Burke, O'Neill, Leonard & O'Brien, Ltd.
Representative Clients: Commercial State Bank of Minnesota; Prudential Capital Corp.; Premier Banks; Princeton State Bank; First American Bank Metro; Resolution Trust Corp.; Federal Deposit Insurance Corp.; ITT Commercial Finance Corp.; The St. Paul Companies; Mid-America Bank; numerous closely held corporations, business organizations, and many creditors' committees, creditors, debtors, and trustees in bankruptcy proceedings.
Professional Associations: ABA; MSBA (Bankruptcy Section); RCBA; State Bar of Wisconsin.
Community Involvement: Minnesota Literacy Council, Inc. (Board of Directors); Southeast Metro YMCA (Fund-raiser); Suburban Literacy Project (Tutor).
Firm: O'Neill, Burke, O'Neill, Leonard & O'Brien, Ltd., has 23 lawyers and offices in Minneapolis and St. Paul. The firm provides legal services in a broad range of finance, business, corporate, banking, restructuring, workout, and real estate transactions together with civil and bankruptcy litigation. *See additional listings in Banking Law and Publicly Held Corporations Law Chapters.*

JOHN R. MCDONALD

Robins, Kaplan, Miller & Ciresi
2800 LaSalle Plaza
800 LaSalle Avenue
Minneapolis, MN 55402

Phone: (612) 349-8500
Fax: (612) 339-4181
800 number: (800) 553-9910

Admitted: 1985 Minnesota;
1986 US Dist. Ct. (MN)
Birthdate: 07/17/58

•**JOHN R. MCDONALD:** Mr. McDonald specializes in bankruptcy, insolvency, and reorganization, representing secured and unsecured creditors, creditors' committees, and debtors in Chapter 11 cases and in complex financial restructurings. Mr. McDonald also represents both plaintiffs and defendants in commercial litigation matters. He frequently lectures both locally and nationally on bankruptcy, secured transactions, and creditors' rights.
Education: JD 1985 with honors, Hamline University; MA 1982 cum laude, University of New Hampshire; BA 1981 cum laude, College of St. Thomas.
Employment History: Partner 1992-present, Robins, Kaplan, Miller & Ciresi; Associate 1989-92, Robins, Kaplan, Miller & Ciresi; Associate 1986-89, Fabyanske, Svoboda, Westra & Davis, P.A.; Associate 1985-86, LeFevere, Lefler, Kennedy, O'Brien & Drawz, P.A.
Representative Clients: Banking and other financial institutions, including Citicorp North America, Inc.; Norwest Bank Minnesota, N.A.; and Northern National Bank; creditors' committees, including those appointed in the Chapter 11 cases of Citi-Equity Group, Inc.; Brooks Hauser; 10,000 Auto Parts; and Monica Scott; and various business entities, including Larken Properties, Inc. and Amdura Corporation.
Professional Associations: American Bankruptcy Institute (1990-present, Mass Tort Task Force; 1990-present, Normal & Small Business Reorg. Committee); MSBA (Chair 1992-present, Bankruptcy Section, Legislative Committee; Chair 1991-present, Bankruptcy Section, Small Business Reorg. Committee); RCBA (1986-present); HCBA (1985-present).
Community Involvement: Children's Home Society of Minnesota (Crisis Nursery/Foster Parent); American Cancer Society (Volunteer); American Diabetes Foundation (Volunteer); Sharing and Caring Hands (Volunteer).
Firm: Robins, Kaplan, Miller & Ciresi is a national law firm with offices in eight major metropolitan areas throughout the country. The firm's lawyers provide a wide range of transactional and litigation services to a diverse group of clients including Fortune 500 companies, banks and lending institutions; property insurers; Big Six accounting firms; and foreign, state, and municipal governments. *See additional listing in Banking Law Chapter.*

•**MICHAEL L. MEYER:** Mr. Meyer has practiced business bankruptcy and workout law since 1975. Prior to 1991, Mr. Meyer represented both debtors and creditors. Since 1991, he exclusively represents debtors and unsecured creditors, including committees. Mr. Meyer, with his partner Michael McGrath, represented the debtor in the following recent chapter 11 cases in the District of Minnesota: R.L. Johnson (real estate developer); Retail Holdings Group, Inc. (chain of 130 women's clothing stores); Consul Restaurant Corp. (publicly traded restaurant franchisee); Country Club Markets, Inc. (grocery store chain); Lumber Exchange Building L.P. (office building); Harry A. Johnson, Jr. (real estate and hotel developer); and various single and multiple asset commercial real estate cases. Representation of these clients included all aspects of bankruptcy practice including several contested plan confirmation processes and a variety of commercial litigation matters in bankruptcy and nonbankruptcy courts. In addition, Mr. Meyer is a frequent lecturer at programs sponsored by Minnesota Continuing Legal Education and Minnesota Institute of Legal Education and a speaker on a variety of bankruptcy topics.
Education: JD 1974 cum laude, University of Minnesota; BA 1971, University of Minnesota.
Employment History: Shareholder 1991-present, Ravich, Meyer, Kirkman & McGrath, P.A.; Partner 1981-91, Associate 1975-81, Robins, Kaplan, Miller & Ciresi.
Professional Associations: MSBA (Bankruptcy Section); ABA (Business Bankruptcy Committee, Business Law Section); American Bankruptcy Institute.
Firm: Ravich, Meyer, Kirkman & McGrath, P.A., was formed in 1991 to represent businesses and individuals in financial and real estate matters and provide general business counseling. The firm consists of the four named shareholders, a legal assistant, and staff. The firm's philosophy is to provide services in its specialized areas with a minimum of delegation and reassignment. Many times the firm's representation is coordinated with and supplements that provided by the client's corporate lawyers.

MICHAEL L. MEYER

Ravich, Meyer, Kirkman & McGrath, P.A.
4545 IDS Center
80 South Eighth Street
Minneapolis, MN 55402

Phone: (612) 332-8511
Fax: (612) 332-8302

Admitted: 1975 Minnesota; 1975 US Dist. Ct. (MN); 1983 Massachusetts; 1983 US Dist. Ct. (MA); 1991 US Ct. App. (8th Cir.)
Birthdate: 03/28/49

•**HOWARD A. PATRICK:** Mr. Patrick represents debtors, financial institutions, creditors, creditors' committees, and plan sponsors in Chapter 11 cases and out-of-court restructuring matters and has been involved in major bankruptcy proceedings throughout the country for the past 30 years. He recently completed work on the reorganization of International Broadcasting Corporation where he represented IBC's largest creditor, National Westminster Bank, USA. Mr. Patrick is coauthor of "An Overview of the Bankruptcy Reform Act of 1978," reprinted in 1 *B. R.* 1, and is a frequent lecturer on bankruptcy, insolvency, workouts, and creditors' remedies.
Education: JD 1961, University of Minnesota; BS 1961, University of Minnesota.
Employment History: 1962-present, Robins, Kaplan, Miller & Ciresi; Law Clerk 1961-62, US District Court, District of Minnesota.
Professional Associations: ABA; American Bankruptcy Institute; Commercial Law Foundation (past President; Board member); Commercial Law League of America (Bankruptcy and Insolvency Section); Federal Bar Assn.; HCBA; MSBA (past Chair, Bankruptcy and Insolvency Section).
Firm: Robins, Kaplan, Miller & Ciresi is a national litigation and business practice firm with offices in eight major metropolitan areas throughout the country. The firm's lawyers provide a range of transactional and litigation services to a diverse group of clients including Fortune 500 companies, banks, and lending institutions; property insurers; Big Six accounting firms; and foreign, state, and municipal governments. *See additional listing in Banking Law Chapter.*

HOWARD A. PATRICK

Robins, Kaplan, Miller & Ciresi
2800 LaSalle Plaza
800 LaSalle Avenue
Minneapolis, MN 55402

Phone: (612) 349-8500
Fax: (612) 339-4181
800 number: (800) 553-9910

Admitted: 1961 Minnesota; 1962 US Dist. Ct. (MN); 1982 US Ct. App. (8th Cir.)
Birthdate: 07/13/31

Chapter 9: Bankruptcy & Workout Law

JACK L. PRESCOTT

Prescott & Pearson, P.A.
P.O. Box 120088
New Brighton, MN 55112

Phone: (612) 633-2757
Fax: (612) 633-7562

Admitted: 1951 Minnesota
Birthdate: 04/23/27

•**JACK L. PRESCOTT:** Mr. Prescott practices exclusively in bankruptcy debtor law, with 90 percent of his practice dealing with consumer cases and 10 percent with small business cases. Mr. Prescott currently files the highest percentage of all Minnesota bankruptcy filings, with over 27,000 bankruptcy cases filed to date. For consumer cases, he has established a payment policy of "nothing down except clerk fee," followed by an affordable payment plan. In addition, Mr. Prescott lectures on consumer bankruptcy for Minnesota Continuing Legal Education.
Education: LLB, JD 1947-51, St. Paul College; BSL 1945-46, Hamline University, 1946-47, University of Minnesota.
Employment History: Currently President & Owner, Prescott & Pearson, P.A.; Municipal Judge, New Brighton, Minnesota (12 years).
Representative Clients: 3000 consumer debtors filed in each of the last several years.
Professional Associations: MSBA (Bankruptcy Section); RCBA.
Firm: Prescott & Pearson, P.A., consists of two attorneys, six paralegals, and seven clerical persons. The firm provides its clients with many years of experience, especially in consumer Chapter 7 and Chapter 13 cases.

CHARLES W. RIES

Farrish, Johnson & Maschka
201 North Broad Street, Suite 200
P.O. Box 550
Mankato, MN 56002-0550

Phone: (507) 387-3002
Fax: (507) 625-4002

Admitted: 1981 Minnesota
Birthdate: 06/01/52

•**CHARLES W. RIES:** Mr. Ries practices principally in the areas of bankruptcy and taxation, banking and commercial law, and related litigation. He is also experienced in corporations, partnerships, sole proprietorships, and limited liability companies. Mr. Ries is a Panel Trustee for the District of Minnesota. In addition, he lectures at continuing legal education seminars in agricultural law, bankruptcies, and the tax consequences of agricultural liquidations and bankruptcies.
Education: JD 1981 cum laude, William Mitchell; CPA 1977; BS 1974 cum laude, Mankato State University.
Employment History: 1980-present, Farrish, Johnson & Maschka; Clerk 1978-79, Lamm, Lamm & Nelson; Accountant 1974-77, Broker Hendrikson (Certified Public Accountants).
Professional Associations: Sixth District Bar Assn.; MSBA (Chair, Bankruptcy Section (past Vice Chair, Secretary-Treasurer)); MN Society of Certified Public Accountants (President 1987-88, Southern Chapter); National Assn. of Bankruptcy Trustees.
Community Involvement: All Saints Parish (Chair, Finance Board; past Trustee, Endowment Fund); Madison Lake American Legion Post 269 (Adjutant); Lions Club; MN Valley Regional Library (past library Officer; past Trustee, Endowment Fund); Southern MN Chapter American Red Cross; Mankato and Rochester Jaycees.
Firm: Founded in the late 1800s, Farrish, Johnson & Maschka is a general practice firm comprised of 11 lawyers experienced in civil litigation for both plaintiffs and defendants, real estate, estate planning, bankruptcy, and family law. *See additional listing in Business Tax Law Chapter.*

RANDI ILYSE ROTH - Farmers' Legal Action Group, Inc. - 1301 Minnesota Building, 46 East Fourth Street - St. Paul, MN 55101 - Phone: (612) 223-5400, Fax: (612) 223-5335 - *See complete biographical profile in Agricultural Law Chapter.*

JAMES A. RUBENSTEIN

Moss & Barnett, A Professional Association
4800 Norwest Center
90 South Seventh Street
Minneapolis, MN 55402-4129

Phone: (612) 347-0300
Fax: (612) 339-6686

Admitted: 1974 Minnesota
Birthdate: 01/12/48

•**JAMES A. RUBENSTEIN:** Mr. Rubenstein specializes in the areas of business bankruptcy and workouts and is certified as a Business Bankruptcy Law Specialist by the American Bankruptcy Board of Certification. Jim has substantial experience in all aspects of legal problems of financially troubled businesses including Chapter 11 and Chapter 7 cases under the US Bankruptcy Code, out-of-court reorganizations, and receiverships. He represents secured and unsecured creditors, shareholder committees, potential buyers of troubled companies, landlords, debtors, and trustees. He has also served as a receiver of companies in situations where management is accused of defrauding creditors and shareholders. Jim also works closely with the firm's banking clients in the areas of general civil litigation and workouts and with landlords of commercial properties in civil litigation and tenant relations. He speaks frequently on bankruptcy and commercial leasing topics.
Education: JD 1973 cum laude, National Law Center, George Washington University; BA 1970 cum laude, Williams College.
Employment History: Shareholder 1994, Moss & Barnett; Partner/Associate 1974-94, O'Connor & Hannan; Law Clerk 1973-74, Hon. Miles W. Lord, US District Court, District of Minnesota.
Professional Associations: ABA; MSBA.
Firm: Moss & Barnett is a full service law firm. Each attorney strives to develop individually in his or her respective area of law, while building a firm known for its cohesive, cooperative approach to diverse and complex legal issues. They represent local, regional, and national clients in a broad range of specialized areas of law including administrative, banking and financial services, bankruptcy, business, communications, employment, energy, environmental, family, health care, insurance, legislation, litigation, real estate, taxation, and trusts and estates. *See additional listings in Commercial Real Estate Law and Commercial Litigation Chapters.*

Bankruptcy & Workout Law Leading Attorneys

ALLEN I. SAEKS - Leonard, Street and Deinard Professional Association - 150 South Fifth Street, Suite 2300 - Minneapolis, MN 55402 - Phone: (612) 335-1548, Fax: (612) 335-1657 - *See complete biographical profile in Commercial Litigation Chapter.*

•**GROVER C. SAYRE III** - O'Neill, Burke, O'Neill, Leonard & O'Brien, Ltd. - 100 South Fifth Street, Suite 1200 - Minneapolis, MN 55402 - Phone: (612) 332-1030, Fax: (612) 332-2740 - *See complete biographical profile in Publicly Held Corporations Law Chapter.*

•**PAUL J. SCHEERER:** Mr. Scheerer practices in the area of financial transactions, principally representing financial institutions in connection with loan restructurings, reorganizations, workouts, and bankruptcies. He has been a partner in the Banking and Commercial Department of Dorsey & Whitney since 1978 and is a former professor at William Mitchell College of Law in the areas of torts, creditor's remedies, and bankruptcy.
Education: JD 1970 magna cum laude, Order of the Coif, University of Minnesota; AB 1967, University of Michigan.
Employment History: Partner 1978-present, Associate 1970-71, 1974-77 Dorsey & Whitney; Professor of Law 1972-1974, William Mitchell College of Law.
Firm: Dorsey & Whitney is the largest law firm in Minnesota and one of the largest firms in the United States with over 350 lawyers in 12 offices. The depth and breadth of the experience of its lawyers enables it to provide a broad range of services to meet the diverse legal needs of its client base, which includes Fortune 500 companies, public agencies, banks and other financial institutions, nonprofit organizations, individual investors, family owned businesses, and high-tech and low-tech, growth oriented companies. *See additional listing in Publicly Held Corporations Law Chapter.*

PAUL J. SCHEERER

Dorsey & Whitney
Pillsbury Center South
220 South Sixth Street
Minneapolis, MN 55402-1498

Phone: (612) 340-2883
Fax: (612) 340-2643

Admitted: 1970 Minnesota; 1970 US Dist. Ct. (MN)

ROBERT J. SEFKOW - Pemberton, Sorlie, Sefkow, Rufer & Kershner - 110 North Mill Street, P.O. Box 866 - Fergus Falls, MN 56538-0866 - Phone: (218) 736-5493, Fax: (218) 736-3950 - *See complete biographical profile in Banking Law Chapter.*

•**BARBARA G. STUART:** Ms. Stuart was appointed by Attorney General Janet Reno to the position of U.S. Trustee for Region 12, which consists of the five federal judicial districts in Minnesota, Iowa, North Dakota, and South Dakota. She was previously a shareholder and chair of Moss & Barnett's Bankruptcy and Workout practice. Ms. Stuart has extensive experience in bankruptcy and workout law, commercial and business litigation, and corporate and finance law. She is recognized for successfully representing clients in a broad range of sophisticated and complex business, litigation, and bankruptcy matters involving a broad range of issues including business reorganizations, debt restructuring, loan workouts, debtor-in-possession financing, secured and unsecured creditor remedies, preferential and fraudulent transfers, landlord and tenant remedies, and asset purchases. She successfully defended debtors in actions by creditors to foreclose interests in multimillion dollar securities and real estate holdings. She successfully represented creditors in nationally prominent cases including *In re Texaco, Inc.* and *In re A.H. Robins Company*. Ms. Stuart has served as a Chapter 7 trustee for the District of Minnesota, adjunct professor for the University of Minnesota Law School, and frequent author and lecturer for continuing legal education seminars.
Education: JD 1980, William Mitchell; BA 1971 cum laude, Macalester College (Phi Beta Kappa).
Employment History: Oct. 3, 1994-present, U.S. Trustee, Region 12; 1980-94, Moss & Barnett.
Professional Associations: ABA; Federal Bar Assn. (Board of Directors, Minnesota Chapter); American Bankruptcy Institute; MSBA (Board of Governors and Bankruptcy Section); HCBA (Ethics Committee, Diversity Committee, Urban Youth Internship Committee); Minnesota Women Lawyers; Historical Society of US Courts of Eighth Circuit.
Community Involvement: Children's Defense Fund (Advisory Committee); Minnesota Literacy Council; French-American Chamber of Commerce. *See additional listing in Publicly Held Corporations Law Chapter.*

BARBARA G. STUART

U.S. Trustee-Region 12
Law Building, Suite 400
225 Second Street SE
Cedar Rapids, IA 52401

Phone: (319) 364-2211
Fax: (319) 364-7370

Admitted: 1980 Minnesota; 1980 US Dist. Ct. (MN)
Birthdate: 04/02/49

1994/1996 ◆ Minnesota Edition

Chapter 9: Bankruptcy & Workout Law

KENNETH T. TYRA - Dorsey & Whitney - Pillsbury Center South, 220 South Sixth Street - Minneapolis, MN 55402-1498 - Phone: (612) 340-8869, Fax: (612) 340-7800 - *See complete biographical profile in Commercial Real Estate Law Chapter.*

CASS S. WEIL

Moss & Barnett, A Professional Association
4800 Norwest Center
90 South Seventh Street
Minneapolis, MN 55402

Phone: (612) 347-0300
Fax: (612) 339-6686

Admitted: 1980 Minnesota; 1984 Wisconsin; 1980 US Dist. Ct. (MN); 1980 US Ct. App. (8th Cir.); 1984 US Ct. App. (7th Cir.)
Birthdate: 11/06/46

•**CASS S. WEIL:** Mr. Weil practices primarily in debtor/creditor law with an emphasis in bankruptcy and workout matters and commercial litigation. His special expertise is in bankruptcy fraud. He also handles commercial litigation matters, including employment law, restrictive covenants, fraudulent transfers, and contract claims. Mr. Weil is one of the first lawyers in the United States to be certified in both Business and Consumer Bankruptcy Law by the American Bankruptcy Board of Certification. In addition, he is the editor of *Minnesota Legal Forms Bankruptcy Manual*. He is listed in *Who's Who in American Law*, 1987, 1989, 1991, and 1993.

Education: JD 1980 cum laude, Order of Barristers, William Mitchell (Phi Alpha Delta); BA 1968, State University of New York at Stony Brook.

Employment History: Currently, Moss & Barnett; 1991-93 O'Connor & Hannan; 1983-91, Peterson, Franke & Riach, P.A.; 1983, Zohlman & Weil; 1981-83, Wagner, Rutchick & Trojack, P.A.; 1980-81, J. R. Kotts & Associates.

Representative Clients: FCC National Bank (Chicago, IL); Maryland National Bank (Baltimore, MD); MicroComponent Technology, Inc.

Professional Associations: MSBA (past Secretary 1983-85, Bankruptcy Section; Vice Chair 1985-88; Chair 1988-1989); HCBA; State Bar of Wisconsin; American Bankruptcy Institute; Commercial Law League of America (Bankruptcy and Insolvency Section).

Community Involvement: Habitat for Humanity; Democratic Farmer-Labor Party; Home Foreclosure Prevention Task Force.

Firm: Moss & Barnett and its predecessor firms have provided legal service in Minneapolis and the surrounding multistate area continuously since before 1900. It is a large firm providing legal services to individuals and all types of business entities in personal, business, governmental, and all types of dispute resolution matters. *See additional listing in Commercial Litigation Chapter.*

Complete listing of all attorneys nominated in Bankruptcy & Workout Law

CRAIG W. ANDRESEN, Attorney at Law, Edina; **JAMES L. BAILLIE,** Fredrikson & Byron, P.A., Minneapolis; **IAN TRAQUAIR BALL,** Attorney at Law, Minneapolis; **LARRY J. BERG,** Fredrikson & Byron, P.A., Minneapolis; **EDWARD W. BERGQUIST,** Attorney at Law, Minneapolis; **PHILLIP W. BOHL,** Gray, Plant, Mooty, Mooty & Bennett, P.A., Minneapolis; **PAUL W. BUCHER,** Dunlap & Seeger, P.A., Rochester; **JAMES F. CHRISTOFFEL,** Christoffel, Elliott & Albrecht, P.A., Minneapolis; **JOHN J. CONNELLY,** Lindquist & Vennum, Minneapolis; **KATHERINE A. CONSTANTINE,** Dorsey & Whitney, Minneapolis; **JAMES J. DAILEY,** Dailey Law Office, Mankato; **TED E. DEANER,** O'Brien, Ehrick, Wolf, Deaner & Maus, Rochester; **FREDERICK A. DUDDERAR,** Hanft, Fride, O'Brien, Harries, Swelbar & Burns, P.A., Duluth; **SHAWN M. DUNLEVY,** Fryberger, Buchanan, Smith & Frederick, P.A., Duluth; **CHRISTOPHER A. ELLIOTT,** Christoffel, Elliott & Albrecht, P.A., Minneapolis; **JAMES FITZMAURICE,** Faegre & Benson, Minneapolis; **JOHN D. FRENCH,** Faegre & Benson, Minneapolis; **MALIN D. GREENBERG,** Attorney at Law, Minneapolis; **DOUGLAS B. GREENSWAG,** Leonard, Street and Deinard Professional Association, Minneapolis; **PATRICK B. HENNESSY,** Best & Flanagan, Minneapolis; **ROBERT F. HENSON,** Henson & Efron, P.A., Minneapolis; **THOMAS E. HOFFMAN,** Norwest Corporation-Law Division, Minneapolis; **RICHARD D. HOLPER,** Holper Welsh & Mitchell, Ltd., Minneapolis; **MICHAEL J. IANNACONE,** Iannacone Law Office, St. Paul; **GEOFFREY P. JARPE,** Maun & Simon, St. Paul; **MARK J. KALLA,** Oppenheimer, Wolff & Donnelly, Minneapolis; **WILLIAM I. KAMPF,** Kampf & Associates, Minneapolis; **FAYE KNOWLES,** Fredrikson & Byron, P.A., Minneapolis; **GARY W. KOCH,** Gislason, Dosland, Hunter & Malecki, P.A., New Ulm; **JOHN M. KONECK,** Fredrikson & Byron, P.A., Minneapolis; **HART KULLER,** Winthrop & Weinstine, P.A., St. Paul; **PHILLIP L. KUNKEL,** Hall, Byers, Hanson, Steil & Weinberger, P.A., St. Cloud; **THOMAS J. LALLIER,** Foley & Mansfield, Minneapolis; **DOUGLAS M. LAWRENCE,** Moss & Barnett, A Professional Association, Minneapolis; **BRIAN F. LEONARD,** O'Neill, Burke, O'Neill, Leonard & O'Brien, Ltd., Minneapolis; **JOHN R. McDONALD,** Robins, Kaplan, Miller & Ciresi, Minneapolis; **MICHAEL L. MEYER,** Ravich, Meyer, Kirkman & McGrath, P.A., Minneapolis; **THOMAS F. MILLER,** Attorney at Law, Minneapolis; **TIMOTHY D. MORATZKA,** Mackall, Crounse & Moore, Minneapolis; **DAVID A. ORENSTEIN,** Parsinen, Bowman & Levy, P.A., Minneapolis; **MELVIN I. ORENSTEIN,** Lindquist & Vennum, Minneapolis; **HOWARD A. PATRICK,** Robins, Kaplan, Miller & Ciresi, Minneapolis; **JACK L. PRESCOTT,** Prescott & Pearson, P.A., New Brighton; **CHARLES W. RIES,** Farrish, Johnson & Maschka, Mankato; **JAMES A. RUBENSTEIN,** Moss & Barnett, A Professional Association, Minneapolis; **ROBERT L. RUSSELL,** Svingen, Athens & Russell, Fergus Falls; **GROVER C. SAYRE III,** O'Neill, Burke, O'Neill, Leonard & O'Brien, Ltd., Minneapolis; **PAUL J. SCHEERER,** Dorsey & Whitney, Minneapolis; **MICHAEL R. STEWART,** Faegre & Benson, Minneapolis; **T. CHRIS STEWART,** Dunkley Bennett & Christensen, P.A., Minneapolis; **BARBARA G. STUART,** U.S. Trustee-Region 12, Cedar Rapids, IA; **DONALD C. SWENSON,** Lindquist & Vennum, Minneapolis; **JOHN C. THOMAS,** Oppenheimer, Wolff & Donnelly, Minneapolis; **RONALD J. WALSH,** Ronald J. Walsh, P.A., St. Paul; **CASS S. WEIL,** Moss & Barnett, A Professional Association, Minneapolis; **JANE S. WELCH,** Rider, Bennett, Egan & Arundel, Minneapolis.

CHAPTER 10

BUSINESS TAX LAW

Businesses are responsible for paying a variety of local, state and federal taxes, depending in part on how the business is organized, the services the business provides, and the products it sells. In general, businesses are liable for federal and state income taxes, state sales tax, Social Security and Medicare tax (FICA), federal unemployment tax (FUTA), and state unemployment tax. Businesses involved in the sale of alcohol, tobacco, or fuel and those that generate hazardous waste are liable for additional taxes. Businesses that have employees are responsible for withholding taxes from the pay of employees. This chapter discusses some of these liabilities and responsibilities.

TAXES AND THE FORM OF ORGANIZATION

Minnesota businesses are responsible for different types of taxes depending on the way they are organized. The three common forms of business organization—sole proprietorships, partnerships, and corporations—are discussed here. Limited liability companies that are recognized as partnerships in Minnesota are treated as partnerships for tax purposes. For more information on the forms of business organization, see the Closely Held Business Law Chapter.

SOLE PROPRIETORSHIP

Under a sole proprietorship, the owner is the taxpayer. Thus, the individual tax rate applies, rather than the higher corporate rate. The owner reports income and expenses from the business on his or her individual federal income tax return, using federal Schedule C with Form 1040. Generally, a sole proprietor cannot claim personal insurance, such as health, dental, and life insurance, as a business expense. Most sole proprietors are liable for self-employment tax, discussed in this chapter in the Employment Taxes section, which is filed with federal Form SE. Usually, sole proprietors make estimated tax payments in quarterly installments during the year, using federal Form 1040-ES and Minnesota Form M-14. There is no special form for reporting sole-proprietorship income to the state. Instead, copies of the federal forms and schedules are attached to Minnesota's individual return, Form M-1.

PARTNERSHIP

A partnership itself does not pay taxes; each partner reports his or her income and deductions individually on federal Form 1040, Schedule E, and Minnesota Form M-1. Thus, the individual tax rate rather than the higher corporate rate applies. Generally, benefits such as health, dental, and life insurance are not deductible by individual partners. Partners are usually liable for self-employment tax, and they generally make quarterly estimated tax payments toward their year-end tax liability, using federal Form 1040-ES and Minnesota Form M-14. Even though it does not pay taxes directly, a partnership is required to file a federal "information return" (Form 1065) which reports partnership income and distributions to the partners. Other forms and schedules may be required. A partnership is also required to file an information return (Form M-3) with the Minnesota Department of Revenue (MDOR). Partnerships with combined Minnesota payroll, property, and sales of $500,000 or greater are subject to a graduated minimum fee to the state.

CORPORATION

A corporation is an association of shareholders created under law and regarded by the courts as an "artificial person" with its own legal identity. There are two kinds of corporations, C corporations and S corporations, and each is subject to different tax laws. At the federal level, a C corporation is taxed under the provisions of Subchapter C of the Internal Revenue Code, and it is subject to a tax rate that is higher than the individual rate. For 1993, the corporate tax rate ranged from 15 percent for corporations with incomes of $50,000 or less to 35 percent for those with incomes over $10 million. Corporations use federal Form 1120 or Form 1120-A to report income, deductions, and credits, and to compute tax. Other forms may also be required.

A C corporation's taxable income is determined prior to distribution of shareholder dividends. A shareholder reports dividend income from a C corporation on his or her individual Form 1040. Thus, profits that are distributed as dividends are taxed twice—once on the C corporation's tax return and again on an individual shareholder's tax return. Shareholders are not able to use a corporation's losses for their individual tax purposes. However, dividends may be accumulated to certain limits by a corporation to postpone the double taxation. For state taxes, a C corporation uses Minnesota Form M-4 and is liable for a minimum fee based on property, payroll, and sales attributable to Minnesota.

For purposes of the state income tax, C corporations are permitted to deduct:

- Contributions to the state or its political subdivisions for exclusively public purposes

- Contributions to Minnesota charities

- Contributions to a non-Minnesota charity, in proportion to the charity's activity in Minnesota, provided the charity conducts a large portion of its activities in Minnesota

- Gifts to the federal government of Minnesota real property

Subchapter S of the Internal Revenue Code applies to an S corporation, which generally is not directly liable for federal income tax. Instead, each shareholder pays tax on his or her share of the S corporation's income and deductions by including it on federal Form 1040. However, an S corporation is required to file federal Form 1120-S with supporting schedules. Also, an S corporation files Minnesota Form M-3S-4, and it must pay a minimum fee to the state based on property, payroll, and a proportion of its sales attributable to Minnesota. Corporations that do business in Minnesota or own property in Minnesota may be subject to Minnesota taxes if they are determined to have a sufficient connection or nexus with the state. Some activities that justify imposition of Minnesota tax laws are:

- Having a place of business in Minnesota

- Having employees or independent contractors conducting business in Minnesota

- Owning or leasing tangible personal property in Minnesota

- Obtaining or regularly soliciting business from within Minnesota

A C corporation that expects to be liable for $500 or more in taxes must make estimated tax payments. Federal estimated tax payments are made quarterly to an authorized financial institution or Federal Reserve Bank, using Form 1120-W. Minnesota estimated tax payments are also due quarterly. They are made with Form M-18 to the MDOR. Penalties may be assessed for failure to pay estimated taxes promptly. S corporations are required to pay estimated tax on any income that is not passed to shareholders. For purposes of state income tax, a corporation may carry forward a net operating loss 15 years, and may use the loss to offset future years' income. However, a net operating loss cannot be used to offset tax paid on personal income in previous years.

BUSINESSES THAT OPERATE INSIDE AND OUTSIDE OF MINNESOTA

Firms that do business both inside and outside of Minnesota are assessed state income tax based on a weighted formula that takes into account the percentage of property, payroll, and total sales that is attributable to the business's Minnesota operations. A sale is considered subject to Minnesota taxes if its destination was Minnesota. Minnesota does not follow a "throwback rule," which means that sales made to states that do not assess tax are not subject to Minnesota taxes.

TAX CREDITS

Various federal tax credits are available to certain businesses. Some examples that were effective for 1993 include:

- Businesses that had 30 or fewer full-time employees or $1 million or less in gross receipts were eligible for credit for expenses related to complying with the Americans with Disabilities Act.

- Employers of persons from targeted groups with particularly high unemployment rates or special employment needs were eligible for credits for wages paid to members of the targeted groups.

- Some businesses that increased their research activities over a base amount were eligible for a credit of about 20 percent of the amount of increase.

The state of Minnesota also provides a number of tax credits to businesses to encourage them to engage in socially beneficial endeavors. An enterprise zone credit is available to partnerships and corporations, and this credit may be passed through to partners and S corporation shareholders. Enterprise zones are areas that have been designated for encouragement of business growth. Enterprise zone businesses may qualify for certain sales tax exemptions, as well as income and property tax credits. Other credits currently available are alternative minimum tax carryover credit, alternative minimum credit for individuals, and research and experimental expenditures credit. The MDOR is the contact office for more information on these credits.

TAXPAYER IDENTIFICATION NUMBERS

There are three types of taxpayer identification numbers that apply to Minnesota businesses: the Federal Employer Identification Number (EIN), the Minnesota Taxpayer Identification Number (TIN), and the Unemployment Compensation Employer Identification Number. An EIN is required for all businesses. A sole proprietor generally uses his or her personal Social Security number as the EIN. However, certain sole proprietors, and all partnerships and corporations must apply for an EIN from the Internal Revenue Service (IRS) using Form SS-4. Sole proprietors must apply if they have employees or have a retirement plan, or if they are liable for federal excise taxes, such as for alcohol, tobacco, or firearms. A TIN is required for all Minnesota businesses. Sole proprietors who do not have employees, who are not required to file information returns, and who do not make retail sales that are subject to Minnesota sales and use tax generally may use their Social Security number. Other businesses must submit an Application for Business Registration (Form ABR) to the MDOR. There is a $100 penalty for failure to obtain the number. Businesses with employees are required to get an Unemployment Compensation Employer Identification Number by registering with the Minnesota Department of Jobs and Training.

Selecting the Tax Year

A tax return is based on an accounting period called a tax year. A tax year may be either a calendar year or a fiscal year. A calendar year is 12 consecutive months from January 1st through December 31st. A fiscal year is generally composed of any other 12 consecutive months. Once a tax year is established, a business needs IRS approval to change it. Businesses use the same tax year for federal and state tax returns. Sole proprietorships usually use a calendar tax year. A partnership generally must use the same tax year as the partners who own a majority interest. If the majority partners' years differ, the business must use the same tax year as the principal partners—those with a 5 percent or greater interest in partnership profits or capital. If the principal partners' years conflict, a partnership generally uses a calendar tax year. A fiscal tax year can be used if either of the following is true:

- The IRS agrees that there is a business purpose for using a fiscal year

- The partnership files IRS Form 8716, Election to Have a Tax Year Other than a Required Tax Year, also known as a "Section 444 election." In this case, a business may have to pay a fee that represents the amount of tax deferral benefit that results from using a fiscal, rather than calendar, year.

A C corporation's first income tax return establishes its tax year. The first tax year must not be greater than 12 months from the date of incorporation. A C corporation that provides personal services must use a calendar tax year unless it has IRS approval to use a fiscal year or it makes a Section-444 election. An S corporation must use a calendar tax year unless it gets IRS approval. In some cases, S corporations may make a Section-444 election.

EMPLOYMENT TAXES

A number of taxes are of interest to businesses with employees.

Payroll Taxes

The taxes discussed here are often called payroll taxes because employers are responsible for deducting an employee's share from his or her earnings before the employee is paid.

FICA Taxes

Taxes under the Federal Insurance Contributions Act (FICA) help pay for Social Security and Medicare benefits. Businesses without employees do not pay FICA tax. Instead, most sole proprietors and partners in partnerships without employees pay a self-employment tax, which is discussed later in this chapter. Businesses that have employees contribute half of the total FICA tax, and are responsible for collecting the other half from employees through payroll deductions. For 1993, the tax rate for the Social Security portion of FICA tax was 6.2 percent each for employers and employees (a total of 12.4 percent). The maximum wage that was subject to the tax (the wage base) was $57,600; for 1994, the wage base is $60,600. Wage base limits usually change annually. The 1993 tax rate for the Medicare portion of FICA tax was 1.45 percent each for employers and employees (2.9 percent total). For 1994 there is no wage base limit; all covered wages are subject to Medicare tax. Special rules apply to employees who receive tips, to persons who receive both wages and self-employment income, and to non-wage payments to employees for items such as meals, lodging, clothing, and some services. The employer's share of FICA taxes is deductible as a business expense.

Income Tax Withholding

Along with the employee's share of FICA tax, employers must withhold federal and state income tax from the employee's pay. The amount to withhold is determined by the employee's pay and by the number of withholding allowances that the employee claims on federal Form W-4, Withholding Allowance Certificate. Employees are required to complete Form W-4 when hired, and generally the employer retains the form. However, the form must be filed with the IRS if the employee claims more than ten withholding allowances, or the employee claims exemption from withholding and his or her wages normally exceed $200 per week. A monetary penalty may be assessed against the employer for any form that is not filed when required.

Employees who reside in North Dakota, Wisconsin, or Michigan may claim exemption from withholding Minnesota state tax. To do so, the employee must complete Form MW-R, Reciprocity Exemption from Minnesota Withholding each year. Employers of truck drivers, bus drivers, and railroad workers who cross state borders while working must withhold taxes for the employee's state of residence. Payments to entertainers who are not residents of Minnesota for performances in Minnesota are subject to a 2 percent compensation tax. This tax must be withheld from the entertainer's pay and remitted to the state by the end of the month following the performance.

Employers must furnish a statement of wages and taxes (federal Form W-2) to employees by January 31st of each year, or, if requested by the employee, within 30 days of termination. The federal copy of Form W-2 must be submitted to the IRS, accompanied by federal Form M-3, Transmittal of Income and Tax Statements. The state copy must be sent to the MDOR by February 28th, accompanied by either Minnesota Form MW-3, Annual Reconciliation of Income Tax Withheld, or Form MW-1A, Annual Return/Reconciliation.

Payroll Tax Return

Generally, employers report FICA taxes and withheld federal income tax together on federal Form 941, Employer's Quarterly Federal Tax Return, which as the name implies, is filed at the end of each calendar quarter. There are different forms to be used for agricultural and household workers and for employees who are not subject to FICA taxes. Most employers are required to make deposits for payroll taxes before returns are actually due. How often deposits must be made is determined in part by how much tax liability a business has accrued in the past. For example, a business that owed

$50,000 or less in payroll taxes during a specific previous 12-month period may be designated a monthly depositor; a business that owed $50,000 to $100,000 during the specific period may be designated a semi-weekly depositor. The depositor designation is reevaluated annually. A business's actual tax liability at the end of each deposit period determines whether it must actually make a deposit. If the amount of accumulated undeposited liability reaches $100,000 in any period, taxes must be deposited the day after that volume is reached, and if the business's deposit status was monthly, it is immediately changed to semi-weekly.

SELF-EMPLOYMENT TAX

Self-employment tax is a Social Security and Medicare tax for individuals who work for themselves. This includes sole proprietors and most partners in partnerships without employees. Net earnings of $400 or more are subject to self-employment tax. For 1993, there were ceilings on the amount of earnings subject to the tax: $57,600 for the Social Security portion of the tax; $135,000 for the Medicare portion. The Social Security portion was assessed at 12.4 percent of earnings, and Medicare at 2.9 percent, for a total self-employment tax of 15.3 percent. Federal Schedule SE is used to calculate self-employment tax, which is then added to one's total tax liability on Form 1040. One-half of the self-employment tax is deductible as an adjustment to gross income on Form 1040.

UNEMPLOYMENT TAX

Both the federal and state governments have programs to help support able workers who lose their jobs. Tax under the Federal Unemployment Tax Act (FUTA) is reported by eligible employers once per year on federal Form 940 or 940-EZ. The form is usually due one month after the end of a calendar year. However, deposits toward the annual payment are required at the end of any quarter in which the employer accrues $100 or more in FUTA tax liability. Penalties may be imposed for late filing and late deposits. Most employers, even those with part-time employees, are responsible for paying FUTA tax. The general rule is that a business is subject to FUTA tax if the business pays wages of $1500 or more in any calendar quarter, or the business had a least one part-time employee in each of 20 different (not necessarily consecutive) calendar weeks. In addition, FUTA tax is due on cash wages of $1000 or more paid in any calendar quarter to domestic workers who work in a private home, local college club, or local fraternity or sorority house.

A business that employs farm workers is subject to FUTA tax on their wages if the wages total $20,000 or more in any calendar quarter, or if there was at least one day in each of 20 different calendar weeks when the business had ten or more at least part-time farm workers. The tax is figured at a rate of 6.2 percent of the wages paid to the employee up to $7000. Tip income reported by an employee to an employer for FICA tax purposes is considered wages for calculating FUTA tax. However, the tax does not apply to some payments, such as Workers' Compensation payments, nor does it apply to certain types of employment, such as earnings paid to cooperative education students. A business is credited for up to 5.4 percent of the amount it pays for state unemployment tax, which can reduce the actually tax liability to 0.8 percent. The IRS administers the FUTA tax.

The state has its own unemployment program and corresponding taxes. Any employer that conducts business in Minnesota is required to submit Form DJT-13, Report to Determine Liability, to the Minnesota Department of Jobs and Training (MDJT) within a month of initiating business in the state. The MDJT then informs the business whether it is liable for the tax. Liability is based on the number and type of employees, the amount of wages paid, and other factors. The tax rate for new employers is generally the state's benefit cost rate, which is 1.9 percent. Construction businesses are assigned a separate rate, which cannot be less than 1.0 percent or more than 9.0 percent. The maximum benefit cost rate for all other businesses is 5.4 percent. Once a business has paid unemployment tax for a period of time, the tax rate will be based on the business's experience. Minimum experience rates range from 0.1 percent to 0.6 percent. The maximum experience rate is 9.0 percent. An employer's experience rate is redetermined annually, just after June 30th.

If the state unemployment fund falls below a certain amount as of June 30th of any year, a business becomes liable for a "solvency assessment" of 10 to 15 percent of their regular annual contributions. The assessment is payable with the following year's contributions. All employers that pay unemployment tax are also liable for a special assessment for the Dislocated Worker Fund, calculated as 0.1 percent of taxable payroll. The tax is due on the first $15,100 of each covered employee's earnings (base wages). Wages include cash wages, salary, commissions, S corporation dividends when credited to shareholders as services, and the reasonable value of meals and housing provided to an employee. Wages contributed to deferred income plans, such as a "401(k)" plan, and "cafeteria" or flexible benefit plans are also taxable. Certain payments are not taxable, such as Workers' Compensation and retirement payments. Minnesota requires that businesses pay unemployment taxes quarterly. The quarterly tax return has two parts: the Contribution Report contains summarized information; the Wage Detail Report shows information for each employee. There are penalties and fines that can be imposed on businesses that fail to file on time, do not pay the necessary employment taxes, or fail to keep accurate employment records. MDJT audits employer records periodically. The business can deduct unemployment taxes as business expenses.

ACQUIRED BUSINESSES

A firm that acquires an existing business that has been subject to unemployment tax is required to file Form DJT-13S, Report to Determine Succession. The new business may be eligible to have an experience rate computed based on all or part of the predecessor's experience; in some cases, an acquired business may be required to use the predecessor's experience rating. By statute, an individual or business that acquires all or part of an existing Minnesota employer's business or assets is jointly and severally liable for the predecessor's unpaid tax, interest, and liabilities.

SALES AND USE TAXES

Minnesota sales tax is due on the gross receipts from selling, leasing, or renting tangible personal property at the retail level. Some services, such as building cleaning, lawn and garden maintenance, and tailoring, are also subject to state sales tax. Generally, retail sales do not include transactions where the customer buys items either to resell them or to incorporate them into something new for sale at retail. A general sales tax rate of 6.5 percent applies to most retail sales. Some exceptions to this are alcohol sales, which are taxed at a rate of 9 percent, and sales of some farm machinery, logging equipment, and agriculture production equipment, which are taxed at a 2.5 percent rate. The use tax applies to purchases of goods that are not subject to Minnesota sales tax but will be stored, used, or consumed in the state. This includes items that are purchased outside of Minnesota, items that were originally purchased for resale but then used directly, and items that are purchased in Minnesota where sales tax is not collected. Items become subject to the use tax when they enter Minnesota, are taken from inventory for use, or are purchased from a Minnesota seller. The use tax rate is the same as the sales tax rate, 6.5 percent.

Anyone who makes retail sales or who provides taxable services in Minnesota must have a sales and use tax permit. This includes any seller located outside of Minnesota who meets any of the following conditions:

- Is a corporation authorized to do business in Minnesota

- Has a place of business in Minnesota, either directly or by a subsidiary

- Has any type of temporary or permanent agent in Minnesota for any purpose, including repair, delivery, or installation of taxable items

- Solicits sales of tangible personal property in Minnesota

Businesses obtain the sales and use tax permit from the MDOR using Form ABR, Application for Business Registration. Generally, sales and use tax returns are due monthly. A business may file annually if it averages less than $25 per month in taxes, or quarterly, if less than $250 per month. However, it must file Form ST-12, Application to File Quarterly or Annual Returns, to obtain authorization. MDOR provides preprinted sales-tax returns to permit holders. The return, Form ST-1, must be postmarked by the 20th day of the month following the end of a reporting period to be considered timely. A business is required to collect sales tax even if it has not yet received its permit.

EXEMPTIONS

Certain customers are not required to pay Minnesota sales tax at the time of purchase. The MDOR requires that these customers present a properly completed exemption certificate to the seller. Certificates are subject to inspection by MDOR, and thus, the seller should keep them on file to substantiate sales where tax was not collected. Customers who frequently make exempt purchases can obtain a blanket exemption certificate that applies to future purchases.

LOCAL SALES TAX

In addition to the sales tax imposed by the state, a number of cities have been granted authority to impose local sales taxes as well. Also, all towns or cities in Minnesota have the right to impose a "lodging tax" on hotels and motels for the purpose of funding a convention or tourism bureau to promote tourism to the city. Bloomington, Duluth, Minneapolis, Rochester, St. Cloud, and St. Paul impose a lodging tax. Duluth, Minneapolis, Rochester, St. Cloud, and St. Paul also impose general sales taxes. Minneapolis also taxes restaurants and liquor in its downtown area. Permits and filing forms for the sales taxes imposed by Minneapolis, Rochester, and St. Cloud are obtained from the MDOR, Business Tax Unit; information on sales taxes in the other cities is available directly from the cities.

OTHER TAXES

Business owners also need to be aware of a variety of miscellaneous taxes.

OTHER STATE TAXES

An excise tax of 6.5 percent is assessed on the sale of most motor vehicles. A lower or special rate may apply to passenger vehicles ten years old or older, collector vehicles, and certain other vehicles. This tax is administered by the Minnesota Department of Public Safety, Driver and Vehicle

Services Division. Any business that generates more than 100 pounds of hazardous waste per year is subject to a hazardous waste tax based on the quantity of waste and the disposal method used. For a discussion of hazardous waste, see the Environmental Law Chapter. The rate for very small quantity generators is a flat $50; the tax for other generators begins at $200 for small quantities and at $500 for large quantities. The tax is payable annually to the MDOR, using Form HZ-1, Minnesota Hazardous Waste Tax Generator Annual Tax Return. Tax revenues are used to clean up hazardous waste in the state. Businesses that sell gasoline, propane, or diesel fuel and wholesalers and distributors of cigarettes and alcohol are responsible for collecting appropriate taxes for those items from customers and remitting the taxes to the state.

OTHER FEDERAL TAXES

The federal government assesses various excise taxes. For example, excise taxes are imposed on the sale, use, or lease of the following articles by the manufacturer, producer, or importer: sport fishing equipment, electric outboard motors and certain sonar devices, bows and arrows, highway-type tires, gas guzzling automobiles, certain vaccines, coal, and alcohol sold as fuel but not used as fuel. There are environmental excise taxes, such as taxes on the sale or manufacturing use of certain ozone-depleting chemicals and there are luxury taxes, such as a tax on the sale of passenger vehicles that cost over $30,000.

Many of these taxes are reported with federal Form 720, Quarterly Federal Excise Tax Return. Although the return is filed quarterly, the taxes generally must be deposited before the return is due. There are additional excise taxes that are reported separately from those described above. For example, certain heavy vehicles are subject to a federal highway use tax. This includes buses, truck tractors, and trucks with gross vehicle weights of 55,000 pounds or more. Pickup and panel trucks are not subject to the tax. Generally, the vehicles must be used on public roads more than 5,000 miles per year. This tax is reported on IRS Form 2290, Heavy Vehicle Use Tax Return. There are also taxes on alcohol, tobacco, and firearms that are filed with the Bureau of Alcohol, Tobacco, and Firearms.

RESOURCES

The Internal Revenue Service, the Minnesota Department of Revenue, and the Minnesota Department of Jobs and Training jointly present free workshops every month. For information and registration, call the IRS at (612) 644-7515 or, from outstate Minnesota, (800) 829-1040.

Employer's Tax Guide (Circular E), Pub 15. Available from the Internal Revenue Service.

Unemployment Insurance Information for Employers, DJT-130. Available from the Minnesota Department of Jobs and Training, 390 North Robert Street, St. Paul, MN 55101, (612) 296-3674.

Taxpayer Bill of Rights. Two pamphlets, with the same name, describe the laws which standardize audit, appeal, and collection procedures, and clarify taxpayer rights and protections. The federal version is available from the IRS. The state version is available from the Minnesota Department of Revenue, Mail Station 4453, St. Paul, MN 55146-4453, (612) 296-6181. From outstate Minnesota, call (800) 657-3777.

Chapter 10: Business Tax Law

BUSINESS TAX LAW LEADING ATTORNEYS

Selected by Attorneys for **GUIDEBOOK**
Law & Leading Attorneys
MINNESOTA

The attorneys profiled in this section were nominated by their peers in a statewide survey conducted in 1993 in which several thousand Minnesota attorneys were asked to name the lawyer to whom they would send a friend or family member in need of legal assistance in the area of *Business Tax Law*.

Because the survey resulted in a list of less than five percent of Minnesota's practicing attorneys, this should not be construed as a complete list. Nevertheless, it is an excellent source of highly qualified and reputable attorneys, who, if unable to assist can in most cases make quality referrals.

The attorneys profiled below were recommended by their peers in a statewide survey.

A list of all attorneys nominated in this category is found at the end of this section. For information on the survey methodology see page ix.

Please note that the shorter, two line attorney listings in this section are of attorneys who practice in this area but whose full biographical profile appears in another section of this book. A bullet "•" preceeding name indicates the attorney was nominated in this particular area of law. For information on the format of these profiles, consult the section "Using the *Business Guidebook*" found on page xiv. Note that the following abbreviations are used throughout these profiles:

App.	- Appellate	ABA	- American Bar Association
Cir.	- Circuit	ATLA	- American Trial Lawyers Association
Ct.	- Court	HCBA	- Hennepin County Bar Association
Dist.	- District	MDLA	- Minnesota Defense Lawyers Association
Hon.	- Honorable	MSBA	- Minnesota State Bar Association
JD	- Law degree (Juris Doctor)	MTLA	- Minnesota Trial Lawyers Association
LLB	- Law degree	NBTA	- National Board of Trial Advocacy
LLM	- Master in Law degree	RCBA	- Ramsey County Bar Association
Sup.	- Supreme		

KIMBALL J. DEVOY

Doherty, Rumble & Butler
Professional Association
2800 Minnesota World Trade Center
30 East Seventh Street
St. Paul, MN 55101-4999

Phone: (612) 291-9333
Fax: (612) 291-9313

Admitted: 1972 Minnesota
Birthdate: 08/02/41

•**KIMBALL J. DEVOY:** Mr. Devoy has been a shareholder of Doherty, Rumble & Butler since 1984. He practices primarily in the areas of taxation and representation of closely held businesses. He has extensive experience in taxation of real estate; S corporations; partnerships; business formation; corporate acquisitions, mergers, and liquidations; and IRS ruling applications. Mr. Devoy is frequently involved in Doherty Rumble's extensive practice in cooperative law and cooperative taxation. He also is a certified public accountant (he received the Utley Award (first place, MN, 1970 CPA Exam) and the Sells Certificate of Honorable Mention (top 25 in nation, 1970 CPA Exam). He is listed in *The Best Lawyers in America* 1983, '87, '89, '91, '93, and '95 editions and in *Who's Who in American Law*.
Education: JD 1972 magna cum laude, Order of the Coif, University of Minnesota (member 1970-72, *Minnesota Law Review*); BS 1963, St. John's University.
Employment History: 1984-present, Doherty, Rumble & Butler, P.A.; Associate/Partner 1972-84, Oppenheimer, Wolff & Donnelly; Accountant 1968-69, Broeker Hendrickson & Company; IRS Agent 1966-68; 1st Lt. 1963-65, US Army.
Representative Clients: The Toro Company; American Crystal Sugar; R. D. Offutt Company; First Trust; Florists' Transworld Delivery Assn.; Buckman Farmers Cooperative; Viking Electronics, Inc.; Minnesota Mutual Life.
Professional Associations: MSBA (Chair 1987-88, Tax Section; Chair 1983-87, Income Tax Committee).
Community Involvement: Kiwanis Club of St. Paul and Kiwanis Foundation (Director; Treasurer); St. John's University; Visitation School; Mendota Heights Youth Athletics.
Firm: Doherty, Rumble & Butler has extensive knowledge in the areas of planning and structuring simple and complex corporate, cooperative, partnership, and estate and trust transactions. The firm's attorneys have the experience to promptly recognize tax issues and work with their clients to resolve them in a beneficial and efficient manner. Their tax lawyers assist clients in the areas of corporate and partnership taxation, cooperative taxation, individual taxation, tax-exempt organizations, state taxation, IRS and state administrative matters, criminal matters, collection matters, employment tax matters, and estate and gift taxation. *See additional listing in Closely Held Business Law Chapter.*

•**JOHN J. ERHART:** An officer and shareholder at Fredrikson & Byron, Mr. Erhart works primarily with closely held corporations and partnerships on business planning and taxation. He is currently chair of Fredrikson & Byron's Tax and Business Planning Group. He frequently functions as general counsel to business clients and advises them with respect to the formation and operation of their businesses. His practice includes all phases of corporate and state taxation. A significant part of his practice relates to the purchase and sale of businesses. In the last ten years, Mr. Erhart has also developed expertise in tax issues related to workouts and reorganizations. He is a frequent lecturer for various groups, including the Minnesota State Bar Association and the Minnesota Society of Certified Public Accountants.
Education: JD 1977, Georgetown University (member and Editor 1975-77, *The Tax Lawyer*); BA 1974 summa cum laude, St. John's University.
Employment History: Judicial Clerk 1977-79, Hon. Gerald W. Heaney, US Court of Appeals, Eighth Circuit; Intern 1976-77, The Securities and Exchange Commission; Intern 1975-76, Offices of Congressman James L. Oberstar.
Representative Clients: Closely held businesses, professional corporations, partnerships, and individuals.
Professional Associations: ABA; MSBA.
Firm: Mr. Erhart serves on Fredrikson & Byron's Board of Directors. He is one of 13 attorneys in Fredrikson & Byron's Tax and Business Planning Group, which focuses on working with businesses to develop creative structures and strategies to minimize taxes and regulatory problems. The group combines a solid foundation in tax law with practical knowledge of business organizations and the issues that accompany the formation, operation, purchase, sale, and termination of businesses. They actively advise clients on all aspects of federal and state income taxes, sales and use taxes, real estate taxes, and employment taxes. Other types of services include advice in shareholder and partner disputes; business, tax, and legal aspects of mergers and acquisitions; tax free reorganizations; leveraged buyouts; international transactions; coordination of personal, estate, and corporate planning matters; debt and equity financing of businesses; and drafting and implementing agreements. *See additional listing in Closely Held Business Law Chapter.*

JOHN J. ERHART

Fredrikson & Byron, P.A.
1100 International Centre
900 Second Avenue South
Minneapolis, MN 55402

Phone: (612) 347-7035
Fax: (612) 347-7077

Admitted: 1977 Minnesota;
1977 US Dist. Ct. (MN);
1978 US Ct. App. (8th Cir.);
1980 US Tax Ct.
Birthdate: 05/20/52

ALAIN FRECON - Frécon & Associates - 902 Foshay Tower, 821 Marquette Avenue South - Minneapolis, MN 55402 - Phone: (612) 338-6868, Fax: (612) 338-6878 - *See complete biographical profile in International Business Law Chapter.*

TODD I. FREEMAN - Larkin, Hoffman, Daly & Lindgren, Ltd. - 1500 Norwest Financial Center, 7900 Xerxes Avenue South - Bloomington, MN 55431 - Phone: (612) 835-3800, Fax: (612) 896-3333 - *See complete biographical profile in Closely Held Business Law Chapter.*

•**NICK HAY:** Mr. Hay practices business tax law with a primary emphasis on federal and state income tax planning including structuring mergers, acquisitions, and business sales; C-corporation, S-corporation, partnership, and limited liability company structuring and taxation; and taxation of other business transactions. He has extensive experience in tax controversy work including audits, appeals, civil and criminal tax litigation, and tax collection matters. Mr. Hay represents clients in administrative appearances before state and federal tax authorities including sales and use tax, offers in compromise, private letter rulings and exemption applications, unemployment compensation, excise tax, and trust-fund recovery penalty (formerly 100% penalty) matters. He also represents closely held businesses and their owners on a wide range of general business, financial, and corporate matters.
Education: JD 1973 magna cum laude, University of Minnesota; BSBA 1970 magna cum laude, University of North Dakota.
Employment History: Shareholder 1990-present, Moss & Barnett, A Professional Association; Partner 1984-90, O'Connor & Hannan; Shareholder/Associate 1977-84, Head & Truhn, P.A.; Associate 1973-77, Dorsey & Whitney; Adjunct Professor of Tax Law 1976-85, William Mitchell College of Law.
Professional Associations: ABA (1991-present); MSBA (1985-present); HCBA (1985-present); North Dakota Society of Certified Public Accountants (1970-present).
Firm: See firm profile in Appendix C. *See additional listings in Closely Held Business Law and Publicly Held Corporations Law Chapters.*

NICK HAY

Moss & Barnett, A Professional Association
4800 Norwest Center
90 South Seventh Street
Minneapolis, MN 55402-4129

Phone: (612) 347-0443
Fax: (612) 339-6686

Admitted: 1973 Minnesota;
1977 US Tax Ct.;
1978 US Dist. Ct. (MN);
1978 US Ct. App. (8th Cir.);
1982 US Sup. Ct.
Birthdate: 06/21/49

JOHN S. HIBBS - Dorsey & Whitney - Pillsbury Center South, 220 South Sixth Street - Minneapolis, MN 55402-1498 - Phone: (612) 340-2661, Fax: (612) 340-8827 - *See complete biographical profile in Health Law Chapter.*

WILLIAM H. HIPPEE, JR.

Dorsey & Whitney
Pillsbury Center South
220 South Sixth Street
Minneapolis, MN 55402-1498

Phone: (612) 340-2665
Fax: (612) 340-8827

Admitted: 1972 Minnesota;
US Dist. Ct. (MN)

•**WILLIAM H. HIPPEE, JR.**: Mr. Hippee practices in the areas of business taxation and related transactional work. He serves as tax counsel for corporate and partnership clients and advises with respect to mergers, acquisitions, restructurings, and general tax matters. He also represents clients in tax controversies, including administrative appeals and litigation in federal and state courts. Mr. Hippee has been a partner in the Tax Department at Dorsey & Whitney since 1978.
Education: JD 1972, Stanford University; BS 1968 cum laude, University of Pennsylvania, Wharton School of Finance and Commerce.
Employment History: Partner 1978-present, Associate 1972-77, Dorsey & Whitney.
Professional Associations: ABA (Tax Section); MSBA (Tax Section); HCBA.
Firm: Dorsey & Whitney is the largest law firm in Minnesota and one of the largest firms in the United States with over 350 lawyers in 12 offices. The depth and breadth of the experience of its lawyers enables it to provide a broad range of services to meet the diverse legal needs of its client base, which includes Fortune 500 companies, public agencies, banks and other financial institutions, nonprofit organizations, individual investors, family owned businesses, and high-tech and low-tech, growth oriented companies. *See additional listing in Closely Held Business Law Chapter.*

WILLIAM A. JONASON - Dorsey & Whitney - 201 First Avenue SW, Suite 340 - Rochester, MN 55902 - Phone: (507) 288-3156, Fax: (507) 288-6190 - *See complete biographical profile in Closely Held Business Law Chapter.*

MICHAEL C. KARP - Blethen Gage & Krause - 127 South Second Street, P.O. Box 3049 - Mankato, MN 56002-3049 - Phone: (507) 345-1166, Fax: (507) 345-8003 - *See complete biographical profile in Closely Held Business Law Chapter.*

PAUL J. LINSTROTH

Popham, Haik, Schnobrich & Kaufman, Ltd.
222 South Ninth Street
Suite 3300
Minneapolis, MN 55402

Phone: (612) 333-4800
Fax: (612) 334-8888

Admitted: 1986 Minnesota;
1980 US Tax Ct.
Birthdate: 04/21/53

•**PAUL J. LINSTROTH:** Mr. Linstroth advises individuals, partnerships, and corporations on the planning and structuring of a wide range of business, tax, and financial transactions. His extensive experience is in the areas of domestic and international corporate taxation and tax litigation, with an emphasis on acquisitions, divestitures, and exchanges of real estate; the corporate and tax issues arising in mergers, acquisitions, and reorganizations of foreign and domestic corporations; the successful resolution of state and federal tax controversies; and estate planning. Mr. Linstroth lectures on federal income tax developments in the areas of mergers and acquisitions, and the taxation of real estate transactions, particularly in the area of tax-deferred like-kind exchanges of real estate. He is currently the chair of the firm's Tax Practice Group.
Education: JD 1979, Creighton University (Executive Editor, *Creighton Law Review*); LLM 1980, New York University; BA 1975, University of St. Thomas.
Representative Clients: The Prudential Home Mortgage Company and Securitized Asset Sales, Inc.
Professional Associations: MSBA (Chair 1994-95, Tax Section Council; past Editor, *Tax Section News*); ABA (Corporate Tax Committee, Tax Section); HCBA; Illinois State Bar Assn.; The Florida Bar.
Community Involvement: Rotary Club of Minneapolis (Board of Directors).
Firm: Popham, Haik, Schnobrich & Kaufman, Ltd., is a firm of more than 230 attorneys with offices in Denver, Miami, Minneapolis, Washington, D.C., and international affiliations in Beijing, China and Leipzig and Stuttgart, Germany. The firm represents clients nationally and internationally on issues relating to corporate and business law, administrative law, and litigation.

•**PHILLIP H. MARTIN:** Mr. Martin practices in the area of corporate and individual taxation, including tax litigation and tax controversies before the Internal Revenue Service, mergers and acquisitions, reorganizations and capitalizations, and business succession planning for closely held businesses. Cases he has tried include *Sally O. Irvine Estate v. Comm'r* (issues involved the refund of a $30 million gift tax deficiency; US Supreme Court held disclaimer was a taxable gift); *Lois P. Cotrell v. Comm'r* (issues involved a $4.5 million plus interest gift tax deficiency overturned by 8th Circuit; disclaimer was held not to constitute a taxable gift); *Deluxe Corporation v. US* (Federal Circuit overturned Court of Claims holding, finding that corporation was not liable for self-dealing penalty taxes); *Calvin Griffith v. Comm'r* (Tax Court: issues in this case involved the favorable valuation of Minnesota Twins stock for federal gift tax purposes). Mr. Martin has also represented Jeno's Inc. in the sale of their pizza business to the Pillsbury Company; Hormel Foods in its acquisition of Jenny-O and several other acquisitions; as well as representing SUPERVALU INC. in its acquisition of Charlie Brothers Grocery, West Coast Grocery Company, Pantry Pride, Food Giant, Wetterau, Inc., and Sweet Life Foods and in its disposition of County Seat. Mr. Martin has been listed in *The Best Lawyers in America* since 1989 in the Tax Section.
Education: JD 1964 cum laude, Order of the Coif, University of Minnesota (President 1963-64, *Minnesota Law Review*); BS 1961 magna cum laude, University of Minnesota (Phi Beta Kappa).
Employment History: Partner 1970-present, Associate 1964-69, Dorsey & Whitney.
Representative Clients: Hormel Foods Corp.; SUPERVALU INC.; Deluxe Corp.; stockholders and/or families at Cargill, Inc.; Pella Corp.; and Schwan's Sales Enterprises, Inc.
Firm: Dorsey & Whitney is the largest law firm in Minnesota and one of the largest firms in the United States with over 350 lawyers in 12 offices. The depth and breadth of the experience of its lawyers enables it to provide a broad range of services to meet the diverse legal needs of its client base, which includes Fortune 500 companies, public agencies, banks and other financial institutions, nonprofit organizations, individual investors, family owned businesses, and high-tech and low-tech, growth oriented companies.

PHILLIP H. MARTIN

Dorsey & Whitney
Pillsbury Center South
220 South Sixth Street
Minneapolis, MN 55402-1498

Phone: (612) 340-2845
Fax: (612) 340-8827

Admitted: 1964 Minnesota;
1968 US Dist. Ct. (MN);
1972 US Ct. App. (8th Cir.);
1989 US Ct. App. (7th Cir.);
1988 US Ct. App. (Fed. Cir.);
1967 US Tax Ct.;
1981 US Sup. Ct.
Birthdate: 01/04/40

•**THOMAS R. MUCK:** An officer in Fredrikson & Byron's Litigation Group and Tax & Business Planning Group, Mr. Muck concentrates in tax litigation and disputes, including representation in state and federal courts on income, sales, and property tax matters. He also provides representation and counseling in tax appeals, protests, and other prelitigation stages of disputes. Mr. Muck is an accomplished administrative law litigator as well, with experience in securities, banking, and insurance matters. In addition, he has been awarded the Minnesota State Bar Association Tax Section Distinguished Service Award.
Education: JD 1972 cum laude, University of Minnesota (staff member 1970-71, Primary Editor 1971-72, *Minnesota Law Review*); BA 1969, University of Michigan.
Employment History: Formerly, Chief Litigator, Minnesota Department of Revenue, representing the State in complex corporate tax cases involving unitary taxation and other constitutional issues.
Representative Clients: Public companies, closely held businesses, professional corporations, financial institutions, utilities, partnerships, and individuals.
Professional Associations: MSBA (Secretary, Tax Section Council; Administrative Law Section & its Council); RCBA (Tax Section); HCBA (Tax Section).
Firm: Fredrikson & Byron's litigators are highly skilled, experienced and aggressive. Each lawyer has developed several specific areas of expertise. They have substantial experience before state and federal administrative agencies with alternative dispute resolution. Mr. Muck combines his litigation experience with his expertise in tax and business planning. He is one of 13 attorneys in the Tax & Business Planning Group, which focuses on working with businesses to develop creative structures and strategies to minimize taxes and regulatory problems. The group combines a solid foundation in tax law with practical knowledge of business organizations and the issues that accompany the formation, operation, purchase, sale, and termination of businesses. They actively advise clients on all aspects of federal and state income taxes, sales, and use taxes, real estate taxes, and employment taxes. Other types of services include advice in shareholder and partner disputes; business, tax, and legal aspects of mergers and acquisitions; tax free reorganizations; leveraged buyouts; coordination of personal, estate, and corporate planning matters; debt and equity financing of businesses; and drafting and implementing agreements. *See additional listing in Commercial Litigation Chapter.*

THOMAS R. MUCK

Fredrikson & Byron, P.A.
1100 International Centre
900 Second Avenue South
Minneapolis, MN 55402

Phone: (612) 347-7045
Fax: (612) 347-7077

Admitted: 1972 Minnesota;
1972 US Dist. Ct. (MN);
1973 US Ct. App. (8th Cir.);
1991 US Tax Ct.;
1984 US Sup. Ct.
Birthdate: 03/21/47

SUE ANN NELSON

Doherty, Rumble & Butler
Professional Association
3500 Fifth Street Towers
150 South Fifth Street
Minneapolis, MN 55402

Phone: (612) 340-5590
Fax: (612) 340-5584

Admitted: 1979 Minnesota;
1979 New York;
1987 District of Columbia;
1979 US Tax Ct.;
1987 US Ct. Fed. Claims;
1979 US Dist. Ct. (MN);
1984 US Ct. App. (8th Cir.);
1992 US Ct. App. (Fed. Cir.)
Birthdate: 02/22/53

•**SUE ANN NELSON:** Ms. Nelson's tax and tax litigation practice focuses on counseling corporations, partnerships, estates, trusts, and individuals on federal and state tax issues and representing clients in all facets of state and federal administrative and litigation tax matters. Her past experience as counsel to the Internal Revenue Service provides her with unique qualifications for handling federal and state tax controversies, as evidenced by the results-oriented accomplishments for her clients. For example, Ms. Nelson recently obtained innovative IRS administrative rulings for a publicly-traded trust and the cooperative industry and precedent setting court victories in such diverse areas as the tax treatment of cooperatives under Section 277 of the Internal Revenue Code, the reversal of an attempt by the IRS to subject small banks to the accrual method of accounting, the invalidation of a state sales and use tax provision singling out railroads, and a determination prohibiting the IRS from levying upon discretionary trust assets. Ms. Nelson was recently featured in the article "Antidote to the IRS" in *Corporate Report Minnesota*.

Education: JD 1978, State University of New York at Buffalo; BS 1975, St. Bonaventure University.
Employment History: Associate/Shareholder 1985-Present, Doherty, Rumble & Butler, P.A.; Associate 1984-85, Stolpestad, Brown & Smith, P.A.; Trial Attorney 1978-84, Office of Chief Counsel, IRS (St. Paul).
Professional Associations: ABA (Tax Section); MSBA (Tax Section (Tax Council 1988-93)); District of Columbia Bar.
Community Involvement: Southern MN Regional Legal Services, Inc. (volunteer attorney/Board member, 1981-92); Minneapolis Chamber of Commerce Economic Task Force (1993).
Firm: Doherty, Rumble & Butler's tax and tax litigation practice provides diverse expertise in a broad spectrum of tax planning and tax controversy areas. The firm's tax attorneys have extensive knowledge in planning and structuring simple and complex transactions in the corporate, cooperative, partnership, and estate and trust areas with the experience to promptly recognize and resolve tax issues in a cost-effective and beneficial manner. The tax litigation attorneys include former government lawyers who can implement the appropriate strategies to address government tax audits and civil and criminal tax investigations. Ms. Nelson serves as head of the firm's tax and tax litigation group which includes Kimball J. Devoy, Terrance A. Costello, and Tracy M. Smith. *See additional listing in Commercial Litigation Chapter.*

CHARLES W. RIES - Farrish, Johnson & Maschka - 201 North Broad Street, Suite 200, P.O. Box 550 - Mankato, MN 56002-0550 - Phone: (507) 387-3002, Fax: (507) 625-4002 - *See complete biographical profile in Bankruptcy & Workout Law Chapter.*

BRUCE J. SHNIDER

Dorsey & Whitney
Pillsbury Center South
220 South Sixth Street
Minneapolis, MN 55402-1498

Phone: (612) 340-2862
Fax: (612) 340-8827

Admitted: 1977 Minnesota;
1977 US Dist. Ct. (MN);
1980 US Ct. App. (8th Cir.);
1978 US Tax Ct.;
1981 US Sup. Ct.
Birthdate: 10/16/50

•**BRUCE J. SHNIDER:** Mr. Shnider practices in the area of federal income taxation, including executive compensation, structured financing, lease financing, and mergers and acquisitions. He provides general tax advice to several investment banking companies, venture capital funds, financial institutions, and public companies. He has been a partner in Dorsey & Whitney's Tax Department since 1983.

Education: JD 1977 magna cum laude, Harvard University; MPP 1977, Kennedy School of Government - Harvard University (Administration Fellowship); AB 1972 magna cum laude, Dartmouth College (Phi Beta Kappa; Public Service Fellow).
Employment History: Partner 1983-present, Associate 1977-82, Dorsey & Whitney.
Professional Associations: ABA (Tax Section); MSBA (Tax Section); HCBA (Tax Section); Minnesota Justice Foundation (Board member 1989-91).
Community Involvement: Guthrie Theatre (Quest Fund 1993-94); DFL Education Foundation (Special Counsel).
Firm: Dorsey & Whitney is the largest law firm in Minnesota and one of the largest firms in the United States with over 350 lawyers in 12 offices. The depth and breadth of the experience of its lawyers enables it to provide a broad range of services to meet the diverse legal needs of its client base, which includes Fortune 500 companies, public agencies, banks and other financial institutions, nonprofit organizations, individual investors, family owned businesses, and high-tech and low-tech, growth oriented companies.

JAMES H. STEWART - Fryberger, Buchanan, Smith & Frederick, P.A. - 302 West Superior Street, Suite 700 - Duluth, MN 55802 - Phone: (218) 722-0861, Fax: (218) 722-9568 - *See complete biographical profile in Probate, Estate Planning & Trusts Law Chapter.*

JON E. STRINDEN - Gunhus, Grinnell, Klinger, Swenson & Guy, Ltd. - 512 Center Avenue, P.O. Box 1077 - Moorhead, MN 56561-1977 - Phone: (218) 236-6462, Fax: (218) 236-9873 - *See complete biographical profile in Closely Held Business Law Chapter.*

•**PAUL M. TORGERSON** - Dorsey & Whitney - Pillsbury Center South, 220 South Sixth Street - Minneapolis, MN 55402-1498 - Phone: (612) 340-8700, Fax: (612) 340-8827 - *See complete biographical profile in Health Law Chapter.*

MICHAEL TRUCANO - Dorsey & Whitney - Pillsbury Center South, 220 South Sixth Street - Minneapolis, MN 55402-1498 - Phone: (612) 340-2673, Fax: (612) 340-8738 - *See complete biographical profile in Closely Held Business Law Chapter.*

•**JOHN W. WINDHORST, JR.:** Mr. Windhorst, a partner in the Tax Department at Dorsey & Whitney, practices in the area of corporate and individual taxation, including tax litigation and tax controversies, with an emphasis upon state and local taxation. These state and local tax cases, in Minnesota and other Midwestern states, have involved income, sales, property, mining, and utility taxation, and have raised a variety of nexus, apportionment, exemption, and other issues. He has also represented clients in major federal employment tax cases before the national offices of the IRS and Social Security Administration. Several cases in which Mr. Windhorst has appeared before the Minnesota Supreme Court are *Metropolitan Sports Facilities Commission v. County of Hennepin* (1991); *Erie Mining Company v. Commissioner of Revenue* (1984); *Village of Burnsville v. Onischuk* (1974); and *Transport Leasing Corp. v. State* (1972). Mr. Windhorst is a continuing legal education lecturer on tax topics. He is listed in *The Best Lawyers in America* and *Who's Who in America*.
Education: LLB 1965 magna cum laude, Order of the Coif, University of Minnesota (Note Editor 1964-65, *Minnesota Law Review*); AB 1962 magna cum laude, Harvard College.
Employment History: Partner 1971-present, Associate 1966-70, Dorsey & Whitney; 1967 and 1969 legislative sessions - Staff of the Revisor of Statutes of the State of Minnesota (legislative bill drafting); Legal Writing Instructor 1966-1970, University of Minnesota Law School; Law Clerk 1965-66, Hon. Harry A. Blackmun, Judge, US Court of Appeals, Eighth Circuit.
Professional Associations: MSBA (past Governing Council member, Tax Section).
Community Involvement: Legal Advice Clinics (volunteer attorney); Harvard Club of Minnesota (President 1977-78); St. Paul Chamber Orchestra (Board member 1980-86).
Firm: Dorsey & Whitney is the largest law firm in Minnesota and one of the largest firms in the United States with over 350 lawyers in 12 offices. The depth and breadth of the experience of its lawyers enables it to provide a broad range of services to meet the diverse legal needs of its client base, which includes Fortune 500 companies, public agencies, banks and other financial institutions, nonprofit organizations, individual investors, family owned businesses, and growth oriented companies.

JOHN W. WINDHORST, JR.

Dorsey & Whitney
Pillsbury Center South
220 South Sixth Street
Minneapolis, MN 55402-1498

Phone: (612) 340-2645
Fax: (612) 340-8827

Admitted: 1965 Minnesota; 1967 US Dist. Ct. (MN); 1965 US Ct. App. (8th Cir.); 1975 US Sup. Ct.; US Tax Ct.
Birthdate: 07/06/40

Chapter 10: Business Tax Law

Complete listing of all attorneys nominated in Business Tax Law

JOHN P. BYRON, Fredrikson & Byron, P.A., Minneapolis; **JACK W. CARLSON,** Thomsen, Nybeck, Johnson, Bouquet, Van Valkenburg, Ohnstad & Smith, P.A., Edina; **MARTIN A. CULHANE III,** Oppenheimer, Wolff & Donnelly, Minneapolis; **KIMBALL J. DEVOY,** Doherty, Rumble & Butler Professional Association, St. Paul; **JOHN J. ERHART,** Fredrikson & Byron, P.A., Minneapolis; **MYRON L. FRANS,** Gray, Plant, Mooty, Mooty & Bennett, P.A., Minneapolis; **JEROME, A. GEIS,** Briggs and Morgan, P.A., St. Paul; **BARRY A. GERSICK,** Maun & Simon, Minneapolis; **NICK HAY,** Moss & Barnett, A Professional Association, Minneapolis; **DAVID N. HAYNES,** Leonard, Street and Deinard Professional Association, Minneapolis; **WILLIAM H. HIPPEE JR.,** Dorsey & Whitney, Minneapolis; **PAUL J. LINSTROTH,** Popham, Haik, Schnobrich & Kaufman, Ltd., Minneapolis; **WARREN E. MACK,** Fredrikson & Byron, P.A., Minneapolis; **PHILLIP H. MARTIN,** Dorsey & Whitney, Minneapolis; **THOMAS R. MUCK,** Fredrikson & Byron, P.A., Minneapolis; **SUE ANN NELSON,** Doherty, Rumble & Butler Professional Association, Minneapolis; **THOMAS M. REGAN,** Felhaber, Larson, Fenlon & Vogt, P.A., Minneapolis; **BURTON G. ROSS,** Ross, Rosenblatt & Wilson, Ltd., Minneapolis; **CLINTON A. SCHROEDER,** Gray, Plant, Mooty, Mooty & Bennett, P.A., Minneapolis; **BRUCE J. SHNIDER,** Dorsey & Whitney, Minneapolis; **PAUL M. TORGERSON,** Dorsey & Whitney, Minneapolis; **JOHN A. TRENTI,** Trenti Law Firm, Virginia; **HONNEN S. WEISS,** Felhaber, Larson, Fenlon & Vogt, P.A., Minneapolis; **JOHN W. WINDHORST JR.,** Dorsey & Whitney, Minneapolis; **ALAN J. YANOWITZ,** Attorney at Law, Rochester.

CHAPTER 11

CLOSELY HELD BUSINESS LAW

A business that is closely held is one that is owned by a single individual or small number of persons. It is a business whose stocks are not traded or easily available for purchase on a stock exchange or, under Minnesota law, one that does not have more than 35 shareholders. Attorneys who specialize in helping small and closely held businesses can help companies decide how best to organize. They also can help owners understand the consequences of the various organizational structures for governmental regulation, day-to-day operation, and tax purposes. This chapter discusses the legal aspects of starting, operating, and selling small and closely held businesses.

ORGANIZATION

One of the first, and possibly most important, decisions a person starting a small business will make is how to organize the business. This decision is an important one because it can have important tax consequences and can affect the way the business operates. There are many ways to organize a closely held business, including sole proprietorships, partnerships, franchises, corporations, and limited liability companies.

SOLE PROPRIETORSHIP

The simplest way to own a closely held business is the sole proprietorship, in which the business is owned and controlled by one person who reports the debts and profits of the business on his or her personal income tax return. One person owns, manages, and controls the business. A sole proprietorship may have employees, but only the owner is in charge of the business. The owner receives the business profits and losses. The owner is also personally responsible for any debts the business may incur. Income, expenses, and losses are reported on the business owner's individual tax return.

A sole proprietorship is relatively easy to organize. The business owner is responsible for getting appropriate licenses, if any, and tax identification numbers, and must register the business name. There are no specific state filing requirements for this business option.

The benefits of the sole proprietorship include having complete control over the business, ease of the initial set-up, and having business profits taxed at the individual taxpayer rate, which is lower than the rate charged to corporations. The drawbacks to sole proprietorship include being personally responsible for debts and liabilities of the business. For example, if a business owner has debts that are not being paid, the creditors can reach the personal assets of the business owner, such as a personal checking account, house, or car. A business owner may obtain insurance to minimize this drawback. Other drawbacks include lack of continuity—when the business owner dies, the business ceases to exist—and generally not being able to deduct benefits like health, dental, and life insurance on a sole proprietor's income tax return as business expenses.

PARTNERSHIP

A partnership is formed anytime two or more people who have not filed for incorporation agree to carry on a business together and to share profits and liability. A partnership is relatively easy to form and can be valid even without a written agreement setting forth its terms.

There are two types of partnerships, general and limited. In a general partnership each partner has an equal voice in how the business is run. Minnesota courts have ruled that a partnership can be formed merely by the act of two people running a business together, whether or not they ever had a formal agreement to do so. Usually, however, the partners draw up an agreement which specifies how the partnership will make decisions, when and how the partners can withdraw profits, and how each will be required to make contributions to the business. A chief advantage to forming a general partnership is that it is relatively inexpensive to start, as the agreement need not be filed with any governmental entity. In a general partnership, each partner is equally liable for the agreements and debts of the business.

A limited partnership sets limits on the power of partners to conduct business and affords limited liability to each partner. A limited partner is prohibited from managing or making day-to-day-decisions concerning the business but is shielded from most debts incurred by the company. More legal formalities must be met under this type of arrangement than in a general partnership. In Minnesota, a limited partnership can only be formed in accordance with the Uniform Limited Partnership Act. State and federal tax codes make a number of distinctions between limited and general partnerships. In general, neither kind of partnership has to pay federal income tax, instead, each partner pays tax at the individual tax rates on his or her share of the profits.

CORPORATION

A corporation differs from a partnership in that it is treated as a separate legal entity in and of itself rather than as a collection of individuals. A corporation is owned by one or more shareholders and must meet certain legal requirements spelled out in its articles of incorporation. The corporation is managed by a board of directors, who are elected from the shareholders of the corporation.

The corporation is taxed as a separate entity, and shareholders are not liable for the corporation's losses nor for any claims against the company. Under both state and federal tax laws, the corporation reports its income, losses, and expenses on a corporate income tax return.

One of the biggest drawbacks to incorporating a business is double taxation. Double taxation occurs because a corporation's income is taxed before dividends are paid to shareholders, but shareholders also have to report the gains as taxable income on their own individual tax returns.

All corporations, whether small or large, are expected to adhere to certain formalities, such as holding regular meetings of the board of directors and of shareholders. However, the small size of most closely held corporations and the tendency for shareholders to take active roles in the operation and management of the corporation often mean that many small and closely held corporations ignore such formalities. The failure to observe corporate formalities can be very unwise.

Sometimes, individuals use the corporate entity to insulate themselves from personal liability and the consequences of their actions. In such cases, where creditors find themselves unable to pursue their claims against closely held corporations, creditors may ask a court to ignore the organization's corporate status and impose liability upon the shareholders. Courts are more likely to take this action, called "piercing the corporate veil," in cases where shareholders have not regularly conducted the business like a corporation or where the business has a seriously inadequate financial base for operation.

Professional Corporation

Professional corporations are formed by professionals such as doctors, lawyers, and accountants for the purpose of saving money on their taxes through pension plans and deferred-income programs.

A professional corporation is much like any other corporation except that it can be formed by only one person and can engage in only one category of professional service. Also, only other individuals licensed to practice in that particular profession can own shares in such a corporation. The shares cannot be easily transferred. Although forming a professional corporation does not shield the individual from liability for professional malpractice, it can shield an individual from liability for malpractice committed by other persons with whom he or she associates.

Limited Liability Company

As of January 1, 1993, companies in Minnesota have another option for organization. They can organize as a limited liability company, which allows them to take advantage of the favorable tax treatment of a partnership while preserving the limited liability of a corporation. A limited liability company must have at least two members and a limited lifetime, and ownership of the company cannot be transferred freely. This type of company limits the amount an investor in the corporation can lose, either from a lawsuit against the corporation or from other losses. Generally, the amount the investor can lose is limited to the amount he or she invests in the limited liability corporation. In addition, the liability of the corporation itself is limited to the value of its assets. Instead of being taxed as a single organization, the limited liability company is taxed through the income of its owners. All stockholders are allowed to participate in the decision-making process of the company, unlike members of a limited partnership.

Franchise

A franchise is an agreement, sometimes in the form of a contract, which allows the franchisee (the person buying the franchise) to use a marketing system that has been designed by the franchisor (the seller). The business is closely associated with the trademark or commercial identity of the franchisor and the franchisee must pay a fee for the use of the marketing system.

Some prognosticators have predicted that by the year 2000 more than one-half of all retail stores in America will be franchises. There is generally less of a financial risk associated with the purchase of a franchise because the marketing strategy has been proven successful in the past. It is often easier for a franchise to obtain financing than it is for another independent business even if both want financing for the same reason.

While a franchise fee does not guarantee success in business, the purchaser of a franchise can usually expect some help, services, and support from the franchisor. Among other things, the purchaser might receive help choosing a site for the business in the form of feasibility studies of the location and the demographics of the area where he or she hopes to locate the business. A franchisee might also expect to receive help in negotiating a lease for the business and financial assistance with the start-up and initial operating costs. Finally, a franchisor often provides a franchisee with training, support, advertising, product discounts, and further assistance.

In Minnesota, there are three specific elements that must be present with a franchise: a fee, a name, and a community of interest. Any offer that meets this definition may be subject to regulations found in the Minnesota Franchise Act. A franchise must be registered with the Minnesota Department of Commerce before any sales are made. In addition, certain fees are owed, such as a $400 application fee and several additional filing fees.

There are some exemptions to registration and a wide variety of state regulations with which franchises must comply. Copies of the Minnesota Franchise Act, the rules of the Department of Commerce, and the Uniform Franchise Offering Circular (a form of franchise guidelines accepted in almost every state) are all available from the State of Minnesota Bookstore.

BUYING OR SELLING A CLOSELY HELD BUSINESS

Buying or selling a business is like buying or selling anything else, only much more complicated. In many closely held businesses, family concerns can influence, even dominate, business decision making. The decision to buy or sell a business can be motivated by a divorce, death, or personal animosities between business associates so emotions may override prudent business judgment. The advice of professionals can be invaluable before buying or selling any business, especially a closely held business.

TRANSFERABILITY

The ease of transferability of ownership varies depending on the way a business is organized. The assets of a sole proprietorship are easy to transfer. A sole proprietorship can be sold by selling all the assets of the business to another person, who then becomes the new sole proprietor of the business. A partnership is not easily transferable. Unless otherwise specified, no person can become a partner unless all of the other partners agree. Thus, if a partner sells his or her share in the business to someone who is not already a partner, the purchaser does not then become a partner but merely earns the profits that the seller otherwise would have received. To avoid this situation, most partnership agreements specify the conditions under which partnership status can be transferred. Sometimes partners have buy-sell agreements between themselves that obligate remaining partners to buy out the interest of a partner who wants to sell his or her interest. Buy-sell agreements can be mandatory, that is, requiring remaining partners to buy out a departing partner, or optional, giving the remaining partner or partners the right of first refusal should one partner want to sell his or her interest.

Shares in a corporation are usually the easiest to transfer because, by definition, a corporation is made up of shareholders who may transfer ownership of their shares to others. However, in the case of small and closely held corporations, there may not be much of a market for shares that are not publicly traded. Other shareholders may want to prevent the frequent sale of shares by strictly limiting such sales in their articles of incorporation. Members of limited liability companies can sell their rights to share in the profits and losses of the company unless there is an agreement to the contrary. As with a partnership, the rights to participate in the decision making of the company cannot be sold unless all of the members agree.

Non-Compete Agreements

Usually when a business is sold, the buyer wants the seller to agree not to compete with the business being sold. Non-compete agreements are enforceable in Minnesota so long as they are reasonable in geographic scope and duration. Non-compete agreements are especially important in the context of small and closely held companies because often goodwill and name recognition are the most significant items the buyer is paying for. Without an effective non-compete agreement, the seller might set up a new business in direct competition with the old one and transfer the loyalty of longtime customers to the new enterprise. A buyer may want to get non-compete agreements from the seller's spouse and children or anyone else who worked closely with the seller in operating the business and who might go into competition with the buyer.

Consulting Agreements

Another common component of an agreement to sell a closely held business is a consulting agreement. Often, the advice of the former business owner is a valuable asset for a new owner during a transitional period. The former owner can give advice on how business has been conducted, where supplies are kept, how to operate machinery, working effectively with suppliers, and generally keeping customers happy. Both parties to the agreement need to be clear on the extent and duration of the consulting arrangement. The advice of an attorney can be especially helpful when drafting a consulting agreement because the seller may be able to realize certain tax advantages by re-characterizing a portion of the purchase price as a consulting fee.

BUSINESS SUCCESSION

Succession can actually be more complicated for closely held companies than for large publicly held companies. The ways a business is transferred following the death or withdrawal of an owner depends on how the business is organized.

In a sole proprietorship, the business ceases to exist when the proprietor dies. In a general partnership, the business can be continued after one of the partners dies, but the remaining partners have to pay the beneficiary of the deceased partner the fair market value of his or her partnership. If a partner in a limited partnership dies, his or her ownership in the corporation may be inherited and all attendant rights exercised by the new owner.

Because a corporation is a freestanding legal entity, the death of an owner technically has no effect on the operation of the business. Many smaller corporations, however, take out life insurance policies on certain key employees, such as the founder or CEO of the business. The shares held by those persons may be transferred to descendants or, by previous agreement, to remaining key individuals.

In a limited liability company, the company dissolves unless there was prior agreement to continue in the event of a death. Also, if the remaining members of a company with more than one remaining member unanimously consent to continue operations, the company may do so.

Because interests in a small and closely held business often lack liquidity and can be difficult to evaluate, they can be difficult to transfer before or after the death of the owner. Estate planning concerns for owners of small and closely held businesses are addressed in the Probate, Estate Planning & Trusts Law Chapter.

RESOURCES

Internal Revenue Service, Minnesota District Office, 708 Federal Building, 316 North Robert Street, St. Paul, MN 55101, (612) 644-7515.

Minnesota Department of Revenue, Minnesota Business Assistance Group, Mail Station 4453, St. Paul, MN 55146-4453, (612) 296-6181 or (800) 657-3777.

Minnesota Secretary of State, 180 State Office Building, 100 Constitution Avenue, St. Paul, MN 55155-1299, (612) 296-2803.

Small Business Administration, 610C Butler Square, 100 N Sixth Street, Minneapolis, MN 55403, (612) 370-2324.

Minnesota Small Business Assistance Office, 500 Metro Square, 121 Seventh Place East, St. Paul, MN 55101-2146, (612) 296-3871 or (800) 657-3858. The organization publishes *A Guide to Starting a Business in Minnesota*, a helpful resource that is available for no charge.

CLOSELY HELD BUSINESS LAW LEADING ATTORNEYS

The attorneys profiled in this section were nominated by their peers in a statewide survey conducted in 1993 in which several thousand Minnesota attorneys were asked to name the lawyer to whom they would send a friend or family member in need of legal assistance in the area of *Closely Held Business Law.*

Because the survey resulted in a list of less than five percent of Minnesota's practicing attorneys, this should not be construed as a complete list. Nevertheless, it is an excellent source of highly qualified and reputable attorneys, who, if unable to assist can in most cases make quality referrals.

A list of all attorneys nominated in this category is found at the end of this section. For information on the survey methodology see page ix.

Please note that the shorter, two line attorney listings in this section are of attorneys who practice in this area but whose full biographical profile appears in another section of this book. A bullet "•" preceeding name indicates the attorney was nominated in this particular area of law. For information on the format of these profiles, consult the section "Using the *Business Guidebook*" found on page xiv. Note that the following abbreviations are used throughout these profiles:

Selected by Attorneys for GUIDEBOOK
Law & Leading Attorneys
MINNESOTA

The attorneys profiled below were recommended by their peers in a statewide survey.

App.	- Appellate	ABA	- American Bar Association
Cir.	- Circuit	ATLA	- American Trial Lawyers Association
Ct.	- Court	HCBA	- Hennepin County Bar Association
Dist.	- District	MDLA	- Minnesota Defense Lawyers Association
Hon.	- Honorable	MSBA	- Minnesota State Bar Association
JD	- Law degree (Juris Doctor)	MTLA	- Minnesota Trial Lawyers Association
LLB	- Law degree	NBTA	- National Board of Trial Advocacy
LLM	- Master in Law degree	RCBA	- Ramsey County Bar Association
Sup.	- Supreme		

•TIMOTHY M. BARNETT: Mr. Barnett practices closely held and emerging business law; mergers and acquisitions; general corporate finance and securities law; and franchise law. He serves as general corporate counsel to successful national, regional, and local businesses in a variety of industries, most notably, aerospace, waste processing and waste-to-energy, machining and manufacturing, and restaurant development and franchising. His background as a Certified Public Accountant is the basis of strong analytical and negotiation skills and, since early in his career, he has been the lead attorney on numerous merger and acquisition matters, including management-led buy-outs. In the last four years he has served as lead counsel (both corporate and tax counsel) on more than 20 acquisitions and dispositions, accounting for approximately 35-40% of his time. In the closely held business arena, his entrepreneurial spirit has benefited him in the representation of dozens of new and emerging companies, and he possesses special expertise in counseling entrepreneurs on the organization, financing, and development of their closely held businesses, helping them convert business opportunities into reality. A unique area of his practice involves the representation of companies involved in the development of waste processing and waste-to-energy facilities. This area demands a unique blend of sophisticated contract negotiation and drafting and corporate finance expertise. Mr. Barnett's extensive experience in many different types of business transactions has also led to his nomination as one of Minnesota's leading attorneys in the area of tax law.
Education: JD 1982 magna cum laude, University of Minnesota; BBA 1979 with highest honors, University of Notre Dame; Certified Public Accountant, Minnesota 1980.
Employment History: Shareholder 1993-present, Winthrop & Weinstine, P.A.; Associate/Partner 1982-93, Mackall, Crounse & Moore.
Representative Clients: World Aerospace Corp.; Towle Real Estate Company; Daneco, Inc. (waste processing); Legend Foods, Inc.; Safe Link Corp. (cellular radio networks).
Professional Associations: HCBA; MSBA; ABA.
Community Involvement: Notre Dame Alumni Club.
Firm: See firm profile in Appendix C. *See additional listing in Publicly Held Corporations Law Chapter.*

TIMOTHY M. BARNETT

Winthrop & Weinstine, P.A.
3000 Dain Bosworth Plaza
60 South Sixth Street
Minneapolis, MN 55402

Phone: (612) 347-0700
Fax: (612) 347-0600

Admitted: 1982 Minnesota
Birthdate: 10/12/57

Chapter 11: Closely Held Business Law

WILLIAM J. COSGRIFF - Doherty, Rumble & Butler Professional Association - 2800 Minnesota World Trade Center, 30 East Seventh Street - St. Paul, MN 55101-4999 - Phone: (612) 291-9333, Fax: (612) 291-9313 - *See complete biographical profile in Commercial Real Estate Law Chapter.*

KENNETH L. CUTLER - Dorsey & Whitney - Pillsbury Center South, 220 South Sixth Street - Minneapolis, MN 55402-1498 - Phone: (612) 340-2740, Fax: (612) 340-8738 - *See complete biographical profile in Publicly Held Corporations Law Chapter.*

KIMBALL J. DEVOY - Doherty, Rumble & Butler Professional Association - 2800 Minnesota World Trade Center, 30 East Seventh Street - St. Paul, MN 55101-4999 - Phone: (612) 291-9333, Fax: (612) 291-9313 - *See complete biographical profile in Business Tax Law Chapter.*

MORRIS DICKEL - Dickel, Johannson, Taylor, Rust & Tye, P.A. - 407 North Broadway, P.O. Box 605 - Crookston, MN 56716 - Phone: (218) 281-2400, Fax: (218) 281-5831 - *See complete biographical profile in Agricultural Law Chapter.*

FREDERICK A. DUDDERAR - Hanft, Fride, O'Brien, Harries, Swelbar & Burns, P.A. - 1000 First Bank Place, 130 West Superior Street - Duluth, MN 55802 - Phone: (218) 722-4766, Fax: (218) 720-4920 - *See complete biographical profile in Bankruptcy & Workout Law Chapter.*

DEAN R. EDSTROM - Doherty, Rumble & Butler Professional Association - 3500 Fifth Street Towers, 150 South Fifth Street - Minneapolis, MN 55402-4235 - Phone: (612) 340-5575, Fax: (612) 340-5584 - *See complete biographical profile in Publicly Held Corporations Law Chapter.*

DAVID B. EIDE - Frommelt & Eide, Ltd. - 580 International Centre, 900 Second Avenue South - Minneapolis, MN 55402 - Phone: (612) 332-2200, Fax: (612) 342-2761 - *See complete biographical profile in Commercial Real Estate Law Chapter.*

JOHN J. ERHART - Fredrikson & Byron, P.A. - 1100 International Centre, 900 Second Avenue South - Minneapolis, MN 55402 - Phone: (612) 347-7035, Fax: (612) 347-7077 - *See complete biographical profile in Business Tax Law Chapter.*

TODD I. FREEMAN

Larkin, Hoffman, Daly & Lindgren, Ltd.
1500 Norwest Financial Center
7900 Xerxes Avenue South
Bloomington, MN 55431

Phone: (612) 835-3800
Fax: (612) 896-3333

Admitted: 1978 Minnesota;
1980 US Dist. Ct. (MN);
1980 US Tax Ct.
Birthdate: 11/24/53

•**TODD I. FREEMAN:** Mr. Freeman is a shareholder with Larkin, Hoffman, Daly & Lindgren, Ltd., and heads its Personal Service Corporation Group. He practices law in the areas of benefits and tax planning with a special emphasis on medical practices, closely held businesses, and professional corporations. Mr. Freeman is also a Certified Public Accountant. His articles on corporate and tax subjects have appeared in publications such as *The Tax Advisor*, *The Practical Accountant*, and *The Practical Tax Lawyer*. Mr. Freeman regularly speaks at seminars to numerous groups including the Minnesota Medical Association, Minnesota Dental Association, Minnesota Society of Certified Public Accountants, American Bar Association, Independent Bankers Association of Minnesota, and National Business Institute and Twin Cities Association of Financial Planning. Mr. Freeman is listed in *Who's Who of American Lawyers*.
Education: JD 1978 cum laude, University of Minnesota; BS 1974 magna cum laude, University of Colorado.
Employment History: Currently, Larkin, Hoffman, Daly & Lindgren, Ltd.; Accountant 1977-80, Coopers & Lybrand.
Representative Clients: Shapco Printing; Spartan Products; Jerry's Enterprises; Minneapolis Radiation Oncology; Sundance Medical Clinic; Baldinger Baking Co.
Professional Associations: ABA (Chair 1990-92, Personal Service Organization Committee); MSBA; HCBA; American Institute of Certified Public Accountants; MN Society of Certified Public Accountants.
Community Involvement: Edina Chamber of Commerce (President 1984-85; Director 1983-93); Sholom Home, Inc. (Director 1983-89); Temple of Aaron (Director & Counsel 1983-present).
Firm: Larkin, Hoffman, Daly & Lindgren, Ltd., has served the legal and business counseling needs of clients since 1958. The firm's entrepreneurial spirit and understanding of the challenges facing growing businesses has been key to its success. The firm serves small and middle-market growing business and individual clients, as well as providing its special expertise to Fortune 500 companies. The firm's Bloomington location allows it to deliver legal services to clients in the most convenient and cost-effective manner possible. *See additional listings in Health Law and Business Tax Law Chapters.*

•**F. KELTON GAGE:** Mr. Gage has practiced in Mankato since 1950. His practice has been general with an emphasis on business law, business litigation, and securities law. He has represented the State of Minnesota in judicial disciplinary proceedings and represented a Governor's Commission which investigated the office of the Scott County Attorney. Mr. Gage has served the community as a member of the Mankato School Board, the Minnesota State College Board, and the Minnesota State Senate.
Education: JD 1950, University of Minnesota; BSL 1948, University of Minnesota.
Employment History: Attorney 1950-present, Blethen Gage & Krause.
Representative Clients: Michigan Millers Insurance Company; Norwest Bank of Minnesota South Central, N.A.; Phenix Composites, Inc.; Waseca Mutual Insurance Company.
Professional Associations: MSBA; Board of Professional Responsibility (1974-81); American Bar Foundation (Life Fellow).
Community Involvement: Minnesota State Senator, 11th Legislative Dist. (1966-72); Metropolitan Sports Facilities Commission (1978-85); Immanuel-St. Joseph's Hospital (Director); Mankato Kiwanis Club; Mankato Area Riverblenders; Centenary United Methodist Church.
Firm: Founded in 1896, Blethen Gage & Krause is a general practice law firm. *See additional listings in Commercial Litigation and Securities & Venture Finance Law Chapters.*

F. KELTON GAGE

Blethen Gage & Krause
127 South Second Street
P.O. Box 3049
Mankato, MN 56002-3049

Phone: (507) 345-1166
Fax: (507) 345-8003

Admitted: 1950 Minnesota; 1954 US Dist. Ct. (MN); 1970 US Ct. App. (8th Cir.); 1973 US Tax Ct.
Birthdate: 06/20/25

•**LEE W. HANSON:** Mr. Hanson practices in the area of closely held business law, including acquisitions, mergers, and sales; estate planning; farm matters; business; commercial real estate; and tax planning.
Education: JD 1969, University of Minnesota; BA 1966 magna cum laude, Concordia College.
Employment History: Clerk, Hon. Urban Steimann, Judge, Minnesota District Court; Tax Researcher 1968-69, Coopers & Lybrand, Certified Public Accountants; Tax Researcher 1967-68, Hendrickson n/k/a McGladrey & Pullen, Certified Public Accountants.
Representative Clients: Arvig Telcom Inc.; Big Bear Enterprises; Bauerly Brothers; Hardrives, Inc.
Professional Associations: ABA; Stearns-Benton Bar Assn.; MSBA (Vice President, Business Section; Board member, Continuing Legal Education); Seventh District Bar Assn. (past Chair, Fee Arbitration Committee); ADR Committee Fee Arbitration Mediation.
Community Involvement: United Way (past President, Executive Committee); St. Cloud State University Foundation (past President, Vice President, Board member); Central Minnesota Boy Scout Council (Executive Committee & past President); St. Cloud Area Boy's and Girl's Club (Executive Committee); Bishop's Task Force on Economic Reform; North Star University Foundation (Board member).
Firm: The law firm of Hall, Byers, Hanson, Steil & Weinberger was founded in 1931 by Lawrence M. Hall, former Speaker of the Minnesota House of Representatives, and has operated continuously to the present time. Since the founding of the firm, the legal system and the practice of law have grown in size and complexity. To meet this growth, Hall, Byers, Hanson has also grown in size and ability to handle a wide variety of complex legal matters. At present the firm employs 41 persons, consisting of 17 attorneys and 24 support staff. Minneapolis address: 2904 Plaza VII, 45 South Seventh Street, Minneapolis, MN 55402. Phone: (612) 339-2553. Fax: (612) 339-4775. *See additional listings in Commercial Real Estate Law and Publicly Held Corporations Law Chapters.*

LEE W. HANSON

Hall, Byers, Hanson, Steil & Weinberger, P.A.
1010 West St. Germain
Suite 600
St. Cloud, MN 56301

Phone: (612) 252-4414
Fax: (612) 252-4482

Admitted: 1969 Minnesota
Birthdate: 02/01/44

NICK HAY - Moss & Barnett, A Professional Association - 4800 Norwest Center, 90 South Seventh Street - Minneapolis, MN 55402-4129 - Phone: (612) 347-0443, Fax: (612) 339-6686 - *See complete biographical profile in Business Tax Law Chapter.*

WILLIAM H. HIPPEE, JR. - Dorsey & Whitney - Pillsbury Center South, 220 South Sixth Street - Minneapolis, MN 55402-1498 - Phone: (612) 340-2665, Fax: (612) 340-8827 - *See complete biographical profile in Business Tax Law Chapter.*

Chapter 11: Closely Held Business Law

JOEL D. JOHNSON

Dosland, Nordhougen,
Lillehaug & Johnson, P.A.
730 Center Avenue, Suite 203
P.O. Box 100
Moorhead, MN 56561-0100

Phone: (218) 233-2744
Fax: (218) 233-1570

Admitted: 1976 Minnesota;
1982 North Dakota
Birthdate: 11/15/48

•**JOEL D. JOHNSON:** Mr. Johnson practices law in the following areas: corporate and commercial; probate, estates, and trusts; and real estate. He is certified by the Minnesota State Bar Association as a Real Estate Specialist.
Education: JD 1976, University of North Dakota; BA 1970, Concordia College.
Employment History: 1976-present, Dosland, Nordhougen, Lillehaug & Johnson, P.A.
Professional Associations: MSBA; ABA; Clay County Bar Assn.; State Bar Assn. of North Dakota.
Community Involvement: F-M Soccer Assn., Inc. (Board member 1980-83; President 1980-82); F-M Soccer Assn. (Coach 1979-present); Moorhead Chamber of Commerce Ambassadors (Chair 1987); Moorhead Parks Advisory Board (1987-93); Regional International Trade Assn. (Board member 1992-present; President 1992-94).
Firm: The firm of Dosland, Nordhougen, Lillehaug & Johnson, P.A., is a regional law firm in the general practice of law that has served clients in North Dakota and Minnesota for more than 100 years. *See additional listings in Probate, Estate Planning & Trusts Law and Commercial Real Estate Law Chapters.*

WILLIAM A. JONASON

Dorsey & Whitney
201 First Avenue SW
Suite 340
Rochester, MN 55902

Phone: (507) 288-3156
Fax: (507) 288-6190

Admitted: 1983 Minnesota;
1984 US Dist. Ct. (MN);
1984 US Ct. App. (8th Cir.);
1988 US Tax Ct.
Birthdate: 02/06/58

•**WILLIAM A. JONASON:** Mr. Jonason specializes in business advice for closely held companies. He serves as general counsel for numerous small and medium-size businesses, and has substantial experience in advising clients on corporate formations, financings, mergers and acquisitions, shareholder agreements, shareholder disputes, estate planning, and tax controversies. Mr. Jonason has been with the firm since 1984 and a partner in the Tax and General Business Group since 1991.
Education: JD 1983 with distinction, University of Iowa (Senior Articles Editor 1982-83, *Iowa Law Review*); BA 1980 with honors, St. Olaf College.
Employment History: Partner 1991-present, Associate 1984-90, Dorsey & Whitney; Adjunct Professor of Law, Corporations 1988-89, Hamline Law School; Law Clerk 1983-84, Hon. Donald P. Lay, Chief Judge, US Court of Appeals, Eighth Circuit.
Firm: Dorsey & Whitney is the largest law firm in Minnesota and one of the largest firms in the United States with over 350 lawyers in 12 offices. The depth and breadth of the experience of its lawyers enables it to provide a broad range of services to meet the diverse legal needs of its client base, which includes Fortune 500 companies, public agencies, banks and other financial institutions, nonprofit organizations, individual investors, family owned businesses, and high-tech and low-tech, growth oriented companies. *See additional listing in Business Tax Law Chapter.*

Closely Held Business Law Leading Attorneys

•**MICHAEL C. KARP:** Mr. Karp has extensive experience in representing closely held businesses and routinely assists them in documenting major transactions. His experience extends to real estate matters and taxation, including employee benefit and ERISA matters. Mr. Karp is certified as a Real Property Law Specialist by the Minnesota State Bar Association.
Education: JD 1980, Oklahoma City University (Articles Editor, *Oklahoma City Law Review*); BS 1978, Bemidji State University.
Employment History: Attorney 1981-present, Blethen Gage & Krause.
Representative Clients: Winco, Inc.; Norwest Bank Minnesota South Central, N.A.; River Valley Truck Centers, Inc.
Professional Associations: MSBA; Minnesota State Society of CPA's.
Community Involvement: United Way (Chair); Coach for youth sports and program leader for youth scouting programs.
Firm: Founded in 1896, Blethen Gage & Krause is a general practice law firm. *See additional listings in Business Tax Law and Employee Benefits Law Chapters.*

MICHAEL C. KARP

Blethen Gage & Krause
127 South Second Street
P.O. Box 3049
Mankato, MN 56002-3049

Phone: (507) 345-1166
Fax: (507) 345-8003

Admitted: 1981 Minnesota; 1981 US Dist. Ct. (MN); 1989 US Tax Ct.
Birthdate: 12/25/55

•**JOHN J. KILLEN:** Mr. Killen practices medical malpractice defense, legal malpractice defense, and product liability defense. He has been listed in *The Best Lawyers in America* since 1987.
Education: LLB 1955 Order of the Coif, University of Minnesota (Delta Theta Phi); BA 1949, University of Minnesota.
Representative Clients: The St. Paul Insurance Companies; Travelers Insurance Companies; St. Mary's Medical Center; CPC International; Wal-Mart Stores.
Professional Associations: 11th District Bar Assn. (President 1981-82); MSBA (Board of Governors 1982-84); ABA; American College of Trial Lawyers; International Academy of Trial Lawyers; International Assn. of Insurance Counsel; Federation of Insurance and Corporate Counsel; American Board of Trial Advocates; American Society of Hospital Attorneys; MDLA.
Community Involvement: Duluth Transit Authority (President 1969-71).
Firm: Founded in 1888, Johnson, Killen, Thibodeau & Seiler, P.A., is the oldest firm in northern Minnesota. Today the firm's 18 lawyers provide a wide range of services for consumers, businesses, and companies in commercial, toxic tort, environmental, and insurance litigation; commercial and residential real estate; probate, estate planning, and trusts; employment law; closely held business law; and Workers' Compensation. S*ee additional listings in Commercial Litigation and Publicly Held Corporations Law Chapters.*

JOHN J. KILLEN

Johnson, Killen, Thibodeau & Seiler, P.A.
811 Norwest Center
230 West Superior Street
Duluth, MN 55802

Phone: (218) 722-6331
Fax: (218) 722-3031

Admitted: 1955 Minnesota
Birthdate: 05/04/27

FREDERICK A. KUEPPERS, JR. - Kueppers, Hackel & Kueppers, P.A. - 1350 Capital Centre, 386 North Wabasha Street - St. Paul, MN 55102 - Phone: (612) 228-1104, Fax: (612) 297-6599 - *See complete biographical profile in Commercial Real Estate Law Chapter.*

TIMOTHY J. KUNTZ - LeVander, Gillen & Miller, P.A. - 633 South Concord Street, Suite 402 - South St. Paul, MN 55075 - Phone: (612) 451-1831, Fax: (612) 450-7384 - *See complete biographical profile in Federal, State & Local Government Law Chapter.*

W. CHARLES LANTZ - Dorsey & Whitney - 201 First Avenue SW, Suite 340 - Rochester, MN 55902 - Phone: (507) 288-3156, Fax: (507) 288-6190 - *See complete biographical profile in Commercial Real Estate Law Chapter.*

GARY D. MCDOWELL - Lindquist & Vennum - 4200 IDS Center, 80 South Eighth Street - Minneapolis, MN 55402 - Phone: (612) 371-3211, Fax: (612) 371-3207 - *See complete biographical profile in Probate, Estate Planning & Trusts Law Chapter.*

ERIC O. MADSON - Winthrop & Weinstine, P.A. - 3000 Dain Bosworth Plaza, 60 South Sixth Street - Minneapolis, MN 55402 - Phone: (612) 347-0700, Fax: (612) 347-0600 - *See complete biographical profile in Securities & Venture Finance Law Chapter.*

SEYMOUR J. MANSFIELD - Mansfield & Tanick, P.A. - 1560 International Centre, 900 Second Avenue South - Minneapolis, MN 55402-3383 - Phone: (612) 339-4295, Fax: (612) 339-3161 - *See complete biographical profile in Commercial Litigation Chapter.*

JANICE M. NELSON

Nelson Oyen Torvik
221 North First Street
P.O. Box 656
Montevideo, MN 56265

Phone: (612) 269-6461
Fax: (612) 269-8024

Admitted: 1982 Minnesota
Birthdate: 07/10/50

•**JANICE M. NELSON:** Ms. Nelson is in general practice in a rural county seat and primarily serves clients in the surrounding counties in the areas of probate, estate planning, real estate, banking, corporate, municipal, and family law. She is originally from Montevideo, MN.
Education: JD 1982, University of Minnesota; BA 1972, Augsburg College.
Employment History: Currently, Nelson Oyen Torvik; Banker 1972-78, Northwestern State Bank of Montevideo.
Representative Clients: Minnwest Bank Montevideo; Minnesota Valley Cooperative Light & Power Assn.; Co-op Credit Union; Metropolitan Federal Bank Montevideo; Prudential Insurance Company; Prairie State Bank of Milan and Appleton; Klein National Bank of Madison; Cargill, Inc.; Farmers Union Oil Company; Farmers & Merchants State Bank of Clarkfield; Lac qui Parle-Yellow Bank Watershed District; State Bank of Bellingham; Cliff Viessman, Inc.; Chandler Industries; Tri-Line Farmers Cooperative.
Professional Associations: 12th District Bar Assn. (Ethics Committee); MSBA (Real Property Council).
Community Involvement: Volunteer attorney; City of Montevideo (City Attorney); City of Watson (City Attorney); Our Savior's Lutheran Congregation.
Firm: Founded in 1941 as Nelson & Oyen, the firm of Nelson Oyen Torvik has established a strong reputation for providing high quality legal services to clients in west central Minnesota. Members of the firm have served as Chippewa County Attorney since 1977. The firm has attorneys specializing in all areas of litigation, corporate, business, and consumer law. The firm consists of four partners and two associate attorneys and has offices in Montevideo and Clarkfield, MN. *See additional listings in Probate, Estate Planning & Trusts Law and Commercial Real Estate Law Chapters.*

CURTIS A. NORDHOUGEN

Dosland, Nordhougen,
Lillehaug & Johnson, P.A.
730 Center Avenue, Suite 203
P.O. Box 100
Moorhead, MN 56561-0100

Phone: (218) 233-2744
Fax: (218) 233-1570

Admitted: 1966 Minnesota;
1961 North Dakota
Birthdate: 01/10/36

•**CURTIS A. NORDHOUGEN:** Mr. Nordhougen practices primarily in real estate; corporate and business; probate and estate planning; commercial; and agricultural law. In addition, from 1969 through 1986, he served as general counsel for the Housing and Redevelopment Authority of the City of Moorhead Urban Renewal Program. Since 1986, Mr. Nordhougen has served as special counsel to the Moorhead Economic Development Authority in connection with economic development and tax increment financing matters.
Education: LLB 1961, University of North Dakota; BS 1958, University of North Dakota.
Employment History: Currently, Dosland, Nordhougen, Lillehaug & Johnson, P.A.
Representative Clients: American Crystal Sugar Company; Moorhead Economic Development Authority; American Bank Moorhead.
Professional Associations: MSBA; ABA; State Bar Assn. of North Dakota; Clay County Bar Assn.
Community Involvement: Lutheran Church of Christ the King (Church Council 1970-73); Moorhead Youth Hockey Assn. (President 1974-75); Moorhead Area Chamber of Commerce (Director 1979-83; Treasurer 1981-82).
Firm: The firm of Dosland, Nordhougen, Lillehaug & Johnson, P.A., is a regional law firm in the general practice of law that has served clients in North Dakota and Minnesota for more than 100 years. *See additional listings in Probate, Estate Planning & Trusts Law and Commercial Real Estate Law Chapters.*

•**JAMES E. O'BRIEN** - Moss & Barnett, A Professional Association - 4800 Norwest Center, 90 South Seventh Street - Minneapolis, MN 55402 - Phone: (612) 347-0273, Fax: (612) 339-6686 - *See complete biographical profile in Publicly Held Corporations Law Chapter.*

Closely Held Business Law Leading Attorneys

•**DAVID T. PETERSON:** Mr. Peterson serves as an advisor for business clients on a variety of subjects including employment law issues. Recently, his practice has included the sale and acquisition of numerous business entities of varying sizes.
Education: JD 1971 cum laude, University of Minnesota; BS 1966, University of Minnesota.
Employment History: Attorney 1971-present, Blethen Gage & Krause.
RepresentativeClients: Hickory Tech Corp.; The Creative Company; The Child's World, Inc.; Tire Associates Warehouse, Inc.
Professional Associations: ABA; MSBA.
Community Involvement: Mankato Rehabilitation Center (Director 1972-present; President 1976-77); Valley Opportunities, Inc. (Director 1987-present; President 1987-91); Venture Capital Club (Director from inception to 1990; Vice Chair 1990, 1992, 1994); Loyola Alumni Assn. (Director 1989-present); St. John's Church in Mankato (Finance Committee); Schola Foundation (original charter member 1975-85).
Firm: Founded in 1896, Blethen Gage & Krause is a general practice law firm. *See additional listings in Employment Law and Publicly Held Corporations Law Chapters.*

DAVID T. PETERSON

Blethen Gage & Krause
127 South Second Street
P.O. Box 3049
Mankato, MN 56002-3049

Phone: (507) 345-1166
Fax: (507) 345-8003

Admitted: 1971 Minnesota
Birthdate: 05/18/42

MICHAEL PRICHARD - Dorsey & Whitney - Pillsbury Center South, 220 South Sixth Street - Minneapolis, MN 55402-1498 - Phone: (612) 340-2633, Fax: (612) 340-8738 - *See complete biographical profile in International Business Law Chapter.*

•**JOHN E. REGAN:** Mr. Regan concentrates his practice on closely held and family businesses. His experience includes client acquisitions of businesses throughout Minnesota, in other states, and in Canada, as well as follow-up consolidations and mergers; buy-sell-redemption agreement transactions for closely held and family business owners; business sale and retirement planning for closely held business owners; estate and tax planning for family and closely held business owners in manufacturing, banking, wholesale, retail, real estate, agricultural businesses, and professional practices; and the administration and probate of estates of closely held business owners.
Education: JD 1967, William Mitchell; BBA 1962, University of Notre Dame.
Employment History: Partner 1967-present, Regan, Regan & Meyer; Certified Public Accountant 1962-67, Arthur Andersen & Co. (Minneapolis).
Representative Clients: Taylor Corporation; The Thro Company; The Dotson Company; Corporate Graphics International, Inc.; Mankato Implement, Inc.; Mankato Clinic, Ltd.; Taylor Bancshares, Inc.; Lutz-Lloyd Enterprises, Inc.; Feed Service Company; Paper Service Company; Valley Bank; Holiday Inn of Mankato.
Professional Associations: ABA; MSBA; Sixth District Bar Assn. (President 1977-78); American Institute of Certified Public Accountants; Minnesota Society of Certified Public Accountants.
Community Involvement: Mankato City Council (1969-70); Mankato Charter Commission (Chair 1971-81); Immanuel-St. Joseph's Hospital (Board member 1977-86); Mankato Area Catholic Schools (Board member 1984-90; Finance Committee 1990-present); St. Joseph's Church (Trustee 1972-78; Finance Council member 1991-present); Schola Foundation (Trustee 1975-84); Mankato Symphony (Board member 1972-74).
Firm: Regan, Regan & Meyer was founded in 1910 by John E. Regan's grandfather, John E. Regan, who practiced until his death in 1946. The firm was continued by Regan's father, Robert M. Regan, from 1939 until his retirement in 1990. Both active law partners, John E. Regan and Daniel H. Meyer, are also certified public accountants with "Big Six" firm experience and maintain active licenses in both professions. The firm concentrates on business, tax, and estate planning as well as acquisitions, sales, and mergers for closely and family held business clients, including intergenerational and intra-family business transitions and transfers. *See additional listing in Probate, Estate Planning & Trusts Law Chapter.*

JOHN E. REGAN

Regan, Regan & Meyer
115 East Hickory Street
P.O. Box 967
Mankato, MN 56001

Phone: (507) 345-1179
Fax: (507) 345-1182

Admitted: 1967 Minnesota;
1971 US Dist. Ct. (MN);
1971 US Tax Ct.
Birthdate: 06/24/40

•**THOMAS E. ROHRICHT** - Doherty, Rumble & Butler Professional Association - 2800 Minnesota World Trade Center, 30 East Seventh Street - St. Paul, MN 55101-4999 - Phone: (612) 291-9333, Fax: (612) 291-9313 - *See complete biographical profile in Publicly Held Corporations Law Chapter.*

•**THOMAS P. SANDERS** - Leonard, Street and Deinard Professional Association - 150 South Fifth Street, Suite 2300 - Minneapolis, MN 55402 - Phone: (612) 335-1614, Fax: (612) 335-1657 - *See complete biographical profile in Publicly Held Corporations Law Chapter.*

Chapter 11: Closely Held Business Law

ROGER V. STAGEBERG

Lommen, Nelson, Cole & Stageberg, P.A.
1800 IDS Center
80 South Eighth Street
Minneapolis, MN 55402

Phone: (612) 339-8131
Fax: (612) 339-8064
800 number: (800) 752-4297

Admitted: 1966 Minnesota; 1969 US Sup. Ct.
Birthdate: 10/13/41

•**ROGER V. STAGEBERG:** Mr. Stageberg leads the corporate, securities, and tax department at Lommen, Nelson, Cole & Stageberg. He represents numerous small and medium sized corporations, several of which are publicly held. From 1967 to 1978 he practiced corporate and securities law and litigation. Since 1979 he has concentrated in corporate and securities law, representing many companies in mergers and acquisitions, including mergers with foreign companies, and handling private placements and new venture financings. With an engineering background, Mr. Stageberg attracts clients such as electronics, computer, and medical products companies. He is listed in *The Best Lawyers in America*, 1987-93.
Education: JD 1966 cum laude, Order of the Coif, University of Minnesota (*Minnesota Law Review*); B Math 1963 with distinction, Institute of Technology, University of Minnesota.
Employment History: Officer and shareholder 1986-present, Lommen, Nelson, Cole & Stageberg; Partner 1970-86 and Associate 1966-70, Mackall, Crounse & Moore.
Representative Clients: Northgate Computer Systems, Inc.; Astrocom Corp.; Dacomed Corp.; Connect Computer Corp.; Ross Resorts, Inc.; Micro Dynamics Corp.
Professional Associations: HCBA (past President, Treasurer, and Secretary; Securities Law Section (past Chair)); MSBA (President 1993-94, Board of Governors 1989-present; Business and Professional Corporations Committee (past Chair)).
Community Involvement: Minneapolis Legal Aid Society (Director 1970-present and past officer); Fund for the Legal Aid Society (Director 1980-present); MSBA Legal Assistance to the Disadvantaged Committee (1980-present); Colonial Church and Colonial Church Foundation (past officer and trustee); Minneapolis Foundation (past officer and trustee); Commander (retired), US Naval Reserve, JAG Corps.
Firm: Lommen, Nelson, Cole & Stageberg, a firm with 38 lawyers, is a general practice firm with a strong emphasis on business litigation, representing both plaintiffs and defendants, and the defense of medical and legal malpractice actions. The eight-lawyer corporate and business group is known for its representation of small and medium size businesses in connection with all of their business, corporate, securities, tax, and real estate needs. *See additional listings in Securities & Venture Finance Law and Publicly Held Corporations Law Chapters.*

•**JAMES H. STEWART** - Fryberger, Buchanan, Smith & Frederick, P.A. - 302 West Superior Street, Suite 700 - Duluth, MN 55802 - Phone: (218) 722-0861, Fax: (218) 722-9568 - *See complete biographical profile in Probate, Estate Planning & Trusts Law Chapter.*

JON E. STRINDEN

Gunhus, Grinnell, Klinger, Swenson & Guy, Ltd.
512 Center Avenue
P.O. Box 1077
Moorhead, MN 56561-1977

Phone: (218) 236-6462
Fax: (218) 236-9873

Admitted: 1983 Minnesota; 1982 North Dakota; 1983 US Dist. Ct. (ND); 1983 US Ct. App. (8th Cir.); US Tax Ct.
Birthdate: 02/02/57

•**JON E. STRINDEN:** Mr. Strinden practices business law with emphasis in tax and business planning, employee fringe benefits, employment law, IRS representation, and mergers and acquisitions. He is a frequent speaker at continuing legal education seminars on business and tax topics.
Education: JD 1982, University of North Dakota; BSBA 1979, University of North Dakota.
Employment History: 1989-present, Gunhus, Grinnell, Klinger, Swenson & Guy; Associate Attorney 1986-89, Zuger & Bucklin; Tax Supervisor 1982-86, Eide Helmeke & Co. CPA's.
Representative Clients: Gate City Federal Savings Bank; Heartland Medical Center; Nodak Mutual Insurance Company; Champion Health Care; Blue Cross Blue Shield of North Dakota; Medical Arts Clinic; Heartland Trust Company; Concordia College; First Trust Company of North Dakota.
Professional Associations: Clay County Bar Assn.; MSBA; Cass County Bar Assn.; State Bar Assn. of North Dakota; North Dakota Society of Certified Public Accountants (Chair, Legislative Committee); North Dakota Limited Liability Company Act (Drafting Committee); American Institute of Certified Public Accountants (Legislation Committee); ABA (Taxation Section).
Community Involvement: Fargo-Moorhead Chamber of Commerce (Public Affairs and International Trade Committees); Rotary; Olivet Lutheran Church (Board member).
Firm: Founded in 1914, Gunhus, Grinnell, Klinger, Swenson & Guy, Ltd., is a general practice law firm with offices in Moorhead, MN and Fargo, ND. The firm handles matters primarily in the western half of Minnesota and all of North Dakota, offering a wide range of litigation and commercial services. *See additional listings in Business Tax Law and Publicly Held Corporations Law Chapters.*

GERALD L. THOREEN - Hughes, Thoreen & Knapp, P.A. - 110 South Sixth Avenue - St. Cloud, MN 56302-1718 - Phone: (612) 251-6175, Fax: (612) 251-6857 - *See complete biographical profile in Probate, Estate Planning & Trusts Law Chapter.*

Closely Held Business Law Leading Attorneys

•**MICHAEL TRUCANO:** Mr. Trucano practices in the corporate, finance, and general business areas, with a focus on the legal representation of emerging, growth-oriented companies. He has significant experience in the representation of companies at all stages of their corporate and financial life cycles, from start-up to public ownership. Mr. Trucano also has over 15 years of experience in venture capital financing, both as legal counsel for venture capital investment funds and portfolio companies. With his background in tax and securities laws, Mr. Trucano has handled over 150 business acquisitions and divestitures during his career. He has also been involved in significant project financings (including the construction of the Miami Dolphins Stadium), private securities offerings, and the representation of agricultural cooperatives. Mr. Trucano is a principal of Dorsey's emerging companies group, is a partner in the Corporate Department, and was affiliated with the Tax Department from 1970-77. He has been a lecturer at William Mitchell and University of Minnesota law schools, Minnesota Continuing Legal Education and Bar Association seminars, and entrepreneur forums on a variety of topics, including business planning, tax issues, venture capital financing, acquisitions and divestitures, private financings, and agricultural cooperatives.
Education: JD 1970, New York University (Editor 1969-70, *Annual Survey of American Law*); BA 1967 cum laude, Carleton College.
Employment History: Partner 1976-present, Associate 1970-75, Dorsey & Whitney.
Representative Clients: National Computer Systems, Inc.; ANCOR COMMUNICATIONS, Inc.; Ringer Corp.; Cherry Tree Ventures; The Food Fund; Southern Minnesota Beet Sugar Cooperative; Twin Cities Stores, Inc.; Orphan Medical, Inc.; LEARN PC, Inc.
Professional Associations: MSBA; HCBA.
Firm: Dorsey & Whitney is the largest law firm in Minnesota and one of the largest firms in the United States with over 350 lawyers in 12 offices. The depth and breadth of the experience of its lawyers enables it to provide a broad range of services to meet the diverse legal needs of its client base, which includes Fortune 500 companies, public agencies, banks and other financial institutions, nonprofit organizations, individual investors, family owned businesses, and high-tech and low-tech, growth oriented companies. *See additional listings in Business Tax Law and Securities & Venture Finance Law Chapters.*

MICHAEL TRUCANO

Dorsey & Whitney
Pillsbury Center South
220 South Sixth Street
Minneapolis, MN 55402-1498

Phone: (612) 340-2673
Fax: (612) 340-8738

Admitted: 1970 Minnesota;
1974 US Dist. Ct. (MN);
1974 US Ct. App. (8th Cir.);
1971 US Tax Ct.
Birthdate: 05/28/45

KENNETH T. TYRA - Dorsey & Whitney - Pillsbury Center South, 220 South Sixth Street - Minneapolis, MN 55402-1498 - Phone: (612) 340-8869, Fax: (612) 340-7800 - *See complete biographical profile in Commercial Real Estate Law Chapter.*

NEIL A. WEIKART - Fredrikson & Byron, P.A. - 1100 International Centre, 900 Second Avenue South - Minneapolis, MN 55402 - Phone: (612) 347-7025, Fax: (612) 347-7077 - *See complete biographical profile in Publicly Held Corporations Law Chapter.*

•**CRAIG W. WENDLAND:** Mr. Wendland is experienced in all aspects of commercial law, including business formations, acquisitions, mergers, sales, and general corporate matters. In addition, he represents commercial lenders in loan documentation and in workouts and restructuring. Mr. Wendland also has extensive commercial and residential real estate experience in the areas of sales, purchases, leasing, and exchange. Mr. Wendland is an author and lecturer on contract law for Minnesota Continuing Legal Education seminars and a frequent lecturer before business and professional groups on legal issues related to business formation and relationships and estate planning techniques.
Education: JD 1976, UCLA; BA 1972, University of Minnesota (Phi Beta Kappa).
Employment History: Currently, Shareholder, Dingle & Wendland, Ltd.; Associate 1976-79, Price, Postel & Parma (Santa Barbara, CA).
Representative Clients: Norwest Bank Minnesota Southeast, N.A.; First Bank National Assn.; Southern Minnesota Broadcasting Co.; North Star Foods, Inc.; Palmer-Soderberg, Inc.; Ranfranz Funeral Home, Inc.; Vine Funeral Home, Inc.; S & S Moving & Storage, Inc.; Bouquet Builders, Inc.; Grande Construction, Inc.; Home Federal Savings & Loan; Norwest Mortgage Company; B & F Distributing, Inc.; Halcon, Inc.; Rochester Software Connection, Inc.; Whitings Flowers & Greenhouse, Inc.; NAPA Auto Parts, Inc.; Rochester Meats, Inc.
Professional Associations: Olmsted County Bar Assn.; MSBA; ABA; State Bar of California.
Community Involvement: YMCA Camp Olsen (Board member); Rochester Fund for Educational Excellence; Rochester Amateur Sports Commission; Rochester Youth Hockey and Soccer (Coach). Past Board member of: Olmsted County Legal Aid; Cronin Homes, Inc.; Rochester Community College Foundation; Early Risers Exchange Club; Rochester Area Builders, Inc.; Tax Roundtable; Rochester Estate Planning Council.
Firm: Founded in 1957 by Joseph H. Dingle and Harold G. Krieger, current Judge for Third Judicial District of MN, Dingle & Wendland, Ltd., continues a community based, sophisticated practice in the areas of business, real estate, commercial law, and civil litigation (including sophisticated commercial and personal injury matters). The firm emphasizes a team approach to facilitating resolution of legal problems and makes extensive use of paraprofessionals and computer equipment to provide efficient service. *See additional listings in Commercial Litigation and Commercial Real Estate Law Chapters.*

CRAIG W. WENDLAND

Dingle & Wendland, Ltd.
Suite 300, Norwest Center
P.O. Box 939
Rochester, MN 55903

Phone: (507) 288-5440
Fax: (507) 281-8288

Admitted: 1979 Minnesota;
1976 California;
1980 US Dist. Ct. (MN)
Birthdate: 02/16/50

Complete listing of all attorneys nominated in Closely Held Business Law

CHARLES BANS, Maun & Simon, Minneapolis; **TIMOTHY M. BARNETT,** Winthrop & Weinstine, P.A., Minneapolis; **DANIEL E. BERNDT,** Dunlap & Seeger, P.A., Rochester; **CHARLES C. BERQUIST,** Best & Flanagan, Minneapolis; **PAUL W. CHAMBERLAIN,** Chamberlain, Neaton, and Johnson, Wayzata; **J. MICHAEL DADY,** J. Michael Dady & Associates, P.A., Minneapolis; **WAYNE P. DORDELL,** Hansen, Dordell, Bradt, Odlaug & Bradt, St. Paul; **STANLEY EFRON,** Henson & Efron, P.A., Minneapolis; **ROLF ENGH,** Valspar Corporation Counsel, Minneapolis; **TODD I. FREEMAN,** Larkin, Hoffman, Daly & Lindgren, Ltd., Bloomington; **F. KELTON GAGE,** Blethen Gage & Krause, Mankato; **PHILIP S. GARON,** Faegre & Benson, Minneapolis; **THOMAS H. GARRETT III,** Lindquist & Vennum, Minneapolis; **AVRON L. GORDON,** Briggs and Morgan, P.A., Minneapolis; **WILLIAM L. GUY III,** Gunhus, Grinnell, Klinger, Swenson & Guy, Ltd., Moorhead; **LEE W. HANSON,** Hall, Byers, Hanson, Steil & Weinberger, P.A., St. Cloud; **JOEL D. JOHNSON,** Dosland, Nordhougen, Lillehaug & Johnson, P.A., Moorhead; **MICHAEL D. JOHNSON,** Frundt Johnson & Roverud, Blue Earth; **WILLIAM A. JONASON,** Dorsey & Whitney, Rochester; **SAMUEL L. KAPLAN,** Kaplan Strangis & Kaplan P.A., Minneapolis; **MICHAEL C. KARP,** Blethen Gage & Krause, Mankato; **JOHN J. KILLEN,** Johnson, Killen, Thibodeau & Seiler, P.A., Duluth; **GARY W. KOCH,** Gislason, Dosland, Hunter & Malecki, P.A., New Ulm; **WILLIAM S. LAPP,** Lapp, Laurie, Libra, Abramson & Thomson, Chartered, Minneapolis; **RICHARD G. LAREAU,** Oppenheimer, Wolff & Donnelly, Minneapolis; **G. THOMAS MACINTOSH II,** Mackall, Crounse & Moore, Minneapolis; **GERALD E. MAGNUSON,** Lindquist & Vennum, Minneapolis; **JOHN W. MOOTY,** Gray, Plant, Mooty, Mooty & Bennett, P.A., Minneapolis; **BRIAN J. MURPHY,** Quarnstrom Doering Pederson Leary & Murphy, P.A., Marshall; **JANICE M. NELSON,** Nelson Oyen Torvik, Montevideo; **CURTIS A. NORDHOUGEN,** Dosland, Nordhougen, Lillehaug & Johnson, P.A., Moorhead; **KENNETH J. NORMAN,** Miller Norman & Kenney, Ltd., Moorhead; **JAMES E. O'BRIEN,** Moss & Barnett, A Professional Association, Minneapolis; **DENNIS L. O'TOOLE,** Lano, Nelson, O'Toole & Bengtson, Ltd., Grand Rapids; **DAVID T. PETERSON,** Blethen Gage & Krause, Mankato; **JOHN E. REGAN,** Regan, Regan & Meyer, Mankato; **THOMAS E. ROHRICHT,** Doherty, Rumble & Butler Professional Association, St. Paul; **BARBARA J. RUNCHEY,** Runchey Louwagie & Wellman, Marshall; **LEHAN J. RYAN,** Oppenheimer, Wolff & Donnelly, St. Paul; **THOMAS P. SANDERS,** Leonard, Street and Deinard Professional Association, Minneapolis; **BRIAN B. SCHNELL,** Gray, Plant, Mooty, Mooty & Bennett, P.A., Minneapolis; **MORRIS M. SHERMAN,** Leonard, Street and Deinard Professional Association, Minneapolis; **PAUL O. SKATVOLD,** Gjevre McLarnan Hannaher Vaa Skatvold & McLarnan, Moorhead; **ROGER V. STAGEBERG,** Lommen, Nelson, Cole & Stageberg, P.A., Minneapolis; **JOHN K. STEFFEN,** Faegre & Benson, Minneapolis; **LEON I. STEINBERG,** Maslon, Edelman, Borman & Brand, Minneapolis; **JAMES H. STEWART,** Fryberger, Buchanan, Smith & Frederick, P.A., Duluth; **RALPH L. STRANGIS,** Kaplan Strangis & Kaplan, P.A., Minneapolis; **ROBERT F. STRAUSS,** Mackall, Crounse & Moore, Minneapolis; **JON E. STRINDEN,** Gunhus, Grinnell, Klinger, Swenson & Guy, Ltd., Moorhead; **RUSSELL J. SUDEITH JR.,** Felhaber, Larson, Fenlon & Vogt, P.A., St. Paul; **MICHAEL TRUCANO,** Dorsey & Whitney, Minneapolis; **STEVEN C. WELLMAN,** Runchey Louwagie & Wellman, Marshall; **CRAIG W. WENDLAND,** Dingle & Wendland, Ltd., Rochester; **C. THOMAS WILSON,** Gislason, Dosland, Hunter & Malecki, P.A., New Ulm; **SHERMAN WINTHROP,** Winthrop & Weinstine, P.A., St. Paul.

CHAPTER 12

COMMERCIAL LITIGATION

The phrase "commercial litigation" covers a broad spectrum of cases stemming from business conduct. The other chapters in this *Guidebook* that have nominated attorney listings focus on particular areas of substantive law. For instance, a business leader with a dispute involving securities laws might turn to the Securities & Venture Finance Law Chapter to better understand those laws, or a CEO whose company is being sued for products liability might read the Personal Injury Defense Law Chapter for a discussion of the basic principals of personal injury defense. This chapter is different because it focuses on a style of practice rather than a particular area of substantive law. This chapter covers issues common to many different kinds of commercial disputes and ways that businesses might use the adversarial system more effectively or avoid it altogether.

WHAT IS A COMMERCIAL LITIGATOR?

A majority of the attorneys listed in this *Guidebook* could be considered commercial litigators—at least part-time commercial litigators—because most of the nominated attorneys will litigate a commercial matter at least occasionally. But most of the attorneys nominated for this *Guidebook* do not bill themselves as commercial litigators either because they concentrate on transactional work more than litigated matters, or because they normally litigate only a limited range of issues. For example, a wills and trusts attorney may be able to litigate occasional disputes arising out of a will, or an attorney whose primary specialty is litigating disputes over commercial agricultural contracts may call his or her practice area "agricultural law" rather than "commercial litigation" especially if he or she also does a significant amount of transactional work. Most of these attorneys (for whom litigation makes up only a small part of their practice) were nominated in practice areas covered by other chapters of this *Guidebook*. For example, an attorney who handles commercial real estate disputes may be profiled in the Commercial Real Estate Law Chapter; an attorney who only litigates commercial employment disputes may be profiled in the Employment Law Chapter.

The attorneys nominated in Commercial Litigation differ from those in other chapters either because they handle a broad variety of commercial disputes (and thus do not wish to be described by a narrow practice group title) or because they focus on honing the craft of effective courtroom representation and are rarely involved in transactional work. This is not to say that commercial litigators spend the majority of their time in a courtroom. The idea that litigators spend most of their day arguing before a judge or making impassioned appeals to juries is a creation of Hollywood. Effective courtroom representation requires extensive behind-the-scenes preparation. Commercial litigators spend the majority of their time outside the courtroom reviewing documents, taking depositions, writing briefs, interviewing potential witnesses, visiting the sight of a dispute, and counseling clients.

QUALITIES OF A GOOD COMMERCIAL LITIGATOR

A good commercial litigator will be able to play two roles—advocate and advisor. Many businesspersons fail to see how important it is that the attorney they hire be able to play both of these roles. Some commercial litigators who are very good in the courtroom are poor advisors outside the courtroom and thus fail to suggest alternatives to costly court battles. Too often, especially if a businessperson feels offended by a lawsuit and sees an attorney while still feeling indignant, he or she will wind up hiring an attorney who feels as indignant over a case as the client. Too often that attorney is simply arguing the case to the client and telling the client everything he or she wants to hear. The problem with this is that what a client needs to hear is not always what he or she wants to hear.

Today many commercial disputes can be time-consuming and costly. No party should initiate one or continue to fight one solely because he or she is offended or indignant at the other party's actions. Often, there is too much money at stake to allow emotions to rule over rational judgment. It is the responsibility of a good commercial litigator to tell his or her clients the benefits and risks of taking a case to trial and to act as an advisor in the office. The advocacy role should be saved for trial or for settlement negotiations. This distinction between the two roles of a good commercial litigator may seem obvious, but many decisionmakers do not really understand it. An attorney who never sees any way out of a problem other than fighting in court is an attorney who learned the advocacy role but failed to learn the advisor role. If that attorney is going to represent a client it is important that the client also have other counsel who can recognize the risks and occasionally suggest alternate courses of action.

WHEN TO SUE

Eventually it may be necessary to sue another party. Litigation has become a routine cost of doing business for many companies in this country. Of course, litigation is not painless, even for a party that eventually wins a lawsuit. It is a skill to know when to turn to the courts to settle commercial disputes.

SEEK LEGAL ADVICE EARLY

As discussed below, the best way to use lawyers is to involve them in the early stages of a deal. Often, if legal advice is sought early enough in putting together a deal, it will be unnecessary later to ask lawyers to "fix" something that has gone wrong. If legal advice has not been sought early, or a deal looks like it will sour despite earlier legal advice, it is wise to seek legal counsel again. Most importantly, our legal system is full of statutes of limitation that require a plaintiff to bring a lawsuit within a set time or lose forever the right to do so. Different statutes of limitation have different time periods and different events can start the clock ticking. Even if a dispute is later settled peacefully to the satisfaction of all sides, it may be necessary to file a commercial lawsuit in order to preserve the right to go to court if other forms of dispute resolution are not effective.

WHAT TO DO WHEN SUED

At first glance it may seem that getting sued is a world away from suing someone else, thus it may come as a surprise that responding to a lawsuit is similar to initiating one.

SEEK LEGAL ADVICE EARLY

It is no coincidence that the first heading under this category is identical to the first heading under the category "When to Sue." Lawyers are essential to protecting business interests in litigation. The first chapter of this *Guidebook,* Selecting and Managing Counsel, describes an intelligent process for finding the right legal counsel for a business's needs. Individuals are always permitted to represent themselves in court, but representing oneself is only appropriate in cases where there is very little money involved or where the factual disputes are very plain. In all other disputes it is wise to hire counsel. In a number of situations, a corporation is required to hire an attorney to represent itself in court.

APPOINT SOMEONE TO BE IN CHARGE

For larger companies, this is rarely a problem. Most large companies have in-house legal counsel that handles routine legal matters. In-house attorneys are often able to handle litigated matters. If there is no in-house legal counsel, someone in the company should be delegated to work closely with outside lawyers in coordinating company strategy and responses.

If a business turns to independent counsel to handle a commercial dispute, the in-house legal department can often supervise the outside lawyers and be involved in preparation for the lawsuit. Not only can the in-house lawyers offer insight into the company and suggest the best sources of information about company policy, but they can handle some parts of the litigation in order to keep costs down. A good strategy when selecting counsel is to ask how outside lawyers will cooperate with a business's in-house attorney and/or staff to control costs and effectively represent the business.

THE BEST DEFENSE IS A GOOD OFFENSE

Many commercial disputes involve counterclaims, crossclaims, and joinder of third parties. "Counterclaims" are claims brought against the original plaintiff, "joinder" is a way to bring third parties into a dispute, and "crossclaims" are claims between an original defendant and third parties joined to the dispute. Good legal counsel may be able to suggest claims that a company may have against the party bringing a lawsuit or against third parties. Assuming a more offensive posture can help convince another side to settle a dispute or drop one altogether.

MOVE THE FIGHT TO YOUR BACKYARD AND PLAY BY YOUR RULES

One of the worst facts about commercial disputes is that a company can be forced to defend itself far from home in a court applying unfamiliar rules. If a business is sued in a faraway court, it may be possible to force the plaintiff to transfer its complaint to a court closer to the company's home base. The rules about when this is possible are complex, but attorneys experienced in handling commercial disputes will know these rules well. Forcing a plaintiff to travel to another jurisdiction to bring a claim is sometimes enough to convince him or her to drop the claim altogether. For this reason, many businesses include forum selection clauses in routine business contracts.

WAYS TO AVOID LITIGATION

It is the nature of most commercial disputes that attorneys are brought into a matter only after something has gone wrong. A deal has fallen through, an account is overdue, or a disgruntled customer has filed a lawsuit. While these are certainly appropriate times to call upon a lawyer, most commercial litigators could, if asked, offer plenty of advice on how to avoid these problems in the first place. One of the results of years of litigating commercial disputes in court is that commercial litigators become keenly aware of relatively simple steps that, if taken early, can prevent much larger headaches later. The trouble is that most businesses do not ask their lawyers the right questions in advance. The point of this section on avoiding litigation is not to help the reader avoid litigators, but instead is intended to help the reader use legal resources more efficiently and cost-effectively.

USE COMMON SENSE

Many businesses discover too late that they could have avoided the expense and trouble of commercial litigation had they exercised even a little common sense in the beginning of a business relationship. Wise businesses do credit checks on new customers unless payment is in full at the time of delivery or receipt of a service. Business partners can often be liable for each other's debts, so the prudent businessperson avoids partners about whom he or she knows very little. Businesses should learn about a potential business partner's litigation history before jumping into a joint venture. A company that has been quick to litigate in the past may be a company with which to avoid entanglements. At the very least, if a potential customer or business partner has a history of taking disputes to court, it may be wise to insist upon mandatory arbitration for any disputes that arise out of the relationship. The Alternative Dispute Resolution Chapter describes many forms of alternative dispute resolution available to business.

PROVE IT

It is amazing how many business leaders fail to understand how often a right or privilege can be lost for lack of a way to prove the contents of a business agreement. Many executives have learned the rule that most oral contracts are as enforceable as written contracts. What they have not learned is the corollary to this rule that, without a way to prove what was orally agreed upon, there is no mechanism for enforcing one's rights under the oral agreement. In the real world, it makes no difference at all what a vendor promised if there is no record of the promise and the vendor denies his or her earlier statements. In the American legal system facts that cannot be proven are not facts at all, they are mere allegations. In every business transaction, it is wise to spend some time imagining how one's actions might look in the future in a courtroom. Would there be evidence of an offer? of an agreement? of delivery? of acceptance? What about changes to an earlier written agreement? An agreement may have been in writing originally but the parties to it may make numerous oral modifications that substantially affect its terms. How much of the altered agreement could be proven in court?—probably very little if neither side makes an effort to record changes in writing.

USE LANGUAGE CLEARLY

It should be clear to most business managers that the law at times takes words very literally. A decisionmaker may feel awkward being blunt with clients, employees, or vendors but a little clear language at the start of a business relationship can prevent a lot of headaches down the road. Courts can sometimes interpret unclear language in a way the parties never intended. Is it necessary to fire an employee? If so, that employee should know that he or she is being terminated and should be told the legally permissible reason for doing so. An employee told he or she is being terminated because "things are not working out" is an employee who is being invited to infer a sinister reason for the termination. Is a vendor's offer unacceptable? The reply to the offer should be clear—"No, those terms are unacceptable to this company, what about the following terms…."

When people deal with each other in person, facial expressions and nuances of language communicate a significant portion of their intentions. In phone conversations or written documents, the literal words alone have to carry all the intent. Thus, it is important for business persons to develop habits of using language precisely.

Develop a Healthy Dose of Skepticism

Many commercial disputes can be avoided if business managers develop a more realistic sense of reading people and the promises they make. Just because a person learns to use precise language himself or herself does not mean that other parties will do the same. A salesperson eager to close a sale may promise "100% satisfaction" but is the salesperson actually giving a warranty that if any part of a deal is not perfect, the deal is off?—probably not. More than likely, the salesperson is just puffing. One way to tell the difference between a warranty and mere puffing is to ask if the person making the claim is willing to put it into writing. Often, being asked to commit to a promise in writing is enough to make the other side back away from its original rosy estimates. A vendor may make an unrealistic "guesstimate" of how soon he or she can deliver a product, but a little persistent probing may show that he or she is unlikely to be able to deliver on the promise. If someone cannot guarantee an estimate it may be best to do business with a vendor who makes a more realistic estimate and stands by it.

Be Careful about Making Promises

Think carefully about making promises that will be difficult to keep. The business world is full of uncertainties and no one can ever be perfectly positive that they can fulfill their end of a bargain. Key employees can leave, computer systems can go down, suppliers can be hit by labor strikes, weather can foul up the best laid plans. When the unexpected happens, and a company is unable to deliver what it promised, is there a way out?—not if the person making the promise gave an ironclad promise. The point of this discussion is to help businesspersons understand that the promises they give are like little insurance policies given to the other side in a deal. When a company promises to produce a product or provide a service by a given date and does not leave itself a way out, it is effectively assuming responsibility for any unanticipated occurrences that may intervene to prevent performance. It is a wise policy to have experienced counsel review agreements to determine whether a business is assuming more risk than it is aware of. After all, if a business is going to give out little insurance policies with every contract, then the price of the good or service ought to reflect the additional insurance.

Have an Attorney Draft Preventive Forms and Procedures

It is unreasonable to expect employees to know all the intricacies of the law and how they might apply to every business transaction, but litigators experienced in unraveling commercial disputes are often an excellent source of preventive advice for avoiding disputes in the first place. Often they can recommend simple language and phrases to add to routine forms used by a business. These simple additions can save countless headaches and costly litigation. In addition, many law firms are happy to help businesses conduct in-house training seminars for employees to help them understand the important role they play in enforcing company policies and properly documenting all transactions.

DO NOT LET EMOTIONS INTERFERE WITH SOUND BUSINESS JUDGMENT

Too many business managers feel uncomfortable when lawyers describe the preventive acts that can prevent legal trouble from developing. The attitude of many managers is that if they are too cautious they will lose sales or scare away suppliers. It would be wrong to say that emotions have no role to play in business. Good relations with a customer are important to create and preserve. A good attorney should be able to offer suggestions on how preventive legal practices can be implemented without offending customers, business partners, or suppliers. This advice goes hand in hand with the earlier discussion of how a good commercial litigator is both a good advocate and advisor. In his or her advisor role, he or she should be able to help a business see when emotions may interfere with sound business judgment.

RESPECT AND EDUCATE EMPLOYEES

It does a company little, if any, good to have a board of directors following every letter of the law if its employees do not know or care enough to do so. Employees are the front line dealing with customers and handling complaints. Satisfied employees who have an interest in their company's future work to keep customers happy and avoid disputes. On the other hand, disgruntled employees are an excellent source of liability for any company. A clientele that feels poorly treated by a business's employees is fertile ground for lawsuits. If employees are respected and educated about the business's legal concerns they are more likely to follow company policies and provide better customer service. Furthermore, employees who are educated about the reasons behind company policies will make better witnesses if called upon to testify in court about the company's operations.

RESOURCES

Liability: The Legal Revolution and its Consequences. Peter W. Huber, Basic Books, Inc., New York, NY, 1988.

What Every Executive Better Know about the Law. Michael G. Trachtman, Simon and Schuster, New York, NY, 1987.

The 96 Billion Dollar Game: You are Losing, How Personal Injury Litigation has Become a Costly Game to You. Philip J. Hermann, Legal Information Publications, Inc., Beachwood, OH, 1993. Although written from the perspective of a personal injury attorney, this book contains an insightful analysis and criticism of the American dispute resolution system applicable to all commercial litigation.

COMMERCIAL LITIGATION LEADING ATTORNEYS

The attorneys profiled in this section were nominated by their peers in a statewide survey conducted in 1993 in which several thousand Minnesota attorneys were asked to name the lawyer to whom they would send a friend or family member in need of legal assistance in the area of *Commercial Litigation*.

Because the survey resulted in a list of less than five percent of Minnesota's practicing attorneys, this should not be construed as a complete list. Nevertheless, it is an excellent source of highly qualified and reputable attorneys, who, if unable to assist can in most cases make quality referrals.

A list of all attorneys nominated in this category is found at the end of this section. For information on the survey methodology see page ix.

Please note that the shorter, two line attorney listings in this section are of attorneys who practice in this area but whose full biographical profile appears in another section of this book. A bullet "•" preceeding name indicates the attorney was nominated in this particular area of law. For information on the format of these profiles, consult the section "Using the *Business Guidebook*" found on page xiv. Note that the following abbreviations are used throughout these profiles:

Selected by Attorneys for
GUIDEBOOK
Law & Leading Attorneys
MINNESOTA

The attorneys profiled below were recommended by their peers in a statewide survey.

App.	- Appellate	ABA	- American Bar Association
Cir.	- Circuit	ATLA	- American Trial Lawyers Association
Ct.	- Court	HCBA	- Hennepin County Bar Association
Dist.	- District	MDLA	- Minnesota Defense Lawyers Association
Hon.	- Honorable	MSBA	- Minnesota State Bar Association
JD	- Law degree (Juris Doctor)	MTLA	- Minnesota Trial Lawyers Association
LLB	- Law degree	NBTA	- National Board of Trial Advocacy
LLM	- Master in Law degree	RCBA	- Ramsey County Bar Association
Sup.	- Supreme		

•**CARL BAER:** Mr. Baer is a civil litigation trial lawyer who also handles business litigation and construction mediation. He was the 1992 recipient of the Legal Services of Northwest Minnesota Advocacy Achievement Award.
Education: JD 1975, University of Minnesota; BA 1971, Bemidji State University.
Employment History: Partner 1979-present, Kief, Fuller, Baer, Wallner & Rodgers, Ltd.; 1975-78, Powell, Drahos, Baer & Anderson; Clerk 1975, Ninth Judicial District Court.
Representative Clients: Security Bank of Bemidji; Naylor Electric.
Professional Associations: Beltrami County Bar Assn. (past President); 15th District Bar Assn. (past President); MSBA; ABA; MTLA; ATLA; University of Minnesota School of Law (Board of Visitors); Minnesota State Board of Law Examiners; American Arbitration Assn. (Arbitrator).
Community Involvement: Bemidji State University Foundation (Board member).
Firm: Mr. Baer is a partner in the Kief, Fuller, Baer, Wallner & Rodgers, Ltd. seven attorney law firm which is presently the largest in north central Minnesota. The partners in the firm each emphasize specific areas of law. Paul Kief concentrates on criminal defense; Steve Fuller on plaintiffs personal injury and divorce litigation; Bob Wallner on plaintiffs personal injury work and criminal defense; Mark Rodgers on Workers' Compensation. Kief, Fuller, Baer, Wallner & Rodgers, Ltd. offers a full range of legal services through its partners, two associates, and four paralegals. *See additional listings in Banking Law and Personal Injury Defense Law Chapters.*

CARL BAER

Kief, Fuller, Baer, Wallner & Rodgers, Ltd.
P.O. Box 880
514 America Avenue
Bemidji, MN 56601

Phone: (218) 751-2221
Fax: (218) 751-2285
800 number: (800) 552-6881

Admitted: 1975 Minnesota; 1976 US Dist. Ct. (MN); 1981 US Sup. Ct.
Birthdate: 06/21/45

JAMES L. BAILLIE - Fredrikson & Byron, P.A. - 1100 International Centre, 900 Second Avenue South - Minneapolis, MN 55402 - Phone: (612) 347-7013, Fax: (612) 347-7077 - *See complete biographical profile in Bankruptcy & Workout Law Chapter.*

BRYAN BAUDLER - Baudler, Baudler, Maus & Blahnik - 110 North Main Street - Austin, MN 55912 - Phone: (507) 433-2393, Fax: (507) 433-9530 - *See complete biographical profile in Personal Injury Defense Law Chapter.*

Chapter 12: Commercial Litigation

BAILEY W. BLETHEN - Blethen Gage & Krause - 127 South Second Street, P.O. Box 3049 - Mankato, MN 56002-3049 - Phone: (507) 345-1166, Fax: (507) 345-8003 - *See complete biographical profile in Employment Law Chapter.*

•RICHARD A. BOWMAN - Bowman and Brooke - 150 South Fifth Street, Suite 2600 - Minneapolis, MN 55402 - Phone: (612) 339-8682, Fax: (612) 672-3200 - *See complete biographical profile in Personal Injury Defense Law Chapter.*

FREDERICK C. BROWN, JR. - Popham, Haik, Schnobrich & Kaufman, Ltd. - 222 South Ninth Street, Suite 3300 - Minneapolis, MN 55402 - Phone: (612) 333-4800, Fax: (612) 334-8888 - *See complete biographical profile in Personal Injury Defense Law Chapter.*

•RONALD J. BROWN - Dorsey & Whitney - Pillsbury Center South, 220 South Sixth Street - Minneapolis, MN 55402-1498 - Phone: (612) 340-2879, Fax: (612) 340-2868 - *See complete biographical profile in Intellectual Property Law Chapter.*

CRAIG R. CAMPBELL - Gunhus, Grinnell, Klinger, Swenson & Guy, Ltd. - 512 Center Avenue, P.O. Box 1077 - Moorhead, MN 56561-1077 - Phone: (218) 236-6462, Fax: (218) 236-9873 - *See complete biographical profile in Personal Injury Defense Law Chapter.*

•KEVIN S. CARPENTER - Quinlivan, Sherwood, Spellacy & Tarvestad, P.A. - P.O. Box 1008 - St. Cloud, MN 56302-1008 - Phone: (612) 251-1414, Fax: (612) 251-1415 - *See complete biographical profile in Personal Injury Defense Law Chapter.*

MICHAEL V. CIRESI

Robins, Kaplan, Miller & Ciresi
2800 LaSalle Plaza
800 LaSalle Avenue
Minneapolis, MN 55402

Phone: (612) 349-8500
Fax: (612) 339-4181
800 number: (800) 553-9910

Admitted: 1971 Minnesota;
1971 US Ct. App. (8th Cir.);
1974 US Dist. Ct. (MN);
1986 US Ct. App. (2nd Cir.);
1987 US Ct. App. (9th Cir.);
1981 US Sup. Ct.;
1990 US Ct. App. (10th Cir.)
Birthdate: 04/18/46

•MICHAEL V. CIRESI: Mr. Ciresi is a named partner and a member of the Executive Board of Robins, Kaplan, Miller & Ciresi. The firm, with its principal office in Minneapolis, is internationally recognized for its expertise in litigation. Mr. Ciresi's trial practice and consulting is focused in the areas of product liability, intellectual property, business, and commercial litigation. He has obtained a number of multimillion dollar verdicts and settlements in a variety of cases. His verdicts and settlements on behalf of his clients exceed one billion dollars. Some of his more visible cases include the Dalkon Shield litigation, *Honeywell v. Minolta,* Copper-7 litigation, and the *Government of India v. Union Carbide* in which Mr. Ciresi was chief counsel to the Government of India. During the course of his career he has taught and lectured nationally and internationally to various professional and business groups. Mr. Ciresi is one of the few lawyers who have been recognized on two occasions in the *National Law Journal*'s annual list of "Ten of the Nation's Top Trial Lawyers." He has also been listed in *The Best Lawyers in America* since 1989 and was honored by the Australian National Consumer Law Association as "Product Liability Lawyer of the Year" in 1989. He is also a member, among other professional organizations, of the Inner Circle of Advocates and the American Board of Trial Advocates.
Education: JD 1971, University of Minnesota; BA 1968, College of St. Thomas.
Employment History: 1971-present, Robins, Kaplan, Miller & Ciresi.
Representative Clients: Honeywell; Ecolab; Pitney Bowes; 3M.
Professional Associations: MSBA; ABA; HCBA; RCBA; ATLA; American Board of Trial Advocates; MTLA; Centre of Advanced Litigation at Nottingham Law School (Advisory Board).
Community Involvement: University of St. Thomas (Board of Trustees).
Firm: Robins, Kaplan, Miller & Ciresi is a national litigation and business practice firm with offices in eight major metropolitan areas throughout the country. The firm's lawyers provide a range of transactional and litigation services to a diverse group of clients including Fortune 500 companies, banks, and lending institutions; property insurers; Big Six accounting firms; and foreign, state, and municipal governments. *See additional listing in Intellectual Property Law Chapter.*

Commercial Litigation Leading Attorneys

•PHILLIP A. COLE: Mr. Cole's special emphasis is on professional liability issues and complex commercial disputes, although he also handles securities, antitrust, and complex insurance coverage issues. Mr. Cole is certified as a Trial Specialist by the National Board of Trial Advocacy and is certified by the American Board of Professional Liability Attorneys. He is listed in *Who's Who of American Lawyers* and in *The Best Lawyers in America*.
Education: JD 1964, Georgetown Law Center; BA 1961, University of Maryland.
Employment History: 1968-present at Lommen Nelson firm and its predecessors.
Representative Clients: St. Paul Fire & Marine Insurance Company; Alexander and Alexander; Fairview Hospitals; Minnesota Lawyers Mutual Insurance Company.
Professional Associations: ABA; International Assn. of Defense Counsel; MSBA; National Board of Trial Advocacy.
Community Involvement: Legal Advice Clinics (volunteer attorney).
Firm: Lommen, Nelson, Cole & Stageberg, P.A., a firm with 38 lawyers, is a general practice firm with a strong emphasis on business litigation, representing both plaintiffs and defendants, and the defense of medical malpractice and legal malpractice actions. The eight-lawyer corporate and business group is known for its representation of small and medium size businesses in connection with all of their business, corporate, securities, tax, and real estate needs. A large number of its clients are involved in the insurance, construction, electronics, computer, and medical products industries. Partner Thomas F. Dougherty has an LLM in taxation from New York University and advises businesses and individuals on tax matters of every nature. The firm has also represented businesses and individuals in numerous substantial real estate transactions, including tax increment financing, apartment projects, resort development, and general commercial real estate matters. *See additional listings in Personal Injury Defense Law and Professional Malpractice Defense Law Chapters.*

PHILLIP A. COLE

Lommen, Nelson, Cole & Stageberg, P.A.
1800 IDS Center
80 South Eighth Street
Minneapolis, MN 55402

Phone: (612) 339-8131
Fax: (612) 339-8064
800 number: (800) 752-4297

Admitted: 1964 Maryland;
1968 Minnesota;
1968 US Dist. Ct. (MN);
1968 US Ct. App. (8th Cir.)
Birthdate: 03/03/40

•J. MICHAEL DADY - J. Michael Dady & Associates, P.A. - 4000 IDS Center, 80 South Eighth Street - Minneapolis, MN 55402-2204 - Phone: (612) 359-9000, Fax: (612) 359-3507 - *See complete biographical profile in Franchise & Dealership Law Chapter.*

CHARLES K. DAYTON - Leonard, Street and Deinard Professional Association - 150 South Fifth Street, Suite 2300 - Minneapolis, MN 55402 - Phone: (612) 335-1500, Fax: (612) 335-1657 - *See complete biographical profile in Environmental Law Chapter.*

•JOHN M. DEGNAN: Mr. Degnan practices in the areas of professional liability defense, commercial litigation, and personal injury, as well as hospital law and professional disciplinary matters. Mr. Degnan is certified as a Civil Trial Specialist by the National Board of Trial Advocacy and the Minnesota State Bar Association Civil Litigation Section.
Education: JD 1976, William Mitchell; BA 1970, University of Minnesota.
Employment History: 1977-present, Bassford, Lockhart, Truesdell & Briggs; 1973-76, Marsh & McLennan; Lieutenant 1970-72, US Army (Republic of Vietnam 1971-72).
Representative Clients: The St. Paul Companies; Minnesota Lawyers Mutual Insurance Company; Midwest Medical Insurance Company; The Dentists' Insurance Company; Methodist Hospital; Riverside Medical Center; Park Nicollet Medical Center; Group Health, Inc.; Emergency Physicians, P.A.
Professional Associations: ABA; MSBA; HCBA; MDLA (President 1991-92); American Society of Law and Medicine; Defense Research Institute; Minnesota Society of Hospital Attorneys; International Assn. of Defense Counsel; Creative Dispute Resolution (CDR) (Board member); Mediation Center (past Board member).
Community Involvement: Hennepin County Public Libraries (past Board member); Richfield Jaycees (past President).
Firm: Founded in 1882, Bassford, Lockhart, Truesdell & Briggs and its predecessor firms have been serving clients in Minnesota for more than 110 years. Today, the Bassford firm's 27 trial lawyers provide a broad range of litigation services for clients around the country, handling all areas of civil and business litigation. *See additional listings in Professional Malpractice Defense Law and Personal Injury Defense Law Chapters.*

JOHN M. DEGNAN

Bassford, Lockhart, Truesdell & Briggs, P.A.
3550 Multifoods Tower
33 South Sixth Street
Minneapolis, MN 55402-3787

Phone: (612) 333-3000
Fax: (612) 333-8829

Admitted: 1976 Minnesota
Birthdate: 04/02/48

Chapter 12: Commercial Litigation

FREDERICK A. DUDDERAR - Hanft, Fride, O'Brien, Harries, Swelbar & Burns, P.A. - 1000 First Bank Place, 130 West Superior Street - Duluth, MN 55802 - Phone: (218) 722-4766, Fax: (218) 720-4920 - *See complete biographical profile in Bankruptcy & Workout Law Chapter.*

SHAWN M. DUNLEVY - Fryberger, Buchanan, Smith & Frederick, P.A. - 302 West Superior Street, Suite 700 - Duluth, MN 55802 - Phone: (218) 722-0861, Fax: (218) 722-9568 - *See complete biographical profile in Banking Law Chapter.*

•**JAMES F. DUNN** - Dunn & Elliott, P.A. - 1510 Minnesota World Trade Center, 30 East Seventh Street - St. Paul, MN 55101-4901 - Phone: (612) 221-9048, Fax: (612) 223-5797 - *See complete biographical profile in Personal Injury Defense Law Chapter.*

•**J. MARQUIS EASTWOOD** - Dorsey & Whitney - Pillsbury Center South, 220 South Sixth Street - Minneapolis, MN 55402-1498 - Phone: (612) 340-2856, Fax: (612) 340-8800 - *See complete biographical profile in Employment Law Chapter.*

DAVID R. FAIRBAIRN - Kinney & Lange, P.A. - 625 Fourth Avenue South, Suite 1500 - Minneapolis, MN 55415-1659 - Phone: (612) 339-1863, Fax: (612) 339-6580 - *See complete biographical profile in Intellectual Property Law Chapter.*

GEORGE W. FLYNN - Cosgrove, Flynn & Gaskins - 2900 Metropolitan Centre, 333 South Seventh Street - Minneapolis, MN 55402 - Phone: (612) 333-9500, Fax: (612) 333-9579 - *See complete biographical profile in Personal Injury Defense Law Chapter.*

•**MICHAEL J. FORD** - Quinlivan, Sherwood, Spellacy & Tarvestad, P.A. - P.O. Box 1008 - St. Cloud, MN 56302-1008 - Phone: (612) 251-1414, Fax: (612) 251-1415 - *See complete biographical profile in Employment Law Chapter.*

JOHN D. FRENCH

Faegre & Benson
2200 Norwest Center
90 South Seventh Street
Minneapolis, MN 55402

Phone: (612) 336-3000
Fax: (612) 336-3026
800 number: (800) 328-4393

Admitted: 1963 Minnesota; 1960 District of Columbia
Birthdate: 06/26/33

•**JOHN D. FRENCH:** Mr. French, a partner at Faegre & Benson, focuses his practice on antitrust and FTC counseling and litigation and other government regulation of business; legal malpractice; first amendment work; corporate takeover work; counseling and litigation with regard to advertising claims, employee and business covenants not to compete, trade associations, and professional and amateur sports teams and leagues; and representation before various administrative agencies. He has been lead counsel on many large antitrust cases representing clients including IBM, the National Football League, and the Pillsbury Company. His corporate takeover work includes involvement with several large cases, including *PJ Acquisition Corp. v. Minnesota Vikings*, Grand Metropolitan's takeover of The Pillsbury Company, and Horner Waldorf Corporation's successful resistance to a takeover attempt by dissident shareholders. Mr. French represents Cowles Media in connection with first amendment issues and has represented law firms and lawyers against multimillion dollar malpractice claims. He has handled a number of constitutional law cases, has undertaken internal legal audits for several clients, and has successfully engaged on several occasions in lobbying for and against proposed legislation at the State Capitol. He has been a member of Faegre & Benson's Management Committee since 1975 and has been the chair for over four years.
Education: JD 1960 magna cum laude, Harvard University (President 1959-60, *Harvard Law Review*); BA 1955 summa cum laude, University of Minnesota.
Employment History: Partner 1967-present, Associate 1963-67, Faegre & Benson; Associate 1962-63, Ropes & Gray (Boston); Legal Assistant 1961-62, Federal Trade Commissioner Philip Elman; Law Clerk 1960-61, Hon. Felix Frankfurter, Associate Justice, US Supreme Court.
Representative Clients: ADC Telecommunications, Inc.; Archer Daniels Midland; UPS; Brunswick Corp., The St. Paul Companies; Minnegasco; Norwest Bank; NW Bell.
Professional Associations: Lawyer's Committee for Civil Rights Under Law (Executive Committee member); Lawyers Alliance for World Security.
Community Involvement: University of Minnesota Alumni Assn. (past President); Twin Cities Public Television (former Trustee); Minnesota Business Partnership (Executive Committee member). *See additional listing in Publicly Held Corporations Law Chapter.*

F. KELTON GAGE - Blethen Gage & Krause - 127 South Second Street, P.O. Box 3049 - Mankato, MN 56002-3049 - Phone: (507) 345-1166, Fax: (507) 345-8003 - *See complete biographical profile in Closely Held Business Law Chapter.*

ROY A. GINSBURG - Dorsey & Whitney - Pillsbury Center South, 220 South Sixth Street - Minneapolis, MN 55402-1498 - Phone: (612) 340-8761, Fax: (612) 340-2868 - *See complete biographical profile in Employment Law Chapter.*

JOHN B. GORDON - Faegre & Benson - 2200 Norwest Center, 90 South Seventh Street - Minneapolis, MN 55402 - Phone: (612) 336-3000, Fax: (612) 336-3026 - *See complete biographical profile in Environmental Law Chapter.*

•**PAUL E. GRINNELL** - Gunhus, Grinnell, Klinger, Swenson & Guy, Ltd. - 512 Center Avenue, P.O. Box 1077 - Moorhead, MN 56561-1077 - Phone: (218) 236-6462, Fax: (218) 236-9873 - *See complete biographical profile in Personal Injury Defense Law Chapter.*

Commercial Litigation Leading Attorneys

•**GUNDER D. GUNHUS** - Gunhus, Grinnell, Klinger, Swenson & Guy, Ltd. - 512 Center Avenue, P.O. Box 1077 - Moorhead, MN 56561-1077 - Phone: (218) 236-6462, Fax: (218) 236-9873 - *See complete biographical profile in Personal Injury Defense Law Chapter.*

KAREN HANSEN - Popham, Haik, Schnobrich & Kaufman, Ltd. - 222 South Ninth Street, Suite 3300 - Minneapolis, MN 55402 - Phone: (612) 333-4800, Fax: (612) 334-8888 - *See complete biographical profile in Environmental Law Chapter.*

•**PETER S. HENDRIXSON:** Mr. Hendrixson practices in the areas of antitrust, securities, accountant malpractice, and other complex civil litigation. He has been with Dorsey & Whitney since 1973 and a partner in the firm since 1978. Representative litigation includes *National Association of Review Appraisers and Mortgage Underwriters v. The Appraisal Foundation*; *Marisch v. Dain Bosworth*; *Midwest Properties v. Minnesota Twins*; *Inter-Regional Financial Group v. Deloitte & Touche*; *In re Workers' Compensation Insurance Antitrust Litigation*; and *In re Hormel Trust Litigation*. Mr. Hendrixson is listed in *The Best Lawyers in America*, 1993-94. Mr. Hendrixson served as chair of the Trial Department for 1989-93 and is now group head of the Trial, Employment, Environmental, and Intellectual Property Departments. Mr. Hendrixson is a member of the firm's Management Committee.
Education: JD 1972 magna cum laude, Harvard University (Editor and Officer 1970-72, *Harvard Law Review*); BA 1969, Northwestern University (Phi Beta Kappa).
Employment History: Partner 1978-present, Associate 1973-77, Dorsey & Whitney; Law Clerk 1972-73, Hon. Bailey Aldrich, US Court of Appeals, First Circuit.
Professional Associations: MSBA (Section on Antitrust Law (past Chair)); ABA (Antitrust Section); Harvard Law School Assn. (past President).
Community Involvement: Children's Home Society (Board member 1990-present); La Creche Early Learning (Board member 1989-present); Children's Theatre of Minneapolis (Board member 1987-92).
Firm: Dorsey & Whitney is the largest law firm in Minnesota and one of the largest firms in the United States with over 350 lawyers in 12 offices. The depth and breadth of the experience of its lawyers enables it to provide a broad range of services to meet the diverse legal needs of its client base, which includes Fortune 500 companies, public agencies, banks and other financial institutions, nonprofit organizations, individual investors, family owned businesses, and high-tech and low-tech, growth oriented companies. *See additional listing in Securities & Venture Finance Law Chapter.*

PETER S. HENDRIXSON

Dorsey & Whitney
Pillsbury Center South
220 South Sixth Street
Minneapolis, MN 55402-1498

Phone: (612) 340-2917
Fax: (612) 340-8800

Admitted: 1973 Minnesota; 1973 US Dist. Ct. (MN); 1977 US Ct. App. (8th Cir.); 1978 US Sup. Ct.
Birthdate: 04/09/47

DANIEL J. HEUEL - Muir, Heuel, Carlson & Spelhaug, P.A. - 404 Marquette Bank Building, P.O. Box 1057 - Rochester, MN 55903 - Phone: (507) 288-4110, Fax: (507) 288-4122 - *See complete biographical profile in Personal Injury Defense Law Chapter.*

GARY W. HOCH - Meagher & Geer - 4200 Multifoods Tower, 33 South Sixth Street - Minneapolis, MN 55402 - Phone: (612) 338-0661, Fax: (612) 338-8384 - *See complete biographical profile in Personal Injury Defense Law Chapter.*

BARRY P. HOGAN - Jeffries, Olson, Flom, Oppegard & Hogan, P.A. - 1325 23rd Street South - Fargo, ND 58103 - Phone: (701) 280-2300, Fax: (701) 280-1880 - *See complete biographical profile in Personal Injury Defense Law Chapter.*

KEVIN J. HUGHES - Hughes, Mathews & Didier, P.A. - 110 Sixth Avenue South, Suite 200, P.O. Box 548 - St. Cloud, MN 56302-0548 - Phone: (612) 251-4399, Fax: (612) 251-5781 - *See complete biographical profile in Health Law Chapter.*

MICHAEL J. IANNACONE - Iannacone Law Office - 101 East Fifth Street, Suite 1614 - St. Paul, MN 55101 - Phone: (612) 224-3361, Fax: (612) 297-6187 - *See complete biographical profile in Bankruptcy & Workout Law Chapter.*

•**RICHARD N. JEFFRIES** - Jeffries, Olson, Flom, Oppegard & Hogan, P.A. - 403 Center Avenue, P.O. Box 9 - Moorhead, MN 56561-0009 - Phone: (218) 233-3222, Fax: (701) 280-1880 - *See complete biographical profile in Professional Malpractice Defense Law Chapter.*

Chapter 12: Commercial Litigation

ELLIOT S. KAPLAN

Robins, Kaplan, Miller & Ciresi
2800 LaSalle Plaza
800 LaSalle Avenue
Minneapolis, MN 55402

Phone: (612) 349-8500
Fax: (612) 339-4181
800 number: (800) 553-9910

Admitted: 1961 Minnesota;
1961 US Dist. Ct. (MN);
1961 US Ct. App. (8th Cir.);
1978 US Sup. Ct.
Birthdate: 11/28/36

•**ELLIOT S. KAPLAN:** Mr. Kaplan is a named partner and chair of the Executive Board of Robins, Kaplan, Miller & Ciresi. He has represented clients before numerous state and federal courts at the trial and appellate levels, the US Supreme Court, and various federal and state regulatory agencies. Mr. Kaplan, former chair of the firm's Business Litigation Department, oversees and handles a variety of business litigation matters. He also counsels clients on preventative measures, evaluating potential and actual litigation, and drafting numerous compliance programs. He has been responsible for several multidistrict complex class action litigations, including plumbing fixture antitrust litigation; price-fixing litigation concerning aluminum, chlorine, the alcoholic beverage industry, hearing aids, and real estate; and numerous securities and RICO class action litigations. Additionally, he has handled unfair trade practice cases, lender liability cases, employment cases, franchise litigation, trade secret cases, intellectual property litigation, and monopolization and unfair competition cases. Mr. Kaplan has also provided expert testimony to the US Senate Committee on Franchise Legislation. He has lectured on business litigation and antitrust matters and written articles on antitrust and employment issues.
Education: LLB 1961, University of Minnesota; BA 1957, University of Minnesota.
Employment History: 1959-present, Robins, Kaplan, Miller & Ciresi.
Representative Clients: E & J Gallo Winery; Kaiser Aluminum and Chemical Corp.; Honeywell; KPMG Peat Marwick; Polaris Industries; Hormel; Textron; Guardian Industries; The Scotts Company; Norwest Bank; Factory Mutual Research Corp.; Budget Rent-A-Car; Burlington Northern; Best Buy Company, Inc.
Professional Associations: University of Minnesota Law School Alumni Assn. (President 1991); Minnesota Business Partnership (1987); MSBA (Chair 1977-79, Antitrust Section); ABA (Antitrust Section); MN Institute of Legal Education (Board member); HCBA.
Community Involvement: Involved with various civic, cultural, and religious boards of directors; Cochair of the Anne Frank exhibit in St. Paul, MN.
Firm: Robins, Kaplan, Miller & Ciresi is a national litigation and business practice firm with offices in eight major metropolitan areas throughout the country. The firm's lawyers provide a range of transactional and litigation services to a diverse group of clients including Fortune 500 companies, banks, and lending institutions, property insurers, Big Six accounting firms, and foreign, state, and municipal governments. *See additional listings in Publicly Held Corporations Law and Franchise & Dealership Law Chapters.*

JOHN D. KELLY

Hanft, Fride, O'Brien, Harries, Swelbar & Burns, P.A.
1000 First Bank Place
130 West Superior Street
Duluth, MN 55802

Phone: (218) 722-4766
Fax: (218) 720-4920

Admitted: 1974 Minnesota;
1986 Wisconsin;
1975 US Dist. Ct. (MN);
1984 US Ct. App. (8th Cir.)
Birthdate: 11/14/46

•**JOHN D. KELLY:** Mr. Kelly practices civil trial law, representing insurance companies and corporate clients in tort actions and commercial disputes, including antitrust, professional liability, product liability, contract, employment, and personal injury matters. His most recent cases include: the defense of multiple personal injury claims arising out of pipeline spills (*Anderson v. Western Lake Superior Sanitary District*); the defense of an action challenging the operating practices of a medical center (*Vezina v. Miller Dwan Medical Center*); the representation of a school district in extended proceedings involving issues ranging from sexual harassment to suspension (*Silvestrini v. ISD 695 (Chisholm)*); the defense of a man camp management firm in action arising out of a labor riot in International Falls (*ATCO, Inc. v. Ogden-Burtco, Inc.*); and the defense of a logging equipment manufacturer in a product liability case involving failure of boom component (*Luecken v. Hood Equipment, Inc.*). Mr. Kelly is a frequent trial advocacy instructor.
Education: JD 1974 cum laude, University of Minnesota; BA 1968, Harvard University.
Employment History: 1975-present, Hanft, Fride, O'Brien, Harries, Swelbar & Burns, P.A.; Law Clerk 1974, Minnesota Attorney General's Office, Department of Natural Resources; 1972, Minnesota Department of Economic Development; Infantry Officer 1968-70, US Army.
Representative Clients: Eveleth Taconite Company; Miller Dwan Medical Center; Gateway Foods, Inc.; Minnesota Lawyers Mutual; Employers Mutual Casualty Company; Continental Insurance Company.
Professional Associations: ABA; MSBA; 11th District Bar Assn.; International Assn. of Defense Counsel.
Community Involvement: Minnesota Board of Law Examiners (President); Duluth United Way Campaign (Chair-Elect); Duluth YMCA (Board).
Firm: Founded in 1899, Hanft, Fride, O'Brien, Harries, Swelbar & Burns, P.A, is a full service law firm specializing in business and trial work. The firm's 17 attorneys serve clients throughout Minnesota, northern Wisconsin, and beyond. *See additional listings in Personal Injury Defense Law and Professional Malpractice Defense Law Chapters.*

•**CHARLES R. KENNEDY** - Kennedy & Nervig - 503 Jefferson Street South, P.O. Box 647 - Wadena, MN 56482 - Phone: (218) 631-2505, Fax: (218) 631-9078 - *See complete biographical profile in Personal Injury Defense Law Chapter.*

WILLIAM J. KEPPEL - Dorsey & Whitney - Pillsbury Center South, 220 South Sixth Street - Minneapolis, MN 55402-1498 - Phone: (612) 340-2745, Fax: (612) 340-2644 - *See complete biographical profile in Environmental Law Chapter.*

H. MORRISON KERSHNER - Pemberton, Sorlie, Sefkow, Rufer & Kershner - 110 North Mill Street, P.O. Box 866 - Fergus Falls, MN 56538-0866 - Phone: (218) 736-5493, Fax: (218) 736-3950 - *See complete biographical profile in Personal Injury Defense Law Chapter.*

•**JOHN J. KILLEN** - Johnson, Killen, Thibodeau & Seiler, P.A. - 811 Norwest Center, 230 West Superior Street - Duluth, MN 55802 - Phone: (218) 722-6331, Fax: (218) 722-3031 - *See complete biographical profile in Closely Held Business Law Chapter.*

FAYE KNOWLES - Fredrikson & Byron, P.A. - 1100 International Centre, 900 Second Avenue South - Minneapolis, MN 55402 - Phone: (612) 347-7054, Fax: (612) 347-7077 - *See complete biographical profile in Bankruptcy & Workout Law Chapter.*

TIMOTHY J. KUNTZ - LeVander, Gillen & Miller, P.A. - 633 South Concord Street, Suite 402 - South St. Paul, MN 55075 - Phone: (612) 451-1831, Fax: (612) 450-7384 - *See complete biographical profile in Federal, State & Local Government Law Chapter.*

GERALD T. LAURIE - Lapp, Laurie, Libra, Abramson & Thomson, Chartered - One Financial Plaza, Suite 1800, 120 South Sixth Street - Minneapolis, MN 55402 - Phone: (612) 338-5815, Fax: (612) 338-6651 - *See complete biographical profile in Employment Law Chapter.*

JOHN C. LERVICK - Swenson, Grover, Lervick, Syverson, Battey & Anderson, Ltd. - 710 Broadway, Box 787 - Alexandria, MN 56308 - Phone: (612) 763-3141, Fax: (612) 763-3657 - *See complete biographical profile in Personal Injury Defense Law Chapter.*

•**GREER E. LOCKHART** - Bassford, Lockhart, Truesdell & Briggs, P.A. - 3550 Multifoods Tower, 33 South Sixth Street - Minneapolis, MN 55402-3787 - Phone: (612) 333-3000, Fax: (612) 333-8829 - *See complete biographical profile in Professional Malpractice Defense Law Chapter.*

GARY D. MCDOWELL - Lindquist & Vennum - 4200 IDS Center, 80 South Eighth Street - Minneapolis, MN 55402 - Phone: (612) 371-3211, Fax: (612) 371-3207 - *See complete biographical profile in Probate, Estate Planning & Trusts Law Chapter.*

•**ROGER J. MAGNUSON:** Mr. Magnuson represents corporate clients in three principal areas of litigation: regulatory/white-collar crime, securities, and shareholder cases. He has tried a variety of other complex cases, including litigation related to business torts, antitrust, medical malpractice, copyright, RICO, ERISA, constitutional litigation (Section 1983), and inverse condemnation, as well as other substantive areas. Mr. Magnuson is a frequent speaker on securities litigation and class actions, white collar crime and compliance programs, litigation techniques, shareholder disputes, limited partnerships, the closing argument, RICO, the representation of financial institutions, punitive damages, and a variety of other subjects at national and international programs for lawyers and CEO's. Mr. Magnuson is also listed in *Who's Who in America* and *Who's Who in American Law.*
Education: JD 1971, Harvard University (Board of Editors 1970-71, *Harvard Law Review*; Officer of the Harvard Corporation); BCL 1972, Oxford University; BA 1967 with honors, Stanford University (Phi Beta Kappa).
Employment History: Partner 1978-present, Associate 1972-77, Dorsey & Whitney; Chief Public Defender 1973, Hennepin County Municipal Court.
Professional Associations: Supreme Court Commission on Attorneys' Registration Fees; Minnesota Chamber of Commerce and Industry (AIDS Steering Committee).
Firm: Dorsey & Whitney is the largest law firm in Minnesota and one of the largest firms in the United States with over 350 lawyers in 12 offices. The depth and breadth of the experience of its lawyers enables it to provide a broad range of services to meet the diverse legal needs of its client base, which includes Fortune 500 companies, public agencies, banks and other financial institutions, nonprofit organizations, individual investors, family owned businesses, and high-tech and low-tech growth oriented companies. *See additional listings in Criminal Law and Securities & Venture Finance Law Chapters.*

ROGER J. MAGNUSON

Dorsey & Whitney
Pillsbury Center South
220 South Sixth Street
Minneapolis, MN 55402-1498

Phone: (612) 340-2738
Fax: (612) 340-2868

Admitted: 1973 Minnesota

SEYMOUR J. MANSFIELD

Mansfield & Tanick, P.A.
1560 International Centre
900 Second Avenue South
Minneapolis, MN 55402-3383

Phone: (612) 339-4295
Fax: (612) 339-3161

Admitted: 1978 Minnesota;
1969 Illinois;
1978 US Dist. Ct. (MN);
1970 US Dist. Ct. (N. Dist. IL);
1971 US Ct. App. (7th Cir.);
1975 US Sup. Ct.;
1992 US Ct. App. (8th Cir.);
1994 US Ct. App. (3rd Cir.)
Birthdate: 03/30/45

•**SEYMOUR J. MANSFIELD:** Mr. Mansfield has extensive litigation and alternative dispute resolution (ADR) experience in commercial and business litigation, business fraud, breach of business contracts, shareholders' and partners' business disputes, employment law, securities, RICO, class action, and other complex litigation. He has extensive experience with structuring and negotiating complex deals and transactions. Mr. Mansfield frequently represents smaller companies in transactions or disputes with much larger corporations. He also frequently lectures and writes on business law related issues. He received the 1994 Pro Bono Publico Distinguished Service Award (Hennepin County Bar) and is listed in *Who's Who in American Law*.

Education: JD 1969 with honors, DePaul University (Editor-in-Chief 1969, *DePaul Law Review*); BA 1966, University of Illinois.

Employment History: Partner 1989-present, Mansfield & Tanick; Principal & Owner 1981-89, Seymour J. Mansfield & Associates; Executive Director & Chief Counsel 1978-81, Central MN Legal Services and Legal Aid Society of Mpls.; Supervising Attorney 1970-78, Legal Assistance Foundation of Chicago; Clinical Law Instructor 1969-70, Northwestern University Legal Assistance Clinic.

Representative Clients: American Harvest; American Wireless System of Mpls.; GME Consultants; Motel 6; Possis Medical; Reliable Automotive Corp.; Resource Bank & Trust Co.

Professional Associations: MSBA (Board of Governors 1988-present); HCBA (Board of Governors 1988-present); ABA (Editorial Advisory Board 1992-present, *Leadership and Management Directions*, Law Practice Management Section).

Community Involvement: Fund for the Legal Aid Society (Board member 1982-present); MN Fund for Bosnia (Steering Committee 1994); American Jewish Committee (Board member).

Firm: Mansfield & Tanick, P.A., provides a broad range of litigation and ADR services, as well as representing clients in deals and transactions, in Minnesota, the upper Midwest, and around the country, through its legal staff of 12 attorneys. All are licensed in Minnesota, and some attorneys are licensed in Illinois, Wisconsin, California, and the District of Columbia. Mansfield and Tanick is committed to finding legal solutions for their clients through superior competence, hard work, responsiveness, and dedicated advocacy. *See additional listings in Closely Held Business Law and Employment Law Chapters.*

•**KURT J. MARBEN** - Charlson, Marben & Jorgenson, P.A. - 119 West Second Street, P.O. Box 506 - Thief River Falls, MN 56701-0506 - Phone: (218) 681-4002, Fax: (218) 681-4004 - *See complete biographical profile in Personal Injury Defense Law Chapter.*

DAVID S. MARING

Maring Law Office, P.C.
1220 Main Avenue, Suite 105
P.O. Box 2103
Fargo, ND 58107

Phone: (701) 237-5297
Fax: (701) 235-2268

Admitted: 1975 Minnesota;
1974 North Dakota;
1975 US Dist. Ct. (MN);
1974 US Dist. Ct. (ND)
Birthdate: 06/13/49

•**DAVID S. MARING:** Mr. Maring's litigation experience spans 20 years, covering the areas of construction law, agricultural law, franchise law, shareholder and business disputes, professional liability, and personal injury. He is licensed in Minnesota and North Dakota and is admitted to practice in state and federal courts in both jurisdictions. His primary practice is in eastern North Dakota and northwestern Minnesota. Mr. Maring is certified as a Civil Trial Specialist by the National Board of Trial Advocacy and the Minnesota State Bar Association. He also lectures at seminars on litigation topics.

Education: JD 1974 with distinction, University of North Dakota (Note Editor, *North Dakota Law Review*); BS 1971, North Dakota State University.

Employment History: Private Practice 1976-present (Fargo, ND/Moorhead, MN area); Law Clerk 1975-76, Hon. Donald D. Alsop, Judge, US District Court. Mr. Maring was raised on a family farm and is involved in the management/ownership of the family farm.

Representative Clients: Bristol-Myers Squibb Company; Amoco Oil Company; Plaza Development Company; Minnesota Lawyers Mutual Insurance Company; National Chiropractic Insurance Company; Great American Insurance Company.

Professional Associations: MSBA (Ethics and Disciplinary Committee; past member, Board of Governors, Civil Litigation Section); State Bar Assn. of North Dakota; ATLA; North Dakota Trial Lawyers Assn.

Community Involvement: Youth soccer and basketball (Coach); North Dakota State University Alumni Assn. (Board member); North Dakota Citizens for Safety Belts (past Chair).

Firm: Maring Law Office, P.C., is a relatively new association of experienced litigators concentrating in the areas of professional liability, business and commercial, public interest, and personal injury law. The firm's attorneys are all licensed in Minnesota and North Dakota. The Maring firm is strongly committed to client satisfaction created by quality legal services and prompt, meaningful communications with clients. *See additional listing in Personal Injury Defense Law Chapter.*

•**JAMES T. MARTIN:** Mr. Martin has been practicing law since 1974 as a civil trial lawyer. His experience includes insurance defense matters in the automobile negligence, product liability, municipal defense, fire subrogation, and coverage areas. Mr. Martin also has considerable experience representing businesses in litigation involving employment and civil rights claims, minority shareholder suits, environmental issues, and breach of contract claims. He is certified as a Civil Trial Specialist by the National Board of Trial Advocacy (1984) and is a member of the American Board of Trial Advocates.
Education: JD 1974, William Mitchell; BA 1967, University of Minnesota.
Representative Clients: Western National Mutual Insurance Company; Commercial Union Insurance Companies; Transamerica Insurance Group; Hartford Insurance Company; Orion Group; Home Insurance Company; Nodak Mutual Insurance Company; Chrysler Corp.; The London Agency; Austin Mutual Insurance Company; Great American Insurance Company; Great Central Insurance Company; MSI Insurance Company; Crum & Forster Insurance Company; Integrity Mutual Insurance Company.
Professional Associations: MDLA; HCBA; MSBA.
Community Involvement: St. Steven's Homeless Shelter; Minneapolis Legal Aid Society; and a multitude of church activities.
Firm: Gislason, Martin & Varpness, P.A., is a civil litigation firm handling a wide range of cases. Its practice includes an insurance defense practice in automobile, product liability, construction, asbestos, and other environmental matters. It has substantial experience in defending potentially responsible parties and generator defendants in state and federal hazardous waste/landfill claims. It provides litigation services to businesses for their commercial claims in a wide range of matters including employment, civil rights, contract, environmental, and construction issues. The firm prides itself in its delivery of top flight legal services which are performed on the basis of what needs to be done to fully protect the client's interests compared to what will generate the largest fee. Upon request, client references will be furnished. *See additional listings in Professional Malpractice Defense Law and Personal Injury Defense Law Chapters.*

JAMES T. MARTIN

Gislason, Martin & Varpness, P.A.
7600 Parklawn Avenue South
Suite 444
Minneapolis, MN 55435

Phone: (612) 831-5793
Fax: (612) 831-7358

Admitted: 1974 Minnesota; 1974 US Dist. Ct. (MN); 1974 US Ct. App. (8th Cir.)
Birthdate: 11/23/45

•**GERALD L. MASCHKA** - Farrish, Johnson & Maschka - 201 North Broad Street, Suite 200, P.O. Box 550 - Mankato, MN 56002-0550 - Phone: (507) 387-3002, Fax: (507) 625-4002 - *See complete biographical profile in Personal Injury Defense Law Chapter.*

GORDON G. (JEFF) MOHR - Attorney at Law - 5001 West 80th Street, Suite 1020 - Bloomington, MN 55437 - Phone: (612) 831-0944, Fax: (612) 831-6625 - *See complete biographical profile in Criminal Law Chapter.*

THOMAS R. MUCK - Fredrikson & Byron, P.A. - 1100 International Centre, 900 Second Avenue South - Minneapolis, MN 55402 - Phone: (612) 347-7045, Fax: (612) 347-7077 - *See complete biographical profile in Business Tax Law Chapter.*

ROSS MUIR - Muir, Heuel, Carlson & Spelhaug, P.A. - 404 Marquette Bank Building, P.O. Box 1057 - Rochester, MN 55903 - Phone: (507) 288-4110, Fax: (507) 288-4122 - *See complete biographical profile in Personal Injury Defense Law Chapter.*

CHARLES N. NAUEN - Schatz Paquin Lockridge Grindal & Holstein - 2200 Washington Square, 100 Washington Avenue South - Minneapolis, MN 55401 - Phone: (612) 339-6900, Fax: (612) 339-0981 - *See complete biographical profile in Environmental Law Chapter.*

SUE ANN NELSON - Doherty, Rumble & Butler Professional Association - 3500 Fifth Street Towers, 150 South Fifth Street - Minneapolis, MN 55402 - Phone: (612) 340-5590, Fax: (612) 340-5584 - *See complete biographical profile in Business Tax Law Chapter.*

THOMAS F. NELSON

Popham, Haik, Schnobrich & Kaufman, Ltd.
222 South Ninth Street
Suite 3300
Minneapolis, MN 55402

Phone: (612) 333-4800
Fax: (612) 334-8888

Admitted: 1983 Minnesota; 1983 US Dist. Ct. (MN); 1983 US Ct. App. (8th Cir.)
Birthdate: 07/10/47

•**THOMAS F. NELSON:** Mr. Nelson is a commercial and corporate attorney and experienced trial lawyer. His practice focuses on commercial counseling, contract negotiations and disputes, and professional liability. Mr. Nelson is a shareholder in the Minneapolis office and is currently serving as chair of the firm's Design and Construction Practice Group. In addition, Mr. Nelson has chaired and lectured for several continuing education seminars, focusing on general commercial matters as well as design professional and construction project liability.
Education: JD 1977 with honors, University of Connecticut (Editor, *Connecticut Law Review*); MA 1971, Yale University; BA 1969, St. Olaf College (Phi Beta Kappa).
Employment History: 1983-present, Popham, Haik, Schnobrich & Kaufman, Ltd.; 1979-83, Tyler, Cooper, Grant, Bowerman & Keefe (New Haven, CT); Judicial Clerk 1977-79, Hon. Thomas J. Meskill, US Court of Appeals, Second Circuit (New York, NY); former teacher and administrator, New Haven, CT public schools.
Representative Clients: Corporations and commercial enterprises, including financial institutions, insurance brokerage and consulting companies; design professionals and construction industry participants; and public institutions.
Professional Associations: Federal Bar Assn. (Board member); MSBA (Construction Law Section Council).
Community Involvement: Playwright Center (Board member); Izaak Walton League (Board member); B.A.A. Baseball (coach).
Firm: Popham, Haik, Schnobrich & Kaufman, Ltd., is a firm of more than 230 attorneys with offices in Denver, Miami, Minneapolis, Washington, D.C., and international affiliations in Beijing, China and Leipzig and Stuttgart, Germany. The firm represents clients nationally and internationally on issues relating to corporate and business law, administrative law, and litigation. *See additional listings in Professional Malpractice Defense Law and Publicly Held Corporations Law Chapters.*

•**MICHAEL T. NILAN** - Popham, Haik, Schnobrich & Kaufman, Ltd. - 222 South Ninth Street, Suite 3300 - Minneapolis, MN 55402 - Phone: (612) 333-4800, Fax: (612) 334-8888 - *See complete biographical profile in Securities & Venture Finance Law Chapter.*

•**JOHN N. NYS** - Johnson, Killen, Thibodeau & Seiler, P.A. - 811 Norwest Center, 230 West Superior Street - Duluth, MN 55802 - Phone: (218) 722-6331, Fax: (218) 722-3031 - *See complete biographical profile in Publicly Held Corporations Law Chapter.*

•**BRIAN B. O'NEILL** - Faegre & Benson - 2200 Norwest Center, 90 South Seventh Street - Minneapolis, MN 55402 - Phone: (612) 336-3000, Fax: (612) 336-3026 - *See complete biographical profile in Environmental Law Chapter.*

DENNIS L. O'TOOLE - Lano, Nelson, O'Toole & Bengtson, Ltd. - 115 East Fifth Street, P.O. Box 20 - Grand Rapids, MN 55744 - Phone: (218) 326-9603, Fax: (218) 326-1565 - *See complete biographical profile in Personal Injury Defense Law Chapter.*

•**BRUCE A. PETERSON** - Popham, Haik, Schnobrich & Kaufman, Ltd. - 222 South Ninth Street, Suite 3300 - Minneapolis, MN 55402 - Phone: (612) 333-4800, Fax: (612) 334-8888 - *See complete biographical profile in Criminal Law Chapter.*

H. JEFFREY PETERSON - Cope & Peterson, P.A. - 415 South First Street, P.O. Box 947 - Virginia, MN 55792 - Phone: (218) 749-4470, Fax: (218) 749-4783 - *See complete biographical profile in Personal Injury Defense Law Chapter.*

•**JOHN D. QUINLIVAN** - Quinlivan, Sherwood, Spellacy & Tarvestad, P.A. - P.O. Box 1008 - St. Cloud, MN 56302-1008 - Phone: (612) 251-1414, Fax: (612) 251-1415 - *See complete biographical profile in Personal Injury Defense Law Chapter.*

•**THOMAS J. RADIO** - Popham, Haik, Schnobrich & Kaufman, Ltd. - 222 South Ninth Street, Suite 3300 - Minneapolis, MN 55402 - Phone: (612) 333-4800, Fax: (612) 334-8888 - *See complete biographical profile in Federal, State & Local Government Law Chapter.*

•**FRANK J. RAJKOWSKI** - Rajkowski Hansmeier, Ltd. - 11 Seventh Avenue North, P.O. Box 1433 - St. Cloud, MN 56302 - Phone: (612) 251-1055, Fax: (612) 251-5896 - *See complete biographical profile in Personal Injury Defense Law Chapter.*

•**LEWIS A. REMELE, JR.:** Mr. Remele practices civil trial law in both tort and commercial matters. He has substantial experience in shareholder disputes and closely held corporations, family businesses, and partnerships. He represents numerous entrepreneurs and small businesses as both plaintiffs and defendants in corporate disputes. Mr. Remele also successfully defends major financial institutions, their trustees and professional fiduciaries, and lawyers and law firms in professional liability and partnership disputes. In addition, he represents insurance companies in numerous personal injury and coverage cases and defends corporate clients in diverse commercial suits, including employment claims, contract claims, securities claims, professional and fiduciary claims, directors' and officers' liability, shareholder litigation, class action suits, and debtor/creditor litigation. Mr. Remele is listed in *The Best Lawyers in America,* 1991-94 editions.
Education: JD 1975 cum laude, Creighton University; BA 1970 magna cum laude, Harvard University.
Employment History: Associate/Partner 1975-88, Rider, Bennett, Egan & Arundel; Law Clerk 1975-77, Hon. Miles W. Lord, Judge, US District Court.
Representative Clients: United Healthcare Corp.; American National Can Corp.; Minnesota Lawyers Mutual; The St. Paul Companies.
Professional Associations: ABA; HCBA (President 1989-90); MSBA (President-elect 1994-95, Secretary 1992-93).
Community Involvement: Legal Advice Clinics (volunteer attorney and Board member); Hennepin County Bar Foundation (Board member); American Bar Foundation; Harvard/Radcliffe Club of MN (past President).
Firm: Founded in 1882, Bassford, Lockhart, Truesdell & Briggs and its predecessor firms have been serving clients in Minnesota for more than 110 years. Today, the Bassford firm's 27 trial lawyers provide a broad range of litigation services for clients around the country, handling all areas of civil and business litigation. *See additional listings in Professional Malpractice Defense Law and Personal Injury Defense Law Chapters.*

LEWIS A. REMELE, JR.

Bassford, Lockhart, Truesdell & Briggs, P.A.
3550 Multifoods Tower
33 South Sixth Street
Minneapolis, MN 55402-3787

Phone: (612) 333-3000
Fax: (612) 333-8829

Admitted: 1975 Minnesota
Birthdate: 11/25/48

•**CARVER RICHARDS** - Trenti Law Firm - P.O. Box 958 - Virginia, MN 55792 - Phone: (218) 749-1962, Fax: (218) 749-4308 - *See complete biographical profile in Personal Injury Defense Law Chapter.*

SCOTT E. RICHTER - Popham, Haik, Schnobrich & Kaufman, Ltd. - 222 South Ninth Street, Suite 3300 - Minneapolis, MN 55402 - Phone: (612) 333-4800, Fax: (612) 334-8888 - *See complete biographical profile in Securities & Venture Finance Law Chapter.*

JAMES M. RILEY - Meagher & Geer - 4200 Multifoods Tower, 33 South Sixth Street - Minneapolis, MN 55402 - Phone: (612) 338-0661, Fax: (612) 338-8384 - *See complete biographical profile in Personal Injury Defense Law Chapter.*

JOSEPH J. ROBY, JR. - Johnson, Killen, Thibodeau & Seiler, P.A. - 811 Norwest Center, 230 West Superior Street - Duluth, MN 55802 - Phone: (218) 722-6331, Fax: (218) 722-3031 - *See complete biographical profile in Labor Law Chapter.*

•**JAMES F. ROEGGE** - Meagher & Geer - 4200 Multifoods Tower, 33 South Sixth Street - Minneapolis, MN 55402 - Phone: (612) 338-0661, Fax: (612) 338-8384 - *See complete biographical profile in Professional Malpractice Defense Law Chapter.*

JAMES A. RUBENSTEIN - Moss & Barnett, A Professional Association - 4800 Norwest Center, 90 South Seventh Street - Minneapolis, MN 55402-4129 - Phone: (612) 347-0300, Fax: (612) 339-6686 - *See complete biographical profile in Bankruptcy & Workout Law Chapter.*

ALLEN I. SAEKS

Leonard, Street and Deinard
Professional Association
150 South Fifth Street
Suite 2300
Minneapolis, MN 55402

Phone: (612) 335-1548
Fax: (612) 335-1657

Admitted: 1956 Minnesota;
1956 US Dist. Ct. (MN);
1956 US Ct. App. (8th Cir.);
1958 US Sup. Ct.
Birthdate: 07/14/32

•**ALLEN I. SAEKS:** Mr. Saeks practices civil trial law, concentrating in commercial and business litigation, including bankruptcy, banking, legal malpractice defense, RICO, white collar crime, and public contracts litigation. His substantial experience in bankruptcy litigation arises out of his handling of various real estate developments. In addition to significant bank and securities litigation, he has handled shareholder disputes in closely held corporations and law firm break-ups. Mr. Saeks represents defendants in complicated hostile takeover litigation and has successfully defended major financial institutions and their officers and trustees. He is a member of the national SWAT (Settlement Workout Asset) Team for the Resolution Trust Corporation, handling complex real estate issues. Mr. Saeks received the Pro Bono Publico Attorney Award in 1985.

Education: JD 1956, University of Minnesota; BSL 1954, University of Minnesota.

Employment History: 1960-present, Leonard, Street and Deinard; 1957-60, Judge Advocate General Corps, US Army; Assistant US Attorney 1956-57, US District Court, District of Minnesota.

Representative Clients: National City Bank of Minneapolis; TCF Bank Minnesota; Ollig Utilities Company; Medical Evaluations, Inc.; Napco International, Inc.; Resolution Trust Corp.

Professional Associations: ABA (1990-93, Commission on Interest on Lawyers Trust Accounts); HCBA (President 1983-84); Lawyers Professional Responsibility Board (1970-75); MSBA; National Conference of Bar Presidents; American Bar Foundation; Minnesota Supreme Court Lawyer Trust Account Board (Chair, 1985-87).

Community Involvement: US Consumer Product Safety Commission Advisory Council (Chair 1976-78); Minnesota Public Interest Research Group (Cofounder); Jewish Community Relations Council (President); Fund for the Legal Aid Society (Executive Committee).

Firm: Leonard, Street and Deinard is a full service commercial law firm of approximately 125 attorneys. Approximately half of the firm's practice concerns commercial, securities, and other business oriented litigation. *See additional listings in Bankruptcy & Workout Law and Banking Law Chapters.*

JOHN R. SCHULZ - Collins, Buckley, Sauntry & Haugh - 332 Minnesota Street, Suite W1100 - St. Paul, MN 55101 - Phone: (612) 227-0611, Fax: (612) 227-0758 - *See complete biographical profile in Personal Injury Defense Law Chapter.*

•**ROBERT J. SEFKOW** - Pemberton, Sorlie, Sefkow, Rufer & Kershner - 110 North Mill Street, P.O. Box 866 - Fergus Falls, MN 56538-0866 - Phone: (218) 736-5493, Fax: (218) 736-3950 - *See complete biographical profile in Banking Law Chapter.*

ROBERT K. SEVERSON

Brink, Sobolik, Severson,
Vroom & Malm, P.A.
217 Birch Avenue South
P.O. Box 790
Hallock, MN 56728

Phone: (218) 843-3686
Fax: (218) 843-2724
800 number: (800) 962-6281

Admitted: 1959 Minnesota;
1981 North Dakota
Birthdate: 01/09/32

•**ROBERT K. SEVERSON:** Mr. Severson practices in the areas of Workers' Compensation law, personal injury law, civil litigation, insurance law, and banking law. He represents commercial and business clients and personal injury clients in all areas of tort and commercial disputes, including product liability, automobile accidents, contracts, and construction law. His commercial litigation cases cover areas such as defective concrete, building contracts, soil borings, and other aspects of defective construction. He has represented severely injured people: quadriplegics, paraplegics, the brain-injured, and amputees. Recent liability issues concern power take-off, tractor roll-over, motorcycle, and snowmobile accidents.

Education: JD 1959, University of North Dakota (Phi Alpha Delta); BA 1954, University of Minnesota.

Employment History: Attorney 1965-present, Brink, Sobolik, Severson, Vroom & Malm, P.A.; Assistant County Attorney 1967-90, Kittson County; Assistant County Attorney 1959-65, Beltrami County; Private practice 1959-65, Olson, Kief & Severson.

Representative Clients: Representative clients furnished upon request.

Professional Associations: Kittson County Bar Assn. (President 1975-76); 14th District Bar Assn.; MSBA; ABA; ATLA; MTLA; State Bar Assn. of North Dakota.

Community Involvement: Kittson County Salvation Army (Chair); Hallock Development Commission (Executive Secretary); Kittson County Republicans (past Chair); Seventh District Republican Party (past Secretary).

Firm: The lawyers of Brink, Sobolik, Severson, Vroom & Malm, P.A., are all licensed to practice in all courts of Minnesota and North Dakota. Members travel extensively in northern Minnesota and northeastern North Dakota. The firm also has an aircraft to provide service throughout Minnesota and North Dakota. Brink, Sobolik, Severson, Vroom & Malm maintains offices in Karlstad and Argyle, MN. Services include an exceptional in-house library and computerized research capabilities. Referrals from other attorneys represent a substantial part of the firm's present work load. *See additional listings in Banking Law and Personal Injury Defense Law Chapters.*

•**DAVID A. SHULMAN:** Mr. Shulman practices civil litigation and municipal law. He is certified as a Civil Trial Specialist by the National Board of Trial Advocacy and by the Minnesota State Bar Association and is an arbitrator with the American Arbitration Association. Mr. Shulman was appointed as City Justice of the Peace (Rochester), as Special County Court Judge (Olmsted County), and to the Supreme Court Advisory Committee on Rules of Evidence. In addition to his practice, Mr. Shulman hosts the "Legal Eagle" radio show on KWEB in Rochester and spoke at the 1994 Vail Law Education Institute-Divorce Law. He is also a past business law instructor for the Rochester Vocational School and continuing legal education seminars. Mr. Shulman is an airline-transport-rated pilot with type rating in the citation jet as well as a multi-engine flight instructor.
Education: JD 1968, University of Minnesota; BA & BS 1960, Michigan State University (East Lansing, MI).
Employment History: General partner, Gartner & Shulman, Ltd.; Continuing Legal Education Coordinator 1980-82, Hamline University School of Law; Instructor in Family Law 1979, University of Minnesota - General Extension Division.
Representative Clients: Peoples State Bank of Plainview; Plainview School Board; Lake City Federal Savings and Loan; Lake City School Board; Professional Skaters Guild of America; Cities of Lake City, Byron, Pine Island, and Elgin.
Professional Associations: ABA; MSBA (Mock Trial Program (Judge, 1992-94)); Olmsted County Bar Assn.; ATLA; MTLA; Colorado Criminal Trial Lawyers Assn.; State Bar of Wisconsin; Academy of Certified Trial Lawyers of Minnesota.
Community Involvement: Rochester Cablevision Committee. A former USFSA Figure Skating Gold Medalist (Pairs), Mr. Shulman has devoted his time as instructor, coach, judge, referee, rating examiner, and legal counsel for various figure skating organizations.
Firm: The office of Gartner & Shulman, Ltd., is unique in offering the combined expertise of municipal law and civil litigation. Strategically located in Rochester and Lake City, the firm offers a full range of litigation needs as well as advice on litigation avoidance. Representing business claimants, city government, and high profile product liability claims has been standard fare for the firm's attorneys. All litigation in the firm is handled by National Board of Trial Advocacy and Minnesota State Bar Association Board Certified Trial Specialists. In addition, the firm represents the interests of local banks and school boards.

DAVID A. SHULMAN

Gartner & Shulman, Ltd.
Ironwood Square, Suite 302
300 Third Avenue SE
Rochester, MN 55904

Phone: (507) 288-3078
Fax: (507) 288-9599
800 number: (800) 788-6439

Admitted: 1968 MN;
1986 CO; 1986 WI;
1971 US Dist. Ct. (MN);
1984 US Ct. App. (8th Cir.);
1969 US Tax Ct.;
1981 US Sup. Ct.;
1994 Arbitration Neutral
Roster-MN
Birthdate: 11/20/36

•**PETER W. SIPKINS:** Mr. Sipkins practices in the areas of product liability, construction and engineering litigation, environmental litigation, and other complex civil litigation. Cases he has tried include *Metcalf & Eddy v. Puerto Rico Aqueduct & Sewer Authority* (lead plaintiff's counsel on $55 million engineering/construction case); *Mergentime v. Hazen & Sawyer and Metcalf & Eddy* (lead defense counsel on $52 million engineering malpractice case pending in US District Court, Southern District of New York); Showa Denko L-tryptophan litigation (lead local counsel for defendant in 80+ product liability cases); *State of Minnesota v. Philip Morris, et al.* (tobacco industry litigation); *CPT Corp. v. Tandon*; *Marvin Windows v. Norton Co.*; *In re: New York & New Jersey Powerhouse Asbestos* cases (counsel for defendant in over 800 cases). Mr. Sipkins also represented Weyerhaeuser Company, from 1978-89, as national formaldehyde trial counsel. He coordinated 180+ cases and personally tried two cases to verdict. Mr. Sipkins has been a partner in the Litigation Department since 1984 and was a Practice Development partner from 1991 to 1992.
Education: JD 1969, University of Minnesota; BA 1966, University of Minnesota.
Employment History: Partner 1984-present, Dorsey & Whitney; Partner 1977-84, Briggs and Morgan; State of Minnesota Solicitor General 1973-76; Assistant Attorney General 1973; Special Assistant Attorney General 1971-73.
Professional Associations: MSBA (Litigation Section Governing Council (Chair 1991)).
Firm: Dorsey & Whitney is the largest law firm in Minnesota and one of the largest firms in the United States with over 350 lawyers in 12 offices. The depth and breadth of the experience of its lawyers enables it to provide a broad range of services to meet the diverse legal needs of its client base, which includes Fortune 500 companies, public agencies, banks and other financial institutions, nonprofit organizations, individual investors, family owned businesses, and high-tech and low-tech, growth oriented companies. *See additional listing in Personal Injury Defense Law Chapter.*

PETER W. SIPKINS

Dorsey & Whitney
Pillsbury Center South
220 South Sixth Street
Minneapolis, MN 55402-1498

Phone: (612) 343-7903
Fax: (612) 340-2807

Admitted: 1969 Minnesota;
1971 US Dist. Ct. (MN);
1970 US Ct. App. (8th Cir.);
1974 US Ct. App. (10th Cir.);
1978 US Ct. App. (5th Cir.);
1991 US Ct. App. (1st Cir.);
1972 US Sup. Ct.

•**STEPHEN J. SNYDER** - Winthrop & Weinstine, P.A. - 3200 Minnesota World Trade Center, 30 East Seventh Street - St. Paul, MN 55101 - Phone: (612) 290-8400, Fax: (612) 292-9347 - *See complete biographical profile in Employment Law Chapter.*

GEORGE W. SOULE - Bowman and Brooke - 150 South Fifth Street, Suite 2600 - Minneapolis, MN 55402 - Phone: (612) 339-8682, Fax: (612) 672-3200 - *See complete biographical profile in Personal Injury Defense Law Chapter.*

CHARLES E. SPEVACEK - Meagher & Geer - 4200 Multifoods Tower, 33 South Sixth Street - Minneapolis, MN 55402 - Phone: (612) 338-0661, Fax: (612) 338-8384 - *See complete biographical profile in Environmental Law Chapter.*

BYRON E. STARNS - Leonard, Street and Deinard Professional Association - 150 South Fifth Street, Suite 2300 - Minneapolis, MN 55402 - Phone: (612) 335-1516, Fax: (612) 335-1657 - *See complete biographical profile in Environmental Law Chapter.*

Chapter 12: Commercial Litigation

•GAYLORD W. SWELBAR - Hanft, Fride, O'Brien, Harries, Swelbar & Burns, P.A. - 1000 First Bank Place, 130 West Superior Street - Duluth, MN 55802 - Phone: (218) 722-4766, Fax: (218) 720-4920 - *See complete biographical profile in Personal Injury Defense Law Chapter.*

THOMAS R. THIBODEAU - Johnson, Killen, Thibodeau & Seiler, P.A. - 811 Norwest Center, 230 West Superior Street - Duluth, MN 55802 - Phone: (218) 722-6331, Fax: (218) 722-3031 - *See complete biographical profile in Personal Injury Defense Law Chapter.*

•JAMES J. THOMSON - Holmes & Graven, Chartered - 470 Pillsbury Center, 200 South Sixth Street - Minneapolis, MN 55402 - Phone: (612) 337-9300, Fax: (612) 337-9310 - *See complete biographical profile in Federal, State & Local Government Law Chapter.*

•MADGE S. THORSEN - Popham, Haik, Schnobrich & Kaufman, Ltd. - 222 South Ninth Street, Suite 3300 - Minneapolis, MN 55402 - Phone: (612) 333-4800, Fax: (612) 334-8888 - *See complete biographical profile in Personal Injury Defense Law Chapter.*

THOMAS W. TINKHAM

Dorsey & Whitney
Pillsbury Center South
220 South Sixth Street
Minneapolis, MN 55402-1498

Phone: (612) 340-2829
Fax: (612) 340-2807

Admitted: 1969 Minnesota; 1969 US Dist. Ct. (MN)
Birthdate: 06/29/44

•THOMAS W. TINKHAM: Mr. Tinkham has been a partner in the Litigation Department since 1975. He practices in the areas of contract, complex technology, and employment litigation. Cases Mr. Tinkham has tried include *University of Minnesota v. Medical, Inc.* (issues in this case involved the validity and infringement by a manufacturer of the Lillehei-Kaster Heart Valve; jury found the University's patents valid and infringed, upheld on appeal); *University of Minnesota v. Applied Innovations* (case concerning validity of the copyright to the Minnesota Multiphasic Personality Inventory; declaration of validity and judgment for the University of Minnesota, upheld by the Eighth Circuit Court of Appeals); *Northwest Airlines v. American Airlines* (issues concern alleged trade secrets of American Airlines in the pricing and yield management areas - case pending); *Sondel v. Northwest Airlines* (class action sex discrimination allegations by flight attendants); *Durell v. Mayo Clinic* (medical malpractice and related issues); *Datacard v. AMI* (issues involved environmental and bankruptcy law). Mr. Tinkham is also listed in the civil litigation section of the current edition of *The Best Lawyers in America*.
Education: JD 1969 cum laude, Harvard University; BS 1966 with honors, University of Wisconsin.
Employment History: Partner 1975-present, Associate 1969-74, Dorsey & Whitney.
Professional Associations: HCBA (President 1980-81); MSBA (President 1990-91); ABA; Legal Advice Clinics (Board member; past President); Minnesota Supreme Court Gender Bias Task Force (Committee Chair 1989, 1991).
Community Involvement: Minneapolis Athletic Club (Board member); Minnesota Mental Health Commitment Task Force.
Firm: Dorsey & Whitney is the largest law firm in Minnesota and one of the largest firms in the United States with over 350 lawyers in 12 offices. The depth and breadth of the experience of its lawyers enables it to provide a broad range of services to meet the diverse legal needs of its client base, which includes Fortune 500 companies, public agencies, banks and other financial institutions, nonprofit organizations, individual investors, family owned businesses, and high-tech and low-tech, growth oriented companies. *See additional listings in Employment Law and Intellectual Property Law Chapters.*

STEPHEN TORVIK - Nelson Oyen Torvik - 221 North First Street, P.O. Box 656 - Montevideo, MN 56265 - Phone: (612) 269-6461, Fax: (612) 269-8024 - *See complete biographical profile in Publicly Held Corporations Law Chapter.*

LYNN G. TRUESDELL

Bassford, Lockhart, Truesdell & Briggs, P.A.
3550 Multifoods Tower
33 South Sixth Street
Minneapolis, MN 55402

Phone: (612) 333-3000
Fax: (612) 333-8829

Admitted: 1961 Minnesota
Birthdate: 08/01/36

•LYNN G. TRUESDELL: Mr. Truesdell practices in the areas of professional liability defense, insurance law, commercial litigation, and personal injury. His litigation involvement has included shareholder and partner disputes, Uniform Commercial Code issues, securities law, professional negligence, contract disputes, insurance coverage, personal injury, and product liability. He has been a lecturer and participant in various litigation-related legal education programs. Mr. Truesdell is listed in *The Best Lawyers in America*, from the 1989 through the 1995-96 editions.
Education: LLB 1961, University of Minnesota (staff 1960-61, *Minnesota Law Review*); BA 1958 cum laude, Amherst College.
Employment History: 1961-present, Bassford, Lockhart, Truesdell & Briggs, P.A.
Representative Clients: The St. Paul Companies; Minnesota Lawyers Mutual; Midwest Medical Insurance Company; The Medical Protective Company; John Hancock Mutual Life Insurance Company; National Union Fire Insurance Company.
Professional Associations: American College of Trial Lawyers (State Committee); American Board of Trial Advocates; MDLA (past President; past Board member); Defense Research Institute; Minnesota Society of Hospital Attorneys; American Society of Law and Medicine; ABA; MSBA; HCBA.
Community Involvement: Plymouth Congregational Church (past Moderator; past Board member); United Theological Seminary (past Board member); Milkweed Editions, Inc. (Board member); Minikahda Club (Board of Governors).
Firm: Founded in 1882, Bassford, Lockhart, Truesdell & Briggs, P.A., and its predecessor firms have been serving clients in Minnesota for more than 110 years. Today, the Bassford firm's 27 trial lawyers provide a broad range of litigation services for clients around the country, handling all areas of civil and business litigation. *See additional listings in Professional Malpractice Defense Law and Personal Injury Defense Law Chapters.*

Commercial Litigation Leading Attorneys

CASS S. WEIL - Moss & Barnett, A Professional Association - 4800 Norwest Center, 90 South Seventh Street - Minneapolis, MN 55402 - Phone: (612) 347-0300, Fax: (612) 339-6686 - *See complete biographical profile in Bankruptcy & Workout Law Chapter.*

•ROBERT R. WEINSTINE: Mr. Weinstine specializes in commercial litigation including antitrust, securities, banking, professional liability, and product liability litigation. In addition, he lectures for the Practicing Law Institute and Minnesota Continuing Legal Education. Mr. Weinstine is named in *The Best Lawyers in America,* 1991-92 and 1993-94.

Education: JD 1969 cum laude, Order of the Coif, University of Minnesota (Phi Beta Kappa); BA 1966, University of Minnesota.

Employment History: Shareholder 1979-present, Winthrop & Weinstine, P.A.; Associate/Partner 1969-1979, Oppenheimer, Wolff & Donnelly.

Representative Clients: Golden Valley Microwave Foods, Inc.; Marvin Lumber and Cedar Co.; Wick Building Systems, Inc.; Fireman's Fund Insurance Companies; G.F.I. America; Coopers & Lybrand; American Coating Technology, Inc.; NJK Associates Corp.; Red Line HealthCare Corporation; Commercial Acceptance Insurance Company; M.G.I.C. Indemnity Corporation; BancInsure, Inc.; M.F. Bank & Company, Inc.

Professional Associations: RCBA; MSBA; ABA; State Bar of Wisconsin; ATLA; MTLA.

Community Involvement: University of Minnesota Law School (Board of Visitors; Alumni Board); United Jewish Fund and Council; Temple of Aaron Synagogue; Oak Ridge Country Club.

Firm: Winthrop and Weinstine has talented and experienced litigators who have participated in sophisticated and complex commercial litigation in Minnesota, as well as nationally and internationally. Over the years, the litigation group has specialized in several areas including general corporate, financial institution, antitrust trade regulation and unfair competition, securities, employment, environmental, insurance, and product liability. *See additional listings in Employment Law and Labor Law Chapters.*

ROBERT R. WEINSTINE

Winthrop & Weinstine, P.A.
3000 Dain Bosworth Plaza
60 South Sixth Street
Minneapolis, MN 55402

Phone: (612) 347-0700
Fax: (612) 347-0600

Admitted: 1969 Minnesota; 1982 Wisconsin
Birthdate: 04/21/44

CRAIG W. WENDLAND - Dingle & Wendland, Ltd. - Suite 300, Norwest Center, P.O. Box 939 - Rochester, MN 55903 - Phone: (507) 288-5440, Fax: (507) 281-8288 - *See complete biographical profile in Closely Held Business Law Chapter.*

•G. MARC WHITEHEAD - Popham, Haik, Schnobrich & Kaufman, Ltd. - 222 South Ninth Street, Suite 3300 - Minneapolis, MN 55402 - Phone: (612) 333-4800, Fax: (612) 334-8888 - *See complete biographical profile in Publicly Held Corporations Law Chapter.*

Complete listing of all attorneys nominated in Commercial Litigation

DOUGLAS P. ANDERSON, Rosenmeier, Anderson & Vogel, Little Falls; **JOSEPH W. ANTHONY,** Fruth & Anthony, Minneapolis; **WALTER BACHMAN,** Lindquist & Vennum, Minneapolis; **CARL BAER,** Kief, Fuller, Baer, Wallner & Rodgers, Ltd., Bemidji; **ALLEN D. BARNARD,** Best & Flanagan, Minneapolis; **ROBERT BENNETT,** Bennett, Ingvaldson & Coaty, P.A., Bloomington; **MICHAEL BERENS,** Kelly & Berens, P.A., Minneapolis; **CHARLES A. BIRD,** Bird & Jacobsen, Rochester; **RICHARD A. BOWMAN,** Bowman and Brooke, Minneapolis; **GENE P. BRADT,** Hansen, Dordell, Bradt, Odlaug & Bradt, St. Paul; **RICHARD H. BREEN,** Breen & Person, Ltd., Brainerd; **LAWRENCE C. BROWN,** Faegre & Benson, Minneapolis; **RONALD J. BROWN,** Dorsey & Whitney, Minneapolis; **TYRONE P. BUJOLD,** Robins, Kaplan, Miller & Ciresi, Minneapolis; **WILLIAM M. BURNS,** Hanft, Fride, O'Brien, Harries, Swelbar & Burns, P.A., Duluth; **JAMES D. CAHILL,** Cahill & Marquart, P.A., Moorhead; **KARL L. CAMBRONNE,** Chestnut & Brooks, P.A., Minneapolis; **ALAN G. CARLSON,** Merchant, Gould, Smith, Edell, Welter & Schmidt, P.A., Minneapolis; **KEVIN S. CARPENTER,** Quinlivan, Sherwood, Spellacy & Tarvestad, P.A., St. Cloud; **JOSEPH F. CHASE,** O'Brien, Ehrick, Wolf, Deaner & Maus, Rochester; **MICHAEL V. CIRESI,** Robins, Kaplan, Miller & Ciresi, Minneapolis; **PHILLIP A. COLE,** Lommen, Nelson, Cole & Stageberg, P.A., Minneapolis; **THEODORE J. COLLINS,** Collins, Buckley, Sauntry & Haugh, St. Paul; **LAWRENCE R. COMMERS,** Mackall, Crounse & Moore, Minneapolis; **JOHN F. COPE,** Cope & Peterson, P.A., Virginia; **G. ALAN CUNNINGHAM,** Faegre & Benson, Minneapolis; **J. MICHAEL DADY,** J. Michael Dady & Associates, P.A., Minneapolis; **R. SCOTT DAVIES,** Briggs and Morgan, P.A., Minneapolis; **JOHN M. DEGNAN,** Bassford, Lockhart, Truesdell & Briggs, P.A., Minneapolis; **JAMES F. DUNN,** Dunn & Elliott, P.A., St. Paul; **J. MARQUIS EASTWOOD,** Dorsey & Whitney, Minneapolis; **ROBERT T. EDELL,** Merchant, Gould, Smith, Edell, Welter & Schmidt, P.A., Minneapolis; **THOMAS L. FABEL,** Lindquist & Vennum, Minneapolis; **MARVIN T. FABYANSKE,** Fabyanske, Svoboda, Westra, Davis & Hart, Minneapolis; **HAROLD D. FIELD JR.,** Leonard, Street and Deinard Professional Association, Minneapolis; **DAVID F. FITZGERALD,** Rider, Bennett, Egan & Arundel, Minneapolis; **JAMES FITZMAURICE,** Faegre & Benson, Minneapolis; **TERRENCE J. FLEMING,** Lindquist & Vennum, Minneapolis; **MICHAEL J. FORD,** Quinlivan, Sherwood, Spellacy & Tarvestad, P.A., St. Cloud; **DAVID C. FORSBERG,** Briggs and Morgan, P.A., St. Paul; **JOHN D. FRENCH,** Faegre & Benson, Minneapolis; **TERENCE M. FRUTH,** Fruth & Anthony, Minneapolis; **STEVEN M. FULLER,** Kief Fuller Baer Wallner & Rodgers, Ltd., Bemidji; **CRAIG W. GAGNON,** Oppenheimer, Wolff & Donnelly, Minneapolis; **LUDWIG B. GARTNER JR.,** Gartner & Schupp P.A., Minneapolis; **EDWARD M. GLENNON,** Lindquist & Vennum, Minneapolis; **CLIFFORD M. GREENE,** Greene Espel, Minneapolis; **WILLIAM L. GREENE,** Leonard, Street and Deinard Professional Association, Minneapolis; **PAUL E. GRINNELL,** Gunhus, Grinnell, Klinger, Swenson & Guy, Ltd., Moorhead; **GUNDER D. GUNHUS,** Gunhus, Grinnell, Klinger, Swenson & Guy, Ltd., Moorhead; **RAYMOND A. HAIK,** Popham, Haik, Schnobrich & Kaufman, Ltd., Minneapolis; **SAMUEL L. HANSON,** Briggs and Morgan, P.A., Minneapolis; **PETER S. HENDRIXSON,** Dorsey & Whitney, Minneapolis; **LARRY R. HENNEMAN,** Rider, Bennett, Egan & Arundel, Minneapolis; **DAVID F. HERR,** Maslon, Edelman, Borman & Brand, Minneapolis; **ROBERT W. IRVINE,** Irvine Ramstad Briggs & Karkela P.A., Detroit Lakes; **JON K. IVERSON,** Erstad & Riemer P.A., Bloomington; **GEOFFREY P. JARPE,** Maun & Simon, St. Paul; **RICHARD N. JEFFRIES,** Jeffries, Olson, Flom, Oppegard & Hogan, P.A., Moorhead; **BRIAN N. JOHNSON,** Popham, Haik, Schnobrich & Kaufman, Ltd.,

Minneapolis; **THOMAS P. KANE,** Oppenheimer, Wolff & Donnelly, St. Paul; **ELLIOT S. KAPLAN,** Robins, Kaplan, Miller & Ciresi, Minneapolis; **JAMES H. KASTER,** Nichols Kaster & Anderson, Minneapolis; **DOUGLAS A. KELLEY,** Douglas A. Kelley, P.A., Minneapolis; **JOHN D. KELLY,** Hanft, Fride, O'Brien, Harries, Swelbar & Burns, P.A., Duluth; **TIMOTHY D. KELLY,** Kelly & Berens, P.A., Minneapolis; **CHARLES R. KENNEDY,** Kennedy & Nervig, Wadena; **JEFFREY J. KEYES,** Briggs and Morgan, P.A., Minneapolis; **JOHN J. KILLEN,** Johnson, Killen, Thibodeau & Seiler, P.A., Duluth; **D. RANDALL KING,** Merchant, Gould, Smith, Edell, Welter & Schmidt, P.A., Minneapolis; **JAMES R. KORMAN,** Attorney at Law, Faribault; **RAYMOND C. KRAUSE,** Blethen Gage & Krause, Mankato; **ELTON A. KUDERER,** Erickson Zierke Kuderer Madsen & Wollschlager, P.A., Fairmont; **EDWARD M. LAINE,** Oppenheimer, Wolff & Donnelly, St. Paul; **NEAL A. LANO,** Lano Nelson O'Toole & Bengtson Ltd., Grand Rapids; **JOHN D. LEVINE,** Of Counsel, Dorsey & Whitney, Minneapolis; **GREER E. LOCKHART,** Bassford, Lockhart, Truesdell & Briggs, P.A., Minneapolis; **ERIC J. MAGNUSON,** Rider, Bennett, Egan & Arundel, Minneapolis; **GERALD E. MAGNUSON,** Lindquist & Vennum, Minneapolis; **GEORGE F. MCGUNNIGLE JR.,** Leonard, Street and Deinard Professional Association, Minneapolis; **ROGER J. MAGNUSON,** Dorsey & Whitney, Minneapolis; **SEYMOUR J. MANSFIELD,** Mansfield & Tanick, P.A., Minneapolis; **KURT J. MARBEN,** Charlson, Marben & Jorgenson, P.A., Thief River Falls; **DAVID S. MARING,** Maring Law Office, Fargo, ND; **JAMES T. MARTIN,** Gislason, Martin & Varpness, P.A., Minneapolis; **GERALD L. MASCHKA,** Farrish, Johnson & Maschka, Mankato; **JOHN M. MASON,** United States Magistrate Judge (Retired, Dorsey & Whitney, Minneapolis); **TERENCE L. MAUS,** O'Brien, Ehrick, Wolf, Deaner & Maus, Rochester; **RONALD I. MESHBESHER,** Meshbesher & Spence, Ltd., Minneapolis; **MALCOLM L. MOORE,** Moore & Hansen, Minneapolis; **JOAN S. MORROW,** Joan S. Morrow, P.A., Minneapolis; **WILLIAM E. MULLIN,** Maslon, Edelman, Borman & Brand, Minneapolis; **THOMAS F. NELSON,** Popham, Haik, Schnobrich & Kaufman, Ltd., Minneapolis; **DONALD H. NICHOLS,** Nichols Kaster & Anderson, Minneapolis; **MICHAEL T. NILAN,** Popham, Haik, Schnobrich & Kaufman, Ltd., Minneapolis; **RICHARD J. NYGAARD,** Rider, Bennett, Egan & Arundel, Minneapolis; **JOHN N. NYS,** Johnson, Killen, Thibodeau & Seiler, P.A., Duluth; **TERENCE J. O'LOUGHLIN,** Geraghty O'Loughlin & Kenney P.A., St. Paul; **BRIAN B. O'NEILL,** Faegre & Benson, Minneapolis; **VANCE K. OPPERMAN,** West Publishing Corporation, Eagan; **REBECCA PALMER,** Maslon, Edelman, Borman & Brand, Minneapolis; **WILLIAM Z. PENTELOVITCH,** Maslon, Edelman, Borman & Brand, Minneapolis; **JUSTIN H. PERL,** Maslon, Edelman, Borman & Brand, Minneapolis; **BRUCE A. PETERSON,** Popham, Haik, Schnobrich & Kaufman, Ltd., Minneapolis; **HUGH V. PLUNKETT III,** Popham, Haik, Schnobrich & Kaufman, Ltd., Minneapolis; **WAYNE G. POPHAM,** Popham, Haik, Schnobrich & Kaufman, Ltd., Minneapolis; **ROMAINE R. POWELL,** Powell, Powell & Aamodt, Bemidji; **JOHN C. QUAM,** Thorwaldsen Quam Beeson Malmstrom & Sorum, Detroit Lakes; **JOHN D. QUINLIVAN,** Quinlivan, Sherwood, Spellacy & Tarvestad, P.A., St. Cloud; **THOMAS J. RADIO,** Popham, Haik, Schnobrich & Kaufman, Ltd., Minneapolis; **FRANK J. RAJKOWSKI,** Rajkowski Hansmeier, Ltd., St. Cloud; **CHARLES J. RAMSTAD,** Irvine Ramstad Briggs & Karkela P.A., Detroit Lakes; **THOMAS J. REIF,** Thornton Hegg Reif Johnston & Dolan, Alexandria; **LEWIS A. REMELE JR.,** Bassford, Lockhart, Truesdell & Briggs, P.A., Minneapolis; **CARVER RICHARDS,** Trenti Law Firm, Virginia; **JOHN M. RIEDY,** McLean Peterson Law Firm, Mankato; **JAMES F. ROEGGE,** Meagher & Geer, Minneapolis; **ALLEN I. SAEKS,** Leonard, Street and Deinard Professional Association, Minneapolis; **DAVID B. SAND,** Briggs and Morgan, P.A., Minneapolis; **PETER C. SANDBERG,** Dunlap & Seeger P.A., Rochester; **WILLIAM M. SCHADE,** Somsen Schade & Shaffer P.A., New Ulm; **ROBERT L. SCHNELL JR.,** Faegre & Benson, Minneapolis; **TIMOTHY R. SCHUPP,** Gartner & Schupp P.A., Minneapolis; **ROBERT J. SEFKOW,** Pemberton, Sorlie, Sefkow, Rufer & Kershner, Fergus Falls; **ROBERT K. SEVERSON,** Brink, Sobolik, Severson, Vroom & Malm, P.A., Hallock; **LEE E. SHEEHY,** Popham, Haik, Schnobrich & Kaufman, Ltd., Minneapolis; **JOHN M. SHERAN,** Leonard, Street and Deinard Professional Association, Minneapolis; **DANIEL R. SHULMAN,** Shulman, Gainsley & Walcott, Minneapolis; **DAVID A. SHULMAN,** Gartner & Shulman, Ltd., Rochester; **MARTHA M. SIMONETT,** Rider, Bennett, Egan & Arundel, Minneapolis; **JAMES S. SIMONSON,** Gray, Plant, Mooty, Mooty & Bennett, P.A., Minneapolis; **PETER W. SIPKINS,** Dorsey & Whitney, Minneapolis; **JERRY W. SNIDER,** Faegre & Benson, Minneapolis; **STEPHEN J. SNYDER,** Winthrop & Weinstine, P.A., St. Paul; **MARK N. STAGEBERG,** Attorney at Law, Shorewood; **ROGER V. STAGEBERG,** Lommen, Nelson, Cole & Stageberg, P.A., Minneapolis; **JAN STUURMANS,** Stuurmans & Karan, P.A., Minneapolis; **TIMOTHY A. SULLIVAN,** Best & Flanagan, Minneapolis; **GERALD L. SVOBODA,** Fabyanske, Svoboda, Westra, Davis & Hart, Minneapolis; **GAYLORD W. SWELBAR,** Hanft, Fride, O'Brien, Harries, Swelbar & Burns, P.A., Duluth; **FRANK A. TAYLOR,** Popham, Haik, Schnobrich & Kaufman, Ltd., Minneapolis; **THOMAS R. THIBODEAU,** Johnson, Killen, Thibodeau & Seiler, P.A., Duluth; **JOE E. THOMPSON,** Schmidt Thompson Johnson & Moody P.A., Willmar; **JAMES J. THOMSON JR.,** Holmes & Graven, Chartered, Minneapolis; **MADGE S. THORSEN,** Popham, Haik, Schnobrich & Kaufman, Ltd., Minneapolis; **THOMAS W. TINKHAM,** Dorsey & Whitney, Minneapolis; **TIMOTHY P. TOBIN,** Gislason, Dosland, Hunter & Malecki, P.A., Hopkins; **ELMER B. TROUSDALE,** Oppenheimer, Wolff & Donnelly, St. Paul; **LYNN G. TRUESDELL,** Bassford, Lockhart, Truesdell & Briggs, P.A., Minneapolis; **JAMES B. VESSEY,** Of Counsel, Dorsey & Whitney, Minneapolis; **ROBERT M. WALLNER,** Kief Fuller Baer Wallner & Rodgers, Ltd., Bemidji; **ROBERT R. WEINSTINE,** Winthrop & Weinstine, P.A., Minneapolis; **GREGORY M. WEYANDT,** Rider, Bennett, Egan & Arundel, Minneapolis; **G. MARC WHITEHEAD,** Popham, Haik, Schnobrich & Kaufman, Ltd., Minneapolis; **DOUGLAS J. WILLIAMS,** Merchant, Gould, Smith, Edell, Welter & Schmidt, P.A., Minneapolis; **GREGORY L. WILMES,** Briol and Wilmes, Minneapolis; **RICHARD G. WILSON,** Maslon, Edelman, Borman & Brand, Minneapolis; **STEPHEN R. YOUNG,** Drahos & Young, Bemidji; **ROBERT ZEGLOVITCH,** Leonard, Street and Deinard Professional Association, Minneapolis.

CHAPTER 13

COMMERCIAL REAL ESTATE LAW

Corporate real estate transactions invariably have far-reaching business and economic repercussions. This chapter explains frequently used real estate terminology and considers some of the issues common to commercial real estate transactions in Minnesota. Landlord liability for personal injuries occurring on business property is discussed in the Personal Injury Defense Law Chapter. The Real Estate Law Chapter of the *Consumer Guidebook to Law & Leading Attorneys* covers residential real estate, dealing with real estate agents, and landlord-tenant issues.

TERMINOLOGY

A stumbling block for many persons entering the real estate market is the unfamiliar terminology frequently used by real estate professionals. Real estate law uses many old terms and concepts because many real estate laws have ancient roots. However, many rights and responsibilities regarding real estate have evolved and been updated over time as societal and business needs have changed. The following are some of the most frequently encountered real estate terms:

ASSESSMENT

An assessment is a value placed on real property by a local taxing authority for purposes of levying taxes. Real estate taxes are calculated by multiplying the assessed value of a piece of property by the tax rate. Most properties are reassessed periodically, but a property's assessed value may not be the same as its actual market value.

CO-OWNERSHIP

Co-ownership is ownership of property by more than one person. The two common ways in which two or more parties can co-own a piece of property are joint tenancy and tenancy in common, both discussed below. Although there are advantages to co-owning property, there are drawbacks as well. If co-owners cannot agree on use, sale, or possession of a piece of property, they may have to go to court to resolve the matter in a partition action. In a partition action a joint tenant or tenant in common asks the court to split the property in a fair and just manner. Because real property may be difficult to divide and partial interests may be difficult to sell, a court will usually order that the property be sold and proceeds from the sale distributed to the co-owners in relation to their interests.

Deed

A deed is a written instrument that transfers the title of property from one person to another. The two most common types of deeds are general warranty deeds and quitclaim deeds.

Deed Restriction

Deed restrictions are usually imposed on a buyer of land when the property is sold and the restrictions are included in the seller's deed to the buyer. Restrictions are generally imposed by a property developer to maintain certain standards. Restrictions may include limits on the color an owner may paint a building, what trees one may plant, or the size of structures to be built on the property. Deed restrictions may also be known as covenants or conditions.

Easement

An easement is the right to use another person's land for a particular purpose. There are many forms of easements. Public utility companies frequently have utility easements that permit them to run gas, water, or electrical lines through particular property. The owner of property on a lake shore might sell to the owner of an adjacent lot without lake access an easement to cross over to the shore. A person who owns property that is landlocked may receive an easement from an adjacent land owner to have access in and out of the property. This kind of easement is also called a right of way.

Encumbrance

An encumbrance is an obligation attached to a piece of real property. It is a right or interest held by a party who is not the owner of the property. An encumbrance is not an ownership interest in real property, and the property may be bought and sold even though there are encumbrances attached to the property. Because encumbrances attach to property, not the property owners, a person who buys property with an encumbrance is bound by the encumbrance. Easements and deed restrictions are examples of encumbrances.

General Warranty Deed

Generally, in Minnesota, title is transferred by a general warranty deed. A general warranty deed provides the greatest protection to the purchaser because the seller pledges or warrants that he or she legally owns the property and that there are no outstanding liens, mortgages, or other encumbrances against it. A warranty deed is also a guaranty of title, which means that the seller may be held liable for damages if the buyer discovers that the title is defective. A warranty deed is no substitute for title insurance, however, as a warranty from a seller who later dies or goes bankrupt may have little, if any, value.

Joint Tenancy

Joint tenancy is a form of co-ownership. Although usually thought of as a way for a husband and wife to own property, there is no requirement that joint tenants be married to one another or that there be only two joint tenants. Each individual owner in joint tenancy has a right to sell, encumber, and possess the entire property. Regardless of the number of joint tenants, when one joint tenant dies, the remaining joint tenants automatically take the deceased joint tenant's share of the property by right of survivorship. In such cases, the surviving joint tenants are required to file a death certificate and an affidavit with the county recorder without having to pay transfer taxes. A principal advantage of joint tenancy is that it allows the surviving joint tenant to avoid probate and death taxes.

LIEN

A lien is a charge against property that provides security for a debt or obligation of the property owner. The lien holder does not own the property. The owner of property may voluntarily agree to a lien, perhaps by taking out a mortgage, or a lien can be imposed, perhaps for nonpayment of taxes. One of the most common liens is the mechanics lien. A mechanics lien arises when someone furnishes labor or materials to improve a piece of property. If the worker or supplier is not paid by the property owner, he or she can file a notice of lien with the county recorder and the property owner and collect the amount owed from a subsequent sale of the property. If a property owner has paid the general contractor in full but the general contractor has not paid the subcontractors, the owner will not have to pay for the services a second time.

QUITCLAIM DEED

A quitclaim deed is a deed that relinquishes to the buyer whatever interest, if any, the seller may have in the property. A quitclaim deed gives the buyer the least protection of any deed. If the seller is the sole owner of the property, the quitclaim deed is enough to transfer title, but the buyer takes a risk by accepting a quitclaim deed because it offers the buyer no guarantee that the title is valid. Quitclaim deeds are used frequently during the property settlement phase of a marriage dissolution.

RECORDING

In Minnesota, real estate records are kept in each county. Owners and parties with real estate interests are required to file, in the county, all documents affecting their interest in property in order to give public notice of the interest. Titles in Minnesota may be registered under the abstract system or the Torrens system. Abstract records go back hundreds of years and an abstract of title is a record of all the entries for that property. Torrens or registered property is much simpler, more modern, and more efficient. Instead of a thick abstract of title, Torrens property has a simple certificate of title.

SPECIAL ASSESSMENT

A special assessment is a tax levied on a piece of property to pay for improvements that benefit the particular property. These taxes are frequently used to pay for improvements such as streets, sidewalks, and street lighting. Special assessments are liens on the property until they are paid.

SUBLEASE

Subleasing is having someone else take over a tenant's rights and obligations under a lease before the original lease expires. The tenant has a right to sublet a unit if the lease does not prohibit doing so. If the new tenant does not pay rent, damages the unit, leaves before the lease expires, or breaches another condition of the lease, the landlord can hold the original tenant responsible. The original tenant can then sue the new tenant for those costs.

TENANCY IN COMMON

Tenancy in common is a form of co-ownership. Tenants in common, like joint tenants, share the right to possess, sell, and encumber the property. Unlike joint tenants, tenants in common do not have a right of survivorship. Upon the death of one tenant in common, his or her ownership interest passes to his or her heirs as part of the estate.

TITLE

Title to real estate is the right to, or ownership of, the property. Title may refer to the actual ownership or to the documentary evidence of that ownership. In order to sell a piece of property, all title matters must be cleared. Usually, this is accomplished through a title search, in which a diligent search is made of all records relating to the property to determine whether the owner can sell the property and whether there are any claims against it. If any defects in title are discovered during the title search, the seller is usually given time to cure the defect. Title insurance is often taken out to protect against any hidden defects in the title. There are two types of title insurance. One type protects the lender's interest in the property and the second protects the owner's interest.

PURCHASING REAL ESTATE

Most real estate purchases are fairly complex transactions. Because a purchaser may later be held liable for such things as environmental hazards and injuries caused due to the condition of the structure, it is imperative that a prospective buyer make a thorough investigation of the property before buying. A good purchase agreement should provide the buyer with ample opportunity to assess such risks and verify all terms of the lease. If the purchaser is acquiring rental property, it is his or her responsibility to verify the terms of the tenant leases and to explore any claims tenants may have against the seller, as these claims may later become the legal responsibility of the purchaser. Only an experienced real estate attorney can adequately advise on the many issues of concern to parties buying and selling real estate.

ENVIRONMENTAL LIABILITY

Of increasing concern to businesses are environmental hazards associated with acquiring real estate. Whether in the form of leaking underground oil storage tanks or hazardous emissions, such concerns may, under state and federal environmental laws, become the cleanup responsibility of a new owner, even a new owner who neither contributed to or knew of the contamination. The new owner may be required under Superfund and other laws to pay for the cost of cleanup of contamination that occurred even under a former owner.

LEASING REAL ESTATE

By Minnesota law, a rental agreement does not have to be in writing but it usually is in the form of a lease. If the lease is an agreement to rent the property for an unspecified length of time, it is considered a periodic tenancy, or month-to-month lease. Either the tenant or the landlord may end this type of lease with a one-month notice. A lease which specifically states the amount of time for which the lease is good is called a definite term lease. By law, if the duration of this type of lease is for more than a year, it must be in writing. Often, a tenant will be required to provide a written notice to end the tenancy.

Periodic versus Term Leases

There are two general types of leases—periodic leases and term leases. A periodic lease continues for a specific time period and is automatically renewed at the end of the period for an indefinite time without a specific end date. For example, parties may agree on a month-to-month lease without specifying how many months the renter will stay and the lease continues until one party terminates it. Most periodic leases will state the timing of notice and the form the notice must take. If the periodic lease does not specify when or how notice is to be given, state law requires that notice be given at least one full rental period plus one day before the lease ends.

A term lease is a rental agreement specifying a definite time period. For example, a lease for one year is a term lease. Term leases are almost always written. If they are for more than one year, the law requires that they be in writing. If the parties to the lease do not state when and what kind of notice is required, the lease automatically ends on the last day of the time period.

Negotiating a Lease

Some novices in real estate negotiations assume that the terms of a lease are non-negotiable. It is in a property owner's best interest to give potential renters printed forms presented in a "take it or leave it" manner. Contrary to the impression many rental property owners give tenants, most leases are negotiable, especially in today's overbuilt commercial real estate market. Many businesses will have specific needs that cannot be satisfied by a standardized lease agreement, so it is important that a prospective tenant identify its needs and negotiate a lease agreement that meets them. Of particular and increasing concern in commercial lease agreements is the operating expenses provisions of the lease. It is not unheard-of for a landlord to negotiate a lucrative cut in rent, only to compensate for the price break by loading costs onto operating expenses.

The following items should be addressed in negotiations:

- Amount of and conditions for recovering the security deposit

- Maintenance of fixtures, appliances, and common areas of the property; who is responsible for maintenance and what standards apply

- Renewal rights at the end of the lease

- Cancellation rights

- Circumstances under which the owner can enter leased premises; who has access to keys

- Which party is obligated to insure the property and which party is named beneficiary under the policies

- Subleasing rights or prohibitions

- Whether the landlord will agree not to rent adjacent space to competing businesses

It is wise to keep in mind that it is a rare business that will be able to negotiate a lease in which all of these items are decided in its favor, but the list can serve as a checklist for negotiations.

SECURITY DEPOSIT

Landlords have a right to insist that renters pay a security deposit before moving in. The security deposit is used to pay for any damage beyond ordinary wear and tear that the tenant might cause to the rental property, or to satisfy any debts between the tenant and landlord under an agreement or to cover any unpaid rent. There is no limit to how much the landlord can require for a security deposit. The landlord can increase the security deposit at any time during a periodic lease if the tenant is given proper notice—generally, one rental period plus one day. If the lease is a term lease, no changes can be made to the deposit until the lease comes up for renewal or the parties agree otherwise. At the end of the tenancy, the landlord must return the deposit to the renter with interest (4 percent non-compounded per year). The landlord is allowed to keep the amount of deposit necessary to repair damages, or to pay off debts owed to the landlord as part of the lease.

REAL ESTATE DEVELOPMENT

Until 1916, there were no controls over how a property owner could use his or her land. But as population grew and cities became more crowded, the number of controls on land use became more and more extensive. Today, almost every city and town has some type of land use plan. In Minnesota, regional commissions oversee development according to the plans drafted by their respective cities.

A property owner has many land ownership rights, but these rights are also restricted by controls from the local, state and federal government. It is important to understand exactly what regulations apply to certain properties and to the rights of the property owners. In any transaction, it is important for a developer to understand what government regulations are in force and how they affect the property.

CONSTRUCTION CONTRACTS

Construction contracts are a highly specialized subcategory of contract law. Most construction projects involve many parties, each with unique expectations, deadlines, and responsibilities. Architects, engineers, contractors, subcontractors, and lenders all have to understand their rights and responsibilities. Failure to have an experienced real estate attorney negotiate and draft documents can lead to numerous headaches and unplanned expenses. Good planning should include discussion of mechanics liens, provide for periodic inspections, provide for bonding, discussion of timetables and appropriate rewards or punishments for early or late completion.

MORTGAGE FINANCING

Many attorneys practicing real estate law spend a substantial portion of their practices negotiating mortgages secured by real property. These negotiations are often quite complex. Mortgage financing for new real estate can be as difficult to obtain for an established business as for one that is starting up. To help move the process along, a business often has to give up a degree of control over business decisions that affect the property. A lender may want to impose liabilities onto the borrower for the property, while at the same time retaining a say in how the property is managed.

It is important for a borrower to try and retain as much flexibility and control as is possible. For example, a borrower may want to retain control of insurance proceeds in the event of damage to the property so that the property can be restored, while a lender may want to require that such proceeds go toward debt owed.

Foreclosure

Foreclosure is a legal action in which property that has been used as security for a debt is sold in order to pay off that debt. It must be initiated by the grantor of the mortgage, must occur in the county in which the property is located, and must follow a default by the debtor on the terms of the mortgage. Mortgages provide for foreclosure in order to give lenders the right to recover the money they previously lent. In Minnesota, most mortgages include a power-of-sale clause which gives the lender authority to conduct the foreclosure without taking the matter to court. Although there are various forms of foreclosure available, the most common method in Minnesota is foreclosure by advertisement, in which a notice that the property is up for sale is posted in advance of the sale and the property owner is served a notice.

Zoning

Zoning regulations are a particular type of land use control. Their purpose is to control and regulate development and growth of a community in a way that is best for the general public. They attempt to accomplish this task by dividing a community into areas (zones) that can be used only for certain purposes.

Zoning laws are generally divided into four basic categories—residential, commercial, industrial, and agricultural. Most cities further divide property into much more intricate specifications, such as single-family houses within a residential area, or zones that allow for the building of condominiums or apartments. Furthermore, an industrial section of a city might be split between areas zoned for light-industrial and heavy-industrial operations.

It is important to find out exactly how a property is zoned, for this could have serious consequences on how the property can be used both at the present time and in the future. Zoning ordinances can be changed through amendments. Such changes can be sought by an individual property owner or by local governments. The changes must be determined to be in the best interest of the community, and the opinions of those persons affected must be sought through public hearings.

Another way to seek relief from zoning laws is through the form of a variance permit. Such permits make exceptions for uses of property that are not otherwise allowed under the zoning laws. Still, other ways around zoning laws include conditional use promises which allow special permission for an inconsistent use that benefits the community, and spot zoning which re-zones a small area or even one plot of land. Again, this is only allowed if it benefits the community.

Land Use Law

In addition to zoning laws, there are other laws that mandate how a building can be built, how big or small it can be, and where it may be placed on the property. These specifications may be laid out in local regulations or in building codes. Building codes are developed to protect public health and safety. To ensure compliance with building codes, many municipalities require that property owners get building permits before they begin any type of construction or development. Thus the city can ensure that the proposed building meets the applicable codes before construction begins. Another way communities enforce codes is by issuing a certificate of occupancy (without which a building cannot legally be occupied) to buildings that pass code requirements.

As stated before, communities often regulate the size and shape of buildings as well as their locations on lots. On shoreline areas, the state adds other rules to these local regulations. The additional regulations are intended to avoid adverse environmental consequences resulting from building construction.

Other kinds of land-use regulations serve to protect the environment. Any development that may have an effect on the environment must conform to local, state, and federal regulations. For example, the National Environmental Policy Act is a federal law that requires federal agencies to create environmental impact statements and secure approval before proceeding with projects that could adversely affect the environment. Such statements detail the effects of projects on areas such as air and water quality, safety, and wildlife. More information about these rules are provided in the Environmental Law Chapter.

WATER LAW

With the purchase or sale of real estate comes certain rights. These include air rights, mineral rights and water rights. In the land of 10,000 lakes, water issues are not as serious as in arid states. Nonetheless, there are some issues to be aware of. Water rights include the use of underground water as well as water that touches the owner's property. Landowners whose property touches flowing water are "riparian owners," which means they have the right to use the bordering water for reasonable and beneficial use. This use includes boating, swimming and other recreational purposes. Riparian owners may not, however, legally divert the water to land that does not adjoin the stream or lake. An owner may also not use the adjoining water in a way that affects the quality or availability of the water further upstream, downstream, or down the coast. Thus an owner cannot pollute the water or change its flow.

RESOURCES

Landlords and Tenants: Rights and Responsibilities. Minnesota Attorney General, Consumer Division, 1400 NCL Tower, 445 Minnesota Street, St. Paul, MN 55101.

Commercial Real Estate Transactions. Stuart M. Saft, Shepard's/McGraw Hill, Inc. Colorado Springs, CO, 1989.

Real Estate Financing in a Nutshell. Jon W. Bruce, West Publishing, St. Paul, MN, 1991.

Minnesota Real Estate. 2d Ed., Richard Larson, Bruce Harwood, Reston Publishing Co., Reston, VA, 1984.

COMMERCIAL REAL ESTATE LAW LEADING ATTORNEYS

The attorneys profiled in this section were nominated by their peers in a statewide survey conducted in 1993 in which several thousand Minnesota attorneys were asked to name the lawyer to whom they would send a friend or family member in need of legal assistance in the area of *Commercial Real Estate Law*.

Because the survey resulted in a list of less than five percent of Minnesota's practicing attorneys, this should not be construed as a complete list. Nevertheless, it is an excellent source of highly qualified and reputable attorneys, who, if unable to assist can in most cases make quality referrals.

A list of all attorneys nominated in this category is found at the end of this section. For information on the survey methodology see page ix.

Please note that the shorter, two line attorney listings in this section are of attorneys who practice in this area but whose full biographical profile appears in another section of this book. A bullet "•" preceeding name indicates the attorney was nominated in this particular area of law. For information on the format of these profiles, consult the section "Using the *Business Guidebook*" found on page xiv. Note that the following abbreviations are used throughout these profiles:

Selected by Attorneys for
GUIDEBOOK
Law & Leading Attorneys
MINNESOTA

The attorneys profiled below were recommended by their peers in a statewide survey.

App.	- Appellate	ABA	- American Bar Association
Cir.	- Circuit	ATLA	- American Trial Lawyers Association
Ct.	- Court	HCBA	- Hennepin County Bar Association
Dist.	- District	MDLA	- Minnesota Defense Lawyers Association
Hon.	- Honorable	MSBA	- Minnesota State Bar Association
JD	- Law degree (Juris Doctor)	MTLA	- Minnesota Trial Lawyers Association
LLB	- Law degree	NBTA	- National Board of Trial Advocacy
LLM	- Master in Law degree	RCBA	- Ramsey County Bar Association
Sup.	- Supreme		

•**CHARLES H. (HUCK) ANDRESEN:** Mr. Andresen is certified as a Real Property Law Specialist by the Minnesota State Bar Association. His real estate practice includes residential, commercial, mining, and mineral law; boundary and title correction matters; condominiums; and housing and development law. Mr. Andresen also practices in corporate and business law. Mr. Andresen has spoken frequently at legal seminars on real estate and mining matters.
Education: JD 1966, University of Minnesota; BA 1963 magna cum laude, University of Minnesota (Delta Theta Phi).
Employment History: 1989-present, Crassweller, Magie, Andresen, Haag & Paciotti, P.A.; 1966-89, Bye, Boyd & Andresen.
Representative Clients: Cleveland Cliffs, Inc.; Great Lakes Gas Transmission Company; Inland Steel Company; National Steel Corp.; Lakehead Pipe Line Company; London Development Corp.; Northern Land Company; The Nature Conservancy; Trust for Public Land; US Forest Service.
Professional Associations: Real Property Council (Chair 1973-76); Annual Real Estate Institute; Real Property Certification Council (Chair 1991-94); 11th District Bar Assn.; MSBA (Real Property Section, Council member, Secretary, Vice Chair, and Chair); ABA.
Community Involvement: Duluth Area Chamber of Commerce (Chair 1993-94, Board of Directors); Duluth Entertainment Convention Center (Chair 1992-94, Board of Directors); Alworth Memorial Fund (Secretary & Counsel); National Ski Patrol (Regional counsel); Chromaline Corp. (Board member).
Firm: Crassweller, Magie, Andresen, Haag & Paciotti, P.A., was formed in 1891. Approximately half of the firm's practice relates to nonlitigation business, mining, pipeline, real estate, corporate, and estate planning and trust matters. The other half of the firm concentrates on litigation, including insurance defense, Workers' Compensation, and real estate litigation. The real estate group practices in all areas of real estate law and has extensive experience in mining and mineral matters and oil and gas pipeline law.

CHARLES H. (HUCK) ANDRESEN

Crassweller, Magie, Andresen, Haag & Paciotti, P.A.
1000 Alworth Building
306 West Superior Street
Duluth, MN 55801

Phone: (218) 722-1411
Fax: (218) 720-6817

Admitted: 1966 Minnesota
Birthdate: 01/25/41

Chapter 13: Commercial Real Estate Law

JOHN F. BANNIGAN, JR.

Bannigan & Kelly, P.A.
1750 North Central Life Tower
445 Minnesota Street
St. Paul, MN 55101

Phone: (612) 224-3781
Fax: (612) 223-8019

Admitted: 1961 Minnesota
Birthdate: 10/26/36

•**JOHN F. BANNIGAN, JR.:** Mr. Bannigan practices civil trial law concentrating in real estate litigation, with expertise in eminent domain, zoning, land use litigation, and property tax appeal. His experience in the field of municipal law includes both private and public sector clientele. He has over 25 reported appellate decisions in the above areas including *Parranto Bros., Inc. v. City of New Brighton*; *BBY Investors v. City of Maplewood*; and *County of Anoka v. Esmaihzadeh*. He frequently serves as consultant to other attorneys in these areas.
Education: LLB 1961, University of Minnesota (Gamma Eta Gamma); BA 1958 cum laude, University of St. Thomas.
Employment History: 1970-present, Bannigan & Kelly, P.A.; Staff Counsel 1963-70, Housing & Redevelopment Authority of the City of St. Paul; Adjunct Professor 1962-63, University of St. Thomas (contracts, agency, negotiable instruments).
Representative Clients: Cities of Maplewood, New Brighton, and Taylors Falls; towns of Grey Cloud Island and White Bear; Port Authority of the City of St. Paul; Drovers First American Bank; Fina Oil & Chemical Co.; Centex Real Estate Corporation; Rottlund Homes, Inc.; Tilsen Homes, Inc.
Professional Associations: RCBA; MSBA (Local Law Section); ABA (Urban, State and Local Government Law Section); HCBA (Eminent Domain Section); MTLA.
Community Involvement: Cretin-Derham Hall High School (past Board member) and St. Mark's Parochial School (past Board member).
Firm: Founded in April 1970 as Lais & Bannigan, the firm of Bannigan & Kelly, P.A. has four shareholders: John F. Bannigan, Jr., Patrick J. Kelly, James J. Hanton, and Janet M. Wilebski. The firm's general practice includes state and federal courts; municipal law; zoning, planning, and eminent domain law; land use litigation; real estate law; estate planning and administration; personal injury law; employment law; and administrative hearings. *See additional listing in Federal, State & Local Government Law Chapter.*

PETER K. BECK - Larkin, Hoffman, Daly & Lindgren, Ltd. - 1500 Norwest Financial Center, 7900 Xerxes Avenue South - Bloomington, MN 55431 - Phone: (612) 835-3800, Fax: (612) 896-3333 - *See complete biographical profile in Federal, State & Local Government Law Chapter.*

LARRY J. BERG

Fredrikson & Byron, P.A.
1100 International Centre
900 Second Avenue South
Minneapolis, MN 55402

Phone: (612) 347-7052
Fax: (612) 347-7077

Admitted: 1978 Minnesota;
1978 US Dist. Ct. (MN)
Birthdate: 05/22/53

•**LARRY J. BERG:** An officer in Fredrikson & Byron's Real Estate Group, Mr. Berg has in-depth experience in real estate development, land use, and construction law. He concentrates in the areas of purchase and sale of property; leasing; subdivision of land/real estate development work; representing borrowers/lenders regarding real estate based loans; easements; examination of title; and representing clients before city councils, planning commissions, and other regulatory bodies for various municipal and regulatory approvals such as zoning changes and subdivisions. Mr. Berg has earned his reputation as a "problem-solver." He emphasizes service, attention to detail, and loyalty to his clients. He has represented individuals, corporations, and institutional clients in the acquisition and disposition of office, industrial, manufacturing, research, and service sites in numerous states; a wide range of clients in obtaining municipal and regulatory approvals for the development and/or use of real property; developers in the purchase and development of property for commercial and residential projects; landlords and tenants in leasing office, industrial, mixed-use, and residential space; hospitals, medical groups, corporations, and other clients for the construction of buildings, homes, and other facilities.
Education: JD 1978 cum laude, University of Minnesota; BA 1975, University of Minnesota.
Employment History: Lecturer in business law and real estate law, University of Minnesota.
Representative Clients: Small and large institutions and businesses, individual owners and investors, banks and other institutional lenders, municipalities, property managers and real estate developers including Northco Corporation, H.B. Fuller Company, and Cooperative Power Association.
Professional Associations: MSBA (Cochair, Board of Editors, *Minnesota Real Property Survey*, Real Property Section); HCBA (Construction Law Section; Vice Chair, Real Property Section); Minnesota Shopping Center Assn.
Community Involvement: St. Joseph's School of Music (Board of Trustees); active with various committees of the Twin Cities Marathon, the United Jewish Fund and Council, and other charitable organizations.
Firm: Larry Berg is one of ten attorneys in Fredrikson & Byron's Real Estate Group which focuses on working with clients in developing, financing, leasing, management, sale, and acquisition of industrial and commercial projects of all types, including the largest hotel in Minnesota, and major mixed use complexes in downtown Minneapolis and St. Paul. They counsel real estate clients in tax and business planning, property tax issues, environmental and land-use concerns, condemnation proceedings, mortgage foreclosures, loan restructuring and workouts, and general real estate dispute resolution. The group takes pride in being able to understand the diverse concerns of their clients.

•**PHILIP F. BOELTER:** Mr. Boelter has been a partner in the Real Estate Department of Dorsey & Whitney since 1974 and is certified as a Real Property Law Specialist by the Real Property Section of the Minnesota State Bar Association. He practices in all aspects of real property law, including assisting owners, developers, tenants, and contractors in the acquisition, construction, leasing, financing, and sale of office, retail, residential, medical, resort, farming, commercial, and industrial properties throughout the United States. He also assists individuals and companies in estate and business succession planning, restructuring, mergers, and acquisitions. Mr. Boelter has been listed in *The Best Lawyers in America* and in *Who's Who in American Law*.
Education: JD 1968 with high distinction, Order of the Coif, University of Iowa (Associate Editor 1967-68, *Iowa Law Review*); BS 1965 with high distinction, Iowa State University.
Employment History: Partner 1974-present, Associate 1968-73, Dorsey & Whitney.
Representative Clients: Kraus-Anderson, Incorporated.
Firm: Dorsey & Whitney is the largest law firm in Minnesota and one of the largest firms in the United States with over 350 lawyers in 12 offices. The depth and breadth of the experience of its lawyers enables it to provide a broad range of services to meet the diverse legal needs of its client base, which includes Fortune 500 companies, public agencies, banks and other financial institutions, nonprofit organizations, individual investors, family owned businesses, and high-tech and low-tech, growth oriented companies.

PHILIP F. BOELTER

Dorsey & Whitney
Pillsbury Center South
220 South Sixth Street
Minneapolis, MN 55402-1498

Phone: (612) 340-2649
Fax: (612) 340-7800

Admitted: 1968 Minnesota; 1968 Iowa

•**LORENS Q. BRYNESTAD:** Drawing from 30 years of practical legal experience, Larry Brynestad is a recognized expert in all phases of real estate transactions, from the initial planning stages through subdivision, title examination, acquisition, financing, and construction. Larry is adept at the drafting and negotiation of real estate agreements and contracts, whether they concern land purchases, development or redevelopment, construction financing, or complex commercial leases. His practice covers every aspect of real estate law, from helping people buy their first home to the development of shopping centers and the creation of townhouse and condominium projects. Because of Larry's reputation for successfully resolving complex real estate title problems, attorneys statewide consult him on such matters as questions of marketability of title, contract for deed cancellations, and land registration issues. The Minnesota State Bar Association has called upon Larry to help in drafting and publishing guidelines for Minnesota real estate practice and probate proceedings.
Education: JD 1961, University of Chicago; BA 1958, St. Olaf College (Phi Beta Kappa).
Employment History: Currently in private practice and Of Counsel to the law firm of Jensen & Swanson, P.A., of Brooklyn Park and to the law firm of Strobel & Hanson, P.A., of Red Wing; Partner/Attorney 1965-93, Mackall, Crounse & Moore (Minneapolis); Judge Advocate 1961-65, US Air Force.
Representative Clients: Businesses, individuals, and other attorneys seeking assistance with real estate, environmental, and estate planning matters including inter and intrastate banks and mortgage lenders, real estate developers, condominium and townhouse associations, trucking companies, manufacturing firms, service firms, governmental agencies, and economic development authorities.
Professional Associations: ABA; MSBA (Real Property Section and Governing Council (Officer); Title Standards Committee (Chair)); HCBA (Real Property Section (past Chair)).
Community Involvement: Minneapolis Downtown Kiwanis Club (past President). Board member of: Ebenezer Society; Vision Loss Resources; Minneapolis Society for the Blind; Crossroads Aftercare Program, Inc.; and Greater Twin Cities Youth Symphonies. *See additional listings in Environmental Law and Probate, Estate Planning & Trusts Law Chapters.*

LORENS Q. BRYNESTAD

Brynestad Law Offices
8525 Edinbrook Crossing
Suite 201
Brooklyn Park, MN 55443

Phone: (612) 424-8811
Fax: (612) 493-5193

Admitted: 1961 Minnesota; 1970 US Dist. Ct. (MN); 1963 US Sup. Ct.
Birthdate: 04/02/36

•**WILLIAM M. BURNS** - Hanft, Fride, O'Brien, Harries, Swelbar & Burns, P.A. - 1000 First Bank Place, 130 West Superior Street - Duluth, MN 55802 - Phone: (218) 722-4766, Fax: (218) 720-4920 - *See complete biographical profile in Publicly Held Corporations Law Chapter.*

Chapter 13: Commercial Real Estate Law

JAMES F. CHRISTOFFEL

Christoffel, Elliott & Albrecht, P.A.
100 South Fifth Street
Suite 1250
Minneapolis, MN 55402

Phone: (612) 672-0900
Fax: (612) 341-2835

Admitted: 1980 Minnesota;
1980 US Dist. Ct. (MN)
Birthdate: 05/15/54

•**JAMES F. CHRISTOFFEL:** Mr. Christoffel practices in the areas of banking, real estate, and commercial law. He represents all types of lending clients, including national banks, state chartered banks, asset based lenders, venture capital funds, construction lenders, permanent lenders, and equipment lessors. Mr. Christoffel has been lead counsel on multibank loan transactions ranging from $30 million to $234 million. He is conversant in all aspects of secured and unsecured lending, with a special emphasis on real estate lending, representing both lenders and development entities. He is also extensively experienced in loan workouts and restructurings from both lender's and borrower's perspectives. Mr. Christoffel is certified as a Real Property Specialist by the Real Property Section of the Minnesota State Bar Association.
Education: JD 1980 cum laude, William Mitchell; BA 1976, University of Minnesota.
Employment History: Founding Partner 1989-present, Christoffel, Elliott & Albrecht, P.A.; Associate/Partner 1983-89, Fabyanske, Svoboda, Westra & Davis, P.A.; Associate 1981-83, Briggs & Morgan, P.A.; Law Clerk, 1980-81, Hon. Lawrence Yetka, Minnesota Supreme Court Justice.
Representative Clients: Eastern Heights Bank; TCF Bank Minnesota FSB; First American Banks; E.J. Plesko & Associates, Inc.; Canal Capital Corporation; Frandsen Financial Corp. and affiliated banks; Bor-Son Construction Company; Brutger Equities, Inc.; Supervalu Stores, Inc.
Professional Associations: RCBA; MSBA (Real Property Section); ABA.
Firm: Mr. Christoffel is one of the original partners of Christoffel, Elliott & Albrecht, P.A., founded in 1989. In addition to Mr. Christoffel's areas of expertise, the firm concentrates on bankruptcy, reorganization, creditor's rights, and commercial litigation. Christopher Elliott has been lead counsel in bankruptcy proceedings involving debtors with assets exceeding $150 million. Gary Albrecht leads the firm's commercial litigation practice which includes representation of lenders, investors, and telecommunications industry clients. *See additional listings in Bankruptcy & Workout Law and Banking Law Chapters.*

PETER L. COOPER

McGrann Shea Franzen
Carnival Straughn & Lamb,
Chartered
2200 LaSalle Plaza
800 LaSalle Avenue
Minneapolis, MN 55402

Phone: (612) 338-2525
Fax: (612) 339-2386

Admitted: 1972 Minnesota;
1973 US Dist. Ct. (MN)
Birthdate: 02/26/46

•**PETER L. COOPER:** Mr. Cooper practices in the areas of real estate and public finance law with McGrann Shea Franzen Carnival Straughn & Lamb, Chartered. His practice includes the purchase and sale of real estate, governmental development projects, commercial real estate development, real estate and commercial financing, and condominium and other common interest ownership projects. He also acts as bond counsel and underwriters' counsel for government-financed projects.
Education: JD 1972, University of Minnesota; BA 1969 magna cum laude, University of Minnesota.
Employment History: 1990-present, McGrann Shea Franzen Carnival Straughn & Lamb, Chartered; 1986-89, O'Connor & Hannan; 1975-86, private practice; 1972-75, Minneapolis Legal Aid Society.
Representative Clients: Minneapolis Community Development Agency; Metropolitan Sports Facilities Commission; US WEST Real Estate, Inc.; Morgan Stanley Incorporated; American Commercial Bank; Franklin National Bank; Montgomery Ward & Co., Inc.
Professional Associations: MSBA; HCBA; National Assn. of Bond Lawyers.
Firm: McGrann Shea Franzen Carnival Straughn & Lamb, Chartered, provides a broad range of legal services in real estate, corporate, banking, commercial and public financing, municipal utilities, employee benefits, government relations, commercial litigation, environmental, and other areas of commercial law. The firm strives to provide the personal service that enables its clients to compete in the current business climate. *See additional listing in Federal, State & Local Government Law Chapter.*

•**WILLIAM J. COSGRIFF:** Mr. Cosgriff practices real estate law, including commercial and residential real estate development. He represents owners and developers of apartment complexes, condominiums, townhouses, and single family homes; office buildings, office warehouses, retail centers, industrial, and recreational properties; landlords and tenants; limited and general partnerships; placement of equity and debt financing; transaction negotiations; land and building acquisition, financing, development, and disposition; architects' contracts; construction contracts; leasing; and numerous other real estate issues. Mr. Cosgriff is certified as a Real Property Law Specialist by the Minnesota State Bar Association. He also practices business law, representing both publicly and privately held corporations and nonprofit corporations in such diverse areas as radio, microelectronics, computer graphics, franchises, construction, beverage wholesalers, accounting, health care, manufacturing, publishing and the arts. He also counsels clients regarding equity and debt financing; mergers and acquisitions; asset purchases and sales; organization, financing, and development of new businesses; restructuring of existing businesses; and general corporate matters.
Education: JD 1966 cum laude, University of Minnesota; BA 1963 cum laude, University of St. Thomas.
Employment History: 1969-present, Doherty, Rumble & Butler; 1966-69, US Navy Judge Advocate Corps.
Representative Clients: Construction 70; Dan Dolan Development; Federal Land Company; MN Public Radio; NewMech Companies; North Oaks Company; Resistance Technology; Stuart Companies; Walser Automotive Group; Westminster Corp.
Professional Associations: MSBA; RCBA.
Community Involvement: Boards of: MN Museum of American Art; HealthEast Foundation; Catholic Services for the Elderly. Past Board member of: The Minnesota Club; United Arts Council; St. Paul Winter Carnival; Westminster Corp.; MN Public Radio.
Firm: Some of the most visible office buildings and retail complexes in the Twin Cities area were developed with assistance from Doherty, Rumble & Butler. The firm's attorneys represent developers of hotels; office buildings; shopping centers; industrial, manufacturing, and agricultural projects; and residential developments. Doherty, Rumble & Butler is highly skilled at interdisciplinary real estate transactions, handling complicated leases, development, tax, environmental, and financing issues. The emphasis each lawyer brings to the real estate practice never overshadows the fundamental real estate needs of clients including entity formation, contract drafting, platting and zoning, title examination and registration, and basic residential transactions. *See additional listings in Closely Held Business Law and Publicly Held Corporations Law Chapters.*

WILLIAM J. COSGRIFF

Doherty, Rumble & Butler
Professional Association
2800 Minnesota World Trade Center
30 East Seventh Street
St. Paul, MN 55101-4999

Phone: (612) 291-9333
Fax: (612) 291-9313

Admitted: 1966 Minnesota;
1969 US Dist. Ct. (MN);
1967 US Ct. App. (8th Cir.);
1967 Ct. Military App.;
1967 Ct. App. (Fed. Cir.);
1967 US Claims Ct.;
1967 US Sup. Ct.;
1970 US Tax Ct.
Birthdate: 03/03/41

ROLLIN H. CRAWFORD - LeVander, Gillen & Miller, P.A. - 633 South Concord Street, Suite 402 - South St. Paul, MN 55075 - Phone: (612) 451-1831, Fax: (612) 450-7384 - *See complete biographical profile in Federal, State & Local Government Law Chapter.*

•**TED E. DEANER** - O'Brien, Ehrick, Wolf, Deaner & Maus - Marquette Bank Building, Suite 611, P.O. Box 968 - Rochester, MN 55903 - Phone: (507) 289-4041, Fax: (507) 281-4778 - *See complete biographical profile in Bankruptcy & Workout Law Chapter.*

•**DAVID B. EIDE:** Mr. Eide has practiced for over 20 years in the areas of real estate and corporate law, with an emphasis on the financing, development, and operation of multifamily housing. Mr. Eide is a frequent speaker locally and nationally regarding community association law and multifamily housing issues. He was a principal drafter of the Minnesota Uniform Condominium Act and the Minnesota Common Interest Ownership Act.
Education: JD 1964, University of Minnesota; BA 1961, University of Minnesota.
Employment History: Has practiced in the areas of real estate and corporate law in Minneapolis since 1969, with an emphasis on multifamily housing and development since 1973; US Judge Advocate (Lt.) 1965-69, US Navy Judge Advocate General Corps.
Representative Clients: Acts as legal counsel for residential and commercial developers, property managers, owners and owners associations involving over 10,000 dwelling units, primarily in the Minneapolis-St. Paul metropolitan area.
Professional Associations: ABA; MSBA (Real Estate Law Section; Business Law Section; Uniform Condominium Act Committee; MN Common Interest Ownership Act Committee (Chair)); HCBA (Real Estate Law Section); Community Assns. Institute, Minnesota Chapter (founding member; past Trustee; Treasurer); MN Multi-Housing Assn. (Board member 1977-79; Secretary 1981-82).
Community Involvement: Minnetonka Charter Commission (former member).
Firm: Mr. Eide is a founding partner of Frommelt & Eide, Ltd., a small law firm which provides primarily business-related legal services involving community associations, real estate, business formation, securities offerings, corporations, and commercial transactions. Mr. Eide heads a group of three attorneys who focus on the financing, development, and operation of condominium, townhouse and cooperative projects, and the representation of the homeowners associations which govern those types of developments. *See additional listing in Closely Held Business Law Chapter.*

DAVID B. EIDE

Frommelt & Eide, Ltd.
580 International Centre
900 Second Avenue South
Minneapolis, MN 55402

Phone: (612) 332-2200
Fax: (612) 342-2761
800 number: (800) 332-2296

Admitted: 1964 Minnesota;
1971 US Dist. Ct. (MN);
1980 US Ct. App. (8th Cir.);
1968 US Tax Ct.;
1969 US Sup. Ct.;
1972 US Ct. of Military App.
Birthdate: 06/02/39

Chapter 13: Commercial Real Estate Law

CHRISTOPHER A. ELLIOTT - Christoffel, Elliott & Albrecht, P.A. - 100 South Fifth Street, Suite 1250 - Minneapolis, MN 55402 - Phone: (612) 672-0900, Fax: (612) 341-2835 - *See complete biographical profile in Bankruptcy & Workout Law Chapter.*

JOSEPH M. FINLEY

Leonard, Street and Deinard
Professional Association
150 South Fifth Street
Suite 2300
Minneapolis, MN 55402

Phone: (612) 335-1500
Fax: (612) 335-1657

Admitted: 1980 Minnesota;
1980 US Dist. Ct. (MN)
Birthdate: 10/21/52

•**JOSEPH M. FINLEY:** Mr. Finley is chair of Leonard, Street and Deinard's Real Estate Department. His current practice concentrates mainly on acquisition and financing transactions involving real estate and mortgage portfolios held by investment companies and real estate investment trusts. He also spends portions of his time dealing with real estate development and litigating real estate related issues arising out of condemnations, foreclosures, and land use disputes. He also assists title insurance companies in dealing with claims that have been made on their policies. Finally, he devotes part of his practice to representing start-up corporations.
Education: JD 1980, University of Minnesota; MCP 1977, Harvard University; BA 1974, Harvard University.
Employment History: Shareholder 1986-present, Associate 1980-85, Leonard, Street and Deinard.
Representative Clients: Carlson Real Estate Company; The Shidler Group; Robinson, Blake & George, Inc.; First Industrial Financing Partnership (Chicago); RD Management (New York); Aldrich, Eastman & Waltch (Boston); Finger Enterprises (Houston); Old Republic National Title Insurance Company; Chicago Title Insurance Company; MedIntell, Inc.; MedAmicus, Inc.; Five Star Food Base Company.
Professional Associations: ABA; MSBA; HCBA; Urban Land Institute; American Planning Assn.; Metropolitan Council (1985-93, Transportation Advisory Board); Dual Track Airport Study Task Force (1993-present).
Community Involvement: Edgecumbe Community Center Hockey Booster Club (President; Treasurer); Youth Hockey (Coach); Youth Baseball (Coach).
Firm: Leonard, Street and Deinard is a full service commercial law firm of approximately 125 attorneys. The firm's 15-member Real Estate Department handles the full spectrum of real estate related matters, including purchases and sales; leases; land development and land use issues; tax-increment financing; mortgage financing; secondary mortgage market transactions; mortgage loan servicing; all phases of construction; and related environmental, income tax, and bankruptcy issues.

LINDA FISHER - Larkin, Hoffman, Daly & Lindgren, Ltd. - 1500 Norwest Financial Center, 7900 Xerxes Avenue South - Bloomington, MN 55431 - Phone: (612) 835-3800, Fax: (612) 896-3333 - *See complete biographical profile in Environmental Law Chapter.*

HAROLD A. FREDERICK - Fryberger, Buchanan, Smith & Frederick, P.A. - 302 West Superior Street, Suite 700 - Duluth, MN 55802 - Phone: (218) 722-0861, Fax: (218) 722-9568 - *See complete biographical profile in Health Law Chapter.*

ROGER H. FROMMELT - Frommelt & Eide, Ltd. - 580 International Centre, 900 Second Avenue South - Minneapolis, MN 55402 - Phone: (612) 332-2200, Fax: (612) 342-2761 - *See complete biographical profile in Securities & Venture Finance Law Chapter.*

CHERYL L. GRASMOEN

Petersen, Tews & Squires, P.A.
4800 IDS Center
80 South Eighth Street
Minneapolis, MN 55402

Phone: (612) 344-1600
Fax: (612) 344-1650

Admitted: 1978 Minnesota;
1978 US Dist. Ct. (MN);
1978 US Ct. App. (8th Cir.)
Birthdate: 03/18/51

•**CHERYL L. GRASMOEN:** Ms. Grasmoen, a shareholder at Petersen, Tews & Squires, P.A., practices in the areas of commercial real estate law and loan origination with extensive experience in all facets of development, leasing, construction and acquisition financing, workouts, and sales and acquisitions of real estate holdings throughout the United States. She is certified as a Real Property Law Specialist by the Minnesota State Bar Association and is a trained mediator under the Minnesota Civil Mediation Act.
Education: JD 1978 cum laude, William Mitchell (Editor, *William Mitchell Law Review*); BA 1972 cum laude, Macalester College.
Employment History: 1984-present, Petersen, Tews & Squires, P.A.; 1984-88, 1979-82 Adjunct Professor, William Mitchell College of Law; 1979-84, Dorsey & Whitney.
Professional Associations: MSBA (Title Standards Committee; Coeditor, MSBA *Real Property Law Survey*); HCBA (Vice President, Real Property Law Section; Real Property Law Section Council); Annual CLE Real Estate Institute (Planning Committee); MN Supreme Court (appointee to Committee on Legal Assistant Specialization).
Firm: Petersen, Tews & Squires, celebrating its 20th year, is a business law firm that provides a broad range of commercial legal services. The firm's clients include Fortune 500 companies, government agencies, partnerships, individuals, and closely and publicly held corporations. By name, they include SUPERVALU INC.; United Healthcare Corp.; Lutheran Brotherhood; TCF Bank, fsb.; Marquette Bank; Norwest Bank Minnesota, N.A.; Software, Etc. Stores, Inc.; North Coast Mortgage; Kuempel Chime Clock Works; Dorso Trailers, Inc.; Braun Fashions, Inc.; Dakota's Children, Inc.; RTC/FDIC; and Computype, Inc. Petersen, Tews & Squires provides legal counsel in the areas of commercial litigation, securities and venture finance law, employment law, commercial real estate, bankruptcy and workout law, and closely held business law. In addition to Ms. Grasmoen, the firm has four other Real Property Law Specialists and four other trained mediators. Ms. Grasmoen's fellow shareholders are J. Dixon Tews, Rodger D. Squires, Charles C. Jensch, John Paul Martin, Jeffrey G. Stephenson, Bradley J. Martinson, Valdis A. Silins, and Joseph L. Nuñez. Petersen, Tews & Squires is committed to providing quality cost-effective legal services to its clients. *See additional listing in Environmental Law Chapter.*

WILLIAM L. GUY III - Gunhus, Grinnell, Klinger, Swenson & Guy, Ltd. - 512 Center Avenue, P.O. Box 1077 - Moorhead, MN 56561-1077 - Phone: (218) 236-6462, Fax: (218) 236-9873 - *See complete biographical profile in Probate, Estate Planning & Trusts Law Chapter.*

•**MARK E. HAMEL:** Mr. Hamel has focused his practice exclusively on real estate law since 1979 and is certified as a Real Property Law Specialist by the Real Property Section of the Minnesota State Bar Association. He represents clients of all sizes on real estate transactions and issues of all kinds. Mr. Hamel concentrates his practice on transactions involving commercial real estate, including acquisitions and sales, development, construction, financing, leasing, and securitization. His projects have included office, mixed-use, retail, shopping center, industrial, health care, and commercial condominium projects. Mr. Hamel represents owners, developers, lenders, landlords, and tenants. He also supports other departments in his firm in matters affecting real estate, including business mergers, acquisitions, sales, and financings. Mr. Hamel is listed in *Who's Who in American Law* and is a frequent lecturer at continuing legal education seminars.
Education: JD 1978 cum laude, Harvard University; BA 1975 summa cum laude, Carroll College.
Employment History: Partner 1985-present, Associate 1979-84, Dorsey & Whitney; Law Clerk 1978-79, Hon. Walter F. Rogosheske, Minnesota Supreme Court.
Professional Associations: MSBA (Real Property Section); HCBA (Real Property Section).
Community Involvement: Accessible Space, Inc. (ASI) (Chair 1991-present, Board of Directors; Chair, Statewide Expansion Campaign). ASI is a nonprofit corporation providing accessible, affordable housing and personal care services to over 400 persons with a mobility-impairment and/or traumatic brain-injury in 34 locations in four states.
Firm: Dorsey & Whitney is the largest law firm in Minnesota and one of the largest firms in the United States with over 350 lawyers in 12 offices. The depth and breadth of the experience of its lawyers enables it to provide a broad range of services to meet the diverse legal needs of its client base, which includes Fortune 500 companies, public agencies, banks and other financial institutions, nonprofit organizations, individual investors, family owned businesses, and high-tech and low-tech, growth oriented companies.

MARK E. HAMEL

Dorsey & Whitney
Pillsbury Center South
220 South Sixth Street
Minneapolis, MN 55402-1498

Phone: (612) 340-8716
Fax: (612) 340-7800

Admitted: 1979 Minnesota; 1979 US Dist. Ct. (MN)
Birthdate: 04/09/53

KAREN HANSEN - Popham, Haik, Schnobrich & Kaufman, Ltd. - 222 South Ninth Street, Suite 3300 - Minneapolis, MN 55402 - Phone: (612) 333-4800, Fax: (612) 334-8888 - *See complete biographical profile in Environmental Law Chapter.*

•**LEE W. HANSON** - Hall, Byers, Hanson, Steil & Weinberger, P.A. - 1010 West St. Germain, Suite 600 - St. Cloud, MN 56301 - Phone: (612) 252-4414, Fax: (612) 252-4482 - *See complete biographical profile in Closely Held Business Law Chapter.*

•**GILBERT W. HARRIES** - Hanft, Fride, O'Brien, Harries, Swelbar & Burns, P.A. - 1000 First Bank Place, 130 West Superior Street - Duluth, MN 55802 - Phone: (218) 722-4766, Fax: (218) 720-4920 - *See complete biographical profile in Environmental Law Chapter.*

ROBERT A. HEIBERG

Dorsey & Whitney
Pillsbury Center South
220 South Sixth Street
Minneapolis, MN 55402-1498

Phone: (612) 340-2751
Fax: (612) 340-7800

Admitted: 1968 Minnesota
Birthdate: 06/29/43

•**ROBERT A. HEIBERG:** Mr. Heiberg has focused his practice almost exclusively on commercial real estate matters since 1970. He has represented a wide variety of local and national clients, including (a) national banks in connection with permanent loans, construction loans, tax-exempt loans, loan modifications, and workouts in Minnesota and at least 20 other states; (b) real estate syndicators in acquiring, managing, selling, financing, refinancing, working out, and converting to condominium, apartment, shopping center, office building, off/warehouse, motel, and hotel properties in Minnesota and at least 18 other states; (c) local and regional grocery store chains in leasing and developing store buildings; (d) life insurance companies in connection with permanent loans, loan modifications, property acquisitions, workouts, and foreclosures in Minnesota and at least 12 other states; and (e) most other types of complex commercial real estate transactions. He is listed in *The Best Lawyers in America*, 1991-93 edition in real estate.

Education: JD 1968 summa cum laude, Order of the Coif, University of Minnesota (Articles Editor 1967-68, *Minnesota Law Review*); BA 1965 summa cum laude, University of Minnesota (Phi Beta Kappa).

Employment History: Partner 1973-present, Associate 1969-73, Dorsey & Whitney; Instructor 1972-76, Real Estate Law for Paralegals, University of Minnesota General College; Instructor 1968-72, Legal Writing and Appellate Advocacy, University of Minnesota Law School; Law Clerk 1968-69, Hon. Walter F. Rogosheske, Justice, Minnesota Supreme Court.

Professional Associations: ABA (Real Property, Probate and Trust Law Section); MSBA (Member, Real Property Section); HCBA.

Community Involvement: Legal Advice Clinics (past volunteer attorney); Pro bono transactional real estate work for nonprofit organizations; University of Minnesota Legal Assistants Program (Advisory Committee 1974-78); University of Minnesota Law School (Board of Visitors 1990-present). Avid rose-grower and exhibitor: American Rose Society (Rose Judge); Royal National Rose Society (Great Britain); Minnesota Rose Society; North Star Rose Society; Minneapolis Men's Garden Club. Edina High School football (Statistician 1985-present); youth baseball, hockey, and volleyball (Coach and Manager).

Firm: Dorsey & Whitney is the largest law firm in Minnesota and one of the largest firms in the United States with over 350 lawyers in 12 offices. The depth and breadth of the experience of its lawyers enables it to provide a broad range of services to meet the diverse legal needs of its client base, which includes Fortune 500 companies, public agencies, banks and other financial institutions, nonprofit organizations, individual investors, family owned businesses, and high-tech and low-tech, growth oriented companies.

ROBERT L. HOFFMAN - Larkin, Hoffman, Daly & Lindgren, Ltd. - 1500 Norwest Financial Center, 7900 Xerxes Avenue South - Bloomington, MN 55431 - Phone: (612) 835-3800, Fax: (612) 896-3333 - *See complete biographical profile in Federal, State & Local Government Law Chapter.*

CRAIG W. JOHNSON

Hoversten, Strom, Johnson & Rysavy
807 West Oakland Avenue
Austin, MN 55912

Phone: (507) 433-3483
Fax: (507) 433-7889

Admitted: 1972 Minnesota
Birthdate: 10/22/45

•**CRAIG W. JOHNSON:** Mr. Johnson is certified as a Real Property Specialist by the Minnesota State Bar Association. His real estate practice includes residential, commercial, and agricultural real estate transactions, condominiums, and housing and development law. Mr. Johnson also practices in corporate and business law, estate planning and probate, and employment and labor law. In addition he is a lecturer and panelist on real estate for Minnesota Continuing Legal Education seminars.

Education: JD 1971, University of Minnesota; BA 1968, University of Minnesota.

Employment History: Currently, Hoversten, Strom, Johnson & Rysavy; Law Clerk 1970-71, MN Attorney General's Office.

Representative Clients: Sterling State Bank; Farmers State Bank of Adams; Farmers State Bank of Elkton; St. Olaf Hospital Assn.; Adams Health Care Center; St. Mark's Lutheran Home; Austin Housing and Redevelopment Authority; Development Corporation of Austin; Cities of Austin, Adams, and Lyle; Akkerman Mfg., Inc.; King Company of Owatonna.

Professional Associations: Real Estate Title Standards Committee (1980-present); Real Estate Institute (Planning Committee); Real Property Council (Chair); Mower County Bar Assn. (President 1975-76); Tenth District Bar Assn. (Treasurer); ABA (Real Property, Probate and Trust Law Section; Business Law Section).

Community Involvement: Development Corporation of Austin (Board member; Vice President); Austin Symphony Orchestra (Business Manager); St. Olaf Lutheran Church Foundation (Board member); Austin United Way (Board member); Austin Rotary Club (Vice President); Austin Community Scholarship Committee (Board member); Austin Country Club (Board member; current Vice President).

Firm: Hoversten, Strom, Johnson & Rysavy of Austin is one of the largest law firms in southeastern Minnesota. The firm provides a wide range of litigation services including personal injury, product liability, and insurance defense and engages in the general practice of law, handling all areas of real estate, commercial, family, employment and labor, estate planning, probate, trusts, municipal, and governmental law.

•JEFFREY S. JOHNSON: Mr. Johnson concentrates his practice on commercial real property and banking law, representing owners, asset managers, and lenders. In the commercial real property area, he represents condominium and townhouse developers, land developers, property purchasers, and landlords and tenants. Mr. Johnson is certified as a Real Property Law Specialist by the Minnesota State Bar Association and is a licensed Real Estate Broker with the Anoka County Board of Realtors. His representation of banks encompasses all aspects of document drafting, commercial paper issues, and federal and state bank statutes and regulations. He is an author and a frequent lecturer on real estate topics for Minnesota Continuing Legal Education.
Education: JD December 1978, Hamline University; BA 1975, University of Minnesota.
Employment History: 1979-present, Barna, Guzy & Steffen, Ltd.
Professional Associations: MSBA (Board of Governors 1993-present; Real Property Council (member 1985-present, Chair 1990-91); Real Property Certification Council (Chair 1988-90)); HCBA (Board of Governors; Real Property Section (Chair 1986-87); Title Standards Committee (Chair 1983)); Anoka County Bar Assn. (Real Property Section (Chair 1987-88)); ABA (Section of Real Property Probate and Trust Law); MN Bankers Assn.
Community Involvement: Totino-Grace High School (Board member 1980-83); Northeast YMCA (Board member 1983-86; Capital Campaign Chair 1993-present); Northeast Kiwanis (Chair 1987-88); Columbia Heights Chamber of Commerce (Chair 1987).
Firm: Barna, Guzy & Steffen, Ltd., offers a spectrum of legal services, including corporate/business, banking, real estate, commercial litigation, labor and employment law (including discrimination), estate planning and probate, family law, criminal defense, and personal injury. By having experienced attorneys in a variety of areas, the firm is able to offer clients the precise legal expertise to suit their needs. *See additional listing in Banking Law Chapter.*

JEFFREY S. JOHNSON

Barna, Guzy & Steffen, Ltd.
400 Northtown Financial Plaza
200 Coon Rapids Boulevard
Minneapolis, MN 55433

Phone: (612) 780-8500
Fax: (612) 780-1777

Admitted: April 1979
Minnesota;
1979 US Dist. Ct. (MN)

JOEL D. JOHNSON - Dosland, Nordhougen, Lillehaug & Johnson, P.A. - 730 Center Avenue, Suite 203, P.O. Box 100 - Moorhead, MN 56561-0100 - Phone: (218) 233-2744, Fax: (218) 233-1570 - *See complete biographical profile in Closely Held Business Law Chapter.*

•DAVID KANTOR: Mr. Kantor is chair of Leonard, Street and Deinard's Banking and Business Reorganization Department, which concentrates on representing financial institutions and other lenders. He handles banking, regulatory compliance, residential mortgage lending, and consumer credit matters for numerous lenders. Mr. Kantor also has special expertise in real estate loans and workouts and in developing standard forms and procedures and new banking products. He regularly advises banks regarding deposit operations and regulatory compliance. He is editor of the *Minnesota Bankers Association Deposit Accounts Procedure Manual* and frequently lectures to the Minnesota Bankers Association on Uniform Commercial Code issues, garnishments, levies and executions, and various regulatory matters.
Education: JD 1980, University of Michigan; MA 1975, Stanford University; BA 1974, University of Michigan.
Employment History: 1987-present, Leonard, Street and Deinard; 1980-87, O'Connor & Hannan.
Representative Clients: National City Bank of Minneapolis; TCF Bank Minnesota; Knutson Mortgage Corporation; United of Omaha Life Insurance Company; Eberhardt Company; Preferred Credit, Inc.
Professional Associations: ABA; HCBA; MSBA; American Bankers Assn. (Service member); Mortgage Bankers Assn. of America (Service member).
Community Involvement: Legal Advice Clinics (volunteer attorney 1980-94).
Firm: Leonard, Street and Deinard is a full service commercial law firm of approximately 125 attorneys. Half of the firm's practice concerns commercial, securities, and other business litigation; the other half of the practice concerns nonlitigated business matters, including corporate, public and private finance, real estate, mergers and acquisitions, banking, trade regulation, distribution, intellectual property, health, tax, and estate planning. The firm has a long history of representing family held, entrepreneurial, publicly held, and institutional businesses. The firm prides itself on its reputation for excellence and efficiency, and on the long term relationships it consistently builds with clients. *See additional listings in Bankruptcy & Workout Law and Banking Law Chapters.*

DAVID KANTOR

Leonard, Street and Deinard
Professional Association
150 South Fifth Street
Suite 2300
Minneapolis, MN 55402

Phone: (612) 335-1500
Fax: (612) 335-1657

Admitted: 1980 Minnesota
Birthdate: 08/10/52

Chapter 13: Commercial Real Estate Law

DAVID W. KELLEY

Leonard, Street and Deinard
Professional Association
150 South Fifth Street
Suite 2300
Minneapolis, MN 55402

Phone: (612) 335-1500
Fax: (612) 335-1657

Admitted: 1979 Minnesota
Birthdate: 04/05/52

•**DAVID W. KELLEY:** Mr. Kelley is a shareholder in Leonard, Street and Deinard's Banking and Business Reorganization Department. His practice is concentrated in the area of secured lending, including commercial real estate and asset-based loans. Mr. Kelley's clients include national and state banks, insurance companies, investment banks, and municipal agencies. He also represents buyers, sellers, and developers of commercial real estate. Mr. Kelley is a Real Property Law Specialist certified by the Minnesota State Bar Association.
Education: JD 1979 cum laude, University of Minnesota (Senior Editor, *Minnesota Law Review*; author, "Letters of Credit: Injunction as a Remedy for Fraud," 63 *Minn. L. Rev.* 487); BA 1974 magna cum laude, St. Olaf College.
Employment History: 1986-present, Leonard, Street and Deinard; 1979-86, O'Connor & Hannan.
Representative Clients: National City Bank of Minneapolis; Minneapolis Community Development Agency; Marquette Capital Bank; Piper Jaffray, Inc.; The Lander Group; Theatre de la Jeune Lune.
Professional Associations: ABA (Real Property, Probate and Trust Law Section); MSBA; HCBA (Real Property and Corporation, Banking and Business Law Sections); National Assn. of Industrial Office Parks.
Community Involvement: Board member, Red Eye Collaboration (nonprofit theater).
Firm: Leonard, Street and Deinard is a full service law firm of approximately 125 attorneys. About half of the firm's practice concerns commercial, securities, and other business oriented litigation. The other half concerns nonlitigated business matters, including corporate, public and private finance, real estate, mergers and acquisitions, banking, trade regulation, product distribution, intellectual property, health care, tax, and estate planning. The firm has a long history of representing family held and entrepreneurial businesses (a number of which have grown into large, multinational concerns), as well as publicly held and institutional businesses. Leonard, Street and Deinard prides itself on its reputation for excellence and efficiency, and on the long-term relationships it is consistently able to build with clients. *See additional listings in Bankruptcy & Workout Law and Banking Law Chapters.*

JOHN M. KONECK

Fredrikson & Byron, P.A.
1100 International Centre
900 Second Avenue South
Minneapolis, MN 55402

Phone: (612) 347-7038
Fax: (612) 347-7077

Admitted: 1979 Minnesota;
1978 North Dakota;
1979 US Dist. Ct. (MN);
1980 US Dist. Ct. (ND);
1978 US Ct. App. (8th Cir.)
Birthdate: 08/16/53

•**JOHN M. KONECK:** An officer and chair of Fredrikson & Byron's Real Estate Dispute Resolution and Litigation Group and cochair of the Real Estate Department. Mr. Koneck's unique focus combines the areas of real estate, litigation, and bankruptcy, which allows him to solve complex real estate problems in the best way for his clients whether through negotiations or litigation. He handles all aspects of real estate transactions, including purchases, sales, development contracts, leasing and real estate, bankruptcy, debtor-creditor law, and real estate related litigation, including leasing and contract disputes, mortgage foreclosures, property tax disputes, eminent domain, mechanics' lien actions, zoning and land use disputes, and complicated transactions. Mr. Koneck is certified as a Real Property Law Specialist by the Minnesota State Bar Association. He frequently lectures and writes about real estate, bankruptcy, and ethical issues for lawyers, accountants, lenders, and real estate professionals, and teaches business law for college students.
Education: JD 1978, Yale University; BS 1975 with honors, North Dakota State University.
Employment History: Judicial Clerk 1978, Hon. Robert Vogel, North Dakota Supreme Court and 1978-79, Hon. Gerald W. Vandle Walle, North Dakota Supreme Court.
Representative Clients: Small and large institutions and businesses; individual owners and investors; banks and other institutional lenders; municipalities; property managers; real estate developers.
Professional Associations: ABA (Vice Chair 1991-present and Chief Editor of newsletter, Litigation and Dispute Resolution Committee, Section of Real Property, Probate and Trust Law). MSBA (Real Property and Bankruptcy Sections; Rules of Professional Conduct Committee; 1990, Real Property Certification Council); State Bar Assn. of North Dakota; HCBA (Rules of Professional Conduct Committee); Hennepin County Legal Advice Clinics, Inc.
Community Involvement: State Board of Legal Certification, Supreme Court of Minnesota; Legal Advice Clinics, Ltd. (Board of Directors); Lawyers Professional Responsibility Board (supervisor of disciplined attorneys).
Firm: Mr. Koneck works with Fredrikson & Byron attorneys in bankruptcy, real estate, and litigation to assist clients with avoiding real estate disputes and resolving them when they do occur. He is one of eight attorneys in the Bankruptcy Group, one of 24 attorneys in the Commercial Litigation Group, and one of ten in the Real Estate Group. The Real Estate Group counsels clients in developing, financing, leasing, management, sale, and acquisition of industrial and commercial projects of all types. The group takes pride in being able to understand the diverse concerns of their clients. *See additional listing in Bankruptcy & Workout Law Chapter.*

Commercial Real Estate Law Leading Attorneys

•**FREDERICK A. KUEPPERS, JR.:** Mr. Kueppers primarily represents purchasers, sellers, and developers of commercial or residential real estate and is certified as a Real Property Law Specialist by the Real Property Section of the Minnesota State Bar Association. He also handles mechanic lien filings and foreclosures, mortgage foreclosures and contract cancellations, and formation of condominium and townhouse projects and serves as general counsel to a residential mortgage lender. In addition, Mr. Kueppers represents borrowers in commercial loan transactions and assists clients in the formation of corporations and partnerships. He also handles estate planning, wills and trusts, and probating of estates.
Education: LLB 1958, William Mitchell; BA 1954, St. Mary's College of Minnesota.
Representative Clients: St. Paul Area Assn. of Realtors; The Catholic Aid Assn.; Hermes Floral Company; Ankeny, Kell, Richter, Walsh Architects, Inc.; Fuel Oil Service Company, Inc.; Murray Properties, Inc.
Professional Associations: MSBA (Chair 1967-69, Ethics Committee; Secretary 1963-69, Real Property Section); speaker at Realtor education courses; American College of Real Estate Lawyers (charter member 1980); RCBA; ABA.
Community Involvement: Catholic Services for the Elderly, Inc. (Board member 1978-present; President 1990-93); St. Paul Area United Way (member of community study task forces); Volunteer Attorney Programs (volunteer attorney).
Firm: The firm of Kueppers, Hackel & Kueppers, P.A., and its predecessors have maintained offices in downtown St. Paul continuously since 1927. Presently the firm is comprised of three attorneys and two paralegal assistants. The several attorneys practice in the areas of residential and commercial real estate; family law (including dissolution of marriage, postdissolution matters, support, custody, and adoption); personal injury claims and other claims involving litigation; probate of estates, estate planning, wills, trusts, and guardianships; and general business matters. *See additional listings in Probate, Estate Planning & Trusts Law and Closely Held Business Law Chapters.*

FREDERICK A. KUEPPERS, JR.

Kueppers, Hackel & Kueppers, P.A.
1350 Capital Centre
386 North Wabasha Street
St. Paul, MN 55102

Phone: (612) 228-1104
Fax: (612) 297-6599

Admitted: 1958 Minnesota
Birthdate: 09/09/32

HART KULLER - Winthrop & Weinstine, P.A. - 3200 Minnesota World Trade Center, 30 East Seventh Street - St. Paul, MN 55101 - Phone: (612) 290-8400, Fax: (612) 292-9347 - *See complete biographical profile in Bankruptcy & Workout Law Chapter.*

•**PHILLIP L. KUNKEL** - Hall, Byers, Hanson, Steil & Weinberger, P.A. - 1010 West St. Germain, Suite 600 - St. Cloud, MN 56301 - Phone: (612) 252-4414, Fax: (612) 252-4482 - *See complete biographical profile in Bankruptcy & Workout Law Chapter.*

•**W. CHARLES LANTZ:** Mr. Lantz practices in the area of real estate and general business, with emphasis on commercial and real estate-based financing for lenders and borrowers, commercial landlord and tenant leasing, land development, utility law, and business contracts.
Education: JD 1971 summa cum laude, Order of the Coif, University of Minnesota (Board of Editors 1970-71, *Minnesota Law Review*); BA summa cum laude 1968, Hamline University (Editor 1967-68, *Hamline Oracle*).
Employment History: Partner 1981-present, Associate 1975-80, Dorsey & Whitney; Lieutenant 1972-75, USNR (rank at release from active duty), US Navy Judge Advocate General's Corp.
Firm: Dorsey & Whitney is the largest law firm in Minnesota and one of the largest firms in the United States with over 350 lawyers in 12 offices. The depth and breadth of the experience of its lawyers enables it to provide a broad range of services to meet the diverse legal needs of its client base, which includes Fortune 500 companies, public agencies, banks and other financial institutions, nonprofit organizations, individual investors, family owned businesses, and high-tech and low-tech, growth oriented companies. *See additional listings in Banking Law and Closely Held Business Law Chapters.*

W. CHARLES LANTZ

Dorsey & Whitney
201 First Avenue SW
Suite 340
Rochester, MN 55902

Phone: (507) 288-3156
Fax: (507) 288-6190

Admitted: 1971 Minnesota
Birthdate: 07/03/46

JANICE M. NELSON - Nelson Oyen Torvik - 221 North First Street, P.O. Box 656 - Montevideo, MN 56265 - Phone: (612) 269-6461, Fax: (612) 269-8024 - *See complete biographical profile in Closely Held Business Law Chapter.*

CURTIS A. NORDHOUGEN - Dosland, Nordhougen, Lillehaug & Johnson, P.A. - 730 Center Avenue, Suite 203, P.O. Box 100 - Moorhead, MN 56561-0100 - Phone: (218) 233-2744, Fax: (218) 233-1570 - *See complete biographical profile in Closely Held Business Law Chapter.*

Chapter 13: Commercial Real Estate Law

JOHN W. PERSON

Breen & Person, Ltd.
510 Laurel Street
P.O. Box 472
Brainerd, MN 56401

Phone: (218) 828-1248
Fax: (218) 828-4832

Admitted: 1975 Minnesota
Birthdate: 08/16/47

•**JOHN W. PERSON:** Thirty percent of Mr. Person's practice involves personal injury representation of injured plaintiffs, with another 50% as counsel in Workers' Compensation claims. He is certified as a Civil Trial Specialist by the Minnesota State Bar Association. The remaining 20% involves representation of two area banks, two municipalities, and work with clients involving real estate, as well as estate planning and probate matters.
Education: JD 1975 cum laude, University of Minnesota; BS 1969 magna cum laude, Augsburg College.
Employment History: Currently, Breen & Person, Ltd.; Real estate sales; US Army Band.
Representative Clients: City Attorney for the Cities of Baxter and Pillager, MN; Attorney for the Security State Bank of Staples in Staples and Pillager, MN, and a great number of workers and other individuals with various types of injuries and various other clients in matters involving real estate, estate planning, and probate.
Professional Associations: ATLA; MTLA; MSBA.
Community Involvement: Brainerd Jaycees (past President); Brainerd Lions Club (past President); Lions Club International (Melvin Jones Fellow); church and church choir; Brainerd Elks Club; Chamber of Commerce; other miscellaneous organizations and activities.
Firm: The firm of Breen & Person, Ltd., consists of two lawyers who are both Certified Trial Specialists and whose work largely involves various types of litigation, primarily in matters involving injury in both work and nonwork settings. *See additional listing in Personal Injury Defense Law Chapter.*

PAUL H. RAVICH

Ravich, Meyer, Kirkman & McGrath, P.A.
80 South Eighth Street
Suite 4545
Minneapolis, MN 55402-2225

Phone: (612) 332-8511
Fax: (612) 332-8302

Admitted: 1964 Minnesota
Birthdate: 08/27/39

•**PAUL H. RAVICH:** Mr. Ravich practices business law in the Twin Cities area and has done so since 1966. His special emphasis is real estate and finance law, representing real estate users, developers, investors, managers, and syndicators. In recent years, due to the difficulties in the real estate industry, Mr. Ravich has devoted a great deal of his practice to distressed real estate owners and projects. Examples include the restructuring of limited partnerships that own the Whitney Hotel, Ceresota Office Building, and Crown Roller Mill Office Building, and the restructuring of numerous apartments, industrial properties, hotels, and retail properties. His business counseling skills are frequently utilized by his clients to provide them with a disinterested, experienced viewpoint. Mr. Ravich is listed in every edition of *The Best Lawyers in America.*
Education: JD 1964 cum laude, University of Minnesota; BBA 1961 cum laude, University of Minnesota.
Employment History: President/Shareholder 1991-present, Ravich, Meyer, Kirkman & McGrath, P.A.; Partner 1985-91, Robins, Kaplan, Miller & Ciresi; Partner 1973-85, Stacker & Ravich; Partner 1966-73, Rosen, Ravich, Summers & Holmes; 1964-66, US Army.
Representative Clients: Dominium Group, Inc.; Frauenshuh Companies; The Stuart Corp.; R.L. Johnson Investment Company; Sentinel Management Company; Klodt Companies; Roseville Properties; Hoyt Properties, Inc.; Ron Clark Construction, Inc.; Universal International, Inc.; Game Financial Corp.
Professional Associations: ABA (Real Property Section); MSBA (Real Property Law Section); HCBA (Real Estate Section).
Firm: Ravich, Meyer, Kirkman & McGrath, P.A., was formed in 1991 to represent businesses and individuals in financial and real estate matters and provide general business counseling. The firm consists of the four named shareholders, a legal assistant, and staff. The firm's philosophy is to provide services in its specialized areas with a minimum of delegation and reassignment. Many times the firm's representation is coordinated with and supplements that provided by the client's corporate lawyers.

JAMES A. RUBENSTEIN - Moss & Barnett, A Professional Association - 4800 Norwest Center, 90 South Seventh Street - Minneapolis, MN 55402-4129 - Phone: (612) 347-0300, Fax: (612) 339-6686 - *See complete biographical profile in Bankruptcy & Workout Law Chapter.*

GROVER C. SAYRE III - O'Neill, Burke, O'Neill, Leonard & O'Brien, Ltd. - 100 South Fifth Street, Suite 1200 - Minneapolis, MN 55402 - Phone: (612) 332-1030, Fax: (612) 332-2740 - *See complete biographical profile in Publicly Held Corporations Law Chapter.*

DAVID C. SELLERGREN - Doherty, Rumble & Butler Professional Association - 3500 Fifth Street Towers, 150 South Fifth Street - Minneapolis, MN 55402-4235 - Phone: (612) 340-5555, Fax: (612) 340-5584 - *See complete biographical profile in Federal, State & Local Government Law Chapter.*

•**ROBERT J. SILVERMAN:** Mr. Silverman, a partner in the Real Estate Department of Dorsey & Whitney, represents lenders and owners of commercial real estate in the areas of purchase and sales, financing, condemnation, and loan workouts with emphasis on housing including syndications, major tenant leasing, and securitization. Recently he has had extensive experience in the acquisition and financing of multistate loan pools. Mr. Silverman is a lecturer for Minnesota Continuing Legal Education seminars and a former lecturer at William Mitchell College of Law (1977-78) and Hamline Law School (1992-94). Mr. Silverman is listed in *The Best Lawyers in America*, *Who's Who in American Law*, and *Who's Who in America*.
Education: JD 1967 cum laude, Order of the Coif, University of Minnesota (Assistant Editor 1966-67, *Minnesota Law Review*); BA 1964, University of Minnesota.
Employment History: Partner 1973-present, Associate 1967-72, Dorsey & Whitney.
Representative Clients: First Bank National Assn.; Cargill Financial Services Corp.; Thies & Talle Enterprise; The Northwestern Mutual Life Insurance Corp.
Professional Associations: ABA; MSBA; HCBA.
Community Involvement: Courage Center (Board member 1982-present; Board Chair 1989-90).
Firm: Dorsey & Whitney is the largest law firm in Minnesota and one of the largest firms in the United States with over 350 lawyers in 12 offices. The depth and breadth of the experience of its lawyers enables it to provide a broad range of services to meet the diverse legal needs of its client base, which includes Fortune 500 companies, public agencies, banks and other financial institutions, nonprofit organizations, individual investors, family owned businesses, and high-tech and low-tech, growth oriented companies.

ROBERT J. SILVERMAN

Dorsey & Whitney
Pillsbury Center South
220 South Sixth Street
Minneapolis, MN 55402-1498

Phone: (612) 340-2742
Fax: (612) 340-7800

Admitted: 1967 Minnesota; 1967 US Dist. Ct. (MN)
Birthdate: 04/04/42

•**RALPH T. SMITH** - Smith Law Firm, P. A. - 115 Fifth Street, P.O. Box 1420 - Bemidji, MN 56601 - Phone: (218) 751-3130, Fax: (218) 751-3132 - *See complete biographical profile in Labor Law Chapter.*

•**WILLIAM R. SOTH:** Mr. Soth, a partner in real estate law at Dorsey & Whitney since 1973, practices in the area of general real estate, with experience in municipal law. He represents developers, sellers, purchasers, landlords, tenants, mortgage lenders, and cities. Mr. Soth's experience includes the acquisition, development, financing, leasing, and sale of major office buildings, retail facilities, residential developments, and corporate real estate, and zoning, condemnation, redevelopment projects, tax-increment financing, and real estate tax abatement.
Education: JD 1966 cum laude, University of Minnesota (staff member 1965-66, *Minnesota Law Review*); BS 1963, Iowa State University.
Employment History: Partner 1973-present, Associate 1966-67 and 1969-72, Dorsey & Whitney; Captain, Artillery 1967-69, US Army.
Representative Clients: Development & user representation: IDS Financial Services, Inc.; Graco Inc.; Northrup King; SUPERVALU INC.; Rosemount Inc.; Fingerhut Companies, Inc.; Minneapolis Public Schools. Leasing & operations: MEPC American Properties Inc.; Ceridian Corp.; The Equitable Life Assurance Society of the United States. Real estate sales & acquisitions: IDS Financial Corp.; Travelers Companies; California real estate partnerships. Mortgage lending: Builders Development & Finance, Inc. Municipal law: Cities of St. Anthony, Deephaven, and Woodland.
Professional Associations: MSBA (Real Property and Public Law Sections); HCBA.
Community Involvement: Minneapolis Downtown Council (Board member); Friends of the Minneapolis Mounted Patrol (Board member).
Firm: Dorsey & Whitney is the largest law firm in Minnesota and one of the largest firms in the United States with over 350 lawyers in 12 offices. The depth and breadth of the experience of its lawyers enables it to provide a broad range of services to meet the diverse legal needs of its client base, which includes Fortune 500 companies, public agencies, banks and other financial institutions, nonprofit organizations, individual investors, family owned businesses, and high-tech and low-tech, growth oriented companies. *See additional listing in Federal, State & Local Government Law Chapter.*

WILLIAM R. SOTH

Dorsey & Whitney
Pillsbury Center South
220 South Sixth Street
Minneapolis, MN 55402-1498

Phone: (612) 340-2969
Fax: (612) 340-7800

Admitted: 1966 Minnesota
Birthdate: 06/11/41

Chapter 13: Commercial Real Estate Law

ROBERT O. STRAUGHN

McGrann Shea Franzen
Carnival Straughn & Lamb,
Chartered
2200 LaSalle Plaza
800 LaSalle Avenue
Minneapolis, MN 55402

Phone: (612) 338-2525
Fax: (612) 339-2386

Admitted: 1976 Minnesota;
1978 US District Court (MN)
Birthdate: 11/01/42

•**ROBERT O. STRAUGHN:** Mr. Straughn practices in the areas of real estate, commercial financing, and environmental law with McGrann Shea Franzen Carnival Straughn & Lamb, Chartered. His practice includes the purchase and sale of real estate, architectural and construction contracts, governmental zoning and development approvals, leasing matters, real estate financing, corporate and partnership matters, and environmental issues. He is certified as a Real Property Law Specialist by the Minnesota State Bar Association, and is also registered as a professional engineer in the state of Minnesota.
Education: JD 1976 cum laude, William Mitchell; MS 1971, University of Minnesota; BS 1965, University of Minnesota.
Employment History: 1990-present, McGrann Shea Franzen Carnival Straughn & Lamb, Chartered; 1984-90, O'Connor & Hannan; 1979-84, Oxford Properties, Inc.; Assistant City Attorney 1977-79, City of St. Paul. Prior to practicing law, Mr. Straughn was employed as an environmental engineer.
Representative Clients: Frauenshuh Companies; BetaWest, Inc.; U S WEST Real Estate, Inc.; Montgomery Ward & Co., Incorporated; The Palmer Group, Ltd.; American Commercial Bank; Franklin National Bank; St. Anthony Park State Bank; Minneapolis Community Development Agency; Beltmann North American Company, Inc.; Centrum Design Building Corp.
Professional Associations: ABA; MSBA; HCBA; Christian Legal Society.
Community Involvement: Greater Minneapolis Building Owners and Managers Assn. (BOMA); University UNITED Local Development Company (Director); LRT Business Partnership; Midway Chamber of Commerce (past President and Director); St. Paul Area Chamber of Commerce (past Director); St. Anthony Park Community Council (past Chair); Ramsey County Historical Society (past Secretary and Director).
Firm: McGrann Shea Franzen Carnival Straughn & Lamb, Chartered, provides a broad range of legal services in real estate, corporate, banking, commercial and public financing, municipal utilities, employee benefits, government relations, commercial litigation, environmental, and other areas of commercial law. The firm strives to provide the personal service that enables its clients to compete in the current business climate. *See additional listing in Environmental Law Chapter.*

•**STEPHEN TORVIK** - Nelson Oyen Torvik - 221 North First Street, P.O. Box 656 - Montevideo, MN 56265 - Phone: (612) 269-6461, Fax: (612) 269-8024 - *See complete biographical profile in Publicly Held Corporations Law Chapter.*

KENNETH T. TYRA

Dorsey & Whitney
Pillsbury Center South
220 South Sixth Street
Minneapolis, MN 55402-1498

Phone: (612) 340-8869
Fax: (612) 340-7800

Admitted: 1982 Minnesota;
1986 Michigan;
1986 US Dist. Ct. (W. Dist. MI)
Birthdate: 09/03/57

•**KENNETH T. TYRA:** Mr. Tyra practices in all real estate areas, including leasing, financing, workouts, sales and acquisitions, development, and municipal law. Representative transactions include development, financing, and leasing of several major downtown Minneapolis office buildings and several regional shopping centers; financing for an international airline; financings for shopping center REITs; real estate aspects of several large bank mergers; representation of numerous corporations regarding headquarters leases and regional office, manufacturing, distribution, and sales facilities; general representation of a grocery store chain; and general representation of several real estate developers.
Education: JD 1982, University of Michigan; AB 1979 with highest distinction, University of Michigan (Phi Beta Kappa).
Employment History: Partner 1990-present, Associate 1982-85 and 1987-89, Dorsey & Whitney; Associate 1985-87, Dykema Gossett (Ann Arbor, Bloomfield Hills, and Grand Rapids, MI).
Representative Clients: ADC Telecommunications, Inc., and affiliates; Apertus Technologies Incorporated; Canon USA, Inc., and affiliates; Cargill, Inc., and affiliates; First Bank System, Inc., and affiliates; Gage Marketing Group, LLC; Green Tree Financial Corp.; Lunds, Inc., and affiliates; Northwest Airlines, Inc., and affiliates.
Professional Associations: Building Owners and Managers Assn.; Sensible Land Use Coalition.
Firm: Dorsey & Whitney is the largest law firm in Minnesota and one of the largest firms in the United States with over 350 lawyers in 12 offices. The depth and breadth of the experience of its lawyers enables it to provide a broad range of services to meet the diverse legal needs of its client base, which includes Fortune 500 companies, public agencies, banks and other financial institutions, nonprofit organizations, individual investors, family owned businesses, and high-tech and low-tech, growth oriented companies. *See additional listings in Bankruptcy & Workout Law and Closely Held Business Law Chapters.*

•**PETER L. VOGEL:** Mr. Vogel, a partner in the firm Rosenmeier, Anderson & Vogel, is engaged in the general practice of law, concentrating in real estate. Since 1992, he has been certified by the Minnesota State Bar Association as a Real Property Specialist. Peter Vogel is married to Deborah Ginder, and they have two children.
Education: JD 1978 cum laude, University of Minnesota; BA 1974 summa cum laude, Carleton College.
Employment History: Partner 1982-present, Rosenmeier, Anderson & Vogel; Associate 1979-82, Rosenmeier & Simonett; Law Clerk 1978-79, Hon. Warren F. Plunkett, Third Judicial District (Austin, MN).
Representative Clients: Community Federal Savings & Loan Assn. of Little Falls; City of Little Falls; City of Upsala; American National Bank of Little Falls.
Professional Associations: MSBA (Real Property Section).
Community Involvement: Community Federal Savings & Loan Assn. (Board member); Musser Fund (Board member); Cass Gilbert Depot Society, Inc. (Board member).
Firm: Rosenmeier, Anderson & Vogel has been engaged in the general practice of law in Little Falls since the early 1920s. The firm was founded by Christian Rosenmeier and continued after his death by his son, A. Gordon Rosenmeier (deceased 1989). Gordon Rosenmeier served with distinction in the Minnesota State Senate for over 30 years, ending his career as majority leader. John E. Simonett was a partner in the firm for over 25 years before his elevation to the Minnesota Supreme Court. The present partners of the firm are Douglas Anderson, Peter Vogel, and Brigid Fitzgerald. The firm is engaged in traditional general practice which includes civil litigation of all sorts, personal injury claims, Workers' Compensation, residential, commercial and recreational real estate transactions, family law, probate, banking, and social security claims and related matters. In addition to representing individuals, the firm represents institutional clients including cities in Morrison County, state and federally chartered lending institutions, central Minnesota school districts, and insurance companies.

PETER L. VOGEL

Rosenmeier, Anderson & Vogel
210 Second Street NE
Little Falls, MN 56345

Phone: (612) 632-5458
Fax: (612) 632-5496

Admitted: 1978 Minnesota
Birthdate: 01/16/52

•**CRAIG W. WENDLAND** - Dingle & Wendland, Ltd. - Suite 300, Norwest Center, P.O. Box 939 - Rochester, MN 55903 - Phone: (507) 288-5440, Fax: (507) 281-8288 - *See complete biographical profile in Closely Held Business Law Chapter.*

SHERMAN WINTHROP - Winthrop & Weinstine, P.A. - 3200 Minnesota World Trade Center, 30 East Seventh Street - St. Paul, MN 55101 - Phone: (612) 290-8400, Fax: (612) 292-9347 - *See complete biographical profile in Publicly Held Corporations Law Chapter.*

Chapter 13: Commercial Real Estate Law

Complete listing of all attorneys nominated in Commercial Real Estate Law

Charles H. Andresen, Crassweller, Magie, Andresen, Haag & Paciotti, P.A., Duluth; **John F. Bannigan Jr.**, Bannigan & Kelly, P.A., St. Paul; **Charles Bans**, Maun & Simon, Minneapolis; **Timothy M. Barnett**, Winthrop & Weinstine, P.A., Minneapolis; **Larry J. Berg**, Fredrikson & Byron, P.A., Minneapolis; **Philip F. Boelter**, Dorsey & Whitney, Minneapolis; **John E. Brandt**, Murnane, Conlin, White & Brandt, St. Paul; **Lorens Q. Brynestad**, Brynestad Law Offices, Brooklyn Park; **William M. Burns**, Hanft, Fride, O'Brien, Harries, Swelbar & Burns, P.A., Duluth; **John R. Carroll**, Best & Flanagan, Minneapolis; **James F. Christoffel**, Christoffel, Elliott & Albrecht, P.A., Minneapolis; **Angela M. Christy**, Leonard, Street and Deinard Professional Association, Minneapolis; **Daniel J. Cole Jr.**, Briggs and Morgan, P.A., St. Paul; **Peter L. Cooper**, McGrann Shea Franzen Carnival Straughn & Lamb, Chartered, Minneapolis; **William J. Cosgriff**, Doherty, Rumble & Butler Professional Association, St. Paul; **Stephen J. Davis**, Attorney at Law, Minneapolis; **Ted E. Deaner**, O'Brien, Ehrick, Wolf, Deaner & Maus, Rochester; **James B. Druck**, Southwest Casino & Hotel Ventures, Inc., Minneapolis; **Frederick A. Dudderar**, Hanft, Fride, O'Brien, Harries, Swelbar & Burns, P.A., Duluth; **James A. Dueholm**, Faegre & Benson, Minneapolis; **Ward G. Edgerton**, Edgerton & Theobald, Duluth; **David B. Eide**, Frommelt & Eide, Ltd., Minneapolis; **Orrin S. Estebo**, Estebo, Schnobrich & Frank, Ltd., Redwood Falls; **Charles S. Ferrell**, Faegre & Benson, Minneapolis; **Joseph M. Finley**, Leonard, Street and Deinard Professional Association, Minneapolis; **Roger D. Gordon**, Winthrop & Weinstine, P.A., Minneapolis; **N. Walter Graff**, Best & Flanagan, Minneapolis; **Cheryl L. Grasmoen**, Petersen, Tews & Squires, P.A., Minneapolis; **Andrew E. Hagemann Jr.**, Mork H. Darling Hagemann & Kohler, Worthington; **Mark E. Hamel**, Dorsey & Whitney, Minneapolis; **Lee W. Hanson**, Hall, Byers, Hanson, Steil & Weinberger, P.A., St. Cloud; **Gilbert W. Harries**, Hanft, Fride, O'Brien, Harries, Swelbar & Burns, P.A., Duluth; **William A. Haug**, Moss & Barnett, A Professional Association, Minneapolis; **Charles R. Haynor**, Briggs and Morgan, P.A., Minneapolis; **John D. Healy Jr.**, Oppenheimer, Wolff & Donnelly, St. Paul; **Robert A. Heiberg**, Dorsey & Whitney, Minneapolis; **Karl K. Heinzerling**, Foley & Mansfield, Minneapolis; **John H. Herman**, Leonard, Street and Deinard Professional Association, Minneapolis; **Gordon L. Jensen**, Jensen & Swanson, Brooklyn Park; **Craig W. Johnson**, Hoversten, Strom, Johnson & Rysavy, Austin; **Jeffrey S. Johnson**, Barna, Guzy & Steffen, Ltd., Minneapolis; **Michael D. Johnson**, Frundt Johnson & Roverud, Blue Earth; **David Kantor**, Leonard, Street and Deinard Professional Association, Minneapolis; **David W. Kelley**, Leonard, Street and Deinard Professional Association, Minneapolis; **John M. Koneck**, Fredrikson & Byron, P.A., Minneapolis; **Frederick A. Kueppers Jr.**, Kueppers, Hackel & Kueppers, P.A., St. Paul; **Phillip L. Kunkel**, Hall, Byers, Hanson, Steil & Weinberger, P.A., St. Cloud; **W. Charles Lantz**, Dorsey & Whitney, Rochester; **James F. Marrin**, Schmitt, Marrin & Janson, St. Cloud; **Kathleen M. Martin**, Popham, Haik, Schnobrich & Kaufman, Ltd., Minneapolis; **Richard H. Massopust Jr.**, Oppenheimer, Wolff & Donnelly, Minneapolis; **Thomas M. Mayerle**, Faegre & Benson, Minneapolis; **Hugh M. Maynard**, Lundgren Brothers Real Estate, Wayzata; **Theodore J. Meyer**, Oppenheimer, Wolff & Donnelly, St. Paul; **William G. Meyer**, Meyer Meyer & Pottratz, Melrose; **Franklin Michaels**, Dunlap & Seeger, P.A., Rochester; **John E. Molle**, Molle Law Office, Marshall; **Timothy D. Moratzka**, Mackall, Crounse & Moore, Minneapolis; **Allan E. Mulligan**, Larkin, Hoffman, Daly & Lindgren, Ltd., Bloomington; **Scott C. Neff**, Trenti Law Firm, Virginia; **Roger D. Neils**, Hoolihan & Neils, P.A., St. Cloud; **James M. Neilson**, Babcock, Locher, Neilson & Mannella, Anoka; **Donald P. Norwich**, Oppenheimer, Wolff & Donnelly, Minneapolis; **Bruce G. Odlaug**, Maun & Simon, Minneapolis; **Charles A. Parsons Jr.**, Moss & Barnett, A Professional Association, Minneapolis; **Michael J. Patchin**, Colosimo Patchin Aronsen & Kearney, Ltd., Virginia; **John W. Person**, Breen & Person, Ltd., Brainerd; **David T. Peterson**, Blethen Gage & Krause, Mankato; **Richard A. Peterson**, Best & Flanagan, Minneapolis; **Paul H. Ravich**, Ravich, Meyer, Kirkman & McGrath, P.A., Minneapolis; **Lewis J. Rotman**, Popham, Haik, Schnobrich & Kaufman, Ltd., Minneapolis; **Jonathan P. Scoll**, Doherty, Rumble & Butler, P.A., St. Paul; **Robert J. Silverman**, Dorsey & Whitney, Minneapolis; **James D. Sinclair**, Hummel Sinclair Pearson Evans Hunt & Heisler, P.A., Detroit Lakes; **Ralph T. Smith**, Smith Law Firm, P.A., Bemidji; **William R. Soth**, Dorsey & Whitney, Minneapolis; **David J. Spencer**, Briggs and Morgan, P.A., Minneapolis; **Howard G. Stacker**, Fredrikson & Byron, P.A., Minneapolis; **James P. Stephenson**, Faegre & Benson, Minneapolis; **Robert H. Stephenson**, Trenti Law Firm, Virginia; **Michael R. Stewart**, Faegre & Benson, Minneapolis; **Robert O. Straughn**, McGrann Shea Franzen Carnival Straughn & Lamb, Chartered, Minneapolis; **Jon E. Strinden**, Gunhus, Grinnell, Klinger, Swenson & Guy, Ltd., Moorhead; **Cindy K. Telstad**, Streeter, Murphy, Gernander, Forsythe, Winona; **Greig R. Tennis**, Tennis Casterton & Sicheneder, Forest Lake; **John W. Thiel**, Gray, Plant, Mooty, Mooty & Bennett, P.A., Minneapolis; **Frederick L. Thorson**, Mackall, Crounse & Moore, Minneapolis; **Stephen Torvik**, Nelson Oyen Torvik, Montevideo; **Ralph H. Tully**, Strong, Tully, Tully & Crouch, Minneapolis; **Kenneth T. Tyra**, Dorsey & Whitney, Minneapolis; **Marinus W. Van Putten Jr.**, Best & Flanagan, Minneapolis; **Peter L. Vogel**, Rosenmeier, Anderson & Vogel, Little Falls; **Steven C. Wellman**, Runchey Louwagie & Wellman, Marshall; **Craig W. Wendland**, Dingle & Wendland, Ltd., Rochester; **Mark W. Westra**, Fabyanske, Svoboda, Westra, Davis & Hart, Minneapolis; **John R. Wheaton**, Faegre & Benson, Minneapolis; **Stephen R. Young**, Drahos & Young, Bemidji.

CHAPTER
14

CRIMINAL LAW

Business owners increasingly need to be aware of how they can run afoul of criminal laws in the operation of their businesses. Newspapers today are so full of reports of corporate criminal investigations and prosecutions that most business owners do not even realize that there was once a time that business entities were thought to be incapable of committing crimes. Under the common law, corporations were considered artificial constructs without minds of their own and, thus, incapable of forming the intent necessary to be guilty of a crime. All this has changed. Today, businesses and the people who run them risk substantial criminal liability for their business activities. During the last two decades, both the federal and state governments have dramatically increased the number of criminal investigations of businesses and the people who run them.

There are many reasons for the increased attention paid to business crimes. Political pressures often force public prosecutors to pursue corporate defendants in order to avoid the public perception that criminal laws punish only the poor and disadvantaged. High profile prosecutions of large corporations are applauded by the press, consumers, and special interest groups. Such cases can help politicians win re-election and often help to advance the careers of ambitious young public prosecutors. All signs point to a continued interest in business prosecutions, so business owners and corporate executives need to have a basic understanding of how criminal laws can impact their businesses.

A myriad of regulatory laws can trip up even a conscientious business owner or manager. This chapter is designed to acquaint the reader with criminal statutes that most affect businesses and the steps that businesses can take to avoid criminal liability.

CRIMINAL LIABILITY OF A CORPORATION

As mentioned earlier, corporations were once thought to be incapable of forming the intent necessary to commit a crime. This attitude has now been swept away and corporations can be found guilty even of crimes requiring specific intent. The Minnesota Supreme Court typically uses a three-part test to determine whether a corporation is guilty of a crime committed by one of its agents. First, the corporation's employee must have had authority to act for the corporation and must have been acting within the scope of his or her authority when the allegedly criminal activity took place. Second, the employee must have been acting to further the corporation's business interests. Third, for crimes not requiring specific intent, the employee's actions must have been authorized, tolerated, or ratified by the corporation's management.

Additionally, the Minnesota Supreme Court has held that for a corporation to be vicariously liable for the actions of one of its employees, the employee's actions must not have been a personal aberration on the part of the employee acting alone, but must, in some way, reflect a corporate policy. However, it is possible that the corporation can be held criminally liable even if the employee was acting contrary to corporate policies at the time of the infraction. This corporate responsibility applies in cases where the employee was acting to benefit the corporation and in which the corporation was not the victim of the crime.

CRIMINAL LIABILITY OF A CORPORATE OFFICER OR AGENT

In addition to the corporation's liability, corporate officers and agents can be personally liable for their criminal conduct. Some businesspersons mistakenly believe that criminal liability is an either/or proposition—that if their actions subject the business to criminal liability, they personally will be free of liability. This belief is incorrect, as many criminal statutes allow prosecutors to go after the business and the individuals who run it. Individual and corporate liability are cumulative, not exclusive.

Participation in business criminal activity does not, by itself, make a person criminally liable. Usually the prosecution must show that the participating officer or agent consciously promoted the illicit scheme. Ordering a subordinate to commit a crime or silently acquiescing to another's commission of a crime can make almost any officer or agent personally liable for the crime. In addition, some officers within a corporation have even been held responsible for criminal activity of which they were unaware because they had an obligation to ensure compliance with the law or to detect and prevent violations of criminal regulations. The law does not look kindly on corporate officers who claim to have been asleep at the helm while their subordinates were engaging in criminal activity. Especially in the context of environmental regulations, with their substantial penalties, the defenses "I did not know" and "I was not aware" fall on deaf ears if the court or jury believes the officer should have known or had an obligation to be aware of what was happening in the company.

WHITE COLLAR CRIME

White collar crime is the most common type of business crime. The term "white collar crime" is generally used to describe crimes that have cheating and dishonesty as their common basis. These crimes are typically committed by professionals or entrepreneurs under cover of legitimate business activity. Such crimes can be difficult to prosecute because of their complexity, and they can carry lesser penalties because they are not associated with violence. However, as discussed in the introduction to this chapter, political and public pressures are leading to more frequent prosecutions for a wide variety of white collar crimes.

As a practical matter, it is impossible to describe every activity that can fit within the definition of white collar crime, because white collar crime can take so many forms.

SPECIFIC WHITE COLLAR CRIMINAL LAWS
Some criminal actions are prohibited by specific laws narrowly drawn to outlaw a particular activity.

Antitrust

Most businesspersons with experience in antitrust law have learned two things: antitrust laws are complicated, and the federal government's enthusiasm for enforcing antitrust laws comes and goes with political changes in Washington, D.C. In times of strict enforcement, a person can violate antitrust laws in many areas: mergers and acquisitions, pricing policy, terms of trade, customer and territory selection, bundling of services, and even advertising and sales technology. In periods of lax enforcement, it can seem that a business can do anything it wants to its competitors. The truth is that antitrust legislation and caselaw are very complex and although enforcement has never entirely died, it has varied widely as political winds have shifted direction. Only an experienced antitrust attorney who stays abreast of current developments in this area can adequately advise businesses how to avoid antitrust problems.

Persons found in violation of certain aspects of the Sherman Antitrust Act—the primary antitrust law—can be fined or jailed. Violations of this act include making contracts that unreasonably restrain trade and attempts to form and maintain a monopoly in an industry. In practice, however, these violations are generally handled with civil, rather than criminal, lawsuits.

Securities Fraud & Insider Trading

A broad range of illegal behavior is prosecuted under securities fraud statutes. Persons who violate securities laws can be subject to criminal penalties, civil penalties, or both; criminal prosecutions require the prosecutor to show that the accused acted willfully. The securities fraud statutes recognize that deception can take many forms and thus are broadly worded as to prohibit "any device, scheme or artifice to defraud" in securities sales. There are two general categories of securities fraud. The first involves the sale of securities to investors for far more than their actual value. The second involves the sale of legitimate securities for illegal purposes. An example of the first type of fraud is selling shares in dry oil wells. An example of the second type of fraud is a brokerage house selling a legitimate stock but concealing information about its own involvement with the company, thus acting in violation of rules established by the Securities and Exchange Commission.

Insider trading prosecutions have been some of the most publicized white collar prosecutions of the 1980s and 90s. Surprisingly, "insider trading" is not defined in any specific statute; it is a colloquial term used to describe a category of wrongdoings whereby insiders take unfair advantage of information to make money or avoid losing money in securities. Generally, insider trading means that an insider (such as an officer of a corporation) with material, non-public information engages in trading without first disclosing that information to the public. Insider trading cases are typically prosecuted under the Securities and Exchange Act of 1934. Further information about that act can be found in the Securities & Venture Finance Law Chapter.

Prosecutors are not confined to using specific securities fraud statutes to prosecute securities fraud. General anti-fraud statutes are frequently used instead of, or in addition to, specific securities fraud laws. For example, parties engaged in securities fraud can be charged with violating mail and wire fraud statutes, discussed below in this chapter.

Computer Crime

Computer crime is an area of the law where the government appears to be perpetually playing catch-up with the growth in new technologies. Some variations of computer crime are so new that laws drafted specifically to combat them do not exist and more general laws without a computer emphasis fit the facts poorly.

Today, six types of conduct are specifically outlawed by federal statute:

- Knowingly accessing a computer without authorization or exceeding authorization, and thereby obtaining confidential national security information

- Intentionally accessing a computer without authorization or exceeding authorization, and thereby obtaining the financial information of a financial institution or of a credit card issuer

- Intentionally, without authorization, accessing a computer of a federal department or agency used exclusively by that department or agency or affecting the government's use thereof

- Knowingly, and with intent to defraud, accessing a federal interest computer without authorization or exceeding authorization to further a fraud or obtain anything of value

- Intentionally accessing a federal interest computer without authorization to alter, damage, or destroy information and thereby causing a loss of $1000 or, if medical information is affected, any amount

- Knowingly, and with intent to defraud, trafficking in any password or similar information through which a computer is accessed without authorization if such computer affects interstate or foreign commerce or is used by or for the government

Catch-All White Collar Criminal Laws

Some actions are not covered by one of the above specific laws but instead are prosecuted under one or more "catch-all" laws criminalizing dishonest behavior generally. Most of these laws have parameters so broad that they can be made to fit a wide variety of dishonest actions.

Perjury

Federal perjury laws penalize anyone who willfully or knowingly makes false statements under oath. The sworn statements may be written or oral and need not be made in court; a person can perjure himself or herself in depositions and written testimony. A related law against subornation of perjury makes it illegal for anyone to procure another person to commit perjury.

Travel Act

Under the federal Travel Act, it is a criminal offense to use interstate travel or facilities in interstate commerce to distribute the proceeds from any unlawful activity, to commit a crime of violence to further any unlawful activity, or to otherwise promote or facilitate unlawful activity.

Hobbs Act

Under the federal Hobbs Act, it is a crime for anyone to obstruct, delay, or affect commerce by extortion, robbery, or threats of physical violence. The terms "robbery" and "violence" are very broadly defined to cover a wide variety of violent actions against people or property.

Racketeer Influenced and Corrupt Organizations Act

The Racketeer Influenced and Corrupt Organizations Act (RICO) was established to combat the influence of organized crime on legitimate businesses. Under federal criminal law, defendants can be found guilty of violating RICO if they are found to have engaged in "racketeering activity" under the auspices of an enterprise that affects interstate commerce, or if they are involved in the collection of an unlawful debt. There are nine state and 35 federal offenses specifically listed as racketeering activity. The nine listed state offenses are murder, kidnapping, gambling, robbery, arson, bribery, dealing in obscene materials, and dealing in narcotics or other dangerous drugs. RICO has a civil-law dimension that accompanies its criminal provisions. While drug smuggling, murder, bribery, and extortion of "protection money" are examples of the activities to which RICO was originally applied, more recently it has been used to prosecute a bewildering variety of criminal actions.

In the first years after it was passed, RICO was a rarely used criminal law. Today, RICO charges are quite common, largely because its provisions have been interpreted expansively to cover many situations where there is no allegation whatsoever that the defendant has any connection to organized crime.

In addition to its criminal provisions, RICO gives private parties and the federal government civil causes of action against violators. Because RICO prosecutions have grown so unpredictably in recent years, calls are frequently heard to redraft the law more narrowly. Civil RICO provisions especially have received extensive criticism and are the most likely to be changed.

Embezzlement

To embezzle means to take another's money and property through abuse of an official job or position of trust. Embezzlement can take many forms. An accountant might use sophisticated methods to falsify records and skim profits, while a bank teller might simply walk home with an extra $20 from his or her drawer.

Fraud

Fraud is intentionally lying in order to induce someone into relying upon the lie to part with something of value. Like embezzlement, fraud can be either complex or simple. The federal government has three general anti-fraud statutes for mail fraud, bank fraud, and wire fraud.

Mail fraud is a broad crime punished under the United States Code. Mail fraud has two elements: 1) a scheme devised or intending to defraud or for obtaining property or money by fraudulent means, and 2) using the mails in furtherance of that fraudulent scheme.

Because the mail fraud statute uses such broad language and because it is relatively easy to prove, mail fraud is one of the most common charges brought by federal prosecutors. Observers sometimes chuckle when notorious criminals suspected of committing heinous crimes are charged with mere mail fraud, but procedurally, it is easier to get a conviction under the mail fraud statute than under more complex criminal statutes. Charges of mail fraud are frequently brought even in cases where more specific charges are brought. The two can exist side by side. The "scheme to defraud" element of mail fraud is deliberately broad. It encompasses a wide variety of criminal activity, including credit card fraud, securities fraud, medical drug fraud, and frauds based on political malfeasance.

The federal wire fraud statute is similar to the mail fraud statute, but requires an interstate or foreign transmittal of a communication by wire, radio, or television. This interstate requirement sets wire fraud apart from mail fraud; an intrastate mailing is sufficient to trigger liability for mail fraud, while an intrastate wire, radio, or television communication is insufficient grounds for wire fraud liability.

The federal bank fraud statute criminalizes the conduct of any party who "knowingly executes, or attempts to execute, a scheme or artifice to defraud a financial institution, by means of false or fraudulent pretenses, representations, or promises." The federal bank fraud statute is much newer than either the mail fraud or wire fraud statutes, so it has not received a great deal of interpretation in the courts. Because its language is so similar to that which is used in the mail and wire fraud statutes, it is expected to be similarly broadly applied and interpreted.

Conspiracy

Conspiracy is the term for a broad category of crimes involving multiple actors coming together to engage in concerted criminal activity. A person or business is generally guilty of conspiracy to commit a crime if that person or business either (a) with the purpose of facilitating or promoting its commission, agrees with another person or business that they will engage in conduct that constitutes a crime or an attempt or solicitation of a crime, or (b) agrees to aid another person or business in planning, committing, or attempting to solicit a crime. Specific federal anti-conspiracy statutes can be found throughout the United States Code. Minnesota Statutes also contain many anti-conspiracy laws. In recent years, a growing number of white collar criminal prosecutions have included allegations of conspiracy.

Bringing a conspiracy charge offers the prosecution several distinct advantages. Prosecutors usually learn of a conspiracy while it is in an early stage; thus, they can prosecute before the underlying crime takes place. In addition, prosecutors are often able to charge many defendants simultaneously and present evidence against the group. When several defendants stand trial together, juries often perceive individual defendants to be guilty by virtue of their association with the others. Several technical procedural rules also give prosecutors distinct advantages against defendants in conspiracy cases.

Often the key element in prosecuting a defendant for conspiracy is proving the agreement. The agreement that forms the basis for conspiracy need not be written, oral, or even explicit, but is often inferred from the facts of the specific case. If the parties meet and reach an understanding to work for a common purpose, there is an agreement. For example, if the producers of a particular product meet to exchange information on prices, and later they set identical prices, a prosecutor may be able to prove they conspired to set prices even though there was never an explicit agreement to do so. Most criminal conspiracy statutes also require that at least one of the parties has committed an overt act in furtherance of the conspiracy.

A procedural issue of great importance to parties accused of conspiracy is whether government prosecutors try to frame the conspiracy as a "hub-and-spoke conspiracy" or a "chain conspiracy." In a hub-and-spoke conspiracy, many parties (the spokes), conspire with one person (the hub) but not with other defendants. It is advantageous for a defendant to have its actions characterized as part of a hub-and-spoke conspiracy because that means that the conspiracies are separate and disconnected.

In contrast to a hub-and-spoke conspiracy, a chain conspiracy involves several parties as links in one long criminal chain. Defendants in chain conspiracies are responsible for the actions of all participants in the chain, even if they never met some of the other participants in the chain.

Obstruction of Justice

Obstruction of justice is a category of offenses that interfere with the three branches of government. Obstruction of justice can take many forms, including assaulting a process server, improperly influencing a juror, stealing or altering a record of process, obstructing a criminal investigation by officers of a financial institution, and picketing, parading, or using sound amplification devices in front of a courthouse, a building or residence occupied by a judge, juror, witness, or court officer.

Bribery & Extortion

A number of federal statutes prohibit bribery and extortion. A common goal of most bribery statutes is to prevent people from improperly seeking preferential treatment from public officials and to prevent public officers from using their office for personal gain. Under a statute prohibiting bribery of federal government officials, both the official and the person offering the bribe are subject to prosecution if the official is offered or seeks anything of value for himself or herself in exchange for being influenced to perform any official act; committing, aiding, conspiring, or allowing a fraud to be committed upon the United States; or being induced to do or omitting to do anything in violation of his or her official duty. Promises and offers are equally prohibited, so there is no requirement that the bribe actually occur. A separate federal statute, known as the Foreign Corrupt Practices Act, prohibits bribery of foreign officials.

AVOIDING WHITE COLLAR CRIMINAL LIABILITY

No company can ever ensure that every one of its employees will always be perfectly virtuous and perfectly vigilant in doing his or her job. Many businesspeople are tempted at least once to violate some minor law, and some laws are so complex that even knowing one's legal responsibilities under it can be difficult. For these reasons, most business owners and executives need to know how they can avoid white collar criminal liability.

In the area of white collar crimes, an ounce of prevention is worth a pound of cure. Attorneys experienced in handling white collar criminal matters can be a good source of information for helping businesses establish internal procedures to prevent wrongdoing by employees. An attorney experienced in the regulatory area can be an excellent source of information for helping managers understand their responsibilities for overseeing corporate employee's actions and reporting accidents and wrongdoing.

Internal investigations are an integral part of the defense of almost all businesses accused of criminal wrongdoing. Whenever a company learns that it may be the subject of a criminal prosecution, it is important to notify management quickly and to act to resolve the situation. Sometimes a business can avoid criminal liability altogether if it can show that it took proper action to correct a situation as soon as managers were made aware of a problem. Prosecutors often treat leniently companies that can show they acted responsibly after being informed of a problem in the organization.

The internal investigation carries risks of its own, however. It may be wisest to have the investigation conducted by outside legal counsel. Using an attorney from outside the company can prevent the ultimate report from being used at trial as evidence against the company. Attorney-client privilege and the work product doctrine may ensure that the corporation's officers will not be required to reveal the contents of the final report to prosecutors.

No business should ever try to obstruct a government investigation into its affairs by using a tactic that could conceivably look like a cover-up or obstruction of justice. Being honest with all employees, if secrecy is necessary, and fully explaining the employees' responsibilities can be excellent preventive medicine against criminal liability. Any employee asked to keep anything secret for reasons he or she does not understand may assume his or her employer is involved in illegal activity and so testify later.

RESOURCES

Business Crime—Criminal Liability of the Business Community. Matthew Bender, 1994.

Internal Corporate Investigations—Conducting Them, Protecting Them. Brad D. Brian & Barry F. McNeil, editors, Section of Litigation, American Bar Association, 1989.

Antitrust for Business—Questions & Answers. Eliot G. Disner, Federal Legal Publications, Inc., 1989.

CRIMINAL LAW LEADING ATTORNEYS

The attorneys profiled in this section were nominated by their peers in a statewide survey conducted in 1993 in which several thousand Minnesota attorneys were asked to name the lawyer to whom they would send a friend or family member in need of legal assistance in the area of *Criminal Law*.

Because the survey resulted in a list of less than five percent of Minnesota's practicing attorneys, this should not be construed as a complete list. Nevertheless, it is an excellent source of highly qualified and reputable attorneys, who, if unable to assist can in most cases make quality referrals.

A list of all attorneys nominated in this category is found at the end of this section. For information on the survey methodology see page ix.

Please note that the shorter, two line attorney listings in this section are of attorneys who practice in this area but whose full biographical profile appears in another section of this book. A bullet "•" preceeding name indicates the attorney was nominated in this particular area of law. For information on the format of these profiles, consult the section "Using the *Business Guidebook*" found on page xiv. Note that the following abbreviations are used throughout these profiles:

Selected by Attorneys for GUIDEBOOK
Law & Leading Attorneys
MINNESOTA

The attorneys profiled below were recommended by their peers in a statewide survey.

App.	- Appellate	ABA	- American Bar Association
Cir.	- Circuit	ATLA	- American Trial Lawyers Association
Ct.	- Court	HCBA	- Hennepin County Bar Association
Dist.	- District	MDLA	- Minnesota Defense Lawyers Association
Hon.	- Honorable	MSBA	- Minnesota State Bar Association
JD	- Law degree (Juris Doctor)	MTLA	- Minnesota Trial Lawyers Association
LLB	- Law degree	NBTA	- National Board of Trial Advocacy
LLM	- Master in Law degree	RCBA	- Ramsey County Bar Association
Sup.	- Supreme		

•**BAILEY W. BLETHEN** - Blethen Gage & Krause - 127 South Second Street, P.O. Box 3049 - Mankato, MN 56002-3049 - Phone: (507) 345-1166, Fax: (507) 345-8003 - *See complete biographical profile in Employment Law Chapter.*

•**JOSEPH P. BLUTH:** Mr. Bluth concentrates primarily on serious felony cases, including sexual misconduct, environmental, white collar, alcohol (DWI) and drug related, child abuse, and other complex cases. As a member of the American Academy of Matrimonial Lawyers, Mr. Bluth handles cases with an emphasis on custody disputes and cases involving dysfunction in the family due to alcoholism, addiction, or abuse. He is also very experienced in handling high profile cases involving professionals and sensitive matters.
Education: JD 1977 cum laude, Hamline University; BA 1975, Mankato State University.
Employment History: Currently, Manahan & Bluth Law Office, Chartered; Assistant County Attorney, Todd County Attorney's Office; US Army 1968-71, Vietnam: 1969-71, Citations: Paratrooper, Bronze Star, Army Medal of Commendation.
Professional Associations: American Academy of Matrimonial Lawyers, Minnesota Chapter (Board of Governors); Minnesota Society for Criminal Justice (past President); ATLA; MTLA; National Assn. of Criminal Defense Lawyers; Todd County Child Protection Team (past member).
Community Involvement: Litchfield Chapter of Rotary International (past President); Cub Scouts (past Packmaster for Troop 98); School District 77 (past lecturer on Art Masterpieces).
Firm: Founded in 1972, Manahan & Bluth is a professional corporation specializing in complex trial work, civil and criminal, including automobile accidents, environmental, white collar crime, and family law. The firm has handled numerous appeals to the Supreme Court and serves clients in southern Minnesota and Wisconsin. Manahan & Bluth uses advanced computers and a vast network of resources to assist in difficult cases. The firm's staff is adept at communications and the use of technology to provide cost-effective service. *See additional listing in Environmental Law Chapter.*

JOSEPH P. BLUTH

Manahan & Bluth Law Office, Chartered
416 South Front Street
P.O. Box 287
Mankato, MN 56001

Phone: (507) 387-5661
Fax: (507) 387-2111

Admitted: 1978 Minnesota;
1991 Wisconsin;
1978 US Dist. Ct. (MN);
1994 US Sup. Ct.
Birthdate: 01/05/50

Chapter 14: Criminal Law

FREDERIC BRUNO

Frederic Bruno & Associates
5500 Wayzata Boulevard
Suite 730
Minneapolis, MN 55416

Phone: (612) 545-7900
Fax: (612) 545-0834

Admitted: 1980 Minnesota;
1980 US Dist. Ct. (MN)
Birthdate: 11/14/55

•**FREDERIC BRUNO:** Mr. Bruno practices trial and appellate law exclusively in the area of criminal defense, with emphasis on complex financial, political, and constitutional cases. Mr. Bruno is a faculty member of the Criminal Justice Institute, the Judicial Trial Skills Training Program at the University of Minnesota Law School, an advisor for the ABA Criminal Trial Competition at Hamline University Law School, and serves as a referee (1985-present) for the Hennepin County District Court. Mr. Bruno is the author of numerous articles, including "Disorder in the Court: Probation Violations in Minnesota," *Challenger*, Summer 1993 and currently, "Notes & Trends," *Bench & Bar*. He is listed in the *Bar Register of Preeminent Attorneys*.
Education: JD 1980, St. Louis University; BA 1977, Stanford University.
Employment History: 1980-present, self-employed; Clerk 1978-80, Law Office of Thomas R. Green (St. Louis, MO); Clerk 1978, Rhode Island Attorney General (major felony prosecution).
Representative Clients: Successful outcomes to the following high-profile cases: *US v. Bolstad, Nichols and Newhouse* (savings and loan fraud); *US v. Anderson* (money laundering); *State v. Green* (election fraud, perjury); *State v. Clausen* (controlled substance penalties); *State v. Lov* (bond reinstatement); *State v. Moran* (boating while intoxicated); *South Dakota In re J.A.* (manslaughter); *State v. Gilbert* (felony assault on police officer); *State v. Grengs* (gang rape); *State v. Officer Gary Lotton* (illegal home search).
Professional Associations: MSBA (Chair 1993-94, Criminal Section; Editor-in-Chief, *Criminal Law News*); HCBA (Criminal Committee); Minnesota Society for Criminal Justice (past President); National Assn. of Criminal Defense Lawyers; Minnesota Assn. of Criminal Defense Lawyers.
Firm: Frederic Bruno has been actively engaged in criminal defense for 14 years. Mr. Bruno is a frequent speaker at criminal law seminars for attorneys, prosecutors, and judges, and has been a commentator on WCCO radio, Minnesota Public Radio, and the Fox network.

DANIEL A. ELLER

Eller Law Office
925 First Street South
St. Cloud, MN 56302

Phone: (612) 253-3700
Fax: (612) 253-5105

Admitted: 1970 Minnesota;
1970 US Dist. Ct. (MN)
Birthdate: 01/19/41

•**DANIEL A. ELLER:** Mr. Eller has over 20 years experience in criminal and civil trial practice in central Minnesota. In addition to his private practice, he served from 1973 through 1990 as Public Defender, with 13 years as District Public Defender for the Seventh Judicial District. In both his private practice and as Public Defender, Mr. Eller has represented individuals charged with murder, assault, robbery, criminal sexual conduct, drug-related crimes and alcohol-related traffic offenses. Mr. Eller has tried cases of statewide notoriety, including *State v. Karr* (pipe bomber) and *State v. Rairdon* (First Degree Murder). Some of his successful defenses include *State v. Neu* (First Degree Murder), *State v. Barnes* (attempted First Degree Murder), *State v. Morris* (attempted First Degree Murder), *State v. Brist* (First Degree Murder), and *State v. Wipper* (First Degree Murder). Since resigning as District Public Defender in 1990, Mr. Eller has continued in St. Cloud in private practice, specializing in criminal defense. His practice also includes civil trial and family law.
Education: JD 1969, Georgetown University; BA 1965, St. John's University.
Employment History: Private Practice, 1970-present; Seventh District Public Defender, 1976-90; Law Clerk 1969-70, Hon. Miles Lord, US District Court, District of Minnesota.
Community Involvement: Frequent guest speaker at local schools and organizations covering legal topics and concerns; lecturer at St. Cloud State University; instructor in criminal law at St. John's University. Mr. Eller has volunteered his time to various charitable and service organizations.

Criminal Law Leading Attorneys

•**JOSEPH S. FRIEDBERG:** Mr. Friedberg is a well known, highly respected trial lawyer who has litigated both common law and white collar criminal cases in state and federal courts across the US. He has attained acquittals in many notable cases including the only two homicide acquittals by the use of the insanity defense in Hennepin County in the last 50 years. Mr. Friedberg has participated in complex litigation and was lead counsel in *Breland v. Aetna*, the first major class action settlement of a product liability/personal injury action in history. *Breland v. Aetna* brought about the Dalkon Shield Trust which is paying out millions of dollars to women injured by the Dalkon Shield. He is certified by the National Board of Trial Advocacy as a Criminal Trial Specialist. He lectures on trial tactics and skills, and has served as adjunct professor of law at William Mitchell College and as guest lecturer at the University of Minnesota School of Law.
Education: JD 1963 with honors, Order of the Coif, University of North Carolina (Recipient 1963, Justice Clark Award; Associate Editor 1962-63, *University of North Carolina Law Review*; Best Individual Oral List 1963, Phillip Jessup Competition); BS 1959, University of North Carolina.
Employment History: 1974-present, Joseph S. Friedberg, Chartered; Of counsel 1992-present, Winthrop & Weinstein, P.A.; 1972-74, Thomson, Wylde, Norby, Friedberg & Rapoport; Teaching Fellow 1963-64, Stanford University Law School.
Professional Associations: HCBA (Chairman 1979-80, Criminal Law Committee, Criminal Law Section); MSBA (Criminal Law Section); ABA (Section on Criminal Justice); National Assn. of Criminal Defense Lawyers; Minnesota Assn. of Criminal Defense Lawyers; Assn. of Trial Lawyers of America; American Board of Trial Advocates; American Board of Criminal Lawyers (1987-present, Executive Committee); 1980-present, Eighth Circuit Practice Committee.

JOSEPH S. FRIEDBERG

Friedberg Law Office
250 Second Avenue South
Suite 205
Minneapolis, MN 55401

Phone: (612) 339-8626
Fax: (612) 339-8627

Admitted: 1966 Minnesota; 1970 US Dist. Ct. (MN); 1975 US Ct. App. (8th Cir.); 1974 US Sup. Ct.
Birthdate: 03/02/37

•**BRUCE H. HANLEY:** Mr. Hanley practices criminal defense trial law in state and federal court, concentrating in white collar criminal defense, specifically, money laundering, bank fraud, environmental crimes, racketeering, continuing criminal enterprise, conspiracy, and Medicare/Medicaid fraud. His clients include corporations and professionals accused of criminal activity. Mr. Hanley is certified as a Criminal Trial Specialist by the National Board of Trial Advocates and has been a member of the Academy of Certified Trial Lawyers of Minnesota since 1986. He is the author of articles on sentencing guidelines and has been an adjunct professor of law at William Mitchell and Hamline University. He was profiled as a "Champion" in *Champion*, June 1991, by the National Association of Criminal Defense Lawyers.
Education: JD 1976, William Mitchell; BSB 1972 with honors, University of Minnesota.
Employment History: Of Counsel 1985-present, Dunkley, Bennett & Christensen; Attorney 1979-85, Hanley, Hergott & Hunziker; Sole practitioner 1976-78.
Representative Clients: Joseph Balzer in *US v. Prouse* (second officer, flying while under the influence); Steven Goethke in *US v. Long* (money laundering charges); defendants in the following cases: *US v. John Martin Wood* (allegations of manufacturing fentanyl), *US v. John Richard Sazenski* (bank fraud, false statements, money laundering), *US v. Technical Ordinance* (allegations of violations of the importation, manufacture, dealing, storage, and distribution of explosive materials; false statements; and conspiracy), *State of Minnesota v. John Heinz, MD* (criminal sexual conduct).
Professional Associations: MN Assn. of Criminal Defense Lawyers (President 1992-93, Treasurer 1990-91, Vice President 1991-92, Board of Directors 1990-93); ABA; MSBA; HCBA; Federal Bar Assn.; National Assn. of Criminal Defense Lawyers; MTLA; MN Advocates for Human Rights; US Federal Court Public Defender Panel.
Community Involvement: Breck High School (advisor, Mock Trial Court).
Firm: Bruce H. Hanley, P.A., with lawyers Bruce Hanley and Lisa Dejoras, is a criminal defense law firm practicing primarily in the areas of white collar criminal defense in state and federal court.

BRUCE H. HANLEY

Bruce H. Hanley, P.A.
701 Fourth Avenue South
Suite 700
Minneapolis, MN 55415

Phone: (612) 339-1290
Fax: (612) 339-7509

Admitted: 1976 Minnesota; 1976 US Dist. Ct. (MN); 1985 US Ct. App. (8th Cir.); 1983 US Sup. Ct.; admitted Pro Hac Vice to eight other district courts and to US Ct. App. (5th Cir.)
Birthdate: 05/31/50

Chapter 14: Criminal Law

DOUGLAS A. KELLEY

Douglas A. Kelley, P.A.
701 Fourth Avenue South
Suite 500
Minneapolis, MN 55415

Phone: (612) 337-9594
Fax: (612) 371-0574

Admitted: 1974 Minnesota;
1974 US Dist. Ct. (MN);
1979 US Ct. App. (8th Cir.)
Birthdate: 09/29/46

•**DOUGLAS A. KELLEY:** Mr. Kelley is a trial attorney who practices in federal and state courts concentrating primarily in the areas of white collar crime defense and complex civil litigation. He represents corporations and individuals in a wide range of areas, including mail fraud, bank fraud, health care fraud, RICO, breach of contract, and gaming law. Mr. Kelley is involved in high-profile litigation. He represented the plaintiffs in *La Société Générale Immobilière (LSGI) v. The City of Minneapolis*, in which a federal jury awarded $34 million to LSGI for breach of contract. As an Assistant US Attorney, he received the Department of Justice Meritorious Achievement Award for prosecuting *US v. Deil Gustafson and Joseph Agosto*, a Las Vegas casino bank fraud case involving the mafia. Mr. Kelley also corepresents the plaintiffs in a federal class action against Edina Realty.
Education: JD 1974 cum laude, University of Minnesota (President, *Minnesota Law Review* and author, "Sex Discrimination in High School Athletics," 57 *Minn. L. Rev.* 339 (1974)); BA 1968 summa cum laude, University of Minnesota (Phi Beta Kappa).
Employment History: Currently, Douglas A. Kelley, P.A.; Partner and Senior Trial Attorney 1989-91, Mahoney, Walling & Kelley; Chief of Staff 1985-89, US Senator Dave Durenberger; Partner 1984-85, Mauzy and Kelley, P.A.; Assistant US Attorney 1978-84, District of Minnesota; Trial Attorney 1974-78, Holmes, Eustis, Kircher & Graven.
Representative Clients: First Bank Minneapolis; La Société Générale Immobilière; Katun Corporation; Northwest Airlines; Little Six, Inc.; Grand Casino; US West; HealthSpan.
Professional Associations: Federal Bar Assn.; ABA; MSBA; HCBA.
Community Involvement: Outward Bound (Board of Trustees); Minnesota Orchestral Assn. (Board of Trustees).
Firm: Douglas A. Kelley, P.A. is a three lawyer firm. Doug Kelley and John Lee are former federal fraud and major crimes prosecutors. Steve Wolter is a former state prosecutor with federal regulatory experience. They form the nucleus of this boutique litigation firm that contracts with a number of ex-federal agents (IRS, FBI, Postal Inspectors) to conduct its investigations. The firm is uniquely situated to conduct investigations into civil or criminal fraud and conduct internal corporate investigations. *See additional listings in Publicly Held Corporations Law and Health Law Chapters.*

ROGER J. MAGNUSON - Dorsey & Whitney - Pillsbury Center South, 220 South Sixth Street - Minneapolis, MN 55402-1498 - Phone: (612) 340-2738, Fax: (612) 340-2868 - *See complete biographical profile in Commercial Litigation Chapter.*

ROBERT G. MALONE

Attorney at Law
386 North Wabasha Street
Suite 780
St. Paul, MN 55102

Phone: (612) 227-6549
Fax: (612) 224-6151

Admitted: 1978 Minnesota;
1978 MN Sup. Ct.;
1979 US Dist. Ct (MN);
1989 US Ct. App. (8th Cir.);
1993 US Ct. App. (7th Cir.)
Birthdate: 01/30/52

•**ROBERT G. MALONE:** Mr. Malone specializes in criminal defense and is one of 19 certified Criminal Trial Specialists in the state. He has more than 20 jury acquittals on cases ranging from minor offenses, to complex bank fraud, to first degree murder.
Education: JD 1978, William Mitchell; BA 1974, University of Minnesota.
Employment History: Solo practice since leaving practice with Joseph S. Friedberg in 1989.
Representative Clients: Mr. Malone has extensive experience representing accountants, architects, attorneys, bankers, chief executive officers, dentists, comptrollers, educators, nurses, pharmacists, physicians, policemen, realtors, and stockbrokers, both in criminal and professional misconduct accusations.
Professional Associations: MSBA; RCBA; MTLA; National Assn. of Criminal Defense Lawyers; Minnesota Assn. of Criminal Defense Lawyers (Cochair, Lawyers Strike Force); Minnesota Society for Criminal Justice; Federal Defender Panel.

•**RONALD I. MESHBESHER:** Mr. Meshbesher practices criminal law in state and federal courts nationwide. Among the many major cases he has won are the Dalkon Shield Fraud trial, Long Cadillac money laundering case, and the Weisberg gambling case. He has authored several publications on trial practice including the acclaimed *Trial Lawyers Handbook for Minnesota* (1992) and has held several leadership positions in professional trial organizations. Mr. Meshbesher lectures frequently to lawyers' organizations including the American Bar Association, the Association of Trial Lawyers of America, the National Association of Criminal Defense Lawyers, the Atlanta Bar Association Super Star Seminars 1982-84, the National College of Advocacy, and the National Institute of Trial Advocacy. He is listed in every edition of *The Best Lawyers in America*; "Best Lawyers in the United States," *Town & Country*, June 1985; *Who's Who in American Law*; and *Who's Who in the World*. He was recognized as one of Minnesota's Winningest Trial Lawyers by *Minnesota Lawyer* (1991) and was awarded Minnesota Lawyer's Judges' Choice Awards, *Minnesota Lawyer* (1991).
Education: JD 1957, University of Minnesota; BSL 1955, University of Minnesota.
Employment History: Permanent Lecturing Faculty, National College of Criminal Defense; Assistant Hennepin County Attorney 1958-61; Assistant Legal Research Instructor 1956-57, University of Minnesota.
Professional Associations: MN Supreme Court Advisory Committee on Rules of Criminal Procedure (1971-91); ABA; The Assn. of Trial Lawyers of America (Board of Governors 1970-71); National Assn. of Criminal Defense Lawyers (President 1984-85); International Academy of Trial Lawyers (membership limited to 500 lawyers in the US); American College of Trial Lawyers (membership limited to 1% of trial lawyers in each state); American Board of Trial Advocates; American Board of Criminal Lawyers (Vice-president 1983-84; Board of Governors 1980-83, 1990-93); MTLA (President 1973-74); MN Assn. of Criminal Defense Lawyers (First President 1990-91).
Firm: Meshbesher & Spence, Ltd. 1616 Park Avenue South, Minneapolis, Minnesota 55404. Phone (612) 339-9121. Fax (612) 339-9188. Branch offices in St. Paul (612) 227-0799, Minnetonka (612) 476-9941, St. Cloud (612) 656-0484, and Rochester (612) 339-9121.

RONALD I. MESHBESHER

Meshbesher & Spence, Ltd.
1616 Park Avenue South
Minneapolis, MN 55404

Phone: (612) 339-9121
Fax: (612) 339-9188
800 number: (800) 274-1616

Admitted: 1957 Minnesota;
1960 US Dist. Ct. (MN);
1965 US Ct App. (8th Cir.);
1966 US Sup. Ct.
Birthdate: 05/18/33

•**GORDON G. (JEFF) MOHR:** Mr. Mohr practices primarily in the area of criminal defense. His experience with offenses includes homicide, possession and sale of drugs, alcohol related traffic offenses, criminal sexual conduct, theft related offenses, fraud, forgery, all traffic matters, environmental crimes, and other white collar crimes. He has also prosecuted police misconduct litigation for individuals who have suffered harm by improper action of public officials, including police officers and matters involving excessive force or where police officers have deprived someone of other constitutionally protected rights. Mr. Mohr is a frequent lecturer on the trial of DWI cases for Minnesota Continuing Legal Education, a former adjunct professor of the criminal clinical programs at William Mitchell and Hamline University law schools, and a former instructor of "Use of Deadly Force and Trial Tactics" at the Law Enforcement Training Center, "Prosecution and Defense of Crime" at Northwestern University School of Law, and "Vehicular Homicide & Driving Under the Influence of Alcohol or Drugs" at Northwestern University Traffic Institute. He is also a frequent guest lecturer on the Bloomington Police cable television show, "Laws in Perspective." In 1980 he received the Certificate of Achievement from the Minnesota Institute of Criminal Justice.
Education: JD 1977, William Mitchell; BA 1973, University of Minnesota.
Employment History: Attorney 1984-present, Gordon G. Mohr Law Offices; Chief Prosecutor 1977-84, City of Bloomington.
Representative Clients: Individuals including several professional or former professional athletes; businesses, including establishments holding licenses threatened by governmental action; and several local corporations, their officers, and employees.
Professional Associations: ABA; MSBA (Criminal Law Committee); HCBA (past Vice Chair, Criminal Law Committee); MN Society for Criminal Justice; Police Misconduct Litigation Assn.
Community Involvement: Bloomington Crime Prevention Assn. (past President; current Board member).
Firm: Gordon (Jeff) G. Mohr Law Offices, Of Counsel relationship with Henry Wieland (practicing areas of criminal defense and police misconduct) and Michael J. Hollenhorst (practicing in areas of criminal defense, personal injury, and business law). *See additional listing in Commercial Litigation Chapter.*

GORDON G. (JEFF) MOHR

Attorney at Law
5001 West 80th Street
Suite 1020
Bloomington, MN 55437

Phone: (612) 831-0944
Fax: (612) 831-6625

Admitted: 1977 Minnesota;
1981 US Dist. Ct. (MN)
Birthdate: 09/06/51

Chapter 14: Criminal Law

BRUCE A. PETERSON

Popham, Haik, Schnobrich & Kaufman, Ltd.
222 South Ninth Street
Suite 3300
Minneapolis, MN 55402

Phone: (612) 333-4800
Fax: (612) 334-8888

Admitted: 1978 Minnesota; 1981 District of Columbia; 1978 US Dist. Ct. (MN); 1978 US Ct. App. (8th Cir.); 1989 US Sup. Ct.
Birthdate: 04/04/51

•**BRUCE A. PETERSON:** Mr. Peterson defends individuals and corporations in government investigations, criminal prosecutions, and a wide variety of related civil proceedings involving white collar crimes such as fraud, environmental violations, and government contract offenses. He also represents police departments and police officers throughout Minnesota in lawsuits alleging negligent pursuit, excessive force, false arrest, violations of federal civil rights statutes, and discriminatory conduct. Mr. Peterson lectures to business and bar groups on white collar crime issues, especially government contracting and environmental crimes, and conducts training sessions for corporations on responding to allegations of crime within the company. He has extensive experience training law enforcement officers on civil liability issues and in trial advocacy programs. He is also the Supervisor of Popham Haik's Pro Bono Death Penalty Project.
Education: JD 1978, Yale University; BA 1972, Cornell University.
Employment History: Associate/Partner 1987-present, Popham, Haik, Schnobrich & Kaufman, Ltd.; Assistant US Attorney 1981-1986, District of Columbia; Special Assistant 1979-1980, Deputy Assistant Attorney General Irvin Nathan, Department of Justice, Criminal Division; Law Clerk 1978-1979, Hon. Robert Sheran, Chief Justice of the MN Supreme Court.
Representative Clients: Major Minnesota corporations in confidential grand jury proceedings and FBI investigations. Civil: City of Minneapolis; League of Minnesota Cities Insurance Trust; Honeywell Inc.; Yamaha Motor Corporation, U.S.A.
Professional Associations: ABA; MSBA; HCBA; MN Assn. of Criminal Defense Lawyers (Cochair, Ethics Strike Force); MN Federal Public Defender Panel.
Firm: Popham, Haik, Schnobrich & Kaufman, Ltd., is a firm of more than 230 attorneys with offices in Denver, Miami, Minneapolis, Washington, D.C., and international affiliations in Beijing, China and Leipzig and Stuttgart, Germany. The firm represents clients nationally and internationally on issues relating to corporate and business law, administrative law, and litigation. *See additional listings in Federal, State & Local Government Law and Commercial Litigation Chapters.*

PHILIP G. VILLAUME

Philip G. Villaume & Associates
7900 International Drive
Suite 675
Bloomington, MN 55425

Phone: (612) 851-0823
Fax: (612) 851-0824

Admitted: 1979 Minnesota; 1984 Wisconsin; 1984 US Sup. Ct.
Birthdate: 09/07/49

•**PHILIP G. VILLAUME:** Mr. Villaume is one of the country's leaders in defending business people and other professionals accused of employment-related misconduct. He defends, investigates, and prosecutes sexual, racial, and religious harassment and abuse claims nationally. Since 1986 he has defended over 500 business people and other professionals, including over 300 educators. Mr. Villaume conducts workshops and seminars throughout the US on diversity, harassment, and prevention in the workplace as well as schools and colleges. He teaches as an adjunct professor at Hamline University School of Law, University of Minnesota Department of Vocational Education and the University of St. Thomas and lectures across the country on professionals at risk. He is the coauthor of *Teachers at Risk* and the author of *The Law & Procedure Handbook for Minnesota Educators*. He has been featured in multiple national media for his work in diversity, harassment, and prevention.
Education: JD 1979, Hamline University; BA 1971 magna cum laude, Macalester College.
Employment History: 1979-present, Philip G. Villaume & Associates; Legal Investigator 1977-79, Villaume Investigative Services; Probation Officer 1972-76, Ramsey County Dept. of Community Corrections.
Representative Clients: Professional Advocacy Network (National Legal Advisor) and professionals including educators, law enforcement officers, clergy, lawyers, physicians and other health care providers, business executives, corporations, educational institutions, professional associations, and labor organizations.
Professional Associations: MSBA; HCBA; State Bar of Wisconsin; Resource Center for Professionals (Cofounder & Executive Director).
Firm: Philip G. Villaume & Associates has been providing legal services to professionals and business organizations since 1979, handling several of Minnesota's high-profile cases involving allegations of professional misconduct. The law firm successfully defended before the Minnesota Supreme Court the leading teachers' rights case in the US, *State v. Gruhl* (1986), and a precedent-setting religious freedom case, *State v. Hershberger* (1990), involving the Amish and the slow-moving vehicle emblem. Recently, the firm argued before the MN Court of Appeals the ground-breaking constitutional case, *Dr. Diane Bay Hunenansky v. The MN Board of Medical Examiners*, with issues impacting all health care providers in MN. *See additional listings in Employment Law and Professional Malpractice Defense Law Chapters.*

•**MARK S. WERNICK:** With a criminal trial and appellate practice in federal and state courts, Mr. Wernick represents individuals either under investigation for or charged with white collar offenses, controlled substance offenses, homicide, and other felony and misdemeanor offenses. He also represents businesses before various licensing authorities. One of his distinctions is having argued before the US Supreme Court in the case of *Minnesota v. Murphy* (probation officer need not give *Miranda* warnings to murder suspect during noncustodial interrogation). Mr. Wernick is certified as a Criminal Trial Specialist by the National Board of Trial Advocacy. He is also the author of "Money Laundering: Let the Seller Beware," 61 *Hennepin Lawyer*, No. 2 (1991) and a lecturer for Minnesota Continuing Legal Education criminal law seminars on topics such as "Brainstorming for Themes and Theories of Defense for Federal Criminal Cases," "Discovery in Complex Criminal Cases," "Money Laundering and Forfeiture," "Bail and Pretrial Detention Issues," "Immigration Consequences in Criminal Law," and "Recent Cases—Search and Seizure."
Education: JD 1975 with honors, Order of the Coif, Drake University; BA 1972, University of Minnesota.
Employment History: Private practice, 1977-present; Assistant Hennepin County Public Defender 1975-77.
Representative Clients: Principals of Endotronics, Inc. and Long Cadillac, Inc.
Professional Associations: Academy of Certified Trial Lawyers of MN; National Assn. of Criminal Defense Lawyers; HCBA (Cochair 1991-93, Criminal Law Section); MSBA (Chair 1994-95, Criminal Law Section).
Community Involvement: Legal Rights Center, Sabathani Community Center (Board member); Minneapolis Civilian Review Working Committee (Chair 1989)—advisory committee to Minneapolis City Council regarding civilian review of police misconduct.
Firm: Since leaving the Hennepin County Public Defender's Office in 1977, Mr. Wernick has been self-employed, practicing almost exclusively in the area of criminal defense. While in private practice, Mr. Wernick has had a 71% acquittal rate in state court jury trials.

MARK S. WERNICK

Attorney at Law
2520 Park Avenue
Minneapolis, MN 55404

Phone: (612) 871-8456
Fax: (612) 871-0960

Admitted: 1975 Minnesota
Birthdate: 03/27/50

•**PETER B. WOLD:** Mr. Wold has a criminal trial practice in both state and federal courts, representing corporations and individuals charged with any crimes. His typical cases include tax fraud, bank fraud, wire fraud, securities fraud, mail fraud, commercial theft, false statements by government contractors, and conspiracy. Mr. Wold has represented Minnesota corporations and businesses, their agents, or employees through trial in federal courts. He can be retained hourly to represent individuals or corporations subpoenaed to appear before grand juries.
Education: JD 1979, University of Minnesota; BA 1976, North Dakota State University.
Employment History: Shareholder 1984-present, Wold, Jacobs & Johnson, P.A.; Partner 1981-83, Wold & Jacobs; Private practice 1979-81.
Representative Clients: References available upon request.
Professional Associations: ABA; HCBA; National Assn. of Criminal Defense Lawyers; MN Assn. of Criminal Defense Lawyers; MN Society of Criminal Justice (past President; Executive Committee).
Community Involvement: Red Eye Theatre (Board President); North Dakota State University Bottineau Development Foundation (Executive Committee).
Firm: The firm of Wold, Jacobs & Johnson, P.A., prides itself on the aggressive representation of their clients in a wide range of litigation. In addition to Mr. Wold's criminal practice, other attorneys represent civil litigants in personal injury cases and business litigation of all types. The firm also operates Elder Legal Services, providing a wide range of legal assistance to senior citizens. Shareholder Keith Johnson is certified as a Civil Trial Specialist by the Minnesota State Bar Association and is available to assist in any civil aspects of criminal prosecutions. Criminal investigators, forensic accountants, and other experts are available for case preparation.

PETER B. WOLD

Wold, Jacobs & Johnson, P.A.
Barristers Trust Building
247 Third Avenue South
Minneapolis, MN 55415

Phone: (612) 341-2525
Fax: (612) 341-0116

Admitted: 1979 Minnesota;
1979 North Dakota;
1980 US Dist. Ct. (MN)
Birthdate: 05/09/54

Chapter 14: Criminal Law

Complete listing of all attorneys nominated in Criminal Law

CARL BAER, Kief, Fuller, Baer, Wallner & Rodgers, Ltd., Bemidji; **K. SCOTT BELFRY**, Belfry Law Office, Cloquet; **BAILEY W. BLETHEN**, Blethen Gage & Krause, Mankato; **JOSEPH P. BLUTH**, Manahan & Bluth Law Office, Chartered, Mankato; **FREDERIC BRUNO**, Frederic Bruno & Associates, Minneapolis; **DANIEL F. BYRNE**, Hennepin County Attorney's Office, Minneapolis; **PETER A. CAHILL**, Cahill Law Offices, Wayzata; **COLIA F. CEISEL**, Attorney at Law, St. Paul; **MICHAEL J. COLICH**, Colich & Associates, Minneapolis; **THEODORE J. COLLINS**, Collins, Buckley, Sauntry & Haugh, St. Paul; **STEPHEN W. COOPER**, Cooper Law Office, Minneapolis; **MICHAEL F. CROMETT**, Attorney at Law, St. Paul; **JOHN E. DESANTO**, St. Louis County Attorney's Office, Duluth; **MICHAEL J. DOLAN**, Thornton, Hegg, Reif, Johnston & Dolan, Alexandria; **DANIEL A. ELLER**, Eller Law Office, St. Cloud; **PAUL ENGH**, Attorney at Law, Minneapolis; **MICHAEL F. FETSCH**, Duckstad & Fetsch, St. Paul; **JOSEPH S. FRIEDBERG**, Friedberg Law Office, Minneapolis; **FRED T. FRIEDMAN**, Chief Public Defender, Sixth Judicial District, Duluth; **EARL P. GRAY**, E.P. Gray & Associates, St. Paul; **BRUCE H. HANLEY**, Bruce H. Hanley, P.A., Minneapolis; **CHARLES L. HAWKINS**, Attorney at Law, Minneapolis; **JOHN D. HOLBROOK**, Kandiohi County Public Defender's Office, Willmar; **PETER IRVINE**, Irvine Ramstad Briggs & Karkela, P.A., Perham; **JAMES R. KEATING**, Keating Law Office, Faribault; **DAVID C. KEEGAN**, Attorney at Law, Duluth; **DOUGLAS A. KELLEY**, Douglas A. Kelley, P.A., Minneapolis; **THOMAS M. KELLY**, Attorney at Law, Minneapolis; **PAUL A. KIEF**, Kief, Fuller, Baer, Wallner & Rodgers, Ltd., Bemidji; **THOMAS W. LIES**, Schroeder Pennington & Lies, St. Cloud; **PATRICK A. LOWTHER**, Mueller Lowther & Vickery, Sleepy Eye; **ROBERT E. LUCAS**, Attorney at Law, Duluth; **KEVIN A. LUND**, Lund & Patterson, Rochester; **JOHN W. LUNDQUIST**, Thompson Lundquist & Sicoli Ltd., Minneapolis; **ROBERT G. MALONE**, Attorney at Law, St. Paul; **JAMES H. MANAHAN**, Manahan & Bluth Law Office, Chartered, Mankato; **WILLIAM J. MAUZY**, Mauzy Law Firm, Minneapolis; **RONALD I. MESHBESHER**, Meshbesher & Spence, Ltd., Minneapolis; **GORDON G. MOHR**, Attorney at Law, Bloomington; **DANIEL M. MOHS**, Daniel Mohs & Associates, Ltd., Minneapolis; **THOMAS M. NEUVILLE**, Grundhoefer & Neuville, Northfield; **DANIEL W. O' BRIEN**, Assistant Public Defender, Minneapolis; **BRUCE A. PETERSON**, Popham, Haik, Schnobrich & Kaufman, Ltd., Minneapolis; **GARY M. PETERSON**, Attorney at Law, Faribault; **JOHN C. QUAM**, Thorwaldsen Quam Beeson Malmstrom & Sorum, Detroit Lakes; **LARRY G. RAPOPORT**, Attorney at Law, Minneapolis; **ANN REMINGTON**, Hennepin County Public Defenders Office, Minneapolis; **PHILLIP S. RESNICK**, Resnick & Associates, Minneapolis; **BRUCE N. RINGSTROM**, Ringstrom Law Office, Moorhead; **DAVID G. ROSTON**, Segal & Roston, Minneapolis; **PETER J. SCHMITZ**, Schmitz & Ophaug, Northfield; **ROBERT J. STREITZ**, Hennepin County Attorney's Office, Minneapolis; **VERNON D. SWANUM**, St. Louis County Attorney's Office, Duluth; **HEATHER L. SWEETLAND**, Fillenworth & Sweetland, Ltd., Duluth; **PETER J. THOMPSON**, Thompson Lundquist & Sicoli, Ltd., Minneapolis; **DOUGLAS W. THOMSON**, Thomson Law Firm, St. Paul; **PAUL R. THORWALDSEN**, Thorwaldsen Quam Beeson Malmstrom & Sorum, Detroit Lakes; **JOHN D. UNDEM**, Maturi & Undem, Grand Rapids; **PHILIP G. VILLAUME**, Philip G. Villaume & Associates, Bloomington; **MARK S. WERNICK**, Attorney at Law, Minneapolis; **PETER B. WOLD**, Wold, Jacobs & Johnson, P.A., Minneapolis; **RENEE L. WORKE**, Rietz, Rietz, Owatonna.

CHAPTER 15

EMPLOYEE BENEFITS LAW

In addition to paying monetary compensation, many employers choose to provide a variety of employee benefits to their workers. Although not required to provide most employee benefits, once an employer decides to do so, he or she must comply with numerous state and federal laws regulating employee benefits programs. This chapter will consider some of the most basic areas of state and federal laws regulating voluntary employee benefits plans. Topics such as wage and hour regulations, Social Security, and termination rights are discussed in the Employment Law Chapter. Unemployment compensation is discussed in the Business Tax Law Chapter. Issues of concern to employers of labor union members are discussed in the Labor Law Chapter.

EMPLOYEE BENEFIT PACKAGES

Employee benefits packages can span a broad spectrum of possibilities. Some employee benefits packages are fully taxable, like paid vacations or cash bonuses for meeting sales goals. Others qualify for special tax treatment, like health insurance or free childcare. Some benefits packages are more attractive for small businesses than large corporations. A business with mostly younger employees might choose to offer a different benefits package than would a business with mostly older employees. An employer with high employee turnover can structure a benefits package one way to minimize his or her contributions or another way in order to encourage employees to stay longer. Fortunately, employee benefits is an area of law where business owners enjoy a great deal of flexibility to structure packages that meet the needs of employers and employees and comply with the law.

The growth in popularity of employee benefits packages has led to a concomitant growth in legislation regulating benefits packages. Familiarity with these regulations can be an important business tool because employee benefits laws frequently influence how businesses are run and intelligently crafted benefits packages often give a business a competitive edge in attracting the most promising workers.

ERISA

The Employment Retirement Income Security Act (ERISA) is a federal law that attempts to standardize pension plans and medical, surgical, sickness, disability, and death benefits plans and to ensure that the plans are financially sound and equitable. To comply with ERISA, plans must provide for broad employee participation. ERISA further requires that businesses provide employees with detailed information regarding benefits plans and sets minimum standards governing eligibility for participation, benefits rights and accrual, vesting, employer and employee contributions, payment of benefits, plan termination, mergers, and survivors' benefits.

A number of benefits plans are specifically exempt from ERISA requirements, including:

- Government plans
- Church plans
- Plans administered outside the United States for non-resident aliens
- Many severance pay plans

Several federal agencies play a role in enforcing ERISA's provisions. These regulations are expansive and complex and failure to follow them can expose an employer to civil liability. ERISA imposes strict fiduciary duties upon employers to oversee their plans. Compliance with ERISA is often a prerequisite for the employer to claim a tax deduction for amounts contributed to a benefits plan. Therefore, employers who wish to establish benefits plans should consult an attorney who is experienced in ERISA compliance issues.

COBRA

Under the Consolidated Omnibus Budget Reconciliation Act of 1985 (COBRA), employers who sponsor group health plans must give covered employees the option to continue group coverage after they leave employment under a number of circumstances. Under COBRA, employers who offer group health plans must provide an employee and that employee's spouse or dependents (if covered) with notice of their right to continue coverage if the employee's job is terminated, the marriage is terminated, or a dependent child ceases to be a dependent under the terms of the plan. A covered employee terminated for gross misconduct cannot elect COBRA continuation coverage, although the terminated employees' spouse and dependents may still elect to continue coverage. The covered individual can elect to continue, for a limited period, the coverage that he or she had before the termination. The employer can require that the covered individual pay up to 102 percent of the cost of coverage.

Generally, an employer with 20 or more employees on a typical business day during the preceding calendar year must comply with COBRA's requirements. All employees of employers under common control (such as subsidiaries of a common parent) are added together to reach this number. Full-time and part-time employees are counted, as are independent contractors, if they are eligible for the group health plan. Churches and government agencies are exempt from COBRA, although government agencies must comply with similar rules under the Public Health Services Act.

As with other employee benefits discussed in this chapter, COBRA requirements are quite technical. Even the definition of what constitutes gross misconduct sufficient to deny a terminated employee continuation coverage is murky. A terminated employee improperly denied COBRA rights can seek substantial penalties from the employer. An attorney experienced in this area can advise an employer how to comply with COBRA's notice requirements.

MINNESOTA LAWS REGULATING GROUP HEALTH PLANS

Minnesota employers who want to offer group health insurance, health maintenance coverage, or group life insurance must comply with a number of state statutes and regulations. This area is a complex thicket of regulations because often the employer is covered both by Minnesota laws and federal ERISA laws. The two sources of law can overlap, even contradict each other, although in some cases the federal law preempts state regulation. Nonetheless, the state regulation is still on the law books. The Minnesota laws regulating group health plans, are similar to ERISA in that they establish minimum standards for coverage, limitations on cancellation and conversion, and procedures to follow upon termination of employment.

Any Minnesota employer with two or more employees can participate in a group health insurance purchasing program by the state. Under the program, employers can offer a wide variety of plans for lower cost than if they were to negotiate their plans alone because the state is able to negotiate on behalf of a large pool of employers. Employers are required to pay at least 50 percent and not more than 100 percent of the lowest cost plan available.

Under Minnesota law employers who provide group life insurance coverage issued within the state must permit a covered employee to elect to continue coverage for himself or herself and any dependents if the employee is voluntarily or involuntarily terminated, has his or her hours reduced to the point that he or she is no longer eligible for coverage, or is laid off.

401(K) PLAN

A 401(k) plan is a salary-reduction plan that is often used alone or to complement other profit-sharing or stock bonus plans. This type of plan takes its name from a section of the Internal Revenue Code and is often referred to as a CODA, which stands for "cash or deferred arrangement." Workers are allowed to choose whether to receive their entire pay in cash or to have a portion of their pay set aside for retirement and taxed only when they retire or withdraw the money. Employers may, but are not required to, match a percentage of the employee contribution. Deferred amounts are invested in a plan and can grow tax free until distribution. A worker can access the funds in a 401(k) account before retiring but must pay taxes upon distribution at his or her current tax rate.

In order to take advantage of Section 401(k) treatment, a plan must meet specific nondiscrimination tests which compare the treatment of "highly compensated employees" and "nonhighly compensated employees". Employers may not discriminate in favor of highly compensated employees.

EMPLOYEE STOCK OWNERSHIP PLAN

An Employee Stock Ownership Plan (ESOP) is a stock-bonus plan designed to provide employees with benefits that invest in the stock of the employer. There are advantages to the employer, such as the ability to conserve cash for other uses, and for the employee, who can take advantage of tax breaks. ESOPs allow employees to share in the ownership and growth of the companies they work for, while giving the company tax deductions for the value of the stock it contributes.

An important advantage to ESOPs is that the shares are voted by the ESOP's trustee. Because the company picks the trustee, management retains control, with two exceptions. Corporate decisions requiring a super-majority vote must be voted on directly by the participants in the ESOP, and participants who choose to take shares at distribution (rather than money) can then vote their own shares. ESOPs are not available to subchapter S corporations.

INDIVIDUAL RETIREMENT ACCOUNT

An individual retirement account (IRA) is a retirement plan that permits employees to pay a specified amount of their compensation into an account—which is not taxed until the individual withdraws the money. There is generally a penalty of 10 percent of the account in addition to the tax if the funds are withdrawn from the account before the individual is age 60.

KEOGH PLAN

A Keogh plan is a retirement plan established for the use of unincorporated small business owners, or professionals such as writers, lawyers, doctors, and other self-employed persons. A Keogh offers a tax shelter, up to a ceiling, for amounts contributed toward retirement. An employee covered by another retirement plan at work can set up a Keogh if he or she earns income from a sideline business. If retirement plans are set up correctly by an employer they may allow the employer to use the money as a tax deduction. Qualified pension plans allow the employer to pay into a trust fund a set amount or percentage each pay period.

QUALIFIED VERSUS NON-QUALIFIED PLANS

There are two categories of employee benefits plans that permit employees to defer taxation of income until retirement or termination of employment. These two categories are referred to as "qualified plans" and "non-qualified plans." A qualified plan is one that meets several requirements in the Internal Revenue Code and ERISA, described above. A non-qualified plan is one that does not meet these requirements and usually refers to a deferred compensation plan for key executives.

Qualified plans enjoy several advantages. Subject to limited exceptions, employers contributing to qualified plans are entitled to a tax deduction when the contribution is made. In contrast, employer contributions to non-qualified plans are non-deductible until the employer is taxed on the benefit. Contributions made to qualified plans can accumulate earnings on a tax-deferred basis while amounts contributed to a non-qualified plan are taxed along with the employer's other income for the year. A qualified plan can protect assets from creditors. Finally, employees who participate in a qualified plan are not taxed on their employer's contribution until they actually receive their benefits from the plan. Participants in a non-qualified plan generally pay tax on employer contributions unless the employee can show that the non-qualified plan includes a substantial risk of forfeiture.

The primary advantage of non-qualified plans is that they need not comply with many of the government regulations governing qualified plans. "Discrimination rules" that require qualified plans to provide benefits to all employees on a generally equivalent basis do not apply to non-qualified plans. A small business owner can concentrate benefits on himself or herself or on key employees.

WHEN TO SEE AN EMPLOYEE BENEFITS ATTORNEY

Lawyers who practice employee benefits law usually operate in a proactive mode helping businesses avoid problems rather than reacting after they arise. Experienced employee benefits attorneys can provide a business with an employee benefits review that can help spot problems before they become significant workplace and financial strains. Such reviews can help ensure that businesses maintain up-to-date required files, that they comply with all new IRS rules, that they are communicating effectively with employees about their benefits, and that none of their plans or practices are illegally discriminatory.

RESOURCES

Internal Revenue Service. For forms and information call (612) 644-7515 in the Twin Cities metropolitan area or (800)-829-1040 elsewhere in greater Minnesota. For forms only, call (800) 829-3676. Walk-in assistance and forms can also be obtained at Taxpayer Assistance Offices at IRS filed offices throughout the state.

Minnesota Department of Revenue, Taxpayer Information Division, Mail Station 4453, St. Paul, MN 55146-4453, (612) 296-6181, (800)-657-3777.

Employee Benefits Law Leading Attorneys

DON L. BYE - Halverson, Watters, Bye, Downs, Reyelts & Bateman, Ltd. - 700 Providence Building, 332 West Superior Street - Duluth, MN 55802 - Phone: (218) 727-6833, Fax: (218) 727-4632 - *See complete biographical profile in Labor Law Chapter.*

GREGG M. CORWIN - Gregg M. Corwin & Associates - 1660 South Highway 100, Suite 508 East - St. Louis Park, MN 55416-1534 - Phone: (612) 544-7774, Fax: (612) 544-7151 - *See complete biographical profile in Labor Law Chapter.*

STEPHEN D. GORDON - Gordon Miller O'Brien - 1208 Plymouth Building, 12 South Sixth Street - Minneapolis, MN 55402 - Phone: (612) 333-5831, Fax: (612) 342-2613 - *See complete biographical profile in Labor Law Chapter.*

MICHAEL C. KARP - Blethen Gage & Krause - 127 South Second Street, P.O. Box 3049 - Mankato, MN 56002-3049 - Phone: (507) 345-1166, Fax: (507) 345-8003 - *See complete biographical profile in Closely Held Business Law Chapter.*

MAURICE W. (BILL) O'BRIEN - Gordon Miller O'Brien - 1208 Plymouth Building, 12 South Sixth Street - Minneapolis, MN 55402 - Phone: (612) 333-5831, Fax: (612) 342-2613 - *See complete biographical profile in Labor Law Chapter.*

FRANK J. RAJKOWSKI - Rajkowski Hansmeier, Ltd. - 11 Seventh Avenue North, P.O. Box 1433 - St. Cloud, MN 56302 - Phone: (612) 251-1055, Fax: (612) 251-5896 - *See complete biographical profile in Personal Injury Defense Law Chapter.*

CHAPTER 16

EMPLOYMENT LAW

Business owners today must be more aware than ever of issues surrounding employment law. No decision is as easy as it may appear. Even the seemingly simple determination of who is legally an employee can be tricky, and mistakes can have serious and costly consequences. Decisions of whom to hire and fire are subject to numerous state and federal laws and can open an employer to liability. This chapter offers a brief introduction to legal issues concerning employers and workers.

THE EMPLOYMENT RELATIONSHIP

Many of the rights and responsibilities of both employers and workers turn on the legal relationship that exists between the worker and his or her employer. The distinction between employee and independent contractor status and the concept of "employment at will" are important to defining an employment relationship.

EMPLOYEE VERSUS INDEPENDENT CONTRACTOR

When a worker gets paid to do a task or provide a service for another person, the worker is either an independent contractor or an employee. The distinction is not always clear, but it is important for both the business and the worker. The classification determines whether a business must withhold taxes and what records it must keep, the benefits a worker is entitled to, whether an injured worker can file a workers' compensation claim, and whether a worker is protected by federal and state wage and hour regulations.

Whether a worker is an independent contractor or an employee is based on the work performed, not the worker's title. The more control an employer has over a worker, the more likely it is the worker is an employee. The more a worker acts like an independent business enterprise, the more likely the worker is an independent contractor. In some cases, the status is clear: a worker who arrives at a set time every day, is trained by the employer, uses the boss's tools or equipment, and is paid by the hour, week, or month, is most likely an employee. Someone who works for more than one company at a time, can set his or her own hours, and realizes a profit or risks a loss is most likely an independent contractor.

An employer could be subject to fines if the Internal Revenue Service, Minnesota Department of Revenue, or Minnesota Department of Jobs and Training finds a worker has been an employee when the employer treated him or her as an independent contractor. An employer who is unsure about a worker's status can ask the federal and state agencies for an opinion based on the respective agency's guidelines. Guidelines vary from agency to agency, and one agency may classify someone as an employee even though another considers the same worker an independent contractor.

EMPLOYMENT AT WILL

The state of Minnesota recognizes the traditional rule of employment at will. This means that, in the absence of an agreement to the contrary, an employer can discharge an employee at any time for any reason other than an illegal reason, such as racial or gender discrimination. It also means that an employee can resign at any time, for any reason, with or without giving notice.

Most workers in Minnesota are at will employees. Generally, an employee is hired at will unless an employer specifically does something to change the status of the relationship. There are several ways an employer can alter the relationship. An employer may enter into an oral or written contract guaranteeing to employ someone for a specific period of time or promising to terminate the employee only for specified reasons. An employee handbook or collective bargaining agreement can limit the employer's right to terminate employees. An employer can inadvertently limit his or her right to fire an employee if the employer, by his or her own actions, gives the employee reason to believe the job will continue. For example, if an employer promises a job to someone from out of state and that person moves to Minnesota specifically to take the job, the employment relationship is probably not at will because the employee has gone to the trouble and expense of moving after reasonably relying on the promise of new employment.

GOVERNMENT ADMINISTERED BENEFITS

Three programs administered by the state and federal government are of interest to employers: Unemployment Compensation Insurance, Workers' Compensation Insurance, and Social Security. Each of these programs provides benefits to a worker based on the terms and conditions of his or her employment, and the cost of the benefits is paid, at least in part, by the employer.

UNEMPLOYMENT INSURANCE

Unemployment insurance provides benefits to employees who are laid off, fired, or otherwise forced to leave their jobs. Most employees are covered by unemployment insurance, a program administered by the state and funded by employer contributions. The Business Tax Law Chapter discusses the unemployment tax more fully.

Unemployment benefits are not automatic; the worker must apply for them through the Minnesota Department of Jobs and Training. After gathering information about an applicant, the department makes an initial determination about the person's eligibility for benefits. If the department's decision is that the individual is eligible, the department informs the former employer. Because the former employer contributes to the benefits, the employer has the right to know what the ex-employee told the department and has an opportunity to present the employer's side of the story.

An applicant cannot receive benefits if any one of the following conditions applies:

- The applicant is fired for misconduct.

- The applicant fails to apply for or accept suitable work.

- The applicant is a commission-only salesperson.

- The applicant participates in a labor strike.

- The applicant refuses an offer to work again for the former employer.

- The applicant quits for any reason other than an illegal or otherwise intolerable work environment.

- The applicant is a student hired by the educational institution in which he or she was enrolled.

Because employers and employees often have different ideas of what constitutes a reasonable work environment, the issue in most disputes over unemployment claims is whether the employer created an intolerable workplace environment. Only certain kinds of employer actions give someone a legitimate reason to quit a job and still collect unemployment benefits. Some valid reasons are: sexual harassment by an employer or inaction by an employer who was informed of instances of sexual harassment, a substantial cut in pay or benefits, drastic changes in working conditions or hours without an employee's consent, and requiring an employee to break the law or work under obviously unsafe conditions.

Workers' Compensation

Workers' compensation provides benefits to employees injured in the workplace. With only a few limited exceptions, all Minnesota employers must abide by the Minnesota Workers' Compensation Law. Under the law, all employers in Minnesota are required to purchase insurance against compensation claims from a company authorized by the state. With state permission, some employers can qualify for self-insurance. Any insurance broker should be able to help a business obtain workers' compensation insurance. An employer can also seek help by contacting the State of Minnesota Workers' Compensation Division.

The cost of premiums for compensation insurance is determined by factors such as the number of employees a business has, how safe the record of the workplace proves to be, and how much employees are paid. Generally, the greater the payroll or the higher the risk, the higher the premium. However, an employer may be able to lower premiums by establishing programs to provide for a safer workplace and by working with injured employees to minimize lost work time.

Employers are required to post a notice in the workplace informing workers of their rights to workers' compensation. If an employee is injured, the employer must report the injury immediately to the insurance carrier. A "First Report of Injury" form must be sent out as soon as possible, but it does not mean that the employer is admitting that the injury is covered by workers' compensation or that the injury even occurred.

It is illegal for an employer to refuse to hire an individual because he or she has a disabling condition from a prior injury. However, employers who hire workers with pre-existing conditions are protected from some liability. If an employee suffers an injury that is made greater because of a pre-existing condition at the time of hiring, the employer's liability is limited under the Minnesota Second Injury Law. The purpose of this law is to encourage employers to hire people who may have disabilities resulting from a previous injury.

SOCIAL SECURITY

Social Security was established in 1935 to provide workers and their dependents with retirement and other benefits. Social Security benefits are financed through taxes on wages paid by both employers and workers. Under the Federal Insurance Contribution Act (FICA), an employer is responsible for withholding the appropriate taxes from an employee's pay, in addition to submitting its own share of FICA taxes. Withholding requirements are discussed in more detail in the Business Tax Law Chapter.

CIVIL RIGHTS IN THE WORKPLACE

Four major federal laws—the Civil Rights Acts of 1964 and 1991, the Age Discrimination in Employment Act of 1967, and the Americans with Disabilities Act of 1990—protect the rights of American workers to be free from workplace discrimination. Minnesota workers also have additional protection under the Minnesota Human Rights Act.

Many federal civil rights laws only apply to employers with a minimum number of employees. The federal Americans with Disabilities Act, for example, only applies to employers with 15 or more employees after July 26, 1994. The Minnesota Human Rights Act, however, applies to all Minnesota employers who have one or more employees who are not close relatives. In addition, the Minnesota act covers more types of discrimination than do the federal laws.

IN GENERAL

Most employment discrimination is outlawed by two major civil rights acts passed by Congress in 1964 and 1991 and by the Minnesota Human Rights Act. Through a combination of these laws, Minnesota workers are protected against discrimination based on race, color, creed, religion, national origin, sex, sexual orientation, marital status, status with regard to public assistance, membership or activity in a local commission, age, or disability. People frequently refer to "Title VII" rights when they are talking about a particular section of the Civil Rights Act of 1964. Title VII prohibits discrimination in a wide number of employment areas including hiring, firing, recruitment, transfers, promotions, testing, layoffs, recalls, fringe benefits, training, apprenticeship programs, and job advertisements. Title VII specifically prohibits retaliation against a person who files a charge of discrimination, participates in an investigation of discrimination, or opposes an unlawful employment practice.

Under certain extremely limited circumstances these civil rights acts allow employers to base their employment decisions or practices on a person's race, marital status, sex, etc., if the employer can demonstrate a truly legitimate need. For example, it is not impermissible sex discrimination to refuse to hire a man to be an attendant in a women's locker room. Religious institutions can refuse to hire individuals based on their religious beliefs, but only for positions that are directly related to the performance of religious duties. Religious institutions are generally not allowed to discriminate when hiring individuals for secular tasks such as secretarial or janitorial work.

Certain employers, such as police departments, can base employment decisions on an applicant's physical abilities. Other types of pre-employment exams are allowed under Minnesota law if they measure skills that are truly essential for an applicant to have in order to perform a particular job and are not applied in a selective or discriminatory way.

Both state and federal agencies handle discrimination complaints.

Age Discrimination

The Age Discrimination in Employment Act (ADEA) expands Title VII prohibitions against age discrimination. Most employers cannot enforce mandatory retirement policies, except under a few very specific circumstances where age is truly a qualification for doing a particular job, such as firefighting, police work, or flying airplanes. Anyone age 40 or over who works for an employer with 20 or more employees is protected by the ADEA and cannot be retired against his or her will, regardless of age, as long as he or she can do the job. Any Minnesota employer employing fewer than 20 employees is prohibited by Title VII and other federal and state laws from discrimination based on age, but such an employer can force an employee aged 70 or older to retire.

Discrimination Against Persons with Disabilities

The Americans with Disabilities Act (ADA) is a federal law that prohibits discrimination based on physical and mental ability. The ADA requires employers to make reasonable accommodations for physically or mentally disabled employees, including modifying facilities and work schedules and providing special training. Using pre-employment tests that identify and exclude disabled applicants is permissible only where the tests are unequivocally job-related.

The ADA does not change in any way an employer's right to hire people who have the skills to perform the "essential duties" of a job. The ADA makes it illegal to refuse to hire an applicant or to fire a current employee because that person lacks physical or mental abilities that are not essential to the job.

ADA requires employers to make "reasonable accommodations" for disabled applicants or employees. A reasonable accommodation is one that does not place an undue burden on the employer. Reasonable accommodations include modifying work schedules, changing the work environment, buying or modifying special equipment, and reassigning to another position a disabled employee who can no longer do the "essential duties" of a job. The ADA protects from discrimination only those people with permanent conditions that limit a major life activity. Thus, an employee who has a sprained ankle that is expected to heal fully is not protected under the ADA, even though that employee is disabled for a period of time. However, a person with a permanent disabling condition that is controlled by drugs, physical therapy, or by some other treatment is covered by the ADA. People with AIDS or HIV are also covered by the ADA.

The ADA prohibits discriminating against individuals who have completed or are still participating in drug rehabilitation programs. However, an applicant or employee currently using illegal drugs is not protected by the ADA.

Sexual Harassment

Everyone, male or female, has the right to be free from sexual harassment in the workplace. Sexual harassment can take many forms:

- Someone says something sexual about a coworker's appearance or an employer enforces a mandatory dress code that provokes others to make sexually explicit comments.

- Someone makes unwanted sexual contact.

- Someone makes sexual jokes or explicit sexual comments that embarrass a coworker.

- Someone displays or passes around pornographic pictures.

Although there is no federal or state act that specifically outlaws sexual harassment, sexual harassment is punishable as an illegal form of sex discrimination under Title VII of the Civil Rights Act of 1964 and under the Minnesota Human Rights Act. Sexual harassment is illegal if participation in any of the above activities is required to get or keep a job, to be promoted, or to qualify for benefits, or if the activities make it harder for a worker to do his or her job by creating a hostile environment.

The law requires that unwelcome behavior be both undesirable and offensive to be considered sexual harassment. Of these two criteria, the most problematic is determining what kind of behavior is offensive. Because of the diversity of sexual attitudes in this country, what is sexually offensive to one person may be just harmless sexual banter to another. The law uses the "reasonable person" standard to determine what is offensive: if a reasonable person would find an action offensive, then it is offensive.

In addition to laws designed to give victims a civil remedy against sexual harassment, criminal laws provide remedies against the most serious forms of unwanted sexual contact. If a harasser's behavior crosses the line into assault, battery, or rape, the victim can file criminal charges against the perpetrator. Anyone fired or forced to leave a job because of sexual harassment may be entitled to receive unemployment insurance benefits while searching for a new job.

Pregnancy Discrimination

Title VII protects pregnant workers and pregnant job applicants from discrimination. Employers cannot refuse to hire a woman because she is pregnant, fire a woman because she is pregnant, take away benefits or accrued seniority because a woman takes maternity leave, or fire or refuse to hire a woman who has an abortion.

Generally, an employer must treat pregnant women the same as other workers who cannot perform their jobs for short periods of time. Thus, if an employer allows employees to take a leave for a broken leg or short-term illness, he or she must allow pregnant women to take a leave under the same terms and conditions. Pregnancy leave is also protected under the Family and Medical Leave Act discussed below.

OTHER WORKPLACE RIGHTS AND RESPONSIBILITIES

The workplace is also governed by a number of other laws.

Workplace Safety and Health

Workplace issues in Minnesota are governed by federal standards under the Occupational Safety and Health Act (OSHA) in combination with Minnesota Occupational Safety and Health Codes. Under these laws, an employer is responsible for making sure working conditions are safe and healthful. More specifically, an employer is responsible for creating working conditions free from recognized hazards that are causing, or are likely to cause, death or serious injury. All places of employment are subject to inspection for compliance with Minnesota safety and health standards, and monetary and criminal penalties can be assessed for noncompliance.

Employers must alert employees to their OSHA rights by displaying an "Occupational Safety and Health Protection on the Job" poster. In addition, employers cannot charge employees for protective equipment required under OSHA standards.

Employers also have certain rights under OSHA. For example, employers may request a variance from an OSHA standard in some situations, may participate in the process of developing or revising standards, or may go before the Occupational Safety and Health Review Board to request that a citation or penalty be reviewed and changed. In addition, under the act, trade secrets or privileged communications are protected.

PARENTING, FAMILY, AND MEDICAL LEAVE

Both the state of Minnesota and the federal government require certain employers to provide parenting, family, and medical leave to qualified employees. The federal law in this area preempts state law only where the federal law provides greater benefits. In areas for which Minnesota provides greater benefits, Minnesota law is controlling. Accordingly, it pays to be familiar with both laws.

The Family and Medical Leave Act of 1993 (FMLA) is a federal law that allows qualified employees to take up to 12 weeks of unpaid leave to attend to family matters, including health emergencies. Under the act, a qualified employee may take an unpaid leave following the birth or adoption of a child, after acquiring a foster child, to care for an immediate family member with a serious health condition, or to care for his or her own serious health condition. Men and women are equally entitled to take these leaves. Thus, a father can take paternity leave.

Not every worker is qualified to take these leaves of absence. A person must be a full-time employee of a company with 50 or more employees and have worked for the company at least 12 months. In addition, an employee must have worked at the company for at least 1250 hours during the 12 months immediately prior to taking a leave under the FMLA.

Under the act, during periods of unpaid FMLA leave, an employer must maintain the employee's health benefits at the same level and in the same manner as they would have been if the employee had continued to work. Under most circumstances, an employee may elect or the employer may require the use of any accrued paid leave for periods of unpaid leave under the FMLA.

When the leave is foreseeable, an employee must provide the employer with at least 30 days notice of the need for the leave. If the leave is not foreseeable, then the notice must be given as soon as it is practical. An employer may require the employee to provide medical certification of a serious health condition and may require periodic reports during the leave of the employee's status and intent to return to work. In addition, an employer may require a fitness-for-duty certification upon return to work in appropriate situations.

When an employee returns from a leave under the FMLA, the employee is entitled to be restored to the same job the employee left when the leave began. If the same job is not available, the employer must place the employee in an equivalent job with equivalent pay, benefits, duties, and responsibilities. The employee is not entitled to accrue benefits such as vacation time or sick leave during a leave under the FMLA. But the employee must be returned to employment with the same benefits at the same levels as existed when the leave began. Any benefits accrued by the employee at the time the leave begins must stay with the employee. Under the act, employers are prohibited from discriminating against or interfering with employees who take FMLA leaves.

Under the Minnesota Family Leave Act, employers with 20 or more employees are required to provide qualified employees with up to six weeks unpaid leave for the birth or adoption of a child. During the employee's absence, the employer must make insurance benefits available to the employee, although the employee can be required to pay the premiums for that insurance. Upon return, the employee is entitled to his or her previous job or a comparable position. A worker choosing not to return to work at the end of a leave period may be considered to have voluntarily quit and be denied unemployment benefits. Employers with 20 or more employees must allow employees to use their own accrued sick, disability, or medical leave to care for a sick or injured child for a reasonable period.

PRIVACY

Employees' right to privacy while at work is a hotly debated issue today as increasing numbers of employers turn to searches, surveillance, and eavesdropping in an attempt to better monitor their employees' activities. Some employers use hidden cameras, unannounced searches, even wiretaps to keep tabs on employees. The law in this area is evolving and still largely unsettled, but it is fair to say that an employee surrenders some of his or her right to privacy at the workplace door. However, the number of employees who are challenging employer practices is growing.

The controlling factor courts look to in deciding if an employee has a right of privacy is whether an employee's expectation of privacy in a particular situation is reasonable. For example, the expectation of privacy is more reasonable for items in a locked desk drawer than for items left out on a desk. Similarly, the expectation is more reasonable for private phone calls made on a pay phone than for work-related calls.

The reasonable expectation standard is not a very strong guarantor of employee privacy. An employer can dramatically expand his or her right to searches, monitoring, and surveillance simply by giving notice to employees. Once an employee receives notice that the employer reserves the right to monitor calls, search offices, read electronic mail, or film the workplace, there is very little reasonable expectation of privacy. In addition to the surveillance and search activities previously mentioned, areas in which the right to privacy is an issue include lie detector tests; drug and alcohol testing; AIDS testing; smoking in the workplace; rights of free speech; rules governing dress and personal appearance; and disclosure of employee records.

SUBSTANCE ABUSE IN THE WORKPLACE

The Minnesota Human Rights Act, under some conditions, protects alcoholics and drug addicts from discrimination. The protection is not absolute; an alcoholic or drug addict can be disciplined or fired if the drug or alcohol addiction prevents the addict from performing essential job duties. In addition, an employer can discipline or fire an addict if his addiction endangers the safety of others.

Under certain circumstances, employers in Minnesota can compel employees to pass drug and alcohol tests as a condition of employment. These tests must not be given in a discriminatory way, and if passing a drug or alcohol test is a job requirement, then all employees performing that job must submit to the testing requirement.

An employer can test an employee for drugs and alcohol only under the following conditions:

- Reasonable suspicion: when an employer notices obvious signs (slurred speech, glazed eyes, etc.) that an employee is under the influence of drugs or alcohol; when an employee injures himself or herself or another worker while on the job, or has an accident while operating a vehicle to perform a work-related task; when an employee has unmistakably violated workplace rules on drugs or alcohol while operating an employer's machinery, equipment, or vehicle.

- Safety-sensitive positions: when an employee performs a task in which impairment by drugs or alcohol directly affects the safety of other workers or the general public.

- Routine physical exams: when conducting a routine physical exam, provided that giving such an exam is directly related to job performance. In addition, such a test can not be required more than once a year and employees must be given at least two weeks' written notice of the exam.

- Treatment program follow-up: at any time in the two years after an employee completes a drug or alcohol treatment program, provided the treatment was covered by an employee benefits plan or if the employer directed the employee to complete the treatment. Any such testing must be done in accordance with a written policy, and the policy must be made available in advance to all employees. Also, under the law, an individual who fails a substance test must be given a chance to go through rehabilitation before being fired.

WHISTLEBLOWER STATUTES

Minnesota and the federal government both have several laws that forbid an employer from retaliating against an employee for reporting a violation of a law or for refusing to participate in activity the employee believes to be illegal. If an employee acts in good faith and reports suspected illegal activities to the employer, a governmental agency, or law enforcement officer, the employee cannot be fired or be treated adversely. The employee need not go through internal employer-sponsored channels to report suspected illegal activity. The law does not permit an employee to make statements or disclosures knowing they are false or that they are in reckless disregard of the truth. Employers must notify employees of their whistleblower rights by posting a summary of the law.

VETERANS' REEMPLOYMENT RIGHTS

Certain veterans returning from active duty are entitled to be re-employed by their pre-service employer. A veteran must meet the following five requirements to be covered by the Veterans' Reemployment Rights Act:

- Held an "other than temporary" (not necessarily "permanent") civilian job

- Left the civilian job for the purpose of going on active duty

- Did not remain on active duty longer than four years, unless the period beyond four years (up to an additional year) was "at the request and for the convenience of the Federal Government"

- Was discharged or released from active duty "under honorable conditions"

- Applied for reemployment with the pre-service employer or successor in interest within 90 days after separation from active duty

Reinstatement must be within a reasonable period of time to a position of like seniority, status, and pay. In addition, the seniority level must be set at the point it would have been had the veteran kept the position continuously during military service.

EMPLOYEE ACCESS TO PERSONNEL RECORDS

Minnesota statutes give employees of most private organizations the right to review personnel records kept on that employee by the employer. An employer must have at least 20 employees to be subject to the law. An employee is anyone currently working for the company or who has been separated from the company for less than one year. Independent contractors are not covered. The personnel record includes:

- Application
- Wage or salary history
- Commendations, warnings, discharge or termination letters
- Employment history and job titles
- Performance evaluations

In most situations, the personnel record does not include:

- Written references
- Information regarding allegations of criminal misconduct
- Results of employer administered tests
- Statements or portions of statements by coworkers concerning job performance that would disclose the identity of the coworker by name, inference, or otherwise

NON-COMPETE AGREEMENTS AND TRADE SECRETS

A non-compete agreement is a type of restrictive covenant that limits an employee's right to work in a particular industry after he or she leaves a company. The ex-employee may be prevented from doing one or all of the following:

- Working for a competitor of the former employer
- Starting a business that competes with the former employer
- Contacting former or current customers or employees of the former employer

A non-compete agreement is generally enforceable only if executed when the worker is initially hired or at a time when the employee receives a raise, broader sales territory, or new or expanded responsibilities. The chances of enforcement are enhanced if the agreement is limited to the geographic area in which the employee actually worked; at most it may cover the employer's trade area. The possibility of enforcement is also improved if the activities the former employee is prevented from doing are specified and if the agreement expires within six months to one year of termination. Non-compete agreements are assignable upon sale of a business.

Another type of restrictive covenant prevents an employee from using trade secrets and other confidential or privileged information learned on the job after termination. Factors in the enforceability of confidentiality agreements include the ability of the former employer to prove that the information is indeed confidential, precautions that were taken to guard the information, and the reasonableness of the time and geographic limitations imposed.

TERMINATION

Firing a worker is usually an emotional situation for both the employer and employee, and employers need to recognize that an involuntarily terminated employee may seek legal action. When a company appears to have been fair to the worker, he or she will have less reason to be angry when fired and less likely to sue.

Recognizing whether or not an employee was hired "at will" is critical to proceeding properly with termination. As stated earlier, if a worker has been employed at will, he or she may be discharged at any time for any reason other than an illegal one (some illegal reasons are discussed below). If the employment relationship is not at will, such as when an employer has promised to employ someone for a specific period of time, termination must be "for cause." Causes which justify job termination include habitual lateness or absence, theft of the company's or a co-worker's property, and falsifying records.

When a written employment contract exists, it may include requirements that relate to termination. A common requirement is that an employee be notified at least 30 days in advance of the termination. If an employee belongs to a union, the negotiated contract governs the process for involuntary termination. In the case of independent sales agents who work on commission, Minnesota statute requires that any earnings due the employee be paid within three working days after the last day of work. The penalty for failure to do so is the commission amount plus one-fifteenth of the commission for each day of nonpayment.

Rights and protections given to employees through an employee manual may be enforceable against employers in post-termination lawsuits as "implied contracts." For example, some courts have found that company retirement, sick leave, and fringe-benefits plans described in employee manuals were enforceable promises of compensation. Oral promises made at the hiring interview also may be recognized as implied contracts.

As stated earlier, fired employees are usually eligible for unemployment benefits. Since unemployment tax for some businesses is based on their experience with unemployment claims, it can be important to know how and when to contest claims. Unemployment claims may have ramifications for any discharge-related lawsuits an ex-employee may file. For example, if a company chooses not to oppose a former employee's claim for unemployment benefits, the company could be found to have waived a legitimate reason for the firing or to be tacitly admitting wrongdoing. Thus, an ex-employee who wins an unemployment case may then find it easier to file a lawsuit for wrongful discharge.

PROHIBITIONS TO FIRING

Dismissals are illegal when based on age, sex, race, national origin or religion, or disability (see earlier discussion under Civil Rights in the Workplace). In addition, statute or public policy prohibits firing an employee for reporting alleged violations of the law (see Whistleblower Statutes, above); participating in union activity, such as a strike; joining with others to protest unsafe working conditions; refusing to commit an unlawful act on the employer's behalf, such as committing perjury or fixing prices; reporting to jury duty; reporting railroad accidents; or engaging in legal activities off-premises and after working hours. It is also prohibited to fire an employee whose wages have been garnished or whose pension rights under the Employment Retirement Security Act (ERISA—discussed in the Employee Benefits Law Chapter) may be affected.

DEFAMATION RELATED TO TERMINATION

Fired employees are increasingly suing former employers for libel (defamation in written form) and slander (defamation in oral form). A defamatory statement is one that harms a person's reputation by lowering his or her standing in the community or deterring others from associating with him or her. Defamation occurs when the statement is false, communicated to a third party, and no special privilege exists.

Discussing a decision to terminate or criticizing a fired employee in front of non-essential third parties are actions that can increase an employer's vulnerability to defamation charges. Successful lawsuits have been based on statements in discharge letters and negative references to prospective employers. Truth is an absolute defense in any defamation lawsuit, and thus, it is important that an employer always state truthful reasons for any termination. A Minnesota employee whose employment is involuntarily terminated has the right to request that the employer provide the truthful reason for termination in writing.

RESOURCES

The Americans with Disabilities Act: Questions and Answers/Your Responsibilities as an Employer/Your Employment Rights as an Individual with a Disability. U.S. Equal Employment Opportunity Commission, U.S. Department of Justice, Civil Rights Division, Washington, D.C.

An Employer's Guide to Employment Law Issues in Minnesota. A free book available from the Minnesota Small Business Assistance Office, 500 Metro Square Building, 121 E. Seventh Place, St. Paul, MN 55101-2146, (612) 296-3871 or (800) 657-3858.

A Guide to Starting a Business in Minnesota. Available free from the Minnesota Small Business Assistance Office.

Small Business Handbook: Laws, Regulations and Technical Assistance Services. The U.S. Department of Labor, 1993.

EMPLOYMENT LAW LEADING ATTORNEYS

The attorneys profiled in this section were nominated by their peers in a statewide survey conducted in 1993 in which several thousand Minnesota attorneys were asked to name the lawyer to whom they would send a friend or family member in need of legal assistance in the area of *Employment Law.*

Because the survey resulted in a list of less than five percent of Minnesota's practicing attorneys, this should not be construed as a complete list. Nevertheless, it is an excellent source of highly qualified and reputable attorneys, who, if unable to assist can in most cases make quality referrals.

A list of all attorneys nominated in this category is found at the end of this section. For information on the survey methodology see page ix.

Please note that the shorter, two line attorney listings in this section are of attorneys who practice in this area but whose full biographical profile appears in another section of this book. A bullet "•" preceeding name indicates the attorney was nominated in this particular area of law. For information on the format of these profiles, consult the section "Using the *Business Guidebook*" found on page xiv. Note that the following abbreviations are used throughout these profiles:

The attorneys profiled below were recommended by their peers in a statewide survey.

App.	- Appellate	ABA	- American Bar Association
Cir.	- Circuit	ATLA	- American Trial Lawyers Association
Ct.	- Court	HCBA	- Hennepin County Bar Association
Dist.	- District	MDLA	- Minnesota Defense Lawyers Association
Hon.	- Honorable	MSBA	- Minnesota State Bar Association
JD	- Law degree (Juris Doctor)	MTLA	- Minnesota Trial Lawyers Association
LLB	- Law degree	NBTA	- National Board of Trial Advocacy
LLM	- Master in Law degree	RCBA	- Ramsey County Bar Association
Sup.	- Supreme		

EMERY W. BARTLE - Dorsey & Whitney - Pillsbury Center South, 220 South Sixth Street - Minneapolis, MN 55402-1498 - Phone: (612) 340-2819, Fax: (612) 340-2643 - *See complete biographical profile in Labor Law Chapter.*

•BAILEY W. BLETHEN: Mr. Blethen has a broad litigation practice and has handled numerous civil and criminal trials and appeals. In recent years, his emphasis has been in employment law, commercial litigation, and criminal defense. Mr. Blethen is a regular lecturer at Mankato State University on the subject of liability of coaches and trainers.
Education: JD 1963 cum laude, University of Minnesota (Case Editor, *Minnesota Law Review*); AB 1960 cum laude, Brown University.
Employment History: Attorney 1963-present, Blethen Gage & Krause.
Representative Clients: Hickory Tech Corp.; Norwest Bank of Minnesota South Central, N.A.; Graybar Electric; Winco, Inc.; Minnesota Valley Action Council; KFC of Shakopee, Inc.; Waseca Mutual Insurance Company.
Professional Associations: MSBA; MTLA; ATLA; Minnesota Assn. of Criminal Defense Lawyers.
Community Involvement: Mankato State University Classic Committee (Chair); First Bank Tip-Off Classic Tournament (Chair); Mankato State University Maverick Booster Club (Director); YMCA Brother-Sister Program (Advisory Committee); Mankato State University Men's Basketball Team (Volunteer Assist. Coach); National Assn. of Basketball Coaches.
Firm: Founded in 1896, Blethen Gage & Krause is a general practice law firm. *See additional listings in Commercial Litigation and Criminal Law Chapters.*

BAILEY W. BLETHEN

Blethen Gage & Krause
127 South Second Street
P.O. Box 3049
Mankato, MN 56002-3049

Phone: (507) 345-1166
Fax: (507) 345-8003

Admitted: 1963 Minnesota; 1963 US Dist. Ct. (MN); 1970 US Ct. App. (8th Cir.); 1989 US Tax Ct.; 1993 US Sup. Ct.
Birthdate: 10/19/37

Chapter 16: Employment Law

RICHARD L. BREITMAN - The Breitman Immigration Law Firm - 701 Fourth Avenue, Suite 1700 - Minneapolis, MN 55415-1818 - Phone: (612) 822-4724, Fax: (612) 339-8375 - *See complete biographical profile in Immigration Law Chapter.*

ROBERT S. BURK - Popham, Haik, Schnobrich & Kaufman, Ltd. - 222 South Ninth Street, Suite 3300 - Minneapolis, MN 55402 - Phone: (612) 333-4800, Fax: (612) 334-8888 - *See complete biographical profile in Labor Law Chapter.*

GREGG M. CORWIN - Gregg M. Corwin & Associates - 1660 South Highway 100, Suite 508 East - St. Louis Park, MN 55416-1534 - Phone: (612) 544-7774, Fax: (612) 544-7151 - *See complete biographical profile in Labor Law Chapter.*

MATTHEW E. DAMON

Popham, Haik, Schnobrich & Kaufman, Ltd.
222 South Ninth Street
Suite 3300
Minneapolis, MN 55402

Phone: (612) 333-4800
Fax: (612) 334-8888

Admitted: 1984 Minnesota; 1984 Wisconsin; 1984 US Dist. Ct. (MN); 1984 US Dist. Ct. (W. Dist. WI); 1989 US Ct. App. (8th Cir.)
Birthdate: 10/18/59

•**MATTHEW E. DAMON:** Mr. Damon handles administrative and litigation matters in labor and employment law, representing both private and public sector management in prevention and defense of claims. His practice emphasizes discrimination, including both individual and class actions, and employment contract/restrictive covenant matters as well as traditional labor law. Mr. Damon practices before the National Labor Relations Board, US Department of Labor, EEOC, and state equal employment agencies, as well as federal and state courts.
Education: JD 1984, University of Wisconsin; BA 1981, St. Olaf College.
Employment History: Associate/Shareholder 1985-present, Popham, Haik, Schnobrich & Kaufman, Ltd.
Representative Clients: EBP Health Plans; Taylor Corp.; Shannon Group of Wisconsin; Residential Services Corp. of America; Heinrich Envelope Corp.; Tokos Medical Corp.; Leisure Hills Health Center, Inc.
Professional Associations: ABA (Committees on Equal Employment Opportunity and Practice and Procedure under the National Labor Relations Act, Labor and Employment Law Section); MSBA (Labor and Employment Law Section); State Bar of Wisconsin (Labor and Employment Law Section); HCBA (Labor and Employment Law Section); RCBA (Labor and Employment Law Section).
Community Involvement: Legal Advice Clinics (volunteer attorney); pro bono work.
Firm: Popham, Haik, Schnobrich & Kaufman, Ltd., is a firm of more than 230 attorneys with offices in Denver, Miami, Minneapolis, Washington, D.C., and international affiliations in Beijing, China and Leipzig and Stuttgart, Germany. The firm represents clients nationally and internationally on issues relating to corporate and business law, administrative law, and litigation. *See additional listing in Labor Law Chapter.*

•**BARBARA JEAN D'AQUILA:** Ms. D'Aquila, a partner and litigator with Cosgrove, Flynn & Gaskins, is chair of the firm's Employment and Labor Law Practice. Ms. D'Aquila defends corporations, officers, directors, managers, and supervisors in lawsuits and administrative claims brought by aggrieved employees and job applicants. Her litigation background includes jury trials and significant summary judgment and appellate experience. Her practice encompasses discipline and discharge, protected class discrimination, harassment, defamation, disabilities and reasonable accommodation, alcohol/drug testing, and other employment claims. Ms. D'Aquila also conducts or coordinates investigations in critical matters such as sexual harassment and assists clients in responding to sensitive inquiries from the media. She also provides advice on various administrative and management-employee issues. Ms. D'Aquila lectures, publishes articles, and cochairs annual seminars relating to labor and employment law. She is listed in *Who's Who in American Law*.
Education: JD Dec. 1979 cum laude, University of Minnesota (1978-79 International Moot Court; 1978-79 Dean's Board of Student Advisors); BBA 1977 magna cum laude, University of Notre Dame; 1983 Admitted as a Certified Public Accountant (MN).
Employment History: Partner, Cosgrove, Flynn & Gaskins; Associate and shareholder at other law firms; Law Clerk, Minnesota Supreme Court; Accountant for two national public accounting firms.
Representative Clients: Federal Express Corp.; Estee Lauder Companies; Carl Bolander & Sons Co.; Honeywell/Alliant Techsystems Federal Credit Union; Realtors Credit Union; Brainerd BN Credit Union; Miller Manufacturing; restaurants and other retail establishments; automobile dealerships; individual managers and supervisors.
Professional Associations: ABA (EEO Comm., Section of Labor and Employment Law); Federal Bar Assn. (officer); University of Minnesota Law School (Board); MSBA (past Governing Council member, Labor and Employment Law Section); HCBA; RCBA; MDLA; ATLA; American Institute of CPAs; MN Society of CPAs.
Community Involvement: MN Safety Council (Board and Devel. Comm.); Domestic Abuse Project (Board and Devel. Comm.); American Heart Assn., MN Affiliate (past Board Chair); United Way of Minneapolis.
Firm: Cosgrove, Flynn & Gaskins, a litigation firm, represents clients nationally and locally on a variety of issues, including product liability; insurance coverage, defense, and subrogation; employment and labor matters; corporate and commercial litigation; construction litigation; and personal injury. The lawyers in the firm's Employment and Labor Practice provide practical, substantive, and preventive advice and effective, outstanding defense of administrative claims and lawsuits. *See additional listing in Labor Law Chapter.*

BARBARA JEAN D'AQUILA

Cosgrove, Flynn & Gaskins
2900 Metropolitan Centre
333 South Seventh Street
Minneapolis, MN 55402

Phone: (612) 333-9527
Fax: (612) 333-9579

Admitted: 1980 Minnesota;
1980 US Dist. Ct. (MN);
1981 US Ct. App. (8th Cir.);
1982 US Tax Ct.
Birthdate: 08/02/55

•**TED E. DEANER** - O'Brien, Ehrick, Wolf, Deaner & Maus - Marquette Bank Building, Suite 611, P.O. Box 968 - Rochester, MN 55903 - Phone: (507) 289-4041, Fax: (507) 281-4778 - *See complete biographical profile in Bankruptcy & Workout Law Chapter.*

•**J. MARQUIS EASTWOOD:** Mr. Eastwood practices in the areas of employment law, complex and commercial civil litigation, (including class actions), and construction litigation. He has been a partner in the Litigation Department at Dorsey & Whitney since 1981, was chair of the Recruiting Committee from 1989-91, and is currently chair of the Trial Department. His cases include *Rajender, et al., v. University of Minnesota, et al.* (defense of Title VII Class Action Consent Decree Claims); *Anderson, et al., v. Ford Motor Company, et al.* (defense of claims by 54 plaintiffs for wrongful discharge, breach of oral contract, fraud, promissory estoppel, negligence, and a breach of the covenant of good faith and fair dealing arising out of layoffs); *Hobbs v. Pacific Hide & Fur Depot* (jury verdict for defense in wrongful discharge case after four weeks of trial); *Toussignant v. Nelson Bros. Construction* (favorable settlement of sexual harassment and defamation claims); *Jacob Leinenkugel Brewing Co. and Miller Brewing Company v. College City Distributing* (lead counsel in recently filed suit challenging constitutionality of Minnesota's brand extension law); *Beer Wholesalers Inc. v. Miller Brewing Company and Philip Morris Inc.* (summary judgment obtained on 13 counts arising out of nonrenewal of beer distributorship agreement); *Rex Distributing Co., Inc. v. Miller Brewing Co.*; *Arnold Beeler v. Miller Brewing Company*; and *James A. Pumper v. Rosemount*.
Education: JD 1975, Stanford; BA 1972, University of Wisconsin (Phi Beta Kappa).
Employment History: Partner 1981-present, Associate 1975-80, Dorsey & Whitney.
Representative Clients: Miller Brewing Company; Jacob Leinenkugel Brewing Company; Dain Bosworth Inc.; First Trust N.A.; Automatic Systems Company.
Professional Associations: ABA (Construction and Labor & Employment Sections); MSBA (Construction and Labor & Employment Sections).
Community Involvement: MELD, a nonprofit organization dedicated to improving parenting skills (Board member and President); United Way (Executive Fund Raising Volunteer); Volunteer Coach for Odyssey of the Mind and for YMCA youth basketball and Little League baseball.
Firm: Dorsey & Whitney is the largest law firm in Minnesota and one of the largest firms in the United States with over 350 lawyers in 12 offices. The depth and breadth of the experience of its lawyers enables it to provide a broad range of services to meet the diverse legal needs of its client base, which includes Fortune 500 companies, public agencies, banks and other financial institutions, nonprofit organizations, individual investors, family owned businesses, and high-tech and low-tech, growth oriented companies. *See additional listing in Commercial Litigation Chapter.*

J. MARQUIS EASTWOOD

Dorsey & Whitney
Pillsbury Center South
220 South Sixth Street
Minneapolis, MN 55402-1498

Phone: (612) 340-2856
Fax: (612) 340-8800

Admitted: 1975 Minnesota;
1976 US Dist. Ct. (MN);
1984 US Ct. App. (8th Cir.);
1985 US Tax Ct.;
1989 US Sup. Ct.

Chapter 16: Employment Law

MICHAEL J. FORD

Quinlivan, Sherwood, Spellacy
& Tarvestad, P.A.
P.O. Box 1008
St. Cloud, MN 56302-1008

Phone: (612) 251-1414
Fax: (612) 251-1415

Admitted: 1979 Minnesota
Birthdate: 05/17/48

•**MICHAEL J. FORD:** Mr. Ford handles all areas of civil litigation, personal injury, and civil appeals, concentrating in insurance coverage, employment litigation, governmental liability, and product liability. He represented parties in *Satre vs. State* (constitutional law), *Hille vs. Wright County* (government liability), *Hoover by Hoover vs. Opatz* (government liability), *Buetz vs. A.O. Smith Harvestore Products, Inc.* (RICO). Mr. Ford's lectures include "Trial Lawyers and Litigators," Minnesota Defense Lawyers Association 17th Annual Trial Techniques Seminar (1992); "Recent Cases of Note on Insurance, Employment, Workers' Compensation, Underinsured Motorist and Uninsured Motorist," Minnesota Defense Lawyers Association 1992 Mid-Winter Meeting; "It's Cold Out There—Lawyer Employment Opportunities; Managing a Law Practice for Fun, and Profit," Seventh District Bar Assn. Annual Meeting (1993).
Education: JD 1979, William Mitchell; BS 1970, St. John's University.
Employment History: Currently, Quinlivan, Sherwood, Spellacy & Tarvestad, P.A.; Law Clerk 1976-79, Hon. J. Jerome Plunkett, State District Court Judge; Captain 1970-74, US Army (Major 1974-87, USAR).
Professional Associations: Defense Research Institute (MN Delegate 1992, State & Local Defense Organization); MDLA (President 1992-93); ABA; MSBA (Board of Governors 1993-94); Seventh District Bar Assn. (MSBA Delegate 1991-present); Stearns-Benton Bar Assn. (President 1987-88); American Arbitration Assn. (Panel of Arbitrators); Fourth District Bar Assn. (Panel of Arbitrators); MN Supreme Court No-Fault Advisory Committee.
Firm: Founded in 1923, Quinlivan, Sherwood, Spellacy & Tarvestad, P.A. is a highly respected law firm devoting its practice to civil litigation and dispute resolution of all types at the state and federal levels. *See additional listings in Commercial Litigation and Professional Malpractice Defense Law Chapters.*

MICHAEL J. GALVIN, JR. - Briggs and Morgan, P.A. - W-2200 First National Bank Building - St. Paul, MN 55101 - Phone: (612) 223-6600, Fax: (612) 223-6450 - *See complete biographical profile in Labor Law Chapter.*

ROY A. GINSBURG

Dorsey & Whitney
Pillsbury Center South
220 South Sixth Street
Minneapolis, MN 55402-1498

Phone: (612) 340-8761
Fax: (612) 340-2868

Admitted: 1980 Minnesota;
1980 US Dist. Ct. (MN);
1980 US Ct. App. (8th Cir.)

•**ROY A. GINSBURG:** Mr. Ginsburg practices in the areas of employment litigation, including age, race, sex, and disability discrimination, sexual harassment, and common law employment claims; insurance litigation; and general commercial litigation. Representative litigation includes: *Matson v. Cargill, Inc.* (lead counsel for defendant; reduction-in-force age discrimination claim; summary judgment granted for defendant); *Chong, et al. v. Cedarfair Limited Partnership* (lead counsel for defendant; nine plaintiffs alleging disability discrimination against Valleyfair amusement park; case settled without any payment by defendant); *Portlance v. Golden Valley State Bank* (lead counsel for defendant; common law employment claims; after denial of summary judgment, sought interlocutory appeal to Minnesota Supreme Court; lower court reversed, judgment entered for defendant); *Smith, et al. v. The Goodyear Tire & Rubber Co.* (lead counsel for defendant; age discrimination claim against Goodyear; tried to jury and plaintiff prevailed; Eight Circuit reversed; judgment entered for defendant); *Glass, et al. v. IDS Financial Services Inc., et al.* (class action age discrimination lawsuit involving 32 managers; case settled); *Mary Flaa v. Ricky Schroder, et al.* (lead counsel for defendant Schroder; sexual harassment litigation against television and movie actor; case settled following submission of defendant's summary judgment motion). Mr. Ginsburg has been a partner in Dorsey & Whitney's Trial Department since 1986 and has been cochair of the firm's Employment Law Practice Group since 1990.
Education: JD 1980, University of Virginia; BA 1975 magna cum laude, Carleton College.
Employment History: Partner 1986-present, Associate 1980-85, Dorsey & Whitney; Adjunct Faculty Member, Hamline University Law School.
Representative Clients: Alliant Techsystems, Inc.; American Cyanamid Company; Apertus, Inc.; Denny's, Inc.; Goodyear Tire & Rubber Company; IDS Financial Services Inc.; International Multifoods, Inc.; Kmart Corp.; MEPC American Properties, Inc.; Marquette Bank Golden Valley; Massachusetts Mutual Life Insurance; Mutual of New York; Pacific Mortgage Inc.; Valleyfair, Inc.; Walmart Corp.; Xerox Corp.
Professional Associations: ABA (Litigation and Labor & Employment Law Sections).
Firm: Dorsey & Whitney is the largest law firm in Minnesota and one of the largest firms in the United States with over 350 lawyers in 12 offices. The depth and breadth of the experience of its lawyers enables it to provide a broad range of services to meet the diverse legal needs of its client base, which includes Fortune 500 companies, public agencies, banks and other financial institutions, nonprofit organizations, individual investors, family owned businesses, and high-tech and low-tech, growth oriented companies. *See additional listing in Commercial Litigation Chapter.*

BARBARA J. GISLASON - Barbara J. Gislason & Associates - 219 SE Main Street, Suite 506 - Minneapolis, MN 55414 - Phone: (612) 331-8033, Fax: (612) 331-8115 - *See complete biographical profile in Arts, Entertainment, Advertising & Media Law Chapter.*

STEPHEN D. GORDON - Gordon Miller O'Brien - 1208 Plymouth Building, 12 South Sixth Street - Minneapolis, MN 55402 - Phone: (612) 333-5831, Fax: (612) 342-2613 - *See complete biographical profile in Labor Law Chapter.*

•**DANIEL J. HEUEL** - Muir, Heuel, Carlson & Spelhaug, P.A. - 404 Marquette Bank Building, P.O. Box 1057 - Rochester, MN 55903 - Phone: (507) 288-4110, Fax: (507) 288-4122 - *See complete biographical profile in Personal Injury Defense Law Chapter.*

•**ROBERT L. HOBBINS** - Dorsey & Whitney - Pillsbury Center South, 220 South Sixth Street - Minneapolis, MN 55402-1498 - Phone: (612) 340-2919, Fax: (612) 340-2643 - *See complete biographical profile in Labor Law Chapter.*

•**KATHLEEN A. HUGHES:** An officer and shareholder of Fredrikson & Byron, Ms. Hughes chairs the firm's Labor and Employment Law Group. She is listed in *The Best Lawyers in America*. Ms. Hughes practices exclusively in labor and employment law, which involves counseling managers and supervisors about all aspects of employment law to prevent problems wherever possible. She advises clients on how to create policies and procedures, how to handle disciplinary problems, and how to discharge employees. Ms. Hughes drafts employment contracts, policy manuals, and severance agreements and advises on compensation systems and procedures. She conducts supervisory training on managing personnel problems, discipline, sexual harassment, and developments in laws affecting the workplace. Ms. Hughes represents clients in the defense of discrimination charges and administrative audits and charges, such as minimum wage and overtime audits and affirmative action audits. She also assists clients in collective bargaining and responding to union organization. Ms. Hughes is considered one of the community's leading experts in the area of wage and hour law as well as in the area of discrimination law. She is a frequent speaker on a wide range of topics involving the workplace.
Education: JD 1979 magna cum laude, Order of the Coif, University of Minnesota (1977-79, *Minnesota Law Review*); BA 1974 cum laude, Carleton College.
Employment History: Administrative Analyst, Minnesota State Department of Administration; Senior Administrative Analyst, Minnesota State Department of Public Welfare; Intern, Minnesota House of Representatives.
Representative Clients: Marigold Foods; Cooperative Power Association; LIFETOUCH Inc.; Multicare Associates of the Twin Cities, P.A.; North Memorial Medical Center; Despatch Industries.
Professional Associations: ABA (Labor & Employment Section); MSBA (Chair 1991-92, Labor & Employment Law Section); HCBA (Chair 1990-91, Labor & Employment Law Section).
Community Involvement: Legal Advice Clinics of Hennepin County (volunteer attorney 1980-present; Board of Directors 1984-86); Fund for the Legal Aid Society (Board of Directors 1988-90); Working Opportunities for Women (Board of Directors 1991-94).
Firm: Ms. Hughes in one of eight attorneys in Fredrikson & Byron's Labor & Employment Law Group, which focuses on preventing and resolving legal problems in the workplace. The group handles a full range of employment law issues including preventative advice and defense of lawsuits and administrative actions against employers. This practice group includes Richard Ross, Anne Radolinski, Robert Boisvert, Jr., Mary Anne Colovic, Mary Krakow, Mary Hanton, and Paul Landry. S*ee additional listing in Labor Law Chapter.*

KATHLEEN A. HUGHES

Fredrikson & Byron, P.A.
1100 International Centre
900 Second Avenue South
Minneapolis, MN 55402

Phone: (612) 347-7037
Fax: (612) 347-7077

Admitted: 1979 Minnesota;
1979 US Dist. Ct. (MN)
Birthdate: 02/09/53

KEVIN J. HUGHES - Hughes, Mathews & Didier, P.A. - 110 Sixth Avenue South, Suite 200, P.O. Box 548 - St. Cloud, MN 56302-0548 - Phone: (612) 251-4399, Fax: (612) 251-5781 - *See complete biographical profile in Health Law Chapter.*

ROGER A. JENSEN - Peterson, Bell, Converse & Jensen, P.A. - 3000 Metropolitan Centre, 333 South Seventh Street - Minneapolis, MN 55402-2441 - Phone: (612) 342-2323, Fax: (612) 344-1535 - *See complete biographical profile in Labor Law Chapter.*

H. MORRISON KERSHNER - Pemberton, Sorlie, Sefkow, Rufer & Kershner - 110 North Mill Street, P.O. Box 866 - Fergus Falls, MN 56538-0866 - Phone: (218) 736-5493, Fax: (218) 736-3950 - *See complete biographical profile in Personal Injury Defense Law Chapter.*

LAWRENCE R. KING - King & Hatch - The St. Paul Building, 6 West Fifth Street, Suite 800 - St. Paul, MN 55102 - Phone: (612) 223-2856, Fax: (612) 223-2847 - *See complete biographical profile in Personal Injury Defense Law Chapter.*

Chapter 16: Employment Law

GERALD T. LAURIE

Lapp, Laurie, Libra, Abramson
& Thomson, Chartered
One Financial Plaza
Suite 1800
120 South Sixth Street
Minneapolis, MN 55402

Phone: (612) 338-5815
Fax: (612) 338-6651

Admitted: 1967 Minnesota;
US Dist. Ct. (MN);
1971 US Ct. App. (8th Cir.);
1987 US Ct. App. (Fed. Cir.);
1970 US Tax Ct.
Birthdate: 01/22/42

•**GERALD T. LAURIE:** Mr. Laurie, a Civil Trial Specialist certified by the Minnesota State Bar Association, has practiced law for over 25 years. His focus for the past 10 years has been employment law in the areas of discrimination (age, race, gender, and disability), whistle-blowing, sexual harassment, wrongful termination, executive severance packages, noncompete agreements, trade secrets, and other commercial litigation. He has represented many small to medium size companies in employment law cases and has defended small companies and individual clients in sexual harassment cases. He has argued several complex trade secret and noncompete cases. Mr. Laurie is a frequent lecturer and writer on employment law. His articles include "Non-Compete Agreements: Are They Valid?" *Minnesota Business Journal*, July 1983; "The Latest Look at Wrongful Termination," *Minnesota Trial Lawyer*, 1985 Vol. 10, No. 2 (coauthor); and "Court Rules That Employment Discrimination Claims Survive the Claimant's Death," *Minnesota Trial Lawyer*, Spring 1990 (coauthor).

Education: JD 1967, University of Minnesota (1966-67, *Minnesota Law Review*); BA 1964 cum laude, University of Minnesota.

Employment History: Founder & Shareholder 1970-present, Lapp, Laurie, Libra, Abramson & Thomson, Chartered; Special Assistant Attorney General 1968-69, MN Attorney General's Office (Department of Revenue).

Representative Clients: Employers, supervisory personnel, and coemployees in employment law matters. His clients include business persons and small to medium sized businesses in manufacturing, retail, and service industries (including medical and dental clinics and other professionals).

Professional Associations: HCBA (Chair 1973-74, Community Relations Committee); MSBA; ABA; ATLA; MTLA (Board of Governors 1981-88; Cochair 1979-85, Commercial Litigation Section); National Employment Lawyers Assn.; Academy of Certified Trial Lawyers of MN.

Firm: With 12 lawyers, Lapp, Laurie, Libra, Abramson & Thomson, Chartered, is also involved in business and corporate law, commercial litigation, real estate law, commercial leases, tax planning and representation, financial reorganization, bankruptcy, securities, personal injury, medical malpractice and wrongful death, retirement planning, estate planning and administration, and family law. *See additional listing in Commercial Litigation Chapter.*

CHARLES L. LEFEVERE - Holmes & Graven, Chartered - 470 Pillsbury Center, 200 South Sixth Street - Minneapolis, MN 55402 - Phone: (612) 337-9300, Fax: (612) 337-9310 - *See complete biographical profile in Federal, State & Local Government Law Chapter.*

SEYMOUR J. MANSFIELD - Mansfield & Tanick, P.A. - 1560 International Centre, 900 Second Avenue South - Minneapolis, MN 55402-3383 - Phone: (612) 339-4295, Fax: (612) 339-3161 - *See complete biographical profile in Commercial Litigation Chapter.*

MAURICE W. (BILL) O'BRIEN - Gordon Miller O'Brien - 1208 Plymouth Building, 12 South Sixth Street - Minneapolis, MN 55402 - Phone: (612) 333-5831, Fax: (612) 342-2613 - *See complete biographical profile in Labor Law Chapter.*

•**RICHARD L. PEMBERTON** - Pemberton, Sorlie, Sefkow, Rufer & Kershner - 110 North Mill Street, P.O. Box 866 - Fergus Falls, MN 56538-0866 - Phone: (218) 736-5493, Fax: (218) 736-3950 - *See complete biographical profile in Personal Injury Defense Law Chapter.*

•**DAVID T. PETERSON** - Blethen Gage & Krause - 127 South Second Street, P.O. Box 3049 - Mankato, MN 56002-3049 - Phone: (507) 345-1166, Fax: (507) 345-8003 - *See complete biographical profile in Closely Held Business Law Chapter.*

•**MICHAEL R. QUINLIVAN:** Mr. Quinlivan focuses his practice on insurance defense matters involving personal injury, employment, professional liability, and product liability law. He is certified as a Civil Trial Specialist by the National Board of Trial Advocacy after having successfully tried numerous cases to verdict in the state and federal courts of Minnesota and Iowa. Mr. Quinlivan is past chair of the firm's Employment Law Practice Group and is a frequent contributing author to the firm's publications on employment law, professional liability, and other insurance defense matters. In addition, Mike lectures at various seminars of the Minnesota Institute of Legal Education and has authored materials for such seminars. He frequently serves as an arbitrator for the American Arbitration Association and is active in the Minnesota Defense Lawyers Association, serving on its Professionalism Committee.
Education: JD 1983, Drake; BBA 1980, University of Notre Dame.
Employment History: Shareholder, Arthur, Chapman, McDonough, Kettering & Smetak, P.A.
Representative Clients: National Farmers Union Insurance Companies; Affirmation Place, Ltd.; Jewelers Mutual Insurance Company; American International Group; Midwest Family Mutual Insurance Company; Rural Insurance Companies.
Professional Associations: Defense Research Institute; MDLA (Professionalism Committee); MSBA; HCBA; The Iowa State Bar Assn. (Litigation Section).
Firm: Founded in 1974, Arthur, Chapman, McDonough, Kettering & Smetak, P.A., is a 30 attorney civil litigation firm. The firm's practice is focused on product liability, environmental law, employment law, automobile law, professional liability, governmental liability, Workers' Compensation, and general insurance law. The firm has established Practice Groups in several of these areas of the law devoted to publishing on the law's development and keeping clients current. The firm is committed to quality service to its clients through utilizing the most cost-effective methods of dispute resolution, use of the latest computer and network technology, a high legal assistant/attorney ratio, regularly provided focused seminars and publications on the developing law, as well as cost-effective case management techniques.
See additional listings in Personal Injury Defense Law and Professional Malpractice Defense Law Chapters.

MICHAEL R. QUINLIVAN

Arthur, Chapman, McDonough, Kettering & Smetak, P.A.
500 Young Quinlan Building
81 South Ninth Street
Minneapolis, MN 55402-3214

Phone: (612) 339-3500
Fax: (612) 339-7655

Admitted: 1983 Minnesota;
1983 Iowa;
1983 US Dist. Ct. (MN);
1985 US Dist. Ct. (IA);
1983 US Ct. App. (8th Cir.)
Birthdate: 06/21/58

JOSEPH J. ROBY, JR. - Johnson, Killen, Thibodeau & Seiler, P.A. - 811 Norwest Center, 230 West Superior Street - Duluth, MN 55802 - Phone: (218) 722-6331, Fax: (218) 722-3031 - *See complete biographical profile in Labor Law Chapter.*

JOHN R. RODENBERG - Berens, Rodenberg & O'Connor, Chartered - 519 Center Street, P.O. Box 428 - New Ulm, MN 56073 - Phone: (507) 354-3161, Fax: (507) 354-7297 - *See complete biographical profile in Personal Injury Defense Law Chapter.*

RICHARD A. ROSS - Fredrikson & Byron, P.A. - 1100 International Centre, 900 Second Avenue South - Minneapolis, MN 55402 - Phone: (612) 347-7022, Fax: (612) 347-7077 - *See complete biographical profile in Labor Law Chapter.*

DONALD E. RYSAVY - Hoversten, Strom, Johnson & Rysavy - 807 West Oakland Avenue - Austin, MN 55912 - Phone: (507) 433-3483, Fax: (507) 433-7889 - *See complete biographical profile in Personal Injury Defense Law Chapter.*

•**DOUGLAS P. SEATON:** Mr. Seaton concentrates in labor and employment law, representing employers and trade associations. He provides counseling and preventive law advice on employment policies, practices, and problem-solving of all kinds, and defends and represents employers in labor and employment related litigation, administrative proceedings, and arbitrations. He also advises and represents employers in connection with union organizing, collective bargaining, strike management, and National Labor Relations Board proceedings. As a Legislative Analyst and Counsel, he worked on all the significant employment and labor legislation passed in Minnesota in the late 1970s and early 1980s and counseled the Legislature on state labor relations and review of state employee labor contracts. Mr. Seaton frequently lectures on employment and labor law topics to employer and bar groups, writes often for legal and trade periodicals, and is a past chair of Popham Haik's Labor and Employment Law Section which includes more than 25 lawyers.
Education: JD 1981, William Mitchell; PhD 1975, Rutgers University; MA 1970, Rutgers University; BA 1969, Princeton University.
Employment History: Senior Attorney/Shareholder 1982-present, Popham, Haik, Schnobrich & Kaufman, Ltd.; previously, Legislative Analyst/Counsel, Minnesota House of Representatives Labor-Management Relations Committee and Joint House-Senate Legislative Commission on Employee Relations.
Professional Associations: HCBA (past Chair, Employment and Labor Law Section); MSBA (Governing Council and Secretary/Treasurer, Employment and Labor Law Section); ABA (Employment and Labor Section).
Firm: Popham, Haik, Schnobrich & Kaufman, Ltd., is a firm of more than 230 attorneys with offices in Denver, Miami, Minneapolis, Washington, D.C., and international affiliations in Beijing, China and Leipzig and Stuttgart, Germany. The firm represents clients nationally and internationally on issues relating to corporate and business law, administrative law, labor and employment law, and litigation.
See additional listing in Labor Law Chapter.

DOUGLAS P. SEATON

Popham, Haik, Schnobrich & Kaufman, Ltd.
222 South Ninth Street
Suite 3300
Minneapolis, MN 55402

Phone: (612) 333-4800
Fax: (612) 334-8888

Admitted: 1981 Minnesota;
1982 US Dist. Ct. (MN);
1985 US Ct. App. (8th Cir.);
1987 US Sup. Ct.
Birthdate: 03/31/47

STEPHEN J. SNYDER

Winthrop & Weinstine, P.A.
3200 Minnesota World Trade Center
30 East Seventh Street
St. Paul, MN 55101

Phone: (612) 290-8400
Fax: (612) 292-9347

Admitted: 1972 Minnesota; 1976 US Dist. Ct. (MN); 1977 US Sup. Ct.; 1980 US Ct. App. (8th Cir.)
Birthdate: 12/09/46

•**STEPHEN J. SNYDER:** Mr. Snyder, cochair of the firm's Employment Law Practice Group, handles the full spectrum of employment and business law matters for a wide variety of clients, though he is best known for his experience in the area of multiparty, classwide claims. He has handled class action claims in federal and state courts in Minnesota and elsewhere, as well as at administrative proceedings. Mr. Snyder is a frequent lecturer to attorneys as part of the Minnesota Continuing Legal Education program. In 1993 he spoke at the Minnesota Continuing Legal Education annual Employment Law Institute on the topic, "Taking the Mystery Out of Class Actions: Comparing the Class Action Case to an Individual Discrimination Claim."
Education: JD 1972 cum laude, Harvard University; B Physics 1969 with high distinction, University of Minnesota (Phi Beta Kappa).
Employment History: Shareholder 1986-present, Winthrop & Weinstine, P.A.; Partner/Associate 1972 and 1976-85, Gray, Plant, Mooty, Mooty & Bennett, P.A.; Attorney 1973-75, US Navy Judge Advocate General's Corps.
Representative Clients: Alliant Techsystems, Inc.; Arch Financial Services, Inc.; Bunge Corp.; Embers Restaurants.
Professional Associations: ABA (Labor and Employment Law Sections); MSBA; HCBA.
Community Involvement: Minnesota Center for Environmental Advocacy (Board member).
Firm: See Winthrop & Weinstine, P.A.'s firm profile in Appendix C. *See additional listing in Commercial Litigation Chapter.*

MARY E. STUMO

Faegre & Benson
2200 Norwest Center
90 South Seventh Street
Minneapolis, MN 55402

Phone: (612) 336-3000
Fax: (612) 336-3026
800 number: (800) 328-4393

Admitted: 1980 Minnesota
Birthdate: 06/05/51

•**MARY E. STUMO:** Ms. Stumo has been with Faegre & Benson since 1985. During most of her years in practice, Ms. Stumo has provided advice to employers on a variety of employment issues and has managed and tried employment cases. She has defended clients in employment law suits involving claims of age, race, sex, sexual harassment, and disability discrimination; breach of contract; promissory estoppel; defamation; and a variety of claims of violations of state and federal employment laws. Ms. Stumo's successful defenses in jury trials include obtaining a defense verdict in a suit in which the plaintiff alleged a pattern and practice of race discrimination including racial epithets, assaults, discriminatory work assignments, and constructive discharge; obtaining a defense verdict in a suit alleging that a supervisor sexually harassed a female employee he supervised; and obtaining a defense verdict in a suit alleging that an employer engaged in race discrimination against a union and an employee of the union. Ms. Stumo also obtained a summary judgment on behalf of several employers in a case alleging various types of discrimination, breach of contract, and tort claims. Ms. Stumo recently represented Eveleth Mines in a sex discrimination class action that included hire through promotion claims and was the first class certified as to hostile environment allegations. In a bench trial the judge dismissed seven of the nine class claims. In addition to her practice with Faegre & Benson, Ms. Stumo has taught and lectured extensively on employment law.
Education: JD 1980 cum laude, University of Minnesota; BS 1972 with high honors, University of Wisconsin - Madison.
Employment History: Partner 1989-present, Associate 1985-89, Faegre & Benson.
Representative Clients: Abbott-Northwestern Hospital; Augsburg College; Metropolitan Waste Control Commission; Norwest Bank Minnesota, N.A.

•**MARSHALL H. TANICK:** Mr. Tanick is certified as a Civil Trial Specialist by the Minnesota State Bar Association with special emphasis on representation of individuals and business organizations in connection with employment law, defamation and media law, constitutional law, and other matters. He has represented many individuals and companies in dealing with resolution of workplace disputes, including contract negotiations, labor-management matters, discrimination, sexual harassment, and wrongful termination. He helped pioneer the structuring of severance arrangements on nontaxable basis for benefit of business and individual clients. Mr. Tanick has written several dozen publications concerning a variety of constitutional and employment law issues, including "Taxation of Employment Damages," 1993 *Minnesota Trial Lawyer* magazine and "How to Use Arbitration to Your Advantage" and "Six Tips to Avoid Wrongful Termination Lawsuits," *Minnesota Ventures*. Among his awards for writing and editing are: Author's Award (1985 & 1992) from the Minnesota State Bar Association, Lifetime Achievement Award from the University of Minnesota School of Journalism, and the First Amendment Award from the Society of Professional Journalists. He has also received President Bush's Points of Light Award, the Award of Excellence from the University of Minnesota Alumni Association, and the Keystone Award from the Twin Cities Chamber of Commerce. Mr. Mansfield is an adjunct professor in construction law at the University of Minnesota and a visiting professor in constitutional law at William Mitchell. He is listed in *Who's Who in American Law*.
Education: JD 1973 Order of the Coif, Stanford University; BA 1969, University of Minnesota.
Employment History: Partner 1989-present, Mansfield & Tanick, P.A.; Attorney 1976-89, Tanick & Heins; Attorney 1974-76, Robins, Davis & Lyons; Law Clerk 1973-74, Hon. Earl R. Larson, Judge, US District Court, District of Minnesota.
Professional Associations: ABA (Editor, *Litigation* magazine); MSBA; HCBA (Editor, *Hennepin Lawyer*); American Arbitration Assn.
Community Involvement: Minnesota News Council; University of Minnesota Alumni Assn.; American Dog Owners Assn.
Firm: Mansfield & Tanick, P.A., is a full service law firm with emphasis on civil litigation, employment and workplace matters, discrimination, and harassment, including defamation, privacy, media law, and other matters. *See additional listings in Arts, Entertainment, Advertising & Media Law and Labor Law Chapters.*

MARSHALL H. TANICK

Mansfield & Tanick, P.A.
1560 International Centre
900 Second Avenue South
Minneapolis, MN 55402-3383

Phone: (612) 339-4295
Fax: (612) 339-3161

Admitted: 1974 Minnesota;
1974 California;
1974 US Dist. Ct. (MN);
1992 US Ct. App. (3rd Cir.);
1974 US Ct. App. (8th Cir.);
1990 US Sup. Ct.
Birthdate: 05/09/47

THOMAS W. TINKHAM - Dorsey & Whitney - Pillsbury Center South, 220 South Sixth Street - Minneapolis, MN 55402-1498 - Phone: (612) 340-2829, Fax: (612) 340-2807 - *See complete biographical profile in Commercial Litigation Chapter.*

ALAN R. VANASEK - Jardine, Logan & O'Brien - 2100 Piper Jaffray Plaza, 444 Cedar Street - St. Paul, MN 55101 - Phone: (612) 290-6500, Fax: (612) 223-5070 - *See complete biographical profile in Personal Injury Defense Law Chapter.*

PHILIP G. VILLAUME - Philip G. Villaume & Associates - 7900 International Drive, Suite 675 - Bloomington, MN 55425 - Phone: (612) 851-0823, Fax: (612) 851-0824 - *See complete biographical profile in Criminal Law Chapter.*

ROBERT R. WEINSTINE - Winthrop & Weinstine, P.A. - 3000 Dain Bosworth Plaza, 60 South Sixth Street - Minneapolis, MN 55402 - Phone: (612) 347-0700, Fax: (612) 347-0600 - *See complete biographical profile in Commercial Litigation Chapter.*

JOHN C. ZWAKMAN - Dorsey & Whitney - Pillsbury Center South, 220 South Sixth Street - Minneapolis, MN 55402-1498 - Phone: (612) 340-2786, Fax: (612) 340-2643 - *See complete biographical profile in Labor Law Chapter.*

Chapter 16: Employment Law

Complete listing of all attorneys nominated in Employment Law

Lawrence R. Altman, Attorney at Law, Minneapolis; **Bailey W. Blethen,** Blethen Gage & Krause, Mankato; **Reid Carron,** Faegre & Benson, Minneapolis; **Catherine A. Cella,** Oppenheimer, Wolff & Donnelly, Minneapolis; **Carolyn Chalmers,** Attorney At Law, Minneapolis; **Stephen W. Cooper,** Cooper Law Office, Minneapolis; **Matthew E. Damon,** Popham, Haik, Schnobrich & Kaufman, Ltd., Minneapolis; **Barbara Jean D'Aquila,** Cosgrove, Flynn & Gaskins, Minneapolis; **Ted E. Deaner,** O'Brien, Ehrick, Wolf, Deaner & Maus, Rochester; **J. Marquis Eastwood,** Dorsey & Whitney, Minneapolis; **Michael J. Ford,** Quinlivan, Sherwood, Spellacy & Tarvestad, P.A., St. Cloud; **Terence M. Fruth,** Fruth & Anthony, Minneapolis; **Roy A. Ginsburg,** Dorsey & Whitney, Minneapolis; **Kathleen M. Graham,** Leonard, Street and Deinard Professional Association, Minneapolis; **Douglas A. Hedin,** Hedin & Rubenstein, Minneapolis; **Daniel J. Heuel,** Muir, Heuel, Carlson & Spelhaug, P.A., Rochester; **Robert L. Hobbins,** Dorsey & Whitney, Minneapolis; **Donald E. Horton,** Horton & Associates, Minneapolis; **Kathleen A. Hughes,** Fredrikson & Byron, P.A., Minneapolis; **R. Ann Huntrods,** Briggs and Morgan, P.A., St. Paul; **James H. Kaster,** Nichols Kaster & Anderson, Minneapolis; **Judith B. Langevin,** Gray, Plant, Mooty, Mooty & Bennett, P.A., Minneapolis; **Gerald T. Laurie,** Lapp, Laurie, Libra, Abramson & Thomson, Chartered, Minneapolis; **Timothy J. McCoy,** Sieben, Grose, Von Holtum, McCoy & Carey, Ltd., Minneapolis; **Susan A. McKay,** McRae and McRae, Bemidji; **Patrick E. Mahoney,** Mahoney, Dougherty & Mahoney, P.A., Minneapolis; **William J. Mavity,** Mavity & Ryan, Minneapolis; **Dennis J. Merley,** Felhaber, Larson, Fenlon & Vogt, P.A., Minneapolis; **Eric R. Miller,** Oppenheimer, Wolff & Donnelly, St. Paul; **Thomas D. Mottaz,** Attorney at Law, Anoka; **Martin D. Munic,** Hennepin County Attorney's Office, Minneapolis; **Rebecca Palmer,** Maslon, Edelman, Borman & Brand, Minneapolis; **Richard L. Pemberton,** Pemberton, Sorlie, Sefkow, Rufer & Kershner, Fergus Falls; **David T. Peterson,** Blethen Gage & Krause, Mankato; **Michael R. Quinlivan,** Arthur, Chapman, McDonough, Kettering & Smetak, P.A., Minneapolis; **Robert R. Reinhart Jr.,** Oppenheimer, Wolff & Donnelly, Minneapolis; **Elinor C. Rosenstein,** Lindquist & Vennum, Minneapolis; **Andrea F. Rubenstein,** Hedin & Rubenstein, Minneapolis; **James M. Samples,** Faegre & Benson, Minneapolis; **Ellen G. Sampson,** Leonard, Street and Deinard Professional Association, Minneapolis; **Mark W. Schneider,** Rider, Bennett, Egan & Arundel, Minneapolis; **Douglas P. Seaton,** Popham, Haik, Schnobrich & Kaufman, Ltd., Minneapolis; **Ronald L. Seeger,** Dunlap & Seeger, P.A., Rochester; **Susan L. Segal,** Gray, Plant, Mooty, Mooty & Bennett, P.A., Minneapolis; **Stephen J. Snyder,** Winthrop & Weinstine, P.A., St. Paul; **Paul C. Sprenger,** Sprenger and Lange, Minneapolis; **Leon I. Steinberg,** Maslon, Edelman, Borman & Brand, Minneapolis; **Gregory J. Stenmoe,** Briggs and Morgan, P.A., Minneapolis; **Susan B. Stingley,** Attorney at Law, Minneapolis; **Mary E. Stumo,** Faegre & Benson, Minneapolis; **Marshall H. Tanick,** Mansfield & Tanick, P.A., Minneapolis; **Stephen R. Van Drake,** Van Drake Law Office, Brainerd; **Nancy L. Vollertsen,** Dunlap & Seeger, P.A., Rochester; **Karin L. Wille,** Briggs and Morgan, P.A., Minneapolis; **Richard T. Wylie,** Attorney at Law, Minneapolis; **Paul J. Zech,** Felhaber, Larson, Fenlon & Vogt, P.A., Minneapolis; **Robert Zeglovitch,** Leonard, Street and Deinard Professional Association, Minneapolis.

CHAPTER 17

ENVIRONMENTAL LAW

State and federal environmental laws can touch many areas of business. Some business owners have become so concerned over potential liability that environmental concerns can make or break deals. These laws regulate not only obvious concerns such as the handling of dangerous chemicals and the disposal of toxic waste, but also many less noticeable areas such as the building of new facilities and the rights of workers to know which chemicals are present in the workplace. Awareness of laws and regulations in this area can help a savvy business owner avoid substantial future costs and liability. This chapter identifies and describes some of the main environmental issues of concern to business owners.

REGULATORY AGENCIES

Various governmental agencies are responsible for establishing and implementing environmental law in Minnesota. Central among these is the Minnesota Pollution Control Agency (MPCA) which administers programs covering air and water quality, management of hazardous and solid waste, and noise pollution. By designation or agreement with the federal Environmental Protection Agency (EPA), the MPCA has responsibility for a number of federal environmental programs, including Superfund. The MPCA enforces state environmental laws and standards in addition to federal ones, monitors environmental conditions throughout the state, responds to pollution emergencies, and provides technical assistance with environmental problems and planning. The MPCA's Office of Planning and Review reviews the Environmental Assessment Worksheets that are required for projects that have known or potential significant environmental effects, as well as the Environmental Impact Statements that are required for major projects, such as paper mills and power plants. A nine-member Citizens Board, appointed by the Governor, directs the MPCA.

Other state agencies that administer environmental regulations include the Minnesota Department of Natural Resources (DNR), Department of Health (DOH), Department of Agriculture, Environmental Quality Board (EQB), Board of Water and Soil Resources, and Office of Waste Management. More state agencies are mentioned throughout this chapter. A regional body, the Metropolitan Council of the Twin Cities Area, establishes broad environmental policies for the Twin Cities area.

BROAD CATEGORIES OF ENVIRONMENTAL CONCERN

Four categories of environmental concern are lumped together and treated under the same broad regulatory structure. These categories include water quality, air pollution, hazardous waste, and solid waste.

WATER QUALITY

Businesses are responsible for the effect their operations may have on water quality. Water quality is governed by a number of different governmental entities and regulations. Business disposal of waste water is regulated by the MPCA, while other business practices are governed by the United States Army Corps of Engineers or the DNR.

Minnesota pollution requirements prohibit anyone from discharging untreated sewage into state waters, which include all streams, lakes, and ponds, and any other bodies of water both above and below ground. Regulations also prohibit the discharge into state waters of any waste that would cause "nuisance conditions." In addition to these standard regulations, the state has set aside areas of "critical concern," which are subject to stricter water quality laws. This distinction currently applies to the Mississippi River Corridor, protecting it from development that could cause irreversible damage. Thus, administrative rules in addition to laws of the state and federal governments govern the treatment of an area. Another area of the state which is subject to special treatment is the Boundary Waters Canoe Area (BWCA). The BWCA comprises several hundreds of thousands of acres of land and water, and is protected against mining, peat harvesting, and leasing. The area is also subject to rules governing the use of vehicles in the area, treatment of campsites, and use of trails and even beverage containers.

National Pollution Discharge Elimination System (NPDES) permits are required for anyone who intends to emit any pollutant into state surface waters, including noncontact cooling water and air-conditioning or heat-pump water. If the discharge goes to a public sewer, NPDES permits are not required, except for certain types of industries. These "categorical" industries, such as companies producing leather, glass, asbestos, rubber, and timber products, are subject to EPA requirements. State disposal system (SDS) permits are required for non-surface-water disposal of wastewater, such as large septic tanks. NPDES and SDS permits can be obtained from the MPCA. Categorical permits for businesses in some cities can be obtained from the city or sanitary district; otherwise, the MPCA is the issuer.

AIR POLLUTION

Laws regulating air pollution are designed to limit industry emission of airborne pollutants which may be harmful to people, plants, and animals. In Minnesota, these air quality standards are enforced by the MPCA. The standards were established by the federal government through the Clean Air Act.

As required by the EPA, the MPCA reports an air pollution standards index (PSI) for cities with 200,000 or more residents. The index is based on measured levels of major air pollutants, such as particulates, ozone, carbon monoxide, and sulfur dioxide, and—during summer—mold and pollen counts. In other areas, levels may be estimated through computer modeling. The levels are a major factor in the State Implementation Plan (SIP) that the MPCA must file with the EPA to demonstrate attainment of federal air quality standards. Attainment or nonattainment in turn affects the issuance of permits to businesses that emit pollutants.

Emission of pollutants can occur either directly or indirectly. Indirect sources include roads and the emissions of heavy traffic drawn to certain businesses locations, such as hotels and shopping centers. Direct emissions are those that come from buildings, machines, or processes that emit pollutants. A person who owns or operates a facility that emits pollutants must comply with all applicable air pollution controls, which often involves getting a permit. In most cases, at least 180 days are needed for processing a permit application.

Some MPCA rules apply even though the business does not have direct air emissions that require permits. Businesses are liable for air pollutants such as odors, dust that may be carried by the winds as a result of business operations, and smoke caused by open burning. Businesses must notify the MPCA immediately of any releases to the air that might endanger human health, damage property, or create a public nuisance, and the business must take any steps necessary to prevent such releases. Businesses that should be particularly aware of air quality rules include those that use boilers, incinerators, generators, and solvent-borne coatings, as well as grain elevators, concrete plants, and sand and gravel and building demolition operations.

Indoor air quality has received more emphasis in recent years. "Sick-building syndrome" is more likely to occur in buildings constructed between 1973 and 1990, due in part to inadequate ventilation. Contributors to indoor air pollution include formaldehyde in particle board, plywood, furniture, and carpets; benzene in synthetic fibers, plastics and cleaning supplies; mercury and lead in paint; asbestos; dust; pollen; mold; and tobacco smoke. Under the Minnesota Clean Indoor Air Act, the DOH has established rules governing smoking in the workplace. Generally, smoking is prohibited in the workplace except in designated areas. Asbestos is discussed in more detail later in this chapter.

HAZARDOUS WASTE

Hazardous waste is waste in any form that may cause serious illness or death or is otherwise dangerous to human health. Under Minnesota Hazardous Waste Rules, each industry generating waste is required to determine whether or not that waste is hazardous, which is usually done by either checking a list in the Minnesota Hazardous Waste Rules or by conducting tests to determine if the waste exhibits one or more hazardous characteristics. A waste is said to exhibit a hazardous characteristic if it is flammable, oxidizable, corrosive, reactive, or toxic.

The MPCA is the regulating authority for hazardous waste. It regularly updates its rules to incorporate changes in the EPA program, but there may be lag time in accomplishing this. Generators and transporters of hazardous waste, as well as operators of treatment, storage, and disposal facilities (TSD facilities), must comply with all applicable rules, including any federal rules not yet incorporated into the state rules.

TSD facilities must apply for an MPCA identification number, and comply with numerous rules that apply specifically to their operations. Transporters of hazardous waste must have an EPA identification number and be registered to haul hazardous waste in the destination state. An experienced environmental law attorney should be familiar with other very technical rules that apply.

Generators are required to have an EPA identification number and a license (renewable annually), and they must submit an annual disclosure statement. Generators located in the seven-county Twin Cities metropolitan area submit license applications and disclosures to their county's hazardous waste staff; outstate businesses, to the MPCA. License fees are based on the amount of waste generated and the disposal method. Additional fees may be assessed if a permit is required for treatment, storage, or disposal activities. Businesses that generate more than 100 pounds of hazardous waste per year are subject to a hazardous waste tax. See the Business Tax Law Chapter for more information.

All generators must name an emergency coordinator who is on-call for disasters; large quantity generators are subject to additional emergency requirements. All generators must post emergency notification information and locations of emergency control equipment and alarms. If a spill occurs, the emergency coordinator or person in control must contain it and cleanup, and also call the National Response Center (800-424-8802), the MPCA emergency response line (612-296-8100), and the local fire department.

Superfund

Superfund laws were enacted to identify and clean up sites which have been contaminated by hazardous substances. States, as well as the federal government, have enacted superfund laws. Minnesota's version is the Minnesota Environmental Response and Liability Act (MERLA). Superfund laws impose liability on those responsible for release of a hazardous substance, pollutant, or contaminant. The liability is "strict," meaning that it does not matter if the company was negligent, merely that it was the cause of the contamination. Further, this liability can be enacted retroactively so that the persons responsible can be liable even though the contamination occurred before the law was enacted. Penalties for noncompliance with federal and state statutes in this area are severe.

Generally, persons who owned or operated a facility when it was contaminated, or who transported or disposed of the contaminant can be held responsible. However, under the "innocent landowner exclusion," an owner of contaminated property may not be liable if he or she did not know or had no reason to know of the contamination and was in no way associated with the contamination. In addition to the persons named by statute as "responsible" for the contamination, courts have extended liability to those who held interest in any corporation responsible for the contamination and who had the power to prevent the damage from occurring. Therefore, corporate officers, directors, and even shareholders can be held personally liable for the cleanup. In addition, parent and successor corporations have also been held liable under Superfund. An employee may be liable only if he or she knew the substance was hazardous and acted negligently, but an employer is responsible regardless of the degree of care exercised by an employee. Responsible persons are also referred to as "potentially responsible parties" or PRPs.

PRPs may have to pay the costs incurred by the state to clean up and remove the damage or contamination. In the case of release of hazardous substances, which MERLA distinguishes from contaminants, PRPs may be liable for economic loss and personal injury. The only defense to the Superfund laws recognized by the courts is that the release of contaminants was caused by an act of God, an act of vandalism or war, or an act of a third party.

Once a contaminated site has been discovered, an extensive system of assessment, cleanup, and monitoring begins. Researchers must determine the total scope and effect of the contamination as well as the best way to conduct the cleanup. Also, monitoring of the site may go on for many years after the initial cleanup has been completed.

Employee Right-To-Know

Under the Employee Right-To-Know Act, all Minnesota employers—regardless of size—are required to evaluate their workplaces for any hazardous substances, harmful physical agents, or infectious agents (applies only to hospitals and clinics), and to provide information and training to workers about the substances that they may encounter. Written information on the hazards must be readily available to staff, and the labeling of substances must conform to certain requirements. The standard established under the act includes lists of hazardous substances and harmful physical agents to assist employers in evaluating their worksites. The Employee Right-To-Know Act is administered by the Minnesota Occupational Safety and Health Division.

Community Right-To-Know

Under federal law, businesses that manufacture, store, or use hazardous substances must report their inventories to local emergency-planning agencies to help these agencies in the event of an unplanned release, fire, or similar disaster. In Minnesota, the agency that collects the information is the Emergency Response Commission in the Department of Public Safety. In addition to inventories, employers are required to report estimates of maximum combined quantities of hazardous substances and the name of a responsible person who is always on-call in case of emergency. Filing fees are determined by a formula based on the number of chemicals reported.

SOLID WASTE

Solid waste is defined as garbage, refuse, sludge, and other waste materials resulting from industrial activities, including mining and agricultural operations. Certain wastes are specifically excluded from the definition because they are covered by different regulations. These include hazardous waste, earthen fill, and sewage sludge.

Solid waste management in Minnesota is the subject of numerous legislative acts and the responsibility of a host of administrative agencies, but jurisdiction lies with each county, which sets local ordinances, zoning rules, and land-use controls. The Office of Waste Management, the Legislative Commission on Waste Management, and the EQB review various aspects of solid waste management and policy. Also, regional organizations, such as the Metropolitan Council of the Twin-Cities metropolitan area, have authority to make rules in their districts. The MPCA is responsible for issuing permits to solid waste management facilities. Facilities with state permits are allowed to operate subject to state operating requirements and environmental monitoring regulations.

Minnesota law prohibits placing waste tires, lead-acid batteries, used motor oil, major appliances, yard waste, used fluorescent lightbulbs, and phone books in landfills. Often the rules regulating what can be placed in the trash are more strict for businesses than for households. Disposal of ash from solid waste incinerators is regulated, and rules governing the use of ash, such as in road paving, have been proposed.

SPECIAL CATEGORIES OF ENVIRONMENTAL CONCERN

Some categories of pollutants or environmental nuisance that might fit into one of the above definitions of broad areas of environmental concern are treated separately under the law because of some special characteristic of the pollutant or the generator or simply because political pressures force the government to treat a type of pollutant or nuisance differently from other similar pollutants.

INFECTIOUS WASTE

Infectious waste includes laboratory waste, blood and blood products, certain body fluids, research animal waste, and sharp instruments, such as needles and scalpel blades. The DOH regulates infectious waste within a facility; the MPCA regulates the waste after it leaves the generating facility. The regulations governing infectious wastes are quite technical. Generators of this type of waste should seek expert advice in devising collection, storage, marking, transportation, and disposal of infectious wastes.

ASBESTOS

Asbestos is listed as a hazardous substance covered by the Superfund Act. Different federal and state agencies regulate asbestos outside of the workplace. The EPA regulates the reporting of commercial and industrial uses of asbestos and the control and abatement of asbestos-containing materials in schools. Emissions of asbestos into the air are regulated under the federal Clean Air Act and by Minnesota air pollution control standards. Various federal and state laws regulate discharge of asbestos into waters.

Asbestos exposure in the workplace is governed by the federal Occupational Safety and Health Administration (OSHA) and is enforced by the Minnesota Department of Labor and Industry and the DOH. In most instances, state laws mirror federal laws, but they have stricter penalties imposed on violators and require greater employee access to information.

The basic legal requirement for all areas of business except construction is to maintain a workplace that is free of asbestos hazards. If the concentration of airborne asbestos fibers rises above a certain level (the "threshold level"), a business must begin air monitoring and medical surveillance of employees. If the levels rise above specified maximum levels ("permissible exposure limits"), businesses must provide employees with protective clothing and equipment, such as respirators, and make sure that they are used. The protective gear must be removed only in designated changing rooms and stored in closed containers to prevent spreading asbestos in the air. The gear must be cleaned weekly, taking care not to release asbestos.

Requirements for construction, including alteration, repair, painting, and decorating, are somewhat different from general industry standards. The strictest rules apply to asbestos abatement activities, while short-term, small-scale activities and construction operations where asbestos does not exceed a threshold level for more than 30 days per year are exempt from some requirements. Medical surveillance is required less often under the construction standard than under the general industry standard. Demolition of buildings, except for apartment buildings with fewer than four units, must be reported to the MPCA and the EPA at least ten days prior to the start of asbestos removal or, if there is no asbestos involved, at least ten days prior to demolition.

Under both the general industry and construction standards, employers must institute a training program for employees who may be exposed to asbestos concentrations above a threshold level. Violations of asbestos standards may result in monetary and criminal penalties.

Storage Tanks

Abandoned or leaking storage tanks are common sources of water and ground pollution. Many tanks that once held toxic substances such as petroleum were buried, poorly maintained, and eventually forgotten. Years after they were last used, they continue to pollute the soil surrounding them and can be a major liability for property owners. Federal and state storage tank regulations are intended to prevent the release of substances that may be hazardous to human health and the environment. The regulations also contain provisions for the cleanup of leaks and damage caused by these storage tanks.

In Minnesota, water quality rules require that persons who own any stored liquid substance that may cause pollution obtain a storage permit from the MPCA. Storage tank owners are also subject to rules governing the operation of the tanks to prevent overfilling or spilling. Other regulations control the number of years that an underground tank can remain in the ground and the ways in which these tanks can be repaired. All new and existing underground tanks must possess a device to indicate if they are leaking, and they must be monitored every month to check for releases, which must immediately be reported and mitigated. In addition, the MPCA requires ten days notice of installation or removal of an underground tank, and only MPCA-certified contractors can perform installation and removal. Certain information about new tanks must be reported after installation. Aboveground liquid storage tanks need a "general permit," which requires meeting several criteria covering spill containment and emergency response. Information and forms are available from the MPCA's Tanks and Spills Unit.

In Minnesota, owners and operators of storage tanks are encouraged to clean up petroleum releases through a system of reimbursement for cleanup. The Petroleum Tank Release Cleanup Act established a fund called the "Petrofund," which owners can tap to help with cleanup costs. Under the same act, the person responsible for the tank is also responsible for any liability incurred from leaks.

ELECTROMAGNETIC FIELDS

Electrical and magnetic fields surround all electrical conductors, such as radio, television, and microwave transmitters, transmission lines, and personal computers. Building materials shield electrical fields, but magnetic fields pass easily through almost anything, including buildings and the human body. Some research studies suggest that electromagnetic fields (EMFs) may play a role in diseases such as cancer and Alzheimer's disease. Concern over possible deleterious health effects has resulted in job-related litigation involving claims of detrimental on-the-job exposures to EMFs.

As of July 1994, OSHA does not regulate EMF exposure in the workplace. In Minnesota, the EQB has authority to regulate electrical and magnetic fields, but currently regulates only electrical fields in certain projects. Minnesota is one of several states that have established electric field limits that apply in or at the edge of electric transmission lines. As more research on the topic is completed, it is expected that litigation and regulation related to EMFs will increase.

Large commercial buildings often have transformer and switching rooms that can generate extremely strong electromagnetic fields, and office wiring can produce high fields. Computer monitors and copy machines are two common pieces of office equipment that produce intense magnetic fields. The fields projected by computer monitors are much stronger at the backs and sides of the monitor than at the front. Offices can be designed to minimize workers' exposure to the sides and backs of other workers' monitors, and thus, their exposure to EMFs.

STRAY VOLTAGE

Stray voltage is a phenomenon that has become an issue in dairy farming. Under certain circumstances, electrical usage and distribution lines on a farm can result in low voltage electrical current that flows through cows, affecting the animals in various ways and often resulting in a decrease in milk production. Dairy farmers have successfully sued electrical utilities for their responsibility in the production loss. In many cases, the source of the problem is incorrect or improper wiring, faulty electrical equipment, improper grounding, dirt or moisture, or bad connections. The EQB has statutory authority to provide assistance in the identification or mitigation of stray voltage. The Public Utilities Commission has been involved in both the technical and regulatory considerations of the stray voltage issue. A Public Utilities Commission engineer is available to respond to public inquiries and conduct limited on-farm investigations.

TOXIC TORTS

A "toxic tort" is personal injury or property damage caused by exposure to toxic substances. Various legal theories that may apply to toxic torts are discussed below. In Minnesota, a fund administered by the Harmful Substances Compensation Board (HSCB) exists to compensate certain toxic torts to a maximum of $250,000. Personal injuries that are compensable through the HSCB include diseases, disabilities, or death caused by hazardous substances. Three types of property damage are also compensable: the cost of replacing or decontaminating a primary source of drinking water, the depleted worth of a hardship-sale of a home on the open market, and losses resulting from the inability under hardship circumstances to sell a property damaged by toxics. Compensation for property damage is limited to $25,000 for each loss.

The legal theory of "strict liability" often arises in toxic torts. In Minnesota, a person who keeps a potentially dangerous substance on his or her land is held strictly liable if the substance escapes and causes injury, regardless of whether the escape resulted from negligence. Negligence, trespass, and nuisance are other theories that may apply to environmentally-caused injuries and damage.

There are certain limits on the toxic tort claims that can be brought against municipalities in Minnesota. For example, the tort liability of municipalities is limited to $200,000 for wrongful death or other tort injuries, and limited to $600,000 for claims arising from any single occurrence, and awards for punitive damages are not permitted. Also limited is the time within which a tort action can be filed. The limitation generally ranges from three to six years, depending on the nature of claim.

RECYCLING

Recycling in Minnesota is governed by numerous state, county and municipal regulations. Recently, municipalities have dramatically increased their involvement in recycling by directly entering the market as recyclers, by contracting out for recycling services, and by putting more regulations on recycling businesses.

The Minnesota Legislature enacted extensive recycling regulations in 1989 which, in part, established goals for metropolitan counties to recycle at least 35 percent of their solid waste and for rural counties to recycle at least 25 percent of their solid waste. These regulations were based on the recommendations of the governor-appointed Select Committee On Recycling and the Environment (SCORE). Another regulation resulting from SCORE's recommendations holds each county responsible for its own recycling, including curbside collection for metropolitan areas and recycling facilities and information campaigns for all counties. The law also encourages state agencies to purchase recycled materials, and requires schools and local agencies to develop recycling programs. The Minnesota Office of Waste Management administers several grant and low interest loan programs designed to encourage recycling.

REAL ESTATE TRANSACTIONS

Under Minnesota law, the owner of contaminated property or property that has been used for hazardous waste disposal must file—prior to transfer of ownership—an affidavit with the county where the property is located. State law does not require that the owner certify property to be clean prior to transfer.

As stated earlier, "innocent landowners" have some protection from liability related to contamination of real property. However, to use this defense, an owner must have exercised "due diligence" in determining the condition of the property at the time of purchase. An environmental site assessment can apprise a purchaser of a site's condition and any potential liability. A review of MPCA and EPA records relating to the property and adjacent land is a mandatory part of a site investigation. At the request of the parties involved in a property transfer, the MPCA will conduct the review of its records. The MPCA will also assist with cleanup by commenting on investigation plans and reviewing cleanup plans. Participants are charged for the agency's costs. Businesses that participate in this MPCA program may be eligible for release from some liability connected with contaminated sites.

Often, an ounce of prevention is worth a pound of cure when it comes to environmental problems stemming from real estate deals. It can be very wise to have a thorough site investigation performed before purchasing any property that may be contaminated or that might contain an underground storage tank. An experienced environmental law attorney can advise on how best to protect one's business in routine real estate transactions.

RESOURCES

A Guide to Starting a Business in Minnesota. Available from: Minnesota Small Business Assistance Office (see below for address).

Business Wastes: What You Don't Know May Cost You. A guidebook for generators of very small quantities of waste. Available from: Minnesota Pollution Control Agency (see below for address).

Minnesota Employee Right-To-Know Standard. Available from: Minnesota Bookstore, 117 University Avenue, St. Paul, MN 55155, (612) 297-3000.

Minnesota Environmental Law Handbook, William J. Keppel and Steven M. Christenson, eds. Available from: Government Institutes, Inc., 966 Hungerford Drive #24, Rockville, MD 20850-1714, (301) 251-9250.

Emergency Response Commission, Department of Public Safety, 175 Bigelow Building, 450 Syndicate Street, St. Paul, MN 55104, (612) 643-3000.

Minnesota Small Business Assistance Office, 500 Metro Square, 121 Seventh Place East, St. Paul, MN 55101-2146, (612) 296-3871. From outstate Minnesota (800) 657-3858.

Minnesota Pollution Control Agency (MPCA), 520 Lafayette Road, St. Paul, MN 55155, (612) 296-6300. From outstate Minnesota, (800) 657-3864.

Minnesota Technical Assistance Program (MnTAP), 1313 5th Street SE, Suite 207, Minneapolis, MN 55414-4504, (612) 627-4646. From outstate Minnesota, (800) 247-0015. This office provides free help on pollution prevention and waste management.

Chapter 17: Environmental Law

ENVIRONMENTAL LAW LEADING ATTORNEYS

Selected by Attorneys for GUIDEBOOK
Law & Leading Attorneys
MINNESOTA

The attorneys profiled below were recommended by their peers in a statewide survey.

The attorneys profiled in this section were nominated by their peers in a statewide survey conducted in 1993 in which several thousand Minnesota attorneys were asked to name the lawyer to whom they would send a friend or family member in need of legal assistance in the area of *Environmental Law.*

Because the survey resulted in a list of less than five percent of Minnesota's practicing attorneys, this should not be construed as a complete list. Nevertheless, it is an excellent source of highly qualified and reputable attorneys, who, if unable to assist can in most cases make quality referrals.

A list of all attorneys nominated in this category is found at the end of this section. For information on the survey methodology see page ix.

Please note that the shorter, two line attorney listings in this section are of attorneys who practice in this area but whose full biographical profile appears in another section of this book. A bullet "•" preceeding name indicates the attorney was nominated in this particular area of law. For information on the format of these profiles, consult the section "Using the *Business Guidebook*" found on page xiv. Note that the following abbreviations are used throughout these profiles:

App.	- Appellate	ABA	- American Bar Association
Cir.	- Circuit	ATLA	- American Trial Lawyers Association
Ct.	- Court	HCBA	- Hennepin County Bar Association
Dist.	- District	MDLA	- Minnesota Defense Lawyers Association
Hon.	- Honorable	MSBA	- Minnesota State Bar Association
JD	- Law degree (Juris Doctor)	MTLA	- Minnesota Trial Lawyers Association
LLB	- Law degree	NBTA	- National Board of Trial Advocacy
LLM	- Master in Law degree	RCBA	- Ramsey County Bar Association
Sup.	- Supreme		

MICHAEL J. AHERN

Moss & Barnett, A Professional Association
4800 Norwest Center
90 South Seventh Street
Minneapolis, MN 55402

Phone: (612) 347-0274
Fax: (612) 339-6686

Admitted: 1977 Minnesota; 1977 US Dist. Ct. (MN); 1991 US Ct. App. (8th Cir.)
Birthdate: 08/20/51

•MICHAEL J. AHERN: Mr. Ahern has over 17 years of experience representing and counseling businesses on environmental and a wide range of other regulatory matters before state and federal agencies and courts and the Minnesota Legislature. His state regulatory experience began in 1973 as legislative staff drafting many of Minnesota's pioneering environmental and health care laws. Mr. Ahern's practice includes representing gas, electric, and telecommunications companies before the Minnesota Public Utilities Commission, the MPCA, EPA, EQB, and other regulatory bodies. He also represents insurance, health care, and financial institutions on regulatory issues and is legal counsel to the Minnesota property and casualty guaranty fund. Illustrative of Mr. Ahern's experience is his role as chief outside counsel on a successful nuclear storage project which required environmental, utility regulatory, and legislative approval, as well as significant state and federal litigation. His column on administrative law appears in *Bench and Bar of Minnesota*, and he is a contributing author to *Minnesota Administrative Procedure*. Mr. Ahern is chair of Moss & Barnett's Communications, Energy and Governmental Relations Department.
Education: JD 1977, William Mitchell; BA 1973, University of Minnesota.
Employment History: Shareholder, Moss & Barnett. Employed with firm since 1976.
Representative Clients: Northern States Power Company; Minnesota Telephone Assn.; ENRON; USX Corp.; Mayo Foundation; Minnesota Insurance Guaranty Assn.
Professional Associations: ABA (member of various sections); MSBA (Governing Council 1993-present, Environmental Law Section; Chair and Governing Council member 1980-93, Administrative Law Section); HCBA (Chair 1984-85, Environmental Law Committee); MN Governmental Relations Council (President 1989); National Conference on Insurance Guaranty Funds (1989-present, Legal Committee).
Community Involvement: Group Health, Inc. (HealthPartners) (past Board Chair and Director); Legal Advice Clinics (volunteer attorney); William Mitchell mentor program.
Firm: Moss & Barnett and its predecessor firms have provided legal service in Minneapolis and the surrounding multistate area continuously since before 1900. It is a firm providing legal services to individuals and business entities in personal, corporate, governmental, and all types of dispute resolution matters. Many of its attorneys have been nominated for inclusion in this publication. *See additional listings in Federal, State & Local Government Law and Health Law Chapters.*

Environmental Law Leading Attorneys

•JOHN M. ANDERSON - Bassford, Lockhart, Truesdell & Briggs, P.A. - 3550 Multifoods Tower, 33 South Sixth Street - Minneapolis, MN 55402-3787 - Phone: (612) 333-3000, Fax: (612) 333-8829 - *See complete biographical profile in Personal Injury Defense Law Chapter.*

PETER K. BECK - Larkin, Hoffman, Daly & Lindgren, Ltd. - 1500 Norwest Financial Center, 7900 Xerxes Avenue South - Bloomington, MN 55431 - Phone: (612) 835-3800, Fax: (612) 896-3333 - *See complete biographical profile in Federal, State & Local Government Law Chapter.*

JOSEPH P. BLUTH - Manahan & Bluth Law Office, Chartered - 416 South Front Street, P.O. Box 287 - Mankato, MN 56001 - Phone: (507) 387-5661, Fax: (507) 387-2111 - *See complete biographical profile in Criminal Law Chapter.*

•MARTHA C. BRAND: Ms. Brand is a shareholder with Leonard, Street and Deinard, and is a leading expert in environmental matters relating to real estate transactions, federal and state Superfund, compliance with state and federal regulations relating to storage tanks, and water law. She is also experienced in advising clients regarding environmental compliance issues, including those relating to development or redevelopment, and issues relating to permitting and wetlands preservation. Ms. Brand served as a citizen member of the Minnesota Environmental Quality Board from 1984 to 1990 and chaired the Water Resources Committee of the Board from 1985 to 1990. She participated in the enactment of the state Land Recycling Act and groundwater legislation and is a frequent lecturer and author on environmental topics. Ms. Brand is experienced in the use of alternative dispute resolution and has been approved for inclusion on the statewide neutrals roster for mediation and arbitration. She is on the board of American Rivers, a national river conservation group, and is currently treasurer of the Environmental and Natural Resources Law Section of the Minnesota State Bar Association.
Education: JD 1974, Boston University; BA 1971, Wellesley College.
Employment History: Shareholder 1983-present, Associate 1981-82, Leonard, Street and Deinard; Associate 1977-80, Miller & Chevalier (Washington, D.C.); Attorney-Advisor 1976-77, Commissioner of the Federal Trade Commission (FTC); Assistant to the Director of the FTC's Bureau of Competition 1975-76; Staff Attorney 1974-75, FTC's Bureau of Competition.
Representative Clients: National and local companies in the construction, development, publishing, container reuse, pharmaceutical, equipment sales, and beverages industries.
Professional Associations: MSBA (Council Delegate 1991-92; Treasurer 1993-present, Environmental and Natural Resources Law Section); HCBA (Environmental Law Section); ABA (Natural Resources, Energy & Environmental Law and Real Property Law Sections); Minnesota Women Lawyers (Board member 1983-86).
Community Involvement: American Rivers (Board member 1992-present); Environmental Quality Board (citizen member 1984-90).
Firm: Leonard, Street and Deinard is a full service commercial law firm of approximately 125 attorneys. The firm includes a specialized section devoted to environmental matters, of which Ms. Brand is a member.

MARTHA C. BRAND

Leonard, Street and Deinard
Professional Association
150 South Fifth Street
Suite 2300
Minneapolis, MN 55402

Phone: (612) 335-1500
Fax: (612) 335-1657

Admitted: 1981 Minnesota; 1974 District of Columbia
Birthdate: 12/02/48

LORENS Q. BRYNESTAD - Brynestad Law Offices - 8525 Edinbrook Crossing, Suite 201 - Brooklyn Park, MN 55443 - Phone: (612) 424-8811, Fax: (612) 493-5193 - *See complete biographical profile in Commercial Real Estate Law Chapter.*

ROBERT S. BURK - Popham, Haik, Schnobrich & Kaufman, Ltd. - 222 South Ninth Street, Suite 3300 - Minneapolis, MN 55402 - Phone: (612) 333-4800, Fax: (612) 334-8888 - *See complete biographical profile in Labor Law Chapter.*

REBECCA A. COMSTOCK

Dorsey & Whitney
Pillsbury Center South
220 South Sixth Street
Minneapolis, MN 55402-1498

Phone: (612) 340-2987
Fax: (612) 340-2644

Admitted: 1978 Minnesota;
1978 US Dist. Ct. (MN)
Birthdate: 03/13/50

•**REBECCA A. COMSTOCK:** Ms. Comstock has been a partner in the Environmental and Regulatory Affairs Department since 1985 and has served as chair to the Environmental & Regulatory Affairs Department since 1989. Ms. Comstock practices exclusively in the area of environmental law, including federal and state Superfund administrative actions and litigation. She represents clients before federal, state, and local agencies on permitting, rulemaking, and regulatory compliance. Ms. Comstock also advises clients on environmental issues in corporate, real estate, and commercial transactions. Representative litigation includes *US v. Reilly Tar & Chemical Corporation* (US District Court, D. Minn.) 1981 and *US v. Arrowhead Refining Company* (US District Court, D. Minn.) 1989. Additionally, she is a frequent speaker on environmental issues and is listed in *Who's Who in America*.
Education: JD 1977 with high honors, Order of Saint Ives University of Denver ; BA 1973 summa cum laude, University of Minnesota.
Employment History: Partner 1985-present, Associate 1982-84, Dorsey & Whitney; 1978-82 Broeker, Hartfeldt, Hedges & Grant.
Professional Associations: ABA (Natural Resources, Energy and Environmental Law and Administrative Law Sections); MSBA (Administrative Law Section (Chair 1990-91); Environmental and Natural Resources Law Section (Executive Council 1992-94)); HCBA (Environmental Law Committee; Local Government Law Committee (Chair 1980-81); Legal Aid Society of Minneapolis (Board member 1987-93); American Arbitration Assn. (Panel of Arbitrators and Mediators); Minnesota Women Lawyers, Inc.
Firm: Dorsey & Whitney is the largest law firm in Minnesota and one of the largest firms in the United States with over 350 lawyers in 12 offices. The depth and breadth of the experience of its lawyers enables it to provide a broad range of services to meet the diverse legal needs of its client base, which includes Fortune 500 companies, public agencies, banks and other financial institutions, nonprofit organizations, individual investors, family owned businesses, and high-tech and low-tech, growth oriented companies. *See additional listing in Federal, State & Local Government Law Chapter.*

CHARLES K. DAYTON

Leonard, Street and Deinard
Professional Association
150 South Fifth Street
Suite 2300
Minneapolis, MN 55402

Phone: (612) 335-1500
Fax: (612) 335-1657

Admitted: 1964 Minnesota;
1988 Wisconsin;
1965 US Dist. Ct. (MN);
1974 US Ct. App. (8th Cir.);
1978 US Sup. Ct.
Birthdate: 05/16/39

•**CHARLES K. DAYTON:** Mr. Dayton is a shareholder with Leonard, Street and Deinard, where he specializes in environmental litigation and administrative practice. He is the current cochair of the Hennepin County Bar Association Environmental Law Committee. Mr. Dayton's environmental law experience includes representation of a wide spectrum of clients, including commercial and industrial firms as well as environmental groups and government. His experience includes most of the significant environmental issues of the past 25 years in Minnesota, including environmental legislation and rulemaking, reserve mining, Boundary Waters Wilderness issues, wetlands controversies, and garbage incineration, at all levels of state and federal courts and agencies. His current practice deals with issues of air, water, and groundwater quality, land use development, waste management, utility regulation, environmental review issues, and pro bono representation of environmental groups. Mr. Dayton was named an "Environmentalist of the Decade" by the Minnesota Chapter of the Sierra Club in 1983.
Education: JD 1964 with distinction, University of Michigan (Editor, *Michigan Law Review*); BA 1961 with honors, Dartmouth College.
Employment History: 1988-present, Leonard, Street and Deinard; Partner/Founding Partner 1973-88, Pepin, Dayton, Herman & Graham (merged with Leonard, Street and Deinard).
Representative Clients: Tower Asphalt, Inc.; American Lung Assn. of Hennepin County; Hennepin Energy Resource Corp.; Dakota County; Encampment Forest Assn.; The Nature Conservancy; Hennepin County Regional Railroad Authority; City of Lake Elmo; Herzog Waste Management, Inc.; Crown CoCo, Inc.; Buffalo Bituminous Corp.; LS Power, Inc.; Lundgren Bros. Construction Company; Rein Midway L.P.; Blount, Inc.; Trussbilt Inc.
Professional Associations: HCBA (Cochair 1994-present, Environmental Law Committee); ABA (Section on Natural Resources, Energy & Environmental Law).
Community Involvement: Committee for the National Institute for the Environment (Board member 1993-present).
Firm: Leonard, Street and Deinard is a full service commercial law firm of approximately 125 attorneys. The firm includes a specialized section devoted to environmental matters, of which Mr. Dayton is a member. *See additional listings in Commercial Litigation and Federal, State & Local Government Law Chapters.*

Environmental Law Leading Attorneys

•**LINDA FISHER:** Ms. Fisher is a shareholder and Board member of Larkin, Hoffman, Daly & Lindgren, Ltd. She practices law in the areas of zoning and land use approvals; real estate development; and federal, state, and local environmental permitting, with a special emphasis on wetlands, environmental assessments, and environmental impact statements. Ms. Fisher is the author of "Minnesota Water Management Law and Section 404 Permits: A Practitioner's Perspective," 7 *Hamline L. Rev.* 249 (1984) and "The Land Use Approval Log - Creating A Record to Take to Court," *Minnesota Real Estate Journal*. She frequently speaks and lectures on land use and environmental law and real estate development.
Education: JD 1975, Albany Law School of Union University and New York University; BA 1972 cum laude with highest honors, Smith College (Phi Beta Kappa).
Employment History: Currently, Larkin, Hoffman, Daly & Lindgren, Ltd.; Assistant Attorney 1976, City of St. Paul.
Representative Clients: Carlson Real Estate Company; Trammell Crow Company; Amoco Oil Company; Circuit City Stores; Lundgren Bros. Construction Company; Meridian Aggregates Company; Rottlund Homes; Perkins Restaurants; Chilis Restaurant; City of Woodbury; Scott County; City of Eden Prairie.
Professional Associations: ABA (Urban & Local Government Law, Real Property, Probate & Trust Law, and Natural Resources, Energy & Environmental Law Sections); MSBA; HCBA (past Chair, Environmental Law Committee); American Planning Assn.
Community Involvement: American Jewish Committee, Minneapolis-St. Paul Chapter (Board member); United Way (past member, Allocations Panel).
Firm: Larkin, Hoffman, Daly & Lindgren, Ltd., has served the legal and business counseling needs of clients since 1958. The firm's entrepreneurial spirit and understanding of the challenges facing growing businesses has been key to its success. The firm serves small and middle-market growing business and individual clients, as well as providing its special expertise to Fortune 500 companies. The firm's Bloomington location allows it to deliver legal services to clients in the most convenient and cost-effective manner possible. *See additional listing in Commercial Real Estate Law Chapter.*

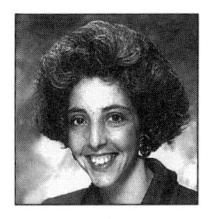

LINDA FISHER

Larkin, Hoffman, Daly & Lindgren, Ltd.
1500 Norwest Financial Center
7900 Xerxes Avenue South
Bloomington, MN 55431

Phone: (612) 835-3800
Fax: (612) 896-3333

Admitted: 1978 Minnesota; 1976 New York
Birthdate: 03/06/50

•**JOHN B. GORDON:** Mr. Gordon has represented many major corporate clients in the upper Midwest since the mid-1970s. He is particularly active in environmental law, including compliance with federal, state, and local regulations, permitting, litigation of Superfund issues, underground storage tanks, and the environmental aspects of corporate and real estate transactions. He also represents corporations in the retail sector, including department stores, discount stores, and convenience stores, and their particular problems such as assaults, false arrest and imprisonment cases, and store security systems. His counseling and litigation experience includes copyrights and trademarks, unfair competition, trade secrets litigation, insurance coverage, construction, age and race discrimination and retaliation issues, general breach of contract, covenants not to compete, and premises liability. Mr. Gordon has a strong background in product liability, having litigated cases involving drugs and medical devices, garage door operators, swimming pools, athletic equipment, playground equipment, toys, motorbikes, carbonated beverages, fabrics, small electric appliances such as fry pans and deep fryers, furnaces, water heaters, mobile homes, elevators, escalators, and industrial machinery. Mr. Gordon has also been active in the area of alternative dispute resolution. He has participated in Faegre & Benson's ADR committee and has served as an arbitrator for the American Arbitration Association and in many private arbitrations. He helped draft the rules and served as the first arbitrator for the Hennepin County District Court's mandatory court-annexed arbitration system. He has served on the US District Court Local Rules Committee for the District of Minnesota, and has been a frequent lecturer at continuing legal education courses in areas such as product liability, trial practice, appellate procedure, liquor liability, construction law, and environmental law.
Education: JD 1973, Harvard University (staff member 1972-73, *Harvard International Law Journal*); AB 1969 cum laude, Princeton University.
Employment History: Partner 1981-present, Associate 1974-80, Faegre & Benson; Law Clerk 1973-74, Hon. Lewis R. Morgan, Judge, US Court of Appeals, Fifth Circuit.
Professional Associations: MSBA; HCBA (past President); MDLA; International Assn. of Defense Counsel; Voluteer Lawyers Network, Ltd.
Community Involvement: Fund for the Legal Aid Society (Board member); Edina Human Relations Commission; various arts organizations (Board member). *See additional listing in Commercial Litigation and Personal Injury Defense Law Chapter.*

JOHN B. GORDON

Faegre & Benson
2200 Norwest Center
90 South Seventh Street
Minneapolis, MN 55402

Phone: (612) 336-3000
Fax: (612) 336-3026

Admitted: 1974 Minnesota
Birthdate: 11/21/47

CHERYL L. GRASMOEN - Petersen, Tews & Squires, P.A. - 4800 IDS Center, 80 South Eighth Street - Minneapolis, MN 55402 - Phone: (612) 344-1600, Fax: (612) 344-1650 - *See complete biographical profile in Commercial Real Estate Law Chapter.*

Chapter 17: Environmental Law

LLOYD W. GROOMS

Winthrop & Weinstine, P.A.
3200 Minnesota World Trade Center
30 East Seventh Street
St. Paul, MN 55101

Phone: (612) 290-8529
Fax: (612) 292-9347

Admitted: 1987 Minnesota; 1990 US Dist. Ct. (MN); 1990 US Ct. App. (8th Cir.); 1991 US Sup. Ct.
Birthdate: 09/17/53

•**LLOYD W. GROOMS:** Mr. Grooms is a shareholder of Winthrop & Weinstine, P.A., with principal responsibility for the firm's environmental practice. He represents a broad spectrum of clients including national corporations and regional lenders, as well as small companies and local governments. Mr. Grooms provides counseling on permit applications and compliance, administrative enforcement actions and private litigation, and commercial and real estate transactions. He also regularly represents his environmental clients before the Minnesota Legislature. In addition to being responsible for the firm's environmental practice, Mr. Grooms is an occasional speaker at environmental seminars.
Education: JD 1985 cum laude, University of Notre Dame; MA 1977, University of Essex (England); BS 1975 with high honors, Indiana University.
Employment History: Associate/Shareholder 1987-present, Winthrop & Weinstine, P.A.; Associate 1985-87, Strauss & Troy.
Representative Clients: City of Albertville; Boise Cascade; Champion Paper; Circuit City, Inc.; Dayton Rogers Mfg.; Eastman Kodak; Hoyt Construction; Liesch & Associates; Marvin Cedar & Lumber; Norwest Bank; TCB, Inc.; Winona Township.
Professional Associations: MSBA (Environment and Natural Resources and Administrative Law Sections); ABA (Natural Resources, Energy & Environmental Law Section).
Firm: Winthrop & Weinstine's environmental practice is integrated with the firm's strong general corporate and commercial litigation practices. The firm is fortunate to have corporate shareholders who can provide invaluable assistance in structuring any corporate and real estate transaction and a strong core of litigators headed by outstanding attorneys who are qualified to handle civil or criminal matters in both state and federal court. In addition, Winthrop & Weinstine, P.A., has the ability to pursue and secure regulatory and legislative alternatives. In the end, Winthrop & Weinstine, P.A., strives to provide its clients with the most timely, cost-effective solutions to their environmental problems. *See additional listing in Publicly Held Corporations Law Chapter.*

RAYMOND A. HAIK

Popham, Haik, Schnobrich & Kaufman, Ltd.
222 South Ninth Street
Suite 3300
Minneapolis, MN 55402

Phone: (612) 333-4800
Fax: (612) 334-8888

Admitted: 1953 Minnesota; 1953 US Dist. Ct. (MN); US Ct. App. (8th Cir.)
Birthdate: 10/22/28

•**RAYMOND A. HAIK:** Mr. Haik practices municipal and administrative law with an emphasis on natural resource and environmental litigation, representing public interest, industry, and governmental clients. He represented the Minnesota Conservation Federation and the Izaak Walton League in *Johnson v. Seifert*, successfully redefining Public Waters, thereby ensuring public use of Minnesota's nonmeandered water areas for hunting, fishing, and recreation. He served as special counsel for the State of Minnesota in the US Supreme Court case involving diversion of waters from the Great Lakes and as legal counsel for the Minneapolis Park & Recreation Board in the successful effort to oppose the taking of Minnehaha and other city park lands for highways. He has also served on federal committees and advisory boards regarding environmental issues. Mr. Haik lectures at Minnesota Continuing Legal Education seminars and writes articles on natural resource issues. He received the "54 Founders Award" from the Izaak Walton League and the "American Motors Citizen Conservation Award" for his work in conservation.
Education: JD 1953, University of Minnesota; BSL 1951, University of Minnesota.
Employment History: Founding Partner 1958-present, Popham, Haik, Schnobrich & Kaufman, Ltd.; Special Assistant Attorney General for the Dept. of Conservation 1953-58, Minnesota Attorney General's Office.
Representative Clients: Municipalities and special water and related land resource agencies.
Professional Associations: MSBA; ABA (House of Delegates; Section of Natural Resources, Energy and Environmental Law (past Chair)).
Community Involvement: Izaak Walton League of America (past President and Board Chair); Minnesota Private College Fund (Board of Trustees).
Firm: Popham, Haik, Schnobrich & Kaufman, Ltd., is a firm of more than 230 attorneys with offices in Denver, Miami, Minneapolis, Washington, D.C., and international affiliations in Beijing, China and Leipzig and Stuttgart, Germany. The firm represents clients nationally and internationally on issues relating to corporate and business law, administrative law, and litigation. *See additional listing in Federal, State & Local Government Law Chapter.*

Environmental Law Leading Attorneys

•**KAREN HANSEN:** Ms. Hansen practices exclusively in environmental law. Her practice involves advising businesses, local government units, and individuals regarding regulatory compliance and enforcement matters, management strategies, business transactions, and litigation concerning environmental issues. Ms. Hansen has a wide range of experience regarding solid and hazardous waste management issues, as well as toxic release reporting, community right to know, water and groundwater matters, and air issues stemming from federal and state programs. In addition, she represents clients before the state legislature on environmental issues and was actively involved with significant environmental enforcement and landfill cleanup programs enacted in 1991 and 1994, respectively. Ms. Hansen also writes and speaks for legal and business publications and interests regarding environmental issues.
Education: JD 1987, University of Texas; BA 1984 cum laude, Trinity University (San Antonio, TX).
Employment History: Currently, Popham, Haik, Schnobrich & Kaufman, Ltd.; previously, McKenna, Conner & Cuneo (Washington, D.C.).
Representative Clients: Businesses, local governments, individuals.
Professional Associations: MSBA (Natural Resources Section Council); State Bar of Texas; ABA (Solid and Hazardous Waste Committee of SONREEL (Vice Chair); Liaison to National Assn. of Attorneys General for the Natural Resources, Energy & Environmental Law Section); Environmental Law Institute; MN Government Relations Council; National and International Air & Waste Management Assn.; National Assn. of Women Business Owners; MN Women Lawyers.
Community Involvement: MN Chamber of Commerce (Solid and Hazardous Waste and Air Quality Committees; Landfill Task Force; Legislative Seminar).
Firm: Popham, Haik, Schnobrich & Kaufman, Ltd., is a firm of more than 230 attorneys with offices in Denver, Miami, Minneapolis, Washington, D.C., and international affiliations in Beijing, China and Leipzig and Stuttgart, Germany. The firm represents clients nationally and internationally on issues relating to corporate and business law, administrative law, and litigation. *See additional listings in Commercial Real Estate Law and Commercial Litigation Chapters.*

KAREN HANSEN

Popham, Haik, Schnobrich & Kaufman, Ltd.
222 South Ninth Street
Suite 3300
Minneapolis, MN 55402

Phone: (612) 333-4800
Fax: (612) 334-8888

Admitted: 1987 Texas;
1989 Minnesota;
1989 US Dist. Ct. (MN);
1989 US Ct. App. (8th Cir.)
Birthdate: 11/21/61

•**GILBERT W. HARRIES:** Mr. Harries concentrates his practice on environmental law, including environmental compliance, CERCLA, and toxic tort litigation; air, water, and wetlands permits; environmental assessment worksheets; environmental impact statements; mineral leases; and mineral and surface titles for mining companies and utilities. In addition, he handles estate planning, probate, and trust administration.
Education: LLB 1955, University of Minnesota; BS 1953, University of Minnesota.
Employment History: Currently, Hanft, Fride, O'Brien, Harries, Swelbar & Burns, P.A.; Law Clerk, Minnesota Supreme Court.
Representative Clients: Oglebay Norton Company; Eveleth Mines; Ordean Foundation; fee owners; bank trust departments.
Professional Associations: ABA; MSBA; 11th District Bar Assn. (past President).
Community Involvement: Duluth Community Trust (Board Chair); Duluth Public Library Foundation; Duluth Public Library (past Board Chair); United Way of Duluth (past President); St. Paul's Episcopal Church (past Warden).
Firm: Founded in 1899, Hanft, Fride, O'Brien, Harries, Swelbar & Burns, P.A., is a full service law firm engaged primarily in business and trial work. The firm's 17 attorneys serve clients throughout Minnesota, northern Wisconsin, and beyond. *See additional listings in Probate, Estate Planning & Trusts Law and Commercial Real Estate Law Chapters.*

GILBERT W. HARRIES

Hanft, Fride, O'Brien, Harries, Swelbar & Burns, P.A.
1000 First Bank Place
130 West Superior Street
Duluth, MN 55802

Phone: (218) 722-4766
Fax: (218) 720-4920

Admitted: 1955 Minnesota;
1984 Wisconsin
Birthdate: 01/15/32

Chapter 17: Environmental Law

G. ROBERT JOHNSON

Popham, Haik, Schnobrich & Kaufman, Ltd.
222 South Ninth Street
Suite 3300
Minneapolis, MN 55402

Phone: (612) 333-4800
Fax: (612) 334-8888

Admitted: 1968 Minnesota; 1968 US Dist. Ct. (MN); 1971 US Ct. App. (8th Cir.)
Birthdate: 07/02/40

•**G. ROBERT JOHNSON:** Mr. Johnson leads Popham, Haik, Schnobrich & Kaufman's Environmental Law Section and practices in all facets of environmental law before federal and state administrative, legislative, and judicial forums. He is past chair of the firm's Administrative Law Department.
Education: JD 1968, University of Minnesota; BA 1965, University of Minnesota.
Employment History: 1975-present, Popham, Haik, Schnobrich & Kaufman, Ltd.; 1971-75, Johnson & Associates, Ltd.; 1968-71, Minnesota Special Attorney General and counsel to the Minnesota Pollution Control Agency.
Representative Clients: Multinational, regional, and local corporations.
Professional Associations: MSBA (past Chair, Environmental Law Section); ABA (Administrative Law Section; Litigation Section; Natural Resources, Energy and Environmental Law Section (Liaison to National Conference of State Legislatures 1987-present; Governing Council (past member); Environmental Quality Committee (past Chair); Continuing Legal Education Committee (past Chair)).
Community Involvement: Greater Minneapolis Chamber of Commerce (Director 1990-present; Division Vice Chair, Public Policy Committee); Minnesota Chamber of Commerce (Environmental Policy Committee).
Firm: Popham, Haik, Schnobrich & Kaufman, Ltd., is a firm of more than 230 attorneys with offices in Denver, Miami, Minneapolis, Washington, D.C., and international affiliations in Beijing, China and Leipzig and Stuttgart, Germany. The firm represents clients nationally and internationally on issues relating to corporate and business law, administrative law, and litigation.

WILLIAM J. KEPPEL

Dorsey & Whitney
Pillsbury Center South
220 South Sixth Street
Minneapolis, MN 55402-1498

Phone: (612) 340-2745
Fax: (612) 340-2644

Admitted: 1970 Minnesota; 1970 US Dist. Ct. (MN); 1979 US Dist. Ct. (W. Dist. WI); 1992 US Dist. Ct. (E. Dist. WI); 1973 US Ct. App. (8th Cir.); 1979 US Sup. Ct.; 1982 US Ct. of Claims; 1979 Interstate Commerce Commission Register
Birthdate: 09/25/41

•**WILLIAM J. KEPPEL:** Mr. Keppel represents clients before federal and state courts and administrative agencies involving Superfund, licensing, regulatory compliance, rulemaking, insurance coverage, FIFRA registration, toxic tort, product liability, health, land use, environmental impact statement, wetland, and administrative law issues. He has chaired and served on steering, allocation, and technical committees of PRP Superfund groups. He also advises clients on regulatory compliance, supervises environmental site assessments, and negotiates contracts in real estate and business transactions. Mr. Keppel is a member of the Environmental and Regulatory Affairs Department (Cofounder 1981, Chair 1984-89), the Litigation Department, and the Indian Law Practice Group and has served on several committees at Dorsey & Whitney. He has lectured at legal seminars and law schools and has written numerous books, articles, and monographs, including *Minnesota Civil Practice* (4 vols.), *Minnesota Environmental Law Handbook*, and *Minnesota Administrative Practice and Procedure*. He is listed in *The Best Lawyers in America* and *Who's Who in American Law*.
Education: JD 1970, University of Wisconsin; AB 1963, Marquette University.
Employment History: Partner 1979-present, Associate 1970-75, Dorsey & Whitney; Professor 1976-79, Hamline University School of Law; Chief Public Defender, Hennepin County Public Defender's Office for Municipal Court (on leave of absence from Dorsey & Whitney); Hearing Examiner and Consultant (under contract) 1977-79, MN Office of Administrative Hearings.
Representative Clients: Large and small corporations, municipalities, utilities, Indian tribes, individuals, and citizen groups.
Professional Associations: ABA (Litigation, Administrative Law, and Natural Resources, Energy & Environmental Law Sections); MSBA (Litigation, Administrative Law, and Environmental and Natural Resource Sections); HCBA (Litigation Section; Governing Council; *The Hennepin Lawyer* (Editorial Board)); Legal Advice Clinics, Ltd. (past President; Board member); Joint Legislative Task Force on the MN Administrative Procedure Act; Hennepin County Conciliation Court (Referee 1973-79).
Firm: Dorsey & Whitney is the largest law firm in Minnesota and one of the largest firms in the United States with over 350 lawyers in 12 offices. The depth and breadth of the experience of its lawyers enables it to provide a broad range of services to meet the diverse legal needs of its client base, which includes Fortune 500 companies, public agencies, banks and other financial institutions, nonprofit organizations, individual investors, family owned businesses, and high-tech and low-tech, growth oriented companies. *See additional listings in Commercial Litigation and Federal, State & Local Government Law Chapters.*

JOHN A. KNAPP - Winthrop & Weinstine, P.A. - 3200 Minnesota World Trade Center, 30 East Seventh Street - St. Paul, MN 55101 - Phone: (612) 290-8400, Fax: (612) 292-9347 - *See complete biographical profile in Federal, State & Local Government Law Chapter.*

Environmental Law Leading Attorneys

CHARLES L. LEFEVERE - Holmes & Graven, Chartered - 470 Pillsbury Center, 200 South Sixth Street - Minneapolis, MN 55402 - Phone: (612) 337-9300, Fax: (612) 337-9310 - *See complete biographical profile in Federal, State & Local Government Law Chapter.*

•**CHARLES N. NAUEN:** Mr. Nauen practices environmental law and litigation, as well as complex commercial and class action litigation. His experience in environmental matters runs the gamut from permitting and compliance counseling to large scale litigation in federal court. He has prosecuted citizen environmental lawsuits, toxic tort class actions, and private Superfund cost recovery litigation involving several hundred parties. He has defended corporate and governmental clients in enforcement actions and private disputes under the various environmental laws. Mr. Nauen lectures and writes on environmental law issues and is an adjunct professor of advanced environmental law at the University of Minnesota Law School. Additionally, he represents parties in complex commercial litigation, including antitrust, bankruptcy, discrimination, and other areas.
Education: JD 1980 cum laude, University of Minnesota; BA 1976 cum laude, Baylor University.
Employment History: 1981-present, Schatz Paquin Lockridge Grindal & Holstein (formerly Opperman & Paquin); Law Clerk 1980-81, Hon. O. Russell Olson and Hon. Daniel F. Foley, MN District Court Judges (Rochester).
Representative Clients: The Foundation Press; Hennepin County; Metropolitan Council; Metropolitan Waste Control Commission; Midway National Bank; Oak Grove Sanitary Landfill Site Trust; Pine Valley Meats; Scrap Metal Processors; United States Gypsum Company; West Publishing Company.
Professional Associations: ABA; ATLA; Federal Bar Assn.; HCBA; MSBA.
Community Involvement: District 12 Neighborhood Council, City of St. Paul (1986-87); St. Anthony Park Block Nurse Program (Board member).
Firm: Schatz Paquin practices in four major areas: sophisticated civil litigation with an emphasis on antitrust, employment, environmental, intellectual property, and securities issues; general corporate counseling in antitrust, employment, environmental, intellectual property, and telecommunications matters; government relations at the local, state, and federal levels; and health care matters involving corporate, commercial, and governmental interests. The firm employs 30 attorneys and maintains offices in Minneapolis and Washington, D.C. *See additional listing in Commercial Litigation Chapter.*

CHARLES N. NAUEN

Schatz Paquin Lockridge
Grindal & Holstein
2200 Washington Square
100 Washington Avenue South
Minneapolis, MN 55401

Phone: (612) 339-6900
Fax: (612) 339-0981

Admitted: 1980 Minnesota;
1981 US Dist. Ct. (MN)
Birthdate: 09/27/54

•**FORREST D. (DICK) NOWLIN:** Mr. Nowlin is the Chair of the Environmental Law Department at Doherty, Rumble & Butler, P.A., where he handles environmental regulatory, administrative, legislative, and litigation matters. His practice also involves waste and land use law. Mr. Nowlin represents private and public entities in securing authorizations for complex land and water uses; handling regulatory and Superfund matters for waste generating, processing, and disposal facilities; and resolving contaminated land issues. He also provides substantive assistance on environmental and land use cases and appears before the Metropolitan Council on Metro Urban Service Area and sewer extension issues; and before the Minnesota Pollution Control Agency on enforcement, solid waste, NPDES, air quality, and hazardous waste matters. Mr. Nowlin taught land use at Hamline Law School from 1980 to 1984 and is a frequent lecturer on solid and hazardous waste and environmental compliance issues.
Education: JD 1968, University of Minnesota; BA 1964, University of the South.
Employment History: Associate/Partner 1989-present, Doherty, Rumble & Butler, P.A.; Associate/Partner 1979-89, Larkin, Hoffman, Daly & Lindgren, Ltd.; Chief Counsel 1973-79, Metropolitan Council; Associate Counsel 1971-73, Land O'Lakes, Inc.; Instructor 1969-71, Nkumbi International College.
Representative Clients: East Bethel and Ponderosa Landfills; CF Industries; DeZurik Corp.; Anagram International; Minneapolis Refuse, Inc.; Upper River Services; Bayport Marina; St. Paul Port Authority; cities of Hopkins, Woodbury, and Cottage Grove; Waseca County; MN Counties Insurance Trust.
Professional Associations: MSBA (Executive Council 1989-93, Environmental Law Section; Executive Council 1994-present, Administrative Law Section); Environmental Law Institute; ABA (Natural Resources, Energy & Environmental Law Section).
Community Involvement: Prospect Park Improvement Assn. (past President); Sensible Land Use Coalition (Executive Director 1981-90); Citizens League; St. Marks Cathedral vestry member.
Firm: Doherty, Rumble & Butler's Environmental and Land Use Law Department provides high quality, innovative legal services to government, business, and individuals. The ten attorneys in the Department assist clients on matters ranging from workplace health and safety to environmental clearances, regulatory permitting, solid and hazardous waste, asbestos, wetlands, shorelands, land use/zoning, agricultural issues, and the Superfund. Problems are solved efficiently and expeditiously using innovative approaches, including complex applications, negotiation, legislative amendment, and/or aggressive litigation. *See additional listing in Federal, State & Local Government Law Chapter.*

FORREST D. (DICK) NOWLIN

Doherty, Rumble & Butler
Professional Association
2800 Minnesota World Trade Center
30 East Seventh Street
St. Paul, MN 55101-4999

Phone: (612) 291-9333
Fax: (612) 291-9313

Admitted: 1968 Minnesota;
1972 US Dist. Ct. (MN)
Birthdate: 12/02/42

1994/1996 ◆ *Minnesota Edition*

Chapter 17: Environmental Law

BRIAN B. O'NEILL

Faegre & Benson
2200 Norwest Center
90 South Seventh Street
Minneapolis, MN 55402

Phone: (612) 336-3000
Fax: (612) 336-3026
800 number: (800) 328-4393

Admitted: 1974 Michigan;
1977 Minnesota;
1977 US Dist. Ct. (MN);
1977 US Ct. App. (8th Cir.);
1974 US Ct. Military App.;
1977 US Claims Ct.;
1980 US Sup. Ct.
Birthdate: 06/07/47

•**BRIAN B. O'NEILL:** Mr. O'Neill is a litigation partner at Faegre & Benson. He has tried securities, antitrust, environmental, admiralty, bankruptcy, contract, patent, trademark, copyright, constitutional, products, trade secrets, and bank robbery cases. He has appeared before the various Minnesota and California state courts, federal district courts across the country, and the US Claims Court. He has argued appeals at the state and federal levels in many jurisdictions, including the US Supreme Court. Mr. O'Neill was lead trial counsel for over 800 Alaskan fisherman in *In re the Glacier Bay* and lead trial cousel *In re the Exxon Valdez* where he obtained 5.3 billion dollar verdict. He tried Minnesota's first CERCLA/MERLA (Superfund) jury case in 1990. In 1985, he received the national Sierra Club's William O. Douglas Award. He lectures regularly on environmental topics and has written law review articles on the environment. Mr. O'Neill is listed in the 1989-90, 1991-92, and 1993-94 editions of *The Best Lawyers in America*. He is a Fellow of the American College of Trial Lawyers.
Education: JD 1974 magna cum laude, Order of the Coif, University of Michigan (Managing Editor 1973-74, *Michigan Law Review*); BS 1969, US Military Academy.
Employment History: 1977-present, Faegre & Benson; 1974-77 Assistant to the General Counsel, US Army.
Representative Clients: Significant trials include: *In re the Exxon Valdez* (Anchorage, AK); *In re the Glacier Bay* (Anchorage, AK); *Gopher Oil Co. v. Union Oil Co.* (Minneapolis, MN); *Jurgens v. McKasy* (St. Paul, MN); *Faribo Cap-Tech, Inc. v. Capspray, Inc.* (St. Paul, MN); *Mentor Corp. v. Cox-Uphoff Corp.* (Los Angeles, CA); *Medical Engineering Corp. v. Mentor Corp.* (Minneapolis, MN). Significant environmental cases of Mr. O'Neill's which have resulted in published judicial precedent include *Lujan v. Defenders of Wildlife* (application of Endangered Species Act to US projects overseas); *Sierra Club and Defenders of Wildlife v. Clark* (the Minnesota wolf case); and *Minnesota v. Bergland and Sierra Club* (dealing with the constitutionality of the 1978 Boundary Waters Canoe Area Wilderness Act).
Community Involvement: Defenders of Wildlife (Board member); Friends of the Boundary Waters Wilderness (Board member); Committee for an International Wolf Center (Board member). *See additional listing in Commercial Litigation Chapter.*

DENNIS L. O'TOOLE - Lano, Nelson, O'Toole & Bengtson, Ltd. - 115 East Fifth Street, P.O. Box 20 - Grand Rapids, MN 55744 - Phone: (218) 326-9603, Fax: (218) 326-1565 - *See complete biographical profile in Personal Injury Defense Law Chapter.*

JAMES A. PAYNE

Popham, Haik, Schnobrich & Kaufman, Ltd.
222 South Ninth Street
Suite 3300
Minneapolis, MN 55402

Phone: (612) 333-4800
Fax: (612) 334-8888

Admitted: 1976 Minnesota
Birthdate: 12/31/45

•**JAMES A. PAYNE:** Mr. Payne is a shareholder in the Minneapolis office practicing in the area of environmental law and regulation. He is also experienced in land use issues and in the environmental aspects of business and real estate transactions. Mr. Payne lectures at and chairs seminars for the Minnesota Institute of Legal Education and other professional organizations. He is also the author of articles on environmental law, including "Minnesota Environmental Law," *Environmental Law Practice Guide* (1992) and "Landowner Liability for Hazardous Substance Disposal Sites under the Minnesota Environmental Response and Liability Act," *Minnesota Real Estate Law Journal*, Vol. 1, No. 14 (Sept/Oct 1983). Mr. Payne is a former adjunct professor of environmental law at the University of Minnesota Law School.
Education: JD 1975 cum laude, University of Minnesota (President, *Minnesota Law Review*); AB 1968 cum laude, Dartmouth College (Phi Beta Kappa; Dartmouth Senior Fellowship).
Employment History: Shareholder 1984-present, Popham, Haik, Schnobrich & Kaufman, Ltd.; Partner 1976-84, Pepin, Dayton, Herman, Graham & Getts.
Representative Clients: University of Minnesota; The Interlake Corp.; Reynolds Metals Company.
Professional Associations: ABA (Section on Natural Resources, Energy and Environmental Law; Special Committee on Biotechnology (Chair 1991-93, Vice Chair 1990-91 & 1993-)); MSBA (Environmental Law Section (Council member 1988-94)).
Community Involvement: Minnesota Environmental Quality Board (Advisory Committee on Genetically Engineered Organisms (Chair 1989-91)); Civic Leadership Foundation (Board member 1994-); University of Minnesota Law School (Environmental Moot Court (Faculty Advisor 1990-91)).
Firm: Popham, Haik, Schnobrich & Kaufman, Ltd., is a firm of more than 230 attorneys with offices in Denver, Miami, Minneapolis, Washington, D.C., and international affiliations in Beijing, China and Leipzig and Stuttgart, Germany. The firm represents clients nationally and internationally on issues relating to corporate and business law, administrative law, and litigation.

Environmental Law Leading Attorneys

DAVID C. SELLERGREN - Doherty, Rumble & Butler Professional Association - 3500 Fifth Street Towers, 150 South Fifth Street - Minneapolis, MN 55402-4235 - Phone: (612) 340-5555, Fax: (612) 340-5584 - *See complete biographical profile in Federal, State & Local Government Law Chapter.*

KEVIN A. SPELLACY - Quinlivan, Sherwood, Spellacy & Tarvestad, P.A. - P.O. Box 1008 - St. Cloud, MN 56302-1008 - Phone: (612) 251-1414, Fax: (612) 251-1415 - *See complete biographical profile in Personal Injury Defense Law Chapter.*

•CHARLES E. SPEVACEK: Mr. Spevacek has a broad-based civil, regulatory, and governmental practice, serving his clients locally and nationally. His expertise is representation of the insurance industry in matters involving environmental and natural resources law. His environmental practice focuses on advising and counseling the insurance industry on claims, underwriting, and marketing issues; and in the trial and appeal of insurance coverage disputes, including breach of contract, declaratory judgment, and bad faith actions. He has shared his expertise on environmental issues before the Minnesota Legislature. Mr. Spevacek has considerable civil trial experience in both tort and commercial matters, including personal injury cases; professional negligence claims involving the defense of attorneys, architects, and engineers; and product liability claims. He has authored articles published in *Minnesota Defense*, *Hamline Law Review*, and *Indiana Law Review*, and has lectured on a wide range of topics at professional seminars throughout the United States.
Education: JD 1980, Indiana University (Associate Editor, *Indiana Law Review*); BS 1977, Purdue University.
Employment History: Partner 1986-present, Associate 1980-86, Meagher & Geer.
Representative Clients: Allstate Insurance Group; CNA Insurance Companies; Federated Insurance Companies; ITT Hartford Insurance Group; The St. Paul Companies, Inc.; State Farm Insurance Companies.
Professional Associations: ABA; Defense Research Institute; MDLA.
Community Involvement: The Purdue Alumni Assn. (past Board member).
Firm: Nineteen ninety-four marks Meagher & Geer's 65th year. The Minneapolis law firm is recognized as one of the Midwest's most reputable; Meagher & Geer attorneys have long been considered among the preeminent trial lawyers in the state of Minnesota and throughout the country. In addition to a practice that encompasses all aspects of insurance law, civil litigation, and business and commercial law, the firm has a separate practice group devoted to the appellate practice. Mr. Spevacek is a member of Meagher & Geer's Management Committee. *See additional listings in Commercial Litigation and Professional Malpractice Defense Law Chapters.*

CHARLES E. SPEVACEK

Meagher & Geer
4200 Multifoods Tower
33 South Sixth Street
Minneapolis, MN 55402

Phone: (612) 338-0661
Fax: (612) 338-8384

Admitted: 1981 Minnesota;
1981 US Dist. Ct. (MN);
1994 US Dist. Ct. (C.D. IL);
1981 US Ct. App. (8th Cir.);
1993 US Ct. App. (9th Cir.);
1989 US Sup. Ct.
Birthdate: 05/17/56

•BYRON E. STARNS: Mr. Starns specializes in environmental and other regulatory litigation and counseling and is chair of Leonard, Street and Deinard's Public Law Department. He has tried cases to conclusion in municipal, state, and federal trial courts, tried administrative contested case and rulemaking proceedings, tried commercial arbitrations, and represented parties in successful mediations. Mr. Starns has also argued appeals in Minnesota appellate courts, the Court of Appeals for the Eighth Circuit, and the US Supreme Court.
Education: JD 1969, University of Chicago; BA 1966, Duke University.
Employment History: Partner/Shareholder 1979-present, Leonard, Street and Deinard; 1969-79, Minnesota Attorney General's Office: Chief Deputy Attorney General 1974-1979; Deputy Attorney General 1973-1974, Pollution Control Agency; Assistant Attorney General 1972-73, Solicitor General's Division; Assistant Attorney General 1970-1972, Opinions and Local Government Division; Special Assistant Attorney 1969-1970, Minnesota Department of Transportation.
Representative Clients: Terra International, Inc.; Howard, Needles, Tammen & Bergendoff.
Professional Associations: ABA; MSBA; HCBA; RCBA; Illinois State Bar Assn.
Community Involvement: Minnesota Harmful Substances Compensation Board (Chair 1985-1991); Cub Scout Pack Master; Messiah Episcopal Church (Secretary/Clerk of Vestry).
Firm: Leonard, Street and Deinard is a full service commercial law firm of approximately 125 attorneys. Half of the firm's practice concerns commercial, securities, and other business litigation; the other half of the practice concerns nonlitigated business matters, including corporate, public and private finance, real estate, mergers and acquisitions, banking, trade regulation, distribution, intellectual property, health, tax, and estate planning. The firm has a long history of representing family held, entrepreneurial, publicly held, and institutional businesses. The firm prides itself on its reputation for excellence and efficiency, and on the long term relationships it consistently builds with clients. *See additional listings in Commercial Litigation and Federal, State & Local Government Law Chapters.*

BYRON E. STARNS

Leonard, Street and Deinard
Professional Association
150 South Fifth Street
Suite 2300
Minneapolis, MN 55402

Phone: (612) 335-1516
Fax: (612) 335-1657

Admitted: 1969 Minnesota;
1969 Illinois;
1969 US Dist. Ct. (MN);
1974 US Ct. App. (8th Cir.);
1974 US Sup. Ct.
Birthdate: 12/14/43

ROBERT O. STRAUGHN - McGrann Shea Franzen Carnival Straughn & Lamb, Chartered - 2200 LaSalle Plaza, 800 LaSalle Avenue - Minneapolis, MN 55402 - Phone: (612) 338-2525, Fax: (612) 339-2386 - *See complete biographical profile in Commercial Real Estate Law Chapter.*

Chapter 17: Environmental Law

•**THOMAS R. THIBODEAU** - Johnson, Killen, Thibodeau & Seiler, P.A. - 811 Norwest Center, 230 West Superior Street - Duluth, MN 55802 - Phone: (218) 722-6331, Fax: (218) 722-3031 - *See complete biographical profile in Personal Injury Defense Law Chapter.*

JOHN B. VAN DE NORTH, JR.

Briggs and Morgan, P.A.
W-2200 First National Bank Building
St. Paul, MN 55101

Phone: (612) 223-6600
Fax: (612) 223-6450

Admitted: 1971 Minnesota; US Dist. Ct. (MN)
Birthdate: 03/07/45

•**JOHN B. VAN DE NORTH, JR.:** Mr. Van de North is a member of the Briggs and Morgan Environmental Law Section. His environmental work has focused on air, water, and hazardous waste regulatory compliance, toxic torts, and environmental issues in commercial and real estate transactions. Mr. Van de North regularly appears in both state and federal courts and before administrative agencies. He is also a member of the firm's ADR Practice Group which focuses on environmental disputes through mediation and arbitration. Mr. Van de North is a frequent lecturer at continuing legal education programs on environmental issues.
Education: JD 1970, University of Notre Dame; BS 1967, St. John's University.
Employment History: 1977-present, Briggs and Morgan; 1976-77, Holmes and Graven; Special Assistant Attorney General 1970, 1973-76, Minnesota Attorney General's Office.
Representative Clients: Quebecor Printing Company; Domtar Inc.; City of Bemidji; Port Authority of the City of St. Paul; A.G. Processing; ConAgra; Schwing America, Inc.
Professional Associations: MSBA; ABA; RCBA.
Community Involvement: St. John's University Board of Regents; Canada/Minnesota Business Council; Indianhead Council Law Exploring.
Firm: Briggs and Morgan, P.A., was established in 1882 and now has over 150 lawyers in its St. Paul and Minneapolis offices. The firm handles a broad range of legal areas for its business, governmental, and individual clients. *See additional listing in Agricultural Law Chapter.*

Complete listing of all attorneys nominated in Environmental Law

MICHAEL J. AHERN, Moss & Barnett, A Professional Association, Minneapolis; **JOHN M. ANDERSON,** Bassford, Lockhart, Truesdell & Briggs, P.A., Minneapolis; **MARTHA C. BRAND,** Leonard, Street and Deinard Professional Association, Minneapolis; **REBECCA A. COMSTOCK,** Dorsey & Whitney, Minneapolis; **CHARLES K. DAYTON,** Leonard, Street and Deinard Professional Association, Minneapolis; **LINDA FISHER,** Larkin, Hoffman, Daly & Lindgren, Ltd., Bloomington; **JOHN B. GORDON,** Faegre & Benson, Minneapolis; **LLOYD W. GROOMS,** Winthrop & Weinstine, P.A., St. Paul; **RAYMOND A. HAIK,** Popham, Haik, Schnobrich & Kaufman, Ltd., Minneapolis; **KAREN HANSEN,** Popham, Haik, Schnobrich & Kaufman, Ltd., Minneapolis; **GILBERT W. HARRIES,** Hanft, Fride, O'Brien, Harries, Swelbar & Burns, P.A., Duluth; **JOHN H. HERMAN,** Leonard, Street and Deinard Professional Association, Minneapolis; **MACLAY R. HYDE,** Gray, Plant, Mooty, Mooty & Bennett, P.A., Minneapolis; **G. ROBERT JOHNSON,** Popham, Haik, Schnobrich & Kaufman, Ltd., Minneapolis; **THOMAS L. JOHNSON,** Gray, Plant, Mooty, Mooty & Bennett, P.A., Minneapolis; **WILLIAM J. KEPPEL,** Dorsey & Whitney, Minneapolis; **GEORGE O. LUDCKE,** Best & Flanagan, Minneapolis; **DAVID C. MCDONALD,** Briggs and Morgan, P.A., St. Paul; **CHARLES N. NAUEN,** Schatz Paquin Lockridge Grindal & Holstein, Minneapolis; **FORREST D. (DICK) NOWLIN,** Doherty, Rumble & Butler Professional Association, St. Paul; **JAMES A. PAYNE,** Popham, Haik, Schnobrich & Kaufman, Ltd., Minneapolis; **CHARLES E. SPEVACEK,** Meagher & Geer, Minneapolis; **BYRON E. STARNS,** Leonard, Street and Deinard Professional Association, Minneapolis; **THOMAS R. THIBODEAU,** Johnson, Killen, Thibodeau & Seiler, P.A., Duluth; **LISA R. TIEGEL,** Minnesota Attorney General's Office, St. Paul; **JOHN B. VAN DE NORTH JR.,** Briggs and Morgan, P.A., St. Paul.

CHAPTER 18

FEDERAL, STATE & LOCAL GOVERNMENT LAW

Some businesses deal exclusively with one or more branches of government, while others only have to deal with the government to get permission to embark on certain projects. This chapter focuses on areas where businesses frequently come into contact with federal, state, and local governments, such as public financing, government contracts, lobbying, and dealing with administrative agencies. The Environmental Law Chapter examines issues relating to business interaction with agencies protecting the environment. The Intellectual Property Law Chapter discusses how a business registers a trademark with federal and state authorities. The Commercial Real Estate Law Chapter covers zoning and land use variances.

PUBLIC FINANCING

One of the government's primary interests is to expand the economy and increase opportunities for a wider cross-section of the population to participate in the economy. In a poor economy, businesses lay off employees, and people without jobs tend to vote against incumbent politicians. Therefore, politicians have created a variety of government programs that aim to promote the interests of businesses. One of the most important means by which the government seeks to help businesses is by making available various forms of public financing so that businesses can expand and grow. Public financing is available from state, local and federal sources.

FEDERAL FINANCING

The federal government offers a number of assistance programs primarily through an organization called the Small Business Administration (SBA). Created by Congress in 1953 to help small businesses, the SBA provides financial, procurement, advocacy and management assistance. Every year, the SBA guarantees bank loans totaling over 3 billion dollars for small businesses. Small businesses that qualify for SBA loans can usually receive far more favorable terms than they would otherwise be able to get. Most SBA loans are for a lengthy period of time and qualify for a relatively low interest rate. Despite their advantages, SBA loans are not right for all businesses: the SBA loan process usually takes longer than the conventional loan process, the SBA can require more personal guarantees and collateral, and the SBA sometimes restricts a business's ability to get additional financing as a pre-condition to the SBA loan.

Chapter 18: Federal, State & Local Government Law

STATE FINANCING

In Minnesota there are various public sources of financing under the direction of the Minnesota Department of Trade and Economic Development. One such program is a private/public partnership called Opportunities Minnesota Incorporated (OMNI) whose goal is to help provide financing for businesses that purchase buildings or capital assets that they plan to use for more than 15 years.

OMNI is certified by the SBA as a development company charged with helping to package and process federal loans. The program can be used to finance such things as land, buildings, renovation and machinery purchases. OMNI can lend no more than 40 percent of the cost of a project or $750,000, whichever is less. The remaining money must be provided by the company seeking the financing (10 percent) and a local lending organization (50 percent).

Other sources of public financing from the state include the Economic Development Program, Rural Development Board, Minnesota Public Facilities Authority, Tourism Loan Program, Capital Access Program, Minnesota Technology, Inc., Technology Information Services, Indian Business Loan Program, and Solid Waste Management Financial Assistance Program. Each of these programs has its own standards for determining who qualifies for economic assistance and how much money is available for which ventures. Information on all of them is available from the Minnesota Department of Trade and Economic Development.

LOCAL FINANCING

Many local government units provide assistance in various forms to new businesses. Some offer technical assistance or financial services, while others offer tax credits or loan packaging assistance. The cities of Minneapolis, St. Paul, Bloomington, and Duluth have the most experience assembling financial packages to encourage businesses to locate within their boundaries, but many other municipalities are amenable to negotiating with potential businesses. A businessperson interested in programs offered in a given area should contact the business services or planning unit of the county or city in which the business is or will be located.

GOVERNMENT CONTRACTS AND TECHNICAL ASSISTANCE

Of all the corporations in the United States, the single largest is the federal government. Likewise, of all the corporations in Minnesota, the single largest is the state government. Despite these figures, government entities are frequently overlooked by business managers as a source of business opportunities. There are a number of ways a business can secure government contracts at the federal, state, and local levels.

On the federal level, each individual federal agency receives requests for bids from small businesses. To receive copies of various federal agencies' requests for bids, a business files an application with each federal agency that the business wants to do business with. Many of these federal agencies have special programs specifically designed to assist small and minority owned businesses because regulations require that a certain percentage of all government contracts be reserved for small or minority owned businesses. The SBA provides assistance to small businesses in this regard by publishing a list called the Small Business Subcontracting Directory. The directory lists the major contractors to the federal government and which are most likely to be in need of subcontracting.

One of the missions the SBA takes most seriously is its goal of management assistance. To this end, the SBA offers a number of different programs that businesses can turn to for advice in such areas as marketing, buying, financial management and administration. Among these programs is the Service Core of Retired Executives (SCORE) which puts small businesses in touch with retired executive volunteers who offer counseling and advice. There is also the Small Business Institute, a coalition of college business schools and small business people, which offers management training seminars and various other services. The SBA's Office of Procurement Assistance helps businesses get information and develop strategies concerning selling to the federal government. The SBA also lobbies Congress and other federal organizations on behalf of small businesses.

There are several other government agencies that a small business should be aware of. For example, the various branches of the armed services offer assistance to businesses in securing defense-related contracts. Also, the General Services Administration (GSA) helps businesses that want to sell their products directly to the government by providing information on which government agencies wish to purchase products. The U.S. Army maintains an office known as the Defense Logistics Agency to assist small businesses with contracts.

LOBBYING

Lobbying is the business of persuading politicians to pass laws that are favorable to a particular person or agency and to defeat potential laws that are unfavorable to lobbyists or their clients. Despite the negative image that some lobbyists have, lobbying government on behalf of business is a long respected tradition in this country. Not only have lobbyists been around for many years, but many government agencies and departments rely on lobbyists to provide them with information necessary to make decisions and set policy. The government is not the large faceless machine it sometimes appears to be. There are people behind every decision and every regulation, and many of these people are sincerely concerned about staying abreast of changes in the law and industry and in promoting the economic vitality of the area they oversee.

There are laws governing lobbying at both the state and federal level, including requirements for lobbyists to identify the clients on whose behalf they lobby. Lobbyists who lobby the United States Congress are governed by federal lobbyist registration statutes. These laws require lobbyists to maintain and periodically file with the Clerk of the House of Representatives detailed records of major contributors and all expenditures made by the lobbyist or lobbying organization. Lobbyists are also required to register with both the Secretary of the Senate and the Clerk of the House of Representatives.

Lobbyists who lobby the Minnesota State Legislature must register with the Minnesota Ethical Practices Board. They must also inform the board about themselves and about the party they intend to represent to the Legislature, and must provide the board with quarterly reports thereafter. The initial registration form provides the Board with information about the lobbyists and the parties they intend to represent. Quarterly reports must be filed thereafter detailing how much money was spent in efforts to persuade elected officials, how that money was raised, and exactly how the money was spent. Supervision and enforcement of these regulations has become tighter in recent years.

Many law firms have attorneys who specialize in lobbying. In addition, there are non-legal political consulting firms available to perform lobbying services. Their employees are often experts at influencing government.

DEALING WITH ADMINISTRATIVE AGENCIES

When the average person imagines how the government makes decisions, he or she envisions the House or the Senate deliberating in session or the Chief Executive sitting in his or her office poring over papers. While it might be nice to have direct input into these decisions, few business managers will ever be asked to testify before Congress or to personally advise the President. Instead, the decisions that most directly affect the average business are usually made by one of a variety of government administrative agencies set up to formulate rules and oversee their implementation. Because administrative agencies deal with a wide variety of substantive problems, it would be impossible to summarize, here, all the work they do. However, because administrative procedures are so similar from agency to agency, a business manager should have a basic grasp of how agencies make decisions and the role he or she can play in dealing with administrative agencies.

The Limited Role of Administrative Agencies

It is easier to understand the role of administrative agencies if one understands their Constitutional limitations. Theoretically, it is Congress that makes all federal laws and the Minnesota State Legislature that makes state laws. Realistically, it would be impossible for either of these two legislative bodies to handle every detail of the laws they create. Legislatures are forced to rely heavily on the advice of numerous administrative agencies in suggesting new laws and implementing existing laws. Frequently, Congress or the state legislature establishes an agency, gives it broad outlines to follow in regulating an industry, then delegates to that agency the power to make rules that industry must follow.

There are limits on how much authority Congress or the state legislature can delegate to administrative agencies. Once they are created, federal agencies must follow the federal Administrative Procedure Act and state agencies must follow the Minnesota Administrative Procedure Act. The statutes creating the agency can sometimes be attacked as an overly broad delegation of legislative power or a particular agency action can be attacked as overstepping the proper bounds of the agency's authority. Thus, an important first step in challenging an agency action is to ask whether the agency has been properly delegated power and whether that power is being properly exercised. The next step in challenging an administrative action is to ask whether the agency has followed the procedures required by the federal or state Administrative Procedure Act.

The Administrative Process

Understanding how agencies work is easier if one understands that all agency actions must fit into one of three broad categories—rulemaking, adjudication, or informal agency action. Each of these categories has unique rules that apply to it, and each offers affected parties a different degree of input into the agency's decision making process. Thus, the first step for any business wanting input into a particular agency action is to determine which category the action fits into. The determination of what to call the agency action is rarely simple. The category that the particular action fits into determines how many procedural safeguards the agency must observe. An agency may try to avoid the cumbersome procedure required for one type of action by trying to fit it into another category of administrative action that requires less formal procedure. Many legal disputes over agency action have centered around how to characterize what the agency is doing, rather than the actions themselves.

Rulemaking is usually done quite informally after a period of notice and comment. An agency gives notice that it is considering adopting a proposed rule and gives notice to interested parties that may want to comment on the rule. The agency considers the comments and then can promulgate a final rule. Commenting on a proposed rule is one of the most direct ways in which businesses can have a voice in formulating new rules. Unfortunately, an agency is not required to heed comments received. Because the agency is not required to follow any of the comments received, an affected party will often try to argue that what the agency is doing is not rulemaking at all, but instead is adjudication. In a few instances, a new rule can only be made after the agency follows detailed procedures known as formal rulemaking.

Adjudication is a procedure very much like a civil court trial. Court rules and agency rules are not identical, but agency adjudication allows for direct examination of witnesses, testimony under oath before an administrative law judge and the development of a substantial written record upon which the agency's decision must be based.

Informal agency action is a very broad category in which the procedures vary considerably. Parties to informal agency action often have minimal procedural protection. For example, an agency might merely be required to give the reason for taking a particular action. It need not allow for public comments or other input into the process.

THE ROLE OF COURTS

Although most administrative decisions are subject to judicial review, few are ever overturned on review. At the federal level, the Supreme Court has sent very strong signals to lower courts that they are not to overturn agency decisions absent very strong evidence that the agency acted erroneously. A business manager would be foolish to treat administrative agencies lightly because he or she assumes that a reviewing court will correct any mistakes the agency might make. The ability of reviewing courts to overturn agency action is so limited that the only sensible strategy is to assume that a case must be won at the agency level or not at all.

FREEDOM OF INFORMATION ACT

The Federal Administrative Procedure Act gives individuals, businesses, and organizations a very powerful tool to use in obtaining information from government agencies—the Federal Freedom of Information Act (FOIA). The FOIA gives unprecedented access to government information. Under FOIA, an agency must make available to the public:

- Final opinions, including concurring and dissenting opinions, as well as orders made in the adjudication of cases

- Statements of policy and interpretation adopted by the agency but not published in the Federal Register

- Administrative staff manuals and instructions to staff that affect a member of the public

This general list is only a starting point, however, as there are a number of specific exceptions to what agencies must provide to the public:

- National security information
- Internal personnel rules and files
- Information specifically exempted by another statute
- Commercial information
- Financial Information
- Trade secrets
- Inter- or intra-agency memoranda
- Personnel, medical, or other files, the disclosure of which would violate personal privacy
- Law enforcement and investigation files
- Data about financial institutions
- Geological and geophysical information on oil and natural gas wells

The definition of agencies subject to the FOIA is quite broad and includes independent regulatory commissions, the executive office of the President, other executive departments, all government corporations, the Central Intelligence Agency, and the Federal Bureau of Investigation.

FOIA requests are usually made in writing to the agency. Most agencies process so many FOIA requests that they have designated an officer to process the requests. The Code of Federal Regulations publishes the names and addresses of FOIA contacts in many agencies. Procedures for seeing these documents are very informal and no written request is necessary. The party making the request is obligated to describe the records reasonably well and to pay photocopying and search fees. Frequently requested documents may be made available at established Information Reading Rooms.

RESOURCES

Opportunities Minnesota Incorporated (OMNI), (612) 296-5005.

General Services Administration, 17th & D St. SW, Washington, D.C. 20407.

U.S. Government Purchasing and Sales Directory, United States Small Business Administration. The SBA offers government publications on all aspects of business planning and organization, available by sending a self-addressed stamped envelope to the Small Business Administration Office of Procurement and Technical Assistance, P.O. Box 15434, Forth Worth, Texas 76119.

Guide to Starting a Small Business in Minnesota. Minnesota Department of Trade and Economic Development, 900 American Center, 150 East Kellogg Boulevard, St. Paul, MN 55101.

Doing Business with Government; Federal, State, Local & Foreign Government Purchasing Practices for Every Business & Public Institution. Susan A. McManus, Paragon House, New York, 1992.

The Entrepreneur's Guide to Doing Business with the Federal Government; A Handbook for Small and Growing Businesses. Charles R. Bevers, Linda Gail Christie, Lynn Rollins Price, Prentice Hall, New York 1989.

Proposals that Win Federal Contracts; How to Plan, Price, Write, and Negotiate Your Fair Share of Government Business. Barry L. McVay, Panoptic Enterprises, Woodbridge, VA, 1989.

Loan Guarantee Program for Firms Involved in Agri-Business or Qualified Energy Projects, Office of Business Energy Finance, Minnesota Department of Energy and Economic Development, 900 American Center Building, 150 East Kellogg Blvd., St Paul, MN 55101.

Chapter 18: Federal, State & Local Government Law

FEDERAL, STATE & LOCAL GOVERNMENT LAW LEADING ATTORNEYS

Selected by Attorneys for GUIDEBOOK
Law & Leading Attorneys
MINNESOTA

The attorneys profiled below were recommended by their peers in a statewide survey.

The attorneys profiled in this section were nominated by their peers in a statewide survey conducted in 1993 in which several thousand Minnesota attorneys were asked to name the lawyer to whom they would send a friend or family member in need of legal assistance in the area of *Federal, State & Local Government Law*.

Because the survey resulted in a list of less than five percent of Minnesota's practicing attorneys, this should not be construed as a complete list. Nevertheless, it is an excellent source of highly qualified and reputable attorneys, who, if unable to assist can in most cases make quality referrals.

A list of all attorneys nominated in this category is found at the end of this section. For information on the survey methodology see page ix.

Please note that the shorter, two line attorney listings in this section are of attorneys who practice in this area but whose full biographical profile appears in another section of this book. A bullet "•" preceeding name indicates the attorney was nominated in this particular area of law. For information on the format of these profiles, consult the section "Using the *Business Guidebook*" found on page xiv. Note that the following abbreviations are used throughout these profiles:

App.	- Appellate	ABA	- American Bar Association
Cir.	- Circuit	ATLA	- American Trial Lawyers Association
Ct.	- Court	HCBA	- Hennepin County Bar Association
Dist.	- District	MDLA	- Minnesota Defense Lawyers Association
Hon.	- Honorable	MSBA	- Minnesota State Bar Association
JD	- Law degree (Juris Doctor)	MTLA	- Minnesota Trial Lawyers Association
LLB	- Law degree	NBTA	- National Board of Trial Advocacy
LLM	- Master in Law degree	RCBA	- Ramsey County Bar Association
Sup.	- Supreme		

•MICHAEL J. AHERN - Moss & Barnett, A Professional Association - 4800 Norwest Center, 90 South Seventh Street - Minneapolis, MN 55402 - Phone: (612) 347-0274, Fax: (612) 339-6686 - *See complete biographical profile in Environmental Law Chapter.*

•JOHN F. BANNIGAN, JR. - Bannigan & Kelly, P.A. - 1750 North Central Life Tower, 445 Minnesota Street - St. Paul, MN 55101 - Phone: (612) 224-3781, Fax: (612) 223-8019 - *See complete biographical profile in Commercial Real Estate Law Chapter.*

•PETER K. BECK: Mr. Beck is a shareholder and serves as chair of the Land Use, Municipal and Environmental Law Department at Larkin, Hoffman, Daly & Lindgren, Ltd. He practices in the areas of land use law, municipal law, and environmental review and approvals. Mr. Beck represents property owners and developers in obtaining local, regional, state and federal land use and environmental approvals for the development and use of land. Mr. Beck represents the City of Elk River, MN, as City Attorney, as well as a number of other Minnesota municipalities on environmental, public financing, and other issues. He has written numerous articles and spoken at seminars in his areas of expertise.
Education: JD 1977 with honors, George Washington University; BA 1973 with highest honors, Hamline University.
Employment History: Currently, Larkin, Hoffman, Daly & Lindgren, Ltd.; Staff Lawyer, Office of the Clerk, Supreme Court of the United States.
Representative Clients: City of Elk River; McCaw Cellular Communications; Norwest Bank; Mid-America Entertainment Company; City of St. Paul; CSM Corp.; Business Centers.
Professional Associations: HCBA (Local Government Law Committee); MSBA (Local Government Law Section); Environmental Law Institute.
Community Involvement: Minneapolis Heritage Preservation Commission (Commissioner 1986-93).
Firm: Larkin, Hoffman, Daly & Lindgren, Ltd., has served the legal and business counseling needs of clients since 1958. The firm's entrepreneurial spirit and understanding of the challenges facing growing businesses has been key to its success. The firm serves small and middle-market growing businesses and individual clients, as well as providing its special expertise to Fortune 500 companies. The firm's Bloomington location allows it to deliver legal services to clients in the most convenient and cost-effective manner possible. *See additional listings in Commercial Real Estate Law and Environmental Law Chapters.*

PETER K. BECK

Larkin, Hoffman, Daly & Lindgren, Ltd.
1500 Norwest Financial Center
7900 Xerxes Avenue South
Bloomington, MN 55431

Phone: (612) 835-3800
Fax: (612) 896-3333

Admitted:
1977 Minnesota;
1977 Virginia;
1977 District of Columbia;
1978 US Dist. Ct. (MN, VA, DC)
Birthdate: 04/14/51

•**JACK W. CLINTON:** Mr. Clinton has practiced law for over 18 years and has extensive experience in the representation of government clients in areas including land acquisitions through negotiations or condemnation, development projects, and issues involving the Data Practices Act and Open Meeting Law. He is also experienced in residential and commercial real estate transactions. In addition, Mr. Clinton handles corporate, probate and estate planning matters, and litigation related to his areas of practice.
Education: JD 1976 cum laude, Hamline University; BA 1973, St. Ambrose University.
Employment History: Private practice since 1978; Assistant County Attorney 1976-78, Washington County.
Representative Clients: City of Cottage Grove (since 1978); South Washington Watershed District; Cottage Grove Economic Development Authority; South Communities Counseling Service, Inc.; served as special counsel for several cities in Washington, Dakota, and Ramsey counties.
Professional Associations: Minnesota City Attorneys Assn. (President 1994-95); MSBA (Chair 1988-89, Urban, State and Local Government Section); 19th District Bar Assn. (1985-91, Ethics Committee); Washington County Bar Assn. (President 1979-80).
Community Involvement: Southeast YMCA (Board member); Cottage Grove Athletic Assn. (volunteer attorney).
Firm: The firm has maintained its office in Cottage Grove since 1978. It is comprised of three attorneys and two legal assistants offering legal services with an emphasis in residential and commercial real estate, probate of estates, estate planning and drafting of wills and trusts, guardianships, personal injury claims, and general business matters, in addition to the representation of government clients. The firm also serves as special counsel in conflict situations and conducts independent, internal investigations. F. Joseph Taylor's practice includes areas of civil litigation, personal injury, real estate, and probate and estate planning. Eric C. Thole's practice includes areas of real estate, business, and probate and estate planning. *See additional listing in Probate, Estate Planning & Trusts Law Chapter.*

JACK W. CLINTON

Jack W. Clinton, P.A.
8750 90th Street South
Suite 201
Cottage Grove, MN 55016-3301

Phone: (612) 459-6644
Fax: (612) 459-4719

Admitted: 1976 Minnesota;
1976 US Ct. App. (8th Cir.);
1976 US Sup. Ct.
Birthdate: 05/17/51

REBECCA A. COMSTOCK - Dorsey & Whitney - Pillsbury Center South, 220 South Sixth Street - Minneapolis, MN 55402-1498 - Phone: (612) 340-2987, Fax: (612) 340-2644 - *See complete biographical profile in Environmental Law Chapter.*

PETER L. COOPER - McGrann Shea Franzen Carnival Straughn & Lamb, Chartered - 2200 LaSalle Plaza, 800 LaSalle Avenue - Minneapolis, MN 55402 - Phone: (612) 338-2525, Fax: (612) 339-2386 - *See complete biographical profile in Commercial Real Estate Law Chapter.*

•**ROLLIN H. CRAWFORD:** Mr. Crawford is an experienced municipal, real estate, and association lawyer and has successfully represented clients in these areas for more than 25 years.
Education: LLB 1965, University of Minnesota; BA 1962, Macalester College.
Employment History: Partner/Shareholder 1988-present, LeVander, Gillen & Miller, P.A.; private practice Attorney and Consultant 1986-87 (in land use, general business, and health care); Principal & President 1966-84, Crawford and Anderson, P.A. (a general suburban type practice with emphasis on small business representation and municipal and land use law); Law Clerk 1965-66, Hon. Oscar R. Knutson, MN Supreme Court Justice.
Representative Clients: City of West St. Paul; Minnesota Dental Assn.; Minnesota Grocers Assn.
Professional Associations: Dakota County Bar Assn.; First District Bar Assn; MSBA.
Community Involvement: Mayor of West St. Paul (1966-70); Metropolitan Section, League of Minnesota Municipalities (Board member 1968-69; Chair 1968-69, Government Finance Committee); Citizens League (Board member 1971-77, 1981-84; Vice President 1972-75; President 1976-77; Committee Member 1971-present); Riverview Memorial Hospital (Board member 1972-79; Executive Committee 1974-79; Vice President 1976-77; President 1978-79); State Planning Advisory Committee (1969-70); United Hospital of St. Paul (Board member 1981-90; Vice Chair 1982-84; Chair 1984-86); HealthOne (Board member & Corporate Secretary 1986-93); Healthspan (Board member 1993-94).
Firm: LeVander, Gillen & Miller, P.A., is a 65 year old law firm practicing primarily in commercial, municipal, probate, estate planning, and condemnation areas. The firm does litigation and appellate work on behalf of its clients and presently has 11 lawyers who represent clients with interests throughout Minnesota and the upper Midwest. *See additional listings in Commercial Real Estate Law and Nonprofit Corporations Law Chapters.*

ROLLIN H. CRAWFORD

LeVander, Gillen & Miller, P.A.
633 South Concord Street
Suite 402
South St. Paul, MN 55075

Phone: (612) 451-1831
Fax: (612) 450-7384

Admitted: 1965 Minnesota;
1965 US Dist. Ct. (MN);
1981 US Sup. Ct.
Birthdate: 06/13/40

CHARLES K. DAYTON - Leonard, Street and Deinard Professional Association - 150 South Fifth Street, Suite 2300 - Minneapolis, MN 55402 - Phone: (612) 335-1500, Fax: (612) 335-1657 - *See complete biographical profile in Environmental Law Chapter.*

JAMES F. DUNN - Dunn & Elliott, P.A. - 1510 Minnesota World Trade Center, 30 East Seventh Street - St. Paul, MN 55101-4901 - Phone: (612) 221-9048, Fax: (612) 223-5797 - *See complete biographical profile in Personal Injury Defense Law Chapter.*

JAMES C. ERICKSON

Larkin, Hoffman, Daly & Lindgren, Ltd.
1500 Norwest Financial Center
7900 Xerxes Avenue South
Bloomington, MN 55431

Phone: (612) 835-3800
Fax: (612) 896-3333

Admitted: 1969 Minnesota
Birthdate: 12/30/43

•**JAMES C. ERICKSON:** Mr. Erickson is the President of Larkin, Hoffman, Daly & Lindgren, Ltd., a prominent Twin Cities law firm. He joined the firm in 1972 after serving as a Special Assistant under Attorney General Warren Spannaus and on the campaign staff of Governor Wendell Anderson. Mr. Erickson has practiced primarily in the Government Relations Group of Larkin Hoffman, serving clients at the federal, state, and local levels in government problem solving. He developed and led the firm's legislative and lobbying department, which now includes eight full time practitioners. In addition to his governmental relations practice, Mr. Erickson has special expertise in the representation of cable television and casino and Indian gaming management companies.
Education: JD 1969, University of Minnesota; BA 1966, St. Olaf College.
Employment History: Currently, Larkin, Hoffman, Daly & Lindgren, Ltd.; Special Assistant Attorney General 1971-72, MN Attorney General's Office.
Representative Clients: Minnesota Cable Communications Assn.; Miller and Schroeder Financial; Naegele Outdoor Advertising; Northwestern Business Travel; DreamCatcher Gaming Group; Mall of America; Coca Cola, Inc.
Professional Associations: MSBA; HCBA.
Community Involvement: Minnesota Cooperation Office (Board member); Bridge for Runaway Youth (past President); Voyager Outward Bound School (past Board member); Good Shepherd Lutheran Church.
Firm: Larkin, Hoffman, Daly & Lindgren, Ltd., has served the legal and business counseling needs of clients since 1958. The firm's entrepreneurial spirit and understanding of the challenges facing growing businesses has been key to its success. The firm serves small and middle-market growing businesses and individual clients, as well as providing its special expertise to Fortune 500 companies. The firm's Bloomington location allows it to deliver legal services to clients in the most convenient and cost-effective manner possible.

HAROLD A. FREDERICK - Fryberger, Buchanan, Smith & Frederick, P.A. - 302 West Superior Street, Suite 700 - Duluth, MN 55802 - Phone: (218) 722-0861, Fax: (218) 722-9568 - *See complete biographical profile in Health Law Chapter.*

•**H. THEODORE GRINDAL** - Schatz Paquin Lockridge Grindal & Holstein - 2200 Washington Square, 100 Washington Avenue South - Minneapolis, MN 55401 - Phone: (612) 339-6900, Fax: (612) 339-0981 - *See complete biographical profile in Health Law Chapter.*

•**RAYMOND A. HAIK** - Popham, Haik, Schnobrich & Kaufman, Ltd. - 222 South Ninth Street, Suite 3300 - Minneapolis, MN 55402 - Phone: (612) 333-4800, Fax: (612) 334-8888 - *See complete biographical profile in Environmental Law Chapter.*

GEORGE C. HOFF

Hoff, Barry & Kuderer, P.A.
7901 Flying Cloud Drive
Suite 260
Eden Prairie, MN 55344

Phone: (612) 941-9220
Fax: (612) 941-7968

Admitted: 1977 Minnesota; 1986 Wisconsin; 1980 US Dist. Ct. (MN); 1990 US Ct. App. (8th Cir.); 1993 US Sup. Ct.
Birthdate: 06/11/48

•**GEORGE C. HOFF:** Mr. Hoff has over 17 years experience as a city attorney and civil litigation trial attorney specializing in the areas of municipal and commercial law. As the appointed city attorney or as specially retained counsel, he has represented public entities and their officials throughout Minnesota on matters including complex land use cases, condemnations, special assessments, civil rights and RICO claims, permit and zoning denials, and personnel matters in state and federal trial and appellate courts. As independent counsel to cities, Mr. Hoff has also investigated charges of employee mismanagement and misconduct in city departments, written reports, and made recommendations. In addition to his advisory and various litigation work, Mr. Hoff regularly lectures at seminars in the areas of law related to local government. Topics have included liability of city officials, conflict of interest, and land use issues.
Education: JD 1977 cum laude, William Mitchell; BA 1970, University of Minnesota.
Representative Clients: The League of Minnesota Cities Insurance Trust; the cities of Red Wing, Victoria, Dayton, and Young America; Local 70 International Union of Operating Engineers; Fargo Electronics, Inc.; Minnesota AquaFarms; Shuffle Master, Inc.; Orbit Interactive Communications, Inc.
Professional Associations: MSBA; State Bar of Wisconsin; ABA.
Firm: Hoff, Barry & Kuderer, P.A., has eight lawyers with varied experience enabling the firm to service clients on a wide range of legal matters. In addition to municipal work, the firm represents companies and individuals on various matters, ranging from complex commercial litigation, incorporation, and business advice, to estate planning, real estate, family matters, and personal injury claims in state and federal court.

•**ROBERT L. HOFFMAN:** Mr. Hoffman is a cofounder of Larkin, Hoffman, Daly & Lindgren, Ltd., and its past Chair of the Board and President. Mr. Hoffman has been extensively involved in land use and development for the last 25 years as both a policy maker and lawyer. This includes serving as a 14-year member of the Bloomington City Council; a 7-year member of the Metropolitan Council and Chair of its Physical Development Committee; Chair of the Bloomington Economic Development Commission; Land Use Law instructor at Hamline University; member of the Urban Land Institute Development Policies and Regulations Council; and member of the Land Use Advisory Group of the Public Technology Institute of Washington, D.C.
Education: JD 1955, University of Minnesota; BA 1952, Carleton College.
Employment History: Currently, Larkin, Hoffman, Daly & Lindgren, Ltd.
Representative Clients: Mall of America Company; Carlson Real Estate Company; Homart Development Company; Eckankar; Ag-Chem Equipment Company, Inc.; AmeriBank; Interstate Inn, Inc.; Burger King; Triple Five Corp.
Professional Associations: Urban Land Institute (Development Policies and Regulations Council); Public Technology Institute of Washington, D.C. (Land Use Advisory Group); Bloomington City Council (1958-71); Metropolitan Council (Chair 1971-77, Physical Development Committee).
Firm: Larkin, Hoffman, Daly & Lindgren, Ltd., has served the legal and business counseling needs of clients since 1958. The firm's entrepreneurial spirit and understanding of the challenges facing growing businesses has been key to its success. The firm serves small and middle-market growing business and individual clients, as well as providing its special expertise to Fortune 500 companies. The firm's Bloomington location allows it to deliver legal services to clients in the most convenient and cost-effective manner possible. *See additional listing in Commercial Real Estate Law Chapter.*

ROBERT L. HOFFMAN

Larkin, Hoffman, Daly & Lindgren, Ltd.
1500 Norwest Financial Center
7900 Xerxes Avenue South
Bloomington, MN 55431

Phone: (612) 835-3800
Fax: (612) 896-3333

Admitted: 1955 Minnesota; 1956 US Dist. Ct. (MN); 1956 US Dist. Ct. (SD)
Birthdate: 09/16/28

BARRY P. HOGAN - Jeffries, Olson, Flom, Oppegard & Hogan, P.A. - 1325 23rd Street South - Fargo, ND 58103 - Phone: (701) 280-2300, Fax: (701) 280-1880 - *See complete biographical profile in Personal Injury Defense Law Chapter.*

ROGER A. JENSEN - Peterson, Bell, Converse & Jensen, P.A. - 3000 Metropolitan Centre, 333 South Seventh Street - Minneapolis, MN 55402-2441 - Phone: (612) 342-2323, Fax: (612) 344-1535 - *See complete biographical profile in Labor Law Chapter.*

•**WILLIAM A. JOHNSTONE:** Mr. Johnstone has been a partner in the Public Finance Department since 1975. He practices in the area of state and local finance and project finance as bond counsel, issuer's counsel, and underwriter's counsel in connection with the issuance of general obligation and revenue bond financing and other forms of project financing for various governmental purposes and health care, economic development, transportation, and housing development activities. He is the group head of the Corporate/Finance Group, which consists of 80 lawyers, and a member of the Management Committee since 1988.
Education: JD 1969 magna cum laude, Order of the Coif, University of Minnesota (Board of Editors 1968-69, *Minnesota Law Review*); BS 1966 with honors, Montana State University.
Employment History: Partner 1975-present, Associate 1970-74, Dorsey & Whitney.
Representative Clients: Northwest Airlines, Inc., on $500 million financing for loans and facilities involving the State of Minnesota and local governments; various health care, economic development, and multifamily housing financings in Minnesota, Iowa, North Dakota, and Montana through issuance of governmental bonds and project financings; bond counsel to State of Montana and its agencies on various governmental and health care projects.
Professional Associations: National Assn. of Bond Lawyers; Minnesota Institute of Public Finance.
Community Involvement: Lake Minnetonka Conservation District (Chair); Citizens League (President).
Firm: Dorsey & Whitney is the largest law firm in Minnesota and one of the largest firms in the United States with over 350 lawyers in 12 offices. The depth and breadth of the experience of its lawyers enables it to provide a broad range of services to meet the diverse legal needs of its client base, which includes Fortune 500 companies, public agencies, banks and other financial institutions, nonprofit organizations, individual investors, family owned businesses, and high-tech and low-tech, growth oriented companies.

WILLIAM A. JOHNSTONE

Dorsey & Whitney
Pillsbury Center South
220 South Sixth Street
Minneapolis, MN 55402-1498

Phone: (612) 340-2815
Fax: (612) 340-2644

Admitted: 1970 Minnesota

DAVID J. KENNEDY

Holmes & Graven, Chartered
470 Pillsbury Center
200 South Sixth Street
Minneapolis, MN 55402

Phone: (612) 337-9300
Fax: (612) 337-9310

Admitted: 1960 Minnesota
Birthdate: 01/29/32

•**DAVID J. KENNEDY:** Mr. Kennedy is an expert in local government finance and representation and is a nationally recognized bond approving counsel. Mr. Kennedy also has long experience in legislative drafting, ordinance code preparation, city charter commission work, including charter and charter amendment drafting, and with joint powers organizations. Mr. Kennedy has written several published articles in the field of local government law and administration and is a frequent lecturer on the subject.
Education: LLB 1960, University of Minnesota; BA 1954 cum laude, University of Notre Dame.
Employment History: Currently, Director at Holmes & Graven, Chartered; formerly President of LeFevere, Lefler, Kennedy, O'Brien & Drawz (merged with Holmes & Graven in 1989); 1969-71, Minnesota Senate Counsel office; Director 1967-69, Office of Local and Urban Affairs, State of Minnesota; Staff Attorney 1960-67, League of Minnesota Cities.
Representative Clients: City Attorney for cities of Crystal and Sandstone; Local Government Systems Assn.; Bond Counsel for Brainerd, Burnsville, Bloomington, Chanhassen, Minnetonka, Champlin, plus numerous cities, counties, and special districts in Minnesota; Special Counsel to numerous economic development agencies, housing and redevelopment agencies, and other governmental units.
Professional Associations: ABA; MSBA; HCBA; National Assn. of Bond Lawyers; National Institute of Municipal Law Officers; Minnesota Assn. of City Attorneys.
Community Involvement: Community Reinvestment Fund (Board member and Trustee); US Naval Reserve (retired naval aviator).
Firm: The firm, Holmes & Graven, Chartered, provides services in the areas of municipal finance, housing and redevelopment, tax increment financing, and all areas of local government representation.

WILLIAM J. KEPPEL - Dorsey & Whitney - Pillsbury Center South, 220 South Sixth Street - Minneapolis, MN 55402-1498 - Phone: (612) 340-2745, Fax: (612) 340-2644 - *See complete biographical profile in Environmental Law Chapter.*

JOHN D. KIRBY

Dorsey & Whitney
Pillsbury Center South
220 South Sixth Street
Minneapolis, MN 55402-1498

Phone: (612) 340-5665
Fax: (612) 340-2644

Admitted: 1968 Minnesota
Birthdate: 07/18/44

•**JOHN D. KIRBY:** Mr. Kirby acts primarily as bond counsel and underwriters counsel in tax exempt financings. He has particular experience in housing, health care, and industrial development financings, and in advance refunding transactions. Mr. Kirby has been a partner in the Public Finance Department since 1975 and department chair since 1991.
Education: JD 1968 Order of the Coif, Duke University (Note Editor 1967-68, *Duke Law Journal*); BA 1965 with honors, Carleton College.
Employment History: Partner 1975-present, Associate 1968-74, Dorsey & Whitney.
Representative Clients: State of Minnesota; Minnesota Housing Finance Agency; South Dakota Housing Development Authority; Iowa Finance Authority; numerous cities and school districts in the upper Midwest.
Professional Associations: ABA; MSBA; National Assn. of Bond Lawyers (Chair 1991, Judicial Action Committee).
Community Involvement: Dorsey & Whitney Pro Bono Program.
Firm: Dorsey & Whitney is the largest law firm in Minnesota and one of the largest firms in the United States with over 350 lawyers in 12 offices. The depth and breadth of the experience of its lawyers enables it to provide a broad range of services to meet the diverse legal needs of its client base, which includes Fortune 500 companies, public agencies, banks and other financial institutions, nonprofit organizations, individual investors, family owned businesses, and high-tech and low-tech, growth oriented companies.

•**JOHN A. KNAPP:** Mr. Knapp practices administrative law; legislative representation; arts, entertainment, advertising, and media law; insurance regulation; financial institutions law; environmental and natural resources law; state and local government law; and utility regulation. He frequently represents clients before the Minnesota Legislature, state and federal regulatory agencies, and city and county governments. His areas of special expertise include representation on securities, insurance, and banking law matters before the Department of Commerce and comparable federal agencies, and representation on environmental and natural resources matters before the MPCA, EPA, and DNR. Mr. Knapp has frequently appeared before the Minnesota Public Utilities Commission on gas, electric, and telephone utility matters. Mr. Knapp represents the interests of the Direct Marketing Association on legislative, tax, regulatory, and business issues affecting this industry. In addition, he is an adjunct professor in telecommunications regulation at St. Mary's College Graduate School in Minneapolis, a lecturer for Minnesota Continuing Legal Education and Minnesota Institute for Legal Education seminars, and an author of articles, including "Minnesota Foreclosure Relief Act: How it Works," 190 *Minnesota Real Estate Law Journal*, 1983. Mr. Knapp is listed in *Who's Who in American Law*.
Education: JD 1974 with distinction, University of Iowa; BA 1971, St. John's University.
Employment History: Shareholder 1985-present, Winthrop & Weinstine, P.A.; 1977-85, Hessian, McKasy & Soderberg; Assistant Revisor of Statutes 1974-77, Minnesota Legislature.
Representative Clients: Aetna Life and Casualty; American Insurance Assn.; Boise Cascade Corp.; Burlington Northern Railroad; Minnesota Business Partnership; Mortgage Bankers Assn. of Minnesota; Travelers Insurance Companies.
Professional Associations: RCBA; The Iowa State Bar Assn.; MSBA (Executive Council 1989-92, Administrative Law Section); ABA; District of Columbia Bar; Minnesota Governmental Relations Council (President, 1993 and 1994).
Firm: Mr. Knapp heads Winthrop & Weinstine's Public Law Practice Group. *See additional listings in Arts, Entertainment, Advertising & Media Law and Environmental Law Chapters.*

JOHN A. KNAPP

Winthrop & Weinstine, P.A.
3200 Minnesota World Trade Center
30 East Seventh Street
St. Paul, MN 55101

Phone: (612) 290-8400
Fax: (612) 292-9347

Admitted: 1974 Minnesota;
1974 Iowa;
1975 US Dist. Ct. (MN);
1982 District of Columbia
Birthdate: 06/14/49

•**TIMOTHY J. KUNTZ:** Mr. Kuntz represents municipal clients in the areas of eminent domain, zoning and subdivision, special assessments, hazardous buildings, civil damage claims, and zoning enforcement actions. He is very experienced at the trial and appellate levels and has successfully argued client cases before the Minnesota appellate and supreme courts. Other areas of concentration include business litigation, closely held corporations, and estate planning. Mr. Kuntz has lectured for the League of Cities and the Government Training Services.
Education: JD 1975, University of Minnesota (staff 1974-75, *Minnesota Law Review*; Editor, "Minnesota Cases"); BA 1972 summa cum laude, University of Notre Dame (Phi Beta Kappa; Ford Merit Scholar; Dean's List; Chair of University Judicial Appellate Board).
Employment History: 1975-present, Levander, Gillen & Miller, P.A.
Representative Clients: Cities of Inver Grove Heights, South St. Paul, and Sunfish Lake; Schanno Properties; Cemstone Products Company; Twin City Concrete Products Company; Vendmark, Inc.; FD Oil Company; Linn Enterprises, Inc.; Petro Plus, Inc.; Dakota Conservators, Inc.
Professional Associations: MSBA (past member of Board of Governors); Dakota County Bar Assn.; Minnesota City Attorneys Assn. (past President); First District Bar Assn.
Community Involvement: All Saints Church of Lakeville, MN (Finance Council).
Firm: LeVander, Gillen & Miller, P.A., is a 65 year old law firm practicing primarily in commercial, municipal, probate, estate planning, and condemnation areas. The firm does litigation and appellate work on behalf of its clients and presently has 11 lawyers engaged in the practice. LeVander, Gillen & Miller represents clients with interests throughout Minnesota and the upper Midwest. *See additional listings in Closely Held Business Law and Commercial Litigation Chapters.*

TIMOTHY J. KUNTZ

LeVander, Gillen & Miller, P.A.
633 South Concord Street
Suite 402
South St. Paul, MN 55075

Phone: (612) 451-1831
Fax: (612) 450-7384

Admitted: 1975 Minnesota
Birthdate: 06/06/50

Chapter 18: Federal, State & Local Government Law

CHARLES L. LEFEVERE

Holmes & Graven, Chartered
470 Pillsbury Center
200 South Sixth Street
Minneapolis, MN 55402

Phone: (612) 337-9300
Fax: (612) 337-9310

Admitted: 1975 Minnesota;
1979 US Dist. Ct. (MN);
1978 US Ct. App. (8th Cir.)
Birthdate: 12/21/46

•**CHARLES L. LEFEVERE:** Mr. LeFevere practices exclusively in representing public and private clients on municipal law matters. As city attorney for three cities, he has extensive experience in a broad range of municipal matters, including planning and zoning, city charters, public improvements and special assessments, employment law, open meeting law, data practices, environmental law, public bidding, municipal litigation, and municipal finance. In addition, Mr. LeFevere has served as counsel to joint powers organizations, HRAs, EDAs, port authorities, charter commissions, and special purpose governmental units. He lectures frequently on municipal law topics such as use of mediation by governmental bodies, special assessments, financing of storm water improvements, and municipal regulation of landfills.

Education: JD 1975 cum laude, University of Minnesota; BA 1968, St. Olaf College.
Employment History: Executive Committee Director 1989-present, Holmes & Graven, Chartered; Director 1975-1989, LeFevere, Kennedy, O'Brien & Drawz; Line Officer 1969-1972, US Naval Reserve.
Representative Clients: City Attorney for New Brighton (1982-present), Brooklyn Center (1987-present), Rosemount (1994-present); Lake Minnetonka Conservation Dist. (1978-present); MN Police Recruitment System; League of MN Cities Insurance Trust.
Professional Associations: ABA (Section of Urban, State and Local Government Law); MSBA; HCBA; Hennepin County Local Government Law Committee; MN Assn. of City Attorneys; Assn. of Metropolitan Municipalities (Committee on Alternative Dispute Resolution).
Community Involvement: Mediation Center (Chair, Board of Directors); Brooklyn Center Rotary (Vice President); Minnetonka Board of Zoning Adjustment (past Chair); Wayzata Youth Hockey Assn. (past President); Twin Cities Chapter Ruffed Grouse Society (past Board member); Coach for youth athletic teams.
Firm: Holmes & Graven, Chartered, is a firm of 25 attorneys with a client base in both public and private industry. Founded in 1973, the firm has focused primarily in municipal finance, governmental representation, real estate, litigation, and employment/labor law. Supporting the attorneys is a highly skilled staff of paralegals, laws clerks, and administrative personnel, each equipped with the latest in computer technology for cost efficient research and document production. Holmes & Graven is an Equal Opportunity Employer. *See additional listings in Employment Law and Environmental Law Chapters.*

•**JOHN C. LERVICK** - Swenson, Grover, Lervick, Syverson, Battey & Anderson, Ltd. - 710 Broadway, Box 787 - Alexandria, MN 56308 - Phone: (612) 763-3141, Fax: (612) 763-3657 - *See complete biographical profile in Personal Injury Defense Law Chapter.*

JERRY (C.D.) MAHONEY

Dorsey & Whitney
Pillsbury Center South
220 South Sixth Street
Minneapolis, MN 55402-1498

Phone: (612) 340-2813
Fax: (612) 340-2644

Admitted: 1955 Minnesota;
1957 US Dist. Ct. (MN)
Birthdate: 09/20/31

•**JERRY (C.D.) MAHONEY:** Mr. Mahoney practices in the area of public and corporate debt financing of virtually all types. He counsels underwriters, banks, and borrowers concerning public offerings, private placements, syndications, and project and structured financings, secured and unsecured. He is a partner in the firm's Corporate/Finance Department.

Education: LLB 1955, University of Minnesota (1953-55, *Minnesota Law Review*); BSL 1953, University of Minnesota.
Employment History: Partner 1963-present, Associate 1957-63, Dorsey & Whitney.
Professional Associations: ABA (Sections on Business Law and State and Local Government Law); National Assn. of Bond Lawyers; HCBA.
Firm: Dorsey & Whitney is the largest law firm in Minnesota and one of the largest firms in the United States with over 350 lawyers in 12 offices. The depth and breadth of the experience of its lawyers enables it to provide a broad range of services to meet the diverse legal needs of its client base, which includes Fortune 500 companies, public agencies, banks and other financial institutions, nonprofit organizations, individual investors, family owned businesses, and high-tech and low-tech, growth oriented companies.

•**FORREST D. (DICK) NOWLIN** - Doherty, Rumble & Butler Professional Association - 2800 Minnesota World Trade Center, 30 East Seventh Street - St. Paul, MN 55101-4999 - Phone: (612) 291-9333, Fax: (612) 291-9313 - *See complete biographical profile in Environmental Law Chapter.*

•**BRUCE A. PETERSON** - Popham, Haik, Schnobrich & Kaufman, Ltd. - 222 South Ninth Street, Suite 3300 - Minneapolis, MN 55402 - Phone: (612) 333-4800, Fax: (612) 334-8888 - *See complete biographical profile in Criminal Law Chapter.*

•WAYNE G. POPHAM: Mr. Popham concentrates his practice in the area of commercial litigation, including litigation involving environmental and intellectual property matters.
Education: LLB 1953, University of Minnesota (*Minnesota Law Review*); BSL 1951, University of Minnesota.
Employment History: Founding member, Popham, Haik, Schnobrich & Kaufman, Ltd.
Representative Clients: Browning-Ferris Industries; NordicTrack, Inc.; Minneapolis Community Development Agency; Soo Line Railroad; SciMed Life Systems, Inc.
Professional Associations: ABA (Eighth Circuit Chair, Legislation Committee, Litigation Section); HCBA; MSBA (past Chair, Intermediate Court of Appeals Committee; past Chair, Legislation Committee).
Community Involvement: Minnesota Senate (1963-72); US District Judge Nominating Commission for Minnesota (1979-81; Chair 1981); Minnesota Chamber of Commerce (Board member 1981-87); Greater Minneapolis Chamber of Commerce (Vice Chair 1977-83; Board member 1984-86).
Firm: Popham, Haik, Schnobrich & Kaufman, Ltd., is a firm of more than 230 attorneys with offices in Denver, Miami, Minneapolis, Washington, D.C., and international affiliations in Beijing, China and Leipzig and Stuttgart, Germany. The firm represents clients nationally and internationally on issues relating to corporate and business law, administrative law, and litigation.

WAYNE G. POPHAM

Popham, Haik, Schnobrich & Kaufman, Ltd.
222 South Ninth Street
Suite 3300
Minneapolis, MN 55402

Phone: (612) 333-4800
Fax: (612) 334-8888

Admitted: 1953 Minnesota
Birthdate: 10/23/29

´•THOMAS J. RADIO: Mr. Radio is a trial lawyer in government, construction, and product liability matters. He also practices in all aspects of municipal law, including general representation of cities, special assessments, eminent domain, land use applications, and civil rights litigation. Mr. Radio currently serves as the city attorney for the cities of Afton and Minnetrista. He is a past chair of the firm's Public Law Practice Group and currently serves as chair of the Litigation Department.
Education: JD 1979 with honors, University of Iowa (Editor 1978-79, *Iowa Law Review*); BS 1976 with distinction, Iowa State University (Phi Beta Kappa).
Employment History: Shareholder 1982-present, Popham, Haik, Schnobrich & Kaufman, Ltd.; Special Assistant Attorney General, Land Use, 1992-93, MN Attorney General's Office; Law Clerk 1980-82, Hon. Robert G. Renner, US District Court, District of Minnesota; Law Clerk 1979-80, Hon. Allen L. Donielson, Iowa Court of Appeals.
Representative Clients: City of Afton; City of Minnetrista; Schindler Elevator Corp.; League of Minnesota Cities Insurance Trust.
Professional Associations: ABA; Federal Bar Assn.; MDLA; MSBA (Board of Governors; Governing Council of the Civil Litigation Section; past Chair, Urban, State, and Local Government Section); HCBA (Ethics Committee Investigator; past Chair, Eminent Domain Section); National Institute of Municipal Legal Officers; US District Court, District of MN (Local Rules Committee).
Community Involvement: House of Hope Presbyterian Church (1987-89, 1991-93, Board of Deacons; Chair 1993, New Member Committee); Calvin Christian School (1993-94, Development Committee).
Firm: Popham, Haik, Schnobrich & Kaufman, Ltd., is a firm of more than 230 attorneys with offices in Denver, Miami, Minneapolis, Washington, D.C., and international affiliations in Beijing, China and Leipzig and Stuttgart, Germany. The firm represents clients nationally and internationally on issues relating to corporate and business law, administrative law, and litigation. *See additional listings in Commercial Litigation Chapter and Personal Injury Defense Law Chapters.*

THOMAS J. RADIO

Popham, Haik, Schnobrich & Kaufman, Ltd.
222 South Ninth Street
Suite 3300

Minneapolis, MN 55402

Phone: (612) 333-4800
Fax: (612) 334-8888

Admitted: 1982 Minnesota;
1979 Iowa;
1980 US Ct. App. (8th Cir.);
1984 US Sup. Ct.
Birthdate: 12/07/53

•PIERRE N. REGNIER - Jardine, Logan & O'Brien - 2100 Piper Jaffray Plaza, 444 Cedar Street - St. Paul, MN 55101 - Phone: (612) 290-6500, Fax: (612) 223-5070 - *See complete biographical profile in Personal Injury Defense Law Chapter.*

RANDI ILYSE ROTH - Farmers' Legal Action Group, Inc. - 1301 Minnesota Building, 46 East Fourth Street - St. Paul, MN 55101 - Phone: (612) 223-5400, Fax: (612) 223-5335 - *See complete biographical profile in Agricultural Law Chapter.*

DAVID C. SELLERGREN

Doherty, Rumble & Butler
Professional Association
3500 Fifth Street Towers
150 South Fifth Street
Minneapolis, MN 55402-4235

Phone: (612) 340-5555
Fax: (612) 340-5584

Admitted: 1968 Iowa;
1968 Minnesota
Birthdate: 02/03/43

•**DAVID C. SELLERGREN:** Mr. Sellergren's practice focuses on local, state, and federal regulation of land use and development. In addition, he represents many clients during the process of buying, selling, financing, and leasing real estate. He has particular expertise with respect to environmental assessments and impact statements, wetland fill permits, mobile source air quality permits, planned unit developments, subdivisions, conditional use permits, highway access permits, golf course development, takings, and exactions law. Mr. Sellergren is an adjunct professor of law and urban affairs at the Hubert H. Humphrey Institute of Public Affairs, University of Minnesota.
Education: LLM Environmental Law 1972, The National Law Center, George Washington University; JD 1968, University of Minnesota; AB 1965, Grinnell College.
Employment History: 1992-present, Doherty, Rumble & Butler, P.A.; 1975-92, Larkin, Hoffman, Daly & Lindgren, Ltd.; 1972-75, Douglas, Bell, Donlin, Shultz & Peterson; 1968-72, US Navy Judge Advocate General's Corps.
Representative Clients: MEPC American Properties, Inc.; ITT Hartford; Citicorp Real Estate, Inc.; The Rottlund Company; Midwest Asphalt Corp.; Sienna Corp.; Charles C. Cudd Company; Mills Fleet Farm; North Oaks Company; Bloomington Housing and Redevelopment Authority.
Professional Associations: MN Chapter of National Assn. of Industrial and Office Parks (Program Committee); Sensible Land Use Coalition; Urban Land Institute.
Community Involvement: St. Paul YMCA Camp du Nord, Ely, MN (Chair, Board of Directors).
Firm: Doherty, Rumble & Butler attorneys provide assistance to cities and counties and port and housing authorities, as well as other governmental entities, in environmental and land use law and by acting as general counsel. Both public and private sector clients are assisted with environmental clearances on contaminated land, environmental permits and litigation, targeted legislative solutions, and real estate, financing, sale, and lease matters. Attorneys in the firm's Environmental and Land Use Law Department also provide assistance to businesses and other entities in securing all forms of regulatory authorizations for land use and development, including assistance with rezonings, plan amendments, conditional use permits, PUDs, state and federal permits, and tax increment and bond financing. Services in this area range from assistance with application preparation to presentation for permit approvals and environmental review documentation and litigation. *See additional listings in Commercial Real Estate Law and Environmental Law Chapters.*

LEE E. SHEEHY

Popham, Haik, Schnobrich & Kaufman, Ltd.
222 South Ninth Street
Suite 3300
Minneapolis, MN 55402

Phone: (612) 333-4800
Fax: (612) 334-8888

Admitted: 1977 Minnesota;
1977 US Dist. Ct. (MN);
1977 US Ct. App. (8th Cir.);
1993 US Sup. Ct.
Birthdate: 07/27/51

•**LEE E. SHEEHY:** Mr. Sheehy practices in the areas of public and telecommunications law before state and local officials. He has represented cable, telecommunications, and media companies for over a decade in contract and regulatory matters and litigation. Lee also serves as General Counsel to Public Radio International and the Twin Cities Cable Consortium. Mr. Sheehy is also the City Attorney for the City of St. Louis Park, MN. He is coauthor of several articles, including "Rulemaking with a Hearing," *MN Administrative Procedure,* 1987, and "FCC Intensifies its Crackdown on 'Indecent' Radio Broadcasts," *National Law Journal,* Jan. 29, 1990, and is a lecturer at Minnesota State Bar Association Regional Communications Forums.
Education: JD 1977 cum laude, University of Minnesota; BA 1973 with honors, Harvard College.
Employment History: Shareholder/Associate 1980-present, Popham, Haik, Schnobrich & Kaufman, Ltd.; Special Assistant Attorney General 1977-80, Office of Minnesota Attorney General; Investigator 1973-74, US Senate Select Committee on Presidential Campaign Activities.
Representative Clients: US Counsel for Rogers Communications; Continental Cablevision of St. Paul; Meredith Cable; Public Radio International.
Professional Associations: MSBA.
Community Involvement: Alan Page for Justice Committee (Chair); Headwaters Fund; Harvard Club of MN (past President); National Staff of Carter-Mondale Campaign and Mondale-Ferraro Presidential Election Campaign.
Firm: Popham, Haik, Schnobrich & Kaufman, Ltd., is a firm of more than 230 attorneys with offices in Denver, Miami, Minneapolis, Washington, D.C., and international affiliations in Beijing, China and Leipzig and Stuttgart, Germany. The firm represents clients nationally and internationally on issues relating to corporate and business law, administrative law, and litigation. *See additional listing in Arts, Entertainment, Advertising & Media Law Chapter.*

•**LOUIS N. SMITH:** Mr. Smith is a senior attorney and shareholder with Popham, Haik, Schnobrich & Kaufman, Ltd., whose practice is devoted to government litigation and immigration law. Mr. Smith's immigration practice focuses primarily on political asylum. He has successfully represented over 50 asylum clients from 16 countries. Mr. Smith has testified concerning human rights matters before the United States Congress, the Inter-American Commission on Human Rights, and the Mexican Human Rights Commission in Mexico City. He also represents governmental agencies and private clients in a wide variety of federal, state, and local proceedings. In 1991-92, Mr. Smith took a sabbatical from the firm to serve as Deputy Hennepin County Attorney, where he was second in command of an office of 125 attorneys responsible for felony prosecution and civil representation of a county of 1,000,000 people. He is also coauthor with Victor Kramer of "The Special Prosecutor Act: Proposals for 1983," 66 *Minnesota Law Review*.
Education: JD 1983 cum laude, University of Minnesota (Associate Editor, *Minnesota Law Review*); BA 1979 magna cum laude, St. Olaf College (Phi Beta Kappa).
Employment History: 1985-present, Popham, Haik, Schnobrich & Kaufman, Ltd.; Deputy Attorney 1991-92, Hennepin County; Law Clerk 1983-85, Hon. Gerald W. Heaney, US Court of Appeals for the Eighth Circuit.
Professional Associations: HCBA; MSBA (Immigration Section); ABA; American Immigration Lawyers Assn.; Minnesota Lawyers International Human Rights Committee (President 1991-92).
Community Involvement: Center for Victims of Torture (Board member).
Firm: Popham, Haik, Schnobrich & Kaufman, Ltd., is a firm of more than 230 attorneys with offices in Denver, Miami, Minneapolis, Washington, D.C., and international affiliations in Beijing, China and Leipzig and Stuttgart, Germany. The firm represents clients nationally and internationally on issues relating to corporate and business law, administrative law, and litigation. *See additional listing in Immigration Law Chapter.*

LOUIS N. SMITH

Popham, Haik, Schnobrich & Kaufman, Ltd.
222 South Ninth Street
Suite 3300
Minneapolis, MN 55402

Phone: (612) 333-4800
Fax: (612) 334-8888

Admitted: 1983 Minnesota; 1992 US Dist. Ct. (MN); 1983 US Ct. App. (8th Cir.)
Birthdate: 09/19/57

WILLIAM R. SOTH - Dorsey & Whitney - Pillsbury Center South, 220 South Sixth Street - Minneapolis, MN 55402-1498 - Phone: (612) 340-2969, Fax: (612) 340-7800 - *See complete biographical profile in Commercial Real Estate Law Chapter.*

BYRON E. STARNS - Leonard, Street and Deinard Professional Association - 150 South Fifth Street, Suite 2300 - Minneapolis, MN 55402 - Phone: (612) 335-1516, Fax: (612) 335-1657 - *See complete biographical profile in Environmental Law Chapter.*

ANTHONY M. TARVESTAD - Quinlivan, Sherwood, Spellacy & Tarvestad, P.A. - P.O. Box 1008 - St. Cloud, MN 56302-1008 - Phone: (612) 251-1414, Fax: (612) 251-1415 - *See complete biographical profile in Professional Malpractice Defense Law Chapter.*

•**JAMES J. THOMSON:** Mr. Thomson practices in the areas of governmental law and litigation. Formerly an attorney with the San Diego City Attorney's Office, he is currently City Attorney for the City of Mounds View and a past President of the Minnesota City Attorney's Association. Since graduating from law school, Mr. Thomson's practice has focused on municipal law and civil litigation on behalf of governmental entities. He also represents clients in commercial litigation matters. He is a frequent lecturer at both state and federal levels, primarily in topics dealing with land use, open meeting law, and general litigation matters.
Education: JD 1976 magna cum laude, University of San Diego (Editor-in-chief 1975-76, *San Diego Law Review*); BA 1969, University of Notre Dame.
Employment History: Director 1989-present, Holmes & Graven, Chartered; Associate/Director 1982-89, LeFevere, Lefler, Kennedy, O'Brien & Drawz; Deputy City Attorney 1976-82, San Diego City Attorney's office; Infantry Officer 1969-73, US Marine Corps.
Representative Clients: City of Mounds View; City of Bloomington; City of Minneapolis; League of Minnesota Cities Insurance Trust.
Professional Associations: ABA (Section of Urban, State and Local Government Law); National Institute of Municipal Law Officers; San Diego Bar Assn. (past Chair, Eminent Domain Committee); MSBA; HCBA; State Bar of California.
Community Involvement: Legal Advice Clinics (volunteer attorney); Notre Dame Club of San Diego (past President).
Firm: Holmes & Graven, Chartered, is a firm of 25 attorneys with a client base in both public and private industry. Founded in 1973, the firm has focused primarily in municipal finance, governmental representation, real estate, litigation, and employment/labor law. Supporting the attorneys is a highly skilled staff of paralegals, law clerks, and administrative personnel, each equipped with the latest in computer technology for cost efficient research and document production. Holmes & Graven is an Equal Opportunity Employer. *See additional listing in Commercial Litigation Chapter.*

JAMES J. THOMSON

Holmes & Graven, Chartered
470 Pillsbury Center
200 South Sixth Street
Minneapolis, MN 55402

Phone: (612) 337-9300
Fax: (612) 337-9310

Admitted: 1976 California; 1976 US Dist. Ct. (S. Dist. CA); 1982 Minnesota; 1982 US Dist. Ct. (MN); 1992 US Ct. App. (8th Cir.); 1994 US Sup. Ct.
Birthdate: 06/26/47

Chapter 18: Federal, State & Local Government Law

Complete listing of all attorneys nominated in Federal, State & Local Government Law

MICHAEL J. AHERN, Moss & Barnett, A Professional Association, Minneapolis; **JOHN F. BANNIGAN JR.,** Bannigan & Kelly, P.A., St. Paul; **PETER K. BECK,** Larkin, Hoffman, Daly & Lindgren, Ltd., Bloomington; **JACK W. CLINTON,** Jack W. Clinton, P.A., Cottage Grove; **ROLLIN H. CRAWFORD,** LeVander, Gillen & Miller, P.A., South St. Paul; **JAMES C. ERICKSON,** Larkin, Hoffman, Daly & Lindgren, Ltd., Bloomington; **RICHARD A. FORSCHLER,** Faegre & Benson, Minneapolis; **F. KELTON GAGE,** Blethen Gage & Krause, Mankato; **MICHAEL J. GALVIN JR.,** Briggs and Morgan, P.A., St. Paul; **ROGER D. GORDON,** Winthrop & Weinstine, P.A., Minneapolis; **H. THEODORE GRINDAL,** Schatz Paquin Lockridge Grindal & Holstein, Minneapolis; **RAYMOND A. HAIK,** Popham, Haik, Schnobrich & Kaufman, Ltd., Minneapolis; **TRUDY J. HALLA,** Briggs and Morgan, P.A., Minneapolis; **ROBYN L. HANSEN,** Leonard, Street and Deinard Professional Association, St. Paul; **JOHN H. HERMAN,** Leonard, Street and Deinard Professional Association, Minneapolis; **GEORGE C. HOFF,** Hoff, Barry & Kuderer, P.A., Eden Prairie; **ROBERT L. HOFFMAN,** Larkin, Hoffman, Daly & Lindgren, Ltd., Bloomington; **WILLIAM A. JOHNSTONE,** Dorsey & Whitney, Minneapolis; **DAVID J. KENNEDY,** Holmes & Graven, Chartered, Minneapolis; **JOHN D. KIRBY,** Dorsey & Whitney, Minneapolis; **JOHN A. KNAPP,** Winthrop & Weinstine, P.A., St. Paul; **ROGER N. KNUTSON,** Campbell Knutson Scott & Fuchs, P.A., Eagan; **TIMOTHY J. KUNTZ,** LeVander, Gillen & Miller, P.A., South St. Paul; **CHARLES L. LEFEVERE,** Holmes & Graven, Chartered, Minneapolis; **JOHN C. LERVICK,** Swenson, Grover, Lervick, Syverson, Battey & Anderson, Ltd., Alexandria; **DAVID L. LILLEHAUG,** United States District Attorney's Office, Minneapolis; **JERRY (C. D.) MAHONEY,** Dorsey & Whitney, Minneapolis; **BRUCE D. MALKERSON,** Popham, Haik, Schnobrich & Kaufman, Ltd., Minneapolis; **RICHARD H. MARTIN,** Leonard, Street and Deinard Professional Association, Minneapolis; **FORREST D. NOWLIN,** Doherty, Rumble & Butler Professional Association, St. Paul; **J. DENNIS O'BRIEN,** Rider, Bennett, Egan & Arundel, Minneapolis; **FLOYD B. OLSON,** Deputy City Attorney, Minneapolis; **DAVID R. ORNSTEIN,** Bloomington City Attorney, Bloomington; **CURTIS A. PEARSON,** Wurst Pearson Larson Underwood & Murtz, P.A., Minneapolis; **BRUCE A. PETERSON,** Popham, Haik, Schnobrich & Kaufman, Ltd., Minneapolis; **DESYL L. PETERSON,** Minnetonka City Attorney, Minnetonka; **WAYNE G. POPHAM,** Popham, Haik, Schnobrich & Kaufman, Ltd., Minneapolis; **THOMAS J. RADIO,** Popham, Haik, Schnobrich & Kaufman, Ltd., Minneapolis; **PIERRE N. REGNIER,** Jardine, Logan & O'Brien, St. Paul; **STEPHEN C. ROSHOLT,** Faegre & Benson, Minneapolis; **PETER H. SEED,** Briggs and Morgan, P.A., St. Paul; **DAVID C. SELLERGREN,** Doherty, Rumble & Butler Professional Association, Minneapolis; **LEE E. SHEEHY,** Popham, Haik, Schnobrich & Kaufman, Ltd., Minneapolis; **LOUIS N. SMITH,** Popham, Haik, Schnobrich & Kaufman, Ltd., Minneapolis; **DAVID P. SULLIVAN,** Sullivan & Setterlund Ltd., Duluth; **JAMES J. THOMSON JR.,** Holmes & Graven, Chartered, Minneapolis; **FRANK E. VILLAUME III,** St. Paul City Attorney's Office, St. Paul.

CHAPTER 19

FRANCHISE & DEALERSHIP LAW

Franchises have become a popular option for many prospective business owners. Especially for a person starting out in the business world, a franchise offers a relatively simple way to run a business without having to develop new marketing strategies, logos, products, services, or a corporate identity. The person or company who grants the right to a franchise (the franchisor) and the person or company who is granted a franchise (the franchisee) invest a great deal of time, money, and energy into the relationship. Franchises are not trouble-free, however, and even a sophisticated businessperson can seriously overestimate the earning potential of a new franchise or the amount of operational support he or she can expect from the franchisor.

Two areas generate most disputes in franchise law—the initial offer and the termination decision. Franchisors and franchisees who want to stay on the right side of the law and have mutually satisfactory business relations need to be aware of state and federal laws that require disclosure by the franchisor of the most significant terms of the franchise relationship and the penalties for not following these disclosure requirements. Franchisors and franchisees also need to be aware of the complex legal framework surrounding termination of franchises.

WHY THE NEED FOR DISCLOSURE?

Failure to understand the risks involved in opening a franchise can be a costly mistake. A key to understanding American franchise regulations is that the law does not try to eliminate risk for investors. In keeping with our capitalist economic ideals, the law does not seek to prevent businesspersons from making poor business decisions, rather it seeks to ensure that businesspersons are able to make informed decisions regarding franchise opportunities. If after learning all the facts about a franchise opportunity, an investor still wants to undertake the risks inherent in opening a franchise, that is his or her decision to make.

FEDERAL REQUIREMENTS

The Federal Trade Commission (FTC) enforces federal laws and rules regulating franchises. These rules only apply to franchises that are "in or affecting interstate commerce." It does not matter what the written agreement is called as long as the relationship meets the FTC's definition of a franchise. This means that if a business is entering into what it calls a limited partnership, it may also be entering into a franchise agreement for purposes of the FTC's franchise regulations. The FTC rules define a franchise as a "continuing commercial relationship" between two or more parties.

There are three basic types of "continuing commercial relationships" covered by the FTC rules. They are:

- Package franchises, defined as prepackaged business programs developed and identified by the franchisor. McDonald's is an example of a package franchise, also called a "business format" franchise.

- Product franchises, defined as arrangements where the franchisor sells goods that bear his or her trade name to a franchisee, who in turn sells them to the public under that same name. The franchisor maintains some degree of control over the selling of the goods by the franchisee in this arrangement.

- Business opportunity ventures, defined as arrangements where the franchisee is required to buy and sell the goods or services of the franchisor or another business. Furthermore, the franchisor arranges the location of the business, seeks out business for the junior partner, and may even provide employees. An example of this type of arrangement is a vending machine route, where a company finds a place to put the machines and sells the candy to the franchisee, but the franchisee collects the money and restocks the machines.

FEDERAL TRADE COMMISSION RULE

The FTC requires franchisors and sellers of certain other business opportunities to disclose several material facts before a sale can be closed. These disclosure requirements officially are titled "Disclosure Requirements and Prohibitions Concerning Franchising and Business Opportunity Ventures" and are frequently referred to as the "FTC Rule." The FTC Rule's coverage is quite broad, but certain narrow exceptions are available. For example, certain presentations at business opportunity trade shows are specifically exempt from the FTC Rule and some franchises have been exempted from coverage by informal advisory opinions issued by the FTC staff. A lawyer familiar with this area of practice should be able to advise whether a particular venture would qualify for an exemption.

There are two official forms that a franchisor can use to meet the disclosure requirements of the FTC Rule—the FTC Disclosure Document (FTC document) and the newer Uniform Franchise Offering Circular (UFOC). Although either form is acceptable for compliance with the FTC Rule, the FTC document does not meet the requirements of most state disclosure laws. The UFOC is acceptable (with minor alterations) in all states with franchise disclosure laws. The two documents have some similar sections, but the franchisor may not pick and choose sections from each document; either the entire FTC document or the entire UFOC must be completed.

The FTC Document
The FTC document must contain information in four broad categories—information about the franchisor, information about the franchisee, details of the franchise agreement, and supporting facts for any earnings claims made by the franchisor.

Information about the Franchisor
The FTC document must contain the following information about the franchisor:

- The business history of the Franchisor
- The employment history of the officers and executives of the company
- The litigation history of the officers and executives of the company
- The history of the company and certain key individuals with regard to filing for bankruptcy
- Financial statements

Information about the Franchisee
The FTC document must contain the following information about the franchised business:

- Detailed description of the franchised business
- Initial investment to be made by the franchisee
- Any requirements that the franchisee make certain purchases or use specific suppliers
- Details of any finances provided by the franchisor
- Services that the franchisor is obligated to perform on behalf of the franchisee
- Right to use trademarks, patents, and copyrights
- Restrictions, if any, on sales
- Details about both current and terminated franchisees
- Site selection
- Employee and management training

Details of the Franchise Agreement
The disclosure statement must contain the following information about the franchise agreement:

- Required fees
- Exclusive right to serve an area
- Extent of the franchisee's personal participation in the business
- Renewal, repurchase, and termination rights and responsibilities
- Procedures for modifying the agreement
- Covenants not to compete
- Term of the agreement
- Arrangements upon the death of the franchisee

Supporting Facts for any Earnings Claims Made by the Franchisor

Information to support earnings claims is only required where the franchisor has made such claims, typically in promotional materials to prospective franchisees. Some franchisors have been tripped up by this requirement because they have not understood how broadly the term "earnings claim" is interpreted by the FTC. Earnings claims include oral, written, or visual representations which can be used to calculate, state, or even suggest sales, income, or profit levels. Also included are claims of past or potential future earnings, or data presented in such a way that income or costs could be calculated by arbitrarily selecting a sales figure. An attorney experienced in this area of compliance can help a potential franchisor understand which of his or her statements might be considered earnings claims.

The UFOC

The UFOC (Uniform Franchise Offering Circular) was developed by the Midwest Securities Commissioner's Association with the goal of making franchise disclosure statements shorter, easier to read and understand, and to require disclosure of additional helpful information while eliminating information of little use but still required by the FTC document. The UFOC has 21 major items:

Item 1—Background Information
Item 1 of the offering circular must describe basic information about the franchisor and franchise offering, as well as define terms used in the circular and describe regulations specific to the industry in which the franchise will operate.

Item 2—Business Experience
Item 2 requires disclosure of the business experience of the franchisor's directors, officers and executives.

Item 3—Litigation History
Item 3 must detail the litigation history of the franchisor, predecessors, and affiliates selling franchises under the franchisor's principal trademark, including confidential settlement terms of concluded litigation.

Item 4—Bankruptcy History
Item 4 must describe whether the franchisor, any predecessor, or general partner has been involved in a bankruptcy or reorganization within the past 10 years.

Item 5—Initial Fee
Item 5 must describe the initial fees to be paid by the franchisee, including whether payable in a lump sum or in installments, and under what conditions, if any, the initial fee is refundable.

Item 6—Ongoing Fees
Item 6 must describe, in tabular form, all additional, ongoing fees to be paid by the franchisee including but not limited to royalties, service charges, lease payments, and advertising fees.

Item 7—Initial Investment
Item 7 requires the use of tables to identify initial costs and expenses, an estimate of any additional funds necessary to operate the business during a reasonable startup period, and the factual basis for that figure.

Item 8—Required Purchases
Item 8 must include:

- Restrictions on sources of products and services, including required purchases by the franchisee

- Disclosure of any franchisor or affiliate revenues from any required purchases or leases

- The existence of any purchasing or distribution cooperatives

- Disclosure of any consideration the franchisor receives from any required sales or leases of supplies by the franchisee

- Disclosure of any requirement that the franchisor negotiate purchase agreements with suppliers on behalf of franchisees

Item 9—Franchisee's Obligations
Item 9 requires the franchisor to list in tabular form all the franchisee's obligations under the franchise and other related agreements.

Item 10—Financing
Item 10 must disclose all direct or indirect offers of financing, and franchisee's potential liabilities upon default. It is strongly suggested that disclosure be in tabular form and all financing documents must be attached as exhibits.

Item 11—Franchisor Obligations
Item 11 must give a detailed description of the franchisor's obligations to the franchisee, both pre-opening and ongoing during the operation of the business. These obligations may include site location, training, record-keeping, and advertising. Specific non-technical disclosure of any electronic cash register or computer systems must be made.

Item 12—Territorial Limitations
Item 12 must describe any exclusive rights granted to the franchisee to serve a particular geographic area, whether such exclusive rights are dependent upon meeting set sales goals, and the conditions under which they can be altered. Item 12 also must describe whether the franchisor operates company-owned units or distributes products through other methods of distribution using the principal or different trademarks.

Item 13—Trademarks
Item 13 must describe the principal trademarks, service marks, trade names, logotypes, or any other commercial symbols to be licensed to the franchisee.

Item 14—Patents & Copyrights
Item 14 must describe all patents and copyrights to be licensed to the franchisee and the terms, conditions, and duration thereof.

Item 15—Operation of Business
Item 15 must describe the obligation of the franchisee to participate personally in the direct operation of the business and whether the franchisor recommends such participation.

Item 16—Restrictions on Goods and Services Sold by the Franchisee
Item 16 requires the franchisor to describe limits on the goods and services that the franchisee may sell under the agreement, and any restrictions on parties to whom the franchisee may sell.

Item 17—Termination and Other Events
Item 17 must disclose, in tabular form, the conditions for termination, renewal, repurchase, modification, or assignment of rights under the franchise agreement. Termination is discussed further below.

Item 18—Public Figures
Item 18 must disclose the names of public figures whose images are used in the promotion of franchise sales. The information must include compensation given to the public figure, his or her actual interest in the franchise and the extent of his or her actual involvement in the business.

Item 19—Earnings Claims
Item 19 requires that any earnings claims made in the franchisor's offer must be included in the UFOC and must be reasonable at the time they are made. If no earnings claims are made, the UFOC must contain a negative disclosure, the wording of which is specified in the UFOC Guidelines.

Item 20—Statistics
Item 20 requires the franchisor to provide statistics about the total number of franchises, broken down by location, type of franchise agreement, and owner. The information must include the names of terminated franchisees, dates of termination and reasons for termination.

Item 21—Financial Statements
Item 21 requires that the franchisor provide detailed financial statements conforming to Generally Accepted Accounting Principles and audited by an independent public accountant.

MINNESOTA REQUIREMENTS

Under the Minnesota Franchise Act, a franchise is either:

- A contract or agreement between two parties that gives the franchisee a right to do business using the franchisor's trade name, trademark, service mark, logotype, advertising, or other commercial symbol, for which the franchisee pays a franchise fee

or

- Any business opportunity in which a seller sells or leases products or services to a purchaser and represents that the seller will assist in finding locations for the buyer or represents that the seller will purchase products made under the agreement, or guarantees that the buyer will make a profit.

Most proposed offers or sales of a franchise are subject to registration and disclosure requirements (similar to those described above for the UFOC) set by the Minnesota Franchise Act and rules established by the Minnesota Department of Commerce. Under the Minnesota Franchise Act, a company can request an interpretive opinion from the Department of Commerce as to whether a particular business is a franchise for the purposes of Minnesota laws, whether registration is required, and whether any exemptions apply. An attorney who practices in this area of law should be familiar with these requirements.

OTHER STATES' REQUIREMENTS

Several other states have franchise or general business opportunity statutes that can require disclosure by the offeror. At this writing, the following states have disclosure requirements:

- California
- Connecticut
- Florida
- Georgia
- Hawaii
- Illinois
- Indiana
- Iowa
- Kentucky
- Maine
- Maryland
- Michigan
- Nebraska
- New Hampshire
- New York
- North Carolina
- North Dakota
- Ohio
- Oklahoma
- Oregon
- Rhode Island
- South Carolina
- South Dakota
- Texas
- Utah
- Virginia
- Washington
- Wisconsin

Chapter 19: Franchise & Dealership Law

There is little uniformity among states' regulations, although several make a franchisor's failure to provide an offering circular or disclosure document an automatic violation of state law. Some state laws only apply to limited types of franchises, some apply only to transactions within their borders while others apply to franchisors located within their borders even if the offer is made to someone in another state. It is wise to check the requirements in each jurisdiction in which one is planning to offer a franchise or general business opportunity. An attorney experienced in representing franchisors should be familiar with the complexities of multi-state offerings.

FEDERAL PENALTIES FOR FAILURE TO DISCLOSE

The FTC has authority to impose fines of up to $10,000 per day and can order rescission, reformation, payment of refunds and damages, and can issue cease and desist orders against franchisors who fail to follow these disclosure requirements. Persons liable for failure to properly disclose can include directors, officers, brokers, subfranchisors, attorneys, accountants, and other individuals. Currently, there is no private cause of action provided under federal law, although Congress is considering legislation that would provide a private cause of action for injunctive relief and damages.

THE TERMINATION DECISION

Manufacturers and distributors or dealers, and their attorneys, too often wrongly assume that the respective rights and responsibilities of the parties are completely defined in the written agreement and by federal antitrust laws. In fact, both manufacturers and dealers or distributors have rights and responsibilities that may be different from or even contrary to the specific language of the written documents or federal antitrust laws.

A proper evaluation of a dealer termination requires the following six-step analysis: (1) determine the reasons for the termination, (2) review the written agreement, (3) evaluate potential antitrust concerns, (4) analyze potentially applicable dealer protection statutes, (5) consider the potential for common law contract and tort claims, and (6) do a damages analysis. Manufacturers typically do a good job on steps 1 through 3, then skip steps 4 and 5 entirely and thus underestimate their damages exposure in step 6. Such oversights can be very costly.

STEP ONE: DETERMINE THE REASONS FOR THE TERMINATION

The first step in analyzing the termination decision is to determine all actual and arguable reasons for the termination, because the ultimate determination as to whether the termination is lawful will depend on the factfinder's conclusion as to the real reason or reasons for the termination. From the manufacturer's perspective, it is crucial that the manufacturer's attorney be involved in the termination planning process, so that the array of potential and arguable reasons for termination can be examined in light of the other factors listed below, and a course of action can be planned which will minimize the likelihood of litigation. Documents which could arguably support or refute any potential reason for the termination should also be reviewed as a part of this first step.

Step Two: Review the Written Agreement

The second step in analyzing the termination decision is to review the written agreement, if any, between the manufacturer and dealer. The primary focus in reviewing the written agreement should be on the provisions concerning termination. However, choice of law and forum selection provisions, arbitration clauses, and clauses limiting liability or damages also should be reviewed because these provisions may have a profound effect on the outcome of the dispute, particularly in light of the trend in recent years toward increased enforcement of these types of provisions.

Termination Provisions
Termination clauses in written dealer agreements tend to fall into two broad categories: termination at will clauses and termination for good cause clauses.

Common Termination at Will Language:
"The Dealer's appointment may be terminated at any time by written notice by either the Company or the Dealer to the other party given at least one hundred twenty (120) days prior to the effective date specified in such notice."

Common Termination for Good Cause Language:
"Company may terminate this Agreement by giving Dealer not less than sixty (60) days prior written notice of termination in the event of any of the following:
Dealer does not maintain a level of sales of products and parts to the satisfaction of Company as required by this Agreement.
Dealer does not perform satisfactorily its obligations listed in this Agreement.
Failure of Dealer to perform any of the promises given or obligations undertaken in this Agreement.
Any dispute, disagreement or controversy between or among principals, partners, managers, officers or shareholders of Dealer, which in the opinion of Company may adversely affect the business of Dealer or Company."

"Company may terminate this Agreement immediately by delivering to Dealer or its representative written notice of such termination in the event of any of the following:
Any transfer or assignment, or attempted transfer or assignment of this Agreement or any right or oblation hereunder or any sale or transfer of any interest in the ownership or active management of Dealer without prior written approval of Company; or
the insolvency of Dealer; the filing of a petition for bankruptcy or for reorganization, whether voluntary or involuntary; if Dealer makes an assignment for the benefit of creditors; if a receiver is appointed for a Dealer or its property if Dealer defaults in the payment of any obligation owing to Company or its affiliates, successors or assigns; or, upon demand fails to account to Company, or its affiliates, successors or assigns for the proceeds from the sale of goods for which Dealer is indebted to Company or its affiliates, successors or assigns.
Dealer makes any material written or oral statement or representation which is false or otherwise misleading."

Forum Selection, Arbitration, Choice of Law, and Integration Clauses

Increasingly within the last five years, manufacturers and franchisors have used, and courts have increasingly enforced, contractual provisions intended to modify or circumvent statutory requirements.

Choice of Law Provisions

A choice of law provision in a contract is an agreement that any dispute arising out of the agreement will be determined applying the laws of a particular state. An enforceable choice of law provision can dramatically affect the rights of those on both sides of the distribution relationship, but there is a wide variety of state laws regulating the termination or substantial alteration of distribution relationships, and a great disparity in the nature and amount of regulation.

Historically, state statutes regulating the conduct of parties to a franchise or dealership agreement have been viewed as the embodiment of the state's public policy and, as such, the statutes prevailed over conflicting language in agreements between the parties. Recent cases, however, have dramatically eroded this view and led to the development of a four-part test to determine whether conflicting contractual provisions, such as choice of law provisions designating the law of a different state to govern, should eliminate otherwise available statutory protection:

- Did the parties agree to the choice of law in advance?

- Are the parties evenly divided between the chosen state and the plaintiff's state?

- Are the parties of relatively equal bargaining strength?

- Is the application of the law chosen repugnant to the public policy of the franchisor's state?

Not all jurisdictions have followed this trend, however and some states' courts are resisting the trend toward enforcement of choice of law provisions that effectively take away franchisees' and dealers' statutory protections. The Minnesota state legislature actually strengthened the language of the Minnesota Franchise Act in reaction to this trend. The Act was amended expressly to state that choice of law provisions which have the effect of waiving compliance with the provisions of the Act are void.

Forum Selection Clauses

As a practical matter, a terminated dealer may be much less willing or financially able to pursue litigation in a far-distant forum than in the dealer's home state. Also, the manufacturer's or dealer's home forum may have more sympathetic judges and juries. Forum selection clauses therefore may also have a profound effect on the ultimate consequences of termination. Like choice of law provisions, the courts seem increasingly willing to enforce forum selection clauses.

Arbitration Clauses

Arbitration clauses are proliferating in franchise and dealer agreements, and for the most part continue to be received warmly by federal courts, even where state laws designed to protect dealers and franchisees specify that arbitration cannot be required.

Integration Clauses

Manufacturers often assume that if a contract contains an "integration clause"—a clause indicating that the written document is the "entire agreement" between the parties—they need not consider other communications or practices that might otherwise affect the agreement. While integration clauses are often effective against some types of claims, it remains a dangerous and often erroneous assumption that an integration clause will erase the effect of promises and conduct not contained in the written document. Courts often take into account, under a variety of legal theories, what the parties' "real agreement" is. Courts frequently consider the parties' oral communications, course of dealing, custom and practice, and other conduct and statements outside of the written agreement—even when it contains an integration clause or oral commitments to attempt to prove its promissory estoppel claim.

Contractual Statutes of Limitation

A troubling development in recent decisions, from the franchisee's perspective, is judicial willingness to enforce contractual limitations on the time a franchisee or dealer has to bring a claim. Several recent cases have found provisions requiring claims to be asserted in periods of as little as one year enforceable.

STEP THREE: EVALUATE POTENTIAL ANTITRUST CONCERNS

Even when federal antitrust laws pose no problem, state antitrust laws may differ, or may be interpreted differently, than their federal counterparts. The best antitrust insurance is to have a good reason for terminating a relationship or a bad reason may well be inferred.

STEP FOUR: ANALYZE POTENTIALLY APPLICABLE DEALER PROTECTION STATUTES

States have a number of ways that they can protect dealers from unfair termination decisions. An attorney experienced in representing dealers or manufacturers should be familiar with how a particular state regulates dealer terminations.

State Franchise Acts

As mentioned above, many states have statutes that govern franchise relationships, often prohibiting termination of the relationship by the franchisor except for good cause. The definition of franchise varies from state to state. Most, but not all, of the states require the payment of consideration from the franchisee to the franchisor in order to qualify as a franchise relationship.

The Minnesota Franchise Act defines prohibited "unfair and inequitable" practices, which may be enjoined, as follows:

"It is an unfair and inequitable practice for a person to . . . :

(b) terminate or cancel a franchise except for good cause. "Good cause" means failure by the franchisee to substantially comply with the material and reasonable franchise requirements imposed by the franchisor including, but not limited to:

(1) the bankruptcy or insolvency of the franchisee;

(2) assignment for the benefit, of creditors or similar disposition of the assets of the franchise business;

(3) voluntary abandonment of the franchise business;

(4) conviction or a plea of guilty or no contest to a charge of violating any law relating to the franchise business; or

(5) any act by or conduct of the franchisee which materially impairs the good will associated with the franchisor's trademark, trade name, service mark, logotype or other commercial symbol. The Act also prohibits unfair and inequitable practices with respect to nonrenewal of a franchise."

Minn. Stat. §80C.14, Subd. 4 provides as follows:

"Failure to renew. Unless the failure to renew a franchise is for good cause as defined in subdivision 3, paragraph (b), and the franchisee has failed to correct reasons for termination as required by subdivision 3, no person may fail to renew a franchise unless (1) the franchisee has been given written notice of the intention not to renew at least 180 days in advance of the expiration of the franchise; and (2) the franchisee has been given an opportunity to operate the franchise over a sufficient period of time to enable the franchisee to recover the fair market value of the franchise as a going concern, as determined and measured from the date of the failure to renew. No franchisor may refuse to renew a franchise if the refusal is for the purpose of converting the franchisee's business premises to an operation that will be owned by the franchisor for its own account."

Industry Specific Legislation

Several industries have industry-specific statutes that govern their particular manufacturer-dealer relationships. Among the industries with industry-specific dealer protections are petroleum (i.e., the Petroleum Marketing Practices Act plus approximately 8 states with petroleum franchise regulations), automobiles (i.e., Automotive Dealer Franchise Act, plus various states' statutes), farm implements (approximately 38 states have statutes), beer (approximately 30 states) and construction and industrial equipment.

Typically these statutes have arisen out of prior terminations and litigation in those particular industries. Accordingly, if the particular industry has had a recent rash of terminations and litigation, the chances are good that an industry specific statute has been passed to regulate it. For example, the Minnesota Agricultural Equipment Dealership Act requiring good cause for cancellation, failure to renew or substantially changing the competitive circumstances of farm equipment dealerships all arose out of a rash of terminations in that industry in Minnesota.

What Industry's Laws Apply?

The definitions in industry-specific statutes are often broad, and the titles of those statutes can be misleading. For example, the Minnesota Agricultural Equipment Dealership Act is expressly applicable to "skid-steer" loader dealerships, although "skid-steer" loaders are wheeled loaders more commonly used in the construction and landscaping businesses, at least in metropolitan areas. "Wheel loaders," by contrast, are considered "heavy and utility equipment" and are governed by a different statute, as are "backhoes." If a dealer sells skid-steer loaders with backhoe attachments the dealer could conceivably be governed by both statutes. It is imperative, therefore, that all potentially applicable industry-specific statutes be consulted in order to determine whether they apply.

What State's Laws Apply?

The search for potentially applicable state dealer protection statutes must go beyond the state where the distributor or dealer has its principal place of business, and must also include (1) the other states in which the distributor or dealer is doing business, (2) the state where the manufacturer has its principal business location, and (3) any other state mentioned in any choice of law clause in the written dealer agreement.

Does the Statute Apply to Preexisting Agreements?

Many dealer and franchise statutes have been enacted relatively recently, and their applicability to existing contracts is often in dispute. These disputes frequently arise either under statutes which do not address retroactive application, or under statutes which provide that they apply to agreements with no expiration date which were in effect at the time the statute was enacted. Even if a statute purports to apply to a contract existing prior to its enactment, the court may decline to apply the statute because of concerns over the constitutionality of its retroactive application.

Is There Good Cause for Termination?

Assuming that either an industry-specific or a general termination protection statute, such as a franchise statute, applies, the next question is whether there is a violation. Since the statutes generally require "good cause" for termination, cancellation, nonrenewal, or in some cases for the substantial change in competitive circumstances, the first question is what is "good cause"? The statute itself often spells out at least some of the acts, omissions, or circumstances which constitute good cause. If the statutory "laundry list" is not applicable to a particular situation, the following are common issues that arise in determining "good cause":

- Failure to meet performance criteria: To constitute good cause, the performance criteria must be reasonable. Additionally, there is a developing body of law to the effect that, in order for the failure to meet reasonable performance criteria to constitute good cause, the criteria must be both essential and applied in a non-discriminatory way.

- System-wide changes: A non-discriminatory, reasonable change in all dealerships of a manufacturer compelled by business considerations may constitute good cause under certain circumstances.

- Violations of contract or law.

- Market withdrawal: There are conflicting decisions as to whether a manufacturer's withdrawal from a market constitutes good cause. However, a change in distribution allegedly made necessary by economic necessity is not good cause for termination of existing dealers absent withdrawal from the market.

Who is Liable?

A question arising with increasing frequency in these days of mergers and acquisitions is the liability of successor manufacturers for their predecessors' obligations to their dealers. In the agricultural and construction equipment industries, a common phenomenon in recent years has been the acquisition of one manufacturer's business by another through an asset purchase transaction. In these transactions, the purchasing manufacturer typically disclaims any assumption of the selling manufacturer's agreements with its dealers. A dealer terminated by the selling manufacturer which ceases business because it has sold its assets to another manufacturer is faced with what appears to be a no-win scenario: the terminated dealer can pursue a judgment against an entity that no longer exists or no longer is solvent; or the terminated dealer can attempt to impose liability on the purchasing manufacturer, who undoubtedly will disclaim any obligation to the dealer.

Generally, attempts to establish common law successor liability on manufacturers in asset purchase situations fare poorly. However, some courts have attempted to find, and some legislatures have attempted to impose, statutory successor liability under unforgiving circumstances.

"Little FTC" and Deceptive Trade Practices Acts

In addition to statutes regulating certain types of distribution relationships or distribution relationships in certain industries, another potentially applicable source of statutory rights and duties is found in statutes regulating business conduct in general. These statutes commonly include deceptive trade practices acts and "Little FTC" acts.

Deceptive Trade Practices Acts

Most, if not all, states have consumer protection statutes, many of which are modeled after the Uniform Deceptive Trade Practices Act. These statutes generally prohibit "deceptive" trade practices and therefore may encompass conduct which might not be found fraudulent. However, they frequently provide only for injunctive relief, not damages.

"Little FTC" Acts

Many states have statutes patterned after Section 5 of the Federal Trade Commission Act, which prohibit unfair methods of competition and unfair or deceptive acts or trade practices. Unlike most deceptive trade practices acts, these "Little FTC" acts prohibit "unfair" conduct as well as "deceptive" conduct, and often allow private actions for damages, attorney's fees, and sometimes multiple damages. These claims have been successfully advanced in some dealer termination cases.

STEP FIVE: COMMON LAW CONSIDERATIONS

The fifth step concerns taking into account common law considerations. This is the step that very few manufacturers and dealers or their counsel complete, but it frequently is the most important. Even where a written agreement states that it is the entire agreement between the parties, and that it may be terminated without cause on short notice, where no protective state legislation applies, and where the termination takes place under circumstances that are unlikely, in today's regulatory environment, to be successfully challenged under antitrust laws, termination without good cause may still be unlawful.

What is the Contract?

The contract consists of all of the parties' various expressions of interest, and is not necessarily limited to the written agreement. For example, the standard jury instruction given in Minnesota on elements of a contract includes the following:

"For a contract to exist the parties must agree with reasonable certainty about the same thing, and on the same terms. In other words, there must be an agreement between the parties as to all the essential terms and conditions of the contract. In determining whether or not there was an agreement you may consider the parties' words, written or oral, their actions and conduct, and all of the circumstances surrounding their dealings. A contract may be formed orally, in writing, by the actions of the parties, or by a combination of all three methods. The usual way in which a contract is formed is through the process of an offer by one party and an acceptance of that offer by the other party."

Unwritten Terms

The enforceable agreement may be different than, or even contrary to, the written contract for several reasons. Often, there are oral communications between "field" or "territory" representatives of the manufacturers and dealers concerning the duration of the dealership or the circumstances under which it could be terminated. These communications, if enforced, may prevent termination even when the written agreement does not.

Parol evidence is admissible to explain or clarify ambiguous writings in all jurisdictions. If the language used in a contract is "reasonably susceptible of more than one meaning" it is ambiguous and parol evidence may be introduced. Evidence of the custom and practice in the industry with respect to dealer terminations, and the course of dealing between the particular manufacturer and dealer, is commonly admissible to assist the jury in determining what the agreement was. Courts have interpreted these provisions to permit introduction of evidence of course of performance, dealing and usage of trade where that evidence does not completely negate the terms of a written contract.

Terms Implied by Operation of Law

Additional, contrary terms may even be implied by operation of law. An obligation of good faith is implied by the common law of most states, and often provides rights not found in the written contracts. It continues to be the law, however, that the covenant of good faith and fair dealing cannot be extended to contradict specific contract terms.

Estoppel

Promissory or equitable estoppel may also operate to prevent a manufacturer from invoking a clause in its written contract where it has, by its conduct, led the dealer to believe it would not rely on that clause against that dealer.

Recoupment

Essentially, recoupment implies a minimum term in an at-will agreement defined as the length of time in which the dealer can reasonably be expected to recoup its investment, and holds that it is a breach of contract if the agreement is terminated before that.

A few courts have interpreted the recoupment doctrine to apply only to exclusive dealers. In calculating unrecouped expenditures recoverable in recoupment, the court must "tak[e] into account, of course, the value of any benefits it may have derived from the arrangement during its existence or may derive thereafter."

Fraudulent Inducement

Fraudulent inducement generally requires a misrepresentation of a material fact made with knowledge of its falsity (or made as of one's own knowledge without knowing whether it is true or false) with the intent that the other party rely on the misrepresentation, and on which the other party in fact relies.

Principal issues for making a claim of fraudulent inducement include: did the person making the promise appear to have the authority to make it; was the promise or statement with respect to when termination would occur false when made; was there a failure to disclose material facts that should have been made at the time to avoid misleading the dealer?

Incredibly, franchisors are having increasing success in asserting that the integration clauses contained in the written agreements operate to bar, as a matter of law, fraudulent inducement claims.

Another issue that is frequently overlooked is whether the conduct of the manufacturer satisfies the elements of tortious interference with contracts and prospective contractual relationships. By introducing a tort theory of liability into dealer termination litigation, the possibility of punitive damages follows. This often has a substantial effect on the manufacturer's potential exposure and the terminated dealer's potential recovery. Tortious interference theories may successfully be employed in dealer termination litigation, and may give rise to liability under circumstances where no obligation can be found in the relevant agreements or statutes.

Contracts

"One who intentionally and improperly interferes with the performance of a contract between another and a third person by inducing or otherwise causing the third person not to perform the contract is subject to liability to the other for the pecuniary loss resulting to the other from the failure of the third person to perform the contract." Restatement (2d) of Torts §766.

This section is generally construed to require (1) a contract, (2) defendant's intentional interference with the performance of the contract, (3) no justification for defendant's actions, and (4) resulting damage. The interference need not be directed at the person with whom plaintiff has a contract, but may be directed at the plaintiff.

Prospective Contractual Relationships

Many jurisdictions also recognize a cause of action for tortious interference with prospective business relationships. Elements of this tort are generally defined to include (1) the existence of a valid business relationship or expectancy, (2) knowledge of the relationship or expectancy on the part of the interferor, (3) an intentional interference causing a breach or termination of the relationship or expectancy, and (4) resulting damage to the party whose relationship or expectancy has been disrupted. There are three types of interference: first, interference with the dealer/distributor contractual relationships with its customers and prospective customers; second, interference with contractual relationship existing between individual owners or operators and the corporate entity itself; third, manufacturer refusal to provide customary and reasonable assistance to the dealer during time between notice of termination and the effective date.

STEP SIX: DO A DAMAGE ANALYSIS

Manufacturers may be too quick to minimize potential liability problems because of an assumption that damages will be limited to a standard formula, such as a multiplier of the pro rata net profits of the dealership. There are at least two reasons why this common assumption is not valid.

First, different liability theories justify different types of damages recoveries. Statutory violations typically permit the recovery of attorneys' fees. The recoupment theory permits the recovery of unrecouped (i.e., unrecovered) investments in the dealership (such that, for example, a dealership which has never made a profit, but instead has lost $500,000 over the years in an effort to build up a market for the manufacturer's product may be able to recover that amount, plus interest). Tort theories create the possibility of punitive damages (in an amount sufficient to punish the wrongdoer for its conduct and to deter others from engaging in similar conduct in the future). Second, even in those cases where the measure of damages is limited to the value of what has been lost, the courts have allowed calculations which yield a far greater damages award than would a simple multiplier of the pro rata net profits of the dealership. For example, a dealer who carried five lines of equipment may often cover his overhead with the first four and make his profit on the fifth. The loss of that fifth line represents the difference between profit and loss to the dealer, a loss much greater than the proportion of his profit that is represented by revenues from the terminating manufacturer's product. Some courts have therefore recognized that a dealer whose overhead was not substantially reduced by a termination may recover damages on the basis of its anticipated gross profits which were attributable to the terminating manufacturer's products.

Injunctive or Declaratory Relief

A strategic consideration for both sides in the dealer termination setting is whether to seek injunctive relief (for a dealer being terminated) or a declaratory judgment (for a terminating manufacturer). Courts often recognize that a dealer threatened with termination does not want to live on the income from a damages award, but rather would prefer to continue to operate the business. Courts therefore will often permit the entry of injunctive relief preserving the relationship pending trial where the injunction is sought before the termination becomes effective. However, courts generally are unwilling to grant injunctive relief after the termination becomes effective.

RECOMMENDATIONS FOR DISTRIBUTORS AND DEALERS

- Assuming the parties have unequal bargaining power, do without a written agreement if possible.

- Ask good questions as to how the termination provision will really work and obtain a side letter with respect to termination concerns.

- Pay close attention to forum selection, arbitration, choice of law, limitation of damages, and contractual "statute of limitation" clauses, and try to obtain a side letter stating that they do not apply to you.

- If you see a termination coming, try and negotiate reasonable performance criteria as an alternative to termination.

- Consider commencing a lawsuit and seeking injunctive relief in advance of the effective date of the termination and seek to negotiate an extension of the termination date to allow you to try and negotiate a resolution of the dispute, allowing continuation of the distributorship or dealership subject to meeting reasonable performance criteria.

RECOMMENDATIONS FOR MANUFACTURERS

- Terminate for good reasons only, and communicate those reasons in advance of the termination, giving the distributor or dealer a reasonable opportunity to correct any correctable reasons for termination.

- Do the above six-step analysis before implementing a termination decision

- Most importantly, have a written agreement, which should contain:

- Definite duration

- Reservation of rights to the manufacturer, such as the right to appoint other dealers within the territory; rights to terminate the relationship upon sale of assets or a decision to go to direct distribution, even if those rights are not presently exercised

- Disclaimer of any franchise relationship

- Choice of law provision

- Forum selection clause

- Possibly an arbitration clause in a specified forum

- Limitation of damages and contractual statute of limitations clause

- Integration clause, with references to how ongoing relationships, including day-to-day business agreements, will be handled

- Authority clause limiting those who can bind the corporation

- Possibly a two-way street provision requiring payment of attorneys' fees by losing party

- Possibly a "good cause" requirement for termination, specifically allowing termination for a reasonable array of good business reasons

RESOURCES

Minnesota Department of Commerce, Franchise Registration (612) 296-6328.

Business Franchise Guide. Commerce Clearing House Inc., Chicago, IL, 1988. This useful resource, updated periodically, contains state and federal regulations.

Evaluating a Franchise Opportunity (With Checklist). David Laufer & Patrick Carter, 40 The Practical Lawyer 59 (April 1994).

FRANCHISE & DEALERSHIP LAW LEADING ATTORNEYS

The attorneys profiled in this section were nominated by their peers in a statewide survey conducted in 1993 in which several thousand Minnesota attorneys were asked to name the lawyer to whom they would send a friend or family member in need of legal assistance in the area of *Franchise & Dealership Law*.

Because the survey resulted in a list of less than five percent of Minnesota's practicing attorneys, this should not be construed as a complete list. Nevertheless, it is an excellent source of highly qualified and reputable attorneys, who, if unable to assist can in most cases make quality referrals.

A list of all attorneys nominated in this category is found at the end of this section. For information on the survey methodology see page ix.

Please note that the shorter, two line attorney listings in this section are of attorneys who practice in this area but whose full biographical profile appears in another section of this book. A bullet "•" preceeding name indicates the attorney was nominated in this particular area of law. For information on the format of these profiles, consult the section "Using the *Business Guidebook*" found on page xiv. Note that the following abbreviations are used throughout these profiles:

The attorneys profiled below were recommended by their peers in a statewide survey.

App.	- Appellate	ABA	- American Bar Association
Cir.	- Circuit	ATLA	- American Trial Lawyers Association
Ct.	- Court	HCBA	- Hennepin County Bar Association
Dist.	- District	MDLA	- Minnesota Defense Lawyers Association
Hon.	- Honorable	MSBA	- Minnesota State Bar Association
JD	- Law degree (Juris Doctor)	MTLA	- Minnesota Trial Lawyers Association
LLB	- Law degree	NBTA	- National Board of Trial Advocacy
LLM	- Master in Law degree	RCBA	- Ramsey County Bar Association
Sup.	- Supreme		

•J. MICHAEL DADY: Mr. Dady, a former senior partner in the 110-member Minneapolis law firm of Lindquist & Vennum, is a nationally certified civil trial specialist. Since 1975, he has spent the majority of his time representing dealers, distributors, and franchisees in different parts of the United States in business-threatening disputes with their suppliers. Two recently reported decisions in which he was successful are presently the last word on the law of injunctive relief for dealers in Minnesota. In *TCBY Systems, Inc. v. RSP Company, Inc.*, Michael successfully established that the implied covenant of good faith and fair dealing applies to franchise agreements. He has written and spoken in the Midwest, and nationally, on franchise and distribution law issues. Michael is a contributing author to *Corporate Counsel's Guide to Distribution Counseling* and serves on the National Governing Committee of the ABA Forum on Franchising. Cases Michael has successfully concluded have been cited by other continuing legal education lecturers as models. His opening statement and closing argument in the case of *Koeppe v. Philbrick, et al.* are featured in *Persuasive Trial Arguments* (MTLA, 1991). One of his appellate briefs is featured as a model in *Art of Advocacy* (Matthew Bender, 1991). Michael devotes the balance of his trial practice to representing personal injury victims. He is listed in *The Best Lawyers in America* and has been listed in Minnesota's *Journal of Law & Politics* as one of Minnesota's "Super Lawyers."
Education: JD 1975, University of Minnesota (Editor, *Minnesota Law Review*); BS 1971, St. John's University.
Employment History: Founding Partner 1994, J. Michael Dady & Associates, P.A.; Senior Partner/Associate 1975-94, Lindquist & Vennum.
Representative Clients: Among the franchisees, dealers, and distributors whom Michael has successfully represented over the past several years are restaurant, fast food, dessert, automobile, video, weight loss, and copier franchisees; numerous construction and agricultural implement dealers; and beer, wine, and soft drink distributors.
Professional Associations: ABA Forum on Franchising (National Governing Committee); MTLA (Board member); American Creativity Assn. (Board member).
Community Involvement: St. John's University Board of Regents (Chair). *See additional listing in Commercial Litigation Chapter.*

J. MICHAEL DADY

J. Michael Dady & Associates, P.A.
4000 IDS Center
80 South Eighth Street
Minneapolis, MN 55402-2204

Phone: (612) 359-9000
Fax: (612) 359-3507

Admitted: 1975 Minnesota;
1983 South Dakota;
1985 North Dakota;
1985 Wisconsin;
1976 US Ct. App. (8th Cir.)
Birthdate: 03/09/49

Chapter 19: Franchise & Dealership Law

•**ELLIOT S. KAPLAN** - Robins, Kaplan, Miller & Ciresi - 2800 LaSalle Plaza, 800 LaSalle Avenue - Minneapolis, MN 55402 - Phone: (612) 349-8500, Fax: (612) 339-4181 - *See complete biographical profile in Commercial Litigation Chapter.*

•**PAUL VAN VALKENBURG** - Moss & Barnett, A Professional Association - 4800 Norwest Center, 90 South Seventh Street - Minneapolis, MN 55402 - Phone: (612) 347-0300, Fax: (612) 339-6686 - *See complete biographical profile in Publicly Held Corporations Law Chapter.*

Complete listing of all attorneys nominated in Franchise & Dealership Law

J. MICHAEL DADY, J. Michael Dady & Associates, P.A., Minneapolis; **ELLIOT S. KAPLAN,** Robins, Kaplan, Miller & Ciresi, Minneapolis; **JEFFREY J. KEYES,** Briggs and Morgan, P.A., Minneapolis; **G. THOMAS MACINTOSH II,** Mackall, Crounse & Moore, Minneapolis; **BRIAN B. SCHNELL,** Gray, Plant, Mooty, Mooty & Bennett, P.A., Minneapolis; **PAUL VAN VALKENBURG,** Moss & Barnett, A Professional Association, Minneapolis.

CHAPTER 20

HEALTH LAW

Health law is a relatively new and rapidly expanding area of legal specialization. Many lawyers are attracted by the dynamic character of this constantly evolving area of practice. Clients range from health care consumers seeking assistance to pay for health care to large corporate health care providers seeking to buy a chain of nursing homes. Because of the diversity of clients, the health law practice area has numerous subspecialties. This chapter covers subjects of most interest to businesses and health care providers. Employee benefits plans are discussed in the Employee Benefits Law Chapter. Medical malpractice is discussed in the Professional Malpractice Defense Law Chapter.

ACCESS TO THE HEALTH CARE SYSTEM

The most important health care issue for many individuals is access to the health care system. The state of Minnesota has some of the world's finest health care providers and facilities, yet Minnesotans can face a number of hurdles before receiving treatment. Patients, their families, and health care institutions all need to be aware of the legal framework that exists to guarantee access to health care.

PAYING FOR HEALTH CARE

The most important health care issue for individuals and their health care providers is often paying for health care. The three primary government-sponsored health care programs are Medicaid, Medicare, and MinnesotaCare.

Medicaid

Medicaid, also called medical assistance (MA) in Minnesota, should not be confused with Medicare. Despite their similar names, the two programs are substantially different. Medicare, described below, is a program funded and administered entirely by the federal government (Social Security Administration) to provide health care to elderly and disabled persons. Medicare coverage is uniform throughout the country. Medicaid is a cooperative program partly funded by the federal government, partly by the individual states, and mostly run by the states to provide health care to indigent persons. Each state has wide latitude in deciding how Medicaid operates within the state. In Minnesota, Medicaid provides a wider range of medical goods and services than in some other states.

The federal government's role in Medicaid is quite limited. It pays a percentage of the cost of each state's health care program for indigents and ensures that every state's program complies with various federal requirements. The amount of money a state receives from the federal government is called the Federal Financial Participation (FFP). Each state's FFP is determined by a formula based on the state's per capita income and the amount of medical services the state chooses to provide to its needy persons.

For an individual to receive Medicaid, the county applies a complex formula which considers the applicant's unique situation. The individual applicant must have few assets and very low income. A person generally cannot have more than $3000 in assets or more than $420 income per month. There are several assets the formula does not count. Assets not counted include:

- Homestead (of any value)

- Automobile under $4500 in value, if necessary for employment, receiving health care, modified for a handicapped person, or essential for performing daily tasks

- Burial funds

- Household goods and personal effects (of any value)

- Capital and operating assets of a business necessary to earn an income

Certain other unavailable assets are not counted, such as jointly held real estate if the other joint owner refuses to sell, or property tied up in probate.

A person can intentionally reduce his or her assets to the point where he or she qualifies for Medicaid. As long as transfers are compensated, it is legal to restructure one's assets and income with the intent of qualifying for Medicaid. For example, it is permissible for a person to invest all of his or her available cash in a larger homestead or in expanding a business in order to reduce his or her counted assets to below $3,000. It is not permissible simply to give the available cash to family members or friends. Lawyers who specialize in Medicaid are often experienced in advising clients how to restructure their assets and income to qualify for Medicaid.

Anyone whose income is above Medicaid limits might still receive Medicaid with a spend-down provision. The spend-down is equal to the amount a person's income exceeds Medicaid limits. Medicaid occasionally agrees to cover the amount that a person's medical bills exceed a patient's spend-down.

Restructuring assets to qualify for Medicaid can be an especially attractive option for senior citizens, even if they already qualify for Medicare. Medicaid coverage is better for persons living in nursing homes because Medicaid pays for a wider variety of nursing care and for a longer period of time than does Medicare.

Medicare
Medicare is a federal program administered entirely by the Social Security Administration and is designed to cover some basic medical and health care costs of eligible individuals over age 65 and some disabled individuals under age 65 regardless of financial need. Medicare has become an enormous federal program, providing billions of dollars in coverage every year.

Medicare should not be confused with Medicaid. Medicaid is a program administered by the Social Security Administration to pay doctor and hospital bills of people with limited income and assets. Unlike Medicaid, Medicare benefits are available to qualified individuals regardless of financial need.

Parts A & B

Medicare has two primary divisions, called Part A and Part B. Medicare Part A, commonly known as Hospital Insurance, covers medically necessary hospital and related health care. Included in Part A are costs for such expenses as inpatient hospital care necessitated by acute illness, skilled nursing home care, certified hospice care for the terminally ill, inpatient psychiatric care, and care in the home by a certified home health care provider.

Medicare Part B, commonly known as Supplemental Medical Insurance, is a voluntary health insurance program designed to cover some of the costs not covered by Medicare Part A, such as outpatient hospital services, outpatient physical therapy, speech pathology services, necessary ambulance service, and medical equipment. Unlike Part A, which is paid for out of Social Security taxes and is free to anyone qualifying for it, Part B is an optional program that carries small monthly premiums.

The federal government contracts with private insurance companies to handle routine claims processing, payment, and other functions under Part A and B. Private insurance companies contracted under Part A are called fiscal intermediaries. The fiscal intermediary for almost all of Minnesota is Blue Cross/Blue Shield of St. Paul. Private insurance companies contracted under Part B are called carriers. The Travelers of Bloomington is the carrier for the counties around the Twin Cities metropolitan area and Rochester. Blue Cross/Blue Shield is the carrier for the rest of Minnesota. The Travelers Insurance Company of Salt Lake City is the carrier for Railroad Retirement beneficiaries in Minnesota.

Anyone eligible to receive RSI or Railroad benefits is eligible to receive Medicare Part A coverage, although the person need not actually be receiving financial benefits through either of these two programs in order to receive Medicare benefits. Anyone age 65 or older not eligible for RSI or Railroad benefits can still receive Medicare Part A coverage by paying a monthly premium. Medicare Part B coverage is automatically available to anyone who qualifies for Medicare Part A benefits. In fact, all applicants for Medicare Part A benefits are automatically enrolled in Medicare Part B unless they opt out of Part B coverage which carries a small monthly premium.

Costs Not Covered by Medicare

Medicare was never intended to provide comprehensive coverage for all medical needs of America's elderly population, but rather was intended to supplement private resources. Many health services are not covered by Medicare. For example, Medicare does not pay for:

- Custodial care that could reasonably be given by someone without medical training and is generally intended to help the patient with his or her daily living needs. Examples include help with bathing, walking, or exercising.

- Dentures or routine dental care

- Eyeglasses, hearing aids, and examinations to prescribe or fit them

- Nursing home care (except skilled nursing care)
- Prescription drugs
- Routine physical checkups and related tests

Insurance Issues Related to Medicare

Many seniors look for some form of private insurance to supplement Medicare coverage. Some seniors are able to get continuation or conversion coverage from group policies they had at their workplace. Under these plans, seniors continue to be covered by the policies that covered them while they were working. Another popular option for seniors is to join a Health Maintenance Organization or HMO. HMO coverage is similar to continuation or conversion coverage, but many HMO's have more complicated rules for persons who are covered by Medicare, so it pays to learn about a particular HMO's policies regarding Medicare benefits before signing up.

In addition, there are private insurance policies for seniors intended to cover gaps in Medicare coverage, such as deductibles, co-payments, or procedures not covered by Medicare. These policies are commonly referred to as Medigap policies. Medigap policies have been a source of much confusion and outright fraud in Minnesota. As a result, the state legislature has created a complex scheme to regulate them. The two types of Medigap policies are basic policies and extended basic policies. The state of Minnesota requires that basic Medigap coverage offered in the state include coverage for several preventative health care procedures and that extended Medigap coverage cover everything covered by basic Medigap coverage plus 100 percent of the cost of several routine cancer screening procedures, immunizations, and many more preventative tests and measures. In Minnesota, most dread disease policies—policies designed to cover a particular type of illness, such as cancer or heart disease—are illegal to sell to Medicare beneficiaries. For certain indigent elderly, Medicaid is available, and therefore private insurance is financially inadvisable.

MinnesotaCare

In response to the growing number of Minnesotans unable to afford private health insurance, the Minnesota legislature created a subsidized health insurance program known as MinnesotaCare. The program is administered by the Minnesota Department of Human Services and is open to permanent Minnesota residents who are not eligible to receive Medicaid (Medical Assistance, or MA, discussed above) and who are also unable to get employer-paid health insurance and are not covered by any other health insurance plan.

MinnesotaCare works like many private health insurance plans. Eligible applicants pay monthly premiums based on family size and income. In return, they receive a variety of health care services, equipment, supplies, and prescriptions from private or public providers. Many of these items have co-payments associated with them.

MinnesotaCare's eligibility requirements are complex. When originally begun, the program covered only children, parents, and dependents. As funding increases, MinnesotaCare's coverage umbrella is slowly expanding to include single adults and married couples without children. Many persons originally ineligible to enroll have become or will soon become eligible, so it is wise to check the latest eligibility requirements with the Minnesota Department of Human Services by calling 1-800-657-3672 or 297-3862 in the Twin Cities metro area.

Access to Facilities

Hospitals rarely refuse to treat a patient if the patient has health care insurance, but it can happen either because of prejudices or a hospital's concern about being reimbursed through Medicare or Medicaid. Several federal and state laws exist to guarantee a patient's access to health care. The Internal Revenue Service requires hospitals to admit all paying members of their communities in order to enjoy tax exempt status. The Hill-Burton Act, which provides construction grants to many hospital projects, requires hospitals receiving grants under its programs to admit all paying patients. Both Medicare and Medicaid require all hospitals participating in these programs to care for all covered patients.

Most of these laws guaranteeing access to health care facilities are rarely ever needed because hospitals are eager to admit paying patients. The AIDS epidemic has made accessibility an issue in some recent cases because some hospitals are concerned with the potentially enormous costs of fighting the disease, worried about spreading the disease, or because some decision makers object to the lifestyles of some AIDS sufferers. Laws governing the medical industry clearly forbid health care providers from using personal bias to decide whom to treat.

Access to Medical Records

A patient's right of access to his or her own medical and psychological records is an important tool for making wise decisions about health care. In Minnesota, a health care institution must provide a patient with the originals or copies of medical or psychological records kept on file. The patient may be required to pay reasonable copying charges. The health care provider can withhold the records only if he or she believes release would be detrimental to the patient's physical or mental well-being or could cause the patient to inflict self harm or to harm another person.

PATIENT CONTROL OVER HEALTH CARE DECISIONS

Once a patient has gained access to the health care system, the law guarantees the patient's right to be kept informed of his or her status and involved in decisions affecting his or her care. Health care providers need to be aware of their responsibilities under these laws.

Right to Consent to Care

In general, a doctor cannot diagnose or treat a patient without first obtaining that person's informed consent. A doctor need not obtain a client's consent to treat mental illness, mental retardation, or chemical dependency. However, failure to obtain informed consent for any other kind of treatment can subject the doctor to charges of battery, invasion of privacy, or malpractice. If the person cannot consent for himself or herself, a guardian, conservator, or close relative can give permission to treat a patient. In an emergency, the head of a health care facility can give consent to treatment for a patient if the patient's close relatives cannot be reached. A patient's consent to treatment will be implied if the patient is unable to give consent and an emergency exists or if the patient can give consent but there is not sufficient time to properly inform the patient of all risks and alternatives.

Minors generally need to have the approval of a parent or guardian to undergo a medical or surgical procedure. Exceptions to this rule are emergencies, certain reproductive matters, testing and

Chapter 20: Health Law

treatment for certain sexually-transmitted diseases, and emancipated minors. In Minnesota, a minor is considered emancipated and able to consent to medical treatment if he or she is living apart from guardians and is managing his or her personal finances.

Most doctors are smart enough to know that they should not treat a patient without any permission, so disputes in this area rarely center on whether a doctor had permission. More often, disputes turn on whether the doctor disclosed sufficient information for the patient's consent to be informed or whether the doctor went beyond the consented actions.

To give informed consent in Minnesota a patient must be given information about:

- Diagnosis
- Nature and purpose of proposed treatment
- Risks and consequences of proposed treatment
- Likelihood of success
- Alternative treatments and likely prognosis if not treated

All of these points must be communicated in language the patient is likely to understand.

In addition, a patient must be informed as to whether his or her treatment is experimental. Experimental research cannot be performed on a patient without the patient's consent. The consent or refusal to participate in experimental research must be recorded in the patient's permanent record.

RIGHT TO REFUSE TREATMENT

Minnesota statutes also give patients the right to refuse treatment, medication, or dietary restrictions. Patients who refuse recommended treatments must be informed of the likely medical and psychological results of their refusal, and documentation must be placed in their record.

ANATOMICAL GIFTS

Many people want to donate their bodies to science when they die. Donated human organs can be transplanted into other people, giving the recipient a chance at a longer or more productive life. A wide variety of institutions also need bodies and organs for scientific, medical, and educational purposes. Unfortunately, many potential transplant recipients and many scientific and educational institutions are unable to secure sufficient donations because too few people are willing to donate or because potential donors do not know how to make their wishes known. To solve this problem, the state of Minnesota adopted the Uniform Anatomical Gift Act to govern the donation of bodies and body parts for transplant, medical, and scientific purposes.

Under this law, a person of sound mind, who is at least 18 years of age, may donate all or part of his or her own body. There are several ways for a donor to record his or her wish to make a donation. The donor may make the donation a provision in a will. If part of a will, the provision becomes effective immediately upon death, unlike other provisions of the will which need to go through probate before they become effective. However, a will is not the best place for a donation provision because its terms may not be known immediately upon death. If the terms of a will are not read for several days after the donor dies, it may be too late to make an effective donation. A more common form of recording one's wish to make a donation is through use of a donor card often carried in a wallet. Drivers in Minnesota can also indicate their wish to be a donor on their driver's license. In addition, one can make a written document of donation which must be signed by the donor and witnessed by at least two other people. A donation can also be made orally. Oral donations are effective if witnessed by at least two other people. A dying patient can communicate his or her wish to make a donation to an attending physician who can act as one of the required witnesses. However, the attending physician must not be the physician who removes or transplants the organ. An intent to make a gift can be revoked orally or in writing.

If there is no donation information in a client's file, doctors and hospitals in Minnesota are required, at or near the time of death, to ask the patient or his or her family about making a donation. Doctors and hospital administrators are required to use reasonable discretion and sensitivity and are not required to make a request if they feel that a body or part is not suitable for current needs.

If a dying person is unable to communicate and has not made his or her donation wishes known, a family member or guardian can make a gift of all or part of that person's body. The following categories of people are authorized to make the gift:

- Spouse
- Adult child
- Parent
- Adult sibling
- Guardian

The order of the list is important. A person in one category can authorize or object to a gift only if no one from the previous category has objected or if all persons in the previous category are unavailable. If two persons in one category disagree on whether to make a gift, the gift cannot be made.

The law forbids the sale of body parts. The recipient cannot pay for the anatomical gift but can and does pay for the cost of transportation and transplant. Only the following are allowed to receive bodies or body parts: hospitals, surgeons, physicians, educational institutions involved in medical or dental research, a storage facility for any of these persons or institutions, or any specified individual who needs the organ personally for therapy or transplantation.

PATIENT RIGHTS INSIDE THE HEALTH CARE SYSTEM

Patients are guaranteed several rights inside the health care system. Patients need to be aware of these rights and their health care providers need to understand their responsibilities under the law.

PATIENT BILL OF RIGHTS

Patients and residents of health care facilities must be informed of their rights as patients and be given a written copy of the following rights:

- Know the identity of all physicians treating them
- Receive all appropriate health care
- Know the identity of all outside health care providers
- Receive complete and current information regarding their diagnosis, treatment, alternative treatments, and risks
- Participate in planning their health care
- Right to refuse care (unless not competent)
- Privacy regarding their health care
- Right to be free from isolation and restraints unless other less restrictive measures are ineffective or not feasible

CONFIDENTIALITY

There are two principal forms of protection for patients worried about the confidentiality of their medical records or information they provide to their health care providers. Minnesota Rules of Evidence prohibit the introduction in court of confidential communications between a patient and a health care provider. The public policy behind this rule is the promotion of full and complete communication between doctors and their patients. Minnesota also recognizes a civil legal action for patients whose doctors release patient records without patient authorization. Under Minnesota law, a health care provider must have the patient's consent to release records to a third person. This general law does not prevent a doctor from releasing records to another doctor in an emergency for the purpose of treating the patient. Neither does it prevent the release of records to the Minnesota Department of Health.

Both of these protections will yield if they conflict with other public policies. For example, a doctor who is told by a patient that the patient plans to kill a particular person has a legal obligation to warn that person. Also, doctors have an obligation to report to the police anyone who comes for treatment of a suspicious wound, such as a stab or gunshot wound.

The AIDS epidemic has tested the boundaries of patients' rights to confidentiality. All health care providers who know that a person has HIV have a legal obligation to warn anyone with whom the carrier is intimate. The state of Minnesota requires that a diagnosis of HIV-positive status be reported to the State Department of Health. A person who is HIV-positive has an obligation to warn potential partners and to practice safe sex. Lying, misrepresenting, or failing to reveal one's HIV positive status could leave a person open to charges of fraud, misrepresentation, battery, and civil lawsuits.

EMPLOYEE HEALTH CARE

A business owner or manager is perhaps most concerned with getting legal help to understand the complexities of employee health care and the many state and federal regulations governing it.

Health care costs are rising exponentially and many businesses are finding it impossible to continue to give their employees the same level of benefits they once had. At the same time, individual health policies have become prohibitively expensive. As a result, more than 34 million

Americans remain uninsured and the cost of health care has become one of the major reasons for strikes and other labor disputes. These are two of the primary factors creating increasing political and social pressure for health care reform and which have moved politicians to begin the difficult process of reshaping the way medical care is purchased and delivered in this country.

How these reforms progress and the shape they eventually assume will have a tremendous effect on businesses and their relationships with their employees and insurers. Many employers, whether large or small, will need to seek an attorney's help to keep track of the many changes taking place.

STATE REFORMS

The 1992 Minnesota Legislature began the state's effort to redesign health care when it passed a sweeping bill designed both to finance health care for the uninsured and to control health care costs. The ultimate aim of the plan, known as MinnesotaCare, is to provide health insurance coverage to slightly less than half of the uninsured people in the state. MinnesotaCare extends coverage to people with enough income to make them ineligible for Medicaid but who are still unable to afford to buy their own insurance. Funding for the reforms is to be raised through new taxes on health care providers and health maintenance organizations (HMOs), and higher cigarette taxes.

The 1993 Legislature modified the 1992 health care proposals with an equally sweeping reform bill that encourages physicians, clinics, hospitals and insurers to organize networks of health care providers into associations called integrated service networks, or ISNs. Only nonprofit corporations will be allowed to form ISNs, and they must provide a full array of health services and participate in the General Assistance, Medical Assistance and MinnesotaCare programs. By creating ISNs, legislators hoped to regulate more closely the health care industry and to reduce health care costs.

RESOURCES

Minnesota Health Department, 717 Delaware Street, Box 9441, Minneapolis, MN 55440, (612) 623-5460.

Health Care Law. Practicing Law Institute, Chairmen Bennett J. Yankowitz & Richard A. Feinstein, 1993.

Patient Care Decision Making, A Legal Guide for Providers. Claire C. Obade, Clark, Boardman, Callaghan, 1993.

Health Care Law, A Practical Guide, Michael G. Macdonald, Kathryn C. Meyer, Beth Essio, Matthew Bender, 1993.

Chapter 20: Health Law

HEALTH LAW LEADING ATTORNEYS

Selected by Attorneys for GUIDEBOOK
Law & Leading Attorneys
MINNESOTA

The attorneys profiled in this section were nominated by their peers in a statewide survey conducted in 1993 in which several thousand Minnesota attorneys were asked to name the lawyer to whom they would send a friend or family member in need of legal assistance in the area of *Health Law*.

Because the survey resulted in a list of less than five percent of Minnesota's practicing attorneys, this should not be construed as a complete list. Nevertheless, it is an excellent source of highly qualified and reputable attorneys, who, if unable to assist can in most cases make quality referrals.

The attorneys profiled below were recommended by their peers in a statewide survey.

A list of all attorneys nominated in this category is found at the end of this section. For information on the survey methodology see page ix.

Please note that the shorter, two line attorney listings in this section are of attorneys who practice in this area but whose full biographical profile appears in another section of this book. A bullet "•" preceeding name indicates the attorney was nominated in this particular area of law. For information on the format of these profiles, consult the section "Using the *Business Guidebook*" found on page xiv. Note that the following abbreviations are used throughout these profiles:

App.	- Appellate	ABA	- American Bar Association
Cir.	- Circuit	ATLA	- American Trial Lawyers Association
Ct.	- Court	HCBA	- Hennepin County Bar Association
Dist.	- District	MDLA	- Minnesota Defense Lawyers Association
Hon.	- Honorable	MSBA	- Minnesota State Bar Association
JD	- Law degree (Juris Doctor)	MTLA	- Minnesota Trial Lawyers Association
LLB	- Law degree	NBTA	- National Board of Trial Advocacy
LLM	- Master in Law degree	RCBA	- Ramsey County Bar Association
Sup.	- Supreme		

MICHAEL J. AHERN - Moss & Barnett, A Professional Association - 4800 Norwest Center, 90 South Seventh Street - Minneapolis, MN 55402 - Phone: (612) 347-0274, Fax: (612) 339-6686 - *See complete biographical profile in Environmental Law Chapter.*

•WILLIAM M. BURNS - Hanft, Fride, O'Brien, Harries, Swelbar & Burns, P.A. - 1000 First Bank Place, 130 West Superior Street - Duluth, MN 55802 - Phone: (218) 722-4766, Fax: (218) 720-4920 - *See complete biographical profile in Publicly Held Corporations Law Chapter.*

JOHN E. DIEHL

Larkin, Hoffman, Daly & Lindgren, Ltd.
1500 Norwest Financial Center
7900 Xerxes Avenue South
Bloomington, MN 55431

Phone: (612) 835-3800
Fax: (612) 896-3333

Admitted: 1969 Minnesota; 1969 Iowa; 1969 US Dist. Ct. (MN)
Birthdate: 12/18/41

•JOHN E. DIEHL: Mr. Diehl practices in the areas of strategic legal planning; negotiation, development, and documentation of relationships and transactions; and general legal consultation in the health care field. He represents health care professionals and institutions as well as insurance companies and their trade associations in systems development, business and professional relationships, and legislative and regulatory compliance matters.
Education: JD 1969, University of Iowa; BBA 1964, University of Iowa.
Employment History: 1982-present, Larkin, Hoffman, Daly & Lindgren, Ltd.; General Counsel 1975-83, University of MN Hospital and Clinics; First Chief 1973-75, MN Dept. of Health, HMO Section (developed first HMO development and regulatory system in America); Special Assistant Attorney General 1969-72, MN Attorney General's Office (Counsel to MN Dept. of Commerce, Insurance Division, and MN Regulator of nonprofit health service plans).
Representative Clients: Ridgeview Medical Center; Douglas County Hospital; HealthEast; HealthSpan; Northwest Anesthesia, P.A.; Hudson Physicians; Midwest Health Care Group, Inc.; Minnesota Hospital Assn.
Professional Associations: MSBA (Governing Council; Health Law Section); American Academy of Hospital Attorneys; MN Society of Hospital Attorneys (Founder; Board member 1976-80; President 1978-80); National Assn. of HMO Regulators (Founder; first President 1974).
Community Involvement: American Cancer Society—MN Division (Board member 1981-present; Chair 1988-90); Grotto Foundation (Board member); Model Cities Health Center (Board member); Gillette Children's Hospital (Board member); Chimera Theatre; active with various political offices and activities.
Firm: Larkin, Hoffman, Daly & Lindgren, Ltd., has served the legal and business counseling needs of clients since 1958. The firm's entrepreneurial spirit and understanding of the challenges facing growing businesses has been key to its success. The firm serves small and middle-market growing business and individual clients, as well as providing its special expertise to Fortune 500 companies. The firm's Bloomington location allows it to deliver legal services to clients in the most convenient and cost-effective manner possible.

•**HAROLD A. FREDERICK:** Mr. Frederick practices in the areas of governmental regulation and licensing of emergency ambulance service providers, hospital planning and financing, administrative and governmental law, municipal bonds, zoning and planning law, condemnation law, municipal and school law, and environmental and natural resources law. Mr. Frederick has extensive experience in representing hospitals, business, industry, and special governmental districts in dealing with government agencies. His expertise includes obtaining environmental permits and managing the preparation of environmental impact statements; Minnesota Environmental Rights Act litigation; state and local planning, zoning variances, and land use permits; gravel and mining permits; wastewater, solid waste, paper mill, and forest products regulation; railyard relocation; wetlands regulation; shoreland management; BWCA use and regulation; and highway and other condemnation proceedings.
Education: JD 1961, University of Minnesota; BA 1958 cum laude, University of Minnesota.
Employment History: Currently, Fryberger, Buchanan, Smith & Frederick, P.A.; City Attorney 1966-68, City of Duluth.
Representative Clients: St. Luke's Hospital of Duluth; Lake Superior Paper Industries; Minnesota Forest Industries; Western Lake Superior Sanitary District; Lakehead Constructors, Inc.; City of Duluth; Gold Cross Ambulance Services; University of Minnesota-Duluth.
Professional Associations: 11th District Bar Assn. (President 1980-81); MSBA (Board of Governors 1982-83); ABA; National Assn. of Bond Lawyers.
Community Involvement: Chair 1966-70 Duluth Charter Commission; Duluth Arena Auditorium (Board 1968-71); Duluth School Board (past member and Chair 1971-78) ; Duluth Downtown Development Corporation (President 1982); railyard relocation consultant (1979-86); Greater Downtown Council (President 1987-89); Duluth-Superior Symphony Assn. (Board 1987-92); Minnesota Public Radio (Board 1989-92); Building for Women (advisor 1993-94); Duluth Lighthouse for the Blind (Board 1994).
Firm: Please see firm profile in Appendix C. *See additional listings in Commercial Real Estate Law and Federal, State & Local Government Law Chapters.*

HAROLD A. FREDERICK

Fryberger, Buchanan, Smith & Frederick, P.A.
302 West Superior Street
Suite 700
Duluth, MN 55802

Phone: (218) 722-0861
Fax: (218) 722-9568

Admitted: 1961 Minnesota;
1971 US Dist. Ct. (MN);
1980 US Tax Ct.;
1984 US Claims Ct.
Birthdate: 10/26/36

•**TODD I. FREEMAN** - Larkin, Hoffman, Daly & Lindgren, Ltd. - 1500 Norwest Financial Center, 7900 Xerxes Avenue South - Bloomington, MN 55431 - Phone: (612) 835-3800, Fax: (612) 896-3333 - *See complete biographical profile in Closely Held Business Law Chapter.*

•**H. THEODORE GRINDAL:** Mr. Grindal is the partner in charge of the Health Care and Government Relations practice groups at Schatz Paquin Lockridge Grindal & Holstein. His reputation within Minnesota's health care community is as an attorney who understands the intricacies and needs of providers in today's evolutionary marketplace, especially the potential impact of health reform on our current system. Mr. Grindal also leads a government relations team of ten professionals dedicated to achieving successful results for clients before governmental bodies in the areas of health care, environment, tax, telecommunications, and general business issues. Mr. Grindal is listed in *The Best Lawyers in America*, 1993 edition.
Education: JD 1979, University of Minnesota; BA 1976 cum laude, Augsburg College.
Employment History: Associate/Partner 1983-present, Schatz Paquin Lockridge Grindal & Holstein; Special Assistant Attorney General 1980-1983, Minnesota Attorney General's Office.
Representative Clients: Delta Dental of Minnesota; Mille Lacs Band of Ojibwe; Health Span, Inc.; Procter and Gamble; Minnesota Society of Anesthesiologists; Good Samaritan of Minnesota; West Publishing Company; Minnesota Public Radio; Minnesota Medical Group Managers Assn.; Minnegasco—Service Plus; Hennepin County.
Professional Associations: ABA; MSBA (Governing Board 1991-94, Health Law Section); National Health Lawyers (1985-present); MN Society of Hospital Attorneys (1990-present); MN Government Affairs Council (1984-present).
Community Involvement: Smoke Free Coalition (volunteer lobbyist and legal counsel 1992-present); International Hearing Foundation (Board member 1990-present); MN Center for Arts Education (Board member 1988-92).
Firm: Schatz Paquin Lockridge Grindal & Holstein provides clients with litigation, intellectual property, environmental, health care, and government relations services. The firm is known for its ability to litigate complex commercial matters in federal court in Minnesota and around the United States. The firm currently has 30 lawyers and an office in Washington, D.C. *See additional listing in Federal, State & Local Government Law Chapter.*

H. THEODORE GRINDAL

Schatz Paquin Lockridge Grindal & Holstein
2200 Washington Square
100 Washington Avenue South
Minneapolis, MN 55401

Phone: (612) 339-6900
Fax: (612) 339-0981

Admitted: 1980 Minnesota;
 1980 US Dist. Ct. (MN);
1988 US Ct. App. (8th Cir.);
1988 US Sup. Ct.
Birthdate: 12/16/53

Keith J. Halleland

Popham, Haik, Schnobrich & Kaufman, Ltd.
222 South Ninth Street
Suite 3300
Minneapolis, MN 55402

Phone: (612) 333-4800
Fax: (612) 334-8888

Admitted: 1981 Minnesota
Birthdate: 10/22/55

•**KEITH J. HALLELAND:** Mr. Halleland practices health law exclusively, advising insurers, managed care companies, physicians, hospitals, and employers in the areas of regulatory compliance, health related litigation, and corporate and contracting matters. His special emphasis is on benefit and administrative services contracting, administrative appeals, antitrust litigation, joint ventures, regulatory matters involving state agencies, and Medicare and Medicaid issues. Most recently, he advised a group of over 300 Minnesota physicians on developing an Integrated Service Network (ISN). Mr. Halleland is a frequent lecturer on health law topics and, for the past three years, has chaired the annual "Health Care" seminar sponsored by the Minnesota Institute of Legal Education (MILE). Among Mr. Halleland's articles are, "The MinnesotaCare 2 Percent Tax," *Minnesota Medicine*, March 1994; "The Health Security Act of 1993: A Blueprint for Reform," *Minnesota Medicine*, Nov. 1993, with Aaron Rodriguez; "AIDS, Discrimination and the Americans with Disabilities Act," *Minnesota Physician*, Oct. 1993, with Andrew Seitel; "Physician Liability for Failure to Remove Breast Implants," *Minnesota Medicine*, July 1992; "Litigation Risks for Self-Insured Plans," Minnesota Institute of Legal Education, Feb. 1992; "Physicians With AIDS: The CDC Guidelines and Related Liability Issues," Minnesota Institute of Legal Education, Nov. 1991; "Experimental Cures, Excruciating Choices," *Legal Times*, Nov. 1991; "The Health Care Crisis Enters the Courtroom," 48 *Bench and Bar of Minnesota* No. 4, April 1991.

Education: JD 1981, University of Puget Sound; BA 1978, University of Iowa.
Employment History: Judicial Clerk, Hon. Floyd E. Boline (Judge) and Hon. Miles W. Lord (Chief Judge), US District Court, District of MN.
Professional Associations: MN Institute of Legal Education (past chair, annual health care seminar); ABA (Vice Chair, Health Care Litigation Committee of the Litigation Section); MSBA (Health Law Section Governing Council); National Health Lawyers Assn.
Firm: Popham, Haik, Schnobrich & Kaufman, Ltd., is a firm of more than 230 attorneys with offices in Denver, Miami, Minneapolis, Washington, D.C., and international affiliations in Beijing, China and Leipzig and Stuttgart, Germany. The firm represents clients nationally and internationally on issues relating to corporate and business law, administrative law, and litigation.

Bruce E. Hanson

Doherty, Rumble & Butler
Professional Association
2800 Minnesota World Trade Center
30 East Seventh Street
St. Paul, MN 55101-4999

Phone: (612) 291-9333
Fax: (612) 291-9313

Admitted: 1966 Minnesota;
1966 US Dist. Ct. (MN);
1973 US Ct. App. (8th Cir.);
1983 US Ct. App. (Fed. Cir.);
1970 US Sup. Ct.;
1973 US Tax Ct.
Birthdate: 08/25/42

•**BRUCE E. HANSON:** Throughout his career, Bruce Hanson's practice has been devoted to the representation of HMOs, PPOs, hospitals, and other health care organizations. He offers creative and constructive advice to health care clients across the spectrum of complex and unique legal issues faced by such organizations in developing an integrated delivery system, reimbursement and finance, peer review, antitrust, and all aspects of the regulatory process affecting health care. He also counsels them with respect to operational and contract issues similar to those faced by other types of organizations. Mr. Hanson is listed in *The Best Lawyers in America*, *Who's Who in American Law*, *Who's Who in the Midwest*, and *Who's Who in the World*.

Employment History: 1966-present, Doherty, Rumble & Butler, P.A.
Professional Associations: American Academy of Hospital Attorneys; MN Society of Hospital Attorneys (past Director; past President); MSBA (past Chair, Health Law Section).
Firm: Providing health care to the nation is increasingly difficult and costly. Equally demanding is the challenge of providing skillful and creative legal solutions to health care organizations. Doherty, Rumble & Butler represents hospitals, ambulatory surgery centers, peer review organizations, health maintenance organizations, and medical device manufacturers. The firm's lawyers provide advice on reimbursement, self-insured plans, joint ventures, antitrust, operational and contract issues, and all aspects of health care and medical technology regulation. Doherty, Rumble & Butler also helps structure new health care companies and reconfigure existing organizations to capitalize on service payment reforms. They draw on in-depth knowledge of managed care principles to satisfy employer requirements without compromising quality of care.

•**JOHN S. HIBBS:** Mr. Hibbs practices in the area of general business, regulatory, legislative, corporate, and tax matters for a broad array of entities involved in the health care field, including medical specialty societies and certifying boards, allied health professional certifying boards, hospitals, nursing homes, medical clinics, medical education and research foundations, retirement homes, substance abuse centers, a professional liability insurance company manager, and a major life insurance company. He is the author of a textbook on Minnesota nonprofit corporations and more than 100 professional papers. He has been named in every edition of *The Best Lawyers in America*. Mr. Hibbs is a partner in the Dorsey & Whitney's Tax/Health Department.
Education: JD 1960 cum laude, University of Minnesota (Board of Editors 1958-60, Recent Case Editor 1959-60, *Minnesota Law Review*); BBA 1956, University of Minnesota.
Employment History: Partner 1967-present, Associate 1960-66, Dorsey & Whitney.
Representative Clients: American Academy of Ophthalmology; Park Nicollet Medical Center; American Board of Ophthalmology; Assn. of University Professors of Ophthalmology; American Registry of Radiologic Technologists.
Professional Associations: American College of Tax Counsel (Fellow); Legislative Advisory Task Force on drafting new MN Chapter 302A Business Corporation Law (Chair 1979-82); MSBA (Section on Corporate, Banking, and Business Law (Chair 1978-79); Nonprofit Corporations Committee Section of Corporate, Banking, and Business Law (Chair 1970-83)); ABA (Committee on Corporate Laws in the development of the revised Model Business Corporation Act (Special Consultant)); Legal Section of American Society of Assn. Executives (Charter member); American Academy of Hospital Attorneys; MN Society of Hospital Attorneys; National Health Lawyers Assn.; American Society of Medical Assn. Counsel.
Firm: Dorsey & Whitney is the largest law firm in Minnesota and one of the largest firms in the United States with over 350 lawyers in 12 offices. The depth and breadth of the experience of its lawyers enables it to provide a broad range of services to meet the diverse legal needs of its client base, which includes Fortune 500 companies, public agencies, banks and other financial institutions, nonprofit organizations, individual investors, family owned businesses, and high-tech and low-tech, growth oriented companies. *See additional listings in Business Tax Law and Nonprofit Corporations Law Chapters.*

JOHN S. HIBBS

Dorsey & Whitney
Pillsbury Center South
220 South Sixth Street
Minneapolis, MN 55402-1498

Phone: (612) 340-2661
Fax: (612) 340-8827

Admitted: 1960 Minnesota;
1960 US Dist. Ct. (MN);
1963 US Ct. App. (8th Cir.);
1965 US Tax Ct.;
1970 US Sup. Ct.
Birthdate: 09/19/34

•**KEVIN J. HUGHES:** Mr. Hughes is an experienced lawyer in health care issues, including medical staff, data release, corporate organization, accreditation, Medicare, tax, contracting, and state antitrust. He also practices in the areas of employment, financial, commercial, corporate, and general business law. His litigation experience, before state and federal courts, is in constitutional and civil rights, contracts, employment, fraud, and various business agreements, including formation, computers, product distribution, bond liability, commercial transactions, and shareholder rights.
Education: JD 1962, University of Minnesota; BA 1958, St. John's University.
Employment History: Currently, Hughes, Mathews & Didier, P.A.; Law Clerk 1962-63, Hon. Walter F. Rogosheske, MN Supreme Court Justice; Active Duty 1959-60, US Army.
Representative Clients: St. Cloud Hospital; St. John's University; College of St. Benedict; First American National Bank (St. Cloud); First National Bank (Cold Spring); First National Bank (Milaca); Minnesota Business Finance, Inc.; Stearns County National Bank; Citizens Savings Bank; Anderson Trucking Service; Crosier Fathers and Brothers; Tri-County Hospital (Wadena); Memorial Community Nursing Home (Osakis).
Professional Associations: MSBA (Health Law Section); Stearns-Benton Bar Assn.; Seventh District Bar Assn. (past President); American Academy of Hospital Attorneys; National Assn. of Health Lawyers; MN Society of Hospital Attorneys; National Assn. of College & University Attorneys.
Community Involvement: St. Cloud Area United Way (past Board member); Chamber of Commerce; YMCA; St. John's University (past Board member); Crosier Seminary Prep, Onamia (past Board member); Governor's Commission on Promoting MN Health Care Resources (past member); Central MN Community Foundation (Board member).
Firm: The firm of Hughes, Mathews & Didier, P.A. has wide experience in planning, negotiating, and litigating in business, corporate, commercial, financing, employment, real estate, partnership, tax exempt and taxable bond financing, nonprofit institution, health, and education areas of law. The firm has appeared in trial and appellate court at the state and federal levels. Specific members are admitted to the bar in the states of Wisconsin and Iowa as well as Minnesota. *See additional listings in Commercial Litigation and Employment Law Chapters.*

KEVIN J. HUGHES

Hughes, Mathews & Didier, P.A.
110 Sixth Avenue South
Suite 200
P.O. Box 548
St. Cloud, MN 56302-0548

Phone: (612) 251-4399
Fax: (612) 251-5781

Admitted: 1962 Minnesota
Birthdate: 07/27/36

Chapter 20: Health Law

DOUGLAS A. KELLEY - Douglas A. Kelley, P.A. - 701 Fourth Avenue South, Suite 500 - Minneapolis, MN 55415 - Phone: (612) 337-9594, Fax: (612) 371-0574 - *See complete biographical profile in Criminal Law Chapter.*

GREER E. LOCKHART - Bassford, Lockhart, Truesdell & Briggs, P.A. - 3550 Multifoods Tower, 33 South Sixth Street - Minneapolis, MN 55402-3787 - Phone: (612) 333-3000, Fax: (612) 333-8829 - *See complete biographical profile in Professional Malpractice Defense Law Chapter.*

RUTH A. MICKELSEN

Allina Health System
5601 Smetana Drive
Minnetonka, MN 55343

Phone: (612) 936-1609
Fax: (612) 936-6858

Admitted: 1981 Minnesota
Birthdate: 10/16/54

•**RUTH A. MICKELSEN:** Ms. Mickelsen is Associate General Counsel for Allina Health System, an integrated delivery system which includes a 600,000 member health maintenance organization, 17 hospitals, 45 medical groups, and 7,000 physicians and allied health care providers. In addition, she is an adjunct professor of health law at William Mitchell College of Law and is a writer and lecturer on health law. She is coauthor of *Law and Mental Health Professionals*, American Psychological Association (1993) and coauthor of a monthly column entitled "Medicine and Law," *The Minnesota Physician* (1987-92). She lectures for the Minnesota Institute of Legal Education and the National Health Lawyers Association as well as speaks before other professional associations.
Education: JD 1981 cum laude, William Mitchell (staff, *William Mitchell Law Review*); MPH 1986, Harvard University (1986 Samdperil Health Law Essay Award); BA 1976 cum laude, University of Minnesota (Phi Kappa Phi).
Employment History: Associate General Counsel 1992-present, Allina Health System; Partner 1989-92, Popham, Haik, Schnobrich & Kaufmann; Director of Legal and Policy Affairs 1988-89, MN Department of Health; Associate 1986-88, Rider, Bennett, Egan & Arundel; Special Assistant Attorney General 1981-85, MN Attorney General's Office.
Professional Associations: ABA; MSBA (Chair 1992-93, Health Law Section); American Public Health Assn.; American Society of Law and Medicine; National Health Lawyers Assn.
Community Involvement: Legal Advice Clinics (volunteer attorney). *See additional listing in Nonprofit Corporations Law Chapter.*

STEVEN J. SEILER

Johnson, Killen, Thibodeau & Seiler, P.A.
811 Norwest Center
230 West Superior Street
Duluth, MN 55802

Phone: (218) 722-6331
Fax: (218) 722-3031

Admitted: 1969 Minnesota
Birthdate: 01/23/44

•**STEVEN J. SEILER:** Mr. Seiler practices general business law, representing major nonprofit health care systems in financial transactions, fraud and abuse, antitrust, contracts, and general corporate matters. He also handles estate planning and probate matters.
Education: JD 1969 Order of the Coif, Drake University (Author, "Case Notes," 17 *Drake Law Review* 1967 & 1968; Phi Alpha Delta); BA 1966, University of Minnesota.
Representative Clients: St. Mary's Medical Center; St. Mary's Regional Health Center; Benedictine Health System; Benedictine Sisters Benevolent Assn.; Bowman Properties; Mesabi Regional Medical Center.
Professional Associations: American College of Trust and Estate Counsel; Arrowhead Estate Planning Counsel.
Community Involvement: Duluth-Superior Area Community Foundation.
Firm: Founded in 1888, Johnson, Killen, Thibodeau & Seiler, P.A., is the oldest firm in northern Minnesota. Today the firm's 18 lawyers provide a wide range of services for consumers, businesses, and companies in commercial, toxic tort, environmental, and insurance litigation; commercial and residential real estate; probate, estate planning, and trusts; employment law; closely held business law; and Workers' Compensation. *See additional listings in Publicly Held Corporations Law and Probate, Estate Planning & Trusts Law Chapters.*

•**PAUL M. TORGERSON:** Mr. Torgerson counsels public, private, nonprofit, and business entities involved in the health care field on corporate issues (with emphasis on nonprofit corporations), regulatory, antitrust, licensing, employment, legislative, general business and health law matters, Medicare/Medicaid laws and regulation, including fraud and abuse issues and reimbursement, and taxation and tax-exemption matters. Mr. Torgerson has substantial experience in transactional work involving hospital and clinic acquisitions and mergers and formation of integrated health care delivery systems. Mr. Torgerson served on the ad hoc committee which in 1989 completely revised the Minnesota nonprofit corporation law and on the state Department of Health advisory committee regarding the antitrust provisions of the MinnesotaCare legislation. He has lectured on health law, tax, and nonprofit corporation topics and has taught at the University of Minnesota and at William Mitchell College of Law. He is listed under Health Law in *The Best Lawyers in America*. Mr. Torgerson has been a partner in the Tax/Health Department of Dorsey & Whitney since 1985 and currently chairs that department.

Education: JD 1979 cum laude, University of Minnesota; BA 1973 magna cum laude, Luther College.
Employment History: Partner 1985-present, Associate 1979-84, Dorsey & Whitney; CPA 1973-76, Peat, Marwick, Mitchell & Co.
Representative Clients: Multihospital systems, including Fairview Hospital and Healthcare Services and the Mayo Foundation; large, small, urban, and rural hospitals; large and small medical clinics; home health organizations; medical education and research organizations; managed care organizations; nursing and retirement homes; joint ventures, individual professionals.
Professional Associations: American Academy of Hospital Attorneys; MN Society of Hospital Attorneys; MSBA (Health Law Section); MN Society of Certified Public Accountants.
Community Involvement: King of Kings Lutheran Church (past President & Board member); University of St. Thomas Health Care Advisory Council.
Firm: Dorsey & Whitney is the largest law firm in Minnesota and one of the largest firms in the United States with over 350 lawyers in 12 offices. The depth and breadth of the experience of its lawyers enables it to provide a broad range of services to meet the diverse legal needs of its client base, which includes Fortune 500 companies, public agencies, banks and other financial institutions, nonprofit organizations, individual investors, family owned businesses, and high-tech and low-tech, growth oriented companies. *See additional listings in Business Tax Law and Nonprofit Corporations Law Chapters.*

PAUL M. TORGERSON

Dorsey & Whitney
Pillsbury Center South
220 South Sixth Street
Minneapolis, MN 55402-1498

Phone: (612) 340-8700
Fax: (612) 340-8827

Admitted: 1979 Minnesota; 1980 US Dist. Ct. (MN); 1981 US Tax Ct.
Birthdate: 08/28/51

NEIL A. WEIKART - Fredrikson & Byron, P.A. - 1100 International Centre, 900 Second Avenue South - Minneapolis, MN 55402 - Phone: (612) 347-7025, Fax: (612) 347-7077 - *See complete biographical profile in Publicly Held Corporations Law Chapter.*

Chapter 20: Health Law

Complete listing of all attorneys nominated in Health Law

William M. Burns, Hanft, Fride, O'Brien, Harries, Swelbar & Burns, P.A., Duluth; **Jay D. Christiansen,** Faegre & Benson, Minneapolis; **John E. Diehl,** Larkin, Hoffman, Daly & Lindgren, Ltd., Bloomington; **Harold A. Frederick,** Fryberger, Buchanan, Smith & Frederick, P.A., Duluth; **Todd I. Freeman,** Larkin, Hoffman, Daly & Lindgren, Ltd., Bloomington; **Konrad J. Friedemann,** Fredrikson & Byron, P.A., Minneapolis; **H. Theodore Grindal,** Schatz Paquin Lockridge Grindal & Holstein, Minneapolis; **Keith J. Halleland,** Popham, Haik, Schnobrich & Kaufman, Ltd., Minneapolis; **Jan D. Halverson,** Felhaber, Larson, Fenlon & Vogt, P.A., Minneapolis; **Bruce E. Hanson,** Doherty, Rumble & Butler Professional Association, St. Paul; **John S. Hibbs,** Dorsey & Whitney, Minneapolis; **Benjamin R. Hippe,** Mayo Clinic Legal Department, Rochester; **Kevin J. Hughes,** Hughes, Mathews & Didier, P.A., St. Cloud; **Daniel J. McInerney Jr.,** Leonard, Street and Deinard Professional Association, Minneapolis; **Kathleen A. Meyerle,** Mayo Clinic Legal Department, Rochester; **Ruth A. Mickelsen,** Allina Health System, Minnetonka; **Mark G. Mishek,** Health One Corporation, Minneapolis; **Robert M. Moore Jr.,** Mayo Clinic Legal Department, Rochester; **Warren E. Mack,** Fredrikson & Byron, P.A., Minneapolis; **Kevin H. Roche,** United Healthcare Corporation, Minnetonka; **Stuart E. Schmitz,** Stuart E. Schmitz & Associates, St. Paul; **Steven J. Seiler,** Johnson, Killen, Thibodeau & Seiler, P.A., Duluth; **James H. Stewart,** Fryberger, Buchanan, Smith & Frederick, P.A., Duluth; **John F. Stone,** Oppenheimer, Wolff & Donnelly, Minneapolis; **Margo S. Struthers,** Oppenheimer, Wolff & Donnelly, Minneapolis; **Paul M. Torgerson,** Dorsey & Whitney, Minneapolis.

CHAPTER 21

IMMIGRATION LAW

For centuries, people from around the world have been coming to America. Many come to work, to escape oppression, start a new life, do business, visit friends, or sightsee. Over the years, the United States has seen tremendous diversity in the countries immigrants come from and their reasons for coming to this country. In response to the incredible demand for permission to enter this country, the federal government has established a complex set of laws that determine who may enter this country and for what reasons. This chapter discusses legal immigration and travel to the United States and the responsibilities of employers under these laws.

U.S. CITIZENSHIP

U.S. citizens have a right to travel to and live in the United States and enjoy the fullest protection of U.S. laws. Those who are not U.S. citizens, aliens, usually require a visa to enter the U.S. and may not enjoy the protection of all U.S. laws.

A person can become a U.S. citizen either through birth or through a process known as naturalization. A person can be a U.S. citizen from birth either by being born here or by being born in a foreign country to a U.S. citizen. Anyone born in the U.S. is an American citizen, regardless of the parents' citizenship. Even if both parents are living in this country illegally at the time of their child's birth, the child is a U.S. citizen if born on U.S. soil. The only exception is that children born to foreign diplomats in the U.S. do not get automatic citizenship. A second way to be born a U.S. citizen is to be born to a parent who is a U.S. citizen at the time of a child's birth on foreign soil. Anyone not born a citizen must be naturalized to become a citizen. Occasionally, a group of people is naturalized by treaty or by act of Congress. Usually, a person goes through the process individually.

ALIENS, IMMIGRANTS, NONIMMIGRANTS, AND RESIDENTS

An alien is a citizen of any country other than the U.S. A person who comes to the U.S. to stay permanently is called an immigrant. Someone who intends to return to his or her country of origin is called a nonimmigrant, even if he or she intends to stay in the U.S. for a substantial period of time.

For example, a student might stay in the U.S. many years to complete an education and still be considered a nonimmigrant. The distinction between immigrant and nonimmigrant is crucial. Permission to enter as a nonimmigrant is often much easier to get than permission to enter as an immigrant, so some people are tempted to claim they intend to return to their home country in order to get into the U.S. The Immigration and Naturalization Service (INS) is aware of this temptation and will often deny a nonimmigrant visa application to anyone it suspects wants to remain permanently. Also, being granted a nonimmigrant visa can sometimes make it more difficult to get an immigrant visa later. A permanent resident is an alien who has been given permission to live permanently in the U.S.

In a dispute with the INS over an applicant's true intent, the applicant always bears the burden of proving temporary intent. For some people, this burden is nearly impossible to overcome. For example, the spouse of a permanent resident normally must wait over two years for available immigrant visas. If he or she claims to want to visit only temporarily, he or she must overcome the presumption that a married person would naturally want to remain permanently with his or her spouse.

THE VISA SYSTEM

A visa is a stamp in a person's passport that gives him or her conditional approval to enter the United States. Most matters involving visas are handled by the INS. For most aliens, the process of traveling to the U.S. is begun by applying for a visa from a U.S. consulate or embassy in the alien's home country.

Citizens of some countries, primarily European countries and Japan, may enter the U.S. for up to 90 days without a visa. To be eligible, citizens of these countries must show the INS that they have a return ticket home and that they intend to engage in a type of business or tourist activity that would be allowed under a B visa, described below. Canadian citizens generally do not need visas to enter the U.S. temporarily. In some instances, they must obtain INS approval in advance if they are coming here to work in the U.S.

Congress establishes a complex set of quotas that limit the number that can be granted for most types of visas. Whether an applicant receives a visa turns on the type of visa requested, the applicant's reason for traveling to the U.S., and the applicant's country of origin. Probably the most important element to successfully getting a visa is knowing for which visa category to apply. For certain categories of visas and certain countries of origin, an applicant can wait many years before he or she will even be considered for a visa. Sometimes the wait would be much shorter if the applicant applied for a different type of visa. Unfortunately, once an applicant applies for one type of visa, it can be difficult to change one's application to another class of visa. For this reason, it is wise to consult an immigration attorney before applying for any kind of visa.

NONIMMIGRANT VISAS

There are 18 different kinds of nonimmigrant visas, identified by the letters A–R, available for persons who do not intend to remain in the U.S. permanently. All nonimmigrant visas are based on what the applicant intends to do in this country. It is important that employers be aware of the variety of visas that exist.

A Visas: A visas are for diplomats and their families.

B Visas: B-1 visas are for aliens coming to this country to do business but not for employment or labor for hire and are commonly used by aliens coming to do business research, engage in litigation, or negotiate contracts. B-2 visas, the most common nonimmigrant visas, allow aliens to enter the country temporarily to engage in tourism, visit with friends or relatives, or to receive medical treatment.

C Visas: C visas allow persons to enter the U.S. only for immediate and continuous transit through the country to a third country.

D Visas: D visas are for crew members of foreign vessels.

E Visas: E visas are for traders and investors covered by commercial treaties between the U.S. and foreign countries. Spouses and children of an E visa holder generally also receive E visas.

F Visas: F visas are for students in full-time academic programs. These visas are not only for university-level students. They are for students from the elementary school level up to the post-graduate level. Spouses and children of F visa holders are usually also given F visas. Unlike most nonimmigrant visa holders, students with F visas may be employed for fewer than 20 hours a week, mainly at certain on-campus jobs typically done by students.

G Visas: G visas are for representatives of foreign countries to international organizations.

H Visas: H visas are for workers needed by U.S. employers to fill immediate and temporary openings. An H-1B visa is commonly held by aliens working in professional-level jobs.

I Visas: I visas are for media representatives and their families.

J Visas: J visas are designed to bring foreigners to the U.S. to receive training in exchange programs designated by the U.S. Information Agency.

K Visas: K visas allow an alien engaged to a U.S. citizen, as well as any minor children of the alien, to enter the U.S. to marry the citizen.

L Visas: L visas are for intracompany employee transfers (e.g., for employees of multinational corporations).

M Visas: M visas are for students in vocational or nonacademic study programs.

N Visas: N visas are for relatives of certain international organization employees here on G visas.

O Visas: O visas are for outstanding artists, entertainers, athletes, scientists, and certain business professionals. O-1 visas are for aliens with extraordinary ability in their field. The standards for getting an O-1 visa are very high and must be shown through extensive documentation of international acclaim. O-2 visas are for person who are needed to accompany and assist an O-1 alien.

P Visas: P visas are for performing artists, entertainers and athletes. P visas are somewhat similar to O visas, but they are usually easier to get and intended more for group entertainers or athletes who come here for a specific performance or tour.

Q Visas: Q visas are for participants in international cultural exchanges.

R Visas: R visas are for religious workers and their families.

IMMIGRANT VISAS

An applicant who intends to stay in this country permanently is generally admitted either on the basis of employment or family connections. The main exception is for political asylum seekers.

Employment-Based Immigration

An alien can receive permission to immigrate to this country on the basis of his or her employment. There are five categories of employment, known as preferences, through which an alien can be permitted to immigrate.

First Preference: Individuals of extraordinary ability (artists, scientists, business people, teachers or athletes); outstanding professors or researchers; and multinational executives. The standards for this category are very high.

Second Preference: Professionals with advanced degrees and aliens with exceptional abilities in science, art, or business. (Note: The terminology is confusing, but "exceptional ability" is a different standard from "extraordinary ability.")

Third Preference: Skilled workers, professionals, and other workers for which there is a shortage of workers in the U.S.

Fourth Preference: Certain special workers, usually religious workers, juvenile court dependents, or employees of U.S. government or international organizations, qualify for the fourth preference.

Fifth Preference: Employment creation aliens. These aliens can gain admission to the U.S. by virtue of their ability to create new jobs here through substantial investment of between $500,000 and $1,000,000.

Family-Based Immigration

An alien can get a visa as an immediate relative of a U.S. citizen if he or she is a child, spouse, or parent of the citizen. In addition, there are five different family-based immigrant visa categories:

1: Unmarried children of U.S. citizens

2a: The spouses and minor children of lawful permanent residents

2b: Adult unmarried children of lawful permanent residents

3: Married children of U.S. citizens

4: Siblings of adult U.S. citizens

These five categories are grouped into preferences, and each preference is allotted a total number of visas. Generally speaking, the lower an applicant's preference number, the shorter the wait to get a visa. For example, Preference One applicants face significantly shorter waits for visas than do Preference Four applicants.

Special Classes of Immigrants
Some groups of immigrants receive special treatment and fall outside the preference system described above.

Diversity Immigrants
In 1986 Congress established a pilot lottery program for visa applicants from countries deemed under-represented in the applicant pool. The pilot program becomes permanent in 1995. Under this program, applicants from under-represented countries can enter a random lottery for a limited number of visas reserved specifically for those countries.

Refugees and Asylees
A person is a refugee if he or she is outside the U.S., is fleeing or has fled his or her country, and has a well-founded fear that if returned to his home country, he or she will be persecuted because of race, religion, nationality, membership in a particular social group, or political opinion. An asylee is an alien already in the U.S. who, like a refugee, has a well-founded fear of persecution if returned to his or her home country. The President and Congress decide each year the total number of refugees and asylees to accept into the country. Congress occasionally grants immigrant visas allotted for individuals from specific countries according to political factors. Recent programs have included Tibet, Hong Kong, and China.

ENTRY AND EXCLUSION

A visa only gives conditional approval to enter the country. Once an alien arrives in the U.S. with a visa, he or she must apply for entry from INS officials at the point of entry. For most aliens, this is a mere formality, but INS can exclude persons with valid visas for a variety of reasons including communicable diseases, physical or mental disorders that pose a threat to others, drug addiction, or criminal history. Involvement in espionage or terrorist activity against the U.S. government or its people is grounds for exclusion. The Secretary of State also has broad discretion to bar entry for anyone whose presence would adversely affect the foreign policy of the U.S. Waivers are sometimes available for aliens who would otherwise be denied entry for certain reasons. For example, the child of a U.S. citizen may be granted a waiver to enter to receive treatment for drug addiction.

GETTING A GREEN CARD AND BECOMING A NATURALIZED CITIZEN

Becoming a permanent resident is the first step that an alien must take to become a naturalized American citizen. Persons with permission to live permanently in the U.S. are issued "green cards" that allow them to work with few restrictions. A permanent resident can apply to become a naturalized American citizen after five years (three years if married to a U.S. citizen).

The INS is diligent in investigating marriages between U.S. citizens and aliens to ensure that aliens do not become permanent residents through sham marriages. Immigration law specifies that an alien seeking permanent residence based on a marriage to a U.S. citizen of less than two years is first granted conditional permanent resident status. This classification exists for two years, and after two years the husband and wife must apply to the INS to remove this conditional status.

DEPORTATION

Deportation is the expulsion of an alien who either entered illegally or entered legally but has done something to become deportable. With few exceptions, any violation of the conditions of a visa, no matter how minor, is grounds for deportation to a person's country of origin. Conviction for anything but the most minor crime is also grounds for deportation. Deportation can severely delay an alien whose long-term goal is to live permanently in this country. After being deported, aliens are forbidden to re-enter the country for five years. Aliens deported for aggravated felonies, such as drug smuggling, are barred from re-entry for 20 years or may even be permanently barred. The delay in returning to the U.S. may even be greater for aliens from countries with long waiting lists, as returning home under a deportation order may result in the U.S. embassy's refusing to entrust the individual with any more temporary visas.

There are a number of remedies to deportation, especially if the deportable person has lived in the U.S. for a long time, building a life here that includes proof of good moral character. Even if the deportable individual has not been here long, there may be certain waivers or defenses to deportation. Among the most common is asking the court for "voluntary departure," which allows the individual to depart the U.S. on his or her own without being deported. In any case, anyone facing deportation is strongly urged to seek the advice of counsel well in advance of a deportation hearing.

BUSINESS CONCERNS WITH IMMIGRATION LAW

Businesses often recruit foreign citizens with specialized skills to come to the United States and work for their companies. As discussed earlier in the description of visa categories, whether an employee can get a work visa depends, to a great extent, on his or her skills. Some immigration lawyers specialize in helping businesses meet the legal requirements for prospective employees to work in the United States.

All employers must verify that all their employees are legally authorized to work in the United States, according to federal immigration laws. This verification is accomplished by having all employees complete an immigration document, Form I-9, at the time employees are hired. If employers fail to verify that employees are eligible to work in the United States, they may be subject to warnings, penalties, fines, and even criminal prosecution. However, employers must also be careful that their procedure for verifying legal authorization does not discriminate on the basis of race, national origin, or citizenship status. Employers cannot hold a certain group of employees to tighter scrutiny than other employees, and they should not take national origin or citizenship status into account when making hiring decisions. There are a number of traps into which an employer might fall if procedures are not carefully established and implemented. For example, some employers have been fined for applying stricter application procedures to job applicants who did not speak English, were members of minority groups, or who had not lived in the United States for long. An experienced immigration attorney can advise on how to establish procedures that verify the legal status of all employees without illegally discriminating.

RESOURCES

Amnesty International, 705 G Street SE, Washington, D.C. 20003. Minnesota chapter: 1929 South 5th Street, Minneapolis, MN 55454, (612) 332-4574.

Immigration and Naturalization Service St. Paul District Office, 2901 Metro Drive, Bloomington, MN 55425, (612) 854-7754. This office has recorded messages that answer the most common questions concerning immigration laws.

IMMIGRATION LAW LEADING ATTORNEYS

The attorneys profiled in this section were nominated by their peers in a statewide survey conducted in 1993 in which several thousand Minnesota attorneys were asked to name the lawyer to whom they would send a friend or family member in need of legal assistance in the area of *Immigration Law*.

Because the survey resulted in a list of less than five percent of Minnesota's practicing attorneys, this should not be construed as a complete list. Nevertheless, it is an excellent source of highly qualified and reputable attorneys, who, if unable to assist can in most cases make quality referrals.

A list of all attorneys nominated in this category is found at the end of this section. For information on the survey methodology see page ix.

Please note that the shorter, two line attorney listings in this section are of attorneys who practice in this area but whose full biographical profile appears in another section of this book. A bullet "•" preceeding name indicates the attorney was nominated in this particular area of law. For information on the format of these profiles, consult the section "Using the *Business Guidebook*" found on page xiv. Note that the following abbreviations are used throughout these profiles:

The attorneys profiled below were recommended by their peers in a statewide survey.

App. - Appellate	ABA - American Bar Association
Cir. - Circuit	ATLA - American Trial Lawyers Association
Ct. - Court	HCBA - Hennepin County Bar Association
Dist. - District	MDLA - Minnesota Defense Lawyers Association
Hon. - Honorable	MSBA - Minnesota State Bar Association
JD - Law degree (Juris Doctor)	MTLA - Minnesota Trial Lawyers Association
LLB - Law degree	NBTA - National Board of Trial Advocacy
LLM - Master in Law degree	RCBA - Ramsey County Bar Association
Sup. - Supreme	

Chapter 21: Immigration Law

RICHARD L. BREITMAN

The Breitman Immigration Law Firm
701 Fourth Avenue, Suite 1700
Minneapolis, MN 55415-1818

and at INS Building:

2901 Metro Dr., Suite 208
Bloomington, MN 55425

Phone: (612) 822-4724
Fax: (612) 339-8375
Fax: (612) 332-3751

Admitted: 1981 Minnesota;
1982 US Dist. Ct. (MN);
1982 US Ct. App. (8th Cir.);
1986 US Dist. Ct. (E. Dist. & W. Dist. WI)
Birthdate: 07/04/47

•**RICHARD L. BREITMAN:** Practicing exclusively in all areas of immigration law since 1984, with expertise in employment visas for nonimmigrants and immigrants, family visas, medical visa matters, and deportation proceedings and appeals. He frequently provides advice to foreign students on employment matters after graduation and to employers hiring foreign graduates. Mr. Breitman has taught immigration classes at William Mitchell and the University of Minnesota law schools and has spoken at national and local immigration law seminars. He conducts monthly national teleconferences on immigration law for attorneys throughout the US and Canada. He also organized a continuing pro bono panel of attorneys in 1991 to assist people at deportation hearings in Minnesota and organized pro bono assistance for individuals from the People's Republic of China, 1989-94.
Education: JD 1981 cum laude, William Mitchell; MBA 1982 with honors, University of Minnesota; BA 1969 magna cum laude, University of Minnesota.
Employment History: Attorney 1986-present, Breitman Immigration Law Firm; Attorney 1984-86, Jerome B. Ingber & Associates; Attorney 1982-84, Maslon, Edelman, Borman & Brand; Law Clerk 1981-82 term to the Hon. Rosalie E. Wahl, MN Supreme Court Justice; Law Clerk 1981, MN Attorney General.
Representative Clients: Fortune 500 companies, smaller corporations, and individuals, including Pfizer, Inc.; University of Minnesota; University of Wisconsin; US Army High Performance Computer Research Center; Theatre de la Jeune Lune; Fingerhut; Advance Machine Corp.; Tescom Corp.
Professional Associations: American Immigration Lawyers Assn. (1985-present; past Board member and past Chair, MN/Dakotas Chapter); MN Advocates for Human Rights (Supervising Attorney on asylum cases).
Community: People, Inc. (Board member 1988-present); MN International Institute (Information Attorney 1986-present).
Firm: The Breitman Immigration Law Firm practices immigration law exclusively with offices in downtown Minneapolis and at the Immigration Service's Building in Bloomington. Mr. Bretiman represents individuals and corporations throughout the US and is experienced in administrative matters before the Immigration Service, immigration litigation in deportation proceedings, and immigration matters before US Federal District Courts and Federal Courts of Appeal. The firm sponsors free informational messages which you can hear by calling (612) 362-3611 and then pressing ("1") for Student Practical Training; ("2") for H-1B Temporary Workers Status; ("3") for Deportation & Custody; ("4") for Immigrant Visas Through Work; ("5") for Immigrant Visas Through Family; and ("6") for Labor Certification. *See additional listings in Employment Law and International Business Law Chapters.*

LAURA J. DANIELSON

Patterson & Keough, P.A.
1200 Rand Tower
527 Marquette Avenue South
Minneapolis, MN 55402

Phone: (612) 349-5740
Fax: (612) 349-9266

Admitted: 1989 Minnesota;
1994 US Dist. Ct. (MN)
Birthdate: 09/08/55

•**LAURA J. DANIELSON:** Ms. Danielson represents clients in immigration and arts and entertainment matters, with special emphasis on arts and business related immigration. She represents foreign artists, entertainers, athletes, engineers, scientists, medical personnel, and other professionals in nonimmigrant and immigrant visa matters. Ms. Danielson also handles family immigration, asylum, and copyright, license, and contract cases for individual artists and arts organizations. She teaches law at William Mitchell and Hamline law schools; lectures for the Minnesota Continuing Legal Education program, Resources and Counseling for the Arts, University of Minnesota immigration classes, University of St. Thomas, and student groups at area law schools; is a former legal writing instructor at William Mitchell and University of Minnesota law schools; and is a consulting editor for the book, *The Practical Musician.*
Education: JD 1989 cum laude, University of Minnesota; BA 1977, Carleton College.
Employment History: Attorney 1994-present, Patterson & Keough, P.A.; Attorney 1991-1994, Danielson & Begley, P.A.; Attorney 1989-91, John M. Roth & Associates.
Representative Clients: Numerous businesses, arts organizations, individuals.
Professional Associations: Midwest Center for Arts, Entertainment and the Law (Vice Chair 1991-present); MSBA (Treasurer, Vice Chair 1991-93, Arts and Entertainment Section); American Immigration Lawyers Assn.
Community Involvement: MN Advocates for Human Rights (volunteer attorney 1989-present); Southern Theatre (Board member 1991-present).
Firm: Patterson & Keough, P.A. provides services in intellectual property, representing clients in the areas of copyrights, trademarks, patents, trade secrets, related litigation, licensing, and immigration. The firm services a broad spectrum of clients ranging from individual creative people to Fortune 500 companies. Since its inception in 1991, Patterson & Keough's practice has focused on meeting the needs of a full range of intellectual property clients—from inventors and engineers to artists and entertainers. *See additional listings in Arts, Entertainment, Advertising & Media Law and Intellectual Property Law Chapters.*

•**PATRICIA G. MATTOS:** Ms. Mattos handles all areas of immigration and nationality law, including immigrant visas, labor certifications, family-based immigration, asylum, and investment. She has worked extensively with corporate clients and individuals. Her work with corporations includes bringing managers and executives, as well as investors, into the United States. She works with individuals seeking employment-creation immigrant visas and with corporations seeking labor certification for employees and with subsequent applications for permanent resident status. In addition ,Ms. Mattos works closely with parents, spouses, and children to assist them in immigrating and helping their relatives to immigrate. Her expertise includes H & L visas, E visas, employment creation visas, and R visas as well as all areas of naturalization law, including claims to citizenship through parents. Ms. Mattos is a lecturer on immigration and asylum law for the Minnesota Institute for Legal Education and the Minnesota Advocates for Human Rights.
Education: JD 1982, William Mitchell; BA 1976, Augsburg College.
Employment History: 1982-present, private practice; Law Clerk 1981-82, Robins, Kaplan, Miller & Ciresi; Legal Assistant 1979-81, Dorsey & Whitney.
Professional Associations: MSBA (Chair 1988-90, Immigration Section); American Immigration Lawyers Assn. (Secretary/Treasurer 1990-91, Minnesota Dakotas Chapter).
Community Involvement: Minnesota Advocates for Human Rights (consulting lawyer, pro bono asylum project and lecturer on immigration and asylum law); joint MSBA and American Immigration Lawyers Assn. project (volunteer attorney, pro bono master calendar project).
Firm: Ms. Mattos is in solo practice in St. Paul and has worked exclusively in immigration and naturalization law since 1982. She has developed expertise in all facets of the immigration practice and has successfully represented clients at every stage of proceedings.

PATRICIA G. MATTOS

Attorney at Law
1539 Grand Avenue
St. Paul, MN 55105

Phone: (612) 698-8841
Fax: (612) 698-5703

Admitted: 1982 Minnesota;
1982 US Dist. Ct. (MN);
1983 US Ct. App. (8th Cir.)

•**HOWARD S. (SAM) MYERS III:** Mr. Myers is a senior attorney at Popham Haik. Since 1977 his practice has focused on all areas of immigration law, particularly emphasizing employment-based immigration. He was selected for inclusion in *The Best Lawyers in America* for his work in this field. Mr. Myers is a permanent board member and past president of the American Immigration Lawyers Association, the only professional association of immigration lawyers in the US. During the 101st Congress, Mr. Myers helped direct the Association's legislative strategy which contributed to the passage of the Immigration Act of 1990. Mr. Myers was on the legislative negotiating team of the Business Immigration Coalition. He has been quoted in the *Wall Street Journal* and *The New York Times* on business and investment related immigration. He served as an adjunct professor at William Mitchell where he taught a pro bono immigration law clinic, which he founded. Examples of his published articles include "A General Practitioner's Guide to Principles of Immigration, Non-Immigrant Visas and Employment of the Alien," (received MSBA Author's Award); "US Immigration Reform: 'A Weather Prediction'," *Federal Immigration Laws, Regulations & Forms*, West Publishing Co., 1993 edition; and "IRCA—'86: The Immigration Reform and Control Act," *Bench & Bar of Minnesota*, 1987, Vol. 44, No. 1, coauthored with Elizabeth A. Thompson.
Education: JD 1972, University of Virginia; BA 1969, University of North Dakota.
Representative Clients: Fortune 500 companies; employers and employees in high technology and medical industries.
Professional Associations: American Immigration Lawyers Assn. (permanent Board member; past President, Section on Congressional and Public Affairs; past Chair, Committee on Administrative Law and Immigration Procedure); liaison committees with agencies in the Departments of State, Labor, Commerce, and Justice.
Community Involvement: International Institute of Minnesota (past President and Board member); Minnesota Human Rights Advocates (Board member).
Firm: Popham, Haik, Schnobrich & Kaufman, Ltd., is a firm of more than 230 attorneys with offices in Denver, Miami, Minneapolis, Washington, D.C., and international affiliations in Beijing, China and Leipzig and Stuttgart, Germany. The firm represents clients nationally and internationally on issues relating to corporate and business law, administrative law, and litigation.

HOWARD S. (SAM) MYERS III

Popham, Haik, Schnobrich & Kaufman, Ltd.
222 South Ninth Street
Suite 3300
Minneapolis, MN 55402

Phone: (612) 333-4800
Fax: (612) 334-8888

Admitted: 1976 Minnesota;
1972 Virginia
Birthdate: 09/23/47

MICHAEL PRICHARD - Dorsey & Whitney - Pillsbury Center South, 220 South Sixth Street - Minneapolis, MN 55402-1498 - Phone: (612) 340-2633, Fax: (612) 340-8738 - *See complete biographical profile in International Business Law Chapter.*

•**LOUIS N. SMITH** - Popham, Haik, Schnobrich & Kaufman, Ltd. - 222 South Ninth Street, Suite 3300 - Minneapolis, MN 55402 - Phone: (612) 333-4800, Fax: (612) 334-8888 - *See complete biographical profile in Federal, State & Local Government Law Chapter.*

Complete listing of all attorneys nominated in Immigration Law

Robert D. Aronson, Ingber & Aronson, P.A., Minneapolis; **Richard L. Breitman,** The Breitman Immigration Law Firm, Minneapolis; **Laura J. Danielson,** Patterson & Keough, P.A., Minneapolis; **Karim G. El-Ghazzawy,** Attorney at Law, Minneapolis; **Phillip F. Fishman,** Attorney at Law, Minneapolis; **Jerome B. Ingber,** Ingber & Aronson P.A., Minneapolis; **Patricia G. Mattos,** Attorney at Law, St. Paul; **Howard S. Myers III,** Popham, Haik, Schnobrich & Kaufman, Ltd., Minneapolis; **Louis N. Smith,** Popham, Haik, Schnobrich & Kaufman, Ltd., Minneapolis; **Elizabeth A. Thompson,** Popham, Haik, Schnobrich & Kaufman, Ltd., Minneapolis.

CHAPTER 22

INTELLECTUAL PROPERTY LAW

The creative ideas generated by businesses are among their most important strategic competitive weapons. This creative output is afforded protection under the law, but if not properly managed, a company's ideas can be used by others and result in a loss of competitive advantage. The law gives different protection to different categories of intellectual property. Which category applies depends on the particular subject matter in question. This chapter summarizes three types of intellectual property protection: copyright, patents, and trademarks. The Arts, Entertainment, Advertising & Media Law Chapter discusses intellectual property issues of concern to persons in those fields.

COPYRIGHT

A copyright is an exclusive legal right given to a creator of original literary or artistic work. Copyright protection is provided by federal law.

COVERAGE

Copyright protection is granted to original works of "authorship" fixed in a tangible form of expression. Authorship includes literary works, such as novels, poems, and short stories; musical works, including any accompanying words; dramatic works, including any accompanying music, dance works, paintings, photographs, sculptures, movies and sound recordings; and architectural works. Copyright protection applies to a wide range of expression, from computer software to advertisements. What all of these items have in common is an original expression of an idea. Copyright applies to the expression of the idea, not the idea. Whether something infringes on a copyright is difficult to discern and a great deal of case law has been written on the subject. For example, in a written work outright plagiarism—that is, the exact copying of words—is infringement but a copyright does not prevent others from using the facts and ideas used in that work.

Copyright is separate from the subject matter of the copyright. For example, if a person buys a painting from an artist, he or she buys the painting only and not the copyright. If the buyer makes copies of the painting and sells them, the buyer is infringing on the artist's copyright. Copyright gives the creator of the work the exclusive right to reproduce the work, prepare other works based upon copyrighted work, distribute copies, perform the work, and display the work. An owner of a copyright can sell one, some, or all of these exclusive rights. For example, an author of a novel can sell the movie rights to one person and the paperback rights to another.

CREATION

Copyright protection originates from the time the work is created. A work does not have to be published in order to receive copyright protection. There are no applications to fill out in order to have copyright protection. Copyright protection lasts a limited time. The time period depends on when the work is created and whether or not it was published. Generally, works created on or after January 1, 1978, have copyright protection from the time of creation throughout the creator's life, plus an additional 50 years. For works made during the course of employment, the duration of copyright is 75 years from publication or 100 years from creation, whichever is shorter.

OWNER

The owner of a copyright is typically the creator of the work. However, if a person is employed by another and creates the work while on the job, the copyright is owned by the employer, not the employee. This is known as work made for hire. If a person hires an independent contractor to create a work, he or she should address the copyright ownership up front. One does not necessarily own the copyright for an item that an independent contractor creates on the job. In this situation, the parties should decide who owns the copyright and whether the work is work made for hire.

NOTICE & REGISTRATION

As stated previously, copyright protection arises when a work is created and does not require registration or notice. However, a person may give notice that the work is copyrighted and register a copyright. For works created after March 1, 1989, it is no longer required to place a copyright notice on the work. However, it is a good idea to place the copyright notice on all creative works to give notice of the copyright claim. If there is an infringement of a copyright, a court will not allow the party who infringed to claim that he or she did not know that the work was copyrighted if a notice was placed on the work.

A copyright notice contains three parts:

- The word "Copyright," the abbreviation "Copr.," or the © symbol

- The year the work was first published

- The name of the copyright owner

The federal law states that the notice should be placed in a manner and location to give reasonable notice of the copyright claim. When one places a copyright notice on a work, it should be in a conspicuous location.

Besides placing a copyright notice on an original work, a person may also register the copyright. Registering a copyright is not required, but it provides three benefits: first, a presumption that the copyright claim is valid; second, the award of attorney fees and statutory damages in an infringement case; and finally, copyright registration is a prerequisite to bringing an action for copyright infringement.

Registering a copyright is relatively straightforward. In general, the registration should be done within three months of publication. A person must complete an application supplied by the Library of Congress, Copyright Office. This form is sent to the Office with a filing fee and copies of the work. The number of copies to be supplied depends on whether the work has been published, whether the work has been published outside the United States, or if the work is a contribution to a collective work.

FAIR USE

Although a copyright gives its owner exclusive rights, fair use of a copyrighted work is not considered an infringement of copyright. Fair use includes copying for purposes such as news reporting, teaching, research, and comments and criticisms. Factors to be considered in determining whether use is fair use include purpose of use, whether for profit or not, amount of work used, and effect of the use upon the value of the work. There are also exceptions for libraries and teachers.

PATENT

A patent is a right granted by the federal government to an inventor to exclude others from making, using, or selling an invention. The invention must be novel, non-obvious and utilitarian in order to qualify for a patent. The rationale behind patents is to reward an inventor for the time and efforts used in the creation of an invention. A patent is granted for a limited time period. After a patent expires, the inventor loses the exclusive rights to the invention. A patent protects an invention only in this country. If an inventor wants to have protection in other countries, those countries' patent procedures must be followed.

PATENT CATEGORIES

An invention must be new, useful (except for design patents that must be ornamental), and not obvious in order to be granted a patent. There are three categories of patents—utility patents, design patents, and plant patents. A utility patent is granted to anyone who invents or discovers any new or useful process, method, machine, manufacture, compositions of matter, or any improvement thereof. A new industrial or technical process may be patented. Manufacture refers to the articles that are made. Composition of matter relates to chemical compositions and includes mixtures of ingredients as well as new compounds. A utility patent is granted for a term of 17 years. A design patent is granted to anyone who invents a new, original, and ornamental design for an article of manufacture. The appearance of the article is protected under this patent. A design patent is granted for a term of 14 years. A plant patent is granted to any person who invents or discovers and asexually reproduces any distinct and new variety of plant. The plants may include any mutants, hybrids, and newly found seedlings, except a tuber-propagated plant or a plant found in an uncultivated state. A plant patent is granted for a term of 17 years.

APPLICATION

In order for a patent to be granted to an inventor, an application for a patent must be filed. Once a patent has been applied for, the inventor may proclaim that his or her product has a patent pending, but this does not provide any protection against infringement, it only serves as a warning to others that a patent may be forthcoming. A patent application is made to the U.S. Patent and Trademark Office, which is part of the U.S. Department of Commerce. A patent application is confidential; however, if a patent is granted, the application becomes public information.

The application includes three components; first, a written document that describes the invention and states the claims of the inventor. The statement must be in such detail that a person knowledgeable in the subject matter area could build and use the invention based upon the information provided. The claims state the patented characteristics of the invention. This document must also contain a declaration by the inventor that he believes himself to be the original and first inventor of the application's subject matter. The declaration must be notarized. The second component of the application is drawings. Drawings of an invention should be furnished to illustrate an invention. An inventor should supply as many drawings as necessary to describe the invention. The third requirement is the filing fee. The fees may be reduced by 50 percent if the patent applicant is an individual, small business, or nonprofit organization.

After a patent application is filed, a patent examiner reviews the application. The examiner can allow the patent, reject the application, or object to the application. A rejection means that the examiner believes the invention should not be granted a patent, while an objection means that there is a problem with the application. A problem with the application can be fixed. An inventor can amend his or her patent application to address the concerns raised by the examiner. An inventor can appeal a patent rejection.

A patent will not be granted if the invention was in public use or on sale in the United States, or the subject of a patent application in another county which has matured more than one year prior to the filing of a patent application. An inventor's own use of the invention may bar him or her from receiving a patent if used for more than one year before application.

Patents are granted only to the inventor; however, an inventor may sell his or her rights to the patent or sell licenses whereby another can pay a fee to use the patent. The license may be exclusive or nonexclusive. If the rights to a patent are assigned, this assignment should be registered with the U.S. Patent and Trademark Office.

Before an inventor applies for a patent, a search should be done to determine whether a patent already has been granted for the invention. This search may be expensive. The Public Search Room of the U.S. Patent and Trademark Office is the primary source of information. Also, a Patent and Trademark Depository Library has been established at the Minneapolis Public Library and Information Center.

When a patent is granted, an inventor must pay an issuance fee. Also, maintenance fees for the patent are paid three times during the patent period to keep the patent in force. Minnesota Statutes require any invention development services in Minnesota to disclose the number of customers who have received additional money by virtue of the work done by the invention developer service.

The U.S. Patent and Trademark Office maintains a register of attorneys and agents who meet the legal, scientific, and technical requirements to practice patent law, and who agree to uphold high standards of professional conduct.

TRADEMARK

Perhaps the best definition of what a trademark is used for was provided by the United States Supreme Court in 1942, which stated that "a trademark is a merchandising shortcut which induces a purchaser to select what he wants, or what he has been led to believe he wants." A trademark is either a word, phrase, symbol, or design, or a combination of those items that identifies and distinguishes the source of the goods or services of one party from those of others. A service mark is the same except that it identifies and distinguishes the source of a service rather than a product. The terms "trademark" and "mark" are often used interchangeably to refer to both trademarks and service marks.

Rights to a trademark arise when a trademark is used or an application to register is made and the applicant intends to use the mark. A trademark gives the owner exclusive use of the trademark as long as it is used to identify goods or services. As is the case with copyrights, federal registration is not necessary for a trademark to be protected. A trademark is good from the first time a product is used in interstate commerce. A mark may lose its trademark significance if it becomes associated with a generic name. For example, the terms "nylon" and "escalator" were once trademarks that became generic. As with a copyright, there are a number of advantages to federal registration. A trademark may be registered with either the U.S. Patent and Trademark Office or the Minnesota Secretary of State. Registration in one office does not register the trademark in the other office.

Federal Trademark Registration

As previously mentioned, federal registration of a trademark is not required; however, there are two benefits from registering. First, the owner of a federal trademark registration is presumed to be the owner of the trademark. Second, the owner of a federal trademark registration is entitled to use the trademark nationwide.

An application for federal trademark registration goes through two stages. First, the application must be accepted, and second, once the application has been accepted, the process to determine trademark registration begins. An application to register a trademark must be filed in the name of the owner. The owner can be an individual, partnership, or corporation. An owner who has already begun using a trademark can file an application based on that use. An owner who has not yet used the trademark may make an application based upon an intention to use the trademark. Use of a trademark in promotion or advertising before the trademark is used with the products or goods does not qualify as use. If an owner files an application based upon intent to use the trademark, she or he must use the trademark and submit proof of this use to the U.S. Trademark and Patent office before the trademark will be registered.

The application consists of a completed application form, a drawing of the mark, and a filing fee. There is a separate filing fee for each class of goods or services listed in the application. The Patent and Trademark Office maintains a list of over 40 class categories, from furniture to clothing to chemicals. If the application is based on the use of the trademark, the application must include three examples per class showing actual use of the trademark. A separate application must be filed for each trademark a person wishes to register. The applicant must be careful when identifying goods and services, because an application may not be amended later to add goods or services not within the scope of the original identification.

After an application is filed, it is reviewed to determine if it meets the minimum requirements. If it does, the application is given a serial number and the applicant is sent a receipt. If minimum requirements are not met, the application and the fee are returned to the applicant. If an application is accepted, an examining patent and trademark attorney reviews the application to determine whether the trademark should be registered. If the attorney decides that the trademark may not be registered, a letter is sent to the applicant stating the grounds for refusal. The applicant must respond within six months or the application will be abandoned. If the applicant's response does not overcome the attorney's objections, a final refusal will be issued. A common reason for refusing to register a trademark is the likelihood of confusion between the applicant's trademark and a trademark that has already been registered.

If there are no objections to the application or the objections have been overcome, the attorney will approve the trademark for publication in the Official/Gazette, a weekly publication of the Patent and Trademark Office. Any party who believes that it may be harmed by the registration of the published trademark has 30 days to file an opposition to the trademark. Oppositions to trademarks are heard before the Trademark Trial and Appeal Board.

If no oppositions are raised, the application continues in the registration process. The next step depends on whether the application is based on actual use of the trademark or intent to use the trademark. If the application is based upon the actual use of the mark, the Patent and Trademark Office registers the mark and issues a registration certificate.

If the application is based on the party's intent to use the trademark, the Patent and Trademark Office issues a Notice of Allowance. The applicant has six months from the date of the notice to either use the trademark and send to the Patent and Trademark Office a Statement of Use with three samples of use per class or request an extension of time. If the Statement of Use is filed and approved, the Patent and Trademark Office then issues a registration certificate. There is an additional fee per class for these filings.

Before a person applies for federal registration of a trademark, a search should be done to determine whether there are any conflicting trademarks. The application fee is not refunded if a conflicting trademark is found. Also, one would not want to spend resources on a trademark that is not available. The Public Search Library of the U.S. Patent and Trademark Office is the primary source of available trademark information. Also, a Patent and Trademark Depository Library has been established at the Minneapolis Public Library and Information Center. The term of a federal trademark registration is ten years, with ten-year renewal terms.

Besides registering a trademark claim, a person may also give notice to the public that trademark rights are claimed. The TM symbol or the SM symbol may be used by anyone to notify the public of the claim. Registration is not required; however, use of the registration symbol ® is permitted only when the trademark has been registered with the Patent and Trademark Office.

STATE TRADEMARK REGISTRATION

A trademark can also be registered with the Minnesota Secretary of State's Office. A state trademark registration is not equivalent to federal registration. A trademark that is federally registered does not need to be registered with a state since federal registration gives the owner the rights to that trademark nationally. However, a party who has not registered a trademark with the Federal Patent and Trademark Office may, in some instances, wish to file the trademark with Minnesota. For example, if a person is operating a small business in Minnesota and has no intention of expanding the business, he or she may consider registering the trademark with the Secretary of State to protect his or her interests only in the state of Minnesota.

A trademark registration in Minnesota takes less time and costs less than federal trademark registration. An applicant must submit an application to the state with the appropriate filing fee. State registration only provides protection in Minnesota, so a person can have a trademark registered with Minnesota and another person could legally use the same trademark in Wisconsin. Trademarks registered in Minnesota can also be protected as long as the trademark continues to be used. The initial term of a trademark registration is ten years with subsequent renewal periods. Registering an assumed name or a corporate name in Minnesota is not trademark registration and does not provide trademark protection.

TRADE SECRET LAW

Minnesota's Uniform Trade Secrets Act provides protection for a broad category of sensitive business information. The act provides both injunctive relief and damages for misappropriation of a trade secret. The act defines a "trade secret" as information, including a formula, pattern, compilation, program, device, method, technique, or process that derives value from not being generally known and about which some effort has been made at keeping the information secret. Note that the definition of a trade secret is not limited to documents or information entered into a computer; trade secrets can be information retained only in a person's head. Thus a trade secret can be passed on simply by a key employee leaving to work at a competitor. Note also that the definition requires the business to take steps to keep the information secret; an employer cannot claim misapproariation of a trade secret if the employer never treated the information as secret.

Case law interpreting Minnesota's Uniform Trade Secrets Act has focused on the steps a business must take to protect a secret before it can claim misappropriation. An attorney experienced

Intellectual Property Law

in this area can advise on the steps appropriate for a particular business to take. Generally, a business can help protect trade secrets by maintaining a strict policy regarding the identification, communication and use of trade secrets. Some practical means by which a company can help protect misappropriation of its secrets include reminding employees about confidential communications, asking them to sign confidentiality agreements, reminding them before and after the discussion of a trade secret to keep the information confidential, and by denoting sensitive communications with the word "secret," or "confidential."

RESOURCES

Copyright Office, Library of Congress, Washington, D.C. 20559-6000. Public Information Office: (202) 707-3000. Form hotline: (202) 707-9100.

U.S. Patent and Trademark Office, U.S. Department of Commerce, Washington, D.C. 20231. General Information: (703) 308-HELP. Automated Information: (703) 557-INFO. TDD: (703) 305-7785.

Minnesota Secretary of State, 180 State Office Building, 100 Constitution Avenue, St. Paul, MN 55155-1299, (612) 296-2803.

INTELLECTUAL PROPERTY LAW LEADING ATTORNEYS

The attorneys profiled in this section were nominated by their peers in a statewide survey conducted in 1993 in which several thousand Minnesota attorneys were asked to name the lawyer to whom they would send a friend or family member in need of legal assistance in the area of *Intellectual Property Law*.

Because the survey resulted in a list of less than five percent of Minnesota's practicing attorneys, this should not be construed as a complete list. Nevertheless, it is an excellent source of highly qualified and reputable attorneys, who, if unable to assist can in most cases make quality referrals.

A list of all attorneys nominated in this category is found at the end of this section. For information on the survey methodology see page ix.

Please note that the shorter, two line attorney listings in this section are of attorneys who practice in this area but whose full biographical profile appears in another section of this book. A bullet "•" preceeding name indicates the attorney was nominated in this particular area of law. For information on the format of these profiles, consult the section "Using the *Business Guidebook*" found on page xiv. Note that the following abbreviations are used throughout these profiles:

Selected by Attorneys for
GUIDEBOOK
Law & Leading Attorneys
MINNESOTA

The attorneys profiled below were recommended by their peers in a statewide survey.

App.	- Appellate	ABA	- American Bar Association
Cir.	- Circuit	ATLA	- American Trial Lawyers Association
Ct.	- Court	HCBA	- Hennepin County Bar Association
Dist.	- District	MDLA	- Minnesota Defense Lawyers Association
Hon.	- Honorable	MSBA	- Minnesota State Bar Association
JD	- Law degree (Juris Doctor)	MTLA	- Minnesota Trial Lawyers Association
LLB	- Law degree	NBTA	- National Board of Trial Advocacy
LLM	- Master in Law degree	RCBA	- Ramsey County Bar Association
Sup.	- Supreme		

Chapter 22: Intellectual Property Law

KENNETH J. ABDO - Abdo & Abdo, P.A. - 710 Northstar West, 625 Marquette Avenue - Minneapolis, MN 55402 - Phone: (612) 333-1526, Fax: (612) 342-2608 - *See complete biographical profile in Arts, Entertainment, Advertising & Media Law Chapter.*

STEPHEN R. BERGERSON - Fredrikson & Byron, P.A. - 1100 International Centre, 900 Second Avenue South - Minneapolis, MN 55402 - Phone: (612) 347-7025, Fax: (612) 347-7077 - *See complete biographical profile in Arts, Entertainment, Advertising & Media Law Chapter.*

RONALD J. BROWN

Dorsey & Whitney
Pillsbury Center South
220 South Sixth Street
Minneapolis, MN 55402-1498

Phone: (612) 340-2879
Fax: (612) 340-2868

Admitted: 1977 Minnesota;
1977 US Dist. Ct. (MN);
1984 US Ct. Claims;
1982 US Ct. App. (8th Cir.);
1989 US Ct. App. (Fed. Cir.);
1978 US Patent & Trademark Office (No. 29016)
Birthdate: 10/05/47

•**RONALD J. BROWN:** Mr. Brown practices in the area of complex technology litigation. Mr. Brown has extensive experience in patent and trade secret litigation, including the following cases: *Amgen v. Chugai*, International Trade Commission (recombinant DNA technology for pharmaceuticals, specifically EPO); *Intermedics and Carbomedics v. St. Jude Medical* (artificial heart valve design and pyrolytic carbon coating technology); *Renal Systems v. Endotronics* (bioreactor and hollow fiber module technology); *3M v. Norton Company* (seeded sol gel abrasive technology); *Schneider USA et al. v. Everest Medical et al.* (catheter manufacture and design); *Imprimis v. Edwards* (magnetic hard disk drive design); *New Generation Foods v. Dairyland Products, Inc.* (batching procedures and formulae for high fat powders); *PPG v. Diametrics et al.* (portable blood gas analyzer technology). Mr. Brown has been chairman of Dorsey & Whitney's Intellectual Property Department since 1991 and a partner in the firm's Litigation Department since 1983. He has been responsible for office automation as Dorsey & Whitney's computer partner.

Education: JD 1977 with honors, University of Iowa (Lead Articles Editor 1976-77, *Iowa Law Review*); PhD 1974, California Institute of Technology (Society of the Sigma Xi); BA 1969 with distinction, Stanford University (Tau Beta Pi).
Employment History: Partner 1983-present, Associate 1977-82, Dorsey & Whitney.
Representative Clients: Seagate Technology; Century Manufacturing; Diametrics Medical, Inc.
Professional Associations: Federal Circuit Bar Assn.; National Institute for Trial Advocacy (1980 Graduate).
Firm: Dorsey & Whitney is the largest law firm in Minnesota and one of the largest firms in the United States with over 350 lawyers in 12 offices. The depth and breadth of the experience of its lawyers enables it to provide a broad range of services to meet the diverse legal needs of its client base, which includes Fortune 500 companies, public agencies, banks and other financial institutions, nonprofit organizations, individual investors, family owned businesses, and high-tech and low-tech, growth oriented companies. *See additional listing in Commercial Litigation Chapter.*

ALAN G. CARLSON

Merchant, Gould, Smith, Edell, Welter & Schmidt, P.A.
3100 Norwest Center
90 South Seventh Street
Minneapolis, MN 55402-4131

Phone: (612) 332-5300
Fax: (612) 332-9081

Admitted: 1971 Minnesota;
1971 US Patent and Trademark Office
Birthdate: 03/02/45

•**ALAN G. CARLSON:** Since he began his legal career, Mr. Carlson has focused his practice on intellectual property litigation. His experience includes jury and bench trials throughout the United States for both plaintiffs and defendants in every type of intellectual property case including patent, trademark, trade dress, trade secret, copyright, contract, and libel cases. He counsels clients on general intellectual property issues related to the obtaining and licensing of rights from a litigation view point. Mr. Carlson also lectures on various areas of intellectual property law. He is listed in *The Best Lawyers in America*, 1991-92 and 1993-94 editions.

Education: JD 1971 cum laude, Ohio State University, University of Minnesota, and William Mitchell; BSME 1967, Purdue University (Pi Tau Sigma).
Employment History: 1971-present (CEO since 1989), Merchant Gould, Smith, Edell, Welter & Schmidt; Law Clerk 1969-71, Honeywell, Inc.; Engineer 1968-69, Honeywell, Inc.
Representative Clients: General Mills, Inc.; Valspar Corp.; Pillsbury; Minnesota Mining and Manufacturing Company; Donaldson Company, Inc.; Honeywell, Inc.; H.B. Fuller Company; Carlson Companies, Inc.; Aveda Corp.
Professional Associations: ABA; MSBA; ATLA.
Community Involvement: Legal Advice Clinics (volunteer attorney and former Board member); District Four Ethics Committee (1992-present); Minneapolis Club; Lafayette Club.
Firm: Merchant, Gould, Smith, Edell, Welter & Schmidt is engaged exclusively in the practice of intellectual property law, including patent, trademark, copyright, unfair competition, trade secret, advertising and computer law, and related litigation including both trials and appeals. With offices in Minneapolis, St. Paul, and Los Angeles and more than 70 practicing attorneys, the firm is one of the largest intellectual property law firms in the United States.

Intellectual Property Law Leading Attorneys

•**MICHAEL V. CIRESI** - Robins, Kaplan, Miller & Ciresi - 2800 LaSalle Plaza, 800 LaSalle Avenue - Minneapolis, MN 55402 - Phone: (612) 349-8500, Fax: (612) 339-4181 - *See complete biographical profile in Commercial Litigation Chapter*

LAURA J. DANIELSON - Patterson & Keough, P.A. - 1200 Rand Tower, 527 Marquette Avenue South - Minneapolis, MN 55402 - Phone: (612) 349-5740, Fax: (612) 349-9266 - *See complete biographical profile in Immigration Law Chapter.*

•**ROBERT T. EDELL:** Mr. Edell has nearly thirty years of experience as a trial lawyer and has worked on several cases involving both US and foreign parties. He has been lead trial counsel for numerous jury and bench trials involving complex matters in patents, trademarks, copyrights, trade secrets, and unfair competition. He is a world renowned expert in the area of intellectual property rights litigation before the US International Trade Commission, and in addition to trying cases before the USITC, he has written and spoken extensively on this subject. Mr. Edell was recognized as one of the best attorneys in America in the area of intellectual property rights in *The Best Lawyers in America*, 1991-92 and 1993-94 editions.
Education: JD 1964 cum laude, William Mitchell; BEE 1960, University of Minnesota.
Employment History: 1964-present, Merchant, Gould, Smith, Edell, Welter & Schmidt.
Representative Clients: Minnesota Mining and Manufacturing Company; Honeywell, Inc.; McNeilus Truck and Manufacturing Company; Dahlberg; DataCard Corp.; Mead Corp.; Munsingwear, Inc.
Professional Associations: HCBA; MSBA; ABA; American Intellectual Property Law Assn. 1974-77, (Board of Managers; Chair 1973-74), Patent Law Committee; 1979-81, Small Business Committee; 1982, Taxation Committee); Minnesota Patent Lawyers Assn. (Secretary 1968-69; President 1971-72).
Firm: Merchant, Gould, Smith, Edell, Welter & Schmidt is engaged exclusively in the practice of intellectual property law, including patent, trademark, copyright, unfair competition, trade secret, advertising and computer law, and related litigation including both trials and appeals. With offices in Minneapolis, St. Paul, and Los Angeles and more than 70 practicing attorneys, the firm is one of the largest intellectual property law firms in the United States.

ROBERT T. EDELL

Merchant, Gould, Smith, Edell, Welter & Schmidt, P.A.
3100 Norwest Center
90 South Seventh Street
Minneapolis, MN 55402-4131

Phone: (612) 332-5300
Fax: (612) 332-9081

Admitted: 1964 Minnesota; 1961 US Patent and Trademark Office
Birthdate: 03/30/32

•**DAVID R. FAIRBAIRN:** David has 25 years of intellectual property law experience and is President and a founder of Kinney & Lange. Dave focuses his practice on intellectual property litigation. He is a frequent lecturer on intellectual property law topics and has also taught "Communications Law" at the College of St. Thomas. Dave and Thomas J. Stueber received the 1993 Elmer H. Wiblishauser Author's Award for Best *Bench & Bar* Article of the Year. The article, "Lawful Photocopying: Where Fair Use Becomes Unfair," 49 *Bench & Bar of Minnesota* 21 (October 1992), was reprinted in the *Iowa Lawyer*. Dave is an avid tournament fisherman who qualified for the 1994 World Walleye Tournament. He also plays bass guitar and collects baseball memorabilia.
Education: JD 1973 cum laude, William Mitchell; BSEE 1969 with distinction, University of Minnesota.
Representative Clients: Empi, Inc.; Friedrich Wilh.Schwing GmbH; 3M; Munsingwear, Inc.; Redmond Products, Inc.; Seagate Technologies, Inc.; SPX Corp.
Professional Associations: ABA; AIPLA; MN Intellectual Property Lawyers Assn. (President-Elect); MSBA; MTLA; HCBA (past Governing Council member).
Firm: Kinney & Lange, P.A., is an energetic, full service, intellectual property law firm practicing patent, trademark, copyright, licensing, unfair competition, advertising, and franchise law. Kinney & Lange litigates and resolves intellectual property disputes in federal and state courts, the US Patent and Trademark Office, foreign patent offices and courts, the International Trade Commission, and arbitration tribunals. The firm's attorneys are skilled in a variety of trade and technical areas including avionics, digital circuits, computer hardware and software, semiconductors, biomedical devices, food technology, cryogenics, biochemistry, microbiology, virology, organic chemistry, plastics, petroleum refining, advertising, publishing, and franchising. Kinney & Lange's clients range from multinational corporations to small and start-up businesses. *See additional listings in Arts, Entertainment, Advertising & Media Law and Commercial Litigation Chapters.*

DAVID R. FAIRBAIRN

Kinney & Lange, P.A.
625 Fourth Avenue South
Suite 1500
Minneapolis, MN 55415-1659

Phone: (612) 339-1863
Fax: (612) 339-6580

Admitted: 1971 US Patent & Trademark Office;
1973 Minnesota;
1978 US Dist. Ct. (MN);
1982 US Ct. App. (Fed. Cir.);
1990 US Ct. App. (8th Cir.)
Birthdate: 08/07/47

ALAIN FRECON - Frécon & Associates - 902 Foshay Tower, 821 Marquette Avenue South - Minneapolis, MN 55402 - Phone: (612) 338-6868, Fax: (612) 338-6878 - *See complete biographical profile in International Business Law Chapter.*

BARBARA J. GISLASON - Barbara J. Gislason & Associates - 219 SE Main Street, Suite 506 - Minneapolis, MN 55414 - Phone: (612) 331-8033, Fax: (612) 331-8115 - *See complete biographical profile in Arts, Entertainment, Advertising & Media Law Chapter.*

JOHN D. GOULD

Merchant, Gould, Smith, Edell, Welter & Schmidt, P.A.
3100 Norwest Center
90 South Seventh Street
Minneapolis, MN 55402-4131

Phone: (612) 332-5300
Fax: (612) 332-9081

Admitted: 1953 Minnesota;
1955 US Patent and Trademark Office
Birthdate: 04/12/27

•**JOHN D. GOULD:** Mr. Gould has 40 years experience as a trial lawyer throughout the United States in the field of intellectual property. He has extensive litigation experience in all phases of contested intellectual property matters. In addition to the numerous cases Mr. Gould has tried as lead counsel, he has assisted in the trial of many others and has also successfully negotiated settlement before trial in a significant number of cases.
Education: JD 1953, University of Minnesota; B Physics 1950 with distinction, University of Minnesota.
Employment History: 1954-present, Merchant, Gould, Smith, Edell, Welter & Schmidt.
Representative Clients: Minnesota Mining and Manufacturing Company; Arctco, Inc.; Sico Inc.
Professional Associations: ABA; MSBA; Minnesota Intellectual Property Law Assn.; American Intellectual Property Law Assn.
Community Involvement: Minneapolis Rotary; Minneapolis Club; St. Stephens Foundation Committee.
Firm: Merchant, Gould, Smith, Edell, Welter & Schmidt is engaged exclusively in the practice of intellectual property law, including patent, trademark, copyright, unfair competition, trade secret, advertising and computer law, and related litigation including both trials and appeals. With offices in Minneapolis, St. Paul, and Los Angeles and more than 70 practicing attorneys, the firm is one of the largest intellectual property law firms in the United States.

CURTIS B. HAMRE

Merchant, Gould, Smith, Edell, Welter & Schmidt, P.A.
3100 Norwest Center
90 South Seventh Street
Minneapolis, MN 55402-4131

Phone: (612) 332-5300
Fax: (612) 332-9081

Admitted: 1979 Minnesota;
1979 Iowa;
1978 US Patent and Trademark Office
Birthdate: 03/11/42

•**CURTIS B. HAMRE:** Mr. Hamre concentrates his practice in the areas of entertainment law and patent, trademark, and copyright prosecution, including licensing and business planning, representing many individual inventors, entrepreneurs, and start-up companies. He has a broad range of engineering, legal, and business experience, both domestic and international. He founded Merchant & Gould's Foreign Filing Department and was initial Chair of the firm's International Section.
Education: JD 1979, Drake University; MA 1967, University of Nebraska; BA 1964 cum laude, Concordia College.
Employment History: 1979-present, Merchant, Gould, Smith, Edell, Welter & Schmidt; Chair 1985-93, Board of Directors, Interlock Structures International, Inc.; Project Engineer 1970-76, Naval Weapons Center; Systems Engineer 1966-70, Honeywell, Inc.; Captain 1967-69, US Army.
Representative Clients: Coda Music Technology, Inc.; Recovery Engineering, Inc.; Gift Certificate Center, Inc.; Donaldson Company; Hyundai Electronics; Nippon Glass Company.
Professional Associations: American Intellectual Property Law Assn.; Minnesota Intellectual Property Law Assn.; MSBA (Entertainment Law Section); HCBA; International Trademark Assn.; Assn. Internationale pour la Protection de la Propriete Industrielle.
Community Involvement: Vision of Glory Lutheran Church (Church Council member); Head Coach for youth baseball and hockey, Wayzata; Instructor, Junior Achievement.
Firm: Merchant, Gould, Smith, Edell, Welter & Schmidt is engaged exclusively in the practice of intellectual property law, including patent, trademark, copyright, unfair competition, trade secret, advertising and computer law, and related litigation including both trials and appeals. With offices in Minneapolis, St. Paul, and Los Angeles and more than 70 practicing attorneys, the firm is one of the largest intellectual property law firms in the United States.

•**ORRIN M. HAUGEN:** Mr. Haugen practices patent, trademark, and copyright law in state and federal courts, including the US Patent and Trademark Office. His undergraduate education in chemical engineering provides him with scientific knowledge that is useful in his work with companies that produce biochemical, chemical, and medical products.
Education: LLB 1951, University of Minnesota; B Chemical Engineering 1948, University of Minnesota.
Representative Clients: Sheldahl, Inc.; The Bergquist Company; Cardiac Pacemakers, Inc.; Fremont Industries, Inc.; Hypro Corp.; Berkley, Inc.; Timesavers, Inc.; Ag-Chem Equipment Company, Inc.; ATS Medical, Inc.; Cortec Corp.; Applied Membrane Technology, Inc.
Professional Associations: ABA (Patent, Trademark and Copyright Law Section); HCBA; MSBA; Minnesota Intellectual Property Law Assn.; American Intellectual Property Law Assn.; MTLA.
Firm: Haugen & Nikolai, P.A., specializes in patent, trademark, copyright, and unfair competition cases. The firm's clients include individuals and firms working in many areas including biomedical, agricultural, defense, computer, electronics, communications, medical, and chemical fields. Their experienced and skilled attorneys have handled many cases in these areas and know precisely what steps to take, what research to conduct, and how to best represent their clients. The firm utilizes state-of-the art computer systems and a network of professionals who provide them with direct access to foreign courts and governmental agencies.

ORRIN M. HAUGEN

Haugen & Nikolai, P.A.
820 International Centre
900 Second Avenue South
Minneapolis, MN 55402

Phone: (612) 339-7461
Fax: (612) 349-6556

Admitted: 1951 Minnesota;
1951 US Dist. Ct. (MN);
1963 US Sup. Ct.;
1966 US Ct. App. (8th Cir.);
1977 US Ct. App. (1st Cir.);
1982 US Ct. App. (Fed. Cir.);
US Patent & Trademark Office
Birthdate: 08/01/27

•**STUART R. HEMPHILL:** Mr. Hemphill practices in the area of intellectual property, including acquisition of patent, trademark, copyright, and trade secret rights; licensing or other transfers of technology and intellectual property rights, particularly for computer hardware and software businesses, publishing/entertainment businesses and authors; and litigation concerning intellectual property rights and unfair competition. His technical expertise in data processing systems, computer software, microprocessor controlled systems, electro-mechanical devices, optical scanning systems, and mechanical devices and systems is an asset to his practice.
Education: JD 1975 cum laude, University of Michigan (staff member 1973-74, *University of Michigan Journal of Law Reform*); AM 1972, University of Michigan; BS 1970 with highest honors, AB 1970 with honors, University of Illinois.
Employment History: Partner 1981-present, Associate 1975-80, Dorsey & Whitney; Adjunct Professor of Copyright Law 1976-79, William Mitchell College of Law; Systems Specialist 1970-72, Bell Telephone Laboratories.
Professional Associations: Minnesota Intellectual Property Law Assn.; MSBA (Computer Law Section); HCBA.
Community Involvement: Minnesota Film Center/University Film Society (Board member, past Board President).
Firm: Dorsey & Whitney is the largest law firm in Minnesota and one of the largest firms in the United States with over 350 lawyers in 12 offices. The depth and breadth of the experience of its lawyers enables it to provide a broad range of services to meet the diverse legal needs of its client base, which includes Fortune 500 companies, public agencies, banks and other financial institutions, nonprofit organizations, individual investors, family owned businesses, and high-tech and low-tech, growth oriented companies. *See additional listing in Arts, Entertainment, Advertising & Media Law Chapter.*

STUART R. HEMPHILL

Dorsey & Whitney
Pillsbury Center South
220 South Sixth Street
Minneapolis, MN 55402-1498

Phone: (612) 340-2734
Fax: (612) 340-2868

Admitted: 1975 Minnesota;
1977 US Dist. Ct. (MN);
1988 US Ct. App. (8th Cir.);
1985 US Ct. App. (Fed. Cir.);
1976 US Patent & Trademark Office
Birthdate: 07/18/47

Chapter 22: Intellectual Property Law

EUGENE L. JOHNSON

Dorsey & Whitney
Pillsbury Center South
220 South Sixth Street
Minneapolis, MN 55402-1498

Phone: (612) 340-2625
Fax: (612) 340-2868

Admitted: 1963 Minnesota; 1965 California; 1963 US Dist. Ct. (MN); 1970 US Ct. App. (8th Cir.); 1963 US Patent & Trademark Office (No. 21028)
Birthdate: 11/30/36

•**EUGENE L. JOHNSON:** Mr. Johnson practices in the area of intellectual property, including the litigation of patent, trademark, trade secret, unfair competition, and copyright claims and the acquisition of intellectual property rights. Mr. Johnson's legal areas of expertise are copyright and trademark licensing and other contracts, intellectual property litigation, and technology transfer agreements. His technical specialties include mechanical and hydraulic technology; mechanical devices and systems; and medical devices, appliances, and methods. Mr. Johnson has been a partner in the Intellectual Property Law Department at Dorsey & Whitney since 1971. He is listed in *The Best Lawyers in America*, *Who's Who in American Law*, and *Who's Who in America*.
Education: LLB 1962, University of Wisconsin; BSCE 1960, University of Wisconsin.
Employment History: Partner 1971-present, Associate 1966-70, Dorsey & Whitney; Associate 1964-66, Mellin, Hanscom & Hirsh; Attorney 1962-64, The Pillsbury Company.
Professional Associations: MSBA (Board of Governors); Minnesota Intellectual Property Law Assn. (past President); American Intellectual Property Law Assn.
Community Involvement: Minneapolis Athletic Club; Lafayette Country Club.
Firm: Dorsey & Whitney is the largest law firm in Minnesota and one of the largest firms in the United States with over 350 lawyers in 12 offices. The depth and breadth of the experience of its lawyers enables it to provide a broad range of services to meet the diverse legal needs of its client base, which includes Fortune 500 companies, public agencies, banks and other financial institutions, nonprofit organizations, individual investors, family owned businesses, and high-tech and low-tech, growth oriented companies. *See additional listing in Arts, Entertainment, Advertising & Media Law Chapter.*

D. RANDALL KING

Merchant, Gould, Smith, Edell, Welter & Schmidt, P.A.
3100 Norwest Center
90 South Seventh Street
Minneapolis, MN 55402-4131

Phone: (612) 332-5300
Fax: (612) 332-9081

Admitted: 1973 Ohio; 1977 Minnesota
Birthdate: 12/23/46

•**D. RANDALL KING:** Mr. King has practiced trademark law for over 20 years, including the selection of trademarks; the prosecution of matters before the US Patent and Trademark Office; the policing of trademarks on behalf of clients; and the practice of civil litigation relating to trademark infringement matters.
Education: JD 1973, University of Akron; BS 1968, University of Akron.
Employment History: 1976-present, Merchant, Gould, Smith, Edell, Welter & Schmidt; Law Clerk and Trademark Attorney 1972-76, Goodyear Tire and Rubber Company.
Representative Clients: Northern States Power; Harvest States Cooperatives; MGI Pharma; Slumberland, Inc.; Stearns Manufacturing; Schwann's Sales Enterprises; McGlynn Bakeries; Burlington Northern Railroad; Snyder's Drug Stores; Colgate-Palmolive.
Professional Associations: ABA; Federal Bar Assn.; American Intellectual Property Law Assn.; MSBA, Minnesota Intellectual Property Law Assn.; International Trademark Assn.
Firm: Merchant, Gould, Smith, Edell, Welter & Schmidt is engaged exclusively in the practice of intellectual property law, including patent, trademark, copyright, unfair competition, trade secret, advertising and computer law, and related litigation including both trials and appeals. With offices in Minneapolis, St. Paul, and Los Angeles and more than 70 practicing attorneys, the firm is one of the largest intellectual property law firms in the United States.

•**DEXTER A. LARSEN:** Mr. Larsen practices business and commercial law, commercial real estate law, securities law, and intellectual property law. He has extensive experience in representing new business ventures, including debt financing, bank loans, equity financing, venture capital, private placements, and local and regional economic development financing. His areas of expertise include structuring and representation of closely held businesses including partnerships, corporations, professional corporations, and limited liability companies; and providing the commercial, business, real estate, and employment law services necessary for a closely held business. Mr. Larsen has strong ties to the Ely, Minnesota area where his family owned a resort and where he worked during his school years as a Boundary Waters Canoe Area guide.
Education: JD 1967, University of Minnesota; BA 1964 summa cum laude, University of Minnesota.
Employment History: 1967-present, Fryberger, Buchanan, Smith & Frederick, P.A.
Representative Clients: Lutsen Mountains Corporation; Lutsen Corporation; The Whitecliff Group; Duluth Lighthouse for the Blind; North Shore Bank of Commerce; Owens Forest Products Company; regional banks and lenders; businesses; private individuals.
Professional Associations: 11th District Bar Assn.; MSBA; ABA; State Bar of Wisconsin.
Community Involvement: Duluth-Superior Symphony Assn. (Officer & Director 1992-present); Duluth Chamber of Commerce (Finance Committee); Kiwanis Club of Duluth; AAD Temple Shrine, Scottish Rite Bodies, Valley of Duluth.
Firm: Please see firm profile in Appendix C. *See additional listing in Publicly Held Corporations Law Chapter.*

DEXTER A. LARSEN

Fryberger, Buchanan, Smith & Frederick, P.A.
302 West Superior Street
Suite 700
Duluth, MN 55802

Phone: (218) 722-0861
Fax: (218) 722-9568

Admitted: 1967 Minnesota; 1986 Wisconsin
Birthdate: 12/28/41

CALVIN L. LITSEY - Faegre & Benson - 2200 Norwest Center, 90 South Seventh Street - Minneapolis, MN 55402 - Phone: (612) 336-3000, Fax: (612) 336-3026 - *See complete biographical profile in Arts, Entertainment, Advertising & Media Law Chapter.*

BRUCE H. LITTLE - Popham, Haik, Schnobrich & Kaufman, Ltd. - 222 South Ninth Street, Suite 3300 - Minneapolis, MN 55402 - Phone: (612) 333-4800, Fax: (612) 334-8888 - *See complete biographical profile in Arts, Entertainment, Advertising & Media Law Chapter.*

•**LAWRENCE M. NAWROCKI:** Mr. Nawrocki has been registered to practice and represent clients before the US Patent and Trademark Office since 1979. He renders counsel in establishing, protecting, and seeking redress for violations of legal rights in the fields of patent, copyright, and trademark. He advises, counsels, and negotiates transfer of intellectual property rights by way of assignment and/or license.
Education: JD 1979 cum laude, William Mitchell; BS 1968, US Naval Academy.
Employment History: Attorney 1993-present, Nawrocki, Rooney & Sivertson, P.A.; Attorney 1983-93, Lawrence M. Nawrocki & Associates, Ltd.; 1979-82, Merchant & Gould.
Representative Clients: Crown Iron Works Company; Marvin Windows & Doors; JohnsTech International; Tandem Products, Inc.; Fargo Electronics, Inc.
Professional Associations: MSBA; Minnesota Intellectual Property Law Assn.; American Intellectual Property Law Assn.
Firm: Nawrocki, Rooney & Sivertson, P.A., counsels clients with regard to all aspects of intellectual property law. The firm employs attorneys who are experienced in all technological areas, and expertise is available, therefore, to represent clients in virtually every field of invention. A broad range of experience in the trademark area is available in the firm. Nawrocki, Rooney & Sivertson also offers in-depth experience in the licensing area.

LAWRENCE M. NAWROCKI

Nawrocki, Rooney & Sivertson, P.A.
401 Broadway Place East
3433 Broadway Street NE
Minneapolis, MN 55413

Phone: (612) 331-1464
Fax: (612) 331-2239

Admitted: 1979 Minnesota; 1979 US Dist. Ct. (MN); 1982 US Ct. App. (8th Cir.); 1979 US Patent & Trademark Office
Birthdate: 10/31/46

Z. PETER SAWICKI

Kinney & Lange, P.A.
625 Fourth Avenue South
Suite 1500
Minneapolis, MN 55415-1659

Phone: (612) 339-1863
Fax: (612) 339-6580

Admitted: 1980 Minnesota;
1981 US Patent & Trademark Office;
1981 US Dist. Ct. (MN);
1981 US Ct. App. (8th Cir.);
1982 US Ct. App. (Fed Cir.);
1994 Canadian Patent Office
Birthdate: 04/13/49

•**Z. PETER SAWICKI:** With more than 14 years of intellectual property law experience, Peter focuses on patent prosecution in both the United States and foreign countries, trademark registration in the United States and foreign countries, and licensing of patents and trademarks. His patent prosecution practice is primarily concentrated in the chemical, mechanical, medical, food technology, and electromechanical technology arts. He is a member of the Board of Directors of the Orono Hockey Boosters Association and is an American Legion member.

Education: JD 1980, Hamline University; MBA 1977, College of St. Thomas; BSChE 1972, Purdue University.

Representative Clients: Land O'Lakes, Inc.; 3M; BMC Industries, Inc.; Luigino's, Inc.; First Team Sports, Inc.; Mentor Corp.; Laser Machining, Inc.; Federated Mutual Insurance Co.; Interplastics Corp.; Resistance Technology, Inc.; Minnesota Scientific, Inc.; Complast, Inc.; Wizard Works, Inc.; Zumbro, Inc.

Professional Associations: ABA; AIPLA; MN Intellectual Property Law Assn. (past Treasurer); International Trademark Assn.; MSBA; HCBA; Delta Theta Phi Legal Fraternity.

Firm: Kinney & Lange, P.A., is an energetic, full service intellectual property law firm practicing patent, trademark, copyright, licensing, unfair competition, advertising, and franchise law. Kinney & Lange litigates and resolves intellectual property disputes in federal and state courts, the United States Patent and Trademark Office, foreign patent offices and courts, the International Trade Commission, and arbitration tribunals. Kinney & Lange attorneys are skilled in a variety of trade and technical areas, including avionics, digital circuits, computer hardware and software, semiconductors, biomedical devices, food technology, cryogenics, biochemistry, microbiology, virology, organic chemistry, plastics, petroleum refining, advertising, publishing, and franchising. Kinney & Lange's clients range from multinational corporations to small and start-up businesses. *See additional listing in Arts, Entertainment, Advertising & Media Law Chapter.*

CECIL C. SCHMIDT

Merchant, Gould, Smith, Edell, Welter & Schmidt, P.A.
1000 Norwest Center
55 East Fifth Street
St. Paul, MN 55101-1785

Phone: (612) 298-1055
Fax: (612) 298-1160

Admitted: 1965 Minnesota;
1966 US Patent and Trademark Office
Birthdate: 08/14/36

•**CECIL C. SCHMIDT:** Mr. Schmidt's practice emphasizes technology transfer (domestic and foreign) and strategic business planning with regard to maximizing the value of intellectual property assets, negotiations, licensing, and employer/employee problems involving inventions and trade secrets. His experience is extensive in domestic and foreign technology transfer, including such diverse matters as the licensing of technology from the former USSR and the establishment of joint ventures in the Far East. Mr. Schmidt is an author and lecturer on various areas of intellectual property law.

Education: JD 1965, Georgetown University; ChE 1959, University of Cincinnati (Tau Beta Pi, Phi Lambda Upsilon).

Employment History: 1968-present, Merchant, Gould, Smith, Edell, Welter & Schmidt; 1966-68, Law Department, Archer Daniels Midland Company (Minneapolis, MN); Patent Office Manager 1964-65, Archer Daniels Midland Company (Washington, D.C.); 1961-64, Patent and Licensing Department, Esso Research and Engineering Company (now known as Exxon) (Washington, D.C.); 1959-61, active service as a commissioned officer with the Army Security Agency; 1959, Patent and Licensing Department, Esso Research and Engineering Company (Elizabeth, NJ).

Representative Clients: Andersen Corp.; Multi-Arc Scientific Coatings; Trail King Industries; H.B. Fuller Company; Ecolab; North Dakota State University; Spinal Designs International.

Professional Associations: Society of International Business Fellows; ABA; MSBA; Minnesota Intellectual Property Law Assn.

Community Involvement: SEED (Cofounder and President); Northern Pines of Minnesota, Inc. (Trustee).

Firm: Merchant, Gould, Smith, Edell, Welter & Schmidt is engaged exclusively in the practice of intellectual property law, including patent, trademark, copyright, unfair competition, trade secret, advertising and computer law, and related litigation including both trials and appeals. With offices in Minneapolis, St. Paul, and Los Angeles and more than 70 practicing attorneys, the firm is one of the largest intellectual property law firms in the United States.

•**DOUGLAS A. STRAWBRIDGE:** Mr. Strawbridge's expertise is in general intellectual property counseling, including patentability studies, new product clearance studies, trademark clearance and registrability studies, and due diligence studies in connection with acquisition and licensing of intellectual property rights. Mr. Strawbridge practices before the US Patent and Trademark Office in connection with the preparation and prosecution of applications for patent, trademark registrations, and reissue and reexamination of patents. His practice also includes civil litigation, representing both plaintiffs and defendants in intellectual property disputes.
Education: JD 1976 cum laude, University of Minnesota; BS 1973 with distinction, University of Colorado, Purdue (Tau Beta Pi).
Employment History: 1976-present, Merchant, Gould, Smith, Edell, Welter & Schmidt; Law Clerk 1974, Corporate Legal Department, TRW, Inc.
Representative Clients: Minnesota Mining & Manufacturing Company; Andersen Corp.; Genmar, Inc.; Smead Manufacturing, Inc.; Anchor Wall Systems, Inc.
Professional Associations: HCBA; MSBA; MN Intellectual Property Assn.; American Intellectual Property Assn.; United States Trademark Assn.; Federal Circuit Bar Assn.; Federal Bar Assn.; ABA.
Community Involvement: Minneapolis Rotary; St. Alban's Church (Outreach Committee); Edina Elementary Girls' Basketball (assistant coach); Braemar Men's Club.
Firm: Merchant, Gould, Smith, Edell, Welter & Schmidt is engaged exclusively in the practice of intellectual property law, including patent, trademark, copyright, unfair competition, trade secret, advertising and computer law, and related litigation including both trials and appeals. With offices in Minneapolis, St. Paul, and Los Angeles and more than 70 practicing attorneys, the firm is one of the largest intellectual property law firms in the United States.

DOUGLAS A. STRAWBRIDGE

Merchant, Gould, Smith, Edell, Welter & Schmidt, P.A.
3100 Norwest Center
90 South Seventh Street
Minneapolis, MN 55402-4131

Phone: (612) 332-5300
Fax: (612) 332-9081

Admitted: 1976 Minnesota; 1977 US Patent & Trademark Office
Birthdate: 04/05/51

•**JOHN S. SUMNERS:** Mr. Sumners' expertise is in general intellectual property practice and counseling, including practice before the US Patent and Trademark Office; practice before the US Copyright Office; securing and maintaining US and international patents, trademark registrations, and copyright registrations; business planning pertaining to intellectual property rights; and licensing and enforcement of patent, trademark, copyright, and trade secret rights. Mr. Sumners presents continuing legal education seminars on intellectual property law and is a former adjunct professor of copyright law at William Mitchell College of Law (1986-90).
Education: LLB 1965, University of Arizona; BS 1962, Arizona State University.
Employment History: 1969-present, Merchant, Gould, Smith, Edell, Welter & Schmidt; 1965-69, Patent Department, Honeywell, Inc.
Representative Clients: Apothecary Products, Inc.; Augsburg Fortress Publishers; Avon Plastics, Inc.; Bachman's, Inc.; Bankers Systems, Inc.; Black Hills Jewelry Manufacturing Company; Dahlberg, Inc.; Department 56, Inc.; Garrison Keillor; Grow Biz International, Inc.; Intek Weatherseal Products, Inc.; ME International; Minnesota Communications Group; Minnesota Monthly Publications, Inc.; Minnesota Public Radio; MNN Radio Networks, Inc.; Paper Warehouse Franchising, Inc.; Rivertown Trading Company; Rocco Altobelli, Inc.; TCF Bank FSB; Tiro Industries, Inc.; TREND Enterprises, Inc.
Professional Associations: ABA; MSBA; HCBA; American Intellectual Property Law Assn.; MN Intellectual Property Law Assn.; International Trademark Assn.
Community Involvement: Lecturer on various areas of intellectual property law to business and community organizations; Bible Study Fellowship; church organist.
Firm: Merchant, Gould, Smith, Edell, Welter & Schmidt is engaged exclusively in the practice of intellectual property law, including patent, trademark, copyright, unfair competition, trade secret, advertising and computer law, and related litigation including both trials and appeals. With offices in Minneapolis, St. Paul, and Los Angeles and more than 70 practicing attorneys, the firm is one of the largest intellectual property law firms in the United States. *See additional listing in Arts, Entertainment, Advertising & Media Law Chapter.*

JOHN S. SUMNERS

Merchant, Gould, Smith, Edell, Welter & Schmidt, P.A.
3100 Norwest Center
90 South Seventh Street
Minneapolis, MN 55402-4131

Phone: (612) 332-5300
Fax: (612) 332-9081

Admitted: 1965 Minnesota; 1966 US Patent & Trademark Office
Birthdate: 12/16/39

THOMAS W. TINKHAM - Dorsey & Whitney - Pillsbury Center South, 220 South Sixth Street - Minneapolis, MN 55402-1498 - Phone: (612) 340-2829, Fax: (612) 340-2807 - *See complete biographical profile in Commercial Litigation Chapter.*

PAUL VAN VALKENBURG - Moss & Barnett, A Professional Association - 4800 Norwest Center, 90 South Seventh Street - Minneapolis, MN 55402 - Phone: (612) 347-0300, Fax: (612) 339-6686 - *See complete biographical profile in Publicly Held Corporations Law Chapter.*

Chapter 22: Intellectual Property Law

NICKOLAS E. WESTMAN

Westman, Champlin & Kelly, P.A.
720 TCF Tower
121 South Eighth Street
Minneapolis, MN 55402

Phone: (612) 334-3222
Fax: (612) 334-3312

Admitted: 1960 Minnesota; 1960 US Dist. Ct. (MN); 1960 US Patent & Trademark Office; 1975 US Ct. App. (8th Cir.); 1978 US Sup. Ct.; 1982 US Ct. App. (Fed. Cir.)
Birthdate: 06/22/32

•**NICKOLAS E. WESTMAN:** Mr. Westman is President of the firm of Westman, Champlin & Kelly, P.A. He has over 30 years of experience in intellectual property law, working in the fields of patents and trademarks. Mr. Westman has prepared and prosecuted patent and trademark applications in the United States and all major foreign countries. He also advises clients on licensing and infringement matters.
Education: LLB 1959, William Mitchell; BS 1954, North Dakota State University (Tau Beta Pi, honorary engineering fraternity).
Employment History: President 1993-present, Westman, Champlin & Kelly, P.A.; 1978-93, Kinney & Lange, P.A.; 1968-78, Dugger Johnson & Westman; 1962-68, Dugger Braddock Johnson & Westman.
Representative Clients: Rosemount, Inc.; Rosemount Aerospace, Inc.; Melroe Company; MTS Systems Corporation; University of Minnesota; Kurt Manufacturing Company; Communication Systems Incorporated; Seagate Technology Incorporated.
Professional Associations: ABA; MSBA; HCBA; American Intellectual Property Law Assn.; Minnesota Intellectual Property Law Assn. (President 1985); Licensing Executives Society.
Firm: Westman, Champlin & Kelly, P.A., provides intellectual property law services focusing on patent and trademark prosecution and copyrights. The firm members are all admitted to practice before the US Patent and Trademark Office. Firm technical background and experience is concentrated on high technology electronic, software, and computer related inventions, and also mechanical and electromechanical inventions. The firm has associates for handling intellectual property matters in all major countries of the world. Prompt, efficient, and reasonably priced services are stressed.

DOUGLAS J. WILLIAMS

Merchant, Gould, Smith, Edell, Welter & Schmidt, P.A.
3100 Norwest Center
90 South Seventh Street
Minneapolis, MN 55402-4131

Phone: (612) 332-5300
Fax: (612) 332-9081

Admitted: 1974 Iowa; 1974 Texas; 1975 Minnesota; 1973 US Patent & Trademark Office
Birthdate: 06/19/50

•**DOUGLAS J. WILLIAMS:** Mr. Williams is Chair of Merchant & Gould's Litigation Practice Group. His practice includes extensive patent litigation experience in various technical disciplines, substantial defense work in patent jury trials in various courts throughout the country, work with trademark and corporate identification development and enforcement programs, and experience with entertainment and the arts. Mr. Williams is the author of various works on copyright protection and a lecturer on intellectual property litigation.
Education: JD 1974, Drake University (1973-74, *Drake Law Review*); BS 1971, University of Iowa.
Employment History: 1975-present, Merchant, Gould, Smith, Edell, Welter & Schmidt; 1974, Exxon Company U.S.A. (Houston, TX).
Representative Clients: Ecolab, Inc.; Dial Corp.; Travellers Express Co.; Major League Baseball Promotions, Inc.; Minnesota Twins.
Community Involvement: Legal Advice Clinics (volunteer attorney and Board member).
Firm: Merchant, Gould, Smith, Edell, Welter & Schmidt is engaged exclusively in the practice of intellectual property law, including patent, trademark, copyright, unfair competition, trade secret, advertising and computer law, and related litigation including both trials and appeals. With offices in Minneapolis, St. Paul, and Los Angeles and more than 70 practicing attorneys, the firm is one of the largest intellectual property law firms in the United States. *See additional listing in Arts, Entertainment, Advertising & Media Law Chapter.*

Complete listing of all attorneys nominated in Intellectual Property Law

HERMAN H. BAINS, Attorney at Law, Minneapolis; RONALD J. BROWN, Dorsey & Whitney, Minneapolis; ALAN G. CARLSON, Merchant, Gould, Smith, Edell, Welter & Schmidt, P.A., Minneapolis; MICHAEL V. CIRESI, Robins, Kaplan, Miller & Ciresi, Minneapolis; ROBERT T. EDELL, Merchant, Gould, Smith, Edell, Welter & Schmidt, P.A., Minneapolis; DAVID R. FAIRBAIRN, Kinney & Lange, P.A., Minneapolis; NORMAN P. FRIEDERICHS, Attorney at Law, Minneapolis; JOHN D. GOULD, Merchant, Gould, Smith, Edell, Welter & Schmidt, P.A., Minneapolis; CURTIS B. HAMRE, Merchant, Gould, Smith, Edell, Welter & Schmidt, P.A., Minneapolis; ORRIN M. HAUGEN, Haugen & Nikolai, P.A., Minneapolis; STUART R. HEMPHILL, Dorsey & Whitney, Minneapolis; EUGENE L. JOHNSON, Dorsey & Whitney, Minneapolis; D. RANDALL KING, Merchant, Gould, Smith, Edell, Welter & Schmidt, P.A., Minneapolis; W. CHARLES LANTZ, Dorsey & Whitney, Rochester; DEXTER A. LARSEN, Fryberger, Buchanan, Smith & Frederick, P.A., Duluth; MALCOLM L. MOORE, Moore & Hansen, Minneapolis; LAWRENCE M. NAWROCKI, Nawrocki, Rooney & Sivertson, P.A., Minneapolis; THOMAS J. NIKOLAI, Haugen & Nikolai, P.A., Minneapolis; HAROLD R. PATTON, Medtronic Legal Department, Minneapolis; Z. PETER SAWICKI, Kinney & Lange, P.A., Minneapolis; CECIL C. SCHMIDT, Merchant, Gould, Smith, Edell, Welter & Schmidt, P.A., St. Paul; DOUGLAS A. STRAWBRIDGE, Merchant, Gould, Smith, Edell, Welter & Schmidt, P.A., Minneapolis; JOHN S. SUMNERS, Merchant, Gould, Smith, Edell, Welter & Schmidt, P.A., Minneapolis; ROBERT O. VIDAS, Vidas, Arrett & Steinkraus, P.A., Minneapolis; NICKOLAS E. WESTMAN, Westman, Champlin & Kelly, P.A., Minneapolis; DOUGLAS J. WILLIAMS, Merchant, Gould, Smith, Edell, Welter & Schmidt, P.A., Minneapolis.

CHAPTER 23

INTERNATIONAL BUSINESS LAW

The days when international transactions and business deals were only the realm of huge multinational corporations are over. Today even a sole proprietorship can obtain a license to buy or sell his or her products and services across national boundaries, just like a mega-conglomerate. There is no simple way to sum up all of the regulations that a company might encounter doing business abroad because there are so many foreign countries, each with unique import/export laws, corporate structures, and cultural norms. At the very least, a U.S. company involved in an international business transaction will be bound by regulations of the United States (the home country), the regulations of the country in which the business is conducted (the host country), and international regulations, which are derived from a variety of sources. This chapter will offer a brief sketch of where and how international businesses are most likely to encounter the legal system.

HOME COUNTRY LAWS

The United States has many laws governing the international transactions in goods and services. Among these laws are export controls, import controls, and the Foreign Corrupt Practices Act.

EXPORT CONTROLS

Generally speaking, United States government regulations make it much easier for businesses to export than to import. Exports are commonly thought to be beneficial for the domestic economy so the government does not want to impede them. Most government involvement in exports is for the purpose of encouraging a greater volume of exports to existing trade partners, tearing down barriers to American exports, and helping businesses find new markets for their products. Nonetheless, controls are sometimes placed on exports to protect national security, advance foreign policy, or protect the domestic economy from the drain of materials in short supply. Export controls include requirements that persons acquire a license to export certain high technology items or other goods that might be used for military or other strategic purposes. In order to export certain sensitive items, it may be necessary for the exporter to make known or "certify" the country of destination of goods for which a license is required.

Most export controls are overseen by the Bureau of Export Administration, an arm of the United States Department of Commerce. Department of Commerce officials are an excellent source of information on complying with general export regulations and licensing procedures.

Certain classes of exports administered by other federal agencies include:

- Endangered fish, wildlife, migratory birds, bald eagles, and golden eagles—Exports are controlled by the Department of the Interior

- Tobacco seed or any live tobacco product—Exports are controlled by the Department of Agriculture

- Arms, ammunition, instruments of war—Exports are controlled by the Department of State, Office of Defense Trade Controls

- Narcotics and dangerous drugs—Exports are controlled by the Department of Justice, Drug Enforcement Administration

Import Controls

As mentioned above, the federal government offers substantially more help to exporters than it offers to importers. A bewildering variety of government agencies are involved in one or more aspects of United States import policies and it can be confusing to know which agency or agencies need to approve an import before it can be legally brought into the country. The United States Customs Service assesses and collects duties, taxes, and fees on most imported goods, enforces customs and related laws, and administers certain navigation laws and treaties. The Customs Service publishes several general guides to help importers understand United States import regulations. These guides are available from regional offices in Minneapolis and Duluth. A number of categories of imports are subject to special treatment before they can be brought into this country:

Agricultural Products

- Cheese, milk, and dairy products—Most dairy products are required to have special import licenses, and are subject to quotas administered by the Department of Agriculture's Foreign Agricultural Service. Milk and cream imports must also meet the requirements of the Food, Drug, and Cosmetic Act and the Import Milk Act. Milk and cream importers need permits from the Department of Health and Human Services, Food and Drug Administration, and the Department of Agriculture.

- Fruits, Vegetable, and Nuts—Many agricultural commodities must meet detailed import requirements related to size, grade, quality, and maturity. Commodities must pass inspection before they are allowed into the United States. Inspection certificates are issued by the Food Safety and Quality Service of the Department of Agriculture. General inquiries about importing fruits, vegetables and nuts can be directed to the Agriculture Marketing Service of the Department of Agriculture, Washington, D.C. 20250.

- Insects—All insects which could be harmful to domestic crops or trees are forbidden entry into the United States unless they are for scientific research. Insects which could not be harmful to domestic crops can be imported only with special approval from the Animal and Plant Health Inspection Service of the Department of Agriculture.

- Livestock and Animals—The Animal and Plant Health Inspection Service imposes a variety of inspection and quarantine requirements on most livestock and animal by-products. Permits for importation into the United States must be obtained before the item is shipped from its country of origin. Only certain ports of entry into the United States are set up to handle animal inspection and quarantine, so arrangement should be made well in advance to ensure that a desired point of entry can perform the appropriate inspection and quarantine. Exceptions to most of these inspection and quarantine requirements are available for imports from Canadian provinces and certain northern Mexican states.

- Meat and Meat Products—Commercial shipments of meat and meat products are regulated by the Department of Agriculture and must be inspected by both the Animal and Plant Health Inspection Service of the Department and the Food Safety and Inspection Service of the Department before they are permitted entry into the United States. Noncommercial shipments of meat are regulated by the Federal Food, Drug, and Cosmetic Act, which is enforced by the Food and Drug Administration.

- Plant and Plant Products—The Department of Agriculture regulates the importation of plants and plant products. Certain endangered species may require special inspection and approval or may be denied entry altogether.

- Poultry and Poultry Products—Imports of poultry and poultry products, including eggs are controlled by the Animal and Plant Health Inspection Service and the Food Safety and Quality Service of the Department of Agriculture. Permits, special markings, labeling, and in some cases foreign inspection certificates are required. Inquiries about other birds can be made to the Fish and Wildlife Service, Washington, D.C. 20240.

- Seeds—Imports of seeds are governed by the Federal Seed Act of 1939 and regulations of the Agricultural Marketing Service of the Department of Agriculture.

Arms, Ammunition, and Radioactive Materials

- Arms, Ammunitions, Explosives, and instruments of war—All of these imports are severely limited and can only be brought into the United States with express permission and license of the Bureau of Alcohol, Tobacco and Firearms of the Department of the Treasury. Even temporary importation or transit across the territory of the United States is prohibited without a license from the Office of Munitions Control, Department of State, Washington, D.C. 20520.

- Radioactive Materials—Most radioactive materials are subject to regulation by the Nuclear Regulatory Commission. License to import these items into the United States can be granted by the Nuclear Regulatory Commission, Washington, D.C. 20520.

Consumer Products

- Appliances—Household appliances must meet energy efficiency standards set by the Department of Energy, Consumer Products Efficiency Branch before they can be brought into the country. In addition, the Federal Trade Commission, Division for Energy and Product Information sets standards for labeling household appliances. Importers intending to bring any common household appliance into the United States should contact both of these agencies for the requirements in effect at the desired date of importation.

- Flammable Fabrics—Fabrics intended for wearing apparel or interior decoration must meet strict standards for non-flammability set by the United States Consumer Products Safety Commission. Some products that do not meet these standards can be brought into the country with special permission, provided they are intended for finishing or processing that will make them meet federal non-flammability standards.

- Radiation Producing Products—Many radiation producing products, such as television sets, microwave ovens, sunlamps, and ultrasound equipment are subject to radiation performance standards set by the Radiation Control for Health and Safety Act of 1968. Any product with a performance standard set by the Act can only be imported into the United States with the permission of the Food and Drug Administration, National Center for Devices and Radiological Health, 1390 Picard Drive, Rockville, MD 20850.

- Radio Frequency Devices—Radios, televisions, tape recorders, and other radio frequency emitting devices can only be imported with documentation from the Federal Communications Commission (FCC) that they are in conformity with, will soon be in conformity with, or are exempt from FCC requirements.

Food, Drugs, Cosmetics and Medical Products

- Foods and Cosmetics—Imports of most foods, beverages, and cosmetics are controlled by the Food and Drug Administration of the Department of Health and Human Services, Rockville, MD 20857. Imports of products regulated by the Food and Drug Administration are subject to inspection, and possible detention, at the border. Prohibited products are any products that are defective, unsafe, filthy, produced under unsanitary conditions, or branded in such a way that they are false, misleading, or improperly labeled. Seafoods are subject to additional standards set by the National Marine Fisheries Service of the Department of Commerce, Washington D.C. 20910.

- Biological Drugs—Import of biological products for human use is regulated by the Public Health Service Act. Foreign producers intending to send their products to the United States must obtain licenses for both their facility and individual shipments from the Food and Drug Administration, Department of Health and Human Services, Rockville, MD 20857. Biological drugs for animal use are regulated by the Virus Serum Toxin Act, which is enforced by the Department of Agriculture. The Virus Serum Toxin Act requires special permits and labels before biological drugs for animal use may be imported into the United States.

- Drug Paraphernalia—Imports are prohibited under the United States Code. Penalties for illegal imports of drug paraphernalia include both jail time and fines. Prohibited items include water pipes, roach clips, miniature spoons, bongs, and cocaine freebase kits.

Gold, Silver, Currency, and Stamps

- Gold and Silver—Imports of gold and silver are subject to detailed quality and marking regulations established by the National Stamping Act and enforced by the Department of Justice, Washington, D.C. 20530.

- Monetary Instruments—Anyone importing into the United States or receiving from overseas more than $10,000 in monetary instruments, including currency, travelers checks, money orders, and negotiable instruments or investment securities must file a report of the transaction with the Customs Service at the point of entry.

- Postage Stamps—It is illegal to import facsimiles of United States postage stamps, unless they are intended for philatelic, educational, historical, or newsworthy purposes. Further information on these regulations can be obtained by contacting the United States Secret Service of the Department of the Treasury, Washington, D.C. 20223.

Pesticides, and Toxic and Hazardous Substances

- Pesticides—Pesticides, fungicides, herbicides, and rodenticides are governed by the Insecticide, Fungicide, and Rodenticide Act of 1947 and the Federal Environment Pesticide Control Act of 1972. All imports of these substances must be registered with the Environmental Protection Agency's Office of Pesticides and Toxic Substances, Washington, D.C. The registration can be completed in advance of shipment. If the shipment is approved by the Agency, the Office of Pesticides and Toxic Substances provides the importer with a Notice of Arrival that must be presented to Customs officials in order for the items to be released from Customs custody.

- Hazardous Substances—Several federal regulations govern imports of hazardous substances packaged for household use. Marking, labeling, and packaging regulations are enforced by the Department of Transportation, Office of Hazardous Materials Transportation, Washington, D.C. 20590.

- Toxic Substances—The Toxic Substances Control Act regulates imports of chemical substances that pose an unreasonable risk of injury to health or the environment. Customs officers are required to impound all imports of toxic substances until the importer can show proof of compliance with or exemption from the requirements of the Toxic Substances Control Act.

Textiles, Wool, and Fur

- Textiles—Textile fiber products imported into the United States are subject to identification and marking requirements set forth in the Textile Fiber Products Identification Act. More information on the Act and regulations promulgated under it can be obtained from the Federal Trade Commission, Washington, D.C. 20580.

- Wool Products—Wool products are regulated by the Wool Products Labeling Act of 1939. The Act requires most wool imports to be clearly labeled to show the total wool weight and content of the product. Pamphlets describing the requirements of the Act can be obtained by contacting the Federal Trade Commission, Washington, D.C. 20580.

- Fur Products—Most fur imports are subject to regulation under the Fur Products Labeling Act. Detailed descriptions of the Act and its requirements can be obtained from the Federal Trade Commission, Washington, D.C. 20580.

Subjects of Voluntary Restraint Agreements

Voluntary Restraint Agreements limit exports to the United States of certain products from certain countries. An example of such an agreement is the limit on steel and machine tools manufactured in Japan and South Korea. Voluntary Restraint Agreements are reached through trade negotiations between the United States government and representatives of foreign countries. The Department of Commerce administers these programs and an export certificate or license from the country of origin is required before the item is permitted entry into the United States.

FOREIGN CORRUPT PRACTICES ACT

The Foreign Corrupt Practices Act (FCPA) is a federal act that forbids any United States citizen or resident of the United States from giving or offering to give gifts, bribes, or anything of value to a foreign official or political figure in an attempt to influence any decision. The text and intent of the FCPA are quite simple but both have been criticized severely by many American business leaders as naive and an unnecessary handicap to American business efforts abroad. Many people believe the FCPA is an awkward, even elitist attempt to impose American values onto foreign transactions that occur in dramatically different cultures. Even the law itself recognizes the difficulty of imposing American ethical norms on overseas transactions. Thus, the law contains an exception for payments made to foreign government officials if the money or goods are "facilitive payments for routine government action." The boundaries of what items constitute "facilitative payments" or what actions are "routine government actions" are hazy at best. Business leaders concerned with how a transaction might be viewed under the FCPA should consult legal counsel experienced in this often confusing area.

HOST COUNTRY LAWS

Host countries have their own laws which U.S. companies must obey when doing business in that country. There can be a variety of tax consequences, restrictions on the movement of capital, merger restrictions and financial disclosure legislation. Furthermore, in some countries a company's capital and property can be nationalized with few, if any, due process protections. American businesses trying to establish a presence in Russia have firsthand experience with what it is like to make deals in a country where laws and monetary exchange rates can change dramatically from day to day.

This chapter cannot summarize all the laws an American business might encounter doing business internationally. However, the United States Department of Commerce operates a Trade Information Center in Washington, D.C. that counsels American businesses wanting to do business overseas. The Trade Information Center can be reached at (800) 872-8723. The Department of Commerce also operates a National Trade Data Bank which collects information on trade with specific countries. The National Trade Data Bank can be reached at (202) 482-1986. The Department of Commerce can direct interested business persons to one of over a hundred different Country Desk Officers who specialize in advising businesses and individuals on a particular country's economy, trade policies, political situation, and United States government policies toward that country.

INTERNATIONAL LAW

A wide variety of international codes and laws regulate international sales. For example, the Convention on International Sale of Goods is similar to the United States Uniform Commercial Code, but does have some significant differences. In addition to the Convention on International Sale of Goods, there are codes of conduct for international businesses which, although not enforced by any one legal body, are generally adhered to by many parties actively engaged in international business. The sources described above for finding more information on host country laws can also be excellent sources of information on international laws applicable to trade with a particular nation or part of the world.

INTERNATIONAL CONTRACT CONSIDERATIONS

Contracts are the basis on which international trade is conducted. In an environment where currencies fluctuate daily, the language may not be English, and the issue of which country's laws are to be followed is not always clear, contracts are vital. Many of the contracts entered into are similar to those used in every domestic business such as employment contracts, distributorship contracts and purchasing contracts. However, there are some issues which are of particular concern in the international arena. For example, an international contract should specify which language will be used to conduct business and specify a set rate of exchange between currencies. In addition, because international business dealings involve governmental regulation at several levels, it is common to include a government approval clause in contracts. Such a clause states which partner in the contract is responsible for obtaining any governmental permission needed for the transaction.

Some preparation must also be made for the handling of any disputes which may arise between the parties. A contract may specify that parties will attempt arbitration before any lawsuit is filed in the event of a grievance. Contracts may also include a choice of forum or a choice of law clause. The former signifies a country in which a lawsuit will be brought in case of a dispute. The latter denotes a set of laws that are to be followed to settle a grievance, regardless of where the grievance occurs.

INTERNATIONAL LETTER OF CREDIT

In some international negotiations, a letter of credit may be necessary to help facilitate the transaction. Unlike most domestic transactions where buyer and seller typically know each other or have easy access to reliable financial data about one another, such as a credit report, in many international transactions buyer and seller know very little about each other and may have a difficult time learning more about each other. The seller may not know how creditworthy a buyer is or how shifts in exchange rates could alter the terms of the agreement. A buyer may not know the seller's reputation for quality and timeliness or whether the seller will be able to handle customs formalities sufficiently well to ship the product to the buyer. Because they are far apart, neither may be able to get adequate assurance from the other without help from third parties. This is usually accomplished through use of letters of credit.

The term "letter of credit" is actually a shorthand way of referring to a complex set of agreements and documents whereby a bank assumes responsibility for paying the seller for the good and for assuring that the good was properly shipped. In a typical letter of credit transaction the buyer contracts with its bank to issue a letter of credit to the seller. The letter of credit is a promise from the bank to pay an amount to the seller if and only if the seller can produce adequate documentation (such as invoices, bills of lading, inspection certificates) proving that the good was shipped properly and will be received as agreed upon. The buyer and its bank make a separate arrangement between them so the bank is reimbursed. In some transactions the seller's bank will also be involved in guaranteeing payment to the seller if seller provides adequate documentation as described above.

RESOURCES

United States Department of Commerce, US & FCS District Office, 108 Federal Building, 110 South Fourth Street, Minneapolis, MN 55401, (612) 349-3338.

United States Small Business Administration, 100 North Sixth Street, Suite 610, Minneapolis, MN 55403, (612) 349-3550.

Minnesota Export Finance Authority, 90 West Plato Boulevard, St. Paul, MN 55107, (612) 297-4659.

Minnesota World Trade Association, 33 Wentworth Avenue, Suite 101, West St. Paul, MN 55118, phone: (612) 457-1035.

Minnesota Trade Office, 90 West Plato Boulevard, St. Paul, MN 55107, (612) 297-4222.

International Trade for the Nonspecialist, Paul H. Vishny, editor, American Law Institute-American Bar Association Committee for Continuing Professional Education, Philadelphia, PA, 1992.

How to Succeed in Exporting and Doing Business Internationally. Eric Sletten, John Wiley & Sons, Inc., New York, NY., 1994.

Start Your Own Import/Export Business. JoAnn Padgett editor, Pfeiffer & Company, San Diego, CA, 1994.

Building an Import Export Business. Kenneth D. Weiss, John Wiley & Sons, Inc., New York, NY 1987.

A Basic Guide to Exporting. United States Department of Commerce, NTC Business Books, Lincolnwood, IL, 1993.

Importing into the United States, Revised second edition. The Official U.S. Customs Service Guide to Importing into the United States, Prima Publishing, Rocklin, CA, 1992.

INTERNATIONAL BUSINESS LAW LEADING ATTORNEYS

The attorneys profiled in this section were nominated by their peers in a statewide survey conducted in 1993 in which several thousand Minnesota attorneys were asked to name the lawyer to whom they would send a friend or family member in need of legal assistance in the area of *International Business Law*.

Because the survey resulted in a list of less than five percent of Minnesota's practicing attorneys, this should not be construed as a complete list. Nevertheless, it is an excellent source of highly qualified and reputable attorneys, who, if unable to assist can in most cases make quality referrals.

A list of all attorneys nominated in this category is found at the end of this section. For information on the survey methodology see page ix.

Please note that the shorter, two line attorney listings in this section are of attorneys who practice in this area but whose full biographical profile appears in another section of this book. A bullet "•" preceeding name indicates the attorney was nominated in this particular area of law. For information on the format of these profiles, consult the section "Using the *Business Guidebook*" found on page xiv. Note that the following abbreviations are used throughout these profiles:

The attorneys profiled below were recommended by their peers in a statewide survey.

App.	- Appellate	ABA	- American Bar Association
Cir.	- Circuit	ATLA	- American Trial Lawyers Association
Ct.	- Court	HCBA	- Hennepin County Bar Association
Dist.	- District	MDLA	- Minnesota Defense Lawyers Association
Hon.	- Honorable	MSBA	- Minnesota State Bar Association
JD	- Law degree (Juris Doctor)	MTLA	- Minnesota Trial Lawyers Association
LLB	- Law degree	NBTA	- National Board of Trial Advocacy
LLM	- Master in Law degree	RCBA	- Ramsey County Bar Association
Sup.	- Supreme		

RICHARD L. BREITMAN - The Breitman Immigration Law Firm - 701 Fourth Avenue, Suite 1700 - Minneapolis, MN 55415-1818 - Phone: (612) 822-4724, Fax: (612) 339-8375 - *See complete biographical profile in Immigration Law Chapter.*

STEVEN E. CARLSON

Dorsey & Whitney
3 Gracechurch Street
London, England EC 3V OAT

Phone: 011-4471-929-3334
Fax: 011-4471-929-3111

Admitted: 1985 Minnesota;
1978 New York;
1978 US Dist. Ct. (NY)
Birthdate: 06/15/52

•**STEVEN E. CARLSON:** Mr. Carlson practices in the areas of banking and international financial and commercial matters. He provides legal assistance to financial institutions and corporations in connection with a wide variety of financial and commercial transactions and bank regulatory matters. Mr. Carlson has been in the London office since 1994 and has been head of the International Practice Group since 1993. He was chair of the Banking and Commercial Department in Minneapolis from 1989-93.
Education: JD 1977 with honors, Columbia University (Editor-in-Chief 1976-77, *Columbia Journal of Transnational Law*); BA 1973 magna cum laude, special distinction, Yale University.
Employment History: Partner 1987-present, Associate 1985-86, Dorsey & Whitney; Assistant General Counsel for the Private Enterprise Bureau 1983-85, Regional Legal Advisor (Tunisia) 1980-82, and Attorney-Advisor (Washington, D.C.) 1979-80, US Agency for International Development (Superior Honor Awards from US AID for work on Private Enterprise and Near Eastern matters); Associate 1977-79, Cleary, Gottlieb, Steen & Hamilton.
Professional Associations: MSBA; American Society of International Law; Council on Foreign Relations (New York, NY); St. Paul-Minneapolis Committee on Foreign Relations.
Community Involvement: Minnesota Advocates for Human Rights (Director 1990-93); Mondale Policy Forum, University of Minnesota (Fellow 1990-91); Export Legal Assistance Network (Minnesota Coordinator 1985-90); Minnesota World Trade Assn. (Director 1988-89).
Firm: Dorsey & Whitney is the largest law firm in Minnesota and one of the largest firms in the United States with over 350 lawyers in 12 offices. The depth and breadth of the experience of its lawyers enables it to provide a broad range of services to meet the diverse legal needs of its client base, which includes Fortune 500 companies, public agencies, banks and other financial institutions, nonprofit organizations, individual investors, family owned businesses, and high-tech and low-tech, growth oriented companies. *See additional listing in Banking Law Chapter.*

•**ALAIN FRECON:** With over 20 years of experience, Mr. Frécon assists clients on a broad spectrum of international business and legal matters. His cross cultural and international business and legal skills serve clients on a worldwide basis through a personal network of local counsels and consultants. Mr. Frécon represents clients in developing, implementing, and restructuring strategies for their international operations. He also handles and manages complex international transactions (exchanges of technology, licensing, and joint ventures) and litigations pertaining to international breach of contract, distributorship termination, and trademark, and copyright infringement matters including counterfeiting and grey market goods. Mr. Frécon is a frequent arbitrator in international arbitrations. Additionally, he has written numerous articles on international business and legal issues and pamphlets on doing business in France, the US, India, and Canada. He chairs the annual Minnesota Institute of Legal Education seminar entitled "Global Markets and the Law." In 1988 he was appointed as a foreign trade advisor to France and in 1994 as Honorary Consul of France in Minnesota.
Education: JD 1982, William Mitchell; LLM 1976, Stanford University; Licence en droit 1972 cum laude, Université de droit de Paris II.
Representative Clients: Businesses involved in international markets, with particular emphasis on the worldwide sale and distribution of products. Clients' profiles include large American or foreign multinationals, as well as small companies.
Professional Associations: ABA (Chair 1992 and 1993, Intellectual Property Section Subcommittees C and D); MSBA (Chair 1991-92, International Business Section; Council member 1985-present); HCBA; Paris Bar (France); International Bar Assn.; American Arbitration Assn. (Chair 1994, International Advisory Committee); William Mitchell International Intellectual Property Advisory Committee (1994).
Community Involvement: French American Chamber of Commerce Minneapolis/St. Paul Chapter (past President; Board member 1984-present); Alliance Française (Board member 1994).
Firm: Frécon & Associates is an international business and legal consulting firm with offices in Minneapolis and Paris (France). *See additional listings in Business Tax Law and Intellectual Property Law Chapters.*

ALAIN FRECON

Frécon & Associates
902 Foshay Tower
821 Marquette Avenue South
Minneapolis, MN 55402

Phone: (612) 338-6868
Fax: (612) 338-6878

Admitted: 1969 Paris, France; 1982 Minnesota
Birthdate: 01/27/46

•**STEVEN C. NELSON:** Mr. Nelson has practiced exclusively in the field of international law and transactions throughout his 25-year career. He has advised and represented scores of companies, most of them based in the upper Midwest, in connection with their international business operations and transactions. His clients have ranged from small start-up companies launching their first export operations to large multinational corporations organizing complex joint ventures in remote parts of the world. Mr. Nelson's experience encompasses the negotiation of international engineering, construction, distribution, and licensing agreements; the formation of foreign joint ventures, consortia, and strategic alliances; the structuring of foreign investments; international mergers, acquisitions, and divestitures; and arbitrations and litigation, both foreign and domestic, relating to such transactions. He is a frequent speaker at national seminars covering topics in these areas.
Education: LLB 1969, Yale University; BA 1966 magna cum laude, honors with exceptional distinction, Yale University.
Employment History: Partner 1985-present, Dorsey & Whitney; Partner 1975-85, Oppenheimer, Wolff, Foster, Shepard & Donnelly; Attorney-Adviser 1969-73, Assistant Legal Adviser 1973-74, Office of the Legal Adviser, US Department of State (Washington, D.C.).
Professional Associations: ABA (Section of International Law & Practice (Chair 1988-89)); Union Internationale des Avocats (First Vice President 1990-93); MSBA; District of Columbia Bar; American Society of International Law; American Foreign Law Assn.
Community Involvement: Yale Alumni Assn. of the Northwest (President 1988-90); NATO Board of Appeals, Brussels (1977-present).
Firm: Dorsey & Whitney is the largest law firm in Minnesota and one of the largest firms in the United States with over 350 lawyers in 12 offices. The depth and breadth of the experience of its lawyers enables it to provide a broad range of services to meet the diverse legal needs of its client base, which includes Fortune 500 companies, public agencies, banks and other financial institutions, nonprofit organizations, individual investors, family owned businesses, and high-tech and low-tech, growth oriented companies.

STEVEN C. NELSON

Dorsey & Whitney
Pillsbury Center South
220 South Sixth Street
Minneapolis, MN 55402-1498

Phone: (612) 340-2942
Fax: (612) 340-8738

Admitted: 1975 Minnesota; 1969 Ct. App. (D.C.); 1973 US Sup. Ct.
Birthdate: 05/11/44

Chapter 23: International Business Law

MICHAEL PRICHARD

Dorsey & Whitney
Pillsbury Center South
220 South Sixth Street
Minneapolis, MN 55402-1498

Phone: (612) 340-2633
Fax: (612) 340-8738

Admitted: 1965 Minnesota
Birthdate: 04/23/37

•**MICHAEL PRICHARD:** Mr. Prichard has practiced in the areas of international business transactions and general corporate matters since 1965. He represents US based clients regarding distribution of goods and services outside the US, technology licensing, establishment of overseas subsidiaries and joint ventures, acquisitions, and regulatory aspects of such activities, including the US Export Administration Regulations. He represents foreign based clients regarding their business activities in the US, including distribution of goods and services in the US, establishment of subsidiaries and joint ventures, acquisitions, regulatory aspects of such activities, and immigration matters. Mr. Prichard also provides tax planning and advice regarding international business transactions and investments. Mr. Prichard is also an experienced general corporate lawyer, handling a broad range of corporate matters, including mergers and acquisitions. Prior to law school, he was a banker for three years with Citibank in New York City and its branches in Caracas, Venezuela. He is fluent in Spanish and has a special interest in Latin American matters.
Education: LLB 1965, University of Minnesota (Student Editorial Board 1963-65, *Minnesota Law Review*); MA 1960, University of Minnesota; BA 1958, Harvard University.
Employment History: 1968-present, Dorsey & Whitney.
Professional Associations: ABA (Section of Taxation, Committee on Foreign Activities of US Taxpayers; Section of International Law and Practice); MSBA (International Business Law Section: Council member, officer 1984-93, Chair 1985-86); Corporate Counsel Assn. of Minnesota.
Community Involvement: Minnesota Parks and Trails Council (Director; President 1991-94; Chair 1994-present); Minnesota World Trade Assn. (1967-present; President 1973-74); St. Croix Valley Health Care Foundation (Director 1993-present). Mr. Prichard counsels several nonprofit organizations on a pro bono basis.
Firm: Dorsey & Whitney is the largest law firm in Minnesota and one of the largest firms in the United States with over 350 lawyers in 12 offices. The depth and breadth of the experience of its lawyers enables it to provide a broad range of services to meet the diverse legal needs of its client base, which includes Fortune 500 companies, public agencies, banks and other financial institutions, nonprofit organizations, individual investors, family owned businesses, and high-tech and low-tech, growth oriented companies. *See additional listings in Closely Held Business Law and Immigration Law Chapters.*

•**G. MARC WHITEHEAD** - Popham, Haik, Schnobrich & Kaufman, Ltd. - 222 South Ninth Street, Suite 3300 - Minneapolis, MN 55402 - Phone: (612) 333-4800, Fax: (612) 334-8888 - *See complete biographical profile in Publicly Held Corporations Law Chapter.*

Complete listing of all attorneys nominated in International Business Law

DAVID R. BRENNAN, Faegre & Benson, Minneapolis; **KEVIN M. BUSCH,** Moss & Barnett, A Professional Association, Minneapolis; **STEVEN E. CARLSON,** Dorsey & Whitney, London; **ALAIN FRECON,** Frécon & Associates, Minneapolis; **EDWARD J. HAYWARD,** Oppenheimer, Wolff & Donnelly, Minneapolis; **FRANKLIN C. JESSE JR.,** Gray, Plant, Mooty, Mooty & Bennett, P.A., Minneapolis; **DAVID KANTOR,** Leonard, Street and Deinard Professional Association, Minneapolis; **DAVID B. MILLER,** Faegre & Benson, Minneapolis; **MICHAEL E. MURPHY,** Faegre & Benson, Minneapolis; **STEVEN C. NELSON,** Dorsey & Whitney, Minneapolis; **JAMES F. PEDERSEN,** Oppenheimer, Wolff & Donnelly, Minneapolis; **MICHAEL PRICHARD,** Dorsey & Whitney, Minneapolis; **JAMES A. RUBENSTEIN,** Moss & Barnett, A Professional Association, Minneapolis; **W. SMITH SHARPE JR.,** Faegre & Benson, Minneapolis; **STEVEN J. TIMMER,** Merritt, Furber & Timmer, Minneapolis; **G. MARC WHITEHEAD,** Popham, Haik, Schnobrich & Kaufman, Ltd., Minneapolis.

CHAPTER 24

LABOR LAW

The term "labor law" encompasses a myriad of workplace issues dealing with how an employer interacts with organized groups of employees, such as a union. This chapter examines the principal federal and state laws governing the relationship between management and organized labor and employee and employer rights and responsibilities during collective bargaining. The Employment Law Chapter covers the rights and obligations of employees as individuals, and discusses such issues as Social Security, Unemployment Compensation Insurance, sexual harassment, and racial discrimination. The Employee Benefits Law Chapter discusses employee benefits programs commonly used by employers to attract new employees and reward their existing employees. It is important to note that while labor law, employment law, and employee benefits law are treated separately in this *Guidebook*, the issues raised in one of these three areas of law often involve issues from the other two. For example, employee benefits packages (an employee benefits law issue) can determine whether an individual worker is an independent contractor or employee (an employment law issue), and are often the subject of union negotiations (a labor law issue). Refusal to provide maternity benefits (an employee benefits issue) may lead to allegations of sexual discrimination (an employment law issue) which are frequently handled by union committees set up to pursue employee complaints (a labor law issue).

FEDERAL LEGISLATION REGARDING UNIONS

The United States has seen the struggle between labor and management played out over a long history. Relations between labor and management in this country have frequently been tense with power seeming to ebb and flow between workers and business owners. Some of the most heated battles in the struggle for workers' rights were fought right here in Minnesota as management and labor fought over the issues that mass industrialization brought to the state. In time, much of the relationship between management and labor came to be governed by federal laws enacted in response to the strife and economic disruption caused by long strikes. The history of federal labor legislation is a story of Congress reacting to the perceived imbalance of power between organized labor and management in this country, stepping in to bolster the labor movement when it perceived organized labor to be too weak, and curtailing the power of organized labor when Congress perceived it had grown too strong or corrupt.

The principal federal laws setting ground rules for how management and labor deal with each other are the Norris-LaGuardia Act, the National Labor Relations Act, the Taft-Hartley Law, and the Landrum-Griffin Act.

Chapter 24: Labor Law

NORRIS-LAGUARDIA ACT

The Norris-LaGuardia Act was one of the first attempts to limit the power of federal courts to impede labor disputes. Prior to the adoption of the Norris-LaGuardia Act in 1932 many courts looked upon any concerted actions by groups of employees, such as strikes, boycotts, and picketing as criminal conspiracies punishable by law. Industrial representatives frequently turned to courts sympathetic to management interests in order to get temporary or permanent injunctions against labor unions to prevent them from organizing workers, calling strikes, picketing, or boycotting. The primary aim of the Norris-LaGuardia Act was to do away with the power of the federal judiciary to use injunctions to stifle the nascent labor movement. The Act so severely limits the use of injunctions (courts are permitted to enjoin union activity in rare instances to prevent violence) that today court-ordered injunctions are almost never a tool for management to use in labor disputes.

The Norris-LaGuardia Act also made illegal the theretofore common practice of requiring new employees to sign pledges not to join unions as a pre-condition of employment. So-called "yellow dog" contracts had been a common tool that management used to squash labor unions.

Even more significant than its literal impact was the policy implication of the Norris-LaGuardia Act. For the first time, Congress said that federal courts were not the proper forum for resolving labor-management disputes. Henceforth government would be more neutral in letting market forces determine the proper balance of power between workers and their employers. Perhaps naively, Congress assumed that simple government neutrality would provide the best environment for union-management negotiations.

NATIONAL LABOR RELATIONS ACT

The National Labor Relations Act of 1935 (NLRA), frequently referred to as the Wagner Act, represented the first substantial effort by the federal government to reshape the balance of power between labor and management in this country. The NLRA explicitly guarantees employees the right to form labor organizations and to bargain collectively through representatives of their own choosing. The NLRA made illegal a number of management practices that had been used to interfere with employee efforts to self-organize. The NLRA provides stiff penalties for employers who interfere with its provisions.

The NLRA also established an administrative agency, the National Labor Relations Board (NLRB) and endowed it with the power to administer and enforce its provisions. The NLRB's five board members are appointed by the United States President with the advice and consent of the Senate for five-year terms. The Board's home is in Washington, D.C. The President also appoints, with the advice and consent of the Senate, a General Counsel responsible for investigating and prosecuting allegations of unfair labor practices.

Most employer-employee interaction with the NLRB is through one of over 30 regional offices throughout the country. Each regional office is headed by a regional director who reports to the General Counsel in Washington.

Under the NLRA, the term "employee" includes a very broad range of workers who earn wages, salaries, or commissions. Specifically exempted from its coverage are agricultural workers, domestic servants, persons employed by their own parent or spouse, railroad employees, and independent contractors. The definition of an independent contractor is discussed in the Employment Law Chapter. Employers should know that courts have generally interpreted "independent contractor" quite narrowly for purposes of deciding whether someone would be protected by the NLRA. Thus, an individual who is considered an independent contractor for purposes of complying with other federal regulations might still be considered an employee for purposes of the NLRA.

The NLRA remains the primary law regulating relations between labor and management in this country. Most post-NLRA legislation sought merely to refine and improve the provisions of the NLRA rather than replace it with another scheme. For instance, the NLRA contained no restrictions on the activities of unions. Later laws would impose rules on how unions operate internally and require labor organizations to submit periodic financial information to the government.

Taft-Hartley Law

The Taft-Hartley Law (officially titled the Labor-Management Relations Act) was an attempt by Congress to limit the abuses of organized labor's power after the Second World War and to reign in the power of the NLRB. The Taft-Hartley Law is a complex piece of legislation. Its most important provisions are:

- Establishment of a general counsel with authority to issue complaints

- Banning of "closed shops" agreements whereby only union members could be hired by a particular employer (the Taft-Hartley law does not prohibit "union shop" agreements whereby anyone hired by a particular employer is required to join the union after a set period of time)

- Prohibition of unfair labor practices by management such as discrimination in hiring and tenure to discourage union membership

- Prohibition of unfair labor practices by labor such as refusal to bargain or illegal strikes or boycotts

- Institution of a 60-day "cooling off" period before a work stoppage at the end of a collective bargaining agreement

- Creation of special powers to limit strikes that could threaten the security of the nation

- Barring Communists from holding office in the union

- Forcing unions to file financial reports with the NLRB

Landrum-Griffin Act

The Landrum-Griffin Act (officially the Labor-Management Reporting and Disclosure Act) was enacted to reform the way that unionized labor and union management interact in an attempt to protect members of labor unions from perceived abuses from corrupt labor leaders. The bill gave union members a "bill of rights" they could assert against union leadership and established procedures to help union members uncover unscrupulous practices of labor leaders. The Landrum-Griffin Act requires certain financial disclosures by unions, establishes procedures that unions must follow to elect officers, provides penalties for financial abuses committed by union officials and strictly limits secondary boycotts and picketing.

FORMING A UNION

An employer whose employees are considering organizing should be aware of what the law requires of all parties.

EMPLOYEE PROCEDURES

A group of employees can form a union by filing a petition at the regional office of the NLRB. The petition should prove that at least 30 percent of the employees of the prospective bargaining unit support the petition to organize. An NLRB official will determine whether the petition is valid and whether any legal obstacles need to be overcome. The board will then hold hearings for company and union representatives and hold an election within the company to vote for or against the union.

An important issue at this stage is what is an appropriate bargaining unit. Different employees have different interests and goals for collective bargaining. If the bargaining unit is too broad, some members of the unit may not be effectively represented, but if the unit is too small, it may lack clout to bargain with management. The following factors are typically considered when deciding upon the appropriate bargaining unit:

- Amount and method of calculating pay
- Similarity of benefits
- Similarity of hours worked
- Type of work performed
- Qualifications, skill, and education required for the position
- Physical proximity of workers and integration of tasks
- Employer's supervisory or organizational structure
- Employee preferences

EMPLOYERS' RIGHTS AND OBLIGATIONS DURING ORGANIZATIONAL DRIVES

The Taft-Hartley Law gives employers substantial freedom to present their views during union organization drives including the expressing of views, arguments, opinions, in unwritten, printed, and graphic forms, so long as such dissemination contains no threat of reprisal or promise of benefit. This right to express one's views on unions generally, to criticize a particular union, or to express a preference for one union over another can quickly lead to problems for employers who are unfamiliar with how courts have interpreted the requirement that there be no threat of reprisal.

It is important that employers realize that their actions will be closely watched during organization drives. An employer should not make unusual wage adjustments, threaten economic reprisals, try to convince employees to sign individual employment agreements, question employees about their union status or activities, or anything else that could be construed as illegal anti-union activity.

When a union is soliciting employees to join a union, the employer is prohibited from pressuring employees against joining or discriminating against those who organize or join the union. The NLRB has heard thousands of complaints accusing employers of discriminating against organizing efforts. Although the complaints are necessarily heard on a case-by-case basis, the following are most often found to constitute illegal discrimination against efforts to organize:

- Refusal to hire anyone involved in a union
- Failure to recall seasonal workers who join a union
- Discharge or layoff of an employee
- Demotion or transfer to a less desirable job or location
- Significantly worse treatment following organizing efforts

NEGOTIATING WITH A UNION

Once the NLRB has certified a union to represent a group of employees, management is required to deal with that union.

The Duty to Engage in Collective Bargaining

The law imposes upon labor and management the obligation to engage in collective bargaining. While neither side is obligated to agree to any proposals made by the other side, both labor and management have an obligation to:

- Meet at reasonable times
- Confer "in good faith" with respect to wages, hours, and other terms and conditions of employment
- Incorporate into a written contract any agreement reached in oral negotiations

If the NLRB has certified a union to represent the employees, the employer must discuss wages and employment conditions with that union. Negotiations usually begin with the union submitting a proposed contract to management, which then submits counterproposals to the union representatives. Employers and employees are usually represented by professionals when entering a collective bargaining agreement.

The Exclusivity Principal

The NLRA contains an exclusivity principal which declares that where the NLRB has recognized a union as the representative of a group of employees or where the employer has privately agreed to so recognize the union, the union has the exclusive right to represent those employees. This exclusivity provision can trip up even well-meaning employers who are not careful to avoid bargaining with other than the union's representatives. Often a problem can develop when an employer is approached by an independent group of employees, acting on their own, bringing to management a specific problem. If he or she attempts to respond to the employee-initiated contact without first going through the union, the employer can run afoul of the NLRA's exclusivity principal.

STRIKES

Strikes can be classified four ways—economic strikes, unfair labor practices strikes, wildcat strikes, and illegal strikes. The law treats each category differently.

Economic Strike

An economic strike results when employees strike after a stalemate in negotiations over a contract with management. The NLRA protects workers against unfair labor practices during an economic strike and guarantees that they retain their status as employees during the strike. After an economic strike, employers may not refuse to re-hire a striker solely because he or she participated in an economic strike.

Unfair Labor Practice Strike

An unfair labor practice strike is a strike over an alleged unfair labor practice. Employees who take part in an unfair labor practice strike retain their status as employees. Once the NLRB determines an employer's actions to be an unfair labor practice, employees are entitled to have their old jobs back, even if their employee has hired replacement workers in the interim.

Wildcat Strike

A wildcat strike is a strike initiated by a group of employees without sanction of their union. Wildcat strikers are not protected by the provisions of the NLRA and may be permanently fired by their employers.

Illegal Strike

A number of categories of strikes are specifically made illegal by the Taft-Hartley Law, including:

- Strikes attempting to force an employer or a self-employed person to join a union

- Strikes attempting to pressure an employer to stop doing business with another person

- Strikes to force an employer to bargain with a minority union after the NLRB has certified a majority union to represent the employees

- Strikes that begin within 60 days preceding the expiration of a labor agreement

Employees who participate in an illegal strike lose their status as employees.

BOYCOTTS AND PICKETING

The Labor Reform Act makes it illegal for a union to go on strike, refuse to work or otherwise threaten an employer if the purpose of its actions is to:

- Force the employer not to handle the goods of another employer

- Stop any person from using, handling, selling, or transporting the products of another employer

- Make another employer recognize or bargain with a union, other than a union certified by the NLRB

- Force the employer to bargain with a union when a different union has already been certified by the NLRB

RESOURCES

National Labor Relations Board, Region 18 Office (responsibile for Minnesota, Iowa, North Dakota, South Dakota, and western Wisconsin), 110 South Fourth Street, Room 316, Minneapolis, MN 55401-2291, (612) 348-1757.

Survey of Labor Relations. Second Edition, Lee Balliet, Bureau of National Affairs, Washington, D.C., 1987.

Labor Relations. Fifth Edition, Arthur A. Sloane, Fred Witney, Prentice-Hall, Englewood Cliffs, NJ, 1989.

Making Unions Unnecessary. Charles A. Hughes, Executive Enterprises Publications Co., Inc., New York, NY, 1990.

LABOR LAW LEADING ATTORNEYS

Selected by Attorneys for GUIDEBOOK
Law & Leading Attorneys
MINNESOTA

The attorneys profiled below were recommended by their peers in a statewide survey.

The attorneys profiled in this section were nominated by their peers in a statewide survey conducted in 1993 in which several thousand Minnesota attorneys were asked to name the lawyer to whom they would send a friend or family member in need of legal assistance in the area of *Labor Law.*

Because the survey resulted in a list of less than five percent of Minnesota's practicing attorneys, this should not be construed as a complete list. Nevertheless, it is an excellent source of highly qualified and reputable attorneys, who, if unable to assist can in most cases make quality referrals.

A list of all attorneys nominated in this category is found at the end of this section. For information on the survey methodology see page ix.

Please note that the shorter, two line attorney listings in this section are of attorneys who practice in this area but whose full biographical profile appears in another section of this book. A bullet "•" preceeding name indicates the attorney was nominated in this particular area of law. For information on the format of these profiles, consult the section "Using the *Business Guidebook*" found on page xiv. Note that the following abbreviations are used throughout these profiles:

App.	-	Appellate	ABA	-	American Bar Association
Cir.	-	Circuit	ATLA	-	American Trial Lawyers Association
Ct.	-	Court	HCBA	-	Hennepin County Bar Association
Dist.	-	District	MDLA	-	Minnesota Defense Lawyers Association
Hon.	-	Honorable	MSBA	-	Minnesota State Bar Association
JD	-	Law degree (Juris Doctor)	MTLA	-	Minnesota Trial Lawyers Association
LLB	-	Law degree	NBTA	-	National Board of Trial Advocacy
LLM	-	Master in Law degree	RCBA	-	Ramsey County Bar Association
Sup.	-	Supreme			

EMERY W. BARTLE

Dorsey & Whitney
Pillsbury Center South
220 South Sixth Street
Minneapolis, MN 55402-1498

Phone: (612) 340-2819
Fax: (612) 340-2643

Admitted: 1968 Minnesota;
1969 New York;
1970 US Dist. Ct. (MN);
1980 US Dist. Ct. (E. Dist.WI);
1982 US Dist. Ct. (W. Dist. TX);
1971 US Ct. App. (8th Cir.);
1987 US Ct. App. (D.C.);
1973 US Sup. Ct.

•**EMERY W. BARTLE:** Mr. Bartle has focused his practice exclusively on representing management clients in connection with labor and employment law issues for 25 years. He is a partner in, and current chair of, the Labor and Employment Law Department at Dorsey & Whitney. Mr. Bartle has substantial experience with employer clients of all sizes in a broad range of industries. This experience includes counseling clients and representing them in litigation in the following areas of labor and employment law: representation cases, negotiation of contracts, labor arbitration, employment discrimination, OFCCP investigations and complaints, proceedings before the National Labor Relations Board, OSHA investigations and citations, wage and hour matters, and common law employment law claims. He has served as the chief negotiator for a number of employers in union contract negotiations. He provides training to management clients on labor and employment law and lectures at legal education seminars. He is also coauthor of the book *Strikes, Lockouts and Boycotts*, (Clark, Boardman & Callahan). Mr. Bartle has been listed in *Who's Who in America* since 1992, in *Who's Who in American Law* since 1990, and in *The Best Lawyers in America* since 1987 under Labor & Employment Law-Management.
Education: JD 1968 cum laude, Order of the Coif, University of Minnesota (Note and Comment Editor 1967-68, *Minnesota Law Review*); BSEE 1965, South Dakota State University (Phi Kappa Phi).
Employment History: Partner 1975-present, Associate 1970-74, Dorsey & Whitney; Attorney 1968-70, International Business Machines Corp.
Professional Associations: MSBA (Section of Labor & Employment Law (Chair 1979-80)); ABA (Section of Labor & Employment Law).
Community Involvement: Speaker before numerous groups and organizations on labor and employment related topics.
Firm: Dorsey & Whitney is the largest law firm in Minnesota and one of the largest firms in the United States with over 350 lawyers in 12 offices. The depth and breadth of the experience of its lawyers enables it to provide a broad range of services to meet the diverse legal needs of its client base, which includes Fortune 500 companies, public agencies, banks and other financial institutions, nonprofit organizations, individual investors, family owned businesses, and high-tech and low-tech, growth oriented companies. *See additional listing in Employment Law Chapter.*

•**ROBERT S. BURK:** Mr. Burk is a senior shareholder at Popham Haik with over 35 years of personnel, labor relations, and environmental experience. He represents clients before federal and state agencies and courts, including the National Labor Relations Board, the Occupational Safety and Health Administration, the Environmental Protection Agency, and the Minnesota Pollution Control Agency. Mr. Burk handles labor negotiations, mediations, arbitrations, labor contract administration, union avoidance, and all aspects of labor/employment and environmental law. Mr. Burk is chair, Board of Trustees, William Mitchell College of Law; was the 1993 recipient of The Honorable Ronald E. Hachey Outstanding Alumnus Award; is listed in *Who's Who in America*, 1994 and 1995; was appointed by the Governor to the Wage Advisory Board for Clerical Operations; was District 15 representative on the Metropolitan Council's §208 Waste Water Management Advisory Committee; was chair of the Industry Task Force on Application of the State's Critical Areas Act to the Mississippi River Corridor; and is past president and CEO of Popham Haik.
Education: LLB 1965, William Mitchell; BBA 1959, University of Minnesota.
Employment History: Currently, Popham, Haik, Schnobrich & Kaufman, Ltd.; Labor Relations Consultant; Manager of Industrial Relations and Environmental Affairs for a major Minnesota corporation.
Representative Clients: VEE Corporation (Sesame Street Live); Sheldahl, Inc.; Koch Refining Company; Fingerhut Corporation; Browning-Ferris Industries; Taylor Corporation.
Professional Associations: ABA (Labor and Environmental Sections); MSBA (Labor and Environmental Sections).
Firm: Popham, Haik, Schnobrich & Kaufman, Ltd., is a firm of more than 230 attorneys with offices in Denver, Miami, Minneapolis, Washington, D.C., and international affiliations in Beijing, China and Leipzig and Stuttgart, Germany. The firm represents clients nationally and internationally on issues relating to corporate and business law, administrative law, and litigation. *See additional listings in Employment Law and Environmental Law Chapters.*

ROBERT S. BURK

Popham, Haik, Schnobrich & Kaufman, Ltd.
222 South Ninth Street
Suite 3300
Minneapolis, MN 55402

Phone: (612) 333-4800
Fax: (612) 334-8888

Admitted: 1966 Minnesota;
1977 US Dist. Ct. (MN);
1989 US Ct. App. (8th Cir.);
1990 US Sup. Ct.
Birthdate: 01/13/37

•**DON L. BYE:** Mr. Bye has represented labor unions and individual employees for over 30 years. He has substantial court experience in varied types of litigation, including accident and personal injury, product liability, and business litigation. He is a speaker at legal seminars, an occasional lecturer at area colleges, and has written several legal articles. Mr. Bye represents unions in all matters: representation and elections, grievance and arbitration, contract interpretation and bargaining, unfair labor practices, injunctive proceedings, and court actions. He has been listed in *The Best Lawyers in America* since 1987.
Education: LLB 1963, University of Minnesota; BA 1963, University of Minnesota; AA 1955, Brainerd Community College.
Employment History: Halverson, Watters, Bye, Downs, Reyelts & Bateman, Ltd. since 1963. He is a former union carpenter.
Representative Clients: Duluth and Iron Range building trade councils, ironworkers, electrical workers, laborers, plumbers, sheetmetal workers, roofers, machinists/woodworkers; service unions—UFCW, Hotel and Restaurant; Teamsters; public employees—AFSCME, SEIU; teachers—MFT and Duluth Federation of Teachers; communications workers; operating engineers; supervisory associations; law enforcement; health care.
Professional Associations: MSBA (Board of Governors 1988-91); ABA; National Employment Lawyers' Assn.; 11th District Bar Assn. (President 1988); University of MN Industrial Relations Advisory Council; original Board of Legal Certification (1987-93); original Public Employment Relations Board (1972-81).
Community Involvement: Kids' Voting USA; Arrowhead Food Bank (Chair 1983-92); SHARE Food Drive (Chair or Cochair 1982-91); National Bone Marrow Donor Bank (1981-85); Duluth Planning Commission (1967-75).
Firm: Halverson, Watters, Bye, Downs, Reyelts & Bateman is a 12 lawyer firm which concentrates its practice in the areas of business and injury litigation. The firm also handles employment disputes of all types. The firm's associates and paralegals devote a substantial portion of their practice to the fields of litigation, labor relations, employment, and employee benefits. *See additional listing in Employee Benefits Law Chapter.*

DON L. BYE

Halverson, Watters, Bye, Downs, Reyelts & Bateman, Ltd.
700 Providence Building
332 West Superior Street
Duluth, MN 55802

Phone: (218) 727-6833
Fax: (218) 727-4632

Admitted: 1963 Minnesota;
1963 US Dist. Ct. (MN);
1967 US Claims Ct.
Birthdate: 11/13/35

Chapter 24: Labor Law

GREGG M. CORWIN

Gregg M. Corwin & Associates
1660 South Highway 100
Suite 508 East
St. Louis Park, MN
55416-1534

Phone: (612) 544-7774
Fax: (612) 544-7151

Admitted: 1972 Minnesota;
1972 US Dist. Ct. (MN);
1976 US Ct. App. (8th Cir.);
1977 US Sup. Ct.
Birthdate: 05/04/47

•**GREGG M. CORWIN**: Mr. Corwin has been practicing in the areas of labor and employment law for over twenty years. With special expertise in the area of union side public sector labor law and discrimination law, he was instrumental in the drafting of the Minnesota Pay Equity Act, the amendments to the Minnesota Public Employment Labor Relations Act, and the Government Data Practices Act. Mr. Corwin is a popular seminar lecturer on the topics of union representation, public sector labor law, sexual harassment, American Disabilities Act, defamation, discrimination, data privacy, and arbitration. He is named in the 1989-90 (third edition), 1991-92 (fourth edition), 1993-94 (fifth edition), and the 1995-96 (sixth edition) of *The Best Lawyers in America*, as well as in the 1993 and 1994 *Bar Register of Preeminent Lawyers* under the area of Labor/Employment Law.
Education: JD 1972 cum laude, University of Minnesota; BA 1969 summa cum laude, University of Minnesota.
Employment History: 1972-present, Gregg M. Corwin & Associates.
Representative Clients: American Federation of State, County and Municipal Employees Councils No. 6, 14 and 65 (statewide); Minnesota Assn. of Professional Employees (statewide); Professional Employees Assn.; Communication Workers of America; Amalgamated Transit Union Local 1005; Minnesota School Employees Assn.; Service Employees International Union; Law Enforcement Labor Services, Inc. (LELS); Minneapolis Police Federation; other unions.
Professional Associations: AFL-CIO Lawyers Coordinating Committee (Charter member 1982-present); HCBA; MSBA (Treasurer 1988-89, Labor & Employment Law Section); ABA; MTLA; ATLA.
Community Involvement: AFSCME Legal Services Plan (Founder).
Firm: Gregg M. Corwin & Associates, representing numerous public employee unions, has established itself as a leader in labor law in Minnesota. In the past several years, the firm has expanded its employment law practice, representing both plaintiffs and defendants in the areas of sexual harassment and discrimination. The firm has obtained six-figure verdicts in two recent employment cases. In addition to representing the firm's labor and employment clients, the associate attorneys have established expertise in the labor and employment area. Karin Peterson concentrates in employment law and cases brought under the Minnesota Government Data Practices Act. Ann Walther concentrates in law enforcement labor law and police misconduct defense. *See additional listings in Employment Law and Employee Benefits Law Chapters.*

MATTHEW E. DAMON - Popham, Haik, Schnobrich & Kaufman, Ltd. - 222 South Ninth Street, Suite 3300 - Minneapolis, MN 55402 - Phone: (612) 333-4800, Fax: (612) 334-8888 - *See complete biographical profile in Employment Law Chapter.*

BARBARA JEAN D'AQUILA - Cosgrove, Flynn & Gaskins - 2900 Metropolitan Centre, 333 South Seventh Street - Minneapolis, MN 55402 - Phone: (612) 333-9527, Fax: (612) 333-9579 - *See complete biographical profile in Employment Law Chapter.*

MICHAEL J. GALVIN, JR.

Briggs and Morgan, P.A.
W-2200 First National Bank Building
St. Paul, MN 55101

Phone: (612) 223-6600
Fax: (612) 223-6450

Admitted: 1957 Minnesota
Birthdate: 07/08/30

•**MICHAEL J. GALVIN, JR.:** Mr. Galvin, a shareholder at Briggs and Morgan, P.A., practices in the areas of labor relations, employment law litigation, administrative law, and municipal law. He has written and spoken extensively on the termination of employees, employment, and developments in labor law. Mr. Galvin is listed in *Who's Who in America*, 47th edition, and *The Best Lawyers in America*, 1987 to date. In addition, he is the author of numerous articles on labor and environmental issues, including "Sexual Harassment Statutory Update," *Minnesota Institute for Legal Education*, March 1993; "Organizing the Unorganized," *18th Annual Labor & Employment Law Institute*, Nov. 1991; "Buying and Selling a Business—Addressing Potential Liability Exposure: Environmental Concerns," *Minnesota Continuing Legal Education*, Nov. 1991.
Education: LLB 1957, University of Minnesota (Phi Delta Phi); BA 1952, College of St. Thomas.
Employment History: Partner 1957-present, Briggs and Morgan, P.A.; 1954-60, US Air Force Reserve; 1st Lieutenant 1952-54, US Air Force; 1950-51, US Army Reserve.
Professional Associations: MSBA (President 1994-95, Treasurer 1990-92, Board of Governors 1985-87, 1990-present; Chair 1985 Labor and Employment Law Section; ABA (Labor and Employment Law Section); Ramsey County Bar Assn. (President 1984); Minnesota Volunteer Attorney Program (President 1993-94).
Community Involvement: American Red Cross, St. Paul Chapter (past Director); University Club of St. Paul (past President); St. Paul Junior Chamber of Commerce (past President); Minnesota Club of St. Paul (past President); St. Paul Area Chamber of Commerce (past Secretary); St. Paul Winter Carnival Assn. (past President); University of St. Thomas (past Trustee); University of St. Thomas Alumni (past President); St. Paul Athletic Club (past President).
Firm: Briggs and Morgan, P.A., was established in 1882 and now has over 135 lawyers in its St. Paul and Minneapolis offices. The firm handles a broad range of legal areas for its business, governmental, and individual clients. *See additional listing in Employment Law Chapter.*

•**STEPHEN D. GORDON:** Since 1967 Steve Gordon has practiced exclusively in the labor and employment areas, representing private and public sector unions in Minnesota and surrounding states, employees in a wide range of professions and occupations, and several international unions as local counsel. Steve has extensive experience in representing unions in federal and state court; representing clients before the National Labor Relations Board; negotiating collective bargaining agreements, including interest arbitration in the public and private sectors; and representing labor organizations before state and federal agencies. In 1994, after a three-week jury trial in Federal District Court, Steve recovered $632,000 in a Section 301 breach-of-contract case. He has been involved in over 500 labor arbitrations involving both contract interpretation and discipline. In addition, he has written on labor law and labor relations and teaches as an adjunct professor at the University of Minnesota. He received the John F. Kennedy Labor Law Award and is listed in *Who's Who in American Law* and *The Best Lawyers in America*.
Education: JD 1967, Georgetown University; LLM 1970 Labor Law, Georgetown University; BS 1964, Cornell University.
Employment History: Founding partner 1985-present, Gordon Miller O'Brien; Partner 1974-85, Robins, Kaplan, Miller & Ciresi; Partner 1967-73, Mozart G. Ratner Law Offices.
Representative Clients: Minnesota State Building & Construction Trades Council; Minnesota Teamsters Joint Council No. 32; over 100 other private and public sector labor organizations.
Professional Associations: ABA (Cochair 1985-88, Committee on Development of Law under the National Labor Relations Act; Council member 1992-present, Section of Labor and Employment Law); National Labor Relations Board (Advisory Council 1994); MSBA (Chair 1976-77, Labor and Employment Law Section); AFL-CIO Lawyers Coordinating Committee.
Firm: Gordon Miller O'Brien lawyers are widely known for representation of labor organizations and employees in all types of employment disputes and also for their work in the Workers' Compensation and personal injury areas. Partners Richard Miller and Michael Bloom head the Workers' Compensation practice as well as practicing in the labor and employment areas. Partner Daniel Froehlich works primarily in the firm's injury practice and represents injured people and people in workplace disputes including disability discrimination. *See additional listings in Employee Benefits Law and Employment Law Chapters.*

STEPHEN D. GORDON

Gordon Miller O'Brien
1208 Plymouth Building
12 South Sixth Street
Minneapolis, MN 55402

Phone: (612) 333-5831
Fax: (612) 342-2613

Admitted: 1973 Minnesota; 1968 District of Columbia; 1974 US Dist. Ct. (MN); 1974 US Ct. App. (8th Cir.); 1973 US Sup. Ct.
Birthdate: 02/11/43

•**ROBERT L. HOBBINS:** Mr. Hobbins practices in all areas of labor and employment law for management including labor arbitration, employment discrimination, union organizing attempts, proceedings before the National Labor Relations Board, OSHA, wage and hour, affirmative action, OFCCP, and common-law employment claims. He also represents a number of Railway Labor Act employers. His cases include *Garlock Equipment Co. v. NLRB* (defense of employer charged with failure to bargain in case presenting question concerning representation); *Arnold, et al. v. Northwest Airlines, Inc.* (defense of RLA carrier in hybrid breach of contract/duty of fair representation case); *Northwest Airlines, Inc. v. International Association of Machinists & Aerospace Workers* (suit for injunction to prevent unauthorized work stoppage under Railway Labor Act); *Foster et al. v. Cargill, Inc.* (representation of employer in class action race/sex discrimination suit under Title VII by private plaintiffs and EEOC, and negotiation of Consent Decree). Mr. Hobbins is listed in *The Best Lawyers in America*, 1992-94, under Labor and Employment Law-Management.
Education: JD 1973, New York University (Root Tilden Scholar; staff member 1971-72, *Annual Survey of American Law*); BA 1970 magna cum laude, Creighton University.
Employment History: Partner 1979-present, Associate 1973-78, Dorsey & Whitney.
Representative Clients: Northwest Airlines, Inc.; Mayo Foundation; First Bank System, Inc.; Cargill Incorporated; Northern States Power Company; Dain Bosworth Incorporated.
Professional Associations: MSBA (Labor and Employment Law Section); ABA (Labor and Employment Law Section); Legal Rights Center, Inc. (Director 1984-90); Legal Advice Clinics (Director 1978-80).
Community Involvement: Creighton University (National Alumni Board).
Firm: Dorsey & Whitney is the largest law firm in Minnesota and one of the largest firms in the United States with over 350 lawyers in 12 offices. The depth and breadth of the experience of its lawyers enables it to provide a broad range of services to meet the diverse legal needs of its client base, which includes Fortune 500 companies, public agencies, banks and other financial institutions, nonprofit organizations, individual investors, family owned businesses, and high-tech and low-tech, growth oriented companies. *See additional listing in Employment Law Chapter.*

ROBERT L. HOBBINS

Dorsey & Whitney
Pillsbury Center South
220 South Sixth Street
Minneapolis, MN 55402-1498

Phone: (612) 340-2919
Fax: (612) 340-2643

Admitted: 1973 Minnesota; 1973 US Dist. Ct. (MN); 1983 US Ct. App. (DC Cir.); 1990 US Ct. App. (8th Cir.)

KATHLEEN A. HUGHES - Fredrikson & Byron, P.A. - 1100 International Centre, 900 Second Avenue South - Minneapolis, MN 55402 - Phone: (612) 347-7037, Fax: (612) 347-7077 - *See complete biographical profile in Employment Law Chapter.*

Chapter 24: Labor Law

ROGER A. JENSEN

Peterson, Bell, Converse & Jensen, P.A.
3000 Metropolitan Centre
333 South Seventh Street
Minneapolis, MN 55402-2441

Phone: (612) 342-2323
Fax: (612) 344-1535

Admitted: 1967 Minnesota
Birthdate: 10/24/42

•**ROGER A. JENSEN:** Mr. Jensen engages in all aspects of labor and employment law practice, including state and federal court proceedings, labor arbitration, and negotiations. He also represents municipalities in all aspects of municipal government law. He is listed in *The Best Lawyers in America*, 1988-94 editions.
Education: JD 1967, Valparaiso University Law School; BA 1964, St. Olaf College.
Employment History: Currently, Partner, Peterson, Bell, Converse & Jensen, P.A.; Judge Advocate 1967-71, US Marine Corps.
Representative Clients: Minnesota Education Assn.; Carpenters' Union; International Assn. of Machinists; United Food and Commercial Workers; Service Employees International Union; City of Roseville; City of White Bear Lake; City of Vadnais Heights; American Family Insurance Company; Mutual Services Insurance Company; Design Professionals Insurance Company.
Professional Associations: MSBA (past Chair, Labor Law Section; past Chair, Consumer Protection Committee); RCBA (Ethics Committee); ABA (Labor Law Section).
Firm: Peterson, Bell, Converse & Jensen, P.A., has been in existence since 1962. The firm represents labor organizations, cities, insurance companies, and a broad range of clients with an emphasis on labor, employment, employee benefits, and municipal criminal and civil practice. *See additional listings in Employment Law and Federal, State & Local Government Law Chapters.*

MAURICE W. (BILL) O'BRIEN

Gordon Miller O'Brien
1208 Plymouth Building
12 South Sixth Street
Minneapolis, MN 55402

Phone: (612) 333-5831
Fax: (612) 342-2613

Admitted: 1981 Minnesota;
1981 US Dist. Ct. (MN);
1981 US Ct. App. (8th Cir.)
Birthdate: 12/31/55

•**MAURICE W. (BILL) O'BRIEN:** Since 1981 Mr. O'Brien has practiced civil trial law exclusively in the labor and employment areas, representing building trades and nonbuilding trades unions, employee associations, and groups. He provides counsel, strategic planning, and representation in collective bargaining negotiations, contract grievances, and arbitrations, and in unfair labor practice and representation cases before the National Labor Relations Board. Mr. O'Brien also represents private and public sector clients before state and federal agencies. In addition, he represents clients under the Public Employees Labor Relations Act; in trial work; and in nonlitigation and prelitigation counseling and strategic positioning concerning workplace disputes, employment agreements, noncompete agreements, and stock option agreements. In employer-employee disputes Mr. O'Brien handles legal claims under federal and state discrimination and sexual harassment statutes, various state employment laws, and common law causes of action. He has a strong commitment to alternative dispute resolution. In 1994 he completed the certified Minnesota General Mediation Training. He is a frequent speaker and lecturer on labor and employment law and is an adjunct professor at William Mitchell College of Law.
Education: JD 1981, Northwestern University; BA 1977, Colgate University.
Employment History: Founding Partner 1985-present, Gordon Miller O'Brien; Associate 1981-85, Law Clerk 1980, Robins, Kaplan, Miller & Ciresi (formerly Robins, Davis & Lyons); Law Clerk 1980, Legal Aid Foundation (Chicago).
Representative Clients: Private and public sector unions, building trades, and nonbuilding trades.
Professional Associations: MSBA (Chair 1989, Labor and Employment Law Section); ABA (Labor and Employment Section); National Employment Lawyers Assn. (President 1992-94, MN Chapter); AFL-CIO Lawyer's Coordinating Committee.
Community Involvement: ACT, Inc. (former volunteer attorney); volunteer mediator.
Firm: The firm's lawyers are widely known for representation of labor organizations and individual employees in all types of employment disputes and for their work in the Workers' Compensation and personal injury areas. Partners Rich Miller and Michael Bloom head the Workers' Compensation practice as well as practicing with partner Kathryn Endahl in the labor and employment area. Partner Daniel Froelich works primarily in the firm's injury practice and represents people with disability discrimination claims. *See additional listings in Employee Benefits Law and Employment Law Chapters.*

•**JOSEPH J. ROBY, JR.:** Mr. Roby practices labor and employment law, including wrongful discharge, discrimination and harassment matters, and commercial and business litigation, representing management and companies. He is experienced in collective bargaining and grievance arbitration. He is certified as a Civil Trial Specialist by the Minnesota State Bar Association and as a Civil Trial Advocate by the National Board of Trial Advocacy. Mr. Roby is an adjunct instructor in Business Law at the College of St. Scholastica, the author of published articles on employment discrimination, and a lecturer on employment law issues.
Education: JD 1979, William Mitchell; BS 1974 with highest honors, South Dakota School of Mines & Technology.
Employment History: Associate/Shareholder 1979-present, Johnson, Killen, Thibodeau & Seiler, P.A.; Director 1978-79, In-Office Compliance, Unclaimed Property Division, Office of the Minnesota State Treasurer.
Representative Clients: Duluth Clinic, Ltd.; Duluth News-Tribune; St. Mary's Medical Center; College of St. Scholastica; Franklin Foods; Woolworth Corp.; Louisiana-Pacific Corp.; Mesabi Regional Medical Center; Benedictine Sisters Benevolent Assn.; Walgreen Company.
Professional Associations: ABA (Labor and Employment Law Section); MSBA (Board of Governors 1986-87); 11th District Bar Assn.; MDLA; State Bar of Wisconsin; Academy of Certified Trial Lawyers.
Community Involvement: Volunteer Attorney Program (volunteer attorney; Board member); Lake Park Little League (President); Human Development Center (Board member 1983-92).
Firm: Founded in 1888, Johnson, Killen, Thibodeau & Seiler, P.A., is the oldest firm in northern Minnesota. Today the firm's 18 lawyers provide a wide range of services for consumers, businesses, and companies in commercial, toxic tort, environmental, and insurance litigation; commercial and residential real estate; probate, estate planning, and trusts; employment law; closely held business law; and Workers' Compensation. *See additional listings in Commercial Litigation and Employment Law Chapters.*

JOSEPH J. ROBY, JR.

Johnson, Killen, Thibodeau & Seiler, P.A.
811 Norwest Center
230 West Superior Street
Duluth, MN 55802

Phone: (218) 722-6331
Fax: (218) 722-3031

Admitted: 1979 Minnesota; 1985 Wisconsin; 1979 US Dist. Ct. (MN); 1985 US Dist. Ct. (WI); 1979 US Ct. App. (8th Cir.); 1983 US Sup. Ct.; 1989 US Ct. App. (7th Cir.)
Birthdate: 07/04/52

•**RICHARD A. ROSS:** Mr. Ross is the senior shareholder in Fredrikson & Byron's Labor & Employment Law Group. His practice includes defense of employers in litigation and administrative proceedings, as well as advice to employers concerning all aspects of employment relations. Mr. Ross defends and advises clients on the full spectrum of employment relation issues including sexual harassment, age, sex, disability, race, and other forms of discrimination, defamation, breach of contract, noncompetition agreements, wrongful discharge, discipline and termination of employees, plant closing, OSHA, wage and hour problems, and general employment policies, practices, and procedures as well as employee handbooks. Mr. Ross is active in labor relations and defends employers before administrative agencies such as the National Labor Relations Board and in arbitrations. He also negotiates and provides general advice regarding collective bargaining agreement interpretations and general labor relation issues. Mr. Ross is an adjunct professor for William Mitchell College of Law and for University of St. Thomas MBA Program.
Education: JD 1976, St. John's University (N.Y.C.); BA 1968, Syracuse University.
Employment History: Partner (Employment Law & Litigation) 1986-88, Robins, Kaplan, Miller & Ciresi; partner (Employment Law & Litigation) 1984-86, Roberts & Finger (New York); associate (Employment Law & Litigation) 1980-84, Simpson, Thacher & Bartlett (New York); staff attorney 1976-80, National Labor Relations Board (New York).
Representative Clients: Clients range from small businesses to multinational corporations, including Caterpillar Paving Products, Inc.; Club Corporation of America; PPG Industries; Fortis Benefit Insurance Co.; Floyd Security Inc.; Domino's Pizza Inc.
Professional Associations: ABA (Labor & Employment Law Section); MSBA (Labor & Employment Law Section); HCBA (Program Chair 1993-94, Labor & Employment Law Section); State Bar of Wisconsin; New York State Bar Assn. (Labor & Employment Law Section); New York State Management Attorneys' Conference.
Firm: Mr. Ross is the senior attorney of eight attorneys in Fredrikson & Byron's Labor & Employment Law Group, which focuses on preventing and resolving legal problems in the workplace. The group handles a full range of employment law issues including preventative advice and defense of lawsuits and administrative actions against employers. This practice group includes Kathleen Hughes, Paul Landry, Anne Radolinski, Robert Boisvert, Jr., Mary Anne Colovic, Mary Krakow, and Mary Hanton. *See additional listing in Employment Law Chapter.*

RICHARD A. ROSS

Fredrikson & Byron, P.A.
1100 International Centre
900 Second Avenue South
Minneapolis, MN 55402

Phone: (612) 347-7022
Fax: (612) 347-7077

Admitted: 1987 Minnesota; 1987 Wisconsin; 1977 New York
Birthdate: 09/04/46

DOUGLAS P. SEATON - Popham, Haik, Schnobrich & Kaufman, Ltd. - 222 South Ninth Street, Suite 3300 - Minneapolis, MN 55402 - Phone: (612) 333-4800, Fax: (612) 334-8888 - *See complete biographical profile in Employment Law Chapter.*

Chapter 24: Labor Law

RALPH T. SMITH

Smith Law Firm, P.A.
115 Fifth Street
P.O. Box 1420
Bemidji, MN 56601

Phone: (218) 751-3130
Fax: (218) 751-3132

Admitted: 1958 Minnesota;
1962 US Sup. Ct.;
1980 US Ct. App. (8th Cir.)
Birthdate: 10/07/33

•**RALPH T. SMITH:** Mr. Smith represents management in public and private sector labor negotiations, human rights claims, and veterans preference proceedings as well as representing employers in civil litigation and administrative proceedings relating to labor and management issues. **Education:** JD 1958 Order of the Coif, University of Minnesota; AB 1955, University of Notre Dame. **Representative Clients:** First Federal Banking and Savings, F.A.; First National Bank of Bemidji; City of Bemidji; City of Bagley; City of Blackduck; North Country Health Services; numerous school districts in northwestern Minnesota. **Professional Associations:** MSBA (Board of Governors 1979-82; Real Property Section); Certified Real Property Specialist, MSBA Real Property Section; MN School Boards Assn. (Council of Attorneys). **Community Involvement:** Judge Advocate General Corps 1959-62, US Army; First Federal Banking and Savings, F.A., Bemidji (Board Chair); North Country Hospital (past Board member & Chair); Bemidji Jaycees Distinguished Service Award. **Firm:** The Smith Law Firm has been established in Bemidji for over 70 years with a primary emphasis on representation of employers in all facets of business law, including labor and employment law. *See additional listings in Probate, Estate Planning & Trusts Law and Commercial Real Estate Law Chapters.*

MARSHALL H. TANICK - Mansfield & Tanick, P.A. - 1560 International Centre, 900 Second Avenue South - Minneapolis, MN 55402-3383 - Phone: (612) 339-4295, Fax: (612) 339-3161 - *See complete biographical profile in Employment Law Chapter.*

ROBERT R. WEINSTINE - Winthrop & Weinstine, P.A. - 3000 Dain Bosworth Plaza, 60 South Sixth Street - Minneapolis, MN 55402 - Phone: (612) 347-0700, Fax: (612) 347-0600 - *See complete biographical profile in Commercial Litigation Chapter.*

JOHN C. ZWAKMAN

Dorsey & Whitney
Pillsbury Center South
220 South Sixth Street
Minneapolis, MN 55402-1498

Phone: (612) 340-2786
Fax: (612) 340-2643

Admitted: 1965 Wisconsin;
1966 Minnesota

•**JOHN C. ZWAKMAN:** Mr. Zwakman practices in the areas of labor and employment law, representing employers in all phases of labor and employment issues, including civil litigation and National Labor Relations Board and other administrative proceedings. He also consults with clients regarding all phases of advice concerning labor law and employment law issues. Mr. Zwakman has been a partner in the Labor and Employment Law Department at Dorsey & Whitney since 1971. **Education:** LLB 1965, University of Wisconsin (Board of Editors 1964-65, *Wisconsin Law Review*); BS 1962, University of Wisconsin. **Employment History:** Partner 1971-present, Associate 1965-71, Dorsey & Whitney. **Professional Associations:** MSBA (Labor and Employment Law Section); ABA (Labor and Employment Law Section). **Firm:** Dorsey & Whitney is the largest law firm in Minnesota and one of the largest firms in the United States with over 350 lawyers in 12 offices. The depth and breadth of the experience of its lawyers enables it to provide a broad range of services to meet the diverse legal needs of its client base, which includes Fortune 500 companies, public agencies, banks and other financial institutions, nonprofit organizations, individual investors, family owned businesses, and high-tech and low-tech, growth oriented companies. *See additional listing in Employment Law Chapter.*

Complete listing of all attorneys nominated in Labor Law

EMERY W. BARTLE, Dorsey & Whitney, Minneapolis; **EDWARD J. BOHRER,** Felhaber, Larson, Fenlon & Vogt, P.A., Minneapolis; **ROBERT S. BURK,** Popham, Haik, Schnobrich & Kaufman, Ltd., Minneapolis; **DON L. BYE,** Halverson, Watters, Bye, Downs, Reyelts & Bateman, Ltd., Duluth; **GREGG M. CORWIN,** Gregg M. Corwin & Associates, St. Louis Park; **JAMES M. DAWSON,** Felhaber, Larson, Fenlon & Vogt, P.A., Minneapolis; **MICHAEL J. GALVIN JR.,** Briggs and Morgan, P.A., St. Paul; **STEPHEN D. GORDON,** Gordon Miller O'Brien, Minneapolis; **ROBERT S. HALAGAN,** Felhaber, Larson, Fenlon & Vogt, P.A., Minneapolis; **ROBERT L. HOBBINS,** Dorsey & Whitney, Minneapolis; **DAVID R. HOLS,** Felhaber, Larson, Fenlon & Vogt, P.A., Minneapolis; **ROGER A. JENSEN,** Peterson, Bell, Converse & Jensen, P.A., Minneapolis; **MAURICE W. O'BRIEN,** Gordon Miller O'Brien, Minneapolis; **ROGER A. PETERSON,** Peterson Engberg & Peterson, Minneapolis; **JOSEPH J. ROBY JR.,** Johnson, Killen, Thibodeau & Seiler, P.A., Duluth; **RICHARD A. ROSS,** Fredrikson & Byron, P.A., Minneapolis; **RALPH T. SMITH,** Smith Law Firm, P. A., Bemidji; **HOWARD B. TARKOW,** Maslon, Edelman, Borman & Brand, Minneapolis; **THOMAS M. VOGT,** Felhaber, Larson, Fenlon & Vogt, P.A., Minneapolis; **JOHN C. ZWAKMAN,** Dorsey & Whitney, Minneapolis.

CHAPTER 25

NONPROFIT CORPORATIONS LAW

Today, many small organizations are interested in the benefits of tax-exempt, nonprofit status. Forming a tax-exempt, nonprofit corporation is a fairly complex endeavor that requires time, money and an understanding of legal and tax technicalities—all of which can be scarce in organizations that would most likely benefit from tax-exempt treatment and nonprofit status. Still, the benefits available to nonprofits are so great that it is often worth the time and hassle to become familiar with the necessary steps. Some of the rules governing how a nonprofit corporation must be formed and run are complex. An organization will likely need professional advice from an attorney to establish the business, and from an accountant to oversee financial matters when the corporation is in operation. This chapter explores the issues uniquely of concern in forming a nonprofit corporation and the process of gaining tax-exempt status for a nonprofit corporation.

BECOMING A TAX-EXEMPT, NONPROFIT CORPORATION

The process of becoming a tax-exempt, nonprofit corporation actually has two distinct phases, first, creating the nonprofit corporation, then, applying for tax-exempt status for the corporation once it has been created. The chronology of these two phases is important. The second phase—applying for tax-exempt status will be far simpler for organizations that keep that goal in mind during the first phase—creating the nonprofit corporation.

BENEFITS OF TAX-EXEMPT, NONPROFIT STATUS

The primary benefits of tax-exempt, nonprofit status are financial. All or most of the money made by a tax-exempt, nonprofit corporation is free of federal, state, and local taxes, so the organization can devote a larger share of its funds to the ends for which it was formed rather than turning it over to the government. Furthermore, nonprofit status is often a prerequisite to obtaining private grants or government funding. Donors are more likely to contribute financially to tax-exempt, nonprofits than to non-exempt organizations because donors can write off their donation on their tax returns. In addition to tax benefits, there may be low-cost postage and advertising rates available to nonprofit organizations and many retail stores offer reduced rates to nonprofits and their employees.

As with all other businesses, nonprofits are open to lawsuits and liability for the way they conduct themselves. Organizing as a nonprofit corporation can shield the individuals who run the organization from personal liability for the debts of their organization.

The often overlooked advantages to forming a tax-exempt, nonprofit organization are the internal benefits that the organization experiences when forced to commit to writing its management structure and corporate purpose. Many nonprofits start out as a small group of committed persons working toward a definite goal. If the organization grows, commitment levels can fall and goals multiply. Having to think through the organization's purposes and management procedures can bring clarity, focus, and structure at an early stage in the organization's life. These qualities can be invaluable as the organization grows, takes on new projects, adds new members, or if internal disputes arise.

DRAWBACKS OF TAX-EXEMPT, NONPROFIT STATUS

Just because an organization qualifies for tax-exempt, nonprofit status does not mean that seeking nonprofit status is the best plan. Tax-exempt, nonprofit status does have drawbacks:

- Profits of the organization cannot be divided among workers or directors (although workers and directors can be paid reasonable salaries).

- Only a small amount of the group's income can be earned from sources unrelated to the organization's reason for receiving tax-exempt status.

- The assets of the group cannot go toward purposes other than those that warranted the tax-exempt status.

Many businesses do not take advantage of tax-exempt, nonprofit status because they prefer the flexibility and possibility of personal financial gain associated with for-profit status. Other organizations that could qualify as nonprofit simply do not incorporate in order to avoid the paperwork. For very small organizations that do not need donations or that have few tax obligations, forming a nonprofit corporation and seeking tax-exempt status may be more trouble than it is worth.

NONPROFIT CORPORATIONS IN MINNESOTA

Most nonprofit corporations in Minnesota are governed by the Minnesota Nonprofit Corporation Act. The Minnesota Nonprofit Corporation Act does not apply to cooperative associations, public cemetery associations and corporations, private cemeteries, and some religious associations. Under the Minnesota Nonprofit Corporation Act, a nonprofit may not be formed for any purpose that involves pecuniary gain, paying dividends or any other pecuniary remuneration, directly or indirectly to its members, other than those members that are nonprofit organizations or subdivisions, units, or agencies of the federal state, or local government. There are many rules to be aware of when forming and running a nonprofit corporation. In addition to the information in this chapter, much of the information in the Publicly Held Corporations Law Chapter is equally applicable to nonprofit corporations.

Necessary Documents

At the very beginning of the process of forming a nonprofit corporation, there are two documents which a group can use to file for incorporation—articles of incorporation and bylaws. The articles are the documents filed with the Secretary of State's Office and form the charter document of the corporation. Articles of incorporation must include:

- Name of the corporation

- Address of the registered office of the corporation and the name of the registered agent, if any, at that address

- Name and address of each incorporator

- Clear statement that the corporation is organized pursuant to the Minnesota Nonprofit Corporation Act

Although the list of required items is short, most articles of incorporation are complex, because incorporators want to craft an organization uniquely suited to the people who form it and the purposes for which it is formed. The Minnesota Nonprofit Corporation Act contains numerous "fallback" provisions detailing how the corporation operates. Some provisions automatically apply unless they are specifically modified in the articles of incorporation or bylaws. Other provisions can only be modified in the articles of incorporation. An attorney experienced in advising nonprofits can help an organization decide how much it wants to alter the "fallback" provisions of the act and whether it is best to do so in the articles of incorporation or bylaws. Incorporators are charged with signing and delivering the articles of incorporation to the Secretary of State's Office.

The nonprofit corporation may, but need not, have bylaws. Bylaws usually define the rules and procedures under which the corporation will operate. Bylaws typically include:

- Number, qualifications, manner of election, powers, duties, and compensation of directors

- Qualifications for membership

- Different classifications for members

- Manner of admission, withdrawal, suspension, and expulsion of members

- Property, voting, and other rights and privileges of members

- Appointment and authority of committees

- Appointment or election, duties, compensation, and tenure of officers

- Time, place, and manner of calling, conducting, and giving notice of member, board, and committee meetings or of conducting mail ballots

- Making of reports and financial statements to members

- Numbers required to establish a quorum for meetings of members, committees and the board

Later, the articles of incorporation and bylaws must be submitted to the IRS when filing for federal tax-exempt status under section 501(c)(3) of the Internal Revenue Code, discussed below. In Minnesota, a nonprofit corporation should file bylaws and articles of incorporation with the Secretary of State's Office. All nonprofit corporations in the state are required to file an annual registration with the Secretary of State's Office. The organization must also register with the Charities Division of the Minnesota Attorney General's Office if it solicits donations within the state.

Required Officers

Corporations governed by the Minnesota Nonprofit Corporation Act must have at least two officers—a president and a treasurer—although the same person can perform both functions. Unless modified by the articles, bylaws, or resolution, the president shall:

- Actively manage the general business of the corporation
- When present, preside at meetings of the board and member meetings
- Ensure that orders and resolutions of the board are carried out
- Sign and deliver deeds, mortgages, bonds, contracts, and other instruments pertaining to the business of the corporation

Unless the corporation modifies the following requirements in its articles, bylaws, or resolution, the treasurer shall:

- Keep accurate financial records for the corporation
- Endorse and/or deposit money, drafts, checks, and notes in the name of the corporation
- Disburse corporate funds in the name of the corporation
- As required, keep the president and board informed of the financial condition of the corporation

Liability of Officers

Incorporating means that a business is considered a legal entity separate from that of its employees and directors, and thus is able to make contracts and incur liability in its own right. But the employees and directors can have legal responsibilities for actions taken on behalf of the corporation.

Minnesota Statutes require that the director of a nonprofit corporation discharge his or her duties in good faith, in a manner he or she reasonably believes to be in the best interest of the corporation, and "with the care an ordinarily prudent person in a like position would exercise under similar circumstances." A director who performed his or her duties in accord with this standard is not liable by reason of having been a director.

GETTING TAX-EXEMPT STATUS FOR A NONPROFIT

A fairly wide variety of businesses and groups can qualify for federal tax-exemption. Some groups such as chambers of commerce, social clubs, and credit unions may be entitled to federal tax-exempt status under very narrowly drawn statutes not discussed here. The most desirable form of tax-exempt status is found in section 501(c)(3) of the Internal Revenue Code. This is the most desirable form of tax-exemption because 501(c)(3) corporations are not only exempt from federal, state, and local taxes, but donors to the organization can qualify for tax write-offs for their contributions to the organization.

Nonprofits that Qualify for 501(c)(3) Status

There are five different purposes for which the IRS allows organizations to file for tax-exempt status as nonprofit corporations under 501(c)(3) of the tax code. They are:

Charitable Purpose

The term "charitable" here is more broadly defined than in common usage, referring to anything that has benefit for the public. Organizations established for a charitable purpose can be intended to benefit only a relatively small group of people, but not so small that the actual beneficiaries are specifically listed. Examples of charitable purposes include the maintenance of public buildings and relief for the poor.

Religious Group

This term is broadly interpreted. "Religious groups" include mainstream organized churches as well as many other organizations that have truly and sincerely held beliefs. The only necessary factor for qualifying as a religious group is that the group be pursuing the advancement of religion. It is more difficult to qualify as a "church" for tax-exempt purposes than it is to qualify as a religious group.

Scientific Organization

Groups whose primary purpose is scientific research in the public interest are also eligible for tax-exempt status. Research is considered to be in the public interest if the results are eventually made available to the public.

Literary Purpose

Literary purpose is a rarely-used category for filing because most literary organizations that could fit this classification file instead as educational organizations. Generally, groups that sell books that promote the public interest, sell them at or below cost, and make them available to the general public would qualify as groups organized for literary purposes.

Educational Organization

Educational organization is another broadly defined filing category in which endeavors that are aimed at self development as well as community benefit are allowed tax-free status for the purpose of education. A person or group may qualify under this purpose to espouse a point of view, provided it is not a political position.

Application for Federal Tax-Exemption

There are four publications and forms available from the IRS that should be used to apply for 501(c)(3) tax exemption.

- Package 1023
Application for Recognition of Exemption

- Form 8708
User Fee for Exempt Organization Determination Letter Request

- Form ss-4
Application for Employer Identification Number

- Publication 557
Tax-Exempt Status for Your Organization

Each of these publications is available free of charge and all come with detailed instructions or advice. The IRS will respond to the application in one of three ways—granting the exemption, requesting further information before making a final decision, or issuing notice of proposed adverse determination. Form 1023 is the nucleus of the application. The 1023 packet includes instructions for responding to a request for further information or notice of proposed adverse determination. If the nonprofit corporation is granted tax exempt status, the determination letter will summarize the basis for the decision and conditions that must be met to maintain it.

QUALIFYING FOR STATE TAX-EXEMPT STATUS

In order to receive state tax-exemption, a nonprofit must file a separate application with the Minnesota Department of Revenue. The state decision of whether to grant a nonprofit corporation state tax-exemption always follows the IRS decision regarding tax-exempt status, so nonprofits should not apply to the Department of Revenue until they receive an official notification letter from the IRS. The state application, known as M-120, is very simple to complete. Applicants must attach to the M-120 form a copy of their federal exemption application and a copy of the federal determination letter. If granted, the Minnesota exemption will be made retroactive to the date of the federal exemption.

RESOURCES

Office of the Secretary of State, Business Services Division, 180 State Office Building, St. Paul, MN 55115, (612) 296-2863.

Minnesota Department of Revenue, P.O. Box 64446, St. Paul, MN 55145-4453. Twin Cities (612) 296-0555, Outstate Minnesota (800) 652-9747.

How to Form a Nonprofit Corporation. 2d national ed., Anthony Mancuso, Nolo Press, Berkeley, CA, 1994.

What Every Executive Better Know About the Law. Michael G. Trachtman, Simon & Schuster, New York, NY, 1987.

The Practical Musician: A Legal Guidebook to the Music Industry. Minnesota Continuing Legal Education, 40 Milton Street North, St. Paul, MN 55104, (612) 227-8266, Toll free: (800) 759-8840.

Forming Corporations and Partnerships. 2d ed., John Cotton Howell, Liberty Hall Press, McGraw Hill, New York, NY, 1991.

Keys to Incorporating. Steven A. Fox, Barrons, Hauppage, NY, 1989.

How to Incorporate, A Key for Entepreneurs & Professsionals. Michael R. Diamond & Julie L. Williams, John Wiley & Sons, New York, NY, 1987.

Forming Corporations & Partnerships, An Easy Do-It-Yourself Guide. John C. Howell, Liberty Hall Press, New York, NY, 1986.

Incorporating, A Guide for Small-Business Owners. Carolyn M. Vella & John J. McMonagle, Jr., American Management Associations, New York, NY, 1984.

How to Incorporate Your Business in Any State. Hoyt L. Barber, Liberty House, New York, NY, 1989.

Nonprofit Organizations, Operations Handbook for Directors and Administrators. Barbara Singer, Callaghan & Company, Wilmette, IL, 1987.

Nonprofit Organizations, Forms for Creation, Operation and Dissolution. Marcia L. Clifford, William B. Glynn, Amy Pat Tyrell, Callaghan & Company, Wilmette, IL, 1987.

Running a One-Person Business. Claude Whitmeyer & Salli Rasberry, Ten Speed Press, Berkeley, CA, 1989.

The Closet Enterpreneur, 337 Ways to Start Your Successful Business With Little or No Money. Neil Balter, Carrie Shook, Career Press, Hawthorne, NJ, 1994.

Resources and Counseling for the Arts, 75 West Fifth Street, Suite 429, St. Paul, MN 55102. (612) 292-4381. *Referrals and information; will provide up to one-half hour of free legal consultation to artists.*

SCORE-The Service Corps of Retired Volunteers (SCORE) is a fraternity of retired business managers who volunteer to help new or existing businesses and nonprofit organizations. Information about the services offered through SCORE can be gained by contacting one of its regional offices throughout the state. A complete list of these offices can be found in Appendix A: Legal Resources. Four of the larger chapters are listed below:

Duluth SCORE Office Chapter #286
Duluth Chamber of Commerce
118 E Superior Street
Duluth, MN 55802
Phone: (218) 722-5501

Rochester SCORE Chapter #406
Rochester Chamber of Commerce
220 S Broadway, Suite 100
Rochester, MN 55904
Phone: (507) 288-1122

Minneapolis SCORE Chapter #2
North Plaza Building, Suite 51
5217 Wayzata Boulevard
Minneapolis, MN 55416
Phone: (612) 591-0539

St. Paul SCORE Chapter #391
St. Paul Chamber of Commerce
101 Norwest Center
55 Fifth Street E
St. Paul, MN 55101
Phone: (612) 223-5010

Nonprofit Corporations Law Leading Attorneys

ROLLIN H. CRAWFORD - LeVander, Gillen & Miller, P.A. - 633 South Concord Street, Suite 402 - South St. Paul, MN 55075 - Phone: (612) 451-1831, Fax: (612) 450-7384 - *See complete biographical profile in Federal, State & Local Government Law Chapter.*

JOHN S. HIBBS - Dorsey & Whitney - Pillsbury Center South, 220 South Sixth Street - Minneapolis, MN 55402-1498 - Phone: (612) 340-2661, Fax: (612) 340-8827 - *See complete biographical profile in Health Law Chapter.*

RUTH A. MICKELSEN - Allina Health System - 5601 Smetana Drive - Minnetonka, MN 55343 - Phone: (612) 936-1609, Fax: (612) 936-6858 - *See complete biographical profile in Health Law Chapter.*

NICK SMITH - Fryberger, Buchanan, Smith & Frederick, P.A. - 302 West Superior Street, Suite 700 - Duluth, MN 55802 - Phone: (218) 722-0861, Fax: (218) 722-9568 - *See complete biographical profile in Publicly Held Corporations Law Chapter.*

GERALD L. THOREEN - Hughes, Thoreen & Knapp, P.A. - 110 South Sixth Avenue - St. Cloud, MN 56302-1718 - Phone: (612) 251-6175, Fax: (612) 251-6857 - *See complete biographical profile in Probate, Estate Planning & Trusts Law Chapter.*

PAUL M. TORGERSON - Dorsey & Whitney - Pillsbury Center South, 220 South Sixth Street - Minneapolis, MN 55402-1498 - Phone: (612) 340-8700, Fax: (612) 340-8827 - *See complete biographical profile in Health Law Chapter.*

CHAPTER 26

PERSONAL INJURY DEFENSE LAW

Personal injuries, as the name implies, are injuries to an individual person. In contrast, crimes are wrongful acts against society. The government punishes those who commit crimes—criminals—with criminal penalties. For personal injuries, the government does not punish the wrongdoer but gives the victim the right to pursue a private, civil lawsuit, called a tort action, against the wrongdoer. Some wrongful acts are both crimes and torts, and can subject the wrongdoer to both criminal penalties imposed by the government and tort remedies sought by the injured party. This chapter outlines the general legal principles courts use to decide most personal injury cases, and gives an overview of the personal injuries that most often lead to lawsuits.

TORT LAW GENERALLY

Most civil suits are determined using theories contained in the law of torts (from the Latin word *tortus*, meaning twisted). Personal injury lawsuits are usually based on the tort law premise that when someone does something that harms another person either physically, mentally or financially, the person who suffers the harm ought to be compensated for the loss and the person who caused the loss should pay. Whether a civil lawsuit based on tort law will succeed depends upon the type of tort committed.

DEGREE OF FAULT

Each of the three kinds of torts—negligence, intentional misconduct, and strict liability—has its own degree of fault (not to be confused with the burden of proof, discussed below) that a plaintiff must show in order to collect from a defendant. Proving that someone else was negligent hinges on the following question: Was the party who allegedly caused the injury behaving at least as carefully as a reasonable person would have behaved under the same circumstances? If not, then that party was negligent and has committed the tort of negligence. Examples of negligence include an automobile accident caused by a reckless driver, or a customer falling and being hurt at a store because a store owner did not repair a defective door or an unsafe escalator. If a reasonable person would have driven more prudently, or if a reasonable store owner would have repaired the defective door or unsafe escalator, then the negligent party could be found liable by a judge or jury. Product liability cases often allege negligence. For example, a plaintiff might allege that a reasonable automotive engineer would have known that a particular type of steering system would cause a driver to lose control of a car and thus should have taken steps to redesign the steering system.

The outcome of lawsuits alleging negligence can be difficult to predict because guessing how much care a reasonable person would have exercised in the same situation is difficult. The reasonable person standard is vague, imprecise, and apt to be interpreted differently by different people. Often, a practice that seemed reasonable in the past may appear unreasonable with the benefit of hindsight. Finding an attorney who has experience with how juries typically interpret the reasonable person standard is therefore one of the most important steps in successfully defending a personal injury lawsuit alleging that a person acted unreasonably.

Intentional misconduct occurs when someone does something to deliberately hurt another person or damage another person's property. For example, if a manufacturer deliberately sells products it knows to be defective, it is causing harm on purpose. A plaintiff alleging intentional misconduct need not compare the defendant's actions to those of a reasonable person, he or she need only show that the defendant intended his or her actions. In a civil lawsuit alleging intentional misconduct, a plaintiff can recover punitive damages in addition to awards for injuries, pain, and suffering. Punitive damages, designed to punish people or organizations for unlawful acts, are often very large sums of money. Until recently, there were few limits on the amount of money a jury could award as punitive damages. However, federal and state legislatures have recently passed laws putting caps on punitive damage awards in certain types of cases, and judges have long had the authority to reduce many types of punitive damage awards. Still, it is to the plaintiff's advantage to convince a jury that his or her injuries were the result of intentional misconduct rather than negligence.

The final theory of tort liability, strict liability, applies only to very dangerous situations. If someone does something extremely dangerous, such as demolish a building, and someone gets hurt as a result, the injured person can sue for damages without having to prove the defendant acted negligently or with intent to cause harm. The principle behind strict liability lawsuits is that some activities are so dangerous that, in exchange for permission to engage in the activity, the actor must assume total responsibility for any results.

BURDEN OF PROOF

The burden of proof in a tort case, as in most civil law cases, is lower than the proof required in criminal law cases. In a criminal case, the state must prove a person's guilt beyond a reasonable doubt. To win a personal injury lawsuit based on tort law, the plaintiff need only show that a majority of the evidence shows that an injury was caused by the defendant's tortious actions. The different burdens of proof mean that a company might be acquitted of criminal charges stemming from its actions and still be found liable in a civil lawsuit stemming from the same actions.

COMPARATIVE FAULT

Tort law attempts to compensate victims if their injury is caused by another person. Where one person clearly causes all of another person's injury, blame is easy to place. In many other cases, however, the victim's actions help cause the injury or make it worse than it would otherwise be. For instance, a negligent driver might injure a pedestrian who is negligently walking in the street, instead of on a sidewalk where a prudent pedestrian normally walks. A prudent person might be slightly injured when using a defective chainsaw, whereas a less prudent person might incur more severe injuries by negligently failing to wear safety goggles while using the chainsaw. In these cases, a judge or jury must calculate how much each party is at fault. Each state has its own rules for calculating damages that can be recovered when a victim is at least partially to blame for his or her own injury.

Minnesota has a comparative fault rule. Under the comparative fault rule, a judge reduces the amount of any damage award by the percent that the victim's own actions contributed to his or her injuries. For example, if a jury finds that a plaintiff suffered $100,000 in damages, but was 30 percent at fault, the judge reduces the damage award by 30 percent, to $70,000. In Minnesota, the reduction is only up to 50 percent. If the victim is more than 50 percent at fault, he or she collects nothing.

VICARIOUS LIABILITY

There are several ways that a business can be held liable for the actions of its actions. All are known as vicarious liability. For example, a company might be held responsible for damage caused by an employee if the company knows that the employee is likely to injure someone and negligently fails to exercise adequate control over the employee. The owner of a vehicle can be held responsible for accidents caused when another person drives the vehicle if the owner negligently entrusts the vehicle to the other driver. The most common form of vicarious liability is known by the Latin term *respondeat superior*. Under *respondeat superior*, an employer is responsible for torts committed by employees within the scope of their employment. A business owner is usually not responsible for acts committed by independent contractors. For example, if a pedestrian is struck and injured by a person driving to a party, the victim has a claim against the driver. If the pedestrian is hit by a person driving a delivery van for his or her employer, then *respondeat superior* allows the pedestrian to bring claims against both the driver and the employer. Frequently, personal injury plaintiffs cannot recover anything from the employee because he or she has no money. Because employers usually have more money or better insurance, plaintiffs often focus their recovery efforts on the employers. An employer may have a cause of action against the employee who exposed the company to liability, but such actions are rarely pursued either because the employee has no money or the employer assumes that to do so would create ill will among remaining employees.

PREMISES LIABILITY

Premises liability is an area of tort law that governs the duties owed by landowners to persons on their property. Generally speaking, a landowner is liable for anyone injured on the landowner's property and a jury can award damages to the injured person. However, a landowner may not be liable if he or she had no way of knowing about a hazard that caused an accident. No one is responsible if an accident was truly unavoidable, and, as described above, a plaintiff cannot recover from someone unless the plaintiff can prove fault (strict liability is the only exception to this principle). In general, a landowner is not liable for injuries to a trespasser, although a landowner must take reasonable care to protect persons who are likely to approach a property for legitimate purposes, such as letter carriers or delivery persons. Anyone, even a trespasser, can sue a landowner if he or she is injured by an unjustified hazard on the property, such as a trap designed intentionally to injure people.

Under a theory known as "attractive nuisance" a landowner can be liable for injuries to small children if the landlord fails to take preventative action to avoid injuries to children he or she should have known would come onto the property. A swimming pool is a classic example of an attractive nuisance. An apartment complex that maintains a private outdoor swimming pool is obligated to take measures designed to keep out trespassers, such as erecting a fence or having a lifeguard present, because the law assumes that the owner of a pool should know that children will be attracted to a pool despite warning signs.

If someone is injured on public land adjacent to a landlord's property, the landlord generally is not legally liable unless he or she did something to cause the injury, such as hitting a passerby with the falling branches of a tree being cut down on the landowner's property.

Business owners can always be sued if their own carelessness or negligence causes others to be injured. Historically this meant landowners were not liable for the actions of third parties they did not control. However, today business owners can sometimes be liable for injuries caused by third parties committing crimes on their property. An increasing number of crime victims are winning lawsuits filed against business owners who did not, in a jury's opinion, take appropriate measures to ensure the safety of their customers. This type of lawsuit extends the landowner's duty to foresee, and take steps to prevent, possible illegal activity on his or her property. An example of this type of case is one in which a person who is attacked in a parking lot sues the lot's owner for failing to provide security measures that might have prevented the attack.

Whether a lawsuit based on premises liability will succeed largely depends on a jury's opinion of whether a reasonable business owner would have foreseen the probability of the crime occurring. For example, if tenants of an apartment building complain several times to their landlord that their security system is not working, and burglars later rob several apartments, the tenants might have grounds for a successful lawsuit against their landlord alleging negligence in failing to fix the security system.

PRODUCT LIABILITY

A common kind of personal injury lawsuit is one that results from an injury caused by a defective product. Product liability lawsuits require the plaintiff to prove that a product was defective and that the defect was the principal cause of the plaintiff's injury. This section describes the most important principles of law governing product liability cases.

KINDS OF DEFECTS

Product liability lawsuits typically allege one or more of three kinds of defects—defective warning, design defect, and manufacturing defect. Often, a single lawsuit will allege all three theories.

Defective Warning

A manufacturer has a duty to provide adequate instructions concerning the safe use of its product and must warn buyers of any dangers associated with the product. If such warnings are not present, the manufacturer may be liable for injuries caused by the product. Manufacturers therefore have a duty to perform safety tests to determine what warning labels need to be put on a product. These tests should simulate conditions under which the product would ordinarily be used. For example, the manufacturer of a hand-held electric hair dryer must anticipate that its product might be used above a sink full of water and therefore must warn buyers that dropping the product in water may lead to electrocution. However, a warning label need not be put on an obviously dangerous product, such as a kitchen knife.

Included in the duty to warn is a duty to provide post sale information. Under Minnesota law, manufacturers must warn consumers of hazards associated with a product discovered after a product has been sold. A manufacturer may also be required to recall products in which defects have been discovered and to redesign the products to make them safe. In Minnesota, these are continual obligations of manufacturers. In other words, a manufacturer must warn consumers about, and possibly recall, an unsafe product, even if the manufacturer stopped making it many years ago.

Design Defect

Sometimes products are built exactly as designed, but are dangerous because of poor engineering, inadequate testing or poor choice of construction materials. A manufacturer is negligent if it fails to take reasonable care to ensure that a product is designed to perform safely. Not only must companies make sure their products are safe when they are used in the intended way, but also in unintended, though foreseeable, ways. If a manufacturer cannot eliminate a danger from a product, or install a guard to protect a user from the danger, then the manufacturer must warn the user of the danger. Most product liability cases attempt to prove that a design defect caused an injury.

Manufacturing Defect

This type of defect occurs when a product is designed well, but through a flaw in the manufacturing process, fails to meet the specifications contained in the design. For example, even if a motorcycle manufacturer ordinarily makes a well-designed gasoline tank for its motorcycles, if it makes a leaking one that causes a fire, then the manufacturer could be liable for injuries caused by that defect.

TYPES OF PRODUCT LIABILITY CLAIMS

Most often, product liability lawsuits are brought under one or more of three theories—strict liability, negligence, and wrongful death. Knowing which theory a plaintiff is pursuing in a particular case is important because each theory applies different standards and has a different statute of limitations.

Strict Liability

Strict liability holds a manufacturer liable for injuries sustained by a person using its product, if the product is found to be unreasonably dangerous. Under Minnesota law, a plaintiff pursuing a claim for strict liability must prove that a product was defective and unreasonably dangerous, that the defect was present while the product was still in the manufacturer's control, and that the defect was the cause of the injury. The statute of limitations in Minnesota for product liability lawsuits based on strict liability is four years from the date of the injury.

Negligence

Product liability lawsuits can allege negligence when a manufacturer fails to exercise the care that would be exercised by a reasonable manufacturer in the same or similar situation. Whereas strict liability focuses on the manufactured product, negligence theory focuses on the conduct of the manufacturer. A manufacturer who implements very strict production controls designed to ensure that products are made properly may be able to avoid committing a negligence tort because all due care was taken that reasonably could be expected.

Minnesota, like some other states, has laws that under certain conditions allows a plaintiff to collect damages from companies that distribute or sell defective products, even if the company did not design, test, or manufacture the product. If distributors or sellers knew that a product was defective but did nothing to keep it from reaching consumers, they could be held liable for damages. In addition, a distributor who damages a product can be held liable for any injuries this causes, and a retailer who incorrectly assembles or installs a product can also be sued. The statute of limitations in Minnesota for product liability lawsuits based on negligence is six years from the date of the injury.

Wrongful Death

A wrongful death lawsuit is usually a lawsuit filed by the surviving relatives of a person killed by a defective product. Although a wrongful death lawsuit can be filed in other types of personal injury cases such as automobile accidents, it is most often associated with product liability cases. Under Minnesota law, any dependent heirs such as sons or daughters of a person killed by a defective product can sue the manufacturer for that person's future income that was lost when he or she died. Surviving relatives cannot, however, sue a manufacturer to collect damages for the pain and suffering of a person wrongfully killed by a manufacturer's defective product. However, the estate of the dead person can sue to collect money needed to pay any bills for medical treatment received by the person before he or she died.

A person who files a wrongful death lawsuit after the death of a spouse can sue for damages to recover for loss of companionship, affection, and sexual relations. Minnesota also has a fetal protection law that allows wrongful death lawsuits to be filed if a manufacturer's defective product (or a car accident) causes the death of a viable fetus, that is, one that would be capable of surviving outside the mother's womb.

DRAM SHOP LAWS

Dram shop laws are laws that can make a business owner liable for injuries caused by an intoxicated person if the business is responsible for causing that person to become intoxicated illegally. The Minnesota Dram Shop Act allows a spouse, child, parent, guardian, or employer of the intoxicated person, or any other person injured by the intoxicated person to bring a civil action for damages against the party that caused the intoxication by illegally selling alcoholic beverages. Cases most commonly brought under the Act allege illegal sale of alcohol to minors or sale of alcohol to persons who were obviously intoxicated at the time of sale.

The only defense specifically permitted by the Act is that the business establishment reasonably and in good faith relied upon proof of age offered by the person who subsequently became intoxicated. The law states that the only proofs of age sufficient for a business owner to rely upon this defense are:

- A valid driver's license or identification card issued by any state or Canadian province

- A valid military identification card issued by the United States Department of Defense

- In the case of a foreign national (from any nation other than Canada), a valid passport

Thus, businesses licensed to serve alcohol can limit their exposure to liability under the Minnesota Dram Shop Act by implementing programs designed to train employees when to refuse to serve alcohol and preventing the illegal sale of alcohol to minors by insisting upon proof of age from the above list.

WORKERS' COMPENSATION

Like many other states, Minnesota has a Workers' Compensation system to compensate workers for any injuries occurring in the workplace. Without a Workers' Compensation system, workers injured while on the job would have to prove that their employer's negligence led to the injury. Because the system does not require proof of negligence, anyone injured while working for an employer subject to the Minnesota Workers' Compensation Act (only a few employers are exempt) has a greater chance of being compensated than if he or she were injured in some other way and had to file a civil lawsuit. Instead of filing suit, a worker notifies his or her employer of the injury, and the employer then contacts its insurance carrier which handles payment of any medical bills and other claims made by the employee. All employers subject to the Minnesota Workers' Compensation Act must either carry Workers' Compensation insurance or demonstrate that they have the financial resources to cover any reasonably anticipated claims.

The Workers' Compensation system operates under rules substantially different from those used to settle other types of personal injury claims. For this reason, many lawyers specialize in handling only Workers' Compensation disputes, while other lawyers who routinely do personal injury work never handle Workers' Compensation claims.

Under the Minnesota Workers' Compensation Act an injured employee may be eligible for some or all of the following:

- Medical services, including all reasonable expenses for care and treatment

- Temporary total disability payments which provide the employee with as much as two-thirds of his or her weekly wage for the time the worker is unable to work

- Temporary partial disability for employees who are able to work part-time but not able to earn the same amount of money as earned at the time the injury happened

- Permanent partial disability if the employee is permanently disabled

- Permanent total disability payments (as high as two-thirds the salary of the worker at the time of the injury) for employees who are totally disabled and unable to work again

- Death benefits (for some burial expenses and benefits to dependents of the deceased employee) in case of fatal work-related injuries

In return for this relatively easy route to compensation, there is a limit to the amount of money that can be awarded for a work-related injury. For example, employers (or their insurers) are only required to pay for medical expenses, permanent injuries and/or lost wages. An employer cannot be made to pay for emotional distress, pain and suffering, and loss of companionship, affection, or sexual relations. There are only a few exceptions to these limits on an employer's liability for a work-related injury; the limits generally apply even if an employer's negligence caused the injury.

SETTLING WORKERS' COMPENSATION DISPUTES

Often a worker contacts an attorney because the employer or its insurance carrier refuses to pay a Workers' Compensation claim, maintaining that either the injury was not work-related or that the benefits demanded exceed those that are justified for the injury. Sometimes a dispute arises over when an employer stops making Workers' Compensation payments. When a dispute arises, a variety of options exist to settle it, including an administrative conference, conciliation court, or as a final option, a hearing before a Workers' Compensation judge.

By far the most common way to resolve disputes is through a semiformal administrative conference subject to the rules established by the state's Department of Labor and Industry. At the conference, a Department representative acts as an informal mediator and referee who decides what kind of evidence can be discussed by those attending. These rules are very liberal, meaning that almost all applicable evidence can be discussed. Typically, the employer, an investigator from the insurance company (if the employer is not self-insured), the Department representative, the injured employee and the employee's attorney (if one has been hired) attend the conference. The goal of such a conference is to reach a voluntary resolution to the dispute, but if one cannot be reached, the Department representative will make a judgment that everyone is obliged to follow. Such a judgment can be appealed to the Department by anyone involved in the conference.

Going to conciliation court is another way to resolve disputes over a Workers' Compensation claim. Both the employer and employee, however, must agree to turn over the dispute to a conciliation court and the amount of the dispute cannot exceed $5,000. Either side can decide whether to be represented by an attorney in such a proceeding, a decision that should not be made lightly because the decision of the conciliation court judge cannot be appealed.

Finally, a dispute over a Workers' Compensation claim can be taken to a special Workers' Compensation court where a judge will formally hear evidence about the injury and will resolve the dispute in a written decision that both sides must follow. Anyone disagreeing with the decision can appeal it to the Minnesota Workers' Compensation Court of Appeals, and if still unsatisfied, to the Minnesota Supreme Court.

Which of the three ways is best to resolve a Workers' Compensation dispute depends on the particular details surrounding the injury and the amount of money involved. In general, the administrative conference can be the best and least expensive way to solve a dispute, but only if employer and employee are willing to negotiate fairly and compromise if necessary. Both the administrative conference and conciliation court are options that can be pursued without lawyers, and therefore either may be a relatively cheap option.

HIRING AND WORKERS' COMPENSATION

It is illegal for an employer to refuse to hire an individual because he or she has a disabling condition from a prior injury. However, employers are protected from some Workers' Compensation liability if an employee is hired with a pre-existing condition. If an employee suffers an injury that is made worse because of a condition existing prior to the time of hiring, the employer is protected from some liability under the Minnesota Second Injury Law. The purpose of this law is to encourage employers to hire people who may have disabilities from a previous injury.

RESOURCES

An Employer's Guide to Employment Law Issues in Minnesota. 3rd Edition, 1993. This book has a good chapter on Workers' Compensation rules. For a free copy, contact the Minnesota Small Business Assistance Office, 500 Metro Square Building, 121 7th Place East, St. Paul, MN 55101-2146, (612) 296-3871 or (800) 657-3858.

A Manufacturer's Guide to Product Liability Law in Minnesota. A free booklet from the Minnesota Small Business Assistance Office at the address listed above.

The Products Liability Resource Manual. James T. O'Reilly and Nancy C. Cody, The American Bar Association, Chicago, IL, 1993.

Personal Injury Defense Law Leading Attorneys

The attorneys profiled in this section were nominated by their peers in a statewide survey conducted in 1993 in which several thousand Minnesota attorneys were asked to name the lawyer to whom they would send a friend or family member in need of legal assistance in the area of *Personal Injury Defense Law.*

Because the survey resulted in a list of less than five percent of Minnesota's practicing attorneys, this should not be construed as a complete list. Nevertheless, it is an excellent source of highly qualified and reputable attorneys, who, if unable to assist can in most cases make quality referrals.

A list of all attorneys nominated in this category is found at the end of this section. For information on the survey methodology see page ix.

Please note that the shorter, two line attorney listings in this section are of attorneys who practice in this area but whose full biographical profile appears in another section of this book. A bullet "•" preceeding name indicates the attorney was nominated in this particular area of law. For information on the format of these profiles, consult the section "Using the *Business Guidebook*" found on page xiv. Note that the following abbreviations are used throughout these profiles:

The attorneys profiled below were recommended by their peers in a statewide survey.

App.	- Appellate	ABA	- American Bar Association
Cir.	- Circuit	ATLA	- American Trial Lawyers Association
Ct.	- Court	HCBA	- Hennepin County Bar Association
Dist.	- District	MDLA	- Minnesota Defense Lawyers Association
Hon.	- Honorable	MSBA	- Minnesota State Bar Association
JD	- Law degree (Juris Doctor)	MTLA	- Minnesota Trial Lawyers Association
LLB	- Law degree	NBTA	- National Board of Trial Advocacy
LLM	- Master in Law degree	RCBA	- Ramsey County Bar Association
Sup.	- Supreme		

•**DOUGLAS P. ANDERSON:** Mr. Anderson handles all types of civil litigation with an emphasis on personal injury claims. He is a no-fault arbitrator for the American Arbitration Association and often acts as a neutral arbitrator in underinsured and uninsured motorist claims.
Education: JD 1975, University of Minnesota; BA 1972 summa cum laude, University of Minnesota-Duluth.
Employment History: Mr. Anderson has been an attorney with Rosenmeier, Anderson & Vogel since 1975 when it was known as Rosenmeier & Simonett. He became a partner in 1978.
Representative Clients: American National Bank of Little Falls; First State Bank of Swanville; School Districts of Pillager, Little Falls, Swanville, Pierz, Royalton, Motley, and Holdingford; and various businesses and individuals for their civil trial needs.
Professional Associations: MSBA; MTLA; Seventh District Bar Assn. (past President; past member, Ethics Committee).
Community Involvement: Central Minnesota Council of the Boy Scouts (past President); Employment Enterprises, Inc. (past President); Morrison County United Way (past President); Community Development Corp. (Board member); Little Falls Area Chamber of Commerce (Board member); American National Bank (Board member).
Firm: Rosenmeier, Anderson & Vogel has been engaged in the general practice of law in Little Falls since the early 1920s. The firm was founded by Christian Rosenmeier and continued after his death by his son, A. Gordon Rosenmeier who also served in the Minnesota State Senate for 30 years. John E. Simonett was a partner in the firm before his elevation to the Minnesota Supreme Court. The present partners of the firm are Douglas P. Anderson, Peter Vogel, and Brigid Fitzgerald. The firm is engaged in traditional general practice which includes civil litigation of all sorts, personal injury claims, real estate transactions, family law, probate, banking, and social security claims. Besides individuals, the firm represents cities in Morrison County, state and federally chartered lending institutions, school districts, and insurance companies.

DOUGLAS P. ANDERSON

Rosenmeier, Anderson & Vogel
210 Second Street NE
Little Falls, MN 56345

Phone: (612) 632-5458
Fax: (612) 632-5496

Admitted: 1975 Minnesota
Birthdate: 10/08/50

Chapter 26: Personal Injury Defense Law

JOHN M. ANDERSON

Bassford, Lockhart, Truesdell & Briggs, P.A.
3550 Multifoods Tower
33 South Sixth Street
Minneapolis, MN 55402-3787

Phone: (612) 333-3000
Fax: (612) 333-8829

Admitted: 1978 Minnesota
Birthdate: 11/30/51

•**JOHN M. ANDERSON:** Mr. Anderson practices civil trial law, representing insurers and corporations in environmental, construction, product liability, insurance coverage, and employment claims. He is certified as a Civil Trial Specialist by the Minnesota State Bar Association Civil Litigation Section. Mr. Anderson is a frequent seminar lecturer on insurance law topics. His significant cases include *Bureau of Engraving v. Federal Insurance Company*; *Sylvester Brothers Development Company v. Great Central Insurance Company*; and *Benson v. Northern Gopher Enterprises*.
Education: JD 1978 cum laude, University of Minnesota; BS 1974 with high distinction, University of Minnesota (Phi Beta Kappa).
Employment History: 1978-present, Bassford, Lockhart, Truesdell & Briggs; Legal Writing Instructor 1976-77, University of Minnesota Law School.
Representative Clients: Commercial Union Insurance Company; American States Insurance Company; General Electric Company; Murphy Oil USA, Inc.; St. Paul Fire & Marine Insurance Company.
Professional Associations: ABA; MSBA; HCBA; MDLA; Defense Research Institute.
Community Involvement: Roosevelt Area Youth Hockey Assn. (past President); Youth Baseball (coach); High School Mock Trial Competition (judge); American Civil Liberties Union; MN Civil Liberties Union.
Firm: Founded in 1882, Bassford, Lockhart, Truesdell & Briggs and its predecessor firms have been serving clients in Minnesota for more than 110 years. Today, the Bassford firm's 27 trial lawyers provide a broad range of litigation services for clients around the country, handling all areas of civil and business litigation. *See additional listing in Environmental Law Chapter.*

•**CARL BAER** - Kief, Fuller, Baer, Wallner & Rodgers, Ltd. - P.O. Box 880, 514 America Avenue - Bemidji, MN 56601 - Phone: (218) 751-2221, Fax: (218) 751-2285 - *See complete biographical profile in Commercial Litigation Chapter.*

BRYAN BAUDLER

Baudler, Baudler, Maus & Blahnik
110 North Main Street
Austin, MN 55912

Phone: (507) 433-2393
Fax: (507) 433-9530

Admitted: 1964 Minnesota
Birthdate: 08/14/40

•**BRYAN BAUDLER:** Mr. Baudler's career covers over 30 years in civil trial practice in state and federal courts. He represents insurance carriers in personal injury, product liability, and coverage cases, and business clients in various commercial suits, including employment claims and contract claims. Mr. Baudler is a certified Civil Trial Specialist. His experience extends into the area of alternative dispute resolution, including mediation and arbitration.
Education: JD 1964 cum laude, University of Minnesota; BS 1963 cum laude, University of Minnesota.
Representative Clients: Farmers Insurance Group; Federated Insurance Company; Grinnell Mutual Reinsurance Company; Northbrook Property and Casualty; Iowa Mutual Insurance; Spring Valley Mutual Insurance; Mower County Mutual Insurance; First Bank Southeast, N.A.; Sterling State Bank; Norwest Mortgage, Inc.; Farmers State Bank of Elkton; First Farmers and Merchants State Banks of Brownsdale, Sargeant, and Grand Meadow; First National Bank LeRoy; Litton Industries; City of Grand Meadow; City of Rose Creek; Woodale Management Services, Inc.; Independent School District #499.
Professional Associations: ABA; MSBA; MDLA; Defense Research Institute; Tenth District Bar Assn. (past President); Mower County Bar Assn. (past President); American Board of Trial Advocates; Academy of Certified Trial Lawyers of MN.
Community Involvement: Austin YMCA (Board member); Cedar Valley Services, Inc. (past President); Austin Kiwanis Club (past President); and Mower County Mental Health Assn. (past President).
Firm: Baudler, Baudler, Maus & Blahnik has served clients in Minnesota since 1928. The firm provides a broad range of legal services in the areas of civil and criminal trial practice, probate and estate planning, real estate law, business law, family law, agricultural law, and elder law. *See additional listings in Agricultural Law and Commercial Litigation Chapters.*

•**J. RICHARD BLAND** - Meagher & Geer - 4200 Multifoods Tower, 33 South Sixth Street - Minneapolis, MN 55402 - Phone: (612) 338-0661, Fax: (612) 338-8384 - *See complete biographical profile in Professional Malpractice Defense Law Chapter.*

•**RICHARD A. BOWMAN:** Mr. Bowman is a founding partner of Bowman and Brooke, a litigation firm with offices in Minneapolis, Phoenix, Detroit, San Jose, and Los Angeles. He has been a trial lawyer for 29 years, trying product liability lawsuits for manufacturers in jurisdictions across the country. Mr. Bowman is author of several articles, including "*Erling David Larsen v. General Motors Corporation*" and "For the Defense," 1969 *Hennepin County Lawyer*, and *The Seat Belt Defense in Practice*, 1980 Defense Research Institute monograph. He is coauthor of "Human Factors in the Defense of a Product Liability Case," 1983 *Southern Methodist University Product Liability Institute*.
Education: LLB 1965 cum laude, Order of the Coif, University of Minnesota (Associate Editor 1964-65, *Minnesota Law Review*); BA 1962 magna cum laude, Cornell College (Phi Beta Kappa).
Employment History: Founding Partner, Bowman and Brooke; Partner, Gray, Plant, Mooty, Mooty & Bennett.
Representative Clients: General Motors Corp.; Honda North America, Inc.; Outboard Marine Corp.; Ford Motor Company; Nissan Motor Co., Ltd.
Professional Associations: HCBA; MSBA; ABA; Defense Research Institute; MDLA; The Product Liability Council (PLAC).
Firm: Bowman and Brooke is an energetic and well established national litigation firm with offices in several large cities. It is strictly a litigation firm, now engaged principally in the defense of product liability actions. It is also engaged in environmental, labor and employment, and franchise and commercial litigation. While the firm's attorneys often appear on behalf of its clients in state and federal courts in Minnesota, Arizona, Michigan, and California, they also serve as trial counsel in courts across the country. The firm has established a nationwide reputation for top quality work on complex litigation matters. It is distinguished by a well developed, highly effective team approach to litigation, employing approximately 75 legal assistants, investigators, and other professionals who efficiently deliver services to clients and allow lawyers to concentrate on the legal and tactical aspects of their cases. The firm is a closely knit group with a warm, cooperative working relationship among attorneys and support staff.
See additional listings in Commercial Litigation *and* Professional Malpractice Defense Law *Chapters.*

RICHARD A. BOWMAN

Bowman and Brooke
150 South Fifth Street
Suite 2600
Minneapolis, MN 55402

Phone: (612) 339-8682
Fax: (612) 672-3200

Admitted: 1965 Minnesota;
1990 California
Birthdate: 10/02/40

•**FREDERICK C. BROWN, JR.:** Mr. Brown is a litigation partner whose practice includes jury trials, court trials, appeals, and ADR procedures in state and federal court and before governmental agencies. His litigation experience includes product liability, municipal and governmental, civil rights, general personal injury, insurance coverage and defense, professional malpractice, toxic tort, intellectual property, and commercial and general litigation. Mr. Brown is certified as a Civil Trial Specialist by the National Board of Trial Advocacy and by the Minnesota Civil Trial Certification Council. Mr. Brown also has extensive experience in alternative dispute resolution procedures and serves as one of the firm's active members in the Center for Public Resources. Mr. Brown was a lecturer at the University of Minnesota from 1973 through 1979. He has been in private practice with Popham Haik since 1971 and is former chair of the firm's Litigation Department. He has an active practice with both the Minneapolis and Denver offices of Popham Haik.
Education: JD 1971 cum laude, University of Minnesota (Managing Editor, *Minnesota Law Review*); BA 1969, University of Minnesota.
Employment History: 1971-present, Popham, Haik, Schnobrich & Kaufman.
Professional Associations: Defense Research Institute; MDLA; ABA; MSBA; HCBA; Society of Law and Medicine; Minnesota Civil Trial Certification Council (Board member).
Firm: Popham, Haik, Schnobrich & Kaufman, Ltd., is a firm of more than 230 attorneys with offices in Denver, Miami, Minneapolis, Washington, D.C., and international affiliations in Beijing, China and Leipzig and Stuttgart, Germany. The firm represents clients nationally and internationally on issues relating to corporate and business law, administrative law, and litigation. *See additional listings in* Commercial Litigation *and* Professional Malpractice Defense Law *Chapters.*

FREDERICK C. BROWN, JR.

Popham, Haik, Schnobrich & Kaufman, Ltd.
222 South Ninth Street
Suite 3300
Minneapolis, MN 55402

Phone: (612) 333-4800
Fax: (612) 334-8888

Admitted: 1971 Minnesota;
1991 Colorado;
1971 US Dist. Ct. (MN);
1971 US Ct. App. (8th Cir.);
1983 US Ct. App. (5th Cir.);
1984 US Sup. Ct.;
1992 US Claims Ct.
Birthdate: 11/12/47

Chapter 26: Personal Injury Defense Law

CRAIG R. CAMPBELL

Gunhus, Grinnell, Klinger,
Swenson & Guy, Ltd.
512 Center Avenue
P.O. Box 1077
Moorhead, MN 56561-1077

Phone: (218) 236-6462
Fax: (218) 236-9873

Admitted: 1986 Minnesota;
1981 North Dakota;
1986 US Dist. Ct. (MN);
1981 US Dist. Ct. (ND);
1988 US Ct. App. (8th Cir.);
1993 US Tax Ct.
Birthdate: 12/04/53

•**CRAIG R. CAMPBELL:** With a civil trial practice in tort and commercial matters, Mr. Campbell represents self-insurance corporations and insurance companies in product liability, errors and omissions, legal malpractice, insurance issues, employment issues, agent disputes, commercial and business disputes, and general casualty/liability claims in state and federal courts in Minnesota and North Dakota. His experience is extensive in managing media coverage in high profile litigation. Mr. Campbell lectures at continuing legal education seminars on topics such as "Issues in Bad Faith in Minnesota and North Dakota," "Tort Law Update," and "Issues in Real Estate Litigation."

Education: JD 1981 Order of Barrister, University of North Dakota; BSPA 1976 cum laude, University of North Dakota.

Employment History: Currently, Gunhus, Grinnell, Klinger, Swenson & Guy, Ltd.; Law Clerk, Chief Justice, North Dakota Supreme Court; Associate, Howe, Hardy, Galloway & Maus (Dickinson, ND); Instructor, Business Law, Dickinson State College.

Representative Clients: Blue Cross Blue Shield of North Dakota; The St. Paul Insurance Companies; Home Insurance; Nodak Insurance Company; Sentry Insurance; Royal Insurance; Milbank Insurance; Maryland Casualty Company; State Auto Insurance Company; Goodyear; Westfield Insurance Company; Gate City Federal Savings Bank; Moorhead Construction Company; Simonson Lumber Company; Jarick Products, Inc.

Professional Associations: American Jurisprudence Society; American Arbitration Assn. (Panel of Arbitrators); Clay County Bar Assn.; MSBA; State Bar Assn. of North Dakota; ABA; Defense Research Institute; MDLA; North Dakota Defense Lawyers Assn.

Community Involvement: Kiwanis Club; Fargo-Moorhead Community Theater (Board member).

Firm: Founded in 1914, Gunhus, Grinnell, Klinger, Swenson & Guy, Ltd., is a general practice law firm with offices in Moorhead, MN and Fargo, ND. The firm handles matters primarily in the western half of Minnesota and all of North Dakota, offering a wide range of litigation and commercial services. *See additional listings in Professional Malpractice Defense Law and Commercial Litigation Chapters.*

KEVIN S. CARPENTER

Quinlivan, Sherwood, Spellacy
& Tarvestad, P.A.
P.O. Box 1008
St. Cloud, MN 56302-1008

Phone: (612) 251-1414
Fax: (612) 251-1415

Admitted: 1979 Minnesota;
1993 North Dakota;
1980 US Dist. Ct. (MN)
Birthdate: 11/03/54

•**KEVIN S. CARPENTER:** Mr. Carpenter practices civil trial law, including appeals, in the areas of motor vehicle accidents, insurance coverage disputes, dram shop, medical malpractice, product liability (including Uniform Commercial Code issues) defamation, breach of contract (including employment contracts) and many different types of personal injuries. Mr. Carpenter is certified as a Civil Trial Specialist by the Minnesota State Bar Association. He is the author of "Discussions of Defendant's Insurance Coverage During Voir Dire: An Analysis of the Current Practice and its Origins," *Wm. Mitchell L. Rev.* Vol. 14, No. 1 (1988).

Education: JD 1979, St. Louis University; BA 1976 cum laude, St. John's University.

Employment History: Currently, Quinlivan, Sherwood, Spellacy & Tarvestad, P.A.; Law Clerk 1979-80, Minnesota District Court, Seventh Judicial District.

Representative Clients: Allied Insurance Group; American Hardware Mutual Insurance Company; American West Insurance Company; Auto-Owners Insurance; Farm Bureau Mutual; Grinnell Mutual Reinsurance Company; The St. Paul Companies; State Farm Insurance Company.

Professional Associations: MSBA; ABA; Stearns-Benton Bar Assn.; Defense Research Institute; Assn. of Defense Trial Attorneys; MDLA; American Arbitration Assn. (Panel of Arbitrators).

Community Involvement: Stearns-Benton Counties Law Libraries, St. Cloud (Trustee 1980-84); Sts. Peter, Paul & Michael School, St. Cloud (Trustee 1986-92); St. Peter's Church (Pastoral Council 1992-present); Central Minnesota Youth Soccer Assn. (Coach 1992-94).

Firm: Founded in 1923, Quinlivan, Sherwood, Spellacy & Tarvestad, P.A. is a highly respected law firm devoting its practice to civil litigation and dispute resolution of all types at the state and federal levels. *See additional listings in Commercial Litigation and Professional Malpractice Defense Law Chapters.*

PHILLIP A. COLE - Lommen, Nelson, Cole & Stageberg, P.A. - 1800 IDS Center, 80 South Eighth Street - Minneapolis, MN 55402 - Phone: (612) 339-8131, Fax: (612) 339-8064 - *See complete biographical profile in Commercial Litigation Chapter.*

•**JOHN M. DEGNAN** - Bassford, Lockhart, Truesdell & Briggs, P.A. - 3550 Multifoods Tower, 33 South Sixth Street - Minneapolis, MN 55402-3787 - Phone: (612) 333-3000, Fax: (612) 333-8829 - *See complete biographical profile in Commercial Litigation Chapter.*

Personal Injury Defense Law Leading Attorneys

•**JAMES F. DUNN:** Mr. Dunn practices exclusively in personal injury litigation and has done so since 1974. His areas of expertise are product liability, insurance litigation, employment litigation, premises liability, automobile liability, and fire appraisal hearings. Mr. Dunn is certified as a Civil Trial Advocate by the National Board of Trial Advocacy and as a Civil Trial Specialist by the Minnesota State Bar Association. He is also an experienced arbitrator and mediator. He is fluent in German.
Education: JD 1974 magna cum laude, William Mitchell; BA 1968, College of St. Thomas.
Employment History: President 1993-present, Dunn & Elliott, P.A.; President 1983-93, James F. Dunn & Associates, P.A.; Partner 1981-83, Dunn & Johnson; Partner 1976-81, Liefschultz & Dunn; Associate 1974-76, Robins, Davis & Lyons (now known as Robins, Kaplan, Miller & Ciresi); Legal Writing Instructor 1974-75, Hamline University School of Law.
Representative Clients: Aetna Casualty & Surety Company; 3M; Ralston Purina Company; Hartford Steam Boiler Inspection & Insurance Company; General Adjustment Bureau; Sara Lee Corp.; Starcraft Corp.; Horace Mann Insurance Company; Colonial Penn Insurance Company; Integrity Mutual Insurance Company.
Professional Associations: ABA; MSBA; State Bar of Wisconsin; RCBA; HCBA; Defense Research Institute; MDLA; MTLA; ATLA; American Arbitration Assn. (Arbitrator); Hennepin County Arbitration System (Arbitrator); Minnesota Supreme Court appointed No-Fault Arbitrator; Equilaw, Inc. (Mediator); Creative Dispute Resolution, Inc. (Arbitrator/Mediator); Ramsey County (Mini-Trial Judge). *See additional listings in Federal, State & Local Government Law and Commercial Litigation Chapters.*

JAMES F. DUNN

Dunn & Elliott, P.A.
1510 Minnesota World Trade Center
30 East Seventh Street
St. Paul, MN 55101-4901

Phone: (612) 221-9048
Fax: (612) 223-5797

Admitted: 1974 Minnesota;
1987 Wisconsin;
1975 US Dist. Ct. (MN);
1989 US Dist. Ct. (W. Dist. WI);
1990 US Dist. Ct. (ND);
1974 US Ct. App. (8th Cir.);
1981 US Sup. Ct.
Birthdate: 11/28/45

•**WILLIAM D. FLASKAMP:** Mr. Flaskamp's civil trial practice includes both commercial and tort matters, with emphasis on personal injury matters, defending churches in alleged sexual abuse cases, aviation law, product liability litigation, class action suits, and plaintiff's personal injury work. He is listed in *The Best Lawyers in America*, 1993 edition.
Education: JD 1951, University of Michigan; BS 1948, University of Michigan; BA 1947, University of Michigan.
Employment History: Partner 1960-present, Associate 1951-60, Meagher & Geer; Brigadier General, United States Air Force (retired).
Representative Clients: Federated Insurance Company; Church Mutual Insurance Company; The St. Paul Companies, Inc.; CNA Insurance Companies.
Professional Associations: International Academy of Trial Lawyers (Advocate); International Society of Barristers (Fellow & Past President); American College of Trial Lawyers (Fellow); American Board of Trial Advocates (Advocate).
Firm: Nineteen ninety-four marks Meagher & Geer's 65th year. The Minneapolis law firm is recognized as one of the Midwest's most reputable; Meagher & Geer attorneys have long been considered among the preeminent trial lawyers in the state of Minnesota and throughout the country. In addition to a practice that encompasses all aspects of insurance law, civil litigation, and business and commercial law, the firm has a separate practice group devoted to the appellate practice. Meagher & Geer's clientele represents the industries of agriculture, aviation, construction, finance, health care, insurance, manufacturing, and real estate. *See additional listing in Professional Malpractice Defense Law Chapter.*

WILLIAM D. FLASKAMP

Meagher & Geer
4200 Multifoods Tower
33 South Sixth Street
Minneapolis, MN 55402

Phone: (612) 338-0661
Fax: (612) 338-8384

Admitted: 1951 Minnesota;
1951 Michigan;
1960 US Sup. Ct.;
1960 US Ct. of Military App.
Birthdate: 05/08/24

Chapter 26: Personal Injury Defense Law

GEORGE W. FLYNN

Cosgrove, Flynn & Gaskins
2900 Metropolitan Centre
333 South Seventh Street
Minneapolis, MN 55402

Phone: (612) 333-9500
Fax: (612) 333-9579

Admitted: 1967 Minnesota
Birthdate: 09/08/42

•**GEORGE W. FLYNN:** Mr. Flynn has acted as national counsel for manufacturing concerns in the defense and management of product liability litigation across the country arising out of manufacture of gas control devices, building materials, and farm equipment. He has tried through verdict cases in Florida, Indiana, Iowa, Kansas, Michigan, Minnesota, Missouri, New York, and Wisconsin and won 14 of 15 cases. He has represented clients in proceedings before the Consumer Product Safety Commission. Mr. Flynn is national counsel for a building materials manufacturer in defense and management of litigation arising out of flammability of building insulation products and managed multidistrict litigation cases. He is also a speaker at seminars for organizations such as Gas Appliance Manufacturers, National Propane Gas Association, National Electrical Manufacturers Association, National Fire Protection Association, the Food & Drug Administration, and AIRMIC (England).
Education: JD 1967, Georgetown University; BA 1964, St. John's University.
Employment History: 1989-present, Cosgrove, Flynn & Gaskins; 1967-89, Faegre & Benson.
Representative Clients: National, regional, and local counsel for numerous manufacturers and insurers in product liability litigation, including Honeywell, Inc.; Belarus Manufacturing, Inc.; The Celotex Corp.; Emerson Electric Company; Square D. Company; Ensign Bickford; Dayton-Hudson Company; Sears Roebuck & Company; Aetna Casualty & Surety Company; Northland Insurance Company; CIGNA, Inc.; Hartford Insurance Company.
Professional Associations: American College of Trial Lawyers (Fellow). *See additional listing in Commercial Litigation Chapter.*

JOHN B. GORDON - Faegre & Benson - 2200 Norwest Center, 90 South Seventh Street - Minneapolis, MN 55402 - Phone: (612) 336-3000, Fax: (612) 336-3026 - *See complete biographical profile in Environmental Law Chapter.*

PAUL E. GRINNELL

Gunhus, Grinnell, Klinger,
Swenson & Guy, Ltd.
512 Center Avenue
P.O. Box 1077
Moorhead, MN 56561-1077

Phone: (218) 236-6462
Fax: (218) 236-9873

Admitted: 1964 Minnesota;
1980 North Dakota;
1970 US Dist. Ct. (MN);
1981 US Dist. Ct. (ND)
Birthdate: 01/26/39

•**PAUL E. GRINNELL:** For over 30 years, Paul Grinnell has practiced civil trial law, including tort litigation representing insurance companies in Minnesota and North Dakota state and federal courts at the trial and appellate levels. He is also active in dispute resolution through arbitration and mediation. Mr. Grinnell is the Managing Partner of Gunhus, Grinnell, Klinger, Swenson & Guy, Ltd.
Education: LLB 1964, University of North Dakota; BSBA 1961, University of North Dakota.
Employment History: Attorney 1967-present, Gunhus, Grinnell, Klinger, Swenson & Guy, Ltd.; County Attorney 1970-79, Clay County, MN; Attorney 1964-67, Erickson & Erie.
Representative Clients: Aetna Life & Casualty; Capitol Indemnity Corp.; Heritage Insurance Company; Home Insurance Company; Grinnell Mutual Reinsurance; USF & G; Milbank Insurance Company; The St. Paul Insurance Companies.
Professional Associations: ABA; MSBA; Clay County Bar Assn.; Seventh District Bar Assn. (President 1991-92); Cass County Bar Assn.; State Bar Assn. of North Dakota.
Community Involvement: Moorhead Jaycees (past President); Minnesota Jaycees (past State Legal Counsel); Church Council (Chair for four years and member for nine years); Toastmasters (past President).
Firm: Founded in 1914, Gunhus, Grinnell, Klinger, Swenson & Guy, Ltd., is a general practice law firm with offices in Moorhead, MN and Fargo, ND. The firm handles matters primarily in the western half of Minnesota and all of North Dakota, offering a wide range of litigation and commercial services. Strong internal communication among the firm's 13 attorneys, together with numerous contacts within the surrounding community, are invaluable assets in providing insight into cases. *See additional listings in Commercial Litigation and Professional Malpractice Defense Law Chapters.*

•GUNDER D. GUNHUS: Mr. Gunhus practices in the areas of tort law, including medical malpractice, legal malpractice, product liability, insurance issues, and general casualty/liability claims in all Minnesota and North Dakota state, federal, trial, and appellate courts.
Education: LLB 1953, University of Minnesota; BSL 1951, Mankato State College.
Employment History: Attorney 1958-present, Gunhus, Grinnell, Klinger, Swenson & Guy, Ltd.; Federal Magistrate 1972-76; Assistant County Attorney 1970-79, Clay County.
Representative Clients: The St. Paul Insurance Companies; Minnesota Medical Insurance Company; Home Insurance Company; PHICO; Crum & Forster; Hartford Insurance Company.
Professional Associations: International Assn. of Insurance Counsel; American College of Trial Lawyers (Fellow); Defense Research Institute; MDLA (Board of Directors 1976-86); Clay County Bar Assn.; Seventh District Bar Assn. (MN)(past President); MSBA; Cass County Bar Assn.; State Bar Assn. of North Dakota; ABA.
Firm: Gunhus, Grinnell, Klinger, Swenson & Guy, Ltd., was founded in 1914 and is a general practice law firm with offices in Moorhead, MN and Fargo, ND. The firm provides counsel to the western half of Minnesota and all of North Dakota, offering a wide range of commercial and litigation services. *See additional listings in Professional Malpractice Defense Law and Commercial Litigation Chapters.*

GUNDER D. GUNHUS

Gunhus, Grinnell, Klinger, Swenson & Guy, Ltd.
512 Center Avenue
P.O. Box 1077
Moorhead, MN 56561-1077

Phone: (218) 236-6462
Fax: (218) 236-9873

Admitted: 1953 Minnesota;
1981 North Dakota;
1979 US Dist Ct. (MN);
1983 US Dist Ct. (ND);
1977 US Ct. App. (8th Cir.)
Birthdate: 09/14/28

•DANIEL J. HEUEL: Mr. Heuel, a Civil Trial Specialist certified by the Minnesota State Bar Association, practices civil trial law in federal and state courts throughout Minnesota. He principally represents insurance companies and their insureds in a wide variety of claims involving personal injury, product liability, professional liability, contract disputes, and business torts. In addition, Mr. Heuel also handles employment law, wrongful discharge, civil rights violations, and defamation. The case of *Hunt v. IBM Mid Am. Employee's Fed. Credit Union*, 384 N.W.2d 853 (Minn. 1986), in which he successfully appeared for the defense, remains an often cited authority on the subject of wrongful termination in the state of Minnesota.
Education: JD 1978, University of Minnesota; BA 1974 summa cum laude, St. Mary's College.
Representative Clients: American Family Insurance Group; Westfield Companies; IBM Mid America Employee's Credit Union; Carolina Freight Corp.
Professional Associations: Third District Bar Assn. (President 1993-94); MSBA; American Arbitrator Assn. (Commercial Arbitrator).
Community Involvement: Interests include raising horses on his farm in rural Olmsted County, sailing, motorcycling, darkroom photography, and playing amateur baseball in a local league.
Firm: Founded by Ross Muir in Rochester in 1966, Muir, Heuel, Carlson & Spelhaug, P.A., began as a firm devoted exclusively to insurance defense. While it continues to limit itself to trial practice, it has evolved over the years, now representing individuals, as well as insurers and corporate clients, in both the prosecution and defense of civil claims. The four partners and staff, including two full-time legal investigators, are uniquely situated to provide for the litigation needs of a broad base of clients. *See additional listings in Commercial Litigation and Employment Law Chapters.*

DANIEL J. HEUEL

Muir, Heuel, Carlson & Spelhaug, P.A.
404 Marquette Bank Building
P.O. Box 1057
Rochester, MN 55903

Phone: (507) 288-4110
Fax: (507) 288-4122

Admitted: 1978 Minnesota;
1980 US Ct. App. (8th Cir.)
Birthdate: 09/20/52

Chapter 26: Personal Injury Defense Law

GARY W. HOCH

Meagher & Geer
4200 Multifoods Tower
33 South Sixth Street
Minneapolis, MN 55402

Phone: (612) 338-0661
Fax: (612) 338-8384

Admitted: 1968 Minnesota;
1984 Wisconsin;
1972 US Sup. Ct.
Birthdate: 01/14/43

•**GARY W. HOCH:** Mr. Hoch's civil trial practice includes both commercial and tort matters. He represents insurance companies in personal injury and coverage cases, and corporate clients on a broad range of matters including product liability, mass tort claims, contract disputes, employment discrimination claims, and defamation actions. He is an approved arbitrator and mediator and presents lectures for legal professionals at institutes and seminars. Mr. Hoch is a member of the firm's Management Committee.
Education: JD 1968, University of Minnesota; BA 1965, University of Minnesota.
Employment History: Partner 1974-present, Associate 1968-74, Meagher & Geer.
Representative Clients: Federated Insurance Company; CNA Insurance Companies; The St. Paul Companies, Inc.; State Farm Insurance Companies.
Professional Associations: ABA; MSBA; State Bar of Wisconsin; MDLA; Defense Research Institute; Fellow, International Academy of Barristers.
Firm: Nineteen ninety-four marks Meagher & Geer's 65th year. The Minneapolis law firm is recognized as one of the Midwest's most reputable; Meagher & Geer attorneys have long been considered among the preeminent trial lawyers in the state of Minnesota and throughout the country. In addition to a practice that encompasses all aspects of insurance law, civil litigation, and business and commercial law, the firm has a separate practice group devoted to the appellate practice. Meagher & Geer's clientele represents the industries of agriculture, aviation, construction, finance, health care, insurance, manufacturing, and real estate. *See additional listings in Professional Malpractice Defense Law and Commercial Litigation Chapters.*

BARRY P. HOGAN

Jeffries, Olson, Flom,
Oppegard & Hogan, P.A.
1325 23rd Street South
Fargo, ND 58103

Phone: (701) 280-2300
Fax: (701) 280-1880

Admitted: 1983 Minnesota;
1981 North Dakota;
1983 US Dist. Ct. (MN);
1982 US Dist. Ct. (ND);
1983 US Ct. App. (8th Cir.);
1988 US Sup. Ct.
Birthdate: 05/19/53

•**BARRY P. HOGAN:** Mr. Hogan practices civil litigation and trial law in tort and commercial matters for insurance defense and self-insured persons and corporations. He handles varied personal injury, property damage and coverage cases, defending claims involving general casualty and liability, product liability, automobile liability, employment and sexual discrimination/harassment, premises liability, errors and omissions, civil rights, and dram shop. He practices before all state and federal courts in Minnesota and North Dakota and in proceedings involving arbitration, mediation, and other methods of alternative dispute resolution. Mr. Hogan is a lecturer at insurance defense seminars on topics such as surveillance of the malingering claimant, admissibility of graphic evidence, medical expense subrogation rights, tort reform, legal updates, innovative settlements, and releases.
Education: JD 1981 with distinction, University of North Dakota; BA, BS, BSEd 1978 magna cum laude, University of North Dakota.
Employment History: Law Instructor 1984-86, Moorhead State University; Law Clerk 1981-83, Hon. Paul Benson, Chief Justice of US District Court; Airborne Infantry US Army (active); Medical Service & JAG Officer 1971-93, USAR.
Representative Clients: The St. Paul Insurance Companies; Home Insurance Company; League of MN Cities Insurance Trust; Auto Owners Insurance Company; State of MN (Special Attorney General); Royal Insurance Company; Milbank Insurance Company; State Auto Insurance Company; GAB Business Services, Inc.
Professional Associations: American Arbitration Assn. (Panel of Arbitrators); Clay County Bar Assn.; Cass County Bar Assn.; Seventh District Bar Assn.; MSBA; State Bar Assn. of North Dakota; Federal Bar Assn.; ABA; Defense Research Institute; MDLA; North Dakota Defense Lawyers Assn.
Community Involvement: Northside Hockey Club; Boy Scouts of America (Troop Leader); Reserve Officers Assn.
Firm: Jeffries, Olson, Flom, Oppegard & Hogan, P.A., is a general practice law firm with offices in Moorhead, MN and Fargo, ND. The firm handles matters primarily in the western half of Minnesota and all of North Dakota, offering a wide range of litigation and commercial services. *See additional listings in Commercial Litigation and Federal, State & Local Government Law Chapters.*

RICHARD N. JEFFRIES - Jeffries, Olson, Flom, Oppegard & Hogan, P.A. - 403 Center Avenue, P.O. Box 9 - Moorhead, MN 56561-0009 - Phone: (218) 233-3222, Fax: (701) 280-1880 - *See complete biographical profile in Professional Malpractice Defense Law Chapter.*

Personal Injury Defense Law Leading Attorneys

•**KENNETH F. JOHANNSON:** Mr. Johannson has practiced law in Crookston, MN all of his professional life. While in law school, Mr. Johannson was awarded a graduate assistantship and served as Assistant Dean of Students. During his senior year, he also served as research assistant to Professor John Crabb. While initially engaged in the general practice of law in his early years of practice, in the last 15 years he has focused exclusively in the field of civil litigation. He has tried over 200 cases to a jury verdict and handled over 50 cases before the Minnesota Court of Appeals, the Minnesota State Supreme Court, the 8th Circuit, and the US Supreme Court. His practice geographically covers northwestern Minnesota and eastern North Dakota.
Education: JD 1962 with distinction, University of North Dakota; BS & BA 1958, University of North Dakota.
Employment History: Associate 1962-65, Partner 1965-present, Dickel, Johannson, Taylor, Rust & Tye, P.A.
Representative Clients: First American National Bank; Crookston National Bank; J.R. Simplot Company; Vigen Construction Company; American Sugar Beet Growers Assn.; Dahlgren, Inc.; Crookston Welding & Machine; Phoenix Industries; Red River Distributors.
Professional Associations: ABA; MSBA; State Bar Assn. of North Dakota; 14th District Bar Assn. (past President); ATLA; MTLA; MDLA; Defense Research Institute; American Society of Law and Medicine.
Community Involvement: The Crookston Rotary Club (past President); Trinity Lutheran Church (past President); Minakwa Country Club (past President).
Firm: The firm of Dickel, Johannson, Taylor, Rust & Tye, P.A., was founded in 1932 by John W. Padden (deceased), a former President of the Minnesota State Bar Association. The firm is now composed of seven lawyers, stockholders, and associates. The firm is engaged in the general practice of law serving northwestern Minnesota and eastern North Dakota. The firm lists over 50 insurance companies as clients in *Best's Directory of Recommended Insurance Attorneys*.

KENNETH F. JOHANNSON

Dickel, Johannson, Taylor, Rust & Tye, P.A.
407 North Broadway
P.O. Box 605
Crookston, MN 56716

Phone: (218) 281-2400
Fax: (218) 281-5831
800 number: (800) 584-7077

Admitted: 1962 Minnesota; 1962 North Dakota
Birthdate: 11/17/36

JOHN D. KELLY - Hanft, Fride, O'Brien, Harries, Swelbar & Burns, P.A. - 1000 First Bank Place, 130 West Superior Street - Duluth, MN 55802 - Phone: (218) 722-4766, Fax: (218) 720-4920 - *See complete biographical profile in Commercial Litigation Chapter.*

•**CHARLES R. KENNEDY:** Mr. Kennedy practices civil trial law and appellate litigation in state and federal court, primarily in insurance defense and coverage; tort claims; and commercial, business, employment (management), and plaintiff personal injury cases. He has successfully defended utilities on claims of stray voltage, electrocution, wrongful death or injury, right of way, and employment discrimination; has defended legal and medical malpractice actions; and has served as an expert witness in legal malpractice cases. Mr. Kennedy utilizes mediation and arbitration (ADR) in all types of claims and is on the MN Supreme Court roster of qualified neutrals.
Education: JD 1962, University of Minnesota (Board of Editors 1961-62, *Minnesota Law Review*); BA 1960 cum laude, University of Minnesota.
Employment History: Senior Partner/Partner 1962-present, Kennedy & Nervig.
Representative Clients: Federated Rural Electric Insurance Corp.; Minnesota Power & Light Company; Dorn & Company Inc.; Capitol Indemnity Corp.; General Star Management Company; Wadena State Bank; First National Bank of Menahga; First National Bank of Bertha-Verndale; Ind. School District #2155; Todd-Wadena Electric Cooperative.
Professional Associations: American Board of Trial Advocates; American College of Trial Lawyers (Fellow); ABA; MSBA; Federal Bar Assn.; MTLA; ATLA; MDLA; Defense Research Institute; American Judicature Society; MN Lawyers Professional Responsibility Board (1982-91; Chair 1989-91); Governor's Commission on Judicial Selection; Supreme Court Advisory Committee on Rules of Civil Procedure (1992-93).
Firm: Kennedy & Nervig and its predecessor firms have been serving the legal needs of clients throughout Minnesota since the early 1900s. The firm's seven lawyers provide a wide range of legal services including civil litigation of all types, trials and appeals, personal injury, probate, real estate, family law, employment law, and educational law. The practice covers a broad area of Minnesota and portions of North and South Dakota. *See additional listing in Commercial Litigation Chapter.*

CHARLES R. KENNEDY

Kennedy & Nervig
503 Jefferson Street South
P.O. Box 647
Wadena, MN 56482

Phone: (218) 631-2505
Fax: (218) 631-9078

Admitted: 1962 Minnesota; 1962 US Dist. Ct. (MN); 1981 US Sup. Ct.
Birthdate: 04/25/38

1994/1996 ◆ *Minnesota Edition* 353

Chapter 26: Personal Injury Defense Law

H. MORRISON KERSHNER

Pemberton, Sorlie, Sefkow,
Rufer & Kershner
110 North Mill Street
P.O. Box 866
Fergus Falls, MN 56538-0866

Phone: (218) 736-5493
Fax: (218) 736-3950

Admitted: 1976 Minnesota
Birthdate: 01/02/48

•**H. MORRISON KERSHNER:** Mr. Kershner practices civil trial law in tort and employment matters, representing insurance companies in personal injury and coverage cases, and defending corporate clients in employment and franchise disputes. Mr. Kershner is certified as a Civil Trial Specialist by the Minnesota State Bar Association.
Education: JD 1976, University of Minnesota; BA 1970 summa cum laude, Luther College.
Representative Clients: North American Crop Underwriters, Inc.; Grinnell Mutual Insurance Company; American Family Insurance Group; Citizens Security Mutual Insurance Company; Coast America II Corp.
Professional Associations: MTLA; Academy of Certified Trial Specialists; MSBA; ATLA.
Firm: Founded in 1882, Pemberton, Sorlie, Sefkow, Rufer & Kershner and its predecessor firms have been serving clients in Minnesota and North Dakota for more than 110 years. Firm members have been active in the profession on a statewide level. Former firm member Roger Dell served as Chief Justice of the Minnesota Supreme Court from 1953 to 1962. Former partner Gerald S. Rufer served as president of the Board of Law Examiners for many years. Richard L. Pemberton was president of the MSBA in 1986-87 and currently serves as chair of the Minnesota Racing Commission. The firm's 12 attorneys are able to provide specialized services commonly associated with big city practices. *See additional listings in Commercial Litigation and Employment Law Chapters.*

LAWRENCE R. KING

King & Hatch
The St. Paul Building
6 West Fifth Street, Suite 800
St. Paul, MN 55102

Phone: (612) 223-2856
Fax: (612) 223-2847

Admitted: 1976 Minnesota; 1983 Wisconsin; 1976 US Dist. Ct. (MN); US Dist. Ct. (W. Dist. WI); US Ct. App. (8th Cir.)
Birthdate: 05/18/51

•**LAWRENCE R. KING:** Mr. King practices civil dispute resolution in defense of various areas of civil litigation, including employment law, product liability, professional liability, governmental liability, insurance coverage issues, commercial and contractual suits, automobile liability, and premises liability. His defense practice and experience includes the trial of cases in state and federal courts of Minnesota and Wisconsin. Mr. King is the coauthor (with Barbara R. Hatch) of "Improvement to Real Property: Defending Actions Under Minn. Stat. §541.051," *Minnesota Defense*, Winter 1990.
Education: JD 1976 cum laude, Hamline University; BA 1973, University of Missouri.
Employment History: King & Hatch.
Representative Clients: Assn. of Minnesota Counties; Berkley Risk Services; Britamco, Inc.; CIGNA; Eagle Manufacturing Company; First Oak Brook Corp.; HealthEast, Inc.; Homelite, Inc., a Division of Textron, Inc.; Kelly Company; League of Minnesota Cities Insurance Trust; Meadowbrook Insurance Group; Medical Protective Group; Midwest Gas Company; Minnesota Counties Insurance Trust; Minnesota Fire & Casualty; National Farmers Union Insurance Company; Northland Insurance Companies; Prudential Insurance Companies; Raymond Corp.; Star Insurance Company; State of Minnesota; 3M; Travelers Insurance Company.
Professional Associations: MDLA (President 1991-92); MSBA (Young Lawyers Section (Chair 1982-83); Board of Governors (1982-85, 1992-93)); American Bar Foundation (Fellow); International Society of Barristers (Fellow); MN Institute of Legal Education (Annual Insurance Law seminar (Chair & Cochair 1989-94); MN Automobile Insurance Claims seminar (Cochair 1993); Complex Settlement seminar (faculty member 1990-93)).
Firm: The law firm of King & Hatch limits its practice to the resolution of civil disputes. The firm, founded in 1993, is dedicated to defending clients in a broad range of civil cases in an effective and efficient manner. The members of the firm represent insurance companies, self-insured corporations, governmental entities, and individuals in resolving disputes through trial or alternative dispute mechanisms. *See additional listings in Professional Malpractice Defense Law and Employment Law Chapters.*

Personal Injury Defense Law Leading Attorneys

•**JOHN C. LERVICK:** Mr. Lervick handles civil litigation, insurance defense, and general practice law in many areas including automobile, property, casualty, and personal injury liability; municipal law; school law; and business law. He is certified as a Civil Trial Specialist by the Civil Litigation Section of the Minnesota State Bar Association. Mr. Lervick has been the City Attorney for Alexandria since 1975.
Education: JD 1970 with distinction, University of North Dakota; BA 1962, University of North Dakota.
Employment History: 1970-present, Swenson, Grover, Lervick, Syverson, Battey & Anderson; Captain 1962-67, US Air Force.
Representative Clients: Auto-Owners Insurance Company; American Family Insurance Company; Horace Mann Insurance Company; Secura Insurance Company; Bituminous Casualty Insurance Company; Alexandria Extrusion Company; Independent School District No. 206; Austin Mutual Insurance Company.
Professional Associations: Douglas County Bar Assn. (past President); Seventh District Bar Assn. (Chair 1989-present, Ethics Committee); MDLA; Defense Research Institute.
Community Involvement: Alexandria Rotary Club (member 1973-present; President 1980-1981); First Lutheran Church in Alexandria (Church Council member and past President); Alexandria Golf Club (Board member 1978-84); volunteer with various community service organizations.
Firm: Founded in 1959, Swenson, Grover, Lervick, Syverson, Battey & Anderson, Ltd., has grown to a six-lawyer general practice firm offering specialized practice areas for its clients. The firm provides litigation, real estate services, and business representation to a wide variety of clients from individuals, insurance companies, and banks to corporations. *See additional listings in Federal, State & Local Government Law and Commercial Litigation Chapters.*

JOHN C. LERVICK

Swenson, Grover, Lervick, Syverson, Battey & Anderson, Ltd.
710 Broadway, Box 787
Alexandria, MN 56308

Phone: (612) 763-3141
Fax: (612) 763-3657

Admitted: 1970 Minnesota
Birthdate: 08/13/40

•**KURT J. MARBEN:** Mr. Marben has a civil trial and appellate practice in personal injury, property damage, product liability, insurance coverage disputes, and commercial litigation. He is certified as a Civil Trial Specialist by the Minnesota State Bar Association.
Education: JD 1977, University of Minnesota; BS 1974, Bemidji State College.
Employment History: 1977-present, Charlson, Marben & Jorgenson, P.A.
Representative Clients: Northern St. Bank of Thief River Falls; American Family Insurance Company; North Star Mutual Insurance Company; Milbank Mutual Insurance Company; Wikstrom Telephone Company; Dairyland Mutual Insurance Company; Preferred Risk Mutual Insurance Company; Home Mutual Insurance Company; Bankers Life Insurance Company; Farm Bureau Insurance Company; Austin Mutual Insurance Company.
Professional Associations: MSBA; ABA; Defense Research Institute; Commission for Judicial Selection.
Community Involvement: Northwest Technical College (Advisory Board); Northland Community College (Advisory Board).
Firm: Founded in 1980, Charlson, Marben & Jorgenson, P.A., and its predecessor firm is a regional law firm practicing throughout northern and central Minnesota. The firm's attorneys concentrate their practice in civil litigation of all types. *See additional listing in Commercial Litigation Chapter.*

KURT J. MARBEN

Charlson, Marben & Jorgenson, P.A.
119 West Second Street
P.O. Box 506
Thief River Falls, MN 56701-0506

Phone: (218) 681-4002
Fax: (218) 681-4004

Admitted: 1977 Minnesota; 1979 US Dist. Ct. (MN)
Birthdate: 11/14/52

DAVID S. MARING - Maring Law Office - 1220 Main Avenue, Suite 105, P.O. Box 2103 - Fargo, ND 58107 - Phone: (701) 237-5297, Fax: (701) 235-2268 - *See complete biographical profile in Commercial Litigation Chapter.*

JAMES T. MARTIN - Gislason, Martin & Varpness, P.A. - 7600 Parklawn Avenue South, Suite 444 - Minneapolis, MN 55435 - Phone: (612) 831-5793, Fax: (612) 831-7358 - *See complete biographical profile in Commercial Litigation Chapter.*

Chapter 26: Personal Injury Defense Law

GERALD L. MASCHKA

Farrish, Johnson & Maschka
201 North Broad Street
Suite 200
P.O. Box 550
Mankato, MN 56002-0550

Phone: (507) 387-3002
Fax: (507) 625-4002

Admitted: 1971 Minnesota
Birthdate: 03/28/41

•**GERALD L. MASCHKA:** Mr. Maschka practices civil trial law in both tort and commercial matters, with his principal experience in auto and product liability defense throughout southern Minnesota. He also handles the defense of clients alleged to have committed professional negligence. Mr. Maschka is certified as a Civil Trial Advocate by the National Board of Trial Advocacy and as a Civil Trial Specialist by the Civil Litigation Section of the Minnesota State Bar Association.
Education: JD 1971, William Mitchell; BS 1963, College of St. Thomas.
Representative Clients: State Farm Automobile Insurance Company; State Farm Fire and Casualty Company; Grinnell Mutual Reinsurance Company; Progressive Insurance Company; AIG; Mutual Service; Midwest Family Mutual; General Casualty Insurance Company; Citizens Security Mutual Insurance Company; Berkley Administrators; Milwaukee Mutual Insurance Company; TCO Insurance Services.
Professional Associations: Sixth District Bar Assn. (past President; past Chair, Ethics Committee); MSBA (Continuing Legal Education Committee 1976-83); ABA; American Board of Trial Advocacy.
Community Involvement: Mankato YMCA (past Director); Mankato Area Girls Fastpitch Softball Assn. (Director); Mankato East Booster Club (Director).
Firm: Founded in 1900, Farrish, Johnson & Maschka and its predecessors have served clients throughout southern Minnesota for more than 90 years. Today, the Farrish firm has 11 lawyers, seven of which are trial lawyers providing its clients with litigation services in all areas of civil and business litigation. *See additional listings in Professional Malpractice Defense Law and Commercial Litigation Chapters.*

REBECCA EGGE MOOS

Bassford, Lockhart, Truesdell & Briggs, P.A.
3550 Multifoods Tower
33 South Sixth Street
Minneapolis, MN 55402-3787

Phone: (612) 333-3000
Fax: (612) 333-8829

Admitted: 1977 Minnesota; 1978 US Dist. Ct. (MN)
Birthdate: 08/08/47

•**REBECCA EGGE MOOS:** Ms. Moos, a trial lawyer in both state and federal courts, concentrates in the areas of professional liability, personal injury, construction, and insurance law. She has also successfully handled a large number of appeals in these areas of law. She is also an active lecturer and course coordinator in legal education for continuing education programs, law students, and clients.
Education: JD 1977, University of Minnesota; BS 1969, College of St. Catherine and University of Minnesota.
Employment History: Currently, Bassford, Lockhart, Truesdell & Briggs.
Representative Clients: Minneapolis Children's Medical Center; HealthSpan Health Systems Corp.; Abbott Northwestern Hospital; Riverside Medical Center; MetLife; The St. Paul Companies; Midwest Medical Insurance Co.; HDR Engineering, Inc.; Minnesota Lawyers Mutual.
Professional Associations: MSBA; HCBA; ABA; MDLA. Ms. Moos has been elected to a number of positions of leadership in various professional organizations, including positions as an officer and board member of the MDLA and Chair of the Hennepin County Ethics Committee.
Community Involvement: Minnesota Lawyers Mutual Insurance Company (Underwriting Committee 1991-present); American Bar Foundation.
Firm: Founded in 1882, Bassford, Lockhart, Truesdell & Briggs and its predecessor firms have been serving clients in Minnesota for more than 110 years. Today, the Bassford firm's 27 trial lawyers provide a broad range of litigation services for clients around the country, handling all areas of civil and business litigation.

Personal Injury Defense Law Leading Attorneys

•**ROSS MUIR:** Mr. Muir practices civil trial law in state and federal courts throughout Minnesota. For the past 35 years he has devoted his practice exclusively to civil trial litigation, representing plaintiffs and defendants in personal injury, commercial litigation, and Workers' Compensation. Mr. Muir founded the firm now known as Muir, Heuel, Carlson & Spelhaug, P.A., in Rochester in 1966. The firm's trial practice includes a substantial appellate practice.
Education: JD 1958, University of Minnesota; BA 1954, Macalester College.
Employment History: Founder & Partner 1966-present, Muir, Heuel, Carlson & Spelhaug, P.A.; Attorney 1958-66, Jardine, Logan & O'Brien.
Representative Clients: On defense, American Family Insurance Group, Westfield Companies, and numerous others.
Professional Associations: MSBA; Olmsted County Bar Assn.; MDLA; MTLA.
Firm: Founded by Ross Muir in Rochester in 1966, Muir, Heuel, Carlson & Spelhaug, P.A., began as a firm devoted exclusively to insurance defense. While it continues to limit itself to trial practice, it has evolved over the years, now representing individuals, as well as insurers and corporate clients, in both the prosecution and defense of civil claims. The four partners and staff, including two full-time legal investigators, are uniquely situated to provide for the litigation needs of a broad base of clients. *See additional listings in Professional Malpractice Defense Law and Commercial Litigation Chapters.*

ROSS MUIR

Muir, Heuel, Carlson & Spelhaug, P.A.
404 Marquette Bank Building
P.O. Box 1057
Rochester, MN 55903

Phone: (507) 288-4110
Fax: (507) 288-4122

Admitted: 1958 Minnesota
Birthdate: 05/17/32

•**DENNIS L. O'TOOLE:** Mr. O'Toole practices civil trial law, including the defense of personal injury and property claims, insurance coverage disputes, litigation and arbitration of business and banking disputes, and environmental issues. He is certified as a Civil Trial Specialist by the Minnesota State Bar Association. Mr. O'Toole is also counsel in business, banking, and environmental transactions.
Education: JD 1976, University of North Dakota; BS 1972, University of North Dakota.
Employment History: 1980-present, Lano, Nelson, O'Toole & Bengtson, Ltd.; Associate 1977-79, Johnson, Fredin, Killen, Thibodeau & Seiler; Law Clerk 1976-77, Hon. Ralph Erickstad, Chief Justice of the North Dakota Supreme Court.
Representative Clients: State Farm Insurance Companies; City of Grand Rapids; Grand Rapids State Bank.
Professional Associations: MSBA (Board of Governors 1992-present); ABA; American Bar Foundation (Fellow).
Community Involvement: Courage Center (Board member); active in the Ruffed Grouse Society and other conservation organizations.
Firm: Lano, Nelson, O'Toole & Bengtson, Ltd., is a regional law firm based in Grand Rapids, MN. The firm's four lawyers concentrate their practices in areas combining litigation and transactions to provide broad-based services to clients, which include businesses, insurers, government bodies, nonprofit organizations, and individuals. The firm and its predecessors have practiced continuously since 1922. *See additional listings in Commercial Litigation and Environmental Law Chapters.*

DENNIS L. O'TOOLE

Lano, Nelson, O'Toole & Bengtson, Ltd.
115 East Fifth Street
P.O. Box 20
Grand Rapids, MN 55744

Phone: (218) 326-9603
Fax: (218) 326-1565

Admitted: 1976 Minnesota
Birthdate: 05/07/50

•**RICHARD L. PEMBERTON**: Mr. Pemberton practices civil trial law in all areas of tort law, including personal injury, employment law, product liability, and professional malpractice. He is listed in *The Best Lawyers in America* in the categories of personal injury and employment law.
Education: JD 1957, University of Minnesota; BS, Macalester College and University of Minnesota.
Representative Clients: PHICO Insurance Companies; Minnesota Lawyers Mutual; American Family Insurance Group; Grinnell Mutual Reinsurance Company; State Farm Fire and Casualty; Progressive Insurance Company; Hawkeye Insurance Company; Citizens Security Insurance Company; Wal-Mart Stores; various Minnesota counties, townships, and school districts.
Professional Associations: American College of Trial Lawyers (Fellow); American Board of Trial Advocates; International Assn. of Defense Counsel; Assn. of Defense Trial Lawyers; Defense Research Institute (past regional Vice President); MDLA (past President); MSBA (President 1986-87); American Bar Foundation; Minnesota State Judicial Selection Commission; Minnesota Racing Commission (current Chair).
Firm: Founded in 1882, Pemberton, Sorlie, Sefkow, Rufer & Kershner and its predecessor firms have been serving clients in Minnesota and North Dakota for more than 110 years. Firm members have been active in the profession on a statewide level. Former firm member Roger Dell served as Chief Justice of the Minnesota Supreme Court from 1953 to 1962. Former partner Gerald S. Rufer served as president of the Board of Law Examiners for many years. The firm's 12 attorneys are able to provide specialized services commonly associated with big city practices. *See additional listings in Employment Law and Professional Malpractice Defense Law Chapters.*

RICHARD L. PEMBERTON

Pemberton, Sorlie, Sefkow, Rufer & Kershner
110 North Mill Street
P.O. Box 866
Fergus Falls, MN 56538-0866

Phone: (218) 736-5493
Fax: (218) 736-3950

Admitted: 1957 Minnesota
Birthdate: 06/14/32

Chapter 26: Personal Injury Defense Law

JOHN W. PERSON - Breen & Person, Ltd. - 510 Laurel Street, P.O. Box 472 - Brainerd, MN 56401 - Phone: (218) 828-1248, Fax: (218) 828-4832 - *See complete biographical profile in Commercial Real Estate Law Chapter.*

H. JEFFREY PETERSON

Cope & Peterson, P.A.
415 South First Street
P.O. Box 947
Virginia, MN 55792

Phone: (218) 749-4470
Fax: (218) 749-4783

Admitted: 1974 Minnesota;
1975 US Dist. Ct. (MN);
1981 US Ct. App. (8th Cir.)
Birthdate: 12/24/47

•**H. JEFFREY PETERSON:** Mr. Peterson practices civil trial law exclusively, with 90% of his work in defense of civil actions for commercial, business, insurance, and self-insured clients. He handles all tort areas including product liability; propane gas explosions; toxic torts; asbestos; construction and industrial accidents; fire claims; medical malpractice; automobile, motorcycle, and snowmobile accidents; and commercial and business claims including subrogation, contribution, and indemnity. Mr. Peterson has tried several significant plaintiff cases and is the only lawyer in northeastern Minnesota who has a plaintiff's verdict in excess of $750,000 as well as a defense verdict where the jury determined damages to be in excess of $2.5 million.
Education: JD 1974, University of North Dakota; AB 1970, Harvard University.
Employment History: Founding Partner 1976-present, Cope & Peterson.
Representative Clients: Insurance and self-insured companies—American Family; Capitol Indemnity; Dart & Kraft (Hobart); Employers Mutual; Fireman's; Horace Mann; PHICO; Pettibone Corp.; PPM Cranes; Ranger Insurance; State Farm; Travelers; Wausau; Western National.
Professional Associations: American Board of Trial Advocates; Assn. of Defense Trial Attorneys (Executive Committee 1994-); Federation of Insurance and Corporate Counsel; International Assn. of Defense Counsel; Lawyer-Pilots Bar Assn.; ABA; MSBA; Propane Gas Defense Assn.; MDLA (Board member 1990-92); Range Bar Assn. (President 1979-80); Ethics Committee (Chair, 1983-present).
Community Involvement: Volunteer attorney; Rotary member; founder, director, and leader in the construction of an ice hockey arena.
Firm: Cope & Peterson, P.A., a three-attorney firm, specializes in the defense of civil lawsuits. Cope & Peterson has been involved in many of the major cases tried in northern Minnesota in the last 20 years. The firm handles cases throughout Minnesota, from Crookston in the west to Grand Marais in the east; from International Falls in the north to Brainerd in the south. *See additional listings in Commercial Litigation and Professional Malpractice Defense Law Chapters.*

ROMAINE R. POWELL

Powell, Powell & Aamodt
713 Beltrami Avenue
P.O. Box 908
Bemidji, MN 56601-0908

Phone: (218) 751-5650
Fax: (218) 751-5658

Admitted:
1949 Minnesota
Birthdate: 03/18/24

•**ROMAINE R. POWELL:** With over 40 years of experience, Mr. Powell practices civil trial litigation exclusively. He predominantly performs insurance defense work, with experience in substantially all tort areas including product liability, and dram shop. He is also experienced in insurance coverage issues and commercial litigation. Mr. Powell has been listed in *The Best Lawyers in America* since 1983.
Education: LLB 1948, University of Minnesota; BSL 1947, University of Minnesota.
Employment History: Private Practice 1950-present; part-time US Magistrate 1971-76; Assistant Attorney 1951-54, Beltrami County; Law Clerk 1949, Minnesota Supreme Court.
Representative Clients: State Farm Insurance; American Family Insurance; Allstate Insurance; Citizens Security; numerous other insurance companies; American Hardware; General Motors; Ford Motor Credit; Chrysler.
Professional Associations: ABA; MSBA (Board of Governors); 15th District Bar Assn. (past President); Assn. of Defense Trial Attorneys; Defense Research Institute; International Society of Barristers; American Board of Trial Advocates; American College of Trial Lawyers.
Community Involvement: Bemidji Chamber of Commerce; Bemidji State University Foundation (past member, Vice President's Club).
Firm: The Powell, Powell & Aamodt Law Office consists of three partners: Romaine R. Powell, Charles R. Powell, and Paul R. Aamodt. Former partner Lois J. Lang has recently been appointed District Court Judge for the Ninth Judicial District.

•**JOHN D. QUINLIVAN:** Mr. Quinlivan practices in all areas of civil litigation and personal injury.
Education: JD 1968, William Mitchell; BSL 1966, William Mitchell, St. Cloud State University.
Employment History: 1968-present, Quinlivan, Sherwood, Spellacy & Tarvestad, P.A.
Representative Clients: Colonial Insurance Company of California; Citizens Security Mutual Insurance Company; Secura Insurance; Waseca Mutual Insurance Company; Western National Insurance Group; Northland Insurance Company; Farm Bureau Mutual Insurance Company; American States Insurance; Ohio Casualty Group; Austin Mutual Insurance Company; The Manitoba Public Insurance Corp.; Tri-State Insurance Company; St. Paul Fire & Marine Insurance Company; Continental Western Insurance Company; Viking Insurance Company of Wisconsin; Catholic Mutual Insurance Company.
Professional Associations: William Mitchell College of Law (1988-91, Board of Trustees); Stearns-Benton County Bar Assn. (President 1972); Seventh District Bar Assn. (President 1975); MSBA; Assn. of Defense Trial Attorneys (President 1981-82); Defense Research Institute (Board member 1986-89); MDLA (Secretary 1973-86); International Assn. of Defense Counsel; American Board of Trial Advocates.
Community Involvement: St. Cloud Chamber of Commerce (Board member 1983-86); St. Cloud Sertoma Club (President 1974-75); Cathedral High School (Board member 1979-85).
Firm: Founded in 1923, Quinlivan, Sherwood, Spellacy & Tarvestad, P.A. is a highly respected law firm devoting its practice to civil litigation and dispute resolution of all types at the state and federal levels. *See additional listings in Commercial Litigation and Professional Malpractice Defense Law Chapters.*

JOHN D. QUINLIVAN

Quinlivan, Sherwood, Spellacy & Tarvestad, P.A.
P.O. Box 1008
St. Cloud, MN 56302-1008

Phone: (612) 251-1414
Fax: (612) 251-1415

Admitted: 1968 Minnesota
Birthdate: 05/22/36

•**MICHAEL R. QUINLIVAN** - Arthur, Chapman, McDonough, Kettering & Smetak, P.A. - 500 Young Quinlan Building, 81 South Ninth Street - Minneapolis, MN 55402-3214 - Phone: (612) 339-3500, Fax: (612) 339-7655 - *See complete biographical profile in Employment Law Chapter.*

THOMAS J. RADIO - Popham, Haik, Schnobrich & Kaufman, Ltd. - 222 South Ninth Street, Suite 3300 - Minneapolis, MN 55402 - Phone: (612) 333-4800, Fax: (612) 334-8888 - *See complete biographical profile in Federal, State & Local Government Law Chapter.*

•**FRANK J. RAJKOWSKI:** Mr. Rajkowski has practiced nearly 20 years, primarily in the area of civil litigation. The trial work he has been involved in is primarily in the personal injury field for both defendants and plaintiffs. Mr. Rajkowski is admitted to practice in the state of Minnesota, Minnesota Federal District Court, and the US Court of Appeals for the 8th Circuit. He is a member of the American Board of Trial Advocates.
Education: JD 1975 cum laude, William Mitchell; BA 1970 cum laude, St. John's University.
Employment History: 1976-present, Rajkowski Hansmeier, Ltd.; Law Clerk 1975, Seventh Judicial District for the State of Minnesota.
Representative Clients: American Family; Catholic Mutual Relief Society; Cenex/Land of Lakes; Employers Mutual; Mutual Service Insurance; North Star Insurance; ISD No. 742; Metropolitan Transit Commission; First American National Bank.
Professional Associations: MSBA (1976-present); Stearns-Benton Bar Assn. (1976-present; President 1978-79); MDLA; American Board of Trial Advocates.
Firm: Rajkowski Hansmeier is a law firm located in Stearns County, MN consisting of 11 lawyers with a primary emphasis in civil litigation. The bulk of the litigation is in the area of personal injury; however, the firm also does a substantial amount of commercial, employment, and environmental litigation. *See additional listings in Commercial Litigation and Employee Benefits Law Chapters.*

FRANK J. RAJKOWSKI

Rajkowski Hansmeier, Ltd.
11 Seventh Avenue North
P.O. Box 1433
St. Cloud, MN 56302

Phone: (612) 251-1055
Fax: (612) 251-5896
800 number: (800) 445-9617

Admitted: 1975 Minnesota; 1975 US Dist. Ct. (MN); 1994 US Ct. App. (8th Cir.)
Birthdate: 10/05/48

Chapter 26: Personal Injury Defense Law

PIERRE N. REGNIER

Jardine, Logan & O'Brien
2100 Piper Jaffray Plaza
444 Cedar Street
St. Paul, MN 55101

Phone: (612) 290-6500
Fax: (612) 223-5070

Admitted: 1968 Minnesota;
1972 US Dist. Ct. (MN);
1976 US Ct. App. (8th Cir.)
Birthdate: 06/27/43

•**PIERRE N. REGNIER:** Mr. Regnier has continuously engaged in negligence and product liability cases, government liability, construction, civil rights cases, dram shop liability litigation, gas explosion litigation, employment law, and medical malpractice litigation.
Education: JD 1968, University of Minnesota; BS 1965 cum laude, St. John's University.
Employment History: 1976-present, Jardine, Logan & O'Brien; 1975-76, City Attorney for City of St. Paul; 1969-76, St. Paul City Attorney's Office.
Representative Clients: All levels of government, including state, counties, cities, school districts, police, and other governmental employees; all types of medical providers; numerous manufacturers, retailers, and insurance companies.
Professional Associations: ABA; MSBA; RCBA.
Community Involvement: Big Brothers/Big Sisters of St. Paul; Minnesota Friends of Orphans, Inc.; HealthEast Hospice.
Firm: Litigation is, and always has been, the primary focus of the Jardine, Logan & O'Brien Law Firm. Throughout the firm's 75-year history, its lawyers have worked on some of the region's largest and most complex disputes with outstanding results. The success of the firm can be traced to a philosophy of file handling that puts the client first. That requires early involvement to understand clients' needs, preferred procedures, and desired roles in their matters; early and accurate evaluation of cases, made simpler by the firm's collective years of experience; aggressive handling in preparation of the files; and frequent communication with clients to keep them informed and answer questions. This approach does not mean that Jardine, Logan & O'Brien does unnecessary work; quite the opposite. By properly evaluating cases and skillfully preparing them, they can resolve clients' disputes by the best and most cost-effective means, whether by settlement, through alternative dispute resolution techniques, or in a trial or hearing. Clients of the firm include individuals, large and small businesses, insurance companies, and self-insured trusts. The firm receives many referrals from peers at other law firms who frequently refer to its attorneys complex litigation matters. *See additional listings in Federal, State & Local Government Law and Professional Malpractice Defense Law Chapters.*

LEWIS A. REMELE, JR. - Bassford, Lockhart, Truesdell & Briggs, P.A. - 3550 Multifoods Tower, 33 South Sixth Street - Minneapolis, MN 55402-3787 - Phone: (612) 333-3000, Fax: (612) 333-8829 - *See complete biographical profile in Commercial Litigation Chapter.*

CARVER RICHARDS

Trenti Law Firm
P.O. Box 958
Virginia, MN 55792

Phone: (218) 749-1962
Fax: (218) 749-4308

Admitted: 1974 Minnesota
Birthdate: 03/24/43

•**CARVER RICHARDS:** Mr. Richards has a civil trial practice in personal injury, property damage, business and commercial litigation, medical malpractice, product liability, dram shop, and professional liability and coverage issues. He has brought over 100 lawsuits to verdict, substantially all of which were jury cases. Mr. Richards is certified as a Civil Trial Advocate by the National Board of Trial Advocacy.
Education: JD 1973, William Mitchell; BA 1968, University of Minnesota.
Employment History: 1973-present, Trenti Law Firm; 1971-73, Continental Western Insurance Company; 1968-71, Fireman's Fund Insurance Company.
Representative Clients: Numerous insurance companies; City of Gilbert, MN; City of Mt. Iron, MN; LTV Steel; Hibbing Taconite Company; Range Mental Health Center, Inc.; East Range Clinics, Ltd.
Professional Associations: ABA; MSBA; American Board of Trial Advocacy; American Trial Lawyers Assn.; MTLA; Academy of Certified Lawyers of MN; Range Bar Assn. (past President); MDLA; Mock Trial Coach.
Community Involvement: Virginia Area Chamber of Commerce (Board member); Eshquaguma Country Club (Board member); Range Mental Health Center, Inc. (Board member); Evereth Gilbert School Board (Board Chair).
Firm: The Trenti Law Firm was founded in 1960. Currently the firm has offices in Virginia, Cook, and Edina. There are nine lawyers providing services for businesses, industry, insurance companies, banks, mining companies, real estate, probate, estates, trusts, employment, and Workers' Compensation. *See additional listings in Commercial Litigation and Professional Malpractice Defense Law Chapters.*

•**JAMES M. RILEY:** Mr. Riley practices civil trial law in both tort and commercial matters. He represents insurance companies on various personal injury matters, including those involving professional liability, dram shop liability, premises liability, and automobile liability. Mr. Riley formerly served as managing partner at Meagher & Geer.
Education: JD 1968, William Mitchell; BSL 1966, College of St. Thomas, St. Cloud State College.
Employment History: Partner 1974-present, Associate 1968-74, Meagher & Geer; Law Clerk 1967-68, Hennepin County District Court.
Representative Clients: American Casualty Company of Reading, PA; Columbia Casualty Company; Continental Casualty Company; National Fire Insurance Company of Hartford; Transportation Insurance Company; State Farm Insurance Companies; Browning-Ferris Industries, Inc.; Woodlake Sanitary Services, Inc.; Metropolitan Insurance Company; Allstate Insurance Company; Federated Insurance Company; Action Disposal, Inc.; The St. Paul Companies, Inc.
Professional Associations: MSBA; HCBA; MDLA; National Assn. of Ski Area Defense Lawyers; International Society of Barristers (Fellow).
Firm: Nineteen ninety-four marks Meagher & Geer's 65th year. The Minneapolis law firm is recognized as one of the Midwest's most reputable; Meagher & Geer attorneys have long been considered among the preeminent trial lawyers in the state of Minnesota and throughout the country. In addition to a practice that encompasses all aspects of insurance law, civil litigation, and business and commercial law, the firm has a separate practice group devoted to the appellate practice. Meagher & Geer's clientele represents the industries of agriculture, aviation, construction, finance, health care, insurance, manufacturing, and real estate. *See additional listings in Commercial Litigation and Professional Malpractice Defense Law Chapters.*

JAMES M. RILEY

Meagher & Geer
4200 Multifoods Tower
33 South Sixth Street
Minneapolis, MN 55402

Phone: (612) 338-0661
Fax: (612) 338-8384

Admitted: 1968 Minnesota
Birthdate: 10/06/40

•**JOHN R. RODENBERG:** Mr. Rodenberg is a Civil Trial Specialist certified by both the National Board of Trial Advocacy (1993) and the Minnesota State Bar Association (1990). He is also a member of the Academy of Certified Trial Lawyers of Minnesota and is an Arbitrator with the American Arbitration Association (1991). Mr. Rodenberg represents a wide variety of litigants in auto and premises liability, agricultural and veterinary litigation, insurance coverage, and other matters. He has tried cases to jury verdict throughout the southern half of Minnesota. Mr. Rodenberg and the firm believe that attention and dedication to client needs must be of paramount importance. That attention and dedication has served this firm and its attorneys well, allowing them to translate their skills to serving client needs in a broad range of legal matters.
Education: JD 1981 cum laude, Hamline University (Honor Society; Editor, *Hamline Law Review*); BA 1978 cum laude, St. Olaf College.
Employment History: 1982-present, Berens, Rodenberg & O'Connor, Chartered.
Representative Clients: In addition to representing people insured by State Farm Insurance Companies, American Family Insurance Group, and North Star Mutual Insurance Company in auto, premises, malpractice, and other litigation, the firm represents those and other insurers in coverage litigation. The firm also represents a diverse group of employers and many agricultural clients, including numerous cooperatives.
Professional Associations: MSBA; ABA; Defense Research Institute; MDLA; Academy of Certified Trial Lawyers of Minnesota.
Community Involvement: Christ the King Lutheran Church (past President and member); Highland Manor Nursing Home (Director & Vice President); Brown County Child Protection Team; Southern Minnesota Regional Legal Services (volunteer attorney).
Firm: Berens, Rodenberg & O'Connor presently consists of eight attorneys functioning as a general practice law firm. They have an active and growing litigation practice in which they emphasize individualized attention to client needs by use of an expert staff of attorneys, legal assistants, and office professionals. Three attorneys practice extensively in the area of agricultural law, with special emphasis on representation of cooperatives. The firm is founded upon the cornerstones of honesty, integrity, dedication, and hard work. *See additional listings in Employment Law and Agricultural Law Chapters.*

JOHN R. RODENBERG

Berens, Rodenberg & O'Connor, Chartered
519 Center Street
P.O. Box 428
New Ulm, MN 56073

Phone: (507) 354-3161
Fax: (507) 354-7297

Admitted: 1981 Minnesota; 1984 US Dist. Ct. (MN)
Birthdate: 06/08/56

Chapter 26: Personal Injury Defense Law

JAMES F. ROEGGE - Meagher & Geer - 4200 Multifoods Tower, 33 South Sixth Street - Minneapolis, MN 55402 - Phone: (612) 338-0661, Fax: (612) 338-8384 - *See complete biographical profile in Professional Malpractice Defense Law Chapter.*

DONALD E. RYSAVY

Hoversten, Strom, Johnson & Rysavy
807 West Oakland Avenue
Austin, MN 55912

Phone: (507) 433-3483
Fax: (507) 433-7889

Admitted: 1973 Minnesota
Birthdate: 12/11/47

•**DONALD E. RYSAVY:** Mr. Rysavy is a civil litigator with 20 years experience in insurance defense and employment related disputes. He has practiced before state and federal courts and has tried multiple actions before courts and juries throughout southeastern Minnesota. His litigation practice is primarily in the areas of employment law and insurance personal injury defense. Mr. Rysavy has also practiced before the federal court in ERISA related defenses.
Education: JD 1973, University of Minnesota; BA 1970, St. Mary's College at Winona.
Employment History: Currently, Hoversten, Strom, Johnson & Rysavy; Prosecutor 1973-75, City of Austin/Mower County.
Representative Clients: Quality Pork Processors, Inc.; Travelers Insurance; Auto Owners Insurance; Hartford Insurance.
Professional Associations: ABA (Litigation Section); MSBA; American Assn. of Arbitrators (Panel of No-Fault Arbitrators); MDLA; Assn. of Defense Trial Attorneys.
Firm: Hoversten, Strom, Johnson & Rysavy, one of the largest law firms in southeastern Minnesota, practices in a wide range of litigation services including personal injury, product liability, and insurance defense. It also engages in the general practice of law, handling all areas of real estate, commercial, family, employment and labor, estate planning, probate, trusts, municipal, and governmental law. *See additional listing in Employment Law Chapter.*

JOHN R. SCHULZ

Collins, Buckley, Sauntry & Haugh
332 Minnesota Street
Suite W1100
St. Paul, MN 55101

Phone: (612) 227-0611
Fax: (612) 227-0758

Admitted: 1983 Minnesota;
1983 US Dist. Ct. (MN);
1983 US Ct. App. (8th Cir.);
1989 US Sup. Ct.
Birthdate: 08/08/54

•**JOHN R. SCHULZ:** Mr. Schulz's civil trial practice includes injury claims, professional malpractice, and business, employment, and commercial disputes, with related involvement in business formation and transactions. Mr. Schulz has represented numerous parties in both minor and complex litigation matters. In the context of injury cases, he has handled cases involving brain injury, wrongful death, and other traumatic injury. He is trained as a civil law mediator, serving both as a mediator and assisting clients choosing to utilize alternative forms of dispute resolution.
Education: JD 1982, William Mitchell; BA 1976 magna cum laude, Concordia College.
Employment History: Managing Partner 1993-present, Attorney/Partner 1983-present, Collins, Buckley, Sauntry & Haugh; Staff Member 1978-80, MN Housing Finance Agency; Executive Director 1976-78, Swift County Housing & Redevelopment Authority, Benson, MN.
Professional Associations: ABA; MSBA; RCBA (Ethics Committee 1988-present); Criminal Defense Services, Inc. of Ramsey County (Board member); National Employment Lawyers Assn.; University of Minnesota Law School trial practice classes (Judge); National Moot Court Competitions (Judge); MSBA High School Mock Trial Competition (Coach and Judge 1989-present).
Community Involvement: Freedom's Foundation of Valley Forge, PA (Recipient of the George Washington Honor Medal); "Leadership St. Paul" (Participant).
Firm: Founded in 1971, the law firm of Collins, Buckley, Sauntry & Haugh is a full-service law firm with special capabilities in trial practice. It serves a broad range of clients in injury and property claims, business and commercial disputes and transactions, employment matters, family law issues, professional misconduct and negligence matters, and tax and real estate issues. Two firm lawyers are also registered CPAs and one holds an MBA degree in finance. The firm's 14 lawyers and more than 20 staff members strive to provide quality representation to clients in Minnesota and around the country. *See additional listings in Professional Malpractice Defense Law and Commercial Litigation Chapters.*

ROBERT K. SEVERSON - Brink, Sobolik, Severson, Vroom & Malm, P.A. - 217 Birch Avenue South, P.O. Box 790 - Hallock, MN 56728 - Phone: (218) 843-3686, Fax: (218) 843-2724 - *See complete biographical profile in Commercial Litigation Chapter.*

PETER W. SIPKINS - Dorsey & Whitney - Pillsbury Center South, 220 South Sixth Street - Minneapolis, MN 55402-1498 - Phone: (612) 343-7903, Fax: (612) 340-2807 - *See complete biographical profile in Commercial Litigation Chapter.*

•**GEORGE W. SOULE:** Mr. Soule is a founding partner of Bowman and Brooke, a litigation firm in Minneapolis and four other cities. He is a trial lawyer, principally in the defense of product liability actions and in commercial litigation. Mr. Soule is a frequent lecturer on civil litigation and product liability and has written several law review and journal articles. In 1992 he was a visiting lecturer of law at Ritsumeikan University in Japan.
Education: JD 1979 magna cum laude, Harvard (Editor, *Harvard Law Review*); BA 1976 summa cum laude, Moorhead State University.
Employment History: Founding partner 1985-present, Bowman and Brooke; Associate 1979-85, Gray, Plant, Mooty, Mooty, & Bennett.
Representative Clients: Navistar International Transportation Corp.; Clark Material Handling Company; General Motors Corp.; PACCAR Inc; Vermeer Manufacturing Company; Wagner Spray Tech Corp.
Professional Associations: ABA; Defense Research Institute; HCBA; MDLA (Chair 1985-92, Products Liability Committee); MSBA (Chair 1994-95, Civil Litigation Section); State Bar of Wisconsin.
Community Involvement: Minnesota Commission on Judicial Selection (Vice Chair 1992-present); Citizens for Chief Justice Sandy Keith (Cochair 1992); Doug Kelley for Governor Campaign (Issues Director 1989-90); Lawyers for Durenberger (Cochair 1988); John Anderson for President Campaign (Minnesota Coordinator 1979-80).
Firm: Bowman and Brooke is a national litigation firm with offices in several large cities. It is strictly a litigation firm engaged principally in the defense of product liability actions. The firm serves as trial counsel in courts across the country. The members of the firm have established a nationwide reputation for top quality work on complex litigation matters. The firm is distinguished by a well-developed, highly effective team approach to litigation. It employs approximately 55 legal assistants, investigators, and other professionals who efficiently deliver services to clients. *See additional listings in Commercial Litigation and Professional Malpractice Defense Law Chapters.*

GEORGE W. SOULE

Bowman and Brooke
150 South Fifth Street
Suite 2600
Minneapolis, MN 55402

Phone: (612) 339-8682
Fax: (612) 672-3200

Admitted: 1979 Minnesota; 1985 Wisconsin
Birthdate: 06/24/54

•**KEVIN A. SPELLACY:** Mr. Spellacy practices civil litigation, including business litigation, defense of attorney and accountant malpractice, product liability, fires, construction litigation, industrial accidents, personal injury, property damage, and other disputes.
Education: JD 1977 cum laude, William Mitchell; BS 1973, St. John's University.
Employment History: Currently, Quinlivan, Sherwood, Spellacy & Tarvestad, P.A.; Law Clerk 1977, Hon. Donald Barbeau, District Court Judge, Fourth Judicial District.
Representative Clients: Cooper Tire & Rubber Company; The St. Paul Companies; Medrad, Inc.; M & P Transport, Inc.; Polar Manufacturing; Whink Products Company; Rheem Manufacturing Company; CNA Insurance Companies; Horace Mann Companies; Farmers Insurance Group; General Casualty; Grinnell Mutual Reinsurance Company; Federated Insurance; American States Insurance Company; Minnesota Joint Underwriting Assn.; Minnesota Lawyers Mutual Insurance Company; Farmers Home Group; Northland Insurance Company; Lumber Insurance Company; Citizens Security Mutual Insurance Company.
Professional Associations: MSBA; Stearns-Benton Bar Assn.; MN Supreme Court Advisory Committee on Rules of Evidence; Seventh District Bar Assn.; MDLA; Defense Research Institute; International Assn. of Defense Counsel.
Community Involvement: St. Cloud United Way; Optimist Club.
Firm: Founded in 1923, Quinlivan, Sherwood, Spellacy & Tarvestad, P.A. is a highly respected law firm devoting its practice to civil litigation and dispute resolution of all types at the state and federal levels. *See additional listings in Professional Malpractice Defense Law and Environmental Law Chapters.*

KEVIN A. SPELLACY

Quinlivan, Sherwood, Spellacy & Tarvestad, P.A.
P.O. Box 1008
St. Cloud, MN 56302-1008

Phone: (612) 251-1414
Fax: (612) 251-1415

Admitted: 1977 Minnesota; 1978 US Dist. Ct. (MN)
Birthdate: 07/12/51

Chapter 26: Personal Injury Defense Law

GAYLORD W. SWELBAR

Hanft, Fride, O'Brien, Harries, Swelbar & Burns, P.A.
1000 First Bank Place
130 West Superior Street
Duluth, MN 55802

Phone: (218) 722-4766
Fax: (218) 720-4920

Admitted: 1970 Minnesota; 1961 Ohio; 1986 Wisconsin; 1986 US Sup. Ct.; 1986 US Tax Ct.
Birthdate: 06/21/32

•**GAYLORD W. SWELBAR:** Mr. Swelbar has a civil trial practice in personal injury, property damage, and commercial matters representing insurance companies and corporate clients in all litigation matters, including condemnation, construction claims, employment claims, and product liability, as well as professional liability and coverage issues.
Education: LLB 1961, Ohio Northern; BS 1958, Ohio State University.
Employment History: Currently, Hanft, Fride, O'Brien, Harries, Swelbar & Burns, P.A.; Private practice 1962-70 in Ohio; Attorney 1960-62, Republic Steel Corporation.
Representative Clients: Numerous insurance companies; Duluth Transit Authority; Duluth, Winnipeg & Pacific Railway Company; Canadian National Railway; American Steamship Company.
Professional Associations: ABA; American Arbitration Assn. (Advisory Committee); Defense Research Institute; Federation of Insurance and Corporate Counsel; International Assn. of Defense Counsel; MSBA; National Assn. of Railroad Trial Counsel; State Bar of Wisconsin.
Firm: Founded in 1899, Hanft, Fride, O'Brien, Harries, Swelbar & Burns, P.A., is a full service law firm engaged primarily in business and trial work. The firm's 17 attorneys serve clients throughout Minnesota, northern Wisconsin, and beyond. *See additional listings in Commercial Litigation and Professional Malpractice Defense Law Chapters.*

•**ANTHONY M. TARVESTAD** - Quinlivan, Sherwood, Spellacy & Tarvestad, P.A. - P.O. Box 1008 - St. Cloud, MN 56302-1008 - Phone: (612) 251-1414, Fax: (612) 251-1415 - *See complete biographical profile in Professional Malpractice Defense Law Chapter.*

THOMAS R. THIBODEAU

Johnson, Killen, Thibodeau & Seiler, P.A.
811 Norwest Center
230 West Superior Street
Duluth, MN 55802

Phone: (218) 722-6331
Fax: (218) 722-3031

Admitted: 1967 Minnesota; 1983 Wisconsin
Birthdate: 02/05/42

•**THOMAS R. THIBODEAU:** Mr. Thibodeau has extensive experience in personal injury, product liability, toxic torts, wrongful death, and dram shop. He is liaison counsel in the Superfund Case, *US v. Arrowhead Refining Co., et al.*, and has been active in the defense of asbestos claims for over 20 years. He was elected an Advocate of the American Board of Trial Advocates and a Fellow of the American College of Trial Lawyers. He is certified as a Civil Trial Advocate by the National Board of Trial Advocacy and a Civil Trial Specialist by the Minnesota State Bar Association. He is a frequent lecturer to attorneys on wrongful death, personal injury, trial tactics, evidence, CERCLA, and product liability.
Education: JD 1967, University of Minnesota; BA 1964 cum laude, University of St. Thomas.
Representative Clients: Abex Corp.; Austin Mutual Insurance Co.; Auto Owners Insurance Co.; Capitol Indemnity Co.; Carolina Casualty Co.; Catholic Mutual Insurance Group; Great American Insurance Co.; Heritage Mutual Insurance Co.; Horace Mann Insurance Co.; J.B. Hunt Transport, Inc.; Louisiana-Pacific Corp.; Minnesota Lawyers Mutual Ins. Co.; Ogleby-Norton Co.; National Indemnity Co.; North American Refractories, Inc.; Transamerica Insurance Co.; USX Corp.; Westbend Mutual Insurance Co.; Western World Insurance Co.
Professional Associations: Academy of Certified Trial Lawyers of MN (President 1993-94); MDLA (past President); MSBA.
Community Involvement: Legal Aid (President 1970-74); St. Louis County Heritage & Art Center (Volunteer Attorney 1980-86); University of Minnesota-Duluth (volunteer attorney); Duluth City Charter Commission (President 1976-78); The Marshall School (Board member 1986-92, President 1990-92).
Firm: Founded in 1888, Johnson, Killen, Thibodeau & Seiler, P.A., is the oldest firm in northern Minnesota. Today the firm's 18 lawyers provide services for consumers, businesses, and companies in commercial, toxic tort, environmental, and insurance litigation; commercial and residential real estate; probate, estate planning, and trusts; employment law; closely held business law; and Workers' Compensation. *See additional listings in Environmental Law and Commercial Litigation Chapters.*

Personal Injury Defense Law Leading Attorneys

•**MADGE S. THORSEN:** Ms. Thorsen's practice concentrates in commercial litigation and drug and medical device litigation on a local, regional, and national basis. Ms. Thorsen has taught product liability law as an adjunct professor at the University of Minnesota and trial practice at William Mitchell College of Law.
Education: JD 1977 magna cum laude, University of Minnesota (President 1976-77, *Minnesota Law Review*); BA 1972 summa cum laude, University of Minnesota.
Employment History: 1991-present, Popham, Haik, Schnobrich & Kaufman, Ltd.; 1978-91, Oppenheimer, Wolff & Donnelly; Judicial Clerk 1977-78, Hon. Earl Larsen, US District Court, District of Minnesota.
Representative Clients: G.D. Searle; Pfizer, Inc.; General Electric Capital Corp.; Thompson Medical Company; Astra Pharmaceuticals; American Medical Systems; American Airlines.
Professional Associations: MSBA; Minnesota Women Lawyers; ABA; Defense Research Institute.
Firm: Popham, Haik, Schnobrich & Kaufman, Ltd., is a firm of more than 230 attorneys with offices in Denver, Miami, Minneapolis, Washington, D.C., and international affiliations in Beijing, China and Leipzig and Stuttgart, Germany. The firm represents clients nationally and internationally on issues relating to corporate and business law, administrative law, and litigation. *See additional listing in Commercial Litigation Chapter.*

MADGE S. THORSEN

Popham, Haik, Schnobrich & Kaufman, Ltd.
222 South Ninth Street
Suite 3300
Minneapolis, MN 55402

Phone: (612) 333-4800
Fax: (612) 334-8888

Admitted: 1977 Minnesota
Birthdate: 02/20/49

LYNN G. TRUESDELL - Bassford, Lockhart, Truesdell & Briggs, P.A. - 3550 Multifoods Tower, 33 South Sixth Street - Minneapolis, MN 55402 - Phone: (612) 333-3000, Fax: (612) 333-8829 - *See complete biographical profile in Commercial Litigation Chapter.*

•**ALAN R. VANASEK:** Mr. Vanasek has over 25 years of specialized experience in the handling of civil litigation matters, with a special emphasis on product liability, medical malpractice, motor vehicle liability, employment claims, and insurance coverage issues.
Education: JD 1969, William Mitchell (Harvey T. Reid Scholar 1966-69).
Employment History: Partner 1969-present, Jardine, Logan & O'Brien.
Representative Clients: Phico Insurance Company; Farmers Insurance Group; American States Insurance Company; St. Paul Ramsey Medical Center; Alexsis; Federated Mutual Insurance Company; GAB Business Services; American Hardware Mutual Insurance Company.
Professional Associations: ABA; American College of Trial Lawyers (Fellow; State Chair 1994); American Board of Trial Advocates; American Society of Law & Medicine; ATLA; International Assn. of Insurance Counsel; MDLA (Board member 1985-86); MN Society of Hospital Attorneys; MSBA (Board of Governors).
Firm: Litigation is, and always has been, the primary focus of the Jardine, Logan & O'Brien Law Firm. Throughout the firm's 75 year history, their lawyers have worked on some of the region's largest and most complex disputes with outstanding results. The success of the firm can be traced to a philosophy of file handling that puts the client first. That requires early involvement to understand clients' needs, preferred procedures, and desired roles in their matters; early and accurate evaluation of cases, made simpler by the firm's collective years of experience; aggressive handling in preparation of the files; frequent communication with clients to keep them informed and answer questions. This approach does not mean that Jardine, Logan & O'Brien does unnecessary work; quite the opposite. By properly evaluating cases and skillfully preparing them, they can resolve clients' disputes by the best and most cost-effective means, whether by settlement, through alternative dispute resolution techniques, or in a trial or hearing. Clients of the firm include individuals, large and small businesses, insurance companies, and self-insured trusts. The firm is the recipient of many referrals from peers at other law firms who frequently refer to its attorneys complex litigation matters. *See additional listings in Professional Malpractice Defense Law and Employment Law Chapters.*

ALAN R. VANASEK

Jardine, Logan & O'Brien
2100 Piper Jaffray Plaza
444 Cedar Street
St. Paul, MN 55101

Phone: (612) 290-6500
Fax: (612) 223-5070

Admitted: 1969 Minnesota; 1969 US Dist. Ct. (MN); US Ct. App. (8th Cir.)
Birthdate: 04/09/42

Chapter 26: Personal Injury Defense Law

Complete listing of all attorneys nominated in Personal Injury Defense Law

DAVID D. ALSOP, Gislason, Dosland, Hunter & Malecki, P.A., Hopkins; **DOUGLAS P. ANDERSON,** Rosenmeier, Anderson & Vogel, Little Falls; **JOHN M. ANDERSON,** Bassford, Lockhart, Truesdell & Briggs, P.A., Minneapolis; **LINDSAY G. ARTHUR,** Arthur, Chapman, McDonough, Kettering & Smetak, Minneapolis; **CARL BAER,** Kief, Fuller, Baer, Wallner & Rodgers, Ltd., Bemidji; **BRYAN BAUDLER,** Baudler, Baudler, Maus & Blahnik, Austin; **J. RICHARD BLAND,** Meagher & Geer, Minneapolis; **RICHARD A. BOWMAN,** Bowman and Brooke, Minneapolis; **CRAIG R. CAMPBELL,** Gunhus, Grinnell, Klinger, Swenson & Guy, Ltd., Moorhead; **KEVIN S. CARPENTER,** Quinlivan, Sherwood, Spellacy & Tarvestad, P.A., St. Cloud; **THEODORE J. COLLINS,** Collins, Buckley, Sauntry & Haugh, St. Paul; **THOMAS M. CONLIN,** Murnane, Conlin, White & Brandt, St. Paul; **G. ALAN CUNNINGHAM,** Faegre & Benson, Minneapolis; **J. MICHAEL DADY,** J. Michael Dady & Associates, P.A., Minneapolis; **JOHN M. DEGNAN,** Bassford, Lockhart, Truesdell & Briggs, P.A., Minneapolis; **C. ALLEN DOSLAND,** Gislason, Dosland, Hunter & Malecki, P.A., New Ulm; **CARL C. DRAHOS,** Drahos & Young, Bemidji; **JAMES F. DUNN,** Dunn & Elliott, P.A., St. Paul; **DAVID F. FITZGERALD,** Rider, Bennett, Egan & Arundel, Minneapolis; **JAMES FITZMAURICE,** Faegre & Benson, Minneapolis; **WILLIAM D. FLASKAMP,** Meagher & Geer, Minneapolis; **GEORGE W. FLYNN,** Cosgrove, Flynn & Gaskins, Minneapolis; **STEVEN M. FULLER,** Kief, Fuller, Bae,r Wallner & Rodgers, Ltd., Bemidji; **STEVEN S. FULLER,** O'Brien, Ehrich, Wolf, Deaner & Maus, Rochester; **DANIEL A. GISLASON,** Gislason, Dosland, Hunter & Malecki, P.A., New Ulm; **EDWARD M. GLENNON,** Lindquist & Vennum, Minneapolis; **PAUL E. GRINNELL,** Gunhus, Grinnell, Klinger, Swenson & Guy, Ltd., Moorhead; **GUNDER D. GUNHUS,** Gunhus, Grinnell, Klinger, Swenson & Guy, Ltd., Moorhead; **DAVID L. HASHMALL,** Popham, Haik, Schnobrich & Kaufman, Ltd., Minneapolis; **W. SCOTT HERZOG,** Moss & Barnett, A Professional Association, Minneapolis; **DANIEL J. HEUEL,** Muir, Heuel, Carlson & Spelhaug, P.A., Rochester; **GARY W. HOCH,** Meagher & Geer, Minneapolis; **BARRY P. HOGAN,** Jeffries, Olson, Flom, Oppegard & Hogan, P.A., Fargo; **LYNN J. HUMMEL,** Hummel Sinclair Pearson Evans Hunt & Heisler, P.A., Detroit Lakes; **DAVID C. HUTCHINSON,** Geraghty O'Loughlin & Kenney, P.A., St. Paul; **PETER IRVINE,** Irvine Ramstad Briggs & Karkela, P.A., Perham; **KENNETH F. JOHANNSON,** Dickel, Johannson, Taylor, Rust & Tye, P.A., Crookston; **BRIAN N. JOHNSON,** Popham, Haik, Schnobrich & Kaufman, Ltd., Minneapolis; **CHARLES R. KENNEDY,** Kennedy & Nervig, Wadena; **H. MORRISON KERSHNER,** Pemberton, Sorlie, Sefkow, Rufer & Kershner, Fergus Falls; **JEFFREY J. KEYES,** Briggs and Morgan, P.A., Minneapolis; **LAWRENCE R. KING,** King & Hatch, St. Paul; **PATRICK M. KRUEGER,** Borden Steinbauer & Krueger, Brainerd; **NEAL A. LANO,** Lano Nelson O'Toole & Bengtson, Ltd., Grand Rapids; **JOHN C. LERVICK,** Swenson, Grover, Lervick, Syverson, Battey & Anderson, Ltd., Alexandria; **D. PATRICK MCCULLOUGH,** McCullough, Smith & Wright, St. Paul; **ROBERT H. MAGIE III,** Crassweller Magie Andresen Haag & Paciotti P.A., Duluth; **PATRICK E. MAHONEY,** Mahoney, Dougherty & Mahoney, P.A., Minneapolis; **RICHARD P. MAHONEY,** Mahoney, Dougherty & Mahoney, P.A., Minneapolis; **KURT J. MARBEN,** Charlson, Marben & Jorgenson, P.A., Thief River Falls; **GERALD L. MASCHKA,** Farrish, Johnson & Maschka, Mankato; **REBECCA EGGE MOOS,** Bassford, Lockhart, Truesdell & Briggs, P.A., Minneapolis; **FREDERICK W. MORRIS,** Leonard, Street and Deinard Professional Association, Minneapolis; **ROSS MUIR,** Muir, Heuel, Carlson & Spelhaug, P.A., Rochester; **TERENCE J. O'LOUGHLIN,** Geraghty O'Loughlin & Kenney P.A., St. Paul; **DENNIS L. O'TOOLE,** Lano, Nelson, O'Toole & Bengtson, Ltd., Grand Rapids; **RICHARD L. PEMBERTON,** Pemberton, Sorlie, Sefkow, Rufer & Kershner, Fergus Falls; **H. JEFFREY PETERSON,** Cope & Peterson, P.A., Virginia; **ROMAINE R. POWELL,** Powell, Powell & Aamodt, Bemidji; **JOHN D. QUINLIVAN,** Quinlivan, Sherwood, Spellacy & Tarvestad, P.A., St. Cloud; **MICHAEL R. QUINLIVAN,** Arthur, Chapman, McDonough, Kettering & Smetak, P.A., Minneapolis; **FRANK J. RAJKOWSKI,** Rajkowski Hansmeier, Ltd., St. Cloud; **SHERYL RAMSTAD-HVASS,** Rider, Bennett, Egan & Arundel, Minneapolis; **PIERRE N. REGNIER,** Jardine, Logan & O'Brien, St. Paul; **CARVER RICHARDS,** Trenti Law Firm, Virginia; **JAMES M. RILEY,** Meagher & Geer, Minneapolis; **JOHN R. RODENBERG,** Berens, Rodenberg & O'Connor, New Ulm; **DONALD E. RYSAVY,** Hoversten, Strom, Johnson & Rysavy, Austin; **JOHN R. SCHULZ,** Collins, Buckley, Sauntry & Haugh, St. Paul; **GEORGE W. SOULE,** Bowman and Brooke, Minneapolis; **KEVIN A. SPELLACY,** Quinlivan, Sherwood, Spellacy & Tarvestad, P.A., St. Cloud; **JAN STUURMANS,** Stuurmans & Karan, P.A., Minneapolis; **GAYLORD W. SWELBAR,** Hanft, Fride, O'Brien, Harries, Swelbar & Burns, P.A., Duluth; **ANTHONY M. TARVESTAD,** Quinlivan, Sherwood, Spellacy & Tarvestad, P.A., St. Cloud; **THOMAS R. THIBODEAU,** Johnson, Killen, Thibodeau & Seiler, P.A., Duluth; **MADGE S. THORSEN,** Popham, Haik, Schnobrich & Kaufman, Ltd., Minneapolis; **TIMOTHY P. TOBIN,** Gislason, Dosland, Hunter & Malecki, P.A., Hopkins; **ALAN R. VANASEK,** Jardine, Logan & O'Brien, St. Paul; **ROBERT T. WHITE,** Murnane, Conlin, White & Brandt, St. Paul; **THOMAS WOLF,** O'Brien, Ehrich, Wolf, Deaner & Maus, Rochester.

CHAPTER 27

PROBATE, ESTATE PLANNING & TRUSTS LAW

Although no one likes to think about dying, there are good reasons to prepare for this inevitable event by setting up a plan to distribute one's estate after death. A person's estate consists of all his or her property and possessions, and includes bank accounts, real estate, furniture, automobiles, stocks, bonds, life insurance policies, retirement funds, pensions, and death benefits. If a person plans well, his or her estate can often be passed on after death quickly, easily, and subject to fewer taxes. This chapter discusses the most common estate planning tools—wills and trusts—and gives special attention to the interests of business owners.

WILLS

A will is the most common document used to specify how an estate should be handled after death. Anyone designated to receive property under a will (or trust) is called a beneficiary. A will can be simple or elaborate, depending upon the size of the estate and the wishes of the person who makes it—the testator. Many types of post-death instructions can be described in a will. A will can describe who should receive specific items of furniture, artwork, or jewelry. A will can name a guardian who will take care of minor children should there be no surviving parent. A will can disinherit a child if the testator does not want the child to receive any part of the estate. The options for what a person can do with a will are varied but limited.

REQUIREMENTS FOR A VALID WILL

Each state sets slightly different formal requirements for the creation of a legal will. In Minnesota, a person must be at least 18 years old in order to make a legal will. In addition, he or she must be of sound mind, which means that the individual has no mental disability that prevents him or her from understanding the full nature of the document he or she signs. In Minnesota, a will must be in writing and must be witnessed and signed by at least two other people. A handwritten will, often called a holographic will, is valid in Minnesota provided that it is witnessed and signed by two people. Individuals must sign their own wills, but if they are illiterate or otherwise incapacitated, they can direct another person, in the presence of witnesses, to sign for them. A will is valid until it is revoked or superseded by a new will. Individual provisions can be changed by a codicil, which is described in the section, "Changing and Updating Wills."

It is not necessary to hire an attorney to create a will. A non-attorney can create a will, but he or she must pay close attention to the details outlined above. Smaller estates can be described simply, and making a will to disperse a smaller estate can be done by almost anyone. The simplest will in history ever to be declared valid by a court contained only three words: "All to wife." However, a lawyer's guidance is very helpful with complicated property holdings or an estate with many assets, especially if they are located in several different places. Small business owners need the advice of an experienced attorney to transfer their assets. In these cases, an attorney's help can ensure that the transfer of property described in the will is done in a way that minimizes the survivor's tax liability. In addition, a complicated estate may require documents other than a will, such as a trust agreement, to ensure that all of a person's wishes are carried out.

PERSONAL REPRESENTATIVE

A will typically appoints someone called a personal representative to carry out the specific wishes of the person who has died—the decedent. The personal representative should be a trusted friend or family member who should be made fully aware of his or her duties before the decedent dies. A personal representative must do many things, including collecting and managing the decedent's assets, collecting any money owed at the time of death, selling any assets, if necessary, to pay estate taxes or expenses, and filing all required tax returns. Because a personal representative is allowed to charge a fee for doing this work, choosing a friend or family member who is also a beneficiary to fill this role may be a good choice, as he or she may not charge the full amount allowed by law. To ensure that one's estate has a personal representative chosen by the decedent, it is wise to name one or more contingent personal representatives who can take over the responsibilities of the primary personal representative if the primary personal representative is unable to assume the responsibilities of the position.

If a person does not name a personal representative in his or her will, state law establishes the order in which a probate court appoints relatives to act as personal representative. If none of these family members agree to be the personal representative, the probate division of the district court may appoint a professional administrator to do the job.

APPOINTING A GUARDIAN FOR CHILDREN

A person with minor or dependent children can name in a will a guardian to care for those children should there be no surviving parent. If a person fails to name someone to assume the role of guardian, the probate court appoints someone. The person chosen by the court will usually be a close relative or friend, but it may not be the person the parent would have chosen. As with the selection of a personal representative, it is important that the potential guardian understands the provisions of the will and is willing to accept the responsibilities of being a guardian. Also, it is wise to name an alternate guardian should the primary guardian be unable to accept the responsibility. Of course, the selection of a guardian for children is likely to influence how the parent wants to distribute his or her property. Otherwise, a decedent's money might go to one person while his or her children go to another person. The parent may want to give property to someone only if the recipient accepts guardianship of a child. In this way, the guardian is given the financial resources to care for the child.

PLANNING FOR INCAPACITY

People drafting wills often use the opportunity to plan for the possibility of their own incapacity. By preparing a document called a durable power of attorney, they can give another person of their choosing full legal authority to act on their behalf should they become unable to handle their personal and financial affairs. Without a durable power of attorney, a person's family might need to go to court to have someone appointed to handle the person's legal affairs. If a power of attorney is made part of the will, it is essential that the will be made known to family members before the testator becomes incapacitated. If a will is kept secret, locked away in a safe deposit box until a person dies, it will be too late for the power of attorney provisions to be useful.

Some people also use a document called a durable power of attorney for health care to make health care decisions in advance should they subsequently become incapacitated.

Restrictions on Wills

In order to protect spouses and dependent children, some laws prevent a person from disinheriting a spouse or child. A married person cannot completely disinherit his or her spouse without the spouse's consent. Occasionally this happens through a prenuptial agreement, for example, in which a second spouse agrees that an entire estate will go to children from a first marriage. In the absence of a contrary agreement, a surviving spouse has the right of election, which allows him or her to take a portion of the spouse's estate. This is used when a spouse is unhappy with the provisions of a will. A person may legally disinherit a child by clearly specifying in a will that the child not receive any of the estate.

There are other limits to a will. Anything owned in joint tenancy with another person will go to the surviving joint tenant. Arrangements must be made to end the joint tenancy before death if one joint tenant does not want the other to inherit the jointly held property. Because there may be significant tax consequences in doing so, these changes should be made only after consulting an attorney. Other possessions are not considered part of the estate because they are already promised to someone else. For example, a testator cannot specify in a will that someone other than the beneficiary of a life insurance policy gets the benefits described in that policy. However, a person can designate his or her estate as the beneficiary of a life insurance policy. In this case, the money from the policy will be added to other estate assets and will be distributed according to the will. Similarly, the money from a retirement plan goes to the persons named on the plan, regardless of whether they are beneficiaries in a will. Laws designed to uphold public policy also limit what can be done with a person's assets after death. For example, conditions in a will encouraging someone to do something illegal or immoral in order to inherit money or property would not be enforced.

Changing and Updating Wills

The provisions of a will are valid until they are changed, revoked, destroyed, or invalidated by the writing of a new will. Changes or additions to a will can be included in a document called a codicil. Codicils must be written, signed, and witnessed in the same way as a will. Wills cannot be changed simply by crossing out existing language or writing in new provisions. In order to avoid making a new will or codicil each time a person's possessions change, a will can specify that personal property is to be distributed according to instructions outlined in a separate document. A person can then revise the separate document as often as necessary, without observing all of the formalities required to change the will itself.

If someone dies with a will that is not up-to-date, people may not be provided for adequately. For example, a person chosen to be a personal representative or guardian may have died or fallen out of favor with the author of the will, or a favorite charity may no longer be in existence. A significant amount of case law has dealt with how a probate court is to proceed with a will that has become unenforceable because of changed circumstances. These headaches can be avoided if a will is reviewed at least every two years and revised for major changes in tax laws or for personal events such as births, deaths, marriages, divorces, or significant changes in the size of the estate. It is also a good idea to review a will if its author moves to another state, because the new state of residency may have different inheritance and tax laws. In Minnesota, a divorce automatically revokes any distribution to the former spouse.

THE RIGHT OF ELECTION

As discussed previously, Minnesota's probate code protects surviving spouses from being entirely disinherited by a decedent spouse. A surviving spouse who is unsatisfied with his or her portion under an otherwise valid will is allowed to exercise the right of election and take one-third of the decedent's estate. Thus, the one-third portion is the minimum amount a surviving spouse may receive. A will can give more to the surviving spouse, but if it gives less, the surviving spouse can simply elect to forego his or her share under the will in favor of this statutorily guaranteed one-third share.

DYING WITHOUT A WILL

If a person does not have a will or has not adequately planned for the distribution of his or her estate at death, survivors can face a complicated, time-consuming, and costly process. Often survivors wind up having to pay more taxes on their inheritance than they would have paid had there been a will or other estate planning tool. To provide for surviving friends and relatives, or to support favorite causes or charities, a person can plan for the distribution of his or her estate after death. With planning, an estate can be distributed as fairly as possible with as little tax burden as legally allowed.

When a decedent leaves no will or other comparable estate planning tool, he or she is said to have died intestate. The division of the state district court system set up to handle wills and trusts is called the probate division. When a person dies intestate, the probate division steps in to divide the decedent's estate, according to a formula known as the state inheritance laws. Under the state inheritance laws, the probate division uses formulas set by the legislature to divide a deceased person's possessions among any surviving relatives.

A probate division applying the state inheritance laws first deducts from the estate funeral expenses, any unpaid medical bills, taxes, family allowance expenses, and any other debts owed. If the decedent has a surviving spouse and no children, the entire estate, after these deductions, goes to the spouse. If there are children, and the family home was not held in joint tenancy, the surviving spouse receives the right to the homestead for his or her life, known as a life estate, and a portion of the remaining estate. Surviving children receive whatever is left of the estate after the spouse's share is deducted, and they inherit the homestead when the surviving spouse dies. In the absence of a will, a surviving spouse with at least one child generally receives a life estate in the homestead, the first $70,000 of the estate, plus one-half of the amount remaining after the first $70,000 is deducted. The other one-half of the estate is divided equally among the decedent's children. If one of the decedent's children dies before the decedent, that child's share passes to his or her living descendants, if any. Anyone entitled to inherit a portion of an intestate decedent's estate is known as an heir.

One problem with relying on a probate division applying state inheritance laws to distribute one's estate is that it may not distribute the estate in the manner the decedent would have wanted. State inheritance laws only recognize relatives. The inheritance laws never permit the probate division to support a decedent's close friend, lover, or favorite charities. If no relatives are found, the estate goes to the state. Clearly, for most people writing a will or creating a trust is advisable.

TRUSTS

A trust is another frequently used estate planning device that manages the distribution of a person's estate.

MECHANICS OF A TRUST

To create a trust, the owner of property (grantor) transfers the property to a person or institution (trustee) who holds legal title to the property and manages it for the benefit of a third party (beneficiary). The grantor can name himself or herself or another person as the trustee. A trust can be either a testamentary trust or a living trust. A testamentary trust transfers the property to the trust only after the death of the grantor. A living trust, sometimes called an inter vivos trust, is created during the life of the grantor and can be set up to continue after the grantor's death or to terminate and be distributed upon the grantor's death.

Unlike a will, which in some cases can be drafted without the help of an attorney, a person should never draft a trust without the aid of a lawyer. Many complex laws regulate trusts depending on the size and composition of the estate. Trusts must be carefully structured if they are to take advantage of beneficial tax treatment. An experienced attorney should always assist in drafting a trust so that it is valid, meets the needs of the estate, and does not conflict with any previously drafted will.

ADVANTAGES AND DISADVANTAGES OF A TRUST

Trusts have many advantages over wills. The advantages depend on whether a living trust or testamentary trust is chosen. All trusts have the advantage of allowing the grantor to determine who receives the benefit of the money, when they receive it, and what conditions must be met. If a spouse is unable or unwilling to manage assets, if children are minors or unable to handle money responsibly, or if a beneficiary is disabled, creating a trust can be a better way of passing on assets. Living and testamentary trusts are an especially popular way of providing for beneficiaries' future educational or medical costs.

Some advantages are particular to living trusts. First, a living trust can give its grantor substantial tax advantages. Second, possessions held in a living trust are not subject to estate administration by the probate division after the grantor dies. Survivors do not have to reveal the details of any possessions held in trust through the public filing process that takes place during probate. In addition, if the grantor owns real estate in another state, establishing a living trust for the title to that property may allow survivors to avoid probate in the other state. A living trust can free the grantor from the burden of overseeing his or her financial affairs because a trustee manages all the assets of a living trust. More importantly, a living trust allows a trustee to manage the trust funds in the event that its creator becomes incapacitated or mentally or physically unable to oversee his or her possessions. If a living trust contains all of a person's assets, then he or she may not need a will, and his or her survivors may be able to avoid probate. If only part of a person's possessions are held in living trust, then a will is necessary to distribute those items in the estate not placed into a trust. However, a pour-over provision in a will can place any possessions remaining upon death into a pre-existing living trust.

The primary disadvantage of a living trust is that it involves the loss of some flexibility and control over one's assets. Unlike wills, which become effective only at death, a living trust becomes effective immediately upon its creation. For the person who wants to retain unrestricted control over his or her estate, a will or a testamentary trust is a better estate planning tool because it can be changed at any time prior to death.

The primary advantage of a testamentary trust is that it allows the grantor to retain unrestricted control over his or her estate. A testamentary trust becomes effective only upon the death of its grantor. Like a will, a testamentary trust can be changed at any time prior to death.

The primary disadvantage to testamentary trusts is that they do not take advantage of the beneficial tax treatment given to living trusts. Because a testamentary trust only takes effect when the grantor dies, the grantor cannot enjoy any tax advantage during his or her life. Also, most testamentary trusts must go through probate.

REVOCABLE AND IRREVOCABLE TRUSTS

A living trust can be either revocable or irrevocable. As implied by their names, a revocable trust can be changed or revoked after its creation, while a person signing an irrevocable trust gives up the right to change or revoke the trust. Revocable trusts are quite often devised to supplement a will and/or to name someone to handle the grantor's affairs should the grantor become incapacitated. A trust usually must be made irrevocable if the grantor wants to avoid income or estate taxes. Tax authorities consider the grantor of a revocable trust to be the owner of the property because he or she still controls the property. For this reason, income from assets held in a revocable trust must be reported as income to the grantor for income tax purposes. At the death of the grantor, property in a revocable trust is included in the estate for calculating estate taxes.

Irrevocable trusts are often designed to be the beneficiary of a life insurance policy. Such a life insurance trust can also spell out how the policy's money is distributed to survivors. In addition, irrevocable trusts are often set up to manage money given to minors and to charities. Finally, an irrevocable trust can be used to transfer assets to another person in the event that the grantor requires expensive medical care. Although doing so may protect the grantor's family by ensuring that the cost of medical care does not wipe out the family fortune, it may also make the grantor ineligible to receive federal and state Medical Assistance. State law prohibits the beneficiary of a trust fund from receiving public assistance or public health care benefits. However, the 1993 Minnesota Legislature passed a law permitting disabled people to receive supplemental needs trusts without jeopardizing their public assistance status. These trusts must be designed to meet the special needs of disabled people that are not met by public assistance benefits; therefore, one should only create this kind of trust after consulting with an attorney.

PROBATE

With few exceptions, the estate of a person who dies owning property in his or her name cannot be legally distributed without first going through probate. Only if all of a decedent's property is held in joint tenancy or in trust can survivors avoid probate. Probate can operate either formally, with court supervision, or informally, without court supervision. Whether formal or informal, the first duty of the probate division is to determine whether the decedent left a valid will. If the decedent left a valid will, the division oversees the process of settling the estate according to the terms of the will. If the decedent did not leave a will or if the probate division determines the will is invalid, the probate division applies the state inheritance laws, described earlier, to the estate.

Informal probate is designed for estates in which court supervision or adjudication is not required because the estate has no uncertainties, legal disputes, or complex administrative requirements. A personal representative can apply for informal probate and become personally responsible for probating the estate completely, correctly, in accordance with state statutes, and promptly. Most personal representatives engage an attorney to handle at least a portion of their duties even with informal probate.

When the probate division formally supervises distribution, its responsibilities may include:

- Overseeing the distribution of estate assets, including payment of state and federal taxes.
- Hearing any contested claims by creditors or others seeking to collect from the estate.
- Choosing a personal representative when one is not named in the will.
- Supervising the actions of the personal representative, including the payment of state and federal taxes.
- Ensuring that the personal representative posts a surety bond to protect creditors and others in the event that the executor acts improperly.
- Deciding which possessions are subject to estate administration and which are not.
- Determining a decedent's true heirs.
- Ruling on the legitimacy of any claims outstanding against the estate.
- Supervising the transfer of assets to beneficiaries named in the will.
- Overseeing a guardian's use of property placed in trust for the benefit of children or dependents.

Making out a will does not guarantee that survivors can avoid all problems of distribution, but a carefully drafted will can mean that their time in court is minimized.

AVOIDING DEATH TAXES

A carefully created estate plan can considerably reduce the tax burden on an estate. Although the state of Minnesota no longer has an inheritance tax, under Minnesota and federal law a decedent with an estate worth more than $600,000 must file an estate tax return and possibly pay federal and Minnesota estate taxes. The federal government's inheritance tax scheme is quite complicated. Under federal tax law a person is allowed to leave $600,000 tax-free to one or more individuals, other than a surviving spouse. The surviving spouse is entitled to receive an unlimited amount tax-free. If the estate is a very large one, however, and the entire estate is left to the surviving spouse, that surviving spouse may lose the option of giving $600,000 tax-free to individuals of his or her own choosing. An experienced tax attorney can create trusts that will allow the two spouses to pass on a total of $1,200,000 free of unnecessary estate taxes. Regardless of whether the recipient pays state or federal estate taxes, there may be income tax consequences for the recipients under a will.

CONCERNS FOR OWNERS OF CLOSELY HELD BUSINESSES

Closely held businesses present unique challenges to the person planning for his or her estate. Often a businessperson's interest in a closely held business is his or her primary source of income and constitutes the bulk of his or her wealth. Because interests in a closely held business often lack liquidity and are difficult to valuate, transferring them before or after death can be difficult and determining the taxes owed can be time consuming.

Only an attorney experienced in estate planning for owners of closely held businesses can adequately advise on all aspects of treating closely held business assets. Before an attorney can prepare a will or trust, however, the person with an interest in a closely held business must consider his or her own need for income until death, the likelihood that someone in the family will want to continue playing an active role in the business, and the ability of a recipient to pay death taxes and administration costs if the business is going to continue after the owner's death.

Some common options chosen by small business owners include partner buyout agreements, gift-leaseback arrangements, life insurance policies, incorporation, or selling the business. In a partner buyout agreement, partners can agree that a surviving partner will buy the interest of a decedent at a price agreed upon in advance. Partner buyout agreements are common but they need to be updated periodically as the value of the business changes. Under a gift-leaseback arrangement, substantial assets are put in trust for the benefit of one or more beneficiaries then leased back to the business. The primary benefit of a gift-leaseback arrangement is that the beneficiary receives financial support but business operations cannot be disrupted. Life insurance policies can provide a recipient with sufficient cash to pay taxes and administration costs without having to sell the business. Incorporating often makes it easier to valuate the business.

Selling the business may seem drastic, but doing so can mean the recipient receives more money. Many small business owners feel strong emotional attachment to businesses they have grown from scratch. Often emotional attachments lead an owner to refuse to sell a business and the family has to sell it later in order to pay off bills or because no one is capable of managing the business. Accepting the need to sell a business while its owner is still alive can be wise because the owner has time to find a suitable buyer. In addition the business is likely to fetch a higher price because its current owners can offer to oversee the transition to new ownership.

RESOURCES

National Senior Citizens Law Center, 2025 M Street NW, Suite 400, Washington, DC, 20036. (202) 887-5280.

Seniors' Legal Rights. This 48-page booklet is available free from the Minnesota Attorney General's Office—Consumer Division, 1400 NCL Tower, 445 Minnesota Street, St. Paul, MN, 55101. (612) 296-3353.

Why You Need a Will. To get a free copy of this pamphlet, send a self-addressed, stamped envelope to the Minnesota State Bar Association, 514 Nicollet Mall, Suite 300, Minneapolis, MN 55402.

Probate, Estate Planning & Trusts Law Leading Attorneys

The attorneys profiled in this section were nominated by their peers in a statewide survey conducted in 1993 in which several thousand Minnesota attorneys were asked to name the lawyer to whom they would send a friend or family member in need of legal assistance in the area of *Probate, Estate Planning & Trusts Law*.

Because the survey resulted in a list of less than five percent of Minnesota's practicing attorneys, this should not be construed as a complete list. Nevertheless, it is an excellent source of highly qualified and reputable attorneys, who, if unable to assist can in most cases make quality referrals.

A list of all attorneys nominated in this category is found at the end of this section. For information on the survey methodology see page ix.

Please note that the shorter, two line attorney listings in this section are of attorneys who practice in this area but whose full biographical profile appears in another section of this book. A bullet "•" preceeding name indicates the attorney was nominated in this particular area of law. For information on the format of these profiles, consult the section "Using the *Business Guidebook*" found on page xiv. Note that the following abbreviations are used throughout these profiles:

Selected by Attorneys for GUIDEBOOK
Law & Leading Attorneys
MINNESOTA

The attorneys profiled below were recommended by their peers in a statewide survey.

App.	- Appellate	ABA	- American Bar Association
Cir.	- Circuit	ATLA	- American Trial Lawyers Association
Ct.	- Court	HCBA	- Hennepin County Bar Association
Dist.	- District	MDLA	- Minnesota Defense Lawyers Association
Hon.	- Honorable	MSBA	- Minnesota State Bar Association
JD	- Law degree (Juris Doctor)	MTLA	- Minnesota Trial Lawyers Association
LLB	- Law degree	NBTA	- National Board of Trial Advocacy
LLM	- Master in Law degree	RCBA	- Ramsey County Bar Association
Sup.	- Supreme		

•**STEVE A. BRAND:** Mr. Brand has practiced in the areas of probate, estate planning, trusts, and estate administration and related tax areas for over 20 years. His practice has included trust litigation on both the trial and appellate court levels. Steve has been named in the last three editions of *The Best Lawyers in America*. He also is recognized in *Who's Who in the World, Who's Who in America, Who's Who in American Law, Who's Who in the Midwest*, and *Who's Who of Emerging Leaders*. Steve has been a frequent lecturer for Minnesota Continuing Legal Education programs on probate, estate planning, and fiduciary income taxation and for estate planning programs for the Minnesota Society of Certified Public Accountants. He also appeared as a lecturer on probate rules before a meeting of the Probate Registrars of Minnesota. He will be lecturing at the 1995 Annual Meeting of ACTEC in Scottsdale, Arizona. Steve is a native of St. Paul.
Education: JD 1973, University of Chicago (Board, *University of Chicago Law Review*); BA 1970 summa cum laude, University of Minnesota (Phi Beta Kappa).
Employment History: Partner 1991-present, Robins, Kaplan, Miller & Ciresi; Shareholder 1978-91, Briggs and Morgan; Associate 1973-78, Briggs and Morgan.
Professional Associations: American College of Trust & Estate Counsel (Fellow 1984-present; MN Chair 1991-present; member, Fiduciary Income Tax Committee); MSBA (Chair 1984-85, Trust & Probate Law Section); MN Supreme Court Advisory Committee on Probate Rules (Reporter for five years).
Community Involvement: Shalom Home, Inc. (Board member 1992-present); Mount Zion Temple (Board member 1976-present & past President); Hebrew Union College-Jewish Institute of Religion (Board of Overseers; Chair 1987-present, Nominating Committee); Sons of Abraham Congregation and Cemetery Assn. (Treasurer 1980-present).
Firm: Robins, Kaplan, Miller & Ciresi is a national litigation and business practice firm with offices in eight major metropolitan areas throughout the country. The firm's lawyers provide a range of transactional and litigation services to a diverse group of clients including Fortune 500 companies, banks, and lending institutions; property insurers; Big Six accounting firms; and foreign, state, and municipal governments.

STEVE A. BRAND

Robins, Kaplan, Miller & Ciresi
2800 LaSalle Plaza
800 LaSalle Avenue
Minneapolis, MN 55402

Phone: (612) 349-8500
Fax: (612) 339-4181
800 number: (800) 553-9910

Admitted: 1973 Minnesota; 1974 US Dist. Ct. (MN); 1976 US Sup. Ct.
Birthdate: 09/05/48

LORENS Q. BRYNESTAD - Brynestad Law Offices - 8525 Edinbrook Crossing, Suite 201 - Brooklyn Park, MN 55443 - Phone: (612) 424-8811, Fax: (612) 493-5193 - *See complete biographical profile in Commercial Real Estate Law Chapter.*

Chapter 27: Probate, Estate Planning & Trusts Law

RICHARD R. BURNS

Hanft, Fride, O'Brien, Harries, Swelbar & Burns, P.A.
1000 First Bank Place
130 West Superior Street
Duluth, MN 55802

Phone: (218) 722-4766
Fax: (218) 720-4920

Admitted: 1976 Minnesota; 1972 California; 1983 Wisconsin
Birthdate: 05/03/46

•**RICHARD R. BURNS:** Mr. Burns' current practice is divided fairly equally between representing small to medium size family-owned businesses and professionals in business and estate planning matters and functioning as general counsel for media companies and a medical center, primarily in the areas of contract and employment and benefit issues as well as libel and privacy matters.
Education: JD 1971 magna cum laude, Order of the Coif, University of Michigan; BA 1968 with distinction, University of Michigan.
Employment History: Currently, Hanft, Fride, O'Brien, Harries, Swelbar & Burns, P.A.; Associate 1971-76, Orrick, Herrington & Sutcliffe (San Francisco, CA, primarily tax and benefit issues).
Representative Clients: Evening Telegram Co. (Superior, WI); Morgan Murphy Stations (Madison, WI); RXL Pulitzer (Spokane, WA); Miller-Dwan Medical Center (Duluth, MN); and has represented 10 or more estates in $5 million to $50 million range.
Professional Associations: ABA (Forum on Communications Law Committee); Arrowhead Estate Planning Council (past President); MSBA (Secretary, Probate & Trust Council); State Bar of Wisconsin; 11th District Bar Assn. (past President); State Bar of California; Fellow, American College of Trust & Estate Counsel.
Community Involvement: Minnesota Council on Foundations (Committee Chair); Duluth-Superior Area Community Foundation (former Chair); United Way of Greater Duluth (Board member); Quetico Lifecare Corp. (Chair).
Firm: Founded in 1899, Hanft, Fride, O'Brien, Harries, Swelbar & Burns, P.A., is a full service law firm engaged primarily in business and trial work. The firm's 17 attorneys serve clients throughout Minnesota, northern Wisconsin, and beyond. *See additional listing in Arts, Entertainment, Advertising & Media Law Chapter.*

JACK W. CLINTON - Jack W. Clinton, P.A. - 8750 90th Street South, Suite 201 - Cottage Grove, MN 55016-3301 - Phone: (612) 459-6644, Fax: (612) 459-4719 - *See complete biographical profile in Federal, State & Local Government Law Chapter.*

MORRIS DICKEL - Dickel, Johannson, Taylor, Rust & Tye, P.A. - 407 North Broadway, P.O. Box 605 - Crookston, MN 56716 - Phone: (218) 281-2400, Fax: (218) 281-5831 - *See complete biographical profile in Agricultural Law Chapter.*

WILLIAM L. GUY III

Gunhus, Grinnell, Klinger, Swenson & Guy, Ltd.
512 Center Avenue
P.O. Box 1077
Moorhead, MN 56561-1077

Phone: (218) 236-6462
Fax: (218) 236-9873

Admitted: 1976 Minnesota; 1976 North Dakota; 1976 US Tax Ct.
Birthdate: 04/27/46

•**WILLIAM L. GUY III:** Mr. Guy primarily handles estate planning, trusts, and probate in North Dakota and Minnesota with an emphasis on large estates, family businesses, family farms, guardianships and conservatorships, supplemental needs trusts, and Medicaid estate planning.
Education: JD 1976, University of North Dakota; BS in BA 1968, North Dakota State University.
Employment History: 1976-present, Gunhus, Grinnell, Klinger, Swenson & Guy, Ltd.; 1968-73, US Naval Supply Corps.
Representative Clients: American Bank of Moorhead; Concordia College; First Trust Company of North Dakota, N.A.; Heartland Trust Company; Lutheran Social Service of Minnesota; Norwest Bank North Dakota, N.A.; Community First National Bank, N.A.
Professional Associations: MSBA; Clay County Bar Assn.; Seventh District Bar Assn.; Cass County Bar Assn.; State Bar Assn. of North Dakota; North Dakota Business Corporation Act (Chair, Revision Committee); North Dakota Limited Liability Company Act (Chair, Drafting Committee); American Institute of Certified Public Accountants; North Dakota Society of Certified Public Accountants; MN Society of Certified Public Accountants; American College of Trust and Estate Counsel.
Community Involvement: Hope Lutheran Church Foundation (Trustee); American Lutheran Church (Vice Chair 1980-88, Board of Pensions); Rotary Club (Director); Concordia College C-400 Club; Moorhead Foundation Task Force (Chair); Northside Raiders Youth Hockey Club (Director); F-M Athletic Youth Football.
Firm: Founded in 1914, Gunhus, Grinnell, Klinger, Swenson & Guy, Ltd., is a general practice law firm with offices in Moorhead, MN and Fargo, ND. The firm handles matters primarily in the western half of Minnesota and all of North Dakota, offering a wide range of litigation and commercial services. *See additional listings in Publicly Held Corporations Law and Commercial Real Estate Law Chapters.*

GILBERT W. HARRIES - Hanft, Fride, O'Brien, Harries, Swelbar & Burns, P.A. - 1000 First Bank Place, 130 West Superior Street - Duluth, MN 55802 - Phone: (218) 722-4766, Fax: (218) 720-4920 - *See complete biographical profile in Environmental Law Chapter.*

•EDWARD G. HEILMAN: Mr. Heilman's practice is limited to estate planning and estate administration, including wills, revocable and irrevocable trusts, powers of attorney, living wills, charitable trusts, and prenuptial agreements, using state-of-the-art computer technology which he has developed for his clients. He is the author of *MINNE PRO® Probate System*™ and *Drafting System*™, computer document assembly software for lawyers and is a frequent lecturer and author for legal educational seminars.
Education: JD 1973, University of CA-Berkeley; MA 1970, University of CA-Berkeley; Woodrow Wilson Graduate Fellow 1968-69, University of CA-Berkeley; Fulbright Graduate Fellow 1967-68, Muenster, West Germany; BA 1967 summa cum laude, Doane College.
Employment History: Attorney 1993-present, Heilman Law Firm; Attorney 1992-93, Law Office of Edward G. Heilman; Associate/Partner 1977-91, Faegre & Benson; Associate 1974-77, Cline, Williams, Wright, Johnson & Oldfather (Lincoln, NE).
Professional Associations: American College of Trust and Estate Counsel (Fellow 1984-present; Board of Regents 1994); ABA (1974-present); Nebraska State Bar Assn.; MSBA Probate & Trust Law Section (Chair 1987-88; Vice Chair 1986-87; Secretary 1985-86; Editor of newsletter 1983-85; Governing Council 1985-88; Chair 1991-present, Law Office Automation & Economics of the Practice Committee); MN Continuing Legal Education (Board member 1988-94).
Community Involvement: Doane College (Board of Trustees 1989-present); Methodist Hospital Foundation (Board member 1983-93; Chair 1986-88); Minneapolis Rotary Club No. 9 (1987-present); Senate District No. 41 DFL, St. Louis Park & Golden Valley (Chair 1979-80).

EDWARD G. HEILMAN

Heilman Law Firm
1221 Nicollet Mall, Suite 206
Minneapolis, MN 55403

Phone: (612) 338-5230
Fax: (612) 338-0910
800 number: (800) 646-3776

Admitted: 1977 Minnesota;
1974 California (currently inactive);
1973 Nebraska
Birthdate: 06/24/45

JOEL D. JOHNSON - Dosland, Nordhougen, Lillehaug & Johnson, P.A. - 730 Center Avenue, Suite 203, P.O. Box 100 - Moorhead, MN 56561-0100 - Phone: (218) 233-2744, Fax: (218) 233-1570 - *See complete biographical profile in Closely Held Business Law Chapter.*

•LARRY W. JOHNSON: Mr. Johnson practices in the area of estate planning and estate and trust administration. He has been a partner in Dorsey & Whitney's Estate Planning and Administration Department since 1968.
Education: LLB 1959 cum laude, University of Minnesota (staff member 1958-59, *Minnesota Law Review*); BSL 1957, University of Minnesota.
Employment History: Partner 1968-present, Associate 1961-67, Dorsey & Whitney; First Lieutenant 1959-61, US Army.
Professional Associations: American College of Trust and Estate Counsel.
Firm: Dorsey & Whitney is the largest law firm in Minnesota and one of the largest firms in the United States with over 350 lawyers in 12 offices. The depth and breadth of the experience of its lawyers enables it to provide a broad range of services to meet the diverse legal needs of its client base, which includes Fortune 500 companies, public agencies, banks and other financial institutions, nonprofit organizations, individual investors, family owned businesses, and high-tech and low-tech, growth oriented companies.

LARRY W. JOHNSON

Dorsey & Whitney
Pillsbury Center South
220 South Sixth Street
Minneapolis, MN 55402-1498

Phone: (612) 340-2619
Fax: (612) 340-8827

Admitted: 1959 Minnesota;
1959 US Dist. Ct. (MN)
Birthdate: 05/21/34

FREDERICK A. KUEPPERS, JR. - Kueppers, Hackel & Kueppers, P.A. - 1350 Capital Centre, 386 North Wabasha Street - St. Paul, MN 55102 - Phone: (612) 228-1104, Fax: (612) 297-6599 - *See complete biographical profile in Commercial Real Estate Law Chapter.*

Chapter 27: Probate, Estate Planning & Trusts Law

BRIDGET A. LOGSTROM

Dorsey & Whitney
Pillsbury Center South
220 South Sixth Street
Minneapolis, MN 55402-1498

Phone: (612) 343-7945
Fax: (612) 340-8827

Admitted: 1983 Minnesota;
1983 US Dist. Ct. (MN)
Birthdate: 02/17/58

•**BRIDGET A. LOGSTROM:** Ms. Logstrom is a partner in the Estate Planning and Administration Department of Dorsey & Whitney. She advises and assists her clients in all estate planning matters, including the preparation of wills, revocable ("living") trusts, powers of attorney, health care declarations ("living wills"), irrevocable tax planning trusts (i.e., gift trusts, life insurance trusts), and prenuptial agreements. In addition, Ms. Logstrom has substantial probate experience, including administering decedents' estates and handling guardianship/conservatorship matters. She is very knowledgeable in the area of trust law, and her practice includes advising clients regarding the funding and administration of trusts, in addition to assisting in resolving disputes among beneficiaries concerning the construction or validity of trusts. Ms. Logstrom is a member of the University of St. Thomas Family Business Program and assists her family business clients with succession planning. Ms. Logstrom is a Policy Committee member, Foundation Board member, former Recruiting Committee member, and former cochair of the Summer Associate Program with Dorsey & Whitney. She frequently speaks to professional and public organizations on a variety of estate planning topics.
Education: JD 1983 magna cum laude, William Mitchell; BA 1980 magna cum laude, University of Minnesota-Duluth.
Employment History: Partner 1991-present, Associate 1983-90, Dorsey & Whitney.
Professional Associations: HCBA (Probate and Estate Law Committee (Secretary)); MSBA (Probate & Trust Law and Elder Law Sections); University of St. Thomas Family Business Program; University of St. Thomas Women in Family Business Program.
Community Involvement: Animal Humane Society of Hennepin County (former Board member); variety of church-related activities.
Firm: Dorsey & Whitney is the largest law firm in Minnesota and one of the largest firms in the United States with over 350 lawyers in 12 offices. The depth and breadth of the experience of its lawyers enables it to provide a broad range of services to meet the diverse legal needs of its client base, which includes Fortune 500 companies, public agencies, banks and other financial institutions, nonprofit organizations, individual investors, family owned businesses, and high-tech and low-tech, growth oriented companies.

GARY D. MCDOWELL

Lindquist & Vennum
4200 IDS Center
80 South Eighth Street
Minneapolis, MN 55402

Phone: (612) 371-3211
Fax: (612) 371-3207

Admitted: 1968 Minnesota;
1968 US Dist. Ct. (MN)
Birthdate: 07/25/39

•**GARY D. MCDOWELL:** Mr. McDowell handles the disposition and sale of businesses and estate and business planning, including drafting of interfamily business transition arrangements and corporate disposition agreements and negotiating buy-sell agreements involving third parties. Mr. McDowell is coauthor of *Drafting Wills and Trust Agreements in Minnesota*, Continuing Legal Education, 1st-4th editions, 1980-94, and editor of *Probate and Trust Law Desk Book*, 1986-94. He also lectures on estate planning for Minnesota Continuing Legal Education.
Education: JD 1968, University of Minnesota; BA 1961, University of South Dakota.
Employment History: Nov. 1994-present, Linquist & Vennum; Founding Partner 1977-Oct. 1994, Arnold & McDowell; Assistant Vice President 1973-77, First Bank Minneapolis; Associate 1968-73, Callinan, Raidt, Haertzen & Ramier.
Representative Clients: Citizens Independent Bank of St. Louis Park; City of Hutchinson; City of Princeton; Modern Machine & Engineering; Core Technologies; Crystal Cabinet Works; Custom Mold & Design; MTI Group International; Coffee Mill, Inc.
Professional Associations: MSBA (past Chair 1989, Probate and Trust Law Section); HCBA; Minneapolis Estate Planning Council; Consumer Protection Committee; American College of Trust and Estate Council (Fellow).
Community Involvement: American Cancer Society MN Division (Legacy and Planned Giving Committee 1968-94); Captain USNR (Retired) and Former Reserve Intelligence Area Commander; Family Hope Services (Lecturer); Legal Advice Clinics (volunteer attorney). *See additional listings in Closely Held Business Law and Commercial Litigation Chapters.*

•**JANICE M. NELSON** - Nelson Oyen Torvik - 221 North First Street, P.O. Box 656 - Montevideo, MN 56265 - Phone: (612) 269-6461, Fax: (612) 269-8024 - *See complete biographical profile in Closely Held Business Law Chapter.*

•**CURTIS A. NORDHOUGEN** - Dosland, Nordhougen, Lillehaug & Johnson, P.A. - 730 Center Avenue, Suite 203, P.O. Box 100 - Moorhead, MN 56561-0100 - Phone: (218) 233-2744, Fax: (218) 233-1570 - *See complete biographical profile in Closely Held Business Law Chapter.*

•**JOHN W. PROVO:** As cochair of the firm's Estate Planning, Probate, and Trust Law Group, Mr. Provo assists both individuals and business clients with wealth preservation and management strategies for highly compensated individuals. His work includes a wide range of lifetime and charitable giving strategies, executive compensation planning, dispute resolution, and tax advantaged estate and succession planning arrangements. Mr. Provo recently represented the estate of a North Dakota based agribusiness majority shareholder in US Tax Court proceedings that resulted in the reduction of the IRS' deficiency assessment against the estate by more than eighty percent. In addition, he writes "Notes & Trends," a bimonthly column in *Bench & Bar of Minnesota* which highlights emerging trends and developments in estate planning, probate, and trust law.
Education: JD 1983 cum laude, University of Minnesota (Article and Book Review Editor, *Journal of Law and Inequality*); AB 1980 summa cum laude, Stanford University.
Employment History: 1986-present, Popham, Haik, Schnobrich & Kaufman, Ltd.; 1982-86, Harstad & Rainbow.
Professional Associations: MSBA (Probate and Trust Law Council; Cochair 1990-92, Education Committee; Editor 1988-90, newsletter of the Probate and Trust Law Section); MN Continuing Legal Education (Advisory Committee, *Drafting Wills and Trust Agreements*).
Firm: Popham, Haik, Schnobrich & Kaufman, Ltd., is a firm of more than 230 attorneys with offices in Denver, Miami, Minneapolis, Washington, D.C., and international affiliations in Beijing, China and Leipzig and Stuttgart, Germany. The firm represents clients nationally and internationally on issues relating to corporate and business law, administrative law, and litigation. *See additional listing in Arts, Entertainment, Advertising & Media Law Chapter.*

JOHN W. PROVO

Popham, Haik, Schnobrich & Kaufman, Ltd.
222 South Ninth Street
Suite 3300
Minneapolis, MN 55402

Phone: (612) 333-4800
Fax: (612) 334-8888

Admitted: 1983 Minnesota;
1984 US Dist. Ct. (MN);
1990 US Tax Ct.
Birthdate: 12/07/57

JOHN E. REGAN - Regan, Regan & Meyer - 115 East Hickory Street, P.O. Box 967 - Mankato, MN 56001 - Phone: (507) 345-1179, Fax: (507) 345-1182 - *See complete biographical profile in Closely Held Business Law Chapter.*

•**JAMES W. ROCKWELL:** Mr. Rockwell has practiced in the estate planning, probate, and trust law area since graduating from law school in 1976. He represents individuals in their personal estate planning, owners of closely held businesses in coordinating their estate and business planning, and fiduciaries and beneficiaries in resolving contested probate and trust matters. Mr. Rockwell has taught wills, estates, and trusts as an adjunct professor at William Mitchell College of Law. He is listed in *The Best Lawyers in America*.
Education: JD 1976, William Mitchell; BA 1971, College of St. Thomas.
Employment History: Shareholder 1990-present, Popham, Haik, Schnobrich & Kaufman, Ltd.; Partner 1976-90, Robins, Kaplan, Miller & Ciresi.
Professional Associations: ABA (Probate and Trust Law Section); MSBA (past Chair, Probate and Trust Law Section); American College of Trust and Estate Counsel (1988-present, Fiduciary Litigation Committee).
Firm: Popham, Haik, Schnobrich & Kaufman, Ltd., is a firm of more than 230 attorneys with offices in Denver, Miami, Minneapolis, Washington, D.C., and international affiliations in Beijing, China and Leipzig and Stuttgart, Germany. The firm represents clients nationally and internationally on issues relating to corporate and business law, administrative law, and litigation.

JAMES W. ROCKWELL

Popham, Haik, Schnobrich & Kaufman, Ltd.
222 South Ninth Street
Suite 3300
Minneapolis, MN 55402

Phone: (612) 333-4800
Fax: (612) 334-8888

Admitted: 1976 Minnesota;
1982 Wisconsin;
1976 US Sup. Ct.
Birthdate: 01/18/49

STEVEN J. SEILER - Johnson, Killen, Thibodeau & Seiler, P.A. - 811 Norwest Center, 230 West Superior Street - Duluth, MN 55802 - Phone: (218) 722-6331, Fax: (218) 722-3031 - *See complete biographical profile in Health Law Chapter.*

•**RALPH T. SMITH** - Smith Law Firm, P.A. - 115 Fifth Street, P.O. Box 1420 - Bemidji, MN 56601 - Phone: (218) 751-3130, Fax: (218) 751-3132 - *See complete biographical profile in Labor Law Chapter.*

DENNIS M. SOBOLIK - Brink, Sobolik, Severson, Vroom & Malm, P.A. - 217 Birch Avenue South, P.O. Box 790 - Hallock, MN 56728 - Phone: (218) 843-3686, Fax: (218) 843-2724 - *See complete biographical profile in Agricultural Law Chapter.*

Chapter 27: Probate, Estate Planning & Trusts Law

JAMES H. STEWART

Fryberger, Buchanan, Smith & Frederick, P.A.
302 West Superior Street
Suite 700
Duluth, MN 55802

Phone: (218) 722-0861
Fax: (218) 722-9568

Admitted: 1967 Minnesota; 1982 Wisconsin
Birthdate: 07/17/39

•**JAMES H. STEWART:** Mr. Stewart practices estate planning, including wills, trusts, estate, gift and generation-skipping transfer tax planning, premortem planning, probate avoidance, qualified retirement plan beneficiary designation, prenuptial agreements, Crummey trusts, grantor-retained annuity trusts, family limited partnerships, life insurance trusts, partnerships and agencies, and charitable giving. His practice also includes estate and trust administration, including probate, settlement of contested estates, postmortem elections, funding trusts, estate tax returns, audits and appeals, and trust construction and interpretation. He also practices in closely held businesses, including formation, financing, operation, and dissolution of all types of business entities, shareholder/partner/member agreements, purchase and sale of all types of business and professional practices, succession planning, discounted transfers, corporate reorganizations, comprehensive tax analysis, and ownership, purchase, and leasing of mineral properties. Mr. Stewart is also listed in *The Best Lawyers in America*.

Education: JD 1967, University of Minnesota (1965-67, *Minnesota Law Review*); BA 1961, St. John's University.
Representative Clients: Super One Foods; North Star Ford; Sonju Motor, Inc.; Du Nord Land Co.; Norman Properties, LLC; Commercial Testing Laboratory, Inc.; Oneida Realty Co.; First Bank, N.A.; North Shore Bank of Commerce; O'Neill Resources Corp.
Professional Associations: ABA; MSBA (Probate & Trust Section; Chair 1993-94, Tax Section Council); American College of Trust & Estate Counsel (Fellow); Arrowhead Estate Planning Council (Director).
Community Involvement: Duluth-Superior Area Community Foundation (Trustee); Duluth Area Family YMCA (Trustee); College of St. Scholastica Deferred Giving Advisory Council (Chair).
Firm: Please see firm profile in Appendix C. *See additional listings in Closely Held Business Law and Business Tax Law Chapters.*

GERALD L. THOREEN

Hughes, Thoreen & Knapp, P.A.
110 South Sixth Avenue
St. Cloud, MN 56302-1718

Phone: (612) 251-6175
Fax: (612) 251-6857

Admitted: 1957 Minnesota; 1960 US Dist. Ct. (MN)
Birthdate: 03/11/33

•**GERALD L. THOREEN:** Mr. Thoreen's practice is concentrated in the area of personal representation, including estate and trust planning, administration, and litigation. His experience covers a wide range of matters, including estate settlement: estate tax planning, valuation of closely held businesses, payment of death costs, financially distressed estates or estate assets, environmental liability, and income tax planning; estate planning: use of trusts to shelter assets from claims and taxation, use of life insurance (irrevocable trusts, split dollar agreements, and taxation), incapacity (powers of attorney, trusts, protective orders, and conservatorships), succession of ownership and control of family businesses (lifetime gifts, entity selection, transfer restriction, buyout, and control agreements), charitable gifts and nonprofit corporations (governance, investment management, and liability and indemnification of officers and directors); qualified plan and IRAs (plan design for estate building and distribution choices, distribution planning); and estate tax reduction planning (annual exclusion gifts, gifts which leverage tax savings on future value, valuation freezes, and valuation discounts in corporations and partnerships).

Education: LLB 1957, University of Minnesota; BSL 1955, University of Minnesota.
Professional Associations: American College of Trust and Estate Counsel; MSBA (Probate and Trust Law Section: Governing Council 1972-76 (Chair 1975-76); Principles of Probate Practice Committee (Chair 1976-79); Probate Court Rules Committee (Chair 1978-85); Special Committee on UPC Article II (1992-94)); President's Committee on the MN Probate Code (1974-75); MN Supreme Court Advisory Committee on Probate Court Rules (1984-89); Central MN Estate Planning Council (1974-present).
Community Involvement: Great River Regional Library (Trustee 1969-71); Sts. Peter, Paul and Michael School (Trustee 1973-75); Cathedral High School (Director 1975-78; Education Foundation Trustee 1978-83); Downtown Council (Director 1992-present).
Firm: Mr. Thoreen is an attorney in Hughes, Thoreen, & Knapp, P.A. With Keith F. Hughes (personal injury, condemnation, and business and employment litigation), Thomas P. Knapp (personal injury and real property and commercial litigation), Jerry O. Relph (real property, land use, bond financing, commercial, and secured transactions), and Bradley W. Hanson (closely held businesses, professional and nonprofit corporations, retirement plans, probate, and elder law), the firm provides a broad range of legal services. *See additional listings in Closely Held Business Law and Nonprofit Corporations Law Chapters.*

•**JOHN R. WICKS:** Mr. Wicks practices in the area of estate planning, individual tax planning, charitable giving, trusts and estates, and family business planning. In addition to being an attorney, he is a Certified Public Accountant. Mr. Wicks is listed in *The Best Lawyers in America*, 1992-93 edition, in the area of estates and trusts. He is a partner in the Estate Planning and Administration Department at Dorsey & Whitney.
Education: JD 1964 cum laude, University of Iowa (Editorial staff 1963-64, *Iowa Law Review*); BSC 1959 magna cum laude,University of Iowa.
Employment History: Partner 1971-present, Dorsey & Whitney; Staff Accountant 1959-61, Coopers & Lybrand (CPA Certificate 1961).
Professional Associations: American College of Trust and Estate Counsel; Iowa Law School Foundation (past President); MSBA (Council (past member); Probate and Trust Law Section); Olmsted County Bar Assn.
Firm: Dorsey & Whitney is the largest law firm in Minnesota and one of the largest firms in the United States with over 350 lawyers in 12 offices. The depth and breadth of the experience of its lawyers enables it to provide a broad range of services to meet the diverse legal needs of its client base, which includes Fortune 500 companies, public agencies, banks and other financial institutions, nonprofit organizations, individual investors, family owned businesses, and high-tech and low-tech, growth oriented companies.

JOHN R. WICKS

Dorsey & Whitney
201 First Avenue SW
Suite 340
Rochester, MN 55902

Phone: (507) 288-3156
Fax: (507) 288-6190

Admitted: 1966 Minnesota;
1964 Iowa
Birthdate: 12/08/37

•**RICHARD A. WILHOIT**
Education: JD 1967, University of Minnesota; BA 1961, Creighton University.
Employment History: 1967-present, Doherty, Rumble & Butler, P.A.
Representative Clients: First Trust National Assn.; Norwest Bank Minnesota; American National Bank; many closely held businesses and their owners.
Professional Associations: RCBA; HCBA; MSBA; ABA; State Bar of Wisconsin; American College of Trust and Estate Counsel.
Community Involvement: Ramsey County Historical Society (Board member); numerous past board memberships and officer positions of church, school, and nonprofit organizations.
Firm: Doherty, Rumble & Butler is committed to providing individuals and families with the best possible service in the areas of estate planning, charitable giving, and administering trusts and decedents' estates. Their lawyers have the expertise and experience necessary to advise business owners, executives, and others whose assets or personal situations call for sophisticated estate planning alternatives. In addition, Doherty, Rumble, & Butler is well-versed in applying charitable remainder trusts and other techniques designed to fulfill charitable aims while preserving wealth for heirs. Beyond the immediate needs of individuals and families, the firm often handles the related needs of family-owned businesses. Consequently, their capabilities include advising executives and business owners in matters of control transition, management succession, and ownership and equity transfers. With decades of experience and knowledge in estate law, Doherty, Rumble & Butler has a focus on probate process and trust management. When appropriate, their lawyers help clients with planning to avoid probate. The firm has extensive experience in shepherding clients through tax audits and tax litigation, including will contests and trust administration disputes.

RICHARD A. WILHOIT

Doherty, Rumble & Butler
Professional Association
2800 Minnesota World Trade Center
30 East Seventh Street
St. Paul, MN 55101-4999

Phone: (612) 291-9333
Fax: (612) 291-9313

Admitted: 1968 Minnesota
Birthdate: 03/17/39

SHERMAN WINTHROP - Winthrop & Weinstine, P.A. - 3200 Minnesota World Trade Center, 30 East Seventh Street - St. Paul, MN 55101 - Phone: (612) 290-8400, Fax: (612) 292-9347 - *See complete biographical profile in Publicly Held Corporations Law Chapter.*

Complete listing of all attorneys nominated in Probate, Estate Planning & Trusts Law

EDWARD M. ARUNDEL, Rider, Bennett, Egan & Arundel, Minneapolis; **STEVE A. BRAND,** Robins, Kaplan, Miller & Ciresi, Minneapolis; **WILLIAM J. BRODY,** Fredrikson & Byron, P.A., Minneapolis; **ANN B. BURNS,** Rider, Bennett, Egan & Arundel, Minneapolis; **RICHARD R. BURNS,** Hanft, Fride, O'Brien, Harries, Swelbar & Burns, P.A., Duluth; **JOHN P. BYRON,** Fredrikson & Byron, P.A., Minneapolis; **ROBERT L. CROSBY,** Best & Flanagan, Minneapolis; **TERENCE N. DOYLE,** Briggs and Morgan, P.A., St. Paul; **PATRICK F. FLAHERTY,** Moss & Barnett, A Professional Association, Minneapolis; **TODD I. FREEMAN,** Larkin, Hoffman, Daly & Lindgren, Ltd., Bloomington; **WILLIAM L. GUY III,** Gunhus, Grinnell, Klinger, Swenson & Guy, Ltd., Moorhead; **ANDREW E. HAGEMANN JR.,** Mork H. Darling Hagemann & Kohler, Worthington; **JOHN E. HARRIS,** Faegre & Benson, Minneapolis; **WILLIAM T. HEDEEN,** Hedeen & Hughes, Worthington; **EDWARD G. HEILMAN,** Heilman Law Firm, Minneapolis; **LAURENCE B. HUGHES,** Hedeen & Hughes, Worthington; **JOHN C. JOHANNESON,** Maun & Simon, St. Paul; **LARRY W. JOHNSON,** Dorsey & Whitney, Minneapolis; **SIDNEY KAPLAN,** Mackall, Crounse & Moore, Minneapolis; **JOHN H. KRAFT,** Kraft Walser Nelson & Hettig, Olivia; **E. JOSEPH LaFAVE III,** Best & Flanagan, Minneapolis; **STEPHEN R. LITMAN,** Leonard, Street and Deinard Professional Association, Minneapolis; **BRIDGET A. LOGSTROM,** Dorsey & Whitney, Minneapolis; **GARY D. McDOWELL,** Arnold & McDowell, Minneapolis; **EDWARD D. McLEAN,** McLean Peterson Law Firm, Mankato; **KRIS L. MASER,** Maser Amundson & Crist, P.A., Minneapolis; **LEIGH D. MATHISON,** Garvey & Mathison P.A., Bloomington; **SCOTT C. NEFF,** Trenti Law Firm, Virginia; **JANICE M. NELSON,** Nelson Oyen Torvik, Montevideo; **J. BRIAN O'LEARY,** O'Leary & Moritz, Springfield; **MICHAEL J. PATCHIN,** Colosimo Patchin Aronsen & Kearney, Ltd., Virginia; **JOHN W. PROVO,** Popham, Haik, Schnobrich & Kaufman, Ltd., Minneapolis; **JAMES O. RAMSTAD,** Irvine Ramstad Briggs & Karkela, P.A., Detroit Lakes; **RAYMOND A. REISTER,** Of Counsel, Dorsey & Whitney, Minneapolis; **JOHN M. RIEDY,** McLean Peterson Law Firm, Mankato; **JAMES W. ROCKWELL,** Popham, Haik, Schnobrich & Kaufman, Ltd., Minneapolis; **RICHARD L. RONNING,** Attorney at Law, Willmar; **LEHAN J. RYAN,** Oppenheimer, Wolff & Donnelly, St. Paul; **HENRY W. SCHMIDT,** Schmidt Thompson Johnson & Moody, P.A., Willmar; **STUART E. SCHMITZ,** Stuart E. Schmitz & Associates, St. Paul; **RICHARD C. SCHMOKER,** Faegre & Benson, Minneapolis; **CLINTON A. SCHROEDER,** Gray, Plant, Mooty, Mooty & Bennett, P.A., Minneapolis; **MARK T. SIGNORELLI,** Brown Andrew Hallenbeck Signorelli & Zallar, Duluth; **RALPH T. SMITH,** Smith Law Firm, P.A., Bemidji; **ROBERT A. STEIN,** University of Minnesota Law School, Minneapolis; **ROBERT H. STEPHENSON,** Trenti Law Firm, Virginia; **JAMES H. STEWART,** Fryberger, Buchanan, Smith & Frederick, P.A., Duluth; **ROSS A. SUSSMAN,** Bernick & Lifson, Minneapolis; **GERALD L. THOREEN,** Hughes, Thoreen & Knapp, P.A., St. Cloud; **ROBERT G. WEBER,** Fredrikson & Byron, P.A., Minneapolis; **HONNEN S. WEISS,** Felhaber, Larson, Fenlon & Vogt, P.A., Minneapolis; **JOHN R. WICKS,** Dorsey & Whitney, Rochester; **RICHARD A. WILHOIT,** Doherty, Rumble & Butler Professional Association, St. Paul; **C. THOMAS WILSON,** Gislason, Dosland, Hunter & Malecki, P.A., New Ulm; **ALAN J. YANOWITZ,** Attorney at Law, Rochester.

CHAPTER 28

PROFESSIONAL MALPRACTICE DEFENSE LAW

Professional malpractice occurs whenever a professional performs his or her duties improperly or unethically out of ignorance, carelessness or intentional misconduct. Professional malpractice is a subcategory of tort law. The Personal Injury Defense Law Chapter examines several key tort law concepts that arise in general personal injury tort litigation, but because professional malpractice lawsuits raise a number of distinct issues, professional malpractice deserves its own chapter. This chapter examines some of the issues involved in professional malpractice suits arising in the medical, legal, engineering, architecture, and accounting professions. It is important to note that professional malpractice is only one way in which professionals can incur liability for their job-related actions. A doctor can be sued for breach of contract if he or she backs out of an agreement to work for a hospital. A nurse might be sued for assault and battery if he or she intentionally harms another person with an improper injection.

Medical malpractice comprises the majority of professional malpractice lawsuits brought in this country. This is not to say that medical professionals are more prone to committing malpractice. Rather, historical and social factors have made it easier to sue doctors than other professionals, so most case law in the professional malpractice arena stems from medical mishaps. As it has become easier and more common to sue other professionals for malpractice, many of the concepts developed in medical malpractice lawsuits are being adopted for use in other professional malpractice lawsuits. Thus, many key concepts in the professional malpractice arena are explained using medical examples. A good understanding of how medical malpractice lawsuits proceed can help one predict how other professional malpractice lawsuits are likely to be decided.

MEDICAL MALPRACTICE

"Medical malpractice" does not apply only to medical doctors; other health care providers are frequently sued for medical malpractice. Psychologists, dentists and nurses are just a few of the numerous types of health care professionals who can be sued for medical malpractice.

DEFENDING AGAINST MEDICAL MALPRACTICE

A key to understanding any medical malpractice lawsuit is comprehending the elements of malpractice. Under Minnesota law a person makes out a prima facie case of medical malpractice by establishing four elements—duty owed to the patient, breach of the standard of care, causation of harm, and damages to the patient. A party accused of medical malpractice can defend itself either by showing that one of these elements is missing and/or by establishing an affirmative defense. An affirmative defense is a legal argument which admits the existence of all required elements, but nonetheless excuses the actions of the medical professional.

Duty Toward the Patient

The first element in any medical malpractice lawsuit is that of a duty owed to the patient. Without a legal duty to act, a medical professional can stand by doing nothing while a person suffers, and still not commit malpractice. Thus, the first question to address in a medical malpractice lawsuit is whether the medical professional had any duty at all to the plaintiff.

Often this question is easily answered. When a patient goes to a doctor with a problem and the doctor agrees to treat the patient, the two have entered into a contract and the doctor has a duty to treat the patient. By agreeing to diagnose or treat a patient the doctor has indicated that he or she has the appropriate training and skill to adequately care for the patient and has assumed a duty toward the patient.

Cases in which the duty owed a patient is contested generally arise in the context of a doctor who has done nothing toward the patient (nonfeasance), rather than having done something incorrectly (malfeasance). Historically, in the American system of jurisprudence, a person generally had no affirmative duty to help others, absent some special relationship between the two parties. A doctor dining out at a restaurant had no general duty to help someone experiencing a heart attack. The doctor could continue his or her meal and do nothing to help the heart attack victim because the law imposed no duty to act in this circumstance. If, however, the person having the heart attack was the doctor's child the law did impose a duty to act because of the parent-child relationship. Despite the apparent callousness of this rule, it remains the law in most states.

Minnesota has altered this rule, but only slightly, with the Minnesota Good Samaritan Law. Under the Good Samaritan Law, any person at the scene of an emergency who knows that another person is exposed to or has suffered grave physical harm must, to the extent he or she can do so without risk to self or others, give reasonable assistance to the exposed person. The person who violates this law is guilty only of a petty misdemeanor. Under the Good Samaritan Law, any person who, without compensation or the expectation of compensation, renders emergency assistance, care, or advice at the scene of an emergency or during transit to an emergency medical care center, is insulated from liability for acts or omissions in rendering that care unless he or she acts in a willful, wanton, or reckless manner in providing the assistance, care, or advice.

Once a person has begun to help another person, the law does impose a continuing duty to help the injured person if ceasing aid would cause harm to the injured person. Thus, if a doctor at a restaurant rushes to help the victim of a heart attack, he or she may have a duty to continue to aid the patient.

An important area of medical malpractice law receiving increased attention in the courts deals with the circumstances under which a doctor owes a duty to persons other than the patient. In some situations, the doctor may owe a duty to persons other than those who undergo his or her treatment. For example, a pedestrian injured when an automobile driver suffers an epileptic seizure while driving might charge that the driver's doctor violated a duty to the general public by failing to properly diagnose the driver's epileptic condition. The victim of a domestic assault might charge that the perpetrator's psychiatrist had a duty to warn the victim of the patient's unstable condition. Under

Minnesota law a psychologist, nurse, or chemical dependency worker licensed by the state must make reasonable efforts to communicate any serious specific threats to a potential victim if the practitioner has reason to believe his or her patient is capable of carrying out the threat.

Breach of the Standard of Care Owed to the Patient

Medical malpractice results if the doctor injures his or her patient by using less skill and care than a reasonably competent doctor would use in diagnosing or treating the same condition. In order to avoid liability for medical malpractice, a physician must—at a minimum—use the same level of care that any other reasonably competent doctor would use under the same circumstances. In most cases, a plaintiff must present expert testimony on what the standard of care should have been. Medical malpractice lawsuits often become battles where each side has expert witnesses declaring wildly different levels of acceptable medical standards.

In practice, a doctor is not considered a reasonably competent doctor if he or she does not keep abreast of current, commonly accepted methods of treatments or uses outmoded methods. However, if there are two or more commonly accepted methods of treatment, a doctor is free to use whichever he or she chooses, so long as the method is accepted by a substantial number of physicians.

A doctor who clearly disregards well-established medical standards or who attempts to perform medical procedures clearly beyond his or her capabilities is not using the same level of care that a reasonably competent physician would use. Anyone injured by such a careless doctor can sue for medical malpractice and would almost certainly recover damages from his or her doctor.

When examining the actions of a generalist, Minnesota courts usually ask whether the physician applied the degree of skill and learning possessed by members of the profession in similar localities or communities. However, when the professional accused of medical malpractice is a specialist, his or her actions are judged against the actions of members of the profession across the nation.

Causation of Harm

The third element of a medical malpractice lawsuit is causation. Causation is frequently divided into two separate inquiries—whether the professional's actions in fact caused the harm to the patient, and whether the professional's actions were the proximate cause of the patient's harm.

The "cause in fact" inquiry is usually answered with a "but for" or "*sine qua non*" test. A doctor's actions caused the patient's harm if, but for that action, the patient would not have been harmed. *Sine qua non* is a Latin expression meaning "without which not". In other words, a doctor's actions caused harm if, without that action, the harm would not have occurred.

The proximate cause inquiry asks whether the professional ought to be held responsible for his or her actions even if those actions did in fact cause the harm. In some rare instances, the physician's actions are so removed from the final harm to the patient that the law cuts off liability for those actions by saying that the tortious conduct was not proximate to the harm.

Sometimes this causation inquiry is answered rather easily—a doctor gives a patient the wrong drug and that drug causes permanent injury. Thorny issues arise when the harm to the patient had more than one cause. For example, two doctors, acting independently, might both prescribe the same wrong medication. If "but for" analysis is applied to each doctor's actions in isolation, it cannot be said that his or her actions were the cause of harm to the patient because the patient would have been harmed through the malpractice of the other doctor. Different jurisdictions have created their own rules to deal with "multiple cause" injuries. In Minnesota the courts have dealt with this issue by holding that when there is more than one person whose conduct may have caused or contributed to an injury or death, proximate causation can be established by showing that a particular defendant's actions were a "substantial factor" in causing the plaintiff's injury.

Damage to the Patient

A person who is the victim of medical malpractice can sue for the injuries and all direct consequences of those injuries. "Direct consequences" include any mental or physical pain and suffering caused by the careless doctor, and any lost wages resulting from the injury. Due to the seriousness of some errors, awards can be quite high.

Breach of Confidentiality

In order to collect a large damage award in a case of a breach of confidentiality, a person must show that the doctor's careless disclosure caused him or her great harm. For example, a patient might be able to collect a great deal of money if a doctor told the patient's rich aunt that the patient had a heroin addiction and the aunt subsequently wrote the patient out of her will. This injury is far greater than if the doctor was overheard at a party asking his or her patient about a wart problem.

AFFIRMATIVE DEFENSES

As described above, a defendant asserting an affirmative defense admits, for the purpose of argument, that the plaintiff can establish the existence of all four elements of a medical malpractice action, but the defendant argues that the existence of some other factor excuses the medical professional's actions.

Conflicting Legal Duty

Generally, a doctor violates a patient's right to confidentiality by releasing information about his or her medical condition to unauthorized persons or organizations. However, there are a few conditions under which a doctor is legally required to inform others of a patient's medical condition. If a patient suffers a gunshot wound, for example, the doctor treating him or her must inform the police. Also, a doctor must inform the Minnesota Department of Health of anyone with a serious communicable disease, including HIV or AIDS. In Minnesota, a doctor treating a minor who appears to be the victim of child abuse must report the child's condition to appropriate authorities.

Consent

Consent is the most frequently asserted affirmative defense in medical malpractice lawsuits. In order to establish the affirmative defense of consent in Minnesota a defendant must show that a patient was informed of all risks associated with a procedure and that the defendant did not go beyond the procedures to which the plaintiff consented.

Doctors and hospitals have tried to protect themselves from medical malpractice lawsuits by having patients sign consent forms before they receive treatment. These consent forms typically include warnings that medicine is an imperfect art and not an exact science, and that patients must assume all the risks of any surgical procedures. By signing a consent form, a person does not give up all his or her rights to sue the medical professional if things go wrong. First, such an agreement may not be valid if the doctor does not fully inform the patient of the risks associated with their particular surgery. In other words, only a complete and informed consent is valid. However, even a valid consent form is no protection for a doctor who either performed surgery that went beyond the consent of the patient or who failed to perform the surgery according to well-accepted medical standards. A patient may also sue a doctor (or a hospital) if a person other than the one named on the consent form performs the surgery.

THE FUTURE OF MEDICAL MALPRACTICE LAWSUITS

Medical malpractice lawsuits have been targeted as one of the factors contributing to the spiraling costs of health care. Medical malpractice suits have increased dramatically both in frequency and in the amount of damages awarded. As a result, the price doctors pay for malpractice insurance has soared. These costs are passed on to patients and their insurers. Of course, insurers then pass the increased costs on to their customers in a seemingly endless cycle. Calls are frequently heard in Congress and in state legislatures to put caps on the amount of money judges or juries can award in medical malpractice lawsuits. The theory behind these proposals is that too many judges and juries fail to see the connection between spiraling malpractice awards and spiraling medical costs. Proponents of this legislation argue that people hurt by bad medical care should be compensated, but that the current system relies too heavily on emotional appeals in the courtroom and less on reasoned analysis of how much the victims of medical malpractice truly need to be compensated for their loss.

LEGAL MALPRACTICE

An increasingly common target of professional malpractice lawsuits are lawyers themselves. Although there is no precise definition of legal malpractice, generally speaking, a lawyer commits legal malpractice when he or she fails to provide quality legal services to a client. Bad conduct that is not unique to lawyers may lead to a lawsuit, but does not constitute legal malpractice. For instance, a lawyer who misses deadlines, does inadequate preparation for a trial, misses numerous court dates, hearings, or appointments with the client, or represents both sides in a dispute without informing both parties, commits legal malpractice. A lawyer who steals funds from the client, assaults, or defrauds the client, has committed a crime but probably has not committed legal malpractice.

DEFENDING AGAINST LEGAL MALPRACTICE CLAIMS

A legal malpractice lawsuit generally has four elements—existence of an attorney-client relationship, breach of the duty owed to the client, injury to the client, and causation between the lawyer's actions and the harm to the client. A judge or jury examines all four elements in a legal malpractice trial and if any element is missing, the plaintiff cannot recover. Thus to understand how an attorney defends himself or herself against a claim of legal malpractice it is necessary to understand how Minnesota courts interpret each of these four elements.

Existence of an Attorney-Client Relationship

The duty that a lawyer owes a client has two components—legal competency and fiduciary obligations. The lawyer must exercise the legal skill that a competent attorney would exercise and must meet all of his or her fiduciary obligations to the client. No lawyer is expected to know the law so well that he or she can give perfect answers to every legal question, but lawyers are expected to know how to research issues and to recognize the limit of their knowledge when they reach an unsettled or unclear area of law. In one early Minnesota case, the Minnesota Supreme Court defined the duty an attorney owes a client: "An attorney is bound to exercise only a reasonable degree of care and skill having reference to the character of the business undertaken, and is not answerable for every error or mistake but will be protected provided he acts honestly and in good faith to the best of his skill and knowledge, or with at least reasonable skill and learning and an ordinary degree of attention and care." *Sjobeck v. Leach*, 6 N.W.2d 819, 213 Minn 360 (Minn. 1943).

A lawyer's fiduciary obligations include a duty of undivided loyalty to the client's interests and confidentiality. As part of this fiduciary duty, a lawyer has an obligation to disclose any conflicts of interest that might impair his or her loyalty to the client or any personal constraints that might affect his or her ability to represent the client.

Many legal malpractice suits have centered on the question of when these duties to a client arise. There is an important distinction between consulting an attorney about a legal matter and retaining that attorney to handle the matter. Generally speaking, only retaining an attorney obligates him or her to act on behalf of a client. Many Minnesotans have learned this lesson the hard way. They thought that consulting a lawyer about their legal problem meant that their case was being handled by that attorney so they stopped taking steps to pursue their claim. Meanwhile the lawyer they consulted allowed the statute of limitations to run out on the claim because the lawyer believed that he or she had not been retained to act on the client's behalf. Many legal malpractice suits have disputed whether an original office visit with a lawyer constituted a consultation or a hiring.

Closely related to the issue of whether an attorney-client relationship has been formed in an initial consultation is that of whether or not an attorney gives legal advice to a potential client during the initial consultation. In one case, the Minnesota Supreme Court upheld a lower court's award of damages to a woman who consulted with an attorney about her husband's medical malpractice claim. At the initial consultation, the lawyer told the woman that he thought she had no claim against her husband's physician and thus the lawyer would not take the case. Relying on the lawyer's opinion, the woman waited too long to file her lawsuit and the statute of limitations expired on her claim. When she sued the attorney for legal malpractice, she alleged that the advice she received was sufficient to establish an attorney-client relationship between herself and the lawyer. The court found that an attorney-client relationship existed, in part, because the attorney had rendered legal advice under circumstances that made it reasonably foreseeable that if the advice were rendered negligently, the person receiving the advice could be injured by acting upon it.

The lesson for lawyers and prospective clients is that before leaving a lawyer's office, the individual and the lawyer should be absolutely clear as to whether the lawyer has or has not been hired. If an attorney declines to handle a case, he or she should be careful about saying that the individual has no case, and take care to suggest perhaps, that the individual seek other counsel. If the individual believes that the attorney has been hired, he or she should be absolutely clear regarding what steps he or she believes the lawyer will take to handle a matter.

Breach of Duty to the Client
Breach of duty is frequently the toughest element to prove in a legal malpractice lawsuit because a lawyer can make mistakes and still not commit legal malpractice. Law is an inexact science. Competent lawyers frequently disagree on the best course of action in a particular legal matter. Sometimes, the strategy that a lawyer chooses to pursue in a particular matter is a combination of

knowledge about the law and guesswork about how a judge or jury will react to the facts of a case. A client may be able to show that another lawyer would have pursued a different strategy, and still the client may be unable to show that the first lawyer committed a breach of duty. Even an error in judgment does not create malpractice liability so long as it is within the bounds of honest exercise of professional judgment. Expert testimony generally is required to establish the standard of care that should be applied to an attorney whose conduct is alleged to constitute legal malpractice. However, there are some behaviors almost any judge or jury could call legal malpractice even in the absence of expert testimony. For example, if an attorney missed a filing deadline and allowed a statute of limitations to expire thereby causing a court to deny a lawsuit, then the client would have a strong case for legal malpractice.

Injury

When a plaintiff claims breach of duty, the plaintiff must show not only the alleged breach of duty, but the injury caused thereby. A lawyer might miss a deadline, but if he or she is subsequently granted an extension, the client is not injured. If missing the deadline bars the plaintiff's claim, he or she might recover damages. A lawyer might forget to assert a claim, but if the claim would have been denied anyway, the client has not been injured. Usually a plaintiff can only recover direct economic losses, such as the money needed to pay another attorney to re-do legal work or any fees or penalties paid, or for any interest income lost because of an attorney's malpractice. It is difficult, although not impossible, to recover for speculative losses (what might have happened if a different lawyer had been hired), emotional losses, or legal expenses incurred hiring a new lawyer to sue the previous lawyer.

Proving legal malpractice can be difficult because merely losing a case is not sufficient grounds to recover for malpractice. Like medicine, the law is not an exact science and many strategic legal decisions are made based on an attorney's background and experience. Even if a lawyer made a significant error in judgment that the client thinks caused the loss of the case, he or she does not automatically have the basis for a legal malpractice lawsuit. The same standard of reasonableness that applies in other areas of tort law also applies here. An attorney's honest mistake will be judged against the course of action a reasonable and knowledgeable attorney would have taken.

All states set statutes of limitations on legal malpractice lawsuits. Some of the time limits begin when someone discovers that he or she has been harmed, while others begin when service by a professional is rendered. Thus, it is important for a person to research this information as soon as one feels they may have a justifiable claim.

Causation

Finally, as is true with medical malpractice claims, the plaintiff in a legal malpractice action must show that the breach was both the actual and proximate cause of the plaintiff's injury. An attorney's actions are the actual cause, or cause in fact, of a client's injury if but for those actions, the client would not have been harmed. Proximate cause is a thorny legal concept that essentially asks whether the breach was sufficiently responsible for, or sufficiently related to, the injury that the lawyer should be held responsible.

Causation is easiest to prove if a lawyer misses a deadline or gives advice that is clearly wrong. In these cases, the client can usually show exactly what would have happened had the lawyer met the deadline or given correct advice. Causation is more difficult to show where a lawyer pursues a wrong course of action in trial. In this case, the client has to show what the judge or jury would have done had the lawyer chosen another strategy. This can be difficult. The client needs to prove, to the judge's or jury's satisfaction, what another lawyer would have done, and how the jury and/or judge would have reacted to that strategy. The first lawyer might argue successfully that even had a different strategy been pursued, the outcome of the case would have been the same.

THE FUTURE OF LEGAL MALPRACTICE LAWSUITS

Attorneys who try legal malpractice cases have had increasing success recently with new theories of liability for legal malpractice. One trend focuses on attorney investments and financial dealings. Courts can find that a lawyer breached a fiduciary duty to a client by failing to reveal stock ownership in an opposing corporate party or by using insider information learned about the client to make profits in the stock market.

A growing trend is for the court to allow claims brought against lawyers by persons other than clients. For example, the beneficiaries under a client's will might bring a legal malpractice action against a lawyer who incorrectly drafted a deceased client's will if the beneficiaries are upset with their share of the estate. Depositors in a failed savings and loan company might sue lawyers who gave advice to the savings and loan.

ACCOUNTANT MALPRACTICE

While the number of professional malpractice lawsuits against doctors is leveling off nationally, the number of professional malpractice lawsuits against accountants is on the rise. There are a number of theories to explain why lawsuits against accountants are becoming more common. Perhaps the most likely explanation is that with the growing number of business insolvencies, lenders and investors are looking to other parties from which to recoup losses. Accountants appear to be an easy target because so often they are close to the heart of business decision making. Whatever the reason for the increasing number of lawsuits against them, accountants need to be aware of the ways they can become liable for the results of their work.

As is true for doctors and lawyers, accountants can be sued for malpractice if they perform a service at a level below that which would be expected of a competent accountant. An accountant cannot be sued merely because of an honest mistake; he or she must be found to have made an error that a reasonable accountant would not have made.

Accountant malpractice lawsuits differ in a number of important ways from medical or legal malpractice lawsuits. One of the most important differences between accountant malpractice lawsuits and medical or legal malpractice lawsuits is the role played by written compilations of standards of conduct for the accounting and auditing professions. These rules, known as Generally Accepted Accounting Principals (GAAP) and Generally Accepted Auditing Standards (GAAS), are frequently used in accountant malpractice lawsuits to judge the actions of defendants. Although mere blind adherence to these standards is not an absolute defense to malpractice liability, it is powerful defense against an allegation of malpractice if a defendant can show that his or her actions complied with a rule found in GAAP or GAAS.

Another way in which accountant malpractice lawsuits differ from medical or legal malpractice lawsuits is that many accountant malpractice cases are based on violations of federal and state statutes relating to the sale of securities. Accountants' financial statements are frequently used in connection with various kinds of securities offerings and are frequently submitted with annual reports or other periodic filings companies must make in order to comply with SEC requirements. If the financial statements are erroneous and lead to negative market impacts, then investors frequently try to recoup their losses by asserting securities claims against the accountants who prepared the statements. The statutes most commonly used to bring claims against accountants are the Securities Act of 1933, the Securities Act of 1934, and Racketeer Influenced and Corrupt Organizations Act (RICO). Each is quite complex and a discussion of their intricacies is beyond the scope of this chapter, but an attorney experienced in defending accountants against charges of professional malpractice can advise accountants of their responsibilities and potential liabilities under these acts.

ENGINEER AND ARCHITECT MALPRACTICE

Engineers and architects can also be sued for malpractice. Engineers and architects can be liable for the actual construction and design of a building itself if the structure proves unsafe or unsound, or they can be liable for negligent review of a building under construction or remodeling. If an engineer or architect reviews a structure and declares it sound to a perspective buyer, and it is discovered later that the building needed structural repairs, the buyer may have grounds for a professional malpractice lawsuit against the engineer or architect.

Lawsuits that allege that an architect or engineer committed professional malpractice differ substantially from medical or legal malpractice lawsuits in that virtually all agreements between an architect or engineer and an owner are in standardized written contracts.

Lawsuits against an engineer or architect alleging professional malpractice hinge more on interpretation of contract than on the application of common law principals. Another factor further distinguishing professional malpractice lawsuits against engineers and architects from professional malpractice lawsuits against doctors and lawyers is that standard contracts used in the engineering and architecture professions often call for disputes to be submitted to binding arbitration. The Contract Law Chapter addresses general issues of contract law interpretation, and the Alternative Dispute Resolution Chapter describes the processes used in arbitration.

The standard contract used by engineers and contractors can be modified. However, architects and engineers should seek advice from an attorney experienced in disputes between owners and architects or engineers before agreeing to modify the terms of a standard form contract. Often, even seemingly innocuous language changes can substantially shift liabilities between the parties. For example, disputes often arise over the standard of care to be applied in judging the professionals' actions. The standard of care against which an engineer's or architect's actions generally are judged is the "ordinary and reasonable skill usually exercised by one in that profession." Some owners suggest changing the language to require the architect or engineer to exercise the "highest professional standards." While these words may appear to be innocuous, they should never be integrated into an agreement as they can set impossibly high standards for any architect or engineer to meet.

RESOURCES

Accountant Liability. Thomas J. Shroyer, Wiley Law Publications, Somerset, NJ, 1991.

Architect and Engineer Liability: Claims Against Design Professionals. Robert F. Cushman & Thomas G. Bottum, editors, Wiley Law Publications, Somerset, NJ, 1987.

Architects and Engineers. James Acret, Shepard's/McGraw-Hill, Colorado Springs, CO, 1993.

Architect-Engineer Liability Under Minnesota Law. Marv Fabyanske, Robert J. Huber, The Cambridge Institute, Vienna, VA, 1988.

Professional Malpractice Defense Law Leading Attorneys

The attorneys profiled in this section were nominated by their peers in a statewide survey conducted in 1993 in which several thousand Minnesota attorneys were asked to name the lawyer to whom they would send a friend or family member in need of legal assistance in the area of *Professional Malpractice Defense Law.*

Because the survey resulted in a list of less than five percent of Minnesota's practicing attorneys, this should not be construed as a complete list. Nevertheless, it is an excellent source of highly qualified and reputable attorneys, who, if unable to assist can in most cases make quality referrals.

A list of all attorneys nominated in this category is found at the end of this section. For information on the survey methodology see page ix.

Please note that the shorter, two line attorney listings in this section are of attorneys who practice in this area but whose full biographical profile appears in another section of this book. A bullet "•" preceeding name indicates the attorney was nominated in this particular area of law. For information on the format of these profiles, consult the section "Using the *Business Guidebook*" found on page xiv. Note that the following abbreviations are used throughout these profiles:

App.	- Appellate	ABA	- American Bar Association
Cir.	- Circuit	ATLA	- American Trial Lawyers Association
Ct.	- Court	HCBA	- Hennepin County Bar Association
Dist.	- District	MDLA	- Minnesota Defense Lawyers Association
Hon.	- Honorable	MSBA	- Minnesota State Bar Association
JD	- Law degree (Juris Doctor)	MTLA	- Minnesota Trial Lawyers Association
LLB	- Law degree	NBTA	- National Board of Trial Advocacy
LLM	- Master in Law degree	RCBA	- Ramsey County Bar Association
Sup.	- Supreme		

J. RICHARD BLAND

Meagher & Geer
4200 Multifoods Tower
33 South Sixth Street
Minneapolis, MN 55402

Phone: (612) 338-0661
Fax: (612) 338-8384

Admitted: 1971 Minnesota;
1971 Iowa
Birthdate: 10/30/46

•J. RICHARD BLAND: Mr. Bland has been active in civil litigation since 1971 in both appellate and trial work. Currently, his practice emphasizes defense of professional liability claims, with a special focus on health professional claims. Mr. Bland is a member of Meagher & Geer's Management Committee and chairs the firm's Health Care Practice Group. He is listed in *The Best Lawyers in America*, 1993 edition and is a frequent lecturer.
Education: JD 1971, Drake University; BA 1968, Augustana College.
Employment History: Partner 1975-present, Associate 1971-75, Meagher & Geer.
Representative Clients: The St. Paul Companies, Inc.; Midwest Medical Insurance Company.
Professional Associations: MDLA; Defense Research Institute; MSBA.
Firm: Nineteen ninety-four marks Meagher & Geer's 65th year. The Minneapolis law firm is recognized as one of the Midwest's most reputable; Meagher & Geer attorneys have long been considered among the preeminent trial lawyers in the state of Minnesota and throughout the country. In addition to a practice that encompasses all aspects of insurance law, civil litigation, and business and commercial law, the firm has a separate practice group devoted to the appellate practice. Meagher & Geer's clientele represents the industries of agriculture, aviation, construction, finance, health care, insurance, manufacturing, and real estate. *See additional listing in Personal Injury Defense Law Chapter.*

RICHARD A. BOWMAN - Bowman and Brooke - 150 South Fifth Street, Suite 2600 - Minneapolis, MN 55402 - Phone: (612) 339-8682, Fax: (612) 672-3200 - *See complete biographical profile in Personal Injury Defense Law Chapter.*

•FREDERICK C. BROWN, JR. - Popham, Haik, Schnobrich & Kaufman, Ltd. - 222 South Ninth Street, Suite 3300 - Minneapolis, MN 55402 - Phone: (612) 333-4800, Fax: (612) 334-8888 - *See complete biographical profile in Personal Injury Defense Law Chapter.*

CRAIG R. CAMPBELL - Gunhus, Grinnell, Klinger, Swenson & Guy, Ltd. - 512 Center Avenue, P.O. Box 1077 - Moorhead, MN 56561-1077 - Phone: (218) 236-6462, Fax: (218) 236-9873 - *See complete biographical profile in Personal Injury Defense Law Chapter.*

Professional Malpractice Defense Law Leading Attorneys

KEVIN S. CARPENTER - Quinlivan, Sherwood, Spellacy & Tarvestad, P.A. - P.O. Box 1008 - St. Cloud, MN 56302-1008 - Phone: (612) 251-1414, Fax: (612) 251-1415 - *See complete biographical profile in Personal Injury Defense Law Chapter.*

PHILLIP A. COLE - Lommen, Nelson, Cole & Stageberg, P.A. - 1800 IDS Center, 80 South Eighth Street - Minneapolis, MN 55402 - Phone: (612) 339-8131, Fax: (612) 339-8064 - *See complete biographical profile in Commercial Litigation Chapter.*

JOHN M. DEGNAN - Bassford, Lockhart, Truesdell & Briggs, P.A. - 3550 Multifoods Tower, 33 South Sixth Street - Minneapolis, MN 55402-3787 - Phone: (612) 333-3000, Fax: (612) 333-8829 - *See complete biographical profile in Commercial Litigation Chapter.*

WILLIAM D. FLASKAMP - Meagher & Geer - 4200 Multifoods Tower, 33 South Sixth Street - Minneapolis, MN 55402 - Phone: (612) 338-0661, Fax: (612) 338-8384 - *See complete biographical profile in Personal Injury Defense Law Chapter.*

MICHAEL J. FORD - Quinlivan, Sherwood, Spellacy & Tarvestad, P.A. - P.O. Box 1008 - St. Cloud, MN 56302-1008 - Phone: (612) 251-1414, Fax: (612) 251-1415 - *See complete biographical profile in Employment Law Chapter.*

PAUL E. GRINNELL - Gunhus, Grinnell, Klinger, Swenson & Guy, Ltd. - 512 Center Avenue, P.O. Box 1077 - Moorhead, MN 56561-1077 - Phone: (218) 236-6462, Fax: (218) 236-9873 - *See complete biographical profile in Personal Injury Defense Law Chapter.*

GUNDER D. GUNHUS - Gunhus, Grinnell, Klinger, Swenson & Guy, Ltd. - 512 Center Avenue, P.O. Box 1077 - Moorhead, MN 56561-1077 - Phone: (218) 236-6462, Fax: (218) 236-9873 - *See complete biographical profile in Personal Injury Defense Law Chapter.*

GARY W. HOCH - Meagher & Geer - 4200 Multifoods Tower, 33 South Sixth Street - Minneapolis, MN 55402 - Phone: (612) 338-0661, Fax: (612) 338-8384 - *See complete biographical profile in Personal Injury Defense Law Chapter.*

•RICHARD N. JEFFRIES: Mr. Jeffries practices civil litigation and trial law in tort and commercial matters for insurance defense, corporations, and self-insured people. He handles varied personal injury, wrongful death, and property damages cases, defending claims including malpractice, civil rights, construction, product liability, casualty, fire, automobile negligence, insurance coverage issues, employment, liquor liability, governmental liability, health law, commercial litigation, and subrogation in all state and federal courts in Minnesota and North Dakota. He also handles arbitration, mediation, and other forms of alternative dispute resolution proceedings. Mr. Jeffries is an author of published articles and a lecturer at insurance claim seminars and continuing legal education seminars.
Education: JD 1970 Order of the Coif, University of North Dakota; BA 1965, Moorhead State University.
Employment History: 1970-present, private law practice.
Representative Clients: AT&T; GAB Business Services, Inc.; 3M; numerous insurance industry companies, such as Aid Association for Lutherans; American Hardware Insurance Company; Citizens Security Insurance Company; Diamond State Insurance Company; Dundee Mutual Insurance Company; Fireman's Fund Insurance Company; General Casualty Insurance Company; Indiana Lumberman's Mutual Insurance Company; John Deere Insurance Company; Meadowbrook Insurance Company; Midwest Medical Insurance Company; Minnesota Counties Insurance Trust; National Farmer's Union; Prudential Insurance Company; Reliance National Risk Specialists; Tri-State Insurance Company; US Fidelity & Guaranty Company.
Professional Associations: American Arbitration Assn. (Panel of Arbitrators); Clay County Bar Assn.; Cass County Bar Assn.; Seventh District Bar Assn.; MSBA; State Bar Assn. of North Dakota; Defense Research Institute; MDLA; North Dakota Defense Lawyers Assn.
Firm: Jeffries, Olson, Flom, Oppegard & Hogan, P.A., is a general practice law firm with offices in Moorhead, MN and Fargo, ND. The firm handles cases primarily in the western half of Minnesota and all of North Dakota, offering a wide range of litigation and commercial services. *See additional listings in Commercial Litigation and Personal Injury Defense Law Chapters.*

RICHARD N. JEFFRIES

Jeffries, Olson, Flom, Oppegard & Hogan, P.A.
403 Center Avenue
P.O. Box 9
Moorhead, MN 56561-0009

Phone: (218) 233-3222
Fax: (701) 280-1880

Admitted: 1970 Minnesota;
1981 North Dakota;
1981 Florida
Birthdate: 10/20/42

JOHN D. KELLY - Hanft, Fride, O'Brien, Harries, Swelbar & Burns, P.A. - 1000 First Bank Place, 130 West Superior Street - Duluth, MN 55802 - Phone: (218) 722-4766, Fax: (218) 720-4920 - *See complete biographical profile in Commercial Litigation Chapter.*

LAWRENCE R. KING - King & Hatch - The St. Paul Building, 6 West Fifth Street, Suite 800 - St. Paul, MN 55102 - Phone: (612) 223-2856, Fax: (612) 223-2847 - *See complete biographical profile in Personal Injury Defense Law Chapter.*

Chapter 28: Professional Malpractice Defense Law

GREER E. LOCKHART

Bassford, Lockhart, Truesdell
& Briggs, P.A.
3550 Multifoods Tower
33 South Sixth Street
Minneapolis, MN 55402-3787

Phone: (612) 333-3000
Fax: (612) 333-8829

Admitted: 1953 Minnesota;
1953 US Dist. Ct. (MN);
1977 US Sup. Ct.
Birthdate: 02/04/29

•**GREER E. LOCKHART:** In practice with Bassford, Lockhart, Truesdell & Briggs, P.A. for over 40 years, Mr. Lockhart's practice is limited to dispute resolution, including all forms of civil litigation, including professional liability defense, hospital law, product liability defense, commercial litigation, and insurance law. He is a frequent seminar lecturer on topics of insurance coverage, court rules, medical malpractice, civil litigation, and alternative dispute resolution. Mr. Lockhart is Chair of the Board of Bassford, Lockhart, Truesdell & Briggs, P.A.
Employment History: Adjunct Professor of Law 1977-81, University of Minnesota Law School.
Education: LLB 1953, University of Minnesota; BSL 1951, University of Minnesota.
Representative Clients: Abbott Northwestern Hospital; Minneapolis Children's Medical Center; The Travelers Insurance Company.
Professional Associations: ABA (Insurance, Negligence and Compensation Law Section; Legal Education Section; Arbitration Committee (past Vice Chair)); MSBA (Court Rules Committee; Judicial Administration Committee; Civil Litigation Section); HCBA; American College of Trial Lawyers; American Board of Trial Advocates; American Arbitration Assn. (1972-present, Minneapolis Accident Claims Advisory Committee).
Community Involvement: Citizens League of Twin Cities Metropolitan Area (past President); Twin Cities Opportunities Industrialization Center (Board member); City of Minneapolis Development Policy Task Force (1976-77); American Civil Liberties Union; MN Civil Liberties Union.
Firm: Founded in 1882, Bassford, Lockhart, Truesdell & Briggs and its predecessor firms have been serving clients in Minnesota for more than 110 years. Today, the Bassford firm's 27 trial lawyers provide a broad range of litigation services for clients around the country, handling all areas of civil and business litigation. *See additional listings in Commercial Litigation and Health Law Chapters.*

•**JAMES T. MARTIN** - Gislason, Martin & Varpness, P.A. - 7600 Parklawn Avenue South, Suite 444 - Minneapolis, MN 55435 - Phone: (612) 831-5793, Fax: (612) 831-7358 - *See complete biographical profile in Commercial Litigation Chapter.*

GERALD L. MASCHKA - Farrish, Johnson & Maschka - 201 North Broad Street, Suite 200, P.O. Box 550 - Mankato, MN 56002-0550 - Phone: (507) 387-3002, Fax: (507) 625-4002 - *See complete biographical profile in Personal Injury Defense Law Chapter.*

ROSS MUIR - Muir, Heuel, Carlson & Spelhaug, P.A. - 404 Marquette Bank Building, P.O. Box 1057 - Rochester, MN 55903 - Phone: (507) 288-4110, Fax: (507) 288-4122 - *See complete biographical profile in Personal Injury Defense Law Chapter.*

THOMAS F. NELSON - Popham, Haik, Schnobrich & Kaufman, Ltd. - 222 South Ninth Street, Suite 3300 - Minneapolis, MN 55402 - Phone: (612) 333-4800, Fax: (612) 334-8888 - *See complete biographical profile in Commercial Litigation Chapter.*

•**RICHARD L. PEMBERTON** - Pemberton, Sorlie, Sefkow, Rufer & Kershner - 110 North Mill Street, P.O. Box 866 - Fergus Falls, MN 56538-0866 - Phone: (218) 736-5493, Fax: (218) 736-3950 - *See complete biographical profile in Personal Injury Defense Law Chapter.*

H. JEFFREY PETERSON - Cope & Peterson, P.A. - 415 South First Street, P.O. Box 947 - Virginia, MN 55792 - Phone: (218) 749-4470, Fax: (218) 749-4783 - *See complete biographical profile in Personal Injury Defense Law Chapter.*

JOHN D. QUINLIVAN - Quinlivan, Sherwood, Spellacy & Tarvestad, P.A. - P.O. Box 1008 - St. Cloud, MN 56302-1008 - Phone: (612) 251-1414, Fax: (612) 251-1415 - *See complete biographical profile in Personal Injury Defense Law Chapter.*

MICHAEL R. QUINLIVAN - Arthur, Chapman, McDonough, Kettering & Smetak, P.A. - 500 Young Quinlan Building, 81 South Ninth Street - Minneapolis, MN 55402-3214 - Phone: (612) 339-3500, Fax: (612) 339-7655 - *See complete biographical profile in Employment Law Chapter.*

PIERRE N. REGNIER - Jardine, Logan & O'Brien - 2100 Piper Jaffray Plaza, 444 Cedar Street - St. Paul, MN 55101 - Phone: (612) 290-6500, Fax: (612) 223-5070 - *See complete biographical profile in Personal Injury Defense Law Chapter.*

LEWIS A. REMELE, JR. - Bassford, Lockhart, Truesdell & Briggs, P.A. - 3550 Multifoods Tower, 33 South Sixth Street - Minneapolis, MN 55402-3787 - Phone: (612) 333-3000, Fax: (612) 333-8829 - *See complete biographical profile in Commercial Litigation Chapter.*

CARVER RICHARDS - Trenti Law Firm - P.O. Box 958 - Virginia, MN 55792 - Phone: (218) 749-1962, Fax: (218) 749-4308 - *See complete biographical profile in Personal Injury Defense Law Chapter.*

JAMES M. RILEY - Meagher & Geer - 4200 Multifoods Tower, 33 South Sixth Street - Minneapolis, MN 55402 - Phone: (612) 338-0661, Fax: (612) 338-8384 - *See complete biographical profile in Personal Injury Defense Law Chapter.*

•JAMES F. ROEGGE: In his civil trial practice, Mr. Roegge represents professional negligence calims, product liability issues, employment matters, and general commercial litigation matters. His practice also includes the handling and defense of fidelity claims and litigation on behalf of the insurance industry. He currently serves on the firm's Management Committee and is an approved arbitrator.
Education: JD 1971, Valparaiso University; BA 1967, Concordia College.
Employment History: Partner 1975-present, Associate 1971-75, Meagher & Geer.
Representative Clients: Chubb & Sons, Inc.; American International Group; The St. Paul Companies, Inc.; Midwest Medical Insurance Company; CNA Insurance Companies; Lutheran Church–Missouri Synod Minneapolis South District.
Professional Associations: MSBA; State Bar of Wisconsin; Defense Research Institute; MDLA; Federation of Insurance and Corporate Counsel; American College of Trial Lawyers (Fellow).
Community Involvement: Board of Directors of various nonprofit corporations; Executive Director, St. Michael Lutheran Church.
Firm: Nineteen ninety-four marks Meagher & Geer's 65th year. The Minneapolis law firm is recognized as one of the Midwest's most reputable; Meagher & Geer attorneys have long been considered among the preeminent trial lawyers in the state of Minnesota and throughout the country. In addition to a practice that encompasses all aspects of insurance law, civil litigation, and business and commercial law, the firm has a separate practice group devoted to the appellate practice. Meagher & Geer's clientele represents the industries of agriculture, aviation, construction, finance, health care, insurance, manufacturing, and real estate. *See additional listings in Commercial Litigation and Personal Injury Defense Law Chapters.*

JAMES F. ROEGGE

Meagher & Geer
4200 Multifoods Tower
33 South Sixth Street
Minneapolis, MN 55402

Phone: (612) 338-0661
Fax: (612) 338-8384

Admitted: 1971 Minnesota; 1985 Wisconsin
Birthdate: 04/22/45

JOHN R. SCHULZ - Collins, Buckley, Sauntry & Haugh - 332 Minnesota Street, Suite W1100 - St. Paul, MN 55101 - Phone: (612) 227-0611, Fax: (612) 227-0758 - *See complete biographical profile in Personal Injury Defense Law Chapter.*

GEORGE W. SOULE - Bowman and Brooke - 150 South Fifth Street, Suite 2600 - Minneapolis, MN 55402 - Phone: (612) 339-8682, Fax: (612) 672-3200 - *See complete biographical profile in Personal Injury Defense Law Chapter.*

KEVIN A. SPELLACY - Quinlivan, Sherwood, Spellacy & Tarvestad, P.A. - P.O. Box 1008 - St. Cloud, MN 56302-1008 - Phone: (612) 251-1414, Fax: (612) 251-1415 - *See complete biographical profile in Personal Injury Defense Law Chapter.*

CHARLES E. SPEVACEK - Meagher & Geer - 4200 Multifoods Tower, 33 South Sixth Street - Minneapolis, MN 55402 - Phone: (612) 338-0661, Fax: (612) 338-8384 - *See complete biographical profile in Environmental Law Chapter.*

GAYLORD W. SWELBAR - Hanft, Fride, O'Brien, Harries, Swelbar & Burns, P.A. - 1000 First Bank Place, 130 West Superior Street - Duluth, MN 55802 - Phone: (218) 722-4766, Fax: (218) 720-4920 - *See complete biographical profile in Personal Injury Defense Law Chapter.*

•ANTHONY M. TARVESTAD: Mr. Tarvestad practices insurance defense law in all areas of civil litigation and personal injury in state and federal courts. He concentrates in professional malpractice (primarily for hospitals, physicians, and other health care providers) employment litigation, governmental liability, and product liability. He also lectures to health care providers on issues relating to the prevention of malpractice suits.
Education: JD 1977, William Mitchell; BA 1973, Winona State University.
Employment History: Currently, Shareholder, Quinlivan, Sherwood, Spellacy & Tarvestad, P.A.
Representative Clients: American States Insurance Company; Austin Mutual Insurance Company; Auto-Owners Insurance Company; CNA Insurance Company; Citizens Security Mutual Insurance; Crawford and Company; The Dentist Insurance Company; Druggist Mutual; Farm Bureau Mutual Insurance Company; Farmers Insurance Group; Federated Mutual; General Casualty Company; General Star Management; Horace Mann Insurance Company; Maryland Casualty Company; Meadowbrook Insurance Group; Medical Protective Insurance Company; Medrad; Midwest Medical Insurance Company; Minnesota Counties Insurance Trust (MCIT); Northland Insurance Company; Progressive Insurance Company; Prudential Property & Casualty; The St. Paul Insurance Companies, Inc.; SECURA Insurance Company; State Farm Insurance Companies; Travelers Group; Western National Insurance Company.
Professional Associations: Defense Research Institute; Federation of Insurance and Corporate Counsel (Medical Malpractice Committee); MDLA; MSBA; HCBA; Stearns-Benton Bar Assn.; Seventh District Bar Assn.; ABA; American Arbitration Assn. (Panel of Arbitrators).
Firm: Founded in 1923, Quinlivan, Sherwood, Spellacy & Tarvestad, P.A. is a highly respected law firm devoting its practice to civil litigation and dispute resolution of all types at the state and federal levels. *See additional listings in Personal Injury Defense Law and Federal, State & Local Government Law Chapters.*

ANTHONY M. TARVESTAD

Quinlivan, Sherwood, Spellacy & Tarvestad, P.A.
P.O. Box 1008
St. Cloud, MN 56302-1008

Phone: (612) 251-1414
Fax: (612) 251-1415

Admitted: 1977 Minnesota; US Dist. Ct. (MN)
Birthdate: 04/26/50

Chapter 28: Professional Malpractice Defense Law

LYNN G. TRUESDELL - Bassford, Lockhart, Truesdell & Briggs, P.A. - 3550 Multifoods Tower, 33 South Sixth Street - Minneapolis, MN 55402 - Phone: (612) 333-3000, Fax: (612) 333-8829 - *See complete biographical profile in Commercial Litigation Chapter.*

ALAN R. VANASEK - Jardine, Logan & O'Brien - 2100 Piper Jaffray Plaza, 444 Cedar Street - St. Paul, MN 55101 - Phone: (612) 290-6500, Fax: (612) 223-5070 - *See complete biographical profile in Personal Injury Defense Law Chapter.*

PHILIP G. VILLAUME - Philip G. Villaume & Associates - 7900 International Drive, Suite 675 - Bloomington, MN 55425 - Phone: (612) 851-0823, Fax: (612) 851-0824 - *See complete biographical profile in Criminal Law Chapter.*

Complete listing of all attorneys nominated in Professional Malpractice Defense Law

J. RICHARD BLAND, Meagher & Geer, Minneapolis; **FREDERICK C. BROWN JR.,** Popham, Haik, Schnobrich & Kaufman, Ltd., Minneapolis; **RICHARD N. JEFFRIES,** Jeffries, Olson, Flom, Oppegard & Hogan, P.A., Moorhead; **GREER E. LOCKHART,** Bassford, Lockhart, Truesdell & Briggs, P.A., Minneapolis; **JAMES T. MARTIN,** Gislason, Martin & Varpness, P.A., Minneapolis; **WILLIAM E. MULLIN,** Maslon, Edelman, Borman & Brand, Minneapolis; **TERENCE J. O'LOUGHLIN,** Geraghty O'Loughlin & Kenney, P.A., St. Paul; **RICHARD L. PEMBERTON,** Pemberton, Sorlie, Sefkow, Rufer & Kershner, Fergus Falls; **CHARLES QUAINTANCE JR.,** Maslon, Edelman, Borman & Brand, Minneapolis; **JAMES F. ROEGGE,** Meagher & Geer, Minneapolis; **ANTHONY M. TARVESTAD,** Quinlivan, Sherwood, Spellacy & Tarvestad, P.A., St. Cloud; **ROBERT T. WHITE,** Murnane, Conlin, White & Brandt, St. Paul; **RICHARD G. WILSON,** Maslon, Edelman, Borman & Brand, Minneapolis.

CHAPTER 29

PUBLICLY HELD CORPORATIONS LAW

The classic definition of a corporation is that a corporation is a fictitious or artificial person. For legal and tax purposes, a corporation is a separate entity from its owners, an entity that can make purchases, enter into contracts, must pay taxes, and can sue and be sued on its own behalf. A publicly held corporation is a corporation that has shares that are held by a large number of people. In contrast, a closely held corporation is one that has shares held by a small number of people.

There is no definitive line that separates a publicly held corporation from a closely held corporation. For certain limited purposes, the Minnesota Business Corporations Act defines a closely held corporation as a corporation with 35 or fewer shareholders. The Minnesota's Workers' Compensation Act, defines a closely held corporation as a corporation whose stock is held by no more than 10 persons. In addition, federal law requires that publicly held corporations with more than $5,000,000 in assets and whose outstanding securities are held by more than 500 shareholders of record must meet several unique requirements of the Federal Securities and Exchange Act of 1934, including a requirement to submit periodic financial information to the Securities and Exchange Commission.

This chapter discusses how to form a publicly held corporation, the advantages and disadvantages of corporate status, and mergers and acquisitions. The Closely Held Business Law Chapter discusses other ways to organize a business and addresses issues uniquely of concern to closely held corporations. The Nonprofit Corporations Law Chapter discusses how to form a nonprofit, tax-exempt corporation. The Securities & Venture Finance Law Chapter discusses securities laws and regulations that affect most publicly held corporations.

FORMING A PUBLICLY HELD CORPORATION

A corporation can only be created by complying with the statutes of its state of incorporation. In most states "incorporators" initially organize the corporation, "shareholders" own the corporation and elect a "board of directors" which is responsible for management and control of the corporation. The board of directors then chooses officers who are responsible for overseeing day-to-day operations of the corporation.

ADVANTAGES OF CORPORATE STATUS

Becoming a corporation gives a business several advantages over other forms of business organization such as sole proprietorship or partnership.

Survivability

One advantage is that because a corporation is an artificial person, its existence does not depend on who its owners are at any given time. A corporation can survive the death of an individual shareholder or director or the transfer of shares. The corporation "dies" only when it is dissolved, either voluntarily or involuntarily. The ability to survive the death or departure of any individual person gives the corporation stability and makes it a more attractive candidate for long-term financing. Survivability also permits the corporation to raise funds by selling shares to new investors because new owners can be added without disturbing the corporate form.

Shareholder Insulation from Debt and Liability

A corporation is liable for its own debts and obligations without limit, but because the corporation can take out loans and be sued in its own name, the shareholders are not personally liable for those debts should the corporation be unable to pay. Absent an agreement to the contrary, a corporation's creditors may not seek to collect debts from the owners of the corporation. In legalese, the shareholders enjoy "limited liability." Limited liability makes investment in a corporation more attractive to potential investors because the most that can be lost is the initial investment.

Incorporators of new corporations may not be able to enjoy limited liability immediately, however, because owners of a new corporation may be required by financial institutions to give personal financial assurances in order to receive funding. Financial institutions understand the risk they take by making loans to young corporations without established credit records and thus they may try to limit their exposure by requiring shareholders to personally guarantee loans should the corporation be unable to make payments.

In addition to the possibility that financial institutions will require personal guarantees for loans to corporations, on rare occasions, a court will ignore a business' corporate status and make its shareholders personally liable for the debts of a corporation. Disregarding corporate status is known as "piercing the corporate veil." In Minnesota, piercing the corporate veil is extremely rare. Minnesota courts use a two-prong test in deciding whether to pierce the corporate veil and ignore a corporation's corporate status.

The first prong considers:

- Shareholders' relationship to the corporation
- Whether there was insufficient capitalization for corporate undertakings
- Observance of corporate formalities such as regular meetings and elections
- Nonpayment of dividends
- Nonsolvency of the corporation at the time of the transaction in question
- Siphoning off of funds by a dominant shareholder
- Absence of corporate records
- Use of the corporation as a facade for individual dealings

The second prong of the test focuses on the plaintiff's relationship to the corporation and asks whether piercing the veil is necessary to prevent injustice or fundamental unfairness.

Centralized Management

Another benefit of corporate status is centralized management. The shareholders of a publicly held corporation are its owners, but management and control of the corporation are the responsibility of the board of directors, who may or may not be shareholders. In contrast, in a partnership, each partner has a right to participate in management.

Transferability of Interest

Shares of stock in a corporation may be freely bought, sold, assigned, or otherwise disposed of by their owners unless there are special circumstances. In contrast, partnership interests are not freely transferable without the permission of remaining partners. The free transferability of shares increase their value because investors know they will be able to sell the shares quickly and easily should they choose to do so.

DISADVANTAGES OF CORPORATE STATUS

Becoming a corporation is not the best course of action for all businesses, as corporate status does have its disadvantages.

Double Taxation

The biggest drawback of corporate status is double taxation. Most publicly held corporations file their own tax returns and pay taxes on corporate profits before paying dividends to the shareholders. When the shareholders receive the dividends, these profits will be taxed on the individual shareholders' tax returns. In contrast, the profits of a partnership are only taxed once because a partnership pays no taxes before distributing profits. Partners only pay taxes on their individual share of the profits.

Cost

Given the more complex nature of organizing and running a corporation as compared to other forms of business organization, most corporations pay more for professional services from accountants and lawyers. In addition, the fees for incorporating are generally higher than fees for other forms of business organization. Finally, a corporation that sells securities faces very substantial costs to comply with a myriad of securities regulations.

Inflexibility

Another significant drawback to corporate status is the loss of flexibility in running a business. In order to avoid the possibility of a court piercing the corporate veil, a corporation needs to observe several formalities, such as regular meetings and elections. For some small businesses, the loss of flexibility may make corporate status more trouble than it is worth.

STATE OF INCORPORATION

Incorporators usually choose to incorporate under the laws of the state in which the corporation is primarily located, although they can choose to incorporate under the laws of another state. For example, close to one-third of the corporations in the United States are incorporated under the laws of the state of Delaware, even though most of them do little, if any, business in Delaware. The state of Delaware has purposefully sought to entice corporations to incorporate under its laws by maintaining an especially efficient, well run, system of courts that exclusively handles corporate matters. Because so many corporations are organized under Delaware laws, the Delaware Corporate Code has been litigated extensively. A result of the extensive amount of case law interpreting the Delaware Corporate Code is that outcomes of lawsuits are often easier to predict in Delaware, so many business operators now feel more comfortable knowing that corporate disputes will be handled in Delaware courts applying Delaware laws.

MINNESOTA REQUIREMENTS FOR CORPORATIONS

Corporations formed under Minnesota law must comply with the requirements set forth in the Minnesota Business Corporations Act (MBCA). Any natural person at least 18 years of age may form a corporation by filing articles of incorporation with the office of the Minnesota Secretary of State.

Articles of Incorporation

The MBCA allows corporations to have very simple articles of incorporation. Articles of incorporation need only include:

- Name of the corporation

- Address of the corporation's registered office and name of the registered agent, if any, at that address

- Aggregate number of shares that the corporation has authority to issue

- Name and address of each incorporator

The reason articles of incorporation can be so simple is that the MBCA contains a long list of provisions that apply to all corporations unless specifically modified in the articles of incorporation, including:

- Board of Directors has power to adopt, amend or repeal bylaws

- Absent directors must be given an opportunity to give written consent or opposition to proposals

- An affirmative vote of a majority of directors present at a meeting is required for board action

- All shares have equal rights and preferences in all matters

- A shareholder has preemptive rights to acquire newly issued shares

Name Registration

Minnesota Statutes require that any business operating in Minnesota under a name other than the full name of the business owner must register the assumed name with the Minnesota Secretary of

State. A "Certificate of Assumed Name" form is available from the Minnesota Secretary of State's office. The business owner must fill out the form and submit it and the accompanying fee to the Secretary of State. After the Secretary of State notifies the owner that the filing has been accepted and the proposed name does not conflict with corporate or partnership names on file, the owner must publish notice of the assumed name in a newspaper. The newspaper chosen must be in the county where the principal office of the business is located. The corporation's name registration is valid for ten years and can be renewed.

Tax Identification Numbers

Corporations in Minnesota must obtain federal and state tax identification numbers. A corporation with employees must also register with the Minnesota Department of Jobs and Training for an Unemployment Compensation Insurance number. Businesses that sell goods or services that are taxable must obtain a sales and use tax permit from the Minnesota Department of Revenue.

FORMS OF CORPORATIONS

Corporations can be formed in a number of different ways.

Subchapter C Corporation

Most large, publicly held corporations are Subchapter C corporations. The Subchapter C corporation takes its name from Subchapter C of the Internal Revenue Code. A Subchapter C corporation is subject to the general corporate taxation rules discussed above.

Subchapter S Corporation

A Subchapter S corporation derives its name from Subchapter S of the Internal Revenue Code. Under Subchapter S, a corporation that meets certain requirements may be treated as a corporation for purposes of insulating its shareholders from personal liability for corporate debts, but treated as a partnership for tax purposes. Shareholders of a Subchapter S corporation receive limited liability protection, and their profits from the business are included on their individual income tax return. Minnesota has similar tax treatment for such corporations.

To be treated as a Subchapter S corporation under federal tax laws, the corporation:

- Must be a domestic corporation (not foreign)

- Must not be part of an affiliated group of corporations

- Must not have more than 35 shareholders

- Must have only one class of stock

- Shareholders must be either an individual, a decedent's estate, or one of a special class of trusts (not corporations or partnerships)

- Shareholders cannot be nonresident aliens

After a business has incorporated, all shareholders must consent to Subchapter S treatment. The election to be treated as a Subchapter S corporation must be filed with the Internal Revenue Service in a timely manner.

Director's Fiduciary Responsibilities

The attitude of lawmakers toward corporate directors is somewhat contradictory. Because directors hold great power in a corporation's management structure, the law imposes upon them a high standard of fidelity and loyalty to the interests of the corporation. On the other hand, because most Americans value the freedom of corporations to take risks and pursue untested ventures, lawmakers are loathe to restrict the actions of directors. In legalese, directors are said to owe the corporation "fiduciary duties." The outlines of directors' fiduciary duties are frequently the subject of lawsuits alleging that a director had a conflict of interest in his or her dealing with the corporation or failed to exercise good business judgment.

Minnesota Statutes require a director to "discharge the duties of the position of director in good faith, in a manner the director reasonably believes to be in the best interest of the corporation, and with the care an ordinarily prudent person in a like position would exercise under similar circumstances."

Directors who perform their duties in compliance with the above standard are not liable for their actions merely by reason of being or having been a director of the corporation. Put another way, directors' decisions made honestly and with reasonable prudence do not subject a director to liability even if they turn out badly for the corporation.

MERGERS AND ACQUISITIONS

There are two ways that a corporation can grow—either it can add new employees and customers of its own, or it can merge with or acquire another business. There are many reasons why merging with or acquiring another business can be preferable to internal growth.

Benefits of Merging and Acquiring

Though there are many possible reasons for mergers and acquisitions, the following are the most common benefits to be gained:

Economies of scale
By consolidating purchasing, advertising, and administrative functions, a larger, merged company often can be more efficient than two smaller companies.

Diversification and Access to Assets
A merger may give a company better access to credit and new products and may help to even out peaks and valleys in cash flow and profits.

Tax Advantages
The Internal Revenue Code provides some incentive for a financially healthy corporation to acquire a troubled business. If the acquiring corporation meets several strict requirements, it may be able to use a limited part of the net operating loss carryover of the acquired business against the acquiring company's taxable income.

Personal Considerations
An owner looking to make assets more liquid, either out of retirement considerations or because of dissent within the company, may look to a sale or merger. Sometimes a business may be growing so quickly that its owners need the skills and resources of a competitor to keep up with the growth. In some instances an older, more stable company may be interested in sharing its experiences in exchange for the higher profit margins of a smaller, up-and-coming business.

WAYS OF MERGING WITH OR ACQUIRING ANOTHER BUSINESS
Generally, businesses are acquired or merged through one of three possible approaches. Which method might be the best in a particular situation depends on such considerations as tax laws, antitrust laws and corporate laws.

Asset Acquisition
In this method, a buyer will purchase some or all of the seller's assets in exchange for securities, cash or property of the acquiring corporation. If the seller is a corporation, the structure of the selling corporation will remain intact until the corporation is dissolved and the proceeds from the sale are distributed to shareholders. Minority shareholders will generally not have a say in the sale of the business and, as the buyer is not purchasing an entire business but rather parts of the whole, the buyer need not assume the liabilities of the seller. Asset acquisition is a way to acquire the physical property and accounts of another business without also acquiring its liabilities.

Acquiring the assets of a business can be more expensive than other types of acquisitions or mergers. There may be some difficulty in transferring contracts, leases and licenses from third parties, and titles to each asset sold must be separately transferred.

Stock Acquisition
Stock acquisitions are frequently called takeovers. A corporation's shareholders, not its management, own the company (although managers often are significant shareholders themselves). Thus, the shareholders are always free to sell their shares of stock to a purchaser. In the event that the management does not approve of the sale, the acquisition is called a hostile takeover.

Under this arrangement, the director's approval is not needed to purchase the corporation and the only documents that need to be transferred are stock certificates (rather than titles), contracts or any other form of consideration by third parties.

There are a number of problems with takeovers. For example, the new majority shareholders may be liable for debts incurred under the old leadership prior to the purchase. In addition, the Securities and Exchange Commission may require registration for the sale, and minority shareholders may be able to hold out and retain positions within the acquired corporation.

Statutory Merger

Under a statutory merger, two corporations agree to combine and form a single corporation under state law. This arrangement must be agreed to by at least two-thirds of the shareholders from each corporation and by both boards of directors. Only one company survives, and it takes over all operations, assets, and liabilities of both companies. The shareholders of the disappearing corporation trade in their shares of stock for an equity position in the surviving business. In a related type of merger, called a statutory consolidation, the two businesses both cease to exist and form an entirely new entity.

A statutory merger is beneficial because all title transfers are automatic if the arrangement follows state guidelines, and because all assets of both companies are retained in the merger.

On the other hand, this type of arrangement runs the risk of assuming all liabilities of the disappearing corporation, and the process can be costly and time-consuming due to the necessity of shareholder meetings and the technicalities of state laws.

CORPORATE BUY-SELL AGREEMENTS

As with any buy-sell agreement, price is the cornerstone of an agreement to buy or sell a corporation or its assets. Determining the worth of a company to be purchased or merged can be accomplished through a variety of means. The price of a company can be determined by the book value of the company, by an independent appraisal, by comparing the price/earnings ratio within the seller's industry, or by any of several other methods. The method of sale can significantly affect the overall cost to the buyer and seller due to tax considerations. Some acquisitions are considered tax-free, while others are taxable. An accountant should be able to help a company understand and take advantage of such tax-minimizing schemes as the pooling-of-interest accounting method.

Employee Considerations

An agreement should guarantee that key employees are retained and that contracts for employment are transferred to the buyer company. The buyer should review any collective bargaining agreements thoroughly, since they may be binding. Retirement plans will likely be transferred to the buyer company as well.

Seller Indemnification

It is common for an agreement to dismiss the buyer from any future unassumed liabilities from an asset purchase.

Securities Regulations

A buyer of a business who offers securities in exchange for the business, or for significant shares of the business, may be considered an "issuer" of the securities and therefore may be required to register with the Securities and Exchange Commission. The buyer may, however, be eligible for exemption under the law. Determining whether a business must register and which kind of registration it must undertake can affect the sellers' ability to resell the securities they receive as payment. There are a number of other considerations under both federal securities laws and state blue-sky laws to be aware of in mergers and acquisitions that involve the exchange of stocks. The advice of a competent attorney is highly recommended.

Buyer-Seller Representations

The buyer in a transaction in which the seller is being paid in stock will generally warrant that the stock is legal, authorized and fully paid. The seller in the same type of exchange will warrant that the stock is legal, and will further note the condition of the business in financial documents.

RESOURCES

Internal Revenue Service, Minnesota District Office, 708 Federal Building, 316 N Robert Street, St. Paul, MN 55101, (612) 644-7515.

Revenue Department—Minnesota, Minnesota Business Assistance Group, Mail Station 4453, St. Paul, MN 55146-4453, (612) 296-6181 or (800) 657-3777.

Secretary of State—Minnesota, 180 State Office Building, 100 Constitution Avenue, St. Paul, MN 55155-1299, (612) 296-2803.

Small Business Assistance Office—Minnesota, 500 Metro Square, 121 Seventh Place E, St. Paul, MN 55101-2146, (612) 296-3871 or (800) 657-3858. The organization publishes *A Guide to Starting a Business in Minnesota*, a great resource which is available free of charge.

PUBLICLY HELD CORPORATIONS LAW LEADING ATTORNEYS

The attorneys profiled in this section were nominated by their peers in a statewide survey conducted in 1993 in which several thousand Minnesota attorneys were asked to name the lawyer to whom they would send a friend or family member in need of legal assistance in the area of *Publicly Held Corporations Law*.

Because the survey resulted in a list of less than five percent of Minnesota's practicing attorneys, this should not be construed as a complete list. Nevertheless, it is an excellent source of highly qualified and reputable attorneys, who, if unable to assist can in most cases make quality referrals.

A list of all attorneys nominated in this category is found at the end of this section. For information on the survey methodology see page ix.

Please note that the shorter, two line attorney listings in this section are of attorneys who practice in this area but whose full biographical profile appears in another section of this book. A bullet "•" preceeding name indicates the attorney was nominated in this particular area of law. For information on the format of these profiles, consult the section "Using the *Business Guidebook*" found on page xiv. Note that the following abbreviations are used throughout these profiles:

The attorneys profiled below were recommended by their peers in a statewide survey.

App. - Appellate	ABA - American Bar Association
Cir. - Circuit	ATLA - American Trial Lawyers Association
Ct. - Court	HCBA - Hennepin County Bar Association
Dist. - District	MDLA - Minnesota Defense Lawyers Association
Hon. - Honorable	MSBA - Minnesota State Bar Association
JD - Law degree (Juris Doctor)	MTLA - Minnesota Trial Lawyers Association
LLB - Law degree	NBTA - National Board of Trial Advocacy
LLM - Master in Law degree	RCBA - Ramsey County Bar Association
Sup. - Supreme	

TIMOTHY M. BARNETT - Winthrop & Weinstine, P.A. - 3000 Dain Bosworth Plaza, 60 South Sixth Street - Minneapolis, MN 55402 - Phone: (612) 347-0700, Fax: (612) 347-0600 - *See complete biographical profile in Closely Held Business Law Chapter.*

WILLIAM M. BURNS

Hanft, Fride, O'Brien, Harries, Swelbar & Burns, P.A.
1000 First Bank Place
130 West Superior Street
Duluth, MN 55802

Phone: (218) 722-4766
Fax: (218) 720-4920

Admitted: 1968 Minnesota
Birthdate: 06/24/43

•**WILLIAM M. BURNS:** Mr. Burns handles private and public financing of business enterprises; multifamily and commercial real estate development; mergers and acquisitions; general business advice; management of litigation and other dispute resolution methodologies; and representation of medical vendors and specialists.
Education: JD 1968 cum laude, Order of the Coif, University of Michigan (Associate Editor, *University of Michigan Law Review*); AB 1965, University of Michigan.
Employment History: Currently, Hanft, Fride, O'Brien, Harries, Swelbar & Burns, P.A.; Associate 1968-70, Oppenheimer, Wolf & Donnelly; Research Assistant 1965-68, Professor Arthur Miller, University of Michigan Law School.
Representative Clients: First Bank, N.A.; Reach-All, Inc.; The Jamar Company; North Shore Bank of Commerce; Johnson-Wilson Constructors, Inc.
Professional Associations: ABA; MSBA.
Community Involvement: College of St. Scholastica, Inc. (past Chair, Board of Trustees); Wolf Ridge Environmental Learning Center (Chair, Board of Trustees); United Way of Greater Duluth (past President); Legal Aid Service of Northeastern Minnesota (past Chair).
Firm: Founded in 1899, Hanft, Fride, O'Brien, Harries, Swelbar & Burns, P.A., is a full service law firm engaged primarily in business and trial work. The firm's 17 attorneys serve clients throughout Minnesota, northern Wisconsin, and beyond. *See additional listings in Health Law and Commercial Real Estate Law Chapters.*

WILLIAM J. COSGRIFF - Doherty, Rumble & Butler Professional Association - 2800 Minnesota World Trade Center, 30 East Seventh Street - St. Paul, MN 55101-4999 - Phone: (612) 291-9333, Fax: (612) 291-9313 - *See complete biographical profile in Commercial Real Estate Law Chapter.*

KENNETH L. CUTLER

Dorsey & Whitney
Pillsbury Center South
220 South Sixth Street
Minneapolis, MN 55402-1498

Phone: (612) 340-2740
Fax: (612) 340-8738

Admitted: 1974 Minnesota; 1973 Georgia;
1974 US Dist. Ct. (MN);
1973 US Dist. Ct. (GA)
Birthdate: 08/08/47

•**KENNETH L. CUTLER:** Mr. Cutler practices in the areas of emerging growth companies, venture capital financing, and corporate finance. He represents private and public companies on general corporate matters, financing transactions, mergers and acquisitions, and SEC registered public offerings and also represents venture capital funds. He has been a partner in the Corporate/Finance Department since 1979.
Education: JD 1973 with honors, Order of the Coif, University of Texas (Articles Editor 1972-73, *Texas International Law Journal*; Legal Writing Instructor 1972-73); MBA 1970, University of Chicago; AB 1970, University of Chicago.
Employment History: Partner 1979-present, Associate 1974-78, Dorsey & Whitney; Associate 1973, Powell, Goldstein, Frazer & Murphy.
Representative Clients: Diametrics Medical, Inc.; CIMA LABS INC.; ShowCase Corp.; Fieldworks, Inc.; InoMet, Inc.; Pathfinder Venture Capital Funds; Medical Innovation Funds; Nutrition Medical, Inc.
Professional Associations: MSBA (Business Law Section (Subcommitte on Partnerships, Limited Partnerships and Limited Liability Companies 1992-present)).
Community Involvement: District 6 Hockey Assn. (President 1994-95); Edina Hockey Assn. (President 1993-94; Board member 1991-94); Ruffed Grouse Society of the Twin Cities (Board member 1985-90); University of Chicago Club of the Twin Cities (President 1980-87).
Firm: Dorsey & Whitney is the largest law firm in Minnesota and one of the largest firms in the United States with over 350 lawyers in 12 offices. The depth and breadth of the experience of its lawyers enables it to provide a broad range of services to meet the diverse legal needs of its client base, which includes Fortune 500 companies, public agencies, banks and other financial institutions, nonprofit organizations, individual investors, family owned businesses, and high-tech and low-tech, growth oriented companies. *See additional listings in Closely Held Business Law and Securities & Venture Finance Law Chapters.*

•**DEAN R. EDSTROM:** Mr. Edstrom has a general corporate and business practice with concentrations in securities offerings, mergers and acquisitions, and international transactions. He represents clients ranging from entrepreneurial ventures to major corporations and investment banking firms. He has represented corporate and limited partnership issuers and underwriters in numerous successful public and private offerings of equity and debt securities, venture capital financings, and exchange offers. Mr. Edstrom has extensive experience in mergers and acquisitions, representing both acquiring and acquired companies in transactions structured as mergers, asset purchases, and stock acquisitions, private and fully registered, taxable and tax-free. He has structured and successfully completed joint ventures, spin-offs, divestitures, and business restructurings. He works with litigators in planning and executing strategic corporate objectives in an adversarial context, including takeover defense, contract disputes, and workouts. Mr. Edstrom's international transactions have included securities offerings and financings, acquisitions, joint ventures, and a variety of contractual matters on behalf of both domestic and foreign clients.
Education: LLM 1966, LLB 1965 cum laude Order of the Coif, New York University (Root-Tilden Scholar; *New York University Law Review*); BA 1962 cum laude, Macalester College.
Employment History: 1967-1973, Davis Polk & Wardwell (New York, NY & Paris, France).
Representative Clients: Cray Research, Inc.; The Toro Company; Piper Jaffray Inc.; Dain Bosworth Incorporated; Upsher-Smith Laboratories, Inc.; Serving Software, Inc.
Professional Associations: ABA; MSBA (Chair 1982-83, International Business Law Section); HCBA; American Society of International Law; International Law Assn.
Community Involvement: Rotary International (District Governor 1983-84; various district and international committees 1979-present); University Children's Foundation (Director 1989-present; Vice Chair 1992-present); Minnesota International Health Volunteers (Director 1986-92); Macalester College (Alumni Assn. Director 1979-85; Alumni Fund Cochair 1985-86); Eden Prairie City Council 1979-82; Eden Prairie Foundation (Director 1981-86; President 1981-82).
Firm: Doherty, Rumble & Butler Professional Association is a 100 member general practice firm with offices in Minneapolis, St. Paul, Denver, and Washington, D.C. With a history dating from 1858, it has a tradition of innovation in major areas of the law and business transactions. *See additional listings in Closely Held Business Law and Securities & Venture Finance Law Chapters.*

DEAN R. EDSTROM

Doherty, Rumble & Butler
Professional Association
3500 Fifth Street Towers
150 South Fifth Street
Minneapolis, MN 55402-4235

Phone: (612) 340-5575
Fax: (612) 340-5584

Admitted: 1965 New York;
1973 Minnesota
Birthdate: 12/31/40

•**ROLF ENGH:** Mr. Engh practiced corporate law in mergers, acquisitions, venture capital, and international law until joining The Valspar Corporation in 1993.
Education: JD 1982 cum laude, William Mitchell; BA 1976, University of Minnesota.
Employment History: General Counsel and Vice President of International Sales 1993-present, The Valspar Corporation; Partner 1986-1993, Associate 1982-1986, Lindquist & Vennum.
Representative Clients: IBM; Carlisle Plastics, Inc.; Norwest Bank; Bolger Publications; VCI Capital; Musicland Stores Corp.; R.L. Cooperman; Spectro-Alloys; Anglo-Chinese Finance Corp.
Professional Associations: ABA; MSBA; HCBA.
Community Involvement: William Mitchell College of Law (Trustee); Westminster Church (Trustee); Minneapolis Club (House Committee); Committee on Foreign Affairs.
Firm: The Valspar Corporation is a Fortune 500 company listed on the New York Stock Exchange. Its principal business is manufacturing and selling of a broad variety of paints and coatings for consumer and industrial applications.

ROLF ENGH

Valspar Corporation Counsel
1101 Third Street South
Minneapolis, MN 55415

Phone: (612) 375-7705
Fax: (612) 375-7313

Admitted: 1982 Minnesota
Birthdate: 10/26/53

•**GREGORY G. FREITAG** - Fredrikson & Byron, P.A. - 1100 International Centre, 900 Second Avenue South - Minneapolis, MN 55402 - Phone: (612) 347-7153, Fax: (612) 347-7077 - *See complete biographical profile in Securities & Venture Finance Law Chapter.*

•**JOHN D. FRENCH** - Faegre & Benson - 2200 Norwest Center, 90 South Seventh Street - Minneapolis, MN 55402 - Phone: (612) 336-3000, Fax: (612) 336-3026 - *See complete biographical profile in Commercial Litigation Chapter.*

ROGER H. FROMMELT - Frommelt & Eide, Ltd. - 580 International Centre, 900 Second Avenue South - Minneapolis, MN 55402 - Phone: (612) 332-2200, Fax: (612) 342-2761 - *See complete biographical profile in Securities & Venture Finance Law Chapter.*

Chapter 29: Publicly Held Corporations Law

ROGER D. GORDON

Winthrop & Weinstine, P.A.
3000 Dain Bosworth Plaza
60 South Sixth Street
Minneapolis, MN 55402

Phone: (612) 347-0700
Fax: (612) 347-0600

Admitted: 1975 Minnesota
Birthdate: 10/17/50

•**ROGER D. GORDON:** Mr. Gordon practices banking and real estate law and acts as underwriter's counsel, bond counsel, issuer's counsel, trustee's counsel, and credit enhancer's counsel in connection with numerous (in excess of 200) tax-exempt and taxable bond financings aggregating in excess of $500 million. He handles other forms of debt financing, including securitized financing transactions, and advises as to state and federal securities laws as applied to debt financings.
Education: JD 1975 magna cum laude, University of Minnesota; BA 1972, University of Minnesota (Phi Beta Kappa).
Employment History: Shareholder 1979-present, Winthrop & Weinstine, P.A.; Associate 1975-79, Oppenheimer, Wolff & Donnelly.
Representative Clients: American National Bank and Trust Company; Norwest Bank; Juran & Moody, Inc.; Norwest Investment Services, Inc.; John G. Kinnard & Company; Park Investment, Inc.; TCB, Inc.; Piper Jaffray; Benchmark Computer Systems, Inc.
Professional Associations: ABA; RCBA; MSBA; National Assn. of Bond Lawyers; Minnesota Institute of Public Finance.
Community Involvement: Evans Scholars Foundation (Trustee); Western Golf Assn. (Executive Committee member and officer); Minnesota Golf Assn. (Executive Committee member and officer).
Firm: Winthrop & Weinstine's 30-person corporate/banking/finance department assists banking and underwriting clients in creatively structuring, documenting, and closing various forms of financing transactions. These include conventional bank financings such as lines of credit, term loans, equipment loans, real estate loans, construction loans, and bank stock loans; tax-exempt financings including revenue bonds for housing (including Section 8 and low-income tax credit projects), manufacturing, hospital, nursing home, and other health care projects, and revenue bonds for 50l(c)(3) organizations; taxable bonds for various types of projects; and securitized financing transactions such as receivables and limited partner investor notes. The firm provides advice with respect to municipal, securities, and tax laws applicable to the transaction. *See additional listings in Banking Law and Securities & Venture Finance Law Chapters.*

LLOYD W. GROOMS - Winthrop & Weinstine, P.A. - 3200 Minnesota World Trade Center, 30 East Seventh Street - St. Paul, MN 55101 - Phone: (612) 290-8529, Fax: (612) 292-9347 - *See complete biographical profile in Environmental Law Chapter.*

WILLIAM L. GUY III - Gunhus, Grinnell, Klinger, Swenson & Guy, Ltd. - 512 Center Avenue, P.O. Box 1077 - Moorhead, MN 56561-1077 - Phone: (218) 236-6462, Fax: (218) 236-9873 - *See complete biographical profile in Probate, Estate Planning & Trusts Law Chapter.*

•**LEE W. HANSON** - Hall, Byers, Hanson, Steil & Weinberger, P.A. - 1010 West St. Germain, Suite 600 - St. Cloud, MN 56301 - Phone: (612) 252-4414, Fax: (612) 252-4482 - *See complete biographical profile in Closely Held Business Law Chapter.*

•**NICK HAY** - Moss & Barnett, A Professional Association - 4800 Norwest Center, 90 South Seventh Street - Minneapolis, MN 55402-4129 - Phone: (612) 347-0443, Fax: (612) 339-6686 - *See complete biographical profile in Business Tax Law Chapter.*

•**TIMOTHY M. HEANEY** - Fredrikson & Byron, P.A. - 1100 International Centre, 900 Second Avenue South - Minneapolis, MN 55402 - Phone: (612) 347-7019, Fax: (612) 347-7077 - *See complete biographical profile in Securities & Venture Finance Law Chapter.*

ELLIOT S. KAPLAN - Robins, Kaplan, Miller & Ciresi - 2800 LaSalle Plaza, 800 LaSalle Avenue - Minneapolis, MN 55402 - Phone: (612) 349-8500, Fax: (612) 339-4181 - *See complete biographical profile in Commercial Litigation Chapter.*

DOUGLAS A. KELLEY - Douglas A. Kelley, P.A. - 701 Fourth Avenue South, Suite 500 - Minneapolis, MN 55415 - Phone: (612) 337-9594, Fax: (612) 371-0574 - *See complete biographical profile in Criminal Law Chapter.*

JOHN J. KILLEN - Johnson, Killen, Thibodeau & Seiler, P.A. - 811 Norwest Center, 230 West Superior Street - Duluth, MN 55802 - Phone: (218) 722-6331, Fax: (218) 722-3031 - *See complete biographical profile in Closely Held Business Law Chapter.*

•**THOMAS R. KING** - Fredrikson & Byron, P.A. - 1100 International Centre, 900 Second Avenue South - Minneapolis, MN 55402 - Phone: (612) 347-7059, Fax: (612) 347-7077 - *See complete biographical profile in Securities & Venture Finance Law Chapter.*

FAYE KNOWLES - Fredrikson & Byron, P.A. - 1100 International Centre, 900 Second Avenue South - Minneapolis, MN 55402 - Phone: (612) 347-7054, Fax: (612) 347-7077 - *See complete biographical profile in Bankruptcy & Workout Law Chapter.*

•**HART KULLER** - Winthrop & Weinstine, P.A. - 3200 Minnesota World Trade Center, 30 East Seventh Street - St. Paul, MN 55101 - Phone: (612) 290-8400, Fax: (612) 292-9347 - *See complete biographical profile in Bankruptcy & Workout Law Chapter.*

•**WILLIAM S. LAPP:** Mr. Lapp is the key person at Lapp, Laurie, Libra, Abramson & Thomson in the corporate, securities, business law, and taxation areas. He helps start-up businesses, assists companies in obtaining public and private financing, and guides companies and their management through public offerings and private placements. He works in securities arbitration as well. Along with Mr. Lapp's substantial experience in negotiating complex business transactions, he also advises individuals and businesses on the many legal issues they face. Mr. Lapp's background, his tremendous negotiating skills, his legal ability, and his desire to get the job done make him a valuable resource for businesses and individuals. His lectures include "Advising Clients on Investing in Tax Shelters," Advanced Legal Education, Hamline University School of Law, 1982 and "Tax Flavored Investments," Annual Tax Seminar, 1979.
Education: JD 1967, University of Minnesota; BA 1964 cum laude, University of Minnesota.
Employment History: Founder & Shareholder, 1970-present, Lapp, Laurie, Libra, Abramson & Thomson, Chartered.
Professional Associations: HCBA (Chair 1983-85, Executive Committee of the Securities Section); MSBA; ABA; member of the National Arbitration Committee of the National Association of Securities Dealers, Inc. (NASD) which committee has the authority to establish appropriate rules regulations to govern the conduct of all arbitration matters before the NASD; MN Technology Board of Directors (Advisory Board for the Minneapolis/St. Paul area); Director of Public Investors Arbitration Bar Association.
Firm: Since the firm's inception in 1970, it has provided legal services of a business nature for many individuals and small-to-medium size public and nonpublic companies. In addition to Mr. Lapp, Mr. Gregory Pusch practices in the business and corporate area. The firm has substantial experience in business planning, formation of corporations, partnerships and joint ventures, purchase and sale of businesses, financial negotiations, shareholder agreements, buy-sell agreements, corporate covenants, employment agreements, confidentiality agreements, noncompetition agreements, acquisitions, licensing agreements, franchise agreements, distribution agreements, and other contracts. The law firm also has a very strong commercial litigation department. The firm also does work in real estate law, leasing, tax planning and representation, financial reorganization and bankruptcy, retirement planning, and estate planning.

WILLIAM S. LAPP

Lapp, Laurie, Libra, Abramson
& Thomson, Chartered
One Financial Plaza
Suite 1800
120 South Sixth Street
Minneapolis, MN 55402

Phone: (612) 338-5815
Fax: (612) 338-6651

Admitted: 1968 Minnesota;
1968 US Dist. Ct. (MN);
1987 US Tax Ct.;
1982 US Sup. Ct.
Birthdate: 04/20/42

•**DEXTER A. LARSEN** - Fryberger, Buchanan, Smith & Frederick, P.A. - 302 West Superior Street, Suite 700 - Duluth, MN 55802 - Phone: (218) 722-0861, Fax: (218) 722-9568 - *See complete biographical profile in Intellectual Property Law Chapter.*

•**BRIAN F. LEONARD** - O'Neill, Burke, O'Neill, Leonard & O'Brien, Ltd. - 100 South Fifth Street, Suite 1200 - Minneapolis, MN 55402 - Phone: (612) 332-1030, Fax: (612) 332-2740 - *See complete biographical profile in Bankruptcy & Workout Law Chapter.*

DAVID J. LUBBEN - Dorsey & Whitney - Pillsbury Center South, 220 South Sixth Street - Minneapolis, MN 55402-1498 - Phone: (612) 340-2904, Fax: (612) 340-8738 - *See complete biographical profile in Securities & Venture Finance Law Chapter.*

ERIC O. MADSON - Winthrop & Weinstine, P.A. - 3000 Dain Bosworth Plaza, 60 South Sixth Street - Minneapolis, MN 55402 - Phone: (612) 347-0700, Fax: (612) 347-0600 - *See complete biographical profile in Securities & Venture Finance Law Chapter.*

•**DAVID B. MILLER** - Faegre & Benson - 2200 Norwest Center, 90 South Seventh Street - Minneapolis, MN 55402 - Phone: (612) 336-3000, Fax: (612) 336-3026 - *See complete biographical profile in Securities & Venture Finance Law Chapter.*

Chapter 29: Publicly Held Corporations Law

LEE R. MITAU

Dorsey & Whitney
Pillsbury Center South
220 South Sixth Street
Minneapolis, MN 55402-1498

Phone: (612) 340-2780
Fax: (612) 340-8738

Admitted: 1972 Minnesota
Birthdate: 10/17/48

•**LEE R. MITAU:** Mr. Mitau specializes in mergers and acquisitions and corporate finance. He also provides general corporate and securities law advice to large and small public and private companies. Additionally, he is a board member of Graco, Inc. and corporate secretary of H.B. Fuller Company. He has been a partner in Dorsey & Whitney's Corporate Department since 1983 and chair of the department since 1989.
Education: JD 1972 magna cum laude, Order of the Coif, University of Minnesota (Note and Comment Editor 1972, *Minnesota Law Review*); AB 1969 cum laude, Dartmouth College.
Employment History: Partner 1983-present, Dorsey & Whitney; Partner 1979-83, Oppenheimer, Wolff and Donnelly; Associate 1973-79, Cleary, Gottlieb, Steen & Hamilton (New York); Judicial Clerk 1972-73, Hon. George E. MacKinnon, US Court of Appeals, Washington, D.C. Circuit.
Professional Associations: ABA; MSBA (Business Law Section (Chair 1993-94); Securities Law Committee (Chair 1982-87)); Corporate Counsel Assn. of Minnesota (Board member); American Society of Corporate Secretaries; National Assn. of Corporate Directors.
Community Involvement: Boundary Waters Wilderness Foundation (Board member 1991-93).
Firm: Dorsey & Whitney is the largest law firm in Minnesota and one of the largest firms in the United States with over 350 lawyers in 12 offices. The depth and breadth of the experience of its lawyers enables it to provide a broad range of services to meet the diverse legal needs of its client base, which includes Fortune 500 companies, public agencies, banks and other financial institutions, nonprofit organizations, individual investors, family owned businesses, and high-tech and low-tech, growth oriented companies. *See additional listing in Securities & Venture Finance Law Chapter.*

•**THOMAS F. NELSON** - Popham, Haik, Schnobrich & Kaufman, Ltd. - 222 South Ninth Street, Suite 3300 - Minneapolis, MN 55402 - Phone: (612) 333-4800, Fax: (612) 334-8888 - *See complete biographical profile in Commercial Litigation Chapter.*

JOHN N. NYS

Johnson, Killen, Thibodeau & Seiler, P.A.
811 Norwest Center
230 West Superior Street
Duluth, MN 55802

Phone: (218) 722-6331
Fax: (218) 722-3031

Admitted: 1973 Minnesota; 1984 Wisconsin
Birthdate: 05/03/48

•**JOHN N. NYS:** Mr. Nys practices general business law, representing national businesses on a regional basis and smaller businesses as general counsel. This includes transactional law, primarily in connection with financing, venture capital, commercial development, and the purchase and sale of businesses; preventative law, primarily advising businesses on all types of legal problems such as environmental, contract, securities law, corporate governance, officers and directors liability, debtor-creditor, and bankruptcy; and litigation, primarily in these same areas.
Education: JD 1973, Stanford University (Managing Editor 1972-73, *Stanford Journal of International Studies*); BA 1970 magna cum laude, Dartmouth College (Phi Beta Kappa).
Employment History: Associate/Partner 1973-present, Johnson, Killen, Thibodeau & Seiler, P.A.; Lieutenant 1970-76, USNR JAG.
Representative Clients: Federal Deposit Insurance Corp.; First Bank; Franklin Foods; Industrial Rubber Applicators; Louisiana Pacific; The Minnesota Companies; Northern Electric Cooperative Assn.; The Rajala Companies; Rhude & Fryberger.
Professional Associations: ABA; MSBA; 11th District Bar Assn. (President 1989-90); MSBA (Secretary 1993-94); Lawyers Professional Responsibility Board (1981-87).
Community Involvement: Dartmouth Alumni Assn. of the Northwest (Director); Morgan Park Community Club (Director-President); Duluth Regional Care Center (Director-President); Duluth Bar Library Assn. (Director); Duluth Volunteer Attorney Program (volunteer attorney & Director); Boy Scouts of America (Cubmaster, Pack 13, Lake Superior Council).
Firm: Founded in 1888, Johnson, Killen, Thibodeau & Seiler, P.A., is the oldest firm in northern Minnesota. Today the firm's 18 lawyers provide a wide range of services for consumers, businesses, and companies in commercial, toxic tort, environmental, and insurance litigation; commercial and residential real estate; probate, estate planning, and trusts; employment law; closely held business law; and Workers' Compensation. *See additional listing in Commercial Litigation.*

•**JAMES E. O'BRIEN:** Mr. O'Brien was nominated for the *Guidebook* in three categories: corporate and financial law, closely held business law, and securities law. He has over 25 years of experience in business law, including extensive experience in business litigation. He represents many businesses in various industries. He has dealt in depth with business formation, financing, taxation, labor and employment relations, securities registration, compliance and proxy regulation, mergers, acquisitions, family transfers, and general operational matters. Mr. O'Brien is a counselor to management and directors, often as a member of a team including management, accounting personnel, and other advisors. He has taught various business law courses at the University of Minnesota and has lectured on corporate, tax, and securities law involving the purchase and sale of a business. Mr. O'Brien is an honor graduate of the Russian language program of the Presidio of Monterey and was a Russian linguist in the US Air Force Security Service.
Education: JD 1965 cum laude, Order of the Coif, University of Minnesota (member 1963-65, Senior Editor 1965, *Minnesota Law Review*); BA 1962, University of Alaska.
Employment History: Chair and Chief Executive Officer, Moss & Barnett. He has been employed there since 1965 and has held all officer positions.
Professional Associations: ABA; MSBA; HCBA.
Community Involvement: Opportunity Workshop, Inc. (Director and former Chair); Fund for the Legal Aid Society (Director); Minneapolis Kiwanis Club; Minneapolis Kiwanis Foundation (former Trustee and President).
Firm: Moss & Barnett and its predecessor firms have provided legal service in Minneapolis and the surrounding multistate area continuously since before 1900. It is a large firm providing legal services to individuals and all types of business entities in personal, business, governmental, and all types of dispute resolution matters. Many of its attorneys have been nominated for inclusion in this publication. *See additional listings in Closely Held Business Law and Securities & Venture Finance Law Chapters.*

JAMES E. O'BRIEN

Moss & Barnett,
A Professional Association
4800 Norwest Center
90 South Seventh Street
Minneapolis, MN 55402

Phone: (612) 347-0273
Fax: (612) 339-6686

Admitted: 1965 Minnesota;
US Dist. Ct. (MN);
US Tax Ct.
Birthdate: 06/10/37

•**DAVID T. PETERSON** - Blethen Gage & Krause - 127 South Second Street, P.O. Box 3049 - Mankato, MN 56002-3049 - Phone: (507) 345-1166, Fax: (507) 345-8003 - *See complete biographical profile in Closely Held Business Law Chapter.*

•**ROBERT K. RANUM** - Fredrikson & Byron, P.A. - 1100 International Centre, 900 Second Avenue South - Minneapolis, MN 55402 - Phone: (612) 347-7067, Fax: (612) 347-7077 - *See complete biographical profile in Securities & Venture Finance Law Chapter.*

•**THOMAS E. ROHRICHT:** In the summer of 1963, Mr. Rohricht joined Doherty, Rumble & Butler as an associate lawyer. After practicing in various areas of law for his first few years, he began to concentrate more and more in the area of general business law, which is now his principal area of practice. The focus of his practice is on commercial and banking transactions; general business counseling; formation of new business entities and restructuring of existing business entities; joint ventures, mergers, acquisitions, or other consolidations of businesses, cooperatives, and associations. Mr. Rohricht has served as consultant to and as a board member of life insurance companies, banks, and small business corporations. He currently serves as a member of the Board of Trustees of The Minnesota Mutual Life Insurance Company and as a member of its Corporate Governance and Public Affairs and Personnel and Compensation Committees. In addition, Mr. Rohricht is a former lecturer for Minnesota Continuing Legal Education seminars on the Uniform Commercial Code.
Education: JD 1963, Duke University (Note Editor 1963, *Duke Law Journal*; Phi Delta Phi) ; BA 1957, University of Minnesota.
Employment History: Partner/Shareholder 1968-present, Associate 1963-68, Doherty, Rumble & Butler, P.A.; Lieutenant 1957-60, US Navy (Active Duty).
Professional Associations: RCBA; MSBA (Business Section (Chair 1983-84, Corporate Council; past Chair, Uniform Commercial Code Committee)); ABA (Business Section).
Community Involvement: St. Anthony Park Assn. (past Treasurer, Secretary, & President); Indianhead Council of the Boy Scouts of America (past member of several committees; past Chair of Advancement Committee); current member of Board of Trustees and Treasurer of his church.
Firm: Doherty, Rumble & Butler's corporate and finance practice provides a wide variety of legal services to large and small banks, other financial institutions, corporations, and individuals in the upper Midwest and throughout the United States. Their corporate clients turn to DRB with needs ranging from lending, leasing and project financing, mergers and acquisitions, branching, compliance with Truth in Lending, home equity and ARM loans, consumer leasing, equal credit opportunity, usury and interest rates, plain language contracts, transactions with affiliates, officers, and directors, and federal and state laws, and services under the Uniform Commercial Code. *See additional listings in Closely Held Business Law and Banking Law Chapters.*

THOMAS E. ROHRICHT

Doherty, Rumble & Butler
Professional Association
2800 Minnesota World Trade Center
30 East Seventh Street
St. Paul, MN 55101-4999

Phone: (612) 291-9333
Fax: (612) 291-9313

Admitted: 1963 Minnesota;
1964 US Dist. Ct. (MN);
1969 US Ct. App. (8th Cir.);
1970 US Sup. Ct.
Birthdate: 11/13/34

THOMAS P. SANDERS

Leonard, Street and Deinard
Professional Association
150 South Fifth Street
Suite 2300
Minneapolis, MN 55402

Phone: (612) 335-1614
Fax: (612) 335-1657

Admitted: 1984 Minnesota
Birthdate: 02/14/57

•**THOMAS P. SANDERS:** Mr. Sanders has a general corporate practice, representing large, medium, and small sized companies on both a local and national basis. He has substantial experience in a broad range of corporate legal matters, including mergers and acquisitions, shareholder relationships and disputes, private debt and equity financings, formation and governance issues, and commercial transactions, with a special emphasis on mergers and acquisitions and representing family businesses and other closely held concerns.
Education: JD 1984 cum laude, Order of the Coif, Northwestern University; BA 1980 with distinction, George Washington University (Phi Beta Kappa).
Employment History: Partner 1992-present, Associate 1984-91, Leonard, Street and Deinard.
Representative Clients: IDS Financial Services, Inc.; PC Express, Inc.; Mary Tjosvold and affiliated businesses.
Professional Associations: ABA; MSBA; HCBA.
Community Involvement: Minneapolis Federation for Jewish Service (Board of Directors and Treasurer); Jewish Community Relations Council of Minnesota and the Dakotas (Board of Directors).
Firm: Leonard, Street and Deinard is a full service commercial law firm of approximately 125 attorneys. About half of the firm's practice concerns commercial, securities, and other business oriented litigation, and about half of the practice concerns nonlitigated business matters, including general corporate matters, public and private finance, real estate, mergers and acquisitions, banking, trade regulation, distribution, intellectual property, health, tax, and estate planning. The firm has a long history of representing family held and entrepreneurial businesses (many of which have grown into large, multinational concerns) as well as publicly held and institutional businesses. The firm prides itself on its reputation for excellence and efficiency, and on the long term relationships it consistently builds with clients. *See additional listing in Closely Held Business Law Chapter.*

GROVER C. SAYRE III

O'Neill, Burke, O'Neill,
Leonard & O'Brien, Ltd.
100 South Fifth Street
Suite 1200
Minneapolis, MN 55402

Phone: (612) 332-1030
Fax: (612) 332-2740

Admitted: 1982 Minnesota
Birthdate: 09/28/55

•**GROVER C. SAYRE III:** Mr. Sayre devotes 40 percent of his practice to lenders and borrowers in the negotiation and preparation of documentation for commercial loan transactions involving secured and unsecured term loans, lines of credit, construction loans, participation agreements, intercreditor agreements, letters of credit, and real estate mortgages; the negotiation and preparation of loan workout agreements for troubled loans and industrial revenue bond transactions; and the handling of foreclosures, bankruptcies, receiverships, and lender-related litigation. Twenty percent of his practice is devoted to the negotiation and preparation of documentation required for industrial revenue bond financing including trust indentures, loan agreements, offering memorandums, and credit enhancement agreements, and another 20 percent is devoted to representing owners, buyers, sellers, and lessors of commercial real estate and negotiating environmental remediation matters with the Minnesota Pollution Control Agency and the EPA. Mr. Sayre also represents owners of real estate with regard to property tax appeals and abatements, including prosecution of property tax appeals and devotes some of his time to general civil litigation involving commercial real estate, debtor-creditor disputes, and general business matters, including inverse condemnation litigation.
Education: JD 1982, William Mitchell; BS 1978, University of Minnesota.
Employment History: Partner/Shareholder, O'Neill, Burke, O'Neill, Leonard & O'Brien; Division Counsel 1980-90, ITT Commercial Finance Corp.
Representative Clients: National City Bank; Firstar Bank; ITT Commercial Finance Corp.; ITT Capital Finance; Lutheran Brotherhood; Towle Realty; College Properties, Inc.; Roseville Properties; Resolution Trust Corp.; The Travelers Insurance Company; Equitable Real Estate Investment; Mid-America Banks; University of Minnesota.
Professional Associations: ABA; MSBA; HCBA; RCBA.
Community Involvement: Boy Scouts of America (volunteer; fund-raiser); Children's Hospital of St. Paul (fund-raiser).
Firm: Founded in 1965, O'Neill, Burke has been serving clients around the country and in Minnesota, handling all areas of civil and business transactions and litigation. Currently, the firm has 23 lawyers.
See additional listings in Bankruptcy & Workout Law and Commercial Real Estate Law Chapters.

•**PAUL J. SCHEERER** - Dorsey & Whitney - Pillsbury Center South, 220 South Sixth Street - Minneapolis, MN 55402-1498 - Phone: (612) 340-2883, Fax: (612) 340-2643 - *See complete biographical profile in Bankruptcy & Workout Law Chapter.*

•**STEVEN J. SEILER** - Johnson, Killen, Thibodeau & Seiler, P.A. - 811 Norwest Center, 230 West Superior Street - Duluth, MN 55802 - Phone: (218) 722-6331, Fax: (218) 722-3031 - *See complete biographical profile in Health Law Chapter.*

•**W. SMITH (KRIS) SHARPE, JR.** - Faegre & Benson - 2200 Norwest Center, 90 South Seventh Street - Minneapolis, MN 55402 - Phone: (612) 336-3000, Fax: (612) 336-3026 - *See complete biographical profile in Securities & Venture Finance Law Chapter.*

•**NICK SMITH:** Chairman of Fryberger, Buchanan, Smith & Frederick, P.A., Mr. Smith has over 30 years experience in representing small and medium-sized businesses, assisting clients with their financing needs ranging from debt of all kinds to private placements of equity and public offerings, and has earned recognition for his positive influence on the business community. He was named 1990 Business Person of the Year by the School of Business and Economics at the University of Minnesota-Duluth. He also received the 1992 Minnesota Financial Services Advocate Award, presented by the United States Small Business Administration. He is the founder and CEO of Northeast Ventures Corporation, a $10 million venture development effort for northeastern Minnesota. Mr. Smith is a graduate of a certified training program in general mediation.
Education: JD cum laude and BSL 1960, University of Minnesota (1958-1960, *Minnesota Law Review*); Amherst College.
Professional Associations: 11th District Bar Assn.; MSBA; ABA; State Bar of Wisconsin.
Community Involvement: Northeast Ventures Corporation (President & CEO); Northeast Venture Development Fund, Inc. (Chair); Northeast Entrepreneur Fund, Inc. (Chair); North Shore Bank of Commerce (Board of Directors), a $100 million independent bank in Duluth; Duluth Improvement Trust (Board of Trustees); Community Reinvestment Trust (Board of Trustees); Society of International Business Fellows, Upper Midwest (Board of Directors); Northeastern Minnesota Development Assn. (Board of Directors); Advantage Minnesota (Board of Directors); National Venture Consortium (Cochair); Minnesota Technology (Equity Fund Board); Minnesota Technology Regional Office (Regional Operating Board); Natural Resources Research Institute (Advisory Board); Arrowhead Growth Alliance; World Trade Office Advisory Committee on Central Europe and the former Soviet Union; Lake Superior Center (founding Chair), an international freshwater education center focusing on the world's largest lakes.
Firm: Please see firm profile in Appendix C. *See additional listing in Nonprofit Corporations Law Chapter.*

NICK SMITH

Fryberger, Buchanan, Smith & Frederick, P.A.
302 West Superior Street
Suite 700
Duluth, MN 55802

Phone: (218) 722-0861
Fax: (218) 722-9568

Admitted: 1960 Minnesota;
1986 Wisconsin;
1986 US Dist. Ct. (MN)
Birthdate: 09/27/36

ROGER V. STAGEBERG - Lommen, Nelson, Cole & Stageberg, P.A. - 1800 IDS Center, 80 South Eighth Street - Minneapolis, MN 55402 - Phone: (612) 339-8131, Fax: (612) 339-8064 - *See complete biographical profile in Closely Held Business Law Chapter.*

JOHN H. STOUT - Fredrikson & Byron, P.A. - 1100 International Centre, 900 Second Avenue South - Minneapolis, MN 55402 - Phone: (612) 347-7012, Fax: (612) 347-7077 - *See complete biographical profile in Arts, Entertainment, Advertising & Media Law Chapter.*

JON E. STRINDEN - Gunhus, Grinnell, Klinger, Swenson & Guy, Ltd. - 512 Center Avenue, P.O. Box 1077 - Moorhead, MN 56561-1977 - Phone: (218) 236-6462, Fax: (218) 236-9873 - *See complete biographical profile in Closely Held Business Law Chapter.*

•**STEPHEN TORVIK:** Mr. Torvik, a partner in the law firm of Nelson Oyen Torvik, engages in corporate, business, and personal injury litigation. He also practices in the areas of estate planning and employment law.
Education: JD 1967, University of Minnesota; BA 1964, Augustana College.
Representative Clients: Minnwest Bank Montevideo; Minnesota Valley Cooperative Light & Power Assn.; Co-op Credit Union; Metropolitan Federal Bank Montevideo; Prudential Insurance Company; Prairie State Bank of Milan and Appleton; Klein National Bank of Madison; Cargill, Inc.; Farmers Union Oil Company; Farmers & Merchants State Bank of Clarkfield; Lac qui Parle-Yellow Bank Watershed District; State Bank of Bellingham; Cliff Viessman, Inc.; Chandler Industries; Tri-Line Farmers Cooperative.
Professional Associations: 12th District Bar Assn. (Chair, Fee Arbitration Board); MSBA; ABA; MTLA; ATLA; American Arbitration Assn. (Arbitrator).
Community Involvement: Chippewa County (Assistant Attorney); Montevideo Housing & Redevelopment Authority (Commissioner); 6-W Community Corrections (Board member).
Firm: Founded in 1941 as Nelson & Oyen, the firm of Nelson Oyen Torvik has established a strong reputation for providing high quality legal services to clients in west central Minnesota. Members of the firm have served as Chippewa County Attorney since 1977. The firm's four partners and two associate attorneys, with their own areas of expertise, provide a full complement of litigation, corporate, business, and consumer law services. The firm has offices in Montevideo and Clarkfield, MN. *See additional listings in Commercial Real Estate Law and Commercial Litigation Chapters.*

STEPHEN TORVIK

Nelson Oyen Torvik
221 North First Street
P.O. Box 656
Montevideo, MN 56265

Phone: (612) 269-6461
Fax: (612) 269-8024

Admitted: 1967 Minnesota
Birthdate: 12/06/42

PAUL VAN VALKENBURG

Moss & Barnett,
A Professional Association
4800 Norwest Center
90 South Seventh Street
Minneapolis, MN 55402

Phone: (612) 347-0300
Fax: (612) 339-6686

Admitted: 1959 Minnesota;
1959 US Dist. Ct. (MN);
1963 US Ct. App. (8th Cir.)
Birthdate: 12/19/33

•**PAUL VAN VALKENBURG:** Mr. Van Valkenburg, a business lawyer, concentrates in corporate and finance law, computer law, distribution law, and intellectual property. He is experienced in organizing, financing, and operating business organizations such as profit, nonprofit, and tax-exempt corporations; partnerships; limited partnerships; registered limited liability partnerships; limited liability companies; and cooperatives. In representing businesses, Mr. Van Valkenburg has extensive experience in executive compensation including deferred compensation, rabbi trusts, and noncompete covenants which he has drafted and enforced. He also handles the acquisition of organizations through merger, exchange, purchase of assets, and purchase of stock. His representation of franchisers, including the issues of antitrust and intellectual property, spans the entire 35 years of his practice. Mr. Van Valkenburg handles the creation of dealerships, distributorships, and sales representative systems and drafts appropriate agreements. Since the 1970s, he practices extensively in the area of computer law, primarily representing end-users in connection with the acquisition of computer hardware and/or software, and handles copyright and trade secret matters. He also writes on business, computer law, and franchise topics. He is listed in the *Directory of Intellectual Property Attorneys*, *Who's Who in America*, and *Who's Who in American Law* and has received several awards from the Minnesota State Bar Association.
Education: JD 1959, University of Wisconsin; BA 1955, Harvard College.
Employment History: Moss & Barnett, A Professional Association, and its predecessors for 35 years: past Director, past Chair of the Business Law Department, past Chair of the Personnel Committee, past Chair of the Ethics Committee.
Representative Clients: Wholesale distributor to over 1,000 franchisees, with sales over $130 million; manufacturers located in the US with operations in Australia, Canada, France, Hong Kong, and South Africa; various retailers, professionals, and providers of services.
Professional Associations: ABA; American Arbitration Assn.; Computer Law Assn.; Corporate Counsel Assn. of Minnesota; HCBA; Lawyers Concerned for Lawyers; Minnesota Intellectual Property Law Assn.; MSBA (Antitrust, Business, Computer, and Tax Law Sections); National Assn. of Corporate Directors.
Firm: See firm profile in Appendix C. *See additional listings in Franchise & Dealership Law and Intellectual Property Law Chapters.*

NEIL A. WEIKART

Fredrikson & Byron, P.A.
1100 International Centre
900 Second Avenue South
Minneapolis, MN 55402

Phone: (612) 347-7025
Fax: (612) 347-7077

Admitted: 1975 Minnesota
Birthdate: 05/17/50

•**NEIL A. WEIKART:** Mr. Weikart handles corporate and commercial law, mergers and acquisitions, corporate finance, and tax and business planning for public and closely held corporations. Neil Weikart's special emphasis and expertise is in representing clients in the health care industry. He has previously acted as an adjunct professor at the University of Minnesota where he taught income taxation for four years. Mr. Weikart is coauthor of the business organization chapters in *Minnesota Methods of Practice*, a reference work published by West Publishing.
Education: JD 1975 magna cum laude, Indiana University; BA 1972, Indiana University.
Representative Clients: Snyder's Drug Stores, Inc.; Thrifty White Stores, Inc.; Columbia Park Medical Group, P.A.; Park Dental Health Centers.
Professional Associations: HCBA; MSBA (Chair 1991-92, Legislative Coordinator 1984-89, Executive Counsel member 1984-85, and Corporation Committee Chair 1984-85, Business Law Section).
Community Involvement: Board of Directors, Edina A Better Chance Foundation.
Firm: Mr. Weikart serves on Fredrikson & Byron's board of directors, is the chair of the firm's Hiring and Diversity Committees, and is a member of the firm's Corporate & Commercial Law Group and its Health Law Group. The Corporate & Commercial Law Group focuses on working with a wide spectrum of clients, from start-up enterprises to large family owned businesses and Fortune 500 companies. The group concentrates on business financings, acquisitions, and divestitures of all sizes and types, from individuals acquiring a business for the first time to complex transactions initiated by the M & A departments of Fortune 500 companies. The Health Law Group focuses on representing the business and personal interests of health care providers and health related businesses. This representation includes structuring businesses, handling transactions, dealing with regulatory and governmental concerns, and advising clients on other problems specific to the health care industry. The group's experience encompasses tax and business planning, provider networks, joint ventures, third party reimbursement (including Medicare and Medicaid), health care contracting, and management of interrelationships among providers and between providers and patients. *See additional listings in Closely Held Business Law and Health Law Chapters.*

•**G. MARC WHITEHEAD:** Mr. Whitehead is Chair Emeritus of Popham, Haik, Schnobrich & Kaufman, Ltd. He is a civil trial practitioner primarily in toxic tort, product liability, and environmental law in the US and has an active international practice in product liability and environmental law. He is a frequent lecturer and author on trial tactics, preventive law, and international liability topics. His articles include "'Daubert' Will Allow More Expert Testimony, Complicate Jurors' Job, Prejudice Defense," Bureau of National Affairs, *Product Safety & Liability Reporter*, Summer/Fall 1993, and "A Comparison of Product Liability Law in the United States and The European Community," Bureau of National Affairs, *Product Safety & Liability Reporter*, Feb. 1991. In June 1992, Mr. Whitehead cochaired a national *Symposium on the Future of the Civil Jury System in the United States* with The Brookings Institute.
Education: JD 1964, Yale University; BA 1961, Princeton University.
Employment History: Chair and CEO 1986-94, Popham, Haik, Schnobrich & Kaufman, Ltd.; Chair and Founding Director 1993-present, Global Liability Management.
Representative Clients: Honeywell, Inc.; Motorola; SCM Corp.; Hanson Industries; The Glidden Company; W.R. Grace.
Professional Associations: ABA (past Chair, Environmental Litigation Committee; past Council member, past Division Director, Litigation Section); American Bar Foundation (Fellow); American Board of Trial Advocates; International Assn. of Defense Counsel; International Bar Assn. (Environmental Law Committee); MDLA; MSBA (founding member and past Chair, Civil Litigation Section); *European Environmental Law Review* (Editorial Advisory Board); *European Business Law Journal* (Board of Editors); Bureau of National Affairs' *Product Liability Journal* (Board of Editors); *Inside Litigation* (Board of Editors).
Community Involvement: Fund for Legal Aid Society (1987-present, Board and Executive Committee member).
Firm: Popham, Haik, Schnobrich & Kaufman, Ltd., is a firm of more than 230 attorneys with offices in Denver, Miami, Minneapolis, Washington, D.C., and international affiliations in Beijing, China and Leipzig and Stuttgart, Germany. The firm represents clients nationally and internationally on issues relating to corporate and business law, administrative law, and litigation. *See additional listing in International Business Law Chapter.*

G. MARC WHITEHEAD

Popham, Haik, Schnobrich & Kaufman, Ltd.
222 South Ninth Street
Suite 3300
Minneapolis, MN 55402

Phone: (612) 333-4800
Fax: (612) 334-8888

Admitted: 1964 Minnesota; 1979 US Ct. App. (8th Cir.)
Birthdate: 05/20/40

•**SHERMAN WINTHROP:** Mr Winthrop specializes in banking law, general corporate law, securities law, real estate law, tax law, and estate planning law. He has special expertise in counseling corporations and business clients and with respect to business mergers and acquisitions. Mr. Winthrop has been named in *The Best Lawyers in America*, 1987-93.
Education: JD 1955, Harvard Law School; BBA 1952 with distinction, University of Minnesota.
Employment History: Shareholder 1979-present, Winthrop & Weinstine, P.A.; Associate/Partner 1956-79, Oppenheimer, Wolff & Donnelly; Law Clerk 1955-56, Chief Justice Roger L. Dell of the Supreme Court, State of Minnesota.
Representative Clients: Zytec Corp. (Secretary and Board member); St. Paul Progress Corp. (Secretary); Otto Bremer Foundation; Bremer Financial Corp.; Autocon Industries, Inc.; McMillan Electric Company; Tradehome Shoe Stores, Inc.; Minnesota Knitting Mills, Inc.
Professional Associations: RCBA, MSBA (Chair 1992-93, Business Law Section); ABA; Minnesota Lawyers Professional Responsibility Board (1976-82).
Community Involvement: Past Board member of St. Paul Rehabilitation Center; St. Paul Athletic Club; Mt. Zion Temple; Sholom Home; Friends of the St. Paul Public Library.
Firm: Winthrop & Weinstine, P.A., is an entrepreneurial law firm founded by six attorneys in 1979. Since its inception, the firm has had a strong practice in the areas of general corporate law, estate planning and probate, banking, and litigation services for clients both large and small. The firm has advised many business owners and managers on issues as diverse as public and private stock offerings, employment disputes, tax problems, and mergers and acquisitions. Winthrop & Weinstine's approach – innovative and cost effective legal solutions focused on producing results – has fostered the successful growth and excellent reputation of the firm. *See additional listings in Probate, Estate Planning & Trusts Law and Commercial Real Estate Law Chapters.*

SHERMAN WINTHROP

Winthrop & Weinstine, P.A.
3200 Minnesota World Trade Center
30 East Seventh Street
St. Paul, MN 55101

Phone: (612) 290-8400
Fax: (612) 292-9347

Admitted: 1955 Minnesota
Birthdate: 02/03/31

Chapter 29: Publicly Held Corporations Law

Complete listing of all attorneys nominated in Publicly Held Corporations Law

TIMOTHY R. BAER, Assistant General Counsel, Dayton Hudson Corp., Minneapolis; TIMOTHY M. BARNETT, Winthrop & Weinstine, P.A., Minneapolis; DANIEL E. BERNDT, Dunlap & Seeger, P.A., Rochester; CHARLES C. BERQUIST, Best & Flanagan, Minneapolis; JOHN E. BRANDT, Murnane, Conlin, White & Brandt, St. Paul; WILLIAM M. BURNS, Hanft, Fride, O'Brien, Harries, Swelbar & Burns, P.A., Duluth; KEVIN M. BUSCH, Moss & Barnett, A Professional Association, Minneapolis; KENNETH L. CUTLER, Dorsey & Whitney, Minneapolis; J. MICHAEL DADY, J. Michael Dady & Associates, P.A., Minneapolis; WILLIAM T. DOLAN, Briggs and Morgan, P.A., Minneapolis; FREDERICK A. DUDDERAR, Hanft, Fride, O'Brien, Harries, Swelbar & Burns, P.A., Duluth; DEAN R. EDSTROM, Doherty, Rumble & Butler Professional Association, Minneapolis; STANLEY EFRON, Henson & Efron, P.A., Minneapolis; ROLF ENGH, Valspar Corporation Counsel, Minneapolis; THOMAS D. FEINBERG, Leonard, Street and Deinard Professional Association, Minneapolis; RICHARD J. FITZGERALD, Lindquist & Vennum, Minneapolis; JAMES FITZMAURICE, Faegre & Benson, Minneapolis; GERALD T. FLOM, Faegre & Benson, Minneapolis; GREGORY G. FREITAG, Fredrikson & Byron, P.A., Minneapolis; JOHN D. FRENCH, Faegre & Benson, Minneapolis; F. KELTON GAGE, Blethen Gage & Krause, Mankato; CRAIG W. GAGNON, Oppenheimer, Wolff & Donnelly, Minneapolis; PHILIP S. GARON, Faegre & Benson, Minneapolis; THOMAS H. GARRETT III, Lindquist & Vennum, Minneapolis; AVRON L. GORDON, Briggs and Morgan, P.A., Minneapolis; ROGER D. GORDON, Winthrop & Weinstine, P.A., Minneapolis; JOEL H. GOTTESMAN, Briggs and Morgan, P.A., Minneapolis; DAVID C. GRORUD, Fredrikson & Byron, P.A., Minneapolis; LEE W. HANSON, Hall, Byers, Hanson, Steil & Weinberger, P.A., St. Cloud; JOHN E. HARRIS, Faegre & Benson, Minneapolis; DAVID L. HASHMALL, Popham, Haik, Schnobrich & Kaufman, Ltd., Minneapolis; NICK HAY, Moss & Barnett, A Professional Association, Minneapolis; CHARLES R. HAYNOR, Briggs and Morgan, P.A., Minneapolis; TIMOTHY M. HEANEY, Fredrikson & Byron, P.A., Minneapolis; ROBERT F. HENSON, Henson & Efron, P.A., Minneapolis; WILLIAM H. HIPPEE JR., Dorsey & Whitney, Minneapolis; JOHN R. HOUSTON, Lindquist & Vennum, Minneapolis; GEOFFREY P. JARPE, Maun & Simon, St. Paul; JOEL D. JOHNSON, Dosland, Nordhougen, Lillehaug & Johnson, P.A., Moorhead; WILLIAM A. JONASON, Dorsey & Whitney, Rochester; SAMUEL L. KAPLAN, Kaplan Strangis & Kaplan, P.A., Minneapolis; JEFFREY J. KEYES, Briggs and Morgan, P.A., Minneapolis; THOMAS R. KING, Fredrikson & Byron, P.A., Minneapolis; GARY W. KOCH, Gislason, Dosland, Hunter & Malecki, P.A., New Ulm; HART KULLER, Winthrop & Weinstine, P.A., St. Paul; WILLIAM S. LAPP, Lapp, Laurie, Libra, Abramson & Thomson, Chartered, Minneapolis; RICHARD G. LAREAU, Oppenheimer, Wolff & Donnelly, Minneapolis; DEXTER A. LARSEN, Fryberger, Buchanan, Smith & Frederick, P.A., Duluth; BRIAN F. LEONARD, O'Neill, Burke, O'Neill, Leonard & O'Brien, Ltd., Minneapolis; KEITH A. LIBBEY, Fredrikson & Byron, P.A., Minneapolis; THOMAS G. LOVETT IV, Lindquist & Vennum, Minneapolis; DAVID C. MCLAUGHLIN, Pfluegel Helseth McLaughlin Anderson & Brutlag, Ortonville; GERALD E. MAGNUSON, Lindquist & Vennum, Minneapolis; GALE R. MELLUM, Faegre & Benson, Minneapolis; DAVID B. MILLER, Faegre & Benson, Minneapolis; LEE R. MITAU, Dorsey & Whitney, Minneapolis; BRIAN J. MURPHY, Quarnstrom Doering Pederson Leary & Murphy, P.A., Marshall; GARY M. NELSON, Oppenheimer, Wolff & Donnelly, Minneapolis; THOMAS F. NELSON, Popham, Haik, Schnobrich & Kaufman, Ltd., Minneapolis; JOHN N. NYS, Johnson, Killen, Thibodeau & Seiler, P.A., Duluth; JAMES E. O'BRIEN, Moss & Barnett, A Professional Association, Minneapolis; WILLIAM J. O'BRIEN, Mackall, Crounse & Moore, Minneapolis; HAROLD R. PATTON, Medtronic Legal Department, Minneapolis; DAVID T. PETERSON, Blethen Gage & Krause, Mankato; J. PATRICK PLUNKETT, Moore, Costello & Hart, St. Paul; CHARLES QUAINTANCE JR., Maslon, Edelman, Borman & Brand, Minneapolis; ROBERT K. RANUM, Fredrikson & Byron, P.A., Minneapolis; JOHN E. REGAN, Regan, Regan & Meyer, Mankato; THOMAS E. ROHRICHT, Doherty, Rumble & Butler Professional Association, St. Paul; BURTON G. ROSS, Ross, Rosenblatt & Wilson Ltd., Minneapolis; THOMAS P. SANDERS, Leonard, Street and Deinard Professional Association, Minneapolis; GROVER C. SAYRE III, O'Neill, Burke, O'Neill, Leonard & O'Brien, Ltd., Minneapolis; PAUL J. SCHEERER, Dorsey & Whitney, Minneapolis; RONALD L. SEEGER, Dunlap & Seeger, P.A., Rochester; STEVEN J. SEILER, Johnson, Killen, Thibodeau & Seiler, P.A., Duluth; W. SMITH SHARPE JR., Faegre & Benson, Minneapolis; MORRIS M. SHERMAN, Leonard, Street and Deinard Professional Association, Minneapolis; NICK SMITH, Fryberger, Buchanan, Smith & Frederick, P.A., Duluth; LEON I. STEINBERG, Maslon, Edelman, Borman & Brand, Minneapolis; MICHAEL R. STEWART, Faegre & Benson, Minneapolis; RALPH L. STRANGIS, Kaplan Strangis & Kaplan, P.A., Minneapolis; ROBERT F. STRAUSS, Mackall, Crounse & Moore, Minneapolis; RUSSELL J. SUDEITH JR., Felhaber, Larson, Fenlon & Vogt, P.A., St. Paul; DONALD C. SWENSON, Lindquist & Vennum, Minneapolis; FRANK A. TAYLOR, Popham, Haik, Schnobrich & Kaufman, Ltd., Minneapolis; STEPHEN TORVIK, Nelson Oyen Torvik, Montevideo; PAUL VAN VALKENBURG, Moss & Barnett, A Professional Association, Minneapolis; NEIL A. WEIKART, Fredrikson & Byron, P.A., Minneapolis; HONNEN S. WEISS, Felhaber, Larson, Fenlon & Vogt, P.A., Minneapolis; STEVEN A. WELLVANG, Oppenheimer, Wolff & Donnelly, Minneapolis; CRAIG W. WENDLAND, Dingle & Wendland, Ltd., Rochester; G. MARC WHITEHEAD, Popham, Haik, Schnobrich & Kaufman, Ltd., Minneapolis; SHERMAN WINTHROP, Winthrop & Weinstine, P.A., St. Paul.

CHAPTER 30

SECURITIES & VENTURE FINANCE LAW

There are two basic ways for a new business to raise money—borrowing money and selling shares of ownership in the company. A brand new business that survives more than a few years is bucking the odds. The vast majority of new businesses do not reach their first anniversary and only a handful reach their fifth. Lenders are keenly aware of these statistics, and thus they view funding startup businesses as highly risky. Conventional banks generally are wary of loaning money to new businesses and usually require a large capital investment by the prospective business owner as well as a personal guarantee from him or her to repay the loan if the business cannot. In practice, securing money for a new venture largely depends on what owners can raise on their own. The following is a discussion of some options for those looking to finance new ventures.

SECURITIES

An option for business owners in need of capital but unable or unwilling to go into debt is to sell equity stakes in the business. Securities such as stocks and bonds are different from other commodities because they have no value by themselves. Rather, they are evidence of a debt owed to their holder. They are written secured promises to pay back money or other payment. From a business owner's point of view, issuing securities is one of two ways to finance a business. The other way is through debt capital, which usually must be repaid with interest.

All offerings of securities can be placed into one of two categories depending on the regulations that govern them. Securities that are exempt from the registration requirements of the Securities Act of 1933 are called private placements, while all other sales of securities are called public placements. Although the majority of business issue securities are exempt from registration requirements, it can be very difficult to discern whether a specific business is exempt.

STOCKS AND BONDS

There are two different types of securities: stocks and bonds. Bonds are documents that signify a debt owed. Selling a bond is like a loan agreement in which the bond holder is promised the return of the original sum loaned out plus interest over time. Generally, bonds are secured with collateral, which ensures that the debt will be satisfied even in the case of default by the party that issued the bonds.

Stocks signify an equity or ownership interest in a company. The unit of ownership is the share, and the holder of one or more shares in a company has some say in how the company is run, how profits are spent, and how the company's assets should be divided upon dissolution of the company. Some, but not all, companies distribute profits to shareholders by paying dividends. Other corporations reinvest the profits within the business, thereby theoretically increasing the value of the stock.

SECURITIES MARKETS

The vehicles through which sales and purchases of securities are conducted are called securities markets. These markets do not necessarily have a physical location, but are sometimes just informal networks through which buyers and sellers of securities make transactions. The largest securities market—in terms of the value traded—is the bond market. The bond market is the means through which the United States government, state and local governments, and corporations borrow money from the public. Because bonds are generally less attractive to individual buyers and more likely to be purchased by professional investors, bond markets are less widely regulated than are markets for common stock.

There are two kinds of markets for stocks—over-the-counter markets and exchange markets. An over-the-counter market is the less rigid of the two. This type of market exists via a network of transactions, with no permanent physical location. Instead the market uses telephone and computer connections. This kind of market allows a wider variety of firms to participate in the trading of securities.

Exchange markets differ from over-the-counter markets in several important ways. Exchange markets operate in a facility in which actual transactions occur between parties on a trading floor. The New York Stock Exchange is the largest such exchange. Exchange markets differ further from over-the-counter markets in that they operate under more strict guidelines governing who can and cannot trade on the exchange. The distinction between the two is blurring because of new technologies which call into question the need for "floor" trading.

A securities firm makes its money in several different ways. In an exchange transaction, the firm charges a commission on the purchase or sale of the stock. In the case of over-the-counter stock, a firm is hired to create a market for a certain stock. In such cases, the firms will sell the stock to customers at a price higher than that sold to other brokers. The firm makes its profit from the difference between its cost for the stock and the price of stock as offered to the public.

PRIVATE PLACEMENTS

Private placements or offerings are sales of securities that are not subject to requirements for registration under the Securities Act of 1933. As these exemptions are fairly complex, and the punishment for breaking securities regulations are severe, seeking legal advice from an expert in the field of securities regulation is highly recommended.

INITIAL PUBLIC OFFERINGS

A business "goes public" when it solicits or concludes a sale of securities from a group of public investors. Although there are exemptions available under both federal and state laws, public offerings generally must comply with registration requirements set forth by the federal Securities and Exchange

Commission and state authorities. An initial public offering, often referred to as an IPO, is the first such public sale by an organization.

REGULATION

Largely because of the nature of securities—that they do not have a value in and of themselves and can therefore be created and sold in unlimited amounts—there has developed a fairly sophisticated network of laws governing their use and sale. Securities law is governed by both state and federal laws, but all these laws have four main purposes:

- Ensure that investors have an accurate idea of what they are getting (and how much) when they purchase securities

- Ensure disclosure of information concerning corporations or other entities which are trading in securities

- Prevent fraud, insider trading, abuse of non-public information, or other price manipulation

- Govern those who buy and sell securities on the secondary market to investors

Securities regulations can be extremely technical. A business seeking to issue securities to finance its business should consult an expert. If the business is not exempt from registration, meeting the registration requirements can be quite expensive. On the other hand, public placements offer distinct advantages over private placements. Securities regulations are complicated rules whose primary objective is to protect the investor or buyer of the securities. For this reason, sales of securities done in violation of state and federal rules are subject to strict civil and criminal penalties, even if the violations are inadvertent or the result of ignorance.

Federal Laws

There are a number of federal laws upon which much of the regulation of the sale of securities is based. The Securities Act of 1933 deals with the initial public offering of securities. The aim of the legislation is to prohibit fraud or deception in the sale of the securities by providing for full disclosure of facts concerning the securities for sale and the business and finances of the issuer.

The Securities Exchange Act of 1934 regulates trading in the secondary market. Like the earlier act, it also requires disclosure of information about the offering. This act established the Securities and Exchange Commission, the principal regulatory body policing securities markets. It also instituted several other restrictions on publicly-held corporations, such as a restriction on the amount of credit that can be extended for the purchase of securities. The act further requires that brokers, dealers, and businesses that deal in securities register with the SEC. It was amended in 1975 to give the government even broader powers over securities exchange and the structure of the market system.

The Trust Indenture Act of 1939 regulates public issues of large securities. The Investment Company Act of 1940 regulates publicly owned businesses that deal primarily in the buying and selling of securities. The Investors Advisers Act of 1940 sets down rules for the registration and regulation of investment advisors, similar to those used in the Securities Exchange Act of 1934. The Securities Investor Protection Act of 1970 established the Securities Investor Protection Corporation, which has the authority to oversee the liquidation of securities firms and to pay off debts owed to their customers.

Minnesota Laws

In addition to federal securities laws, there are state securities laws, generally referred to as "blue sky laws". Like the federal laws, blue sky laws provide for registration of brokers and dealers, require information be made available about securities open for trading, and also mandate penalties for fraudulent or deceptive practices.

Securities offered in Minnesota generally must be registered with both the federal Securities and Exchange Commission and the Minnesota Department of Commerce before they can legally be advertised or sold to investors. However, there are exemptions from the registration requirement under both state and federal laws. Exemptions are discussed in more detail below.

Minnesota Statutes provide that a corporation can issue securities or rights to buy securities only when the corporation has been so authorized by its board of directors acting in accordance with the articles of incorporation. Thus, the first step for any corporation is to determine whether there are sufficient authorized but unissued shares available. If additional shares have not been authorized, then the articles of incorporation may need to be amended to allow for sufficient authorized stock.

Under Minnesota law, unless limited or denied by the articles of incorporation, a shareholder in a Minnesota corporation has a right to buy a certain number of newly offered shares, based on the proportion of previously existing shares that he or she already owns. This "preemptive right" can substantially limit a corporation's ability to restructure itself.

Also under Minnesota law, a corporation can sometimes receive something other than money, such as goods or services, in exchange for shares. The non-monetary consideration must bear a reasonable relation to the value of the shares. This area has been the subject of much litigation and is full of pitfalls for novices. Directors who are present at a meeting when such a transaction is approved can be made personally liable to the corporation if they do not vote against the transaction.

Exemptions

Exemptions from many rules are available under both state and federal laws. Any one security may qualify for exemption under state laws but not federal laws, or vice versa. Examples of such exemptions include offering a key employee of a company a chance to become a shareholder in the company. Placements with large institutional investors, such as insurance companies, may be exempt also. Offerings that do not exceed $5,000,000 can be exempted from regulations by the federal Securities and Exchange Commission. Other exemptions are available to the sale of securities to parties that meet the definition of accredited investors such as a bank, pension fund, or a charitable foundation with assets of at least $5 million, a director or officer of the issuer, or a wealthy individual.

Most smaller businesses are exempt from the registration requirement, which is the most expensive requirement to meet. The federal laws generally exempt any offerings which are confined to any single state. However, the federal courts have interpreted this exemption narrowly and have determined that even some state issuances are subject to federal regulations because they use the federal mailing system. The federal government also provides an exemption to businesses that offer less than $1.5 million worth of securities per year.

Although there are several areas under which companies are exempt from registration requirements, these rules are subject to interpretation and may change. Businesses contemplating offering securities should not rely on the possibility that they may be subject to one or more of the exemptions unless they have received expert legal advice.

DEBT FINANCING

Selling securities is difficult and highly regulated. The cost of meeting these regulations, as well as the difficulty in convincing buyers that a business is a good investment, makes offering securities impractical for many startup companies. Another way of selling ownership in a company—by admitting partners into the deal for a cost (called a limited liability company)—is an option, but a business owner must be willing to forgo some of the profits and convince prospective members they will make money. Further limiting the appeal of memberships in limited liability companies is the fact that they are not freely transferable to third parties. Thus, it is a somewhat easier task to raise money through debt financing, available from banks, credit corporations and local and state loan programs. There are various ways a business can go about finding venture capital from public and private sources.

Anyone trying to use a lender to raise money for a new business will need to give a prospective lender detailed information about the form a new company will take. At a minimum, a prospective business owner will have to provide information about his or her current financial situation, including all business and personal assets and debts. Also, an applicant must be prepared to provide information about how the money requested will be spent and a full description of the intent of the business, along with information about the experience and management capabilities of the owner and those expected to be employed in top positions. A lender will also want to know how much money the owner plans to invest in the business and any projections of how much the project is expected to earn in its first year.

Retail and service-oriented businesses often have more difficulty obtaining financing because the funding for these types of businesses is used for expenses such as inventory, fixtures and working capital—collateral that usually does not meet a lender's criteria for resale recovery. Often, these endeavors are financed primarily, if not fully, through equity. With that background in mind, here are various types of debt financing options that are available.

CONVENTIONAL BANK LOANS

Bank loans are a common way of financing new ventures. The most advantageous to young businesses, but toughest to obtain, are unsecured loans. These are usually available only for short term loans to borrowers with strong balance sheets, ample cash flow, and a low debt-to-equity ratio. Unsecured loans are usually made for less than one year, and the interest rate is a factor of the size of the loan, financial health of the borrower, and the type of industry or business in which the borrower engages. Easier to obtain are a variety of secured loans, which can be structured in a variety of ways and which can give the lender a security interest in accounts receivable, inventory, or raw materials.

It is almost impossible to finance a business with 100 percent debt. Cautious bankers—and bankers are a cautious bunch—typically require that at least half of the startup costs be covered by the owner, and nearly any source of financing will require at least a 20 percent equity stake by the owner.

As noted above, financiers are more willing to provide funding for projects in which there is collateral that can be easily sold if necessary to recoup the lender's investment. Thus, manufacturing and industrial operations are historically easier ventures to finance than retail and service businesses.

A bank is a corporation that earns money by maintaining savings and checking accounts, issuing loans and credit, and dealing in negotiable securities for governments and corporations. Banks invest the money entrusted to them by their customers. The investments that banks are allowed to make are regulated and banks are defined by the limitations put upon them. The types of banks, from least to most regulated, are commercial banks, savings banks and savings and loans.

Commercial banks are the most common and most loosely regulated type of bank. These banks must have more deposits on hand than other types of banks in order to handle the daily transactions of the bank and prevent a money shortage (and the panic that can result). These types of banks are often publicly held corporations.

Savings banks are a rarer form of bank, although they are fairly common in the midwest. These are limited-service banks that were originally formed to encourage people to save their money. To this end, savings banks traditionally offered as their major service "time" savings accounts that prevented withdrawal of money deposited until a set period of time had elapsed. In modern times, the services of this type of bank have expanded somewhat. A business person looking for a lender should note that a savings bank will sometimes offer higher interest rates on accounts than a commercial bank. This is because a savings bank does not have to keep as high a portion of its deposits in reserve as do commercial banks. Savings banks are usually owned in the form of a partnership among depositors who receive dividends in the form of interest on their accounts.

The third type of bank is a savings and loan association. Despite news of scandals and problems in recent years, savings and loan banks have traditionally been highly regulated, conservative organizations whose primary purpose, other than encouraging savings, is to provide loans for homes and businesses.

ASSET BASED LENDERS

Asset based lenders use assets as collateral to lend money to businesses that would not ordinarily qualify for a bank loan. Businesses that are growing fast but have not established a credit history with a bank might find these lenders helpful. Generally, businesses that seek asset based loans are high risks, so asset based lenders charge a premium for their service. Some asset based lenders will use a business' receivables and inventory as collateral. Others may prefer to use real estate or equipment as collateral.

Commercial Finance Companies

Commercial finance companies specialize in financing higher risk applicants unable to obtain conventional bank financing. Their interest rates can be substantially higher than those offered by conventional banks because of the increased risks. Commercial finance companies often are more willing to finance riskier applicants because they have more experience evaluating the liquidation value of failed businesses.

Venture Capital Companies

Venture capital companies provide capital to businesses that might not be eligible for straight bank loans but have high potential in their market. These companies assess the viability of an emerging business and fund it by taking a stake in the company. Thus, the success of the venture capital firm depends on the success of the business. Many investors demand a say in management decisions for their investment capital—a demand that is anathema to some entrepreneurs.

Only about one out of every ten investments reaps profits for venture capital companies, so they are choosy about where they place their money. Many firms specialize in certain areas in which they have expertise. Before approaching a venture capitalist, a business owner should prepare a solid business plan that takes into account marketing plans, cash flow and research needs.

Venture capital companies specialize in lending to startup companies or established companies expanding into new risky markets. Venture capital companies may be the only option available to some businesses. Venture capital companies frequently prefer to acquire stock in the company as a way to finance the loan, insist on playing a substantial role in managing the company, and can have substantial involvement in the day-to-day operations of the business.

Public Financing

There are many government programs charged with helping businesses succeed. One of the ways the government encourages new businesses is by making loans easier to obtain. The U.S. Small Business Administration (SBA) helps qualified small businesses get loans by offering guarantees to banks for those loans. The SBA will guarantee 85 to 90 percent of a loan depending on the size of the loan (the maximum is $750,000). It is difficult to receive the SBA's help, however, without sizable investment capital from investors.

In addition to SBA help, there are a number of other government programs, from local and federal sources, designed to help specific kinds of businesses such as minority-owned businesses.

FRANCHISES

Strictly speaking, franchising is not a type of new venture financing, but it can be a way for an existing business to expand rapidly and move into new markets for a reasonable cost. A franchise is a right given to a private person or corporation to market a given product within a certain area. When a business with a trademark sells the rights to that trademark for use in distributing products or services, their relationship can be a franchise. Usually the business selling the franchise also provides market assistance to the buyer.

Franchises are governed by both state and federal law. It is extremely important to know these laws before starting a business that may franchise or if a business is considering becoming a franchisee for another business. The laws are drafted using broad language and some people find themselves in violation of the laws, even though they are not engaged in activities they consider to be franchising.

The Federal Trade Commission enforces laws and rules regulating franchises. These rules do not require a business to register with or seek the approval of the FTC before offering or selling a franchise. The rules only apply to franchises that are "in or affecting interstate commerce." Although there are differences between the laws that govern state and federal franchise law, it is most important to remember that the name of a company is not important as long as the relationship meets the definition of a franchise. This means that if a business is entering into a limited partnership, it may also be entering into a franchise agreement. The FTC rules define a franchise as a "continuing commercial relationship" between two or more parties. This continuing relationship is further defined as one in which supplies for reorder are made available to the purchaser after the first required inventory is purchased.

There are three basic types of "continuing commercial relationships" covered by the rules:

- Package franchises, defined as prepackaged business programs developed and identified by the franchisor. McDonald's is an example of this type, also called a "business format" franchise.

- Product franchises, arrangements where the franchisor sells goods that bear his or her trade name to a franchisee, who in turn sells them to the public under that same name. The dealer company maintains a degree of control over the selling of the goods by the franchisee in this arrangement.

- Business opportunity ventures, in which the franchisor retains more control than in either of the previous arrangements. In this type of franchising agreement, the franchisee is required to buy and sell the goods or services of the franchisor or another business. Furthermore, the franchisor arranges the location of the business, seeks out business for the junior partner, and even provides employees. An example of this type of arrangement is a vending machine route, where a company finds a place to put the machines and sells the candy to the franchisee, but the franchisee collects the money and restocks the machines.

Franchises are also discussed in the Closely Held Business Law Chapter and the Franchise & Dealership Law Chapter.

RESOURCES

Minnesota Department of Commerce—Securities Registration, 1337 7th Street E., St. Paul, MN 55101, (612) 296-4973.

A Guide to Starting a Business in Minnesota. This very thorough manual is updated annually. It is available from the Minnesota Small Business Assistance Office. (612) 296-3871 or (800)-657-3858.

SECURITIES & VENTURE FINANCE LAW LEADING ATTORNEYS

The attorneys profiled in this section were nominated by their peers in a statewide survey conducted in 1993 in which several thousand Minnesota attorneys were asked to name the lawyer to whom they would send a friend or family member in need of legal assistance in the area of *Securities & Venture Finance Law*.

Because the survey resulted in a list of less than five percent of Minnesota's practicing attorneys, this should not be construed as a complete list. Nevertheless, it is an excellent source of highly qualified and reputable attorneys, who, if unable to assist can in most cases make quality referrals.

A list of all attorneys nominated in this category is found at the end of this section. For information on the survey methodology see page ix.

Please note that the shorter, two line attorney listings in this section are of attorneys who practice in this area but whose full biographical profile appears in another section of this book. A bullet "•" preceeding name indicates the attorney was nominated in this particular area of law. For information on the format of these profiles, consult the section "Using the *Business Guidebook*" found on page xiv. Note that the following abbreviations are used throughout these profiles:

The attorneys profiled below were recommended by their peers in a statewide survey.

App.	- Appellate	ABA	- American Bar Association
Cir.	- Circuit	ATLA	- American Trial Lawyers Association
Ct.	- Court	HCBA	- Hennepin County Bar Association
Dist.	- District	MDLA	- Minnesota Defense Lawyers Association
Hon.	- Honorable	MSBA	- Minnesota State Bar Association
JD	- Law degree (Juris Doctor)	MTLA	- Minnesota Trial Lawyers Association
LLB	- Law degree	NBTA	- National Board of Trial Advocacy
LLM	- Master in Law degree	RCBA	- Ramsey County Bar Association
Sup.	- Supreme		

KENNETH L. CUTLER - Dorsey & Whitney - Pillsbury Center South, 220 South Sixth Street - Minneapolis, MN 55402-1498 - Phone: (612) 340-2740, Fax: (612) 340-8738 - *See complete biographical profile in Publicly Held Corporations Law Chapter.*

•**DEAN R. EDSTROM** - Doherty, Rumble & Butler Professional Association - 3500 Fifth Street Towers, 150 South Fifth Street - Minneapolis, MN 55402-4235 - Phone: (612) 340-5575, Fax: (612) 340-5584 - *See complete biographical profile in Publicly Held Corporations Law Chapter.*

•**GREGORY G. FREITAG:** Mr. Freitag is an officer in the Securities Law Group at Fredrikson & Byron. He represents broker-dealers, investors, and owners of public and private corporations in general corporate, Securities and Exchange Commission, NASD, investment banking, and transactional matters. His transactional experience includes acquisitions and mergers, venture capital, private and public securities offerings, and leveraged buy-outs. Mr. Freitag combines his business background, which includes being a Certified Public Accountant, with his extensive transactional and corporate law experience to bring not only legal and investment expertise, but good business sense, to his clients. This includes the understanding that exceptional service, delivered in an efficient manner, is paramount to successful representation.
Education: JD 1987, University of Chicago; BA 1984 magna cum laude, Macalester College (Phi Beta Kappa, Omicron Delta Epsilon and recipient of the 3M Scholar award and the John M. Dozier prize).
Representative Clients: Black Hawk Holdings, Inc.; Champps Entertainment, Inc.; Clipper Alliance Corporation; Craig Hallum, Inc.; Equity Securities Trading Company, Inc.; Garment Graphics, Inc.; John G. Kinnard and Company, Inc.; Peterson Brothers Securities Company; Qrantech, Ltd.; Skytech Robotics, Inc.
Professional Associations: MSBA; HCBA; 1991 Securities Advisory Committee, Minnesota Commissioner of Commerce.
Firm: Gregory Freitag is one of eleven attorneys in Fredrikson & Byron's Securities Law Group which focuses on working with publicly owned and closely held corporate clients in the US and overseas. The group has experience in a full range of transactions including the sale of securities by corporations and shareholders, mergers, acquisitions, and dispositions, SEC and NASD compliance matters, solicitation of proxies, and representation of broker-dealers and underwriters. In addition to Mr. Freitag, this practice group is comprised of highly experienced securities attorneys including Timothy Heaney, Robert Ranum, John Stout, Thomas King, John Wurm, and David Grorud. These individuals work in teams with a dedicated group of associates and legal assistants: Melodie Rose, Timothy Dordell, Daniel Yarano, Elizabeth Reiskytl, Dianne Maciosek, and Diane Heney. *See additional listing in Publicly Held Corporations Law Chapter.*

GREGORY G. FREITAG

Fredrikson & Byron, P.A.
1100 International Centre
900 Second Avenue South
Minneapolis, MN 55402

Phone: (612) 347-7153
Fax: (612) 347-7077

Admitted: 1987 Minnesota
Birthdate: 02/24/62

1994/1996 ♦ Minnesota Edition **425**

Chapter 30: Securities & Venture Finance Law

ROGER H. FROMMELT

Frommelt & Eide, Ltd.
580 International Centre
900 Second Avenue South
Minneapolis, MN 55402

Phone: (612) 332-2200
Fax: (612) 342-2761
800 number: (800) 332-2296

Admitted: 1965 Minnesota;
1968 US Dist. Ct. (MN);
1968 US Tax Ct.;
1969 US Sup. Ct.;
1972 US Ct. Military App.;
1980 US Ct. App. (8th Cir.)
Birthdate: 09/13/36

•**ROGER H. FROMMELT:** Mr. Frommelt is a founding partner of Frommelt & Eide, Ltd. Mr. Frommelt has over 27 years experience representing numerous corporations and other entities with respect to general business matters, with a primary concentration in the area of securities law. He has represented underwriters and corporations in connection with over two hundred public offerings of securities since 1967, including offerings involving mergers and acquisitions, and debt as well as equity securities. Mr. Frommelt has acted as an advisor to the board of directors of a number of public and privately held corporations and has also represented numerous entrepreneurs and start-up companies.
Education: JD 1965, University of Minnesota (1964-65, *Minnesota Law Review*; Phi Delta Phi); B Chem E 1959, University of Minnesota.
Employment History: 1974-present, Frommelt & Eide, Ltd.; 1969-74, Katz, Taube, Lange & Frommelt; 1968, private practice; 1965-68, Best & Flanagan.
Representative Clients: Casino Magic Corp.; Summit Investment Corp.; Sparta Foods, Inc.; Brainerd International, Inc.; Certified Technologies Corp.; Concourse Corp.; North Atlantic Technologies, Inc.; Copy Duplicating Products, Inc.
Professional Associations: ABA (International Law and Practice Section; Business Law Section); HCBA (Securities Law Section (past Chair); Dist. IV Ethics Committee); MSBA (Business Law Section; Tax Section); Minnesota Lawyers Mutual Insurance Company (Board member; Executive Committee; Underwriting Committee).
Firm: Founded in 1974, Frommelt & Eide, Ltd. is a small law firm which is able to give entrepreneurs and growing businesses personal attention. The firm provides a variety of services including business formation, private placements, public offerings, commercial transactions, mergers and acquisitions, franchises, licensing, real estate, community association, employee matters, contracts, and commercial litigation. *See additional listings in Publicly Held Corporations Law and Commercial Real Estate Law Chapters.*

F. KELTON GAGE - Blethen Gage & Krause - 127 South Second Street, P.O. Box 3049 - Mankato, MN 56002-3049 - Phone: (507) 345-1166, Fax: (507) 345-8003 - *See complete biographical profile in Closely Held Business Law Chapter.*

ROGER D. GORDON - Winthrop & Weinstine, P.A. - 3000 Dain Bosworth Plaza, 60 South Sixth Street - Minneapolis, MN 55402 - Phone: (612) 347-0700, Fax: (612) 347-0600 - *See complete biographical profile in Publicly Held Corporations Law Chapter.*

TIMOTHY M. HEANEY

Fredrikson & Byron, P.A.
1100 International Centre
900 Second Avenue South
Minneapolis, MN 55402

Phone: (612) 347-7019
Fax: (612) 347-7077

Admitted: 1972 Minnesota
Birthdate: 06/25/46

•**TIMOTHY M. HEANEY:** Mr. Heaney is an officer and the chair of Fredrikson & Byron's Securities Law Group. He represents start-up and publicly held corporations, broker-dealers, and venture capital funds. Mr. Heaney works with entrepreneurs who are building businesses based on proprietary technology. His primary focus is on financing corporations through private and public equity offerings. He works with clients on a broad range of corporate issues, including mergers, acquisitions, and compensation and incentive plans. Mr. Heaney's representation of broker-dealers involves all aspects of underwriter representation, compliance matters, and customer dispute resolution. He is also an author and lecturer on securities law topics for MN Venture Collaborative, *Star Tribune*, continuing legal education seminars, and *Broker Focus*. His articles include "Positioning to Go Public," Business Law Focus, *Minnesota Ventures*, March/April 1992.
Education: JD 1972 cum laude, University of Minnesota; BA 1968 cum laude, St. John's University.
Representative Clients: Public and closely held companies, development stage companies, broker-dealers, investment advisors, shareholders, limited partnerships, and venture capital companies.
Professional Associations: ABA (Federal Regulation of Securities Committee, Business Law Section); MSBA (Business Law Section); HCBA; arbitrator, National Association of Securities Dealers; National Society of Compliance Professionals; past trustee, Securities Investor Protection Corporation.
Firm: Mr. Heaney is one of eleven attorneys in Fredrikson & Byron's Securities Law Group which focuses on working with publicly owned and closely held corporate clients in the US and overseas. The group has experience in a full range of transactions including the sale of securities by corporations and shareholders, mergers, acquisitions and dispositions, SEC and NASD compliance matters, solicitation of proxies, and representation of broker-dealers and underwriters. Other highly experienced securities attorneys in this group are Thomas King, Robert Ranum, John Stout, John Wurm, David Grorud, and Gregory Freitag. These individuals work in teams with a dedicated group of associates and legal assistants: Melodie Rose, Timothy Dordell, Daniel Yarano, Elizabeth Reiskytl, Dianne Maciosek, and Diane Heney. *See additional listing in Publicly Held Corporations Law Chapter.*

PETER S. HENDRIXSON - Dorsey & Whitney - Pillsbury Center South, 220 South Sixth Street - Minneapolis, MN 55402-1498 - Phone: (612) 340-2917, Fax: (612) 340-8800 - *See complete biographical profile in Commercial Litigation Chapter.*

•THOMAS R. KING: An officer in Fredrikson & Byron's Securities Law Group, Mr. King has been active in management. Mr. King has extensive experience in counseling entrepreneurs, especially those involved in high technology enterprises, in all aspects of corporate formation and financing. His special emphasis is on the representation of public corporations and emerging private companies seeking to raise capital through exempt or public offerings and underwriters of public offerings.
Education: Graduate work 1966, University of Minnesota; LLB 1965, University of Minnesota; BA 1962, University of Minnesota.
Representative Clients: Datakey, Inc.; Empi, Inc.; First Team Sports; Orthomet, Inc.; Sunrise Leasing Corporation; Everest Medical Corporation; Garment Graphics, Inc.; Scicom Data Services, Inc.; Teltech Resource Network Corporation.
Professional Associations: ABA (Antitrust and Business Law Sections); MSBA; HCBA (Securities and General Corporate Sections).
Community Involvement: Fund for the Legal Aid Society (past Chair, Executive Committee); Director, Children's Home Society of Minnesota.
Firm: Mr. King is one of eleven attorneys in Fredrikson & Byron's Securities Law Group which focuses on working with publicly owned and closely held corporate clients in the US and overseas. The group has experience in a full range of transactions, including the sale of securities by corporations and shareholders, mergers, acquisitions, and dispositions, SEC and NASD compliance matters, solicitation of proxies, and representation of broker-dealers and underwriters. This practice group is comprised of highly experienced securities attorneys including Timothy Heaney, Robert Ranum, John Stout, John Wurm, David Grorud, and Gregory Freitag. These individuals work in teams with a dedicated group of associates and legal assistants, including Melodie Rose, Timothy Dordell, Daniel Yarano, Elizabeth Reiskytl, Dianne Maciosek, and Diane Heney. *See additional listing in Publicly Held Corporations Law Chapter.*

THOMAS R. KING

Fredrikson & Byron, P.A.
1100 International Centre
900 Second Avenue South
Minneapolis, MN 55402

Phone: (612) 347-7059
Fax: (612) 347-7077

Admitted: 1965 Minnesota
Birthdate: 05/18/40

•DAVID J. LUBBEN: Mr. Lubben represents public and private companies on general corporate, securities, and merger & acquisition matters and also represents underwriters in connection with registered public offerings and private placement transactions, involving equity, debt, and receivables-backed securities. He has represented United HealthCare Corporation in connection with various acquisitions and dispositions, including HMO America, Inc., Complete Health Services, Inc., Ramsay-HMO, Inc., and the sale of United's subsidiary, Diversified Pharmaceutical Services, Inc.; Green Tree Financial in connection with the public offering of 2.5 million shares of common stock.; Olympic Financial Ltd. in connection with its first public offering of automobile receivables asset backed securities; and Universal Hospital Services, Inc. in its initial public offering. In addition he has represented Goldman Sachs & Co.; Montgomery Securities; Wessels, Arnold & Henderson; Piper Jaffray Inc.; Dain Bosworth Incorporated; Needham & Company, Inc.; and others on various public offerings of equity and debt securities. Mr. Lubben is a partner in the Corporate Department at Dorsey & Whitney.
Education: JD 1977 with high honors, Order of the Coif, University of Iowa (Editor 1976-77, *Iowa Law Review*); BA 1974 magna cum laude, Luther College.
Employment History: Partner 1983-present, Associate 1977-82, Dorsey & Whitney.
Representative Clients: General corporate counsel to United HealthCare Corp.; Green Tree Financial Corp.; MGI PHARMA, Inc.; Medical Graphics Corp.; United Market Services, Inc.; Camax Manufacturing Technologies.
Firm: Dorsey & Whitney is the largest law firm in Minnesota and one of the largest firms in the United States with over 350 lawyers in 12 offices. The depth and breadth of the experience of its lawyers enables it to provide a broad range of services to meet the diverse legal needs of its client base, which includes Fortune 500 companies, public agencies, banks and other financial institutions, nonprofit organizations, individual investors, family owned businesses, and high-tech and low-tech, growth oriented companies. *See additional listing in Publicly Held Corporations Law Chapter.*

DAVID J. LUBBEN

Dorsey & Whitney
Pillsbury Center South
220 South Sixth Street
Minneapolis, MN 55402-1498

Phone: (612) 340-2904
Fax: (612) 340-8738

Admitted: 1977 Minnesota

Chapter 30: Securities & Venture Finance Law

ERIC O. MADSON

Winthrop & Weinstine, P.A.
3000 Dain Bosworth Plaza
60 South Sixth Street
Minneapolis, MN 55402

Phone: (612) 347-0700
Fax: (612) 347-0600

Admitted: 1977 Minnesota
Birthdate: 08/31/51

•**ERIC O. MADSON:** Mr. Madson practices securities regulation law, corporate and business law, and business finance law. He combines practical business judgment and project management skills with technical expertise to guide clients from initial stages of development to maturity. His principal expertise is in the formation of capital for emerging and established businesses, through public and private securities offerings. In the past two years, he has served as counsel to the issuer or underwriters in more than 15 public offerings ranging in size from less than $5 million to more than $60 million and as counsel to the issuer or placement agent in numerous private offerings. Additionally, Mr. Madson serves as general corporate and securities counsel to businesses in a variety of industries, including manufacturers of consumer products, computer equipment, medical devices, and other technology-based products; financial institutions; and companies engaged in various aspects of the gaming industry.
Education: JD 1977, Harvard University (Phi Beta Kappa); BA 1973 magna cum laude, St. Olaf College.
Employment History: Shareholder 1993-present, Winthrop & Weinstine, P.A.; Associate/Partner 1977-93, Mackall, Crounse & Moore.
Representative Clients: Equity Securities Trading Company, Inc.; Recovery Engineering, Inc.; Rimage Corp.; Acres Gaming Inc.; Phenix Composites Inc.; Wanner Engineering, Inc.
Firm: Winthrop & Weinstine's Corporate Practice Group focuses on the representation of emerging and growing businesses from initial stages of development and financing to maturity. The firm is counsel to numerous publicly held companies, underwriters of equity and debt securities, and other sources of debt financing. Sherman Winthrop, Marvin C. Ingber, and Timothy M. Barnett provide expertise in corporate finance, acquisitions, and dispositions of businesses, and business planning. Roger D. Gordon and Todd B. Urness have expertise in public finance and tax-oriented finance transactions. The firm's representation of lending institutions, led by Richard A. Hoel and David E. Moran, complements the corporate finance practice of other members of the Corporate Practice Group.
See additional listings in Publicly Held Corporations Law and Closely Held Business Law Chapters.

•**ROGER J. MAGNUSON** - Dorsey & Whitney - Pillsbury Center South, 220 South Sixth Street - Minneapolis, MN 55402-1498 - Phone: (612) 340-2738, Fax: (612) 340-2868 - *See complete biographical profile in Commercial Litigation Chapter.*

DAVID B. MILLER

Faegre & Benson
2200 Norwest Center
90 South Seventh Street
Minneapolis, MN 55402

Phone: (612) 336-3000
Fax: (612) 336-3026
800 number: (800) 328-4393

Admitted: 1978 Minnesota

•**DAVID B. MILLER:** Mr. Miller practices primarily in the areas of mergers and acquisitions, securities regulation, venture capital financing, banks and bank holding companies, and general corporate and partnership counseling. In the area of securities regulation, Mr. Miller works extensively with public and private companies and partnerships, underwriters, and placement agents in offerings of securities of all types. Mr. Miller has had primary or significant responsibility for over 35 underwritten public offerings in the last ten years. He also represents issuers in a variety of primary and secondary public offerings involving a range of securities such as notes, preferred stock, asset-backed instruments, limited partnership interests, and units. His experience includes related Securities Exchange Act of 1934 and Securities Act of 1933 matters, such as periodic reporting, trading and disclosure practices, proxy regulation, and resale of restricted securities. With respect to mergers and acquisitions, Mr. Miller represents sellers, buyers, financial advisors, and director committees in a variety of public and private transactions. In the venture capital area, Mr. Miller has worked with both venture capitalists and with companies pursuing venture financing. For his banking clients, he handles mergers and acquisitions, securities activities, financial products, corporate governance, and bank and bank holding company regulation. He also handles general corporate counseling and compensation plan matters. Mr. Miller is a frequent lecturer for continuing legal education programs and has been a member of the Minnesota Commissioner of Commerce Securities Regulation Advisory Committee.
Education: JD 1977 magna cum laude, University of Michigan; AB 1974 magna cum laude, Dartmouth College.
Employment History: Partner 1985-present, Associate 1978-84, Faegre & Benson.
Representative Clients: General Electric Capital Corp.; Piper Jaffray Inc.; Dain Bosworth Incorporated; Wessels, Arnold & Henderson, Inc.; Norwest Corp.; Marquette Bancshares, Inc.; First National Corp.; SBM Company; Computer Network Technology, Inc.; Baukol-Noonan, Inc.; DataServ, Inc.; Norwest Growth Fund, Inc. *See additional listings in Banking Law and Publicly Held Corporations Law Chapters.*

•**LEE R. MITAU** - Dorsey & Whitney - Pillsbury Center South, 220 South Sixth Street - Minneapolis, MN 55402-1498 - Phone: (612) 340-2780, Fax: (612) 340-8738 - *See complete biographical profile in Publicly Held Corporations Law Chapter.*

•**MICHAEL T. NILAN:** Mike Nilan is a trial attorney representing corporate and individual clients in securities and commercial cases and manufacturing defendants in product liability matters. He is certified as a Civil Trial Specialist by the Minnesota State Bar Association. Mr. Nilan has served as an arbitrator for the National Association of Securities Dealers, the New York Stock Exchange, and the American Arbitration Association. He is also an experienced mediator and has been qualified as an Alternative Dispute Resolution Mediator by the Minnesota Supreme Court, ADR Review Board.
Education: JD 1979 cum laude, University of Minnesota (member 1977-78, Research Editor 1978-79, *Minnesota Law Review*); MS 1971, University of Minnesota; BA 1970, University of Minnesota.
Employment History: Attorney & Shareholder 1979-present, Popham, Haik, Schnobrich & Kaufman, Ltd.
Representative Clients: Dean Witter Reynolds, Inc.; Refco, Inc.; PPG, Inc.; Hanson PLC; The Glidden Company; The Kemper Insurance Group.
Professional Associations: MSBA (Civil Litigation Section (past Chair)); International Assn. of Defense Counsel; MDLA.
Community Involvement: Alpha Tau Omega House Corp. (Chair); Mediation Center (Mediator and Instructor).
Firm: Popham, Haik, Schnobrich & Kaufman, Ltd., is a firm of more than 230 attorneys with offices in Denver, Miami, Minneapolis, Washington, D.C., and international affiliations in Beijing, China and Leipzig and Stuttgart, Germany. The firm represents clients nationally and internationally on issues relating to corporate and business law, administrative law, and litigation. *See additional listing in Commercial Litigation Chapter.*

MICHAEL T. NILAN

Popham, Haik, Schnobrich & Kaufman, Ltd.
222 South Ninth Street
Suite 3300
Minneapolis, MN 55402

Phone: (612) 333-4800
Fax: (612) 334-8888

Admitted: 1979 Minnesota; 1979 US Dist. Ct. (MN); 1979 US Ct. App. (8th Cir.); 1993 US Ct. App. (3rd Cir.); 1993 US Ct. App. (1st Cir.)
Birthdate: 09/14/48

•**JAMES E. O'BRIEN** - Moss & Barnett, A Professional Association - 4800 Norwest Center, 90 South Seventh Street - Minneapolis, MN 55402 - Phone: (612) 347-0273, Fax: (612) 339-6686 - *See complete biographical profile in Publicly Held Corporations Law Chapter.*

•**ROBERT K. RANUM:** Mr. Ranum is an officer with Fredrikson and Byron's Securities Group. He advises corporations and their officers and directors on matters involving corporate and securities law, including private and public securities offerings, mergers, acquisitions, proxy solicitations, stock options, and compliance with Securities and Exchange Commission requirements. Mr. Ranum has assisted entrepreneurs in the formation and financing of development stage companies and worked with established corporate clients in a variety of matters. Since 1991, he has served as legislative coordinator for the Minnesota State Bar Association's Business Law Section, assisting in the development and communication of the Section's legislative proposals and positions.
Education: JD 1983 cum laude, University of Minnesota; BA 1980 summa cum laude, St. Olaf College (Phi Beta Kappa).
Representative Clients: Audio King Corporation; Cellex Biosciences, Inc.; Shturman Cardiology Systems, Inc.; Winland Electronics, Inc.
Professional Associations: ABA; MSBA (Business Law Section); HCBA (Securities Law Section).
Firm: Mr. Ranum is one of eleven attorneys in Fredrikson & Byron's Securities Law Group, which focuses on working with publicly owned and closely held corporate clients in the US and overseas. The group has experience in a full range of transactions, including the sale of securities by corporations and shareholders, mergers, acquisitions, and dispositions, SEC and NASD compliance matters, solicitation of proxies, and representation of broker-dealers and underwriters. This practice group is comprised of highly experienced securities attorneys including Timothy Heaney, Thomas King, John Stout, John Wurm, David Grorud, and Gregory Freitag. These individuals work in teams with a dedicated group of associates and legal assistants, including Melodie Rose, Timothy Dordell, Daniel Yarano, Elizabeth Reiskytl, Dianne Maciosek, and Diane Heney. *See additional listing in Publicly Held Corporations Law Chapter.*

ROBERT K. RANUM

Fredrikson & Byron, P.A.
1100 International Centre
900 Second Avenue South
Minneapolis, MN 55402

Phone: (612) 347-7067
Fax: (612) 347-7077

Admitted: 1983 Minnesota
Birthdate: 03/21/58

Scott E. Richter

Popham, Haik, Schnobrich & Kaufman, Ltd.
222 South Ninth Street
Suite 3300
Minneapolis, MN 55402

Phone: (612) 333-4800
Fax: (612) 334-8888

Admitted: 1982 Minnesota; 1982 US Dist. Ct. (MN)
Birthdate: 07/04/56

•**SCOTT E. RICHTER:** Mr. Richter is a trial lawyer concentrating his practice in complex securities and other commercial litigation and in securities arbitrations. He has handled numerous large cases, including class actions involving the liability of corporations, officers and directors, underwriters, accountants, and attorneys. In addition, he has tried numerous securities arbitrations for broker-dealer clients, including suitability, churning, and other claims brought by customers, and claims brought by and against individual brokers, including employment claims. He also has represented the National Association of Securities Dealers in matters before the US Court of Appeals for the Eighth Circuit. Mr. Richter's publications include *Securities Litigation: Forms and Analysis*, Callaghan & Co., 1989 (2 vol.); "Through the Looking Glass: The Eighth Circuit Views Scienter," *Wm. Mitchell L. Rev.*, 1990, Vol 16 No. 3; and with Keith Halleland, "RICO on the Rebound: The Pattern Requirement and Other Developments in the Law of Racketeering," *The Hennepin Lawyer* (Sept.-Oct. 1989).
Education: JD 1982, Stanford University (President, Moot Court Board); MBA 1982, Stanford Business School; AB 1978, Stanford University.
Employment History: 1982-present (Senior attorney since 1987), Popham, Haik, Schnobrich & Kaufman, Ltd.
Representative Clients: Regional counsel for Dean Witter Reynolds, Inc. Other local, regional, and national broker-dealers and the National Assn. of Securities Dealers.
Professional Associations: ABA (Section of Litigation, Committee on Securities Litigation); MSBA; HCBA.
Community Involvement: Minneapolis Paint-a-Thon; Stanford Club of Minnesota.
Firm: Popham, Haik, Schnobrich & Kaufman, Ltd., is a firm of more than 230 attorneys with offices in Denver, Miami, Minneapolis, Washington, D.C., and international affiliations in Beijing, China and Leipzig and Stuttgart, Germany. The firm represents clients nationally and internationally on issues relating to corporate and business law, administrative law, and litigation. *See additional listing in Commercial Litigation Chapter.*

W. Smith (Kris) Sharpe, Jr.

Faegre & Benson
2200 Norwest Center
90 South Seventh Street
Minneapolis, MN 55402

Phone: (612) 336-3000
Fax: (612) 336-3026
800 number: (800) 328-4393

Admitted: 1972 Minnesota
Birthdate: 12/26/46

•**W. SMITH (KRIS) SHARPE, JR.:** Mr. Sharpe focuses his practice on public securities offerings, venture capital representation, mergers and acquisitions, and general corporate counseling. He represents both emerging companies and seasoned issuers in public and private placements of both equity and debt. He also represents underwriters and placement agents in public and private equity and debt financings. Mr. Sharpe counsels public clients regarding ongoing reporting and compliance matters, including disclosure issues, preparation of periodic reports and proxy statements, Rule 144 share sale transactions, and Section 16 reporting and "short-swing" profits questions. He has considerable expertise in helping public clients create so-called medium-term note programs, which facilitate immediate sales of significant amounts of debt securities to the public, and he has significant experience in specialized securities law areas. For many years he has represented a number of the larger venture capital firms in the Twin Cities. In the area of mergers and acquisitions, Mr. Sharpe's clients include buyers, sellers, and institutional investors in various types of public and private transactions, many of which have involved the issuance of securities and/or the solicitation of proxies, with all of the accompanying issues under the Securities Act of 1933 and the Securities Exchange Act of 1934. He has frequently advised corporations regarding fiduciary duties to shareholders, compensation plans and arrangements, financing strategies, charter and bylaw amendments, preparation of annual shareholder reports, director and shareholder resolutions, and other issues requiring detailed knowledge of general corporate law.
Education: JD 1972, Yale University; BA 1969 summa cum laude, Columbia College (Phi Beta Kappa).
Employment History: Partner 1980-present, Associate 1972-1980, Faegre & Benson.
Representative Clients: Hutchinson Technology, Inc.; Fastenal Company; Dayton Hudson Corp.; Archer-Daniels-Midland Company; Norwest Corp.; The NWNL Companies, Inc.; Piper Jaffray, Inc.; Dain Bosworth, Inc.; Goldman, Sachs & Co.; Merrill Lynch, Pierce, Fenner & Smith, Inc.; Smith Barney, Harris Upham & Co., Inc.; Medtronic, Inc.; Tennant Company; International Multifoods Corp.; Northwestern National Life; Lutheran Brotherhood; St. Paul Venture Capital, Inc.; North Star Ventures, Inc.; Edgewater Private Equity Fund, L.P.; Spine-Tech, Inc.; GalaGen, Inc.; Adler Management Corp.; Education Alternatives, Inc.; Martinson & Company, Ltd.; Milestone Growth Fund, Inc.; Stairstep, Inc.; Pioneer Hi-Bred International. *See additional listing in Publicly Held Corporations Law Chapter.*

ROGER V. STAGEBERG - Lommen, Nelson, Cole & Stageberg, P.A. - 1800 IDS Center, 80 South Eighth Street - Minneapolis, MN 55402 - Phone: (612) 339-8131, Fax: (612) 339-8064 - *See complete biographical profile in Closely Held Business Law Chapter.*

JOHN H. STOUT - Fredrikson & Byron, P.A. - 1100 International Centre, 900 Second Avenue South - Minneapolis, MN 55402 - Phone: (612) 347-7012, Fax: (612) 347-7077 - *See complete biographical profile in Arts, Entertainment, Advertising & Media Law Chapter.*

•**FRANK A. TAYLOR:** Mr. Taylor has been, and is, lead trial counsel in over 80 major class actions in which over $7.0 billion of actual damages were at stake. Mr. Taylor was lead trial counsel for at least 15 matters which have published opinions. To date, he has had lead trial counsel responsibility for jury and nonjury actions in 42 different states in both federal and state courts. He has tried numerous and significant commercial, construction, and securities cases in a variety of forums including the AAA, NASD, MSRB, NYSE, and before many local, state, and federal regulatory bodies. Mr. Taylor has used, and participated in, alternative dispute resolution mechanisms with great frequency. Mr. Taylor has extensive experience in work-outs, reorganizations, and restructurings of failed securities or commercial transactions including limited partnerships, initial public offerings, corporate debt offerings, and tax exempt securities. He is an adjunct professor at William Mitchell College of Law teaching Securities Regulation and has served as a panelist and lecturer for the annual meeting of the Legal and Compliance Division of the Securities Industry Association.
Education: JD 1977 with distinction, University of Iowa (Notes and Comments Editor, *Iowa Law Review*); BA 1974 with distinction, University of Iowa (Phi Beta Kappa).
Employment History: Shareholder 1990-present, Popham, Haik, Schnobrich & Kaufman, Ltd.; Partner 1989-90, Winthrop & Weinstine; Partner/Associate 1977-89, Kutak, Rock & Campbell (Omaha, NE and New York, NY offices).
Professional Associations: Federal Bar Council; MSBA; New York State Bar Assn.; Nebraska State Bar Assn.; The Iowa State Bar Assn.; Assn. of the Bar of the City of New York; MN Institute of Legal Education.
Firm: Popham, Haik, Schnobrich & Kaufman, Ltd., is a firm of more than 230 attorneys with offices in Denver, Miami, Minneapolis, Washington, D.C., and international affiliations in Beijing, China and Leipzig and Stuttgart, Germany. The firm represents clients nationally and internationally on issues relating to corporate and business law, administrative law, and litigation. *See additional listing in Publicly Held Corporations Law Chapter.*

FRANK A. TAYLOR

Popham, Haik, Schnobrich & Kaufman, Ltd.
222 South Ninth Street
Suite 3300
Minneapolis, MN 55402

Phone: (612) 333-4800
Fax: (612) 334-8888

Admitted: Iowa; Minnesota; Nebraska; New York; NY Ct. App. (3rd Div.); US Dist. Ct. (AZ); US Dist. Ct. (IA); US Dist. Ct. (MN); US Dist. Ct. (NE); US Dist. Ct. (S. Dist. NY); US Ct. App. (2nd Cir.); US Ct. App. (8th Cir.); US Ct. App. (10th Cir.); US Ct. App. (11th Cir.); US Sup. Ct.

MICHAEL TRUCANO - Dorsey & Whitney - Pillsbury Center South, 220 South Sixth Street - Minneapolis, MN 55402-1498 - Phone: (612) 340-2673, Fax: (612) 340-8738 - *See complete biographical profile in Closely Held Business Law Chapter.*

Chapter 30: Securities & Venture Finance Law

Complete listing of all attorneys nominated in Securities & Venture Finance Law

Joseph W. Anthony, Fruth & Anthony, Minneapolis; **Timothy R. Baer,** Assistant General Counsel, Dayton Hudson Corp., Minneapolis; **Mark J. Briol,** Briol and Wilmes, Minneapolis; **Dean R. Edstrom,** Doherty, Rumble & Butler Professional Association, Minneapolis; **Terrence J. Fleming,** Lindquist & Vennum, Minneapolis; **Gerald T. Flom,** Faegre & Benson, Minneapolis; **Gregory G. Freitag,** Fredrikson & Byron, P.A., Minneapolis; **Roger H. Frommelt,** Frommelt & Eide, Ltd., Minneapolis; **Terence M. Fruth,** Fruth & Anthony, Minneapolis; **Craig W. Gagnon,** Oppenheimer, Wolff & Donnelly, Minneapolis; **Philip S. Garon,** Faegre & Benson, Minneapolis; **Thomas H. Garrett III,** Lindquist & Vennum, Minneapolis; **Avron L. Gordon,** Briggs and Morgan, P.A., Minneapolis; **Deanne M. Greco,** Moss & Barnett, A Professional Association, Minneapolis; **David C. Grorud,** Fredrikson & Byron, P.A., Minneapolis; **Timothy M. Heaney,** Fredrikson & Byron, P.A., Minneapolis; **John R. Houston,** Lindquist & Vennum, Minneapolis; **Reese C Johnson,** Retired, Dorsey & Whitney, Minneapolis; **James H. Kaster,** Nichols Kaster & Anderson, Minneapolis; **Thomas R. King,** Fredrikson & Byron, P.A., Minneapolis; **Edward M. Laine,** Oppenheimer, Wolff & Donnelly, St. Paul; **John C. Levy,** Parsinen, Bowman & Levy, P.A., Minneapolis; **Thomas G. Lovett IV,** Lindquist & Vennum, Minneapolis; **David J. Lubben,** Dorsey & Whitney, Minneapolis; **J. Lawrence McIntyre,** Toro, Minneapolis; **Eric O. Madson,** Winthrop & Weinstine, P.A., Minneapolis; **Roger J. Magnuson,** Dorsey & Whitney, Minneapolis; **Richard H. Massopust Jr.,** Oppenheimer, Wolff & Donnelly, Minneapolis; **Gale R. Mellum,** Faegre & Benson, Minneapolis; **David B. Miller,** Faegre & Benson, Minneapolis; **Lee R. Mitau,** Dorsey & Whitney, Minneapolis; **Gary M. Nelson,** Oppenheimer, Wolff & Donnelly, Minneapolis; **Michael T. Nilan,** Popham, Haik, Schnobrich & Kaufman, Ltd., Minneapolis; **James E. O'Brien,** Moss & Barnett, A Professional Association, Minneapolis; **Robert K. Ranum,** Fredrikson & Byron, P.A., Minneapolis; **Scott E. Richter,** Popham, Haik, Schnobrich & Kaufman, Ltd., Minneapolis; **Jeffrey C. Robbins,** Parsinen, Bowman & Levy, P.A., Minneapolis; **W. Smith Sharpe Jr.,** Faegre & Benson, Minneapolis; **Ralph L. Strangis,** Kaplan Strangis & Kaplan P.A., Minneapolis; **Frank A. Taylor,** Popham, Haik, Schnobrich & Kaufman, Ltd., Minneapolis; **John C. Thomas,** Oppenheimer, Wolff & Donnelly, Minneapolis; **Mark S. Weitz,** Leonard, Street and Deinard Professional Association, Minneapolis; **Steven A. Wellvang,** Oppenheimer, Wolff & Donnelly, Minneapolis; **Gregory L. Wilmes,** Briol and Wilmes, Minneapolis; **Albert A. Woodward,** Maun & Simon, Minneapolis.

APPENDIX A: LEGAL RESOURCES

A variety of sources exist to help corporate decision makers understand the law and use legal resources effectively. The following is an overview of some of the most useful resources for learning more about the law and lawyers.

ADR PROVIDERS

Many services exist which can provide alternative dispute resolution (ADR) services to businesses. The following is a representative list of some ADR providers who routinely offer their services in Minnesota. Some ADR providers listed specialize in one type of dispute or usually work with a particular type of client. Finding a good ADR provider is much like finding a good attorney; it pays to ask a lot of questions and shop around.

American Arbitration Association
514 Nicollet Mall, Suite 600
Minneapolis, MN 55402
Phone: (612) 332-6545

Attorney-Client Fee Arbitration
514 Nicollet Mall, Suite 350
Minneapolis, MN 55402
Phone: (612) 340-0022

Christian Conciliation Services of Minnesota
1433 Utica Avenue S
Suite 70
Minneapolis, MN 55416

Dispute Resolution Center
265 Oneida Street
St. Paul, MN 55102

Dispute Resolution Services
One Financial Plaza, 120 S Sixth Street
Suite 2500
Minneapolis, MN 55402
Family and employment mediation.

Divorce Mediation of Ramsey, Washington and Dakota County, Inc.
411 Main Street, Suite 202
St. Paul, MN 55102
Divorce mediation.

Goldfarb and Associates
5353 Wayzata Boulevard
Minneapolis, MN 55416
Phone: (612) 546-8888

Hennepin County Arbitration, Mediation and Settlement Conference Program
Room 328 City Hall
300 South Fifth Street
Minneapolis, MN 55487

Kaufman Mediation Group, Inc.
2430 Lincoln Centre
333 S Seventh Street
Minneapolis, MN 55402
Phone: (612) 371-0982

Mediation Center
210 Spruce Tree Center
1600 University Avenue
St. Paul, MN 55104
Phone: (612) 644-1453

Mediation Opportunities, Inc.
1000 Water Park Place
5101 Olson Memorial Parkway
Golden Valley, MN 55422
Phone: (612) 545-2720

Midwest Mediation, Inc.
514 Division Street
Northfield, MN 55057
Phone: (507) 663-1241

North Hennepin Mediation Project
3300 County Road 10, Suite 212
Brooklyn Center, MN 55429
Phone: (612) 561-0033

Northland Mediation Service
1000 Torrey Building
314 W Superior Street
Duluth, MN 55405
Phone: (218) 723-4003

Rural Mediation Services
P.O. Box 836
30620 Olinda Trail N
Lindstrom, MN 55045

Appendix A: Legal Resources

THE OFFICE OF THE ATTORNEY GENERAL

The Attorney General is the chief legal officer of the state of Minnesota. Elections for this post are held every four years. The current Attorney General, Hubert H. Humphrey III, was elected in 1982 and reelected in 1986, 1990 and 1994.

The Attorney General represents all state agencies, boards and commissions and appears on behalf of the state in both federal and state courts. He is included in all major questions involving systems of law and justice, and participates in shaping legislative agenda.

Hubert H. Humphrey III

The Attorney General's office handles a vast range of issues such as drug prevention, sexual violence and harassment prevention, environmental protection and consumer education.

In order to deal with the large volume of disputes, the Attorney General's staff consists of more than 200 attorneys operating in 32 divisions and units. Three divisions work exclusively with the public and are described further in this section.

ATTORNEY GENERAL'S OFFICE

The Attorney General's Office is often referred to as "The People's Lawyers." That is true, but more often than not people think of the Attorney General working for taxpayers somewhat indirectly as a lawyer on behalf of state government. The Attorney General also plays an important role as the "People's Advocate." It is in this role that the Attorney General is able to offer some direct legal services to the public and work on behalf of the "little guy."

In Minnesota, Attorney General Hubert "Skip" Humphrey III has developed a vast array of consumer, environmental, and health fraud services that the public can easily access. In fact, Minnesota has become a leader and a model for many states in offering prompt and helpful customer service through the Attorney General's Office, especially in the area of consumer services.

CONSUMER DIVISION

The Consumer Division of the Attorney General's Office consists of professional mediators who handle consumer complaints and consumer specialists who answer between 400 and 500 telephone calls per day. The mediators in the Consumer Division work to resolve disputes between consumers and various types of businesses, such as auto dealers, mortgage companies, landlords, and sweepstakes companies. The specialists who answer the consumer phone lines provide basic information to callers about a wide variety of consumer-related issues, including auto repair and other auto issues, landlord-tenant issues, credit and collection issues, and home repair issues, among others.

The Consumer Division also publishes numerous brochures and booklets on various consumer topics. Some of the most popular are the brochures on landlord-tenant issues, the Minnesota Lemon Law, and the Used Car Warranty Law. Recently, the Consumer Division completed a series of booklets on home ownership, including *"The Home Buyer's Handbook," "The Home Seller's Handbook,"* and *"The Refinancing Handbook."* These booklets are designed to help consumers understand the complexities of buying, selling, and refinancing their homes.

ENVIRONMENT

The Attorney General's Office is involved in a number of environmental programs. Minnesota law provides substantial criminal penalties for several serious environmental violations, particularly those that involve illegal transportation and disposal of hazardous wastes and illegal discharge of hazardous air and water pollutants.

The Attorney General's Office has two environmental crimes investigators on staff to work on these types of cases. Information on suspected criminal violations of environmental laws may be reported by calling or contacting one of the environmental crimes investigators at the following address: Minnesota Attorney General's Office, 1400 NCL Tower, 445 Minnesota Street, St. Paul, MN 55101. The phone number for the environmental crimes program is (612) 296-7575 and the TDD number is (612) 297-7206. The toll free number for voice and TDD is (800) 657-3787.

The Attorney General's Office also serves as legal counsel to state environmental agencies and is frequently involved in civil enforcement activities related to violations of environmental laws. Although the Attorney General's Office cannot provide legal advice or represent individuals, the office frequently answers questions related to the legal aspects of the implementation and enforcement of environmental laws. These questions are most often answered by staff from the Environmental Protection Division at (612) 297-3471 and the Agriculture and Natural Resources Division at (612) 297-2735.

HEALTH CARE FRAUD AND OVERBILLING

The Attorney General's Office investigates and prosecutes health care providers who engage in fraudulent billing practices. If a person reviews the statement of benefits paid by the insurance company to the health care provider (such as a dentist or doctor) and sees that the payment includes services that were never provided, such as getting a tooth pulled or two office visits in one week, the consumer should contact the insurance company or the Attorney General's Office.

Medicaid recipients receive a monthly statement of benefits which lists all of the providers who were paid by the state for services billed in the preceding month. This statement is attached to the MA card they receive every month. If the recipient sees a payment made for something never received, such as a filled prescription or a doctor's visit, the recipient should contact the Department of Human Services at the number listed on the bottom of the statement. The Department of Human Services looks into the matter to find out if it was a negligent error on the part of the provider, or if there is evidence of a pattern of fraud. If it appears that fraud is taking place, the matter is referred to the Attorney General's Office for further investigation.

The Attorney General's Medicaid Fraud Unit has worked with the Travelers Company and Blue Cross/Blue Shield of Minnesota to prosecute health care providers who have billed both the state Medicaid program and the insurance companies for services that were never provided, or for more expensive services than those actually provided.

Although many of the cases the Attorney General's Office prosecutes come as referrals from insurance companies and the Department of Human Services, often employees or former employees who are tired of watching their bosses cheat the system contact the office. Many times they ask to keep their identity confidential so the employer will not know that the illegal practices have been reported by a person who is an employee. Other cases are reported to the Attorney General by concerned family members who feel that their sick loved one is being taken advantage of.

The FBI estimates that as much as one in every ten dollars spent on health care is lost to fraud, overbilling, and abuse. This cost is passed on to consumers in increased premiums and taxes for Medicaid and Medicare. What may appear to be a single error to the consumer may in fact be a broad pattern of fraudulent billing the provider has spread around to many patients. Paying attention to the

Appendix A: Legal Resources

statements the insurance company or Medicaid program issues and questioning discrepancies can save the health care system and taxpayers millions of dollars each year.

The following is a list of the contacts at the Minnesota Attorney General's office:

Attorney General's Office—General Information
102 State Capitol Building
St. Paul, MN 55155
Phone: (612) 296-6196
Fax: (612) 297-4193

Attorney General's Office—Agriculture
520 Lafayette Road, #200
St. Paul, MN 55155
Phone: (612) 297-1075
Fax: (612) 297-4139

Attorney General's Office—Antitrust
445 Minnesota Street, #1400
St. Paul, MN 55101
Phone: (612) 296-1799
Fax: (612) 296-4348

Attorney General's Office—Charities
445 Minnesota Street, #1200
St. Paul, MN 55101
Phone: (612) 297-4613
Fax: (612) 296-7438

Attorney General's Office—Civil Litigation
445 Minnesota Street, #1100
St. Paul, MN 55101
Phone: (612) 282-5700
Fax: (612) 282-5832

Attorney General's Office—Commerce
445 Minnesota Street, #1200
St. Paul, MN 55101
Phone: (612) 296-9412
Fax: (612) 296-7438

Attorney General's Office—Construction
445 Minnesota Street, #1100
St. Paul, MN 55101
Phone: (612) 282-5700
Fax: (612) 282-5832

Attorney General's Office—Consumer Protection
1400 NCL Tower, 445 Minnesota Street
St. Paul, MN 55101
Phone: (612) 296-3353
Fax: (612) 296-9663

Attorney General's Office—Corrections
445 Minnesota Street, #1100
St. Paul, MN 55101
Phone: (612) 282-5700
Fax: (612) 282-5832

Attorney General's Office—Criminal
445 Minnesota Street, #1400
St. Paul, MN 55101
Phone: (612) 296-7575
Fax: (612) 296-9663

Attorney General's Office—Education
445 Minnesota Street, #1200
St. Paul, MN 55101
Phone: (612) 296-9412
Fax: (612) 296-7438

Attorney General's Office—Employment Law
445 Minnesota Street, #1100
St. Paul, MN 55101
Phone: (612) 282-5700
Fax: (612) 282-5832

Attorney General's Office—Gambling
445 Minnesota Street, #1100
St. Paul, MN 55101
Phone: (612) 296-9412
Fax: (612) 282-5832

Attorney General's Office—Human Rights
445 Minnesota Street, #1200
St. Paul, MN 55101
Phone: (612) 296-9412
Fax: (612) 296-7438

Attorney General's Office—Labor Law
520 Lafayette Road, Second Floor
St. Paul, MN 55155
Phone: (612) 297-1075
Fax: (612) 297-4139

Attorney General's Office—Licensing
525 Park Street, Fifth Floor
St. Paul, MN 55103-2106
Phone: (612) 297-2040
Fax: (612) 297-2576

Attorney General's Office—Natural Resources
520 Lafayette Road, #200
St. Paul, MN 55155
Phone: (612) 297-1075
Fax: (612) 297-4139

Attorney General's Office—Opinions
445 Minnesota Street, #1100
St. Paul, MN 55101
Phone: (612) 282-5700
Fax: (612) 282-5832

Legal Resources

Attorney General's Office—Public Finance
525 Park Street, Fourth Floor
St. Paul, MN 55103
Phone: (612) 297-2040
Fax: (612) 297-2576

Attorney General's Office—Public Safety
525 Park Street, Fourth Floor
St. Paul, MN 55103
Phone: (612) 297-2040
Fax: (612) 297-2576

Attorney General's Office—Public Utilities Commission
350 Metro Square
Seventh Place and Robert Street
St. Paul, MN 55103
Phone: (612) 296-7940
Fax: (612) 297-7073

Attorney General's Office—Residential Utilities Users
1200 NCL Tower
445 Minnesota Street
St. Paul, MN 55101
Phone: (612) 296-6504
Fax: (612) 296-7438

Attorney General's Office—Solicitor General
445 Minnesota Street, #1100
St. Paul, MN 55101
Phone: (612) 282-5700
Fax: (612) 282-5832

Attorney General's Office—Tax Litigation
10 River Park Plaza, Eighth Floor
St. Paul, MN 55146
Phone: (612) 296-3421
Fax: (612) 297-8265

Attorney General's Office—Tort Claims
445 Minnesota Street, #1100
St. Paul, MN 55101
Phone: (612) 282-5700
Fax: (612) 282-5832

Attorney General's Office—Transportation
525 Park Street, #S-500
St. Paul, MN 55103
Phone: (612) 297-2040
Fax: (612) 297-2576

BAR ASSOCIATIONS

Bar associations are professional groups for attorneys. Bar associations view helping the public as an important part of their mission. The largest bar association in Minnesota is the Minnesota State Bar Association (MSBA), an organization with almost 14,000 members. Each member of the MSBA also belongs to one of 21 district bar associations. These associations serve their members by providing continuing legal education and a forum for discussing concerns of the legal profession. They also serve the public, providing lawyer referrals, informational booklets and pamphlets, a telephone information service, and a variety of public education programs. Most of these services are available at little or no cost. Members of the public should consider taking advantage of bar association services when they are seeking general information. Although they cannot provide legal advice, bar associations can help people decide whether to pursue a case, what actions to take, and what type of lawyer to contact. A list of state bar associations in states other than Minnesota appears in Appendix B of this *Guidebook*. The following bar associations can provide information about the law, lawyers, and other legal resources in Minnesota.

American Bar Association
750 N Lake Shore Drive
Chicago, IL 60611
Phone: (312) 988-5000
Fax: (312) 988-6281

American Immigration Lawyers Association
701 Fourth Avenue S, Suite 1440
Minneapolis, MN 55415
Phone: (612) 822-4724

Minnesota American Indian Bar Association
Midland Square Building, Suite 840
Minneapolis, MN 55401
Phone: (612) 282-5708
Fax: (612) 282-5832

Minnesota State Bar Association
514 Nicollet Mall, Suite 300
Minneapolis, MN 55402
Phone: (612) 333-1183

Appendix A: Legal Resources

THE MINNESOTA STATE BAR ASSOCIATION

The Minnesota State Bar Association is a statewide organization for attorneys, with almost 14,000 attorneys members throughout Minnesota. The 1994 president was Roger V. Stageberg, a commercial lawyer with the firm of Lommen Nelson Cole & Stageberg. Its current officers are: Michael J. Galvin Jr., President; Lewis A. Remele Jr., President-Elect; Sheryl Ramstad Hvass, Secretary; and John Nys, Treasurer. Its Executive Director is Timothy Groshens.

In recent years, the Bar Association has worked to improve communication between the legal profession and the public, promoting increased levels of the public's understanding of the law. During Mr. Stageberg's term, the Bar Association developed a successful summer intern program in which inner-city youths work in law-related environments and launched a pilot program to provide reduced-fee legal services to low-income Minnesotans. The Bar Association has also heightened the public's awareness of the numerous positive contributions that lawyers make to the community that often go unnoticed.

Michael J. Galvin, Jr.
President

Roger V. Stageberg
Past President

Also during 1994, the Bar Association has addressed the issue of legal reform, sponsoring a series of consultations on Civil Justice Reform at the University of Minnesota's Humphrey Institute of Public Affairs. A summary report of these consultations is available by contacting the Bar Association.

FINANCING

Business managers should be aware that a variety of sources of business financing exist at federal, state and local levels.

FEDERAL SOURCES OF FINANCING

The following are the most common federal sources of financing for small businesses.

Certified Development Companies

The Small Business Administration operates the 504 program, which makes available to small businesses financing from federal and private sources. Loans are made through regional Certified Development Companies in cooperation with local banks. More information about the 504 program is available from the following Certified Development Companies.

Coon Rapids Development Company
First Bank Coon Rapids Building
P.O. Box 33346
1308 Coon Rapids Blvd., Suite 209
Coon Rapids, MN 55433
Phone: (612) 755-2304

Minneapolis Economic Development Company
Minneapolis Community Development Agency
1215 Marshall Street NE
Minneapolis, MN 55413
Phone: (612) 673-5181

Minnesota Business Finance Inc.
c/o Minnesota Dept. of Trade & Economic Development
500 Metro Square
121 Seventh Place East
St. Paul, MN 55101-2146
Phone: (612) 297-1391

Prairieland Economic Development Corp.
2524 Broadway Avenue
P.O. Box 265
Slayton, MN 56172
Phone: (507) 836-8549

438 *Business Guidebook to Law & Leading Attorneys*

Legal Resources

Region Nine Development Corp.
410 South Fifth Street
P.O. Box 3367
Mankato, MN 56002-3367
Phone: (507) 387-5643

Southern Minnesota 504 Development, Inc.
220 S Broadway, Suite 100
Rochester, MN 55904
Phone: (507) 288-6442

St. Paul Metro East Development Corp.
25 W Fourth Street
St. Paul, MN 55102
Phone: (612) 266-6698

Twin Cities Metro Certified Development Company
Four Seasons Professional Building
Suite 1200
4205 Lancaster Lane
Plymouth, MN 55441
Phone: (612) 551-1825

Farmers Home Administration

The Farmers Home Administration administers a variety of federally funded business and industrial loan programs through its main office and its district offices.

Farmers Home Administration
410 Farm Credit Building
375 Jackson Street
St. Paul, MN 55101-1853
Phone: (612) 290-2842

Alexandria District Office
912 Highway 29 N, Suite 102
Box 1088
Alexandria, MN 56308
Phone: (612) 762-8147

Austin District Office
101 21st Street SE
Austin, MN 55912
Phone: (507) 437-8247

Crookston District Office
528 Strander, Suite C
P.O. Box 25
Crookston, MN 56716
Phone: (218) 281-4815

Grand Rapids District Office
516 "B" Pokegama Avenue S
Grand Rapids, MN 55744
Phone: (218) 326-0561

Marshall District Office
Professional Office Building
104 W Redwood
Marshall, MN 56258
Phone: (507) 532-9671

Waite Park District Office
Marketplace of Waite Park
110 S Second Street, Suite 120
Waite Park, MN 56387-1300
Phone: (612) 255-9111

Willmar District Office
316 SW Becker
P.O. Box 1013
Willmar, MN 56201
Phone: (612) 235-8690

Small Business Administration
610C Butler Square Building
100 N 6th Street
Minneapolis, MN 55403
Phone: (612) 370-2324

STATE SOURCES OF FINANCING

Indian Affairs Council
1819 Bemidji Avenue
Bemidji, MN 56601
Phone: (218) 755-3825

Minnesota Technology, Inc.
111 Third Avenue S, Suite 400
Minneapolis, MN 55401
Phone: (612) 338-7722

Trade and Economic Development, Department of
500 Metro Square
121 Seventh Place E
St. Paul, MN 55101-2146

   Capital Access Program
   Phone: (612) 297-1391

   Community Development Corporation Program
   Phone: (612) 297-1844

   Rural Development Board
   Challenge Grant Program
   Phone: (612) 296-9090

   Tourism Loan Program
   Phone: (612) 296-6858

   Urban Initiative Board
   Phone: (612) 296-9090

Appendix A: Legal Resources

Waste Management, Office of
1350 Energy Lane, Suite 201
St. Paul, MN 55108
Phone: (612) 649-5750
Toll free: (800) 657-3843

Local Sources of Financing
Local Economic Development Programs

In smaller communities, the Economic Development Director of the local unit of government should be able to provide information regarding local economic development programs. In Duluth, Minneapolis, and St. Paul contact the following:

Duluth Area Chamber of Commerce
118 E Superior Street
Duluth, MN 55802
Phone: (218) 722-5501
Request "Economic Development Financing Resource Manual".

Minneapolis Community Development Agency
Business Finance Unit
1215 Marshall Street NE
Minneapolis, MN 55413
Phone: (612) 673-5187
Request "Helping Small Businesses Grow."

St. Paul Department of Planning and Economic Development, Economic Development Division
25 W Fourth Street
St. Paul, MN 55102
Phone: (612) 228-3210
Request "The St. Paul Business Owner's Guide."

GOVERNMENT OFFICES

Addresses of state and federal offices most important to the business community.

Federal Offices

Copyright Office, US Library of Congress
101 Independence Avenue SE
Washington, D.C. 20559
Phone: (202) 707-3000

Equal Employment Opportunity Commission
220 Second Street S
Minneapolis, MN 55401
Phone: (612) 370-3330

Immigration and Naturalization Service
Attn: Employer Relations Officer
2901 Metro Drive, Suite 100
Bloomington, MN 55425
Phone: (612) 335-2255

Internal Revenue Service
Old Federal Building, Room 149
210 Third Avenue S
Minneapolis, MN 55401
For forms and information or inquiries about the field offices, call the Minneapolis office at (612) 644-7515 or (800) 829-1040.

Internal Revenue Service
Duluth Field Office
Room 105 Federal Building
515 First Street W
Duluth, MN 55802

Internal Revenue Service
Fergus Falls Field Office
220 W Washington
Fergus Falls, MN 56537

Legal Resources

Internal Revenue Service
Mankato Field Office
Northwestern Office Building, Suite 408
209 Second Street S
Mankato, MN 56001

Internal Revenue Service
Rochester Field Office
21 Second Street SW
Rochester, MN 55902

Internal Revenue Service
St. Cloud Field Office
720 W Saint Germain, Room 212
St. Cloud, MN 56301

Internal Revenue Service
St. Paul Field Office
Federal Building, Room 385
316 N Robert Street
St. Paul, MN 55101

Internal Revenue Service
Willmar Field Office
Plaza I Shopping Center
1305 First Street S
Willmar, MN 56201

Labor, Department of Employment Standards Administration Wage and Hour Division
Bridge Place, Room 106
220 Second Street S
Minneapolis, MN 55401-2104
Phone: (612) 370-3371

Office of Pension, Welfare and Benefit Programs
815 Olive, Room 338
St. Louis, Missouri 63101
Phone: (314) 539-2691

Patent and Trademark Office, US
Washington, D.C. 20231
Phone: (703) 557-3158

Securities and Exchange Commission Publications Office
450 Fifth Street NW, Room 3C38
Washington, D.C. 20549
Phone: (202) 272-7460

Small Business Administration
610C Butler Square Building
100 Sixth Street N
Minneapolis, MN 55403
Phone: (612) 370-2324

STATE OFFICES

Administration, Department of Materials Management Division
Procurement Helpline
112 Administration Building
50 Sherburne Avenue
St. Paul, MN 55155
Phone: (612) 296-2600

Agriculture, Department of Food Inspection Division
90 West Plato Boulevard
St. Paul, MN 55107
Phone: (612) 296-1592

Bookstore, Minnesota
117 University Avenue
St. Paul, MN 55155
Phone: (612) 297-3000

Commerce, Department of
133 Seventh Street E
St. Paul, MN 55101

    General Information
    Phone: (612) 296-4026

    Franchise Registration
    Phone: (612) 296-6328

    Insurance Information
    Phone: (612) 296-4026

    Securities Registration
    Phone: (612) 296-4973

Economic Security, Department of Tax Processing Unit
390 N Robert Street
St. Paul, MN 55101

    Information
    Phone: (612) 296-3674

    Forms
    Phone: (612) 296-3643

    Posters
    Phone: (612) 296-2536

Environmental Quality Board
300 Centennial Office Building
658 E Cedar Street
St. Paul, MN 55155

    General Information
    Phone: (612) 296-3985

    Environmental Review
    Phone: (612) 296-8253

Appendix A: Legal Resources

Human Rights, Department of
500 Bremer Tower
Seventh Place and Minnesota Street
St. Paul, MN 55101
Phone: (612) 296-5663
TTY: (612) 296-1283
Toll free: (800) 657-3704

Labor and Industry, Department of
443 N Lafayette Road
St. Paul, MN 55155

   Apprenticeship
   Phone: (612) 296-2371

   Labor Standards
   Phone: (612) 296-2282

   OSHA Compliance
   Phone: (612) 296-2116

   Posters
   Phone: (612) 296-1096

   Prevailing Wage Standards
   Phone: (612) 296-6452

   Workplace Safety Consultation
   Phone: (612) 297-2393

OSHA Brainerd Area Office
1991 Industrial Park Road
Baxter, MN 56401
Phone: (218) 828-2455

OSHA Duluth Area Office
108 Government Services Center
320 Second Street W
Duluth, MN 55802
Phone: (218) 723-4678

OSHA Mankato Area Office
Nichols Office Center
410 Jackson Street, Suite 110
Mankato, MN 56001
Phone: (507) 389-6501

Pollution Control Agency
520 Lafayette Road
St. Paul, MN 55155

   Information
   Phone: (612) 296-6300
   Toll free: (800) 657-3864
   TDD: (612) 282-5332

   Air Quality (Asbestos Notification)
   Phone: (612) 297-7152

   Air Quality Permits (Emission Facilities)
   Phone: (612) 296-7723

   Air Quality Permits (Indirect Source)
   Phone: (612) 296-7723

   Air Quality Permits (Small Business Assistance)
   Phone: (612) 296-6300

   Air Quality (Small Business Ombudsman)
   Phone: (612) 297-8615

   Categorical Industry Permits
   Phone: (612) 296-8006

   Disposal System Permits
   Phone: (612) 297-1832

   Environmental Analysis Office
   Phone: (612) 296-8645

   Feedlot Permits
   Phone: (612) 296-7326

   National Pollution Discharge Elimination System Permits
   Phone: (612) 297-1832

   Tanks and Spills Unit
   Phone: (612) 297-8679

   Water Quality Permits
   Phone: (612) 297-1832

Public Safety, Department of Driver and Vehicle Services
Motor Vehicle Excise Tax
Transportation Building
St. Paul, MN 55155
Phone: (612) 296-6911

Revenue, Department of Taxpayer Information Division
Mail Station 4453
St. Paul, MN 55146-4453
Phone: (612) 296-6181
Toll free: (800) 657-3777

   Business Audit Section
   Mail Station 6610
   St. Paul, MN 55146-6610
   Phone: (612) 296-6181
   Toll free: (800) 657-3777

   Collection Enforcement Group
   Mail Station 6522, P.O. Box 64447
   St. Paul, MN 55164
   Phone: (612) 296-8225

   Forms Distribution Office
   Mail Station 4451
   St. Paul, MN 55146-4451
   Phone: (612) 296-6181
   Toll free: (800) 657-3777

Petroleum Tax Office
Mail Station 3333
St. Paul, MN 55146-3333
Phone: (612) 296-0889

Special Taxes Office
Mail Station 3331
St. Paul, MN 55146-3331
Phone: (612) 297-1882

Secretary of State, Office of
180 State Office Building
St. Paul, MN 55155
Phone: (612) 296-2803

Small Business Assistance Office, Minnesota
500 Metro Square, 121 Seventh Place E
St. Paul, MN 55101-2146
Phone: (612) 296-3871 (Twin Cities area)
Toll free: (800) 657-3858 (Outside Twin Cities)

Technical Assistance Program (MnTAP)
1313 Fifth Street SE, Suite 207
Minneapolis, MN 55414-4504
Phone: (612) 627-4646
Toll free: (800) 247-0015

Trade and Economic Development, Department of
500 Metro Square
121 Seventh Place E
St. Paul, MN 55101-2146

General Information
Phone: (612) 297-1291
Toll free: (800) 657-3858

Business and Community Development Division
Phone: (612) 296-5005

Small Business Assistance Office
Phone: (612) 296-3871
Toll free: (800) 657-3858

Small Business Development Centers
Phone: (612) 297-5770
Toll free: (800) 657-3858

Tourism Office
100 Metro Square
121 Seventh Place E
St. Paul, MN 55101
Phone: (612) 296-5029
Toll free: (800) 657-3700

Trade Office
1000 World Trade Center Building
St. Paul, MN 55101-4902
Phone: (612) 297-4222

Workers' Compensation Information
Phone: (612) 296-2432 (Twin Cities)
Toll free: (800) 342-5354 (Twin Cities office)
Phone: (218) 723-4670 (Duluth)
Toll free: (800) 365-4584 (Duluth office)

LAW FIRM NEWSLETTERS

Several of the law firms profiled in this *Guidebook* produce periodic newsletters for clients and friends of the firm. To request a single copy or to learn about how to get on a firm's mailing list, contact the law firm directly, see attorney biographies. The following is a representative sample of law firm newsletters available:

Bank Focus
Fredrikson & Byron and Independent Community Bankers of Minnesota
1100 International Centre
900 Second Avenue S
Minneapolis, MN 55402
Phone: (612) 347-7000
Newsletter for legal developments in the field of banking.

Construction News
Leonard, Street and Deinard Professional Association
150 South Fifth Street, Suite 2300
Minneapolis, MN 55402
Phone: (612) 335-1500
Quarterly newsletter for the construction industry.

Employment Law Review
Leonard, Street and Deinard Professional Association
150 South Fifth Street, Suite 2300
Minneapolis, MN 55402
Phone: (612) 335-1500
Federal and legal developments that affect employers and employees.

EnviroLaw
Heins Schatz & Paquin, Attorneys at Law
2200 Washington Square
100 Washington Avenue S
Minneapolis, MN 55401
Phone: (612) 339-6900
Newsletter of environmental law.

Appendix A: Legal Resources

Lawgram
Popham, Haik, Schnobrich and Kaufman, Ltd.
3300 Piper Jaffray Tower
222 S Ninth Street
Minneapolis, MN 55402
Phone: (612) 333-4800
Newsletter of compensation and benefits.

Marketing Law Focus
Fredrikson & Byron, P.A.
1100 International Centre
900 Second Avenue
Minneapolis, MN 55402
Phone: (612) 347-7000
Newsletter of legal developments in the area of advertising, marketing, sales and distribution.

State and Local Tax News
Dorsey & Whitney
Pillsbury Center South
220 S Sixth Street
Minneapolis, MN 55402
Phone: (612) 340-2600
Newsletter of current developments in tax law.

Workplace Law Notes
Faegre & Benson
2200 Norwest Center
90 S Seventh Street
Minneapolis, MN 55402
Phone: (612) 336-3000
Newsletter for workplace law issues.

LAWYER REFERRAL SERVICES

Persons who are unsure of how to locate an attorney can use this *Guidebook,* and may also consider contacting one of several lawyer referral services operated by bar associations and other organizations. Lawyer referral services attempt to match the client with a lawyer in his or her community. MSBA operates the Statewide Attorney Referral Service, which handles more than 30,000 consumer calls each year. The Service's panel of lawyers includes nearly 300 attorneys who practice throughout Minnesota.

Attorneys who participate in this referral service have agreed to provide a free 30-minute consultation for each case referred to them. The referral service charges clients $20 when there is a consultation with a lawyer. If a client does not consult a lawyer, there is no referral fee. If a client decides to hire a lawyer through the service, the client and lawyer negotiate fees privately between themselves; the service does not set fees for its lawyers.

Separate attorney referral services operate in Hennepin, Ramsey, Dakota, and Washington counties. These services list only lawyers in the particular county. There are fees for these referrals. In addition, Minnesota Women Lawyers will refer cases involving all areas of law to the 120 women lawyers listed on that organization's referral service. Callers are given the names of up to three lawyers, and the referral is free. As with the other referral services, the consumer and the lawyer negotiate fees privately. Most of the lawyers listed in the Minnesota Women Lawyers' Service practice in the Twin Cities area.

Chrysalis Attorney Referral Service
2650 Nicollet Avenue S
Minneapolis, MN 55408
Phone: (612) 871-2603
PTY: (612) 871-3652
Primarily serves women.

Dakota County Bar Association Referral Service
15025 Glazier Avenue, Suite 226
Apple Valley, MN 55124
Phone: (612) 431-3200

Gay and Lesbian Action Council Legal Advocacy Program
310 E 38th Street, Suite 204
Minneapolis, MN 55409
Phone: (612) 822-0127

Hennepin County Bar Association Referral Service
514 Nicollet Mall, Suite 350
Minneapolis, MN 55402
Phone: (612) 339-8777

Lambda Justice Center
332 Minnesota Street, Suite E1324
St. Paul, MN 55101-1314
Phone: (612) 293-1440
Fax: (612) 227-4933
Provides referrals for lesbian, gay, bisexual, transgender, and transsexual people.

MSBA Statewide Referral Service
514 Nicollet Mall, Suite 403
Minneapolis, MN 55402
Phone: (612) 333-4927
Toll free: (800) 292-4152
TDD: (612) 333-1216

Minnesota Women Lawyers Referral Service
514 Nicollet Mall, Suite 305A
Minneapolis, MN 55402
Phone: (612) 338-3205
Fax: (612) 340-9518

Ramsey County Bar Association Referral Service
332 Minnesota Street, Suite E1312
St. Paul, MN 55101
Phone: (612) 224-1775

Resources and Counseling for the Arts
75 W Fifth Street, Suite 429
St. Paul, MN 55102
Phone: (612) 292-4381
Referrals and information; will provide up to one-half hour of free legal consultation to artists.

Washington County Bar Referral Service
3880 Laverne Avenue N, Suite 245
Lake Elmo, MN 55042
Phone: (612) 777-6878

LIBRARIES

LAW LIBRARIES

Law libraries are an excellent source of information about lawyers and the legal system. Althought they cannot give legal advice, most law librarians are happy to help novices learn how to use the resources of Minnesota's primary legal libraries.

The Minnesota State Law Library
25 Constitution Avenue
St. Paul, MN 55155
Phone: (612) 296-2775

Hamline University School of Law
1536 Hewitt Avenue
St. Paul, MN 55104
Phone: (612) 641-2349

Hennepin County Law Library
C-2451 Government Center
Minneapolis, MN 55487
Phone: (612) 348-3022

Ramsey County Law Library
1815 Courthouse
St. Paul, MN 55102
Phone: (612) 298-5208

St. Louis County Law Library
100 N Fifth Avenue W, Room 515
Duluth, MN 55802-1202
Phone: (218) 726-2611

University of Minnesota Law Library
229 19th Avenue South
Minneapolis, MN 55455
Phone: (612) 625-4309

William Mitchell College of Law Library
871 Summit Avenue
St. Paul, MN 55105
Phone: (612) 290-6333

GOVERNMENT DOCUMENT DEPOSITORY LIBRARIES

Government document depository libraries are an excellent resource for gaining access to specified government documents. The following libraries can teach patrons how to access a tremendous number of government resources.

Anoka County Library
707 Highway 10 NE
Blaine, MN 55434-2398
Phone: (612) 784-1100

Bemidji State University Library
Fourteenth and Birchmont
Bemidji, MN 56601
Phone: (218) 755-3342

Carleton College Library
One N College Street
Northfield, MN 55057
Phone: (507) 663-4259

Dakota County Library
1340 Wescott Road
Eagan, MN 55123
Phone: (612) 452-9600

Duluth Public Library
520 W Superior Street
Duluth, MN 55802
Phone: (218) 723-3802

Government Publications Library
University of Minnesota
409 Wilson Library
3091 Ninth Avenue S
Minneapolis, MN 55455
Phone: (612) 624-5073

Appendix A: Legal Resources

Gustavus Adolphus College Library
St. Peter, MN 56082
Phone: (507) 933-7569

Hamline University School of Law Library
1536 Hewitt Avenue
St. Paul, MN 55104
Phone: (612) 641-2125

Hennepin County Library
Southdale Area Library
7001 York Avenue S
Edina, MN 55435
Phone: (612) 830-4933

Mankato State University Memorial Library
P.O. Box 8400
Mankato, MN 56001
Phone: (507) 389-5153

Minneapolis Public Library
300 Nicollet Mall
Minneapolis, MN 55401
Phone: (612) 372-6534

Minnesota Historical Society Research Center
345 Kellogg Boulevard W
St. Paul, MN 55102-1906
Phone: (612) 296-2143

Minnesota State Law Library
25 Constitution Avenue
St. Paul, MN 55155
Phone: (612) 296-2775

Moorhead State University Livingston Lord Library
Moorhead, MN 56563
Phone: (218) 236-2349

St. Cloud State University Learning Resources Center
St. Cloud, MN 56301
Phone: (612) 255-2086

St. John's University Alcuin Library
Collegeville, MN 56321-2500
Phone: (612) 363-3101

St. Olaf College Rolvaag Memorial Library
Northfield, MN 55057
Phone: (507) 663-3601

St. Paul Public Library
90 W Fourth Street
St. Paul, MN 55102
Phone: (612) 292-6178

Southwest State University Library
Marshall, MN 56258
Phone: (507) 537-7210

University of Minnesota Law School Library
229 Nineteenth Avenue S
Minneapolis, MN 55455
Phone: (612) 625-9800

University of Minnesota Duluth
Library, Room 370
10 University Drive
Duluth, MN 55812-2495
Phone: (218) 726-6157

University of Minnesota Morris Library
10 University Drive
Morris, MN 56267
Phone: (612) 589-2211, Ext. 6174

University of Minnesota St. Paul Campus
1984 Buford Avenue
St. Paul, MN 55108
Phone: (612) 624-1212

Washington County Library-Park Grove
7900 Hemingway Avenue
Cottage Grove, MN 55016
Phone: (612) 459-2040

William Mitchell College of Law Library
871 Summit Avenue
St. Paul, MN 55105
Phone: (612) 290-6333

Winona State University Maxwell Library
Johnson and Sanborn Streets
Winona, MN 55987
Phone: (507) 457-5148

MANAGEMENT ASSISTANCE

There are many sources of free or low-cost management assistance for businesses in Minnesota.

SCORE

The Service Corps of Retired Volunteers (SCORE) is a fraternity of retired business managers who volunteer to help new or existing businesses. Information about the services offered through SCORE can be gained by contacting one of its regional offices throughout the state.

Albert Lea SCORE Office
Albert Lea Chamber of Commerce
202 N Broadway
Albert Lea, MN 56007
Phone: (507) 373-3939

Alexandria SCORE
Alexandria Technical College
1601 Jefferson Street
Alexandria, MN 56308
Phone: (612) 762-4502

Anoka SCORE Office
Anoka City Hall
2015 First Avenue
Anoka, MN 55303
Phone: (612) 421-6630, Ext. 166

Austin SCORE Office
Austin Chamber of Commerce
P.O. Box 864
Austin, MN 55912
Phone: (507) 437-4561

Brainerd SCORE Office
Brainerd Chamber of Commerce
Sixth and Washington Street
Brainerd, MN 56401
Phone: (218) 829-2838

Duluth SCORE Office Chapter #286
Duluth Chamber of Commerce
118 E Superior Street
Duluth, MN 55802
Phone: (218) 722-5501

SCORE Office
Hennepin Technical College
Eden Prairie Campus
9200 Flying Cloud Drive
Highway 169 South
Eden Prairie, MN 55344
Phone: (612) 944-2222

Fairmont SCORE Office
Fairmont Area Chamber of Commerce
Box 826
1015 Main Street
Fairmont, MN 56031
Phone: (507) 235-5547

Mankato SCORE Chapter #328
Mankato Chamber of Commerce
P.O. Box 999
220 E Main Street
Mankato, MN 56001
Phone: (507) 345-4519

Marshall SCORE Office
Marshall Chamber of Commerce
501 W Main
Marshall, MN 56258
Phone: (507) 532-4484

Minneapolis SCORE Chapter #2
North Plaza Building, Suite 51
5217 Wayzata Boulevard
Minneapolis, MN 55416
Phone: (612) 591-0539

Ortonville SCORE
Ortonville Economic Development Authority
315 Madison Avenue
Ortonville, MN 56278
Phone: (612) 839-2618

Owatonna SCORE
Owatonna Chamber of Commerce
320 Hoffman Drive
P.O. Box 331
Owatonna, MN 55060
Phone: (507) 451-7970

Red Wing SCORE
Red Wing Technical College
Highway 58 at Pioneer Road
Red Wing, MN 55066
Phone: (612) 388-4079 or 388-8271

Rochester SCORE Chapter #406
Rochester Chamber of Commerce
220 S Broadway, Suite 100
Rochester, MN 55904
Phone: (507) 288-1122

St. Cloud SCORE Office Chapter #468
400 First Street S, Suite 430
St. Cloud, MN 56301
Phone: (612) 255-4955

St. Paul SCORE Chapter #391
St. Paul Chamber of Commerce
101 Norwest Center
55 Fifth Street E
St. Paul, MN 55101
Phone: (612) 223-5010

Small Business Administration SCORE
610-C Butler Square Building
100 N Sixth Street
Minneapolis, MN 55403
Phone: (612) 370-2308 or 370-2339

Winona SCORE Office
Winona Chamber of Commerce
P.O. Box 870
67 Main Street
Winona, MN 55987
Phone: (507) 452-2272

Worthington SCORE
Worthington Chamber of Commerce
Box 608
Worthington, MN 56187
Phone: (507) 372-2919

Small Business Development Centers

Small Business Development Centers are state funded resource centers, administered by the Minnesota Small Business Assistance Office, whose purpose is to provide information and counseling to small businesses and persons wanting to start a small business. In order to qualify for assistance, a business must meet the definition of a "small business" set by the U.S. Small Business Administration.

Bemidji Technical College
Small Business Development Center
905 Grant Avenue SE
Bemidji, MN 56601
Phone: (218) 759-3274

Brainerd Technical College
Small Business Development Center
300 Quince Street
Brainerd, MN 56401
Phone: (218) 828-5302
Toll free: (800) 247-2574

Dakota County Technical College
Small Business Development Center
1300 145th Street E
Rosemount, MN 55068
Phone: (612) 423-8262

Grand Rapids Small Business Development Center
Itasca Development Corporation
19 NE Third Street
Grand Rapids, MN 55744
Phone: (218) 327-2241

Hennepin Technical College
Small Business Development Center
1820 N Xenium Lane
Plymouth, MN 55441
Phone: (612) 550-7218

Hibbing Community College
Small Business Development Center
1515 E 25th Street
Hibbing, MN 55746
Phone: (218) 262-6700

Mankato State University
Small Business Development Center
P.O. Box 145
Mankato, MN 56001
Phone: (507) 389-1648

Mesabi Community College
Small Business Development Center
Ninth Avenue and W Chestnut
Virginia, MN 55792
Phone: (218) 749-7729

Minnesota Project Innovation
111 Third Avenue S, Suite 100
Minneapolis, MN 55401
Phone: (612) 338-3280

Moorhead State University
Small Business Development Center
Box 303
Moorhead, MN 56563
Phone: (218) 236-2289

Normandale Community College
Small Business Development Center
9700 France Avenue S
Bloomington, MN 55431
Phone: (612) 832-6560

Northeast Metro Technical College
Small Business Development Center
70 W County Road B-2
Little Canada, MN 55117
Phone: (612) 779-5764

Pine Technical College
Small Business Development Center
1100 Fourth Street
Pine City, MN 55063
Phone: (612) 629-7340

Rainy River Community College
Small Business Development Center
Highways 11 and 71
International Falls, MN 56649
Phone: (218) 285-2255

Red Wing Technical College
Small Business Development Center
Pioneer Road at Highway 58
Red Wing, MN 55066
Phone: (612) 388-4079
Toll free: (800) 642-3344, Ext. 12

Rochester Community College
Small Business Development Center
Highway 14 East
851 30th Avenue SE
Rochester, MN 55904-4999
Phone: (507) 285-7536

St. Cloud State University
Small Business Development Center
Business Resource Center, Suite 430
400 S First Street
St. Cloud, MN 56301
Phone: (612) 255-4842

Small Business Development Centers Administrative Office
500 Metro Square
121 Seventh Place E
St. Paul, MN 55101
Phone: (612) 297-5770
Toll free: (800) 657-3858

Legal Resources

Southwest State University
Small Business Development Center
ST 105
Marshall, MN 56258
Phone: (507) 537-7386

Thief River Falls Technical College
Small Business Development Center
1301 Highway One East
Thief River Falls, MN 56701
Phone: (218) 681-5424
Toll free: (800) 222-2884

University of Minnesota Duluth
Small Business Development Center
10 University Drive
150 School of Business and Economics
Duluth, MN 55811
Phone: (218) 726-8758

University of St. Thomas
Small Business Development Center
1000 LaSalle Avenue, Suite MPL 100
Minneapoolis, MN 55403
Phone: (612) 962-4500

Wadena Technical College
Small Business Development Center
222 Second Street SE
Wadena, MN 56482
Phone: (218) 631-1502

Winona State University
Small Business Development Center
Winona, MN 55987
Phone: (507) 457-5088

SMALL BUSINESS INSTITUTES

Small business institutes are counseling centers that provide free services and counseling to small businesses for a variety of problems. Students participate in the program by providing assistance under the direction of qualified faculty. The following is a list of small business institutes in Minnesota.

Bemidji State University
Small Business Institute
1500 Birchmont Drive NE
Bemidji, MN 56601-2699
Phone: (218) 755-2750

Bethel College
Small Business Institute
P.O. Box 77
3900 Bethel Drive
St. Paul, MN 55112
Phone: (612) 638-6318

Mankato State University
Small Business Institute
Mankato, MN 56001
Phone: (507) 389-5401

Moorhead State University
Small Business Institute
1104 Seventh Avenue S
Moorhead, MN 56560
Phone: (218) 236-2289

St. Cloud State University
Small Business Institute
First Avenue S and Seventh Street
St. Cloud, MN 56301
Phone: (612) 255-3215

St. Mary's College
Dept. of Business Administration
Small Business Institute
700 Terrace Heights
Winona, MN 55987-1399
Phone: (507) 452-4430

St. Olaf College
Small Business Institute
Department of Economics
Northfield, MN 55057
Phone: (507) 663-3152

University of Minnesota Duluth
Small Business Institute
150 School of Business and Economics
Duluth, MN 55812
Phone: (218) 726-8761

University of St. Thomas
Small Business Institute
2115 Summit Avenue
St. Paul, MN 55105
Phone: (612) 647-5621

Winona State University
Small Business Institute
Somsen Hall
Eighth and Jackson
Winona, MN 55987
Phone: (507) 457-5176

Appendix A: Legal Resources

COMMUNITY COLLEGES, SMALL BUSINESS MANAGEMENT

All community colleges in Minnesota offer courses in small business management. Course descriptions can be obtained by contacting one of the following community college campuses directly.

Austin Community College
1600 NW Eighth Avenue
Austin, MN 55912
Phone: (507) 433-0505
Toll free: (800) 747-6941

Anoka-Ramsey Community College Cambridge Center
151 SW County Road 70
Cambridge, MN 55008
Phone: (612) 689-1536

Anoka-Ramsey Community College
11200 Mississippi Boulevard
Coon Rapids, MN 55433
Phone: (612) 427-2600

Brainerd Community College
501 W College Drive
Brainerd, MN 56401
Phone: (218) 828-2525

Fergus Falls Community College
1414 College Way
Fergus Falls, MN 56537
Phone: (218) 739-7500

Hibbing Community College
1515 E 25th Street
Hibbing, MN 55746
Phone: (218) 262-6700

Inver Hills Community College
8445 College Trail
Inver Grove Heights, MN 55076
Phone: (612) 450-8500

Itasca Community College
1851 East Highway 169
Grand Rapids, MN 55744
Phone: (218) 327-4460

Lakewood Community College
3401 Century Avenue
White Bear Lake, MN 55110
Phone: (612) 779-3200

Mesabi Community College
Ninth Avenue and W Chestnut Street
Virginia, MN 55792
Phone: (218) 749-7700
Toll free: (800) 657-3860

Minneapolis Community College
1501 Hennepin Avenue
Minneapolis, MN 55403
Phone: (612) 341-7000

Normandale Community College
9700 France Avenue S
Bloomington, MN 55431
Phone: (612) 832-6000

North Hennepin Community College
7411 85th Avenue N
Brooklyn Park, MN 55445
Phone: (612) 424-0811

Northland Community College
101 Highway One East
Thief River Falls, MN 56701
Phone: (218) 681-2181
Toll free: (800) 628-9918

Rainy River Community College
Highway 11-71 and 15th Street
International Falls, MN 56649
Phone: (218) 285-7722
Toll free: (800) 456-3996

Rochester Community College
851 30th Avenue SE
Highway 14 East
Rochester, MN 55904-4999
Phone: (507) 285-7210
Toll free: (800) 383-5421

Vermillion Community College
1900 E Camp Street
Ely, MN 55731
Phone: (218) 365-7200
Toll free: (800) 657-3608

Willmar Community College
County Road 24
P.O. Box 797
Willmar, MN 56201
Phone: (612) 231-5102

Worthington Community College
1450 College Way
Worthington, MN 56187
Phone: (507) 372-2107
Toll free: (800) 652-3966

Technical Colleges, Small Business Management

Alexandria Technical College
1601 Jefferson Street
Alexandria, MN 56308
Phone: (612) 762-0221
Toll free: (800) 253-9884

Albert Lea Technical College
2200 Tech Drive
Albert Lea, MN 56007
Phone: (507) 373-0656
Toll free: (800) 333-2584

Anoka Technical College
1355 West Highway 10
Anoka, MN 55303
Phone: (612) 427-1880
Toll free: (800) 247-5588

Bemidji Technical College
905 Grant Avenue SE
Bemidji, MN 56601
Phone: (218) 759-3200
Toll free: (800) 942-8324

Brainerd Technical College
300 Quince Street
Brainerd, MN 56401
Phone: (218) 828-5380
Toll free: (800) 547-2574

Dakota County Technical College
1300 E 145th Street
Rosemount, MN 55068
Phone: (612) 423-8301
Toll free: (800) 548-5502

Detroit Lakes Technical College
Highway 34 E
Detroit Lakes, MN 56501
Phone: (218) 847-1341
Toll free: (800) 492-4836

Duluth Technical College
2101 Trinity Road
Duluth, MN 55811-3399
Phone: (218) 722-7897
Toll free: (800) 432-2844

Faribault Technical College
1225 SW Third Street
Faribault, MN 55021
Phone: (507) 334-3965
Toll free: (800) 422-0391

Hennepin Technical College
1820 N Xenium Lane
Plymouth, MN 55441
Phone: (612) 559-3535

Hibbing Technical College
2900 E Beltline
Hibbing, MN 55746
Phone: (218) 262-6688
Toll free: (800) 422-0829

Hutchinson Technical College
2 Century Avenue
Hutchinson, MN 55350
Phone: (612) 587-3636, Ext. 251
Toll free: (800) 222-4424

Mankato Technical College
1920 Lee Boulevard
Mankato, MN 56003
Phone: (507) 625-3441
Toll free: (800) 722-9359

Minneapolis Technical College
1415 Hennepin Avenue
Minneapolis, MN 55403-1778
Phone: (612) 370-9438
Toll free: (800) 247-0911

Moorhead Technical College
1900 28th Avenue S
Moorhead, MN 56560
Phone: (218) 236-6277
Toll free: (800) 426-5603

Northeast Metro Technical College
3554 White Bear Avenue N
White Bear Lake, MN 55110
Phone: (612) 779-5800

Pine Technical College
1000 Fourth Street
Pine City, MN 55063
Phone: (612) 629-6764
Toll free: (800) 521-7463

Red Wing Technical College
Highway 58 and Pioneer Road
Red Wing, MN 55066
Phone: (612) 388-8271
Toll free: (800) 642-3344

Riverland Technical College
1926 College View Road
Rochester, MN 55904
Phone: (507) 285-8618
Toll free: (800) 247-1296

Riverland Technical College
1900 NW Eighth Avenue
Austin, MN 55912
Phone: (507) 433-0600
Toll free: (800) 247-5039

Appendix A: Legal Resources

St. Cloud Technical College
1540 Northway Drive
St. Cloud, MN 56301
Phone: (612) 252-0101

St. Paul Technical College
235 Marshall Avenue
St. Paul, MN 55102
Phone: (612) 221-1431
Toll free: (800) 227-6029

**Southwestern Technical College
Canby Campus**
1011 First Street W
Canby, MN 56220
Phone: (507) 223-7252
Toll free: (800) 658-2535

**Southwestern Technical College
Granite Falls Campus**
1593 11th Avenue
Granite Falls, MN 56241
Phone: (612) 564-4511
Toll free: (800) 657-3247

**Southwestern Technical College
Jackson Campus**
401 West Street
Jackson, MN 56143
Phone: (507) 847-3320
Toll free: (800) 658-2522

**Southwestern Technical College
Pipestone Campus**
N Hiawatha Avenue
Pipestone, MN 56164
Phone: (507) 825-5471
Toll free: (800) 658-2330

Thief River Falls Technical College
1301 Highway 1 East
Thief River Falls, MN 56701-2599
Phone: (218) 681-5424
Toll free: (800) 222-2884

University of Minnesota Extension Service
Education Development System
405 Coffey Hall
St. Paul, MN 55108-1030
Phone: (612) 625-2787

Wadena Technical College
405 Colfax Avenue SW
Wadena, MN 56482
Phone: (218) 631-3530
Toll free: (800) 247-2007

Willmar Technical College
Box 1097
Willmar, MN 56201
Phone: (612) 235-5114
Toll free: (800) 722-1151

Winona Technical College
1250 Homer Road
Winona, MN 55987
Phone: (507) 454-4600
Toll free: (800) 372-8164

MANAGEMENT ASSISTANCE FOR MINORITY BUSINESSES

ESB (Emerging Small Business) Clearing House
1121 Glenwood Avenue North
Minneapolis, MN 55405
Phone: (612) 374-5129

Metropolitan Economic Development Association
2021 E Hennepin Avenue, Suite 370
Minneapolis, MN 55413
Phone: (612) 378-0361

Minneapolis/St. Paul Minority Business Development Center (MBDC)-MEDA
2021 E Hennepin Avenue, Suite LL35
Minneapolis, MN 55413
Phone: (612) 331-5576

Minnesota Chippewa Tribe Indian Business Development Center
P.O. Box 217
Cass Lake, MN 56633
Phone: (218) 335-8583

Minnesota Minority Supplier Development Council
2021 E Hennepin Avenue, Suite 370
Minneapolis, MN 55413
Phone: (612) 378-0361

Women Venture
2324 University Avenue, Suite 200
St. Paul, MN 55114
Phone: (612) 646-3808

NEW BUSINESS DEVELOPMENT

The Collaborative
10 S Fifth Street, Suite 415
Minneapolis, MN 55402
Phone: (612) 338-3828
The Collaborative is a 600-member organization of entrepreneurs, investors, managers and advisors involved in developing new and emerging companies. The Collaborative hosts over 30 programs per year and publishes a newsletter and a quarterly business journal.

PROCUREMENT ASSISTANCE

Assistance in procuring government contracts is available from the following sources:

Federal Procurement
Minnesota Project Innovation
Procurement Assistance Center
111 Third Avenue S, Suite 410
Minneapolis, MN 55401-2554
Phone: (612) 341-0641

Twin Cities Procurement
City of Minneapolis
Purchasing Department
250 South Fourth Street
Room 414
Public Health Building
Minneapolis, MN 55415
Phone: (612) 673-2500

City of St. Paul/Ramsey County Joint Purchasing
233 City Hall
St. Paul, MN 55102
Phone: (612) 298-4225

City of St. Paul/Ramsey County Joint Purchasing Targeted Vendor Development Program
233 City Hall
St. Paul, MN 55102
Phone: (612) 292-7516

W/MBE Clearinghouse
1121 Glenwood Avenue N
Minneapolis, MN 55405
Phone: (612) 374-1781

Metropolitan Agencies
Metropolitan Airports Commission
6040 28th Avenue S
Minneapolis, MN 55450
Phone: (612) 726-1892

Metropolitan Council
230 E Fifth Street
Mears Park Center
St. Paul, MN 55101
Phone: (612) 291-6359

Metropolitan Transit Commission
515 N Cleveland
St. Paul, MN 55114
Phone: (612) 642-2600

Metropolitan Waste Control Commission
230 E Fifth Street
Mears Park Center
St. Paul, MN 55101
Phone: (612) 222-8423

Counties
Anoka County Accounting and Central Services
325 E Main
Anoka, MN 55303
Phone: (612) 421-4760

Dakota County Purchasing
1560 Highway 55 West
Hastings, MN 55033
Phone: (612) 438-4383

Hennepin County Purchasing
A-2205 Government Center
301 S Sixth Street
Minneapolis, MN 55487
Phone: (612) 348-4295

PUBLICATIONS

The MSBA offers free pamphlets that provide a quick overview of 11 common legal issues. Topics include adult abuse and neglect, bankruptcy, buying a home, wills, child abuse and neglect, coming of age, getting a divorce, getting married, and being a witness. Two particularly helpful pamphlets discuss lawyers and how to work with them. The pamphlet "Selecting a Lawyer" offers suggestions on finding and selecting an attorney. "Helping Your Lawyer Help You" gives hints on working effectively with a lawyer and avoiding wasted time and money. Single copies of these pamphlets are free; there is a small charge for larger quantities. To order call: (612) 333-1183 or (800) 882-6722, or send a SASE to:

Pamphlets, MSBA
514 Nicollet Mall, Suite 300
Minneapolis, MN 55402

Other organizations offer more specialized information. The Hennepin County Bar Association (HCBA) publishes two booklets that focus on the health care decisions facing senior citizens. The first is a booklet on living wills. The booklet describes how living wills are used and includes a form that the reader can use to write such a will. The second publication is a booklet on the durable power of attorney for health care decisions. The booklet describes how people can use these documents to control how health care decisions will be made for them if they become incapacitated. This booklet includes the necessary forms for making the designation. The booklets can be ordered from the HCBA for $2 each or $3.50 for a set of both.

Other publications of interest to businesses are available from a variety of sources:

A Guide to Starting a Business in Minnesota - Eleventh Edition
Minnesota Small Business Assistance Office
500 Metro Square Building
121 E Seventh Place
St. Paul, MN 55101

Bench & Bar of Minnesota
Minnesota State Bar Association
514 Nicollet Mall, Suite 300
Minneapolis, MN 55402

Corporate Legal Times
Corporate Legal Times Corporation
222 Merchandise Mart Plaza, #1513
Chicago, IL 60654
The national monthly on managing in-house corporate legal departments.

Minnesota's Journal of Law & Politics
BRJG Publishing
Lumber Exchange Building, Suite 415
10 S Fifth Street
Minneapolis, MN 55402
Phone: (612) 338-3828
A somewhat irreverent monthly tabloid reporting on Minnesota's legal and political scene.

APPENDIX B: STATE BAR ASSOCIATIONS

It is important to keep in mind that laws can vary drastically from state to state. Rarely is it safe to assume that what holds true under Minnesota state law will hold true in another state. A good place to start researching law or attorneys in states other than Minnesota is to contact a state bar association in that jurisdiction. Many state bar associations refer callers to member attorneys and several will provide basic summaries of state laws, free of charge. Below is a list of state bar associations around the country. Note that a few states have more than one bar association listed.

Alabama State Bar
415 Dexter Street
P.O. Box 671
Montgomery, AL 36104
Phone: (205) 269-1515
Fax: (205) 261-6310

Alaska Bar Association
510 L, Street No. 602
P.O. Box 100279
Anchorage, AK 99510
Phone: (907) 272-7469
Fax: (907) 272-2932

State Bar of Arizona
363 North First Avenue
Phoenix, AZ 85003
Phone: (602) 252-4804
Fax: (602) 271-4930

Arkansas Bar Association
400 West Markham
Little Rock, AR 72201
Phone: (501) 375-4605
Fax: (501) 375-4901

State Bar of California
555 Franklin Street
San Francisco, CA 94102
Phone: (415) 561-8200
Fax: (415) 561-8305

The Colorado Bar Association
1900 Grant Street, No. 950
Denver, CO 80203
Phone: (303) 860-1115
Fax: (303) 894-0821

Connecticut Bar Association
101 Corporate Place
Rocky Hill, CT 06067
Phone: (203) 721-0025
Fax: (203) 257-4125

Delaware State Bar Association
1225 King Street
Wilmington, DE 19801
Phone: (302) 658-5279
Fax: (302) 658-5212

District of Columbia Bar
Sixth Floor-1250 H Street N.W.
Washington, D.C. 20005-3908
Phone: (202) 737-4700
Fax: (202) 626-3488

Bar Association of the District of Columbia
Twelfth Floor-1819 H Street, N.W.
Washington, D.C. 20006-3690
Phone: (202) 223-6600
Fax: (202) 293-3388

The Florida Bar
The Florida Bar Center
650 Apalachee Parkway
Tallahassee, FL 32399-2300
Phone: (904) 561-5600
Fax: (904) 561-5827

State Bar of Georgia
800 The Hurt Building
50 Hurt Plaza
Atlanta, GA 30303
Phone: (404) 527-8700
Fax: (404) 527-8717

Appendix B: State Bar Associations

Hawaii State Bar Association
Penthouse, Ninth Floor
1136 Union Mall
Honolulu, HI 96813
Phone: (808) 537-1868
Fax: (808) 521-7936

Idaho State Bar
P.O. Box 895
Boise, ID 83701
Phone: (208) 342-8958
Fax: (208) 342-3799

Illinois State Bar Association
424 South Second Street
Springfield, IL 62701
Phone: (217) 525-1760
Fax: (217) 525-0712

Indiana State Bar Association
Fourth Floor
230 East Ohio Street
Indianapolis, IN 46204
Phone: (317) 639-5465
Fax: (317) 266-2588

The Iowa State Bar Association
521 East Locust
Des Moines, IA 50309
Phone: (515) 243-3179
Fax: (515) 243-2511

Kansas Bar Association
1200 Harrison Street
Topeka, KS 66612
Phone: (913) 234-5696
Fax: (913) 234-3813

Kentucky Bar Association
514 West Main Street
Frankfort, KY 40601-1883
Phone: (502) 564-3795
Fax: (502) 564-3225

Louisiana State Bar Association
601 St. Charles Avenue
New Orleans, LA 70130
Phone: (504) 566-1600
Fax: (504) 566-0930

Maine State Bar Association
124 State Street
P.O. Box 788
Augusta, ME 04330
Phone: (207) 622-7523
Fax: (207) 623-0083

Maryland State Bar Association, Inc.
520 West Fayette Street
Baltimore, MD 21201
Phone: (410) 685-7878
Fax: (410) 837-0518

Massachusetts Bar Association
20 West Street
Boston, MA 02111
Phone: (617) 542-3602
Fax: (617) 426-4344

State Bar of Michigan
306 Townsend Street
Lansing, MI 48933-2083
Phone: (517) 372-9030
Fax: (517) 482-6248

Minnesota State Bar Association
Suite 300
514 Nicollet Mall
Minneapolis, MN 55402
Phone: (612) 333-1183
Fax: (612) 333-4927

The Mississippi State Bar
643 North State Street
Jackson, MS 39202
Phone: (601) 948-4471
Fax: (601) 355-8655

The Missouri Bar
326 Monroe
Jefferson City, MO 65102
Phone: (314) 635-4128
Fax: (314) 635-2811

State Bar of Montana
46 North Last Chance Gulch
P.O. Box 577
Helena, MT 59624
Phone: (406) 442-7660
Fax: (406) 442-7763

Nebraska State Bar Association
Second Floor
635 South 14th Street
Lincoln, NE 68508
Phone: (402) 475-7091
Fax: (402) 475-7098

State Bar of Nevada
Suite 200
201 Las Vegas Boulevard
Las Vegas, NV 89101
Phone: (702) 382-2200
Fax: (702) 385-2878

New Hampshire Bar Association
112 Pleasant Street
Concord, NH 03301
Phone: (603) 224-6942
Fax: (603) 224-2910

New Jersey State Bar Association
New Jersey Law Center
One Constitution Square
New Brunswick, NJ 08901-1500
Phone: (908) 249-5000
Fax: (908) 249-2815

State Bar Associations

State Bar of New Mexico
121 Tijeras Street, N.E.
Albuquerque, NM 87102
Phone: (505) 842-6132
Fax: (505) 843-8765

New York State Bar Association
One Elk Street
Albany, NY 12207
Phone: (518) 463-3200
Fax: (518) 463-4276

North Carolina State Bar
208 Fayetteville Street Mall
Raleigh, NC 27611
Phone: (919) 828-4620
Fax: None

North Carolina Bar Association
1312 Annapolis Drive
P.O. Box 12806
Raleigh, NC 27608
Phone: (919) 828-0561
Fax: (919) 821-2410

State Bar Association of North Dakota
Suite 101
515 1/2 East Broadway
Bismarck, ND 58502
Phone: (701) 255-1404
Fax: (701) 224-1621

Ohio State Bar Association
1700 Lake Shore Drive
Columbus, OH 43216-0562
Phone: (614) 487-2050
Fax: (614) 487-1008

Oklahoma Bar Association
1901 North Lincoln
Oklahoma City, OK 73105
Phone: (405) 524-2365
Fax: (405) 524-1115

Oregon State Bar
5200 SW Meadows Road
P.O. Box 1689
Lake Oswego, OR 97035
Phone: (503) 620-0222
Fax: (503) 684-1366

Pennsylvania Bar Association
100 South Street
P.O. Box 186
Harrisburg, PA 17108
Phone: (717) 238-6715
Fax: (717) 238-1204

Puerto Rico Bar Association
P.O. Box 1900
San Juan, PR 00903
Phone: (809) 721-3358
Fax: (809) 725-0330

Rhode Island Bar Association
115 Cedar Street
Providence, RI 02903
Phone: (401) 421-5740
Fax: (401) 421-2703

South Carolina Bar
950 Taylor Street
P.O. Box 608
Columbia, SC 29202
Phone: (803) 799-6653
Fax: (803) 799-4118

State Bar of South Dakota
222 East Capital
Pierre, SD 57501
Phone: (605) 224-7554
Fax: (605) 224-0282

Tennessee Bar Association
3622 West End Avenue
Nashville, TN 37205
Phone: (615) 383-7421
Fax: (615) 297-8058

State Bar of Texas
1414 Colorado
P.O. Box 12487
Austin, TX 78711
Phone: (512) 463-1400
Fax: (512) 473-2295

Utah State Bar
Suite 310
645 South 200 East
Salt Lake City, UT 84111
Phone: (801) 531-9077
Fax: (801) 531-0660

Vermont Bar Association
P.O. Box 100
Montpelier, VT 05601
Phone: (802) 223-2020
Fax: (802) 223-1573

Virginia State Bar
Suite 1500
707 East Main Street
Richmond, VA 23219-2803
Phone: (804) 775-0500
Fax: (804) 775-0501

Virginia Bar Association
Suite 1515
701 East Franklin Street
Richmond, VA 23219
Phone: (804) 644-0041
Fax: (804) 644-0052

Virgin Islands Bar Association
P.O. Box 4108
Christiansted, VI 00822
Phone: (809) 778-7497
Fax: (809) 778-7497

Appendix B: State Bar Associations

Washington State Bar Association
500 Westin Building
2001 Sixth Avenue
Seattle, WA 98121-2599
Phone: (206) 727-8200
Fax: (206) 727-8320

West Virginia State Bar
2006 Kanawha Blvd. E.
Charleston, WV 25311
Phone: (304) 558-2456
Fax: (304) 558-2467

West Virginia Bar Association
904 Security Building
100 Capitol Street
Charleston, WV 25301
Phone: (304) 342-1474
Fax: (304) 345-5864

State Bar of Wisconsin
402 West Wilson Street
Madison, WI 53703
Phone: (608) 257-3838
Fax: (608) 257-5502

Wyoming State Bar
500 Randall Avenue
Cheyenne, WY 82001
Phone: (307) 632-9061
Fax: (307) 632-3737

APPENDIX C

ATTORNEYS & LAW FIRMS BY REGION

The following index is intended to enable quick identification of an appropriate attorney and law firm by location. The area of practice in which the attorney was nominated appears following their address. If more than one area is listed, the boldface indicates the section of the *Guidebook* where their full biography can be found. This index also contains profiles of most of the law firms that were supporters of the *Business Guidebook*.

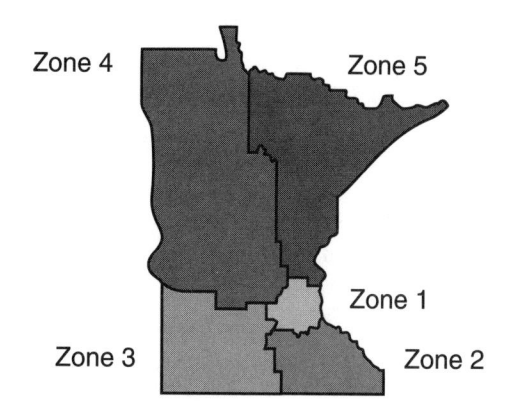

ZONE 1:

Including listings in Bloomington, Brooklyn Park, Cottage Grove, Minneapolis, New Brighton, South St. Paul, St. Louis Park, and St. Paul

Abdo, Kenneth J. - Abdo & Abdo, P.A. - 710 Northstar West, 625 Marquette Avenue, Minneapolis, MN 55402 - **Arts, Entertainment, Advertising & Media Law** - (612) 333-1526

Ahern, Michael J. - Moss & Barnett, A Professional Association - 4800 Norwest Center, 90 South Seventh Street, Minneapolis, MN 55402 - Federal, State & Local Government Law - **Environmental Law** - (612) 347-0274

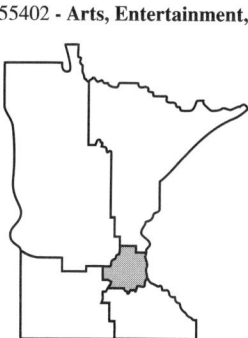

Anderson, John M. - Bassford, Lockhart, Truesdell & Briggs, P.A. - 3550 Multifoods Tower, 33 South Sixth Street, Minneapolis, MN 55402-3787 - Environmental Law - **Personal Injury Defense Law** - (612) 333-3000

Baillie, James L. - Fredrikson & Byron, P.A. - 1100 International Centre, 900 Second Avenue South, Minneapolis, MN 55402 - **Bankruptcy & Workout Law** - (612) 347-7013

Bannigan, John F. - Bannigan & Kelly, P.A. - 1750 North Central Life Tower, 445 Minnesota Street, St. Paul, MN 55101 - Federal, State & Local Government Law - **Commercial Real Estate Law** - (612) 224-3781

Barnett, Timothy M. - Winthrop & Weinstine, P.A. - 3000 Dain Bosworth Plaza, 60 South Sixth Street, Minneapolis, MN 55402 - Publicly Held Corporations Law - **Closely Held Business Law** - (612) 347-0700

Bartle, Emery W. - Dorsey & Whitney - Pillsbury Center South, 220 South Sixth Street, Minneapolis, MN 55402-1498 - **Labor Law** - (612) 340-2819

Beck, Peter K. - Larkin, Hoffman, Daly & Lindgren, Ltd. - 1500 Norwest Financial Center, 7900 Xerxes Avenue South, Bloomington, MN 55431 - **Federal, State & Local Government Law** - (612) 835-3800

Berg, Larry J. - Fredrikson & Byron, P.A. - 1100 International Centre, 900 Second Avenue South, Minneapolis, MN 55402 - Bankruptcy & Workout Law - **Commercial Real Estate Law** - (612) 347-7052

Bergerson, Stephen R. - Fredrikson & Byron, P.A. - 1100 International Centre, 900 Second Avenue South, Minneapolis, MN 55402 - **Arts, Entertainment, Advertising & Media Law** - (612) 347-7025

Bland, J. Richard - Meagher & Geer - 4200 Multifoods Tower, 33 South Sixth Street, Minneapolis, MN 55402 - Personal Injury Defense Law - **Professional Malpractice Defense Law** - (612) 338-0661

Appendix C: Attorneys & Law Firms by Region

Boelter, Philip F. - Dorsey & Whitney - Pillsbury Center South, 220 South Sixth Street, Minneapolis, MN 55402-1498 - **Commercial Real Estate Law - (612) 340-2649**

Bowman, Richard A. - Bowman and Brooke - 150 South Fifth Street, Suite 2600, Minneapolis, MN 55402 - Commercial Litigation - **Personal Injury Defense Law - (612) 339-8682**

Brand, Martha C. - Leonard, Street and Deinard Professional Association - 150 South Fifth Street, Suite 2300, Minneapolis, MN 55402 - **Environmental Law - (612) 335-1500**

Brand, Steve A. - Robins, Kaplan, Miller & Ciresi - 2800 LaSalle Plaza, 800 LaSalle Avenue, Minneapolis, MN 55402 - **Probate, Estate Planning & Trusts Law - (612) 349-8500**

Breitman, Richard L. - The Breitman Immigration Law Firm - 701 Fourth Avenue, Suite 1700, Minneapolis, MN 55415-1818 - **Immigration Law - (612) 822-4724**

Brown, Ronald J. - Dorsey & Whitney - Pillsbury Center South, 220 South Sixth Street, Minneapolis, MN 55402-1498 - Commercial Litigation - **Intellectual Property Law - (612) 340-2879**

Brown, Frederick C. - Popham, Haik, Schnobrich & Kaufman, Ltd. - 222 South Ninth Street, Suite 3300, Minneapolis, MN 55402 - **Personal Injury Defense Law - (612) 333-4800**

Bruno, Frederic - Frederic Bruno & Associates - 5500 Wayzata Boulevard, Suite 730, Minneapolis, MN 55416 - **Criminal Law - (612) 545-7900**

Brynestad, Lorens Q. - Brynestad Law Offices - 8525 Edinbrook Crossing, Suite 201, Brooklyn Park, MN 55443 - **Commercial Real Estate Law - (612) 424-8811**

Burk, Robert S. - Popham, Haik, Schnobrich & Kaufman, Ltd. - 222 South Ninth Street, Suite 3300, Minneapolis, MN 55402 - **Labor Law - (612) 333-4800**

Carlson, Steven E. - Dorsey & Whitney - 3 Gracechurch Street, London, England EC 3V OAT - **International Business Law - 011-4471-929-3334**

Carlson, Alan G. - Merchant, Gould, Smith, Edell, Welter & Schmidt, P.A. - 3100 Norwest Center, 90 South Seventh Street, Minneapolis, MN 55402-4131 - Commercial Litigation - **Intellectual Property Law - (612) 332-5300**

Christoffel, James F. - Christoffel, Elliott & Albrecht, P.A. - 100 South Fifth Street, Suite 1250, Minneapolis, MN 55402 - Bankruptcy & Workout Law - **Commercial Real Estate Law - (612) 672-0900**

Ciresi, Michael V. - Robins, Kaplan, Miller & Ciresi - 2800 LaSalle Plaza, 800 LaSalle Avenue, Minneapolis, MN 55402 - Intellectual Property Law, Personal Injury Law - **Commercial Litigation - (612) 349-8500**

Clinton, Jack W. - Jack W. Clinton, P.A. - 8750 90th Street South, Suite 201, Cottage Grove, MN 55016-3301 - **Federal, State & Local Government Law - (612) 459-6644**

Cole, Phillip A. - Lommen, Nelson, Cole & Stageberg, P.A. - 1800 IDS Center, 80 South Eighth Street, Minneapolis, MN 55402 - **Commercial Litigation - (612) 339-8131**

Comstock, Rebecca A. - Dorsey & Whitney - Pillsbury Center South, 220 South Sixth Street, Minneapolis, MN 55402-1498 - **Environmental Law - (612) 340-2987**

Constantine, Katherine A. - Dorsey & Whitney - Pillsbury Center South, 220 South Sixth Street, Minneapolis, MN 55402-1498 - **Bankruptcy & Workout Law - (612) 340-8792**

Cooper, Peter L. - McGrann Shea Franzen Carnival Straughn & Lamb, Chartered - 2200 LaSalle Plaza, 800 LaSalle Avenue, Minneapolis, MN 55402 - **Commercial Real Estate Law - (612) 338-2525**

Corwin, Gregg M. - Gregg M. Corwin & Associates - 1660 South Highway 100, Suite 508 East, St. Louis Park, MN 55416-1534 - **Labor Law - (612) 544-7774**

Cosgriff, William J. - Doherty, Rumble & Butler Professional Association - 2800 Minnesota World Trade Center, 30 East Seventh Street, St. Paul, MN 55101-4999 - **Commercial Real Estate Law - (612) 291-9333**

Crawford, Rollin H. - LeVander, Gillen & Miller, P.A. - 633 South Concord Street, Suite 402, South St. Paul, MN 55075 - **Federal, State & Local Government Law - (612) 451-1831**

Cutler, Kenneth L. - Dorsey & Whitney - Pillsbury Center South, 220 South Sixth Street, Minneapolis, MN 55402-1498 - **Publicly Held Corporations Law - (612) 340-2740**

Dady, J. Michael - J. Michael Dady & Associates, P.A. - 4000 IDS Center, 80 South Eighth Street, Minneapolis, MN 55402-2204 - Commercial Litigation, Publicly Held Corporations Law, Personal Injury Defense Law, Closely Held Business Law - **Franchise & Distribution Law - (612) 359-9000**

Damon, Matthew E. - Popham, Haik, Schnobrich & Kaufman, Ltd. - 222 South Ninth Street, Suite 3300, Minneapolis, MN 55402 - **Employment Law - (612) 333-4800**

Danielson, Laura J. - Patterson & Keough, P.A. - 1200 Rand Tower, 527 Marquette Avenue South, Minneapolis, MN 55402 - Arts, Entertainment, Advertising & Media Law - **Immigration Law - (612) 349-5740**

D'Aquila, Barbara J. - Cosgrove, Flynn & Gaskins - 2900 Metropolitan Centre, 333 South Seventh Street, Minneapolis, MN 55402 - **Employment Law - (612) 333-9427**

Dayton, Charles K. - Leonard, Street and Deinard Professional Association - 150 South Fifth Street, Suite 2300, Minneapolis, MN 55402 - **Environmental Law - (612) 335-1500**

Degnan, John M. - Bassford, Lockhart, Truesdell & Briggs, P.A. - 3550 Multifoods Tower, 33 South Sixth Street, Minneapolis, MN 55402-3787 - Personal Injury Defense Law - **Commercial Litigation - (612) 333-3000**

Zone 1

Devoy, Kimball J. - Doherty, Rumble & Butler Professional Association - 2800 Minnesota World Trade Center, 30 East Seventh Street, St. Paul, MN 55101-4999 - **Business Tax Law** - **(612) 291-9333**

Diehl, John E. - Larkin, Hoffman, Daly & Lindgren, Ltd. - 1500 Norwest Financial Center, 7900 Xerxes Avenue South, Bloomington, MN 55431 - **Health Law** - **(612) 835-3800**

Dunn, James F. - Dunn & Elliott, P.A. - 1510 Minnesota World Trade Center, 30 East Seventh Street, St. Paul, MN 55101-4901 - Commercial Litigation - **Personal Injury Defense Law** - **(612) 221-9048**

Eastwood, J. Marquis - Dorsey & Whitney - Pillsbury Center South, 220 South Sixth Street, Minneapolis, MN 55402-1498 - Commercial Litigation - **Employment Law** - **(612) 340-2856**

Edell, Robert T. - Merchant, Gould, Smith, Edell, Welter & Schmidt, P.A. - 3100 Norwest Center, 90 South Seventh Street, Minneapolis, MN 55402-4131 - Commercial Litigation - **Intellectual Property Law** - **(612) 332-5300**

Edstrom, Dean R. - Doherty, Rumble & Butler Professional Association - 3500 Fifth Street Towers, 150 South Fifth Street, Minneapolis, MN 55402-4235 - Securities & Venture Finance Law - **Publicly Held Corporations Law** - **(612) 340-5575**

Eide, David B. - Frommelt & Eide, Ltd. - 900 Second Avenue South, Suite 580, Minneapolis, MN 55402 - **Commercial Real Estate Law** - **(612) 332-2200**

Elliott, Christopher A. - Christoffel, Elliott & Albrecht, P.A. - 100 South Fifth Street, Suite 1250, Minneapolis, MN 55402 - **Bankruptcy & Workout Law** - **(612) 672-0900**

Engh, Rolf - Valspar Corporation Counsel - 1101 Third Street South, Minneapolis, MN 55415 - Merger & Acquisition Law, Closely Held Business Law - **Publicly Held Corporations Law** - **(612) 375-7705**

Erhart, John J. - Fredrikson & Byron, P.A. - 1100 International Centre, 900 Second Avenue South, Minneapolis, MN 55402 - **Business Tax Law** - **(612) 347-7035**

Erickson, James C. - Larkin, Hoffman, Daly & Lindgren, Ltd. - 1500 Norwest Financial Center, 7900 Xerxes Avenue South, Bloomington, MN 55431 - **Federal, State & Local Government Law** - **(612) 835-3800**

Fairbairn, David R. - Kinney & Lange, P.A. - 625 Fourth Avenue South, Suite 1500, Minneapolis, MN 55415-1659 - **Intellectual Property Law** - **(612) 339-1863**

Finley, Joseph M. - Leonard, Street and Deinard Professional Association - 150 South Fifth Street, Suite 2300, Minneapolis, MN 55402 - **Commercial Real Estate Law** - **(612) 335-1500**

Fisher, Linda H. - Larkin, Hoffman, Daly & Lindgren, Ltd. - 1500 Norwest Financial Center, 7900 Xerxes Avenue South, Bloomington, MN 55431 - **Environmental Law** - **(612) 835-3800**

Flaskamp, William D. - Meagher & Geer - 4200 Multifoods Tower, 33 South Sixth Street, Minneapolis, MN 55402 - **Personal Injury Defense Law** - **(612) 338-0661**

Flynn, George W. - Cosgrove, Flynn & Gaskins - 2900 Metropolitan Centre, 333 South Seventh Street, Minneapolis, MN 55402 - **Personal Injury Defense Law** - **(612) 333-9500**

Frécon, Alain - Frécon & Associates - 902 Foshay Tower, 821 Marquette Avenue South, Minneapolis, MN 55402 - **International Business Law** - **(612) 338-6868**

Freeman, Todd I. - Larkin, Hoffman, Daly & Lindgren, Ltd. - 1500 Norwest Financial Center, 7900 Xerxes Avenue South, Bloomington, MN 55431 - Health Law, Probate, Estate Planning & Trusts Law - **Closely Held Business Law** - **(612) 835-3800**

Freitag, Gregory G. - Fredrikson & Byron, P.A. - 1100 International Centre, 900 Second Avenue South, Minneapolis, MN 55402 - Publicly Held Corporations Law - **Securities & Venture Finance Law** - **(612) 347-7153**

French, John D. - Faegre & Benson - 2200 Norwest Center, 90 South Seventh Street, Minneapolis, MN 55402 - Publicly Held Corporations Law, Bankruptcy & Workout Law - **Commercial Litigation** - **(612) 336-3000**

Friedberg, Joseph S. - Friedberg Law Office - 250 Second Avenue South, Suite 205, Minneapolis, MN 55401 - **Criminal Law** - **(612) 339-8626**

Frommelt, Roger H. - Frommelt & Eide, Ltd. - 900 Second Avenue South, Suite 580, Minneapolis, MN 55402 - **Securities & Venture Finance Law** - **(612) 332-2200**

Galvin, Michael J. - Briggs and Morgan, P.A. - W-2200 First National Bank Building, St. Paul, MN 55101 - Federal, State & Local Government Law - **Labor Law** - **(612) 223-6600**

Ginsburg, Roy A. - Dorsey & Whitney - Pillsbury Center South, 220 South Sixth Street, Minneapolis, MN 55402-1498 - **Employment Law** - **(612) 340-8761**

Gislason, Barbara J. - Barbara J. Gislason & Associates - 219 SE Main Street, Suite 506, Minneapolis, MN 55414 - **Arts, Entertainment, Advertising & Media Law** - **(612) 331-8033**

Gordon, John B. - Faegre & Benson - 2200 Norwest Center, 90 South Seventh Street, Minneapolis, MN 55402 - **Environmental Law** - **(612) 336-3000**

Gordon, Stephen D. - Gordon Miller O'Brien - 1208 Plymouth Building, 12 South Sixth Street, Minneapolis, MN 55402 - **Labor Law** - **(612) 333-5831**

Gordon, Roger D. - Winthrop & Weinstine, P.A. - 3000 Dain Bosworth Plaza, 60 South Sixth Street, Minneapolis, MN 55402 - Commercial Real Estate Law, Federal, State & Local Government Law - **Publicly Held Corporations Law** - **(612) 347-0700**

Appendix C: Attorneys & Law Firms by Region

Gould, John D. - Merchant, Gould, Smith, Edell, Welter & Schmidt, P.A. - 3100 Norwest Center, 90 South Seventh Street, Minneapolis, MN 55402-4131 - Civil Litigation - **Intellectual Property Law - (612) 332-5300**

Grasmoen, Cheryl L. - Petersen, Tews & Squires, P.A. - 4800 IDS Center, 80 South Eighth Street, Minneapolis, MN 55402 - **Commercial Real Estate Law - (612) 344-1600**

Greenswag, Douglas B. - Leonard, Street and Deinard Professional Association - 150 South Fifth Street, Suite 2300, Minneapolis, MN 55402 - **Bankruptcy & Workout Law - (612) 335-1527**

Grindal, H. Theodore - Schatz Paquin Lockridge Grindal & Holstein - 2200 Washington Square, 100 Washington Avenue South, Minneapolis, MN 55401 - Federal, State & Local Government Law - **Health Law - (612) 339-6900**

Grooms, Lloyd W. - Winthrop & Weinstine, P.A. - 3200 Minnesota World Trade Center, 30 East Seventh Street, St. Paul, MN 55101 - **Environmental Law - (612) 290-8529**

Haik, Raymond A. - Popham, Haik, Schnobrich & Kaufman, Ltd. - 222 South Ninth Street, Suite 3300, Minneapolis, MN 55402 - Commercial Litigation, Federal, State & Local Government Law - **Environmental Law - (612) 333-4800**

Halleland, Keith J. - Popham, Haik, Schnobrich & Kaufman, Ltd. - 222 South Ninth Street, Suite 3300, Minneapolis, MN 55402 - **Health Law - (612) 333-4800**

Hamel, Mark E. - Dorsey & Whitney - Pillsbury Center South, 220 South Sixth Street, Minneapolis, MN 55402-1498 - **Commercial Real Estate Law - (612) 340-8716**

Hamre, Curtis B. - Merchant, Gould, Smith, Edell, Welter & Schmidt, P.A. - 3100 Norwest Center, 90 South Seventh Street, Minneapolis, MN 55402-4131 - **Intellectual Property Law - (612) 332-5300**

Hanley, Bruce H. - Bruce H. Hanley, P.A. - 701 Fourth Avenue South, Suite 700, Minneapolis, MN 55415 - **Criminal Law - (612) 339-1290**

Hansen, Karen - Popham, Haik, Schnobrich & Kaufman, Ltd. - 222 South Ninth Street, Suite 3300, Minneapolis, MN 55402 - **Environmental Law - (612) 333-4800**

Hanson, Bruce E. - Doherty, Rumble & Butler Professional Association - 2800 Minnesota World Trade Center, 30 East Seventh Street, St. Paul, MN 55101-4999 - **Health Law - (612) 291-9333**

Haugen, Orrin M. - Haugen & Nikolai, P.A. - 820 International Centre, 900 Second Avenue South, Minneapolis, MN 55402 - **Intellectual Property Law - (612) 339-7461**

Hay, Nick - Moss & Barnett, A Professional Association - 4800 Norwest Center, 90 South Seventh Street, Minneapolis, MN 55402-4129 - Publicly Held Corporations Law - **Business Tax Law - (612) 347-0443**

Heaney, Timothy M. - Fredrikson & Byron, P.A. - 1100 International Centre, 900 Second Avenue South, Minneapolis, MN 55402 - Publicly Held Corporations Law - **Securities & Venture Finance Law - (612) 347-7019**

Heiberg, Robert A. - Dorsey & Whitney - Pillsbury Center South, 220 South Sixth Street, Minneapolis, MN 55402-1498 - **Commercial Real Estate Law - (612) 340-2751**

Heilman, Edward G. - Heilman Law Firm - 1221 Nicollet Mall, Suite 206, Minneapolis, MN 55403 - **Probate, Estate Planning & Trusts Law - (612) 338-5230**

Hemphill, Stuart R. - Dorsey & Whitney - Pillsbury Center South, 220 South Sixth Street, Minneapolis, MN 55402-1498 - Arts, Entertainment, Advertising & Media Law- **Intellectual Property Law - (612) 340-2734**

Hendrixson, Peter S. - Dorsey & Whitney - Pillsbury Center South, 220 South Sixth Street, Minneapolis, MN 55402-1498 - **Commercial Litigation - (612) 340-2917**

Hibbs, John S. - Dorsey & Whitney - Pillsbury Center South, 220 South Sixth Street, Minneapolis, MN 55402-1498 - **Health Law - (612) 340-2661**

Hippee, William H. - Dorsey & Whitney - Pillsbury Center South, 220 South Sixth Street, Minneapolis, MN 55402-1498 - Publicly Held Corporations Law - **Business Tax Law - (612) 340-2665**

Hobbins, Robert L. - Dorsey & Whitney - Pillsbury Center South, 220 South Sixth Street, Minneapolis, MN 55402-1498 - Employment Law - **Labor Law - (612) 340-2919**

Hoch, Gary W. - Meagher & Geer - 4200 Multifoods Tower, 33 South Sixth Street, Minneapolis, MN 55402 - **Personal Injury Defense Law - (612) 338-0661**

Hoff, George C. - Hoff, Barry & Kuderer, P.A. - 7901 Flying Cloud Drive, Suite 260, Eden Prairie, MN 55344 - **Federal, State & Local Government Law - (612) 941-9220**

Hoffman, Robert L. - Larkin, Hoffman, Daly & Lindgren, Ltd. - 1500 Norwest Financial Center, 7900 Xerxes Avenue South, Bloomington, MN 55431- **Federal, State & Local Government Law - (612) 835-3800**

Holper, Richard D. - Holper Welsh & Mitchell, Ltd. - 750 Pillsbury Center, 200 South Sixth Street, Minneapolis, MN 55402 - **Bankruptcy & Workout Law - (612) 373-2200**

Hughes, Kathleen A. - Fredrikson & Byron, P.A. - 1100 International Centre, 900 Second Avenue South, Minneapolis, MN 55402 - **Employment Law - (612) 347-7037**

Iannacone, Michael J. - Iannacone Law Office - 101 East Fifth Street, Suite 1614, St. Paul, MN 55101 - **Bankruptcy & Workout Law - (612) 224-3361**

Jensen, Roger A. - Peterson, Bell, Converse & Jensen, P.A. - 3000 Metropolitan Centre, 333 South Seventh Street, Minneapolis, MN 55402-2441 - **Labor Law - (612) 342-2323**

Johnson, Jeffrey S. - Barna, Guzy & Steffen, Ltd. - 400 Northtown Financial Plaza, 200 Coon Rapids Boulevard, Minneapolis, MN 55433 - Commercial Real Estate Law - **Commercial Real Estate Law - (612) 780-8500**

Johnson, Eugene L. - Dorsey & Whitney - Pillsbury Center South, 220 South Sixth Street, Minneapolis, MN 55402-1498 - **Intellectual Property Law - (612) 340-2625**

Johnson, Larry W. - Dorsey & Whitney - Pillsbury Center South, 220 South Sixth Street, Minneapolis, MN 55402-1498 - **Probate, Estate Planning & Trusts Law - (612) 340-2619**

Johnson, G. Robert - Popham, Haik, Schnobrich & Kaufman, Ltd. - 222 South Ninth Street, Suite 3300, Minneapolis, MN 55402 - **Environmental Law - (612) 333-4800**

Johnstone, William A. - Dorsey & Whitney - Pillsbury Center South, 220 South Sixth Street, Minneapolis, MN 55402-1498 - **Federal, State & Local Government Law - (612) 340-2815**

Kantor, David - Leonard, Street and Deinard Professional Association - 150 South Fifth Street, Suite 2300, Minneapolis, MN 55402 - International Business Law - **Commercial Real Estate Law - (612) 335-1500**

Kaplan, Elliot S. - Robins, Kaplan, Miller & Ciresi - 2800 LaSalle Plaza, 800 LaSalle Avenue, Minneapolis, MN 55402 - **Commercial Litigation - (612) 349-8500**

Kelley, Douglas A. - Douglas A. Kelley, P.A. - 701 Fourth Avenue South, Suite 500, Minneapolis, MN 55415 - Commercial Litigation - **Criminal Law - (612) 337-9594**

Kelley, David W. - Leonard, Street and Deinard Professional Association - 150 South Fifth Street, Suite 2300, Minneapolis, MN 55402 - **Commercial Real Estate Law - (612) 335-1500**

Kennedy, David J. - Holmes & Graven, Chartered - 470 Pillsbury Center, 200 South Sixth Street, Minneapolis, MN 55402 - **Federal, State & Local Government Law - (612) 337-9300**

Keppel, William J. - Dorsey & Whitney - Pillsbury Center South, 220 South Sixth Street, Minneapolis, MN 55402 -1498 - **Environmental Law - (612) 340-2745**

King, Thomas R. - Fredrikson & Byron, P.A. - 1100 International Centre, 900 Second Avenue South, Minneapolis, MN 55402 - Publicly Held Corporations Law - **Securities & Venture Finance Law - (612) 347-7059**

King, Lawrence R. - King & Hatch - The St. Paul Building, 6 West Fifth Street, Suite 800, St. Paul, MN 55102 - **Personal Injury Defense Law - (612) 223-2856**

King, D. Randall - Merchant, Gould, Smith, Edell, Welter & Schmidt, P.A. - 3100 Norwest Center, 90 South Seventh Street, Minneapolis, MN 55402-4131 - Commercial Litigation - **Intellectual Property Law - (612) 332-5300**

Kirby, John D. - Dorsey & Whitney - Pillsbury Center South, 220 South Sixth Street, Minneapolis, MN 55402-1498 - **Federal, State & Local Government Law - (612) 340-5665**

Knapp, John A. - Winthrop & Weinstine, P.A. - 3200 Minnesota World Trade Center, 30 East Seventh Street, St. Paul, MN 55101 - Arts, Entertainment, Advertising & Media Law - **Federal, State & Local Government Law - (612) 290-8400**

Knowles, Faye - Fredrikson & Byron, P.A. - 1100 International Centre, 900 Second Avenue South, Minneapolis, MN 55402 - **Bankruptcy & Workout Law - (612) 347-7054**

Koneck, John M. - Fredrikson & Byron, P.A. - 1100 International Centre, 900 Second Avenue South, Minneapolis, MN 55402 - Bankruptcy & Workout Law - **Commercial Real Estate Law - (612) 347-7038**

Kueppers, Frederick A. - Kueppers, Hackel & Kueppers, P.A. - 1350 Capital Centre, 386 North Wabasha Street, St. Paul, MN 55102 - **Commercial Real Estate Law - (612) 228-1104**

Kuller, Hart - Winthrop & Weinstine, P.A. - 3200 Minnesota World Trade Center, 30 East Seventh Street, St. Paul, MN 55101 - Publicly Held Corporations Law - **Bankruptcy & Workout Law - (612) 290-8400**

Kuntz, Timothy J. - LeVander, Gillen & Miller, P.A. - 633 South Concord Street, Suite 402, South St. Paul, MN 55075 - **Federal, State & Local Government Law - (612) 451-1831**

Lapp, William S. - Lapp, Laurie, Libra, Abramson & Thomson, Chartered - One Financial Plaza, Suite 1800, 120 South Sixth Street, Minneapolis, MN 55402 - Closely Held Business Law - **Publicly Held Corporations Law - (612) 338-5815**

Laurie, Gerald T. - Lapp, Laurie, Libra, Abramson & Thomson, Chartered - One Financial Plaza, Suite 1800, 120 South Sixth Street, Minneapolis, MN 55402 - **Employment Law - (612) 338-5815**

Lawrence, Douglas M. - Moss & Barnett, A Professional Association - 4800 Norwest Center, 90 South Seventh Street, Minneapolis, MN 55402 - **Bankruptcy & Workout Law - (612) 347-0349**

LeFevere, Charles L. - Holmes & Graven, Chartered - 470 Pillsbury Center, 200 South Sixth Street, Minneapolis, MN 55402 - **Federal, State & Local Government Law - (612) 337-9300**

Leonard, Brian F. - O'Neill, Burke, O'Neill, Leonard & O'Brien, Ltd. - 100 South Fifth Street, Suite 1200, Minneapolis, MN 55402 - Publicly Held Corporations Law - **Bankruptcy & Workout Law - (612) 332-1030**

Linstroth, Paul J. - Popham, Haik, Schnobrich & Kaufman, Ltd. - 222 South Ninth Street, Suite 3300, Minneapolis, MN 55402 - **Business Tax Law - (612) 333-4800**

Appendix C: Attorneys & Law Firms by Region

Litsey, Calvin L. - Faegre & Benson - 2200 Norwest Center, 90 South Seventh Street, Minneapolis, MN 55402 - **Arts, Entertainment, Advertising & Media Law** - **(612) 336-3000**

Little, Bruce H. - Popham, Haik, Schnobrich & Kaufman, Ltd. - 222 South Ninth Street, Suite 3300, Minneapolis, MN 55402 - **Arts, Entertainment, Advertising & Media Law** - **(612) 333-4800**

Lockhart, Greer E. - Bassford, Lockhart, Truesdell & Briggs, P.A. - 3550 Multifoods Tower, 33 South Sixth Street, Minneapolis, MN 55402-3787 - Commercial Litigation - **Professional Malpractice Defense Law** - **(612) 333-3000**

Logstrom, Bridget A. - Dorsey & Whitney - Pillsbury Center South, 220 South Sixth Street, Minneapolis, MN 55402-1498 - **Probate, Estate Planning & Trusts Law** - **(612) 343-7945**

Lubben, David J. - Dorsey & Whitney - Pillsbury Center South, 220 South Sixth Street, Minneapolis, MN 55402-1498 - **Securities & Venture Finance Law** - **(612) 340-2904**

McDonald, John R. - Robins, Kaplan, Miller & Ciresi - 2800 LaSalle Plaza, 800 LaSalle Avenue, Minneapolis, MN 55402 - **Bankruptcy & Workout Law** - **(612) 349-8500**

McDowell, Gary D. - Arnold & McDowell - 5881 Cedar Lake Road, Minneapolis, MN 55416 - **Probate, Estate Planning & Trusts Law** - **(612) 545-9000**

Madson, Eric O. - Winthrop & Weinstine, P.A. - 3000 Dain Bosworth Plaza, 60 South Sixth Street, Minneapolis, MN 55402 - **Securities & Venture Finance Law** - **(612) 347-0700**

Magnuson, Roger J. - Dorsey & Whitney - Pillsbury Center South, 220 South Sixth Street, Minneapolis, MN 55402-1498 - Securities & Venture Finance Law - **Commercial Litigation** - **(612) 340-2738**

Mahoney, Jerry C.D. - Dorsey & Whitney - Pillsbury Center South, 220 South Sixth Street, Minneapolis, MN 55402-1498 - **Federal, State & Local Government Law** - **(612) 340-2813**

Malone, Robert G. - Attorney at Law - 386 North Wabasha Street, Suite 780, St. Paul, MN 55102 - **Criminal Law** - **(612) 227-6549**

Mansfield, Seymour J. - Mansfield & Tanick, P.A. - 1560 International Centre, 900 Second Avenue South, Minneapolis, MN 55402-3383 - **Commercial Litigation** - **(612) 339-4295**

Martin, Phillip H. - Dorsey & Whitney - Pillsbury Center South, 220 South Sixth Street, Minneapolis, MN 55402-1498 - **Business Tax Law** - **(612) 340-2845**

Martin, James T. - Gislason, Martin & Varpness, P.A. - 7600 Parklawn Avenue South, Suite 444, Minneapolis, MN 55435 - Professional Malpractice Defense Law - **Commercial Litigation** - **(612) 831-5793**

Mattos, Patricia G. - Attorney at Law - 1539 Grand Avenue, St. Paul, MN 55105 - **Immigration Law** - **(612) 698-8841**

Meshbesher, Ronald I. - Meshbesher & Spence, Ltd. - 1616 Park Avenue South, Minneapolis, MN 55404 - Commercial Litigation - **Criminal Law** - **(612) 339-9121**

Meyer, Michael L. - Ravich, Meyer, Kirkman & McGrath, P.A. - 4545 IDS Center, 80 South Eighth Street, Minneapolis, MN 55402 - **Bankruptcy & Workout Law** - **(612) 332-8511**

Mickelsen, Ruth A. - Allina Health System - 5601 Smetana Drive, Minnetonka, MN 55343 - **Health Law** - **(612) 936-1609**

Miller, David B. - Faegre & Benson - 2200 Norwest Center, 90 South Seventh Street, Minneapolis, MN 55402 - Publicly Held Corporations Law, International Business Law, Securities & Venture Finance Law - **(612) 336-3000**

Mitau, Lee R. - Dorsey & Whitney - Pillsbury Center South, 220 South Sixth Street, Minneapolis, MN 55402-1498 - Securities & Venture Finance Law - **Publicly Held Corporations Law** - **(612) 340-2780**

Mohr, Gordon G. - Attorney at Law - 5001 West 80th Street, Suite 1020, Bloomington, MN 55437 - **Criminal Law** - **(612) 831-0944**

Moos, Rebecca Egge - Bassford, Lockhart, Truesdell & Briggs, P.A. - 3550 Multifoods Tower, 33 South Sixth Street, Minneapolis, MN 55402-3787 - **Personal Injury Defense Law** - **(612) 333-3000**

Morris, Ralph K. - Doherty, Rumble & Butler Professional Association - 2800 Minnesota World Trade Center, 30 East Seventh Street, St. Paul, MN 55101-4999 - **Agricultural Law** - **(612) 291-9333**

Muck, Thomas R. - Fredrikson & Byron, P.A. - 1100 International Centre, 900 Second Avenue South, Minneapolis, MN 55402 - **Business Tax Law** - **(612) 347-7045**

Myers, Howard S. - Popham, Haik, Schnobrich & Kaufman, Ltd. - 222 South Ninth Street, Suite 3300, Minneapolis, MN 55402 - **Immigration Law** - **(612) 333-4800**

Nauen, Charles N. - Schatz Paquin Lockridge Grindal & Holstein - 2200 Washington Square, 100 Washington Avenue South, Minneapolis, MN 55401 - **Environmental Law** - **(612) 339-6900**

Nawrocki, Lawrence M. - Nawrocki, Rooney & Sivertson, P.A. - 401 Broadway Place East, 3433 Broadway Street NE, Minneapolis, MN 55413 - **Intellectual Property Law** - **(612) 331-1464**

Nelson, Sue Ann - Doherty, Rumble & Butler Professional Association - 3500 Fifth Street Towers, 150 South Fifth Street, Minneapolis, MN 55402 - **Business Tax Law** - **(612) 340-5590**

Nelson, Steven C. - Dorsey & Whitney - Pillsbury Center South, 220 South Sixth Street, Minneapolis, MN 55402-1498 - **International Business Law** - **(612) 340-2942**

Nelson, Thomas F. - Popham, Haik, Schnobrich & Kaufman, Ltd. - 222 South Ninth Street, Suite 3300, Minneapolis, MN 55402 - **Commercial Litigation** - (612) 333-4800

Nilan, Michael T. - Popham, Haik, Schnobrich & Kaufman, Ltd. - 222 South Ninth Street, Suite 3300, Minneapolis, MN 55402 - Commercial Litigation - **Securities & Venture Finance Law** - (612) 333-4800

Nowlin, Forrest D. - Doherty, Rumble & Butler Professional Association - 2800 Minnesota World Trade Center, 30 East Seventh Street, St. Paul, MN 55101-4999 - Federal, State & Local Government Law - **Environmental Law** - (612) 291-9333

O'Brien, Maurice W. - Gordon Miller O'Brien - 1208 Plymouth Building, 12 South Sixth Street, Minneapolis, MN 55402 - **Labor Law** - (612) 333-5831

O'Brien, James E. - Moss & Barnett, A Professional Association - 4800 Norwest Center, 90 South Seventh Street, Minneapolis, MN 55402 - Securities & Venture Finance Law, Closely Held Business Law - **Publicly Held Corporations Law** - (612) 347-0273

O'Neill, Brian B. - Faegre & Benson - 2200 Norwest Center, 90 South Seventh Street, Minneapolis, MN 55402 - Commercial Litigation - **Environmental Law** - (612) 336-3000

Patrick, Howard A. - Robins, Kaplan, Miller & Ciresi - 2800 LaSalle Plaza, 800 LaSalle Avenue, Minneapolis, MN 55402 - **Bankruptcy & Workout Law** - (612) 349-8500

Payne, James A. - Popham, Haik, Schnobrich & Kaufman, Ltd. - 222 South Ninth Street, Suite 3300, Minneapolis, MN 55402 - **Environmental Law** - (612) 333-4800

Peterson, Bruce A. - Popham, Haik, Schnobrich & Kaufman, Ltd. - 222 South Ninth Street, Suite 3300, Minneapolis, MN 55402 - Federal, State & Local Government Law, Commercial Litigation - **Criminal Law** - (612) 333-4800

Popham, Wayne G. - Popham, Haik, Schnobrich & Kaufman, Ltd. - 222 South Ninth Street, Suite 3300, Minneapolis, MN 55402 - Commercial Litigation - **Federal, State & Local Government Law** - (612) 333-4800

Prescott, Jack L. - Prescott & Pearson, P.A. - P.O. Box 120088, New Brighton, MN 55112 - **Bankruptcy & Workout Law** - (612) 633-2757

Prichard, Michael - Dorsey & Whitney - Pillsbury Center South, 220 South Sixth Street, Minneapolis, MN 55402-1498 - **International Business Law** - (612) 340-2633

Provo, John W. - Popham, Haik, Schnobrich & Kaufman, Ltd. - 222 South Ninth Street, Suite 3300, Minneapolis, MN 55402 - **Probate, Estate Planning & Trusts Law** - (612) 333-4800

Quinlivan, Michael R. - Arthur, Chapman, McDonough, Kettering & Smetak, P.A. - 500 Young Quinlan Building, 81 South Ninth Street, Minneapolis, MN 55402-3214 - Personal Injury Defense Law - **Employment Law** - (612) 339-3500

Radio, Thomas J. - Popham, Haik, Schnobrich & Kaufman, Ltd. - 222 South Ninth Street, Suite 3300, Minneapolis, MN 55402 - Commercial Litigation - **Federal, State & Local Government Law** - (612) 333-4800

Ranum, Robert K. - Fredrikson & Byron, P.A. - 1100 International Centre, 900 Second Avenue South, Minneapolis, MN 55402 - Publicly Held Corporations Law - **Securities & Venture Finance Law** - (612) 347-7067

Ravich, Paul H. - Ravich, Meyer, Kirkman & McGrath, P.A. - 80 South Eighth Street, Suite 4545, Minneapolis, MN 55402-2225 - **Commercial Real Estate Law** - (612) 332-8511

Regnier, Pierre N. - Jardine, Logan & O'Brien - 2100 Piper Jaffray Plaza, 444 Cedar Street, St. Paul, MN 55101 - Federal, State & Local Government Law - **Personal Injury Defense Law** - (612) 290-6500

Remele, Lewis A. - Bassford, Lockhart, Truesdell & Briggs, P.A. - 3550 Multifoods Tower, 33 South Sixth Street, Minneapolis, MN 55402-3787 - **Commercial Litigation** - (612) 333-3000

Richter, Scott E. - Popham, Haik, Schnobrich & Kaufman, Ltd. - 222 South Ninth Street, Suite 3300, Minneapolis, MN 55402 - **Securities & Venture Finance Law** - (612) 333-4800

Riley, James M. - Meagher & Geer - 4200 Multifoods Tower, 33 South Sixth Street, Minneapolis, MN 55402 - **Personal Injury Defense Law** - (612) 338-0661

Rockwell, James W. - Popham, Haik, Schnobrich & Kaufman, Ltd. - 222 South Ninth Street, Suite 3300, Minneapolis, MN 55402 - **Probate, Estate Planning & Trusts Law** - (612) 333-4800

Roegge, James F. - Meagher & Geer - 4200 Multifoods Tower, 33 South Sixth Street, Minneapolis, MN 55402 - Commercial Litigation - **Professional Malpractice Defense Law** - (612) 338-0661

Rohricht, Thomas E. - Doherty, Rumble & Butler Professional Association - 2800 Minnesota World Trade Center, 30 East Seventh Street, St. Paul, MN 55101-4999 - Closely Held Business Law - **Publicly Held Corporations Law** - (612) 291-9333

Ross, Richard A. - Fredrikson & Byron, P.A. - 1100 International Centre, 900 Second Avenue South, Minneapolis, MN 55402 - **Labor Law** - (612) 347-7022

Roth, Randi Ilyse - Farmers' Legal Action Group, Inc. - 1301 Minnesota Building, 46 East Fourth Street, St. Paul, MN 55101 - **Agricultural Law** - (612) 223-5400

Rubenstein, James A. - Moss & Barnett, A Professional Association - 4800 Norwest Center, 90 South Seventh Street, Minneapolis, MN 55402-4129 - International Business Law - **Bankruptcy & Workout Law** - (612) 347-0300

Saeks, Allen I. - Leonard, Street and Deinard Professional Association - 150 South Fifth Street, Suite 2300, Minneapolis, MN 55402 - **Commercial Litigation** - (612) 335-1548

Sanders, Thomas P. - Leonard, Street and Deinard Professional Association - 150 South Fifth Street, Suite 2300, Minneapolis, MN 55402 - Closely Held Business Law - **Publicly Held Corporations Law** - (612) 335-1614

Appendix C: Attorneys & Law Firms by Region

Sawicki, Z. Peter - Kinney & Lange, P.A. - 625 Fourth Avenue South, Suite 1500, Minneapolis, MN 55415-1659 - **Intellectual Property Law** - (612) 339-1863

Sayre, Grover C. - O'Neill, Burke, O'Neill, Leonard & O'Brien, Ltd. - 100 South Fifth Street, Suite 1200, Minneapolis, MN 55402 - Bankruptcy & Workout Law - **Publicly Held Corporations Law** - (612) 332-1030

Scheerer, Paul J. - Dorsey & Whitney - Pillsbury Center South, 220 South Sixth Street, Minneapolis, MN 55402-1498 - Publicly Held Corporations Law - **Bankruptcy & Workout Law** - (612) 340-2883

Schmidt, Cecil C. - Merchant, Gould, Smith, Edell, Welter & Schmidt, P.A. - 1000 Norwest Center, 55 East Fifth Street, St. Paul, MN 55101-1785 - **Intellectual Property Law** - (612) 298-1055

Schulz, John R. - Collins, Buckley, Sauntry & Haugh - 332 Minnesota Street, Suite W1100, St. Paul, MN 55101 - Family Law - **Personal Injury Defense Law** - (612) 227-0611

Seaton, Douglas P. - Popham, Haik, Schnobrich & Kaufman, Ltd. - 222 South Ninth Street, Suite 3300, Minneapolis, MN 55402 - **Employment Law** - (612) 333-4800

Sellergren, David C. - Doherty, Rumble & Butler Professional Association - 3500 Fifth Street Towers, 150 South Fifth Street, Minneapolis, MN 55402-4235 - **Federal, State & Local Government Law** - (612) 340-5555

Sharpe, W. Smith - 2200 Norwest Center, 90 South Seventh Street, Minneapolis, 55402 - Publicly Held Corporations Law - **Securities & Venture Finance Law** - (612) 336-3000

Sheehy, Lee E. - Popham, Haik, Schnobrich & Kaufman, Ltd. - 222 South Ninth Street, Suite 3300, Minneapolis, MN 55402 - Commercial Litigation, Arts, Entertainment, Advertising & Media Law - **Federal, State & Local Government Law** - (612) 333-4800

Shnider, Bruce J. - Dorsey & Whitney - Pillsbury Center South, 220 South Sixth Street, Minneapolis, MN 55402-1498 - **Business Tax Law** - (612) 340-2862

Silverman, Robert J. - Dorsey & Whitney - Pillsbury Center South, 220 South Sixth Street, Minneapolis, MN 55402-1498 - **Commercial Real Estate Law** - (612) 340-2742

Sipkins, Peter W. - Dorsey & Whitney - Pillsbury Center South, 220 South Sixth Street, Minneapolis, MN 55402-1498 - **Commercial Litigation** - (612) 343-7903

Smith, Louis N. - Popham, Haik, Schnobrich & Kaufman, Ltd. - 222 South Ninth Street, Suite 3300, Minneapolis, MN 55402 - Immigration Law - **Federal, State & Local Government Law** - (612) 333-4800

Snyder, Stephen J. - Winthrop & Weinstine, P.A. - 3200 Minnesota World Trade Center, 30 East Seventh Street, St. Paul, MN 55101 - Commercial Litigation - **Employment Law** - (612) 290-8400

Soth, William R. - Dorsey & Whitney - Pillsbury Center South, 220 South Sixth Street, Minneapolis, MN 55402-1498 - **Commercial Real Estate Law** - (612) 340-2969

Soule, George W. - Bowman and Brooke - 150 South Fifth Street, Suite 2600, Minneapolis, MN 55402 - **Personal Injury Defense Law** - (612) 339-8682

Spevacek, Charles E. - Meagher & Geer - 4200 Multifoods Tower, 33 South Sixth Street, Minneapolis, MN 55402 - **Environmental Law** - (612) 338-0661

Stageberg, Roger V. - Lommen, Nelson, Cole & Stageberg, P.A. - 1800 IDS Center, 80 South Eighth Street, Minneapolis, MN 55402 - Commercial Litigation - **Closely Held Business Law** - (612) 339-8131

Starns, Byron E. - Leonard, Street and Deinard Professional Association - 150 South Fifth Street, Suite 2300, Minneapolis, MN 55402 - **Environmental Law** - (612) 335-1516

Stout, John H. - Fredrikson & Byron, P.A. - 1100 International Centre, 900 Second Avenue South, Minneapolis, MN 55402 - **Arts, Entertainment, Advertising & Media Law** - (612) 347-7012

Straughn, Robert O. - McGrann Shea Franzen Carnival Straughn & Lamb, Chartered - 2200 LaSalle Plaza, 800 LaSalle Avenue, Minneapolis, MN 55402 - **Commercial Real Estate Law** - (612) 338-2525

Strawbridge, Douglas A. - Merchant, Gould, Smith, Edell, Welter & Schmidt, P.A. - 3100 Norwest Center, 90 South Seventh Street, Minneapolis, MN 55402-4131 - **Intellectual Property Law** - (612) 332-5300

Stuart, Barbara G. - U.S. Trustee-Region 12 - Law Building, Suite 400, 225 Second Street SE, Cedar Rapids, IA 52401 - **Bankruptcy & Workout Law** - (319) 364-2211

Stumo, Mary E. - Faegre & Benson - 2200 Norwest Center, 90 South Seventh Street, Minneapolis, MN 55402 - Labor Law - **Employment Law** - (612) 336-3000

Sumners, John S. - Merchant, Gould, Smith, Edell, Welter & Schmidt, P.A. - 3100 Norwest Center, 90 South Seventh Street, Minneapolis, MN 55402-4131 - **Intellectual Property Law** - (612) 332-5300

Tanick, Marshall H. - Mansfield & Tanick, P.A. - 1560 International Centre, 900 Second Avenue South, Minneapolis, MN 55402-3383 - **Employment Law** - (612) 339-4295

Taylor, Frank A. - Popham, Haik, Schnobrich & Kaufman, Ltd. - 222 South Ninth Street, Suite 3300, Minneapolis, MN 55402 - Commercial Litigation, Publicly Held Corporations Law - **Securities & Venture Finance Law** - (612) 333-4800

Thomson, James J. - Holmes & Graven, Chartered - 470 Pillsbury Center, 200 South Sixth Street, Minneapolis, MN 55402 - Commercial Litigation - **Federal, State & Local Government Law** - (612) 337-9300

Thorsen, Madge S. - Popham, Haik, Schnobrich & Kaufman, Ltd. - 222 South Ninth Street, Suite 3300, Minneapolis, MN 55402 - Commercial Litigation - **Personal Injury Defense Law - (612) 333-4800**

Tinkham, Thomas W. - Dorsey & Whitney - Pillsbury Center South, 220 South Sixth Street, Minneapolis, MN 55402-1498 - **Commercial Litigation - (612) 340-2829**

Torgerson, Paul M. - Dorsey & Whitney - Pillsbury Center South, 220 South Sixth Street, Minneapolis, MN 55402-1498 - Business Tax Law - **Health Law - (612) 340-8700**

Trucano, Michael - Dorsey & Whitney - Pillsbury Center South, 220 South Sixth Street, Minneapolis, MN 55402-1498 - **Closely Held Business Law - (612) 340-2673**

Truesdell, Lynn G. - Bassford, Lockhart, Truesdell & Briggs, P.A. - 3550 Multifoods Tower, 33 South Sixth Street, Minneapolis, MN 55402 - **Commercial Litigation - (612) 333-3000**

Tyra, Kenneth T. - Dorsey & Whitney - Pillsbury Center South, 220 South Sixth Street, Minneapolis, MN 55402-1498 - **Commercial Real Estate Law - (612) 340-8869**

Van de North, John B. - Briggs and Morgan, P.A. - W-2200 First National Bank Building, St. Paul, MN 55101 - **Environmental Law - (612) 223-6600**

Van Valkenburg, Paul - Moss & Barnett, A Professional Association - 4800 Norwest Center, 90 South Seventh Street, Minneapolis, MN 55402 - **Publicly Held Corporations Law - (612) 347-0300**

Vanasek, Alan R. - Jardine, Logan & O'Brien - 2100 Piper Jaffray Plaza, 444 Cedar Street, St. Paul, MN 55101 - **Personal Injury Defense Law - (612) 290-6500**

Villaume, Philip G. - Philip G. Villaume & Associates - 7900 International Drive, Suite 675, Bloomington, MN 55425 - **Criminal Law - (612) 851-0823**

Weikart, Neil A. - Fredrikson & Byron, P.A. - 1100 International Centre, 900 Second Avenue South, Minneapolis, MN 55402 - **Publicly Held Corporations Law - (612) 347-7025**

Weil, Cass S. - Moss & Barnett, A Professional Association - 4800 Norwest Center, 90 South Seventh Street, Minneapolis, MN 55402 - **Bankruptcy & Workout Law - (612) 347-0300**

Weinstine, Robert R. - Winthrop & Weinstine, P.A. - 3000 Dain Bosworth Plaza, 60 South Sixth Street, Minneapolis, MN 55402 - **Commercial Litigation - (612) 347-0700**

Wernick, Mark S. - Attorney at Law - 2520 Park Avenue, Minneapolis, MN 55404 - **Criminal Law - (612) 871-8456**

Westman, Nickolas E. - Westman, Champlin & Kelly, P.A. - 720 TCF Tower, 121 South Eighth Street, Minneapolis, MN 55402 - **Intellectual Property Law - (612) 334-3222**

Whitehead, G. Marc - Popham, Haik, Schnobrich & Kaufman, Ltd. - 222 South Ninth Street, Suite 3300, Minneapolis, MN 55402 - Commercial Litigation, International Business Law - **Publicly Held Corporations Law - (612) 333-4800**

Wilhoit, Richard A. - Doherty, Rumble & Butler Professional Association - 2800 Minnesota World Trade Center, 30 East Seventh Street, St. Paul, MN 55101-4999 - **Probate, Estate Planning & Trusts Law - (612) 291-9333**

Williams, Douglas J. - Merchant, Gould, Smith, Edell, Welter & Schmidt, P.A. - 3100 Norwest Center, 90 South Seventh Street, Minneapolis, MN 55402-4131 - Commercial Litigation, Arts, Entertainment, Advertising & Media Law - **Intellectual Property Law - (612) 332-5300**

Windhorst, John W. - Dorsey & Whitney - Pillsbury Center South, 220 South Sixth Street, Minneapolis, MN 55402-1498 - **Business Tax Law - (612) 340-2645**

Winthrop, Sherman - Winthrop & Weinstine, P.A. - 3200 Minnesota World Trade Center, 30 East Seventh Street, St. Paul, MN 55101 - Closely Held Business Law - **Publicly Held Corporations Law - (612) 290-8400**

Wold, Peter B. - Wold, Jacobs & Johnson, P.A. - Barristers Trust Building, 247 Third Avenue South, Minneapolis, MN 55415 - **Criminal Law - (612) 341-2525**

Zwakman, John C. - Dorsey & Whitney - Pillsbury Center South, 220 South Sixth Street, Minneapolis, MN 55402-1498 - **Labor Law - (612) 340-2786**

Bassford, Lockhart, Truesdell & Briggs, P.A.

3550 Multifoods Tower, 33 South Sixth Street - Minneapolis, MN 55402-3787 - Phone: (612) 333-3000 - Fax: (612) 333-8829

Founded in 1882, the law firm now known as Bassford, Lockhart, Truesdell & Briggs, P.A. has been serving clients in Minnesota for more than 110 years. The Bassford firm is one of the oldest law firms in the Twin Cities. Since Fred Snyder and Robert Jamison formed Snyder and Jamison in 1882, the firm has undergone several name changes. Although its name has changed over the years, the firm's strong commitment to client services has not changed, nor has its litigation expertise. Many of the firm's founding lawyers were known as outstanding trial lawyers and community leaders. Fred Snyder's 39 years as member plus 37 years as chairman of the University of Minnesota Board of Regents are the longest service on record. Bergmann Richards' reputation as an outstanding trial lawyer developed during his 60 years of practice. Charles Bassford was one of the first Minnesota lawyers inducted into the American College of Trial Lawyers.

The Bassford firm's 27 lawyers have expertise in civil and business litigation and provide a broad range of litigation services for clients in Minnesota and around the country. The areas include:

- Appellate practice
- Business torts
- Construction law
- Environmental claims
- General liability
- Healthcare litigation and risk management
- Insurance coverage and related claims
- Labor and employment law
- Personal injury
- Premises liability
- Product liability
- Professional ethics and disciplinary matters
- Professional liability:
   legal
   financial
   medical
   architects
   fiduciaries
   engineers
   insurance agents and brokers
   directors and officers
- Securities
- Shareholder and related corporate litigation
- Workers' compensation

During the Bassford firm's second century, the firm continues its commitment to quality service to its clients. The firm has kept abreast and at the forefront of dispute resolution as it expands beyond the traditional trial format. The Bassford firm offers creative approaches to all forms of dispute resolution, while maintaining its tradition of providing quality service at the greatest value for its clients.

Bowman and Brooke

100 South Fifth Street, Suite 2600 - Minneapolis, MN 55402 - Phone: (612) 339-8682 - Fax: (612) 672-3200

Bowman and Brooke is an energetic and well-established national litigation firm with offices in Minneapolis, Phoenix, Detroit, San Jose, and Los Angeles. The firm began practice on February 1, 1985 with seven partners and seven associates who left a large Minneapolis law firm. Since then, the firm has grown to over 70 lawyers. The firm began its practice with a large group of clients with whom the attorneys had long-standing relationships, and this client base has expanded, assuring continued growth into the future.

Bowman and Brooke is strictly a litigation firm. The firm's practice areas include:

- Products liability defense
- Environmental law
- Labor and employment litigation
- Commercial litigation
- White collar criminal defense and compliance
- Product liability prevention

With bases in Minneapolis, Phoenix, Detroit, San Jose and Los Angeles, the firm's practice is truly nationwide. While Bowman and Brooke attorneys often appear on behalf of its clients in state and federal courts in Minnesota, Arizona, Michigan, and California, they also serve as trial counsel in courts across the country. Bowman and Brooke attorneys have now handled cases in virtually every state.

The firm acts as national or regional counsel for several manufacturers in special subject matter litigation. Bowman and Brooke represents clients in defending claims involving park-to-reverse transmissions, post-collision fuel-fed fires, all-terrain vehicles, brake balance, unwanted acceleration, rollover-roof crush, and boat propeller guarding. The firm has become efficient in compiling and analyzing all available information on complex technical issues, organizing and analyzing historical documents on a technical issue, and developing innovative ways to present these issues in trial and settlement negotiations.

Clients include General Motors Corporation, Ford Motor Company, Navistar International Transportation Corp., Outboard Marine Corporation, Toyota Motor Sales, USA, Inc., Nissan Motor Corporation in USA, American Honda Motor Co., Inc.

CHRISTOFFEL, ELLIOTT & ALBRECHT, P.A.
Suite 1250, 100 South Fifth Street - Minneapolis, MN 55402 - Phone: (612) 672-0900 - Fax: (612) 341-2835

Since its inception in 1989, Christoffel, Elliott & Albrecht, P.A. has provided top quality legal services to entrepreneurs and businesses. The firm was established by experienced lawyers with the goal of providing comprehensive legal services to clients with a wide variety of business problems. The firm has successfully achieved this goal throughout its existence.

Christoffel, Elliott & Albrecht, P.A. provides clients with legal expertise in all phases of business development. The firm handles matters on a spectrum ranging from business formation on the one end to reorganization and bankruptcy on the other. Specifically, the firm's practice is concentrated in the following areas:

- Banking and Commercial Finance
- Real Estate
- Corporate and Business Planning
- Bankruptcy and Creditor's Rights
- Commercial Litigation
  - Contract Disputes
  - Employment Matters

The firm has respected lawyers that competently handle both transactional work as well as litigation. Both Mr. Elliott and Mr. Christoffel were recognized in 1994 as top attorneys in their respective fields by a survey of peers published in the *Minnesota Journal of Law & Politics*.

One of the firm's greatest strengths is its moderate size which allows for greater personal attention and contact with clients.

The firm is attentive to its clients' needs, not only providing excellent legal services but also keeping clients well informed and aware at all stages of a legal matter. The firm has offices in both Minneapolis and St. Paul, to further facilitate accessibility with its clients.

In the future, Christoffel, Elliott & Albrecht, P.A. will continue to provide top quality legal services, producing positive results that clients have come to expect.

COSGROVE, FLYNN & GASKINS
2900 Metropolitan Centre, 333 South Seventh Street - Minneapolis, MN 55402 - Phone: (612) 333-9500 - Fax: (612) 333-9579

Cosgrove, Flynn & Gaskins is an aggressive, efficient civil litigation law firm serving as national and local counsel to product manufacturers, various other corporations, financial institutions, insurers, owners, officers, directors and supervisory personnel nationwide, and in Minnesota. The firm's litigation practice includes products liability; insurance coverage, defense and subrogation; employment and labor defense; corporate and commercial litigation; construction litigation; and personal injury litigation. Within the firm's practice areas, subspecialities exist, e.g., gas equipment liability, fire loss and flammable fabrics litigation. In its vigorous representation of its clients, Cosgrove, Flynn & Gaskins places high emphasis on the provision of ethical, outstanding legal services. This approach to the practice of law has become the firm's hallmark.

To ensure the provision of high quality, efficient and affordable legal representation, Cosgrove, Flynn & Gaskins attracts and employs highly skilled, motivated attorneys who aggressively pursue their clients' interest. The firm's litigators possess extensive experience in handling complex matters, including multi-state litigation involving a common product. Whether disputes involve class-actions, multi-district litigation, single plaintiff litigation in federal or state court, government administrative proceedings, arbitration, mediation or other alternative disputes resolution forums, the firm's lawyers provide excellent representation. Cosgrove, Flynn & Gaskins' numerous trial verdicts, summery judgements, successful appellate decisions and effective settlements attest to the firm's preeminence in multiple areas of litigation.

The firm is committed to capable, but cost effective representation. Cosgrove, Flynn & Gaskins does not transfer cases between attorneys and/or paralegals and does not believe the client should pay for more than one lawyer reading and responding to discovery, and attending depositions or conferences. The firm's policy is to try cases with one attorney in attendance. If the size or complexity of the matter requires it, we add trial attorneys and paralegal staff as necessary.

Representative clients of Cosgrove, Flynn & Gaskins include: Honeywell Inc.; Minnesota Mining and Manufacturing Co.; Emerson Electric Co.; Grayco, Inc.; Federal Express Corp.; Target, a division of Dayton Hudson; Celotex Corp.; Union Carbide Corp.; Belarus Machinery of USA, Inc.; Maytag Corp.; Realtors Credit Union; Cigna; Fireman's Fund-American Insurance Cos.; The Hartford; The Traveler's Ins. Cos.; Prudential Insurance Co.; The St. Paul Companies; State Farm Insurance Cos.; and Minnesota Mutual Fire & Casualty.

DOHERTY, RUMBLE & BUTLER, P.A.

2800 Minnesota World Trade Center - 30 East Seventh Street - St. Paul, MN 55101 - Phone: (612) 291-9333 - Fax: (612) 291-9313

Doherty, Rumble & Butler (DRB) is a 100-attorney firm which brings more than 135 years of experience and expertise to address and solve the complex legal issues that confront our clients. Although based in Saint Paul, the firm has offices in Minneapolis, Washington, D.C., and Denver to better meet the needs of clients.

DRB's clientele spans Fortune 500 corporations, growing companies, service organizations, start-ups and emerging businesses, public utilities, sole proprietorships, and individuals. Our attorneys provide a results-oriented approach in the areas of:

- commercial and non-commercial litigation
- environmental and land use law
- cooperative law
- tax law
- banking, commercial, and corporate finance law
- bankruptcy and creditor/debtor law
- corporate and securities law
- health care law
- real estate law
- trust and estate law
- pension and employee benefits law
- labor and employment law

The firm prides itself on innovative approaches to business problems with a focus on client service. We work with clients to best meet their needs in an efficient, aggressive, and cost-effective manner. DRB respects its clients' business sense and consistently turns to them to learn how to improve service. In 1992, the firm officially adopted a commitment to Continuous Quality Improvement and annually surveys clients to determine their level of satisfaction.

It is imperative that outside counsel understand the business of its clients. This involves not only knowing the client's business, but more importantly, having an overall knowledge of the client's long-term objectives and how it intends to attain them. DRB is prepared to absorb the expense of learning the business of a new client. Our goal is to become familiar with the client's business, develop a strategy or plan, and build a solid working relationship.

Doherty, Rumble & Butler strives at providing savings on quality legal services. DRB offers Alternative Dispute Resolution (ADR) services to be used in litigation or independently. In instances where the client chooses these procedures, the cost and burden of litigation can be significantly reduced with innovative and practical solutions.

As an annual participant in the National Price Waterhouse Survey of law firm economics, Doherty, Rumble & Butler continues to stay below the means and averages on our billing rates, as compared to other firms our size. DRB also provides a variety of billing format options for our clients. We can easily invoice subsidiary business units of companies in separate formats, invoices by areas of practice, provide extensive detail or less detail, and/or tailor invoicing to fit client needs.

Doherty, Rumble & Butler is proud of its clients, and grateful. The firm's healthy longevity would not have been possible without our clients' energy, spirit and vision, which in turn inspire in our attorneys enthusiasm, creativity, technical excellence, and a commitment to serve our clients and our communities.

OFFICES

St. Paul:
2800 Minnesota World Trade Center
30 East Seventh Street
St. Paul, MN 55101-4999
Phone: (612) 291-9333
Fax: (612) 291-9313

Minneapolis:
3500 Fifth Street Towers
150 South Fifth Street
Minneapolis, MN 55402-4235
Phone: (612) 340-5555
Fax: (612) 340-5584

Washington, D.C.:
Magruder Building
1625 M Street NW
Washington, D.C. 20036-3203
Phone: (202) 293-0555
Fax: (202) 659-0466

Denver, CO:
2370 One Tabor Center
1200 Seventeenth Street
Denver, CO 80202-5823
Phone: (303) 572-6200
Fax: (303) 572-6203

DORSEY & WHITNEY

Pillsbury Center South, 220 South Sixth Street - Minneapolis, MN 55402-1498 - Phone: (612) 340-2600 - Fax: (612) 340-2868

Dorsey & Whitney traces its history as a law firm to the formation in 1912 of a partnership between William Atwood Lancaster, former judge of the Hennepin County, Minnesota, District Court, and David Ferguson Simpson, former justice of the Minnesota Supreme Court. Since its formation in Minneapolis over 80 years ago, Dorsey & Whitney has grown into the largest law firm between Chicago and the West Coast. Dorsey & Whitney has 350 lawyers in active practice and a support staff of more than 500 persons. Dorsey & Whitney's principal office is located in Minneapolis, but it has established itself as the preeminent law firm in the Upper Midwest and Rocky Mountain region with offices in Rochester, Minnesota; Des Moines, Iowa; Denver, Colorado; Fargo, North Dakota; and Billings, Great Falls, and Missoula, Montana. Dorsey & Whitney also has offices in New York City, Washington, D.C., Costa Mesa, California, London, and Brussels which enable Dorsey to service the legal needs of its clients on a national and international basis.

With approximately 1,100 Apple Macintosh personal computers on the desks of lawyers, legal assistants and support staff in all of Dorsey & Whitney's offices, and in the legal departments of over 60 of the firm's largest clients, Dorsey & Whitney has the largest installation of networked Macintosh computers of any law firm in the world. The electronic mail, computer assisted research, document communications, document assembly systems and litigation support that are part of this integrated system have significantly enhanced efficiencies and quality control capabilities and have improved the firm's ability to respond quickly and consistently to client needs.

Dorsey & Whitney has a wide variety of corporate, governmental, and individual clients, ranging from Fortune 500 companies, non-profit organizations and governmental entities, to a broad base of small and medium-sized corporate and individual clients. The firm's varied practice has enabled Dorsey & Whitney to develop practice groups oriented to satisfying the full range of clients' needs. It is able to provide expertise in transactions that reflect optimum levels of senior partner, junior partner and associate attention. All clients have access to the attorneys necessary to establish a balance between experience and economical execution, regardless of client or transaction size. Dorsey & Whitney takes pride in providing efficient and cost-effective services.

Dorsey & Whitney's practice groups include all of the legal specialties that are required to service a sophisticated corporate clientele, and its litigation, corporate, real estate, tax, banking, employee benefits, acquisitions, corporate securities, and public finance lawyers have a depth and breadth of expertise that is the equal of any firm in the Midwest and Rocky Mountain regions. In addition, the firm has a number of other specialty practice groups that enable it to distinguish itself from most of the other firms in these regions. Specialty practice groups include environmental regulation and litigation, international trade regulation, emerging companies, employment law, intellectual property, and investment companies.

Litigation - Handles all aspects of trial and appellate work with specialties in antitrust, banking, commercial, commodities, construction, intellectual property, patent/copyright/trademark/trade secrets, defamation, education, employment law, environmental, insurance, malpractice, product liability, securities, shareholder, tax, unfair competition, and white collar crime.

Corporate - Provides services in all aspects of general corporate and securities law, corporate financing, and acquisitions and divestitures with extensive experience in representing underwriters, investment bankers, venture capital firms and other professionals specializing in raising capital, as well as corporations and other business organizations.

Banking & Commercial - Represents lenders in the negotiation and drafting of loan and related security agreements, participation agreements and similar financing agreements; advises national banks and multi-bank holding companies on regulatory matters; and represents creditors in bankruptcy and reorganization proceedings.

Real Estate - Handles the purchase, sale and leasing of residential, commercial and industrial properties; development of properties; representation before government bodies; creation of ownership programs; condominium conversions; construction and long term financing; agriculture and agribusiness financing; construction contracts; eminent domain and real estate tax contests; and special assessment matters.

Tax/Health Law - Represents large public corporations, closely held private corporations and individuals in all aspects of tax planning, tax litigation, and dealing with state and federal authorities. Experience includes the initial formation and ongoing operations of health care entities; as well as antitrust, business and tax planning; regulatory compliance; corporate restructuring, mergers, and acquisitions; and foreign and domestic licensing matters. Clients include public and private hospitals, medical societies, medical clinics and providers, research organizations, HMOs, and dependency centers.

Intellectual Property - Provides a full range of intellectual property expertise, including US and foreign patent, trademark, copyright prosecution and litigation; unfair competition and trade secret litigation; and the preparation of license agreements. Special areas of expertise include computer law and licensing in the areas of biotechnology, electronic circuits, and computer hardware and software.

Public Finance - Provides services in all aspects of state and local government unit finance, serving principally as bond counsel, underwriter's counsel, special tax counsel, trustee's counsel, and letter of credit bank counsel. Represents various governmental entities as general or special counsel to other local law matters.

Environmental & Regulatory Affairs - Advises clients on hazardous waste regulatory compliance and land use matters and represents clients before federal, state, regional and local administrative agencies, and federal and state courts. Experience includes major environmental litigation (CERCLA, RCRA, TSCA) in several states, hazardous waste disposal, air emissions, groundwater contamination, and landfill siting.

Labor & Employment - Represents employers in all phases of employer-union relations, including collective bargaining negotiations, arbitrations, NLRB, and judicial proceedings. Also represents employers in OSHA and Fair Labor Standards Act matters, employment discrimination litigation, "wrongful termination" litigation, and representation before state and federal agencies.

continued on page 472

Appendix C: Attorneys & Law Firms by Region

DORSEY & WHITNEY

Pillsbury Center South, 220 South Sixth Street - Minneapolis, MN 55402-1498 - Phone: (612) 340-2600 - Fax: (612) 340-2868

Estate Planning & Administration - Provides services in all aspects of estate planning, including the administration of estates and trusts, generation skipping, and fiduciary and individual income tax laws. Services include probate, estate planning, estate and trust administration, wills, and trusts, litigation, adoptions, conservatorships and guardianships, and premarital agreements.

Employee Benefits - Represents corporate clients in the design, formation, maintenance, IRS qualification, and termination of qualified and nonqualified plans of deferred compensation, including prototype work for financial institutions. Also evaluates the employee benefit aspects of acquisitions and dispositions.

Indian & Gaming Law - Experience in Indian Law includes work on reservation financing and bonding matters, construction, education, gaming, governmental matters, intergovernmental relations, environmental matters, retirement plans, and fringe benefits, income, excise and sales taxation and tax advice, planning, and compliance. Experience in Gaming Law includes representation of manufacturers and distributors of equipment, managers and operators of gaming facilities, state and tribal licensing, financing, and regulatory work. The group also advises business clients who are retained by, or who are doing business with, Indian Tribes.

International - Counsels United States companies in all matters relating to international corporate and commercial transactions, including foreign acquisitions, investments, joint ventures, licensing, and distribution arrangements, and dispute resolution. The London and Brussels offices provide advice on European matters, including financial transactions in the London market, as well as the laws and regulations of the European Economic Community (EEC). The Washington office represents foreign manufacturers and domestic importers in import-related proceedings before the Department of Commerce, the International Trade Commission, and various courts. In cooperation with the Washington and New York offices, the group advises in such regulatory matters as customs and immigration, export controls, and restrictions on foreign investment in the United States.

Dorsey & Whitney has offices in the following locations:

Minneapolis, Minnesota
Phone: (612) 340-2600
Fax: (612) 340-2868

Billings, Montana
Phone: (406) 252-3800
Fax: (406) 252-9480

Brussels, Belgium
Phone: 32-2-504-4611
Fax: 32-2-504-4646

Costa Mesa, California
Phone: (714) 662-7300
Fax: (714) 662-5576

Denver, Colorado
Phone: (303) 629-3400
Fax: (303) 629-3450

Des Moines, Iowa
Phone: (515) 283-1000
Fax: (515) 283-1060

Fargo, North Dakota
Phone: (701) 235-6000
Fax: (701) 235-9969

Great Falls, Montana
Phone: (406) 727-3632
Fax: (406) 727-3638

London, England
Phone: 44-71-929-3334
Fax: 44-71-929-3111/929-0099

Missoula, Montana
Phone: (406) 721-6025
Fax: (406) 543-0863

New York, New York
Phone: (212) 415-9200
Fax: (212) 888-0018

Rochester, Minnesota
Phone: (507) 288-3156
Fax: (507) 288-6190

Washington, D.C.
Phone: (202) 857-0700
Fax: (202) 857-0569

MANAGEMENT COMMITTEE ATTORNEYS

Thomas O. Moe
Managing Partner

William H. Hippe, Jr.

William A. Johnstone

Peter S. Hendrixson

John R. Wicks

FREDRIKSON & BYRON, P.A.

1100 International Centre, 900 Second Avenue South - Minneapolis, MN 55402-3397 - Phone: (612) 347-7000 - Fax: (612) 347-7077

Fredrikson & Byron, P.A. was established in 1948, and has grown steadily to become one of the region's largest business law firms, with approximately 120 lawyers and 180 staff. The mission of Fredrikson & Byron is to provide excellent advice and service to enable clients to achieve their business and personal objectives.

The firm's lawyers represent publicly and closely-held businesses, financial institutions, municipalities, professional corporations, nonprofit organizations, partnerships and individuals, including: new ventures, small and medium-sized companies, family-controlled operations, and national and multinational corporations traded on established stock exchanges.

Fredrikson & Byron lawyers take a proactive, problem-solving approach to serving clients, and are committed to providing high quality, cost-effective legal and business advice. They focus on the business implications of each client's situation, not just the legal details—that's why our clients look to Fredrikson & Byron as partners to solve their problems and facilitate growth. It is of paramount importance to the attorneys and staff of Fredrikson & Byron that their clients feel well served.

Fredrikson & Byron trial lawyers are skilled in all areas of business litigation. They represent clients in court, before administrative agencies, and in arbitrated disputes.

PRACTICE GROUPS

Fredrikson & Byron's highly specialized Practice Groups are organized to meet clients' many needs.

Advertising, Media & Entertainment Law
Co-chairs: S. Bergerson, A. Herbst, P. Landry, J. Stout

Alternative Dispute Resolution
Chair: K. Harbison

Banking Law
Co-chairs: J. Kost, R. Whitlock

Bankruptcy
Chair: J. Baillie

Business Litigation
Chair: T. Fraser

Corporate/Commercial/Insurance
Chair: J. Satorius

Corporate/Securities Law
Chair: T. Heaney

Compensation Planning/Employee Benefits
Chair: J. Merkle

Compliance & Risk Management
Chair: J. Stout

Director & Officer Services
Chair: J. Stout

Environmental Law
Co-chairs: D. Coyne, L. Stern

Estates & Trust
Chair: J. Byron

Family Law
Chair: R. Lazar

Family Business
Chair: G. Ayres

Health Law
Chair: K. Friedemann

Intellectual Property
Chair: J. Haller

International Business
Co-chairs: G. Giombetti, L. Koslow, J. Stout

Labor & Employment
Chair: K. Hughes

Mergers & Acquisitions
Chair: D. West

Nonprofit Organizations
Chair: R. Greener

Property Tax
Chair: T. Wilhelmy

Real Estate
Co-chairs: E. Anderson, J. Koneck

Real Estate Dispute Resolution
Chair: J. Koneck

Tax & Business Planning
Chair: J. Erhart

Tax Disputes & Litigation
Co-chairs: J. James, S. Kaplan, T. Muck

Technology & Software
Co-chairs: S. Root, J. Satorius

FREDRIKSON & BYRON KEEPS CLIENTS INFORMED

The more clients know about legal requirements and options, the more effective we can be. Therefore, the firm produced a series of FOCUS newsletters as a complimentary service to clients and colleagues. Written by Fredrikson & Byron lawyers in plain language, each newsletter has practical information on subjects ranging from hiring and firing to environmental compliance to protecting product ideas in foreign markets. Call (612) 336-4041 to request a list of newsletter titles and to subscribe.

FACILITIES

Fredrikson & Byron's headquarters office is in the International Centre in downtown Minneapolis, at the corner of Second Avenue South and Ninth Street. The London office is centrally located near the business and financial districts at 79 Knightsbridge.

CALL FREDRIKSON & BYRON WITH YOUR QUESTIONS

When you have tough questions or a situation that may require legal assistance, call one of the Practice Group Chairs listed above at (612) 347-7000. They will direct you to the appropriate lawyer or talk with you briefly to give you some options on how to proceed.

LONDON ADDRESS

Fredrikson & Byron, P.A.
79 Knightsbridge
London SW1X 7RB, England
Phone: (011) 44-171-823-2338

FROMMELT & EIDE, LTD.

580 International Centre, 900 Second Avenue South - Minneapolis, MN 55402 - Phone: (612) 332-2200 - Fax: (612) 342-2761

Frommelt & Eide, Ltd., has been providing legal services to entrepreneurs and emerging businesses in the Twin Cities and around the United States since 1974.

The firm provides a variety of legal services in areas which include:

- Business Formation
- Private Placements
- Public Offerings
- Commercial Transactions
- Mergers/Acquisitions
- Franchises
- Licensing
- Real Estate
- Community Associations
- Employee Matters
- Contracts
- Commercial Litigation

Because of the firm's experience Frommelt & Eide is able to quickly understand and anticipate the needs of emerging businesses and entrepreneurs.

As a small law firm of eight attorneys, Frommelt & Eide, Ltd. is able to give entrepreneurs and growing businesses the personal attention they require in a cost-effective manner without "over- lawyering."

Roger H. Frommelt is a founding partner of Frommelt & Eide, Ltd. and a graduate of the University of Minnesota Law School. Mr. Frommelt has over 27 years of experience representing start-up and emerging companies located in the Twin Cities and across the United States, and is well known in the legal community. Mr. Frommelt heads the business organizations and finance group at Frommelt & Eide, Ltd. which is comprised of a small number of highly-skilled attorneys with many years of experience representing growing public and private companies.

David B. Eide is a founding partner of Frommelt & Eide, Ltd. A graduate of the University of Minnesota Law School, Mr. Eide has practiced for over 20 years in the areas of real estate and corporate law, with emphasis on multi-family housing. A substantial part of Mr. Eide's real estate practice focuses on the development of condominiums, townhouses and cooperatives and the representation of the homeowners associations which govern those types of developments. Mr. Eide is a founding member of the Minnesota Chapter of the Community Associations Institute and is a frequent speaker locally and nationally regarding community association law and issues. He was a principal drafter of the Minnesota Uniform Condominium Act and is chair of the Minnesota Bar Committee which obtained passage of the Minnesota Common Interest Ownership Act.

HOLMES & GRAVEN CHARTERED

470 Pillsbury Center - Minneapolis, MN 55402 - Phone: (612) 337-9300 - Fax: (612) 337-9310 -
1616 Pioneer Building, 336 North Robert Street - St. Paul, MN 55101 - Phone: (612) 225-4938 -

Founded in 1973, Holmes & Graven has represented a broad spectrum of public and private industry clientele in Minnesota and nationally. Attorneys at Holmes & Graven and their specialties are:

James S. Holmes - *Municipal Finance; Gov. Law*
John R. Larson - *Municipal Finance; Securities*
David J. Kennedy - *Municipal Finance; Local Gov. Representation*
Robert A. Alsop - *Litigation*
Ronald H. Batty - *Local Gov. Representation*
Stephen J. Bubul - *Municipal Finance*
Robert C. Carlson - *Corporate Law*
Robert L. Davidson - *Real Estate Development*
John B. Dean - *Local Gov. Representation*
Mary G. Dobbins - *Litigation*
Stefanie N. Galey - *Municipal Finance*
Corrine A. Heine - *Local Gov. Representation*
Wellington H. Law - *Construction Law*
Charles L. LeFevere - *Local Gov. Representation*
John M. LeFevre, Jr. - *Litigation; Employment Labor Law*
Robert J. Lindall - *Eminent Domain; Environmental Law*
Robert C. Long - *Municipal Law*
Laura K. Mollet - *Municipal Finance*
Barbara L. Portwood - *Municipal Finance*
T. Jay Salmen - *Commercial Law*
James M. Strommen - *Litigation; Public Utilities*
James J. Thomson - *Litigation*
Larry M. Wertheim - *Real Estate*
Bonnie L. Wilkins - *Litigation*
Gary P. Winter - *Municipal Law; Real Estate*

Holmes & Graven is recognized nationally and has served as municipal finance bond counsel for over 1,000 municipal bond issues in the states of Minnesota, Wisconsin, North Dakota, South Dakota, Arizona, Georgia, Illinois, and California; is a member of The National Association of Bond Lawyers; and is listed in the Municipal Bond Attorneys of the US section of "The Bond Buyer's Directory."

Holmes & Graven attorneys are city attorneys for Richfield, Lauderdale, Medina, New Brighton, Robbinsdale, Brooklyn Center, Crystal, Sandstone, Loretto, Rosemount, Moundsview, and Independence, and general counsel to Local Government Information Systems, Lake Minnetonka Conservation District, White Bear Lake Conservation District, Hennepin Recycling Group, Suburban Rate Authority, Minnesota Police Recruitment System, and the Housing and Redevelopment Authorities of Dakota County, Washington County, Stearns County, the City of St. Cloud, and the City of Columbia Heights.

Holmes & Graven also serves as special counsel to many governmental entities, including Bloomington, Brainerd, Burnsville, Minneapolis, Minneapolis Community Development Agency, Minneapolis Public Housing Authority, and the Economic Development Agencies in Brooklyn Park, Duluth, and Hibbing.

JARDINE, LOGAN & O'BRIEN

2100 Piper Jaffray Plaza, 444 Cedar Street - St. Paul, MN 55101-2160 - Phone: (612) 290-6500 - Fax: (612) 223-5070

Litigation is, and has always been, the primary focus of the Jardine, Logan & O'Brien law firm. Throughout the firm's 75-year history, its lawyers have worked on some of the region's largest and most complex disputes with outstanding results.

The success of the firm can be traced to a philosophy of file handling that puts the client first. This means:

- Early involvement, to understand clients' needs, preferred procedures, and desired roles in their cases

- Early and accurate valuation of cases, made simpler by the firm's collective years of experience

- Aggressive handling and preparation of the files

- Frequent communication with clients, to keep them informed and answer questions

This approach does not mean that Jardine, Logan & O'Brien does unnecessary work; quite the opposite. By properly evaluating cases and skillfully preparing them, the firm can resolve clients' disputes by the best and most cost-effective means, whether by settlement, through alternative dispute resolution techniques, or in a trial or hearing. In addition, the firm continues to represent clients after these steps, in negotiations and appeals.

Clients at the firm include individuals, large and small businesses, insurance companies, and self-insured trusts. Jardine, Logan & O'Brien feels honored to be the recipient of many referrals from their peers at other law firms, who frequently refer complex litigation matters to them. The firm believes this is attributable to excellent results and professionalism; they treat people with civility and respect.

The 40 civil litigators at Jardine, Logan & O'Brien are divided into sub-specialty groups, allowing them to concentrate their practices. At the same time, they can draw upon the experience of their colleagues in an environment which encourages communication and support. The firm's practice includes the following areas of expertise:

- Employment law and civil rights
- Government liability
- Products liability
- Personal injury
- General liability and negligence
- Workers' compensation
- Medical and professional malpractice
- Insurance coverage
- Arson, fraud, and property damage claims
- Environmental liability
- Construction claims
- Subrogation
- Arbitration and mediation
- Appeals

Solving client problems ethically, cost-effectively, and with a good result is the ultimate goal at Jardine, Logan & O'Brien.

KINNEY & LANGE, P.A.

625 Fourth Ave South, Suite 1500 - Minneapolis, MN 55415 - Phone: (612) 339-1863 - Fax: (612) 339-6580

Kinney & Lange is an energetic, full-service intellectual property law firm. The firm was founded in 1977 and has since grown to be one of the largest intellectual property law firms in Minnesota with more than 30 attorneys. Kinney & Lange identifies, obtains, and protects domestic and international rights of its clients through patent, trademark, copyright, licensing, unfair competition, advertising, and franchise law. Its attorneys are capable and experienced in litigating and resolving intellectual property disputes in Federal and State courts, the United States Patent and Trademark office, foreign patent offices and courts, the International Trade Commission, and arbitration tribunals.

Kinney & Lange has a national reputation for providing innovative and responsive counsel. Additionally, the firm regularly conducts seminars to educate other professionals about various aspects of intellectual property law. Kinney & Lange presently provides its *Overview of Intellectual Property for Business Lawyers* annually in Minneapolis and in Milwaukee free of charge. Topics addressed in the most recent seminar included "Obtaining a Patent," "Trade Secrets, Unfair Competition Under § 43(a)," "Counseling a Start-Up Business," "International Protection of Intellectual Property," and "Intellectual Property in Financial and Business Transactions."

Kinney & Lange attorneys are skilled in a variety of trade and technical areas including avionics; digital circuits; computer hardware and software; semiconductors; biomedical devices; cryogenics; biochemistry; microbiology; virology; organic chemistry; petrochemicals, including plastics; petroleum refining; food chemistry and technology; advertising; publishing; and franchising. Kinney & Lange legal professionals are supported by a state-of-the-art computer network. Members of the firm use the network for communications, word processing, legal research, litigation support and docketing.

The firm has a diverse client base ranging from small and start-up businesses to large multinational corporations. These clients design manufacture and market industrial products, and consumer goods and services including sensors, integrated control and manufacturing systems; computer components and software; automotive diagnostic products; construction equipment; pumping equipment; prepared foods; cosmetics; adhesives; recreational products; advertising, publishing, financial, and insurance products such as catheters, ophthalmic lenses, and pharmaceutical delivery systems; health services; and farm supplies, including animal feeds and herbicides.

Lapp, Laurie, Libra, Abramson & Thomson, Chartered

One Financial Plaza, Suite 1800, 120 South Sixth Street - Minneapolis, MN 55402 - Phone: (612) 338-5815 - Fax: (612) 338-6651

Lapp, Laurie, Libra, Abramson &Thomson, Chartered, provides thoughtful and careful solutions for clients in various areas of business. Their primary resource is people—lawyers and staff who are dedicated to excellent, timely, and economic client service. The firm strives to establish businesslike, friendly, and long-term client relationships and represent individuals and businesses in local, regional, national, and international matters. They are committed to excellence in representing their clients by providing them legal services in the following areas:

- Business and Corporate Law
- Commercial Litigation
- Employment Law
- Civil Rights
- Real Estate Law
- Commercial Leases, Tax Planning, and Representation
- Financial Reorganization and Bankruptcy
- Securities
- Personal Injury
- Medical Malpractice and Wrongful Death
- Retirement Planning
- Estate Planning and Administration
- Family Law

Gerald T. Laurie was a founding member of the law firm in 1970. His practice centers on employment and commercial litigation. As a Civil Trial Specialist certified by the Civil Litigation Section of the MSBA, Jerry has argued numerous cases before the Minnesota Supreme Court, is the author of legal articles, and has lectured at legal education seminars on trade secret litigation, legal malpractice, sexual harassment, non-compete agreements, and whistle blowing.

William S. Lapp is a founder of the firm and is the key person in the corporate, securities, business law, and taxation areas. Bill has substantial experience in negotiating complex business transactions but also spends a significant portion of his time advising individuals and businesses on the many legal issues they face. He is also experienced in securities litigation and arbitration. Bill's background, tremendous negotiating skills, legal ability, and desire to get the job done, make him a valuable resource for businesses and individuals. From 1983 to 1985 he served as Chair of the Executive Committee of the HCBA Securities Section.

David A. Libra practices in the areas of real estate law and business law. He represents businesses and individuals in commercial and residential real estate purchases, financing, and leasing. He also has substantial experience in organizing businesses, commercial contracts, and estate planning for business owners. David is a Real Property Law Specialist, certified by the Real Property Section of the MSBA, and a member of the Real Property Sections of the MBA and ABA. He has been with the firm since 1973.

Frank Abramson's litigation practice focuses primarily on the areas of personal injury, medical negligence, and family law. Frank joined the firm in 1975.

Richard T. Thomson practices in the areas of business and employment litigation, including real estate, corporate, banking, and bankruptcy litigation. His trial court, administrative, and appellate victories include: *Eklund v. Vincent Brass,* one of the most significant wrongful termination cases in Minnesota; *TCF Mortgage Corp. v. Verex Assurance, Inc.*, the leading case in Minnesota on mortgage insurance law; *Bergquist v. Anderson-Greenwood Aviation Corp.*, a major bankruptcy case; and *Ohio Calculating v. CPT Corp.*, an important case covering the rights of distributorships and manufacturers. He is a member of the ABA and the MSBA, and has published articles in legal periodicals concerning employment law and bankruptcy law.

Larkin, Hoffman, Daly & Lindgren, Ltd.

1500 Norwest Financial Center, 7900 Xerxes Avenue South - Bloomington, MN 55431 - Phone: (612) 835-3800 - Fax: (612) 896-3333

Larkin, Hoffman, Daly & Lindgren, Ltd., has served the legal needs of clients since 1958. The firm's entrepreneurial spirit and understanding of the challenges facing both business and individual clients has been the key to its success.

Larkin Hoffman acknowledges the need to provide the specialized expertise necessary in complex and changing areas of the law. The firm's 72 attorneys, combined with the support of over 90 staff members, provide expert counsel to clients in the traditional areas such as corporate law, business financing, securities law, tax and taxation, banking, real estate, family law, and litigation. In addition, the firm has specialized practice groups in Land Use Planning and Development, Zoning, Environmental Regulation, Legislative Lobbying, Franchising, Employment Law, Elder Law, and Intellectual Property.

Larkin Hoffman recognizes the need to be aware of technological innovations that enable the firm to maintain a state-of-the-art capability in high technology equipment necessary for the efficient production of legal work, including client friendly communication techniques.

Yet, the greatest asset Larkin Hoffman offers to its clients is the responsiveness of the experienced lawyers and trained staff it brings to any legal issue. Serving clients is the firm's most important responsibility. The firm hires attorneys who have the ability and desire to serve clients enthusiastically and at a level of personal commitment that distinguishes Larkin Hoffman from other law firms. The firm looks for people who not only have a record of high academic achievement, but "real world" experience, which empowers them to communicate effectively with judges, juries, and especially clients.

In addition to the attorneys profiled in this business law publication (**Linda H. Fisher**, Environmental & Natural Resources; **John E. Diehl and Todd I. Freeman,** Health Law; **Allan E. (Pat) Mulligan**, Real Estate; **Peter K. Beck, James C. Erickson,** and **Robert L. Hoffman**, Urban, State, & Local Government; and **Todd I. Freeman,** Probate, Estate Planning & Trusts, and two attorneys (**Todd I. Freeman**, Probate, Estate Planning & Trusts, and **Kathleen M. Newman** in Family Law) were nominated by their peers for inclusion in the *Consumer Guidebook to Law & Leading Attorneys— 1994-1995 Minnesota Edition.*

LEONARD, STREET AND DEINARD PROFESSIONAL ASSOCIATION

150 South Fifth Street, Suite 2300 - Minneapolis, MN 55402 - Phone: (612) 335-1500 - Fax: (612) 335-1657

Leonard, Street and Deinard is a full service commercial law firm of approximately 125 attorneys. Leonard, Street and Deinard is one of the ten largest law firms as well as one of the oldest law firms in Minnesota.

Since its founding in 1922, two law firms have merged with Leonard, Street and Deinard: Pepin Dayton Herman & Graham (1988) and Gunn & Gunn, Ltd. (1990), thereby enhancing the firm's expertise in administrative, corporate, employment, environmental, governmental relations, labor and real estate law, and in the condemnation and eminent domain areas.

Leonard, Street and Deinard has changed and evolved in many ways since its founding. In the early years, the firm represented primarily Minnesota clients in business transactions and litigation within the state. Today, many of Leonard, Street and Deinard's original "Minnesota" clients have grown into major national and international businesses, taking the firm's attorneys to business conferences throughout North America and Europe. In addition, the firm's client base has grown very substantially and now includes many local and out-of-state clients who have transactions and lawsuits not only in Minnesota, but throughout the country and internationally as well.

The firm has a long history of representing family held, entrepreneurial, publicly held and institutional businesses. The firm prides itself on its reputation for excellence and efficiency, and on the long-term relationships it consistently builds with clients.

Leonard, Street and Deinard is continually exploring ways to better serve its clients; in this regard, the firm regularly solicits the opinions and suggestions of clients to enhance and strengthen the lawyer-client relationship. Members of a select client advisory council meet regularly with the firm's President, Lowell Noteboom.

Leonard, Street and Deinard is committed to exploring cost saving measures for clients. For example, in the coming years the firm will place an even greater emphasis on dispute resolution and dispute management techniques to help clients avoid costly litigation. The firm also invests in state-of-the-art computer equipment to speed research, and in sophisticated word processing to reduce attorney review time.

The firm is proud of its commitment to the community and to providing pro bono services and legal aid. In 1993 the firm established a free legal clinic to serve residents in the Phillips neighborhood, one of Minneapolis' poorest areas. In so doing, it became one of a very few firms that have established similar clinics.

Leonard, Street and Deinard provides clients with a full range of legal services, with litigation comprising approximately half of the practice and nonlitigated matters comprising the other half. Many clients who first turn to Leonard, Street and Deinard with a litigation need later ask the firm to handle their nonlitigated legal problems, and vice versa. About half of the firm's attorneys work in the Litigation Division, while the other half are members of the Business Division.

Litigation Division. Litigation matters at Leonard, Street and Deinard include cases for the firm's regular business clients and cases for referral clients, many of whom are based in Minnesota as well as throughout North America. The firm's litigation attorneys represent both plaintiffs and defendants, and try cases and handle appeals in state and federal courts involving virtually every area of substantive law.

The firm maintains a sophisticated computerized litigation support system that offers considerable savings for its litigation clients and employs a full-time administrator to work with its litigation attorneys on efficiency measures and case budgeting.

Litigation Division: Chair, Charles A. Mays

- **Business Litigation Department:**
  Chair, George F. McGunnigle
- **Commercial Litigation Department:**
  Chair, Charles A. Mays
- **Construction Law Department:**
  Chair, Robert J. Huber
- **Employment Law Department:**
  Chair, Robert Zeglovitch
- **Product Liability Department:**
  Chair, Frederick W. Morris
- **Public Law Department:**
  Chair, Byron E. Starns
- **Real Estate Valuation Litigation Department:** Chair, James R. Dorsey

Business Division. Leonard, Street and Deinard's Business Division attorneys are fully dedicated to the client's business and legal affairs, and are familiar with the client's objectives and method of doing business. Over a period of time, these clients have the satisfaction of establishing a close business relationship with their attorney and enjoying the security of knowing that that attorney is fully familiar with their particular business and legal matters.

Business Division: Chair, George Reilly

- **Banking and Business Reorganization Department:** Chair, David Kantor
- **Corporate Department:**
  Chair, George Reilly
- **Finance Department:**
  Chair, Richard H. Martin
- **Real Estate Department:**
  Chair, Joseph M. Finley
- **Tax, Estate Planning and Probate Department:** Chair, Stephen R. Litman

Primary Practice Areas at Leonard, Street and Deinard:

- Administrative Law
- Advertising and Sales Promotion
- Alternative Dispute Resolution and Mediation
- Antitrust
- Architectural Law
- Banking Law
- Bankruptcy Litigation
- Business Law
- Business Succession Planning
- Commercial Litigation
- Computer Law
- Condemnation and Valuation Litigation
- Construction Law
- Corporations
- Employment Law and Litigation
- Employee Benefits
- Environmental Law
- Estate Planning
- Family Law
- Financial Institutions Law
- Financial Reorganization
- Franchise Law
- Governmental Relations
- Health Law
- Housing Development and Finance
- Immigration Law
- Income Tax
- Intellectual Property
- Labor Relations
- Land Use
- Medical Malpractice
- Mergers and Acquisitions
- Native American Law
- Partnerships
- Private and Emerging Businesses
- Probate and Trust Administration
- Product Distribution and Marketing
- Product Liability
- Professional Liability
- Public Finance
- Public Utility Law
- Real Estate Development/Finance
- Securities Law and Litigation
- Shareholder Disputes
- Taxable and Tax-Exempt Securities
- Trademark and Copyright Law
- White Collar Crime

Legal Assistants and Support Staff. Leonard, Street and Deinard employs approximately 30 legal assistants. The firm's ratio of one legal assistant to every four attorneys is one of the highest for a Twin Cities law firm.

Leonard, Street and Deinard also has a full and able support staff to assist its attorneys. The firm's support personnel, which numbers over 175 individuals, is managed by Mary Des Roches, the firm's Chief Operating Officer.

Conclusion: Whatever the legal problem, transaction or business goal, the firm's energies are focused on finding a way for clients to reach their personal or business objectives. This approach has nurtured the loyalty of Leonard, Street and Deinard's clients and solidifies their confidence in the firm.

Appendix C: Attorneys & Law Firms by Region

LeVander, Gillen & Miller, P.A.
633 South Concord Street, Suite 402 - South St. Paul, MN 55075 - Phone: (612) 451-1831 - Fax: (612) 450-7384

LeVander, Gillen & Miller, P.A. has continued its law practice in Dakota County, Minnesota for 65 years. Founded in 1929, the firm has served clients throughout the State of Minnesota through a wide range of representation.

Arthur F. Gillen (JD University of Minnesota '43) consults with businesses and professional associations and is recognized as a Senior Counselor by the Minnesota State Bar Association.

Roger C. Miller (JD University of Minnesota '52) represents the city of South St. Paul and serves as counsel for utility cooperatives and business enterprises.

Timothy J. Kuntz (JD University of Minnesota '75) represents the cities of Inver Grove Heights and Sunfish Lake and represents firms in acquisitions and sales of business enterprises.

Daniel J. Beeson (JD William Mitchell '77) works with regional and national firms in eminent domain and general litigation matters.

Rollin H. Crawford (LLB University of Minnesota '65) represents the city of West St. Paul, several nonprofit trade and professional associations, and does property tax and real estate valuation work.

As a result of its broad practice, the firm has developed substantial expertise in the areas of business, municipal law, and civil litigation. Members of the firm have participated as instructors in continuing education seminars and derive a substantial portion of their practice from referrals from other attorneys.

The attorneys at LeVander, Gillen & Miller provide a wide range of services to the business community including business acquisitions, property tax appeals, corporate and partnership organization, eminent domain, employment law, land use and individual and business real estate transactions. The firm's clientele represents a solid base in Dakota county, but also includes small and large businesses with operations throughout the Upper Midwest.

The firm's associates: **Kenneth J. Rohlf** (JD University of Minnesota '90); **Elizabeth J. Wolf** (JD William Mitchell '90); **Joseph P. Lally** (JD William Mitchell '92); **Tonetta E. Tollefson** (JD University of Minnesota '92); **Stephen H. Fochler** (JD Hamline University '92); **Thomas R. Lehmann** (JD William Mitchell '87).

Lommen, Nelson, Cole & Stageberg, P.A.
1800 IDS Center, 80 South Eighth Street - Minneapolis, MN 55402 - Phone: (612) 339-8131 - Fax: (612) 339-8064

Lommen, Nelson, Cole & Stageberg, P.A. engages in the general practice of law with offices in Minneapolis, Minnesota and Hudson, Wisconsin. Lommen Nelson's litigation practice includes complex commercial matters; insurance coverage disputes; liability insurance defense; property insurance and subrogation; products liability; employment disputes, including discrimination, harassment, and contract claims; environmental hazards; physician, nursing, and hospital liability defense; lawyer professional liability defense; accounting professional liability defense; construction litigation; automobile and general negligence; personal injury; real estate and title insurance litigation; and workers' compensation.

Lommen Nelson's specialized appellate department handles numerous appeals each year in the Minnesota and Wisconsin state and federal appeals courts. Much of their appellate practice is generated on cases tried by other law firms.

Lommen Nelson also engages in the practice of general corporate law, including corporate finance and securities regulation; mergers and acquisitions; reorganizations; public and private offerings; and federal, state, and local taxation. The firm publishes the "Business Law Letter" covering recent developments in corporate law and other topics of concern.

Workers' compensation, bankruptcy, residential and commercial real estate, condemnation, municipal law, estate planning, probate, and trust matters round out the major emphasis of the firm's practice. Lommen Nelson attorneys have developed areas of special expertise. Teams are often developed to serve the needs of a client who has a variety of legal issues.

Litigation Practice
Phillip A. Cole
Thomas R. Jacobson
John R. McBride
J. Christopher Cuneo
Ehrich L. Koch
James M. Lockhart
Stephen C. Rathke
Linc S. Deter
Paul L. Dinger
Reid R. Lindquist
Jill G. Doescher
James R. Johnson
Terrance W. Moore
Barry A. O'Neil
Mary I. King
Sheila A. Bjorklund
V. Owen Nelson - Of Counsel
Henry H. Feikema - Of Counsel

Workers' Compensation
Richard L. Plagens
Margie R. Bodas
James C. Searls
Adam Levitsky
Kenneth J. Johnson

Business Law
Leonard T. Juster
Alvin S. Malmon
Roger V. Stageberg
Glenn R. Kessel
John M. Giblin
Thomas F. Dougherty
Sherri D. Ulland
David S. Ezrilov

Employment Law
Stacey A. DeKalb
Lynn M. Starkovich
Josh D. Kasdan

Appellate Law
Kay Nord Hunt
Marc A. Johannsen

Hudson, Wisconsin office:
Southside Office Plaza, Suite 2A
1810 Crestview Drive
Hudson, Wisconsin 54016
Phone: (715) 386-8217
Fax: (715) 386-8219
Twin City Line: (612) 436-8085

MANSFIELD & TANICK, P.A.

1560 International Centre, 900 Second Avenue South - Minneapolis, MN 55402-3383 - Phone: (612) 339-4295 - Fax: (612) 339-3161

Mansfield & Tanick, P.A. is a rapidly growing law firm located in downtown Minneapolis. Its practice extends throughout the Twin Cities community and greater Minnesota, the surrounding upper Midwest region, and the entire country in certain specialized litigation areas. The firm provides a full range of services, with special emphasis in business litigation and alternative dispute resolution (ADR), employment law, general business and commercial transaction practice, civil litigation, creditor-debtor relationships, media/defamation law, real estate, estate and tax planning, financial reorganization, and bankruptcy.

The firm's clients include high technology companies, newspapers, banks and consumer service companies. Examples are: American Harvest, Home Farmers Mutual Insurance Association, GME Consultants, Inc., Minnesota Orthopedics, P.A., Motel 6, Possis Medical, Inc., Quest Data Systems, Inc., Reliable Automotive Corp., and Resource Bank & Trust Company.

Employment Law. The firm provides a broad spectrum of legal advice to businesses and individuals relating to workplace issues; for example, in connection with discrimination and harassment claims, employment contracts, severance arrangements, representation in connection with wrongful termination claims, defamation and privacy matters, noncompete and other restrictive covenants, and management/labor relations.

Civil Litigation. The firm has extensive experience in litigation and ADR in commercial and business litigation, business fraud, breach of business contracts, shareholders' and partners' business disputes, employment law, securities, media/defamation law, RICO, class action, and other complex litigation.

Business Disputes. The firm frequently represents smaller companies in disputes with very large corporations. The firm's ADR department resolves legal disputes through alternative means, such as innovative prelitigation negotiations, arbitration, and mediation, which frequently are quicker and less costly than conventional litigation.

General Corporate. The firm also provides a broad range of nonlitigation services, including representation of businesses, in general corporate matters and commercial transactions, as well as financial reorganization and bankruptcy, and representation of individuals in estate and tax planning.

The firm has four partners, including Marshall H. Tanick and Seymour J. Mansfield, both of whom have been selected as Leading Attorneys in Minnesota, and Earl H. Cohen and Robert A. Johnson. The partners have a combined legal practice experience of more than 75 years, and are backed up by a very competent legal staff of six associate attorneys, a number of paralegals, law clerks, and other professional staff. All of their lawyers are licensed in Minnesota, and some are licensed in Illinois, Wisconsin, California, and the District of Columbia. The lawyers in the firm have outstanding academic and professional credentials. They are committed to finding effective legal solutions for their clients through superior competence, hard work, responsiveness, and dedicated advocacy.

MCGRANN SHEA FRANZEN CARNIVAL STRAUGHN & LAMB, CHARTERED

2200 LaSalle Plaza, 800 LaSalle Avenue - Minneapolis, MN 55402 - Phone (612) 338-2525 - Fax: (612) 339-2386

McGrann Shea Franzen Carnival Straughn & Lamb, Chartered, serves the legal needs of clients in a wide variety of commercial matters. Its areas of practice include:

- Administrative Law
- Banking Law
- Commercial Financing
- Corporate Law
- Employee Benefits Law
- Environmental Law
- Governmental Relations
- Legislative Affairs
- Litigation
- Municipal Utilities
- Public Finance
- Real Estate

The firm was founded in December 1989. Most of the members of the firm practiced together for a number of years prior to forming McGrann Shea Franzen Carnival Straughn & Lamb, Chartered. The firm's attorneys and staff strive to provide the high level of personal service that enables its clients to succeed in the current business climate. The firm has been involved in a variety of sophisticated and complex commercial matters and public affairs.

The firm's corporate practice includes representation of large and small businesses, nonprofit corporations, major metropolitan governmental agencies, and municipal utilities.

Commercial projects on which the firm has been engaged include LaSalle Plaza, Minneapolis Hilton Hotel and Towers, Minneapolis Federal Courts Building, Midway Marketplace, Laurel Village, and the Park Nicollet Medical Center expansion. The firm serves as municipal bond attorneys on transactions throughout the State of Minnesota, and is listed in *The Bond Buyer's "Red Book."*

The firm has established itself as a leading advocate in legislative affairs and governmental relations. It represents over 30 major corporations and trade organizations at the Minnesota Legislature and represents clients before state regulatory agencies and metropolitan and local units of government.

The firm also has an extensive commercial litigation practice, including experience in business contracts, environmental, real estate, and tax disputes, professional malpractice matters, and defense of white collar crime.

The current shareholders of the firm are:

    William R. McGrann
    Andrew J. Shea
    Douglas J. Franzen
    Douglas M. Carnival
    Robert O. Straughn
    Peter L. Cooper
    Kathleen M. Lamb
    Richard L. Evans
    Corey J. Ayling
    Henry M. Helgen, III
    Randolph W. Morris

Appendix C: Attorneys & Law Firms by Region

MEAGHER & GEER

4200 Multifoods Tower, 33 South Sixth Street - Minneapolis, MN 55402 - Phone: (612) 338-0661 - Fax: (612) 338-8384

Nineteen ninety-four marks Meagher & Geer's 65th year. The Minneapolis law firm is recognized as one of the Upper Midwest's most reputable engaged in the practice of insurance law, litigation and commercial law. Meagher & Geer attorneys have long been considered among the preeminent trial lawyers in the state of Minnesota and throughout the United States.

Clients of every size entrust Meagher & Geer with matters ranging from the simple to the complex. Each receives responsive, thoughtful legal counsel and the benefits of the firms knowledge and expertise in the specific industries of agriculture, aviation, construction, finance, health care, insurance, manufacturing, real estate, and retail.

Of significant value to Meagher & Geer clients is the firm's practical and innovative use of technology. The utilization of products and systems that improve communication, and streamline the management and organization of information enables the firm to save time and money on behalf of clients.

Meagher & Geer's Appellate Group enjoys a well-earned reputation for excellence in written and oral advocacy. In addition to having earned respect in the courts for their demeanor, the appellate group is known for presenting legal work that is consistently focused, forceful, and succinct.

When in the best interest of clients, Meagher & Geer recommends the use of alternative dispute resolution. Meagher & Geer attorneys have completed training promulgated by the Minnesota Supreme Court and are included on the State Court Administrator's roster to serve as qualified neutrals in arbitrations, mediations, and other venues of alternative dispute resolution.

Areas of Practice

•*General and Commercial Litigation Practice* - Representing insurance companies, their insureds, and business and individual interests in the following areas of the law: admiralty and maritime, alternative dispute resolution, asbestos/toxic tort, appellate, automobile liability, automobile no-fault, aviation, commercial, construction, directors', and officers' liability, environmental, employment and human resources, fidelity and surety bonds, governmental liability, insurance law, liquor liability, motor vehicle law, personal injury, products liability, professional liability, workers' compensation and employers' liability.

• *Business and Commercial Practice* - aviation, bankruptcy, creditor and debtor remedies, employee benefits, employment services, and human resources, environmental counseling, and compliance, equipment leasing, estate planning, intellectual property, mergers, and acquisitions, real estate, start-up ventures and financing, tax matters, and workers' compensation.

•*Insurance Defense and Coverage Practice*- admiralty and maritime, asbestos/toxic tort, aviation, corporate and regulatory matters, defense of insurers', directors', and officers' liability, environmental, employment and human resources, fidelty and surety bonds, insurance coverage, liquor liability, motor vehicle law, personal injury, products liability, professional liability, workers' compensation, and employers' liability.

MERCHANT, GOULD, SMITH, EDELL, WELTER & SCHMIDT, P.A.

3100 Norwest Center, 90 South Seventh Street - Minneapolis, MN 55402-4131 - Phone: (612) 332-5300 - Fax: (612) 332-9081

Merchant, Gould, Smith, Edell, Welter & Schmidt is engaged exclusively in the practice of intellectual property law, including patent, trademark, copyright, unfair competition, trade secret, advertising and computer law, and related litigation including both trials, and appeals.

With offices in Minneapolis, St. Paul, and Los Angeles and more than 78 practicing attorneys, the firm is one of the largest intellectual property law firms in the United States.

Clients:
The firm represents a broad spectrum of clients including individual inventors, emerging companies, Fortune 500 corporations, governmental bodies, and academic institutions. Clients represent diverse industries and technologies including chemistry, biotechnology, computer hardware and software, medicine, and manufacturing.

Technical Expertise:
Merchant & Gould has substantial technical expertise to serve the needs of its clients. A number of attorneys have advanced degrees, including Ph.D.'s, in their areas of expertise. In addition, the firm employs staff engineers, patent agents, legal assistants, and drafting personnel to provide a full range of cost-effective intellectual property legal sevices.

Practice Areas:
Approximately one-half of the firm's practice involves securing, licensing, maintaining and counseling relative to intellectual property matters. The other half involves intellectual property litigation. Merchant & Gould is able to obtain or provide its clients with worldwide legal services in its area of practice through an extensive network of foreign associates.

The Litigation Practice Group represents clients in trials and appeals involving complex patent, trademark, copyright, unfair competition, and false advertising matters. In addition to practice before federal and state courts, the firm has an extensive practice before the International Trade Commission. The firm also provides a full range of services in other contested matters, including patent interferences, re-issues, re-examinations, validity opinions, infringement opinions and licensing. Representative clients of the firm include 3M, General Mills, Honeywell, Pillsbury, Rollerblade, and Toro. **Douglas J. Williams, Chair, (612) 336-4632.**

The General Practice Group handles all nonlitigation matters and consists of four specialized practice areas. **D. Randall King, Chair, (612) 371-5269.**

1) *The Chemical Practice Section* handles all areas of chemistry, medicine, polymer science, biotechnology, compositions, articles of manufacture, and related arts. Representative clients of the firm include Ecolab, Bristol Meyers, Sims Deltec, Scripps Institute, UCLA, and the University of Minnesota. **Albin J. Nelson, Chair, (612) 336-4627.**

2) *The Electronic and Computer Law Practice Section's* main focus is obtaining intellectual property rights in electronic, computer, and software technology through patents, copyrights, trade secrets, licensing and other related forms of protection, as well as enforcement of such rights. Representative clients of the firm include IBM, National Computer Systems, Honeywell and Pacific Bell. **John P. Sumner, Chair, (612) 336-4624.**

3) *The Trademark Section* handles all aspects of searching, registering, protecting and policing trademarks and service marks. Advertising, entertainment law and unfair competition issues are also covered. Representative clients of the firm include Carlson Companies, Golden Valley Microwave Foods, and Minnesota Mutual Life Insurance Company. **John A. Clifford, Chair, (612) 336-4616.**

4) *The International Section* handles intellectual property matters for the firm's international associates and clients. In addition, the International Section represents the firm's domestic clients on various international intellectual property matters in foreign countries. **Michael D. Schumann, Chair, (612) 336-4638.**

OFFICES:

Minneapolis:
3100 Norwest Center
90 South Seventh Street
Minneapolis, MN 55402-4131
Phone: (612) 332-5300
Fax: (612) 332-9081
(58 attorneys; **Paul A. Welter**, Managing Director)

St. Paul:
1000 Norwest Center
55 East Fifth Street
St. Paul, MN 55101-1785
Phone: (612) 298-1055
Fax: (612) 298-1160
(12 attorneys; **Michael L. Mau**, Managing Officer)

Los Angeles:
11150 Santa Monica Blvd.- Suite 400
Los Angeles, CA 90025-3395
Phone: (310) 445-1140
Fax: (310) 445-9031
(8 attorneys; **Gregory B. Wood,** Managing Partner)

MANAGEMENT

Alan G. Carlson
Chairman and Chief Executive Officer-JD 1971 cum laude, Ohio State University, University of Minnesota, William Mitchell; BS 1967 Pi Tau Sigma, Purdue University.

Paul A. Welter
Managing Director-JD 1964 cum laude, William Mitchell; BS 1955 cum laude, Bemidji State University.

D. Randall King
Chair, General Practice Group-JD 1973 and BS 1968, University of Akron.

Douglas J. Williams
Chair, Litigation Practice Group-JD 1974, Drake University; BS 1971, University of Iowa.

Carol E. Cummins
Executive Director-MBA 1983, University of Minnesota; BA 1975 magna cum laude, Phi Beta Kappa, Hamline University.

No. Partners: 35
No. Associates: 43
Support Staff: 155

Moss & Barnett, A Professional Association

4800 Norwest Center - 90 South Seventh Street - Minneapolis, MN 55402 - Phone: (612) 347-0300 - Fax: (612) 339-6686

Moss & Barnett provides high-quality legal representation primarily to emerging, middle-sized and large businesses, and their owners, in the Twin Cities area and nationwide.

The firm's 60 lawyers have demonstrated expertise in the numerous areas of business law and other practice areas including:

- Administration
- Anti-trust
- Banking and thrift
- Bankruptcy
- Business formation and operation
- Construction
- Employment
- Environmental
- Estate planning, probate and family law
- Franchising and product distribution
- Health, intellectual property and insurance
- Labor and employee benefits
- Litigation
- Business
- Personal injury
- Product liability
- Professional malpractice
- Legislative and lobbying
- Mergers, sales and acquisitions
- Securities and taxation
- Telecommunications, cable TV, computer software
- Utility and regulatory

Moss & Barnett's roots go back to the founding of a small law practice in 1892. The firm has grown through numerous mergers and practice consolidations. It is committed to continued growth that is responsive to client needs and the changing practice of law.

O'Neill, Burke, O'Neill, Leonard & O'Brien, Ltd.

100 South Fifth Street, Suite 2100 - Minneapolis, MN 55402 - Phone: (612) 332-1030 - Fax: (612) 332-2740
800 Norwest Center, 55 East Fifth Street - St. Paul, MN 55101 - Phone: (612) 227-9505 - Fax: (612) 297-6641

O'Neill, Burke, O'Neill, Leonard & O'Brien, Ltd., was founded in 1968 and currently has twenty-three attorneys who are dedicated to competent and aggressive representation of its clients. The firm is result oriented, employing creativity, resourcefulness, thoroughness, and tenacity, in representing its clients. The firm has earned a reputation for honesty, integrity, and professionalism in the legal community.

O'Neill, Burke, O'Neill, Leonard & O'Brien, Ltd., provides specialized expertise in such traditional areas of law as banking, corporate law, real estate, civil and personal injury litigation, business financing, taxation, and bankruptcy. In addition, the firm has specialized expertise in employment law, governmental affairs, and zoning and municipal law. The firm also has senior attorneys who are trained in various areas of law to provide mediation and arbitration services.

The success of the firm is grounded in the commitment it makes to each of its clients. Each client matter is handled promptly and efficiently, and with the client being kept constantly informed of all developments in the matter. Each client matter receives the continued and personal attention of a qualified professional in the firm.

The lawyers in the firm include two members of the panel of Chapter 7 Bankruptcy Trustees, both of whom have extensive experience representing creditors, creditor-committees, and debtors in bankruptcy proceedings. In addition, the firm has litigation specialists who have extensive practices in civil and personal injury litigation. The firm also has an active governmental affairs practice, with a senior partner and an of-counsel attorney who served for ten years each in the Minnesota legislature. The firm serves clients before municipalities, city and county boards, and state, federal, and local governmental regulatory bodies. The firm also works extensively with its banking and financial institution clients, in documenting and structuring financial and loan transactions and facilities.

O'Neill, Burke, O'Neill, Leonard & O'Brien, Ltd. considers its mission as one of adding value to its clients' transactions. It tailors its fee arrangements to suit the needs of its clients and offers competitive billing rates for its services.

POPHAM, HAIK, SCHNOBRICH & KAUFMAN, LTD.

222 South Ninth Street, Suite 3300 - Minneapolis, MN 55402-3336 - Phone: (612) 333-4800 - Fax: (612) 334-8888

Few legal firms have made their mark faster than Popham, Haik, Schnobrich & Kaufman, Ltd. Founded in Minneapolis in 1958, it grew slowly but steadily as it established its expertise in business and administrative law and litigation. In the 1980s it hit full stride as a major national firm, doubling in size to a staff of more than 120 attorneys in less than five years and growing out from its Minneapolis roots to establish offices in Washington, D.C., and Denver.

Popham Haik's administrative law practice is national in scope—its attorneys have represented clients on regulatory matters in more than 25 states plus the District of Columbia and Puerto Rico. Its business department includes an international group to ensure that the firm can meet the needs of clients ranging from major corporations to sole proprietors, no matter where in the world they might require legal services. In matters that go to litigation, Popham Haik's attorneys provide expertise in areas ranging from antitrust and environmental matters to real estate and securities law.

One of the first areas in which the firm began to develop a reputation was commercial litigation.

Today its expertise includes specialties in product liability, securities and commodities, antitrust, employment discrimination, hazardous waste, medical device and drug liability, environmental law, government liability, construction law, professional liability (representing architects, engineers, real estate agents, and other attorneys), and white-collar crime.

Popham Haik also has distinguished itself through participation in the public process. It counsels municipalities, development authorities, and regional commissions. It represents clients before local, state, and federal regulatory and legislative bodies. It serves as a resource in matters involving regulated industries, environmental regulations, land use, and commercial development.

Its attorneys are of service to both owners and their organizations, whether closely held or publicly traded. That includes estate and financial planning, real estate transactions, bankruptcy, franchising, and product distribution, as well as legal support on matters involving corporate and individual tax planning, public offerings, private placements, mergers, acquisitions, and SEC compliance.

In addition, Popham Haik has demonstrated ability in labor law, immigration matters, election and campaign finance, libel computer law, trademark and patent law, and trade secret protection. The firm is developing a national reputation in the area of preventive law, a specialty that focuses on helping businesses and individuals minimize the risk of future legal liability by identifying potential problems.

Popham Haik has represented hardship and political asylum cases and has worked with the Minneapolis Housing and Development Authority. Its attorneys do volunteer work in social services and involve themselves in legal education activities.

Popham, Haik, Schnobrich & Kaufman, Ltd., looks back over a record of achievement. In just three decades it has become one of the 5 largest law firms in the Twin Cities—one of the 150 largest in the country. It has a young, aggressive outlook. At Popham Haik, the strength of the practice is the strength of each of its people.

PRACTICE GROUP

Banking and Finance - Paul H. Tietz

Bankruptcy - Paul B. Jones/Douglas M. Tisdale

Communications and Entertainment - Louis N. Smith

Compensation and Benefits - Jeffrey P. Carins/Donald H. Seifman

Design and Construction - Bruce C. King/Thomas F. Nelson

Environmental - Karen Hansen

Estate Planning, Probate and Trust Law - John W. Provo/James W. Rockwell

Globalization/International - Donald H. Seifman

Government Contracts - James P. Gallatin, Jr.

Healthcare - Keith J. Halleland

Immigration and Nationality - Howard S. Myers, III/Elizabeth A. Thompson

Insurance Coverage - Thomas C. Mielenhausen

Intellectual Property and Technology - Allen S. Melser

Labor and Employment - Thomas M. Sipkins/Andrew D. Parker

Large Case Litigation - Frank A. Taylor

Liability Management - Scott A. Smith

Pan-Pacific - John C. Childs/Yi Qian

Product Liability - John D. Golden

Public Law - Suesan L. Pace

Real Estate - Bruce D. Malkerson

Securities - D. William Kaufman/Robert A. Minish

Tax and Business Planning - Paul J. Linstroth

Toxic Tort - Michael T. Nilan

OFFICES

Denver
2400 One Tabor Center
1200 Seventeenth Street
Denver, Colorado 80202
Phone: (303) 893-1200
Fax: (303) 893-2194

Miami
4000 International Place
100 SE Second Street
Miami, FL 33131
Phone: (305) 530-0050
Fax: (305) 530-0055

Minneapolis
222 South 9th Street, Suite 3300
Minneapolis, Minnesota 55402-3336
Phone: (612) 333-4800
Fax: (612) 334-8888

Washington
Metropolitan Square Building
655 Fifteenth Street NW
Suite 800
Washington, D.C. 20005-5701
Phone: (202) 824-8000
Fax: (202) 824-8199

Ravich, Meyer, Kirkman & McGrath, P.A.

4545 IDS Center, 80 South Eighth Street - Minneapolis, MN 55402 - Phone: (612) 332-8511 - Fax: (612) 332-8302

Ravich, Meyer, Kirkman & McGrath, A Professional Association, was formed in 1991 to represent businesses and individuals in financial, bankruptcy, and real estate matters and provide general business counseling. The firm's philosophy is to provide services in its specialized areas with a minimum of delegation and reassignment. Many times the firm's representation is coordinated with and supplements that provided by the client's corporate lawyers.

Paul H. Ravich (JD cum laude Minnesota '64) has practiced principally in the areas of real estate and finance law, representing real estate users, developers, investors, managers, and syndicators. His business counseling skills are frequently utilized by clients to provide them with a disinterested, experienced viewpoint. Mr. Ravich is listed in every edition of *The Best Lawyers in America*.

Michael L. Meyer (JD cum laude Minnesota '74) practices principally in the areas of business bankruptcy and workout law and related commercial litigation. Mr. Meyer's bankruptcy work is concentrated in representing debtors in business Chapter 11 cases.

David E. Kirkman (JD magna cum laude William Mitchell '79) practices in the areas of business and commercial law, emphasizing commercial real estate, development and finance, workouts, and related litigation. Mr. Kirkman is an Adjunct Professor of Law in Commercial Real Estate at William Mitchell.

Michael F. McGrath (JD cum laude Hamline '85) practices principally in the areas of business bankruptcy and workout law and related commercial litigation. He has represented large creditors in major bankruptcy cases around the country. Mr. McGrath's present bankruptcy practice is split between creditor and debtor representation.

Robins, Kaplan, Miller & Ciresi

2800 La Salle Plaza, 800 La Salle Avenue - Minneapolis, MN 55402 - Phone: (612) 349-8500 - Fax: (612) 339-4181

Robins, Kaplan, Miller & Ciresi provides a variety of legal services to individuals and business organizations on regional, national and international levels. The firm has a diverse business and commercial practice and a well-recognized litigation practice.

The firm was founded in 1938 and consists of a professional staff of more than 220 lawyers. The firm offices are strategically located to provide service in various regions of the country, including Atlanta, Boston, Chicago, Minneapolis, St. Paul, San Francisco, Southern California, and Washington, D.C.

The **Business Practice** lawyers concentrate in the following areas: Bankruptcy and Reorganization, Corporate Finance, Corporate Restructuring, Employee Benefits, Employment, Estate Planning and Trusts, General Corporate Law, Government Relations, International Trade, Leasing, Maritime Law, Mergers and Acquisitions, Real Estate Finance and Development, Securities, and Tax. Clients include publicly and closely held companies for whom they handle a variety of regular and complex transactions around the country.

The **Business Litigation** lawyers prosecute and defend matters in all aspects of business law including: Antitrust, Cable Communications, Civil Rights, Construction, Contract Litigation, Employment, Franchising, Intellectual Property, Lender Liability, Real Estate Litigation, RICO, Securities Fraud, Trade Secrets, and Unfair Competition. They represent individuals, accounting firms, Fortune 500 companies, and large banks, in venues throughout the country. They also represent parties before governmental agencies.

SCHATZ PAQUIN LOCKRIDGE GRINDAL & HOLSTEIN

2200 Washington Square, 100 Washington Avenue South - Minneapolis, MN 55401 - Phone: (612) 339-6900 - Fax: (612) 339-0981

Schatz Paquin Lockridge Grindal & Holstein was founded in 1978 and employs 30 attorneys, 11 legislative professionals, and 50 support staff. The firm utilizes a state-of-the-art computer system with integrated research, communications, and automated litigation support services. Partners have been named in *Best Lawyers in America* in Health Care Law, *Minnesota's Journal of Law & Politics* "Superlawyers," *Minnesota Lawyer Magazine's* Winningest Trial Lawyers, and the *National Law Journal's* "100 Most Influential Lawyers in America." Schatz Paquin's attorneys and sophisticated support network combine to serve the firm's straightforward goal: to advance the client's interest.

The firm's sophisticated civil litigation practice consists of:

- Antitrust Law
- Employment Law
- Environmental Law
- Intellectual Property
- Securities Law
- Commercial Law

Schatz Paquin's lawyers are experienced in all aspects of federal and state court litigation, from initial case investigation through pretrial matters to trial and any appeals. The firm's litigators are particularly experienced in large-scale lawsuits, including class-actions, multi-district litigation, and multiple state and federal claims.

The firm's intellectual property practice, an integral part of its corporate and commercial representation, has a national reputation for copyright law, earned through long-time representation of distinguished legal and textbook publishers, software developers, authors, illustrators, and musicians. The firm's lawyers are active members of the ABA's Intellectual Property Law Section.

The firm's health care lawyers guide clients through every stage of the business and delivery of health care, including merger, acquisition, partial integration, joint venture, and contrasting issues such as fee splitting, Medicare/Medicaid fraud and abuse, the Stark Laboratory Referral Act, referral patterns, antitrust, taxation, and negotiations.

Schatz Paquin's extensive government affairs work provides excellent results for clients by working closely with the legislative and administrative branches of government. State and federal government affairs specialists are veteran Democratic and Republican political operatives.

Washington, D.C. Office:
1301 K Street N.W.
East Tower, Suite 650
Washington, D.C. 20005
Phone: (202) 789-3970
Fax: (202) 789-2961

WINTHROP & WEINSTINE, P.A.

3200 Minnesota World Trade Center, 30 East Seventh Street - St. Paul, MN 55101 - Phone: (612) 290-8400 - Fax: (612) 292-9347

Winthrop & Weinstine, P.A. is an entrepreneurial law firm founded by six attorneys in 1979. During the 1980s the firm grew substantially to become one of the most respected law firms in the Twin Cities legal community. Its practice areas cover a wide spectrum of legal services for clients both large and small. Winthrop & Weinstine's approach—innovative and cost effective legal solutions focused on producing results—has fostered the successful growth and excellent reputation of the firm.

Since its inception, Winthrop & Weinstine, P.A. has had a strong practice in the areas of general corporate law, securities, real estate, banking, and litigation. The firm has expanded into virtually all practice areas to meet the diverse needs of its clients. This expansion into other specialized areas has occurred by attracting talented attorneys who bring highly specialized skills and knowledge to each of their practice areas.

Winthrop & Weinstine, P.A. provides a broad range of legal services to large and small business clients and to individuals. The firm has advised many business owners and managers on issues as diverse as public and private stock offerings, employment disputes, tax problems, and mergers and acquisitions.

The firm practices primarily in the following areas:

- Corporate Law/Business Counseling
- Banking and Finance
- Litigation
- Securities
- Bankruptcy and Financial Reorganization
- Legislative, Administrative and Governmental
- Real Estate
- Tax
- Employee Benefits
- Estate and Trust
- Employment Law
- Tax-Exempt Financing

Some of the shareholders of the firm include:

Corporate and Securities: **Richard A. Hoel** (JD cum laude, Harvard University 1972) and **Eric O. Madson** (JD cum laude, Harvard University 1977) practice primarily in the areas of corporate, securities, and banking.

Banking: **Roger D. Gordon** (JD magna cum laude, University of Minnesota 1975) practices primarily in the areas of banking, real estate, and bond finance law; **Richard A. Hoel** (see above); **David E. Moran** (JD magna cum laude, University of Minnesota 1981) practices primarily in the areas of banking, general corporate and finance, and real estate law; **Edward J. Drenttel** (JD magna cum laude, William Mitchell 1985) banking and general corporate law; and **Julie K. Williamson** (JD with distinction, University of Iowa 1986) banking, consumer finance and general corporate law.

Real Estate: **John J. Hoganson** (JD cum laude, University of Minnesota 1981) banking, real estate, general corporate and securities law; **David E. Moran** (see above); and **Todd B. Urness** (JD University of Minnesota 1982) real estate, tax, corporate, business planning and partnership law.

Mergers and Acquisitions: **Timothy M. Barnett** (JD magna cum laude, University of Minnesota 1982) mergers and acquisitions, corporate business finance, securities regulation and franchise law; and **Edward J. Drenttel** (see above).

Commercial Litigation: **Robert R. Weinstine** (JD cum laude, University of Minnesota 1969) is one of the founding shareholders of the firm and practices primarily in the areas of commercial litigation, antitrust, securities, banking and professional liability. **Steven C. Tourek** (Yale University and Cambridge University, BS Law honors 1974; MA Law 1979; LLB honors, 1975) commercial litigation, antitrust, and business, commercial, banking and professional liability litigation.

Bankruptcy: **Hart Kuller** (JD cum laude, University of Minnesota 1976) practices primarily in bankruptcy, reorganization proceedings, workout law, and mergers and acquisitions.

Tax: **Todd B. Urness** (see above); and

Employee Benefits: **Gary W. Schokmiller** (JD cum laude, University of Minnesota 1981) practices primarily in the areas of stock ownership plans, employee benefits, executive compensation, and corporate and business planning law.

Winthrop & Weinstine, P.A. opened its Minneapolis offices in the fall of 1993 at 3000 Dain Bosworth Plaza, 60 South Sixth Street, Minneapolis, MN 55402. Phone (612) 347-0700. Fax (612) 347-0600.

ZONE 2:
Including listings in Austin and Rochester

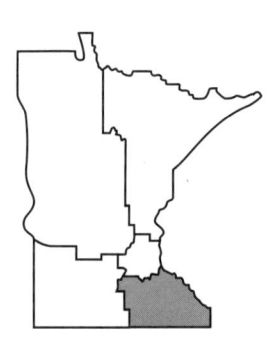

Baudler, Bryan - Baudler, Baudler, Maus & Blahnik - 110 North Main Street, Austin, MN 55912 - **Personal Injury Defense Law - (507) 433-2393**

Deaner, Ted E. - Marquette Bank Building, Suite 611, P.O. Box 968, Rochester, MN 55903 - Employment Law, Commercial Real Estate Law - **Bankruptcy & Workout Law - (507) 289-4041**

Heuel, Daniel J. - Muir, Heuel, Carlson & Spelling, P.A. -404 Marquette Bank Building, P.O. Box 1057, Rochester, MN 55903 - Employment Law - **Personal Injury Defense Law - (507) 288-4110**

Johnson, Craig W. - Hoversten, Strom, Johnson & Rysavy - 807 West Oakland Avenue, Austin, MN 55912 - **Commercial Real Estate Law - (507) 433-3483**

Jonason, William A. - Dorsey & Whitney - 201 First Avenue SW, Suite 340, Rochester, MN 55902 - Publicly Held Corporations Law - **Closely Held Business Law - (507) 288-3156**

Lantz, W. Charles - Dorsey & Whitney - 201 First Avenue SW, Suite 340, Rochester, MN 55902 - Intellectual Property Law - **Commercial Real Estate Law - (507) 288-3156**

Muir, Ross - Muir, Heuel, Carlson & Spelling, P.A. - 404 Marquette Bank Building, P.O. Box 1057, Rochester, MN 55903 - **Personal Injury Defense Law - (507) 288-4110**

Rysavy, Donald E. - Hoversten, Strom, Johnson & Rysavy -807 West Oakland Avenue, Austin, MN, 55912 - Family Law - **Personal Injury Defense Law - (507) 433-3483**

Shulman, David A. - Shulman, Gainsley & Walcott - Ironwood Square, Suite 302, 300 Third Avenue SE, Rochester, MN 55904 - **Commercial Litigation - (507) 288-3078**

Wendland, Craig W. - Dingle & Wendland - Suite 300, Norwest Center, P.O. Box 939, Rochester, MN 55903 - Publicly Held Corporations Law, Commercial Real Estate Law - **Closely Held Business Law - (507) 288-5440**

Wicks, John R. - Dorsey & Whitney - 201 First Avenue SW, Suite 340, Rochester, MN 55902 - **Probate, Estate Planning & Trusts Law - (507) 288-3156**

HOVERSTEN, STROM, JOHNSON & RYSAVY
807 West Oakland Avenue - Austin, MN 55912 - Phone: (507) 433-3483 - Fax: (507) 433-7889

Hoversten, Strom, Johnson & Rysavy of Austin, Minnesota is one of the largest law firms in Southeast Minnesota. The firm provides a wide array of services, with special emphasis in civil litigation including personal injury, product liability, and insurance defense; employment and labor law; real estate and commercial transactions; municipal and government law; and estate planning, probate, and trust. The firm also serves as local agent for Old Republic National Insurance Company and provides title insurance and closing services through the agency.

Senior Partner **Kermit Hoversten** (JD Minnesota '52) engages in a broad general practice and has been retained as attorney for numerous municipalities, governmental agencies, and school districts.

Craig W. Johnson (JD Minnesota '71) works primarily in the areas of real property and business law, employment and labor law, and estate planning. He is certified as a Real Property Law Specialist by the Minnesota State Bar Association.

Donald E. Rysavy (JD Minnesota '73) practices primarily family law, workers' compensation, employment law, and insurance defense. He is a member of the panel of arbitrators, American Arbitration Association, and the Association of Insurance Attorneys.

David V. Hoversten (JD William Mitchell '77) practices in the areas of real estate, commercial law, probate, and estate planning.

John S. Beckmann (JD Minnesota '79) has conducted numerous seminars on legal and related topics, taught business law at Austin Community College, has authored "Limitations of Liability" for the Minnesota Defense Lawyers Association and "Minnesota Statutes of Limitation in Application of Product Liability Cases" for the Minnesota Institute of Legal Education. Mr. Beckmann is active in all fields of litigation, with special emphasis in product liability. He is a member of the Minnesota Defense Lawyers Association.

Fred W. Wellmann (JD William Mitchell '74), former Mower County Attorney and Chief County Prosecutor, practices in the disciplines of civil litigation, social security, criminal law, regulatory, and governmental law.

Steven J. Hovey (JD North Dakota '87) practices in all areas of litigation. He is licensed in both North Dakota and Minnesota. Steve is a member of the Minnesota Defense Lawyers Association and the Defense Research Institute.

The firm's associates: **Mary Carroll Leahy** (JD Hamline University '90). **Daniel L. Scott** (JD William Mitchell '93). Of Counsel is **Kenneth M. Strom** (JD William Mitchell '61). Mr. Strom has been a member of the Federation of Insurance and Corporate Counsel, the American Board of Trial Advocates, and has served on the Board of Directors of William Mitchell College of Law. The firm also employs four paralegals in litigation, probate, and real estate.

MUIR HEUEL CARLSON & SPELHAUG P.A.

404 Marquette Bank Building, P.O. Box 1057 - Rochester, MN 55903 - Phone: (507) 288-4110 - Fax: (507) 288-4122

Dan Heuel, Ross Muir, James Carlson, Robert Spelhaug

Muir, Heuel, Carlson & Spelhaug is unique in southern Minnesota as a firm dedicated exclusively to the representation of individuals and businesses involved in litigation. Founded in 1966 by Ross Muir, the firm has resisted the urge to diversify into a general practice, preferring to remain focused on its trial practice specialty, attracting a reputation as a vigorous and respected advocate for the rights of both plaintiffs and defendants. The four partners, supported by a staff of certified legal investigators, handles a wide array of matters ranging from personal injury to construction to employment to professional liability, including medical malpractice.

Ross Muir, with over 35 years experience, concentrates on representing injured victims of accidents and their families and is well recognized for his expertise in accident reconstruction in all phases of civil litigation. He is a member of both the MTLA and the Minnesota Defense Lawyers Association.

Daniel Heuel joined the firm in 1978 and likewise devotes himself to civil litigation, for both plaintiffs and defendants, and has distinguished himself in the area of employment and discrimination law. He is certified as a Civil Trial Specialist by the Civil Litigation Section of the Minnesota State Bar Association. He was elected President of the Third District of the Minnesota State Bar Association for 1994-95.

James Carlson came to the practice in 1976 and is especially active in the representation of insurance companies and their insureds, with a strong emphasis on workers' compensation and products liability. He is also a Civil Trial Specialist, certified by the Civil Litigation Section of the Minnesota State Bar Association, a member of the Minnesota Defense Lawyers Association, and is licensed to practice in Minnesota and Illinois. He has been president of the Rochester Public Utility Board since 1989.

Robert Spelhaug, with the firm since 1980, rounds out the complement of trial specialists with his own certifications, with both the Civil Litigation Section of the Minnesota State Bar Association as well as the National Board of Trial Advocacy. He is respected for his expertise in the areas of medical malpractice and product liability. He served with the United States Army from 1972-74.

Muir, Heuel, Carlson & Spelhaug is at the forefront of changes in the law, with a strong appellate practice augmented by the latest in computer technology. They are dedicated to retaining their niche as lawyers specialized in trial practice and are well positioned to bring to bear their experience and knowledge on behalf of clients who are confronted with a need for a trial lawyer.

ZONE 3:
Including listings in Clarkfield, Mankato, Montevideo, and New Ulm

Blethen, Bailey W. - Blethen Gage & Krause - 127 South Second Street, P.O. Box 3049, Mankato, MN 56002-3049 - Criminal Law - **Employment Law - (507) 345-1166**

Bluth, Joseph P. - Manahan & Bluth Law Office, Chartered - 416 South Front Street, P.O. Box 287, Mankato, MN 56001 - Family Law - **Criminal Law - (507) 387-5661**

Gage, F. Kelton - Blethen Gage & Krause - 127 South Second Street, P.O. Box 3049, Mankato, MN 56002-3049 - Publicly Held Corporations Law, Business Law, Federal, State & Local Government Law - **Closely Held Business Law - (507) 345-1166**

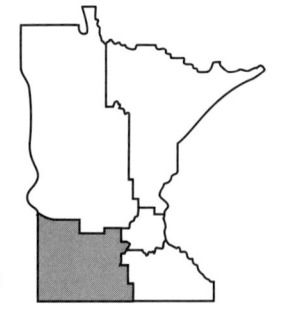

Karp, Michael C. - Blethen Gage & Krause - 127 South Second Street, P.O. Box 3049, Mankato, MN 56002-3049 - Closely Held Business Law - **Closely Held Business Law - (507) 345-1166**

Maschka, Gerald L. - Farrish, Johnson & Maschka - 201 North Broad Street, Suite 200, P.O. Box 550, Mankato, MN 56002-0550 - Commercial Litigation - **Personal Injury Defense Law - (507) 387-3002**

Nelson, Janice M. - Nelson Oyen Torvik - 221 North First Street, P.O. Box 656, Montevideo, MN 56265 - Probate, Estate Planning & Trusts Law - **Closely Held Business Law - (612) 269-6461**

Peterson, David T. - Blethen Gage & Krause - 127 South Second Street, P.O. Box 3049, Mankato, MN 56002-3049 - Commercial Real Estate Law - Employment Law, Publicly Held Corporations Law - **Closely Held Business Law - (507) 345-1166**

Regan, John E. - Regan, Regan & Meyer - 115 East Hickory Street, P.O. Box 967, Mankato, MN 56001 - Publicly Held Corporations Law - **Closely Held Business Law - (507) 345-1179**

Ries, Charles W. - Farrish, Johnson & Maschka - 201 North Broad Street, Suite 200, P.O. Box 550, Mankato, MN 56002-0550 - **Bankruptcy & Workout Law - (507) 387-3002**

Rodenberg, John R. - Berens, Rodenberg & O'Connor - 519 Center Street, P.O. Box 428, New Ulm, MN 56073 - Family Law - **Personal Injury Defense Law - (507) 354-3161**

Torvik, Stephen - Nelson Oyen Torvik - 221 North First Street, P.O. Box 656, Montevideo, MN 56265 - Commercial Real Estate Law - **Publicly Held Corporations Law - (612) 269-6461**

BLETHEN GAGE & KRAUSE

127 South Second Street, P.O. Box 3049 - Mankato, MN 56002-3049 - Phone: (507) 345-1166 - Fax: (507) 345-8003

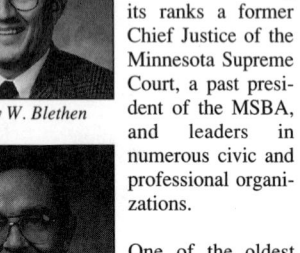

Bailey W. Blethen

Kelton Gage

Blethen, Gage & Krause is a full-service law firm which has included among its ranks a former Chief Justice of the Minnesota Supreme Court, a past president of the MSBA, and leaders in numerous civic and professional organizations.

One of the oldest and largest law firms in southern Minnesota, Blethen Gage & Krause places special emphasis on civil litigation, including personal injury, product liability, and insurance defense, and on business and corporate law. BG&K practices with a "team" approach, creating an in-depth body of knowledge and experience specific to each case. Clients are assured the highest level of service in all areas of the law.

Since its founding in 1896, the firm's philosophy has demanded a strong commitment to professional excellence from its attorneys and encouraged participation in civic, educational, professional, and public service.

Although venerable in years, BG&K is entirely contemporary in maintaining state-of-the-art technology necessary to efficient, cost-effective, highest quality legal services.

The firm has 11 attorneys: **Kelton Gage, Bailey W. Blethen, Richard J. Corcoran, Randall C. Berkland** (also licensed to practice in Iowa), **David T. Peterson, James H. Turk** (certified as a Civil Trial Specialist by the NBTA and MSBA), **Stephen P. Rolfsrad** (certified as a Civil Trial Specialist by the NBTA and MSBA), **Michael C. Karp** (CPA and MSBA-certified Real Property Law Specialist), **William David Taylor III, Ph.D., Julia C. Ketcham, and Silas L. Danielson** (CPA). Its support staff of paraprofessionals and legal secretaries is of the highest caliber.

During the nearly 100 years that BG & K has been a presence in southern Minnesota, the firm has always held to the highest professional and ethical standards and has supported the talent and financial endeavors of local businesses. This commitment to excellence was recognized in 1994 when Blethen Gage & Krause was elected to the Mankato Area Business Hall of Fame.

FARRISH, JOHNSON & MASCHKA

201 North Broad Street, Suite 200 - P.O. Box 550 - Mankato, MN 56002-0550 - Phone: (507) 387-3002 - Fax: (507) 625-4002

Farrish Johnson & Maschka, located in Mankato, traces its roots back to the late 1870s. The firm is committed to providing superior legal assistance for individuals and businesses. Charlotte Farrish (LLM University of Minnesota '26), a pioneer in advancing women in the legal profession, built a notable reputation, first as a civil and criminal defense attorney and in later years as an accomplished probate and estate practitioner. The firm's distinguished history includes four members who were selected to serve as judges. Appointed as Chief Justice of the Minnesota Supreme Court were Henry Gallagher in 1937, and Robert Sheran in 1963, and as District Court judges, Miles Zimmerman in 1974 and Terri Stoneburner in 1989. The tradition of quality legal work continues today. An experienced staff, including six specially trained paralegals, and the latest in law office automation, assist the firm's 11 lawyers in accomplishing the best possible result. The firm offers services in many practice areas: civil litigation, including personal injury and workers' compensation, insurance defense, environmental law, appellate practice, bankruptcy, business law, commercial litigation, real estate, estate planning, and family law.

Gerald Maschka specializes in trials in all courts, and the resolution of disputes by arbitration or mediation. Mr. Maschka is certified as a Civil Trial Advocate by the National Board of Trial Advocacy as well as a Civil Trial Specialist by the Civil Litigation Section of the Minnesota State Bar Association.

Charles Ries practices principally in the areas of bankruptcy and taxation, banking and commercial law, and related litigation. His experience also includes handling corporations, partnerships, sole proprietorships, and limited liability companies. Mr. Ries is a lecturer at Continuing Legal Education seminars in agricultural law, bankruptcies, and in the tax consequences of agricultural liquidations and bankruptcies.

Mary Anne Wray's focus is family law matters including dissolution, custody, paternity, and adoption. She also has a Masters of FamilyTherapy degree and focuses on family dynamics and dysfunction. She is a member of the State Bar Association's Committee for Children and Family Law Section.

David A. Salsbery (JD William Mitchell '75) practices principally in the areas of real estate, closings, title work, and probate and estate planning. He is also a presenter for local estate planning seminars. Mr. Salsbery is a member of the Minnesota State Bar Association's Probate and Trust and Real Estate Sections and of the Sixth District Bar.

NELSON OYEN TORVIK

221 North First Street, P.O. Box 656 - Montevideo, MN 56265 - Phone: (612) 269-6461 - Fax: (612) 269-8024

Nelson Oyen Torvik was founded in 1941 by John P. Nelson and Sigvald B. Oyen, both of whom are now retired. Since that time, the firm has continued to provide quality legal services to residents of Chippewa, Yellow Medicine, Lac qui Parle, and surrounding counties. It has offices in Montevideo and Clarkfield, Minnesota.

In addition to the founders, two other attorneys have left the firm to pursue public service: Bruce Christopherson as a Judge in the Eighth Judicial District, Minnesota; and David Minge as Second District Congressional Representative for Minnesota.

Current firm members provide all types of legal services to the firm's clients. **Stephen Torvik** (JD University of Minnesota '67) practices in the area of personal injury and business litigation, real estate, estate planning, and employment law. **David M. Gilbertson** (JD University of Minnesota '77) is the Chippewa County Attorney and practices in real estate, family, and estate planning. **Janice M. Nelson** (JD University of Minnesota '82) practices in the areas of estate planning, probate, real estate, banking, and corporate law as well as acting as City Attorney for Montevideo and Watson. **Kevin Stroup** (JD University of Minnesota '85) practices in the area of real estate, agricultural, personal injury, and estate planning law and is City Attorney for the City of Clarkfield. **Geoffrey Hathaway** (JD University of Minnesota '92) and **David Torgelson** (JD University of Minnesota '86) are associates with the firm. Mr. Hathaway practices in corporate, business, and banking law, and Mr. Torgelson is engaged in general practice.

As is typical of a small town practice, all of the attorneys engage in general practice of law, continuing the tradition of providing quality, full service legal services for their clients.

Second office:

1020 Tenth Avenue
P.O. Box 656
Clarkfield, MN 56223
Phone: (612) 669-4447
Fax: (612) 669-4675

Zone 4:

Including listings in Alexandria, Bemidji, Brainerd, Crookston, Fergus Falls, Hallock, Little Falls, Moorhead, St. Cloud, Thief River Falls, Wadena, and Fargo, North Dakota

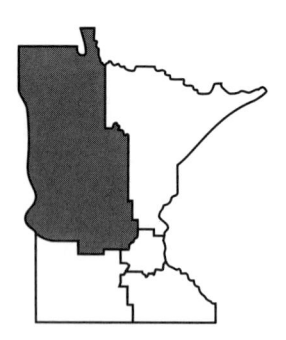

Anderson, Douglas P. - Rosenmeier, Anderson & Vogel - 210 Second Street N.E., Little Falls, MN 56345 - Commercial Litigation - **Personal Injury Defense Law - (612) 632-5458**

Baer, Carl - Kief, Fuller, Baer, Wallner & Rodgers, Ltd. - P.O. Box 880, 514 America Avenue, Bemidji, MN 56601 - Personal Injury Defense Law, Criminal Law - **Commercial Litigation - (218) 751-2221**

Campbell, Craig R. - Gunhus, Grinnell, Klinger, Swenson & Guy, Ltd. - 512 Center Avenue, P.O. Box 1077, Moorhead, MN 56561-1077 - **Personal Injury Defense Law - (218) 236-6462**

Carpenter, Kevin S. - Quinlivan, Sherwood, Spellacy & Tarvestad, P.A. - P.O. Box 1008, St. Cloud, MN 56302-1008 - Commercial Litigation - **Personal Injury Defense Law - (612) 251-1414**

Dickel, Morris - Dickel, Johannson, Taylor, Rust & Tye, P.A. - 407 North Broadway, P.O. Box 605, Crookston, MN 56716 - **Agricultural Law - (218) 281-2400**

Eller, Daniel A. - Eller Law Office - 925 South First Street, St. Cloud, MN 56301 - **Criminal Law - (612) 253-3700**

Ford, Michael J. - Quinlivan, Sherwood, Spellacy & Tarvestad, P.A. - P.O. Box 1008, St. Cloud, MN 56302-1008 - Commercial Litigation - **Employment Law - (612) 251-1414**

Grinnell, Paul E. - Gunhus, Grinnell, Klinger, Swenson & Guy, Ltd. - 512 Center Avenue, P.O. Box 1077, Moorhead, MN 56561-1077 - Commercial Litigation - **Personal Injury Defense Law - (218) 236-6462**

Gunhus, Gunder D. - Gunhus, Grinnell, Klinger, Swenson & Guy, Ltd. - 512 Center Avenue, P.O. Box 1077, Moorhead, MN 56561-1077 - Commercial Litigation - **Personal Injury Defense Law - (218) 236-6462**

Guy, William L. - Gunhus, Grinnell, Klinger, Swenson & Guy, Ltd. - 512 Center Avenue, P.O. Box 1077, Moorhead, MN 56561-1077 - Closely Held Business Law - **Probate, Estate Planning & Trusts Law - (218) 236-6462**

Hanson, Lee W. - Hall, Byers, Hanson, Steil & Weinberger, P.A. - 1010 West St. Germain, Suite 600, St. Cloud, MN 56301 - Publicly Held Corporations Law, Commercial Real Estate Law - **Closely Held Business Law - (612) 252-4414**

Hogan, Barry P. - Jeffries, Olson, Flom, Oppegard & Hogan, P.A. - 1325 23rd Street South, Fargo, ND 58103 - **Personal Injury Defense Law - (701) 280-2300**

Hughes, Kevin J. - Hughes, Mathews & Didier, P.A. - 110 Sixth Avenue South, Suite 200, P.O. Box 548, St. Cloud, MN 56302-0548 - **Health Law - (612) 251-4399**

Jeffries, Richard N. - Jeffries, Olson, Flom, Oppegard & Hogan, P.A. - 403 Center Avenue, P.O. Box 9, Moorhead, MN 56561-0009 - Commercial Litigation - **Professional Malpractice Defense Law - (218) 233-3222**

Johannson, Kenneth F. - Dickel, Johannson, Taylor, Rust & Tye, P.A. - 407 North Broadway, P.O. Box 605, Crookston, MN 56716 - Civil Litigation - **Personal Injury Defense Law - (218) 281-2400**

Johnson, Joel D. - Dosland, Nordhougen, Lillehaug & Johnson, P.A. - 730 Center Avenue, Suite 203, P.O. Box 100, Moorhead, MN 56561-0100 - Publicly Held Corporations Law - **Closely Held Business Law - (218) 233-2744**

Kennedy, Charles R. - Kennedy & Nervig - 503 Jefferson Street South, P.O. Box 647, Wadena, MN 56482 - Commercial Litigation - **Personal Injury Defense Law - (218) 631-2505**

Kershner, H. Morrison - Pemberton, Sorlie, Sefkow, Rufer & Kershner - 110 North Mill Street, P.O. Box 866, Fergus Falls, MN 56538-0866 - Personal Injury Defense Law - **Personal Injury Defense Law - (218) 736-5493**

Kunkel, Phillip L. - Hall, Byers, Hanson, Steil & Weinberger, P.A. - 1010 West St. Germain, Suite 600, St. Cloud, MN 56301 - Agricultural Law, Commercial Real Estate Law - **Bankruptcy & Workout Law - (612) 252-4414**

Lervick, John C. - Swenson, Grover, Lervick, Syverson, Battey & Anderson, Ltd. - 710 Broadway, Box 787, Alexandria, MN 56308 - Federal, State & Local Government Law - **Personal Injury Defense Law - (612) 763-3141**

Marben, Kurt J. - Charlson, Marben & Jorgenson, P.A. - 119 West Second Street, P.O. Box 506, Thief River Falls, MN 56701-0506 - Commercial Litigation - **Personal Injury Defense Law - (218) 681-4002**

Maring, David S. - Maring Law Office - 1220 Main Avenue, Suite 105, P.O. Box 2103, Fargo, ND 58107 - **Commercial Litigation - (701) 237-5297**

Nordhougen, Curtis A. - Dosland, Nordhougen, Lillehaug & Johnson, P.A. - 730 Center Avenue, Suite 203, P.O. Box 100, Moorhead, MN 56561-0100 - Agricultural Law - **Closely Held Business Law - (218) 233-2744**

Pemberton, Richard L. - Pemberton, Sorlie, Sefkow, Rufer & Kershner - 110 North Mill Street, P.O. Box 866, Fergus Falls, MN 56538-0866 - Professional Malpractice Defense Law, Employment Law - **Personal Injury Defense Law - (218) 736-5493**

Person, John W. - Breen & Person, Ltd. - 510 Laurel Street, P.O. Box 472, Brainerd, MN 56401 - **Commercial Real Estate Law - (218) 828-1248**

Powell, Romaine R. - Powell, Powell & Aamodt - 713 Beltrami Avenue, P.O. Box 908, Bemidji, MN 56601-0908 - Commercial Litigation - **Personal Injury Defense Law - (218) 751-5650**

Quinlivan, John D. - Quinlivan, Sherwood, Spellacy & Tarvestad, P.A. - P.O. Box 1008, St. Cloud, MN 56302-1008 - Commercial Litigation - **Personal Injury Defense Law - (612) 251-1414**

Rajkowski, Frank J. - Rajkowski Hansmeier, Ltd. - 11 Seventh Avenue North, P.O. Box 1433, St. Cloud, MN 56302 - Commercial Litigation - **Personal Injury Defense Law - (612) 251-1055**

Sefkow, Robert J. - Pemberton, Sorlie, Sefkow, Rufer & Kershner - 110 North Mill Street, P.O. Box 866, Fergus Falls, MN 56538-0866 - Commercial Litigation - **Banking Law - (218) 736-5493**

Severson, Robert K. - Brink, Sobolik, Severson, Vroom & Malm, P.A. - 217 Birch Avenue South, P.O. Box 790, Hallock, MN 56728 - Commercial Litigation - **Commercial Litigation - (218) 843-3686**

Smith, Ralph T. - Smith Law Firm, P.A. - 115 Fifth Street, P.O. Box 1420, Bemidji, MN 56601 - Probate, Estate Planning & Trusts Law, Commercial Real Estate Law - **Labor Law - (218) 751-3130**

Sobolik, Dennis M. - Brink, Sobolik, Severson, Vroom & Malm, P.A. - 217 Birch Avenue South, P.O. Box 790, Hallock, MN 56728 - **Agricultural Law - (218) 843-3686**

Spellacy, Kevin A. - Quinlivan, Sherwood, Spellacy & Tarvestad, P.A. - P.O. Box 1008, St. Cloud, MN 56302-1008 - **Personal Injury Defense Law - (612) 251-1414**

Strinden, Jon E. - Gunhus, Grinnell, Klinger, Swenson & Guy, Ltd. - 512 Center Avenue, P.O. Box 1077, Moorhead, MN 56561-1977 - Commercial Real Estate Law - **Closely Held Business Law - (218) 236-6462**

Tarvestad, Anthony M. - Quinlivan, Sherwood, Spellacy & Tarvestad, P.A. - P.O. Box 1008, St. Cloud, MN 56302-1008 - Personal Injury Defense Law - **Professional Malpractice Defense Law - (612) 251-1414**

Thoreen, Gerald L. - Hughes, Thoreen & Knapp, P.A. - 110 South Sixth Avenue, St. Cloud, MN 56302-1718 - **Probate, Estate Planning & Trusts Law - (612) 251-6175**

Vogel, Peter L. - Rosenmeier, Anderson & Vogel - 210 Second Street NE, Little Falls, MN 56345 - **Commercial Real Estate Law - (612) 632-5458**

BRINK, SOBOLIK, SEVERSON, VROOM & MALM, P.A.

217 Birch Avenue South, P.O. Box 790 - Hallock, MN 56728 - Phone: (218) 843-3686 - Fax: (218) 843-2724 - (800) 962-6281

When it was founded by Lyman Brink in 1934, the Brink law office provided general practice and litigation services in the Hallock, Minnesota area. Lyman Brink was one of northern Minnesota's most prominent, successful, and aggressive litigators. Through the years, Brink built a reputation as being a hard working, knowledgeable, and effective advocate. He founded his practice largely on plaintiff's personal injury work.

Soon Lyman Brink had far more clients than he could handle. In 1959, Dennis Sobolik was admitted to the bar and joined Brink's practice. By 1965, a third attorney was needed so Robert Severson was brought into the firm. When Lyman Brink died in 1972, Ronald Vroom joined Sobolik and Severson in carrying on Brink's tradition of excellent advocacy.

Through the years, the firm's size, regional influence, and array of legal services have increased dramatically. Now Brink, Sobolik, Severson, Vroom & Malm, P.A. is one of the largest law offices in northwestern Minnesota and northeastern North Dakota. The Brink office operates and maintains its own aircraft for ready access to the Twin Cities, Duluth, Bismarck, and other key forums. In addition, the firm now provides assistance in the areas of:

- Business and Finance Planning
- Probate and Estate Planning
- Business and Agribusiness Issues
- Personal Injuries
- Workers' Compensation
- Municipal Law
- Water Law
- School Litigation
- Product Liability
- Real Estate

All seven attorneys in the Brink firm are licensed to practice in both Minnesota and North Dakota. In addition, each attorney belongs to a number of professional associations. Most of the attorneys are licensed to practice in the federal court as well. Further, the law firm is listed in the 1994 Bar Register of Pre-Eminent Lawyers under the "Civil Trial Practice" and "General Practice" classifications. The Bar Register lists only those law firms that have been designated as outstanding in their field.

The firm's attorneys include:

Dennis M. Sobolik
Robert K. Severson
Ronald C. Vroom
Roger C. Malm
Robert M. Albrecht
Blake S. Sobolik
Jeffrey W. Hane

In addition, the Brink law office employs a full support staff and holds one of the largest private law libraries in northwestern Minnesota and northeastern North Dakota. The firm associates with Canadian counsel for handling international litigation.

DICKEL, JOHANNSON, TAYLOR, RUST & TYE, P.A.

407 North Broadway, P.O. Box 605 - Crookston, MN 56716 - Phone: (218) 281-2400 - Fax: (218) 281-5831

Dickel, Johannson, Taylor, Rust & Tye of Crookston, Minnesota is one of the largest law firms in northwestern Minnesota and eastern North Dakota. The firm provides a broad range of legal services, with special emphasis in civil litigation including personal injury, product liability, medical malpractice, and insurance defense; real estate and commercial transactions; municipal and government law; estate planning, probate and trust; agricultural and family law. The firm serves as general counsel for the Red River Valley Sugar Beet Growers Association and is local counsel for Simplot, Dahlgren & Company and financial institutions in the area.

Morris Dickel (LLB Minnesota 1953) practices in agricultural law, corporate, probate, and estate planning, and has been active in bar association activities and served on the Board of Law Examiners for the State of Minnesota.

Kenneth F. Johannson (JD North Dakota 1967) works primarily in the areas of civil litigation, including personal injury, products liability, insurance defense, and medical malpractice. He is active in all trial bar associations, including plaintiff's and defense bars and is admitted to practice in Minnesota and North Dakota.

Richard C. Taylor (JD North Dakota 1967) practices primarily in the area of civil litigation, including personal injury, products liability, and insurance defense. He is active in all trial bar associations, including plaintiff's and defense bars, and is admitted to practice in Minnesota and North Dakota.

Daniel L. Rust (JD Minnesota 1977) practices in the areas of real estate, commercial law, probate, estate planning, and agricultural law.

Michael J. Tye (JD Minnesota 1977) practices in the areas of real estate, commercial law, probate, estate planning, agricultural law, and family practice.

Dwain E. Fagerlund (JD North Dakota 1989) practices primarily in the area of civil litigation, with special emphasis in insurance defense. He is admitted to practice in Minnesota and North Dakota.

The firm's associates are: **David R. Unkenholz** (JD North Dakota 1992) admitted in Minnesota and North Dakota; **Tamara Hedlund Yon** (JD North Dakota 1994).

DOSLAND, NORDHOUGEN, LILLEHAUG & JOHNSON, P.A.

730 Center Avenue, Suite 203, P.O. Box 100 - Moorhead, MN 56561-0100 - Phone: (218) 233-2744
Fax: (218) 233-1570

Dosland, Nordhougen, Lillehaug & Johnson, P.A., is a regional law firm that has served clients in North Dakota and Minnesota for more than 100 years. The firm was established in 1886 in Moorhead, Minnesota. The firm provides a wide array of legal services, including real estate and commercial transactions; estate planning, probate, and trust; civil litigation, including personal injury, product liability, medical malpractice, employment disputes, and insurance defense.

Attorney J. P. Dosland (JD Minnesota '57), has extensive experience over three decades in the trial courts of Minnesota, North Dakota, and the Federal court system. He is a member of the American Board of Trial Advocates and is certified as a Civil Trial Specialist by the National Board of Trial Advocacy.

Attorney Curtis A. Nordhougen (JD North Dakota '61) has extensive experience in the fields of real estate, corporate law, business, probate and estate planning. Mr. Nordhougen is Secretary and General Counsel for American Crystal Sugar Company. He also served as General Counsel for the Housing and Redevelopment Authority of Moorhead's Urban Renewal Program from 1969 through 1986. Mr. Nordhougen has served as Special Counsel to the Authority in connection with economic development and tax increment financing matters.

Attorney Duane A. Lillehaug (JD North Dakota '77) is certified as a Civil Trial Specialist by the MSBA and is a member of the Board of Governors of the MTLA. Mr. Lillehaug's practice focuses on the preparation and trial of lawsuits, with a significant emphasis on the interpretation of insurance policies. Mr. Lillehaug's trial practice includes practice before the State and Federal courts in Minnesota and North Dakota.

Attorney Joel D. Johnson (JD North Dakota '76) practices primarily in the areas of corporate and commercial law, real estate, estate planning, probate and trust. Mr. Johnson is certified by the Minnesota State Bar Association as a Real Estate Specialist.

Attorney Bruce A. Romanick (JD North Dakota '86) practices primarily in the fields of real estate, commercial, and business transactions, bankruptcy, probate, estate planning, and trust law.

GUNHUS, GRINNELL, KLINGER, SWENSON & GUY, LTD.

512 Center Avenue, P.O. Box 1077 - Moorhead, MN 56561-1077 - Phone: (218) 236-6462 -
Fax: (218) 236-9873

Founded in 1914, Gunhus, Grinnell, Klinger, Swenson & Guy, Ltd., is a general practice firm offering a wide range of litigation and commercial services. With offices in Moorhead, Minnesota and Fargo, North Dakota, the firm handles matters primarily in the western half of Minnesota and all of North Dakota.

The attorneys of Gunhus, Grinnell, Klinger, Swenson & Guy bring diverse and valuable experiences to the firm. Prior to joining the firm, several of our attorneys served as judicial law clerks for courts including the Eighth Circuit Court of Appeals, Federal District Court, and the North Dakota Supreme Court. Some also served as county and city attorneys. All attorneys are members of numerous professional associations. The firm's size, 14 attorneys with total personnel of approximately 50, allows individual attorneys to develop expertise in specific areas of law. Firm attorneys with their areas of concentration are:

Gunder Gunhus - Malpractice; Products Liability; General Insurance Defense
Paul Grinnell - Personal Injury; Business Torts; Workers' Compensation
Edward Klinger - Employment Law; Bankruptcy; Commercial Litigation
Robert Swenson - Real Estate; Health Law; Environmental Law; Commercial Litigation
William Guy III - Probate; Estate Planning; Business Planning; Elder Law
Dean Hoistad - Malpractice; Products Liability; General Insurance Defense; Coverage Issues
Craig Campbell - Products Liability; Insurance Defense; Asbestos and Environmental Litigation; Malpractice
Jon Strinden - Business Law; Tax; Health Law; Banking
Bernie Reynolds - Malpractice; General Insurance Defense; Liquor Liability
Eric Fosaaen - Products Liability; Commercial Litigation; General Insurance Defense
Greg Hammes - Estate Planning; Business Planning; Elder Law
Bruce Schoenwald - Workers' Compensation; Uninsured Motorist; Personal Injury
Mary Locken - Probate; Commercial Law; Estate Planning; Elder Law
David Petrocchi - Commercial Litigation; Business Law; Tax; Employment Law

The firm also employs two full-time investigators with backgrounds in law enforcement and safety inspection, six legal assistants with specialized four year degrees, and two registered nurses.

Among the firm's institutional clients are Concordia College, Gate City Federal Savings Bank, Farm Credit Services, Heartland Medical Center, BlueCross-BlueShield of North Dakota, and Butler Machinery Company. Insurance companies include: Aetna, St. Paul Companies, Home Fireman's Fund, Sentry, and Westfield. The firm is equally proud of the number of small businesses and individuals it serves.

Fargo, North Dakota office:
Gate City Building, Suite 514
Fargo, ND 58102
Phone: (701) 235-2506
Fax: (701) 235-9862

Appendix C: Attorneys & Law Firms by Region

HALL, BYERS, HANSON, STEIL & WEINBERGER, P.A.

1010 West St. Germain, Suite 600 - St. Cloud, MN 56301 - Phone: (612) 252-4414 - Fax: (612) 252-4482

For more than 60 years, Hall, Byers, Hanson, Steil & Weinberger, P.A., has maintained a tradition of personalized client service. They take great pride in that tradition as an integral part of their high professional standards.

As a client-focused law firm they meet the needs of individuals, businesses and governmental units by providing high quality, creative and cost effective legal services. The firm serves its clients and the community with unsurpassed commitment and dedication.

Their clients cover a broad cross-section of business and industry throughout Minnesota. Currently the firm has 17 attorneys serving their clients' needs in the following areas:

- Auto Accidents
- Banking
- Bankruptcy-Financial Planning
- Business & Corporate Law
- Criminal Law
- Employee Benefits
- Environmental Law
- Estate Planning
- Family Law
- Labor & Employment Law
- Municipal Law
- Partnerships
- Real Estate
- Real Estate Development
- Taxation-Income, Estate & Gift
- Trials & Appeals
- Trusts & Guardianships
- Wills
- Wrongful Death

Two of the firm's shareholders are included in the *Business Guidebook to Law and Leading Attorneys:* Lee W. Hanson and Phillip L. Kunkel.

Their goal for each client is to meet their needs efficiently and effectively. They emphasize involvement in and understanding of their clients' special circumstances. This enables them to tailor services for the best results.

Lee W. Hanson - Corporate & Commercial Law
Paul W. Steil - Estates & Trusts
Stanley J. Weinberger, Jr. - Real Estate Development & Public Law
Edward J. Laubach, Jr. - Commercial & Construction Litigation
Robert J. Feigh - Commercial & Personal Injury Litigation
Frank J. Kundrat - Municipal, Labor & Employment Law
Steven B. Kutscheid - Tax & Commercial Law
Phillip L. Kunkel - Banking & Bankruptcy
Lynne M. Ridgway - Family Law
Tom P. Melloy - Bankruptcy & General Litigation
Peter J. Fuchsteiner - Tax, Commercial Law & Estate Planning
Robert J. Walter - Real Estate, Municipal & Criminal Law
Dorraine A. Larison - Bankruptcy, Employment & School Law
Jeffrey M. Mayer - General Litigation
Scott T. Larison - Commercial Law
Susan K. Wyman - Estate Planning & Employee Benefits
William R. Syverson - Corporate/Business Law & Estate Planning

JEFFRIES, OLSON, FLOM, OPPEGARD & HOGAN, P.A.

P.O. Box 9 - Moorhead, MN 56561-0009 - Phone: (218) 233-3222 - Fax: (218) 233-7065

Jeffries, Olson, Flom, Oppegard & Hogan, P.A., concentrates in civil litigation, primarily representing insurance company clients in all facets of modern day tort and contract claims. The firm conducts a trial and appellate practice in all state and federal courts in both Minnesota and North Dakota.

Richard N. Jeffries (JD with distinction University of North Dakota Law School '70) is a member of the honorary legal society, Order of the Coif. During law school, Dick was Articles Editor of the *North Dakota Law Review* and is the author of numerous articles addressing medical, automobile, and catastrophic injury issues.

Thomas R. Olson (JD William Mitchell '81) is licensed to practice in both state and federal courts of Minnesota and North Dakota. He served one year as an Assistant County Attorney with the Clay County Attorney's Office in Moorhead, Minnesota and is certified as a Civil Trial Specialist by the Minnesota State Bar Association.

Joel A. Flom (JD William Mitchell '81). After graduating law school, Joel practiced with Dorsey & Whitney for five years in general litigation with a special emphasis on products liability defense. Joel is certified as a Civil Trial Specialist by the Minnesota State Bar Association.

Paul R. Oppegard (JD William Mitchell '80) is certified by the Minnesota State Bar Association and by the National Board of Trial Advocacy as a Civil Trial Specialist. He is licensed in all state and federal courts in Minnesota and North Dakota and the US Supreme Court.

Barry P. Hogan (JD with distinction University of North Dakota School of Law '81) was a law instructor in Civil Litigation at Moorhead State University (1984-86). He also served as a judicial law clerk (1981-83) for Chief Judge Paul Benson of the US District Court in Fargo.

James R. Bullis (JD University of North Dakota School of Law '92) is an associate with the firm. He is licensed to practice law in both the state and federal courts of Minnesota and North Dakota, and the US Tax Court.

Ronald J. Knoll (JD with distinction University of North Dakota School of Law '92) is an associate with the firm. He is a member of the honorary legal society Order of the Coif.

Michael S. Montgomery (JD with distinction University of North Dakota Law School) is an associate with the firm. He served as an Assistant States Attorney, 1993-94.

Fargo, North Dakota Office:

1325 23rd Street South
Fargo, ND 58103
Phone: (701) 280-2300
Fax: (701) 280-1880

PEMBERTON, SORLIE, SEFKOW, RUFER & KERSHNER

110 North Mill Street, P.O. Box 866 - Fergus Falls, MN 56538-0866 - Phone: (218) 736-5493
Fax: (218) 736-3950

Pemberton, Sorlie, Sefkow, Rufer & Kershner of Fergus Falls, with offices in Rothsay, Henning, and Wheaton, is one of the largest and oldest law firms in west central Minnesota. The firm consists of 11 attorneys and has been providing legal services to a wide area of west central and northern Minnesota and parts of North and South Dakota for over 100 years. Three of its partners have been selected by other Minnesota attorneys as leading attorneys in the state in their particular fields. See the Personal Injury LawChapter for the profiles of Mr. Pemberton and Mr. Kershner. Mr. Sefkow appears in the *Business Guidebook to Law & Leading Attorneys*.

The firm has a major civil trial practice, including personal injury, product liability, and insurance defense. The firm also practices in the areas of employment and labor law, real estate and commercial transactions, municipal and government law, including public law for governmental entities, as well as estate planning, probate, and trust work. The firm is an agent for title insurance and provides closing services for real estate matters.

The other partners in the firm are:
Oscar J. Sorlie, Jr. (JD University of North Dakota '68) engages in a broad general practice and has been retained as attorney for numerous municipalities, governmental agencies, and school districts, and works as well in the areas of real property, business law, employment labor law, and estate planning and probate.

Stephen F. Rufer (JD Minnesota '74) is a Civil Trial Specialist certified by the MSBA and is Secretary of the governing council of the Civil Litigation Section of the MSBA. He has lectured at a number of seminars and has experience in personal injury, aviat-ion law, land use and agriculture, commercial and construction litigation, township and school law, estate planning, and real estate. He has completed certified courses in mediation and arbitration.

Robert W. Bigwood (JD Minnesota '80) is active in the areas of real property law, business and bankruptcy law, and probate and estate planning. He is certified as a Real Property Specialist by the Minnesota State Bar Association.

Michael T. Rengel (JD William Mitchell '85) is active in the areas of litigation, personal injury, products liability, workers' compensation, insurance law, public school law, and employment law.

The firm's associates are **Corenia A. Kollasch** (JD University of South Dakota '91), **Kent D. Mattson** (JD University of Minnesota '93), **Scott E. Dymoke** (JD William Mitchell '91), and **Rachel J. Dymoke** (JD William Mitchell '91).

QUINLIVAN, SHERWOOD, SPELLACY & TARVESTAD, P.A.

P.O. Box 1008 - St. Cloud, MN 56302-1008 - Phone: (612) 251-1414 - Fax: (612) 251-1415

Founded in 1923, Quinlivan, Sherwood, Spellacy & Tarvestad, P.A., has enjoyed a tradition of excellence in the field of litigation of all types. The firm represents individuals, corporations and other organizations in trial and appellate work in virtually all areas of the law. The firm concentrates in the resolution of lawsuits through trial, settlement, arbitration and/or mediation. Founded on the commitment to integrity, confidentiality and excellence, the goal of the firm is to provide clients with efficient, effective and excellent service.

The firm's 18 lawyers have expertise in civil and business litigation and provide a broad range of litigation services for clients in Minnesota. The areas include:

- Appellate practice
- Business torts
- Commercial litigation
- Environment claims
- General liability
- Health care litigation and risk management
- Insurance coverage and related claims
- Labor and employment law
- Personal injury
- Premises liability
- Product liability
- Professional ethics and disciplinary matters
- Professional liability:
  Legal
  Medical
  Architects
  Engineers
  Insurance agents and brokers
  Directors and officers
- Workers' compensation

The firm recognizes the need to be aware of technological innovations that enable the firm to maintain a state-of-the-art capability for the efficient production of legal work. The firm offers creative approaches to all forms of dispute resolution while maintaining a tradition of quality service for its clients.

Appendix C: Attorneys & Law Firms by Region

ROSENMEIER, ANDERSON & VOGEL
210 Second Street NE - Little Falls, MN 56345 - Phone: (612) 632-5458 - Fax: (612) 632-5496

Founded in 1910, the firm became a two attorney partnership in 1951 known as Rosenmeier & Simonett. Gordon Rosenmeier, a state Senator for 30 years and the firm's namesake, practiced until his death in 1989. John Simonett had earlier left the firm in 1980 to become a member of the Minnesota Supreme Court.

The firm currently consists of:

Douglas P. Anderson (JD University of Minnesota '75) who is the primary trial attorney for the firm. His practice includes personal injury litigation from both plaintiff and defense aspects, general civil litigation, banking, and school law. He is a member of the panel of arbitrators of the American Arbitration Association, the Minnesota Trial Lawyers Association, the Minnesota State Bar Association, and frequently serves as an arbitrator in uninsured and underinsured motorist claims.

Peter Vogel (JD University of Minnesota '78) has a broad general practice with emphasis in real estate. He is a certified real property law specialist by the Real Property Section of the Minnesota State Bar Association. He is also City Attorney for the City of Little Falls and the City of Swanville, and is counsel for Community Federal Savings & Loan Association of Little Falls.

Brigid M. Fitzgerald (JD William Mitchell '80) is the third partner in the firm. Her primary practice is with family law, though she also represents Randall State Bank and is City Attorney for the City of Upsala. She is a member of the Minnesota State Bar Association.

For the past 80 years, the law firm has provided all of the legal needs for residents of central Minnesota and has continued a strong commitment to trial excellence and to quality service for its clients.

ZONE 5:
Including listings in Duluth, Grand Rapids, and Virginia

Andresen, Charles H. - Crassweller, Magie, Andresen, Haag & Paciotti, P.A. - 1000 Alworth Building, 306 West Superior Street, Duluth, MN 55801 - **Commercial Real Estate Law** - **(218) 722-1411**

Burns, Richard R. - Hanft, Fride, O'Brien, Harries, Swelbar & Burns, P.A. - 1000 First Bank Place, 130 West Superior Street, Duluth, MN 55802 - **Probate, Estate Planning & Trusts Law** - **(218) 722-4766**

Burns, William M. - Hanft, Fride, O'Brien, Harries, Swelbar & Burns, P.A. - 1000 First Bank Place, 130 West Superior Street, Duluth, MN 55802 - Health Law, Commercial Litigation, Commercial Real Estate Law - **Publicly Held Corporations Law** - **(218) 722-4766**

Bye, Don L. - Halverson, Watters, Bye, Downs, Reyelts & Bateman, Ltd. - 700 Providence Building, 332 West Superior Street, Duluth, MN 55802 - **Labor Law** - **(218) 727-6833**

Dudderar, Frederick A. - Hanft, Fride, O'Brien, Harries, Swelbar & Burns, P.A. - 1000 First Bank Place, 130 West Superior Street, Duluth, MN 55802 - Publicly Held Corporations Law, Commercial Real Estate Law - **Bankruptcy & Workout Law** - **(218) 722-4766**

Dunlevy, Shawn M. - Fryberger, Buchanan, Smith & Frederick, P.A. - 302 West Superior Street, Suite 700, Duluth, MN 55802 - Bankruptcy & Workout Law - **Banking Law** - **(218) 722-0861**

Frederick, Harold A. - Fryberger, Buchanan, Smith & Frederick, P.A. - 302 West Superior Street, Suite 700, Duluth, MN 55802 - **Health Law** - **(218) 722-0861**

Harries, Gilbert W. - Hanft, Fride, O'Brien, Harries, Swelbar & Burns, P.A. - 1000 First Bank Place, 130 West Superior Street, Duluth, MN 55802 - Commercial Real Estate Law - **Environmental Law** - **(218) 722-4766**

Kelly, John D. - Hanft, Fride, O'Brien, Harries, Swelbar & Burns, P.A. - 1000 First Bank Place, 130 West Superior Street, Duluth, MN 55802 - **Commercial Litigation** - **(218) 722-4766**

Killen, John J. - Johnson, Killen, Thibodeau & Seiler, P.A. - 811 Norwest Center, 230 West Superior Street, Duluth, MN 55802 - Commercial Litigation - **Closely Held Business Law** - **(218) 722-6331**

Larsen, Dexter A. - Fryberger, Buchanan, Smith & Frederick, P.A. - 302 West Superior Street, Suite 700, Duluth, MN 55802 - Publicly Held Corporations Law - **Intellectual Property Law** - **(218) 722-0861**

Nys, John N. - Johnson, Killen, Thibodeau & Seiler, P.A. - 811 Norwest Center, 230 West Superior Street, Duluth, MN 55802 - Commercial Litigation - **Publicly Held Corporations Law** - **(218) 722-6331**

O'Toole, Dennis L. - Lano, Nelson, O'Toole & Bengtson, Ltd. - 115 East Fifth Street, P.O. Box 20, Grand Rapids, MN 55744 - Closely Held Business Law - **Personal Injury Defense Law** - **(218) 326-9603**

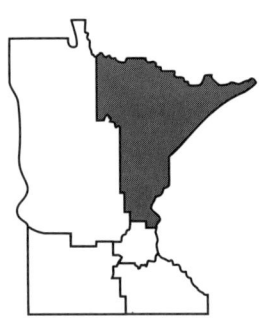

Peterson, H. Jeffrey - Cope & Peterson, P.A. - 415 South First Street, P.O. Box 947, Virginia, MN 55792 - **Personal Injury Defense Law - (218) 749-4470**

Richards, Carver - Trenti Law Firm - P.O. Box 958, Virginia, MN 55792 - Commercial Litigation - **Personal Injury Defense Law - (218) 749-1962**

Roby, Joseph J. - Johnson, Killen, Thibodeau & Seiler, P.A. - 811 Norwest Center, 230 West Superior Street, Duluth, MN 55802 - **Labor Law - (218) 722-6331**

Seiler, Steven J. - Johnson, Killen, Thibodeau & Seiler, P.A. - 811 Norwest Center, 230 West Superior Street, Duluth, MN 55802 - Publicly Held Corporations Law - **Health Law - (218) 722-6331**

Smith, Nick - Fryberger, Buchanan, Smith & Frederick, P.A. - 302 West Superior Street, Suite 700, Duluth, MN 55802 - **Publicly Held Corporations Law - (218) 722-0861**

Stewart, James H. - Fryberger, Buchanan, Smith & Frederick, P.A. - 302 West Superior Street, Suite 700, Duluth, MN 55802 - Closely Held Business Law - **Probate, Estate Planning & Trusts Law - (218) 722-0861**

Swelbar, Gaylord W. - Hanft, Fride, O'Brien, Harries, Swelbar & Burns, P.A. - 1000 First Bank Place, 130 West Superior Street, Duluth, MN 55802 - Commercial Litigation - **Personal Injury Defense Law - (218) 722-4766**

Thibodeau, Thomas R. - Johnson, Killen, Thibodeau & Seiler, P.A. - 811 Norwest Center, 230 West Superior Street, Duluth, MN 55802 - Commercial Litigation, Environmental Law - **Personal Injury Defense Law - (218) 722-6331**

FRYBERGER, BUCHANAN, SMITH & FREDERICK, P.A.

302 West Superior Street, Suite 700 - Duluth, MN 55802 - Phone: (218) 722-0861 - Fax: (218) 722-9568
1190 Capital Centre Building, 386 N. Wabasha Street - St. Paul, MN 55102 - Phone: (612) 221-1044 - Fax: (612) 221-1035

Fryberger, Buchanan, Smith & Frederick, P.A. is the largest law firm serving northern Minnesota and northwest Wisconsin. Although best known as a business law firm, the Fryberger firm offers a complete range of legal services in areas such as general civil, trial, and appellate practice; personal injury, professional malpractice, and workers' compensation; taxation, corporation, business, banking and securities; probate, trusts, and estate planning; municipal law, including municipal and public authority financing; bankruptcy; real estate; mining; maritime law; labor and employment; environmental; trademark and intellectual property law.

The firm has a long, proud history in Duluth, and it remains energetic and dynamic by attracting attorneys with varying backgrounds, education, and interests. Over the years the Fryberger firm has developed a team approach to representing clients. Each attorney concentrates his or her practice in two or three particular areas of the law, and is thus able to sharpen skills and keep abreast of current developments on a focused basis. This approach allows the firm to provide fast, sophisticated legal service at a reasonable cost.

Personal attention is the firm's cornerstone, and that commitment applies to all clients—large regional and national corporations, government entities, small businesses, professional associations, nonprofit organizations, and individuals.

A St. Paul office, which includes legislative lobbying attorneys, was opened in 1992. This important link to the Twin Cities area contributes to the firm's ability to provide comprehensive services not generally available in the region.

History: Founded in 1893 by H.B. Fryberger, Sr. In 1971 the Fryberger law office merged with the Wheeler firm to form Fryberger, Buchanan, Smith & Frederick, P.A. The Fryberger firm has been located on the seventh floor of the Lonsdale Building since 1906.

Other: Three attorneys in the Fryberger firm are graduates of a certified training program in general mediation.

Number of Partners: **14**
Number of Associates: **13**
Of Counsel: 1
Support Staff: 46

Fryberger, Buchanan, Smith & Frederick, P.A. Attorneys

R. Bruce Buchanan	Martha M. Markusen
Nick Smith	Daniel D. Maddy
Harold A. Frederick	Stephanie A. Ball
Dexter A. Larsen	Paul B. Kilgore
James H. Stewart	Mary Frances Skala
Robert E. Toftey	Rolf A. Lindberg
Michael K. Donovan	Kevin T. Walli
Neal J. Hessen	Teresa M. O'Toole
Joseph J. Mihalek	Dean R. Borgh
Shawn M. Dunlevy	Kevin J. Dunlevy
Anne Lewis	James A. Lund
David R. Oberstar	Mark D Britton
Abbot G. Apter	Judith A. Zollar
Michael Cowles	
Herschel B. Fryberger, Jr., Of Counsel	

HANFT, FRIDE, O'BRIEN, HARRIES, SWELBAR & BURNS, P.A.

1000 First Bank Place, 130 West Superior Street - Duluth, MN 55802 - Phone: (218) 722-4766 - Fax: (218) 720-4920

Hanft, Fride, O'Brien, Harries, Swelbar & Burns, P.A. is a full service law firm specializing in business and trial work.

Professionalism has been the firm's cornerstone since 1899 when it was founded. Today, the firm's lawyers define professionalism as dedication to problem solving—working hard and doing the work right; providing sound, objective judgment and advice; and utilizing an outcome-oriented approach to ensure that all work contributes to the client's desired outcome.

The firm's moderate size ensures that clients receive prompt, personal service and have ready access to their lawyer. An unqualified commitment to excellence is demonstrated by the inclusion of six of the firm's seventeen attorneys in this *Guidebook*.

The firm's law practice is concentrated in Minnesota and Northern Wisconsin. Through its membership in Legal Netlink, the firm's clients have access to other high quality moderate sized law firms throughout the United States.

Gaylord W. Swelbar  **John D. Kelly**

Gaylord W. Swelbar and John D. Kelly are experienced civil trial lawyers.

Gilbert W. Harries  **Richard R. Burns**

Gilbert W. Harries has extensive experience with environmental and real estate matters.

William M. Burns  **Frederick A. Dudderar**

William M. Burns is well know for his work with banks, real estate developers, health care providers, and contractors.

Richard R. Burns devotes most of his practice to business and estate planning. He also represents major media interests including television stations in three states, and several newspapers.

Frederick A. Dudderar practices commercial law with an emphasis on bankruptcy and loan workouts.

JOHNSON, KILLEN, THIBODEAU & SEILER, P.A.

230 West Superior Street, 811 Norwest Center - Duluth, MN 55802 - Phone: (218) 722-6331 - Fax: (218) 722-3031

Johnson, Killen, Thibodeau & Seiler, P.A., is the oldest firm in Northern Minnesota having provided legal services to the area since 1888. The firm's 18 lawyers provide specialized service in a broad range of law:

- Personal Injury
- Insurance
- Commercial
- Employment and Labor
- Defamation
- Malpractice
- Workers' Compensation
- Aviation
- Marital
- Estate Planning
- Probate and Trust
- Business, including:
  - Sole Proprietorships
  - Corporations
  - Partnerships
  - Limited Partnerships
  - Financing
  - Mergers
  - Acquisitions
- Hospital Law

- Shopping Centers, involving:
  - Development
  - Financing
  - Leasing for Developers, Landlords, and Tenants
- Bankruptcy
- Banking and Creditors' Rights
- Environmental Law
- Taxation
- Maritime
- Real Estate

Five of the firm's members are included in the *Business Guidebook to Law and Leading Attorneys*: **John J. Killen, Thomas R. Thibodeau, Steven J. Seiler, Joseph J. Roby, Jr. and John N. Nys.** **John J. Killen** and **Thomas R. Thibodeau** are advocates of the ABOTA and fellows of the American College of Trial Lawyers. **Joseph B. Johnson** and **Steven J. Seiler** are fellows of the American Board of Trust and Estate Counsel.

Joseph B. Johnson
John J. Killen

Thomas R. Thibodeau*
Steven J. Seiler
John N. Nys
Robert C. Pearson
James A. Wade*
Joseph J. Roby, Jr.*
Nicholas Ostapenko
Greg C. Gilbert
Sally L. Tarnowski
Faye M. Witt
Greg A. King
David M. Johnson
Jerome D. Feriancek
Alok Vidyarthi
Laura J. Schacht
Timothy A. Costley

Civil Trial Specialist certified by the Minnesota State Bar Association and the National Board of Trial Advocacy.

SUBJECT MATTER INDEX

Acceptance 12
Access to Health Care Facilities ..265
Access to Medical Records 265
Accountant Malpractice 390
Acquired Businesses, Taxes............87
Acquisitions, Corporate 402
ADA (Americans with Disabilities Act)....................................184, 185
Adjudication 226
Administrative Agencies 226
Administrative Process..................226
ADR (Alternative Dispute Resolution) 27
Advertisements................................48
Advertising.........................1, 41, 46
Affirmative Defenses 386
Age Discrimination 185
Agency 13
Agricultural Law 31
Agricultural Production Contracts ..31
Agricultural Production Contracts, General Drafting Issues 33
Agricultural Production Contracts, Minnesota Requirements 33
Agricultural Products Imports 304
AIDS..268
Air Pollution...................................204
Aliens..277
Alternative Dispute Resolution 27
Alternatives to Bankruptcy 68
Americans with Disabilities Act 184, 185
Ammunition Imports 305
Anatomical Gifts 266
Answer 22
Antitrust 161
Appeal Rights, Arbitration..............29
Appliances Imports 306
Application, Patents 289
Appropriate Bargaining Unit 318
Arbitration 28, 33
Arbitration Clauses........................250
Arbitration, Mandatory 16
Architect Malpractice....................391
Arms Imports 305
Articles of Incorporation ..330, 331, 400
Arts Law 41
Asbestos 207
Assessment.....................................135
Asset Acquisition 403
Asset Based Lenders 422
Asylees 281
Attorney-Client Relationship 387

Attractive Nuisance 339
Automotive Dealer Franchise Act ..252
Avoiding Liability, White Collar Crime 165

Background Information, UFOC ..244
Bank Examinations 57
Bank Fraud.....................................164
Bank Funds.......................................58
Banking Law 55
Bankruptcy History, UFOC 244
Bankruptcy Law 63
Bankruptcy, Alternatives 68
Bar 1
Bilateral Contract 12
Biological Drugs Imports..............307
Bonds..417
Booking Contract 42
Boycotts 320
Breach of Confidentiality..............386
Bribery & Extortion 165
Building Codes..............................141
Burden of Proof 338
Business Experience, UFOC 244
Business Opportunity Ventures 242
Business Succession......................101
Business Tax Law 81
Bylaws 330, 331

Capital Access Program 224
Causation of Harm 385
Cause in Fact 385
Certification Standards for Specialization 4
Chain Conspiracy 164
Chapter 7 Bankruptcy 64
Chapter 11 Bankruptcy 65
Chapter 12 Bankruptcy 35
Charitable Purpose 333
Cheese Imports..............................304
Choice of Law Provisions 250
Civil Pretrial Process 22
Civil Process..................................21
Civil Rights in the Workplace 184
Class Action Lawsuits 22
Closely Held Business Law 97
Closely Held Businesses 374
Co-Ownership of Property 135, 138
COBRA 176
CODA...177
Collective Bargaining....................319
Commercial Banks.................55, 422

Commercial Finance Companies ..422
Commercial Litigation 113
Commercial Real Estate Law........135
Community Right-To-Know 206
Comparative Fault 338
Complaint..22
Computer Crime.............................161
Conciliation Court 25
Conditions 136
Confidentiality 268
Consent...386
Consent to Care 265
Consideration 12
Conspiracy 164
Construction Contracts..................140
Consultation 5
Consulting Agreements 101
Consulting an Attorney 5
Consumer Fraud...............................47
Consumer Products Imports..........306
Contests 48
Contingent Fees 8
Contract 11, 256
Contract Termination 14
Contractual Statutes of Limitation ..251
Conventional Bank Loans 421
Conversion, Bankruptcy..................67
Copyright 44, 287
Corporate Agent, Liability 160
Corporate Buy-Sell Agreements ..404
Corporate Farming 35
Corporate Liability 159
Corporate Officer, Liability 160
Corporate Status, Advantages 397
Corporate Status, Disadvantages ..399
Corporation 43, 98
Corporation, Nonprofit..................329
Corporation, Taxes..........................82
Cost, Lawyers...................................7
Counterclaims 22, 115
Court of Appeals 19
Covenants.......................................136
Criminal Law 159
Criminal Liability of a Corporation................................159
Criminal Process 23
Crossclaims 115

Dairy Products Imports 304
Damages..14
Dealership......................................241
Death Taxes 373

1994/1996 ◆ *Minnesota Edition* **501**

Index D: Subject Matter Index

Debt Financing 421
Deceptive Trade Practices 47, 254
Declaring Bankruptcy, Effects of ..68
Deed 136
Deed Restrictions 136
Defamation......................................45
Defective Warning 340
Defenses against Libel 45
Defenses to Contract 13
Delaware Corporations..................400
Deportation.....................................281
Design Defect.................................341
Design Patents 289
Discharge in Bankruptcy 65
Discrimination, Persons with
  Disabilities 185
Dismissal, Bankruptcy 67
Dispute Resolution (ADR).............27
Diversity Immigrants 281
Dram Shop Laws 342
Drug Paraphernalia, Imports 307
Duress..13

Earnings Claims, UFOC 246
Easement 136
Economic Development Program 224
Economic Strike 320
Educating Employees....................118
Educational Organization..............333
Effects of Declaring Bankruptcy 68
Eighth Circuit Court of Appeals 19
Electromagnetic Fields (EMFs) 209
Embezzlement 163
EMFs (Electromagnetic Fields) 209
Employee Benefits 175
Employee Health Care 268
Employee Right-To-Know............206
Employee Stock Ownership Plan
  (ESOP)..177
Employee, Employment Law........181
Employment at Will 182
Employment Law 181
Employment Taxes.........................84
Encumbrance 136
Engineer Malpractice 391
Enterprise Zone Credit...................83
Entertainment Agency Contract......42
Entertainment Law 41
Entry into U.S. 281
Environmental Law 203
Environmental Liability 138
ERISA 175
ESOP (Employee Stock Ownership
  Plan) 177
Estate Planning Law......................367
Estimate of Time 6
Estoppel 255
Exchange Markets 418
Excise Tax 88
Exclusion from U.S. 281

Exclusivity Principal 319
Exemptions, Tax 88
Experience, Lawyers 6
Experts 3
Explosives Imports 305
Export Controls 303

401(k) Plan 177
501(c)(3) Tax-Exemption 332, 333
Fair Use Doctrine 48
Fair Use, Copyright 288
False Statements in Advertising......47
Family and Medical Leave Act of
  1993 (FMLA) 187
Family Leave 187
Farm Bankruptcies 35
FCPA (Foreign Corrupt Practices
  Act)..308
FDIC (Federal Deposit Insurance
  Corporation) 56
Federal Courts 19
Federal Deposit Insurance Corporation
  (FDIC) 56
Federal Employer Identification
  Number (EIN) 83
Federal Financing...........................223
Federal Government Law..............223
Federal Reserve System 56
Federal Trade Commission Rule (FTC
  Rule) 242
Fees..25
Felonies 23
FICA...85
Fiduciary Duties 402
Filing for Bankruptcy 64
Financial Statements, UFOC 246
Financing, UFOC 245
Flammable Fabrics Imports 306
Flat Fees 7
Fleet Factors 59
FMLA (Family and Medical Leave
  Act of 1993) 187
Food, Drugs, Cosmetics and Medical
  Products, Imports 306
Foreign Corrupt Practices Act
  (FCPA) 308
Forming a Union 318
Forum Selection 16
Forum Selection Clauses 115, 250
Franchise 99, 241, 423
Franchisee Obligations, UFOC 245
Franchisor Obligations, UFOC 245
Fraud 14, 163
Fraudulent Conveyances 67
Fraudulent Inducement..................256
Freedom of Information Act 227
Freedom of Speech.........................45
Fruit Imports..................................305
FTC Disclosure Document............242
Fur Products Imports 308

GAAP (Generally Accepted
  Accounting Principals)..............390
GAAS (Generally Accepted Auditing
  Standards)...................................390
Game Promotions..........................48
GATT (General Agreement on Tariffs
  and Trade) 34
General Partnership 43
General Services Administration
  (GSA) 225
General Warranty Deed 136
Generally Accepted Accounting
  Principals (GAAP) 390
Generally Accepted Auditing
  Standards (GAAS) 390
Gift-Leaseback Arrangement 374
Gold Imports 307
Good Samaritan Law 384
Government Contracts 224
Green Card 281
Gross Misdemeanor 23
Group Health Plans 176
GSA (General Services
  Administration) 225
Guardian...368

Hazardous Substances, Imports 307
Hazardous Waste 205
Health Care System, Access to 261
Health Law 261
Hiring, Workers' Compensation ..343
HIV...268
Hobbs Act.......................................162
Home Country 303
Hospital Insurance 263
Host Country 303
Hourly Rates....................................7
Hub-and-Spoke Conspiracy 164
Human Rights, Minnesota 184, 186

Illegal Strike 320
Immigrant Visas 280
Immigrants 277
Immigration and Naturalization
  Service (INS)..............................278
Immigration Law 277
Immigration, Employment-Based ..280
Immigration, Family-Based 280
Import Controls 304
In-House Legal Counsel................115
Incapacity 368
Income Tax....................................85
Incorporation, State of 399
Independent Contractor, Employment
  Law..181
Indian Business Loan Program 224
Individual Retirement Account
  (IRA) 178
Infectious Waste............................207
Informal Agency Action 226, 227
Informal Probate............................373

Subject Matter Index

Initial Fee, UFOC 244
Initial Investment, UFOC 245
Initial Offer, Franchise 241
Initial Public Offerings 418
Injunctive or Declaratory Relief .. 257
INS 278
Insects Imports 305
Insider Trading 161
Instruments of War Imports 305
Integration Clauses 251
Intellectual Property 287
Intentional Misconduct 337, 338
Internal Revenue Code 332
International Agricultural
  Agreements 34
International Business Law 303
International Contract 309
International Letter of Credit 310
Involuntary Bankruptcy 66
IRA (Individual Retirement
  Account) 178
Irrevocable Trusts 372
IRS 331

Joinder 115
Joint Tenancy 136
Jurisdiction 18

Keogh Plan 178

Labor Law 315
Labor Management Relations Act .. 317
Labor-Management Reporting and
  Disclosure Act 317
Land Use Law 141
Landrum-Griffin Act 317
Lanham Act 48
Lawsuit, Process of 21
Leasing Real Estate 138
Legal Fee Provision 26
Legal Malpractice 387
Lender Liability 58
Liability of Officers 332
Libel 45
Lien 137
Limited Liability 398
Limited Liability Company 99
Liquidated Damages 15
Liquidation 65
Liquidation Bankruptcy 64
Literary Purpose 333
Litigation Alternatives 27
Litigation History, UFOC 244
Litigation, Avoiding 116
Little FTC Acts 254
Livestock and Animals Imports 305
Loans 57
Lobbying 225
Local Financing 224
Local Government Law 223

Local Sales Tax 88
Location of Law Firm 4
Lottery 48

Mail Fraud 163
Mailbox Rule 12
Malfeasance 384
Malpractice 383
Malpractice Insurance 6
Management Contract 42
Managing Counsel 1
Mandatory Arbitration 16
Manufacturing Defect 341
Market Specification Contract 32
MBCA (Minnesota Business
  Corporations Act) 400
Meat and Meat Products Imports .. 305
Mechanics Lien 137
Media Law 41, 45
Mediation 29, 33
Mediation-Arbitration 30
Medicaid 261
Medical Assistance 261, 372
Medical Leave 187
Medical Malpractice 383
Medicare 262
Medicare Parts A & B 263
Medicare, Insurance Issues 264
Mergers, Corporate 402
Milk Imports 304
Mini-trials 28
Minnesota Agricultural Equipment
  Dealership Act 252
Minnesota Bar 1
Minnesota Blue Sky Laws 420
Minnesota Business Corporations Act
  (MBCA) 400
Minnesota Department of Trade and
  Economic Development 224
Minnesota Family Leave Act 187
Minnesota Franchise Act 251
Minnesota Human Rights
  Act 184, 186
Minnesota Public Facilities
  Authority 224
Minnesota Requirements,
  Franchises 247
Minnesota Supreme Court 19
Minnesota Taxpayer Identification
  Number (TIN) 83
Minnesota Technology, Inc. 224
Minnesota's Judicial System 17
Minnesota's Legal System 17
MinnesotaCare 264
Miranda Warnings 23
Miscellaneous Expenses 9
Misdemeanor 23
Mistake 13
Moderated Settlement Conferences .. 28
Monetary Instruments Imports 307

Month-to-Month Lease 138
Mortgage Financing 140
Mutual Release Agreement 42

NAFTA (North American Free Trade
  Agreement) 34
Name Registration 400
Narcotics and Dangerous Drugs .. 304
National Banks 55
National Environmental Policy
  Act 142
National Labor Relations Act
  (NLRA) 316
National Labor Relations Board
  (NLRB) 316
National Pollution Discharge
  Elimination System (NPDES) .. 204
National Trade Data Bank 309
Naturalized Citizen 281
Negligence 337, 341
Negotiating a Lease 139
Neutral Fact Findings 28
NLRA (National Labor Relations
  Act) 316
NLRB (National Labor Relations
  Board) 316
Non-Compete Agreements 110, 190
Non-Qualified Plans 178
Nonfeasance 384
Nonimmigrant Visas 278
Nonimmigrants 277
Nonprofit Corporations 329
Norris-LaGuardia Act 316
North American Free Trade
  Agreement (NAFTA) 34
Notice, Copyright 288
NPDES (National Pollution Discharge
  Elimination System) 204
Nuts Imports 305

Obscenity 46
Obstruction of Justice 165
Offer 11
Office of the Comptroller 56
OMNI (Opportunities Minnesota
  Incorporated) 224
Omnibus Hearing 24
Ongoing Fees, UFOC 244
Operation of Business, UFOC 246
Opportunities Minnesota Incorporated
  (OMNI) 224
Organizational Drives 318
Over-the-Counter Markets 418
Owner, Copyright 288

Package Franchises 242
Parenting Leave 187
Partnership 98
Partnership, Taxes 81
Patent 289
Patents & Copyrights, UFOC 246

1994/1996 ♦ Minnesota Edition **503**

Index D: Subject Matter Index

Patient Bill of Rights 267
Payroll Taxes 84, 85
Performance Agreement..................42
Periodic Tenancy 138
Perjury 162
Personal Chemistry...........................5
Personal Injury Defense Law........337
Personal Representative 368
Personnel Records, Employee Access to..189
Pesticides, Imports 307
Petroleum Marketing Practices Act...252
Petty Misdemeanors 23
Picketing.......................................320
Piercing the Corporate Veil 398
Plan Bankruptcy..............................66
Plant and Plant Products Imports..305
Plant Patents 289
Plea Bargaining 24
Pollution Standards Index (PSI)....204
Postage Stamps Imports 307
Potentially Responsible Parties (PRPs)..206
Poultry and Poultry Products, Imports 305
Power-of-Sale Clause....................141
Preferences, Bankruptcy 67
Pregnancy Discrimination 186
Premises Liability.........................339
Prevention of Consumer Fraud Act, Minnesota.....................................47
Preventive Forms and Procedures ..117
Privacy 188
Private Placements 418
Probate 367, 372
Process of a Lawsuit 21
Product Franchises 242
Product Liability...........................340
Production Management Contract ..32
Professional Corporation 99
Professional Malpractice 99, 383
Prohibitions to Firing 191
Prospective Contractual Relationships 256
Proximate Cause 385, 389
PRPs (Potentially Responsible Parties)...206
PSI (Pollution Standards Index)....204
Public Defender 23
Public Figures, UFOC 246
Public Financing 223, 423
Publicly Held Corporations 397
Purchasing Real Estate 138

Qualified Plans 178
Quitclaim deed 137

Racketeer Influenced and Corrupt Organizations Act (RICO)..163, 391

Radiation Producing Products, Imports 306
Radio Frequency Devices Imports..306
Radioactive Materials Imports 305, 306
Reaffirmation of Debt 65
Real Estate Development 140
Real Estate Law 135
Real Estate Transactions, Environmental Concerns 210
Real Estate, Leasing 138
Real Estate, Purchasing 138
Recording 137
Recoupment 255
Recovering Legal Fees 25
Recycling 210
Referral Services 2
Refugees.......................................281
Registering a Copyright 288
Registering a Trademark 44, 291
Religious Group 333
Reorganization Bankruptcy 65
Representation by Counsel.............17
Reputation, Lawyers 3
Required Officers 332
Required Purchases, UFOC 245
Rescission 15
Residents, U.S. 277
Resource Providing Contract 32
Respondeat Superior 339
Restrictions on Goods and Services, UFOC 246
Retainer Fees 7
Retaining an Attorney 5
Revocable Trusts 372
RICO (Racketeer Influenced and Corrupt Organizations Act) ..163, 391
Right of Election 370
Right of Way 136
Right to Refuse Medical Treatment 266
Rulemaking 226, 227
Rural Development Board 224

S Corporation 43
Sales Taxes.....................................87
Savings and Loan Association 422
Savings Banks 422
SBA (Small Business Administration) 423
SBA Loans 223
SBA's Office of Procurement Assistance 225
Scientific Organization 333
SCORE (Service Corps of Retired Executives) 225
Securities Act of 1993 419
Securities Exchange Act of 1934..419
Securities Fraud 161
Securities Law 417

Securities Markets 418
Security Deposit 140
Seeds, Imports 305
Selecting Counsel.............................1
Self-Employment Tax 86
Sentencing Guidelines 23
Service Corps of Retired Executives (SCORE) 225
Settlement......................................28
Settling Disputes 343
Settling Out of Court 26
Sexual Harassment 185
Sexual Harassment Cases in Arbitration 29
Shareholder Insulation from Debt and Liability 398
Shopping Agreement 41
Silver Imports...............................307
Sine Qua Non 385
Size of Law Firm 4
Slander 45
Small Business Administration (SBA) 223, 423
Small Business Subcontracting Directory....................................224
Social Security 184
Sole Proprietorship.........................97
Sole Proprietorship, Taxes 81
Solid Waste 207
Solid Waste Management Financial Assistance Program 224
Special Assessment 137
Special Magistrates 28
Specialization 3
Specific Performance 15
Spend-Down.................................262
State Banks....................................55
State Courts 18
State Financing.............................224
State Franchise Acts 251
State Government Law.................223
Statistics, UFOC...........................246
Statute of Frauds 14
Statutes of Limitation 21
Statutory Merger 404
Stay..64
Stay, Bankruptcy 66
Stock Acquisition 403
Stocks 417
Storage Tanks...............................208
Stray Voltage 209
Strict Liability 337, 338, 341
Strikes..320
Subchapter C Corporation 401
Subchapter S Corporation 82, 401
Sublease 137
Substance Abuse 188
Summary Jury Trials 28
Summons 22
Superfund 206

504 Business Guidebook to Law & Leading Attorneys

Subject Matter Index

Supplemental Medical Insurance ..263
Survivability 398
Suspension, Bankruptcy 67
Sweepstakes 48

Taft-Hartley Law 317
Tax Credits 83
Tax Identification Numbers 401
Tax Year 84
Tax-Exempt Corporation 329
Tax-Exempt Status 332
Taxpayer Identification Numbers ..83
Technical Assistance 224
Technology Information Services ..224
Tenancy in Common 138
Term Leases 139
Termination and Defamation 191
Termination and Other Events, UFOC 246
Termination at Will, Franchise 249
Termination for Good Cause, Franchise 249
Termination of Employment 190
Termination, Contract 14
Termination, Franchise ..241, 248, 253
Terms Implied by Operation of Law 255
Territorial Limitations, UFOC 245
Textiles Imports 308
Title 138
Title Insurance 138
Tort 337
Tourism Loan Program 224
Toxic Substances Imports 308
Toxic Torts 209
Trade Information Center..............309
Trade Secret Law 292
Trade Secrets 190
Trademark 44, 290
Trademark, Federal Registration ..291
Trademark, State Registration 292
Trademarks, UFOC 246
Transferability of Ownership 100
Travel Act......................................162
Trial Process 24
Trust Indenture Act of 1939..........419
Trustee in Bankruptcy 64
Trusts 371
Trusts Law 367

U.S. Citizenship 277
UFOC (Uniform Franchise Offering Circular) 242
Unemployment Insurance 182
Unemployment Tax 86
Unfair Labor Practice Strike 320
Uniform Franchise Offering Circular (UFOC)......................................242
Uniform Interagency Bank Rating System 57

Uniform Trade Secrets Act 292
Unilateral Contract 12
Union Negotiating 319
United States Supreme Court.........20
Unwritten Terms 255
Use Taxes 87
Utility Easements 136
Utility Patents...............................289

Variable Contingent Fees 8
Vegetables Imports........................305
Venture Capital Companies 422
Venture Finance Law 417
Venue 18
Veterans Reemployment Rights....189
Vicarious Liability 339
Visa..278
Voluntary Restraint Agreements ..308

Water Law 142
Water Quality 204
Whistleblower Statutes..................189
White Collar Crime 160
White Collar Crime, Avoiding Liability 165
Wildcat Strike...............................320
Will..367
Will Restrictions............................369
Will, Dying Without 370
Wills, Changing and Updating......369
Wire Fraud 163
Wool Imports 308
Workers' Compensation 183, 342
Workout Law 63
Workouts 68, 69
Workplace Health..........................186
Workplace Safety 186
Wrongful Death 342

Zoning 141

1994/1996 ♦ *Minnesota Edition* **505**

Index E: Listing Attorneys

Abdo, Kenneth J. - Abdo & Abdo, P.A. - Minneapolis - (612) 333-1526 ....**50**, 294
Ahern, Michael J. - Moss & Barnett, A Professional Association - Minneapolis - (612) 347-0274 ....**212**, 230, 270
Anderson, Douglas P. - Rosenmeier, Anderson & Vogel - Little Falls - (612) 632-5458 ....**345**
Anderson, John M. - Bassford, Lockhart, Truesdell & Briggs, P.A. - Minneapolis - (612) 333-3000 ....213, **346**
Andresen, Charles H. - Crassweller, Magie, Andresen, Haag & Paciotti, P.A. - Duluth - (218) 722-1411 ....**143**
Baer, Carl - Kief, Fuller, Baer, Wallner & Rodgers, Ltd. - Bemidji - (218) 751-2221 ....60, **119**, 346
Baillie, James L. - Fredrikson & Byron, P.A. - Minneapolis - (612) 347-7013 ....**70**, 119
Bannigan, John F. Jr. - Bannigan & Kelly, P.A. - St. Paul - (612) 224-3781 ....**144**, 230
Barnett, Timothy M. - Winthrop & Weinstine, P.A. - Minneapolis - (612) 347-0700 ....**103**, 406
Bartle, Emery W. - Dorsey & Whitney - Minneapolis - (612) 340-2600 ....193, **322**
Baudler, Bryan - Baudler, Baudler, Maus & Blahnik - Austin - (507) 433-2393 ....38, 119, **346**
Beck, Peter K. - Larkin, Hoffman, Daly & Lindgren, Ltd. - Bloomington - (612) 835-3800 ....144, 213, **230**
Berg, Larry J. - Fredrikson & Byron, P.A. - Minneapolis - (612) 347-7052 ....**144**
Bergerson, Stephen R. - Fredrikson & Byron, P.A. - Minneapolis - (612) 347-7025 ....**51**, 294
Bland, J. Richard - Meagher & Geer - Minneapolis - (612) 338-0661 ....346, **392**
Blethen, Bailey W. - Blethen Gage & Krause - Mankato - (507) 345-1166 ....120, 167, **193**
Bluth, Joseph P. - Manahan & Bluth Law Office, Chartered - Mankato - (507) 387-5661 ....**167**, 213
Boelter, Philip F. - Dorsey & Whitney - Minneapolis - (612) 340-2600 ....**145**
Bowman, Richard A. - Bowman and Brooke - Minneapolis - (612) 339-8682 ....120, **347**, 392
Brand, Martha C. - Leonard, Street and Deinard Professional Association - Minneapolis - (612) 335-1500 ....**213**
Brand, Steve A. - Robins, Kaplan, Miller & Ciresi - Minneapolis - (612) 349-8500 ....**375**
Breitman, Richard L. - The Breitman Immigration Law Firm - Minneapolis - (612) 822-4724 ....194, **284**, 312
Brown, Frederick C. Jr. - Popham, Haik, Schnobrich & Kaufman, Ltd. - Minneapolis - (612) 333-4800 ....120, **347**, 392
Brown, Ronald J. - Dorsey & Whitney - Minneapolis - (612) 340-2600 ....120, **294**
Bruno, Frederic - Frederic Bruno & Associates - Minneapolis - (612) 545-7900 ....**168**
Brynestad, Lorens Q. - Jensen & Swanson - Brooklyn Park - (612) 424-8811 ....**145**, 213, 375
Burk, Robert S. - Popham, Haik, Schnobrich & Kaufman, Ltd. - Minneapolis - (612) 333-4800 ....194, 213, **323**
Burns, Richard R. - Hanft, Fride, O'Brien, Harries, Swelbar & Burns, P.A. - Duluth - (218) 722-4766 ....**51**, 376
Burns, William M. - Hanft, Fride, O'Brien, Harries, Swelbar & Burns, P.A. - Duluth - (218) 722-4766 ......145, 270, **406**
Bye, Don L. - Halverson, Watters, Bye, Downs, Reyelts & Bateman, Ltd. - Duluth - (218) 727-6833 ....180, **323**
Campbell, Craig R. - Gunhus, Grinnell, Klinger, Swenson & Guy, Ltd. - Moorhead - (218) 236-6462 ....120, **348**, 392
Carlson, Alan G. - Merchant, Gould, Smith, Edell, Welter & Schmidt, P.A. - Minneapolis - (612) 332-5300 ....**294**
Carlson, Steven E. - Dorsey & Whitney - London - (612) 340-2600 ....60, **312**
Carpenter, Kevin S. - Quinlivan, Sherwood, Spellacy & Tarvestad, P.A. - St. Cloud - (612) 251-1414 ....120, **348**, 393
Christoffel, James F. - Christoffel, Elliott & Albrecht, P.A. - Minneapolis - (612) 672-0900 ....60, 71, **146**
Ciresi, Michael V. - Robins, Kaplan, Miller & Ciresi - Minneapolis - (612) 349-8500 ....**120**, 295
Clinton, Jack W. - Jack W. Clinton, P.A. - Cottage Grove - (612) 459-6644 ....**231**, 376
Cole, Phillip A. - Lommen, Nelson, Cole & Stageberg, P.A. - Minneapolis - (612) 339-8131 ....**121**, 348, 393
Comstock, Rebecca A. - Dorsey & Whitney - Minneapolis - (612) 340-2600 ....**214**, 231
Constantine, Katherine A. - Dorsey & Whitney - Minneapolis - (612) 340-2600 ....60, **71**
Cooper, Peter L. - McGrann Shea Franzen Carnival Straughn & Lamb, Chartered - Minneapolis - (612) 338-2525 ....**146**, 231
Corwin, Gregg M. - Gregg M. Corwin & Associates - St. Louis Park - (612) 544-7774 ....180, 194, **324**
Cosgriff, William J. - Doherty, Rumble & Butler Professional Association - St. Paul - (612) 291-9333 ....104, **147**, 406

Crawford, Rollin H. - LeVander, Gillen & Miller, P.A. - South St. Paul - (612) 451-1831 ....147, **231**, 336
Cutler, Kenneth L. - Dorsey & Whitney - Minneapolis - (612) 340-2600 ....104, **406**, 425
Dady, J. Michael - J. Michael Dady & Associates, P.A. - Minneapolis - (612) 359-9000 ....121, **259**
Damon, Matthew E. - Popham, Haik, Schnobrich & Kaufman, Ltd. - Minneapolis - (612) 333-4800 ....**194**, 324
Danielson, Laura J. - Patterson & Keough, P.A. - Minneapolis - (612) 349-5740 ....51, **284**, 295
D'Aquila, Barbara Jean - Cosgrove, Flynn & Gaskins - Minneapolis - (612) 333-9500 ....**195**, 324
Dayton, Charles K. - Leonard, Street and Deinard Professional Association - Minneapolis - (612) 335-1500 ....121, **214**, 231
Deaner, Ted E. - O'Brien, Ehrick, Wolf, Deaner & Maus - Rochester - (507) 289-4041 ....**71**, 147, 195
Degnan, John M. - Bassford, Lockhart, Truesdell & Briggs, P.A. - Minneapolis - (612) 333-3000 ....**121**, 348, 393
Devoy, Kimball J. - Doherty, Rumble & Butler Professional Association - St. Paul - (612) 291-9333 ....**90**, 104
Dickel, Morris - Dickel, Johannson, Taylor, Rust & Tye, P.A. - Crookston - (218) 281-2400 ....**38**, 104, 376
Diehl, John E. - Larkin, Hoffman, Daly & Lindgren, Ltd. - Bloomington - (612) 835-3800 ....**270**
Dudderar, Frederick A. - Hanft, Fride, O'Brien, Harries, Swelbar & Burns, P.A. - Duluth - (218) 722-4766 ....**72**, 104, 122
Dunlevy, Shawn M. - Fryberger, Buchanan, Smith & Frederick, P.A. - Duluth - (218) 722-0861 ....**61**, 72, 122
Dunn, James F. - Dunn & Elliott, P.A. - St. Paul - (612) 221-9048 ....122, 231, **349**
Eastwood, J. Marquis - Dorsey & Whitney - Minneapolis - (612) 340-2600 ....122, **195**
Edell, Robert T. - Merchant, Gould, Smith, Edell, Welter & Schmidt, P.A. - Minneapolis - (612) 332-5300 ....**295**
Edstrom, Dean R. - Doherty, Rumble & Butler Professional Association - Minneapolis - (612) 340-5575 ....104, **407**, 425
Eide, David B. - Frommelt & Eide, Ltd. - Minneapolis - (612) 332-2200 ....104, **147**
Eller, Daniel A. - Eller Law Office - St. Cloud - (612) 253-3700 ....**168**
Elliott, Christopher A. - Christoffel, Elliott & Albrecht, P.A. - Minneapolis - (612) 672-0900 ....61, **72**, 148
Engh, Rolf - Valspar Corporation Counsel - Minneapolis - (612) 375-7705 ....**407**
Erhart, John J. - Fredrikson & Byron, P.A. - Minneapolis - (612) 347-7035 ....**91**, 104
Erickson, James C. - Larkin, Hoffman, Daly & Lindgren, Ltd. - Bloomington - (612) 835-3800 ....**232**
Fairbairn, David R. - Kinney & Lange, P.A. - Minneapolis - (612) 339-1863 ....51, 122, **295**
Finley, Joseph M. - Leonard, Street and Deinard Professional Association - Minneapolis - (612) 335-1500 ....**148**
Fisher, Linda - Larkin, Hoffman, Daly & Lindgren, Ltd. - Bloomington - (612) 835-3800 ....148, **215**
Flaskamp, William D. - Meagher & Geer - Minneapolis - (612) 338-0661 ....**349**, 393
Flynn, George W. - Cosgrove, Flynn & Gaskins - Minneapolis - (612) 333-9500 ....122, **350**
Ford, Michael J. - Quinlivan, Sherwood, Spellacy & Tarvestad, P.A. - St. Cloud - (612) 251-1414 ....122, **196**, 393
Frécon, Alain - Frécon & Associates - Minneapolis - (612) 338-6868 ....91, 295, **313**
Frederick, Harold A. - Fryberger, Buchanan, Smith & Frederick, P.A. - Duluth - (218) 722-0861 ....148, 232, **271**
Freeman, Todd I. - Larkin, Hoffman, Daly & Lindgren, Ltd. - Bloomington - (612) 835-3800 ....91, **104**, 271
Freitag, Gregory G. - Fredrikson & Byron, P.A. - Minneapolis - (612) 347-7153 ....407, **425**
French, John D. - Faegre & Benson - Minneapolis - (612) 336-3000 ....**122**, 407
Friedberg, Joseph S. - Friedberg Law Office - Minneapolis - (612) 339-8626 ....**169**
Frommelt, Roger H. - Frommelt & Eide, Ltd. - Minneapolis - (612) 332-2200 ....148, 407, **426**
Gage, F. Kelton - Blethen Gage & Krause - Mankato - (507) 345-1166 ....**105**, 122, 426
Galvin, Michael J. Jr. - Briggs and Morgan, P.A. - St. Paul - (612) 223-6600 ....196, **324**
Ginsburg, Roy A. - Dorsey & Whitney - Minneapolis - (612) 340-2600 ....122, **196**
Gislason, Barbara J. - Barbara J. Gislason & Associates - Minneapolis - (612) 331-8033 ....**52**, 197, 295
Gordon, John B. - Faegre & Benson - Minneapolis - (612) 336-3000 ....122, **215**, 350
Gordon, Roger D. - Winthrop & Weinstine, P.A. - Minneapolis - (612) 347-0700 ....61, **408**, 426
Gordon, Stephen D. - Gordon Miller O'Brien - Minneapolis - (612) 333-5831 ....180, 197, **325**
Gould, John D. - Merchant, Gould, Smith, Edell, Welter & Schmidt, P.A. - Minneapolis - (612) 332-5300 ....**296**
Grasmoen, Cheryl L. - Petersen, Tews & Squires - Minneapolis - (612) 344-1600 ....**148**, 215
Greenswag, Douglas B. - Leonard, Street and Deinard Professional Association - Minneapolis - (612) 335-1527 ....61, **72**
Grindal, H. Theodore - Schatz Paquin Lockridge Grindal & Holstein - Minneapolis - (612) 339-6900 ....232, **271**
Grinnell, Paul E. - Gunhus, Grinnell, Klinger, Swenson & Guy, Ltd. - Moorhead - (218) 236-6462 ....122, **350**, 393

Index E: Listing Attorneys

Grooms, Lloyd W. - Winthrop & Weinstine, P.A. - St. Paul - (612) 290-8529 ....**216,** 408
Gunhus, Gunder D. - Gunhus, Grinnell, Klinger, Swenson & Guy, Ltd. - Moorhead - (218) 236-6462 ....123, **351,** 393
Guy, William L. III - Gunhus, Grinnell, Klinger, Swenson & Guy, Ltd. - Moorhead - (218) 236-6462 ....149, **376,** 408
Haik, Raymond A. - Popham, Haik, Schnobrich & Kaufman, Ltd. - Minneapolis - (612) 333-4800 ....**216,** 232
Halleland, Keith J. - Popham, Haik, Schnobrich & Kaufman, Ltd. - Minneapolis - (612) 333-4800 ....**272**
Hamel, Mark E. - Dorsey & Whitney - Minneapolis - (612) 340-2600 ....**149**
Hamre, Curtis B. - Merchant, Gould, Smith, Edell, Welter & Schmidt, P.A. - Minneapolis - (612) 332-5300 ....**296**
Hanley, Bruce H. - Bruce H. Hanley, P.A. - Minneapolis - (612) 339-1290 ....**169**
Hansen, Karen - Popham, Haik, Schnobrich & Kaufman, Ltd. - Minneapolis - (612) 333-4800 ....123, 149, **217**
Hanson, Bruce E. - Doherty, Rumble & Butler Professional Association - St. Paul - (612) 291-9333 ....**272**
Hanson, Lee W. - Hall, Byers, Hanson, Steil & Weinberger, P.A. - St. Cloud - (612) 252-4414 ....**105,** 149, 408
Harries, Gilbert W. - Hanft, Fride, O'Brien, Harries, Swelbar & Burns, P.A. - Duluth - (218) 722-4766 ....149, **217,** 377
Haugen, Orrin M. - Haugen & Nikolai, P.A. - Minneapolis - (612) 339-7461 ....**297**
Hay, Nick - Moss & Barnett, A Professional Association - Minneapolis - (612) 347-0300 ....**91,** 105, 408
Heaney, Timothy M. - Fredrikson & Byron, P.A. - Minneapolis - (612) 347-7019 ....408, **426**
Heiberg, Robert A. - Dorsey & Whitney - Minneapolis - (612) 340-2600 ....**150**
Heilman, Edward G. - Heilman Law Firm - Minneapolis - (612) 338-5230 ....**377**
Hemphill, Stuart R. - Dorsey & Whitney - Minneapolis - (612) 340-2600 ....52, **297**
Hendrixson, Peter S. - Dorsey & Whitney - Minneapolis - (612) 340-2600 ....**123,** 427
Heuel, Daniel J. - Muir, Heuel, Carlson & Spelhaug, P.A. - Rochester - (507) 288-4110 ....123, 197, **351**
Hibbs, John S. - Dorsey & Whitney - Minneapolis - (612) 340-2600 ....92, **273,** 336
Hippee, William H. Jr. - Dorsey & Whitney - Minneapolis - (612) 340-2600 ....**92,** 105
Hobbins, Robert L. - Dorsey & Whitney - Minneapolis - (612) 340-2600 ....197, **325**
Hoch, Gary W. - Meagher & Geer - Minneapolis - (612) 338-0661 ....123, **352,** 393
Hoff, George C. - Hoff, Barry & Kuderer, P.A. - Eden Prairie - (612) 941-9220 ....**232**
Hoffman, Robert L. - Larkin, Hoffman, Daly & Lindgren, Ltd. - Bloomington - (612) 835-3800 ....150, **233**
Hogan, Barry P. - Jeffries, Olson, Flom, Oppegard & Hogan, P.A. - Fargo - (701) 280-2300 ....123, 233, **352**
Holper, Richard D. - Holper Welsh & Mitchell, Ltd. - Minneapolis - (612) 373-2200 ....**73**
Hughes, Kathleen A. - Fredrikson & Byron, P.A. - Minneapolis - (612) 347-7037 ....**197,** 325
Hughes, Kevin J. - Hughes, Mathews & Didier, P.A. - St. Cloud - (612) 251-4399 ....123, 197, **273**
Iannacone, Michael J. - Iannacone Law Office - St. Paul - (612) 224-3361 ....**73,** 123
Jeffries, Richard N. - Jeffries, Olson, Flom, Oppegard & Hogan, P.A. - Moorhead - (218) 233-3222 ....123, 352, **393**
Jensen, Roger A. - Peterson, Bell, Converse & Jensen, P.A. - Minneapolis - (612) 342-2323 ....197, 233, **326**
Johannson, Kenneth F. - Dickel, Johannson, Taylor, Rust & Tye, P.A. - Crookston - (218) 281-2400 ....**353**
Johnson, Craig W. - Hoversten, Strom, Johnson & Rysavy - Austin - (507) 433-3483 ....**150**
Johnson, Eugene L. - Dorsey & Whitney - Minneapolis - (612) 340-2600 ....52, **298**
Johnson, G. Robert - Popham, Haik, Schnobrich & Kaufman, Ltd. - Minneapolis - (612) 333-4800 ....**218**
Johnson, Jeffrey S. - Barna, Guzy & Steffen, Ltd. - Minneapolis - (612) 780-8500 ....61, **151**
Johnson, Joel D. - Dosland, Nordhougen, Lillehaug & Johnson, P.A. - Moorhead - (218) 233-2744 ....**106,** 151, 377
Johnson, Larry W. - Dorsey & Whitney - Minneapolis - (612) 340-2600 ....**377**
Johnstone, William A. - Dorsey & Whitney - Minneapolis - (612) 340-2600 ....**233**
Jonason, William A. - Dorsey & Whitney - Rochester - (507) 288-3156 ....92, **106**
Kantor, David - Leonard, Street and Deinard Professional Association - Minneapolis - (612) 335-1500 ....61, 73, **151**
Kaplan, Elliot S. - Robins, Kaplan, Miller & Ciresi - Minneapolis - (612) 349-8500 ....**124,** 260, 408
Karp, Michael C. - Blethen Gage & Krause - Mankato - (507) 345-1166 ....92, **107,** 180
Kelley, David W. - Leonard, Street and Deinard Professional Association - Minneapolis - (612) 335-1500 ....61, 73, **152**
Kelley, Douglas A. - Douglas A. Kelley, P.A. - Minneapolis - (612) 337-9594 ....**170,** 274, 408
Kelly, John D. - Hanft, Fride, O'Brien, Harries, Swelbar & Burns, P.A. - Duluth - (218) 722-4766 ....**124,** 353, 393
Kennedy, Charles R. - Kennedy & Nervig - Wadena - (218) 631-2505 ....125, **353**

Kennedy, David J. - Holmes & Graven, Chartered - Minneapolis - (612) 337-9300 .... **234**
Keppel, William J. - Dorsey & Whitney - Minneapolis - (612) 340-2600 .... 125, **218**, 234
Kershner, H. Morrison - Pemberton, Sorlie, Sefkow, Rufer & Kershner - Fergus Falls - (218) 736-5493 .... 125, 197, **354**
Killen, John J. - Johnson, Killen, Thibodeau & Seiler, P.A. - Duluth - (218) 722-6331 ....**107**, 125, 408
King, D. Randall - Merchant, Gould, Smith, Edell, Welter & Schmidt, P.A. - Minneapolis - (612) 332-5300..............................**298**
King, Lawrence R. - King & Hatch - St. Paul - (612) 223-2856 .... 197, **354**, 393
King, Thomas R. - Fredrikson & Byron, P.A. - Minneapolis - (612) 347-7059..**408**, 427
Kirby, John D. - Dorsey & Whitney - Minneapolis - (612) 340-2600 ....**234**
Knapp, John A. - Winthrop & Weinstine, P.A. - St. Paul - (612) 290-8400 ....52, 218, **235**
Knowles, Faye - Fredrikson & Byron, P.A. - Minneapolis - (612) 347-7054 ....**74**, 125, 408
Koneck, John M. - Fredrikson & Byron, P.A. - Minneapolis - (612) 347-7038 ....74, **152**
Kueppers, Frederick A. Jr. - Kueppers, Hackel & Kueppers, P.A. - St. Paul - (612) 228-1104 ....107, **153**, 377
Kuller, Hart - Winthrop & Weinstine, P.A. - St. Paul - (612) 290-8400 ....**74**, 153, 408
Kunkel, Phillip L. - Hall, Byers, Hanson, Steil & Weinberger, P.A. - St. Cloud - (612) 252-4414 ....**75**, 153
Kuntz, Timothy J. - LeVander, Gillen & Miller, P.A. - South St. Paul - (612) 451-1831 ....107, 125, **235**
Lantz, W. Charles - Dorsey & Whitney - Rochester - (507) 288-3156 ....61, 107, **153**
Lapp, William S. - Lapp, Laurie, Libra, Abramson & Thomson, Chartered - Minneapolis - (612) 338-5815 ....**409**
Larsen, Dexter A. - Fryberger, Buchanan, Smith & Frederick, P.A. - Duluth - (218) 722-0861 ....**299**, 409
Laurie, Gerald T. - Lapp, Laurie, Libra, Abramson & Thomson, Chartered - Minneapolis - (612) 338-5815 ....125, **198**
Lawrence, Douglas M. - Moss & Barnett, A Professional Association - Minneapolis - (612) 347-0300...61, **75**
LeFevere, Charles L. - Holmes & Graven, Chartered - Minneapolis - (612) 337-9300 ....198, 219, **236**
Leonard, Brian F. - O'Neill, Burke, O'Neill, Leonard & O'Brien, Ltd. - Minneapolis - (612) 332-1030 ....61, **76**, 409
Lervick, John C. - Swenson, Grover, Lervick, Syverson, Battey & Anderson, Ltd. - Alexandria - (612) 763-3141 ....125, 236, **355**
Linstroth, Paul J. - Popham, Haik, Schnobrich & Kaufman, Ltd. - Minneapolis - (612) 333-4800 ....**92**
Litsey, Calvin L. - Faegre & Benson - Minneapolis - (612) 336-3000 ....**52**, 299
Little, Bruce H. - Popham, Haik, Schnobrich & Kaufman, Ltd. - Minneapolis - (612) 333-4800 ....**53**, 299
Lockhart, Greer E. - Bassford, Lockhart, Truesdell & Briggs, P.A. - Minneapolis - (612) 333-3000 ....125, 274, **394**
Logstrom, Bridget A. - Dorsey & Whitney - Minneapolis - (612) 343-7945 ....**378**
Lubben, David J. - Dorsey & Whitney - Minneapolis - (612) 340-2600 ....409, **427**
McDonald, John R. - Robins, Kaplan, Miller & Ciresi - Minneapolis - (612) 349-8500..61, **76**
McDowell, Gary D. - Arnold & McDowell - Minneapolis - (612) 545-9000 ....107, 125, **378**
Madson, Eric O. - Winthrop & Weinstine, P.A. - Minneapolis - (612) 347-0700 ....107, 409, **428**
Magnuson, Roger J. - Dorsey & Whitney - Minneapolis - (612) 340-2600 ....**125**, 170, 428
Mahoney, Jerry C.D. - Dorsey & Whitney - Minneapolis - (612) 340-2600 ....**236**
Malone, Robert G. - Attorney at Law - St. Paul - (612) 227-6549 ....**170**
Mansfield, Seymour J. - Mansfield & Tanick, P.A. - Minneapolis - (612) 339-4295 ....107, **126**, 198
Marben, Kurt J. - Charlson, Marben & Jorgenson, P.A. - Thief River Falls - (218) 681-4002 ....126, **355**
Maring, David S. - Maring Law Office - Fargo - (701) 237-5297 ....**126**, 355
Martin, James T. - Gislason, Martin & Varpness, P.A. - Minneapolis - (612) 831-5793 ....**127**, 355, 394
Martin, Phillip H. - Dorsey & Whitney - Minneapolis - (612) 340-2600..**93**
Maschka, Gerald L. - Farrish, Johnson & Maschka - Mankato - (507) 387-3002 ....127, **356**, 394
Mattos, Patricia G. - Attorney at Law - St. Paul - (612) 698-8841 ....**285**
Meshbesher, Ronald I. - Meshbesher & Spence, Ltd. - Minneapolis - (612) 339-9121 ....**171**
Meyer, Michael L. - Ravich, Meyer, Kirkman & McGrath, P.A. - Minneapolis - (612) 332-8511 ....**77**
Mickelsen, Ruth A. - Allina Health System - Minnetonka - (612) 936-1609 ....**274**, 336
Miller, David B. - Faegre & Benson - Minneapolis - (612) 336-3000 ....62, 409, **428**
Mitau, Lee R. - Dorsey & Whitney - Minneapolis - (612) 340-2600 ....**410**, 429
Mohr, Gordon G. - Attorney at Law - Bloomington - (612) 831-0944 ....127, **171**
Moos, Rebecca Egge - Bassford, Lockhart, Truesdell & Briggs, P.A. - Minneapolis - (612) 333-3000 ....**356**

Index E: Listing Attorneys

Morris, Ralph K. - Doherty, Rumble & Butler Professional Association - St. Paul - (612) 291-9333 ....**39**
Muck, Thomas R. - Fredrikson & Byron, P.A. - Minneapolis - (612) 347-7045 ....**93**, 127
Muir, Ross - Muir, Heuel, Carlson & Spelhaug, P.A. - Rochester - (507) 288-4110 ....127, **357**, 394
Myers, Howard S. III - Popham, Haik, Schnobrich & Kaufman, Ltd. - Minneapolis - (612) 333-4800 ....**285**
Nauen, Charles N. - Schatz Paquin Lockridge Grindal & Holstein - Minneapolis - (612) 339-6900 ....127, **219**
Nawrocki, Lawrence M. - Nawrocki, Rooney & Sivertson, P.A. - Minneapolis - (612) 331-1464 ....**299**
Nelson, Janice M. - Nelson Oyen Torvik - Montevideo - (612) 269-6461 ....**108**, 153, 378
Nelson, Steven C. - Dorsey & Whitney - Minneapolis - (612) 340-2600 ....**313**
Nelson, Sue Ann - Doherty, Rumble & Butler Professional Association - Minneapolis - (612) 340-5590 ....**94**, 127
Nelson, Thomas F. - Popham, Haik, Schnobrich & Kaufman, Ltd. - Minneapolis - (612) 333-4800 ....**128**, 394, 410
Nilan, Michael T. - Popham, Haik, Schnobrich & Kaufman, Ltd. - Minneapolis - (612) 333-4800 ....128, **429**
Nordhougen, Curtis A. - Dosland, Nordhougen, Lillehaug & Johnson, P.A. - Moorhead - (218) 233-2744 ....**108**, 153, 378
Nowlin, Forrest D. - Doherty, Rumble & Butler Professional Association - St. Paul - (612) 291-9333 ....**219**, 236
Nys, John N. - Johnson, Killen, Thibodeau & Seiler, P.A. - Duluth - (218) 722-6331 ....128, **410**
O'Brien, James E. - Moss & Barnett, A Professional Association - Minneapolis - (612) 347-0273 ....108, **411**, 429
O'Brien, Maurice W. - Gordon Miller O'Brien - Minneapolis - (612) 333-5831 ....180, 198, **326**
O'Neill, Brian B. - Faegre & Benson - Minneapolis - (612) 336-3000 ....128, **220**
O'Toole, Dennis L. - Lano, Nelson, O'Toole & Bengtson, Ltd. - Grand Rapids - (218) 326-9603 ....128, 220, **357**
Patrick, Howard A. - Robins, Kaplan, Miller & Ciresi - Minneapolis - (612) 349-8500 ....62, **77**
Payne, James A. - Popham, Haik, Schnobrich & Kaufman, Ltd. - Minneapolis - (612) 333-4800 ....**220**
Pemberton, Richard L. - Pemberton, Sorlie, Sefkow, Rufer & Kershner - Fergus Falls - (218) 736-5493 ....198, **357**, 394
Person, John W. - Breen & Person, Ltd. - Brainerd - (218) 828-1248 ....**154**, 358
Peterson, Bruce A. - Popham, Haik, Schnobrich & Kaufman, Ltd. - Minneapolis - (612) 333-4800 ....128, **172**, 236
Peterson, David T. - Blethen Gage & Krause - Mankato - (507) 345-1166 ....**109**, 198, 411
Peterson, H. Jeffrey - Cope & Peterson, P.A. - Virginia - (218) 749-4470 ....128, **358**, 394
Popham, Wayne G. - Popham, Haik, Schnobrich & Kaufman, Ltd. - Minneapolis - (612) 333-4800 ....**237**
Powell, Romaine R. - Powell, Powell & Aamodt - Bemidji - (218) 751-5650 ....**358**
Prescott, Jack L. - Prescott & Pearson, P.A. - New Brighton - (612) 633-2757 ....**78**
Prichard, Michael - Dorsey & Whitney - Minneapolis - (612) 340-2600 ....109, 285, **314**
Provo, John W. - Popham, Haik, Schnobrich & Kaufman, Ltd. - Minneapolis - (612) 333-4800 ....53, **379**
Quinlivan, John D. - Quinlivan, Sherwood, Spellacy & Tarvestad, P.A. - St. Cloud - (612) 251-1414 ....128, **359**, 394
Quinlivan, Michael R. - Arthur, Chapman, McDonough, Kettering & Smetak, P.A. - Minneapolis - (612) 339-3500 ....**199**, 359, 394
Radio, Thomas J. - Popham, Haik, Schnobrich & Kaufman, Ltd. - Minneapolis - (612) 333-4800 ....128, **237**, 359
Rajkowski, Frank J. - Rajkowski Hansmeier, Ltd. - St. Cloud - (612) 251-1055 ....128, 180, **359**
Ranum, Robert K. - Fredrikson & Byron, P.A. - Minneapolis - (612) 347-7067 ....411, **429**
Ravich, Paul H. - Ravich, Meyer, Kirkman & McGrath, P.A. - Minneapolis - (612) 332-8511 ....**154**
Regan, John E. - Regan, Regan & Meyer - Mankato - (507) 345-1179 ....**109**, 379
Regnier, Pierre N. - Jardine, Logan & O'Brien - St. Paul - (612) 290-6590 ....237, **360**, 394
Remele, Lewis A. Jr. - Bassford, Lockhart, Truesdell & Briggs, P.A. - Minneapolis - (612) 333-3000 ....**129**, 360, 394
Richards, Carver - Trenti Law Firm - Virginia - (218) 749-1962 ....129, **360**, 394
Richter, Scott E. - Popham, Haik, Schnobrich & Kaufman, Ltd. - Minneapolis - (612) 333-4800 ....129, **430**
Ries, Charles W. - Farrish, Johnson & Maschka - Mankato - (507) 387-3002 ....**78**, 94
Riley, James M. - Meagher & Geer - Minneapolis - (612) 338-0661 ....129, **361**, 394
Roby, Joseph J. Jr. - Johnson, Killen, Thibodeau & Seiler, P.A. - Duluth - (218) 722-6331 ....129, 199, **327**
Rockwell, James W. - Popham, Haik, Schnobrich & Kaufman, Ltd. - Minneapolis - (612) 333-4800 ....**379**
Rodenberg, John R. - Berens, Rodenberg & O'Connor - New Ulm - (507) 354-3161 ....39, 199, **361**
Roegge, James F. - Meagher & Geer - Minneapolis - (612) 338-0661 ....129, 362, **395**
Rohricht, Thomas E. - Doherty, Rumble & Butler Professional Association - St. Paul - (612) 291-9333 ....62, 109, **411**
Ross, Richard A. - Fredrikson & Byron, P.A. - Minneapolis - (612) 347-7022 ....199, **327**

Roth, Randi Ilyse - Farmers' Legal Action Group, Inc. - St. Paul - (612) 223-5400 ....**39,** 78, 237
Rubenstein, James A. - Moss & Barnett, A Professional Association - Minneapolis - (612) 347-0300 ....**78,** 129, 154
Rysavy, Donald E. - Hoversten, Strom, Johnson & Rysavy - Austin - (507) 433-3483...199, **362**
Saeks, Allen I. - Leonard, Street and Deinard Professional Association - Minneapolis - (612) 335-1548..62, 79, **130**
Sanders, Thomas P. - Leonard, Street and Deinard Professional Association - Minneapolis - (612) 335-1614 ....109, **412**
Sawicki, Z. Peter - Kinney & Lange, P.A. - Minneapolis - (612) 339-1863 ....53, **300**
Sayre, Grover C. III - O'Neill, Burke, O'Neill, Leonard & O'Brien, Ltd. - Minneapolis - (612) 332-1030 ....79, 154, **412**
Scheerer, Paul J. - Dorsey & Whitney - Minneapolis - (612) 340-2600 ....**79,** 412
Schmidt, Cecil C. - Merchant, Gould, Smith, Edell, Welter & Schmidt, P.A. - St. Paul - (612) 298-1055 ....**300**
Schulz, John R. - Collins, Buckley, Sauntry & Haugh - St. Paul - (612) 227-0611 ....130, **362,** 395
Seaton, Douglas P. - Popham, Haik, Schnobrich & Kaufman, Ltd. - Minneapolis - (612) 333-4800 ....**199,** 327
Sefkow, Robert J. - Pemberton, Sorlie, Sefkow, Rufer & Kershner - Fergus Falls - (218) 736-5493..**62,** 79, **130**
Seiler, Steven J. - Johnson, Killen, Thibodeau & Seiler, P.A. - Duluth - (218) 722-6331 ....**274,** 379, **412**
Sellergren, David C. - Doherty, Rumble & Butler Professional Association - Minneapolis - (612) 340-5555 ....154, 221, **238**
Severson, Robert K. - Brink, Sobolik, Severson, Vroom & Malm, P.A. - Hallock - (218) 843-3686...............................62, **130,** 362
Sharpe, W. Smith Jr. - Faegre & Benson - Minneapolis - (612) 336-3000 ....412, **430**
Sheehy, Lee E. - Popham, Haik, Schnobrich & Kaufman, Ltd. - Minneapolis - (612) 333-4800...53, **238**
Shnider, Bruce J. - Dorsey & Whitney - Minneapolis - (612) 340-2600 ....**94**
Shulman, David A. - Gartner & Shulman, Ltd. - Rochester - (507) 288-3078 ....**131**
Silverman, Robert J. - Dorsey & Whitney - Minneapolis - (612) 340-2742 ....**155**
Sipkins, Peter W. - Dorsey & Whitney - Minneapolis - (612) 340-2600 ....**131,** 362
Smith, Nick - Fryberger, Buchanan, Smith & Frederick, P.A. - Duluth - (218) 722-0861 ....336, **413**
Smith, Louis N. - Popham, Haik, Schnobrich & Kaufman, Ltd. - Minneapolis - (612) 333-4800 ....**239,** 285
Smith, Ralph T. - Smith Law Firm, P. A. - Bemidji - (218) 751-3130..155, **328,** 379
Snyder, Stephen J. - Winthrop & Weinstine, P.A. - St. Paul - (612) 290-8400 ....131, **200**
Sobolik, Dennis M. - Brink, Sobolik, Severson, Vroom & Malm, P.A. - Hallock - (218) 843-3686............................**40,** 62, 379
Soth, William R. - Dorsey & Whitney - Minneapolis - (612) 340-2600...**155,** 239
Soule, George W. - Bowman and Brooke - Minneapolis - (612) 339-8682 ....131, **363,** 395
Spellacy, Kevin A. - Quinlivan, Sherwood, Spellacy & Tarvestad, P.A. - St. Cloud - (612) 251-1414...............................221, **363,** 395
Spevacek, Charles E. - Meagher & Geer - Minneapolis - (612) 338-0661 ....131, **221,** 395
Stageberg, Roger V. - Lommen, Nelson, Cole & Stageberg, P.A. - Minneapolis - (612) 339-8131 ....**110,** 413, 431
Starns, Byron E. - Leonard, Street and Deinard Professional Association - Minneapolis - (612) 335-1516......................131, **221,** 239
Stewart, James H. - Fryberger, Buchanan, Smith & Frederick, P.A. - Duluth - (218) 722-0861 ....95, 110, **380**
Stout, John H. - Fredrikson & Byron, P.A. - Minneapolis - (612) 347-7012 ....**54,** 413, 431
Straughn, Robert O. - McGrann Shea Franzen Carnival Straughn & Lamb, Chartered - Minneapolis - (612) 338-2525 ....**156,** 221
Strawbridge, Douglas A. - Merchant, Gould, Smith, Edell, Welter & Schmidt, P.A. - Minneapolis - (612) 332-5300 ....**301**
Strinden, Jon E. - Gunhus, Grinnell, Klinger, Swenson & Guy, Ltd. - Moorhead - (218) 236-6462 ....95, **110,** 413
Stuart, Barbara G. - U.S. Trustee-Region 12 - Cedar Rapids, IA - (319) 364-2211 ....**79**
Stumo, Mary E. - Faegre & Benson - Minneapolis - (612) 336-3000 ....**200**
Sumners, John S. - Merchant, Gould, Smith, Edell, Welter & Schmidt, P.A. - Minneapolis - (612) 332-5300 ....54, **301**
Swelbar, Gaylord W. - Hanft, Fride, O'Brien, Harries, Swelbar & Burns, P.A. - Duluth - (218) 722-4766 ....132, **364,** 395
Tanick, Marshall H. - Mansfield & Tanick, P.A. - Minneapolis - (612) 339-4295 ....54, **201,** 328
Tarvestad, Anthony M. - Quinlivan, Sherwood, Spellacy & Tarvestad, P.A. - St. Cloud - (612) 251-1414...............239, 364, **395**
Taylor, Frank A. - Popham, Haik, Schnobrich & Kaufman, Ltd. - Minneapolis - (612) 333-4800...**431**
Thibodeau, Thomas R. - Johnson, Killen, Thibodeau & Seiler, P.A. - Duluth - (218) 722-6331 ....132, 222, **364**
Thomson, James J. - Holmes & Graven, Chartered - Minneapolis - (612) 337-9300 ....132, **239**
Thoreen, Gerald L. - Hughes, Thoreen & Knapp, P.A. - St. Cloud - (612) 251-6175..110, 336, **380**
Thorsen, Madge S. - Popham, Haik, Schnobrich & Kaufman, Ltd. - Minneapolis - (612) 333-4800 ....132, **365**
Tinkham, Thomas W. - Dorsey & Whitney - Minneapolis - (612) 340-2600 ....**132,** 201, 301

Index E: Listing Attorneys

Torgerson, Paul M. - Dorsey & Whitney - Minneapolis - (612) 340-2600 .... 95, **275**, 336
Torvik, Stephen - Nelson Oyen Torvik - Montevideo - (612) 269-6461 .... 132, 156, **413**
Trucano, Michael - Dorsey & Whitney - Minneapolis - (612) 340-2600 .... 95, **111**, 431
Truesdell, Lynn G. - Bassford, Lockhart, Truesdell & Briggs, P.A. - Minneapolis - (612) 333-3000 .... **132**, 365, 396
Tyra, Kenneth T. - Dorsey & Whitney - Minneapolis - (612) 340-2600 .... 80, 111, **156**
Van de North, John B. Jr. - Briggs and Morgan, P.A. - St. Paul - (612) 223-6600 .... 40, **222**
Van Valkenburg, Paul - Moss & Barnett, A Professional Association - Minneapolis - (612) 347-0300 .... 260, 301, **414**
Vanasek, Alan R. - Jardine, Logan & O'Brien - St. Paul - (612) 290-6590 .... 201, **365**, 396
Villaume, Philip G. - Philip G. Villaume & Associates - Bloomington - (612) 851-0823 .... **172**, 201, 396
Vogel, Peter L. - Rosenmeier, Anderson & Vogel - Little Falls - (612) 632-5458 157
Weikart, Neil A. - Fredrikson & Byron, P.A. - Minneapolis - (612) 347-7025 .... 111, 275, **414**
Weil, Cass S. - Moss & Barnett, A Professional Association - Minneapolis - (612) 347-0300 .... **80**, 133
Weinstine, Robert R. - Winthrop & Weinstine, P.A. - Minneapolis - (612) 347-0700 .... **133**, 201, 328
Wendland, Craig W. - Dingle & Wendland, Ltd. - Rochester - (507) 288-5440 .... **111**, 133, 157
Wernick, Mark S. - Attorney at Law - Minneapolis - (612) 871-8456 173
Westman, Nickolas E. - Westman, Champlin & Kelly, P.A. - Minneapolis - (612) 334-3222 302
Whitehead, G. Marc - Popham, Haik, Schnobrich & Kaufman, Ltd. - Minneapolis - (612) 333-4800 .... 133, 314, **415**
Wicks, John R. - Dorsey & Whitney - Rochester - (507) 288-3156 381
Wilhoit, Richard A. - Doherty, Rumble & Butler Professional Association - St. Paul - (612) 291-9333 381
Williams, Douglas J. - Merchant, Gould, Smith, Edell, Welter & Schmidt, P.A. - Minneapolis - (612) 332-5300 .... 54, **302**
Windhorst, John W. Jr. - Dorsey & Whitney - Minneapolis - (612) 340-2600 95
Winthrop, Sherman - Winthrop & Weinstine, P.A. - St. Paul - (612) 290-8400 .... 157, 381, **415**
Wold, Peter B. - Wold, Jacobs & Johnson, P.A. - Minneapolis - (612) 341-2525 173
Zwakman, John C. - Dorsey & Whitney - Minneapolis - (612) 340-2600 .... 201, **328**

SEND IN THIS CARD

Send in this card for a useful resource that will enable you to more effectively deal with any legal issue that you may confront.

Information for both businesses and consumers.

Making good legal decisions just became a lot easier.

☐ Send me ____ copies of the **Business Guidebook**
Allow two weeks for delivery. For faster service, call us directly at (612) 334-3333.

Name: _____
Address: _____
City, State, Zip: _____
Phone: _____

☐ Check ($52.00) enclosed ☐ Visa ☐ Mastercard
Card# _____ Exp. date _____
Signature _____

GUIDEBOOK
Law & Leading Attorneys
MINNESOTA

$49.95
__2.05__ Shipping, Tax
$52.00

☐ Put me on mailing list to receive updates on future editions.
☐ Send me information on the *Minnesota Consumer Guidebook to Law & Leading Attorneys*.

VISA
MasterCard

Comments on the *Business Guidebook* are encouraged:
_____
_____

☐ Send me ____ copies of the **Consumer Guidebook**
Allow two weeks for delivery. For faster service, call us directly at (612) 334-3333.

Name: _____
Address: _____
City, State, Zip: _____
Phone: _____

☐ Check ($15) enclosed ☐ Visa ☐ Mastercard
Card# _____ Exp. date _____
Signature _____

GUIDEBOOK
Law & Leading Attorneys
MINNESOTA

$12.95
__2.05__ Shipping, Tax
$15.00

☐ Put me on mailing list to receive updates on future editions.
☐ Send me information on the *Minnesota Consumer Guidebook to Law & Leading Attorneys*.

VISA
MasterCard

Comments on the *Business Guidebook* are encouraged:
_____
_____

BUSINESS REPLY MAIL
FIRST-CLASS MAIL PERMIT NO 25074 MPLS MN

AMERICAN RESEARCH CORPORATION
527 MARQUETTE AVENUE-SUITE 2100
MINNEAPOLIS, MN 55402-9765

NO POSTAGE
NECESSARY
IF MAILED
IN THE
UNITED STATES

BUSINESS REPLY MAIL
FIRST-CLASS MAIL PERMIT NO 25074 MPLS MN

AMERICAN RESEARCH CORPORATION
527 MARQUETTE AVENUE-SUITE 2100
MINNEAPOLIS, MN 55402-9765

NO POSTAGE
NECESSARY
IF MAILED
IN THE
UNITED STATES